THE FOREIGN AFFAIRS
50-YEAR BIBLIOGRAPHY

THE FOREIGN AFFAIRS
50-YEAR BIBLIOGRAPHY

NEW EVALUATIONS OF SIGNIFICANT
BOOKS ON INTERNATIONAL RELATIONS
1920–1970

BYRON DEXTER, EDITOR

Assisted by Elizabeth H. Bryant and Janice L. Murray

Published for the Council on Foreign Relations by

R. R. BOWKER COMPANY New York & London 1972

Published by R. R. Bowker Co. (a Xerox company)
1180 Avenue of the Americas, New York, N.Y. 10036
Copyright © 1972 by Council on Foreign Relations, Inc.
All rights reserved
International Standard Book Number: 0-8352-0490-1
Library of Congress Catalog Card Number: 75-163904
Printed and bound in the United States of America.

The Council on Foreign Relations is a nonprofit institution
devoted to the study of political, economic, and strategic
problems as related to American foreign policy. It takes no
stand, expressed or implied, on American policy. The authors
of books published under the auspices of the Council are
responsible for their statements of fact and expressions of
opinion. The Council is responsible only for determining
that they should be presented to the public.

For a partial list of Council publications, see pages 935–936.

FOREWORD

This book will be turned to by librarians and scholars for many years to come. But it is much more than a book of reference; it is a book to be read by everyone interested in the international problems of the past fifty years, so many of which illuminate the problems of today. The 2,130 concise essays printed here in the form of book reviews give a synoptic view of the whole period and provide a starting point for knowledgeable reading in all the main spheres of international relations.

That field is vast under any definition, and its size and complexity have grown enormously with the appearance of new nations, the development of areas which previously attracted little notice, and the attempts to form organizations for regional integration and world coöperation. New dimensions have also been added by amazing developments in science and technology and by new approaches and methods.

It was a staggering task to make a selection of memorable and still useful books from the flood that has poured from the world's presses in fifty years of such unexampled international activity. Byron Dexter, a former Managing Editor of *Foreign Affairs,* may have been staggered but was not dismayed. He assembled a team of 400 experts to make the necessary judgments and write the reviews of the books they chose. It is testimony to the vitality of scholarly life in this country, and in the worldwide community of scholars represented here, that so many distinguished men and women recognized the value of the undertaking and took time from their professional pursuits to ensure its success.

Foreign Affairs bibliographies have been published at the end of each decade in the past fifty years. An editor of one of those bibliographies wrote that the estimates of the books briefly noted there were based on "how they strike a contemporary." This is not the case in this bibliography. The books reviewed here are looked at in a perspective of half a century. Each book selected for review has been the subject of fresh study and is appraised in relation to earlier works and to its influence on later books and events. Each one chosen has been considered as deserving of a place in the ongoing stream of history.

The splendid achievement in the planning and execution of a work of this scope must be the excuse if a note of jubilation creeps into this foreword to a volume which helps celebrate the fiftieth anniversary of the periodical from which it stems.

HAMILTON FISH ARMSTRONG

PREFACE

The quarterly review *Foreign Affairs,* sponsored by the Council on Foreign Relations, will mark its fiftieth year of publication in October 1972. *The Foreign Affairs 50-Year Bibliography* is designed to appear as part of the celebration of that anniversary.

This volume is a selective bibliography of outstanding books on international relations published between 1920 and 1970. Experts in various fields have advised on the selections and written the descriptive and critical evaluations. It is an informal rather than a formal bibliography. The term "international relations" is interpreted broadly. In two respects, indeed, the present volume is quite unorthodox. Not only is it extremely selective, but its reviews are considerably longer than the annotations customary in bibliographies—many, in effect, brief essays. The purpose was to make possible a summarizing volume of manageable size for the fifty-year period, and to gain the flexibility that would permit chosen books to be placed in their setting and reappraised in perspective, with supplementary references to other titles when the contributors so desired. It is hoped that the *50-Year Bibliography* will be a useful instrument of research and teaching over the years.

Though prepared for English-reading users, the bibliography includes titles in other languages, including non-Western. Library of Congress transliterations have been generally followed. Works of reference, including documents, bibliographies, annuals, series, and official histories, are generally not reviewed, nor are journalistic and travel books or very short books. There are exceptions to all these "rules." A brief, selective list of reference works appears in an appendix.

The volume is indexed by authors and by titles. All titles printed in bold face type in the body of the book appear in the index. Entries discussed as cross references within reviews are in bold face but are not accompanied by publication data; readers will find that information, and the cross references, by referring to the titles in the index. Proper names are not indexed unless they are those of authors of books that appear in the index.

The scholars who were asked to aid in the selection and to write the reviews were told that, though the *50-Year Bibliography* did not seek to offer a list of "best" books, the emphasis was to be on works of scholarship of lasting value. What was sought were "landmark" books which, in their opinion, were important in themselves and significant for an understanding of the development of ideas and events of the period; the best available books of something less than landmark quality useful for such an understanding might also be included. Reviews would indicate why books had been selected, for whatever reason. In keeping with the tradition of bibliographical reviewing established in the first issue of *Foreign Affairs,* reviews would be unsigned.

From its first issue *Foreign Affairs* has contained a selected, annotated list of recent books on international relations, and at ten-year intervals the Council has published a "Foreign Affairs Bibliography" based on these lists, revised and expanded. The first volume (1919–1932), which included books published three years before the founding of the review, was prepared by William L. Langer and Hamilton Fish Armstrong; the second (1932–1942) by Robert Gale Woolbert; the third (1942–1952) by Henry L. Roberts; the fourth (1952–1962) by Henry L. Roberts, assisted by Jean Gunther and Janis A. Kreslins; a fifth (1962–1972) is being prepared.

The process of selection for the *50-Year Bibliography* began with the transfer to cards of the entries in these earlier bibliographies, excluding titles published before 1920 and after 1970. After a preliminary sorting out of books in the earlier bibliographies to eliminate those that the annotations suggested were of transient value, the titles were classified according to the three-part scheme followed in the ten-year bibliographies: Part One: General International Relations; Part Two: The World since 1914; Part Three: The World by Regions. Provisional proportions among the various sections and subsections were set to meet a limit of about 2,000 reviews. In the event, the bibliography contains some 2,130 main entries reviewed, plus about 900 books cited without review.

Scholars who made the selections were asked to draw to the extent that they wished on titles from the earlier bibliographies but not to limit themselves to choices among them. They were urged to draw on their own knowledge of books in the field, and to use their own judgment in preparing their lists of choices. When the burden of reviewing was too great, they were asked to invite colleagues to assist them, as many did, and this often meant that those scholars also participated in the process of selection. Some 400 experts, in the United States and abroad, thus took part in the preparation of the volume.

The limitations of so highly selective a bibliography are self-evident. Books that deserve inclusion are undoubtedly absent. The familiar bibliographical problem of overlapping classifications was heightened by the extreme selectivity. Often the same book was sought by different contributors—in the cases of seminal works sometimes by several different contributors—problems settled by lively three-cornered communications among contributors and editor.

The patience, good humor and wonderfully heartening interest with which these 400 men and women contributed their scholarship and their labor to the project made the work of the editor a privilege and a pleasure. In view of the decision for anonymity no credit for specific work can be given to the contributors. The preparation of the bibliography became a collective enterprise; so only could it have been carried through. No distinction can be made between the roles of "reviewers" and "advisers." Advisers were reviewers and reviewers advisers. Some prepared only a few reviews, some many. Some also performed the invaluable service of recommending advisers and reviewers for other sections. No words can adequately express the debt owed by the bibliography to them all.

I venture to believe that the scholars of another generation, for whom these scholars created this book, will, in retrospect, be grateful to them.

The names of advisers and reviewers appear in alphabetical order on the following pages.

Thanks for essential help are due to many other people, and are warmly extended: in particular to Hamilton Fish Armstrong—for fifty years a bookman among so many other useful things—the moving spirit in this and other *Foreign Affairs* bibliographies; to George S. Franklin, Jr., for characteristically kindly support, and to members of the staff of the Council on Foreign Relations; to Donald Wasson, Librarian, and Janet Rigney, Assistant Librarian, and the staff of the Foreign Relations Library; to Janis A. Kreslins for preparing the appendix; and to William L. Langer for counsel in planning the project and aid in finding advisers and reviewers.

I have been fortunate indeed in having as assistants Elizabeth H. Bryant and Janice L. Murray; and I am grateful for the assistance of Sylva Oxenfeld during the first year of the project.

A deeply appreciated grant from the Ford Foundation made possible the preparation of the *50-Year Bibliography*.

BYRON DEXTER

December 1, 1971

ADVISERS AND REVIEWERS

Fredrick Aandahl
Department of State

Edward Allworth
Columbia University

Carl G. Anthon
American University

Olavi Arens
Columbia University

F. Christopher Arterton
Massachusetts Institute of Technology

Abraham Ascher
Brooklyn College, City University of New York

Hans Aufricht
George Washington University

John P. Augelli
University of Kansas

Paul Avrich
Queens College, City University of New York

Donald N. Baker
Michigan State University

Gordon B. Baldwin
University of Wisconsin

Michael Barkun
Syracuse University

M. Searle Bates
New York, N.Y.

R. R. Baxter
Harvard University

A. J. Beattie
London School of Economics and Political Science

Knight Biggerstaff
Cornell University

Thomas E. Bird
Queens College, City University of New York

T. A. Bisson
Renison College

Andrew Blane
Lehman and Hunter Colleges, City University of New York

Boleslaw A. Boczek
Kent State University

Joan V. Bondurant
University of the Pacific

Howard L. Boorman
Vanderbilt University

Dorothy Borg
Columbia University

John Bowditch
University of Michigan

Ralph Braibanti
Duke University

Paul R. Brass
University of Washington

Charles C. Bright
University of Michigan

George Brinkley
University of Notre Dame

Albert S. Britt, III
United States Military Academy

John H. Broomfield
University of Michigan

Ian Brownlie
Wadham College, Oxford

Charles Burdick
San Jose State College

David D. Burks
Indiana University

Vivian C. Bushnell
American Geographical Society

William E. Butler, II
University College, London

Robert J. C. Butow
University of Washington

John F. Cady
Ohio University

Lucius Caflisch
Institut Universitaire de Hautes
Études Internationales, Geneva

John C. Campbell
Council on Foreign Relations

J. M. S. Careless
University of Toronto

Elisa A. Carrillo
Marymount College

Alan Cassels
McMaster University

Alphonso Castagno
Boston University

John Cell
Duke University

Gillian T. Cell
University of North Carolina

Richard D. Challener
Princeton University

D. G. Chandler
Royal Military Academy, Sandhurst

Kang Chao
University of Wisconsin

Carl Q. Christol
University of Southern California

Samuel C. Chu
Ohio State University

Basil Chubb
Trinity College, Dublin

Inis L. Claude, Jr.
University of Virginia

Walter C. Clemens, Jr.
Boston University

O. Edmund Clubb
New York, N.Y.

Paul A. Cohen
Wellesley College

Stephen F. Cohen
Princeton University

Stephen P. Cohen
University of Illinois

Warren I. Cohen
Michigan State University

R. Taylor Cole
Duke University

Robert O. Collins
University of California, Santa
Barbara

Joel Colton
Duke University

Stetson Conn
Department of the Army

Richard Cooley
University of Washington

Alvin D. Coox
San Diego State College

L. Gray Cowan
Columbia University

Gerald M. Craig
University of Toronto

Robert I. Crane
Syracuse University

Robert D. Crassweller
ITT Corporation

J. H. Dales
University of Toronto

Alexander Dallin
Stanford University

Robert V. Daniels
University of Vermont

William M. Darden
United States Naval Academy

Patricia Grady Davies
Washington, D.C.

Vincent Davis
University of Kentucky

W. Phillips Davison
Columbia University

C. Ernest Dawn
University of Illinois

Phyllis Deane
University of Cambridge

Richard T. De George
University of Kansas

Charles F. Delzell
Vanderbilt University

Karl W. Deutsch
Harvard University

William Diebold, Jr.
Council on Foreign Relations

Martin Domke
New York University

William F. Dorrill
University of Pittsburgh

Cora Du Bois
Harvard University

Stephen P. Dunn
Monterey Institute of Foreign
Studies

W. T. Easterbrook
University of Toronto

Lloyd Eastman
University of Illinois

Henry W. Ehrmann
Dartmouth College

Ernst Ekman
University of California, Riverside

Joseph W. Elder
University of Wisconsin

Ainslie T. Embree
Duke University

Rupert Emerson
Harvard University

Salo Engel
University of Tennessee

Howard Erdman
Dartmouth College

Thomas H. Etzold
Yale University

Alona E. Evans
Wellesley College

T. J. D. Fair
Southern Illinois University

David M. Farquhar
University of California, Los Angeles

A. A. Fatouros
Indiana University

Oleh S. Fedyshyn
Richmond College, City University of New York

Gerald D. Feldman
University of California, Berkeley

Roy E. Feldman
Massachusetts Institute of Technology

Charles G. Fenwick
Washington, D.C.

G. Lowell Field
University of Connecticut

Lawrence S. Finkelstein
Harvard University

Wesley Andrew Fisher
Columbia University

William J. Foltz
Yale University

Annette Baker Fox
Columbia University

Paul Fox
University of Toronto

William T. R. Fox
Columbia University

Marcus F. Franda
Colgate University

Francine R. Frankel
University of Pennsylvania

Robert C. Frasure
University of the South

John H. E. Fried
Lehman College and Graduate Faculty, City University of New York

Morton H. Fried
Columbia University

Maurice Friedberg
Indiana University

Erik J. Friis
American-Scandinavian Foundation

Michael Gasster
Rutgers University

Hans W. Gatzke
Yale University

H. Kent Geiger
University of Wisconsin

Federico G. Gil
University of North Carolina

Felix Gilbert
Institute for Advanced Study

Jerome Gilison
Johns Hopkins University

Donald G. Gillin
Vassar College

George Ginsburgs
New School for Social Research

Donald E. Ginter
Sir George Williams University

Zvi Y. Gitelman
University of Michigan

Harvey Glickman
Haverford College

David Goldey
Lincoln College, Oxford

Erich Goldhagen
Brandeis University

Leonard A. Gordon
Columbia University

Wesley L. Gould
Wayne State University

Walter E. Gourlay
Michigan State University

Loren R. Graham
Columbia University

Patricia Albjerg Graham
Barnard College

J. L. Granatstein
York University

C. Hartley Grattan
Austin, Texas

L. C. Green
University of Alberta

Jerome B. Grieder
Brown University

Thomas E. Griess
United States Military Academy

William L. Griffin
Washington, D.C.

Muriel Grindrod
London, England

Ernest A. Gross
New York, N.Y.

Leo Gross
Fletcher School of Law and Diplomacy

Gregory Grossman
University of California, Berkeley

Leo Gruliow
Current Digest of the Soviet Press

Richard F. Gustafson
Barnard College

Ernst B. Haas
University of California, Berkeley

Michael Haas
University of Hawaii

Roger F. Hackett
University of Michigan

William B. Hamilton
Duke University

Darrell P. Hammer
Indiana University

Parker T. Hart
Middle East Institute

Caryl P. Haskins
Carnegie Institution of Washington

Robert D. Hayton
Hunter College, City University of New York

John N. Hazard
Columbia University

Waldo H. Heinrichs, Jr.
University of Illinois

Roger Hilsman
Columbia University

Harold C. Hinton
George Washington University

Erik P. Hoffmann
State University of New York at Albany

Stanley Hoffmann
Harvard University

Paul Hollander
University of Massachusetts

John W. Holmes
Canadian Institute of International Affairs

K. J. Holsti
University of British Columbia

Ole R. Holsti
University of British Columbia

David Hooson
University of California, Berkeley

Alan W. Horton
American Universities Field Staff

Chi-ming Hou
Colgate University

Harry N. Howard
American University

Eric Hula
New School for Social Research

J. C. Hurewitz
Columbia University

Alfred F. Hurley
United States Air Force Academy

Robert A. Huttenback
California Institute of Technology

Irwin T. Hyatt, Jr.
Emory University

James N. Hyde
New York, N.Y.

Max Iklé
Zurich, Switzerland

Akira Iriye
University of Chicago

Graham W. Irwin
Columbia University

Harold R. Isaacs
Massachusetts Institute of Technology

John Israel
University of Virginia

Charles Issawi
Columbia University

Gabriel Jackson
University of California, San Diego

Karl Jackson
Massachusetts Institute of Technology

Larry Jackson
Columbia University

W. A. Douglas Jackson
University of Washington

Gary Jacobson
Yale University

Leonard Jeffries
San Jose State College

Allen W. Johnson
Columbia University

G. Wesley Johnson
Stanford University

John J. Johnson
Stanford University

James Joll
London School of Economics and Political Science

Peter H. Juviler
Barnard College

Joyce K. Kallgren
University of California, Davis and Berkeley

Temma Kaplan
University of California, Los Angeles

Jerzy F. Karcz
University of California, Santa Barbara

George F. Kennan
Institute for Advanced Study

George O. Kent
University of Maryland

Ernest L. Kerley
Department of State

Mark Kesselman
Columbia University

Majid Khadduri
Johns Hopkins University

Christoph M. Kimmich
Columbia University

Anthony King
University of Essex

Klaus Knorr
Princeton University

Stanley A. Kochanek
Pennsylvania State University

Arthur G. Kogan
Department of State

Norman Kogan
University of Connecticut

Janis A. Kreslins
Council on Foreign Relations

H. Peter Krosby
State University of New York at Albany

Arthur Kruger
University of Toronto

Arthur Lall
Columbia University

Betty G. Lall
School of Industrial and Labor Relations, New York City

Richard D. Lambert
University of Pennsylvania

Donald Lammers
Michigan State University

Thomas B. Larson
New York, N.Y.

David M. Leive
Washington, D.C.

Daniel Lerner
Massachusetts Institute of Technology

Warren Lerner
Duke University

Howard S. Levie
St. Louis University

Martin Levin
University of British Columbia

John P. Lewis
Princeton University

John W. Lewis
Stanford University

Robert Lewis
Columbia University

Clara E. Lida
Wesleyan University

Richard B. Lillich
University of Virginia

Leon N. Lindberg
University of Wisconsin

Robert Lipsyte
The New York Times

Oliver J. Lissitzyn
Columbia University

K. C. Liu
University of California, Davis

Francis L. Loewenheim
Rice University

Val R. Lorwin
University of Oregon

C. Leonard Lundin
Indiana University

Michael M. Luther
Hunter College, City University of New York

Jessie G. Lutz
Rutgers University

Jay Luvaas
Allegheny College

Peyton V. Lyon
Carleton University

Robert A. Lystad
School of Advanced International Studies, Johns Hopkins University

Shannon McCune
University of Florida

Charles B. MacDonald
Department of the Army

Vernon McKay
School of Advanced International Studies, Johns Hopkins University

John R. McLane
Northwestern University

John McManus
University of Toronto

Robert H. McNeal
University of Massachusetts

Alvin Magid
State University of New York at Albany

Edward E. Malefakis
Northwestern University

Krystyna Marek
Institut Universitaire de Hautes Études Internationales, Geneva

Laurence W. Martin
King's College, London

Vojtech Mastny
Columbia University

Robert F. Meagher
Fletcher School of Law and Diplomacy

John F. Melby
University of Guelph

Norman Meller
University of Hawaii

Alfred G. Meyer
University of Michigan

John D. Montgomery
Harvard University

Morris David Morris
University of Washington

Henry W. Morton
Queens College, City University of New York

Louis Morton
Dartmouth College

Philip E. Mosely
Columbia University

David Mozingo
Cornell University

Richard A. Musgrave
Harvard University

Peggy B. Musgrave
Northeastern University

H. Blair Neatby
Carleton University

Ralph W. Nicholas
Michigan State University

G. Bernard Noble
Catholic University of America

Emiliana P. Noether
University of Connecticut

F. S. Northedge
London School of Economics and Political Science

Michel Oksenberg
Columbia University

Simon Ottenberg
University of Washington

Norman D. Palmer
University of Pennsylvania

Gustav F. Papanek
Harvard University

Richard L. Park
University of Michigan

Stanley G. Payne
University of Wisconsin

C. Grant Pendill, Jr.
Western Illinois University

Dwight H. Perkins
Harvard University

Ralph Pervan
Duke University

Ray Petridis
Duke University

John A. Petropulos
Amherst College

John N. Plank
University of Connecticut

Ithiel de Sola Pool
Massachusetts Institute of Technology

Margaret Prang
University of British Columbia

Richard A. Preston
Duke University

Pierluigi Profumieri
University of Connecticut

Lucian W. Pye
Massachusetts Institute of Technology

Rouhollah K. Ramazani
University of Virginia

Francis B. Randall
Sarah Lawrence College

James F. Ransone, Jr.
United States Military Academy

David C. Rapoport
University of California, Los Angeles

Tapan Raychaudhuri
University of Pennsylvania

Gordon Reid
Australian National University

Joachim Remak
University of California, Santa Barbara

Norman Rich
Brown University

Barbara A. Ringer
Georgetown University

Benjamin Rivlin
Brooklyn College, City University of New York

Henry L. Roberts
Dartmouth College

Jacek I. Romanowski
University of Washington

Theodore Ropp
Duke University

Eugene J. Rosi
Dickinson College

Robert I. Rotberg
Massachusetts Institute of Technology

Alfred P. Rubin
University of Oregon

Lloyd I. Rudolph
University of Chicago

Susanne Hoeber Rudolph
University of Chicago

Ruth B. Russell
Columbia University

Dankwart A. Rustow
Graduate Center, City University of New York

In-Ho Ryu
Rutgers University

A. E. Safarian
University of Toronto

Nadav Safran
Harvard University

Salvatore Saladino
Queens College, City University of New York

Marwyn S. Samuels
University of Washington

Roland Sarti
University of Massachusetts

Gustav Schachter
Northeastern University

Oscar Schachter
United Nations

William B. Schwab
Temple University

Morton Schwartz
University of California, Riverside

Joseph E. Schwartzberg
University of Minnesota

Egon Schwelb
United Nations

William E. Scott
Duke University

Paul Seabury
University of California, Berkeley

Dieter Senghaas
University of Frankfurt and Harvard University

Robert Sharlet
Union College

James R. Sheffield
Columbia University

James E. Sheridan
Northwestern University

Kalman H. Silvert
New York University

Richard L. Sklar
University of California, Los Angeles

Robert M. Slusser
Johns Hopkins University

Jacob W. Smit
Columbia University

Gaddis Smith
Yale University

Lawrence B. Smith
University of Toronto

T. Lynn Smith
University of Florida

W. I. Smith
Public Archives of Canada

Glenn Snyder
State University of New York at Buffalo

Louis L. Snyder
City College, City University of New York

Louis B. Sohn
Harvard University

Peter H. Solomon, Jr.
University of Toronto

Richard H. Solomon
University of Michigan

Raymond J. Sontag
University of California, Berkeley

Robert M. Spaulding, Jr.
University of Michigan

John H. Spencer
Fletcher School of Law and Diplomacy

C. P. Stacey
University of Toronto

Fritz Stern
Columbia University

John R. Stevenson
Department of State

E-tu Zen Sun
Pennsylvania State University

Paul R. Sweet
Michigan State University

Richard N. Swift
New York University

John E. Talbott
Princeton University

Charles Taquey
Washington, D.C.

Howard J. Taubenfeld
Southern Methodist University

George E. Taylor
University of Washington

Frederick C. Teiwes
Cornell University

Robert Teshera
Western Washington College

John M. Thompson
Indiana University

Willard L. Thorp
Amherst College

Gordon H. Torrey
School of Advanced International Studies, Johns Hopkins University

Robert C. Tucker
Princeton University

Lynn Turgeon
Hofstra University

Henry A. Turner, Jr.
Yale University

Stephen Uhalley, Jr.
Duke University

Joan C. Ullman
University of Washington

Elizabeth K. Valkenier
Columbia University

Lyman P. van Slyke
Stanford University

V. Stanley Vardys
University of Oklahoma

Paul A. Varg
Michigan State University

P. J. Vatikiotis
School of Oriental and African Studies, London

Joseph Velikonja
University of Washington

Klemens von Klemperer
Smith College

Karl von Vorys
University of Pennsylvania

Peter Waite
Dalhousie University

Frederic Wakeman
University of California, Berkeley

Robert E. Ward
University of Michigan

William Watson
University of California, San Diego

Russell F. Weigley
Temple University

Myron Weiner
Massachusetts Institute of Technology

David Welsh
Columbia University

Burns H. Weston
University of Iowa

Douglas L. Wheeler
University of New Hampshire

Urban Whitaker
San Francisco State College

Allen S. Whiting
University of Michigan

C. Martin Wilbur
Columbia University

Wayne Wilcox
Columbia University

Robert K. Woetzel
Boston College

Robert Wohl
University of California, Los Angeles

Thomas W. Wolfe
RAND Corporation

Stanley A. Wolpert
University of California, Los Angeles

Bryce Wood
Social Science Research Council

Gordon Wright
Stanford University

Quincy Wright
Charlottesville, Va.

Theodore P. Wright, Jr.
State University of New York at Albany

Richard Young
Van Hornesville, N.Y.

Walter D. Young
University of British Columbia

George T. Yu
University of Illinois

Mark W. Zacher
University of British Columbia

Raphael Zariski
University of Nebraska

I. William Zartman
New York University

Morris Zaslow
University of Western Ontario

Wilbur Zelinsky
Pennsylvania State University

Earl Ziemke
University of Georgia

Dina Zinnes
Indiana University

Aristide R. Zolberg
University of Chicago

CONTENTS

PART ONE:
GENERAL INTERNATIONAL RELATIONS

PART TWO:
THE WORLD SINCE 1914

PART THREE:
THE WORLD BY REGIONS

CONTENTS

PART ONE:
GENERAL INTERNATIONAL RELATIONS

PART ONE
GENERAL INTERNATIONAL RELATIONS

I. THEORY OF INTERNATIONAL RELATIONS; METHODOLOGY

See also Political Theory, p. 36; War and Peace: General, p. 194; Causes of War, p. 223.

RUSSELL, FRANK MARION. **Theories of International Relations.** New York: Appleton-Century, 1936, 651 p.

This volume contributes to the field of international relations what historical surveys of the "great men" have done for the field of political thought. It describes, abstracts and synthesizes ancient and modern thinkers' explanations about the relations between independent political communities. Anthropological studies of primitive groups and the major international theorists of ancient China, India, Greece, Rome, and of medieval and modern Europe are included. Since the author describes the historical setting of man's speculation about international relationships, the volume also contains interesting information about non-European international systems. The treatment of some of the main intellectual and historical bases of problems and ideologies contemporary to the inter-war period (the "theory" of the League of Nations, imperialism, pacifism, communism, etc.) is less satisfactory because the topics are too complicated to be analyzed successfully in brief fashion.

Kenneth Waltz's **Man, the State, and War** and F. H. Hinsley's **Power and the Pursuit of Peace** (Cambridge: University Press, 1963, 416 p.) follow in Russell's tradition. They systematize and synthesize man's thought on war and peace, but their analyses are tighter, more detailed, and provide a better basis for comparative study because, unlike Russell, they begin with analytical frameworks and examine only the Western tradition. Russell loses depth in order to cover an extensive intellectual history, but the student of international relations theory would do well to cover the first parts of Russell's book to discover the empirical and normative precedents to his own work.

LASSWELL, HAROLD DWIGHT, **World Politics and Personal Insecurity.** New York: McGraw-Hill, 1935, 307 p.

Much of Lasswell's earlier thinking on symbols, élites, propaganda and the psychological roots of politics is applied here to the relations of states and peoples. Insecurity among élites and publics, he suggests, is triggered by changes in the balance of power. However, these insecurities, often manifested in riots, hysteria and prejudice, are to be understood by reference to personality characteristics and élite manipulation of symbols rather than to mere events in the external environment. Lasswell argues that men cannot love their neighbors unless they can hate a distant foe. The problem is that in an economically and technically integrating world, there are few harmless avenues for discharge of collective insecurities. One solution—the development of a universal body of symbols and practices, whether through communist universal appeals or world government ideologies—is not feasible. Hatred and fear of external "enemies" are too deeply embedded in the human psyche, as are national symbols and value systems, to be overcome by universalist propaganda.

This book was received skeptically at the time of publication, perhaps more for aesthetic than intellectual reasons. Yet, Lasswell's insights and proposed methods of analysis did much to expand the scope of international relations studies. His emphasis on psychology and symbols, explored through interviews and content analysis, alerted scholars to the importance of irrational forces working among the populations who ultimately set the tone of foreign policies. Later studies by social psychologists on attitude formation and change, perceptions of threat, prejudice and effects of interpersonal contact across national borders, followed from Lasswell's work. This volume, though often irritating and obscure in style, allows Lasswell to take credit for extending the field of international relations to include phenomena beyond diplomatic interchanges and international organizations.

BERNARD, LUTHER LEE and BERNARD, JESSIE. **Sociology and the Study of International Relations.** St. Louis: Washington University, 1934, 115 p.

The purpose of this slim volume was to demonstrate the sociologist's interest in the study of international relations and to summarize some of the main sociological contributions made toward the study of international relations prior to 1934. Following a brief history of the evolution of sociology as a discipline, the writers show the percentage of papers and Ph.D. theses concerned with different topics of international relations over the years from roughly 1900 to 1933. The definition of international relations topics is particularly interesting. Immigration and race relations, for example, are given as two subjects in international politics that were of greatest concern to the sociologist when this volume was written. The two introductory chapters are followed by three chapters summarizing the main sociological viewpoints on the issues of immigration and assimilation, war and imperialism, and peace and peaceful relations. While most students of international politics will not consider the first a legitimate topic in the field, the latter two, particularly the one on war, present useful annotated bibliographies on major sociological theories of war. The book concludes with a short discussion of international relations in sociology courses and a list of research suggestions that might be profitably investigated.

This volume undoubtedly served as both the inspiration and model for a later article, "The Sociological Study of Conflict," written by Jessie Bernard for the UNESCO Tensions project, "The Nature of Conflict." This article updates the earlier survey and covers not only sociological theories relevant to international relations but a variety of research and methodology that has since developed in the sociology of conflict. It has become a classic introduction to the wide range of sociological contributions in the area.

MORGENTHAU, HANS JOACHIM. **Politics among Nations: The Struggle for Power and Peace.** New York: Knopf, 1948, 489 p.

Professor Morgenthau's famous text is one of the first American efforts to create a systematic explanation of international politics. Starting with the proposition that the search for power and the desire to dominate are "constitutive elements of all human associations," the author views all politics as a struggle for power. Though no evidence is presented for this proposition, the implication for international politics is that the world is comprised of nation-states "continuously preparing for, actively engaged in, or recovering from organized violence." All foreign policies either attempt to maintain the status quo or alter the distribution of power; in the absence of effective restraints, war must result. But how does one explain periods of peace and stability? Two kinds of limitations help render Morgenthau's Hobbesian world occasionally safe: the balance of power and the restraining effects of law, world opinion and international organization. The second portion of the text assesses the conditions under which these restraints succeed or fail.

Morgenthau's book occasioned extensive debate in the 1950s. Those who identified a streak of idealism and moral posturing in American foreign policy could not accept Morgenthau's sanguine vision of diplomatic life. They promoted the "realism of idealism" as an alternative to Morgenthau's advocacy of the prudent use of power. Scholars with an empirical bent attacked what they considered Morgenthau's pretensions of realism and science, saying that he used anecdote rather than data to substantiate generalizations, confused normative and empirical statements, defined power as both end and means, and employed reasoning based on propositions lacking empirical foundations.

This book nevertheless gave a valuable impetus to progress in the field. Indeed, its approach was the "orthodoxy" of the study of international relations for at least a decade. By constructing, in however simple fashion, an analytical framework, Morgenthau superseded the journalistic, event-oriented and legalistic approaches of his predecessors. By emphasizing the need to generalize and to describe and explain patterns of behavior rather than unique events, the work pointed the direction that many theorists of international relations were to take in the 1960s. Morgenthau's methods may be inadequate, but his inquiry helped start a major new direction in the study of international relations: formal and explicit construction of theories of the international system and foreign policy.

WRIGHT, QUINCY. **The Study of International Relations.** New York: Appleton-Century-Crofts, 1955, 642 p.

Working with an extensive knowledge of international relations, history and the social sciences, Wright set himself to synthesize and examine critically types of studies that preceded what may be called the "scientific" approach to the subject, and to point the way to unexplored approaches. Early chapters discuss the development of the field, and the various purposes of the study, namely the theoretical and practical education of citizens, policy-makers, social critics and scholars. The main body of the book then examines the "practical" analyses of the field, such as the arts of war and diplomacy, and the "theoretical" approaches to the subject, found, for example, in sociology and psychology. The last portion of the book—the most rewarding and demanding—spells out the possible form of a scientific and coherent discipline of international relations. Wright suggests that theorists must cease viewing the world as a divine plan, equilibrium (balance of power theories), or organization (administrative and policy-making studies) and regard it instead as a field of constantly fluctuating variables and coördinates. This fundamental shift in "world view" will promote the development of theory based on careful observation and quantification. Though the specific form of a discipline, as proposed by the author, has not come to pass (probably because of problems of measurement), his scientific outlook and concern with identifying and relating significant causal variables underlie many contemporary studies.

Wright's work is in many respects still ahead of some of its successors. His analysis exhibits a commendably universal outlook still lacking in much contemporary writing. Though Wright does not hide his values or some rather old-fashioned assumptions about international life (for example, that there is a tendency of international organizations to develop into federations), the model of the world upon which he bases his proposed discipline is more objective and analytical than many contemporary efforts which equate international relations with the cold war or some modernized version of the balance of power. His book remains a most imaginative and wide-ranging contribution, filled with interesting hypotheses and ideas that deserve further exploration. Professor Wright shows that there is great intellectual reward in broad reading, unhurried speculation and synthesis from many disciplines, not excluding history and philosophy.

MATHISEN, TRYGVE. **Methodology in the Study of International Relations.** New York: Macmillan, 1959, 265 p.

The scope of this book is far broader than is implied by its somewhat misleading title. The author has in fact undertaken a wide-ranging overview of international relations as a discipline, covering topics ranging from basic trends in the literature to methods of presenting research findings.

The discussion is organized into three sections, the first concerned with the development of international relations as a field of study. The second part, ten chapters, is devoted to topics which the author suggests are central to the field: the role of the natural environment; heterogeneity and dynamics of the world society; main structure of the world society; associative and dissociative trends; changing political patterns; standards of conduct; development of institutions; the behavior of states; the role of actors other than states; and the problem of violence. Although these chapters are presented as "a model of analysis," they are in fact much closer to a taxonomy. The final seven chapters are largely devoted to problems of organizing research, collecting data and presenting and using the results.

As a broad overview of international relations as a field of study, Mathisen's book provides a compact summary of major trends. Moreover, the author's familiarity with relevant European writings gives his work a wider scope than similar efforts which sometimes review only American scholarship; almost half of the entries in the short bibliography are by non-American authors.

Despite these merits, many chapters in this book have become dated. In part this is the inevitable result of the outpouring of theoretical, methodological and empirical work which appeared during the 1960s. The author's decision to use textbooks—rather than journals or monographs—as his primary source of data about the developments in the field is a contributing factor. But part of the answer is that Mathisen's book falls between two stools. As a work on methodology it has been surpassed by several books on historical or social science methods. As a survey of the field it lacks the depth and unity of Quincy Wright's **The Study of International Relations** which, although published four years earlier, has stood the test of time better.

KNORR, KLAUS EUGEN and VERBA, SIDNEY, *eds*. **The International System: Theoretical Essays.** Princeton: Princeton University Press, 1961, 237 p.

The first generation of postwar international relations theorists, including Hans Morgenthau, Quincy Wright and Arnold Wolfers, made valuable contributions to the development of a coherent view of the field and conceptual clarification, yet there is still no consensus as to what, exactly, the functions and form of a theory of international relations should be. Thus, without specific guidelines, the chapters in this volume, written by younger theorists at the beginning of the 1960s, cover disparate topics, approached from different viewpoints. The collection is valuable nevertheless because it indicates the developing interest in the concept of international systems, points the way to areas of speculation, such as theory of games and international crisis, which throughout the remainder of the decade engendered an extensive empirical literature, and shows a healthy awareness of the problems involved in developing a "scientific" study of the field.

Chapters by A. L. Burns, Morton Kaplan, Thomas Schelling, Richard Quandt and Sidney Verba, though covering different problems, raise in common important questions about the assumptions of various approaches, analytical methods, theories, the types of variables necessary for theory, and the costs and advantages of forsaking historical detail for increased understanding. The chapter by J. David Singer on the levels of analysis problem has become a classic. Fred Riggs, George Modelski and Stanley Hoffmann make important contributions to the development of typologies of international systems—what criteria one uses to distinguish systems, and what forces account for changes from one system type to another. Charles McClelland's chapter on international crisis, finally, opens up a whole new area for research that today is showing promising results.

HOFFMANN, STANLEY, *ed*. **Contemporary Theory in International Relations.** Englewood Cliffs: Prentice-Hall, 1960, 293 p.

Hoffmann's essay, "International Relations: The Long Road to Theory," originally published in *World Politics,* serves as the core of this book. Following each of the three major sections of that essay are a group of readings which illustrate Hoffmann's major points.

A very brief initial section presents a plea for an autonomous discipline of international relations. Articles by Frederick S. Dunn and Kenneth W. Thompson follow.

The second section is, in the author's own words, a "wrecking operation" performed on some of the more prominent postwar approaches to the study of international politics. Targets of Hoffmann's rapier—he is a perceptive critic who rarely relies upon a bludgeon—include the "realist" school philosophers of history (Toynbee), systems theory, equilibrium theory and decision making. Short excerpts from the writings of Hans Morgenthau, Raymond Aron, Kenneth W. Thompson, Morton Kaplan, Jessie Bernard, George Liska, Richard Snyder, H. W. Bruck and Burton Sapin follow this section of Hoffmann's essay.

The final section represents an effort to develop an "original program of systematic research for the future." Selections from the work of Raymond Aron, Herbert Kelman, Arnold Wolfers, E. H. Carr and Ernst Haas illustrate what Hoffmann generally finds most promising in the literature of international politics.

Hoffmann proposes a "general empirical theory" to bring together the growing number of partial approaches to an autonomous discipline of international relations. Hoffmann's program has both normative and empirical components. The former consists of constructing "relevant utopias" to guide research; historical sociology provides the "conceptual framework" for empirical research by asking relevant questions: What is the structure of the international system? What are the forces which cut across or operate within basic units of the international system? What are the relationships between domestic and foreign policy of the basic units? What are the outcomes of the interaction of these factors? The answers to these questions are to provide the basis for comparison of historical international systems.

Although subsidiary questions are suggested, these categories can include virtually any data, and Hoffmann provides few criteria for selectivity. Nor does he suggest a theory to relate parts of his program. As the targets of Hoffmann's rapier thrusts have no doubt discovered, it is far easier to perform a "wrecking operation," even one as brilliant as Hoffmann's, than to lay even the foundations for a better structure.

ROSENAU, JAMES N., *ed.* **International Politics and Foreign Policy.** New York: Free Press of Glencoe, rev. ed., 1969, 740 p.

A sequel to an earlier highly successful volume having the same title and format, though containing almost entirely new material, this volume collects both articles from journals and previously unpublished studies. The selections are presented under five major headings: (1) the study of international politics and foreign policy—problems of identifying legitimate concerns and issues related to the application of the new research techniques; (2) the structural characteristics of international systems; (3) the decision-making approach—the means-ends question in foreign policy and the relationship of domestic politics to foreign policy; (4) interaction patterns between states—the balance of power, integration, strategy; and (5) "the actions and interactions of states: research techniques and orientations," namely content analysis, survey research, simulation and factor analysis. It is perhaps an indication of the times that 30 percent of the articles fall in the last section.

While the five divisions are not entirely parallel and one might argue that the separation of research techniques from substantive issues leads to the false conclusion that research and substance do not mix, the range and variety of articles is impressive. Each section is introduced by a highly readable summary that integrates the main themes of the articles and attempts to see them against the total development of the field. The only glaring omission is the absence of Rosenau's own important contributions in the theory of domestic sources of foreign policy.

KAPLAN, MORTON A. **System and Process in International Politics.** New York: Wiley, 1957, 283 p.

General agreement tends to divide contemporary research in international politics into two broad complementary approaches: the decision-making approach —the study of the factors influencing national decision makers and their foreign policy decisions—and the systems approach—the analysis of the dynamics of the relationship between states. While traces of either approach can be found in most treatises on international politics, the conscious delineation of the two is part of the behavioral movement and dates from specific works published in the 1950s and 1960s. Snyder, Bruck and Sapin (**Foreign Policy Decision-Making: An Approach to the Study of International Politics**) are the acknowledged originators of the decision-making approach, while Kaplan's **System and Process** marks one of the first discussions of the systems approach in international politics. Although others, most notably McClelland's **Theory and the International System,** have been concerned with the adaptation of systems theory from its biological and communications field backgrounds to international politics, Kaplan's book stands as one of the first attempts to redefine international politics using concepts from systems theory.

System and Process is divided into four parts. In the first two Kaplan proposes his now famous six types of international systems and suggests hypotheses describing consequences within these systems. While the complexity of the hypotheses makes most of them untestable, the delineation of the six systems is both unique and imaginative. Kaplan defines his systems by the rules which govern the behavior of the states in the system. For example, a balance of power system is one in which states attempt to increase their capabilities, fight rather than cease to increase capabilities, but stop fighting before a major state in the system is eliminated. The third section is a somewhat tangential discussion of values, while the fourth attempts to apply the terminology of game theory to international politics. Though the relationship of this last section to the first two remains unclear, the introduction of the terminology to the study of strategy also marked an important contribution.

ROSECRANCE, RICHARD N. **Action and Reaction in World Politics: International Systems in Perspective.** Boston: Little, Brown, 1963, 314 p.

A justifiable characterization of this volume, even though only partially true, would be to call it modern history retold by using the concepts of systems theory. Rosecrance describes the major historical periods since the French Revolution by portraying each as a special network of relationships among the rulers, and between rulers and subjects. Each period is seen as a "system" and its unique system-defining features identified. Thus Rosecrance takes Kaplan's **System and Process in International Politics** one step further—from the abstract definition of different types of systems to the characterization of particular historical periods as international systems.

But the application of systems theory to historical data is only half—indeed, perhaps the smaller half—the aim of this study. The overriding question posed by Rosecrance's analysis is the same raised earlier by a similar study (Karl W. Deutsch and others, **Political Community and the North Atlantic Area**). Rosecrance, like Deutsch and the historians who were his collaborators, wishes to identify the necessary and sufficient conditions for the establishment of a "security community"—a community of states among which recourse to violence is improbable. He is thus asking the age-old question of war and peace. Unfortunately, the questions, and some of the answers proposed, are not always clear because of the heavy use of undefined jargon. Indeed, the contrast between the initial lucid and enjoyable description of each of the historical periods and the subsequent, at times unintelligible, reanalysis of each period using systems theory is startling. Thus the book is noteworthy more for its attempt than its success, in its demonstration of the valuable potential in the use of historical data and the suggestion of how systems theory might be applied.

McCLELLAND, CHARLES A. **Theory and the International System.** New York: Macmillan, 1966, 138 p.

A prominent contemporary theorist on international relations explains the need for, and utility of, building theories about patterns of interaction between states. He surveys and codifies conceptualizations of international politics from many authors, some of whom consider themselves to be behavioralists, and others who have preferred to avoid such a label while making important theoretical contributions to the field of international relations. The main task of theory is viewed as that of accounting for changes and transformations in international systems within a symbolic metalanguage, or paradigm. Power theory is evaluated as one important paradigm but is rejected as having too restricted a vision of the totality of international processes. General systems analysis and communication theory are explicated as alternative methods of conceptualization. Although the book discusses a variety of abstract formulations, its lucidity and eloquence recommend it at once as an introduction to the study of international relations theory and as a source book that will stimulate empirical researchers to investigate its abundant insights and propositions.

HERZ, JOHN HERMANN. **International Politics in the Atomic Age.** New York: Columbia University Press, 1959, 360 p.

This study focuses on the impact which modern means of warfare and bipolarity have had on international politics. It also prescribes policies which will promote international stability under these modern conditions.

Herz states that nuclear weapons and long-range delivery vehicles, economic blockades and propaganda have brought about a fundamental change in the character of international relations. The introduction of these new means of warfare has ended what he calls the "hard shell" or the "impermeability" of the state. Herz anticipates the gradual demise of the nation-state under the pressure of the above forces, although he does not predict precisely what types of political units will emerge. He also believes that the advent of military and ideological bipolarity in the world has undermined the sovereignty of all states in the world—except perhaps of the superpowers—in that it has brought about considerable intervention in their internal affairs by allies and to a certain extent adversaries.

In prescribing policies for the future Herz calls for greater toleration of ideological systems, delimitation of spheres of influence, the defining of aggression (particularly outlawing nuclear attacks), and attempts to achieve modest accords in arms control. He criticizes proposals to change the international system in a radical fashion, reasoning that they only distract attention from attainable goals. In a more general vein he calls for a new attitude of "universalism" which would be based on "the interdependence of doom" and a new comprehension of the need for coöperation in order to avoid mankind's extinction.

The major contributions of Herz's study are the perceptive discussion of forces shaping modern international politics and the thought-provoking challenge to the belief that the present system of nation-states is a permanent fixture in world politics. His prediction of the demise of the nation-state seems at best premature, however, and his general analysis of its evolution fails to consider modest types of international integration which might meet both the dangers wrought by modern technology and the attachment of most people to the nation-state; but his study has helped to undermine the "realist" acceptance of the permanence of the existing structure of world politics and to focus research on possible avenues of its evolution.

ARON, RAYMOND. **Peace and War: A Theory of International Relations.** Garden City: Doubleday, 1966, 820 p.

Aron's massive treatise, one of the most ambitious to appear since World War II, offers interesting contrasts to American conceptions of the field and the approach to it. Aron proposes a theory, but if it is judged by the requirements of carefully elaborated causal statements, operationalized variables, empirical verification and logical consistency, it is not a theory. Unlike American scholars whose recent concerns have been to elucidate the major patterns of behavior in the present international system or to explain limited phenomena such as international integration or foreign policy decision making, Aron looks at a much broader sweep of history and problems. His major concern in the first parts of the book is to explain the goals of foreign policy (power, space, glory) by their "determinants" (geography, population, resources, type of régime). Anecdotes culled from 3,500 years of international history serve as the evidence for establishing relationships between the independent and dependent variables. The virtue of historical perspective, largely lacking in American scholarship, becomes in this case a fault; Aron is unable to establish relationships because of the obviously great technological and social changes occurring in such a historical sweep. He also includes extensive critiques of previous hypotheses (Mackinder; Marxist and liberal theories of foreign policy) and delineates typologies of foreign policy objectives, wars, régimes and international systems, as well as the "relations of forces" that underlie the dynamics of those systems. All of these are questions of major theoretical importance to the field.

In a more contemporary vein, Aron offers some thoughtful commentary on typical forms of statecraft in the cold war and on some problems of military strategy and deterrence.

Unlike most American theorists, Aron also investigates the normative implications of his analysis. His critique of idealism and realism as approaches to foreign policy is rewarding, and he makes a vigorous defense of his own moral position, which he calls prudence. Its essence is to act "in accordance with the particular situation and the concrete data" rather than on the basis of abstract notions of justice or ephemeral and meaningless goals such as "making the world safe for democracy." In this book, Aron again shows himself to be a shrewd observer of contemporary events and a lucid philosopher of international relations. The theory of international relations is best left to others, however.

SNYDER, RICHARD C.; BRUCK, H. W. and SAPIN, BURTON, *eds.* **Foreign Policy Decision-Making.** New York: Free Press of Glencoe, 1962, 274 p.

This monograph, originally published in 1954, has been brought together with a case study of the Korean decision by Snyder and Glenn D. Paige, a review article by Herbert McClosky and Richard A. Brody's comparison of the decision-making approach with Quincy Wright's "field theory," and General Systems Theory.

Snyder and his colleagues distinguish "interaction analysis," which describes and measures the patterns of relations between nations, and decision making, which attempts to explain these patterns. The theoretical works of Kaplan, McClelland, Rosecrance and others have analyzed international relations from the former perspective; Snyder and his associates are mainly responsible for developing a systematic approach to the study of foreign policy.

For purposes of decision-making analysis "state action is the action taken by those acting in the name of the state." The perceptions, choices and expectations of decision makers are the critical variables, and the manner in which these are shaped and constrained by the interaction of individual motivations, the organizational context, and communications and information networks provides the core of decision-making analysis.

Problems with the decision-making approach include the complexity of the scheme, the absence of a general theory to link the many variables, and the relative inattention to policy outputs as compared to processes. These are perhaps the main reasons why relatively few empirical studies have employed the Snyder-Bruck-Sapin scheme in its entirety; Glenn D. Paige's **The Korean Decision** is the most prominent exception. Yet the impact of this book and the monograph upon which it is based has been inestimably greater than such a single-dimensional assessment would suggest. Today students of foreign policy almost routinely employ the ideas of organization and communication theory as well as such key concepts as "definition of the situation," "perception," "role" and many others. That they do so is ample evidence of the indelible impact that Snyder and his colleagues have had on foreign policy analysis.

KELMAN, HERBERT C., *ed*. **International Behavior: A Social-Psychological Analysis.**
New York: Holt, Rinehart and Winston, 1965, 626 p.

This massive volume should not be mistaken for one of the currently fashionable "readers" which brings together a loosely related collection of previously published articles with a maximum of effort by a Xerox machine. During the five years between conception and delivery, the 19 psychologists, anthropologists and political scientists represented in this volume have produced 16 chapters of high quality. These represent an excellent sample of theoretical and empirical work on the "common man's" attitudes and beliefs about international phenomena, as well as newer work on decision making and diplomatic bargaining.

The first group of seven chapters focuses on national and international images. Robert A. Levine, William A. Scott, Ithiel de Sola Pool, Karl W. Deutsch, Richard L. Merritt, Irving L. Janis, M. Brewster Smith, Ralph K. White and Milton J. Rosenberg examine the effects of such factors as socialization, psychological and social attributes, cross-national contact, international events, education and the cold war on such images.

The next seven chapters are grouped under the title "Process of Interaction in International Relations." Nationalism, decision making, bargaining and personal contact are among the foci of attention in papers written by Harold D. Lasswell, Daniel Katz, Dean G. Pruitt, James A. Robinson, Richard C. Snyder, Jack Sawyer, Harold Guetzkow, Chadwick Alger and Anita Mishler.

Not surprisingly, such a diverse group of authors and topics falls short of presenting a wholly integrated view of social-psychological processes relevant to international politics. To the extent that the current state of knowledge makes that possible, Herbert Kelman fills the gap in his excellent introductory and concluding chapters on the scope and relevance of social-psychological approaches to international relations. They are by far the best existing treatments of these issues and should be read by anyone who has been disillusioned by the facile reductionism which has often characterized writings on these topics.

SINGER, J. DAVID, *ed*. **Quantitative International Politics: Insights and Evidence.** New York: Free Press of Glencoe, 1968, 394 p.

Two postwar trends in the study of international relations were the development of "grand theories" to explain types of, and processes in, international systems (systems level of analysis) and the main characteristics of foreign policy decision making (national level of analysis). Another trend has sought to develop studies of more limited phenomena, contained within international systems or foreign policies, exploring hypotheses of limited range through rigorous methods of data gathering and statistical inference. War, crisis and international integration have been subjects commanding the most theoretical and empirical attention of scholars in the past two decades.

Six of the ten research projects reported in this volume concern international crisis and war. The two studies by Dina Zinnes, and Ole R. Holsti, Robert North and Richard Brody, employ content analysis of diplomatic documents preceding the outbreak of World War I to investigate the relationships between policy-makers' perceptions and their actions in crisis situations. Charles McClelland's work reconstructs crises in terms of types and intensities of actions. His study offers an interesting "profile" of crisis action, useful for comparative purposes.

At a different level of analysis, a great deal of time, money and work has gone into exploring, through correlations and factor analysis, the relationship between various national attributes and conflict behavior or war. The mixed findings in the studies by Michael Haas and Rudolph Rummel help to unsettle some intuitive and traditional hypotheses regarding the domestic sources of aggressive foreign policies, though more recent studies have questioned the appropriateness of the methods employed. The study by Singer and Melvin Small looks for a relationship between system structure—in this case alliance membership—and the incidence and magnitude of war.

These and other studies in this volume indicate nicely the major directions of empirical research on problems of war, crisis and integration during the 1960s (more peripheral studies by social psychologists are omitted) and reveal the authors' sensitivity to problems of methodology. They carefully delineate hypotheses and discuss the sources of data, techniques of analysis and procedures for deriving findings. The book also illustrates the painstaking efforts required to produce findings that are, in some cases, meaningful, but in others theoretically insignificant and intellectually unexciting.

HAAS, ERNST B. **Beyond the Nation-State: Functionalism and International Organization.** Stanford: Stanford University Press, 1963, 595 p.

Professor Haas' lengthy study sets forth "an eclectic theory" of international integration. It is based on the theory or ideology of functionalism (developed most notably by David Mitrany) but also draws upon systems theory, the sociological theory of functionalism, organization theory and a case study of the International Labor Organization.

The primary tenet of the traditional theory of functionalism is that the delegation of some economic-social tasks to international organizations in which domestic interest groups and experts have important roles will lead to a constantly increasing bestowal of new tasks on international organizations. This development is then expected to lead slowly to the formation of authoritative political structures in the world and the elimination of international wars. Professor Haas challenges and revises many of the assumptions of this theory—especially, that the political and welfare calculations of nations can be separated, that there is a common good for all nations which can be objectively discerned by experts, and that habits of coöperation learned in the context of one organization and issue are transferred to other contexts. The author stresses that the growth in tasks for international organizations must rest on particular common or converging conception of self-interest by states and that given the heterogeneity of the international environment we can only expect modest developments. In respect to the control of labor conditions in the world by international institutions, Haas specifically notes that support for such activities has come largely from the democratic welfare-oriented states and that the large number in the group of states which falls outside of this category at the present time does not forbode well for international integration in the context of this issue.

Many assumptions, hypotheses and measures of integration are perceptively examined in this study, though tracing Professor Haas' consideration of them throughout the volume offers a problem for the reader. Nevertheless, the book stands as a major contribution by a most influential contemporary student of international integration.

RAPOPORT, ANATOL. **Fights, Games, and Debates.** Ann Arbor: University of Michigan Press, 1960, 400 p.

This is an outstanding book on the analysis of conflicts and on the application of systems theory and game theory to international relations. Rapoport distinguished three basic types of conflicts: fights, games and debates. Fight-type conflicts resemble the behavior of two dogs where the growl of one dog provokes the growl of the other, and then snarl leads to snarl, snap to snap, until an all-out dog fight results. At each stage in such a developing fight the output of behavior by one side becomes the determining input for the behavior of another. Both parties are imprisoned within a single conflict system, the path of which can be simulated by a pair of differential equations. In all pure fight processes both parties have no control over their values and no control over their own actions: everything each of them does is merely a response to what his rival just has done.

Another type of conflicts resembles games. Here each party is free to choose among alternative moves, and each side is expected to make the most rational, *i.e.* profitable move under the given circumstances, but each side inexorably must play to win, or at least not to lose. Though each is free to choose its moves and strategies, neither side can change its own values; each remains imprisoned in the pattern of its original priorities.

Finally, according to Rapoport, there are conflicts that resemble genuine debates. Here each side is free not only to choose its moves, as it would be in a game, but each is also free to change its own values, at least within limits, under the impact of the actions and communications which it is receiving or which it is experiencing from its adversary. Rapoport's book has established a new level in the research on conflict processes. Well written and lucid, despite its abstract character, it is indispensable for all serious students of international relations.

KLINEBERG, OTTO. **Tensions Affecting International Understanding: A Survey of Research.** New York: Social Science Research Council, 1950, 227 p.

This survey by top ranking social psychologists summarizes in a remarkably effective manner the results of about 200 research studies in social psychology and the allied behavioral sciences about human attitudes and actions relevant to international relations. The studies are drawn from the 1930s and the 1940s, and they demonstrate the importance of behavioral science research at that time for the understanding of international relations. Klineberg's more recent book, **The Human Dimension in International Relations** (New York: Holt, Rinehart and Winston, 1964, 173 p.), carries the survey of research forward to the early 1960s, presenting its findings in a somewhat more popular form. Klineberg's original survey represents a milestone in the transformation of the study of international relations under the impact of the behavioral sciences and together with its successor has still much to say to the contemporary reader. More recent books, such as Jerome Frank's **Sanity and Survival** (New York: Random House, 1967, 330 p.), continue this new attention to "human nature" which the behavioral scientists have brought and link it to the vigorous advocacy of policy proposals particularly in such fields as disarmament, arms control and international organizations.

CANTRIL, HADLEY. **The Pattern of Human Concerns.** New Brunswick: Rutgers University Press, 1966, 427 p.

Hadley Cantril was one of the fathers of survey research in the social sciences and of the utilization of polling data for advice to policy-makers. Much of his work has dealt with political problems within various countries, but he was one of the leaders in developing effective comparative methods for gathering and using polling data from different countries. After World War II, he developed with the help of UNESCO such cross-national polling methods to shed light on some fundamental aspects of international relations. As editor of the book **Tensions That Cause Wars** and co-author with William Buchanan of **How Nations See Each Other: A Study in Public Opinion,** he made major contributions to the understanding of psychological aspects of international relations. **The Pattern of Human Concerns** continues and in a sense sums up much of Cantril's work. Here he reports on the results of applying a "self-anchoring scale" of personal expectations, satisfactions and dissatisfactions to respondents from many different countries and cultures. The power of governmental policies and movements, national and international, Cantril found, will depend in large measure on their relation to the expectation and desire of masses of people—desires which social scientists can now identify and measure to a significant extent.

II. GENERAL TREATMENTS:
THE HISTORICAL APPROACH

Toynbee, Arnold Joseph. **A Study of History.** New York: Oxford University Press (for the Royal Institute of International Affairs), 1934–1961, 12 v.

Toynbee's monumental work has remained influential and controversial to this day. Few scholars have read all 11 volumes of text and studied every page of the map volume, but very many have been influenced by ideas they found in one or the other of these volumes. This aspect of Toynbee's reception reminds one sometimes of the Italian peasants who for centuries used the Coliseum as a quarry for blocks of marble to patch their cottages. Toynbee's overall design, to be sure, never aimed at circuses. He intended to trace the development of 21 civilizations which in his view summed up the story of mankind, and he did so from a philosophic and religious perspective. His religious views were not accepted by many of his readers, and his effort to write a serious analysis of the main historical events at all times and places has incurred the wrath of many specialists.

Toynbee's work has been abridged to the dimension of a skeleton by D. C. Somervell (New York: Oxford University Press, 1946–1957, 2 v.). The result is like an X-ray picture of a beautiful girl: the bones and outlines are preserved, but the interesting details have been lost. Much of the merit of Toynbee's work lies precisely in such details and in the middle-range theories about political behavior which he formulates and illustrates. His description of "arrested civilizations" and of the characteristic of growth, given in the first third of volume III, is a classic. Elsewhere, his discussion of challenge and response, of withdrawal and return, of the intoxication of victory, of the tendency of successful cultures to rest on their oars, of the secession of the internal and external proletariat and of the loss of imagination and leadership that turns formerly creative minorities into merely dominant minorities who try to rule by force after their charm has failed—all these are merely examples of a wealth of ideas which should be significant and fruitful for many years to come.

Spengler, Oswald. **The Decline of the West.** New York: Knopf, 1926–28, 2 v.

Spengler tried to develop a morphology of history, *i.e.* a systematic knowledge of cultural forms and of their sequence over time among different populations. His influence can be seen in the emphasis on configurations or patterns of culture by such anthropologists as A. L. Kroeber and Ruth Benedict.

Each culture, as Spengler saw it, developed like an organism, similar to an animal or plant, with characteristic stages of youth, maturity and senile decline. Writing toward the end of World War I, Spengler·was particularly interested in the signs of incipient decline in a culture in the stage of transition from maturity to decay. Like other conservatives, he saw such decline indicated by the rise of the masses in art, politics and culture; the rise of big cities and spectator sports; the breakdown of distinction of locality and rank; the rise of great empires and of latter-day Caesars as the main type of ruler.

By 1932, he made it clear that he considered Adolf Hitler an unimpressive specimen, far below the type of leader Spengler had envisioned. The Western world, Europe as well as North America, he thought, was entering the stage of decline and indeed of its doom. Individuals and even peoples, according to Spengler, could do nothing to modify this inexorable sequence of stages. Men's only choice consisted in how they would accept a fate they could not change, how they would act their part on the stage of history in a play that was already written. For today's readers, Spengler's work belongs more to the philosophy and poetry of world politics than to its history and science; many of his statements of supposed facts, as well as many of his predictions and his consciously amoral judgment of values have been criticized effectively. Yet his book is not dead. By the sweep of its conception, its richness of detail and its unity of mood, Spengler's work remains the most impressive example of that conservative cultural pessimism that has been a persistent ingredient in the thoughts and feelings of our time.

SCHUMAN, FREDERICK LEWIS. **International Politics: Anarchy and Order in the World Society.** New York: McGraw-Hill, 7th ed., 1969, 733 p.

First published in 1933, this book was in its seventh edition in 1969. It is an outstanding example of the historical, literary and polemical approaches to international relations and one of the best written books of its kind. At times it seems to combine the learning of Gibbon, the pragmatism of Machiavelli, the pessimism of Spengler and the indignation of Swift. Given a system of nation-states, Schuman finds that domestic and international politics will largely be ruled by force and fraud. Yet the cynicism of the rulers, Schuman suggests, has been no less riddled with illusions than has been the trustfulness of the ruled. Schuman emphasizes the importance of such political forces as patriotism, nationalism, imperialism, propaganda and, above all, power politics. He gives excellent case studies with quick historical sketches. Political moves are lucidly described and interpreted in a deliberately hard-boiled manner. The mask of disillusionment does little, however, to hide the intense moral concern of the author. Despite all its facts, Schuman's book is normative par excellence, advocating the overcoming of the competitive state system by the voluntary establishment of a World Federal Republic and the overcoming of the gap between the two cultures of science and humanism through a change of heart. Schuman knew little of social science in 1933 and disdained it explicitly in 1969. He relies on intuition, logic and persuasion rather than empirical evidence, systematic proof and cumulative knowledge. Even so, his book still lives, and reading it is an education that should not be missed.

ORTEGA Y GASSET, JOSÉ. **The Revolt of the Masses.** New York: Norton, 1932, 204 p.

Ortega's book has most often been read for its criticism of modern mass culture and modern mass democracy, but it does contain significant ideas about international politics. His thought is largely élitist and conservative in cast, but he is also sensitive to possibilities of cultural and political change within and among nations. People can be united into nations, in Ortega's view, by involving them in great enterprises. Large undertakings of economic construction, geographic expansion, technological change or social revolution—all can create new nations or consolidate old ones. Leaders are less important as individuals than they are through the actions and enterprises to which they give rise. Ortega's ideas are relevant to the interpretation of the historic process that created Spain out of Castile and Aragon at a time of Spain's expansion into the New World, and it may be still relevant in an age of great enterprises such as our own.

NEHRU, JAWAHARLAL. **Glimpses of World History.** New York: Day, 1942, 993 p.

This book represents a remarkable intellectual and human achievement as well as a valuable corrective to such Western views of history as offered by Spengler and Toynbee. It is the work of a Western-educated Indian leader writing in the 1930s in a characteristic Western institution of the time—a British jail in India. There, without the resources of a university and a library to which historians are accustomed, Nehru tried to organize the history of mankind in his head and then to write it down piece by piece in letters to his teenage daughter. The daughter is now Prime Minister of India, and the letters have become a book of enduring value. Its value for us consists in showing us how the history of the world looked to a first-rate mind of Asia, how similar his judgments are to ours on some aspects of man's progress and how different they are in regard to others. It will be some time until we shall be able to read other interpretations of world history from major contemporary Asian writers and scholars. Until then, Nehru's book will continue to offer a significant aid to our understanding of world affairs.

III. POLITICAL FACTORS

GEOGRAPHY

General

HARTSHORNE, RICHARD. **The Nature of Geography.** Lancaster: Association of American Geographers, 1939, 482 p.

A scholarly monograph by one of the profession's most distinguished scholars provides extensive references to the literature in the field to the 1940s. **Perspective on the Nature of Geography** (Chicago: Rand McNally, for the Association of American Geographers, 1959, 201 p.) is an extension and updating of the author's thought in **The Nature of Geography.** It contains a list of key bibliographic items published between 1939 and 1959.

JAMES, PRESTON E. and JONES, CLARENCE F., *eds.* **American Geography: Inventory and Prospect.** Syracuse: Syracuse University Press (for the Association of American Geographers), 1954, 590 p.

A publication of the Association, **American Geography** affords a comprehensive statement of aims and objectives of modern geography, with extensive bibliographic references.

FREEMAN, T. W. **A Hundred Years of Geography.** Chicago: Aldine, 1961, 334 p.

This is the work of a British geographer, which describes and analyzes the changes in geographic thought over the past century. It has extensive notes and references and short biographies of geographers.

CHURCH, MARTHA; HUKE, ROBERT E.; ZELINSKY, WILBUR, *eds.* **A Basic Geographical Library.** Washington: Commission on College Geography, Association of American Geographers, 1966, 153 p.

A useful bibliographic reference containing a listing of general works and works dealing with geographic methodology, topical and regional geography.

Political Geography

KJELLÉN, RUDOLF. **Die Grossmächte vor und nach dem Weltkriege.** Leipzig: Teubner, 22d ed., 1930, 348 p.

Sometime professor of history and government at Upsala and later at Göteborg University, Kjellén's place in the political geographic literature is secure as the founder of *Geopolitik.* For part of his inspiration, Kjellén drew on Friedrich Ratzel's "Politische Geographie," published in Munich in 1897. Ratzel, the "founder" of modern political geography, was the first to speak of states as having organic qualities, but Kjellén carried the implications of the organic theory into geopolitics. His most important theoretical work was "Staten Som Lifsform" (Stockholm, 1916), published in German in 1917 as "Der Staat als Lebensform."

Kjellén believed that laws valid for all states can be developed from the study of individual states. The organic state is manifest in a number of aspects—namely, territory or space, people, economy, society and government. States try to choose geographic units such as a region, he believed, to ally themselves with and through this alliance to transform themselves into natural units. Vitally strong states with a limited area of sovereignty are dominated by the categorical political imperative to enlarge their area by colonization, union with other states or conquests of different types. This is not, he affirmed, the raw instinct of conquest but the natural and necessary trend toward expansion as a means of self-preservation. For Kjellén, Germany was that vitally strong state whose right to natural and necessary growth was clearly justified.

Needless to say, such ideas found fertile ground in post-Versailles Germany and had considerable impact on one defeated Bavarian army officer named Karl Haushofer. In 1924, when the fourth edition of **Die Grossmächte** appeared, Haushofer brought out his magazine, *Zeitschrift für Geopolitik,* whose title was borrowed from Kjellén.

HAUSHOFER, KARL. **Wehr-Geopolitik.** Berlin: Junker und Dünnhaupt, 1932, 138 p.

————. **Weltmeere und Weltmächte.** Berlin: Zeitgeschichte Verlag, 1937, 285 p.

HAUSHOFER, KARL, *ed.* **Raumüberwindende Mächte.** Leipzig: Teubner, 1934, 359 p.

No review of the literature on geopolitics and political geography would be complete without reference to the work of Karl Haushofer, the leading German exponent of *Geopolitik* in the two decades between the world wars. The degree to which Nazi foreign policy drew upon the writings of Haushofer for inspiration may be debated; still, Haushofer's geopolitical institute at Munich served as a factory for the vigorous propagation of German *Lebensraum.*

Influenced by the work of Kjellén and Mackinder, Haushofer attempted to develop a view of world history based on the concept of conflict. Accepting the organic state idea, Haushofer regarded boundaries as biological battlefields in the life of peoples. Germany's path to life, he believed, lay in the consolidation of the Eurasian Heartland under Germany—a gigantic citadel stretching from "the Elbe to the Amur." This would afford Germany the geographic depth without which she could not maintain herself as a great nation.

Haushofer saw the Pacific Ocean as the theater of a major struggle by Britain, Japan, Russia and the United States, a struggle against which all European conflicts would pale. In **Weltmeere und Weltmächte,** he found the basis of conflict to lie in the deep-seated antagonisms of seafaring and land-based states. Amply illustrated with photos of fleets and naval bases, it offers a brief description of the strategic relations of seas and seaports as opposed to land bases. **Raumüberwindende Mächte** offers a series of papers by a number of writers on geopolitical aspects of religion, language and economics.

As Strausz-Hupé has noted, it is futile to look into Haushofer's work for a systematic presentation of geopolitical theory. Still the student of *Geopolitik* would be amiss if he failed to refer to the work of this prolific geopolitician.

MACKINDER, HALFORD J. **Democratic Ideals and Reality.** New York: Holt, 1942, 219 p.

No British geographer has contributed more to what might be termed the geography of political strategy than Sir Halford J. Mackinder. It was in his famous paper, "The Geographical Pivot of History," read before the Royal Geographical Society in 1904, that Mackinder laid down a series of propositions that he believed governed, or would govern, struggles for world hegemony. Mackinder stated that whatever power possessed the Heartland—that north-central part of Eurasia draining into the Arctic Ocean and into landlocked seas—could not be reached effectively by sea power (and the fleets of the western democracies). On the other hand, the Heartland power could, with the improvement of land transportation through the construction of railroads, reach the peripheral regions of the World-Island, the densely inhabited projectories of Eurasia stretching from Japan to Western Europe. Domination of the World-Island would ensue and, ultimately, the world. With further elaboration, the Mackinder hypothesis has come down to us in this book.

First published in 1919, **Democratic Ideals and Reality** was intended as a warning to the peacemakers at Versailles that a new strategic situation had arisen as a result of the war and accompanying revolutions. Faced with the immediate problems of drafting a peace treaty—and in no position to affect the course of events in Soviet Russia—the delegates to Versailles ignored the Mackinder revelation. When **Democratic Ideals and Reality** was reissued in the United States in 1942, Washington had just gone to war with Tokyo. Thereafter, the Heartland theory became an essential component of every major text in political geography.

The basic questions that compel our attention, of course, are the extent to which the hypothesis is viable and to what extent it needs refining as a result of the advent of the jet age and space rocketry. Mackinder in 1904 saw the crossing of Siberia by rail as a factor profoundly transforming world political strategy. Under Soviet control—especially since World War II—Siberia and Soviet Central Asia have been economically transformed, though the Union's "core" still lies to the west, in the Urals and in European Russia. In the space age, the role of sea power has undergone significant revision, but land power, too, has taken on other dimensions. Still, in view of the American role in Korea, Japan, Taiwan, Southeast Asia and the dilemma, above all, that guerrilla warfare on the periphery of Eurasia has posed for the United States, one is inclined to wonder if there is not, indeed, a prophetic element in Mackinder's strategic conclusions. If for no other reason, **Democratic Ideals and Reality** warrants continued examination and thought.

STRAUSZ-HUPÉ, ROBERT. **Geopolitics: The Struggle for Space and Power.** New York: Putnam, 1942, 274 p.

"Geopolitics," Strausz-Hupé notes, "is concerned with power politics," representing a revolutionary attempt to measure and to harness the forces that make for expansionism. With these words, the author launches an attempt to appraise the origins and development of the "pseudoscience," and especially of its German variant, that in the early 1940s was assumed to have contributed substantially to the outbreak of World War II.

While Karl Haushofer was regarded as the immediate founder of German *Geopolitik,* the origins of the latter could be traced back through Friedrich Ratzel, a German, to Rudolf Kjellén. Still, Strausz-Hupé notes that it was not Kjellén who originated the theory of *Lebensraum* but Friedrich List, a German expatriate who came to the United States in 1825. For Germany to achieve economic progress, List believed, she would need "an extended and conveniently bounded territory reaching from the North and Baltic Seas to the Black Sea and the Adriatic."

The author of **Geopolitics** also shows the impact that Mackinder's Heartland thesis had on Haushofer, but under the chapter title "Heartland and Hokum" proceeds to demolish the thesis by raising the question as to whether the struggle for control of the Eurasian heartland was really the one and fundamental issue of world policy, as Mackinder and, later, Haushofer believed it to be. Also laid to rest is the common notion that a high population density is a major cause or prerequisite of expansion. Citing the example of Japan, Strausz-Hupé noted that expansionism can be traced to times of pronounced static trends in national fertility rather than to dynamic increase.

With its attack on some traditional political geographic clichés, together with its general condemnation of geographic environmentalism, **Geopolitics** remains the most comprehensive exposé in English of the pseudoscience that did much to catch the mind and invest the thought of early twentieth-century European man.

MAULL, OTTO. **Politische Geographie.** Berlin: Safari-Verlag, 1956, 624 p.

Although Otto Maull's work spans the Nazi period and reflects some of the geopolitical thinking of that era as well as of an earlier period in German history, it should not be overlooked. The 1925 edition (Berlin: Borntraeger, 1925, 743 p.) is a substantial systematic treatment of the field of political geography, in which Maull deals at length with society and territory. The 1956 edition, on the other hand, is devoted primarily to the major earth regions.

Two basic concepts emerge from Maull's work: *Raumwesen* and *Raumorganis-mus*. *Raumwesen* constitutes the liaison between men in groups and territory; *Raumorganismus* represents the conscious and intense feelings that this relationship generates. Essential to these two concepts is an underlying premise that the state is an organism. Though not identified as a biological entity, the state nevertheless is a "spatial organism" with its own laws of development. It wants to grow and expand, and in the process it comes in conflict with other states. It is this process, indeed, that is the cause for expansion and imperialism, and it is a stage, Maull noted, through which all states must pass. Maull draws heavily from history to illustrate his principle, but he does admit that economic penetration was a perfectly accept-able substitute for territorial expansion and domination.

It was essentially an acceptance of the dynamic element in states that provided the basis in Germany for the differentiation between political geography and geopolitics. The "mother science," political geography, was expected to confine its attention to the state as a phenomenon of nature, its situation, size, form and boundaries—a focus that came to be described in the United States as morphologi-cal. In contradistinction, as Maull reaffirmed in his **Das Wesen der Geopolitik** (Leipzig and Berlin: Teubner, 1936, 57 p.), geopolitics focuses on the state as a living being, investigates the state primarily in relation to its environment and attempts to solve all problems relating from spatial relationships.

Here was the dilemma for postwar political geography. When, at the end of World War II, German *geopolitik* had been thoroughly discredited, all that seemed to remain for political geographical study was state morphology. Only in recent years, by directing their attention to the work of other social scientists and the behavioralists, have Western political geographers found their way out of the impasse.

GOTTMANN, JEAN. **La Politique des États et Leur Géographie.** Paris: Colin, 1952, 228 p.

The work of the French geographer, Jean Gottmann, marks a major turning point in modern political geographical thought, providing above all an alternative to the descriptive, morphological approach that characterized much of political geographical writing after World War II.

Gottmann's focus is on the process of organization of territory or space, which he sees as a reflection of the degree of accessibility of any place on earth. Each place, according to Gottmann, is unique in its position relative to every other place on earth; hence, its accessibility from other places is also unique, the earth being "closed" but not homogeneous. Into his statement of relative accessibility, Gott-mann introduces the notion of "circulation" or movement, a force that makes for displacement and change. Opposing circulation is another force represented by "iconography," the system of symbols in which a people, community or society believe. The interplay of these two forces affects the partitioning of space into organized units.

Unmistakably, however, Gottmann retains the bias of the European in thinking about the political organization of the earth's surface. It is true that it was Africa's accessibility to the technologically superior maritime European powers that led to its delineation into colonial empires, but one may ask if the successor states are destined to remain Africa's reality. What role are the indigenous political com-munities (tribes) that lie astride the relic boundaries of the past to play in the future organization of that vast continent? Gottmann ignores this level of political reality, and the omission weakens his overall presentation. Still, his contribution remains a significant part of the modern political geographic literature.

WHITTLESEY, DERWENT STAINTHORPE. **The Earth and the State: A Study of Political Geography.** New York: Holt, 1939, 618 p.

The late Derwent Whittlesey was the first American geographer to develop political geography as a subject of teaching and research. Although his early work was dominated by the environmentalism of Ellen Churchill Semple and Harlan Barrows, he later presented political geography as the study of "the differentiation of political phenomena from place to place over the earth"—in keeping with the then current ideas about geography. Trained initially as a historian, Whittlesey contributed substantially to the historical approach to politico-geographic analysis.

Whittlesey considered the state, and particularly the nation-state, as the essential focus of political geography. Yet his concern was not narrowly morphologic; and he recognized that governmental systems are not confined to the region of origin but "may spread to other areas and create some degree of political uniformity over contrasted regions"—a feature that many subsequent political geographers often overlooked.

The Earth and the State gives substantial coverage to Africa because, as Whittlesey noted, it "forms a veritable laboratory of colonial experimentation." Prophetically, he recognized that colonial boundaries in Africa were arbitrarily drawn and would likely become axes of stress in the future.

Though much of the politico-geographic material of the book is now of historical interest, the text remains a classic in the literature and of continuing value for the student of political geography. Whittlesey was not a political systems analyst, but he was clearly aware that the dynamic element in human political behavior could not be divorced from its spatial context.

BOGGS, SAMUEL WHITTEMORE. **International Boundaries.** New York: Columbia University Press, 1940, 272 p.

This excellent monograph addresses itself to some basic questions: What are boundaries, how do they work and how may international problems be solved? As Dr. Boggs points out in his preface, his study examines boundaries in two aspects: how and why boundaries and boundary problems vary from place to place and through time; and what the function of international boundaries is. In the subsequent discussion, the text, amply illustrated with diagrams, plates and maps, takes us from one continent to another.

Boggs, who was the Geographer to the Department of State when the volume was prepared, rejected the notion that states are living organisms that must expand or die, placing himself rather in the school that held to the contractual concept of boundaries. Boundaries are, in effect, property lines; they should be agreed to and accepted. Where friction along a boundary occurs, the function of the boundary should be changed, not its location. "Whether a boundary is 'good' or 'bad' depends upon whether it is adapted to serve the purposes for which it is maintained, with maximum efficiency and minimum friction and expense."

This is a useful treatise, replete with extensive appendices dealing with lengths of international boundaries, the United States-Canadian boundary and others, but its coverage is not complete. There is, for example, no discussion of the Sino-Soviet boundary, the Mongolian question nor (though Boggs is aware of the problem) of the potential friction inherent in the system of superimposed European imperial boundaries on African tribal life. Despite omissions and some unevenness, **International Boundaries,** together with **Boundary-Making** by Stephen B. Jones, is an important part of the political geographical literature on boundaries.

JONES, STEPHEN BARR. **Boundary-Making.** Washington: Carnegie Endowment, 1945, 268 p.

The volume is a handbook for statesmen, treaty editors and boundary commissioners, and a scholarly treatise it is. Prepared as World War II was coming to a close, the handbook was regarded as a guide to the fixing and drawing of international boundaries, and, apart from Boggs' work, is the most comprehensive study of boundaries extant.

Jones divided his book into three large parts: General Situation, Delimitation and Demarcation. Under the first part, he discusses boundary classifications, functions and friction, as well as human and physical factors in boundary-making.

Part II is devoted to aims and methods of delimitation, collecting geographical data and types of boundaries. The last part is concerned with boundary commissions—instructions and reports—and survey maps, markers and maintenance. The volume contains extensive appendices, a good bibliography of books, articles, treaties and reports, in addition to an index.

Jones' concept of the boundary, too, was essentially contractual and (as he was later to admit in "Boundary Concepts in the Setting of Place and Time," *Annals of the Association of American Geographers*, v. 49, 1959) ". . . strangely blind to the tumult of forces—the madness of the Nazis, the Communists' vested interest in disorder (outside their own domain), and the power vacuums created by destruction." Still, despite some deficiencies, the study is a classic.

SPROUT, HAROLD and SPROUT, MARGARET. **The Ecological Perspective on Human Affairs.** Princeton: Princeton University Press (for the Princeton Center of International Studies), 1965, 236 p.

By ecological perspective, the Sprouts here refer to that perspective on environmental factors "invoked to help explain past events and predict future trends in patterns of international politics"—that is, the viewing of human groups in associations with one another and with nonhuman conditions and events. With this as their theme, the authors provide a concise and valuable critique of general hypotheses regarding human affairs, especially where international politics are involved.

The book is an outgrowth of an earlier monograph entitled **Man-Milieu Relationship Hypotheses in the Context of International Politics** (Princeton: Princeton University Press, for the Princeton Center of International Studies, 1956, 101 p.). The aim throughout has been to bring the disciplines of geography and politics into more productive relationships, to serve not only the political scientist but the geographer as well.

After carefully defining their terms (the word "milieu" is used in both studies to refer to environment in the broadest possible manner), the authors proceed to evaluate a number of relevant hypotheses: environmental determinism, free-will (or mild) environmentalism, possibilism, probabilism, cognitive behaviorism and other general theories of explanation and prediction. Written before "ecology" became a household word, the Sprouts have made a significant contribution to the field of political geography simply by reminding us that there is an element of truth in every hypothesis and that international politics do not operate in a vacuum. Scholarly in its approach and profile, **The Ecological Perspective** (and its forerunner, **Man-Milieu Relationship Hypotheses**) are essential reading for the student of politics and political geography.

Frontiers and Settlement; Resources

BOWMAN, ISAIAH. **The Pioneer Fringe.** New York: American Geographical Society, 1931, 361 p.

In the middle 1920s, Isaiah Bowman, the dynamic Director of the American Geographical Society, was able to persuade a number of national organizations to support a major project with worldwide participation, designed to lay the basis for a "science of settlement." This book is an "introduction" to another volume, W. L. G. Joerg, *ed.,* **Pioneer Settlement,** written by various regional specialists.

Pioneering was reaching its natural geographical limits, and therefore becoming ever more risky, both to the pioneers and to the land itself, which in marginal conditions and subjected to machine methods was becoming increasingly vulnerable. Moreover, the pioneers were more sophisticated and had "rising expectations," so that the case for scientific preparation, surveys and comparative studies prior to occupation seemed compelling.

The first quarter of this book is devoted to a provocative series of topical chapters on such themes as "The Road to the Border," "Does It Pay?," "Railways as Pioneers," summing up the common pioneering experience and attempting to define its recurring problems. The remainder is devoted to broad regional studies, covering the western United States, Canada, Australia, South Africa, Mongolia and Manchuria, Siberia and South America, concentrating in each case on defining the nature of the fringes and their special problems.

The writing is beautifully vivid and devoid of jargon while retaining scientific control and relevance to its subject. Although in relative terms other topics on the world scene may now have overshadowed this one, it remains a keenly interesting story.

JOERG, W. L. G., *ed.* **Pioneer Settlement.** New York: American Geographical Society, 1932, 473 p.

The historical context of this valuable survey is that of the final stages of the great spread of European settlement, when in general only the less attractive fringes of the main zones of settlement, where special agricultural techniques were generally required, were still available. Along with the companion volume in this series, Isaiah Bowman's **The Pioneer Fringe,** it sought to lay the groundwork for a new "science of settlement." All the contributions in this book are on particular regions of recent settlement, ranging from Mongolia to New Zealand and South Africa, and from the Canadian prairies (given particular prominence) to Patagonia. Since the 26 authors are also from many different nationalities and disciplines, the approaches are naturally quite varied. The volume gives a lively and comprehensive picture of world colonization in its final stages, on the eve of the great Depression.

It would be difficult to assemble today as comprehensive a series of studies with as objective an approach. The contributions from Manchuria, Mongolia and the Soviet Union in particular underline this conclusion, written as they were just before the drastic disruption of pioneer settlement and intellectual inquiry that took place there in the later 1930s. The book is a graphic portrait of the state of world pioneer settlement almost at its climax, and as such should be of wide interest in the settled—but in other ways so unsettled—world of today.

BOWMAN, ISAIAH, *ed.* **Limits of Land Settlement: A Report on Present-Day Possibilities.** New York: Council on Foreign Relations, 1937, 380 p.

Isaiah Bowman was perhaps one of the last of that now unique brand of social scientist whose interests and life's work bore the distinctive mark of universality. It was not simply that he was engaged in a myriad of activities, from the directorship of the American Geographical Society to the presidency of The Johns Hopkins University, but rather that he approached problems and especially broad social problems with a genuinely holistic perspective on the nature of man and the world. As he once phrased his own and the geographic perspective: "The world is not merely a collection of 'factors' or conditions and laws, but a series of processes always but partially worked through and then halted or deflected by new or modified processes. Only by seeing 'life on the run' do we see life at all."

For Bowman, "life on the run" was most dramatic on the frontiers of civilization—in those zones where the raw dynamics of nature collided most directly with the enormous potentials of man. His was a fortunate fascination with the world of deserts and steppe lands, for it was a fascination that resulted in two major studies: **The Pioneer Fringe** and the volume under review. The collection of essays included in **Limits of Land Settlement** addressed itself to the question of whether the then existing limits of settlement might be further extended to compensate for an already recognizable population explosion. The volume retains its relevance because of its conclusion that further development of new land will not adequately offset increasingly high population growth rates. Unfortunately, neither Bowman nor the authors of the various regional essays followed this argument to its logical conclusion and suggested possible alternatives to migration or to the population problem as a whole. **Limits of Land Settlement,** however, serves as a testament to the closing of the frontier and a warning to all those who would see visions of high density settlement throughout the vast "empty" lands of the American West, the Russian East or in the interiors of Africa, Australia, Canada and South America.

PRICE, ARCHIBALD GRENFELL. **White Settlers in the Tropics.** New York: American Geographical Society, 1939, 311 p.

This was the first comprehensive survey of the topic, integrating the findings of a vast body of specialized literature—medical, administrative and economic as well as historical and geographical. The author is an Australian who had previously published several books on the settlement of that country and had also done field work in Central America. It is characterized by detailed precision with respect to particular environments, medical experiments, racial and historical contexts and is notable for its lack of prejudice or deterministic generalizations about the influence of the environment. After a historical introduction, regional case studies of Florida, Costa Rica, Queensland, Panama and parts of Africa are considered, followed by analysis of the various factors involved, prospects for successful acclimatization and even prescriptions for appropriate habits for healthy living in the tropics. A distinction is made between the "moderate tropics," such as the Caribbean islands and North Queensland, where white groups had proved to be able to "reproduce for many generations" and engage in all types of labor, and the more difficult tropical areas. "The early history of white settlement in the tropics was a story of wasted lives, wasted efforts and wasted resources, but the recent years flow with achievement." Although this conclusion has the unmistakable ring of the colonial, prewar period about it, the book broke new ground in the breadth of scope and depth of analysis of its subject. The references, maps, diagrams and photographs are voluminous and well chosen.

FORSYTH, WILLIAM DOUGLASS. **The Myth of Open Spaces.** Melbourne: Melbourne University Press, 1942, 226 p.

This book was written by an Australian at the end of the Depression decade, during much of which he had been studying population and particularly migration problems in Europe and elsewhere. The question of the peopling of "empty" Australia with sufficient numbers of settlers of "suitable" ethnic origin—preferably British—had been critically discussed outside Australia and had become a growing obsession within Australia. This book came out at a low point in Australian morale on this matter, following hard on the heels of the fall of Singapore and at the end both of a deep economic slump and of the great European era of worldwide emigration.

It seems distinctly odd in present days of trepidation about the "population explosion" to read dire and lengthy forebodings about the implications for Australia of the long-term decline of population that was forecast for Britain at the time. The postwar "baby boom" in Britain or the massive assisted Australian immigration program were neither forecast nor promoted. The general conclusion was that, within the traditional "White Australia" framework, the "recovery of population-growth in Australia must be chiefly a matter of social and not of migration policy." In other words, a domestic boost in fertility coupled with an aggressive program of economic growth and overseas trade formed the prescription for postwar recovery in Australia. The book is full of interesting references, figures and diagrams, and includes detailed surveys of general history of British emigration and the character of the Australian environment.

STAMP, SIR L. DUDLEY. **Land for Tomorrow: Our Developing World.** Bloomington: Indiana University Press, rev. ed., 1968, 200 p.

Dudley Stamp was one of a small group of scholars who had maintained an interest in the Malthusian dilemma prior to the public awakening of the late 1960s. **Land for Tomorrow** is primarily an examination of world land resources in terms of their ability to support the demands of a burgeoning population. The population component is examined in a single short chapter which merely sets the stage for an examination of the resource dimension, and Stamp nowhere suggests the management of population growth as a solution to the problem. His assertion that the concept of overpopulation is valid only in the context of potential food supplies must appear naïve to those who view excessive population in absolute dimensions.

The several chapters regarding aspects of food production represent the major contributions of the volume. One may disagree vehemently with Stamp's conclusion that political barriers are the major impediment to assurance of an adequate world food supply and still find value in his discussion of the problems of land inventory, analysis and planning for the maintenance of an adequate food supply. He tends to consider the management of nonrenewable energy and mineral resources in essentially the same context as the food-generating resources, an approach that materially detracts from his discussion of these latter aspects of the land dimension.

A generation that more frequently sees the scientific revolution and the scientific method as causes of current societal problems rather than as potential solutions to the chronic ills of humanity will undoubtedly have difficulty in accepting Stamp's basic optimism. Those who are willing to assess the volume for its discussion of the land as a food-generating resource will find that it contributes to the understanding and amelioration of some aspects of the Malthusian dilemma.

Population Geography; Ecological Problem

THOMPSON, WARREN SIMPSON. **Population Problems.** New York: McGraw-Hill, 4th ed., 1953, 488 p.

From its first edition in 1930 until this final one in 1953, Warren Thompson's general text on demography provided perhaps the best single introduction to the subject for the student with no previous exposure to the population literature. Although superseded to a large extent by two or three recent general texts, it is still of more than passing interest, and the novice would do well to approach this rapidly growing field by way of this well-balanced treatment. Thompson managed to cover all major aspects of the subject and its zones of contact with other academic disciplines, and to do so in lively, readable fashion.

Current population problems are set within the context of historical trends and of various demographic doctrines concerning the causes and consequences of growth in human numbers. Thompson deals equitably with competing schools of thought and is not seeking converts to a particular camp. Particular attention is paid to differential fertility; and throughout most of the volume American material is given special priority, as in the entire chapter given over to the composition of the American Negro population.

Specifically urban phenomena are discussed in two chapters. The most delicate issues are reserved for the concluding section: the definition and possible control of population quality, the whole touchy area of eugenics and national population policies designed to affect number, distribution and quality of inhabitants. In summary, the author's wide knowledge, technical expertise and judiciousness are such that this work can still be recommended without any reservation—except that of general factual obsolescence.

CARR-SAUNDERS, ALEXANDER MORRIS. **World Population: Past Growth and Present Trends.** New York: Oxford University Press, 1936, 336 p.

Carr-Saunders, a leading British demographer, has furnished a sound, comprehensive summary of what was known in the mid-1930s about historical trends in human numbers and migrational flows through the ages and of the immediate and prospective demographic scene as it appeared at that time. So much has happened in the following three decades, in terms of better, more abundant statistics, more sophisticated modes of demographic analysis and, above all, sharply altered trends, that the latter portions of the book are badly dated, but still of substantial historical interest.

The most enduring value of this work lies in its opening chapters with their broad overview of changes in population size and distribution over the centuries, by continent and major country. The field of historical demography has suddenly come into its own within the past ten years or so, with intensive analyses of specific epochs and places (virtually all European in character); but no work of the amplitude of this book has come along to challenge its supremacy, with the possible exception of a parallel work by Marcel Reinhard, **Histoire de la Population Mondiale de 1700 à 1948** (Paris: Domat, 1949, 794 p.). Carr-Saunders' work is still the best to consult in finding out how many persons lived or migrated when and where in ages past.

BEAUJEU-GARNIER, JACQUELINE. **Géographie de la Population.** Paris: Médicis, 1956–1958, 2 v.

This two-volume survey of the contemporary population geography of the world is the first such venture on any extensive scale, and it has yet to be superseded. The work is something of a personal tour de force. Among its obvious virtues are the sheer quantity of skillfully arranged data, the lucid, highly readable prose and the lavish physical production. The text is richly supplemented by innumerable maps, graphs, tables and photographs. Virtually any student concerned with the geography of population—for the world in general or for any specific region—would do well to consult it as a principal starting point; but he must also keep its limitations in mind. Matters of general population theory and demographic methodology are pretty much dismissed after a few introductory pages; no intellectual innovation is attempted; systematic worldwide treatments of individual topics (*e.g.* international migration, occupational structure or journey-to-work) are missing—a deficiency only partially remedied in a rather sketchy, poorly translated volume by the same author, **Geography of Population** (London: Longmans, 1966, 386 p.).

Aside from the analysis of European population history, the temporal dimension is scanty, apart from the recent past. What we do get is a region-by-region panoramic view of the spatial distribution, composition, present dynamics, migrational trends and local demographic problems of the world's peoples that is richly informative in terms of the immediate reality, but one that never dips very far beneath the surface.

Where there are notable problems of racial stress, population pressure or extreme change, these are dealt with at some length. But Mme. Beaujeu-Garnier does so dispassionately, for she has no particular ideological or professional ax to grind.

WOYTINSKY, WLADIMIR S. and WOYTINSKY, EMMA SHADKHAN. **World Population and Production: Trends and Outlook.** New York: Twentieth Century Fund, 1953, 1,268 p.

This book, together with a companion volume by the same authors, **World Commerce and Governments: Trends and Outlook** (New York: Twentieth Century Fund, 1955, 907 p.), "represents an effort to put between the covers of two manageable volumes what amounts to a statistical picture of the collective resources, as well as the economic performance and promise of the full array of the nations of the world." The result of these efforts is an astonishingly encyclopedic, detailed and accurate compendium, taking in not only economic production and consumption but also a wide range of facts about the world's demography and physical resources. It is highly unlikely that the feat can ever be duplicated in terms of sheer breadth and density of coverage by another pair of authors. It seems almost ungrateful to note that the informational grandeur of this ponderous volume is not matched by any theoretical freshness or deep interpretive qualities. None the less, for the student seeking a solid verbal, statistical or graphic purchase on almost any demographic or economic topic where a batch of tangible facts is needed, there is hardly a more ideal place to begin, at least for items predating the early 1950s.

The work proceeds along three parallel tracks; the verbal exposition is invariably supplemented by tabular and graphic presentations. Although some of the tables, maps and diagrams are borrowed intact from previous sources, many are original creations. The effort required to compile some of the more useful tables from scattered materials was obviously prodigious, and many of the maps are ingenious in technique. Throughout the volume, United States data—for the nation and for individual states and regions—are heavily emphasized; but if coverage for the rest of the world is less penetrating, it is still quite conscientious.

The Determinants and Consequences of Population Trends. New York: Department of Social Affairs, Population Division, United Nations, 1953, 394 p.

This is a splendid summation of what was known in the early 1950s about the causes and effects of changes in the size, location and characteristics of human populations in the modern world. Although obviously dated in many respects, it is so thoughtful and monumental an enterprise that it seems certain to retain much of its scholarly value for many years to come. The focus is upon the dynamic aspect of demography; but this strategy involves so much of the substance of the discipline that the result is a volume that serves as a better general introduction than most of the current textbooks.

Following a brief but searching survey of early world population growth and the succession and clash of various schools of population theory, demographic change is attacked from two angles. First, all significant factors affecting mortality, fertility, migration and population structure and distribution are examined with great care and objectivity. Then the process is reversed in a scrutiny of the impact of population makeup and change upon resources, consumption, labor supply and productivity. In the summary chapters, the highly industrialized countries are distinguished from the underdeveloped countries, and rather different conclusions reached for the two groups. Although the members of the U.N. Population Commission who created this treatise were deeply, but not dogmatically, concerned over the negative effects of rapid population increase in the less developed areas, they were relatively sanguine about the capacity of the world in general to support continuing growth for some time to come. Their opinion that in highly industrialized countries "the questions of optimum population size, over-population, and under-population do not appear to be of the first order of importance" seems unduly cheerful in the light of more recent developments.

World Population and Resources: A Report. London: Allen and Unwin (for Political and Economic Planning), 1955, 339 p.

This powerful, sobering document is a broad-ranging diagnosis of the problems confronting the world in the latter half of the twentieth century because of rapid population growth, and it prescribes several preliminary methods for coping with the question. It signals the approaching end of Western self-delusion about perpetual and automatic material progress. This PEP report is perhaps the single most persuasive manifesto yet issued within a rapidly burgeoning library of alarmist and cautionary literature, and it promises to have enduring value. The arguments of an apparently diverse and anonymous committee of scholars are amply fortified with graphs and statistics.

In the first of four sections, there is a review of the capacity of known or probable agricultural, mineral and energy resources to support continuing demographic expansion and of the interrelations between population pressure and economic development. The conclusions are not particularly reassuring. In a second section, 19 countries and islands are surveyed, each selected to represent a significant combination of demographic, physical and economic conditions. This is followed by a discussion of population policy and administration in France, the U.S.S.R., India, Japan, Sweden and the United Kingdom, and of the virtues, shortcomings and possible future efficacy of such programs. Perhaps the most valuable part of the volume is the concluding section with its set of recommendations for study, policy and action in both the advanced and the developing nations. Most of these have been accepted, in principle at least, by international and national agencies, and many have already been put into practice.

BATES, MARSTON. **The Prevalence of People.** New York: Scribner, 1955, 283 p.

The population problem, generated by the disproportionate growth of people in respect to available resources, has received frequent treatment by demographers but has seldom been examined by other scientists in such a clear and comprehensive manner as in this book. A biologist by profession, the author tackles the topics of the numbers, nature and kinds of men, their reproduction and controls, mortality and migration, science and human affairs. This rather optimistic thesis relocates the problem from the strictly biological sphere of human reproduction into a biosphere where the ecological conditions of human existence and reproduction have been molded in all sorts of ways by cultural forces.

Narrowly conceived, the thesis assesses the present relationship of men and existing space as the result of the historical evolution of mankind. The author avoids speculation and projections for the future, deferring to Harrison Brown's **The Challenge of Man's Future** (New York: Viking, 1954, 290 p.), in which the prospects of future development are derived from the past population growth. The relationship between man and environment has undergone and is undergoing drastic changes and is affecting human ecological space with profound cultural as well as physiological constraints.

Addressed to the nonspecialized reader rather than to the demographer or biologist, Bates' discussion extends beyond the traditional limits of a single discipline and provides a refreshing interdisciplinary overview of a generalist who is solidly based on the firm grounds of his own discipline.

PETERSEN, WILLIAM. **Population.** New York: Macmillan, 2d ed., 1969, 735 p.

The book is a refreshing general guide to the study of population and a departure from the standard demographic texts that are widely accepted by sociologists, geographers and anthropologists. It provides a well-integrated although elementary treatment of the structure, growth and movements of the population of the United States, and a comparative demographic assessment of socioeconomic levels in primitive societies and pre-industrial civilizations to the population composition at the time of the industrial revolution, an assessment that leads to an analysis of populations in totalitarian states as well as those in underdeveloped areas. The final part deals with a review of the Malthusian theory, population optima, fertility and birth control, mortality and migration changes. Primarily focused on the United States, the study nevertheless presents a historically reliable and demographically accurate basic picture of populations of the major areas of the world.

The attempt to relate the demographic variables with socioeconomic and cultural conditions departs from the more rigidly structured demographic treatises into a cross-disciplinary narration of the structures, changes and movements of people of the world. As in other similar studies, the information is dated and strongly affected by the views prevailing at the time of first publication in 1961; greater concern is shown for the structural changes of population than for the ecological consequences of its growing number. The second edition was revised, updated and considerably expanded.

BERELSON, BERNARD and OTHERS, *eds.* **Family Planning and Population Programs: A Review of World Developments.** Chicago: University of Chicago Press, 1966, 848 p.

The International Conference on Family Planning Programs, held at Geneva, Switzerland in the summer of 1965 under joint sponsorship of the Population Council and the Rockefeller and Ford Foundations, was convened for the purposes of reviewing the existing national and international family-planning programs and of suggesting recommendations on how to expedite new efforts in spreading information among different disciplines and how to stimulate adoption of existing programs in new geographical areas.

This volume of reports includes an assessment of individual national programs (primarily countries of Asia and Latin America); reviews of administrative aspects of organizational structures; a portrayal of programmatic implications of different contraceptive methods; and summaries of contemporary research efforts, ranging from an assessment of world population growth to the cost of family-planning programs, record-keeping procedures and an evaluation of future research needs. The final part outlines the projects of national and international organizations and stresses the need for a concerted coöperation of private and public agencies.

From the initial rather pessimistic comments on the magnitude of the world population growth and the meager accomplishments of the already existing family-planning programs evident from the national reports, the tone of the volume strikes a more optimistic note when examining the operational aspects: the world already possesses the knowledge of how to curb unregulated and unrestricted growth; it remains to convince the world to adopt new technologies now available, primarily the adoption of birth-control measures by the vast majority.

VOGT, WILLIAM. **People! Challenge to Survival.** New York: Sloane, 1960, 257 p.

If any single individual can be credited with making the general public aware of the so-called population explosion, that person was very probably William Vogt. In numerous articles and speeches, in an influential earlier volume, **Road to Survival,** and finally in the present work, Vogt trumpeted unpalatable truths and awkward questions long before it was socially acceptable to do so. His consistent theme was one of ecological derangement and reproductive madness: that unconsciously or otherwise we have been inflicting major, perhaps irreparable, damage upon our delicate habitat, and that our recent terrific surge in numbers, and the prospect of even more in the future, implies disastrous social as well as physical consequences. Throughout all this, one hears the voice of an ecologist, saying (years before such a notion became fashionable), "The habitat is more important than the species that lives in it—a point that anthropocentric *Homo* finds hard to accept."

This work is calculated to alarm people and to force them to think about the ethics of parenthood. It does so by means of several loosely written, poster-style, even anecdotal chapters that shrilly belabor the evils of irresponsible human proliferation. The book also, perhaps inadvertently, tends to raise the hackles of most scholars with its heavy-handedness and occasional careless treatment of fact. In two pivotal chapters, dramatic contrasts are drawn between the grim outlook in India and the nearly idyllic situation in Scandinavia, where a low, carefully con-trolled fertility pattern has helped produce a balance between people and resources at a high level of civilization—one that is difficult to duplicate in other places or eras. What is perhaps most notably innovative about this volume is a strong insistence on the necessity for halting population growth in the advanced nations, and especially in the United States. In this respect, as in others, Vogt was ahead of his time.

MUDD, STUART, *ed.* **The Population Crisis and the Use of World Resources.** The Hague: W. Junk, 1964, 562 p. (Bloomington: Indiana University Press, dis-tributor.)

This volume, part of a series sponsored by the World Academy of Art and Science, is premised on the assumption that a profound ecological disequilibrium has been brought about by the worldwide application of scientific medicine and public health to reduce death rates without a corresponding reduction of birth rates. The purpose of the book is to offer a balanced discussion of both population and resources by a number of distinguished scholars and public figures. The editor disclaims any attempt to solve the problems posed but does express the hope that some useful guidelines toward rational policies may be offered.

The book is divided into two main parts. The first deals with the population crisis under various headings; the second with the use of world resources. Among the contributors are Bertrand Russell, Julian Huxley, Joseph Spengler, Eugene Black, Hermann Muller, Roger Revelle and Philip Hauser. Most of the papers contributed to the book have either been published previously or have been given as speeches.

As a guide to action the book is inadequate and could have benefited considerably from stronger editorial commentary. The contributions are too uneven in length and quality to provide more than a first introduction to some aspects of world population problems—a comment which should not be allowed to obscure the excellence of some individual papers. For introductory purposes, an abridged edition, Larry K. Y. Ng and Stuart Mudd, *eds.,* **The Population Crisis: Implications and Plans for Action** (Bloomington: Indiana University Press, 1965, 364 p.) is equally valuable.

BROWN, HARRISON SCOTT and OTHERS. **The Next Hundred Years: Man's Natural and Technological Resources.** London: Weidenfeld, 1957, 208 p.

This book stemmed from the concern of Harrison Brown with the application of modern scientific knowledge. Brown, a geochemist who worked on the development of the atomic bomb, helped organize the Emergency Committee of Atomic Scientists and in 1954, after observing living conditions in the British West Indies, published a book on resources and population problems, **The Challenge of Man's Future** (New York: Viking, 1954, 290 p.). **The Next Hundred Years** is based on a series of symposia offered to corporation executives interested in peering into the future. Brown contributed an analysis of the spread and intensification of American industrial culture through the world. James Bonner, a biologist, took up the problem of how to feed increasing numbers of people. John Weir, a psychologist, analyzed the intellectual resources of the world in light of the need to produce creative solutions to technical problems. The demand for raw material in an industrial society, rates of industrialization, world food production, patterns of agricultural change, and energy and manpower resources are among other topics reviewed with the help of numerous charts and diagrams. The conclusions are remarkably optimistic, particularly concerning the lack of technological obstacles to human improvement. The authors' faith in behavioral science as a cure-all for problems science and technology cannot solve is neither carefully evaluated nor borne out by experience to date.

OSBORN, FAIRFIELD. **The Limits of the Earth.** Boston: Little, Brown, 1953, 238 p.

This is the second of two well-received works by the late Fairfield Osborn. The first, **Our Plundered Planet** (Boston: Little, Brown, 1948, 217 p.), was among the best and most dramatic books appearing after World War II to warn of the growing imbalance between human populations and their consumption of the earth's resources. In **The Limits of the Earth,** Osborn linked his concern over the man-land ratio to another pressing problem of the postwar world, the cold war: "The determining question in the future of civilization is whether the supply of resources to be gained from the earth can prove adequate not only to meet the basic needs of people but to support the complex requirements of modern culture and economy." He warned that if the democracies failed to provide the resources necessary for the well-being of people, communism would find ever greater success as the social and political manifestation of need and want.

The book is particularly valuable for its analysis of world population problems on a regional basis, a procedure that does much to qualify a frequently oversimplified view of population issues. Osborn's conclusion emphasizes that the goal of a humanitarian solution to world population problems is not just the quantity but also the quality of living in the future. His call for decisions about the quality of living sustainable within the limits of the earth remains too much ignored. This work of a prophetic leader can be recommended to the generation that must take action.

JACKS, GRAHAM VERNON and WHYTE, ROBERT ORR. **Vanishing Lands: A World Survey of Soil Erosion.** New York: Doubleday, 1939, 332 p.

This book, published in England as **The Rape of the Earth** (London: Faber, 1939, 313 p.), came out in the aftermath of the "Dust Bowl" catastrophes of the inter-war period and is a survey of considerable breadth and depth. A major aim was to show that while accelerated soil erosion in the United States had received the most publicity, the problem was serious in many parts of the world, with roots in antiquity. In the authors' view, Africa was the worst hit of the continents, generally speaking. The book discusses specific features of various environments, from the loess of China to the salt bush of Australia, noting as a major conclusion that the problem had recently become intensified, especially through the increasing mechanized plowing of the semiarid margins of the New World. There are several chapters on conservation techniques and a series of studies on the economic, political and social consequences of erosion, with examples from various countries. National remedial plans, such as the Tennessee Valley Authority and the grandiose Russian plans of the day for river control, are appraised and compared.

The approach of the book is ecological in the best sense, presaging much of the thought that has recently taken hold of American opinion. Readable in style and authoritative and urgent in tone without being unduly sensational, this is still an excellent source book, with a much-needed world view to provide perspective on one of the more serious of our long-term problems.

VOGT, WILLIAM. **Road to Survival.** New York: Sloane, 1948, 335 p.

William Vogt, who has for a number of years been director of the Planned Parenthood Federation, was by training and experience an ecologist and ornithologist. A trip to the Guano Islands on the coast of Peru in 1939, as consulting ecologist to the Peruvian Guano Administration, seems particularly to have aroused Vogt's interest in the relationship between human populations and their environment. At the time this book was published, it was hailed as more fundamental and comprehensive than any previous work on the subject. Although this judgment would now need revision, it is still well worth reading today.

The book is basically optimistic, though Vogt was accused by many of being a pessimist. The questions raised about population and resources are still highly relevant, and Vogt's notion of the earth as a sanctuary without an exit is strikingly similar to the recent notion of the earth as a spaceship. In the 20 or so years since 1948 man has repeatedly been seen in Vogt's terms as a multiplying species that, out of ignorance, is engaged in the suicidal process of making his sanctuary uninhabitable. **Road to Survival** is a landmark study in the rapidly growing awareness of this dilemma, and though the message has been repeated many times few have stated it as cogently or as well.

BORGSTROM, GEORG. **The Hungry Planet.** New York: Macmillan, 1965, 487 p.

When, after World War II, a relatively small number of scholars and writers began to issue warnings about the growing imbalance between world population and resources, the tone of their argument was generally urgent but reasonable. While most people remained ignorant of or unconcerned about the problem, a steadily growing number became informed, excited and even agitated. A feeling of desperation pervades Georg Borgstrom's book. His tone is strident, his style polemical and his criticism of existing institutions sweeping. He assembles impressive evidence about world population trends and treats many countries individually in separate chapters, discussing food and water supplies and the dilemma posed by modern technology, but in the end it is the style rather than the substance of his argument that returns to plague the reader. His questions are good ones, but the answers tend to ignore the complexities he describes.

SCHARLAU, KURT. **Bevölkerungswachstum und Nahrungsspielraum: Geschichte, Methoden und Probleme der Tragfähigkeitsuntersuchungen.** [Population Growth and Food Provision Capacity: The History, Methods and Problems of Population Carrying Capacity Studies.] Bremen-Horn: Dorn (for the Akademie für Raumforschung und Landesplanung), 1953, 391 p.

Scharlau's book is an encompassing review of the literature on the earth's population and capacity to provide food, valuable not only for the scope of the review but also for the author's objective yet analytical evaluations of the ideas and methods of study in the field. The analysis revolves perforce around Malthus and the Malthusian, anti-Malthusian and neo-Malthusian schools of thought. The history of our thought on population and overpopulation appears as a stream of changing values, alternating between optimism and pessimism. Though generally free of bias, Scharlau appears to be among the anti-Malthusian optimists.

Besides its usefulness as a comprehensive and objective review of literature in the field, the book also contains some original contributions. Scharlau's definition and use of the terms "overpopulation," "population density optimum," "relative over-population," "absolute overpopulation" and "population pressure" are excellent analytical tools. In the last chapter, the author reaches the interesting conclusion that "the present production of food does not satisfy the actual needs of the world but rather only its procurement ability." In other words, there is plenty of food for the "economic demand," although there is not enough for the absolute demand.

As a methodological study, there is no doubt that this book will remain a must on the shelves of any serious German-reading scholar in the field.

Human Geography

SPENCER, J. E. and THOMAS, WILLIAM L. **Cultural Geography: An Evolutionary Introduction to Our Humanized Earth.** New York: Wiley, 1969, 591 p.

This highly innovative work, rich in fact, ideas and speculation, departs sharply from earlier textbook traditions in human geography in terms of both intellectual quality and angle of approach. In fact, the volume might be fairly characterized as the magnum opus of two thoughtful geographers, masquerading as an undergraduate text but really addressed to their peers and the brighter young student.

The dominant question throughout the book is the patterning of man's occupancy of the earth—the arrangements within and among human communities and between man and habitat—as it has been evolving through time. It is the emphasis upon an evolutionary framework and a concern with process that makes this book unique and challenging in the geographic literature. As might be expected, Spencer and Thomas are intensely concerned with the implications of the "population spiral" and the social and ecological consequences of man's dominance of the earth; without resorting to hysteria, they provide some intriguing perspectives and food for thought. The maps, either freshly compiled for this work or redrawn from a wide variety of sources, are uniformly well executed, and many are totally unique in subject matter. The photographs, best passed over in silence in most geographic treatises, are thought-provoking and stunning, in the best sense of the term. All in all, this is one of those exceedingly rare books in the geographic realm that have the capacity to trigger major changes in the reader's thought.

BROEK, JAN O. M. and WEBB, JOHN W. **A Geography of Mankind.** New York: McGraw-Hill, 1968, 527 p.

The publication of **A Geography of Mankind** was definitely an occasion for rejoicing, for it was the first general, English-language text on human geography that could be recommended to the college student or the intelligent layman without serious misgivings. Its predecessors were potboiling mediocrities or worse, when they were not tracts pushing rather extreme philosophic viewpoints. Although the gusty winds of change that have been radically transforming the style and substance of human geography during the past few years have scarcely ruffled the surface of this volume, it is none the less an intelligent, stimulating, carefully structured and well-written treatise: a mature and informative statement of many—but hardly all—of the significant ideas and supporting facts in the field, and one obviously aimed at the undergraduate student.

The 20 chapters are arranged into five sections, the first of which is methodological and historical in character, thoughtfully defining the geographic viewpoint and the key concepts in cultural geography, then sketching in the historical geography of technological development from the paleolithic to the present. The second section offers discussion of four dimensions of cultural diversity—racial, linguistic, religious and political—and of the identity of larger cultural realms, all of which are uniquely valuable for the student seeking brief statements on these matters. Except for a very welcome chapter on the geography of economic development, the third section, dealing with livelihood patterns, is relatively humdrum, revealing the authors' lack of a really lively interest in economic geography. The concluding sections, which cover rural and urban settlement and the spatial and temporal dynamics of population, are extremely useful. In fact, the reader would have difficulty in locating a better brief statement on current geographic patterns and problems of a demographic character.

The many maps and diagrams merit special commendation. Not only are they all handsomely and specially created or redrawn for this volume, but a good many cover topics not otherwise readily available in graphic form. The serious student should not overlook the excellently chosen array of books and articles listed at the end of each chapter.

HUNTINGTON, ELLSWORTH. **Mainsprings of Civilization.** New York: Wiley, 1945, 660 p.

The late Ellsworth Huntington, long associated with geography at Yale University, was one of the profession's most scholarly environmentalists. As early as 1915, he had established his reputation with the monumental volume **Civilization and Climate** (New Haven: Yale University Press, 3rd ed., 1924, 453 p.). In **Mainsprings,** Huntington expands upon earlier concepts in an attempt to analyze the role of biological inheritance and physical environment in influencing the course of history. Though today some of his ideas would be untenable and regarded as "unscientific," the remarkable value of the book lies in the author's imaginative range of interest. In its attempt to demonstrate the selective process in history together with the way in which variations in inheritance and physical environment are related to the growth of culture and the advance of civilization, **Mainsprings** deserves a place in classical geographic literature.

It was Huntington's belief that civilization moves forward along certain definite lines, the ratio of advance varying from time to time and place to place. Civilization, he noted, begins when people learn to practice agriculture, live in permanent communities, establish a definite form of government and acquire the art of writing. But civilization is more than a condition; it is also a process. Due to special difficulties imposed by the geographic environment, civilizations in some areas of the earth advanced up blind alleys; there the environment was deficient in possibilities. On the other hand, those societies that are able to make choices make progress so that great civilizations take shape, as for example in China, among the Mayas, in Persia and in Western Europe.

DEFFONTAINES, PIERRE. **Géographie et Religions.** Paris: Gallimard, 1948, 439 p.

This comprehensive study of geography and religion is considered a classic of French geographical literature for originality of approach and completeness of coverage. Published in 1948, it reflects the scheme suggested 40 years earlier by Jean Brunhes for the study of essential facts of human geography—the examination of habitation, settlements, use of resources, movements and style of life and civilization.

Religion is used by Deffontaines as a benchmark and determinant of inhabitation and settlement types, analyzed as a powerful force in population structure, distribution and movements, and presented as an influential agent in the use of resources and style of life, cause of regional interaction, transfer and exchange. His stress on the determining role of religion has procured for the author the label of "cultural determinist." The great wealth of information has to a degree been forced into the preconceived framework and examined, with some repetitions, from different angles, without losing the train of reasoning that aims to explain the occurrences of variations of human phenomena associated with religious beliefs.

The work has been supplemented by other studies, although it remained unchallenged until the appearance of the behavioral studies in geography for which Deffontaines has provided ample empirical and material evidence, though not the theoretical framework. The serious defect of the book is the one-sided assessment of the relationship between geography and religion, in which only the impact of religion on the geographical character of the region has been examined while the influence of physical and human geographical factors upon religion has been omitted.

SOPHER, DAVID E. **Geography of Religion**. Englewood Cliffs: Prentice-Hall, 1967, 118 p.

A landmark item, whose brevity belies the richness and originality of its contents. Despite the obvious importance of religion in fashioning the behavior of men and in molding their mental and terrestrial landscapes, the amount of geographic analysis directed toward this topic has been remarkably slight. Indeed, this is the first book-length treatment in the English language, and by far the best in any. Two factors help account for this apparent oversight: the scarcity and weakness of quantitative data and the inherent intractabilities of religious phenomena for the objective analyst.

In gathering and arranging evidence from a wide variety of sources for his pioneering volume, Sopher has stressed two pervasive themes: the internal spatial attributes of religious systems, and the interplay between religion and other elements as expressed in landscape and behavioral terms. Under the latter rubric are included a broad variety of items, most notably such topics as agricultural, dietary and calendric practice, architecture and settlement morphology and political relations. Sopher has devised a useful typology of religions, the fundamental division being that between the few large universalizing religious systems and the many ethnic varieties. He has traced their spatial careers, the ways in which they are internally segmented and territorially interdigitated; and he has indicated the many ways in which religious systems intersect with other geographic systems. There are only 13 maps but, like the text, they are densely packed with meaning. This is clearly essential reading for the serious student in the fields of either religion or human geography.

GINSBURG, NORTON, *ed.* **Atlas of Economic Development.** Chicago: University of Chicago Press, 1961, 119 p.

The 48 plates in this atlas present a great variety of items that can be quantified and plotted in terms of national units and are thought to be related to the general level of economic performance of a society. This, then, is the first great pioneering effort to map differential levels of socioeconomic achievement on a world scale and also those positive and negative genetic factors that appear to help mold those contours. It is also one of the more valiant attempts to pin down the concepts "developed" and "underdeveloped." Although the maps leave much to be desired aesthetically, they are elegant in a methodological or statistical sense. Many deal with familiar topics—*e.g.* GNP, consumption of energy and steel and per capita cultivated area; but the large group covering population topics are worth noting (quite apart from their relevance to the main theme of the atlas) because of the scarcity of such drawings as those showing literacy, primary and post-primary school enrollment, daily per capita caloric intake or relative numbers of physicians and dentists.

Given the veritable explosion in developmental studies over the past decade, it should now be possible to broaden the range of indicators of socioeconomic status and of relevant genetic factors amenable to cartographic treatment and to update the figures used for the plates in the present atlas. It seems doubtful, however, whether such a revision would very greatly alter the patterns or conclusions achieved in this epochal contribution.

The brief appended essay by Brian Berry on "Basic Patterns of Economic Development," in which four international patterns are detected and mapped by rather advanced methods is correctly regarded as a classic statement.

LACOSTE, YVES. **Géographie du Sous-Développement.** Paris: Presses Universitaires de France, 1965, 285 p.

As the first major essay by a geographer on the nature and implications of socioeconomic underdevelopment, this volume is noteworthy both for its intrinsic merits and for the fact that such an inaugural statement should have come so belatedly. Its only significant predecessors are two works edited by Norton Ginsburg: **Essays on Geography and Economic Development** (Chicago: University of Chicago Press, 1960, 173 p.) and **Atlas of Economic Development.** This prolonged neglect by geographers of an intensely geographic phenomenon has historic and philosophic causes too complex for a brief note.

Lacoste's volume must be classed as a *prologomena* to the geographic study of the subject and a rousing programmatic declaration rather than as any sort of definitive treatise. Thus it is long on theory and definition but short on local specifics. The closely reasoned definitional discussion is of major value to all social scientists in its incisive critique of earlier characterizations of underdevelopment and their partial or total rejection; in the strong emphasis upon the recency and historical uniqueness of the present-day phenomenon; and in the fact that its essential features override the vast physical, cultural, political and social diversity of the less advanced communities of the world. The concepts of imbalance, dislocation, the pathological impact of aggressive, advanced nations upon indigenous societies and economies, or, most generally, an untranslatable *distorsion* recur constantly. In essence, Lacoste claims, underdevelopment must be defined as a persistent *distorsion* between a relatively rapid demographic growth and a relatively slow expansion in the resources effectively available to the population.

BLACHE, JULES. **L'Homme et la Montagne.** Paris: Gallimard, 1933, 190 p.

This study follows in the tradition of the distinctive French school of human geography and particularly that of Raoul Blanchard, professor at Grenoble, who wrote the preface. The general aim was to take a comparative look at the various activities and particular problems of mountain folk throughout the world. The topics described in detail include transhumance and pastoralism in general, depopulation, hydroelectricity and, to some extent, tourism. About half the book is devoted to the Alpine type of mountains, mainly in Eurasia, a predilection that stems from the Grenoble school. The approach might be broadly characterized as cultural and focused on the *genre de vie* theme of the French school. Although it is not surprising that this study did not uncover any startling universal generalizations, it is full of interesting detail and expresses a sort of philosophy of man as an inhabitant of mountainous regions.

Although M. Blache is rather scrupulous in eschewing deterministic interpretations about the influence of environment on man, the choice of topic illustrates nevertheless the strong fascination that situations of highly constricted natural habitats have for the French, and other geographers of the day. Even though the pace of urbanization has accelerated in the meantime and the difficult environments have continued to be depopulated, the curiosity about life in the mountains, in the Arctic and other far reaches of human settlement is a natural one and persists.

BOWMAN, ISAIAH. **Geography in Relation to the Social Sciences.** New York: Scribner, 1934, 382 p.

Bowman's volume was one of the early significant statements by geographers concerned with the nature of their discipline and its relationship to the social sciences as a whole. While only one of the seven chapters is explicitly organized around the techniques of the geographer, the entire volume is essentially a development of geographic perspectives and methods as tools for use in the solution of societal problems. Bowman's humility as a geographer and his commitment to interdisciplinary efforts is evident in his assertion that "no one discipline can furnish the whole analysis"—an assertion even more timely today than when written. It is clear from his selection and development of examples, which range in time from Strabo to Sauer, that Bowman had already adopted the explanatory perspective that Harold Sprout was later to identify as cognitive behaviorism.

The contemporary student of geography will find Bowman's volume to be primarily a contribution to its history. Neophytes who have tended to reject a history of the discipline that they have construed as dominated by deterministic or environmentalistic rhetoric should be pleasantly surprised with the freshness of a work in which the author asserts that "the geographer of today [the 1930s] is primarily interested in breaking down the older generalizations of his subject into the working realities of life as a dynamic thing." Given the emerging emphasis on environmental studies, Bowman's volume may finally, a third of a century after publication, have an appeal to the audience of social scientists for which it was originally designed.

POLITICAL THEORY

See also Theory of International Relations; Methodology, p. 3.

FRIEDRICH, CARL JOACHIM. **Man and His Government: An Empirical Theory of Politics.** New York: McGraw-Hill, 1963, 737 p.

This is a book that synthesizes and sums up a lifetime's work in the study of politics. Professor Friedrich has been responsible for distinguished contributions in nearly all fields of political science: political theory, comparative politics, international relations, constitutional law, to name only the most outstanding. In this work, he has attempted to present in a coherent and systematic form some general conclusions drawn from "the political experiences of mankind." The ambition and scope of his enterprise is indicated by a brief listing of some of the major topics discussed: the political person and the political act, power, rulership, legitimacy, justice and law, equality, élites and freedom, the political order, bureaucracies and parties, sovereignty, empire and federalism, tradition, revolution and reform.

Although Professor Friedrich's work distills and orders considerable recent work in political science (including his own), and although he is very much in the empirical school (as his subtitle indicates), **Man and His Government** is in some ways quite untypical of contemporary political science. At the very beginning of his work, he rejects the fact-value dichotomy and asserts the inseparability of what is referred to today as normative and empirical political theory. His very approach, while empirical, tends to be historical and concrete rather than abstract and quantitative. Strewn throughout the work are cogent criticisms of Weber, Parsons and Almond. Nor does he hesitate to employ currently unfashionable terms such as statesmanship and wisdom. As a book which impressively displays this latter quality combined with immense erudition, it will probably be consulted for a long time.

ELLIOTT, WILLIAM YANDELL. **The Pragmatic Revolt in Politics.** New York: Macmillan, 1928, 557 p.

W. Y. Elliott's book demonstrates what can perhaps be described as the intellectualist fallacy in political science: the belief that political behavior is a function of political philosophy, that theories of the state produce the behavior of states. Thus he reasons that communism, syndicalism and fascism are the fruits—or perversions—of pragmatic philosophy. The threat posed by these movements can be met, he argues, by what he describes as the "co-organic" theory of the state—which is in fact constitutionalism rooted in the ideal of community.

The goal of such an argument is twofold. First, it is to provide a defense against the totalitarianism of the pragmatic progeny, and second, to embody in the theory of liberal democracy the ideas of the pragmatists that could not be dismissed, most notably that of the significance of myth.

The intellectual fascination of such an exercise is great. But it is offset to some degree by the air of unreality which pervades such a study. The philosophers exchange their tablets on Olympus while the world proceeds about its business, heedless, at their feet.

And, of course, the irony of the situation lies in the fact that Elliott, like Laski, MacIver and others, nursed the belief that he was engaging in applied political science, influencing events by the precision of his logic and strength of his evidence. In every case it was bad political science, and in some, not even good philosophy. One cannot help, however, a twinge of envy for the civility and gentility of it all.

LASKI, HAROLD JOSEPH. **The State in Theory and Practice.** New York: Viking, 1935, 299 p.

Harold Laski was no mean practitioner of political science as applied technology. The aims of the discipline, although it is perhaps premature to describe political science in the 1930s as such, were for Laski and others more hortative than heuristic. The goal was the good state, the good law and the good life—not surprising, really, for the background of the English political scientist was, of course, classical philosophy.

Thus in this book it is not enough to demonstrate the flaws in the metaphysical theory of the state as advanced by Hegel and Bosanquet; he must advance a theory and a program of his own, the aim of which is to provide a solid defense against the rising tide of fascism. The premises of Laski's argument are proletarian, the modus operandi a root-and-branch assault on the liberal-capitalist economic order, and the result a vigorous exercise in applied political science.

For Laski the essence of the state "is its power to employ coercion . . . to enforce the will of that group or groups which control the government." Those in the state excluded from ownership must seek to change the system by using the power of the state "to redefine the system of ownership." It is best fitted in the category of building bridges to a better world—or to the New Jerusalem as the Labor Party hymn has it.

MACIVER, ROBERT MORRISON. **The Web of Government.** New York: Macmillan, 1947, 498 p.

Spurred by the events of his own time which seem to him ominous, the political philosopher bends his efforts to the large-scale task of defending the old values or advancing the new. For Plato it was the imminent decay of Athenian social structure; for Hobbes the unrest wrought by civil war; for R. M. MacIver the awesome and growing presence of government in human life.

The Second World War brought about a marked increase in government activity; peace did not produce any very significant diminution. MacIver viewed the growth of government power with alarm. Beginning "at the beginning," arguing from first principles, he examines the basis and structure of authority, forms of government, the state in international affairs and concludes that "there is grave peril when government usurps control over the myths of the community, especially since government is now armed with powers more formidable than before."

The argument is a full-fledged statement of the liberal premise of democracy which finds its cause in the resistance of government intervention in the cultural and economic spheres of life and is a stout defense of the notion of "community" as opposed to "state." Within this context myth is functional in the community, dysfunctional when attached to the state.

This book is emphatically not the product of the sociologist as pamphleteer, however; it is a statement of the intellectual and emotional commitment of the sociologist as philosopher. It is the product of an era when the academic function was seen to include the responsibility to synthesize, teach and lead, but always from the academic framework.

EASTON, DAVID. **The Political System: An Inquiry into the State of Political Science.**
New York: Knopf, 1953, 320 p.

David Easton can perhaps be described as the "father" of systems theory in
political science in the sense that Talcott Parsons fills that role for sociology. In this
book he surveys American political science with a view to "the construction of
systematic theory, the name for the highest order of generalization." In it he
attacks what he describes as "historicist preconceptions" and proposes the alternative of a conceptual framework or general theory as a way of providing criteria by
which political scientists may judge the relevance of data which confront them.

He does not, in this volume, attempt to provide that general theory. He is
content with the elucidation of definitions to enable political scientists to distinguish the political from the nonpolitical in order to begin moving toward the
construction of a general theory. His definition of politics was that it is concerned
with the "authoritative allocation of values." The elaboration of the systems analysis with which his name is inextricably linked came later in his subsequent
publications.

The Political System marked the beginning in many respects of a reëxamination
of political science as a discipline marked not by a variety of approaches which
admitted to the fold, as it were, lawyers, philosophers, historians, but as one with a
central, identifiable body of data and central scheme of analysis. The pace of
movement toward the discipline as a value-free science was quickened by the
appearance of Easton's thoughtful and careful examination of the state of the
discipline and his tentative indications of the direction in which he felt it ought to
move.

SABINE, GEORGE HOLLAND. **A History of Political Theory.** New York: Holt, 1937,
797 p.

As the title clearly indicates, Sabine's work covers the history of Western political thought from ancient Greece to modern fascism and communism and, as such,
stands as the final and full flowering of the historical-descriptive approach in
political philosophy. Sabine's approach was to relate the ideas of the great thinkers
to the social and political setting in which they were generated. And it must be
stated emphatically that he achieved this purpose better than any scholar before or
since. Indeed, few scholars have attempted to duplicate his feat.

The weaknesses of the approach become evident toward the end of the book,
particularly in those chapters that deal with communism and fascism-national
socialism, for it is in the context of recent or contemporary developments in
political thought that historical analysis must of necessity become faulty. Both the
availability and the reliability of historical evidence is clearly crucial. The measure
of philosophical "greatness" and of influence is less certain and the conclusions,
within the context of Sabine's overall approach, less reliable. The descriptive
aspect of the work, however, remains valuable and stimulating.

As a reliable guide to what was thought and the background of the thinkers from
Plato to Hegel, Sabine's work stands as a classic of its kind.

BURNHAM, JAMES. **The Managerial Revolution.** New York: Day, 1941, 285 p.

It must have been somewhere about halfway on his long odyssey from Marxism
to the conservative right that James Burnham paused sufficiently long to write this
book. Its Marxist origins are obvious in the primacy accorded to the relations of
production. The thesis of the book is that individual ownership of the means of
production is inevitably disappearing. But instead of giving rise to socialism and the
classless society, capitalism was being supplanted by the "managerial society." The
growth of large-scale organizations and technological developments rendered,
according to Burnham, the functions of management crucial and more distinctive
to the whole process of production, thereby giving rise to a new class in society:
the managers. They do not own the instruments of production, as capitalists
formerly did, but they will control them indirectly through their control of the state

which in turn will own and control the instruments of production. Examples of these emerging managerial societies, for Burnham writing in 1940, were Stalinist Russia, Nazi Germany and the American New Deal. All three constituted an attack on "individualism," "free enterprise," "economic opportunity" and preached instead the "state," "planning," "coordination," "socialism" and "discipline."

One of the problems with the book's thesis is that Burnham is fuzzy on how the managers actually exercise their political direction; he tends to assume the simple Marxist equation that economic power equals and is automatically translated into political power. He also ignores the fundamental differences in the political traditions and cultures of the various countries he characterizes as embryonic managerial societies. Nevertheless, **The Managerial Revolution** represents one of the first attempts, and a brilliant one, to construct a convergent model of advanced industrial society.

BURNHAM, JAMES. **The Machiavellians: Defenders of Freedom.** New York: Day, 1943, 270 p.

Books often represent attempts at self-education by their authors. The work under review typifies this perhaps more than most. After seven Trotskyist years, James Burnham was trying, in **The Machiavellians,** to shake off the grip of Marxism and forge a new world view, supposedly more "realistic." Substantively the book examines the theories of six men: Dante, as a counterpoint; then Machiavelli, Pareto, Sorel, Mosca and Michels. These last four, all of whom made their contributions at the end of the nineteenth and beginning of the twentieth century, Burnham places in the Machiavellian tradition. Allegedly, they all share a special view of politics inspired by Machiavelli's scientific method and relentless realism. Specifically, the "modern Machiavellians" are said to have derived from their master an élitist understanding of politics and the view that liberty, the right of opposition and democracy generally, depend upon power and not on any legal or constitutional arrangements. Freedom survives only when power is fragmented and dispersed, for "only power restrains power." Hence not the disciples of Locke or Rousseau, but the Machiavellians, as the subtitle of Burnham's book asserts, are the only true "defenders of freedom."

There is a great deal to quarrel with in Burnham's interpretations of the works he examines. The élitist theory, with which he endows Machiavelli, is certainly not there in the contemporary form he argues. Nor do Mosca and Michels, for example, wish to sever politics from ethics. In addition, his discussion of élitism generally lacks rigor and operational utility. However, one can still find in Burnham's thesis that democracy is essentially a function of open and competitive élites one of the earliest and best argued formulations of a pluralist theory of democracy.

DUVERGER, MAURICE. **Les Partis Politiques.** Paris: Colin, 1951, 476 p.

As Leon Epstein has written: "Duverger stands in relation to theories of party development much as Marx does in relation to broader social theories." And just as Marx has suffered the onslaughts of his critics while remaining relevant and useful for much of social science, so Duverger has come under attack from a variety of quarters while his work still constitutes one of the most germinal and comprehensive attempts to describe and analyze the nature and functions of political parties. Duverger, following the path blazed by Ostrogorski and Michels, approaches the study of parties from the perspective of structure and organization. Contemporary parties, he argues, "are distinguished far less by their programme or the class of their members than by the nature of their organization." It is organization, says Duverger, which explains the activity, influence and functions of parties.

Probably no greater testament to Duverger's efforts can be provided than by asserting that even his failures and flaws have been found interesting and productive. His importance to the study of political parties can be measured by the criticisms of his work; he simply cannot be ignored. Wildavsky, for instance, has incisively and persuasively criticized his methodology. Duverger's attempts to formulate "sociological laws," such as "the simple-majority single-ballot system favours the two-party system," and to make important generalizations, such as the two-party system corresponds "to the nature of things," must be considered doubtful, at the very least. Leon Epstein has recently and effectively challenged Duverger's assertion, based on his theory of "organizational contagion" from the left, that "vast centralized and disciplined parties . . . alone suit the structure of contemporary societies." Sartori, among others, has insisted on the necessity for a more refined and elaborate typology of party systems than that provided by Duverger. Yet despite these criticisms, which are largely legitimate, Duverger's book, published in translation as "Political Parties" (New York: Wiley, 1954, 439 p.), remains the most ambitious, systematic and fruitful attempt to describe, classify and explain what are the bones and sinews of contemporary politics: political parties.

BRECHT, ARNOLD. **Political Theory: The Foundations of Twentieth-Century Political Thought.** Princeton: Princeton University Press, 1959, 603 p.

Arnold Brecht was one of the countless German scholars who, forced to leave Germany by the Nazi takeover, took refuge in the United States. It would be difficult indeed to imagine social science in America without the rich and seminal contributions of these scholars. Professor Brecht, in this work, draws on half a century of observation, participation and reflection on two continents. His over-riding preoccupation in the book is to examine the genesis, explicate the theory, and survey the consequences of what he refers to as the "Scientific Method." His account of the origins of social science is very useful, examining as it does the influence of many European scholars whose works have not been translated into English.

Professor Brecht also attempts to formulate a definition of the scientific method and to explore both its assumptions and implications. The distinction of the scientific method, according to Brecht, is that it provides us with "intersubjectively transmissable knowledge." The positive consequence has been to give us immeasurably greater understanding and control over our natural and social world. The negative effect of the scientific method is that it does not allow its practitioners "to determine the superiority of any [moral] ends or purposes over any other ends or purposes in 'absolute' terms." Thus, "scientific value relativism," which is the position Brecht accepts, holds that the validity of ultimate standards of valuation cannot be established through scientific means. Scientific knowledge can contribute to the clarification of alternatives, by indicating that some choices are impractical or too costly, but as to ultimate questions of preference it is, and must be, silent.

While the assumption of a value-free social science has been increasingly called into question, Brecht's book clearly stands as a major work, which thoroughly and incisively analyzes the problem and examines the authorities on all sides of the question.

POWER; REVOLUTION

RUSSELL, BERTRAND RUSSELL, EARL. **Power: A New Social Analysis.** New York: Norton, 1938, 305 p.

The central theme of this influential work is that "the fundamental concept in social science is Power, in the same sense in which Energy is the fundamental concept in physics." Lord Russell argues against those who would reduce power to any one form (for example, economic power) and considers philosophies inspired by love of power to be ultimately self-refuting. Still, the multiplicity of forms of power that he considers—priestly power, kingly power, naked power, revolutionary power, economic power and power over opinion—become so all-inclusive as somewhat to undercut the concept as a tool of analysis. Appearing on the eve of the Second World War, the book now seems slightly remote because of the staggering and savage extensions of power that have afflicted later years, but it is important as a lucid, eminently reasonable effort to grapple with this undoubtedly central feature of international and domestic politics.

DE JOUVENEL, BERTRAND. **On Power.** New York: Viking, 1949, 421 p.

Together with Bertrand Russell's book on the same general theme, this is the most significant recent effort to grapple with the problem of power in societies. What most impressed, and disturbed, De Jouvenel, writing at the end of the Second World War, was the steadily growing power of the state in modern times. For all the advent of democracy and the presumption of popular control, power has not been held in check. The author's basic stance is conservative—"there must be a return to Aristotle, St. Thomas, Montesquieu"—but his views are informed by a profound sense of history combined with great lucidity. It is a valiant attempt to master the Minotaur.

His book **Sovereignty: An Inquiry into the Political Good** (Chicago: University of Chicago Press, 1957, 319 p.) is, as he says, a direct sequel to **On Power.** It is somewhat more difficult and less rewarding reading, but it forms an integral part of this earnest effort to deal with the refractory theme of public authority and its relation to liberty and the public weal.

WITTFOGEL, KARL AUGUST. **Oriental Despotism: A Comparative Study of Total Power.** New Haven: Yale University Press, 1957, 556 p.

This is one of those rare books that are important almost despite themselves. Although the reader is provided with an elaborately articulated table of contents, the actual course of the author's argument is quite meandering. Much of the discussion comprises learned excursions into societies remote in place and time, but Wittfogel's driving impulse is very contemporary and at times polemical. As a whole the book is representative of the years of intense cold war, years productive of numerous works emphasizing the fearful aspects of totalitarian power.

For several reasons the book carries great impact. In the first place, it is the culmination of decades of thought and research, and it displays the peculiar intellectual muscularity of a scholar who has wrestled long both within and against the Marxist cosmos. But centrally it is important in positing a type of social organization—oriental despotism or, more functionally, hydraulic society (*i.e.* based on the controls required for large-scale irrigation)—which creates a "state stronger than society" and massively enduring, a society that leaves for local autonomy only the scraps of a "beggars' democracy," a society in which terror and individual isolation are the norm. The relevance of all this to the more appalling political phenomena of our century is apparent.

It is a book that one may boggle at or quarrel with along the way. Is the hydraulic theme adequate to the author's thesis? Has he in fact scouted out the best path to an understanding of contemporary totalitarianism? The valuable feature of the book is that it does offer an identifiable thesis of major proportions. To judge from echoes one finds in subsequent literature, it is a work that has challenged the imagination and attention of other scholars in the field.

ECKSTEIN, HARRY, *ed.* **Internal War: Problems and Approaches.** New York: Free Press of Glencoe, 1964, 339 p.

In the flood of books on domestic political disorder and revolution that appeared in the early 1960s, this has become one of the more influential and frequently cited. It is not a particularly unified work, being a collection of independent essays addressed to a variety of topics. Still, the book represents a serious effort at relating "internal war" to social science theory, and it is the product of a distinguished group of contributors: Harry Eckstein, the editor, Talcott Parsons, Thomas Perry Thornton, Karl W. Deutsch, Arnold S. Feldman, Andrew C. Janos, William Kornhauser, Lucian W. Pye, Alexander Gerschenkron, Sidney Verba, Gabriel A. Almond, Marion J. Levy, Jr. and Seymour Martin Lipset.

HOBSBAWM, E. J. **Primitive Rebels: Studies in Archaic Forms of Social Movement in the 19th and 20th Centuries.** New York: Praeger, 2d ed., 1963, 208 p.

Despite the author's disclaimer that this brief book is not a work of "exhaustive scholarship," it fills an important gap in the study of social unrest. Hobsbawm is a most able social historian, and his grasp of the subject is obvious even in areas where he feels himself not a specialist. In brief, this is an analytical survey of "primitive" forms of social agitation that have, however, occurred in recent times in some of the remoter areas of Europe. More particularly, he deals with the tradition of social banditry (Robin Hoods), the Mafia in Sicily, various millenarian movements among the Italian and Spanish peasantry, the city mob, labor sects and rituals in social movements. Although Hobsbawm is probably right in his judgment that much of what he describes belongs to the "prehistory" of movements of protest, one finds a remarkable number of clues to behavior in major revolutions and to contemporary unrest in the third world.

BRINTON, CLARENCE CRANE. **The Anatomy of Revolution.** New York: Norton, 1938, 326 p.

First published in 1938, this has probably been the most widely read and influential of all studies on the structure and comparability of revolutions. Directing his attention to four great modern revolutions, the English, American, French and Russian, the author finds a fever chart to be the most convenient "conceptual scheme" in tracing the sequence of signs, symptoms, crises and convalescences. With much sensitivity to historical variety, he none the less urges that there is a discernible pattern to the progress of a major revolution. The American Revolution does not fit his anatomy very comfortably, but the question of the terminus of the revolutionary impulse in Russia is perhaps his most worrisome problem, a central concern in his successive revisions of 1952 and 1965. The book has been criticized for matters of specific detail and for its basic premise of the essential uniformities in revolutions. As is evident in his useful annotated bibliographical appendix, he is somewhat anti-intellectualistic in his approach. This is a corrective to an excess of ideology but presents a danger of underrating the particular flavor and substance of a revolution. The work remains, however, an excellent starting point for the study of revolution and enjoys the distinct advantage of being a pleasure to read.

ARENDT, HANNAH. **On Revolution.** New York: Viking, 1963, 343 p.

Crane Brinton was correct in his observation that this book is "poles apart from the approach" of his **Anatomy of Revolution,** but his wry observation that, if the one book makes sense the other is nonsense, does not give due credit to the notoriously protean nature of the subject: both books are valuable but operate in quite different intellectual universes. For Miss Arendt the problem of revolution (which she limits to the pathos of modernity, the search for political freedom and social justice) is essentially a single vast issue, unfolding in the course of the last two centuries. Her use of comparisons—the American and French Revolutions emerge as protagonists of two divergent, almost opposing lines of development—is chiefly as a device to provide the structure for her argument. Her world is centrally one of ideas and of words; she has a remarkable talent for using the thought of a single person or the evolution of a term as the vehicle for demonstrating a historical process. Not easy reading, the book has many important insights into the quandaries of the contemporary world.

CAMUS, ALBERT. **The Rebel.** New York: Knopf, 1954, 273 p.

No apology is needed for including here (if only as one example of his writings) this extended essay by the French journalist and novelist. For surely his was one of the most seminal minds of the years after the holocaust of the Second World War.

While this work may be described as a "philosophy of politics," it is neither technical nor theoretical but is an effort, with a penetration and clarity of mind that are astonishing, to "understand the times in which we live." His approach is through the theme of rebellion: "Rebellion though apparently negative, since it creates nothing, is profoundly positive, in that it reveals the part of man which must always be defended."

Certainly his perception of, and response to, the contemporary world is an important clue to changes in thought and action in recent years. At the end, however, his concept of rebellion is intimately linked to a sense of limit, of measure: "We all carry within us our places of exile, our crimes, and our ravages. But our task is not to unleash them on the world; it is to fight them in ourselves and in others."

BLACK, CYRIL E. and THORNTON, THOMAS P., eds. **Communism and Revolution: The Strategic Uses of Political Violence.** Princeton: Princeton University Press, 1964, 467 p.

This symposium represents a useful intersection of two themes that became prominent in the 1960s: the study of "internal war" (domestic violence, revolution, etc.) and the comparative study of communism. The particular aim of this book is "to describe the nature of the Communist experience in influencing political change by violent methods." Following an introductory section chiefly on communist revolutionary doctrines, the book is devoted to two major areas of inquiry: (1) the variety of domestic revolutions that may be seen as a direct outcome of the Second World War and (2) the subsequent development of communist revolutionary strategy throughout the world—Asia, the Middle East, Africa, Latin America and the "advanced" countries. The contributors are a distinguished group, but critical rather than friendly interpreters.

HALLGARTEN, GEORGE WOLFGANG FELIX. **Why Dictators? The Causes and Forms of Tyrannical Rule since 600 B.C.** New York: Macmillan, 1954, 379 p.

This study of the forms of dictatorship, which is intimately related to the problem of revolutions, follows Max Weber in attempting to establish some empirical norms of social behavior. In this instance the author discerns four basic types of dictatorship: the "classical," which would include such "saviors of society" as Caesar, Oliver Cromwell and Napoleon; the "ultra-revolutionary," comprising such diverse figures as Savonarola, Robespierre and Lenin; the "counter-revolutionary" (Lucius Cornelius Sulla, Admiral Horthy and General Franco); and the "pseudo-revolutionary," including D'Annunzio, Mussolini and Hitler.

While one might quarrel with some of his personal characterizations (for example, his portrait of Cromwell), and query the appropriateness of all his categories, his scheme definitely has coherence and a logical structure, and is certainly of value in the difficult job of comprehending (and perhaps anticipating) the appearance of tyrannical rule in a society.

CROZIER, BRIAN. **The Rebels.** Boston: Beacon Press, 1960, 256 p.

In a curious way this book is a victim of the author's own acute perception: the cluster of events that attracted his attention in the late 1950s became multiple centers of world attention in the 1960s—with corresponding floods of writing on each. Thus, much of what he has to say will appear quite familiar, occasionally outdated, or overshadowed by subsequent detailed research.

Still, the book retains an important value and unity precisely because of the author's early curiosity about the phenomenon of post-1945 insurrections and rebellions (chiefly anti-colonial). His areas of concern are principally Indochina, Malaya, the Philippines, Kenya, Cyprus, Algeria, Cuba, Palestine and the Suez Canal zone and, significantly, Hungary. Using the comparative method very fruitfully he directs his attention to rebel frustrations ("rebellions are made by rebels"), official shortcomings, the prelude to violence, and the uses and limitations of terrorism and repression.

For all the volume of comparative, reportorial and theoretical writing on revolts and revolutions in recent years, this work still enjoys a fresh quality. There is an excellent concluding chapter of reflections: "The date is all: in the year of rebellion no solution is politically possible (that, indeed, is why there is a rebellion); but earlier it might have been."

PHILOSOPHIES AND IDEOLOGIES

General

NORTHROP, FILMER STUART CUCKOW. **The Meeting of East and West: An Inquiry Concerning World Understanding.** New York: Macmillan, 1946, 531 p.

At the time of this book's appearance it was criticized both for being excessively intellectualistic—in deriving whole cultural patterns from the implications in the thought of selected individuals—and in refurbishing the bipolar East-West antithesis. These criticisms remain valid. It is evident that Northrop is essentially a philosopher, proceeding from the realm of ideas. The multifarious natures of both "East" and "West" have become increasingly apparent. Moreover, in certain key areas, notably in his discussion of Russian communism, his treatment is both inaccurate and unpersuasive. But despite these flaws, this is a major undertaking, a serious and intense effort to grapple with the basic conflicts of the contemporary world as it emerged from the horrors of the Second World War. The author's sense of concern, his intelligence, his search for breadth and for a deeper comprehension of diverse peoples and societies make it a continuing contribution.

SCHUMPETER, JOSEPH ALOIS. **Capitalism, Socialism, and Democracy.** New York: Harper, 3rd ed., 1950, 431 p.

This work by a brilliant Austrian-born economist has had an enormous influence in the academic world. As Schumpeter remarked in his 1942 preface, it is "an effort to weld into a readable form the bulk of almost 40 years thought, observation and research on the subject of socialism." The first part is a penetrating critique of Marxism, debatable at several points but providing one major interpretation—evolutionist at base—of Marx's thought. There follows an inquiry into the viability of capitalism, which he sees in danger of breaking to pieces under the pressure of its own success. He then discusses the question "Can socialism work?" (it can, in its fashion) and finally turns to a sketch of the major socialist parties. Since so many of Schumpeter's ideas have been absorbed into the mainstream, their originality may be less evident now than in the 1940s; the vigor and acuity of the man's perceptions and style remain apparent. It is a book one often refers to.

MOORE, BARRINGTON, JR. **Social Origins of Dictatorship and Democracy: Lord and Peasant in the Making of the Modern World.** Boston: Beacon Press, 1966, 559 p.

The title and subtitle of this book suggest its dual purpose. The author's explicit intent is to "explain the varied political roles played by the landed upper classes and the peasantry in the transformation from agrarian societies . . . to modern industrial ones." But behind this lies the much broader question of the roots of the democratic and dictatorial impulses of the twentieth century. The greater part of the book is devoted to relatively independent essays on the experiences of a selected number of nations: England, France, the United States (a quite interesting and controversial interpretation of the Civil War as "the last Capitalist revolution"), China, Japan and India. There are also several exceptionally interesting chapters of a more theoretical orientation on the democratic route to modern society, revolutions from above, the much vexed issue of peasants as a revolutionary force and finally a most challenging critique of the belief in gradualness and an underlining of the "costs of going without a revolution." In all, a work informed by an original mind at home in both sociology and history.

APTER, DAVID E., *ed*. **Ideology and Discontent.** New York: Free Press, 1964, 342 p.

Published in the mid-1960s, this volume of essays (the fifth in the "International Yearbook of Political Behavior Research" series) could hardly be a definitive treatment of the complex of subjects discussed. Still, by whatever combination of perception, organization and circumstances, it does provide a most illuminating introduction—in the sense of opening for subsequent exploration—to many issues that have proved to be of central interest. The authors range over such themes as "National Loyalties in a Newly Independent State," "Ideology and Modernization: The Japanese Case," "Ideological Foundations of Egyptian-Arab Nationalism," "Ideologies of African Leaders" and "America's Radical Right." The opening and concluding essays wrestle manfully with the meaning and content of the term "ideology" itself.

JOLL, JAMES. **The Anarchists.** Boston: Atlantic (Little, Brown), 1965, 303 p.

This is an exceptionally well-written, fair-minded study of those individuals and groups who are too frequently either dismissed as bearded throwers of bombs or are elevated to a secular sainthood. (Admittedly, some of the figures *are* bizarre enough for the most exotic taste.) After examining the thought and action of such early anarchists as Godwin, Proudhon and Bakunin, Joll turns to late nineteenth-century anarchist and terrorist manifestations, chiefly in Italy, Russia and France, and then to anarchism's twentieth-century crises and failures. Those include the confrontations with Lenin's Bolshevism, the abortive promise of anarcho-syndicalism in France and the United States (IWW) and the heroic and bloody years of the Spanish Civil War. For all his sympathetic approach, Joll is doubtful of the prospects of anarchism as a viable political solution in an industrialized, or industrializing, world. Yet its *jusqu'au boutisme* critique of governments and apparatuses seems likely to have a perennial appeal.

NOLTE, ERNST. **Three Faces of Fascism: Action Française, Italian Fascism, National Socialism.** New York: Holt, Rinehart and Winston, 1966, 561 p.

As the author observes, "as yet no comprehensive and overall account of fascism has been written." This, however, is an ambitious and thoughtful effort to trace and understand certain major strands of fascist thought in their historical setting. Starting with Charles Maurras and Action Française, as a kind of link connecting fascism with much older struggles, the author turns to the history and doctrines of Italian Fascism and German National Socialism. On the whole the stress is upon the realm of ideas. A final chapter, "Fascism as a Metapolitical Phenomenon," attempts to get at the fundamentals of fascism as "resistance to transcendence;" it is rather heavy going.

Totalitarianism

ARENDT, HANNAH. **The Origins of Totalitarianism.** New York: Harcourt, 1951, 477 p.

This has probably been the most influential single book on the theme of totalitarianism. It appeared at that excruciating juncture in the twentieth century when the task of absorbing and comprehending the horrors of the barely vanquished Nazi régime was compounded by the dark prospect of forthcoming conflict with Stalinist Russia: "This moment of anticipation is like the calm that settles after all hopes have died." Linking the Nazi and Stalinist phenomena as essentially identical and as transcending all traditional concepts of "left" and "right," Miss Arendt was instrumental both in preparing the way for a whole series of studies of totalitarianism and in challenging the adequacy of "common-sense" approaches to the malignancy of political pathology.

The book, in its style and tenor, is really an extended essay or, rather, three extended essays: on anti-Semitism (as a blatant outrage to common sense), on imperialism and the prewar "pan-movements" with their undermining of the nation-state, and on totalitarian movements and totalitarian régimes (her distinction between the two is important).

A subject of controversy at the time of its appearance, the book displays both enduring strengths and marked flaws after the passage of two decades. It seems doubtful that the identification of Nazism and Stalinism, for all the parallels, was adequate analytically. Miss Arendt tended to extrapolate unduly from the particular German experience. The post-Stalin evolution of the Soviet Union, for all the backing and hauling, suggests the need of a somewhat different approach to that country. Nor does her apocalyptic sense seem quite appropriate to the 1970s— perhaps because the world has become accustomed to cultivating its gardens on the slopes of the volcano. But whatever one's quibbles, the book remains charged with the perceptions of a highly trained and sensitive mind.

FRIEDRICH, CARL JOACHIM, *ed.* **Totalitarianism.** Cambridge: Harvard University Press, 1954, 386 p.

This volume is the product of a conference on totalitarianism held by the American Academy of Arts and Sciences in 1953. The papers submitted, and the discussion that followed, were by an outstanding array of talents, including George F. Kennan, N. S. Timasheff, Carl J. Friedrich, Alex Inkeles, Franklin H. Littell, Waldemar Gurian, Raymond Bauer, Erik Erikson, H. J. Muller, George de Santillana, Bertram Wolfe, Albert Lauterbach, J. P. Nettl, Karl Deutsch, Paul Kecskemeti, Harold D. Lasswell and Hannah Arendt.

Since totalitarianism, by definition, covers all aspects of human life, the themes of the conference were far-reaching and edged toward the all-inclusive. Perhaps for this reason the current reader may find the book a bit amorphous. The key term, totalitarianism, itself an object of repeated definitions throughout the conference, seems curiously, if inexplicably, dated by the passage of a few years. Still, the intellectual quality of the participants makes this most interesting reading, and the book as a whole well reflects what was a central preoccupation of many able minds in the mid-1950s.

FRIEDRICH, CARL JOACHIM and BRZEZINSKI, ZBIGNIEW KAZIMIERZ. **Totalitarian Dictatorship and Autocracy.** Cambridge: Harvard University Press, 1956, 346 p.

Among the numerous studies of totalitarianism that appeared in the 1950s, this is notable as an effort to provide a general descriptive theory of the phenomenon. Based upon a considerable body of empirical data, it also offers some quite broad generalizations concerning the nature of totalitarian dictatorship. It is the authors' contention that this form of régime is "historically unique and *sui generis*" and is not to be identified with earlier forms of authoritarian government. The six features which they single out as comprising the essential pattern are: "an ideology; a single party, typically led by one man; a terroristic police; a communications monopoly; a weapons monopoly; and a centrally directed economy." The bulk of the book is an extended examination of these features.

At time of writing, the authors felt not only that totalitarian dictatorship was a highly dynamic form of rule but that it was still in process of evolution and stood to thrive on the "endemic conditions" throughout the world that had brought it into being.

A second, revised, edition (1965), prepared by Friedrich, undertakes to take account of a decade's development, of new information and of other contributions in the field—but holds to the central themes presented in the first edition.

FROMM, ERICH. **Escape from Freedom.** New York: Farrar, 1941, 305 p.

Fromm was one of that extraordinary group of young German scholars of the late Weimar era who were forced into exile by the advent of Hitler. Trained in both sociology and psychoanalysis, he has tried persistently in his various writings to relate social processes and individual behavior. The influence of Marx and Freud is central, but his departures from both men have been a source of irritation to the more orthodox of both schools, and the validity of his particular synthesis of these two lines of thought is debatable.

This book, written in the midst of the Second World War, has, however, been extremely influential and has gone through many printings over the years. Indeed, in reëncountering its leading themes—man's isolation in the modern world, the authoritarian character, the effort to evade responsibility, the appearance of automaton conformity—one finds oneself in the midst of much of the intellectual currency of the postwar decades. A notable but hardly surprising exception is the absence of any discussion of Stalinism; Fascism and Nazism here represent the totalitarian extremes in the crisis of post-medieval man.

HOOK, SIDNEY. **Heresy, Yes—Conspiracy, No!** New York: Day, 1953, 283 p.

Although this book is made up of largely independent essays on a variety of topics, it possesses an essential unity, and it has stood up well against the passage of time. There are perhaps two principal reasons for its continuing pertinence. First, the issue of cultural and intellectual freedom—the central theme—was the subject of particularly intense debate and concern in the early 1950s, and although the cast of characters and some of the terms of debate have shifted considerably in subsequent years, the essential nature of the problem is excellently highlighted in the conflicts of those years. Second, Hook's own independence of mind, his capacity simultaneously to criticize both the "cultural vigilantes" and the "ritualistic liberals," gives an integrity to his own position. This, combined with his capacity for clear exposition—and an evident joy in skilled polemic—makes his writing of continued interest. For a younger generation of readers—interested in recapturing the temper of the early post-1945 years and particularly the much vexed and muddied issue of "domestic communism" in the last days of Stalinism—this is remarkably informative and may serve to dissolve some stereotypes. The title admirably expresses Hook's own position.

Marxism; Socialism

See also U.S.S.R.: Soviet Marxism, p. 661.

LABEDZ, LEOPOLD, *ed.* **Revisionism: Essays on the History of Marxist Ideas.** New York: Praeger, 1962, 404 p.

Through most of its history Marxism, like any total system, has been beset by heresies and presumed deviations from the true course of thought and action. One of the earliest and most significant of these was "revisionism," initially associated with the name of Eduard Bernstein, whose life and views were excellently analyzed by Peter Gay, **The Dilemma of Democratic Socialism: Eduard Bernstein's Challenge to Marx** (New York: Columbia University Press, 1952, 334 p.).

Taking off from Bernsteinian revisionism, this group of essays, by very competent scholars, treats a wide variety of persons and positions that have been deemed unorthodox. The first section deals largely with issues relating to the Russian Revolution, in such Marxists as Plekhanov, Rosa Luxemburg, Trotsky and Bukharin. On the more theoretical plane we meet such figures as Bogdanov, Deborin and Lukacs. The second half of the book is devoted to post-1945 manifestations of revisionism in Eastern Europe and among the New Left in Western Europe, the United States and Asia.

It is a complex picture, and, as the editor observes, "There is no one label which can be used to pinpoint the revisionist philosophers' position . . . they represent manifold philosophical tendencies."

WOLFE, BERTRAM D. **Marxism: One Hundred Years in the Life of a Doctrine.** New York: Dial Press, 1965, 404 p.

As Mr. Wolfe observes, this book stems from his work on the intellectual history of the Russian Revolution, studies which necessarily led him into many facets of the Marxist heritage and to an effort to define that heritage. His central emphasis is upon a multiple and really irreducible ambiguity in Marxism: "ambiguity in the spirit of Marx himself, ambiguity in the heritage he left, and ambiguity in those who claimed to be his heirs." This leads the author to a consideration of such dichotomies in Marxism as nationalism versus internationalism, war and peace, democracy versus dictatorship and to such episodes and institutions as the Revolution of 1848, the Paris Commune and the three Internationals.

LICHTHEIM, GEORGE. **Marxism: An Historical and Critical Study.** New York: Praeger, 1961, 412 p.

Although Marx is unmistakably a man of the nineteenth century, a consideration in this bibliography of his views and their evolution in subsequent years hardly needs justification. The literature on the subject is enormous, but certainly one of the best historical introductions is that by Mr. Lichtheim. His work is informed by a major central view: "That Marxism represents a link—possibly the most important link—between the French and the Russian Revolution, has a definite theoretical content, in addition to suggesting a particular understanding of European history between 1789 and 1917." Thus he is particularly concerned to understand Marx and Marxism within the concrete setting of political issues; but this, in his ability to get at the nub of crucial historical problems, gives his critical review a remarkably contemporary flavor. At the end, however, Lichtheim sees the Marxian system of thought and action as in a process of dissolution after 1918, being no longer adequate to the realities.

MITRANY, DAVID. **Marx against the Peasant.** Chapel Hill: University of North Carolina Press, 1952, 301 p.

In the course of his researches in the 1920s on the Rumanian peasantry, **The Land and the Peasant in Rumania,** David Mitrany became acutely aware of the deep-seated and active hostility between Marxist and populist-agrarian currents in Eastern Europe. In 1927 he produced an important essay, "Marx vs. the Peasant." A quarter of a century later, with Eastern Europe under the domination of Stalinist communism, he greatly expanded this essay. In a paperback edition appearing in 1961, he summarized developments in the years following Stalin's death. Throughout the years, however, Mitrany's position was remarkably stable and consistent: a real warmth, perhaps overly romantic, toward the peasant and the village way of life and a clear perception that the Marxist view of the agrarian cosmos was profoundly antipathetic. "In every instance . . . the Marxist agrarian idea has had to be applied by force and to rely on force for its survival, while the Socialists who wanted to remain democrats have in every instance had to abandon it." While the viability of "peasantism" in the twentieth century remains a very troubling question, Mitrany's critique retains its relevance.

For those particularly interested in some of the ramifications of this conflict in Eastern Europe in the 1920s, a valuable supplement to Mitrany is George D. Jackson, Jr., **Comintern and Peasant in East Europe, 1919–1930** (New York: Columbia University Press, 1966, 339 p.).

LUKACS, GEORG. **Geschichte und Klassenbewusstsein.** Berlin: Malik Verlag, 1923, 342 p.

This book, regarded by many as the most significant post-Lenin Marxist work of the twentieth century, has had a curious, almost subterranean history. Comprising a set of essays by a Hungarian-born but German-trained philosopher and literary critic, who joined the Hungarian Communist Party in 1918 and was a member of Béla Kun's government, it was immediately and repeatedly assailed by the Comintern and Soviet ideologues and was repudiated several times by Lukacs himself as an idealistic deviation, among other things. The original German edition, a collector's item for decades, has been republished as volume II of "Georg Lukacs Werke" (Neuwied and Berlin: Hermann Luchterhand Verlag, 1968). The author's 30-page foreword to this 1968 edition is of considerable interest respecting his own attitude toward the book. There is no English translation, and a French translation did not appear until 1960 ("Histoire et Conscience de Classe; Essai de Dialectique Marxiste," Paris: Les Éditions de Minuit, 1960, 381 p.).

And yet this is a major work in Marxist theory and has been an important if "heretical" influence. It carries to a remarkable extreme the old issue of proletarian "consciousness" versus workers' "spontaneity," upholding the need for consciousness and hence for the truth being found, not in the masses, but in the party. Moreover, by his thorough grounding in Hegelianism, Lukacs was able to reveal strands in Marx's thought that had been largely obscured in the nineteenth century. His influence has ranged from Karl Mannheim to a later generation of existentialists.

LANDAUER, CARL and OTHERS. **European Socialism: A History of Ideas and Movements from the Industrial Revolution to Hitler's Seizure of Power.** Berkeley: University of California Press, 1960, 2 v.

This is perhaps the most comprehensive survey of European socialism. Not particularly exciting in thought or style, it is an ambitious effort to bring under one cover the vast and rather loose-jointed evolution of socialist ideas and movements over a period of a century and a half. A former member of the German Social Democratic Party (which receives particular but not inappropriate attention), Landauer clearly reflects the more gradualist and conservative tradition within socialism. Although the British and Balkan socialist movements are omitted from the story, the author, with his associates, conscientiously covers a great deal of ground and seriously considers the succession of debates between socialist and non-socialist economists and amongst the socialists themselves. The book lacks the intellectual brilliance of a Schumpeter or the skill for dealing with ideas of a Lichtheim, but it is a solid contribution.

COLE, GEORGE DOUGLAS HOWARD. **A History of Socialist Thought.** New York: St. Martin's Press, 1953–60, 5 v. in 7 pts.

G. D. H. Cole died (in 1959) with the last volume of this major contribution still in draft, but it is astonishing that he should have come so close to the completion of this enormous work. While originally designed (and titled) as a history of socialist thought, it goes far beyond that to be a full-scale account of the socialist movement, both internationally and in a multitude of countries. Cole himself was an important figure in one of the currents of the movement, Guild Socialism. He defined his own position as among those "left-wing non-Communist Socialists who were strongly critical of reformist parliamentarianism." Certainly this involvement gives the book much of its vitality. Cole was a highly educated, morally sensitive man but not a profound political thinker; it is probably for the best that the work extends beyond "socialist thought" as such.

BRAUNTHAL, JULIUS. **History of the International.** New York: Praeger, 1967, 2 v.

This is a massive and largely successful attempt to achieve a comprehensive history of the successive efforts to create a workers' international. The first volume begins with a useful section on early forerunners in the late eighteenth and early nineteenth centuries, and then turns to the First and Second Internationals. The second volume deals with the shattering impact of the First World War and the split in the international socialist movement, and then follows the vicissitudes of the two rivals, the Labor and Socialist International and the Communist International, to their dissolution in the Second World War. (This tracing of the careers of both internationals in the inter-war years is a principal merit of the study.) The end was dismal in both cases. The socialist international expired in the spring of 1940, with a faint bleat for "lasting peace based on international cooperation." Stalin simply dissolved Comintern in 1943. The author's perspective is that of a "contemporary Socialist."

DRACHKOVITCH, MILORAD M., *ed.* **Marxism in the Modern World.** Stanford: Stanford University Press (for the Hoover Institution on War, Revolution, and Peace), 1965, 293 p.

The singular virtue of this collection of essays is the distinguished quality of its contributors. Raymond Aron reviews and comments on the major phases and crises of Marxist thought in the present century. Bertram D. Wolfe deals with Leninism, Boris Souvarine with Stalinism. Merle Fainsod discusses "Khrushchevism"— though one may doubt whether the latter will be elevated to the pantheon of "isms." Titoism (by Adam B. Ulam) and Maoism (by Arthur A. Cohen) seem more likely candidates as lasting variants in the Marxist tradition. Theodore Draper addresses himself quite subtlely to the question "What is the relationship between Castroism and Communism?": "Historically, then, Castroism is a leader in search of a movement, a movement in search of power, and power in search of an ideology." At the end Richard Lowenthal speculates on the prospects for pluralistic communism.

The general unity of the book, apart from the obvious coherence of the topics, lies perhaps in the fact that the majority of the authors have long been preoccupied with the subject, most at one time or another in their careers had a close connection with the communist movement, and all are essentially critics.

Communism

See also U.S.S.R.: Soviet Marxism, p. 661.

WETTER, GUSTAVO ANDREA. **Dialectical Materialism: A History and Systematic Survey of Philosophy in the Soviet Union.** New York: Praeger, 1959, 609 p.

The English translation of this major work has the advantage of incorporating revisions and additions not in the earlier Italian (1948) and German (1952) editions. Father Wetter, a Jesuit scholar, is admirably equipped to undertake the formidable task of presenting an extended exposition of dialectical materialism as it has developed in the Soviet Union. (The related body of historical materialism is touched on only in passing.) Serious about ideas, prepared to grant the seriousness and scope of the Marxist tradition (though seeing it ultimately as a perversion, anti-church), he provides what is probably the best, most philosophical book on the subject.

The first part is largely historical—tracing the evolution of dialectical materialism from its Hegelian roots, through Mark and Engels (he stresses the differences between the two), to the philosophical strands in Russian Marxism before and after the Revolution. Of particular interest is his view of the movement of Soviet thought under Stalin away from dialectics toward a pattern of concepts akin to the Aristotelian and scholastic traditions.

The second part is systematic and treats such themes as the conception of philosophy, the theory of matter, the laws of the dialectic, the theory of categories, theory of knowledge and the efforts of dialectical materialism to handle the central concepts of modern science.

While certain of these topics have been more thoroughly explored by other writers, this remains the classic study, an indispensable introduction to philosophical thought in the Soviet Union. Wetter has also written a useful, critical account of post-Stalin Soviet ideology: **Soviet Ideology Today** (New York: Praeger, 1966, 334 p.).

DANIELS, ROBERT VINCENT. **The Nature of Communism.** New York: Random House, 1962, 398 p.

In this rewarding effort to establish "what the Communist movement *is*," Professor Daniels, rather than attempting to reduce the phenomenon to any single formula or definition, is content to pursue his examination in a variety of settings, which actually do correspond to the multifaceted character of the movement. "We shall examine Communism first as the orthodox application of Marxist principles; next, as the creature of the Russian Revolution; then as a party conspiracy; as a struggle for world power; as a product of Russian history; as a rebellion against the West; as a form of the industrial revolution; as totalitarian society; and as a secular faith." The book provides numerous *aperçus* and some quite provocative interpretations along the way and has the singular advantage of giving the reader, and especially the non-specialist, a remarkably wide panoramic view.

The student of communism who is reluctant to look at the subject only from without and yet can find no adequate or even reliable communist history of the movement will find much of value in **A Documentary History of Communism,** edited by R. V. Daniels (New York: Random House, 1960, 2 pts. in 1 v.). This extensive selection of documents focuses chiefly on communist thought and doctrine, from Lenin's early writings in the 1890s down to the end of the 1950s. The materials cover domestic developments in Russian Social Democracy before and during the Revolution, in the international communist movement between the wars and in the communist sphere after 1945. Providing a brief introduction to each document, Daniels has shown a very sharp eye in selecting the most appropriate passages to illustrate the extraordinarily complex and schism-ridden evolution of the ideology.

DRAPER, THEODORE. **The Roots of American Communism.** New York: Viking, 1957, 498 p.
————. **American Communism and Soviet Russia: The Formative Period.** New York: Viking, 1960, 558 p.

These volumes, in the series on communism in American life of which Clinton Rossiter is general editor, relate the history of the American Communist Party from its origins at the end of the First World War to the ouster of Jay Lovestone in 1929. (Mr. Draper's continuation of the narrative to 1945 is currently in progress.) Both volumes are the fruit of painstaking research and are well, often dramatically, written. Despite the marginal character of American communism in the 1920s, such exhaustive treatment is warranted. The books catch the flavor of the radical left in those years, presenting a component, though a small one, of the international communist movement in the high days of Comintern and bring out effectively certain themes and qualities of American communism that were to persist into later decades. ("A rhythmic rotation from Communist sectarianism to Americanized opportunism was set in motion at the outset and has been going on ever since.")

The first volume, carrying the story up to 1923, deals with the background, establishment and early career of the Party. Of particular interest is the remarkably high ratio—about 90 percent in 1919—of very recent immigrants, still using their native language, who made up the initial membership. The English-speaking element soon came to provide the enduring core of leadership, but this shift was balanced by an increasing ideological and tactical dependence upon Moscow.

The second volume, as the title indicates, stresses this connection, especially in the setting of the hectic struggle for power among Lenin's lieutenants and their followers. By the end of the 1920s the policies of the CPUSA and the fortunes of its leaders seem to have become wholly dependent upon the twists and turns in the Soviet Union. It all makes for an absorbing if not very edifying story. In the course of his researches Mr. Draper uncovered one of the classic political utterances of the twentieth century. A Zinovievite remarked, after Stalin's victory over his sponsor: *"Eben habe ich entdeckt, dass ich sieben Jahre lang den falschen Arsch geküsst habe!"*

HOWE, IRVING and COSER, LEWIS. **The American Communist Party: A Critical History, 1919–1957.** Boston: Beacon Press, 1958, 593 p.

Viewed in retrospect, the authors' conclusion (written in 1957) that the history of the American Communist Party spanned the 38 years from 1919 to 1957 seems substantially correct. In consequence, their work possesses a real unity; the story has a beginning, a number of climaxes and an appropriate end. The final chapter, "Toward a Theory of Stalinism," strikes one as somewhat dated, but it is certainly central to the writers' preoccupations.

The researches of other scholars, especially Theodore Draper's works on the first decade of American communism and David Shannon's **The Decline of American Communism: A History of the Communist Party of the United States since 1945** (New York: Harcourt, 1959, 425 p.), have since added substantially to our knowledge. Nor are the two authors simply disinterested observers. Their own stance is perhaps best indicated by the dedication of their book to Ignazio Silone and Milovan Djilas. Although a number of judgments may be debated, it is a very satisfactory "effort to write a political, social, and cultural history" of the American Communist Party. The role of the party in espionage and penetration, while not disregarded, is not treated in this book.

LAQUEUR, WALTER ZE'EV and LABEDZ, LEOPOLD, *eds.* **Polycentrism: The New Factor in International Communism.** New York: Praeger, 1962, 259 p.

The term "polycentrism," at least as applied to the communist cosmos, was introduced by the Italian Communist, Palmiro Togliatti, in 1956, at the time of the uproar associated with Khrushchev's anti-Stalin campaign. It was set up as a goal to contrast with the monolithic, enforced unity associated with the Stalin years. The long-term fate of the concept and its application—the achievement of a type of flexible association of communist states capable of averting both centrifugal and centralizing impulses—remains an open question, as it does for most complex forms of social organization.

This book has the virtue of presenting a historical cross section of this question as of the early 1960s: a number of able scholars (writing initially for a special issue of the journal *Survey*) discuss the international and theoretical aspects of polycentrism, Russo-Chinese and Russo-Jugoslav relations, the situations in Eastern Europe, in the French and Italian Communist Parties and in the developing nations of Asia, Latin America, the Middle East and Africa. It is essentially an early "progress report," useful in its broad scope but sharp focus.

CAUTE, DAVID. **Communism and the French Intellectuals, 1914–1960.** New York: Macmillan, 1964, 412 p.

Despite the proletarian emphasis in Marxism, the role of intellectuals in the movement has been important from the beginning, was certainly heightened by the infusion, through Leninism, of the tradition of the Russian revolutionary intelligentsia, and has been a central question in communist movements since 1917. This work, through its choice of setting and the judicious perceptiveness of the author, is a particularly valuable contribution.

The book covers the years from the immediate origins of the French Communist Party in the anguish of the First World War to the confused period that witnessed the collapse of the Fourth Republic, de-Stalinization in Russia and the Hungarian Revolution. The treatment is essentially historical, and properly so, as the quite subjective elements involved in the relations of intellectuals to the Party are best understood as a process through time.

Beyond his general review, Caute undertakes three case studies: André Gide, André Malraux and Jean-Paul Sartre. The final section, a daring one under the heading "Intellectuals and the Intellect," grapples with the enormously intricate problem of what happens to thought, creativity and intellectual integrity through involvement in communism. Happily, the author is no reductionist in considering this important matter.

SETON-WATSON, HUGH. **From Lenin to Khrushchev: The History of World Communism.** New York: Praeger, 2d ed., 1960, 432 p.

Like a number of other students of Eastern Europe, Seton-Watson was necessarily driven to a study of communism as a consequence of the sovietization of that area after 1945, and his approach to a considerable degree is defined by his earlier field of interest. In some respects this is a complement to Borkenau's book on the communist movement, though it carries the story to the end of the 1950s, places less emphasis upon the Comintern (or its pale successor, the Cominform) and is centrally directed toward a comparative history of the "effort of Communists to win recruits, to seize and to wield power in their respective lands." As such it is a valuable introduction to the subsequently flourishing subfield of "comparative communism" and to the growing diversity within communist régimes and parties in the 1960s.

While some account is taken of the early post-Stalin years, the phenomenon of Stalinism, both within and beyond the borders of Russia, is clearly the center of the author's concern.

ALMOND, GABRIEL ABRAHAM and OTHERS. **The Appeals of Communism.** Princeton: Princeton University Press, 1954, 415 p.

This study, made soon after the Second World War, is concerned with "why people join the Communist movement and why they leave it." While the nature of its questions and preoccupations very much reflects the climate of the early 1950s, it remains a significant work and one that has had a considerable methodological impact.

The first part of the book undertakes to create a formal model of the communist movement and to establish the distinction between the "core" and the followers. The second part, based on interviews with former party members (in Western Europe and the United States), deals with the experiences in, and perceptions of, the movement on the part of those who have been involved. The last section deals with actual assimilation into and defection from the movement. Among other things this is a serious effort to integrate rather formal, doctrinal material with information from interviews.

DEGRAS, JANE (TABRISKY), *ed.* **The Communist International, 1919–1943: Documents.** New York: Oxford University Press (for the Royal Institute of International Affairs), 1956–1960, 2 v.

This extensive selection of documents, edited by a leading specialist in the field, is of enormous value to the student of the history of the Comintern. The volumes comprise four general categories of materials: programmatic and theoretical statements; statements on contemporary events; letters to and resolutions concerning the national communist parties; and documents on the internal organization of the International. Each volume contains a useful introductory preface and necessary explanatory notes.

DJILAS, MILOVAN. **The New Class: An Analysis of the Communist System.** New York: Praeger, 1957, 214 p.

The political writings of Milovan Djilas—including, along with this work, **Conversations with Stalin** (New York: Harcourt, Brace and World, 1962, 211 p.) and **The Unperfect Society** (New York: Harcourt, Brace and World, 1969, 267 p.)—present something of a problem for the bibliographer. They have had a considerable impact, and the phrase "New Class" gained much currency as a description of the postwar communist leadership. Yet this impact was in part a result of the fact that the author, formerly a high party official in Tito's Jugoslavia, had turned critic, had fallen out of favor, and was subsequently imprisoned for his criticisms and his refusal to be silent or discreet. Hence his writings appeared newsworthy and somewhat sensationalist. Perhaps in reaction to this, it has been argued that his analysis of communism and of Marxism (in **The Unperfect Society**) were familiar among non-communist scholars, that his revelations of late Stalinism had been largely known already. There is a measure of truth in this criticism: Djilas is not an original or profound political philosopher, and his writings bear the scars both of the spiritual isolation of the Stalinist years and of the physical isolation of his prolonged confinement. Nevertheless, his works have a permanent value as a record of the thoughts and reflections of a man of great personal courage and moral integrity, who has repeatedly been willing to put his own personal safety on the line, and who has emerged with his humanity augmented.

Liberalism; Democracy

VON HAYEK, FRIEDRICH AUGUST. **The Constitution of Liberty.** Chicago: University of Chicago Press, 1960, 569 p.

Whereas the implications for foreign policy of certain ideologies, such as fascism or communism, are more than evident, the relevance of certain other ideologies, such as liberalism, may seem rather less apparent. Yet in the view of this Austrian-born economist (best known for his controversial polemic **The Road to Serfdom**), "Foreign policy today is largely a question of which political philosophy is to triumph over another." Consequently, he departs from the limited role of econo-mist to undertake a general exposition and defense of liberalism in its classic sense ("I am simply an unrepentant Old Whig"). It is a wide-ranging and internally consistent discussion of the principles of individual liberty and of the proper relations between the individual, society and the state. The author has the courage to take a number of positions in explicit opposition to contemporary American "liberal" views, *e.g.* on taxation, education and conservation, not to speak of general economic policy and the role of the state.

It is a carefully reasoned book, and the author's postscript, "Why I am not a Conservative," is altogether appropriate to his position. In a word, this is a major argument explicitly in the tradition of Burke, Macauley, Gladstone, De Tocqueville and Lord Acton—a tradition singularly lacking adequate spokesmen in recent decades.

POLANYI, MICHAEL. **The Logic of Liberty: Reflections and Rejoinders.** Chicago: University of Chicago Press, 1951, 206 p.

Polanyi, a physical scientist turned student of human affairs, has been a remark-able intellectual stimulus in many directions; one is likely to find views of his cited, or contested, in many settings, from discussions of contemporary ideology to the feasibility of central economic planning.

In Polanyi's own judgment these occasional pieces "represent my consistently renewed efforts to clarify the position of liberty in response to a number of ques-tions raised by our troubled period of history." In so doing he defends "pure science" against both materialistic and moralistic attacks, offers the enormously suggestive jigsaw-puzzle method of problem solving, attacks the individualistic justification for liberty, challenges the practicability of central direction in eco-nomic planning and production, and introduces the concept of "polycentricity."

Any student of world affairs would do well to sharpen his wits by an encounter with this humane and highly individual mind. Some flavor of his perceptiveness is conveyed by such a passage as: "A new destructive scepticism is linked here to a new passionate social conscience; an utter disbelief in the spirit of man is coupled with extravagant moral demands. We see at work here the form of action which has already dealt so many shattering blows to the modern world: the chisel of scepticism driven by the hammer of social passion."

LIPSON, LESLIE. **The Democratic Civilization.** New York: Oxford University Press, 1964, 614 p.

This is an ambitious book, with a double purpose: "to examine the democratic form of government and appraise it, and, along with this, to suggest a general theory of the political process." After tracing the discontinuous history of democratic theories, from classical Athens to the nineteenth century, he examines the implica-tions of, and for, democracy in such matters as race relations, religion, geopolitics and economics. A third section deals with the various political, governmental and constitutional expressions of democracy. A final section is a consideration of democratic values. The book, usefully stressing the comparative method, is rather loosely organized and the pace leisurely. While granting that democratic ideals may be self-contradictory and can never be "reconciled with the rigor of metaphysical consistency," Lipson concludes that "they express and summarize the logic of historical experience and political need."

SPITZ, DAVID. **Democracy and the Challenge of Power.** New York: Columbia University Press, 1958, 228 p.

The theme of this thoughtful, and rather somber, book is expressed at the outset: "While democracy is, in principle, a way of controlling abuses of power, such abuses nevertheless persist in the practices of democratic states. And it is this persistence of oppression in a democracy that constitutes what I have called the challenge of power." Limiting himself largely to the American experience, the author examines the various manifestations of oppressive power, in the acts of government itself, in the "tyranny" of public sentiment, in the misuse of private powers. The abuses are deeply rooted, and Spitz finds no magic formula for their eradication, neither through appeal to right principles, nor in the search for the "right" man, nor in institutional tinkering. His conclusion is that, just as there is no single abuse, so there is no single answer but rather "a never-ending quest for particular solutions to the innumerable abuses of power that constantly occur under all forms of political organization." E. M. Forster once wrote "Two Cheers for Democracy;" in this book cheering seems out of place.

NATIONALISM

See also New Nations, p. 355.

HAYES, CARLTON JOSEPH HUNTLEY. **The Historical Evolution of Modern Nationalism.** New York: R. R. Smith, 1931, 335 p.

In 1926 Carlton J. H. Hayes, who later became Seth Low Professor of History at Columbia University, published his **Essays on Nationalism** (New York: Macmillan, 1926, 279 p.), a series of studies on nationalism and its historical development. This pioneer work and its sequel, **The Historical Evolution of Modern Nationalism,** brought him worldwide fame and dedicated disciples.

Hayes' classification of the different types of nationalism in Europe during the last two centuries became the standard treatise on the subject and retains its value today as a basic typology. His formula included these types of nationalism: humanitarian (Bolingbroke, Rousseau, Herder); Jacobin (Robespierre); traditional (Burke, de Bonald, Friedrich von Schlegel); liberal (Bentham, Guizot, Mazzini); and integral (Kipling, Maurras, Treitschke). To these categories Hayes added economic nationalism, which he regarded as reflecting the "recent" tendency to look upon the state as an economic as well as a political unit. He saw economic nationalism as merging with imperialism to form one of the most powerful factors in contemporary civilization.

This study did much to dispel the fog surrounding the phenomenon of nationalism and gave it content and meaning. Hayes was the first to suggest a distinction between original and derived nationalism: every subject nationality in the nineteenth century began its agitation for national liberty in the spirit of a Herder or a Condorcet, but once the oppressed nationality obtained its freedom it transformed its "original" nationalism into a derived form which was reactionary, military and imperialist. Nationalism, in Hayes' view, could be either a blessing or a curse: too often it showed its evil integral form.

HAYES, CARLTON JOSEPH HUNTLEY. **Nationalism: A Religion.** New York: Macmillan, 1960, 187 p.

During his retirement, Hayes decided to write a précis of his lifetime of study, "a brief summing up of what one person . . . has conceived and learned about nationalism, with special regard to its story in Europe and with tentative reflections on its present course on other continents." The result was this small but admirable book, every page of which sparkles with the witty touch of Hayes' pen and reveals his stature as a historian.

Hayes was deeply interested in the religious aspects of a basically political phenomenon. He saw a religious sense exemplified not only in the great surviving religions but also in modern nationalism. Originally an expression of tribalism, nationalism was resurrected in modern times among Christian peoples. It became a religion in revolutionary France, advanced during the time from Napoleon I to Napoleon III, became intensified in the industrial society from 1864 to 1914, was at once the seed and product of the new imperialism, and played an enormously important role in both world wars.

Against the potential pride and selfishness of unlimited nationalism, Hayes pointed to the Christian ideals of humility and altruism. He urged Christians to take their faith seriously and seek to sustain it as a truly world religion superior to the divisive religion of nationalism. Above all, he recommended that a limit be placed on the excesses of nationalism.

KOHN, HANS. **The Idea of Nationalism.** New York: Macmillan, 1944, 735 p.

In this classic study, Hans Kohn presents the history of the idea of nationalism from ancient Hebrew and Greek times to the present. He sees nationalism as first and foremost a state of mind, an act of consciousness, which since the French Revolution has become more and more common to mankind.

The problem of classification is of special interest. In projecting his typology of nationalism, Carlton J. H. Hayes used a vertical conceptualization based on a chronological approach from the French Revolution to the present. Kohn, on the other hand, presents an equally challenging horizontal theme emphasizing the dichotomy between Western and non-Western nationalism. He contrasts two socio-political environments in which nationalism had to grow and develop: the Western world (England, France, the Netherlands and Switzerland); and the non-Western world (central and eastern Europe and Asia). He shows how these two areas provide the poles around which the new age, with its multiplicity of shadings, evolves. Western nationalism was born out of the spirit of the Enlightenment and the struggle for liberty, equality, constitutionalism and a society of free citizens based on laws (the pluralistic, open society). In the non-Western world the Enlightenment was belittled or rejected in favor of an authoritarian uniformity of state and faith, collective power and territorial expansion (the closed society).

In this volume, a masterpiece of historical analysis, Kohn clarifies the plethora of inconsistencies, contradictions and paradoxes which surround nationalism. He shows how the idea of nationalism can be communicated by cultural diffusion, while at the same time its meaning and form take on characteristics dictated by the special aspirations of people.

KOHN, HANS. **The Age of Nationalism: The First Era of Global History.** New York: Harper, 1962, 172 p.

The purpose of Harper's World Perspectives series, of which this volume was an early contribution, was to show that although the present apocalyptic era is one of exceptional tensions, there is also at work an exceptional movement toward a compensating unity. This is the theme of Hans Kohn's brief treatment of the age of nationalism. He regards the record of the past as parochial history but suggests that in the middle of the twentieth century man entered the first stage of global history. He prefers the term "global" to "world" history because "world" has been used indiscriminately to mean the entire cosmos as well as the earth.

Basing his approach and analysis upon his own previous studies, Kohn limits his treatment to the second half of the twentieth century and describes how there appeared for the first time a common attitude including peoples and civilizations all over the globe "under the sign of nationalism." He is aware of the continuing evil: nationalism carries not only a hope and a promise but also a serious threat to the growing unity of mankind. Nationalism still reveals two clear-cut facets: on the one side a human aspiration for equality, and on the other side a passion for power over others. But Kohn, retaining the vigorous optimism of the rationalist, believes that the new age of global history ("pan-nationalism") will find its ultimate justification by transcending itself in a new global order.

HERTZ, FRIEDRICH OTTO. **Nationality in History and Politics.** New York: Oxford University Press, 1944, 417 p.

The original edition of this book appeared in London in 1944 in the International Library of Sociology and Social Reconstruction under the editorship of Karl Mannheim. Its subtitle, "A Psychology and Sociology of National Sentiment and Nationalism," revealed the aim of its author, a sociologist long interested in combining historical investigation with psychological and sociological methods. In scholarly and objective terms and utilizing a topical approach, Hertz examined a wide variety of phases, including the structure and form of national consciousness, nationality and race, nationality and language, religion and nationality, the national territory, national will, national character, social backgrounds and political thought and national ideology. Although he regarded his book as a study in human nature and society, Hertz was careful to avoid sweeping generalizations about so complicated and evasive a subject. Especially valuable are the attempt to present an unambiguous terminology, the able discussion of national character and the explanation of aggressive nationalism. Reprinted in 1945 and 1951, this book remains one of the best standard treatments of nationalism and the complex psychology of nations.

SNYDER, LOUIS L. **The New Nationalism.** Ithaca: Cornell University Press, 1968, 387 p.

Louis L. Snyder, professor of history at City College of The City University of New York, extends the pioneer work of Carlton J. H. Hayes and Hans Kohn to a survey of nationalism since 1945—the new nationalism, which exists on a global scale. In compact, documented chapters, the author commences with a general treatment of the meaning, classification and typology of nationalism, discusses its paradoxes and then treats its development on a regional basis. He describes European fissiparous nationalism, black nationalism in Africa, anticolonialism in Asia, politico-religious nationalism in the Middle East, populist nationalism in Latin America, melting-pot nationalism in the United States and Soviet Russia's messianic nationalism. In the current conflict between nationalism and supranationalism, Snyder sees a persistence of nationalism in its assertive and aggressive form despite rising economic integration. This study serves as a guide not only for the student of contemporary history and international relations but also for the statesman who is concerned with the impact of the strongest and most important of all political emotions.

SNYDER, LOUIS L. **The Meaning of Nationalism.** New Brunswick: Rutgers University Press, 1954, 208 p.

Nationalism, the strongest of contemporary political emotions, is always in flux, changing according to no preconceived pattern. It is multifaceted, part actuality, part myth. It functions in a milieu of historical paradox and is beset with nuances, contradictions and inconsistencies. The problem of clarifying this "ism" has become of major importance to current scholars.

Louis L. Snyder limits his study to the meaning of nationalism. After expressing the problem semantically, he examines the concepts of nation, nationality and nationalism, describes the various classifications, and then appraises economic nationalism, patriotism, national character and the idea of a national soul. Convinced that the historian needs the coöperation of other disciplines and their specific approaches, the author supplies the first introduction to an interdisciplinary inquiry. He devotes attention to work on nationalism in such fields as geography, political science, sociology, economics, psychology, psychiatry and psychoanalysis, surveying the problems and results of different attempts to trace this sentiment to its sources. The study retains its value in the continuing investigation of a powerful but elusive force.

SHAFER, BOYD CARLISLE. **Nationalism: Myth and Reality.** New York: Harcourt, 1955, 319 p.

The bibliography of nationalism is enriched by Boyd C. Shafer's excellent appraisal of the most powerful political force in the modern world. In diligent and carefully documented research, combined with temperate judgments, the author throws light upon a subject too often marred by fallacies and contradictions. After exploring definitions of nationalism, its several dimensions and its variations of structure, Shafer comments on the illusions that have obscured it. He demolishes many contingent metaphysical myths and presents the observation that nations, nationalities and nationalisms exist not because of any inexorable laws or meta-physical phenomena but because of the total culture of modern times. There is no basis, he says, historical, biological or psychological, for the belief that nationalism must be or will be permanent. Men are not born nationalists—they acquire national consciousness because the conditions of their time demand it. Below the surface of their national peculiarities men remain more alike than different. Primarily historical in its approach, the study draws ably upon the findings of other (especially the behavioral) social sciences. This first-rate contribution to a difficult subject takes its place as a standard treatise on nationalism.

BARON, SALO WITTMAYER. **Modern Nationalism and Religion.** New York: Harper, 1947, 363 p.

The author, professor of history at Columbia University, presents a highly original analysis of the fundamental interrelationship between modern nationalism and modern religion. His chief interest is in the attitude of the various churches to worldwide nationalistic trends. After presenting the varieties of nationalistic experi-ence, he discusses the "heroic" nationalism which characterized the ideologies of nationalist fathers from Rousseau to Mazzini. Not until the breakdown of religious sanctions and the accompanying abatement of denominationalism in modern times did ethnic-cultural nationalism emerge as a primary force. By setting up a national state and interdenominational liberty of conscience as related ideals, nationalism relegated both religion and statehood to a secondary position. Within this frame-work the author analyzes such diverse topics as Catholic inter-territorialism, Protes-tant individualism, orthodox Caesaro-Papism and Jewish ethnicism. This chal-lenging and well-written study adds much to our knowledge of modern nationalism.

Nationalism. New York: Oxford University Press, 1940, 360 p.

In 1939, a study group in London of members of the Royal Institute of Inter-national Affairs, under the chairmanship of Edward Hallett Carr, completed an examination of the history and philosophy of nationalism both as a general phenomenon and as a special manifestation among the large and small nations of the world. The goal was an unbiased examination of a phenomenon "which appears to threaten the very future of our civilization." The authors believed that national-ism could not be appreciated properly if it were treated as an isolated political or psychological phenomenon; it was necessary, they said, to regard it as a special case of the more permanent problem of group integration. Within this framework the contributors discussed far-reaching questions of sociology and group psy-chology, "questions which admit of wide differences of opinion and to which scientific methods of study cannot easily be applied." This was a modest description of its procedure, but the group of experts produced one of the most solid studies on nationalism. Of special value is the set of definitions which do much to clarify the complex and often bewildering subject.

CARR, EDWARD HALLETT. **Nationalism and After.** New York: Macmillan, 1945, 76 p.

When he wrote this book at the end of World War II, Edward Hallett Carr, diplomat and historian, was assistant editor of the London *Times*. In his discussion of nationalism he described four periods in international relations: the first was terminated by the French Revolution and the Napoleonic wars; the second, the product of the French Revolution, was undermined from 1870 on, but lasted until 1914; the third period reached its culmination between 1914 and 1939. Carr saw World War II as marking the climax and catastrophe of the third period of modern international relations, leaving us "on the threshold of a fourth period whose character will probably shape the destinies of mankind for a century to come." From this point on Carr treated the future of nationalism as it would exist in what he believed to be an increasingly internationally minded world. He admitted that nationalism *seemed* stronger in 1945, but he felt that nations were in process of undergoing another subtle, though not yet definable, change. The events of 1919 may well have been the last triumph of "the old fissiparous nationalism, of the ideology of the small nation as the ultimate political and economic unit."

From the hindsight of our present-day society, it would seem that Carr was somewhat premature in his judgment made a quarter of a century ago that "small nations can survive only as an anomaly and an anachronism in a world that has moved on to other forms of organization." On the contrary, nationalism has shown a powerful staying capacity in the contemporary world, while the progress of such international organizations as the United Nations remains snail-like.

DOOB, LEONARD W. **Patriotism and Nationalism: Their Psychological Foundations.** New Haven: Yale University Press, 1964, 297 p.

Hans Kohn's reminder that nationalism is first and foremost a state of mind, an act of consciousness, indicates that this vital phenomenon of modern times merits the close attention of psychologists. Unfortunately, however, thus far there has been too little research on nationalism by psychologists. It is for this reason that this study by a professor of psychology at Yale University is a welcome addition to the bibliography of nationalism. The author sees patriotism as merging into nationalism when such a conviction is accompanied by a demand for action. He examines the justifications for the demands and actions of national states and shows them to be similar from country to country. He explores the possibilities for internationalism. He devotes much attention to psychological materials gathered in South Tyrol, which he uses as a "relevant case history."

An otherwise valuable and challenging study is marred by the use of psychological verbiage understandable and meaningful only to fellow members of a special discipline. There is a tendency toward wandering and repetition. A more compact organization, either chronological or topical, as used by historians, would have given this basically first-rate study additional impact.

COLONIALISM

See also New Nations, p. 355.

STRAUSZ-HUPÉ, ROBERT and HAZARD, HARRY W., *eds.* **The Idea of Colonialism.** New York: Praeger, 1958, 496 p.

In this study, planned by the Associates of the Foreign Policy Research Institute, the editors present 15 essays on the history, development and recent trends of colonialism. The overall purpose is to place "colonial problems in perspective," which is the title given to a carefully reasoned essay by Stefan Possony. The book is divided into four parts: an examination of myth and reality in colonialism; historical patterns; new trends of the late 1950s (Bandung Conference, Soviet colonialism, role of the United Nations); and a final assessment of the problems of colonialism. Emphasis is placed upon three categories: national or sub-national groups fallen on evil times, such as Tibet (Communist China), Armenia (Soviet Union) and Algeria (France); the status of political fragments by which distant powers control strategic bases (Gibraltar, Aden, Singapore, Hong Kong); and backward peoples (as, for example, in parts of South America). The contributions are without exception excellent, but especially noteworthy are the opening essay by Hans Kohn devoted to a comparative analysis of colonialism and the concluding contribution by Paul M. A. Linebarger and H. W. Hazard. All in all, this is a carefully organized, interesting and welcome addition to the historiography of colonialism.

EASTON, STEWART COPINGER. **The Twilight of European Colonialism: A Political Analysis.** New York: Holt, Rinehart and Winston, 1960, 571 p.

In this general survey of developments in the colonial world, mainly Africa, to the fall of 1959, Stewart C. Easton, formerly of the department of history of The City College of New York, gives additional evidence of his felicity of style as a textbook writer. He confines his attention almost wholly to political aspects of declining European colonialism and only hints at those social and cultural changes which have led colonial peoples on the road of independence. He considers not only aspects of colonialism as a whole but also the political advances granted by the colonial powers and the rise of political parties to take advantage of the new milieu. He devotes major attention to British independent territories, France overseas, Belgian paternalism and Portuguese colonies. Easton sees imperialism and colonialism reaching their end in an irreversible trend, with only the Portuguese system untouched. Colonialism "will soon be a phase of history to be studied only by historians," and its passing governmental forms "will no longer be of anything but historical interest to students of government." This is an excellent summary of one of the most significant developments of our era.

MANNONI, DOMINIQUE OTARE. **Prospero and Caliban: The Psychology of Colonization.** New York: Praeger, 1956, 218 p.

Translated by Pamela Powesland from the French edition "Psychologie de la Colonisation" (Paris: Éditions du Seuil, 1950, 227 p.), Mannoni's study is devoted to the human side of colonial situations. As a psychologist the author is interested in the more puzzling features of human and social relations in colonial areas, and he has the ability to throw much light on them. Basing his facts and opinions largely on his own experiences in Madagascar, he shows how a colonial situation is created the very instant a white man appears, even alone, in the midst of a tribe. He analyzes the attitudes of primitive, isolated and archaic peoples, pays equal attention to European colonists and examines different aspects of the human relationships which arise in colonies. He is at his best in discussing such topics as psychological dependence, threat of abandonment, inferiority, heredity and personality among colonial peoples. There is an interesting treatment of the conflict between psychological dependence and political independence. A provocative study, unique in its approach.

PLAMENATZ, JOHN PETROV. **On Alien Rule and Self-Government.** New York: Longmans, 1960, 224 p.

In this essay in political philosophy, the author, a don at Nuffield College, Oxford, analyzes the ideas and assumptions of apologists for and critics of European rule over non-Europeans and is successful in uncovering the confusion of thought which makes much of the controversy on colonialism irritating and unprofitable. He is displeased by the circumlocutions and euphemisms used to disclaim a sense of racial or national superiority. Assuming that constitutional government and liberal democracy are desirable, he issues warnings to both sides. He advises the ruler powers: "Beware of European settlers." And: "Don't bother with strategic bases—they are not as important as you think." He cautions the recently independent as well as those who still strive for independence: "Beware of your resentment against white peoples." And: "It is among 'imperialist' people that there is the greatest understanding of your predicament." With affection for his own "backward nation of Montenegro," Plamenatz is well equipped to deal with the perplexing problem of colonialism and its varying facets of claims to domination or independence. This calm and dispassionate study, suffused with common sense, is a useful guide in our era of withering colonialism.

The Colonial Problem. New York: Oxford University Press, 1937, 448 p.

This report by a study group of the Royal Institute of International Affairs, under the chairmanship of Harold Nicolson, is a comprehensive treatment of the entire problem of colonialism as seen from London. Part I concerns international aspects, with attention to the "value" (relative rather than absolute) of colonies politically, militarily and economically. Part II describes diversity in colonial administration, with emphasis upon such topics as open door, dual mandates, individual rule and labor problems. Part III treats the economic aspects of colonial development, with attention to questions of trade, finance, investment and land settlement. There are 15 appendices on such pertinent subjects as "Germans in Mandated Territories" and "Settlement and Development in French North Africa." Although published in 1937, the study recognized the growing sense of national identity among colonized peoples. Included in the judgments is this accurate forecast: "It is possible that the development of self-consciousness may transfer to color areas the militant nationalism for which we suffer in Europe." The authors try valiantly to show that the color problem cannot be reduced to a simple conflict between "haves" and "have-nots." Through the lines of this valuable encyclopedic survey runs a sense of power typical of the late days of Empire, at a time when confident Britain was still "training each community in social and political responsibility."

IMPERIALISM

LENIN, NIKOLAI [VLADIMIR ILICH]. **Imperialism.** New York: International Publishers, 1933, 127 p.

In his famous essay, here translated, Lenin extended the Marxian analysis of modern society to include the tenet that imperialism is "the highest stage of capitalism." Stressing the economic nature of imperialism, Lenin defined it as "capitalism in transition," or more precisely, as "dying capitalism." Imperialism, in Lenin's interpretation, emerged as the growth and direct continuation of the essential qualities of capitalism in general. Imperialism is that phase of capitalism's development in which the domination of monopolies and finance-capital has established itself; in which the export of capital has acquired great importance; in which the division of the world among big international trusts has begun; and in which the partition of the earth among the great capitalist powers has been completed. Lenin saw all efforts to mitigate the oppressive effects of imperialism upon native masses as ineffective and any attempts to resolve the contradictions and dangers of war which imperialism creates among capitalist rivals, on the one side, and between imperialist and anti-imperialist forces, on the other, as futile. Imperialism, said Lenin, contributes to the creation of a revolutionary situation, and revolution is the only method for ending imperialist aggression and its evils. Whether one agrees or disagrees with Lenin's view of imperialism, it is clear that this essay has become a formidable textbook of revolutionary practice. By Marxists of all hues it is regarded as holy writ.

BUKHARIN, NIKOLAI IVANOVICH. **Imperialism and World Economy.** New York: International Publishers, 1929, 173 p.

This is an English translation of the classic Bolshevik indictment of imperialism by Nikolai Bukharin. The book examines the fundamental facts of world economy as related to imperialism and imperialism as a definite stage in the growth of highly developed capitalism. After defining the world economy, Bukharin described its development and organization, tariff policies, world sales markets, relation of the world economy and the national state, the "necessity" of imperialism and ultra-capitalism, the problem of capitalism and war and the juxtaposition of the world economy and proletarian society. In omniscient terms the author indicated his certainty that the capitalist shell would eventually burst, that the contemporary capitalist world would be drenched in blood and that capitalism prepared the way for its own gravediggers. In a glowing introduction, Lenin, using the pseudonym V. Ilyin, praised "the scientific significance" of Bukharin's work and added that "imperialism will eventually explode as capitalism turns into its opposite." Both Bukharin and Lenin wrote in categorical terms with all the confidence of a Galileo or Newton propounding the laws of nature. Despite their brilliance, neither seemed to be fully aware of the enormously complicated nature of economic facts and the difficulty of making them conform to revolutionary aims. They fitted the world economy into a preconceived pattern and denounced any skeptic as either ignorant or prejudiced. Called by Lenin "the darling of the Party," Bukharin had the misfortune of leading the Right Opposition against Stalin, an even more dogmatic custodian of the word, and was executed in 1938 during the Great Purge after serving as the main defendant in a show trial.

MOON, PARKER THOMAS. **Imperialism and World Politics.** New York: Macmillan, 1926, 583 p.

In 1926 Parker Thomas Moon, professor of international relations at Columbia University, published a general account of imperialism, which soon became the standard American textbook on the subject. In clear-cut prose the author discussed the men and motives ("Empire-building is done not by 'nations' but by men").

Foremost in the imperialist scramble were the business interests, whose influential allies included military and naval leaders, diplomats, colonial officials, missionaries, explorers and adventurers. "Sometimes [missionaries] promoted imperialism quite unintentionally; being killed by savages, for example, was a very effective though not a deliberate patriotic service, in as much as it might afford the home country a reason or pretext for conquest." Moon gave special attention to such peripheral subjects as national honor, economic nationalism, surplus population and self-protection, all principles which nerved nations to valiant feats of empire-building. Even today, with imperialism in decline, the book retains much of its value as the best general account of imperialism in the nineteenth and early twentieth centuries. Unfortunately, its brilliant author died at the height of his career.

Curiously, Moon had as much difficulty in defining imperialism as contemporary authors have in eliciting its meaning. An early reviewer of the book counted 17 different uses of the word "imperialism" and complained that "it is certainly mis-leading to describe by the same word, imperialist, both the European statesman who plans cold-bloodedly to seize 1000 square miles of territory in Africa and the university instructor who invests $1000 in a French government bond." The criti-cism merely serves to emphasize the problem of defining any current "ism."

PEFFER, NATHANIEL. **The White Man's Dilemma.** New York: Day, 1927, 312 p.

In a course of lectures at the New School for Social Research in 1926–1927, Nathaniel Peffer traced the growth of imperialism, examined its ideas and discussed its causes and consequences. This well-informed study, written in attractive jour-nalese, is the printed version of that lecture series. Peffer saw twentieth-century imperialists as "Conquistadores—New Style." He devoted much attention to the classic case of the despoliation of China, his special interest. The result of im-perialism, he said, was a world overrun, and the reaction to it led to a turn by the native worm. He saw no happy solution to the accompanying dilemma for the white man. Imperialism does not pay, and it is fallacious to draw any balance sheet. There is a serious problem: "Voluntarily to renounce imperialism requires us to alter the structure of our industrialized society and to recast a fundamental premise of our social philosophy." The inexorable law of history is witness to the fact that conquests so imposed cannot endure forever. Peffer was certain that the Western world was riding a tiger and was unable to stay on or get off. He advised quick liquidation—"cut them off before it is too late." This recommendation is of interest because it was made just after the first quarter of the twentieth century.

WOOLF, LEONARD SIDNEY. **Imperialism and Civilization.** New York: Harcourt, 1928, 182 p.

Originally published in England by Leonard and Virginia Woolf by the Hogarth Press, this brief book, though now outdated, was at the time an exceptionally fine study of imperialism and its aspects in Asia and Africa. After a short but fascinating examination of conflicts of civilization before the nineteenth century, the author discussed the development of imperialism, with special attention to the role of the League of Nations in its history. He saw imperialism as a "menacing problem," one which had always perplexed Europeans. Granting the importance of race, religion and nationality in recent times, he called them secondary to "the collision and maladjustment of different civilizations under the impulse of imperialism." In illuminating terms he described the inverse of imperialism as the relations of Asians and Africans to white men in what may be called white men's countries (in the United States and in South Africa, for example). In the final chapter Woolf expressed hope for the end of imperialism through the agency of the League of Nations, which would mark "a beginning of the synthesis of nations." When writing this book in the late 1920s, the author was not aware of the very real weaknesses of the League and the system of mandates. He knew the nature of imperialism ("Men moralize among ruins"), but he had no workable formula for resolving its abuses.

SCHUMPETER, JOSEPH ALOIS. **Imperialism and Social Classes.** New York: Kelley, 1951, 221 p.

This is a translation by Heinz Norden of the Viennese economist Schumpeter's two important writings, "Zur Soziologie der Imperialismen," which appeared originally in the *Archiv für Sozialwissenschaft und Soziopolitik* (1919), and "Die Sozialen Klassen im Ethnisch Homogenen Milieu" (1927). When he wrote the first essay, Schumpeter, probably at that time unacquainted with Lenin's interpretation of imperialism, attacked the Bauer-Hilferding concept, which was similar to Lenin's—*i.e.* imperialism is an outgrowth of capitalism. Schumpeter regarded imperialism as an atavism, a hangover from conditions of the past. He judged it a basic fallacy to describe imperialism as a necessary phase of capitalism, or even to speak of the development of capitalism into imperialism. "Rather, imperialist and nationalist literature is always complaining vociferously about the debility, the undignified will to peace, the petty commercial spirit, and so on, of the capitalist world." A purely capitalist society, said Schumpeter, can offer no fertile soil to imperialistic impulses. Imperialism has no special object nor does it have any precise limits. Imperialistic conquest is made usually for the sake of conquest, success or activity. Schumpeter's arguments rejected J. A. Hobson's classic assault which saw imperialism as an expression of capitalist desire for profitable investment abroad, and were used later to contradict Lenin's view of imperialism as the final stage of a dying capitalism.

WINSLOW, EARLE MICAJAH. **The Pattern of Imperialism: A Study in the Theories of Power.** New York: Columbia University Press, 1948, 278 p.

This is a valuable exposition of imperialism, with special attention to its economic facets. The author makes a careful distinction between colonialism and imperialism and shows how colonies were established by people innocent of imperialistic aggression. Colonial activity and conflict come under the category of colonialism rather than imperialism, for imperialism suggests something more organized, more military and more self-consciously aggressive. Winslow also makes a careful distinction between imperialism and nationalism. Where some scholars regard the two as virtually synonymous, or perhaps different stages of the same process, the author views nation-building and empire-building as essentially opposed to each other. Nationalism has within it the same feeling as democracy, that of mutuality, but imperialism is an exclusive concept. When the spirit of exclusiveness creeps into a nation, it is a sign that the nation is losing the attributes of nationalism, internationalism and democracy, while setting forth on "an ancient business, the path of empire." A challenging, highly informative book, carefully organized and written in attractive style, this analysis of the various theories of economic imperialism retains much of its original value.

LANGER, WILLIAM L. **The Diplomacy of Imperialism, 1890–1902.** New York: Knopf, 2d ed., 1965, 797 p.

Although primarily a study of international diplomacy in the years between 1890 and 1902 (first published in 1935 in 2 v.), this book concludes a brilliant chapter on the concept of imperialism as it was developed in the debate between its adherents and its critics during that period. In contrast to the purely economic, purely strategic, purely sociological or purely psychological approaches, Langer develops what social scientists would call today a multivariate model of imperialism. The imperialism of the 1890s was produced, he finds, as much as anything by economic interests such as protectionism, desire for armament contracts and particularly by capital glut in England and other advanced countries. This oversupply of capital drove down domestic interest rates and generated strong pressures for opportunities for overseas investment under privileged conditions protected by national military power. These economic pressures coincided with the rise of a new mass reading public, swelled by the first generation of graduates of the new compulsory education system in many European countries. This new mass public, in turn, offered opportunities for the rise of a new popular tabloid or "yellow" press which catered to their tastes with stories featuring blood, sex and the flag of the nation. The same years saw a large expansion of the strata of clerical workers who sought compensation for their tame and boring lives in a new literature of outdoor heroism, violence and war. At the same time, Langer's model of the particular imperialism of the 1890s can be used to note the similarities and differences with other historic epochs.

IV. ECONOMIC FACTORS

GENERAL ECONOMICS

VEBLEN, THORSTEIN. **Absentee Ownership and Business Enterprise in Recent Times.** New York: Huebsch, 1923, 445 p.

Veblen's chief contributions to economic thought came between 1912 and 1915: "Theory of the Leisure Class," "Instinct of Workmanship" and "Theory of Business Enterprise." **Absentee Ownership and Business Enterprise** gave a summary of his ideas concerning those social institutions which create waste and misdirection of economic effort. His heroes were the engineers and technicians; his villains, the captains of industry, the vested interests, the uninterested absentee owners and the anti-social advertisers and salesmen. He scorned classical economics as being at best an unreal schematic exercise and at worst a defense for an indefensible system.

Veblen's influence was reflected at the time in the institutionalist school and has reappeared more recently in such books as C. E. Ayres, **The Theory of Economic Progress** (Chapel Hill: University of North Carolina Press, 1944, 317 p.). An excellent evaluation is to be found in Joseph Dorfman, **Thorstein Veblen and His America** (New York: A. M. Kelley, rev. ed., 1966, 572 p.).

MITCHELL, WESLEY C. **Business Cycles. The Problem and Its Setting.** New York: National Bureau of Economic Research, 1927, 489 p.

Professor Mitchell is the father of modern business cycle analysis. In 1913 he published his massive statistical analysis of the cyclical course of economic activities, "Business Cycles." The work here reviewed, better known but less technical, was the first in a series of business cycle studies undertaken at the National Bureau of Economic Research. In it, Mitchell summarized the complex interactions among a considerable number of economic processes which his earlier study had disclosed, without its elaborate statistical presentation. Much more emphasis was now given to the characteristics of the institutional setting. His analysis rests on the behavior of fairly advanced business economies with monetary mechanisms, price systems and profit incentives. However, it recognizes international differences, particularly in the degree of farming in various countries, the display of enterprise and thrift, the part played by central and local governments in directing economic activity and, most importantly, the uneven development of national business economies.

CHAMBERLIN, EDWARD. **The Theory of Monopolistic Competition.** Cambridge: Harvard University Press, 1933, 208 p.

ROBINSON, JOAN. **The Economics of Imperfect Competition.** London: Macmillan, 1933, 352 p.

These two books must be bracketed, since the two authors independently presented the first theoretical framework for the analysis of price determination under economic conditions falling between perfect competition and complete monopoly. There is no doubt that the new assumptions accord with the conditions under which many products are produced, namely that the number of sellers or buyers in a market is greater than one, yet not great enough to render negligible the influence of any one upon the market price. Price strategy then requires one to take into account the policy of one's rival and his probable reaction to any price change in determining one's price. The result is likely to be a price which more closely resembles that of monopoly than pure competition.

Professor Chamberlin discusses in considerable detail the effort of a seller to protect his position by product differentiation, ranging from legal devices such as patents and trademarks to the provision of special services. Professor Robinson discusses the possibility of the seller discriminating among different buyers, and in turn includes a chapter extending the concept of imperfect competition to the case of markets in which the number of buyers is small. She also discusses the relation of the imperfect competition concept to the labor market, in which monopolistic elements appear with respect both to demand and supply.

Since the publication of these two books, the case of imperfect competition has come to be generally incorporated into economic analysis. The competitive market was impersonal. In a sense, the new refinement introduces the same kind of individual judgment into economic activity as has become familiar in game theory based on action and reaction to anticipated action.

KEYNES, JOHN MAYNARD KEYNES, 1ST BARON. **The General Theory of Employment, Interest and Money.** New York: Harcourt, 1936, 403 p.

Broadening the discussion contained in his highly technical **Treatise on Money** (New York: Harcourt, Brace, 1930, 2 v.), Keynes here develops his general theory of the nature of modern capitalist economy. The classical theory of economic equilibrium was built on assumed market forces which balanced the demand and supply of the factors of production and of final goods and services. Keynes' approach, later to be known as macro-economics, was to consider the forces which determine changes in output and employment as a whole. He placed fresh importance on savings and investment. His analysis had broad implications for public policy and action as well as for economic analysis.

Although his general theory deals with a closed economy, *i.e.* no foreign relations, the theoretical structure has been easily extended into the international field by many writers. Many books have been written about Lord Keynes and his contribution to economic theory and practice, such as Roy Forbes Harrod, **The Life of John Maynard Keynes** (New York: Harcourt, 1951, 674 p.), and his **International Economics;** Seymour Edwin Harris, **John Maynard Keynes: Economist and Policy Maker** (New York: Scribner, 1955, 234 p.); Kenneth K. Kurihara, *ed.,* **Post Keynesian Economics** (New Brunswick: Rutgers University Press, 1954, 442 p.); and in a vigorously critical vein, Henry Hazlitt, **The Failure of the "New Economics": An Analysis of the Keynesian Fallacies** (Princeton: Van Nostrand, 1959, 458 p.).

VARGA, EUGEN. **Two Systems: Socialist Economy and Capitalist Economy.** New York: International Publishers, 1939, 268 p.

This leading Soviet economist presents a comparison of socialism and capitalism which is not merely a theoretical analysis. Rather, he endeavors to demonstrate, often through statistics, that productivity and production in the Soviet Union are increasing much more rapidly than in the capitalist world in which bitter class struggles are raging. The capitalist system is marching inevitably toward its own destruction, he says, capitalism having become "over-ripe" with steadily increasing dissatisfaction of the proletariat. He contrasts the "exploitative" treatment of the colonies with equal treatment of all national territories in the Soviet Union. His comparisons of trends, not of levels, are usually based on statistical series ending in 1936 or 1937, when the West was still suffering from the Depression. As of these years, he is able to argue in true Marxist style that capitalism has a limited power of consumption and that the monopolists are compelled to restrict the development of production and productive forces.

CLARK, JOHN M. **Social Control of Business.** New York: McGraw-Hill, 2d ed., 1939, 537 p.

The importance of this book when it was first published in 1926 was that it presented the picture of a modified capitalism contrasted with the extremes of rugged individualism or socialism. Professor Clark considers the economic scene in terms of community interest, in which case corrective action can properly be taken if and when the public interest requires. He examines controls frequently unrecognized in economic analysis, including legal institutions, government regulation and various forms of extra-legal agreements, and applies his analysis in detail to the fields of public utilities and anti-trust. In the second edition, he rewrote certain chapters and added long sections on depressions, the "New Deal" and economic planning.

SWEEZY, PAUL MARLOR. **The Theory of Capitalist Development.** New York: Oxford University Press, 1942, 398 p.

Dissatisfied with the way in which economists have abstracted from real life by creating an "economic man" who behaves the same way on a desert island or in a metropolitan city, Professor Sweezy argues that the social structure has been disregarded, and he therefore espouses Marxian economics. After discussing the theory of surplus value and the accumulation process, he examines two implications of the theory—crises and depressions, and imperialism. Looking ahead, his hope is that socialism will so demonstrate its superiority that the changeover from capitalism can take place through democratic processes.

A more recent exposition in a similar vein is Leo Huberman and Paul Sweezy, **Introduction to Socialism** (New York: Monthly Review Press, 1968, 127 p.). The ways by which the oligarchy pacifies the proletariat are discussed in Paul A. Baran and Paul Sweezy, **Monopoly Capital: An Essay on the American Economic and Social Order** (New York: Monthly Review Press, 1966, 402 p.).

VON HAYEK, FRIEDRICH AUGUST. **The Road to Serfdom.** Chicago: University of Chicago Press, 1944, 250 p.

Reacting to the increased acceptance of government controls in the 1930s, this is a strong attack on the idea of the managed economy with special emphasis on the evils of planning, social security and more equitable income distribution. Probably more than any other, this book was the handbook of the conservatives who believed in laissez-faire. Aimed more at British developments than American, Professor Hayek argues that attempts by government to improve economic performance not only restrict the free energies of individuals but their civil liberties as well. Hayek does not ask for anarchy or complete laissez-faire but regards the proper function of government in the economic area as limited to setting up rules to ensure a free enterprise system. Totalitarianism is his devil, whether it appeared in Nazi Germany or in the milder form of British socialism.

Professor Hayek recognizes that the family and the small community may be able to plan but insists that the difficulties of planning increase with size. Most difficult of all, therefore, is the international field, where there are no common international ideals, except in the most general terms, nor a willingness to sacrifice. If the object is to achieve maximum individual freedom, he notes that the addition of foreign considerations adds one other area of government interference. This volume was followed by **Individualism and Economic Order** (Chicago: University of Chicago Press, 1948, 271 p.).

SHONFIELD, ANDREW. **Modern Capitalism: The Changing Balance of Public and Private Power.** New York: Oxford University Press (for the Royal Institute of International Affairs), 1965, 456 p.

This remarkable book, by the Director of Studies at the Royal Institute of International Affairs, examines the transition of Western capitalist society from the stagnation and hopelessness of the 1930s and early 1940s to a dynamic and orderly period of rapid economic growth in the 1950s and 1960s. The author suggests that, except in the United States (and one can quarrel over this exclusion), the fear of poverty dominated the prewar period, leading to demands for all kinds of public social security. But he notes that after the war, despite differences in national policies, there was a rapid increase in output per worker, the growth of science-based large industries with more stable employment, the beginning of planning that did not destroy individual initiative, the development of more active and responsible governmental participation in economic activity, a speeding up of the alteration of political and economic institutions to meet current needs, and some movement in the direction of an international society. In the light of these developments, he stresses the need for safeguards against growing governmental power, recommending, for example, that legislative bodies should be better equipped to make independent judgments on policy issues and that pressures by private interests on governments should be brought into the open.

HELLER, WALTER W. **New Dimensions of Political Economy.** Cambridge: Harvard University Press, 1966, 203 p.

The Godkin Lectures at Harvard are expected to deal with "the Essentials of Free Government and the Duties of the Citizen." In 1966 they were given by Walter Heller who, as Chairman of the Council of Economic Advisers from 1961 to 1964, had been a leader in applying economics to the making of economic policy. The author describes the ground to be covered as moving from "yesterday's pleasures of expansion to today's pangs of inflation and tomorrow's promises of fiscal abundance." He feels that a major development required of the federal government is to work out new forms of fiscal support for state and local government. The book is essentially an optimistic view of the economic policy-making process and a declaration of faith in the contribution which economists can make in building modern economic policy.

ROLL, ERIC. **The World after Keynes: An Examination of the Economic Order.** New York: Praeger, 1968, 193 p.

Not many authors dare to present a general survey of the world's economy and its problems, but Professor Roll has essayed this task. Examining the record of economics from 1936, when Keynes' **General Theory of Employment, Interest and Money** was published, the author notes the great changes of the last 30 years through the widespread introduction of economic planning, the use of monetary and fiscal instruments of control, technological advances and many other developments. In the face of this new world, he feels that economics as a discipline has not shown comparable change, with major doctrinal disputes relegated to the background—perhaps in this putting too much weight on controversy as a basis for change. He does not recognize econometrics as a new element nor the new multidiscipline activity resulting from fresh problem areas such as the city.

The most pressing problems as of 1966 are discussed under the headings of regionalism, agriculture, the less-developed countries and the international monetary system. He sees possible steps forward in each area, though with progress impeded by political considerations and the economic consequences of heavy defense burdens.

GALBRAITH, JOHN KENNETH. **The Affluent Society.** Boston: Houghton, 2d rev. ed., 1969, 333 p.

Not a technical economics book nor one dealing directly with international matters, the importance of this essay lies in the problems to which it calls attention. As contrasted with a world of scarcity, Galbraith claims that concern about the production of more goods is no longer essential, and that the way is opening up for choices which are not related to the market place. The needs which he feels are unrecognized in conventional economics are primarily those for public goods and services, such as education, roads, sanitation, hospitals, transportation, parks and playgrounds and the like. The solution suggested is a system of taxation which would automatically provide increasing income to public authority for public purposes, particularly in strengthening state and local services. Specifically, sales taxes would penalize private spending and provide public services. The second edition contains a longish introduction, explaining some of the author's subjective judgments.

SAMUELSON, PAUL A. **Economics.** New York: McGraw-Hill, 8th ed., 1970, 868 p.

Although a textbook, Samuelson's is by all odds the book on economics with the most readers all over the world, and from cover to cover at that. This balanced set of economics lessons is brought up to date about every three years, the latest edition containing new sections on poverty, race and environment. While the chapters on international economic subjects are highly condensed, they do provide the economic background required for examining the behavior of foreign exchange, the balance of payments, international trade and foreign aid. Other related subjects appear elsewhere in the book, such as economic growth and development and alternative systems. There is probably no simpler way to demonstrate the extraordinary development of economics than to compare Samuelson's latest edition with any elementary economics text published in the 1920s. Those of the earlier period were concerned with the working of the price system in hypothetical markets, and government policies entered the picture primarily as enforcers of the competitive system. Samuelson deals with the problems of a modern, industrialized economy, using a greatly augmented structure of economic theory.

Of much greater importance to the evolution of economic theory was the author's **Foundations of Economic Analysis** (Cambridge: Harvard University Press, 1947, 447 p.). Rather than the simple exposition of the textbook, this was written for those well grounded in economic theory and familiar with matrices and differential equations. Not only did it move from statics to dynamics but it brought together into a single system a number of propositions which had not previously been related.

THE INTERNATIONAL ECONOMY

ANGELL, JAMES WATERHOUSE. **The Theory of International Prices.** Cambridge: Harvard University Press, 1926, 571 p.

Impressed by the extraordinary adjustments in economic international relations made necessary by World War I and its aftermath, Professor Angell undertook to examine the part played by international prices. This led to an examination of what forces determine national price levels, and then the determination of the general price relationship between countries. The book is divided into two parts, one historical and critical in which he reviews English (with which he includes the American) and continental thought from mercantilism to 1914, and the second, his own restatement of the theory of international prices.

In his comprehensive historical review, he traces the refinement of the quantity theory, the price-parity theory and the growing recognition of balance of payments, income and national finance considerations. In his own recapitulation, Angell builds upon the classical theory but with major alterations and additions. He rejects the reliance on comparative labor costs or on any other theory of "value" and insists on the use of money prices as the only significant factor in international price theory. Written well in advance of the collapse of currency convertibility in the 1930s, his discussion of ways of dealing with such situations was particularly important.

HARROD, ROY FORBES. **International Economics.** New York: Harcourt, 1933, 211 p.

Professor Harrod's contribution to the Cambridge Economic Handbooks reached its fourth edition in 1957, but the general framework was preserved. He bases his analysis of international trade on comparative costs, disregarding the suggestions of Bertil G. Ohlin as not leading to differences of quantitative importance. However, the analysis also includes the macro-economic approach to economic problems suggested by Lord Keynes. In the 1939 edition, for example, Harrod set forth the doctrine of the "foreign trade multiplier." And at the same time he revised his chapters on the balance of payments and its relation to fluctuations in national employment and investment.

VON HABERLER, GOTTFRIED. **The Theory of International Trade.** New York: Macmillan, 1936, 408 p.

Published in German in 1933, Professor von Haberler's impressive treatise provides a systematic treatment of the main problems arising from international economic transactions. The text and voluminous footnotes are an excellent summary of the related literature. The first part deals with the balance of payments, money and foreign exchange, and the tránsfer problem. As one might expect because of the time of writing, considerable attention is paid to the effect of reparations payments. The rest of the book deals with international trade theory, policy and technique. Von Haberler's basic position is that the international movement of goods and capital, unrestricted by any governmental measures, is economically advantageous. He does admit that tariffs can be defended sometimes on various grounds—as a source of revenue, for purposes of national defense, for protecting certain essential classes such as the farmer, or for economic development (the infant industry argument). He has little sympathy with efforts to deal with dumping, the use of export subsidies or the activities of international cartels. Seeing little prospect of a European customs union, he urges broader negotiations of commercial treaties on a reciprocal basis. In the end, he says, one must fight the spirit of protection and "spread far and wide correct ideas about international trade." In many later articles and pamphlets Professor von Haberler has followed his own advice.

RÖPKE, WILHELM. **International Economic Disintegration.** New York: Macmillan, 1942, 283 p.

Professor Röpke of the Graduate Institute of International Studies in Geneva was convinced in 1937 of the existence of a long-run crisis in international economic relations as part of the general economic, social and political crisis of occidental society. Everywhere he saw rising economic nationalism requiring cumulative interferences with market forces, with industrial protectionism in the agrarian states and agrarian protectionism in the industrial states. He endorses Élie Halévy's conclusion (**The Era of Tyrannies**) that since 1914 it is socialism that has led to the age of tyrannies, since economic planning is the antithesis of freedom. His proposed answer is to break down collectivism by encouraging smaller units of production and greatly limiting state intervention.

MACHLUP, FRITZ. **International Trade and the National Income Multiplier.** Philadelphia: Blakiston, 1943, 237 p.

Among Professor Machlup's contributions to international economics is this early book in which he applied the relatively new concept of the multiplier to international trade and capital movements. The concept (initial spending having a greater economic impact than the immediate transaction) had been presented initially by R. F. Kahn in the *Economic Journal* in 1931 and further developed by Lord Keynes in his **General Theory** in 1936. Starting with the point that changes in disbursements, such as additional investments or exports, have an effect upon a series of subsequent transactions, Machlup applies the concept to foreign trade, demonstrating the step-by-step adjustments of incomes, imports and exports over time. Eleven different models based on different assumptions and with time periods of different lengths are presented. One important conclusion is the beneficial result of the export of capital from countries with an abundant capital supply to countries with meagre resources. He believes that foreign lending may be a generator of national income in the lending country if it activates liquid funds.

MYRDAL, GUNNAR. **An International Economy: Problems and Prospects.** New York: Harper, 1956, 381 p.

Playing his usual role of Cassandra, the eminent Swedish economist develops the thesis that despite increased integration within individual advanced countries, international economic integration is in a bad way indeed, weakened by wars, the Depression and the growth of economic nationalism. Further divisive influences have been the cold war and the emergence of independent underdeveloped countries, themselves often not internally integrated. Moreover, he finds that the international flow of labor and capital are no longer important unifying streams, while imports are restricted.

Foreign aid is described as insignificant and haphazard, even though Myrdal regards the dominant problem of international integration as arising from the tremendous and growing disparities between the industrially advanced nations and the underdeveloped ones. Professor Myrdal notes that the spread of Western ideals of liberty and equality is coming at the moment when the new countries are faced with tremendous internal political problems and when the growing inwardness of the richer countries prevents international human solidarity.

The book was evidently drafted before the concept of the European Economic Community took form, for the author feels that there is little interest in Europe in the development of common policies. However that may be, Myrdal calls for global international coöperation in which the underprivileged nations will join their forces to achieve stronger bargaining power, and much greater use will be made of the international agencies.

MEADE, JAMES EDWARD. **The Theory of International Economic Policy. Volume I: The Balance of Payments.** New York: Oxford University Press (for the Royal Institute of International Affairs), 1951, 432 p. (With **Mathematical Supplement,** 162 p.)
————. **Volume II: Trade and Welfare.** New York: Oxford University Press (for the Royal Institute of International Affairs), 1955, 618 p. (With **Mathematical Supplement,** 128 p.)

These two volumes represent one of the most comprehensive presentations of international economic theory ever published. The first volume deals with the interlocking problems of preserving payments in balance between nations and maintaining full employment domestically within each nation. In his conclusions, Professor Meade relies heavily upon methods of price adjustment. The second volume deals with the same subject matter but, after a lengthy discussion of the theory of economic welfare, analyzes controls over international movements of goods and factors in terms of the efficient use of the world's economic resources, the supply of those resources and the distribution of the total of world income among the various countries. Although the author states his interest to be the formation of economic policy, the book works from abstract models which only partially represent the concrete problems of the policy-maker, and its mass of detail and methodology suit the professional economist much more than the practical operator. Furthermore, the analysis is generally in the form of comparative statics (how variable X changes situation A to situation B) rather than one of continuing dynamics. Nevertheless, the two volumes are an impressive product of pure economic analysis, bringing into play many refinements which have never before been brought into the international relations field. Meade suggests that the value of theoretical inquiry is in finding important factors and relationships, which may be of use in the study of particular problems and where further analysis may combine theory with useful statistical and institutional information.

JOHNSON, HARRY GORDON. **International Trade and Economic Growth.** Cambridge: Harvard University Press, 1958, 204 p.

Professor Johnson deals with a number of theoretical problems in international economics under the general headings of comparative cost, trade and growth, and balance of payments. Much of the book is highly technical, frequently synthesizing and extending the work of previous writers. This is evidenced, for example, in his discussion of the influence of differences in factor supplies on the pattern of trade and of trade on relative factor prices. His analytical ability is particularly evident in his defense of the proposition that a country may gain by imposing a tariff even if other countries retaliate. Perhaps the most important contribution is his discussion of the balance of payments. He distinguishes between "flow" deficits created by the process of exchanging goods and services and "stock" deficits resulting from the purchase of assets. The former are thought of as subject to conventional pressures of interest rates, trade controls and foreign exchange rate adjustments. The behavior of the latter has been much less thoroughly analyzed in international trade theory. Johnson suggests that the conditions which make a "stock" deficit a policy problem indicate that direct control methods are preferable as compared to the price system method of correction applicable to "flow" deficits.

International Economic Relations. Minneapolis: University of Minnesota Press, 1934, 414 p.

The Commission of Inquiry into National Policy in International Economic Relations (Robert M. Hutchins, Chairman, and Alvin H. Hansen, Research Director) was sponsored by the Social Science Research Council. It held public hearings and presented a series of recommendations related to recovery from the Depression. This volume includes the report of the Commission, a separate report by Professor Hansen, 19 expert memoranda and brief summaries of the public hearings. The report struck strongly at the nationalist forces which had undermined the international economic world. It asked for tariff reductions not limited to the 50 percent of the Trade Agreements Act and for a dismissal wage to be paid by government in the case of injury from imports. It endorsed the removal of restrictions on long-term private foreign loans and opposed official foreign lending. It supported authority for the Tariff Commission to lower tariffs presumably on the basis of cost studies. Following so soon after the high Hawley-Smoot Tariff Act of 1930, this report contributed to the reversal in direction in 1934.

VINER, JACOB. **The Customs Union Issue.** New York: Carnegie Endowment, 1950, 221 p.

When the idea of a customs union—an arrangement whereby several countries establish free trade among themselves but maintain a common tariff against the rest of the world—came to the fore after World War II as a possible step toward European integration, its proponents regarded it as a way of knitting countries together short of political union, but its opponents saw it as undermining the non-discrimination principle in the General Agreement on Tariffs and Trade.

Professor Viner's study, regarded as the classic on the subject, sees no necessary incompatibility with GATT principles if the customs union is approximately complete, *i.e.* internal barriers are eliminated. It then is equivalent to a larger country. However, from the economic point of view, he argues that final judgment depends upon whether or not the result is trade diversion or trade creation. The answer will depend on the structure of production and trade of the participating countries and how the customs union operates in practice. Viner points out the particular circumstances to be considered, such as the size of the area, the consequent level of tariffs against the outside world, the possible economies within the area and the nature and distribution of previously protected industries. His views were of major importance in weakening the position of those economists who insisted on the goal of universal nondiscrimination, and thus the book undoubtedly contributed to the acceptance of the European Economic Community.

BALASSA, BELA A. **The Theory of Economic Integration.** Homewood: Irwin, 1961, 304 p.

Professor Balassa's analysis of economic integration starts with established theory on customs unions (see Jacob Viner, **The Customs Union Issue**) and examines more broadly the economic policies which the dynamics of integration would require. He sees integration among industrial countries as aimed at reducing trade-and-payments restrictions, mitigating cyclical fluctuations and accelerating growth. In underdeveloped countries, the emphasis is on economic development. He opposes integration except where political considerations prevent any other, in that such partial arrangements may create internal strains with nonintegrated sectors.

The importance of Professor Balassa's analysis lies in his evaluation of the many elements which enter the integration process, for example, market size, economies of scale, external economies, enhanced competition and risk and uncertainty in foreign transaction. His analysis of the nontrade policy issues which arise as integration becomes more and more complete is particularly valuable. He also discusses the difficult problem of the harmonization of social policies and fiscal operations, and then the problem of monetary unification and a common approach to the balance of payments. Thus Balassa, writing in 1961, forecast the evolution of the European Economic Community, not only in its absorption of the sectoral arrangements but in the series of new problems which it has had to face.

TINBERGEN, JAN. **International Economic Integration.** Amsterdam: Elsevier, 3rd rev. ed., 1964, 141 p.

Tinbergen explains that per capita production varies greatly among countries due to the relative quantities of land and capital available, the education of the population and the institutional framework. The most important forms of intercourse are the transfer of products and of capital. As to trade in products, protection may ease the shock of adaptation or help infant industries, but in the long run it helps to maintain less productive units. However, his main interest is in an international integration in a form which will provide more stability in the financial area and accelerated development in the less-developed countries. But national governments tend to be obstacles to progress, he notes. What is needed is further strengthening of the international organizational structure—international parliamentary and operating agencies. An important conclusion is that "with more centralization in financial policy many other instruments of economic policy can be left decentralized."

THORP, WILLARD L. **Business Annals.** New York: National Bureau of Economic Research, 1926, 380 p.

The National Bureau of Economic Research has included a number of international studies in its series on business cycles. This volume, the first in the series, used comments by contemporary observers as well as statistical material to obtain descriptions of business conditions in 17 countries from 1890 to 1925, for the United States and England since 1790, France since 1840, Germany since 1853 and Austria since 1867. Cycles were present in all cases from the earliest point, those in the United States being more frequent than for any other country. As seen from 1926, there clearly was a common pattern with increasing conformity to a common international cycle.

Among other Bureau studies relating business cycles to international affairs are: Harry Jerome, **Migration and Business Cycles** (New York: National Bureau of Economic Research, 1926, 256 p.); Oskar Morgenstern, **International Financial Transactions and Business Cycles** (Princeton: Princeton University Press, 1959, 591 p.); and Ilse Mintz, **Cyclical Fluctuations in the Exports of the United States since 1879** (New York: National Bureau of Economic Research, 1967, 332 p.).

COPPOCK, JOSEPH DAVID. **International Economic Instability: The Experience after World War II.** New York: McGraw-Hill, 1962, 184 p.

This econometric study aims at measuring the different degrees of instability in international economic relations after World War II and explaining the differences shown to exist among countries by relating their instability indexes to other measurable variables. Professor Coppock used export proceeds for 83 countries, 1946–1958, as the basis for instability indexes, ranging from the widest fluctuations for Iran and Indonesia to the greatest stability for Switzerland and Ireland. In general, trade value was much less stable than trade volume. Instability seems to be relatively highly correlated with physical volume and with rate of growth of exports, and negatively related to foreign trade as a percent of GNP, foreign trade per capita and percent of exports going to the United States.

Professor Coppock makes it clear that there is no single indirectly connected variable which is likely to have much influence on export stability, that stability in a few countries or a few commodities will not make much difference in world trade generally, and that stabilization of a country's imports does not seem to have much effect on its export stability. He suggests that greater availability of short-term credits could be helpful. The work is a forerunner of the extension of correlation analysis made possible by the statistical data explosion and the computer. The quantity of data, however, has far outrun its quality, and his calculations for certain individual countries must be regarded as approximate at best.

MACBEAN, ALASDAIR I. **Export Instability and Economic Development.** Cambridge: Harvard University Press, 1967, 367 p.

This book challenges the long-held and little researched series of propositions that primary products, due to inelasticity of demand and uncertainty of supply, are subject to wide price swings, that as a consequence the countries whose exports depend largely on such products have unstable foreign earnings, and finally that the importance of such exports to such countries gives them a multiplier action which creates unstable domestic earnings and adversely affects the process of investment and growth. MacBean's elaborate econometric study, often limited by inadequate data, indicates that the importance of short-term export instability to underdeveloped countries has probably been exaggerated. There is little evidence to show that their economies have been damaged. He finds the foreign-trade multiplier to be relatively low in most underdeveloped countries. Variations in quantities are so important that price stabilization may actually enhance instability of total earnings.

The author's detailed studies of individual cases lead him to question national stabilization schemes, and he is even less enthusiastic about international commodity agreements. He does suggest that, when temporary balance-of-payments difficulties do appear, an increase in the availability of credit seems likely to be helpful.

Under pressure from certain less-developed countries, the problem of stabilizing export earnings and of compensatory credit arrangements has been high on the U.N. Conference on Trade and Development's agenda. While MacBean denies the general importance of the problem, his studies are useful in indicating what the strategic elements are in the limited number of cases where stabilizing action might be beneficial.

LUNDBERG, ERIK. **Instability and Economic Growth.** New Haven: Yale University Press, 1968, 433 p.

In this book, Professor Lundberg examined cyclical or conjunctural instability from 1950 to 1964 for a number of countries—particularly the United Kingdom, Sweden, the Netherlands, Japan, the United States and Canada—to see to what extent there was any common denominator in their deviations from balanced economic growth. His conclusion is that the national conjuncture patterns have shown little similarity but have varied greatly among the countries examined, due to differences in their institutions and economic structures. He emphasizes the revolution in statistical methods and in techniques of observation which make instability more apparent, and in the sensitivity of governments to the state of the economy. The importance of the book lies in the way in which it tests various theories concerning the destabilizing process and reviews the effectiveness of different policies aimed at stabilization through an examination of the historical record.

ECONOMIC GROWTH AND DEVELOPMENT

General

SCHUMPETER, JOSEPH A. **The Theory of Economic Development.** Cambridge: Harvard University Press, 1934, 255 p.

Professor Schumpeter was not satisfied with the economists' search for equilibrium nor with their insistence that their thinking must end whenever it reaches the boundaries of economics. He sees a circular flow of economic life whereby a stream of goods and a stream of money must be more or less in balance. Development, on the other hand, is spontaneous and brings discontinuous change in the channels of the flow and a disturbance of equilibrium. In this volume he stresses particularly the role played by innovation which often is the result of technology, although other forces, such as the opening of a new market or even a new industrial organization, also continually disturb the circular flows. He points out that all of these require new and different combinations of economic resources. For him the entrepreneur is the key to progress since he is the innovator and the active force. He ends his book by using the same analysis of discontinuous disturbances to explain fluctuations in business conditions.

In the 1930s Schumpeter was among the important economists who insisted that economic thinking should be less concerned with equilibrium and pay more attention to change and development. In a later book, **Capitalism, Socialism, and Democracy,** he compares economic systems in dynamic terms, with a critical section on Marxism.

CLARK, COLIN. **The Conditions of Economic Progress.** New York: Macmillan, 3rd ed., 1957, 584 p.

A provocative examination of masses of data on national income and related topics for the principal countries in an effort to explain the factors of growth. Avowedly limiting himself to economic progress, Clark examines the flow of goods and services, allowing for expenditure of effort (work-time as against leisure) and for inequalities and instability of income. Clark's data, after emphasizing national differences in output and productivity, suggest that most of the richer countries (United States, Canada, France) have had substantial periods of rapid growth after which stagnation in per capita improvement set in, with unemployment and shorter workdays. He was among the first to examine statistically the shift from primary to secondary to tertiary industries. Even though the data available were far from adequate, he produces analyses using the Cobb-Douglas formula for the relation of capital to output, the Pareto coefficient for income distribution and a multiplier function between national income and the value of investment.

NURKSE, RAGNAR. **Problems of Capital Formation in Underdeveloped Countries.** New York: Oxford University Press, 1953, 163 p.

Ragnar Nurkse, in reviewing the requirements for development, emphasized the necessity for balanced growth, the concept with which his name is associated. He argues that an industry, adding its product to the supply, does not create a corresponding demand for the same product and that expansion on many fronts is essential for growth. He emphasizes particularly the importance of expansion in the home market, since he was not optimistic about the elasticity of demand for most less-developed-country exports. Nevertheless, Professor Nurkse suggests that the world is not rich enough to ignore efficiency and certain development needs can be met only with foreign exchange and external capital. His theory of capital movement is that it should be a reaction to the unequal proportions in which capital coöperates with labor and land in the different parts of the world, to technological designs and to fundamental matters such as population growth. Under conditions of balanced growth, the ultimate transfer problem of debt service should, he believes, be manageable. Nurkse later expanded this relatively brief analysis in **Equilibrium and Growth in the World Economy: Economic Essays** (Cambridge: Harvard University Press, 1961, 380 p.). The opposite point of view concerning balance is presented by Albert Hirschman in **The Strategy of Economic Development.**

LEE, DOUGLAS HARRY KEDGWIN. **Climate and Economic Development in the Tropics.** New York: Harper (for the Council on Foreign Relations), 1957, 182 p.

A physiologist and climatologist reports here on the connection between tropical climates and economic underdevelopment. He notes that high temperatures and humidity aid crop production in some cases but more often are disadvantageous. Heavy rainfall depletes the plant nutrients in the soil, diseases and pests are extensive, and storage is difficult. While there are solutions to each difficulty, systems of land tenure, lack of communication, ignorance and poverty all complicate the situation.

Lee believes that the capacity of men for physical work is little changed when acclimatization is complete, but that there is an increased disinclination for work. He suggests that this may reflect the absence of the need to secure food and shelter in advance of cold weather. He does not, however, believe that climate is the main determinant of the level of industrial development in the tropics, though heavy rainfall may interfere with air and land transportation, and bright sunlight and humidity may cause deterioration in materials and products. His conclusion emphasizes the need for organization of research for continuous study of the direct and indirect effects of hot climate.

MEADE, JAMES EDWARD. **A Neo-Classical Theory of Economic Growth.** New York: Oxford University Press, 2d ed., 1961, 185 p.

This is a remarkable theoretical analysis based upon classical assumptions of perfect competition, payments to factors equal to the value of their marginal products, and of a successful Keynesian policy with respect to investment. Within this framework, Meade shows how growth results from population growth, capital accumulation and technical progress. A mathematical appendix discusses the effect of these forces on the price of capital goods in terms of consumption goods. One of the important additions in the second edition is a discussion of growth under conditions where there is a large reserve of unemployed labor. Professor Meade has greatly expanded this analysis in **The Growing Economy** (London: Allen and Unwin, 1968, 512 p.), which is summarized in its subtitle: "A Modern Statement in the Classical Tradition, Elegant and Rigorous, of the Basic Concepts of Economic Analysis."

Capital Formation and Economic Growth. Princeton: Princeton University Press, 1955, 677 p.

This volume consists of a series of papers plus comments with replies by the authors. Subjects include: sources and channels of finance in capitalist countries; savings and finance in the Soviet Union; the influence of enterprise and business organization in advanced countries and then in underdeveloped countries; and the relationship of technology to capital formation. An exploratory conference in 1949 had concluded that both empirical work and theoretical hypotheses concerning economic growth were lacking. The later discussion makes clear that the simple analysis of saving, finance and investment is complicated by the manner in which these activities are carried on in different countries and at different points of time. Furthermore, the old emphasis on interest rates tended to be short-range and to have little concern with rates of growth. Throughout the book runs a continuous thread of the importance of institutions in capital formation and particularly of government policies.

ROSTOW, WALT WHITMAN. **The Stages of Economic Growth: A Non-Communist Manifesto.** New York: Cambridge University Press, 1960, 178 p.

This book has served as a catalytic agent, greatly stimulating interest in the historical process of social change. It describes a society as passing through five stages—the traditional society, the preconditions for takeoff, the takeoff, the drive to maturity and the age of high mass-consumption. Not only is there a discussion of the forces involved in the transitions from one stage to another, but the status of 14 countries is located within the progression.

The idea of the takeoff caught hold, usually without recognition of the author's "massive set of preconditions" but only of the strategic part played by an increase in investment from 5 to 10 percent of the national product. It is usually forgotten that the subtitle of the book is "A Non-Communist Manifesto" and that the last half presents a critique of Marx's description of economic stages.

ROSTOW, WALT WHITMAN, *ed.* **The Economics of Take-Off into Sustained Growth.** New York: St. Martin's Press, 1963, 481 p.

At Konstanz, Germany in 1960, 15 economists and historians from various countries examined Professor Rostow's thesis concerning the stages of economic growth. The papers cannot be summarized; nor can the 175-page summary record of the debate. The definitions of stages were challenged as inexact, and the various national experts all had special difficulties about applying the generalizations to their own countries, virtually never agreeing with Rostow's analysis. Nevertheless, the total is a lively and stimulating discussion by a high-level group of experts on the process and complexities of economic growth as demonstrated by the more advanced countries.

MAIZELS, ALFRED. **Industrial Growth and World Trade.** New York: Cambridge University Press, 1963, 563 p.

The chief aim of this impressive study, heavy with statistics, is to analyze the long-term relationship between industrial growth and international trade in manufactured goods. So far as data permit, it covers all trading nations from 1899 to 1959. In the analysis, Professor Maizels distinguishes between the nonindustrial countries, the industrializing primary-producing countries where a social and economic transformation is involved, and the already industrialized countries where economic development is merely continuing.

Professor Maizels concludes that industrialization is the key to economic progress since it steps up per capita productivity. He adds some specific conclusions. Industrialization first centers on food, textiles and clothing but then moves to capital goods, chemicals and durable consumer goods. As for growth in trade, it has paralleled manufacturing production, except for a break in the 1930s. Primary products prices rose more than those for manufactured goods up to 1939, but the trend has reversed since then. Trade has grown most rapidly among industrial countries and promises to continue to do so. Developing countries should not be expected to be able to meet their capital requirements from increased exports.

Though somewhat skeptical of forecasting, Professor Maizels expects that trade in manufactured goods in the last quarter of the century will be largely, or even mainly, in the development sector of engineering and chemical products. To face this situation, he says, Britain needs to reduce her concentration on exports which are subject to import-substitution and adapt her exporting industry to the changing pattern of world demand. Thus, this volume is an excellent example of how the orderly examination of economic data can produce recommendations for economic policy.

KUZNETS, SIMON. **Modern Economic Growth: Rate, Structure, and Spread.** New Haven: Yale University Press, 1966, 529 p.

It is not surprising that Professor Kuznets, best known for his major contributions in the field of national income, should have moved on to examine the problems of economic growth through international comparisons. His compilations of basic data for many nations have appeared in ten supplements to *Economic Development and Cultural Change* between 1956 and 1965, and selected essays of his were published in **Economic Growth and Structure** (New York: Norton, 1965, 378 p.). The title here listed presents selected data, describes long-term trends, points out national differences, and presents qualifications and questions. He discusses national variations according to population and resources, industrial structure, product and income distribution, international flows, and the economic and social structure of underdeveloped countries. Kuznets raises more questions than he answers, but the net result is an encyclopedic picture of what could be learned from an expert scrutiny of the data available in 1965.

ADELMAN, IRMA and MORRIS, CYNTHIA TAFT. **Society, Politics and Economic Development.** Baltimore: Johns Hopkins Press, 1967, 307 p.

The authors present a systematic statistical analysis of social, political and economic characteristics of nations at varying stages of economic development. Indicators were prepared for 74 countries based upon 41 variables which, in turn, were often composite indexes. For example, the measure for the extent of mass communication, a social indicator, was based upon data for newspapers and radios. The general pattern which the authors found was that as a society evolves, there is progressive differentiation of the social, political and economic spheres from each other and the development of specialized institutions and attitudes within each sphere. In the least developed countries, social factors are dominant and limit progress. With economic growth, the social controls are disrupted, and political forces come more and more into play. In the highly developed countries, the principal obstacles to economic progress are adverse political conditions. This growth pattern suggests that the nature of economic assistance should vary with the level of development. While there can be endless debate over the data and methodology used, the approach is exciting and the general conclusions are less open to challenge.

Less-Developed Countries

STALEY, EUGENE. **The Future of Underdeveloped Countries: Political Implications of Economic Development.** New York: Harper (for the Council on Foreign Relations), 2d rev. ed., 1961, 483 p.

This work, originally published in 1954, was one of the first books about the less-developed countries to set the problem in a political perspective, particularly the dangers of an "aggressive thrust of international communism." Staley argues that the underdeveloped areas are a primary target for communist infiltration and conquest, that countermeasures must be framed with a regard to special sensitivities of the areas concerned, and that economic progress does not necessarily lead to peace, democracy or civil liberties. He suggests that there are grave difficulties with relying upon the "leave it to private enterprise" formula and that an affirmative American policy symbolized by Point Four demonstrates a coöperative desire to help.

Seventy-two pages were added in the revised edition. Staley's approach has not changed, but his fears are intensified. He argues that the revolution of rising expectations is increasing in intensity, that Soviet aid and propaganda have developed substantially since 1953, and that the West must increase its efforts. Specifically, he urges that the United States follow aid and trade policies based on the concept of world community, particularly through much stronger support for the United Nations institutions.

LEWIS, WILLIAM ARTHUR. **The Theory of Economic Growth.** London: Allen and Unwin, 1955, 453 p.

This is a classic analysis among the early books concerning economic growth, dealing with the many factors involved in increasing output per head of population.

It came at a time when the new efforts to assist the less-developed areas had assumed substantial importance on the international stage while the simple ideas of how to do it had been largely discredited. Professor Lewis's analysis recognizes two basic divisions within an economy—the capital-using sector and the subsistence sector. Each has its own characteristics, and one can say that the problem of economic growth is to get more of the first and less of the latter.

Although the book recognizes the importance of natural resources, Professor Lewis's main concern is in reviewing human motivation and the institutions which direct and encourage or discourage action. As might be expected from the central position given to capital, Lewis antedates W. W. Rostow in placing emphasis on the level of savings. Attention is also given to factors contributing to growth in addition to capital, namely knowledge, population and government.

While the subject of the book is economic growth—why are we as well off as we are and why are some nations much better off than others—the interest of the author in social and economic change carries him into many other fields, not only sociology and history but biology, ethics and law. Professor Lewis summarizes his own position as having "fair confidence on how society changes but little or no confidence on the directions in which it is likely to change." An appendix raises the question of whether economic growth is desirable, but ends up with the notion that change is inevitable and it is probably best to try to accelerate the process of growth.

AGARWALA, AMAR NARAIN and SINGH, SAMPAT PAL, eds. **The Economics of Underdevelopment.** New York: Oxford University Press, 1959, 510 p.

Most of the new literature on economic development has been scattered through journals and periodicals. Many of the more significant contributions are brought together in this volume, which includes 21 articles and papers by such a variety of writers as Jacob Viner, Paul Baran, H. Myint, Simon Kuznets, W. W. Rostow, Henry Wallich, P. N. Rosenstein-Rodan, Celso Furtado, Hollis Chenery and M. Bronfenhenner.

All present general and overall analyses of underdevelopment. Of the six groups of articles, several, such as that on external economies and balanced growth, present both thesis and antithesis. In one section different authors discuss economic development first in terms of Schumpeter, then in terms of Keynes and finally in terms of the later group ranging from Harrod to Fellner. The final section gives four models of development, pointing out the strategic points in differing analyses. All in all, it is a book full of general and provocative ideas. While the disagreement among the authors makes it abundantly clear that there is not yet any accepted general theory, it is also evident that many lively minds have accepted the challenge. One might hope that a similar inventory ten years later would show as much progress over the decade as does this book for the period up to 1958.

HIRSCHMAN, ALBERT O. **The Strategy of Economic Development.** New Haven: Yale University Press, 1958, 217 p.

The primary contribution of this book is its defense of unbalanced growth. The author notes that expansion in some particular line, i.e. motor vehicles, forces development in others, such as modern highways and gasoline distribution, and argues that though various investments and economic activities depend on each other, their development does not have to be simultaneous. He reasons that economic planning is likely to emphasize balance and thus lose an important stimulus to growth. Among the applications of this idea is the argument that added overhead capital is less stimulating than investment in directly productive activities and that the deliberate creation of shortages is a more dynamic approach. He notes further that an imbalance of imports often builds local markets and ultimately makes possible domestic production of substitute goods, and that there are geographical imbalances which create regional or national growing points. While he recognizes that the more rapid development of such centers may absorb an undue proportion of private and public resources for development, he reasons that they would nevertheless be a stimulus to other areas.

While there is much to be said for Professor Hirschman's idea of the stimulating effect of imbalance, it is also possible that, if the lagging parts of an economy do not react, they may restrain further progress. In fact, later analysts have reached the point of recognizing that some imbalance is a good thing, if there is not too much of it.

SHONFIELD, ANDREW. **The Attack on World Poverty.** New York: Random House, 1960, 269 p.

Professor Shonfield makes it clear that there are many obstacles to the effective use of foreign aid—political, educational, cultural and technological. Nevertheless, there are some countries, such as India, Mexico and Brazil, where greatly increased assistance might be expected to accelerate their rate of economic growth and ultimate achievement of economic independence. Even in those three cases, his estimate of aid of $1 billion for the three together is less than the actual flow by the mid-1960s. The author follows the Rostow formula that what is required for modernization is a rise in the level of investment from around 5 percent to 10–12 percent of national income. In reviewing the channels of assistance, he finds the United Nations structure and policy-making too much bound by inertia and timidity, and its resources too limited to be effective. The World Bank also has not had a continuous thread of policy and should have done much more for agriculture. The good idea of the International Development Association was frustrated by balance-of-payments troubles of the United States and United Kingdom. The author concludes that these central agencies must be strengthened; and to get more aid, he suggests the use of tied aid, more transfer of obsolescent machinery, and national contributions related to their balance-of-payments positions in a system of "mutual convenience."

HOFFMAN, PAUL GRAY. **World without Want.** New York: Harper and Row, 1962, 144 p.

As administrator of the Marshall Plan, the United Nations Special Fund and the United Nations Development Program, Paul Hoffman has a unique place in the history of programs of foreign assistance. This little book is important because it expresses his credo—that there is seething unrest among peoples in scores of underdeveloped countries and "we cannot sit by and do nothing." He sees the possibility of a major forward thrust in economic development, especially because of advances in science and technology. It is a simple book, drawing on his personal experience and expressing his deeply felt belief that it is possible to create a world by 2000 AD that will have overcome poverty.

Partners in Development: Report of the Commission on International Development. New York: Praeger, 1969, 399 p.

In 1967, the World Bank asked this Commission (of which Lester B. Pearson was chairman) to review the consequences of 20 years of development assistance and propose policies for the future. The report gives a strong endorsement of foreign aid, suggesting a number of ways for increasing its effectiveness. Recognizing that the volume of aid in the last half of the 1960s has increased slowly relative to national income, that terms have hardened, and that conditions such as aid-tying have become more restrictive, the report argues for a new strategy resting on the improved performance of the less-developed countries and the sustained commitment of the richer countries. This strategy would include expanding international trade, encouraging foreign private investment, bringing suppliers and recipients closer in a partnership relation, increasing the volume and softening the terms of aid, slowing the growth of population, emphasizing education and research, and making more use of international agencies. The Commission proposed a target for official development assistance of .7 percent of gross national product. The authority of the members of the Commission and the depth of their examination made this a highly important document in its broad influence, particularly since it was presented at a time when the future of U.S. efforts was uncertain, to say the least.

PINCUS, JOHN. **Trade, Aid and Development: The Rich and Poor Nations.** New York: McGraw-Hill (for the Council on Foreign Relations), 1967, 400 p.

In this contribution to the Atlantic Policy Studies of the Council on Foreign Relations, the author discusses the political and economic interest and policies of the rich nations toward the less-developed world. He reviews general trade and development theory, concluding that trade is necessary but is not necessarily an "engine of development," although foreign exchange availability is likely to be a major constraint on growth. He discusses specific policy issues in the field of trade, especially trade preferences where he sees some limited political and economic advantages, and commodity stabilization programs which he feels might be better accomplished by more general stability in the rich countries than by individual commodity agreements. His conclusions on aid are based on the proposition that there is little prospect for increasing volume but that much can be done to make its use more productive. In the end, he sees the basic problem as ethical in that the present policies of the rich nations are, in effect, a choice that not much assistance will be given to development.

In his discussion, the author makes use of his RAND Corporation study, **Economic Aid and International Cost Sharing** (Baltimore: Johns Hopkins Press, 1965, 221 p.), in which he argues that a loan should be regarded as aid only to the extent that the present value of the future payments of interest and amortization on a discounted basis is less than that which would result from market rates.

MYINT, HLA. **The Economics of the Developing Countries.** New York: Praeger, 1965, 192 p.

Professor Myint challenges much of orthodox economic thought as not being relevant to the conditions of less-developed countries. He insists that more attention should be paid to countries which are at an early stage of development and which do not suffer from population pressure. He regards discontent as not exclusively the result of poverty and also questions the usefulness of capital-output ratios, the concept of the takeoff and the objective of balanced growth. He feels that emphasis on exports encourages a dualistic economic structure, seeing the problem in terms of difficult policy choices: income or stability; consumption or investment; equality or growth; higher incomes or the preservation of traditional social, cultural and religious values. Myint would prefer to have these choices made through the market mechanism, with major efforts focused on raising the level of skills, and foreign aid concentrated on a few countries at a time, beginning with those whose development is most promising. He believes that much more effective assistance could be provided by opening foreign markets and giving more stability to the prices of primary exports.

FURTADO, CELSO. **Development and Underdevelopment.** Berkeley: University of California Press, 1964, 181 p.

In discussing growth problems the author moves easily between the theoretical approaches of Keynes, Marx and classical economists, and the realities as he sees them. In this highly original analysis, based in part on Brazilian experience, he distinguishes between developed economies, where increased productivity must come from technological innovation, and underdeveloped countries, where advance involves the application of techniques already known. As he saw it, the major problem faced by the latter is that progress requires a structural adjustment away from a rigid and traditional social and economic orientation. All too often, he observed the contemporary development process in underdeveloped countries as forming a capitalistic wedge with limited links to the main archaic structure, and as putting great pressure on the balance of payments largely because of the wrong pattern of capital formation.

TINBERGEN, JAN. **Shaping the World Economy: Suggestions for an International Economic Policy.** New York: Twentieth Century Fund, 1962, 330 p.

The main body of this book consists of policy suggestions by Professor Tinbergen to strengthen the international economy. He centered his attention on the development of economically backward countries, which he described as the world's most important economic problem. He saw investment as the core of development policies and urged a world investment program in the form of assistance of at least double existing levels. Furthermore, he argued that trade impediments should be minimal, although he would give some temporary protection for young or small-scale industries, and suggested that tariff reductions be made by commodity groups rather than individual items. He advocated regional or continental groupings for the purpose of economic policy in general and trade policy in particular. Pointing out that financial and monetary policies also are subject to national preoccupations and need to be harmonized, he proposed use of the United Nations agencies in executing the policies advocated.

Tinbergen's general analysis is supplemented by appendices written by specialists dealing with the particular economic development problems of each continent. There are also statistical analyses of world trade flows and of the limited consequences of possible tariff reductions for a number of commodities on imports, government revenue and employment.

PLANNING; FOREIGN AID

ROBBINS, LIONEL CHARLES. **Economic Planning and International Order.** New York: Macmillan, 1937, 330 p.

Noting the ambiguity of the word "planning," Professor Robbins analyzes the significance for international affairs of independent national planning, partial international planning and complete international planning. The international aspects of independent national planning are protectionism, nationalized industry and the control of foreign investment and migration. The author holds that such interferences work against the most efficient use of resources and distribution of products and produce greater instability. He notes also the weaknesses of partial international planning, but he reserves his strongest criticism for complete international planning, which, as he sees it, could only mean international communism. He regards any such system as impractical, for there would be no meaningful price system either reflecting the wants of consumers or the costs of the various factors of production.

Even though he recognized that it will not guarantee the optimum use of resources, Robbins favored a return to laissez-faire and to the gold standard. It was noteworthy that in the middle of the Great Depression, when there was wide discontent with the system, a leading British economist should argue in favor of international liberalism, not strengthened nationalism.

WALLACE, DONALD HOLMES. **Economic Controls and Defense.** New York: Twentieth Century Fund, 1953, 260 p.

In 1950, the Twentieth Century Fund sponsored four studies on how to protect and maintain an effective civilian economy under mobilization pressures. The first three volumes dealt essentially with the avoidance of inflation. The final study, that by Professor Wallace, deals with the use of direct controls over materials, manpower, prices and wages. His task is essentially that of considering ways and means of minimizing the dangers to free, democratic institutions of either inflation or direct controls or both. While the illustrations given are usually from American experience, the conclusions would seem to have universal application. In a concluding chapter, J. M. Clark argues that there should be strong indirect controls to support direct controls, but the entire apparatus should be discarded at the earliest possible moment.

If Professor Wallace were writing on the same subject in 1970, he would not have to change his general analysis, since even the limited mobilization resulting from the Vietnam War led, as he would have predicted, to a dangerous inflation, against which indirect controls alone proved to be singularly ineffective.

BETTELHEIM, CHARLES OSCAR. **Studies in the Theory of Planning.** Bombay: Asia Publishing House, 1959, 451 p.

Prepared especially for Indian readers, the first part of this book is a partial translation of Bettelheim's early book, **Problèmes Théoriques et Pratiques de Planification** (Paris: Presses Universitaires, 1946, 349 p.), in which a systematic approach is presented to the problems of planned economic growth, of investment allocation and of technological choice. The tests which he believes are basic relate to employment, labor productivity, balance in the structure, the standard of living and the volume of saving. In the second part, the author presents a growth model based on the initial establishment of a given rate of increase of aggregate consumption. From this, he is able, at least theoretically, to find the optimum with respect to the five tests noted above. One general conclusion which he reaches is that socialization of the ownership of the means of production is needed for genuine economic planning. Otherwise, not only are available facts insufficient but administrative implementation of any national plan is automatically ruled out. Another of his conclusions is that an efficient economic plan, at least for India, requires substantial institutional change. Professor Bettelheim makes much of the conflict between short-run and long-run.

TINBERGEN, JAN. **Central Planning.** New Haven: Yale University Press, 1964, 150 p.

This relatively small but important discussion of planning contains unique tabular comparisons for 19 countries, covering their planning organizations, personnel, official tasks, roles of the various participants, main aims of official economic policy, sectors covered in detail and the methods used, including statistical techniques and mathematical devices. As might be expected, wide differences appear. On the basis of his own experience, Tinbergen outlines the "best" way of planning for economic policy. It is to start with a notion that the optimum planning régime for a country is one whose decisions coincide with those based on maximizing general well-being and not some single economic indicator. The planning group must be located within the government at the point where it can be effective. The author argues strongly for planning in stages: in a sense, planning should be a series of approximations.

LEWIS, W. ARTHUR. **Development Planning: The Essentials of Economic Policy.** New York: Harper and Row, 1966, 278 p.

Having written in 1955 about economic development in general (**The Theory of Economic Growth**), Professor Lewis turned a decade later to the possibilities and difficulties of planning for development. It is an operational book, some one-third being given over to an arithmetic example demonstrating the statistical framework of a hypothetical national economic plan. However, he insists that good arithmetic is not enough: a plan must be based on wise policy choices and depends for success on sensible politics, good public administration and the improvement of economic institutions—discussed in his earlier book. He argues that the planning agency should not be in a department with a special or limited interest, neither Ministry of Finance nor of Development, but should be directly responsible to the Prime Minister.

This is not a technical book for the actual planner but is intended to explain the process to the intelligent and inquiring layman. The result is a clear presentation of the nature and limitations of the planning process.

MILLIKAN, MAX FRANKLIN and ROSTOW, WALT WHITMAN. **A Proposal: Key to an Effective Foreign Policy.** New York: Harper, 1957, 170 p.

Written ten years after the beginning of large-scale American foreign aid and at a time when there was considerable talk of discontinuing the effort, this little book provided a rallying point for its supporters. It advised a much expanded long-term program of American participation in the economic development of the under-developed areas, reasoning that such action would demonstrate the interest of the United States in developing viable, energetic and confident democratic societies. While the authors argued that little attention should be paid to immediate political orientation, they pointed out that economic programs are one of the few means of influencing political developments, especially when recipients are asked to use the aid effectively to supplement their own efforts in sound development programs.

Millikan and Rostow proposed that the developed world should assure the less developed that it can obtain as much capital and technical assistance as it can use productively. They estimated that this should not be more than two or three billion dollars a year higher than flows as of the middle 1950s. (Actually, the flow in the 1960s increased even more than their estimate, even allowing for increases in the price level.) They insisted that the program should be long-run and contain an important element of international contribution and international administration. The importance of this "proposal" is indicated by the fact that the revised aid legislation of 1961 followed its general outlines closely.

WOLF, CHARLES, JR. **Foreign Aid: Theory and Practice in Southern Asia.** Princeton: Princeton University Press, 1960, 442 p.

This RAND Corporation Research Study uses the record of economic and military aid to Southern Asia, 1951–1957, as a basis for considering how the relative shares in the U.S. foreign aid program should be allocated to different countries and how they should be divided between economic and military assistance. The first half of the book describes the erratic history of aid to Southern Asia from 1945 to 1957, demonstrating that the United States did not appear to follow a clear policy line with respect to either issue. The last half of the book provides an original approach for exploring policy alternatives, even suggesting mathematical models with an aspirations function, an index of political vulnerability, a level-of-living function and an expectations function. The most unusual of these functions is related to the objective of strengthening political stability in recipient countries and measures political vulnerability by indicators of economic and social change such as level of living, literacy, unemployment and several other factors. The author is careful to emphasize that the formula is not calculable, but believes that it can be helpful in organizing the elements of the problem for proper analysis and aid in making judgments among alternatives. This is a thoughtful effort to apply the general approach of purpose-program-cost analysis to a very difficult set of problems.

NELSON, JOAN M. **Aid, Influence, and Foreign Policy.** New York: Macmillan, 1968, 149 p.

A central issue in the field of foreign aid is the conditions that can properly be attached to economic assistance to a less-developed country. Instead of offering ideological generalities about neo-imperialism and the like, this small book is an examination of the relevant experience of the Agency for International Development during the first half of the 1960s. It suggests the wide range of foreign assistance objectives, economic and political, which may apply in individual cases. Dr. Nelson is not concerned with the technical requirements relating to the actual disposition of aid, largely procedural in character, but in aid as a form of influence in broader fields. She approves strongly of the effort to use aid as leverage to promote better domestic economic policies in the recipient country—not only in the allocation of domestic resources but in policy fields such as trade controls, land tenure systems and tax provisions. She finds that this can be done most effectively in connection with commodity loans.

The author is much less certain about the wisdom and propriety of using aid for short-run political purposes, a use which she reports to be only a small fraction of AID activities. Most of the cases have dealt with specific, short-run situations such as budget or crisis support, and the results have varied.

As to using aid to promote long-run political development, Dr. Nelson points out the uncertain relationship between economic growth and democratic institutions. She recommends the introduction of a serious political development dimension as an integral part of the programming process. Since this book was published, the Congress has added in the AID legislation an instruction to the agency to include work in this direction among its objectives.

LITTLE, I. M. D. and CLIFFORD, J. M. **International Aid: A Discussion of the Flow of Public Resources from Rich to Poor Countries.** Chicago: Aldine Publishing Co., 1966, 302 p.

This is an excellent and provocative critique of the flow of public resources from rich to poor countries with particular emphasis on the problems of Africa. It is much more than a descriptive document. The authors are by no means satisfied that aid is being effectively allocated and utilized. They are particularly critical of the donors, holding that improvements in the conditions and forms of aid might do more to raise the rate of economic growth than an increase in the amount. They do suggest that the volume be increased by around $1–1.5 billion, most of this to go to India. They pay little attention to the multilateral agencies, feeling that most governments cannot be expected to give up control over their aid funds, and urge that donor governments set economic development as the goal and have less concern about their own economic or political interests.

The authors are particularly disturbed by aid-tying, by too hard financial terms and by the general lack of coördination. Their discussion of the problem of coördination leads them to urge that it be done at the country level. It is worth noting that officials in national governments and international agencies have also been concerned with these same problems, and considerable progress has been made in dealing with them, though not always along the lines suggested by these authors.

JOHNSON, HARRY GORDON. **Economic Policies toward Less Developed Countries.** Washington: Brookings Institution, 1967, 279 p.

Analyzing the 1964 United Nations Conference on Trade and Development (UNCTAD), Professor Johnson lists the main policy issues between the developed and less-developed countries as the mix of trade and aid, commodity arrangements for primary products, and preferential trade arrangements for manufactures. To these, he adds world monetary reform with the possibility of a more liberal, credit-based international monetary system, preferably an internationally controlled world central bank.

After describing the political and economic problems of economic development, Johnson argues that the developed countries, especially the United States, must shift to a positive policy stance, adjusting to the new political and economic situation rather than persisting in unchanged and essentially negative positions. He does not accept either discrimination or commodity agreements as satisfactory solutions but advocates unilateral reductions in tariffs with stronger domestic adjustment supports and a pledge not to reintroduce protective measures. He argues that trade is not an alternative to aid, that the latter should be increased, and should either be untied or the extra cost provided as a grant. The book ends with the listing of ten policy areas in which further research is needed.

FRIEDMANN, WOLFGANG G.; KALMANOFF, GEORGE and MEAGHER, ROBERT F. **International Financial Aid.** New York: Columbia University Press, 1966, 498 p.

This volume is the product of a five-year research project at the Columbia University Law School and was preceded by individual reports on public international developing financing in 12 countries. The characteristics of aid, the policies of donors and the experiences of recipients are discussed generally and then illustrated by case studies. In presenting the principal policy issues, the recommendations of the authors are presented largely by implication. However, in the final chapter they are clear that much more aid is needed, that terms should be softened, that greater emphasis should be placed on agriculture and small business and on the development of human resources, that a flexible attitude is needed with respect to the division between public and private activity, and that better planning and coördination are required. The detailed case studies on which the analysis is based give this book unusual authority.

TRADE; BALANCE OF PAYMENTS

VINER, JACOB. **Studies in the Theory of International Trade.** New York: Harper, 1937, 650 p.

Most of the considerable work of Professor Viner in the international trade field has consisted of short articles and book reviews which have eventually been collected into single volumes; for example, **International Economics** (Glencoe: Free Press, 1951, 381 p.) and **The Long View and the Short: Studies in Economic Theory and Policy** (Glencoe: Free Press, 1958, 462 p.). He has also contributed authoritative volumes on special subjects such as customs unions and dumping. This volume constitutes a series of studies which examine the theory of international trade from the revolt against English mercantilism through the English currency and tariff controversies of the nineteenth century to the accepted doctrine of 1937. He then subjects the doctrine of comparative costs to detailed scrutiny and in the last chapter considers the effect of trade on real income. For those interested in observing refined theoretical analysis at its best, this is a beautiful demonstration, whether Viner is dealing with the real cost *vs.* opportunity cost controversy or with Edgeworth's mathematical exposition. In the end, Viner emphasizes the dangers of abstraction but insists that the theory of international trade can provide presumptions whose neglect would in most cases lead to wrong policy decisions.

TAUSSIG, FRANK WILLIAM. **International Trade.** New York: Macmillan, 1927, 425 p.

For many years, Professor Taussig was the leading economist in the United States in the field of international trade. Though this book was a general text, it dominated the economics of international trade during the inter-war years. It presented trade theory in simple form along lines traced back to Ricardo and considered the probable consequences of absolute, equal and comparative differences in cost. After thus recognizing the contribution of British economists, the author shifted to the approach of the German historical school to look at what he called the actualities. He expressed dissatisfaction with the results of his examination, finding both conflicts with, and verifications of, the theory, and concluded that economic science needed much more well-sifted material for purposes of confirmation or confutation of its hypothetical generalizations. The final section in the book dealt with international trade under conditions of inconvertible paper money.

It is strange that the book contained no discussion of protection and free trade. Taussig, who had once served as Chairman of the United States Tariff Commission, offered as an excuse that he had already discussed it fully elsewhere (**The Tariff History of the United States,** New York: Putnam, 8th ed., 1931, 453 p.) and that anyway the intellectual problems raised by that issue were relatively simple and clearly implied by the more general discussion.

OHLIN, BERTIL GOTTHARD. **Interregional and International Trade.** Cambridge: Harvard University Press, 1933, 617 p.

Classical international trade theory based on comparative advantage took into account only commodity price-cost differences. The important addition made by

Ohlin was to emphasize the part played by the factors of production in establishing the structure and volume of trade. He reasoned that commodity flows, putting emphasis on the sources where the factors are most plentiful and cheapest, tend to bring about the equalization of the prices of the productive factors, but where mobility is possible, balance can also be achieved by an international flow of labor and capital. Thus the movement of either commodities or factors of production or both will keep international economic flows in balance.

In Ohlin's theoretical analysis, all these flows are controlled by the price mechanism so that "only a study of the whole price system can give a complete explanation of the interregional division of labour." In recent times, Ohlin's thesis has been generally accepted in the body of theory, but the application of the theory is limited by restraints on international movement of labor and, to a lesser degree, of capital and also by interferences with the price mechanism as it operates for major export commodities.

MASON, EDWARD SAGENDORPH. **Controlling World Trade: Cartels and Commodity Agreements.** New York: McGraw-Hill, 1946, 289 p.

Prepared in connection with the program of the Committee for Economic Development to consider possible long-term postwar policies, Professor Mason's study deals first with private international business arrangements (cartels) and then with intergovernmental commodity agreements. Emphasizing the wide divergence between American antitrust policy and the more permissive attitude toward private agreements in Europe, Mason points out that private restrictions are intended to act in behalf of a limited group rather than in the public interest. While he condemns private cartel arrangements, he recognizes that international controls relating to a commodity or industry may be demonstrably necessary, but he insists that in such case they should be intergovernmental, with efforts to balance producer and consumer interests. He proposes an international convention curbing cartels. His recommendations, based upon detailed case studies, were partially followed in the postwar period. Many of the postwar agreements contained provisions looking in this direction, and several countries, including Great Britain, moved closer to American policy. Both in Germany and Japan, the American postwar occupation moved to break up the cartel structure. So far as commodity agreements were concerned, the United States has shared Mason's skepticism, joining rather reluctantly in the few cases in which agreement has been reached.

WILCOX, CLAIR. **A Charter for World Trade.** New York: Macmillan, 1949, 333 p.

This is the authoritative history of the postwar effort to establish an international trade organization, whose objectives had been stated in various intergovernmental agreements and whose details were developed and elaborated in London, Geneva and Havana. The Havana Conference ended in March 1948 with a detailed and technical document embodying agreements reached on trade policy, cartels, commodity agreements, employment, economic development and international investment, and the constitution of a new United Nations agency in the field of international trade. Professor Wilcox outlines the history of the Charter, describes its provisions and the controversies related to their negotiation, and discusses the significance of the whole effort. The book was published before the executive branch of the United States government withdrew the proposal from the Congress, fearing that its defeat would be taken as a declaration against liberalizing trade. However, the provisions relating to commercial policy rose from the ashes and became the basis for the still flourishing General Agreement on Tariffs and Trade.

VINER, JACOB. **Dumping: A Problem in International Trade.** Chicago: University of Chicago Press, 1923, 343 p.

"Dumping" is selling in a distant market at cut prices, *i.e.* price-discrimination between national markets. This simple definition can become complicated if one includes the possible manipulation of foreign exchange, freight costs, different credit terms and the like, or if some small difference is incorporated in the product. In this early book, Professor Viner reviewed the record of dumping in the past, the effects on both parties and the efforts to deal with the problem through protective tariffs, direct legislation and other measures. He saw little difficulty with sporadic or short-run dumping, which can even be regarded as a kind of windfall to the receiving country, but noted that, at the other extreme, predatory dumping represents an effort to destroy competitors by prices which will be raised when that end is achieved. The chief evil of dumping, he feels, is its uncertain duration. In general, he reasoned that there is a sound case for dumping controls because dumping prices are presumptive evidence of abnormal and temporary cheapness, tending to disturb the operation of normal economic forces. Since Viner's book, little has been added on the theoretical aspects of the problem, although there continues to be sporadic interest in the form of appropriate legislation and how best to enforce it.

ELLIOTT, GEORGE ALEXANDER. **Tariff Procedures and Trade Barriers.** Toronto: University of Toronto Press (for the Canadian Institute of International Affairs), 1955, 293 p.

Professor Elliott has studied in detail the restrictions on trade which result from procedural costs and hurdles, sometimes intended to give protection to special groups of domestic producers but often merely the result of government rules and regulations. While many of the general steps which an importer must follow involve costs ranging from the preparation of documents to delay in obtaining delivery of imports, these tend to follow well-worn channels. Elliott, in studying the situation in Canada and the United States, has found that the procedures can hardly be described as endeavors to facilitate trade. The complexity of the tariff schedules and the intricate definitions of value are not only time-consuming but make the amount of duty uncertain. However, protection as such is more clearly involved in the restrictions such as those dealing with marks of origin, health and sanitation and so on. While each such restriction has a basic justification, the author presents a collection of American and Canadian horror stories which go far beyond the intention of the original legislation.

With the general lowering of tariff rates through the GATT machinery, non-tariff barriers have grown relatively in importance, and Elliott's study, though limited to two countries, provides an authoritative description of the problem. An earlier, less detailed study of the American situation is Percy Bidwell, **The Invisible Tariff.**

KINDLEBERGER, CHARLES POOR. **The Terms of Trade: A European Case Study.** Cambridge: Technology Press; New York: Wiley, 1956, 382 p.

An analysis of the terms of trade usually ends in a discussion of how imperfect are the price index numbers used for this purpose. The subject is here examined by Professor Kindleberger on the basis of much wider statistical evidence drawn from the imports and exports of European countries. The analysis is presented by area and commodity group. One of the important findings is the extent to which the adding of indexes of shipping costs and return on foreign capital changes the picture.

Kindleberger finds that favorable terms of trade are not necessarily the result of some basic economic contrast between the behavior of the prices of natural resources and of manufactures, but may come "from luck and flexibility, or from capacity to enter new industries and to quit old." He does not accept the classic idea that manufactured goods have fared better than raw materials, since resource scarcity may appear either in capital or land, and entry may be costly or inexpensive. In summary, he argues that the importance of favorable terms of trade as a kind of subsidy to industrial Europe has been exaggerated. He suggests that in primary-producing countries, on the other hand, trade is likely to be more important to national income and different trends in exports and import prices may therefore be more significant.

While the debate over terms of trade still goes on, made possible in part because different results can be reached for various time periods, Kindleberger's study has helped greatly to explain why it is difficult to draw any simple conclusions. The economic record depicts wide differences by commodity and area.

PATTERSON, GARDNER. **Discrimination in International Trade: The Policy Issues, 1945–1965.** Princeton: Princeton University Press, 1966, 414 p.

In constructing the post-World War II world, the International Monetary Fund and GATT were both built on the principle of equal treatment in international trade and payments, at least among their members. Professor Patterson has made a detailed study of the different forms of discrimination that have in fact been practiced in the period from 1945 to 1965. While he limits his discussion to the economic aspects of the problem, he also notes the use of trade discrimination as a political weapon, not only in the East-West situation including China and Cuba but in the United Nations-induced embargo against Rhodesia.

While a general review of GATT by its members in 1955 did not lead to any change in Article I, which states the principle of nondiscrimination, Patterson believes that by then a great many countries and scholars had concluded that national interests often could best be served through regional blocs. Furthermore, the threat of "market disruption" by products of low-cost countries also militated against completely open markets. Finally, the less-developed countries were asking for access on a discriminatory basis to the richer markets of the developed world. Unhappily, he sees these forces as leading to more and more special situations in which discrimination will appear, implying the maintenance of some relatively high tariffs or other barriers in order to be able to discriminate. In general, the book is a reasoned argument in support of the general policy of nondiscrimination, even though it recognizes the necessity of exceptions.

NEISSER, HANS and MODIGLIANI, FRANCO. **National Incomes and International Trade: A Quantitative Analysis.** Urbana: University of Illinois Press, 1953, 396 p.

This is one of the first demonstrations of the formal use of a macro-economic model in the analysis of foreign trade. The authors were unhappy with the possible conflict between the processes outlined in economic theory for balance-of-payment adjustment and for comparative cost determination. They felt that more attention should be paid to the main relationships between the level of domestic economic activity in the various countries and their international transactions. Supported by extensive statistical studies, they found a high correlation between imports and income, with relative stability for exports, and they examine the implications of such a relationship. They suggest that the occasional failure of the record to correspond to the model may be a reflection of the omission of investment decisions and financial relations among countries. This leads to the need for an even more complex model incorporating financial flows. The authors undoubtedly know (but do not state) that this would be an extremely difficult undertaking.

GARDNER, RICHARD NEWTON. **Sterling-Dollar Diplomacy.** New York: McGraw-Hill, 2d ed., 1969, 423 p.

Professor Gardner has recorded in detail the shifting successes and failures of Anglo-American economic collaboration in the creation of the two Bretton Woods institutions, the Anglo-American Financial Agreement and the Charter for an International Trade Organization. In each case there were advance discussions, then the generalized pronouncements of the statesmen, the struggles of the technicians to prepare a draft, the negotiations ending in compromises and finally the wearisome confrontations with Parliament and Congress. Gardner criticizes these efforts as having too little regard for noneconomic factors, too much loyalty to the idea of universality in disregard of special international relations and too much legalism which in the end led to rigidity and semantic controversy.

In a 78-page introduction to the second edition, the author notes that the relationship between the two countries had become more stable and that the failures which he pointed out earlier had been recouped—convertibility had been achieved, and multilateralism in trade had emerged in the GATT. He also observes that the new facility for special drawing rights in the International Monetary Fund still left untouched the possibility of sterling or dollar crises and therefore did not eliminate the need for sterling-dollar diplomacy, with the same operational problems which he had described before. He does not, perhaps, pay sufficient attention to the fact that the relationship no longer operates through agreements publicly arrived at but is much more a matter of central bank and treasury understandings in which other countries are often included.

IVERSEN, CARL. **Aspects of the Theory of International Capital Movements.** New York: Oxford University Press, 1935, 536 p.

Pointing out that classical trade theory assumes complete mobility of commodities and factors within each country but only commodity flows between them, Carl Iversen undertakes to consider international capital movements in theory and in fact. He attributes capital flows to changes in the cost of transfer, differences in rates of interest between the two countries, or external factors such as the avoidance of taxes or the opening up of new profit opportunities. The process also is affected by shifting anticipations of the future.

After examining the mechanism of international capital movements, particularly their effect on prices, incomes and commodity trade, he examines the record for eight countries. His conclusion is that while there may be direct price effects, the more important impact is the result of the transfer of monetary buying power. His examination of the actual media of transfer brings him to the conclusion that gold movements play a less important role than was assumed by the classical theory and that more importance must be assigned to short-term equalizing capital movements.

In 1952 Professor Iversen made a study of the monetary problems of Iraq for its National Bank where, ironically enough, the situation was one in which the capital movement was the result of oil production and concessionary agreements rather than the usual market forces, and where the real problem was how to put the available capital to work productively within the country (**A Report on Monetary Policy in Iraq,** Copenhagen: Ejnar Munksgaard, 1954, 331 p.).

TRIFFIN, ROBERT. **Europe and the Money Muddle: From Bilateralism to Near-Convertibility.** New Haven: Yale University Press, 1957, 351 p.

This is the first of several books written by Professor Triffin which deal progressively with international monetary problems. It deals with the period from 1947 to 1956, describing Europe's postwar collapse, the failure of the international currency plans, the final emergence of the European Payments Union and the further steps necessary to reach viable convertibility. In an amusing table of contents in which the author advises the reader as to what chapters may be skipped and summarizes the rest, he cites as particularly desirable the creation of a clearinghouse for European central banks and an agreement aimed at a true internationalization of international monetary reserves. He correctly judged that convertibility was around the corner, largely due to growing outflow of dollars, and in his recommendations was concerned with its maintenance, fearing an outburst of deflation or protectionism in the United States. He strongly favored the establishment of the European Community, which he hoped would work in the direction of monetary unification, and he urged a revised system for handling international reserves, now partially accomplished by the new reserve units held by the IMF.

Triffin's later books have included **Gold and the Dollar Crisis: The Future of Convertibility** (New Haven: Yale University Press, rev. ed., 1961, 181 p.) and **Our**

International Monetary System: Yesterday, Today, and Tomorrow (New York: Random House, 1968, 206 p.).

AVRAMOVIĆ, DRAGOSLAV and GULHATI, RAVI. **Debt Servicing Capacity and Postwar Growth in International Indebtedness.** Baltimore: Johns Hopkins Press, 1958, 228 p.

As government assistance shifted from grants to loans, as the new international lending agencies expanded, and as private investment in the less-developed countries revived, not only did total indebtedness increase but the burden of interest and amortization payments on the borrowers became an important element in their balance of payments. Based largely on material provided by the International Bank for Reconstruction and Development, this study traces the record from 1946 to 1955. While grants on public account exceeded loans during the period, the author estimates the public external long-term debt of 52 countries to have reached $23 billion in 1955. If data were available on private debt, it would make a sizeable addition. The general finding was that the increase in indebtedness was accompanied by considerable economic advance by the majority of the borrowers. Foreign exchange earnings increased even more than service payments on the debt and contributed to increased consumption and investment. Unfortunately, there were a few exceptions to the general rule where countries had a poor growth record or suffered some special setback in their exports.

Since 1955, the debt of the less-developed countries has continued to grow, and the problem has been discussed at both sessions of UNCTAD. The developed countries have agreed on a target under which each gives the bulk of its aid on terms substantially below market rates. The basic data are now published and discussed each year in the annual report of the World Bank.

LETICHE, JOHN MARION. **Balance of Payments and Economic Growth.** New York: Harper, 1959, 378 p.

This technical study of the balance of payments begins with the history of theory from the mercantilists through the classicists and Keynes to the "Harvard neo-classicists." By the last category the author means Taussig, Ohlin and Viner, although the latter two had only temporary stays in Cambridge. Letiche's own analysis is primarily in terms of price levels and the forces which affect them. Cyclical, monetary and fiscal pressures lead to internal and external balance or imbalance through their influence on employment, demand, prices and foreign trade. Letiche argued in 1959 that the world dollar shortage was not chronic because the long-term trend was for American imports to grow more rapidly than exports. His outlook for primary-producing countries was also optimistic, but he covered himself by making it clear that he was assuming factor mobility, full employment in the industrial countries, limited inflation in the nonindustrial countries, and reasonably stable terms of trade.

HALM, GEORGE NIKOLAUS. **International Monetary Cooperation.** Chapel Hill: University of North Carolina Press, 1945, 355 p.

This excellent review of the background and birth of the International Monetary Fund was prepared when the experts involved could be consulted and the contemporary documents were still available. The book defends the IMF plan as the only practical way back to convertibility and multilateral clearing, comparing its provisions in some detail with other proposals. The full documentation of the alternative White and Keynes proposals are given in appendices. This early exposition helped greatly to clarify the theory and prospective performance of the new agency in the light of anticipated postwar monetary problems of exchange rates, convertibility and inflation.

CASSEL, GUSTAV. **Money and Foreign Exchange after 1914.** New York: Macmillan, 1922, 287 p.

While Professor Cassel's reputation rests largely on his 1903 work, "Nature and

Necessity of Interest," his position as a monetary expert led the League of Nations to request him to prepare two memoranda about the world's monetary problem. This book is an enlarged version of his analyses, in which he places purchasing-power-parities in the center of the monetary universe. As he saw it, the essential objective of international monetary policy should be stability in exchange rates. Because these are controlled in the long run by purchasing power parities, internal national policies should, he feels, be directed to the stabilization of the internal values of the various currencies. He regarded the gold standard as having been abolished in 1914, never to return as an important element in the world monetary scene: national policy choices had become the determining factors. Cassel suggested that the effort to achieve stability be begun by maintaining parity between the pound and the dollar. While few people in 1922 recognized the effective disappearance of the gold standard, the general lines of the author's analysis came to be widely accepted 20 years later.

FOREIGN INVESTMENT

JENKS, LELAND. **The Migration of British Capital to 1875.** New York: Knopf, 1927, 442 p.

This early book on British foreign investment came before the emphasis on statistical data and is largely a descriptive account of events, attitudes and the development of institutions. Nevertheless, the 87 pages of bibliographical notes and appendices contain enough numbers to backstop some of the generalizations. The record, as Professor Jenks sees it, is one of rapidly shifting capital flows. Thus the collapse of loans to governments and South American mining speculations in 1825 was quickly followed by investments in the United States. The "railway revolution" then went through a cycle. The greatest outflow, chiefly taking the form of government bonds and railway shares and debentures, was during 1850–73, a period of prosperity when prices were rising. All this led not only to a variety of financial institutions—the commission merchant, the bill-discounter and the cosmopolitan banker—but it created a stock and bondholding aristocracy and an economic empire. The book on British investment by A. K. Cairncross, **Home and Foreign Investment, 1870–1913,** takes up where Jenks leaves off.

FEIS, HERBERT. **Europe: The World's Banker, 1870–1914.** New Haven: Yale University Press, 1930, 492 p.

In this early publication sponsored by the Council on Foreign Relations, the author relates the flow of foreign investment to diplomacy before World War I. British investments tended to involve management and control—the entrepreneurial interest—while French investments were those of a lender, frequently made to governments and related to some political purpose. The huge French investment in Russia often included military entries as did those of the Central Powers in other directions. Separate chapters discuss the flows of funds to Italy, Portugal, the Balkans, Turkey, Persia, North Africa, Japan and China. Rather than the more usual emphasis on foreign investment as imperialism with economic exploitation, the borrowing-lending relations are here presented in terms of their connection with political and diplomatic events, shaping the alliances which appeared overtly in World War I. The economic-political interest in this book may explain why the author became one of the first professional economists to enter the employ of the Department of State.

SOUTHARD, FRANK ALLAN, JR. **American Industry in Europe.** Boston: Houghton Mifflin, 1931, 264 p.

This is a pioneering study of American investment in Europe. Even though in the latter part of the nineteenth century the United States was importing capital on balance, American companies were establishing plants in Europe. The number increased greatly in the 1920s, so that when the author began to look for cases in a field where considerable secrecy existed, he was able to get data on 220 corporations with almost 800 subsidiaries in Europe. The first half of the book, which describes these cases, is followed by a discussion of the reasons for foreign investment and the various ways of organizing and operating abroad. Finally, Southard discusses the problems created by American investment abroad, a section which might have been written 30 years later. He describes the growing fear of American invasion, centered in Germany at that time but nevertheless the subject of discussion in the United Kingdom. He notes that the presence of foreign capital in Czechoslovakia was used as an argument for nationalization. The second problem which he discusses is the impact of foreign investment on the balance of payments in the countries involved. This complex situation could be discussed only in general terms since at that time there were no satisfactory statistics indicating quantitative relationships. When this book was written, it was an extraordinary achievement, and was so recognized.

CAIRNCROSS, A. K. **Home and Foreign Investment, 1870–1913.** Cambridge: University Press, 1953, 251 p.

Professor Cairncross's careful statistical studies disclose that, after the initial stages of the industrial revolution, the rapid growth of British investment reflected tremendous demands for railways and steamships plus a growing demand overseas, where the requirements of new communities and new economic ventures were enormous. Foreign investment in the 1870–1913 period dominated the picture, and domestic investment rose relatively slowly. British savings financed more than half the total addition to the stock of capital in Canada, the largest borrower. However, the improved standard of living in the United Kingdom during the period 1870–1913 was largely the result of the reduction in the price of British imports. In terms of industrial fluctuations, Cairncross finds investment and the terms of trade to have provided an "unstable maintenance of stability." This is still the authoritative work in its field.

WHITMAN, MARINA VON NEUMANN. **Government Risk-Sharing in Foreign Investment.** Princeton: Princeton University Press, 1965, 358 p.

Dr. Whitman describes six agencies engaged in sharing the risk with American private investors between 1945 and 1953. Three are American—the Investment Guaranty Program, the Export-Import Bank and the Agency for International Development; three are international—the World Bank, the International Finance Corporation and the Inter-American Bank. The author concludes that they have had an increasing influence on the export of long-term private capital from the United States. To a considerable extent, the agencies undertake various forms of contingency commitments to back up insurance or they hold idle reserves. The potential costs to the government are enormous, and it is quite possible that in the long run the government would be better off to encourage foreign investment by making the rate of return more attractive. Dr. Whitman sees little prospect for a substantial increase in non-subsidized private funds providing development assistance so the problem should be viewed in terms of alternative burdens on the public treasury.

ROBINSON, RICHARD D. **International Business Policy.** New York: Holt, Rinehart and Winston, 1964, 252 p.

Although set in a broad policy framework, this book is addressed to American firms operating in the non-Western world. In a historical section the author points out that those political feelings which broke up empires and ended in nationalistic fervor had their parallel in reactions to Western business enterprise. Professor Robinson describes in some detail the business and political risks in the changed situation. He puts forward criteria which should be met by management to justify a project and its participation in it, as well as tests of operational policies, structure, size and the nature of the product. He admits that on these bases a large proportion of existing international investment would have been ruled out—they were made in the days when Western concepts controlled. The author is careful not to argue that the Western concept of private enterprise is necessarily relevant or meaningful to the underdeveloped countries, but he does say that, given wise private and public policies and performance, a profitable and reasonably secure existence for Western firms in non-Western countries is possible in the coming international era. He deals with the operational aspects of the problem in **International Management** (New York: Holt, Rinehart and Winston, 1967, 178 p.).

REDDAWAY, W. B. **Effects of U. K. Direct Investment Overseas: Interim and Final Reports.** Cambridge: University Press, 1967 and 1968, 2 v.

These reports cover the overseas activities of United Kingdom companies engaged in manufacturing and mining, not including oil. Detailed statistical tables are included. Among the conclusions are that the "true" return to the United Kingdom from these investments overseas was more than 6 percent a year as against a domestic rate of 3 percent. To reach such figures required various adjustments, the overseas figure including nearly one-third as "knowledge-sharing" and the domestic rate being adjusted to a constant price level. Reddaway was unable to assess the effect on balance of payments, since that depends on varying current capital outflows compared with the inflow from past investment. As to international relations, he reasons that foreign investment provides development assistance. Domestic revenues may be somewhat reduced, but that may be offset by taxation on foreign investments in the United Kingdom. The report is particularly valuable in pointing out the difficulties in defining exactly the questions to be asked and then drawing general conclusions from complicated and heterogeneous data.

POLK, JUDD and OTHERS. **U.S. Production Abroad and the Balance of Payments: A Survey of Corporate Investment Experience.** New York: National Industrial Conference Board, 1966, 200 p.

The importance of this volume lies in its exploration of the significance of foreign production by American concerns having direct investment interests abroad. Whereas U.S. exports rose by 5.4 percent per year from 1950 to 1964, U.S. production abroad increased by 10 percent per year over the same period. In part this reflected U.S. needs for foreign products; in part it resulted from foreign demand for U.S.-type products which could not have been paid for in dollars if purchased directly. Looking at the total balance, Polk estimates that the related exports from the United States of U.S. materials and capital goods exceeded the substitution of foreign-made goods for American exports. In his final chapter, he discusses the different implications for policy of short-run and long-run analysis, a distinction which appears in the evaluation of any investment, and concludes that national policy should not be based exclusively on the current state of the balance of payments.

BARLOW, EDWARD ROBERT and WENDER, IRA TENSARD. **Foreign Investment and Taxation.** Englewood Cliffs: Prentice-Hall, 1955, 481 p.

As a background to the tax problem, this study reports on an intensive field study dealing with the growth of foreign investment, and the reported inducements and obstacles to it. It then discusses in detail a number of proposals for changing the tax laws in order to provide increased incentives for foreign investment. The authors express their preference for the establishment of a special class of foreign business corporations, which would be permitted to defer any United States corporate income tax when earned so long as the income was reinvested abroad. While the proposal has never been enacted, it, or a reasonable facsimile, has been repeatedly presented to Congress, and the low level of public aid may lead to new efforts to encourage private foreign investment.

SECTORAL STUDIES

MALENBAUM, WILFRED. **The World Wheat Economy, 1885–1939.** Cambridge: Harvard University Press, 1953, 262 p.

Noting the concern about food shortages after World War II, Wilfred Malenbaum regards the postwar situation of short supply for wheat and other grains as temporary. His study shows that when a similar situation has arisen in the past, grain prices have been high relative to prices of non-food products, wheat supplies have expanded more rapidly than consumption, and surpluses emerged. Higher yields and the opening up of new sources of export contributed to increased wheat output, so that from 1900 to 1939 the world wheat economy was characterized by a growing disequilibrium.

After years of efforts by many countries to maintain production and protect it from competition from lower-cost areas while at the same time encouraging technical advances, public policy was redirected in some cases at holding down output. There still remains great capacity to increase output, but demand is limited. When surpluses and needs exist simultaneously, Professor Malenbaum sees the happiest solution in programs of foreign aid which could be used as a positive tool of foreign economic policy. He proposes that food aid from the United States should move primarily to the other industrial countries on condition that they in turn provide added capital to the less-developed countries. In contrast to his proposal, it should be noted that of the $17.4 billions of foreign assistance provided under the U.S. Food for Peace program 1946–1949, only $1.1 billion went to the developed countries.

PARSONS, KENNETH HERALD and OTHERS, *eds.* **Land Tenure.** Madison: University of Wisconsin Press, 1956, 739 p.

A massive volume recording the proceedings of a large and unusually long conference on world tenure problems held in October 1951. The book contains a number of papers which were specially prepared for the meetings as well as the reports of various working parties which met over a period of some weeks. Of particular interest are the reports which deal with land tenure conditions in various countries and regions, constituting the first major effort to assemble such material in a single volume. The sessions themselves were focused more on problems than on description. Such ticklish subjects as the consolidation of fragmented holdings, the institution of inheritance and the management of public lands received detailed consideration.

This is an excellent illustration of how much can be achieved by a well-planned conference with carefully chosen participants and an expert staff, and when there is enough time for the participants to get beyond initial speech-making.

WHARTON, CLIFTON R., JR., *ed.* **Subsistence Agriculture and Economic Development.** Chicago: Aldine, 1969, 481 p.

This volume is the outgrowth of a week's conference at the University of Hawaii early in 1965. Forty leading social scientists from 11 countries and almost as many disciplines discussed the implications of the fact that 50 to 60 percent of mankind live on subsistence farms, that knowledge about subsistence agriculture is meagre and even less is known of peasant life, and that policies and programs for the transition to commercial agriculture are even more scarce. By definition, this area falls outside the economist's concern with the "market economy," nor have the other disciplines shown much more interest. Starting with eye-opening descriptive material, the conferees proceed through a discussion on productivity to the problem of how to modernize traditional agriculture. Wharton ends the book with a summary of the issues which have emerged in the sessions and a formidable and challenging research agenda.

COCHRANE, WILLARD W. **The World Food Problem: A Guardedly Optimistic View.**
New York: Crowell, 1969, 331 p.

In this work Professor Cochrane did not define the current world food problem
in the usual terms of population, food production and starvation but emphasized
the social and political problems that result when millions of people with inadequate diets have increasing money incomes but are unable to achieve their expected
consumption of food. As he sees it, the problem is less one of crop failures and
regional famines than of unbalanced development. He reasons that what is needed
is greater output and more effective distribution, plus a second set of actions in the
general economy such as the absorption and support of surplus farm labor in non-
farm occupations, the production of appropriate incentive goods, and the development of marketing systems and other related activities. Thus agriculture becomes
one segment of the total problem of development. While success depends on the
leadership in each developing country, substantial technical and financial assistance
will also be required from the developed countries. The author feels that the world
food problem is technically solvable, but as to the actual outcome, as the subtitle
indicates, he is "guardedly optimistic."

LEITH, CHARLES KENNETH. **World Minerals and World Politics.** New York: McGraw-
Hill, 1931, 213 p.
LEITH, CHARLES KENNETH; FURNESS, J. W. and LEWIS, CLEONA. **World Minerals and
World Peace.** Washington: Brookings Institution, 1943, 253 p.

In his 1931 book, Charles K. Leith examined minerals in their political and
international aspects, noting that the rapidly growing consumption of minerals
meant that there was bound to be increased interest in their control. Though he felt
that international controls would be a rational step forward, he expected that
national rivalries would intensify and that nationalization would be the more likely
eventuality.

The second book, **World Minerals and World Peace,** written with J. W. Furness
and Cleona Lewis during World War II, denies the possibility of self-sufficiency in
minerals for any nation and therefore concerns itself with the inevitable international complications. After presenting a statistical summary of the world's
mineral resources, production and international flows, the authors discuss the
efforts to extend control through international arrangements, commercial policy
and closed-door and nationalization policies. Their chief concern is with mineral
needs as a potential source of war.

Looking toward the postwar period, the authors endorse the equal access
promise in the Atlantic Charter but would construe the phrase as removing arbitrary restrictions so far as possible when minerals are required for peacetime
pursuits. They would use mineral control to prevent preparations for war, perhaps
incorporating such controls in the peace settlement. This idea failed to make
headway.

KRANOLD, HERMAN. **The International Distribution of Raw Materials.** New York:
Harper, 1939, 269 p.

The author assembled more than 70 pages of statistical tables concerning what
he calls "internationally interesting raw materials" and discusses the data critically
in his text. His interest is primarily in the national distribution of raw materials,
about which he believes there is much misunderstanding, undue weight being given
to colonial production, the effect of the have-nots and the exploitation of consumers.

After discussing the economic and political forces which work against the
rational supply and use of raw materials, he sets forth a proposal for international
planning. He would have a truce on expansion, since consumption is considerably
less than existing productive capacity. A central economic planning authority
would then promote international agreements aiming at stabilizing production,
reducing trade barriers and helping nations to plan their economic development. In

the end, the credit resources of the world might, he hopes, be used systematically in the further development of raw material production, instead of on a piecemeal basis. The author recognizes not only that he is raising the issue of sovereignty but that any such plan would inevitably involve the armament problem.

It is an interesting comment on Professor Kranold's analysis that while the United Nations family includes a specialized agency to deal with agricultural raw materials, it has no comparable agency in the fields of minerals or electrical energy.

POGUE, JOSEPH E. **The Economics of Petroleum.** New York: Wiley, 1921, 375 p.

This book was important not merely for the light which it shed on an important American industry but as an early example of an industry study in economic terms. There had already been forecasts describing the rapid depletion of the supply of crude petroleum because of expanding demand, and interest in possible foreign sources had grown rapidly. While Professor Pogue shared the general pessimism concerning the imminent exhaustion of petroleum in the United States, he envisaged the supply situation as forcing increased efficiency in the production, refining and use of the products. He pointed out that the variety of products, the rapidly rising demand for some of them and the discovery of new fields might be expected to bring far-reaching changes in the technology and economic structure of the industry. In turn, these changes would reach far beyond the petroleum industry itself. His analysis of the inefficiency of oil-field development, the problem of allocation at the refinery among joint products, the relation of final product prices to those of crude petroleum, the prospective needs for expanding investment, the possible expansion in imports (which at that time meant Mexico) and the extraction of oil from shale, about which he was overly optimistic, not only provided economists with fresh illustrative material for the classroom but put various theoretical problems in a new light.

OWEN, WILFRED. **Strategy for Mobility.** Washington: Brookings Institution, 1964, 249 p.

This is the first volume in Brookings' Transport Research Program. Most of the later volumes in the series are nationally centered, but this book discusses the international aspects of transport. The author points out the critical importance of immobility for problems of poverty, food distribution, industrial development and political unity. Transport usually ranks first or second among all expenditures for national development, but the need for it is still enormous and cost is a major obstacle. Owen notes that foreign aid has been helpful but is far from sufficient. He argues that much can be done by a wise choice of technology, particularly in recognizing that a transport revolution has taken place. Too often, he says, transportation is thought of as an independent sector rather than a service activity which should be integrated with other targets.

This is an eye-opening book, not only to the importance of transport policy but to the many considerations which enter into the making of proper choices. The author suggests that the United Nations can make a major contribution not only in connection with the channels and methods of external assistance but in improving the surveys and plans for developing national programs. In addition, he recommends that a world transport center be established to provide a focal point for research and education. Some of the issues raised are developed further by a number of authors in another book in the same series, **Transport Investment and Economic Development,** edited by Gary Fromm (Washington: Brookings Institution, 1965, 314 p.).

HARBISON, FREDERICK and MYERS, CHARLES A. **Education, Manpower, and Economic Growth: Strategies of Human Resource Development.** New York: McGraw-Hill, 1964, 229 p.

The authors have developed statistical measures of human resource development and applied them to 75 countries. As might be expected, high correlations exist between per capita output and human resource development. The countries were divided into four groups according to the degree of development, and each group was examined in greater detail. Appropriate strategies are suggested for each, since even the most advanced has critical areas of choice with respect to education and training. In the less-developed countries, the authors see the necessity for an initial heavy investment. The least developed have the political imperative of replacing foreigners, building a competent civil service and training teachers. At all levels, persons must be prepared for available jobs, and educational systems need to place more emphasis on vocational and professional training.

The authors are particularly concerned over the fact that national planning has been concerned chiefly with economic projects and frequently has not incorporated any detailed program for the essential development of human resources. They recommend that at a minimum there must be an assessment of manpower requirements, an analysis of the system of formal education and a review of other methods of training.

An indication of how such planning works in reality is presented in essays by various experts covering 11 countries in **Manpower and Education** (New York: McGraw-Hill, 1965, 343 p.), edited by the same authors. While the general importance of education was already recognized, these two books moved the discussion from generalities to specific programs for action.

THOMAS, BRINLEY, ed. **Economics of International Migration.** New York: St. Martin's Press, 1958, 501 p.

This report of an International Economic Conference includes papers on a number of individual emigration and immigration countries, including intra-European movements. The contrast between the large-scale intercontinental migration before 1913 and subsequent years is striking. Luckily, the economic recovery of Western Europe reduced the need for emigration except for displaced persons and refugees. Intra-European migration has substituted for outward movements. Migration in Asia can do little to relieve population pressure, but it is important as a carrier of skills. Of special interest are Professor Spengler's distinction between the income and substitution effects of migration and Professor A. P. Lerner's model demonstrating that immigration can generate a cost inflation. A more detailed examination of the impact on their economies of British migration to the United States is given in Brinley Thomas, **Migration and Economic Growth: A Study of Great Britain and the Atlantic Economy** (New York: Cambridge University Press, 1954, 362 p.).

V. SOCIAL AND CULTURAL FACTORS

GENERAL

MANNHEIM, KARL. **Ideology and Utopia.** London: Routledge, 1936, 318 p.

This sociological classic created, or at least codified, the contemporary field of inquiry called sociology of knowledge. It bridged the gap between traditional normative and evaluative thinking about the social order expressed as "ideology and utopia" and the contemporary quest for empirical and objective solution of social problems expressed as "science."

In analyzing the utopian mentality in terms of such problems as reality and wish-fulfillment, the author differentiates four forms which correspond to successive stages in modern times: 1, the orgiastic chiliasm of the Anabaptists; 2, the liberal-humanitarian idea; 3, the conservative idea; 4, the socialist-communist utopia. There follows a review of utopia in the present situation.

The concluding chapter is devoted to the sociology of knowledge proper, presenting its definition, a classification of subfields and its differentiation from the theory of ideology. The two principal divisions of the sociology of knowledge are its social determination and its epistemological consequences. Mannheim argues for the revision of "the thesis that the genesis of a proposition is under all circumstances irrelevant to its truth."

In his brief concluding historical survey, the author traces one line of development of the sociology of knowledge from Nietzsche through Freud and Pareto with a related current leading from Ratzenhofer through Gumplowicz and Oppenheimer. He concludes that it actually emerged with Marx and was carried forward by Lukacs and Scheler.

CASSIRER, ERNST. **An Essay on Man.** New Haven: Yale University Press, 1944, 237 p.

This is the author's effort to unify his philosophical analyses of various facets of human activity and experience. He reasons that the common center, for man, is self-knowledge. But self-knowledge is the product neither of purely subjective introspection nor of purely objective observation (behaviorism). It is a continuous and interpersonal process of interaction between man and his environment. When he comes to the critical definition of man in terms of human culture, the author states: "We cannot define man by an inherent principle which constitutes his metaphysical essence—nor can we define him by any inborn faculty or instinct that may be ascertained by empirical observation. Man's outstanding characteristic, his distinguishing mark, is not his metaphysical or physical nature--but his *work*."

As it has done with other contemporary thinkers, this conception of man's humanity as integral with his culture leads to a deep stress on the symbolic instrument and the role of communication: "It is the basic function of speech, of myth, of art, of religion that must seek far behind their innumerable shapes and utterances, and that in the last analysis we must attempt to trace back to a common origin."

The book treats these matters. The first part asks: "What is Man?" and the key response is given in the second chapter: "A Clue to the Nature of Man: The Symbol." In part two, which deals with man and culture, the successive chapters focus on myth and religion, language, art, history, science. Cassirer's influence on the older generation of living philosophers is illustrated in F. S. C. Northrop's **The Meeting of East and West.**

ADORNO, THEODOR W.; FRENKEL-BRUNSWICK, ELSE; LEVINSON, DANIEL and NEVITT, SANFORD R. **The Authoritarian Personality.** New York: Harper, 1950, 990 p.

This massive project used a variety of social science techniques to develop a questionnaire that would identify those Americans who had a "potential for fascism." Such people were said to exhibit the following syndrome: conventionalism (rigid adherence to middle-class values); authoritarian submission (uncritical attitude toward idealized moral authorities of the in-group); authoritarian aggression (tendency to be on the lookout for, and to condemn, people who violate conventional values); anti-intraception (opposition to the subjective); superstition and stereotype (the disposition to think in rigid categories); power and "toughness" (preoccupation with leader-follower dimension); destructiveness and cynicism (hostility, vilification of the human); projectivity (the disposition to believe that wild and dangerous things go on in the world); sex (exaggerated concern with sexual "goings-on").

Scales were developed to measure anti-Semitism, ethnocentrism and politico-economic conservatism and then were used to formulate the final scale called the F-scale. Independent validation of the authoritarian personality syndrome was claimed via depth interviews and the results of H. A. Murray's Thematic Apperception Test.

Innumerable social research studies in the years since this volume appeared have used the F-scale, and much debate has centered on its validity. See Richard Christie and Marie Jahoda, *eds.,* **Studies in the Scope and Method of "The Authoritarian Personality"** (Glencoe: Free Press, 1954, 279 p.) and Milton Rokeach's **The Open and Closed Mind** (New York: Basic Books, 1960, 447 p.).

HOFFER, ERIC. **The True Believer: Thoughts on the Nature of Mass Movements.** London: Secker and Warburg, 1952, 192 p.

This short book, or long essay, on political mass movements in contemporary society is animated by a set of theses. The psychological thesis is that there exists a personality type—the "true believer"—which is especially attracted to such movements. The sociological thesis is that mass movements appeal very widely in most societies today; but the true believer is the one whose alienation from what is—and desire for what might be—is so intense that he responds to the appeal and participates actively in the mass movement. The political thesis is that the psychological conditions for participation in all mass movements are so alike that, for true believers, most such movements are interchangeable.

The essay terminates with a discussion of the movers and shapers of contemporary mass movements. It characterizes and contrasts men of words, fanatics and practical men of action. The final section attempts the difficult task of differentiating good and bad mass movements. It concludes, among other things, that there is a category of useful mass movements which awaken and renovate stagnant societies. The final sentence asserts that "this malady of the soul"—fanaticism—can also be "an instrument of resurrection."

Other works that bear centrally and more systematically on this topic are Harold D. Lasswell's **World Politics and Personal Insecurity** and Daniel Bell's **The End of Ideology** (Glencoe: Free Press, 1960, 416 p.). Another psychological portrait is Albert Camus' **The Rebel.**

DAHL, ROBERT ALAN and LINDBLOM, CHARLES EDWARD. **Politics, Economics and Welfare: Planning and Politico-Economic Systems Resolved into Basic Social Processes.** New York: Harper, 1953, 557 p.

This book is a collaborative effort by an economist and a political scientist to address the question: "What are the conditions under which numerous individuals can maximize the attainment of their goals through the use of social mechanisms?"

In order to deal in a generalizing way with the alternative techniques, the authors abbreviated their treatment of the four main institutions through which "vital decisions" are made—business corporation, government bureaucracy, trade union, political party. Instead, they have concentrated on developing a body of theory related to "the future of freedom in the West, and certainly in the United States."

The book, which contains an excellent analytical table of contents, is organized around four central sociopolitical processes—the price system (control of and by leaders); hierarchy (control by leaders); polyarchy (control of leaders); and bargaining (control among leaders). A major chapter considers these processes as "politico-economic techniques" with respect to such matters as choice, allocation and other economizing processes.

DAVIS, HARRY REX and GOOD, ROBERT CROCKER, *eds*. **Reinhold Niebuhr on Politics: His Political Philosophy and Its Application to Our Age as Expressed in His Writings.** New York: Scribner, 1960, 364 p.

Collected here in one volume are Reinhold Niebuhr's thoughts on the nature of political man and his twentieth century dilemmas, drawn from more than 15 major works and numerous articles. The editors' task of selecting Niebuhr's political writing is made more difficult by Niebuhr's insistence that ultimately theology and political theory cannot be separated.

The scholar is directed to the original sources by careful footnoting, while the more casual reader can pursue the argument, hardly aware that the component thoughts and works were spaced over 30 years. Mercifully, the editors commit a violation of some scholarly formalities by omitting the usual dots and brackets of edited compendiums and by slightly altering where necessary their chosen texts to improve continuity. Both scholars and casual readers can content themselves in the knowledge that the author approved the final manuscript.

Davis and Good have structured Niebuhr's political thought into three sections. The first of these focuses on the crisis of modern man and the inadequacies of two utopianisms: liberalism and communism. The second elaborates Niebuhr's dialectical political philosophy. In the third section political theology is applied to contemporary problems, especially those of international relations.

To most political scientists the name Reinhold Niebuhr refers to the notion of **Moral Man and Immoral Society** (New York: Scribner, 1932, 284 p.). However, Niebuhr's thoughts and works have continued to develop since 1934. Davis' and Good's labors provide ease of access to the full range of his thinking.

EISENSTADT, SHMUEL NOAH. **The Political Systems of Empires.** London: Collier-Macmillan, 1963, 524 p.

A pioneering application of sociological analysis to historical phenomena. More particularly, it applies the sociological tradition of structural-functional analysis, elaborated from Max Weber to Talcott Parsons, to the comparative study of a specific type of political system—the bureaucratic empire—found in otherwise different societies. The author says that his book, subtitled "The Rise and Fall of the Historical Bureaucratic Societies," seeks to find some patterns or laws in the structure and development of such political systems.

On all of his comparative indicators, Eisenstadt deals with 32 historical empires, including Greece, Mongols, feudal Europe, Incas, ancient Egypt, Ptolemies, Seleucids, Mogul, Byzantine, Ottomans, Rome, Spanish America, Russia, Prussia, France, England. Tabular materials report comparative data on these widely varied political entities.

After defining bureaucratic polities, the first part deals with their fundamental characteristics, development, economic structure and religious and cultural organization, while the second is concerned with conditions of perpetuation in these empires.

This book claims a prominent place on the very small shelf of contemporary classics in this field, such as K. A. Wittfogel's **Oriental Despotism**.

ERIKSON, ERIK HOMBURGER. **Childhood and Society.** New York: Norton, 2d ed., 1963, 445 p.

This neo-Freudian theory of child development emphasizes the critical importance of the social environment as a determinant of man's behavior. Erikson's theory considers infantile sexuality and also eight stages of human development, during which the successful person exhibits the following characteristics: basic trust *vs.* mistrust; autonomy *vs.* shame and doubt; initiative *vs.* guilt; industry *vs.* inferiority; identity *vs.* role confusion; intimacy *vs.* isolation; generativity *vs.* stagnation; and ego integrity *vs.* despair. The first stage occurs in infancy, and the seventh and eighth represent adulthood and maturity.

The volume is one of the important efforts to apply psychiatric insights to world politics, as in Harold Lasswell's **World Politics and Personal Insecurity.** The chapter on "Reflections on American Identity" utilizes literary analysis and an "ideal type"—a normal boy—to discuss the social and political impact of the immediate family upon the child. Other examples by Erikson are the contemporary Sioux and Yurok, and Hitler's youth and the rise of National Socialism. The author notes that "power spheres [and] spheres of exploitation" are matters pertaining to the social process and not in themselves to be explained as originating in infantile anxiety. He reasons that the problem to be elucidated is that of the extent to which man is apt to project on political and economic necessity those fears, apprehensions and urges which are derived from the arsenal of infantile anxiety.

ANTHROPOLOGY

BENEDICT, RUTH. **Patterns of Culture.** New York: Mentor, 1959, 254 p.

First published in 1934, this beautifully written volume has had a profound impact on the fields of anthropology, political science, psychology and sociology. Generations of students have been exposed to **Patterns of Culture** in introductory sociology and anthropology courses; and the author's hypothesis that each culture has its distinctive themes that permeate the various aspects of personality and culture in a society has, moreover, had a significant impact on recent social theory.

Dr. Benedict examines three distinct cultures (the Zuni Indians of New Mexico, the Kwakiutl of Vancouver Island and the Dobus of Melanesia), each of which, she believes, can be presented and studied as a more or less unique set of behaviors and values, constituting a coherent pattern characterized by a single dominant theme or "configuration." The Zuni are ceremonious and gentle; the Dobu suspicious and distrustful; the Kwakiutl ambitious and competitive. The last two chapters of the book are devoted to a theoretical extrapolation from the case material and can be read independently.

The now familiar hypothesis of cultural relativity—individual behavior must be given meaning in terms of the culture in which it occurs—derives from Dr. Benedict's perspective. Behavior and goals at variance with accepted standards in one culture and, therefore, condemned as abnormal are, in another culture, supported and rewarded by social institutions. In turn, this assertion leads to an examination and a fuller understanding of our own culture and behavior.

LINTON, RALPH, *ed.* **The Science of Man in the World Crisis.** New York: Columbia University Press, 1945, 532 p.

This symposium, produced during World War II, considers a range of policy problems upon which the social sciences, and most particularly anthropology, might bring some helpful guidance. Racial and intercultural relations get most attention, but other topics considered are population, colonial administration, innovation and international relations. A substantial proportion of the authors—such as Clyde Kluckhohn, George Murdock, Melville Herskovits, Julian Steward and Felix Keesing—are anthropologists. But the contributors also include psychologist John Dollard, sociologists Paul Lazarsfeld, Carl Taylor and Louis Wirth and political scientist Grayson Kirk. Sensitivity to the diversity of cultures and also to the profoundly integrated and therefore change-resistant character of cultures is one of the important insights that cultural anthropology has brought into the consciousness of planners of change.

KLUCKHOHN, CLYDE. **Mirror for Man.** New York: Whittlesey House, 1949, 313 p.

Offered as an exposition of anthropology for laymen rather than for professionals, this book is written with unusual lucidity. To begin with, it reviews some of the more conventional areas of classical anthropology, such as folk customs, archaeology, physical anthropology and linguistics. But it moves from the anthropologist's normal preoccupation with the primitive to consider, in the last two chapters, the United States and the world as seen by an anthropologist.

The attempt to refocus anthropology onto the problems of the modern world was a major trend of American anthropology in the 1940s and 1950s. That trend is well represented in this work, subtitled "Anthropology and Modern Life."

REDFIELD, ROBERT. **The Little Community.** Chicago: University of Chicago Press, 1955, 182 p.

Anthropologists tend to write case studies. There are relatively few essays such as this one which synthesize the anthropological perspective on the human experience in the small communities that have been the predominant form of human living arrangements throughout the history of mankind. Redfield draws a good deal on the Mayan villages that he studied at firsthand, but only to provide examples in this general study.

The author states the case for viewing the individual and his behavior in the context of the community in which he grows up and lives, and the focus of the book is the community as a whole in its relation to its parts. Redfield is aware that no community is totally cut off from an enveloping world. But unlike Meyer Fortes and E. E. Evans-Pritchard in **African Political Systems**—the classic anthropological work on a large political system—he treats lightly those corporate, legal and formal structures that make a larger society.

RACE; RELIGION; MIGRATION

DU BOIS, WILLIAM EDWARD BURGHARDT. **Black Folk: Then and Now.** New York: Holt, 1939, 401 p.

The author of this book was a leading formulator of the black view of the Negro's own history for a period of six decades. The volume reviewed here, subtitled "An Essay in the History and Sociology of the Negro Race," is one of a group of books that have laid claim to a distinct cultural identity for American Negroes derived from the African past. The first six chapters present the tribes and culture of Africa as they were before "the trade in men," and the high level of African civilization is emphasized. The next four follow the Africans to the New World, with their struggles, changing culture and achievements. The last chapters portray colonialism in operation in Africa and its impact on the people. Du Bois draws the image that is increasingly popular in contemporary radicalism—the proletariat of the world as predominantly the dark workers of what is now referred to as the third world—and assimilates their rise to the Marxist image of the revolution.

BOAS, FRANZ. **Race, Language and Culture.** New York: Macmillan, 1940, 647 p.

Some essays in this collection by one of America's seminal anthropologists did as much as any other writings to demolish the scientific basis for theories of racial superiority. From 1892 to 1939 a series of physical measurements of dimensions, growth and other anthropometric features showed that race traits, far from being fixed, changed with environment. Children of immigrants to the United States showed body features departing from their ancestry and approaching a common American type.

In essays written in the early 1930s Boas further carefully examined the data on IQ tests, emotional reactions and other nonphysical traits on the basis of which races have often been characterized. He showed to the satisfaction of virtually all social scientists that the data that were sometimes cited as evidences of racial inferiority, or even just of racial differences, were as easily or more easily accounted for by environmental factors.

HERSKOVITS, MELVILLE JEAN. **The Myth of the Negro Past.** New York: Harper, 1941, 374 p.

This book was written at the suggestion of Gunnar Myrdal as part of the inquiry that led to **An American Dilemma,** probably the single most influential book on race in America. Herskovits' book is far more controversial. While Myrdal focused on the contrast between American treatment of the blacks and American consensus values of equality and integration, Herskovits sought to identify a separate and unique cultural heritage of the Negro carried over from Africa. He rejected as myths the notion that the American Negro is a man without a past and that whatever there was in Africa was savage, childlike and lacking any unified core. On the contrary he argues that the slaves came from a highly elaborated civilization which shaped their continuous resistance to slavery and which to varying degrees entered into a distinctive New World Negro culture with values of its own.

ISAACS, HAROLD R. **The New World of Negro Americans.** New York: Viking, 1964, 366 p.

This book deals primarily with the role of Africa in the search for identity of American blacks. Isaacs treats the crisis of feelings posed by the conflict between integration and the establishment of a separate identity. Of special interest is the reaction of American Negroes to the realities of Africa when they go there. Many blacks have gone to Africa with expectations of finding their cultural roots and a sense of belonging. The experience is generally frustrating, for in many ways their experience is that of an American in Africa.

Isaacs considers the interaction of American foreign policy and civil rights in the United States, and notes the impact on the foreign audience of events such as those at Little Rock on both white behavior and black feelings. Much of the book is based upon intensive interviews with a panel of 107 leaders of Negro opinion. The author's conceptual focus is on "identity" and in particular on the Negro's search for a sense of who he is in his world of African origins and an unaccepting American environment.

FANON, FRANTZ. **Black Skin, White Masks.** New York: Grove Press, 1967, 232 p.

Any study of problems of race should take account of the literary expression of Negro self-assertion. This book by Fanon, together with novels such as Richard Wright's "Native Son" or Ralph Ellison's "Invisible Man," memoirs such as Wright's **Black Boy** (New York: Harper, 1966, 288 p.) and essays such as James Baldwin's **Notes of a Native Son** (Gloucester: Smith, 1961, 175 p.) have conveyed to the world some sense of the experience of being black and have formulated for the blacks themselves the commonality of their experience.

Fanon, born in the French Antilles, was a psychoanalyst and revolutionist in the French intellectual milieu. He is a hero of the New Left. Like most of the literary interpreters of the black experience in a white world, he focuses on the psychological meaning of the indignity and denial of humanity that Negroes suffer. He deals with identity, self-hatred, sexual attractions between races, race and class, and the stereotypes whites and blacks have of each other.

SACHAR, ABRAM LEON. **A History of the Jews.** New York: Knopf, 1930, 408 p.

A basic history from earliest times until the eve of the founding of the state of Israel. The text of the volume is divided approximately between the era from the beginnings until Christianity, from that until the nineteenth century, and then developments to 1930. Thus the Biblical era is not stressed. The emphasis is on the origins of modern Zionism and contemporary Jewish attitudes. Much attention is given to social and economic factors and the impact on Jewish life of secular social and cultural trends in the Gentile environment. The author writes readably but with substantial scholarship, from a committedly Jewish and Zionist point of view.

LATOURETTE, KENNETH SCOTT. **History of the Expansion of Christianity.** New York: Harper, 1937–1945, 7 v.

This monumental study is best described by listing the titles of its seven volumes: 1, "The First Five Centuries;" 2, "The Thousand Years of Uncertainty: 500 AD– 1500 AD;" 3, "Three Centuries of Advance: 1500–1800;" 4, "The Great Century: 1800–1914;" 5, "The Great Century in the Americas, Australasia, and Africa: 1800–1914;" 6, "The Great Century in Northern Africa and Asia: 1800–1914;" 7, "Advance through Storm: 1914 and After." The whole is an exhaustive chronicle of missionary activity with some attention to the environment in which it occurred.

BROCKELMANN, CARL. **History of the Islamic Peoples.** New York: Putnam, 1947, 582 p.

This scholarly and detailed volume, highly factual and objective, starts with the time of Muhammad. It was originally published in Germany in 1939; a brief chronology of events from 1939 to 1947 has been added to the American edition by Moshe Perlmann. In addition to a political history, which is the main focus of the book, the author provides some coverage of the cultural and intellectual life of the various eras. Theology is not extensively treated. The history deals mainly with the Islamic heartland in the Middle East and North Africa rather than with the more remote Islamic peoples of Africa and Southeast Asia.

International Migrations. New York: National Bureau of Economic Research, 1929, 1931, 2 v.

The first volume of this monumental study done for the International Labor Office, under the direction of Imre Ferenczi, describes and compiles the data on international migrations from 1846 to 1924, country by country. The second volume, edited by Walter F. Willcox, is devoted to interpretation of the data. Twelve chapters are organized by country of origin of migrants and seven chapters by country to which they immigrated. A typical chapter considers the composition of the migrant population by sex, country and region, race and socioeconomic character; causal factors; and waves and trends in the volume of movement. The various statistical sources on migration are evaluated.

ISAAC, JULIUS. **Economics of Migration.** New York: Oxford University Press, 1947, 285 p.

The object of this analytic study is to examine the economic causes and economic effects of the international migrations of the past century. Causal factors evaluated as explanations for voluntary movement include cost of living and income, unemployment, population pressure and exhaustion of natural resources. The author applies economic theory to clarify such concepts as optimum population and capacity to absorb immigrants and also to examine the case for and against freedom of migration. Among the effects reviewed are the impact of migration on wages, on the quality of the labor force and on capital flows via travel and immigrant remittances.

Between 1846 and 1932 intercontinental migration from Europe totaled 52 million people, of which 35 percent came from the British Isles, even in the 1920s the source of the largest block of migrants. Other large-scale sources of migration include Italy and China.

TAFT, DONALD REED and ROBBINS, RICHARD. **International Migrations: The Immigrant in the Modern World.** New York: Ronald, 1955, 670 p.

This comprehensive sociological review of the process of migration in the modern world treats migration as a pattern of social relations among men. The authors trace a historical trend from "early mass movements, through relatively free individual migration, to nationally and internationally controlled migration, culminating in the compulsory . . . movements of displaced peoples." Migration is examined in relation to population pressure and the structure of the labor force, and its regulation is studied in relation to the "quality of the moving population" and to sentiments of nationalism. Problems of culture contact and assimilation are also analyzed. All of this leads up to a series of historical case studies of which the American experience is the major one. Others include refugee flows from totalitarianism and Jewish migration to Israel.

SCHECHTMAN, JOSEPH B. **The Refugee in the World: Displacement and Integration.** New York: A. S. Barnes, 1964, 424 p.

This book presents an account of all major international refugee movements from 1945 to 1963. In each case the description portrays vividly but without bathos the human plight of the refugees, the political history of their displacement and the more or less successful efforts at relief for and reintegration of the victims in their new homes. The movements described include those of German expellees after the war, Karelians in Finland, Dalmatians and Istrians in Italy, Turks from Bulgaria, North Africans to France, the Hindu-Moslem exchange of population, North to South Vietnam, Korea, the Palestine Arabs, Jews to Israel, Dutch from Indonesia, Chinese, Tibetans, Africans and Cubans to the United States. Several of these chapters are condensed from earlier works by the same author. In his final taking of stock, Schechtman considers the problems of relief integration, and repatriation, coming down strongly for integration rather than repatriation. A similar book with a heavier emphasis on the administration of refugee relief and care is Malcolm J. Proudfoot, **European Refugees: 1939–52** (Evanston: Northwestern University Press, 1956, 542 p.).

EISENSTADT, SHMUEL NOAH. **The Absorption of Immigrants.** New York: Free Press, 1955, 275 p.

While most of this book is devoted to a deep study of the absorption of the various waves of Jewish immigrants into prewar Palestine and postwar Israel, comparative information on various migrations in Europe, to South America, to the United States and by Chinese in Asia is also included. The result is a highly systematic sociological analysis of the conditions that lead to fairly full assimilation into the host culture on the one hand and to continued pluralism on the other. Among the factors Eisenstadt evaluates are the pre-migration organization of the migrants, the cultural affinities between migrants and hosts, economic conditions, the social status of the migrants, their degrees of education as professionals or peasants, the relative achievement motivations of the settlers and hosts, and practices of discrimination and mistreatment toward each other.

NATIONAL MINORITIES; NATIONAL CHARACTER

CLAUDE, INIS LOTHAIR, JR. **National Minorities: An International Problem.** Cambridge: Harvard University Press, 1955, 248 p.

Focusing on the League of Nations and the United Nations, this book reviews the attempts that have been made to find answers to minority problems. Claude concludes that there is no solution to these problems within the confines of unilateral national authority, but that there is little willingness to go to strong international solutions. There may, however, be a growing acceptance of the notion of international recognition of human rights. Most of the book is devoted to a careful historical review of attempts at action by international organizations.

WAGLEY, CHARLES and HARRIS, MARVIN. **Minorities in the New World: Six Case Studies.** New York: Columbia University Press, 1958, 320 p.

The six minorities are: Indians in Brazil and Mexico, Negroes in Martinique and the United States, French Canadians, and Jews in the United States. The authors are anthropologists and approach the description of each group from that perspective. The cases were chosen to represent diversity in regard to historical origins of minority status, degree of assimilation, degree of oppression and racial involvement in minority-majority differentiation. Each of the case studies takes a historical view of the status of the group and how it arrived there.

The authors contend that the appearance of minority groups as a social phenomenon dates only from the emergence of the state form of human organization.

BARKER, SIR ERNEST. **National Character and the Factors in Its Formation.** London: Methuen, 4th rev. ed., 1948, 268 p.

The 1948 edition of **National Character** is essentially an abbreviated edition of the work as published in 1927 and is one of the earliest overtly interdisciplinary approaches to this area. The forces operating on national character are divided into, first, the material factors, which include the genetic factor, territory and climate, and population and occupation; second, what are called the spiritual factors, which include law and government, the religious factor, language, literature and thought; and finally, ideas and systems of education.

National character here refers to the nature of the state as the unit of analysis and not to the individuals or their discrete behavior. Thus, although Sir Ernest Barker has presented an elaborate discussion of factors which influence the existence of Great Britain as a nation and, indeed, may define nationhood, this is a different interpretation of national character from that used more recently which includes psychological makeup and the social behavior of the citizens of a nation. See, for example, H. C. J. Duijker and N. H. Frijda, **National Character and National Stereotypes** (Amsterdam: North-Holland, 1960, 238 p.).

POTTER, DAVID MORRIS. **People of Plenty: Economic Abundance and the American Character.** Chicago: University of Chicago Press, 1954, 219 p.

This book begins with two methodological essays: "The Historians and National Character" and "The Behavioral Scientists and National Character." Potter reviews the treatment of the national character concept by each of the disciplines, noting the disrepute into which the concept has fallen among historians. He suggests how certain conceptual advances of behavioral scientists point to the value of rescuing the concept. Reviewing the works of David Riesman (see **The Lonely Crowd: A Study of the Changing American Character,** New Haven: Yale University Press, 1950, 386 p.), Margaret Mead (see **And Keep Your Powder Dry,** New York: Morrow, 1942, 274 p.) and Karen Horney (see **The Neurotic Personality of Our Time,** New York: Norton, 1937, 299 p.), the author argues that these three views of American character, from the perspectives of sociology, anthropology and psychiatry, respectively, are not incompatible. All emphasize the "competitive spirit." Potter's thesis, then, is that there is a common causal factor for all three perspectives: the economic abundance "of usable goods produced from [natural] resources."

Drawing on both traditional historical material and data from the behavioral sciences, Potter discusses the influence of abundance upon child rearing, mobility and status in America. The role of the advertising industry is presented as functional in perpetuating demand for the goods of an abundant economy. A necessary relationship between abundance and democracy as it exists in the United States is also expounded. Frederick Jackson Turner's frontier hypothesis is discussed as a limited case of Potter's abundance thesis.

ISAACS, HAROLD R. **Scratches on Our Minds: American Images of China and India.** New York: Day, 1958, 416 p.

This is a study of the attitudes and images of Chinese and Indian characteristics held by 181 élite United States opinion makers. Harold Isaacs' sensitive interviews with leaders in such fields as business, mass media, government, academia, religion and information dissemination explore the conscious and unconscious rationales for these images. The interview data are interwoven with relevant historical information about India and China.

With regard to China, the stereotypes discussed include notions of superiority and inferiority, deceit and heroism. Stereotypes about India include "the fabulous Indians," "philosophers," "the lesser breed," ideas about caste and both positive and negative images of Gandhi, Menon and Nehru. Data are analyzed by comparing the stereotypes of those interviewed with their degree of involvement in Asian affairs and with other socially relevant variables such as occupational group and color.

Isaacs traces the sources of his respondents' images to their early roots in childhood experiences, literature, movies and personal contacts. He notes the varied vestigial images that reside in the mind, and how historical events bring one or another of those often contradictory traces to the forefront of attention.

INDUSTRIAL SOCIETY; LABOR

ROETHLISBERGER, FRITZ J. and DICKSON, W. J. **Management and the Worker.** Cambridge: Harvard University Press, 1939, 615 p.

"The Hawthorne effect," so-called as a result of this account of an experiment conducted at the Western Electric Company Hawthorne Works in Chicago, has become a conventional expression among reformers and management planners. It refers to the fact that morale rises in experimental programs seemingly because of the reforms that the program introduces but actually because the very conduct of such a program communicates to the participants the feeling that someone cares.

The studies reported in this volume were pioneering efforts at empirical research on human relations. The authors started out experimenting with the structure of work groups, piecework schemes and other conditions expected to affect productivity and morale. They found that whatever change they introduced, productivity rose. Finally they recognized the Hawthorne effect—that the human relations symbolized by the act of change rather than the content of the change was what made the difference. These studies were the roots of much of the later movement for improved human relations in industry.

TAWNEY, RICHARD HENRY. **Equality.** London: Allen and Unwin, 4th ed., 1964, 255 p.

This twentieth-century classic, first published in 1931, examines the problems of Britain, long the most "developed" society of the world, in terms that are relevant to every developing society. It describes the issues of equality that arise as any society grows more prosperous.

Tawney writes from a perspective characteristic of the British Fabians: a respect for ideas coupled with a dogged concern for reality. Thus, in the first chapters surveying the philosophical and historical context, he traces the fall of legal privilege and the emergent doctrine that stresses equality of opportunity. After acknowledging the various benefits conferred upon poorer people by the newer doctrine, Tawney concludes that recent developments have only raised the old problem in a new guise. The old problem is the continuing inequality of power and "circumstances."

The next chapters, which turn from the past to the future, deal successively with the strategy of equality, the conditions of economic freedom, democracy and socialism. There is close attention to political theory and economic doctrine, but the prevailing pragmatism of the Fabians is shown in the final section entitled "The Task before the Labour Party." Tawney agrees that the party's chief weakness is its inadequate organizational reliance on "the popular forces which should be its strength," according to its own doctrine of democratic socialism. The fourth edition concludes with an "Epilogue, 1938–1950."

FRIEDMANN, GEORGES. **Industrial Society: The Emergence of the Human Problems of Automation.** Glencoe: Free Press, 1955, 436 p.

This book is a model of interdisciplinary writing. As industrialization became pervasive over the past century, so the range of studies devoted to it became more specialized. Industrial engineering, education, physiology were incremented by industrial economics, sociology, psychology. To cope with the ramification of findings produced by these active new disciplines, industrial societies in the postwar years created schools of "industrial management" and firms of "management consultants." Their objective has been to see the industrial enterprise as a whole. This volume systematizes the available findings on nearly every aspect of industrialism—including the rich resources from studies conducted in Europe that were not previously accessible to most English-speaking students of industrial problems.

The author divides his work into three parts. The first deals with the human factor, traditionally conceived since Taylorism as time-motion studies or more generally as the physiology of work, including fatigue, accidents and the work environment. It proposes a reversal of the traditional formula in a chapter entitled "Adapting Machine to Man." The second part is concerned with the limits of the human factor and deals with such supraphysiological problems as monotony, rhythm, assembly-line work, automation, occupational skill and occupational culture.

In part three, "Towards a Social Psychology of the Factory," the author probes such central issues of occupational culture as rationalization, mechanization, integration. The final chapter is a learned and influential assessment of the values and limits of the human relations movement.

ARON, RAYMOND. **The Industrial Society: Three Essays on Ideology and Development.** New York: Praeger, 1967, 183 p.

This book is a distillation of the author's writings on the subject over the preceding decade and thus is to be taken as the expression of his most mature thinking on the problems dealt with.

The first essay begins: "For the first time, all men now share the same history"—the central theme of the author's earlier book, **The Dawn of Universal History** (New York: Praeger, 1961, 70 p.). As applied to the development of industrial society in the world today, this theme is reformulated to explain why "the state of high development of some countries is neither a cause nor a condition of the underdevelopment of other countries." The author describes the essay as mainly concerned with the link between the various phases of development and particular way of interpreting our times.

"Development Theory and Evolutionist Philosophy," the second essay, is a critique of the idea that the total future of mankind is subject to a law of increasing rationality and morality. The author, as a sociologist, exposes the fallacies that underlie "total" analysis and "law" that prescribes both past and future.

The third essay, "The End of Ideology and the Renaissance of Ideas," evolved from the **Eighteen Lectures on Industrial Society** (London: Weidenfeld and Nicolson, 1967, 253 p.), which the author presented as a course at the Sorbonne in 1963, and from subsequent writings. Here the author presents a powerful analysis of what is called convergence theory—namely, the idea that the United States and the Soviet Union are converging, and that the societies oriented to these superpowers are subject to an "inevitable convergence of hostile systems in an intermediary form dubbed 'social democracy.' " The author does not share this theory.

MUMFORD, LEWIS. **Technics and Civilization.** New York: Harcourt, Brace, 1934, 495 p.

This book on the transformation worked by the machine in "the material basis and the cultural forms of Western Civilization" departs from conventional accounts of social change since the industrial revolution in two important ways. First, it projects a much longer time perspective, noting that the machine had been developing for at least seven centuries before the dramatic clustering of industrial applications which have come to be considered as revolutionary. Second, it argues that the transformations worked by the machine were at least as much mental as material, as much cultural as industrial. "Behind all the great material inventions of the last century and a half was not merely a long internal development of technics: there was also a change of mind. Before the new industrial processes could take hold on a great scale, a reorientation of wishes, habits, ideas, goals was necessary."

The development of the machine is perceived to have taken place in three successive phases, the first starting around the tenth century, the second in the eighteenth century, the third in our own day. A sampling of the chapters includes: "The Monastery and the Clock;" "The Primitive Engineer;" "Consumptive Pull and Productive Drive;" Carboniferous Capitalism;" "Class and Nation;" "Purposeless Materialism;" "The Objective Personality;" "Toward an Organic Ideology;" "Toward a Dynamic Equilibrium."

VI. COMMUNICATION

GENERAL

PYE, LUCIAN W., *ed*. **Communications and Political Development.** Princeton: Princeton University Press, 1963, 381 p.

Eleven social scientists—sociologists, psychologists, political scientists, anthropologists—contribute essays on the relationship between institutions of mass communication and nation building. Subjects covered include the economics of mass media, contributions of journalists and other intellectuals to political development in the third world, the part played by media in bringing young people into political life and the role of the press in the politics of developing nations. Case materials are drawn from India, Turkey, Thailand, Communist China and other countries.

The volume is directed primarily to the scholar, although many of the essays, admirably clear, pungent and succinct, recommend themselves to the general reader. A unifying framework for the diverse contributions is provided by the editor's introduction to the book as a whole and by his briefer introductions to individual essays.

As the first stock-taking of knowledge about communication and political development, this anthology defined some of the major problems in the field and has had great influence on subsequent research. Many of the insights it provides remain cogent today. An example: as long as intellectuals in a developing country lack adequate means of exchanging ideas with each other and developing a sense of cohesion, their contribution to the political life of that country will be inhibited.

Daniel Lerner's important **The Passing of Traditional Society: Modernizing the Middle East** should be read in connection with the general theme of **Communications and Political Development.**

INNIS, HAROLD ADAMS. **Empire and Communications.** New York: Oxford University Press, 1950, 230 p.

The author, economic historian at the University of Toronto, addresses himself to the question: How are different modes of communication related to different styles of government? Especially in states covering large areas, he notes, the efficiency with which ideas are recorded and transmitted determines to a large extent the effectiveness of government. As nations or empires grew, "the sword and the pen worked together;" communities were "written into" states, and states into large empires.

Some forms of communication used in ancient times emphasized continuity and stability, thus overcoming the effects of time. Other forms were better at conquering space, enabling reports and instructions to be transmitted rapidly. Civilizations that relied on monuments of stone to transmit their heritage, and kept their records on clay tablets, tended toward decentralization and hierarchical institutions. Those that used lighter papyrus or parchment, enabling them to overcome space, were likely to be more centralized. The conquest of Egypt by Rome, for example, gave access to large supplies of papyrus that became the basis for a huge administrative empire.

Communication methods had an equally large impact in later eras. In medieval Europe, as long as parchment was the material most used for writing, the monas-

111

teries largely controlled education and the transmission of ideas. The advent of relatively cheap and plentiful paper supported the growth of secularism, of trade and cities. The printing press hastened secularization still more and facilitated the rise of nationalism.

Innis tends toward sweeping statements: some well documented, some unsupported and some obscure. Readers who find this annoying may be more than mollified by his obviously enormous erudition, urbanity and perceptiveness.

A very different but equally interesting approach to studying the influence of communication on the formation and aggregation of national states is found in Karl W. Deutsch's **Nationalism and Social Communication.**

ALMOND, GABRIEL ABRAHAM. **The American People and Foreign Policy.** New York: Harcourt, 1950, 269 p.

This study makes a penetrating examination of American attitudes toward foreign policy, the social and psychological environment in which foreign policy decisions are made, and the nature of the groups that have the greatest influence on these decisions. Part of the analysis is based on qualitative observations of historians, anthropologists and other students of American society; part on public opinion research conducted since World War II. Almond finds that foreign policies are initiated and formulated primarily by four "élites": political leaders, bureaucrats, spokesmen for interest groups and influential communicators. These élites are influenced by the "attentive public," an informed and interested stratum—usually a minority—before whom discussion and controversy take place. The general public can approve or disapprove policies, but in view of the complexity of foreign affairs cannot share in making them.

Public education and communication ought therefore not to attempt to make experts of laymen, although improved understanding of policy by the general public is desirable. An effective approach to public information on foreign policy questions should "be directed toward enlarging the attentive public and training the elite cadres." "If there is no 'quantity' market for information about foreign affairs," Almond concludes, "there is an important quality market."

SCHRAMM, WILBUR. **Mass Media and National Development: The Role of Information in the Developing Countries.** Stanford: Stanford University Press, 1964, 333 p.

A handbook for the development administrator and a concise summary of what is known about communication in national development for the student or general reader.

Schramm describes the flow of information throughout the world, how the mass media are distributed among nations and what effects communication can and cannot achieve. He then turns to application, dealing with the structure of information campaigns, methods of using communication research as an arm of social and economic development and the process of building a mass media network. A final chapter presents 15 specific recommendations to developing countries, and an appendix tells how to make a national inventory of basic mass communication facilities.

Written in an engaging and nontechnical style, the book is a leading example of an effort to apply social science research and theory to policy problems. The author, whose writing on journalism and related subjects spans three decades, is Director of the Institute for Communication Research at Stanford University and a long-time consultant to UNESCO.

DAVISON, W. PHILLIPS. **International Political Communication.** New York: Praeger (for the Council on Foreign Relations), 1965, 404 p.

What foreign policy goals can, and should, a nation try to advance through the use of communication? In attacking this question, the author first attempts a summary of what is known about the kinds of effects communication can achieve. This is followed by an examination of the roles of the mass media in industrialized democracies, developing countries and the communist world.

The book's second half addresses the relationship between international communication and national policy more directly. Problems of structuring a propaganda agency and coördinating propaganda with policy in the United States and the Soviet Union are discussed. The work of the United States Information Agency, of other government bodies disseminating information about the United States and of the principal private organizations communicating to foreign audiences is described. Suggestions for improving United States foreign information programs are advanced.

To summarize the author's thesis: the wise user of communication will recognize its limitations, imposed by psychological, social and political factors, and will aim for effects whose attainability has been demonstrated. The United States, committed by its democratic system to freedom of information, should make the most of this by encouraging greater openness in its own official communications and by devoting more resources, public and private, to building two-way communication with other nations.

This volume packages succinctly an enormous quantity of information from the literature of political science, sociology, psychology, history and journalism and also presents a useful schematic model of the communication process. Those who do not accept its conclusions may still find it valuable as a reference work.

HALL, EDWARD T. **The Silent Language.** Garden City: Doubleday, 1959, 240 p.
"In addition to what we say with our verbal language," Hall notes, "we are constantly communicating our real feelings in our silent language—the language of behavior. Sometimes this is correctly interpreted by other nationalities, but more often it is not." His book is devoted to a discussion of nonverbal languages and the cultural systems in which they are rooted. Units of time and space, for instance, have different meanings in different cultures. To be very late for an appointment may be an insult in one society but may be expected in another. Two American acquaintances will usually stand from 20 to 36 inches apart when having a personal conversation; Latin Americans will stand much closer. Techniques for concluding a business deal, patterns of relationships between the sexes and ways of making a living similarly derive meaning from their cultural contexts.

The author, an anthropologist, illustrates his observations with numerous examples, some drawn from everyday experience in the United States and some from the ethnological literature. He also presents a fairly technical scheme that can be used to analyze any given culture or to compare components among cultures. The book may thus be read on two levels: as a popular guide to intercultural communication or as an introduction to the study of culture as a communication system.

During the early years of the United States foreign aid program, Hall was in charge of training technical assistance personnel for overseas service. **The Silent Language** has been widely regarded as basic reading for anyone who wishes to avoid some of the pitfalls involved in trying to communicate with people of other cultures.

PROPAGANDA; PUBLIC OPINION

See also War and Peace: Political and Economic Warfare, p. 219.

LASSWELL, HAROLD DWIGHT and OTHERS. **Propaganda and Promotional Activities.** Minneapolis: University of Minnesota Press, 1935, 450 p.

SMITH, BRUCE LANNES and OTHERS. **Propaganda, Communication, and Public Opinion: A Comprehensive Reference Guide.** Princeton: Princeton University Press, 1946, 435 p.

SMITH, BRUCE LANNES and SMITH, CHITRA M. **International Communication and Political Opinion: A Guide to the Literature.** Princeton: Princeton University Press, 1956, 325 p.

Taken together, these three bibliographies inventory practically all the significant literature on communication and public opinion that appeared prior to 1956. They list approximately 10,000 items. As indicated by the varying titles, each volume has a slightly different emphasis. The first two draw somewhat more from the literature of domestic American communication than the third, which focuses on international politics, but all three cover the basic works in nearly all subdivisions of the field. The concise annotations are enormously helpful.

The categories used to organize the items annotated in the third volume differ from the categories used in the first two, but all categories are related to Lasswell's formula for the study of communication: "Who says what to whom through what channel and with what effect?" In addition, the first two volumes include introductory essays on communication that are of continuing value.

It is unlikely that similarly comprehensive annotated bibliographies covering the literature in this field from 1956 to the present will be prepared. The number of relevant books and articles is now so great that it is time for the computer to take over. Nevertheless, those interested in communication and public opinion can at least be grateful that the literature up to 1956 has been so well described and organized.

BUCHANAN, WILLIAM and CANTRIL, HADLEY. **How Nations See Each Other: A Study in Public Opinion.** Urbana: University of Illinois Press, 1953, 220 p.

At its 1947 meeting in Mexico City, the UNESCO General Assembly authorized a study of "tensions affecting international understanding." This book reports the results of the study, carried out under the direction of Hadley Cantril, Princeton social scientist, and written up by William Buchanan, also at that time a Princeton political scientist.

Parallel public opinion surveys were carried out in Australia, France, Great Britain, Italy, the Netherlands, Norway, the United States, and parts of Mexico and West Germany. Approaches were made to survey organizations in several additional countries, including Czechoslovakia and Hungary, but arrangements could not be completed.

The researchers explored national patterns of class consciousness, the degree of security and satisfaction experienced by people in different countries, the extent of friendship or hostility felt by various peoples toward each other and national stereotypes, including self-images. One of the most suggestive findings is that friendliness or unfriendliness of one people toward another may be attributed largely to relationships between their governments: "stereotypes should not be thought of as causative, but as symptomatic."

These survey results are, of course, now far out of date, and they apply to only a few countries. Nevertheless, the study is of historical interest as one of the first truly international surveys, and it has continuing value as a source of ideas for those interested in exploring the relationship of public opinion and communication to international understanding.

LASSWELL, HAROLD DWIGHT. **Propaganda Technique in the World War.** New York: Knopf, 1927, 233 p.

"So great are the psychological resistances to war in modern nations that every war must appear to be a war of defense against a menacing, murderous aggressor." So wrote Lasswell, then a political scientist at the University of Chicago, after analyzing the propaganda practices of Germany, France, Great Britain and the United States in the First World War.

Systematic propaganda, along with economic and military measures, has become an indispensable instrument of belligerency, Lasswell observes. The primary tasks of wartime propaganda are threefold: to mobilize the will to fight on the home front, to demoralize the enemy and to gain the support of neutrals. These aims are pursued by such techniques as insisting on the ultimate victory of your side, attributing all manner of evil to the enemy, making appeals to special interest groups in all countries and many others. All policies have propaganda aspects. When British Foreign Secretary Balfour committed his government to the establishment of a Jewish National Home in Palestine, General Ludendorff characterized this as a brilliant propaganda coup and regretted that his government had not thought of the idea first, since it appealed powerfully to Jews in all countries, including Germany.

This is not a "how to do it" book, but rather a book on how it is done. Written in a skeptical, urbane style, spiced with telling examples, Lasswell's analysis has scarcely been overtaken by events at all. Indeed, subsequent writing on propaganda has added remarkably little to it.

LINEBARGER, PAUL M. A. **Psychological Warfare.** New York: Duell, Sloan and Pearce, 2d ed., 1954, 318 p.

If parts of **Psychological Warfare** tend to read like a military manual, it is probably because the book developed out of a military manual. The author, formerly a professor at the School for Advanced International Studies of Johns Hopkins University and a long-time resident of China, also prepared a "Syllabus of Psychological Warfare" for the U.S. War Department General Staff.

"Psychological warfare," writes Linebarger, "comprises the use of propaganda against an enemy, together with such military operational measures as may supplement the propaganda. . . . Psychological warfare seeks to win military gains without military force." He includes a large quantity of "how to do it" information but also substantial historical material on military propaganda in ancient times and in both world wars. Linebarger's background in Asia enables him to overcome the "European bias" found in most American authors. His work is profusely illustrated with examples of propaganda leaflets used by the United States, its allies and its enemies in both Europe and Asia.

The first edition of **Psychological Warfare** (Washington: Infantry Journal Press, 1948, 259 p.) proved widely popular; it was translated into several leading languages and was soon out of print in the United States. A chapter which appeared in the first edition, hopefully entitled "Psychological Warfare and Disarmament," was replaced in the second edition by chapters on propaganda in the cold war and in "small wars."

LIPPMANN, WALTER. **Public Opinion.** New York: Macmillan, 1922, 427 p.

Today's reader of Lippmann's **Public Opinion,** like the reader of other classics, will find numerous examples of what appear to be familiar quotations—formulations so apt that they have often been repeated. He will also find freshness and currency in Lippmann's analysis of the role of public opinion and communication in a democracy, even though this analysis is illustrated with examples from World War I, related to the observations of classical thinkers and supported by the psychology and sociology of 50 years ago.

"Whatever we believe to be a true picture, we treat as if it were the environment itself," Lippmann wrote. But to form a true picture, especially in the realm of foreign affairs where most men never have direct contact with reality, is a formidable task. The trickle of messages reaching us from the outside is distorted by censorship and by the limitations of the press and of language. Further distortion occurs when these messages are assimilated into the images and preconceptions we have already formed, and when makers of public opinion seek to create a national will by using simplified formulations that will have mass appeal.

True, the press is bringing the world closer: "this was the first great war in which all the deciding elements of mankind could be brought to think about the same ideas. . . . Without cable, radio, telegraph, and daily press, the experiment of the Fourteen Points would have been impossible." But the press by itself is too frail to carry the whole burden of popular sovereignty. We cannot expect everyone to become an expert on everything. Instead, we should develop and strengthen institutions that can supplement the press in gathering and digesting information about the world. The public should not be asked to form an opinion until it is presented with better organized, more coherent pictures of international affairs.

Lippmann's analysis is often cited; his recommendations have received less attention. They deserve more.

BAUER, WILHELM. **Die Oeffentliche Meinung in der Weltgeschichte** [Public Opinion in World History]. Potsdam: Akademische Verlagsgesellschaft Athenaion, 1929, 402 p.

A historical work of magnificent sweep, tracing public opinion, communication and propaganda from ancient Egypt and Greece, through the Middle Ages to modern times.

Bauer presents a wealth of material on ways of disseminating information and influencing public opinion in societies with a primarily oral tradition; on the early private news services, used mainly by merchants and bankers; on leaflet propaganda during the Thirty Years War; on the first news and advertising publications; on attempts by eighteenth and nineteenth century governments to manipulate the press; and on the rise of modern mass media. Major developments in communication and public opinion are skillfully woven into the context of historical events. The treatment of the period prior to 1900 is especially strong. As the First World War approaches, historical perspective becomes more difficult to achieve and the work tends to fragment. Emphasis is placed on Europe; other areas receive little attention.

Unfortunately, no history of this scope is available in English, though badly needed.

THE PRESS

RESTON, JAMES. **The Artillery of the Press: Its Influence on American Foreign Policy.** New York: Harper and Row (for the Council on Foreign Relations), 1967, 116 p.

Reston characterizes his discussion of the triangular relationship among press, government and public in the field of foreign policy as consisting of "random observations." This description is harsher than necessary, although it is true that he skips rapidly from one subject to another and that his book is a heady combination of lively illustrations from current affairs, wise insights and historical perspectives. Particularly valuable are the sections in which he draws from his own rich experience in covering Washington's foreign policy process for *The New York Times.*

Among the subjects dealt with are the direct and indirect ways in which journalists influence American policy, misuse of the press by officials and misuse of officials by the press, the problem caused by foreign audiences that eavesdrop on the dialogue between the American public and their representatives, and the difficulties of adapting traditional news practices to the complexity of today's world. If there is a central theme it is that the power of the President to set foreign policy with little regard for Congress and the public has grown more rapidly than the power of the press to serve as a check on his actions; the press should stress its watchdog function.

Specific suggestions for improving press performance are modest and constructive. Don't let emphasis on the big event squeeze out careful news analysis. Present great issues in terms of choices that must be made; let the public examine these choices as the President has to. Pay more attention to informing the growing minority of the public that is seriously concerned with world affairs.

This book is based on three Elihu Root Lectures given at the Council on Foreign Relations in 1966.

COHEN, BERNARD C. **The Press and Foreign Policy.** Princeton: Princeton University Press, 1963, 288 p.

The foreign affairs correspondent reports the passing scene, observes Cohen, a University of Wisconsin political scientist, but he is also an important part of that scene. What the correspondent writes about largely determines what questions legislators or private citizens ask the White House and State Department. He thus draws certain issues to the forefront of policy attention. But he also plays other roles in the foreign policy process. Practically all executive and legislative officials in the United States who are concerned with international affairs read *The New York Times* and *The Washington Post* and watch wire service tickers for up-to-the-minute coverage of events abroad; they use the press corps as a loudspeaker to reach the public and rely on the media to bring them indications of public sentiment; some accept senior journalists as confidants or sources of ideas.

The newsman's foreign policy influence is nevertheless limited by the constraints of his profession. He must preserve the confidence of his governmental sources. He must report "the news," but "news" tends to be what is already in the headlines. Room for real innovation in reporting is confined to a relatively few individuals who set the tone for the rest of the press.

Cohen concludes that at best the press contributes only randomly to intelligent policy-making in the democratic context, and at worst is destructive of coherence and planning. His thoughtful analysis is based on more than 220 interviews with journalists and government officials, as well as on an extensive review of the relevant literature.

HOHENBERG, JOHN. **Foreign Correspondence: The Great Reporters and Their Times.** New York: Columbia University Press, 1964, 502 p.

In a succession of lively vignettes, each centered on a distinguished foreign correspondent, the author describes how the great international news events of roughly the past 200 years were covered. There is the enterprising young French reporter, Charles Havas, who broke the Napoleonic government's semaphore code and founded the first of the modern news agencies. There is Daniel H. Craig, who intercepted mail steamers from Europe at Halifax and forwarded European news to his American clients by carrier pigeon. There is Archibald Forbes, whose consistent news beats from the Franco-Prussian War so boosted the circulation of the London *Daily News* that it became profitable almost overnight.

From this series of brief flashes, the main themes of the history of foreign correspondence emerge: the constantly increasing speed of news transmission; the never-ending struggle with government censorship; the growth of international news services; the intense but good-natured competition among foreign correspondents and their employers to be first with the news. There is little analysis or delineation of trends. This the reader must do for himself, but it is an enjoyable task.

The author has relied mainly on English-language sources. As a result, emphasis is given to the British and American press, with relatively little attention devoted to correspondents from other countries.

VII. DIPLOMACY AND DIPLOMATIC PRACTICE

NICOLSON, HAROLD. **Diplomacy.** New York: Harcourt, 1939, 264 p.

Published more than 30 years ago, this work is and will remain a classic, for the author has in uncommon measure the capacity to identify the continuing essentials of diplomacy.

Writing when he did, a less wise man might have yielded to the temptation to define diplomacy as the art of stemming the rising tide of totalitarianism in world affairs. Nicolson remained on much firmer ground: "The function of diplomacy is the management of the relations between independent States by processes of negotiation." The fact that some of these independent states might—and indeed would—have unacceptable forms of government could not alter basic concepts.

In the modest compass of this book are contained not only the essentials of diplomacy but many nuances with a contemporary ring. While "deterrence" is for most commentators a concept of our nuclear age, Nicolson aptly quotes from King Archidamus' address at the Sparta Conference in 432 BC: "It is possible that when they [the Athenians] realise the extent of our rearmament, backed as it will be by equally forceful representations, they will be disposed to give way."

This book is written with clarity, humor and reasonableness. It is an example of the advantage to a writer in this intricate field of considerable firsthand experience in the conduct of foreign affairs.

LALL, ARTHUR. **Modern International Negotiation: Principles and Practice.** New York: Columbia University Press, 1966, 404 p.

Basing himself largely on post-World War II situations and disputes to which diplomacy has been applied, the author deduces some 35 principles of negotiation which may be relevant to the consideration of future international situations calling for diplomatic efforts.

International negotiation is defined widely to include all peaceful methods, other than judicial or arbitral procedures, directed toward the alleviation or resolution of international situations or disputes. Thus the book includes studies of mediatory and other third-party roles as well as of direct negotiation between the parties involved. The analysis also extends to public and closed multilateral diplomacy which has come to be widely practiced both in and around United Nations forums and at the numerous special conferences that have been convened, such as the Indochina Conferences of 1954 and 1961–1962, the Suez Canal Conferences of 1956 and the long series of disarmament conferences throughout the post-World War II era.

The author has had the advantage of an insider's view on many of the cases cited, having led or participated in India's delegations to a large variety of bilateral and multilateral negotiations over a period of some 17 years (1947–1963) during which he served as a delegate to a dozen sessions of the U.N. General Assembly and, at one time or another, to all the organization's major and many of its minor organs.

ACHESON, DEAN GOODERHAM. **Power and Diplomacy.** Cambridge: Harvard University Press, 1958, 137 p.

This survey takes a view of the diplomacy of what has come to be called a superpower in the era when the United States was the leader of a tightly knit alliance against the premised readiness of the other superpower, the U.S.S.R., to pounce wherever there was weakness outside its own alliance system.

With great skill the author constructs the diplomacy of a major alliance system. But the book goes further. For example, its sweep includes the policy to be adopted to strengthen the non-communist world. Taking India as a major case in point, he writes: "The West has the funds and plenty of industrial capacity to turn out the equipment required. What seem to be lacking are understanding of the urgent necessity and the will to act."

Acheson's recipe for successful diplomacy is the discarding of shibboleths and the paring away of inessentials until one is looking unflinchingly at the irreducible realities. In other eras a great power did not need to be this rigorous in its search for a surefooted diplomacy. It could act simplistically—as Palmerston often did. Bluster could be a substitute for analysis and carefully considered action. In a nuclear world this will not work. A superpower, however, will have to use force, the author argues, commitments to the United Nations notwithstanding.

This vigorous book makes a stimulating and important contribution to the unraveling of the diplomacy of the 1950s.

PEARSON, LESTER BOWLES. **Diplomacy in the Nuclear Age.** Cambridge: Harvard University Press, 1959, 114 p.

The author has known diplomacy at firsthand at all its levels. He had some years as a career foreign service officer before he became a parliamentarian and later Foreign Minister, and finally, Prime Minister of Canada. This experience alone would give these lectures richness; there are two other contributory factors.

First, the author speaks for the most part to a distinguished academic school on diplomacy (Fletcher). Second, believing with Lord Strang that "in a world where war is everybody's tragedy . . . diplomacy is everybody's business," he makes a special effort to communicate with a lay audience. "The policies which govern negotiations should be publicly decided and publicly explained."

Speaking of military coalitions—and all through the book Pearson is a staunch NATO man—he says: "But they can never be more than a second-best substitute for the great coalition of the whole United Nations, established to preserve peace." He reasons that "sound policy and astute diplomacy are themselves as much a source of strength as military power." The soundness and astuteness are not easily acquired, but something of these qualities comes through in this short book which deserves to be read and reread.

HAYTER, SIR WILLIAM. **The Diplomacy of the Great Powers.** New York: Macmillan, 1961, 74 p.

Brilliant in style, perceptive in regard to some of the underlying factors that affect world diplomacy, this book merits close attention. Some of its most pregnant comments are made casually. Speaking of the British, Hayter says: "They love foreign travel but when they get home they shut the door and put their feet up. This is not a very attractive characteristic." Then again: "India, for example, which may one day be a Great Power and has meanwhile taken to diplomacy like a swan to water," and perhaps the most charming yet devastating in this category of remarks: "Capitalist diplomats lie too, of course. But they do not like being caught out, whereas Soviet diplomats will tell lies that they know everyone else will know to be lies."

Where the author intends to be more serious and profound, he sometimes hits the mark and sometimes does not. He probably does when he tells us that an elected Minister of Foreign Affairs who has a political standing of his own has advantages over an appointee such as the U.S. Secretary of State. "The former can rely on Parliament, of which he is a part, to protect him against the Press: the latter is likely to be criticized by Congress if he does not yield to all the exigencies of the journalists." He perhaps does not when he says that America's policies on colonialism, "besides annoying the mother countries who are among her principal allies, have been prejudicial to America's own interests (and even sometimes to those of the colonial territories and their inhabitants)."

BAILEY, THOMAS A. **The Art of Diplomacy.** New York: Appleton-Century-Crofts, 1968, 303 p.

The author, a distinguished scholar of diplomacy, enunciates 267 diplomatic guidelines in this book. He hopes that his "book will fall into the hands of the President of the United States, the Secretary of State and other denizens of Foggy Bottom."

Dr. Bailey is firmly convinced of the value of his maxims. In large, they give a useful outline of diplomacy, but they would not help the practitioner who would find the slender evidence adduced for each maxim inadequate. In proliferating his guidelines the author lands himself in contradictions: "Good precepts to keep in mind are 'when in doubt do nothing' and 'doing nothing is better than doing the wrong thing.' " In the very next maxim he tells us: "A statesman should capitalize on the opportunity to fish in troubled waters" and "a statesman should always leave his hands free to exploit these openings as they develop." Cautious action and fishing in troubled waters hardly go together.

However, there are also wise remarks: "Domestic affairs, so called, are increasingly but the reverse side of the shield of foreign affairs" and "Great Powers can afford to lose face."

COT, JEAN-PIERRE. **La Conciliation Internationale.** Paris: Pedone, 1968, 389 p.

This is a rich survey of the development of both conciliation and mediation. Conciliation is distinguished from mediation by assigning the former function to persons or bodies without any authority other than their intelligence, skill and acceptability to the parties. Mediation is assigned to those whose intervention in a dispute or conflict is backed by their political authority and generally also by their power. Cot puts this picturesquely: "le Sage [the conciliator] et le Prince interviennent dans des conditions fondamentalement différentes au cours du règlement du différend. Le Sage a pour toute arme la raison, pour seul appui la confiance des Parties. Le Prince met en balance sa puissance et n'hésite pas, le cas échéant, à utiliser les moyens à sa disposition pour encourager les Parties à accepter la solution qu'il préconise."

Maintaining the distinction has a certain analytical merit, but it misses the necessary mixture of the qualities of the Sage and the Prince which must go into a successful—or even partially successful—exercise in mediation. Indeed, the larger the ingredient of wisdom the greater the likelihood that the mediatory effort will succeed. Nevertheless, this is a book of high value which should certainly be read by all who want to know about third-party efforts in resolving international disputes.

BURTON, JOHN WEAR. **Conflict and Communication: The Use of Controlled Communication in International Relations.** New York: Free Press, 1969, 246 p.

This book introduces an important innovation in the peaceful settlement of disputes between states. The author calls the technique "controlled communication." Representatives of the disputing states meet together with a number of scholars (ten in one of the cases discussed in detail). The process involves the scholars trying to get the parties to focus on their perceptions of the situation, including particularly attention to specific causes of fear. This process of analysis, stimulated by scholars, increases prospects of settlement. Perhaps the most important and innovative sentence in the book is: "parties to a dispute should not be required to compromise."

From "what appears empirically to be the nature of state and system behaviour," the book takes us to "what state and system behaviour is likely to be in conditions in which a third party is present to demonstrate the problems of perception and communication." The book should be read by all practicing diplomats.

HENKIN, LOUIS. **How Nations Behave: Law and Foreign Policy.** New York: Praeger (for the Council on Foreign Relations), 1968, 324 p.

A persuasive account of the importance, acceptability and limitations of international law in the conduct of foreign policy as of the mid-1960s. The author assesses the circumstances under which nations have tended to observe law as well as those when they have tended to violate it. Even when clearly in violation of law, nations have attempted to justify their actions diplomatically in legal terms. Henkin also argues that the observance of international law is probably increasing, with most of the new nations intent on observing and using it to the utmost in their diplomacy as a form of protection against the more powerful nations.

Several chapters discuss national diplomatic behavior and international law, and the extent of the positive influence of the United Nations on the development of international law. The law in operation is evaluated in the Suez crisis of 1956, the abduction of Adolf Eichmann in 1960 from Argentina to Israel and the quarantine of Cuba by the United States in 1962. The author notes that the law against armed intervention is often flouted, concluding, however, that the world "has not abandoned traditional international law or radically departed from its principal tenets. . . . New law for cooperation in the common welfare has taken root."

JOHNSON, E. A. J., *ed.* **The Dimensions of Diplomacy.** Baltimore: Johns Hopkins Press, 1964, 135 p.

To McGeorge Bundy, the first contributor to this rich little book, the pursuit and active use of political power is at the heart of high diplomacy. However, Henry Kissinger's brilliant analysis points out that in our nuclear world diplomacy has become less flexible than in previous eras. Kissinger's view is that restraining and coercive pressures—such as the gunboat—are no longer as effective as in the past. This could imply that less power-intensive diplomatic tools will have to be tried.

National diplomacy tends to be competitive, and W. W. Rostow tells us that even when the nation is not at war "there is a sense in which the Department of State is at war." This lucid essay induces thoughts on the possible alternative of an international diplomacy for our shrinking world.

James R. Killian's contribution is a balanced appraisal of the role of science in foreign policy and diplomacy. His plea is for the use in diplomacy of the constructive tools of science, including systems and models of the softer sciences. Adolf Berle's is a much more trenchant style. Regarding the forces which affect the validity of diplomacy, he writes: "The great change has been in economics." Many would assert that the most startling change had occurred in the military component. However, all would agree with Berle that diplomats cannot regard themselves as too political to get into the economics of international relationships.

Livingston Merchant brings out the advisory functions of an ambassador. He also sees clearly the difficulties which face the diplomat representing a democracy—the watchful eye of a Congress or Parliament, the comments of an alert press and the force of public opinion. He would not, of course, change this state of affairs.

This is a book to be consulted by the diplomat and those interested in his profession.

VIII. INTERNATIONAL LAW

GENERAL

BROWNLIE, IAN. **Principles of Public International Law.** Oxford: Oxford University Press, 1966, 646 p.

Too long to serve as an introduction to international law and too short to be useful as a comprehensive reference work, this book is best suited to the needs of students and of persons seeking aid on the particular subjects that this treatise covers in depth. As the author states, "this book is not a textbook or manual which says something about all aspects of public international law." He has chosen instead "the more basic topics," and he gives full treatment to such matters as personality and recognition, sovereignty, jurisdiction, nationality and state responsibility. But the book is comparatively weak on international organizations, the peaceful settlement of disputes and the law of treaties, and it touches upon the law of war and armed conflict hardly at all. A novel feature of the book is the drawing together of a variety of matters, such as economic aid, Antarctica, access to ports and problems of neighborhood, the essence of which is "sharing," under the rubric of "Common Amenities and Co-operation in the Use of Resources."

Dr. Brownlie is not afraid to take positions on controversial matters, and he is critical of a number of actions of the United Nations. He is sympathetic to many of the positions taken on questions of international law by developing and socialist countries. The legal analysis is rigorously conducted, but occasional difficulties of style detract from the force of some of Dr. Brownlie's arguments.

HYDE, CHARLES CHENEY. **International Law: Chiefly as Interpreted and Applied by the United States.** Boston: Little, Brown, 2d rev. ed., 1945, 3 v.

This great treatise on the whole sweep of international law as seen from an American perspective was written by the late summer of 1941 and therefore stops short a few months prior to the United States entry into World War II. Despite the passage of nearly three decades, it remains the standard work on the American view of international law. However, the book must be read with some caution in view of the many dramatic changes in international law that have taken place since that time.

The late Professor Hyde's statements of the law are illustrated and supplemented by numerous references to specific instances of American practice, often in narrative terms. These are of great value for the light that they shed on diplomatic history as well as on international law. So rich is the annotation and detail that the treatise constitutes virtually a digest in itself. The author's experience as Solicitor for the Department of State and the access he was afforded to the proofs of four of the eight volumes of Hackworth's "Digest of International Law" enabled him to write with particular authority about American views.

The work is written in the measured and weighty style of an earlier era, which is not without its complexities. It must therefore be read and consulted with the same patient care that went into the writing of this great monument to American legal scholarship.

OPPENHEIM, LASSA FRANCIS LAWRENCE. **International Law: A Treatise.** London: Longmans, Green. Vol. I (8th ed.), 1955, 1,071 p.; Vol. II (7th ed.), 1952, 941 p.

Oppenheim-Lauterpacht has been for decades the standard treatise on international law for the English-speaking world, both as a work of reference and as a textbook. Since its first edition in 1905–1906, it has passed through the hands of a succession of distinguished editors, the late Judge Hersch Lauterpacht being responsible for the last four editions. Its only rivals within the Commonwealth are D. P. O'Connell's **International Law** and Georg Schwarzenberger's **International Law as Applied by International Courts and Tribunals.**

The work is comprehensive in its scope and heavily annotated with references to state practice, learned writings and cases decided by national and international courts, the last of which Judge Lauterpacht collected and published in his series, the "International Law Reports." The work is written in a simple and lucid style.

The fact that the treatise was originally written by a positivist and substantially revised by a person deeply critical of that approach to law accounts for a certain inner tension within the volumes. However, the deep concern of Judge Lauterpacht for human rights, his serene confidence in the development of international law through codification, adjudication and resort to the general principles of law, and the emphasis that he placed on the position of the individual in international law are clearly visible in the treatise. His premature death cut off the writing of a completely new text which would have given full expression to his own view of the law.

There have been many developments in international law since the last edition of Oppenheim-Lauterpacht, but the text is so forward-looking that it bears its years lightly.

CORBETT, PERCY E. **Law and Society in the Relations of States.** New York: Harcourt, 1951, 337 p.

This is a general treatment of the old problem of evaluating the law of nations in terms of its relation to the facts and politics of state behavior. However, it is at the same time a general treatise in which the more significant aspects of the law are given perceptive review and illustration. The book's outstanding merits are the vigor and clarity of the writing, the successful selection and arrangement of material and a treatment which has much to offer not only to the novice but also to the expert.

The author is concerned with revealing the interaction of principle and doctrine, on the one hand, and actual practice, on the other hand. He stresses the harm which may result if the law gets out of touch with its surroundings; as he puts it, "attempts to speed law far beyond the living and thinking habits of the entities that it is designed to govern are doomed to failure."

The flavor of the book derives from its measured use of legal material and common-sense evaluation of the material, though it must be said that the author's brand of common sense is somewhat conservative. Moreover, the book naturally reflects the atmosphere in which it was written: an acute phase of the cold war, a world divided into two camps and an acceptance by some at least that the facts warranted the view that a new war was in the offing. Yet this provenance does not infect the whole book, and, in spite of his desire to be realistic at all costs, Professor Corbett is by no means willing to be restricted in his outlook by the political exigencies, as he saw them, of his time. Thus in an interesting final chapter entitled "New Directions" he makes a shrewd long-term prescription for general progress: the definition of human rights and the gradual reorientation of the United Nations around the focus of human rights. He also suggests that priority should be given to the problem of racial discrimination and its relation to other social and economic conditions.

JESSUP, PHILIP CARYL. **A Modern Law of Nations.** New York: Macmillan, 1948, 236 p.

The two principal theses of **A Modern Law of Nations** are that "international law, like national law, must be directly applicable to the individual" and that "breaches of the law must no longer be considered the concern of only the state directly and primarily affected" but of the entire international community. These themes are then spelled out in a critical analysis of the state of the law in 1947, shortly after the adoption of the Charter of the United Nations, and in recommendations for changes in international law. Some progress has been made: for example, the International Bill of the Rights of Man now exists in several forms; there is wider awareness of the variety of forms that international contractual arrangements may take; and colonial questions are no longer regarded as being primarily within the domestic jurisdiction of a state. But collective recognition through the United Nations is still unrealized, and the Security Council's activity in peacekeeping has taken a political course markedly different from the juridical role envisaged by Judge Jessup for that body.

Because progress has been slow on many fronts, a stimulating agenda for action in 1948 remains a lively tract for the 1970s. It is best read on the foundation of some knowledge of international law. While the *lex lata* is clearly spelled out, it is change in the law that counts in this wise book.

JESSUP, PHILIP CARYL. **Transnational Law.** New Haven: Yale University Press, 1956, 113 p.

Although the expression "transnational law" was not invented by Judge Jessup, the Storrs Lectures that he delivered at Yale Law School in 1956 are largely responsible for making the term part of the vocabulary of international law. The term refers to "all law which regulates actions or events that transcend national frontiers" and includes public international law, private international law and certain other rules of national law. Law conceived in these terms is freed from the rigid categories of public and private, civil and criminal, international and municipal law. Problems can be seen whole.

The first lecture draws parallels between domestic life, corporate life and international life to show the universality of human problems. The second lecture on "The Power to Deal with Problems" maintains that separate systems of jurisdictional rules for public and private international law are no longer justifiable. Judge Jessup urges that jurisdiction be dealt out functionally "in the manner most conducive to the needs and convenience of all members of the international community." In the final lecture, he submits that a tribunal should not be bound by such outmoded rubrics as territoriality or domicile and should be permitted to choose from international and municipal law, whether public or private, the rule best suited to the solution of the dispute.

This is a persuasive plea for modernization and liberalization of the law, expressed with great wit and aptness of illustration.

SCHWARZENBERGER, GEORG. **International Law as Applied by International Courts and Tribunals.** London: Stevens, 3rd ed., 1957, 808 p.
————. **The Law of Armed Conflict.** London: Stevens, 1968, 881 p.

Professor Schwarzenberger of the University of London is the principal exponent of the inductive approach to international law, and the two volumes of his treatise thus far published reflect his essentially conservative and positivist view of international law.

Among what are generally regarded to be the sources of customary international law, Professor Schwarzenberger places real confidence only in the decisions of international courts and tribunals, for it is only these law-determining agencies that are substantially free of partiality. Decisions of national courts, general principles of law, borrowings from municipal law and the writings of authorities are therefore left aside. The area of state practice, which Professor Schwarzenberger had originally intended to cover, has been preëmpted by Professor Parry's "British Digest of International Law." However, Professor Schwarzenberger promises a third volume on the law of international institutions.

While the treatise purports to cover the whole area of international law, the exclusion of materials other than the decisions of international courts makes for gaps and thin treatment in areas in which, for example, the application of international law has been delegated to states (*e.g.* the law of diplomatic and consular immunities). Other subjects, such as the law of belligerent occupation, receive heavier emphasis than might otherwise be the case because of the abundance of judicial materials.

Professor Schwarzenberger subjects the cases to critical evaluation and rigorously analyzes their premises and implications. The book is essential to an understanding of the jurisprudence of international courts but, by its very exclusion of other sources that are generally recognized, gives a somewhat lopsided view of the whole of international law. It must be read with a firm understanding of exactly what Professor Schwarzenberger has set about to do.

CHKHIKVADZE, V. M., *ed.* **Kurs Mezhdunarodnogo Prava v Shesti Tomakh.** [Treatise on International Law in Six Volumes.] Moscow: Izdatel'stvo Nauka, 1967–1969, 5 v.

In the longest and most systematic treatise to appear in 50 years of Soviet writing on international law, the editors state their creed: "In addition to the change in fundamental principles, substantial changes have occurred also in the subjects of international law, the law of the sea, consular law, state responsibility and other concrete branches of international law. Taken as a whole, these changes have altered the character of international law and its substance." The volumes document a creed taken from the Communist Party's 1961 program establishing "peaceful coexistence" as the keystone principle of Soviet foreign relations.

The substantive material with profuse documentation, when taken with the Soviet "Yearbooks of International Law" (published in Russian but with English summaries since their initiation in 1958), provides the most comprehensive source yet offered by Soviet authors for study of Soviet attitudes and practice. Their most notable theoretical contribution is in the treatment of the law of relationships among Marxian socialist states. Contrary to the view presented tentatively after the Second World War that in the relations among the then-emerging Marxian socialist states of Eastern Europe and Asia there must develop new norms, more moral than legal, the authors of these volumes argue that although the relationships among Marxian socialist states differ fundamentally from those among states of differing systems, they are nevertheless governed by law. Since practice as evidenced by treaties shows no basic conflict between the two sets of norms—those of traditional international law and those governing relations among Marxian socialist states— the authors believe they can be treated together in their study.

DAHM, GEORG. **Völkerrecht.** Stuttgart: Kohlhammer Verlag, 1958–1961, 3 v.

Professor Dahm adopts a classical form of argumentation in his review and commentary on international law; his methodology resembles that of other major works like Oppenheim-Lauterpacht's **International Law,** albeit with different conclusions in many instances. He cites traditional concepts to endorse or dispute particular applications of law; his interpretations of events since 1945 are controversial, especially of war crimes trials: they do not conform to those of most authors in other countries. Professor Dahm implies, for example, that the Nuremberg trials represented nothing more than "victor's justice" in so far as offenses other than war crimes in the narrow sense were involved, referring obviously to crimes against peace and crimes against humanity.

Volume I deals with general principles, the concept of the state, organs of the state, problems of nationality and jurisdiction on land and sea, in air and space; volume II is concerned with international organizations, peaceful settlement of disputes, economic and social compacts; and volume III treats conventions and violations of international law, sanctions and the liability of individuals for international crimes. Each volume is preceded by a selective bibliography. This work gives an excellent idea of the thinking, especially of German authors, until approximately 1958–1959.

WENGLER, WILHELM. **Völkerrecht.** Berlin: Springer-Verlag, 1964, 2 v.

Professor Wengler's two-volume work on international law represents an intensive effort to combine a review of developments in the field with interesting personal commentary. Unlike many other general works, this examination of principles and rules of international law and organization goes far beyond a recitation of facts. The author quite frankly adopts controversial interpretations which may run counter to the views of other leading analysts. From the very beginning Professor Wengler shuns orthodox endorsements, regrets partisan political approaches, condemns narrow nationalistic educational backgrounds, and seems to espouse the study and teaching of a separate branch of international law which goes beyond national legal preparations whether in his native Germany or elsewhere.

This work is divided into three parts: an introduction tracing basic legal and sociological concepts, the relation of international to municipal law, scientific methodology, historical development, subjects and objects of international law; second, general principles and rules, violations and sanctions, peaceful settlement of disputes; and third, problems of jurisdiction, international organization and laws of war. The work is capped by a selective bibliography referring mainly to major works on the subjects treated. This is a daring analysis in modern terms.

SERENI, ANGELO PIERO. **Diritto Internazionale.** Milan: Giuffre, 1956–1965, 4 v.

Since the publication in 1912 of the magisterial **Corso di Diritto Internazionale** by Dionisio Anzilotti, many Italian authors have made important contributions to the development of the science of international law. Sereni's book contains not only a distillation of this abundant literature within a new analytical framework but also many new ideas and novel approaches to old subjects. In particular, he has succeeded in integrating the new lore of international organizations into traditional international law. At the same time, in such areas as the laws of war, the author's approach is sensible and cautious, weighing the contending opinions of others and trying to find a reasonable compromise. The work is authoritative, bibliographical notes abound, and the footnoting is prodigious.

SCELLE, GEORGES. **Précis de Droit des Gens: Principes et Systématique.** Paris: Sirey, 1932–1934, 2 v.

The work of Georges Scelle, of which this book is the most representative example, is one of the most original and personal contributions to the theory of international law ever put forward, even if it admittedly draws part of its inspiration from the teachings of Durkheim and Duguit.

All law, according to Scelle, is a social fact, necessarily generated by every community. There is thus a *droit objectif,* an objective law which corresponds to the needs and to the social solidarity of the community and of which custom and laws are merely an expression, their validity depending on their conformity with such objective law. Such "realistic" conception of law naturally leaves no room for any sort of voluntarism, which is indeed utterly deprecated by the author. Similarly, the international community generates its own law, even at an unorganized stage when the mechanism of such generation is to be found in Scelle's famous *dédoublement fonctionnel.* This consists in state organs simultaneously performing functions not only on behalf of their respective states but also on behalf of the international legal order. The latter represents the universal, supreme and, indeed, unique legal order, comprising—in a rigorously monist construction—a multitude of lower legal orders (*ordres sous-jacents*), such as states and further subdivisions within states. This supreme order is valid directly for individual human beings who, with the elimination of a distorted, anthropomorphic view of the state, are found to be the only subjects of law, whether they happen to be the "governing" or the "governed" ones within their states. States as such have no sovereignty, which is an "anti-legal principle;" they have merely competences derived from international law.

Here then is a complete and extraordinarily coherent vision of a *Civitas Maxima,* painted not only with passionate conviction but, moreover, with an astonishingly compelling force of persuasion. Yet, in the face of a recalcitrant reality, the argument seems sometimes stretched to the breaking point; and it could be asked whether, in spite of the author's proclaimed realism, the picture he presents is not often rather *de lege ferenda* than *de lege lata,* just as it may be doubted whether the "objective law" is really something fundamentally different from natural law. However, here is a fascinating intellectual achievement, a generous view of international law and community and a source of inspiration which it would be a *testimonium paupertatis* for the world either to overlook or to forget.

EHRLICH, LUDWIK. **Prawo Międzynarodowe.** [International Law.] Warsaw: Wydawnictwo Prawnicze, 4th ed., 1958, 749 p.

This voluminous book by the late Professor Ehrlich, onetime professor of international law at the universities of Lwow and Cracow and Polish national judge in several important cases before the Permanent Court of International Justice, may certainly be considered as the leading Polish treatise on international law. The author's erudition and the resulting wealth of information concerning both the state of positive international law and the writings of publicists to date are truly remarkable, the extensive treatment of the historical background being particularly impressive. But the most prominent single merit of the book is to be found in constant reference to case law. Indeed, large excerpts from, or summaries of, international judicial and arbitral decisions (including more important dissenting opinions), as well as relevant municipal decisions of many countries, serve as ever-present support and illustration of the author's own exposition of each problem to such an extent that the book becomes a combination of a manual and a case-book.

It may be regretted that the author's approach is very conservative, be it in his voluntarism or in his treatment of subjects of international law or of international organizations. What may be even more regretted is the lack of a discussion in depth of problems treated. Professor Ehrlich is obviously less interested in what theoreticians think than in what judges do, but the resulting absence of doctrinal controversy makes the book somewhat unimaginative.

Published in 1958, following the "Polish October" of 1956, when the author broke his self-imposed silence of many years, the book shows not one trace of the political environment of the day, makes not one concession to the powers that be. Indeed, it ignores them totally and consistently. It is thus an achievement not only of a scholar but of a man of integrity.

ANZILOTTI, DIONISIO. **Corso di Diritto Internazionale.** Padova: CEDAM, 4th ed., 1955, 438 p. (French trans.: "Cours de Droit International," Paris: Sirey, 1929; German trans.: "Lehrbuch des Völkerrechts," Berlin: Gruyter, 1929.)

This book had been conceived as the first volume of an all-embracing treatise on international law, to be followed by two more volumes. It remained an unfinished torso, comprising an introduction and a part I. The former covers theoretical problems, such as concept of international law, relations between international and municipal law, sources. The latter deals with subjects and organs of international law, with unilateral acts, the law of treaties and international responsibility.

While the author modestly considered his book as a mere guide for the law students of the Rome University, it immediately achieved the stature of a classic and has retained it ever since. It is not unrealistic to think that this—together with Oppenheim-Lauterpacht—is probably the most widely quoted book on international law of the twentieth century.

That this should be so, despite both its incompleteness and the obvious lack of information about the massive development of international law and organization since its publication, is due to the unsurpassed mastery of the exposition of fundamental problems. Indeed, Latin clarity of thought and style, extraordinary lucidity, apparent simplicity combined with intellectual depth, unerring sense of what is truly important, and legal refinement distinguish Anzilotti as a writer just as they distinguished him as a judge.

The book is a highly important contribution to the theory of international law by one of the most prominent thinkers in this field, and one whose legal *Weltanschauung* left a profound imprint on both legal theory and the practical work of the Permanent Court of International Justice. Next to Triepel, it represents the most emphatic assertion of dualism. It is based on an entirely voluntaristic conception of international law. Yet Anzilotti is too good a positivist to be a doctrinaire— witness his reluctant acceptance of the general principles of law as a third source according to the Statute of the Court, or his admission of the possibility of subjects of international law other than states making their appearance in the future. Even so, the book remains a credo of dualism, voluntarism and state positivism.

KAPLAN, MORTON A. and KATZENBACH, NICHOLAS DEB. **The Political Foundations of International Law.** New York: Wiley, 1961, 372 p.

This is an ambitious but not wholly successful attempt by a political scientist and a lawyer to relate international law and its development to the structure and evolution of the state system, building upon the models of international systems presented by one of the authors, Morton Kaplan, in his earlier work, **System and Process in International Politics,** and upon the conception of international law as a decision-making process elaborated by Professor McDougal (see, for example, Myres S. McDougal and others, **Studies in World Public Order,** New Haven: Yale University Press, 1960, 1,058 p.). The shift from a "balance of power" system to a "loose bipolar" system is seen as having important consequences for international law. Emphasis is on topics most intimately related to the world political process, including recognition, sovereignty, territory, war and neutrality, and international organization. The various chapters are of uneven quality, and the book is marred by questionable generalizations, dogmatic assertions and many factual errors. The roles of economic interests and of technological change in the evolution of international law are barely mentioned, and important topics such as the treatment of aliens and their property are largely ignored. Despite these defects, the book is worthy of attention as a serious and pioneering effort to relate international law to politics.

TUNKIN, GREGORY I. **Voprosy Teorii Mezhdunarodnogo Prava.** [Questions of the Theory of International Law.] Moscow: Gosiurizdat, 1962, 329 p. (French trans.: "Droit International Public: Problèmes Théoriques," Paris: Pedone, 1965, 250 p.)

————. **Ideologicheskaia Bor'ba i Mezhdunarodnoe Pravo.** [Ideological Struggle and International Law.] Moscow: Izdat. Mezhdunarodnye Otnosheniia, 1967, 175 p.

The Soviet Union's most noted international legal author, onetime legal adviser to the Foreign Ministry and currently a professor at Moscow University, in these volumes implements the Communist Party's 1961 declaration that "peaceful coexistence" is the underlying principle of Soviet foreign policy. He polemicizes against outsiders who interpret the theme as denoting something less than coöperation between socialist and capitalist states, although he gives it a place second to proletarian internationalism in governing relations among Marxian socialist states. He sees these relations creating through custom and treaty practice a qualitatively new type of socialist international law in development of norms of traditional international law.

The earlier volume concentrates on sources of law and the process of norm formulation, noting Soviet contributions to what are said to be the novelties of nonaggression, peaceful settlement, self-determination, peaceful coexistence, disarmament and prohibition of warmongering. While Tunkin expects the list to lengthen, not everything is possible, for he recognizes a *jus cogens* to which all norms must conform. What it is cannot yet be stated, for Soviet scholars are held not yet to have explored the problem in depth.

The more polemical later volume seeks to establish that ideological struggle can and must continue between differing systems, but not to the negation of the law of peaceful coexistence. Ultimately, when the struggle has won over the nonbelievers to the superior Marxist system, the new law of proletarian internationalism will reign, but meanwhile traditional norms apply with the specific modifications indicated. A knowledge of Marxist thought is indispensable to appreciation of the reasoning in both volumes.

DE VISSCHER, CHARLES. **Théories et Réalités en Droit International Public.** Paris: Pedone, 3rd rev. and enl. ed., 1960, 534 p.

This is the most sophisticated treatment of the interrelations between the modern state system and international law, the most balanced account of the permanent tension between the political contest of states in the international milieu and the aspiration to a genuine international community. Judge de Visscher's book is the ideal essay for students' first encounter with international law. If they are law students, they will receive an indispensable background of political wisdom and legal theory; if they are students of political science, they will find a judicious assessment—neither utopian nor cynical—of the role of international law.

The first edition appeared in France in 1953, and in this country in 1957, in a distinguished translation by Professor Percy Corbett. The 1968 edition in English ("Theory and Reality in Public International Law," Princeton: Princeton University Press, 1968, 527 p.) is the translation of the 1960 French edition. The main changes (apart from additions to bring the book up to date) are a new chapter on effectivity in international relations and a reorganization of Book IV (the judicial settlement of disputes), which now covers a broader range than in the original edition.

BRIERLY, JAMES LESLIE. **The Law of Nations.** New York: Oxford University Press, 6th ed., 1963, 442 p.

Reviewing the fifth edition (1955), the late Edgar Turlington wrote in the *American Journal of International Law* (v. 50, 1956) that Brierly's introduction to the international law of peace, first published in 1928, "is still the best book of its kind." It is, indeed, as Sir Humphrey Waldock notes in his preface to the present edition, "a masterpiece in its own genre," thanks to "the judgment, vision, and scholarship that characterized all Brierly's work, combined with the simplicity and brevity of his exposition." All these virtues also characterize Professor Waldock's writings, including his changes of and additions to Brierly's own fifth edition. He revised sections dealing with the continental shelf, the high seas and the territorial sea in the light of the 1958 Geneva Conventions on these subjects; the Vienna Convention of 1961 on Diplomatic Relations provided new material for the section on diplomatic immunities. Professor Waldock also added a new chapter on "International Law and Resort to Force" which includes a very close analysis of the relevant parts of the Judgment of the International Court of Justice of 1949 in the *Corfu Channel* case.

The book remains what it was intended to be: "an introduction for students . . . and for laymen who wish to form some idea of the part that law plays . . . in the relations of states." That law, wrote Brierly, "is neither a myth . . . nor a panacea . . . but just one institution among others which we can use for the building of a better international order."

O'CONNELL, DANIEL PATRICK. **International Law.** Dobbs Ferry: Oceana, 1965, 2 v.

Professor O'Connell's **International Law** is the first major attempt to produce a general textbook on international law in the English part of the English-speaking world since Oppenheim. Aimed primarily at practitioners, it is readable, free of paragraph numbers and has footnotes of reasonable length. However, the two volumes contain no discussion of the law of war, and consideration of international organization is minimal.

The author distinguishes clearly between the history of international law and of its doctrine, so that in discussing the development of any rule the significance of the latter is kept to its proper subordinate place. In enunciating the law, Professor O'Connell frequently discusses theory first and then examines the position under English law, United States law and the civil law systems, embodying summaries and extracts from important cases, thus enabling a practitioner to see with ease—and without immediate recourse to other materials—the basis on which any rule purports to rest. To emphasize its practical value, the work proceeds in the sequence of theory, functions, jurisdiction, responsibility and litigation.

Despite a few statements of fact which had been overrun by events before completion of the text, perhaps inevitable in a work of such size, the author pays full attention to historical advances and frequently applies sociological and functional interpretative methods. This is particularly evident in his treatment of the attitude of new states, the interrelationship of custom and treaty, the practical significance of sovereignty, the position of the individual and the political character of recognition. Inevitably, there are points of disagreement and of emphasis, but this work constitutes a major contribution to scholarship in this field.

SØRENSEN, MAX, *ed.* **Manual of Public International Law.** New York: St. Martin's Press, 1968, 930 p.

The trouble with much of the international law literature is the complexity of presentation, making the entire, vital subject impenetrable to the uninitiated. Furthermore, the treatises are written by individual authors, reflecting national attitudes; laid side by side, their divergencies seem unbridgeable. This book, sponsored by the Carnegie Endowment for International Peace, has the double distinction of being a pioneering and an authoritative effort to present to the nonspecialist "objectively, from an *inter*national rather than a *national* point of view, the status and role of international law in the complex world of today." The challenge, then—well met—was to see whether experts of widely different backgrounds could produce a lucid, comprehensive and coherent handbook.

The rather elaborate project was headed by Professor Sørensen (Denmark); his collaborators were from Britain, France, India, Japan, Jugoslavia, Poland, the United Arab Republic, Uganda, Uruguay and the United States. Two British lawyers contributed to the cohesion of the book; that cohesion was also fostered by common working sessions which, however, did not impose uniformity: some (for that matter, remarkably few) divergencies of opinion are not glossed over.

The authors succeeded in covering the whole range of international law—from the law of treaties to that of recognition, from the protection of human rights to atomic energy and outer space, from the rules governing development assistance to international narcotics control, from alliances to collective security, from the law of war to the legal status of aliens. The role and functions of institutional arrangements, from the U.N. system to regional bodies, are properly and realistically woven into the picture.

While primarily designed to fill a widely felt gap for students, government officials and practitioners of newly independent and developing countries, this down-to-earth and yet impeccably craftsmanlike manual has proved useful wherever international problems are seriously studied. Its annotated multilingual bibliography, which includes serial and other publications of the United Nations, merits special mention.

KELSEN, HANS. **Principles of International Law.** New York: Holt, Rinehart and Winston, 2d rev. ed., 1966, 602 p.

When the Viennese creator of the famous Pure Theory of Law first published these Principles in 1952, it was not his first book on international law nor his first work originally to appear in English, but his first comprehensive work on international law. It followed upon two other similar firsts: his fundamental **General Theory of Law and State** (Cambridge: Harvard University Press, 1945, 516 p.) and his monumental **The Law of the United Nations** (New York: Praeger, for the London Institute of World Affairs, 1950, 903 p.), both of which were relevant for the **Principles:** the first because of the basic concepts of law and state developed therein and its two chapters on the elements of the state and on the relations between national and international law—which chapters appear with some variations in the **Principles**—and the second because of the claim of the Charter to be valid also for non-members of the United Nations, *i.e.* because of its emerging character as general international law. While comprehensive, the work is most aptly entitled **Principles of International Law** because it is concerned with the "most important norms which form this branch of law" and because it presents a "theory of international law, that is to say, an examination of its nature and fundamental concepts, an analysis of its structure . . . and of its position in the world of law"—all this on the basis of the author's Pure Theory of Law.

As a distinguished disciple of Kelsen, Professor Robert W. Tucker was eminently qualified for the difficult task of editing and updating such a work. And he has acquitted himself of it very well indeed. He stressed certain developments at the expense of others, an editor's privilege as long as he remains true to the spirit of the work. This Dr. Tucker did. He added *inter alia* judicious discussions of the principle of effectiveness and of the problem of customary law—questions which are of particular importance in international law. The book in its original and revised forms is not easy reading but is an excellent introduction into Kelsen's theory and an indispensable, unique work.

GUGGENHEIM, PAUL. **Traité de Droit International Public: Avec Mention de la Pratique Internationale et Suisse.** Geneva: Georg. Vol. I (2d ed.), 1967; Vol. II, 1953–1954.

The above work covers most of the essential chapters of public international law, including the laws of war and neutrality. It is now widely recognized as being one of the leading treatises on the Law of Nations published on the European continent.

Three aspects of Guggenheim's work must be especially mentioned. First, each chapter contains a highly interesting and erudite historical description; the problems treated by the author are thus put into their proper perspective. Second, the work is firmly rooted in international practice, of which fullest use is made. In this connection, the author concentrates on Swiss practice concerning public international law, thereby following a precedent set by Charles Cheney Hyde in relation to United States practice, in his **International Law: Chiefly as Interpreted and Applied by the United States.** Third, the treatise constitutes one of the first attempts to put Kelsen's Pure Theory of Law to practical use in the field of international law.

It is impossible to review the different chapters of Guggenheim's work within the framework of this summary description. Suffice it to say that thanks to its scholarly qualities, the treatise, though too difficult as a textbook for undergraduate students, has already become a classic which is an indispensable tool for both theorists and practitioners of international law. Guggenheim's work moreover contains an excellent general bibliography, a table of cases and a good index.

DE BUSTAMANTE Y SIRVÉN, ANTONIO SANCHEZ. **Derecho Internacional Público.** Havana: Carasa, 1933–1938, 5 v.

The permanent imprint on the law for which Bustamante undoubtedly will always be remembered is his work in private international law (see among other publications his three-volume work, **Derecho Internacional Privado,** Havana: Cultural s.a., 1943) and above all the still-reigning *Bustamante Code.* None the less, as a jurist and practitioner, he labored prodigiously and prominently in the field of public international law as well. His conflicts of law work kept him close to the working practicalities of personal and commercial relations that cut across state boundaries. He served, too, as a Judge of the Permanent Court of Arbitration and as a Judge of the Permanent Court of International Justice. His academic honors and positions were numerous. Among other things, he founded the American Institute of International Law's *Revista de Derecho Internacional,* published in Havana.

His public international law treatise is still referred to by writers working in Spanish. The first volume, entitled "Constitutional Law," deals with the legal origin, personality and death of states. "Administrative Law," the second volume, emphasizes human rights in a surprisingly modern context. The "Civil Law" volume takes up "contracts" and "obligations," with analogies to municipal systems but dealing with claims and agreements. "Penal Law" is his choice of title for volume IV, in which he examines the law of war and neutrality. The final volume, "Procedural Law," is devoted to the entire spectrum of disputes settlement procedures. Between these covers is a gold mine of theoretical analysis and research, comparing the practice of states with general principles.

Accioly, Hildebrando Pompeo Pinto. **Tratado de Direito Internacional Publico.** Rio de Janeiro: Impr. Nacional, 2d ed., 1956–1957, 3 v.

From his many publications and his long experience as the Counselor of the Brazilian Ministry for Foreign Relations, Professor Accioly earned and has retained a first rank reputation for his encyclopedic knowledge of international law, both as it has been practiced by states and as it is written in the "doctrine." In the classical treatise here reviewed, his tone still tends to the moralistic and his conception of the state is quite traditional. None the less, this is a monumental work that is much relied upon by jurists and researchers as well as by law school students in the Hispano-Luso world. The original edition (1933) was updated and brought out in French (1940) and then again updated for the Spanish translation (1945). In this second Portuguese edition the author substantially reorganized his thinking and adopted a more modern, less abstract approach. The work stands, perhaps, as the epitome of the comprehensive study by jurists of Latin America.

Volume I is dedicated to the theoretical aspects and basic propositions (bases, sources, relationship to municipal law, states as international persons, treaties). Volume II deals with the scope of territorial, maritime and aerial jurisdictions, as well as with international organization. The third volume covers war, neutrality and pacific settlement of disputes. Above all, the reader will find rich documentation and discussion of the Brazilian practice, which is considerable and significant. Brazil's moderate legal posture in international affairs is nowhere as ably presented and explained as in these well-known volumes.

Jiménez de Aréchaga, Eduardo. **Curso de Derecho Internacional Público.** Montevideo: Centro Estudiantes de Derecho, 1959 and 1961, 2 v.

The format for this "teaching treatise" contains no surprises, but the writing is sober, insightful and learned—the distillations of a broadly experienced international lawyer who also has maintained a substantial private practice in Uruguay. The reader is exposed to the leading doctrines, cases and literature from a number of "foreign jurisdictions;" their presentation is open and objective. The first volume deals with "General Theory." His is the best-balanced and most useful general treatment of legal theory, as it pertains to international law, that has appeared in Spanish. The chapter on "The Problem of the Autonomy of Legal Orders" and the one on the "Problem of the Hierarchical Relationship Between the Two Systems" (municipal and international) are especially good explanations. The second volume treats "The States and Their Domain." The chapters on international rivers ("Dominio Fluvial"); the territorial sea, contiguous zone and continental shelf;

and the high seas, including fishing and conservation of living resources, are thorough and modern in outlook.

Professor Aréchaga was elected to the International Court of Justice in 1969, another manifestation of the wide respect he has earned throughout the world. Anyone desirous of acquainting himself with the field as organized and viewed by a highly competent Latin American should take these volumes in hand.

HISTORY

NUSSBAUM, ARTHUR. **A Concise History of the Law of Nations.** New York: Macmillan, rev. ed., 1954, 376 p.

The first edition of this book, published in 1947 (New York: Macmillan, 361 p.), was not well received. The revised edition of 1954 took careful note of the most telling criticisms and became a standard work in the field of international law history within a very few years after publication. Sketching in ancient concepts of international (or inter-tribal, inter-city) propriety in less than 16 pages, the beginnings of modern international law are found in practices and legal concepts arising in medieval Europe and the interactions between the political groups of Europe on the one hand, and the Eastern Roman Empire and its successors (including its Arab successors) and Russia on the other. Having set out this orientation, the book proceeds in the more usual line dividing the history of international law into periods separated by the "watershed" dates of the Peace of Westphalia, the Congress of Vienna and the First World War. The historical survey ends at the Second World War with a short analysis of Soviet practice and doctrine to 1945. Appendices contain a brief survey of some of the leading historiographers of international law and a rather ill-tempered academician's essay strongly disagreeing with the arguments posed by James Brown Scott on the relative merits of the Spanish writers of the sixteenth century and Hugo Grotius as publicists. Professor Nussbaum prefers Grotius.

The book is marked by great erudition and compression. The approach is basically that of the historian tracing the chronological evolution of all the basic concepts at one time. Large sections are devoted to examining in some detail the thought in all areas of international law contributed by leading writers of each period. This can be contrasted to the more recent approaches taken by historians of international law. J. H. W. Verzijl's monumental **International Law in Historical Perspective** (Leyden: Sijthoff, 1968–69, 2 v.) is subject-oriented, tracing each particular doctrine or rule of international law from precedent to historical precedent, aiming at a better understanding of the modern rule, rather than an understanding of the cross section of rules at a given historical moment. Similarly, the publications of the Grotian Society edited by Professor C. H. Alexandrowicz (the first volume of which was published as a part of "The Indian Year Book of International Affairs" in 1964) concentrate on essays dealing with specific doctrines in historical perspective rather than approaches to international law taken at key moments in history.

ALEXANDROWICZ, CHARLES HENRY. **An Introduction to the History of the Law of Nations in the East Indies.** London: Oxford University Press, 1967, 259 p.

Using "East Indies" to include greater India, Nepal, Ceylon, Malaya, Thailand and Burma as well as the Indonesian archipelago, and introducing much material derived from European relations with the Ottoman Empire and Persia, the book analyzes the main outlines of international law as conceived and applied between Europeans and South Asians in the sixteenth, seventeenth and eighteenth centuries. The principal thesis, amply supported by evidence found in treaty practice, diplomatic practice and the writings of European and Asian pre-nineteenth century publicists, is that the "natural" law of nations assumed the sovereign equality of

states regardless of culture or location, and that it was not until the early nineteenth century that positivist approaches to law transformed the universal international society into a European and American family.

There is room for disagreement on several points raised by the book. Some
specialists may feel that Professor Alexandrowicz overstates his case in part, for
example in attributing to Asian experience a significant impact on the European
evolution of the *droit d'Aubaine* and jurisdiction to apply military justice in foreign
territory. There is also some evidence which the book does not include that even in
the seventeenth century European powers were finding legal ways to avoid treating
South Asian communities as sovereign equals by altering the traditional definition
of "piracy" to outlaw some Asian communities otherwise apparently fitting the
definition of "state." But these criticisms are no more than what must be expected
when considering a book as original and as broad in scope as this one.

BUERGENTHAL, THOMAS. **Law-Making in the International Civil Aviation Organization.** Syracuse: Syracuse University Press, 1969, 247 p.

This monograph contains a meticulously accurate and detailed description and
analysis of the little known quasi-legislative activities of the International Civil
Aviation Organization (ICAO). The emphasis is on the development and enactment of the technical International Standards and Recommended Practices for
international air navigation in the form of Annexes to the Chicago Convention on
International Aviation of 1944 and on the extent to which members of ICAO are
required to comply with them, but there are also excellent chapters on membership
in ICAO, on its role in the settlement of disputes between members, and on the
process of amendment of the Chicago Convention. This is the only published study
in English of the quasi-legislative activities of ICAO and is particularly valuable as
a contribution to understanding the increasing role of international organizations in
the international law-making process. Not covered in the book is the work of ICAO
and its Legal Committee in the preparation and drafting of international conventions on air law.

REIBSTEIN, ERNST. **Völkerrecht: Eine Geschichte seiner Ideen in Lehre und Praxis.**
Freiburg: Alber, 1957–1963, 2 v.

The two volumes are part of *Orbis Academicus,* a series of treatises on the
history of the several branches of the social and natural sciences. The author gives
a historical account of the philosophical, political and legal ideas that have played
a significant role in the formation of international law doctrines and in international state practice. The proportion between the analyses of thought and action
naturally varies from chapter to chapter. The more closely the author approaches
the present, the greater attention he pays to the actual conduct of states in international politics. But nowhere does Reibstein lose sight of the interrelation between
theory and practice. The volumes contain often lengthy quotations from political
and legal writings as well as from state documents. The insertion in the text of
pertinent documentary material is indeed a chief feature and a great merit of the
erudite work.

The first volume covers the period of transition from antiquity to the Middle
Ages, the medieval period proper, the epoch of the classics of international law
(Vitoria, Fernandus Vasquius, Suárez, Grotius) and the age of enlightenment.
Much more elaborate is the survey of theory and practice during the last two
hundred years, which fills the whole second volume. The latter also differs
methodologically from the former; the systematic account of the general doctrinal
development which prevails in the first volume gives way, in the second, more and
more to the discussion of special topics, such as codification, international organization, the principle of nationalities and self-determination, imperialism and
colonialism, recognition, the principle *pacta servanda* and intervention. The second
volume is full of highly interesting material drawn from the diplomatic history of

the last two centuries up to the Cuban crisis of October 1962. The 84-page bibliography is not selective enough to serve the layman as an effective guide.

SOURCES; CODIFICATION

ASAMOAH, OBED Y. **The Legal Significance of the Declarations of the General Assembly of the United Nations.** The Hague: Nijhoff, 1966, 274 p.

YEMIN, EDWARD. **Legislative Powers in the United Nations and Specialized Agencies.** Leyden: Sijthoff, 1969, 227 p.

Contemporary history, as Geoffrey Barraclough tells us, does indeed possess a character of its own. Urbanization, decolonization and increasingly rapid rates of technological change, together with other sources of stress, have introduced an unusual degree of uncertainty into world politics. Hence we can look back to the diplomatic history of the nineteenth century with some real envy. On the other hand, the ability of states to deal with stress has been materially affected by the growth of international organizations. This growth, in turn, has placed inevitable strains on traditional conceptions of international law based upon assumptions of state sovereignty. We recognize intuitively that some measure of influence has passed from states to international organizations, but in this as in other aspects of international relations, intuitive judgments must be weighed against more public forms of knowledge. Both Asamoah and Yemin seek in rather different ways to traverse the distance between intuition and publicly transmissible knowledge in this field.

The title of Mr. Asamoah's book notwithstanding, he has attacked a subject of considerable breadth. He asks in effect what significance the ritual acts of the General Assembly possess. What does it mean when a resolution is passed? What mark does an expression of Assembly sentiment leave on the patterns of international relations? The consequences, he finds, are considerable, for he sees resolutions as vehicles for restating and occasionally advancing international customary law. They thus serve, as Wolfgang Friedmann notes in his preface, as potential bridges between customs and treaties. Besides discussing the general jurisprudential problem, the author deals in detail with a series of topics which bulk large in the body of declaratory resolutions: war crimes, natural resources, nuclear weapons, outer space, colonial peoples, human rights, racial discrimination and the rights of children. A full answer to the problem of the consequences of official pronouncements necessarily involves a consideration of issues and resources outside the traditional legal literature. Mr. Asamoah is fully aware of this dimension, so often absent in the literature of international law and organization. He gives due weight to the force of political and social circumstance which, in the end, is the ultimate behavioral source of legal validity. Far more than most writing in this area, he appreciates the absurdity of a hard-and-fast distinction between "law" and "politics." Hence it is a matter of some regret that he appears unfamiliar with the literature of contemporary political science that might provide confirmation for many of his most insightful observations.

While Mr. Yemin's title appears broader, the scope of his monograph is in fact restricted. He seeks to examine the bindingness of international organizational acts. He clearly believes that organizations can and do legislate for states, even after giving due weight to the fact that states continue to find ways of escaping from obligations which they find particularly onerous. One cannot fault Mr. Yemin on his meticulous use of the armamentarium of traditional legal research, yet the answer to his question does not lie wholly within the interstices of legal documents. Michel Virally, in a thoughtful preface, comments that the crisis of contemporary international law is merely the reflection of massive changes in international society; yet Mr. Yemin contents himself with examining the reflection alone. He has not sought direct evidence from the behavior of the human beings who comprise governments and organizations, and by examining their legal artifacts keeps the reader and himself at one more remove from behavioral data. The author's singleminded concentration on traditional legal sources enables him to build and sustain an internally secure argument, but the genuine test of his hypothesis inevitably lies in the realm of political, social and economic data. None the less, he effectively details much of the legal life of the United Nations itself, the International Telecommunications Union, the Universal Postal Union, the International Civil Aviation Organization, the World Meteorological Organization and the World Health Organization.

ROUSSEAU, CHARLES. **Principes Généraux du Droit International Public.** Paris: Pedone, 1944, 975 p.

This work was conceived as the first volume of an *opus magnum* on international law, to be followed by two more volumes. It is to be regretted that this project has not yet materialized and that the volume under review has not had a second edition. For the work is truly a mine of information on the subjects it covers, based on exceptionally wide documentation: state practice, incursions into relevant portions of various constitutional laws, treaty law, judicial decisions both international and municipal, writings of publicists. Every single problem thus receives a much more detailed treatment than is usual in other books.

While aiming chiefly at depicting the state of positive international law, the author deals extensively with all major theories of both the general philosophy of international law and the treatment of particular problems. These theories are expounded with rigorous objectivity and fairness, subjected to critical comment and tested against positive law. The author himself, while refraining from offering a theory of his own, observes a strictly positivist approach, firmly rejecting all natural law in any form.

The law of treaties occupies—not unexpectedly—the greater part of the book. This part is subdivided into two "titres" dealing respectively with the dynamic ("traité au point de vue formel—opération à procédure") and the static ("traité au point de vue matériel—le traité pose une règle juridiquement obligatoire") aspects of a treaty, a distinction rarely made outside the sphere of influence of the Vienna school in spite of its obvious validity.

On the whole, the book is much more a reference and working instrument than a textbook for undergraduates and, as such, is indispensable in any legal library. A very detailed table of contents and a good index help the reader to find his way through the wealth of information.

BRIGGS, HERBERT W. **The International Law Commission.** Ithaca: Cornell University Press, 1965, 380 p.

At the present time, a significant number of public and private organizations are engaged or have recently been engaged in projects for the progressive development of international law and its codification. None, however, has been in a position to emulate the International Law Commission in sustained level of contributions or in ability to elicit critiques, suggestions and commentaries not only from distinguished jurists but also from governments as well as other organs of the United Nations. Professor Briggs' volume on the inner operations, procedures and the decision-making processes of the Commission is, therefore, of particular value to the student of international law. Unfortunately, as the author himself was the first to point out, membership in the Commission required that he reserve his own views on some of the more provocative issues that have arisen during the more than two decades of its existence. The publication, therefore, quite understandably provides a somewhat muted discussion of the relative merits of codification versus "the convention method" versus the "Model Code," or the reasons for which the Commission has so far eschewed such tempting issues as "domestic jurisdiction," or "recognition of acts of foreign states," or why certain proposals, in particular those on Arbitral Procedure, failed to receive the endorsement of the Sixth Committee of the General Assembly. A revised edition might now usefully provide the penetrating insights into these and other issues that the author has never failed to bring forth in his other publications. **The Work of the International Law Commission** (New York: Office of Public Information, United Nations, 1967, 168 p.) is a useful adjunct to this valuable book.

HIGGINS, ROSALYN. **The Development of International Law Through the Political Organs of the United Nations.** New York: Oxford University Press, 1963, 402 p.

In this pioneer study, Dr. Rosalyn Higgins, a gifted young English international lawyer now at Chatham House, has made a major contribution to understanding the elusive "law-making" role of the political processes in the United Nations. At the very outset she faces squarely the contention that the views of governments expressed in the United Nations debates and resolutions can have little legal significance because such positions are generally adopted for political and self-serving interests, rather than on juridical grounds. Her defense is that state practice accepted as law may be evidenced by votes and views in collective bodies just as in diplomatic intercourse, and that in point of fact a near-universal organization such as the United Nations presents a clear, concentrated point for state practice. It matters not that national interests are served: "it would be a curious form of puritanism which insisted that convenience and legality could never run side by side." Yet Mrs. Higgins does not go so far as to abandon the requirement of *opinio juris*. Indeed she rather emphatically asserts that practice cannot become law unless attended by a conviction of legal obligation among a sufficiently large number of states.

To show the impact of United Nations political proceedings on general international law, Mrs. Higgins selected five broad subjects for detailed examination: statehood, domestic jurisdiction, recognition and representation, use of force and law of treaties. In her opening remarks, she seems to have in mind a rather sharp distinction between United Nations practice affecting customary law and the "contractual law" of the Charter; but it becomes evident in her case studies that even though the subjects are topics of customary law they are discussed in the United Nations mainly as questions of Charter interpretation and application. There are advantages in this analysis. It not only recognizes that states are continually creating new norms through interpretation but, more important, it indicates that the test of legality is not so much the semantic links to the Charter as it is the actual practice and behavior of states. Thus, the test of custom provides a useful reminder that a single interpretative resolution or two in the United Nations —even if widely supported—is not necessarily the "law" and that future behavior may have to demonstrate whether or not it expresses an accepted norm.

RECOGNITION; SUCCESSION OF STATES AND GOVERNMENTS

FEILCHENFELD, E. H. **Public Debts and State Succession.** New York: Macmillan, 1931, 922 p.

O'CONNELL, DANIEL PATRICK. **State Succession in Municipal Law and International Law.** Cambridge: Cambridge University Press, 1967, 2 v.

MAREK, KRYSTYNA. **Identity and Continuity of States in Public International Law.** Geneva: Droz, 1954, 613 p.

It is a tribute to the immense, indeed unrivalled, scholarship behind Feilchenfeld's volume that his study of public debts and state succession should, nearly 40 years later, illuminate areas which are only now reappearing on the juridical horizon. While this work had been preceded in 1927 by Alexandre N. Sack's study **Les Effets des Transformations des États sur Leurs Dettes Publiques et Autres Obligations Financières** (Paris: Sirey, 1927, 615 p.), likewise of impressive learning, the latter fails to evoke for the reader the vast historical perspectives and the biting realism that distinguish Feilchenfeld's analysis.

"Succession," he observes, "is a matter of positive law and cannot be established by mere arguments. . . . If the annexing state succeeds by virtue of subsequent acts, his succession is neither a necessary consequence of state succession, nor of general doctrines, but results from voluntary acts of the acquiring state."

His concern lies with the effect of territorial cessions, secessions, annexations and dismemberment of states upon the rights of creditors, vis-à-vis the states participating in such territorial changes. The result is a treatise of vast and challenging complexities but of fresh relevancy today. Devolution agreements and prevalence of the "clean slate" doctrine are at present deflecting attention from the problem which Feilchenfeld explores under the rubric of *droit de poursuite* as well as that concerned with dismemberment which he assigns to *droit de distribution*. Both problems now hang spectrally over the horizon. Questions of decolonization, secession and balkanization must gradually yield in the chaotic third world to those of cessions, annexation of states and partitionings. It is here that the Feilchenfeld study stands with the work of O'Connell to guide the statesmen of the future.

Through continuous research and publication over the space of two decades, and now by his latest two-volume work, Professor O'Connell has attained a position of unique authority and prestige in the field of state succession. Whereas Feilchenfeld treated a somewhat narrower subject within a broad historical and theoretical framework, O'Connell, through immensely impressive research, has functionally brought together all aspects, internal as well as external, of state succession and provided a thorough study of its theoretical underpinnings. External problems include debts, governmental contracts, salaries, pensions and other acquired rights, concessions, delicts, nationality and treaties. Equally illuminating is his analysis of internal problems of continuity as reflected in the evolutionary processes in former British, French and Belgian colonies and, generally, in judicial systems, administration, public property and legislation including the internal legislative effect of treaties.

The author's predilection for natural law leads him, however, in the absence of convincing evidence, to accept such doubtful constructs as servitudes, dispositive régimes, unjust enrichment and an absolutist view of property. Unilateral acknowledgments are frequently accepted as evidence of succession in circumstances where they might more readily be recognized as consensual solutions. Yet, as Rosenne has recently observed, "Succession is almost always regulated by treaties, even in the case of violent decolonization." O'Connell's two volumes will, however, long constitute a classic in the field.

Monism generates difficulties of analysis and treatment for the author of **Identity and Continuity of States in Public International Law,** the principal full-length study of the subject. "A repudiation of what is submitted to be the only correct view of relations between international and State law, namely, monism based on the primacy of the former," she writes, "would necessarily result in the abandonment of this study. . . . Only one of them (primacy of international law and primacy of municipal law) is correct and it is the former." She is thus led to utilize the maxim *ex iniuria ius non oritur* to justify identity and continuity in Ethiopia, Austria, Czechoslovakia, the Baltic States, Albania and Poland (1936–1954), and to reject voluntarism as a criterion for identity and continuity for the period 1914–1919, asserting that a state could otherwise escape obligations by declaring itself "new." Yet the fear of such an escape should not logically exist for the convinced monist. On the other hand, consent is adopted to explain the extinction of Serbia and the appearance of the "new" Jugoslavia. While she accepts Austrian claims (1919) to constitute a new state, no treatment is given to the contemporaneous problems of Hungary and Turkey where a formula of identity and continuity was imposed. It would also have been useful to examine present-day Germany in the same context. The rich literature and jurisprudence concerning the Anschluss might have been further explored, including the International Conference on Austrian External Debts, and the German debt agreements with other European countries. Despite publication of the second edition in 1968, the opportunity to analyze the contradictions of the Austrian State Treaty (1955) has been eschewed as well as questions of continuity so interestingly developed by O'Connell. The problems of Poland from 1939 to 1954, however, receive brilliant treatment.

CHARPENTIER, JEAN. **La Reconnaissance Internationale et l'Évolution du Droit des Gens.** Paris: Pedone, 1956, 357 p.

A thoughtful and original attempt of a French jurist to devise a comprehensive, internally consistent theory of recognition based upon the "opposability" and "non-opposability" of new developments in the international system. Opposable changes are those brought about in a manner compatible with the international order. A development is non-opposable when it constitutes a violation of or is incompatible with either the international order as a whole or the treaty right of another state; however, non-opposable events may have a legal effect upon other states if they are effective or are recognized by them. Recognition, on the other hand, requires a voluntary engagement by the recognizing state and obliges that state to respect the newly recognized event. Thus, recognition of a non-opposable situation would necessarily add significantly to a state's obligations, whereas recognition of an opposable event adds virtually nothing since changes compatible with international law are opposable against all. The author stresses that while recognition is a *condition precedent* to exchange of diplomatic representatives and to functioning as a juridical entity in the recognizing state, these are not necessary consequences. The relationship which follows recognition depends upon a host of extraneous factors.

The flaw of previous theories of recognition, Charpentier argues, lies in their necessary acknowledgment of the relative effect and discretionary nature of recognition, which result from the dissociation of recognition and opposability. Ideally, recognition should be collectivized in an integrated or federated international order with a supreme international authority embracing all collective entities in the world. Short of this, continued individualization or partial collectivization of recognition will necessarily have less than theoretically perfect results.

In addition to his jurisprudential contribution, the author gives an incisive critique of declaratory and constitutive theories of recognition and analyzes an important body of international and state practice, including that relating to the People's Republic of China.

LAUTERPACHT, HERSCH. **Recognition in International Law.** New York: Cambridge University Press, 1947, 442 p.

In his study, **Recognition in International Law,** Professor Lauterpacht reduces the significance of politics in this sphere almost to nothing, contending that recognition is essentially a part of international law. To this end, much of his argument rests upon state practice, and the volume contains a number of nineteenth century opinions by the Law Officers of the Crown which have not been previously published. He discusses the recognition of states and governments, de jure and de facto, belligerency and insurgency. In each case he asserts that the act of recognition is a legal act based on legal principles and effected as a result of the exercise of judicial discretion. He implies that because, generally speaking, in the period preceding the Second World War states according recognition did not give political reasons for the grant, they were therefore motivated by legal principles. However, even the statements he puts forward in this connection, including that by Canning in 1822 indicating that it may be given or withheld at pleasure, do not support his contention. Nor, for that matter, does the application of the Wilsonian principle of consent of the governed or that of the principle of legitimacy.

Professor Lauterpacht's view that non-recognition is not a legal but only a moral obligation as between the signatories of the Kellogg Pact reads strangely in a work published after the judgment of Nuremberg. This is the more so, in view of the fact that the author justifies (in his edition of Oppenheim) American Lend-Lease on the basis of the Pact and contends in this work that a victim of aggressive war would be entitled to regard any peace treaty as null and void. As an advocate of the rule of law, Professor Lauterpacht deplores the fact that a state or government may be recognized and not at one and the same time. He favors a collectivized recognition by the organs of the international community. This is a strange argument, for the United Nations is a political body, and he himself wants the grant made by the political executive organs of the international community.

Whatever our criticisms, **Recognition in International Law,** like everything that comes from Professor Lauterpacht's pen, is a major contribution to the doctrine of international law.

CHEN, TI-CHIANG. **The International Law of Recognition.** London: Stevens, 1951, 461 p.

Perhaps the most significant feature of Dr. Chen's book is the extent to which he acknowledges the significance of politics in this sphere. In the field of theory this leads him virtually to the rejection of the constitutive in favor of the declaratory doctrine, although he tends to accept the view that while a grant of recognition is declaratory of fact it is constitutive of legal consequences. His argument is supported by constant reference to state practice, particularly as it has been shown in Great Britain and the United States, and it has been brought up to date to cover the problems consequential upon the occupation of independent states in Europe by Germany and Italy, and the resuscitation of those states since the defeat of the Axis powers. At the same time, due attention is paid to the fact that since 1945 a number of new states have appeared on the international scene, and the question of the recognition of such states as Ireland, Israel, India and Pakistan is fully analyzed, as is the situation created by the division of Germany and the success of the communist revolution on the mainland of China.

In addition to his examination of state practice in so far as the recognition of states, governments, belligerents and insurgents is concerned, Dr. Chen deals in detail with such matters as modes of recognition, qualified recognition, revocability and retroactivity, and non-recognition. He also pays due attention to the internal effects of recognition, including the right to sue and immunity from suit of both the recognized and the unrecognized entity, as well as the effect of recognition upon such private rights as the status of individuals and corporations, property, marriage and divorce, and even the procedural rights of private litigants.

Although Professor Lauterpacht's book, **Recognition in International Law,** was published while Dr. Chen was preparing his, the decision to go ahead was more than justified. **The International Law of Recognition** is sufficiently different to stand on its own, a fact that is emphasized by the use of recent state practice. Taken with the earlier work, the reader will find virtually all that he needs to know on this subject to date.

DICKINSON, EDWIN DEWITT. **The Equality of States in International Law.** Cambridge: Harvard University Press, 1920, 424 p.

The "sovereign equality" of the members of the United Nations is enshrined in the Charter, but it remains as slippery a concept as it was when the late Professor Dickinson wrote about the subject during World War I.

The history of the equality of states in the writings of publicists shows that the principle did not gain general acceptance until the middle of the eighteenth century. Dickinson found that later writings and practice had not clarified the term; legal equality and political equality, equality before the law and equality of capacity for rights were widely confused, and the practical application of the principle was neglected. States do, in his view, enjoy equality before the law, for without it there can be no stability in the international community. Equality of capacity for rights is only an ideal and not necessary to a legal system. Inequality in this latter respect is the result either of internal limitations under municipal law or of external limitations flowing from the differing relations of a state with other members of the international community. And when states participate in international conferences, organizations and tribunals, they do not necessarily do so on a basis of *political* equality.

In the last half century, equality of capacity for rights has attained much more substance than it had in 1920, while political inequality persists in contemporary international organizations (*e.g.* the veto, weighted voting). The value of Dickinson's book today lies in its historical analysis, which provides a basis of understanding for our contemporary attempts to give content to the principle of equality.

HUMAN RIGHTS

LAUTERPACHT, HERSCH. **International Law and Human Rights.** New York: Praeger, 1950, 475 p.

The late Sir Hersch Lauterpacht, one of the greatest international lawyers of the century and, during the last years of his life, a judge of the International Court of Justice, has presented in this book an analysis of the status of the individual in international law as it had emerged from the history of the dictatorships of the inter-war period, the Second World War, the trials of persons accused of war crimes and crimes against humanity and from the entry into force of the Charter of the United Nations.

It has been Lauterpacht's signal contribution to the state of international law and relations of our time that he has convincingly proved in the book's section "The Law of the Charter" and elsewhere that human rights are now part of positive international law and that the members of the United Nations have undertaken legal obligations in this field, obligations which, though admittedly not defined in great detail, must be interpreted and complied with in good faith. Equally important has been his proof that the terms of Article 2 (7) of the Charter (the domestic jurisdiction clause), interpreted in accordance with the accepted terminology of international law, the history of its drafting and the practice of the United Nations—proof which has become still more conclusive in the 20 years which followed upon the writing of his book—do not imply a decisive or even a substantial restriction of the competence of the United Nations in the matter of human rights and fundamental freedoms.

Lauterpacht criticized sharply the self-denying ordinance adopted by the Commission on Human Rights in 1947 and approved by the Economic and Social Council, to the effect that "the Commission recognizes that it has no power to take action in regard to any complaints concerning human rights." His view was shared by a minority of governments and also by the Secretariat, which in 1949 stated that the ruling was bound to lower the prestige and the authority of the Commission on Human Rights and of the United Nations in the opinion of the general public. However, it was only in 1966–1967 that developments, in particular the situation in the south of the African continent, gave rise to certain initiatives aiming at a reversal of the 1947 ruling, at least in respect of situations which reveal a consistent pattern of gross violations of human rights.

Lauterpacht was a champion of the right of individuals to petition international authorities on the ground of alleged violations of their human rights. He asked: Is it more conducive to the preservation of the sovereignty and the dignity of a state if a complaint concerning the treatment of an individual or of a group of individuals is brought by a foreign state rather than by the person or persons concerned? He most strongly criticized the 1949 draft International Covenant on Human Rights because of the absence of provisions on the right of petition.

In his own "Draft of the International Bill of the Rights of Man" he provided for the right of petition to a "Human Rights Council" and for action by the International Court of Justice or an International Court of Human Right. The International Bill of Rights as completed by the General Assembly in 1966 contains an Optional Protocol to the Covenant on Civil and Political Rights providing for the right of petition (communication), but not for the right of the individual to appeal to an international court.

For Lauterpacht's scholarly work in general, including a detailed evaluation of **International Law and Human Rights,** see: "Hersch Lauterpacht—the Scholar as Prophet," by C. Wilfred Jenks in the *British Yearbook of International Law,* 1960.

WEIL, GORDON LEE. **The European Convention on Human Rights: Background, Development and Prospects.** Leyden: Sijthoff, 1962, 260 p.

ROBERTSON, A. H. **Human Rights in Europe.** Dobbs Ferry: Oceana, 1963, 280 p.

MORRISON, CLOVIS C., JR. **The Developing European Law of Human Rights.** Leyden: Sijthoff, 1967, 247 p.

FAWCETT, J. E. S. **The Application of the European Convention on Human Rights.** New York: Oxford University Press, 1969, 368 p.

VASAK, KAREL. **La Convention Européenne des Droits de l'Homme.** Paris: Pichon et Durand-Auzias, 1964, 327 p.

MONCONDUIT, FRANÇOIS. **La Commission Européenne des Droits de l'Homme.** Leyden: Sijthoff, 1965, 559 p.

ANTONOPOULOS, NICOLAS. **La Jurisprudence des Organes de la Convention Européenne des Droits de l'Homme.** Leyden: Sijthoff, 1967, 262 p.

GOLSONG, HERIBERT. **Das Rechtsschutzsystem der Europäischen Menschenrechtskonvention.** Karlsruhe: Muller, 1958, 115 p.

PARTSCH, KARL JOSEF. **Die Rechte und Freiheiten der Europäischen Menschenrechtskonvention.** Berlin: Duncker and Humblot, 1966, 263 p.

GURADZE, HEINZ. **Die Europäische Menschenrechtskonvention: Kommentar.** Berlin: Vahlen, 1968, 276 p.

The European Convention for the Protection of Human Rights and Fundamental Freedoms, though based on an early draft of the United Nations Covenant on Human Rights, was completed much earlier than the corresponding worldwide instruments elaborated by the United Nations. It was signed in Rome in 1950, entered into force in 1953 and had by the beginning of 1970 been ratified by 16 states, members of the Council of Europe. (The figure of 16 includes Greece which, in 1969, gave notice of withdrawal from the Council of Europe, a fact which will affect Greece's being a party to the Convention.)

The European Convention for the Protection of Human Rights and Fundamental Freedoms (referred to as "the Convention" hereinafter) contains not only a catalogue of rights and freedoms which the states parties have undertaken to secure to everyone within their jurisdiction, but it has also established international organs to ensure the observance of the engagements undertaken by the parties. It is not surprising that an instrument of such novel character has become the object of many books and of innumerable articles. It is proposed to review the more important of those books on the Convention which have appeared in English, French or German.

Weil's is the first book in English devoted exclusively to the Convention. It presents, in addition to a short but very informative outline of the background and history of the Convention, an article-by-article commentary on its provisions in the light of their legislative history and of the case law of the European organs. In general, it covers the materials up to mid-1961.

Robertson wrote an authoritative and reliable guide to the Convention and to the working of its machinery of implementation. The author, who is head of the Directorate of Human Rights in the Secretariat of the Council of Europe, also reports on a number of cases in regard to which decisions on the admissibility of the complaint by a government party to the Convention or by individual petitioners had been taken by the end of 1962. A full account is given of the first great case decided upon by the European Court of Human Rights (*Lawless against Ireland*). A chapter of Robertson's book is devoted to the European Social Charter, signed in Turin in 1961.

When Professor Morrison's book was written the material to be covered, particularly the case law of the European Commission on Human Rights, had considerably increased and permitted him to attempt an evaluation of the developments in the first 12 years of the operation of the Convention. While his overall view is appreciative of the work that has been achieved, he is often very critical of individual decisions rendered.

The work by Mr. Fawcett, the United Kingdom member of the European Commission on Human Rights, is an outstanding and highly original contribution to the literature on the Convention. It describes, article by article and clause by clause, how the Convention has, in fact, been applied from 1954 until the end of 1967, both by the international organs set up by the Convention and by the courts of the states parties. In spite of this pragmatic conception and the author's emphasis on not having aimed at presenting a study of legal or political doctrine, the book is not a dry commentary. It analyzes the practice against the background of the rules of international law, of decisions of the World Court and of national tribunals of very many legal systems. The author makes interesting comparisons between the European Convention and other relevant international instruments, including those elaborated under United Nations auspices.

Vasak's book is the leading French monograph on the Convention. Although the author is a senior official in the Secretariat of the Council of Europe, this is not a secretariat-type instrument. Vasak presents his own, often critical, views of many subjects, however difficult and delicate. His work is a textbook in the legal tradition of the Continent. It analyzes in considerable detail the substantive law of the Convention, the organization and procedure of the Commission and the Court, the role of the Committee of Ministers of the Council of Europe and of the Secretary-General in the application of the Convention. It also summarizes the impact of the Convention on the legal systems of the states parties and its influence outside Western Europe.

The main subjects of Monconduit's book are the organization, internal structure and the various roles and procedures of one of the organs created by the Convention, the European Commission of Human Rights, which the author characterizes as occupying *la position d'un véritable centre moteur* in the system. It is the most elaborate work on the European Commission so far published. However, it also treats important problems of substance and presents a skillful analysis of much of the case law of the Commission.

A very interesting book by a Greek practicing lawyer, Mr. Antonopoulos, is primarily devoted to an analysis and presentation of the case law of the European human rights organs and deals, as a consequence, mainly with the substantive law of the Convention. It is, therefore, a useful complement to the book by Monconduit, which is mainly devoted to procedure.

Golsong's work, which is devoted to the system of the procedures for the protection of the rights guaranteed by the Convention, represents a pioneering effort in the field. It is the first major commentary on the organizational and procedural aspects of the Convention, on the right of individual petition, the inter-state complaints, the actual procedure before the Commission, before the Committee of Ministers and also before the European Court of Human Rights (although the Court was established only in 1959, *i.e.* after the publication of the book). Golsong deals also with the first stage of the protection of human rights under the Convention: their application by the courts of the states parties. It can only be hoped that the author (who was, in succession, Deputy Registrar and Registrar of the European Court of Human Rights and is now the Director of Legal Affairs of the Council of Europe) will find the time to prepare a second edition of this excellent book to absorb the important developments in the European law of human rights—regional and municipal—which have taken place subsequent to 1958.

While Golsong's book is devoted to the adjective law of the Convention, Professor Partsch's outstanding work addresses itself to the status of the Convention in the legal system, both international and municipal, and to its provisions of substantive law. It contains thorough and reliable commentaries on the provisions relating to particular rights and freedoms and on the case law of the European Commission. The author's observations on general questions of substantive law such as the problems of the application of the Convention *ratione loci, ratione personae, ratione materiae* and *ratione temporis,* derogations in time of war or other public emergency, and the protection against "enemies of freedom" are of particular value and interest.

The primary purpose of Professor Guradze's Commentary to the European Convention is to supply the German judge, attorney and civil servant with a manageable and, at the same time, complete book for use in the application of the Convention in the municipal legal system of the Federal Republic of Germany. For this reason, the substantive law of the Convention, the catalogue of the rights guaranteed by it, receives the most thorough treatment. The section which deals with the Commission is also commented upon. The work is far more than a handbook for the German legal practitioner. It presents a thorough, reliable and often critical analysis of the law of the Convention and of its application, and this not only as far as its impact on German law is concerned. It is, therefore, also of great interest outside the Federal Republic.

DROST, PIETER NICOLAAS. **The Crime of State: Penal Protection for Fundamental Freedoms of Persons and Peoples.** Leyden: Sijthoff, 1959, 2 v.

This work by a Dutch jurist, former U.N. official and now professor of international law at Sydney, is dedicated to the proposition that, since the present world order has accepted the promotion of basic rights of individuals and peoples as an international responsibility, major denials of such rights must be made punishable.

A sweeping recital of history's record of brutality and injustice leads him to his two basic premises: that these have been deliberate acts of governmental decision makers; and that it is illusory and, in fact, unfair to expect underlings or populations to prevent them.

Consequently, by analogy to the term "genocide"—the destruction of groups— he coins the term "humanicide"—the destruction of what is *"humanus* in its four meanings of human, humane, civil and civilised . . . intentional violations of the natural rights of life, liberty, safety and integrity of person shall be a penal offense under international criminal law for which the responsible masters and servants of state shall be held answerable before both national and international tribunals." The old notion of "criminal collectivities" must be replaced by the notion of "criminals against the collectivity."

Such proposals, to be sure, will, he notes, be opposed by the majority of states, but he argues that the obligation of U.N. members to coöperate in promoting and encouraging respect for human rights and fundamental freedoms should not allow crimes of state to be sheltered behind the Charter's interdiction of U.N. intervention in essentially domestic matters. There is no prospect for a treaty establishing such international criminal responsibility, but a beginning could be made through a declaration by the General Assembly. Above all, world public opinion must be educated in this sense, and awareness of *personal* national and international criminality be internalized in the decision makers.

Altogether, the work is frankly "pleading." It does not purport to discuss the difficulties facing its thesis. It is animated by a sense of urgency fully validated by subsequent events. Its demands and criticisms may have contributed to the markedly increased interest in the development of international criminal law since the late 1960s.

TERRITORY

McDOUGAL, MYRES S.; LASSWELL, HAROLD D. and VLASIC, IVAN A. **Law and Public Order in Space.** New Haven: Yale University Press, 1963, 1,147 p.

The authors of this book, published just six years after the flight of the first sputnik, sought not only to review the substantial amount of political and legal activity concerning space operations and the vast literature already in existence but to fit the "public order of outer space" into a broader study of the process of "community interaction and authoritative decision" which affects all human activities. In doing so, they dealt with all varieties of claims to use outer space, with accommodation between nations and uses, with minimum order in the earth-space arena, with nationality and control of space vehicles and personnel, with jurisdiction, with resources, enterprises and even interaction with advanced non-earth life. Professors McDougal and Lasswell thus continued here their comprehensive effort to re-analyze the existing system of world public order and to restate international law in terms of international process. To the academic legal scholar, this effort was and is of intrinsic value and provides important insights into the difficulties of resolution of any major international "legal" problem. Other potential users, no doubt, encounter some difficulty in relating this treatment to their specific and inevitably narrower questions. For all, however, this volume, while published before the major U.N. outer space resolution of 1963 and the space treaty of 1968, provides exhaustive analysis of the issues then perceived, and of the authorities then extant, and offers the most insightful treatment even now available of some of the potentially difficult issues created by man's ability to act in outer space, such as that of the utilization of space resources.

MOUTON, MARTINUS WILLEM. **The Continental Shelf.** The Hague: Nijhoff, 1952, 367 p.

The continental shelf doctrine, which recognizes that a coastal state has sovereign rights over submarine areas adjacent to its coast, beyond the limit of its territorial sea, for the purpose of exploring and exploiting the natural resources therein, has been one of the most notable additions to international law since World War II. This study by a distinguished Dutch naval officer and jurist was among the first to examine the concept thoroughly, at a time when it was still regarded as a matter largely *de lege ferenda*. The account ends with 1952, and hence important subsequent developments—most conspicuously, the Convention on the Continental Shelf framed at the 1958 U.N. Conference on the Law of the Sea—must be traced in other sources (*e.g.* McDougal and Burke, **The Public Order of the Oceans**). But the analysis of the scientific, geographical, historical and legal elements involved in the emergence of the doctrine has continuing value, as has the extensive discussion of the proper relationship of shelf rights to traditional freedoms of fishing and navigation in the high seas. The author's conclusion, that the concept has been useful in meeting a new situation created by technological progress but that it is susceptible to abuse if permitted to spread upward from the seabed and subsoil to the superjacent waters, has become the generally accepted view. His cautious but constructive approach was an important forerunner of the views later to prevail at the 1958 Conference.

JESSUP, PHILIP CARYL and TAUBENFELD, HOWARD JACK. **Controls for Outer Space.** New York: Columbia University Press, 1959, 379 p.

While addressed mainly to problems of outer space controls, this study by two international legal scholars illuminates the whole field of international law and organization. Its first part is a historical survey of institutions and arrangements of a multinational character which serve to regulate or administer activities of common interest. The various functional organizations dealing with communications, commodities and technology are described as are the international public companies such as "Eurofima." Part II discusses possible patterns of control for Antarctica, favoring a unified international administration. The actual treaty, adopted soon after publication of this book, revealed still another pattern based on mutual rights of inspection and scientific coöperation. Similarly, the authors' preference in part III for direct international administration of activities in outer space has not been realized and does not seem likely in the foreseeable future. It can hardly be expected that the space powers will turn over their large and costly space projects to international bodies. However, the authors maintain that unless this is done the risk of military use remains great, even if states renounce national claims of sovereignty. Subsequent events cannot be said to have refuted this. In addition to the extensive discussion of the problem of preventing military use of space, the book includes a skillful summary of issues and views on other aspects of space activity. Many of the new developments have overtaken the issues discussed, but several of the legal and political questions remain unresolved and, in respect to them, the book provides a useful summary of positions taken by governments and scholars.

LAY, S. HOUSTON and TAUBENFELD, H. J. **The Law Relating to Activities of Man in Space.** Chicago: University of Chicago Press, 1970, 333 p.

The authors, in examining the space environment consisting of outer space, the moon and celestial bodies, have focused upon man's freedom to use and explore the space environment for the peaceful purposes of the entire community. Such freedom, it may be noted, is by the very nature of things not unlimited. Thus, attention is drawn to a variety of present issues and problems, including national security needs and interests.

Since the nature of the space age and its space law issues and problems cannot remain constant, the present appraisal, including potential solutions, will require reconsideration. None the less, the emerging law is adequately supported by historically well-considered and basic legal principles. As a result of recent reality, a variety of specific rules and acceptable standards of conduct are being derived from such principles. This volume arrives at a critical time. With the acceptance of basic principles and essential policies respecting the environment, and with attention now turning to the formulation of more specific prescriptions for the detailed governance of all space activities, this book faithfully represents the transition from the general to the particular. Its essential contribution will be to hasten that transition.

A series of appendices and an extended bibliography contain a veritable treasure trove of essential data.

JENNINGS, R. Y. **The Acquisition of Territory in International Law.** Dobbs Ferry: Oceana, 1963, 130 p.

The Whewell Professor of International Law in the University of Cambridge provides in this little book in less than 90 pages (the balance is taken up by the Arbitral Award of Judge Max Huber in the *Island of Palmas* case) the best concise exposition of current trends in the law governing the acquisition of territory. The traditional methods—occupation, cession, accretion, subjugation—are succinctly treated. More attention is given to the somewhat controversial method of prescription. This applies to land as well as the sea and "comprehends both a possession of which the origin is unclear or disputed, and an adverse possession of which the origin is demonstrably unlawful." Time is an essential element of this process of acquiring title to territory. The judgment of the International Court of Justice in the *Temple* case is interpreted as evidence of "consolidation of title by lapse of time."

Conquest or cession induced by force, when and if contrary to Article 2, paragraph 4 of the United Nations Charter, will not, in the author's view, create a good title in the future. However, the concept of consolidation may play an important role even here, for if a state has not been dislodged from territory seized illegally by force "it may eventually come about that a title by consolidation is acquired through recognition or other forms of acknowledgment of the position expressive of the will of the international community." The sense of the international community could be expressed by the General Assembly of the United Nations. But the authority of the Assembly in this matter is open to doubt. The old maxim that possession is nine-tenths of the law still seems to hold sway for, as Professor Jennings concludes, "whatever weight may or may not be given to such general expressions of the opinion of States when assessing a *political* claim to territory, it seems that actual possession is still the main catalyst for building a legal title."

VÁLI, FERENC ALBERT. **Servitudes of International Law: A Study of Rights in Foreign Territory.** London: Stevens, 2d ed., 1958, 349 p.

This is a standard work on the concept of servitudes in international law. Although the two works are of comparable merit, the work by Váli has probably been more influential than the only English-language competitor, the work by Helen Dwight Reid, **International Servitudes in Law and Practice** (Chicago: University of Chicago Press, 1932, 254 p.). At any rate Váli's book has the advantage of appearing in a second, enlarged edition. His book has always been regarded as significant and useful even by those who have serious reservations about the analytical structure on which it is based. The fact is, of course, that the various types of rights in foreign territory require systematic study and comparison whether or not the reader accepts the conceptual basis in "servitudes" with the consequent association with analogy from municipal law. Moreover, the author is pragmatic in approach and is not a dogmatic champion of the international servitude. The position of his monograph in the literature is well established. The second edition has a very wide scope with chapters devoted to a great variety of topics ranging from fishing rights and rights of transit to military bases and the Panama Canal Zone.

GARRETSON, A. H.; OLMSTEAD, C. J.; HAYTON, R. D., *eds.* **The Law of International Drainage Basins.** Dobbs Ferry: Oceana, 1967, 916 p.

This book is a collection of monographs on equitable sharing of water, pollution, international basin administration and the régimes of five major international river basins. The Helsinki Rules on the Uses of the Waters of International Rivers adopted by the International Law Association (1966) and the rules on the same subject adopted by *L'Institut de Droit International* (1961) are reproduced. There is an extensive bibliography. The result is a comprehensive analysis of the legal principles and a broad overview of the literature relating to the use of the waters of international rivers.

One has only to compare this book with its classic forerunner, Herbert Arthur Smith's **The Economic Uses of International Rivers** (London: King, 1931, 224 p.), to become aware of the great magnitude of the progressive development of international river law which has taken place in recent years. Significant aspects of this development, fully documented in the book under review, are the transition of the concept of equitable apportionment into one of equitable utilization, pollution as the subject of legal concern and the concept of the integrated basin régime.

JOHNSTON, DOUGLAS M. **The International Law of Fisheries: A Framework for Policy-Oriented Inquiries.** New Haven: Yale University Press, 1965, 554 p.
LEONARD, LEONARD LARRY. **International Regulation of Fisheries.** Washington: Carnegie Endowment, 1944, 201 p.
RIESENFELD, STEFAN ALBRECHT. **Protection of Coastal Fisheries under International Law.** Washington: Carnegie Endowment, 1942, 296 p.

Johnston offers an ambitious, innovative and highly useful reassessment of existing fishery law and practices from a functional point of view in order to develop a system of law adequately balancing national, regional and world community fishery interests. He has assembled an impressive and unique body of legal, economic, sociological, historical, oceanographic and commercial data on fisheries which, when analyzed within the policy framework of Myres McDougal, enables the author to examine the claim and decision-making processes in fisheries and derive a set of preferred principles and assumptions for the allocation, content and execution of exploitation and conservation authority. A strong case for regional fishery schemes is made. The book contains an extensive classified bibliography.

In their respective books, Leonard and Riesenfeld thoroughly summarize the status of doctrinal writing, state practice, decisions of international tribunals and diplomatic history relating to high seas and coastal fishery regulation up to the outbreak of World War II. Each is a useful supplement to Johnston for the period covered; comparable work on the post-1945 era has not been done.

McDougal, Myres Smith and Burke, William T. **The Public Order of the Oceans: A Contemporary International Law of the Sea.** New Haven: Yale University Press, 1962, 1,226 p.

A monumental and provocative work of scholarship applying the policy-oriented jurisprudence developed by McDougal to the law of the sea and drawing creatively from history, philosophy, sociology, science and other disciplines. Although the mode of expression is often prolix and convoluted, the vocabulary so unfamiliar to lawyers is rigorously selected, the arguments are intricate and closely reasoned, and the research is exhaustive. Of particular importance is the detailed treatment of the Geneva Conferences on the Law of the Sea.

However, in undertaking to clarify the common interests of mankind in a public order of the oceans which favors inclusive community interests, the strategies suggested by the authors coincide to a remarkable degree with maritime policy preferences of the United States in the early 1960s.

Gidel, Gilbert. **Le Droit International Public de la Mer.** Paris: Sirey, 1932–1934, 3 v.

A massive, erudite treatise in the finest tradition of French legal scholarship treating the régime of the high seas, internal waters, territorial waters and the contiguous zone in time of peace. Analyzing the marine sphere as a juridical unit with particular reference to the classification schemata for maritime law developed at the 1930 Hague Codification Conference, the author undertakes a detailed and exhaustive study of international legal doctrine and state practice, emphasizing the former. Gidel was one of the earliest exponents of the contiguous zone. A useful source for post-1930 developments is Olivier de Ferron, **Le Droit International de la Mer** (Geneva: Droz, 1958–1960, 2 v.).

Colombos, C. John. **The International Law of the Sea.** London: Longmans, 6th rev. ed., 1967, 886 p.

The standard manual on international maritime law in time of peace and war for scholar, student and practitioner, widely translated into foreign languages and noteworthy for its substantial and clear exposition of the relevant legal rules and their application, particularly with regard to British law and practice but with considerable attention to United States practice as well. Early editions were indebted to the work of A. Pearce Higgins. In an era when Anglo-American practice has become less predominant than in the inter-war period, certain statements of the applicable rules emerge as somewhat provincial and the traditional organization of the materials as increasingly strained, but the book none the less has no peer in its field.

Brüel, Erik. **International Straits: A Treatise on International Law.** London: Sweet and Maxwell, 1947, 2 v.

Strohl, Mitchell P. **The International Law of Bays.** The Hague: Nijhoff, 1963, 426 p.

Brüel is the standard treatise on straits for the period prior to the Second World War; there is no comparable work for subsequent years. With special emphasis on state practice, volume I treats the general legal position of straits prior to, during and following World War I and contains still relevant suggestions for the codification of a straits régime. The second volume is an exhaustive and unmatched account, based on historical and diplomatic materials, of state practice with regard to the Danish, Gibraltar, Magellan and Turkish Straits.

Strohl combines practical naval experience with legal training in his inquiry into the historical development of rules for bays and the economic, political and strategic interests of states influencing the development of those rules. Especially important is the intensive analysis of selected case studies of bays within the littoral of a single state, or two or more states, as well as historic bays. The author concludes by offering a proposed codification for bays.

BAXTER, RICHARD REEVES. **The Law of International Waterways.** Cambridge: Harvard University Press, 1964, 371 p.

A definitive, copiously documented study of those rivers, canals and straits used to a substantial extent by commercial shipping or warships belonging to states other than the riparian nation or nations, with special emphasis on the Suez, Panama and Kiel Canals and the political, technological, fiscal and historical factors shaping the régime of those waterways. Writing with uncommon grace and clarity, the author carefully constructs a framework of the relevant sources of law and evaluates the principles by which treaties and practices have acquired the force of law in this sphere. He concludes that the further gradual development of the common body of customary law already governing international waterways offers greater hope of securing free passage in time of international tension or conflict than do schemes to place interoceanic canals under international administration. A suggested codification of common rules being observed is appended.

TECLAFF, LUDWIK. **The River Basin in History and Law.** The Hague: Nijhoff, 1967, 228 p.

This landmark monograph describes man's awareness of and reaction to the drainage basin from earliest times and tests the validity of the set of physical relationships found therein as the organizing principle for "sweet water" legal and administrative régimes. Dr. Teclaff shows that in the first civilizations a river and its tributaries did receive treatment as a "system," but only where irrigation or navigation were important. The expansion of traditional uses and the burgeoning new uses for industrial, municipal and power generation purposes have, generally speaking, made both the quantity and quality questions highly critical only in this century. Pollution abatement, flood and siltation control, drainage and reclamation, weather modification and other aspects of modern, integrated basin planning are even today not widely undertaken. Above all, perhaps, the necessary administrative machinery for comprehensive water management (including underground waters) is lacking almost everywhere. The author examines the widely varying régimes that have in fact developed, including those affecting international rivers.

But is the "basin" the most fruitful frame within which to erect our water management structures? Is the best institutional basis a spatial or territorial one? If so, is the *whole* basin the optimum unit? There are other alternatives (parts of basins, a region or the continent) and other water relationships—with mineral resource exploitations, electrical power grids, transport nets, crops and recreation, for example—not confined to the drainage area of one river. These critical organizational questions are thoroughly and objectively dealt with here. The volume reads well and is heavily documented. It will be relied upon indefinitely as the overall comparative study of river basin practice.

JURISDICTIONAL IMMUNITIES

LAZAREFF, SERGE. **Le Statut des Forces de l'O.T.A.N. et Son Application en France.** Paris: Pedone, 1964, 548 p.

This is the definitive work on the operation of the treaty governing the juridical relationship with the host government of thousands of foreign military and civilian personnel (and their dependents) stationed in France. For more than a decade problems of criminal jurisdiction, tax power, currency control and claims for damages were solved on the bases established by the multilateral NATO Status of

Forces Agreement. In France, where most of the visiting military and civilian personnel were Americans, the treaty arrangements were complicated by a U.S. Senate reservation regarding criminal trials and by persistent Congressional inquiries. Dr. Lazareff served as Legal Adviser at Headquarters Allied Forces Central Europe and writes from firsthand experience. His book draws upon the *travaux preparatoires* (subsequently published in Joseph M. Snee, *ed.,* **NATO Agreements on Status,** Washington: Government Printing Office, U.S. Naval War College International Law Studies, 1966) and more significantly upon the resolution of actual controversies by French courts, by negotiation and by administrative regulation.

The NATO Status of Forces Agreement became the model for similar arrangements in Germany, Japan, Formosa and Korea. The Lazareff volume is an essential reference for an understanding of how a visiting military force and all of its accompanying personnel can be made accountable to some law and how the prerogative of the host government can be preserved despite the substantial presence of a "friendly" foreign military force.

FALK, RICHARD A. **The Role of Domestic Courts in the International Legal Order.** Syracuse: Syracuse University Press, 1964, 184 p.

In one of the rare monographs on this subject, the author assays the dual status of domestic courts as national institutions and as agents of an emerging international legal order. Challenging "the contemporary tendency to give foreign policy precedence over international law in domestic courts," he makes a powerful plea for a judiciary unwilling to subordinate the outcome of lawsuits to the vagaries of executive policy, but also willing to play a passive role in those areas "where there is no consensus among national units."

The high caliber of the analysis and argument in this volume was recognized by the Supreme Court in the *Sabbatino* case, where the eight-judge majority opinion adopted the author's main thesis lock, stock and barrel. While the test of "consensus" needs much more clarification before it can be applied in areas other than the taking of property, it is a rare book indeed that contains as many fresh insights into old problems as this one does.

CAHIER, PHILIPPE. **Le Droit Diplomatique Contemporain.** Geneva: Droz, 1962, 534 p.

This is a sort of manual for diplomats and others who are called upon to apply the law relating to diplomatic privileges and immunities. It covers the traditional rules of customary international law as well as the 1961 Vienna Convention on Diplomatic Relations. The significance of that Convention would be great in any event (being the first successful codification of this branch of the law), but it is all the greater because so many new states participated in its elaboration and acquired a stake in its application. The usefulness of the book is enhanced by the attention given to more recent forms of diplomacy such as summit conferences of heads of state or government and ad hoc missions. It may be noted that in 1969 the General Assembly of the United Nations adopted a convention on the privilege and immunities of ad hoc missions.

The author is committed to the prevailing functional theory which underlies the Vienna Convention, according to which the immunities and privileges are granted for the sole purpose of enabling diplomats to fulfill their functions effectively. He does not seem to appreciate fully its implications, namely the inevitable erosion of the traditional immunities which surely go beyond what is strictly necessary from that point of view. Moreover, what is necessary is a matter of judgment. The Vienna Conference provides an interesting illustration of differences of opinion. On two points some of the great powers and other states were defeated: first, should the size of the mission be determined by the sending or the receiving state, and second, should the sending or the receiving state determine whether a mission may install and operate a radio transmitter. On both questions the Convention in Articles 11 and 27, paragraph 1, respectively, grants the receiving state a veto. The author agrees with this solution, but surely, from the functional viewpoint, the opposing stand appears as more persuasive. However, all immunities and privileges are in practice subject to reciprocity which, in terms of practical diplomacy, means subject to some hard bargaining.

RONNING, C. NEALE. **Diplomatic Asylum: Legal Norms and Political Reality in Latin American Relations.** The Hague: Nijhoff, 1965, 242 p.

Characterizing the practice of granting asylum in diplomatic missions to political fugitives as a regional institution which has developed as a safety valve in response to unstable political conditions in Latin America, Professor Ronning shows that the practice lacks that basis in obligation which is necessary to the existence of a rule of customary international law and that it has received only limited recognition in the region's multilateral conventional international law.

The book focuses upon significant aspects of diplomatic asylum as practiced by selected Latin American states and by the United States in Latin America, including the fundamental problem of defining the political offense for the purpose of granting asylum. It is based upon official sources as well as the works of publicists. Brief reference is made to grants of diplomatic asylum in the Dominican Republic and Cuba in 1960 and 1961, but there is no consideration of the massive resort to the practice in Guatemala in 1954 nor to the kidnapping of General Tanco from the Haitian Embassy at Buenos Aires in 1956.

This study constitutes a thoughtful and concise, if not definitive, contribution to the literature in English on the subject. The need remains for comprehensive studies of the practice of individual states which would provide the bases for more rigorous evaluation of the nature and function of diplomatic asylum in the international legal system.

SUCHARITKUL, SOMPONG. **State Immunities and Trading Activities in International Law.** New York: Praeger, 1960, 390 p.

Increased participation of governments, state agencies and state-controlled corporations in international trade involves the problem of immunity from foreign jurisdictions which governments often claim. The prevailing trend in many countries now denies protection to commercial transactions. Uncertainty exists, however, on the determination of the commercial character of such transactions. There are conflicting decisions of municipal courts as to whether the state acts thereby as a sovereign or in a private law capacity. The necessary clarification will have to be ascertained from the nature and inherent character of the legal act, from the status of the government agencies involved, or from resulting legal relationships. The author, a legal officer of the Thai government, gives a thorough survey not only of court decisions but also of governmental practice in not less than 36 countries. He also deals with the question of whether attachment and execution against property of the foreign state used in connection with trading activities should be permitted, a question still unsettled in international law. The book analyzes the various legal and economic problems and makes many suggestions on a comparative law basis. It still remains a unique contribution to important legal aspects of international trade relations.

NATIONALITY

WEIS, PAUL. **Nationality and Statelessness in International Law.** London: Stevens (for the London Institute of World Affairs), 1956, 338 p.

Dr. Weis is the legal adviser to the United Nations High Commissioner for Refugees. His book was the first monograph on the public international law of nationality to appear in English, and in the foreword Sir Hersch Lauterpacht described it as "the most comprehensive modern treatment of the law of nationality that has appeared so far in the English language." The later publication of Van

Panhuys, **The Role of Nationality in International Law,** has in no way made the work of Weis redundant since the nature of the treatment is different in a manner which makes the books in a certain way complementary. It is a pity that the volume by Weis is presently out of print.

The book is in some ways conservative in its approach to the relation of municipal and international law in the sphere of nationality, and this disposes the author to reach controversial conclusions on such matters as the effect of territorial changes on nationality. Moreover, the author could not deal adequately with the then lately delivered judgment in the *Nottebohm* case (Second Phase). These factors, together with a rather less than complete use of the available legal materials, incline to the conclusion that the treatment is not definitive. Yet the book deserves to be read and discussed and will doubtless maintain its position as a leading contribution for some time.

Van Panhuys, H. F. **The Role of Nationality in International Law.** Leyden: Sijthoff, 1959, 256 p.

This is the only monograph on nationality in the English language apart from the work of Paul Weis, **Nationality and Statelessness in International Law,** to which it is complementary in that the two writers approach the material in significantly different ways. Given the rarity of monographs in any language on the significance of nationality in international law, this volume and that of Dr. Weis have a leading position in the literature. However, the work of Van Panhuys is important not only in the context of a shortage of other works but for its own considerable intrinsic merit. The author is less concerned with the acquisition and loss of nationality than with its functional importance in international law as a whole. Thus substantial areas of the law are considered, including the treatment of aliens, diplomatic protection, reprisals, collective sanctions and war, criminal jurisdiction and treaties. In general the author is sensible of the implications of the rules and concepts he examines and is conscious of the tension between the nationality concept and development of the protection of individuals as such. A great deal of material is utilized, and the relevant points of private international law are noted, although this aspect of matters is treated as subsidiary to the main purpose. In all, this is a standard work of good quality, showing an admirable learning and sensitivity on the part of the author, a legal adviser at the Netherlands Ministry of Foreign Affairs.

PROTECTION OF PERSONS AND PROPERTY

Lillich, Richard B. **The Protection of Foreign Investment.** Syracuse: Syracuse University Press, 1965, 222 p.

The central thesis of Professor Lillich's presentation of six interrelated studies of various aspects of the protection of United States investors is "that existing protective measures are generally inadequate and often inconsistent and that an expanded and integrated program . . . should assure just compensation to persons whose property is taken while at the same time minimizing the taking's effect on broader foreign policy objectives of the United States."

Professor Lillich urges that the sovereign immunity of foreign governments be restricted to "hard core" sovereign functions and that suggestions of immunity from the State Department not be given conclusive effect on issues such as the extent of immunity required by international law and a foreign government's title to property. An international law exception to the act of state doctrine is the second basis on which Professor Lillich would ground the more activist role in protecting foreign investment he would suggest for United States courts.

Professor Lillich is critical of the Hickenlooper Amendment but generally favorably disposed to the investment guaranty program. However, he does not feel the program should be limited to less-developed countries and suggests "the time may come when Congress will deem it advisable to compel all prospective United States investors in foreign economies to insure their investments."

Pre-adjudication of nationalization claims against foreign states, *i.e.* adjudication by a United States national tribunal in advance of reaching an intergovernmental settlement, is favored as a "laudable first step in the direction of according American investors a measure of formal due process before as well as after the conclusion of lump sum settlement agreements."

BORCHARD, EDWIN MONTEFIORE. **The Diplomatic Protection of Citizens Abroad.** New York: Banks Law Publishing Co., 2d ed., 1928, 988 p.

With the publication of this massive treatise, one of the two or three classic books on international law to appear in English during this century, the field of international claims, previously an unexplored domain known only to private claimants, practicing lawyers and foreign offices, achieved recognition as a separate and distinct area of international law worthy of serious scholarly attention. The first attempt to systematize the myriad of rules relating to diplomatic protection into a coherent body of law, the book established a pattern of classifications and a mode of analysis followed to this day.

Original in concept, the work is also based upon a wealth of original source material found in the practice of the United States and other countries and in the decisions of international claims commissions adjudicating upon pecuniary claims. While subsequent developments in such fields as the nationalization of foreign property have rendered the book less definitive than it once was, no successor volume ever has matched the scope of its coverage, the depth of its research and the originality of its analysis. It remains today what it was acclaimed a half-century ago—namely, the first and foremost book on the law of international claims.

DUNN, FREDERICK SHERWOOD. **The Protection of Nationals.** Baltimore: Johns Hopkins Press, 1932, 228 p.

This short and original volume by a follower of the American legal realists is, in the words of its author, "not a juristic analysis of the rules and principles of international law governing the protection of citizens and their property interests abroad." Rather, using the law of international claims as its subject matter, the book is an experimental study of "the possibility of maintaining a unified economic and social order for the conduct of international trade and intercourse among independent political units of diverse cultures and stages of civilization, different legal and economic systems, and varying degrees of physical power and prestige." In more general terms, it questions the effectiveness of international law as a means of adjusting conflicts of interest between states.

Rejecting a positivistic approach to the subject matter, the author asserts that the law of international claims is predicated upon an underlying common interest by the members of the international community in the orderly carrying on of international affairs. From this perspective, he regards the institution of diplomatic protection as a device for allocating the risks of injuries and losses necessarily associated with international life. Instead of looking for some abstract concept of "justice," under this approach one regards justice "as being whatever the institution can do to aid in maintaining and improving conditions that make for a desirable inter-community life."

The author's thoughtful and imaginative functional approach to the law of international claims makes this book by far the most original in its field. His evenhanded application of his approach results on the one hand in the rejection of some traditional rules supported only by conceptualistic reasoning, and on the other hand in a similar rejection of the oversimplified "imperialistic hypothesis," recently revived by some advocates in developing states, under which this entire body of law would be written off as a product of nineteenth century Western imperialism. At a time when all efforts should be bent toward the reformulation of an acceptable body of law in this area, the author's eloquent plea can be read and reread with profit.

KATZAROV, KONSTANTIN. **Theory of Nationalisation.** The Hague: Nijhoff, 1964, 392 p.

The author of this book, a professor of law in the University of Sofia from 1931 to 1956, believes firmly that nationalization is the panacea for the social, economic and political ills of the world. While his doctrinaire approach to the subject irritates more than it informs, the book nevertheless is the most comprehensive study of nationalization from the Marxist point of view yet published in English. For that reason alone, it deserves to be read widely, especially by economists, lawyers and political scientists.

The book is divided into four parts. The first part, "The Achievement," traces the development of the concept of nationalization from 1917 to 1960. Throughout this part the author seeks to establish that nationalization is a new legal institution distinct from classic expropriation. In part two, entitled "The Legal Structure," he considers various legal aspects of nationalization under a socialist legal order. His principal conclusion is that, since the state may determine the social function of property, it has the unlimited right to decide when it should pay compensation for the taking of property and the amount, if any, of this compensation.

The book's third part covers the "Operation" of nationalized enterprises in the socialist legal order and the impact of the state plan upon the enterprises and economic life in general. The surprising point in this part, after the author's paeans of praise for the concept of nationalization, is his admission that it is "difficult to make an objective assessment of the *practical success* of nationalization."

The fourth and final part considers nationalization from the viewpoint of international law. The author, rightly noting the absence of scholarly studies on the concept of property in public international law, argues that new conceptions of the "social function" of property have influenced the development of the law in this area, which previously had been derived exclusively from municipal law concepts of the Western states. While he thinks a universally accepted rule is indispensable, the author concludes that it will be very difficult to achieve. His book shows why.

WHITE, GILLIAN. **Nationalisation of Foreign Property.** New York: Praeger (for the London Institute of World Affairs), 1962, 283 p.

Although several short monographs on nationalization have appeared in English during the past two decades, this book constitutes the first full-length "attempt at a statement of the relevant rules of international law in the light of the developments both historical and legal since the end of the Second World War." While the author falls short of producing the definitive treatise on the subject, her painstaking search for and thoughtful evaluation of postwar nationalization laws and lump sum settlement agreements make her book an indispensable reference work.

The first part of the book is introductory in nature, consisting of one chapter on the legal and economic background of the subject and another on the right to nationalize foreign property under international law. Part two also contains two chapters, the first covering the concept of nationalization and the second, entitled "The Foreign Owner," describing in detail those persons (natural and juridical) who, should their property be taken by a foreign state, are eligible claimants able to obtain the diplomatic protection of their own government.

Part three comprises six chapters, each taking up a supposed international law limitation on a state's right to nationalize foreign property. The fourth section includes a lengthy chapter on the requirement of compensation, easily the most valuable material in the volume, plus a concluding chapter surveying available protective measures and remedies. Here and throughout the book, in refreshing contrast to many writers on the subject who are content to summarize the various statements of learned writers and foreign offices, Dr. White has fashioned by diligent search and careful analysis a text which both the neophyte and the specialist on nationalization will find rewarding.

LAW, CASTOR H. P. **The Local Remedies Rule in International Law.** Geneva: Droz, 1961, 153 p.

The local remedies rule involves complex relationships between municipal and international law that assume practical importance, especially in negotiations or litigation between governments involving private interests. In his useful and interesting study, Dr. Law collects and systematizes concepts and judicial decisions. His study in depth of these source materials identifies the problems which the rule presents in its application. He considers that its function is to reconcile national and international jurisdictions and to promote the interests of both in the intercourse of states. He concludes, after discussing several conceptual approaches, that the exhaustion of remedies rule remains a procedural rule of international law.

As central to discussion of the subject, there is a detailed consideration of the preliminary objections in the *Interhandel* case in the International Court of Justice. In this litigation between Switzerland and the United States, the International Court held that Interhandel, a Swiss company on whose behalf Switzerland was suing, had not exhausted its remedies in American courts. Dr. Law is critical of the Court's decision because he feels that on the issue of neutral property, American courts would limit themselves to American law and not look to principles of international law which would suggest a different result. Hence, he questions whether exhaustion of local remedies by Interhandel was necessary before consideration of the case on its merits by the International Court.

This book is a fresh and sound contribution to the general subject. It reflects careful scholarship and contains discussion of differences of opinion on the topics discussed. The materials assembled are complete to the date of writing, and they are rounded out by a bibliography. This study is an important introduction to the subject and also represents a valuable source for one working on a specific problem of local remedies.

HARDY, MICHAEL. **Modern Diplomatic Law.** Dobbs Ferry: Oceana, 1968, 150 p.

This book is a clearly written and well-organized study of the law of bilateral diplomatic relations and of relations between states and international organizations. The first four chapters of the book deal cogently with the major aspects of the law of bilateral diplomatic relations as governed by the 1961 Vienna Convention on Diplomatic Relations. The third chapter, dealing with inviolability and jurisdictional immunity, is exceptionally well done and would be of special interest to the general practitioner whose work brings him into contact with diplomatic missions. The author's clear explanation of the discrimination and reciprocity provisions of the Vienna Convention (Article 47) is also an impressive presentation of a difficult subject. The fifth chapter, concerning relations between international organizations and member and non-member states, is less detailed and complete than the preceding chapters, but still useful and well written. Its focus is on the United Nations, though other international organizations are also discussed.

LEE, LUKE T. **Consular Law and Practice.** New York: Praeger (for the London Institute of World Affairs), 1961, 431 p.

————. **Vienna Convention on Consular Relations.** Leyden: Sijthoff, 1966, 315 p.

These two competently researched volumes complement each other in presenting an illuminating and comprehensive statement of the contemporary law of consular relations. The 1961 volume is a thorough study both of the existing state of the law and the factors that shaped its development during the preceding quarter-century. While acknowledging divergent state practice, especially as characterized by the distinct patterns of regional or other groups of states, it seeks to point out generalized trends that could lead to a harmonization of that practice. The principal unifying factor in consular law in recent years is, of course, the Vienna Convention on Consular Relations, and the 1966 volume studies the provisions of that Convention in the light of existing law and practice. Its treatment of existing law and practice is less detailed than that of the 1961 volume, since what was said in the earlier volume is still relevant and valid. The 1966 volume illuminates the meaning of the provisions of the Convention by detailed study of their evolution in the report of the Special Rapporteur (Zourek) to the International Law Commission, the Commission's Report to the General Assembly and the debates at the Vienna Conference.

MARITIME NAVIGATION; CIVIL AVIATION; TELECOMMUNICATIONS; COPYRIGHT

BOCZEK, BOLESLAW ADAM. **Flags of Convenience.** Cambridge: Harvard University Press, 1962, 323 p.

This book deals with the economics and law of "flags of convenience," *i.e.* shipowners' practice of retaining active business control of their ships while operating them with foreign crews under the flag of a state offering more convenient, expedient and profitable conditions of registration than those prevailing under the owner's national law and almost never putting into their ports of registry. As the author points out, the flag of convenience is the shipowners' response to the intensely competitive situation of the world shipping market after World War II, and it has created political and strategic difficulties between the United States and its allies.

The book is well written, comprehensive and amply documented. It therefore provides the necessary background for consideration of alternative solutions of the root problem. However, the book gives the impression that it was written to prove that flags of convenience are a "good" practice. This slant leads the author into a few pitfalls. He cites several United States statutes and policy statements as demonstrating a United States policy favoring flags of convenience. But the Congressional statement of policy particularly relied on might well be considered as ambiguous. In discussing opposition to flags of convenience, the combining of American seamen's unions and European shipowners is described as an "unholy" alliance without distinguishing why it is any more unholy than the alliances of other pressure groups.

The author impales himself on the horns of flag-state control versus owner's-state control. He argues that international law gives the flag state unlimited discretion over registration requirements and that other states have a duty to recognize such registration. He also argues, ultimately on a pragmatic, non-legal basis, that the shipowner's state has a right of effective control.

MEYERS, HERMAN. **The Nationality of Ships.** The Hague: Nijhoff, 1967, 395 p.

This comprehensive study of the nationality of ships fills the gap in the literature of international law of the sea in the area which has become controversial as a result of the rise of the so-called flags of convenience of Liberia, Panama and some other countries.

The author defines nationality of ships or (as he prefers to say) "allocation" as "international rights and duties a state acquires by placing the users of a ship under its authority, that is by 'immatriculating' them." Following the traditional doctrine, the book argues that each state decides upon the conditions of the grant of this allocation and has exclusive jurisdiction over its ships on the high seas. Much space is devoted to the discussion of the celebrated requirement of the "genuine link" in the Convention on the High Seas of 1958, defined by Meyers as "the means required for the establishment and maintenance of sufficient authority of the flag state over its ship-users." The author believes that, because of lack of genuine link, non-recognition of the nationality of a flag-of-convenience ship is possible, although a heavy burden of proof would lie on the state alleging lack of such link. Other issues discussed in the book are loss and change of nationality, stateless ships and ships flying the flag of an international organization. The book concludes with a detailed summary.

CHENG, BIN. **The Law of International Air Transport.** Dobbs Ferry: Oceana (for the London Institute of World Affairs), 1962, 726 p.

A comprehensive treatise by a well-known British specialist on the framework of public international law within which international air transport operates. There is an adequate treatment of the structure and functions of the International Civil Aviation Organization, but the emphasis is on a thorough and uniquely valuable analysis of the multilateral and bilateral treaties under which international air services, scheduled and non-scheduled, obtain transit and traffic rights in foreign countries. Most of the examples of bilateral agreements and their application are drawn from British practice. Unfortunately, there is no comparable work stressing the practice of other major civil aviation countries such as the United States. A few of the author's interpretations and conclusions are open to question. The title is somewhat misleading, since the book does not deal with the private international law of the air. Texts of some treaties are appended, and there is an excellent bibliography.

MATTE, NICOLAS MATEESCO. **Traité de Droit Aérien-Aéronautique.** Paris: Pedone, 2d ed., 1964, 1,021 p.

This is a comprehensive but somewhat superficial treatise along traditional lines covering the entire field of international air law, public and private. The emphasis is on the provisions of various multilateral conventions, past and present, the texts of which occupy about one-third of the volume. Also covered are the major instruments of the International Air Transport Association, an organization which is composed of airlines but performs quasi-public functions. A substantial part of the book is devoted to the emerging law of outer space. The work is of considerable historical as well as contemporary interest, since it deals in some detail with little-known and almost forgotten treaties of the inter-war period. There is an extensive bibliography.

SMITH, DELBERT D. **International Telecommunication Control.** Leyden: Sijthoff, 1969, 231 p.

This book is concerned with the control of international broadcasting, or more precisely, unauthorized broadcasts from the high seas and airspace over the high seas, governmental external broadcasting services and direct broadcasts from satellites to the general public.

Dr. Smith's book recognizes that this complex and important subject has inter-related legal, political, economic and technical aspects and carefully examines a wide variety of institutions, legal rules and practical approaches that are or may become applicable to the control of such broadcasts. The reader thus has available for the first time a wide-ranging and detailed survey summarizing current developments and analyzing prospects for control.

The author's basic thesis is that international broadcasting as defined above will require control, and that such control will necessitate the development and application of new concepts of international law. This view is not, however, adequately buttressed by an analysis of the actual problems that have been caused by such broadcasts.

The book contains brief but valuable sections on the most relevant regional and international institutions and their actual and potential roles in international broadcasting, marred, however, by misconceptions and omissions of a generally minor nature. Dr. Smith concludes with detailed recommendations for a "harmful effects" doctrine and an International Broadcasting Commission to consider and resolve problems of unauthorized broadcasts across national boundaries. While views will naturally differ on the feasibility and merits of this proposal, the important point is that the author has provided a carefully worked out, organizationally flexible and quite specific proposal which merits serious consideration.

BOGSCH, ARPAD. **The Law of Copyright under the Universal Convention.** New York: Bowker, 3rd rev. ed., 1968, 696 p.

This unique and indispensable treatise is divided into two related but independent parts. The first consists of an exhaustive and painstaking analysis of every provision of the Universal Copyright Convention, which was signed at Geneva on September 6, 1952, came into effect on September 16, 1955, and as of 1970 has 58 parties, including the United States. This 150-page section represents as accurate and authoritative a gloss on the convention as exists in any language. It is followed by appendices consisting of the text of the Convention, the report of the Geneva Conference and the rules of procedure of the governing body of the UCC.

Part II consists of an analysis of the national laws of 56 countries party to the Universal Convention. This is broken down into a schematic pattern that not only permits ready reference to the domestic law of a particular country but also facilitates comparison of provisions on a particular point. Both parts of the book are thoroughly documented, accurate and up to date. The index is barely adequate, but the table of contents is sufficiently detailed to offer an acceptable substitute for reference use.

The author of this treatise was Secretary of the 1952 Geneva Conference that adopted the UCC, a former official of UNESCO and of the U.S. Copyright Office and presently is First Deputy Director of BIRPI, the secretariat for the Berne Copyright Convention. Both the Universal and the Berne Copyright Conventions are scheduled for revision in 1971, and Dr. Bogsch's work is therefore not only useful to practitioners but will also provide valuable background in the attempts to solve the current problems plaguing international copyright.

INTERNATIONAL TRIBUNALS

JENKS, C. WILFRED. **The Prospects of International Adjudication.** Dobbs Ferry: Oceana, 1964, 805 p.

This is an important, indeed, monumental book exhibiting scholarship, great thoroughness and fertility of ideas. The work of Dr. Jenks combines a high standard of legal expertise with a strong sense of purpose and great liveliness of mind. Considerable research is presented in a proper perspective: thus the author says, "Throughout the discussion I have attempted to conceive of international adjudication as an adjunct to, and not a substitute for, international organisation, economic policy, and diplomacy."

The enormous scope of this study is not perhaps adequately indicated by its inevitably general title. Separate chapters deal with a variety of related topics. The post-introductory chapter is a very useful and thorough study of the question of compulsory jurisdiction. Chapter 3 is an original and fertile piece on "The Potential Contribution of a Wider Range of Procedures and Remedies to a Further Development of International Adjudication." Other chapters treat such topics as "Proof of Custom in International Adjudication" and "The Authority in English Courts of Decisions of the International Court." The eighth chapter, "The Concept of International Public Policy," is particularly fruitful and concerns, among other things, issues of state responsibility and admissibility of claims. In this and in many other parts of the book, Dr. Jenks deals with matters of general significance for international law. Few monographs on this scale successfully combine readability and a critical sense with the massive provision of information and careful professional analysis.

LAUTERPACHT, HERSCH. **The Function of Law in the International Community.** New York: Oxford University Press, 1933, 469 p.

This is an undoubted classic on the place of the judicial function in international relations and the problems concerning *non liquet* and the distinction between justiciable and non-justiciable disputes. While it is not generally regarded as in all respects persuasive in dealing with the last mentioned question, it will always remain a major contribution on the vexed question of justiciability of disputes. While concerned with a major coherent theme, **The Function of Law** is constructed of well-argued and carefully documented chapters on special questions such as the impartiality of international tribunals, the doctrine *rebus sic stantibus*, abuse of rights, decision *ex aequo et bono* and the nature of international law as a problem of general jurisprudence. An appendix deals with the limitation of the judicial function in disputes between state-members of composite states. Naturally the illustrative material is "out of date," but the themes and arguments are not, and the illustrations for the most part are as pertinent as ever.

LAUTERPACHT, SIR HERSCH. **The Development of International Law by the International Court.** London: Stevens, 1958, 400 p.

This is the latest and possibly the most distinguished of the major works from the hand of one of the world's greatest modern international lawyers. At the end of 1954 Lauterpacht was elected one of the Judges of the International Court, and this circumstance could only enhance the value of the work which was, in fact, almost complete at the time of his election. The book is a second edition and considerable expansion of an essay composed of five lectures delivered in 1933 at the Geneva Graduate Institute of International Studies, published in 1934 under the title **The Development of International Law by the Permanent Court of International Justice** (New York: Longmans, 1934, 111 p.). Dr. C. Wilfred Jenks has written of the second edition: "[It] is neither a treatise on the organisation and procedure of the International Court of Justice nor a systematic digest of its decisions on substantive points of law; it is something far more valuable than either as a contribution to the future development of international law and organisation, namely an appraisal of the international judicial process as a factor in the final development of the law. . . . **The Development of International Law by the International Court** is complementary to **Private Law Sources and Analogies of International Law** [London: Longmans, 1927, 326 p.] and **The Function of Law in the International Community** [New York: Oxford University Press, 1933, 469 p.]. The three volumes constitute together what is in effect a trilogy on the place of the judicial process in international organisation and the development of international law" (*British Yearbook of International Law*, 1960).

Quite apart from the value of the study in this broad sense, it contains acute comment on and analysis of a diversity of matters including treaty interpretation, *forum prorogatum*, abuse of rights, judicial legislation, equality clauses, aspects of state responsibility, issues concerning sovereignty and the formation of customary law. It is important to note that in this book the author was able to some extent to expound his views in a way which was not open to him in the role of editing the rather cramped contents of Oppenheim's **International Law.** The writing is lucid and the exposition, though necessarily judicious, shows the perception and craftsmanship characteristic of Sir Hersch Lauterpacht.

FRANCK, THOMAS M. **The Structure of Impartiality.** New York: Macmillan, 1968, 344 p.

A spirited, learned and argumentative plea for the development of impartial, third-party law in the international milieu, as the only way out of the deadly danger of pure power politics and out of the hazards of power-based two-party (compromise) lawmaking. Professor Franck points out these risks and perils and answers the traditional arguments critical of third-party law. He brings to bear on his subject not only solid and wide legal erudition but a shrewd political and psychological sense and a variety of philosophical references. He realizes the difficulty of finding truly impartial referees but shows persuasively that those obstacles are not fatal and have been overcome in a large number of instances. But the key question remains: Are states, those cold, subjective, committed, competing monsters, at all willing to heed the lawyer's arguments and to entrust their vital interests and concerns to third parties?

ANAND, RAM PRAKASH. **Compulsory Jurisdiction of the International Court of Justice.** New York: Asia Publishing House (for the Indian School of International Studies), 1962, 342 p.

The dubious honor of having initiated the erosion of the compulsory jurisdiction of the International Court of Justice belongs without doubt to the United States. In its Declaration of August 26, 1946, it included the so-called Connally Amendment pursuant to which this declaration does not apply to "disputes with regard to matters which are essentially within the jurisdiction of the United States of America as determined by the United States of America." This clause is not merely self-serving or automatic, which it was intended to be, but also self-defeating, which it was not intended to be. The sorry example set by the United States was imitated by several other governments including France. However, while France had the good sense to drop this reservation, which was turned against her in the *Norwegian Loans* case, the United States has so far failed to do so.

The learned Indian jurist analyzes with great care the evolution and relative decline of the compulsory jurisdiction. He discusses its meaning and range, the variety of reservations attached by states to their declarations and finally the attitude of states toward the Court. In addition to the Connally type of reservations, the most damaging are those of a temporal character permitting states to accept jurisdiction and to terminate their declarations at will. The author quotes with approval Professor P. E. Corbett's view that the practice of attaching such crippling reservations to declarations has "turned this route to generalized compulsory jurisdiction into something of a blind alley." Dr. Anand is not at all hopeful for the future of the Court because "the extreme political tensions in the divided world of today, combined with fluidity of international law itself, have created an atmosphere unfavorable to the development of compulsory jurisdiction of the Court."

There is some truth in this. However, perhaps even more important is the attitude of states, old and new, which—mistakenly—seek security from law rather than security through law.

ROSENNE, SHABTAI. **The Law and Practice of the International Court.** Leyden: Sijthoff, 1965, 2 v.

War and international adjudication stand at opposite extremes of the pursuit of politics "by other means." The prescription of the U.N. Charter registers clear awareness on the part of the organized international community that recourse to judicial process, rather than resort to force, is an imperative of our times. Instruments for lawmaking are amply provided, and institutions for adjudication are comfortably, if not lavishly, endowed. Yet it remains a lethal weakness of the international structure for peace that when disputes become insoluble or unmanageable through political means, the road to force remains wide open; whereas litigation and the application of international norms must thread jurisdictional needles, surmount archaic methods of pleading and, above all, face a cowering reluctance on the part of the Court to grapple with legal implications of major contemporary political and social issues.

The essential importance of Ambassador Rosenne's monumental study of the life and work of the Court lies in its profound analysis of the Court as an institution groping toward a still unfulfilled purpose. The Court's activities are viewed in the political-institutional context of contemporary international society. This approach, outlined in the preface and, more completely, in chapter 3, is admirably developed in chapter 4 on the enforcement of judgments, chapters 8 to 14 on jurisdiction, and in the section on advisory opinions. The basic theme is inherent in the fabric of the book as a whole.

The failure of the Court to fulfill the promise of the Charter and meet the challenge of the present age gives rise to despondency as one follows Rosenne's survey of opportunities lost. Institutions grow with need, however, and it must be hoped that Ambassador Rosenne may yet be able to report that the reconstituted Court is prepared to pursue a bolder and more active course to greatness.

KATZ, MILTON. **The Relevance of International Adjudication.** Cambridge: Harvard University Press, 1968, 165 p.

Three important cases in which the International Court of Justice has been charged with unwillingness to go about the business of adjudication—the *South West Africa* case, the *North Sea Continental Shelf* case and the *Barcelona Traction* case—have led many to wonder what future there is for the Court. This book, originally presented as a series of lectures in a program of instruction for lawyers, takes the first of these cases as a cautionary tale for international adjudication.

An examination of the justiciability of questions arising out of the secession of the southern states during the American Civil War leads Professor Katz to some conclusions about the useful limits of adjudication, which he then applies to cold war disputes and to the *South West Africa* case. In cold war disputes, the only standard which is common ground between the parties is the need for peaceful settlement. In the *South West Africa* case, on the other hand, there was an agreement and a context to provide the standard for adjudication. The International Court withdrew from the field in that case and left the General Assembly to cope—unsuccessfully—with the legal confusion it had occasioned.

The optimum conditions for adjudication exist when the tribunal is an established and respected one, the law applied antedates the dispute and is clear and precise, the issue "has only restricted implications," and "the consequences of a decision one way or the other are easy to foresee." These criteria leave little room for optimism about the ability of the International Court to resolve the major issues dividing states, even though these may be technically justiciable. The sober realism of this little book is a useful corrective to some of the wilder flights of fancy about the ability of international courts to bring about the "world rule of law."

HUDSON, MANLEY OTTMER. **The Permanent Court of International Justice, 1920–1942.** New York: Macmillan, rev. ed., 1943, 807 p.

It may be that the prognosis for the International Court of Justice created in 1945 is uncertain, and in a general way even those "friendly" to the Court are now less prone to stake everything on the growth of its compulsory jurisdiction. Nevertheless, the experience provided by the Court and its predecessor has been invaluable, and this experience has provided guidance indirectly when other types of international tribunal have been set up. The volume by Judge Hudson provides an authoritative and very substantial treatise on the old Court. It is both a major classic and an authority on matters very relevant to current issues. Hudson's first monograph on the Permanent Court, **The Permanent Court of International Justice and the Question of American Participation,** was published in 1925 (Cambridge: Harvard University Press, 389 p.). In 1934 Hudson wrote the first systematic treatise on the entire procedure of the Court, based on the first 12 years of its existence. The volume published in 1943 was a major revision of the last work and was intended to be "a more or less complete record of the establishment, the organisation, and the accomplishment of the Court during the period from 1920 to 1942." It takes into account important developments since the appearance of the earlier work and includes two new chapters. It is the culmination of Hudson's work, a witness to his energy and scholarship, a monument to the Court and a manual of international judicial procedure. Its 29 chapters are supplemented by 14 appendices and a generous subject index. The exposition is enlivened by the clarity of the writing and the critical sense of the writer. It is, among other things, a model of what a monograph should be.

INTERNATIONAL CRIMINAL LAW

JESCHECK, HANS HEINRICH. **Die Verantwortlichkeit der Staatsorgane nach Völkerstrafrecht: Eine Studie zu den Nürnberger Prozessen.** Bonn: Röhrscheid, 1952, 420 p.

German literature on international criminal law and on the punishment of National-Socialist criminality is voluminous; attitudes range from intransigently polemical ("Nuremberg on trial") to sharply critical for laxity and whitewashing ("Nazis still in power"). In so far as it is possible to speak of a "middle" German position, this treatise by the director of the Max Planck Institute at Freiburg on the international criminal responsibility of state organs in the light of the Nuremberg trials can be considered as one of its most authoritative examples. It is also characteristic of the wide historical and multinational research underpinning this type of analysis and of its exclusively legalistic approach, which omits factual description of the policies that formed the substance of the indictments.

Jescheck sees among the merits of Nuremberg the rigorous rejection of any collective guilt of the German people and the reconfirmation of the punishability, in principle, of even highest governmental leaders for violations of the laws and customs of war. Although he has very much to criticize—*i.e.* the Nuremberg position that binding international rules are superior to nationally imposed rules—such war crimes and connected mass atrocities (crimes against humanity) "which actually were committed" should not have remained unpunished; "the esteem (*Achtung*) for those military leaders of our nation to whom grave injustice was done" by the four-power and U.S. tribunals at Nuremberg must not extend to the true criminals who deserved conviction. He argues in particular against punishability of planning or initiating or waging aggressive war: the Allies violated international law by indicting any Germans on this count; the Goering judgment erred by calling such crimes against peace the gravest crime of all; and Nuremberg did not establish any general criminal responsibility of governmental organs for illegal war in the future.

WOETZEL, ROBERT K. **The Nuremberg Trials in International Law.** New York: Praeger, 1960, 287 p.

The book, widely recognized and often quoted, gives a comprehensive description of the trial of Hermann Goering *et al.* by the Nuremberg International Military Tribunal. It traces the history, going back to antiquity, and meaning of the concepts there applied—crimes against peace, war crimes and crimes against humanity—and analyzes the principal criticisms. These were that "victors tried the defeated;" the law was retroactive; the defendants, as top government and military leaders, performed "acts of state" which are immune from penal prosecution by other states; alternatively, although holding top positions, they acted under orders from their own superiors, especially Hitler himself. There is also a succinct discussion of the 12 Nuremberg trials subsequently held before exclusively American tribunals (*Krupp* case, *I. G. Farben* case and others) and of the trial of the major Japanese war criminals by the Tokyo international tribunal. All of these trials applied essentially the law of the Goering tribunal.

Woetzel argues that in view of the unanimous confirmation of the Nuremberg principles by the U.N. General Assembly, the international community acting through the United Nations could at any time bring violators of those principles to justice.

GLUECK, SHELDON. **War Criminals: Their Prosecution and Punishment.** New York: Knopf, 1944, 250 p.

————. **The Nuremberg Trial and Aggressive War.** New York: Knopf, 1946, 121 p.

During World War II, the punishment of German war criminals soon became one of the Allies' formal war aims; and the demand grew in intensity with the ever-mounting Nazi mass atrocities. Yet the U.S.-French-British-Soviet negotiations that led to the London Charter for the joint International Military Tribunal which was to sit at Nuremberg were not concluded until August 8, 1945.

The book **War Criminals** by the Harvard criminologist Sheldon Glueck (completed in September 1944) was one of the first detailed analyses to appear in print of the substantive and procedural aspects of the trials to come. It made a considerable impact and continues to be instructive for several reasons: (a) for the arguments it adduces in favor of basic principles subsequently incorporated into the London Charter and judgment (examples: illegal superior orders are not an absolute defense; no criminal immunity for heads of state or acts of state; absence of preëxisting international penal code no obstacle to punishment); (b) for the expectations that were *not* incorporated into the postwar Allied program (examples: the "super-malefactors to be tried under the auspices of the entire civilized world," including neutrals if they desired; hundreds of thousands of able-bodied convicted war criminals to perform, "for years to come," hard labor "to rebuild what they have destroyed;" strong pressures, including withholding of food and oil, to obtain extradition of gravely incriminated Nazis from neutral states harboring them); (c) the author counseled, in 1944, "for the present" against prosecution for "origination" of or "causing" unjust or aggressive war—arguing that this would drag in a red herring, and that indictment of the "chief malefactors—Hitler, Tojo, Mussolini, their general staffs, and the rest"—for violations of "the laws and customs of legitimate warfare and of criminal law" would suffice.

Glueck's second, shorter work, written during the four-power Nuremberg trial but prior to the Judgment, explains the reasons for revising his views on the last-mentioned point, now agreeing with the principle of personal criminal responsibility for "crimes against peace," as laid down in the Nuremberg Charter and as subsequently applied by the Tribunal. Mr. Justice Jackson strongly supports these arguments in his foreword.

NEUMANN, INGE S., *comp.* **European War Crimes Trials: A Bibliography.** New York: Carnegie Endowment, 1951, 113 p.

Large-scale violations of the law of war and actual and threatened prosecutions for war crimes in the conflict in Vietnam have revived interest in the Nuremberg trial and other proceedings against war criminals after World War II.

This bibliography lists 746 items (with a few duplications), published between 1941 and 1950 and drawn largely from American and West European sources. The two decades since the list appeared have seen the publication of hundreds of additional cases, articles, books and documents of international organizations and conferences. In 1950, the international tribunals convened under Control Council Law No. 10 in Germany had not completed their work, and Germany had barely embarked on its own program of prosecutions. The Geneva Conventions of 1949 for the Protection of War Victims, which were directly responsive to the experience of World War II, are part of this history, as are such matters as the extension of the statute of limitations on the trial of German war criminals. Limited as this bibliography is to one decade and lacking references to the Tokyo trial and other Far Eastern cases, it is of greater assistance to the historian than to the lawyer. But there is no other such list, and this must therefore be the starting point for research.

CYPRIAN, TADEUSZ and SAWICKI, JERZY. **Nuremberg in Retrospect: People and Issues of the Trial.** Warsaw: Western Press Agency, 1967, 246 p.

Of all countries occupied by Hitlerian Germany during World War II, Poland suffered most. The nightmare lasted over five years; with death factories like

Auschwitz, Poland was deliberately made the mass abattoir for all Europe. Condemnation of such policies and of anything conceivably foreshadowing future calamities was then and has remained of fundamental concern to Poles. This is symbolized in the lifework of these two professors. Dr. Sawicki was chief Polish prosecutor at the Nuremberg international tribunal; Dr. Cyprian (now of Poznan University) was for a time Poland's representative on the 17-nation U.N. War Crimes Commission in London that anteceded the great trial. (See **History of the United Nations War Crimes Commission and the Development of the Laws of War,** London: His Majesty's Stationery Office, 1948, 592 p.) Subsequently, they coauthored a number of books on Nuremberg-related subjects, including **Nieznana Norymberga: Dwanascie Procesow Norymberskich** [Unknown Nuremberg: The Twelve Nuremberg Trials] (Warsaw: Ksiazka i Wiedza, 1965, 359 p.), of which **Nuremberg in Retrospect** is the last, for Dr. Sawicki died soon after its publication. They are among the internationally best known Eastern European specialists on these matters.

A succinct, insiders' description of the evolution, course, issues and personalities of the Goering *et al.* trial (emphasizing Polish issues) leads to the core of the book: a sweeping survey and harsh analysis of the polemics *against* the Nuremberg law and Judgment, which started even during the trial itself.

The spectrum of these "attacks" is very wide. They all aim at diminishing the "prestige and political influence" of the basic Nuremberg proposition, the criminality of aggressive policies. The anti-Nuremberg "revisionist" argumentation can be divided into two main types. One type tends to obtain impunity in the *post*-Nuremberg era for the preparation and commission of Crimes against Peace and of large-scale atrocities lumped together at Nuremberg as Crimes against Humanity. The other, even more extreme type of revisionism denies the validity of the Nuremberg law from the outset: it tends to rehabilitate not only the convicted individual major war criminals but especially the German general staff and the SS. Particular apprehension is voiced about the large West German legal and memoir literature aimed at whitewashing the Third Reich, about the role of ex-Nazi generals in NATO and about West German military demands, especially for nuclear weapons.

The book is instructive for the evident depth of feelings it expresses (which feelings do not lead to any general condemnation of "the" Germans; this would be non-Marxist) and because it is not uncharacteristic also of the literature on Nuremberg of Soviet international lawyers. See, for example, A. Poltorak and Y. Zaitsev, **Remember Nuremberg** (Moscow: Foreign Languages Publishing House, 1965, 296 p.).

TREATIES

McNair, Sir Arnold Duncan. **The Law of Treaties.** Oxford: Clarendon Press, 1961, 789 p.

By reason of its authorship, the importance of its subject and the substantial character of the treatment, this book occupies the first rank in the literature. It is a completely revised and essentially independent work and is not a second edition of the author's **The Law of Treaties** (New York: Columbia University Press, 1938, 578 p.), which should now be cited as "The Law of Treaties, 1938." The original work had the subtitle "British Practice and Opinions" and was intended as a statement of the law as understood in the United Kingdom. Thus there was little use of foreign materials or reference to the literature. The present volume, as the preface says, is written "from a more international point of view." There is extensive reference to the literature and to relevant United Nations material. The treatment is more critical and comprehensive, and there is no adherence to the form of a digest. However, the volume is firmly rooted in Anglo-American practice and evidences the author's desire to preserve the common law method in approaching the law. In any case the volume still does give a coherent view of British practice and contains numerous excerpts from the confidential opinions of the Law Officers of the Crown. Thus it provides, in effect, the treaty law section of the **International Law Opinions** (Cambridge: Cambridge University Press, 1956, 3 v.), since in that work the relevant section was left to be filled later.

The volume presents a mass of material with skill, and the writing has a classical economy and clarity. The whole, including major papers reprinted in an appendix, has high value. The treatment is substantial and fairly comprehensive, yet it remains a volume of individual scholarship with its own diversions and emphases, and there is no claim to a formally systematic coverage.

Of course, some of McNair's views have gone out of fashion—for example, his chapter on dispositive and constitutive treaties and the Vienna Convention on Treaties—but this is no less true of many monographs covering less ground than his does. Moreover, in general there is continuity in the problems of treaty law. McNair's book will remain one of the basic texts on the law for the foreseeable future.

BLIX, HANS. **Treaty-Making Power.** New York: Praeger, 1960, 414 p.

Taking account of both practice and theory, this analysis of formal treaty-making procedures gives attention not only to the several procedural stages in the making of various types of international agreements but also to the authorizations required for the performance of each task. The author, a Scandinavian legal scholar, presents a careful analysis of the differences among the powers of heads of states and of governments, foreign ministers, diplomatic agents and administrative department heads negotiating agreements in their agencies' particular areas of competence.

Among the problems discussed is that which arises when one state does not require another state's agent of lower rank than head of state or foreign minister to exhibit his full powers and then finds that in signing an agreement the agent has exceeded his authority. In dealing with this and related questions, Blix provides some plausible explanations of the more difficult situations that can arise in the course of making international agreements. Legalistic in tone and embracing many of the fine points of law, this study is useful for social scientists who would set their studies of international negotiating behavior in the structure in which negotiations occur.

McDOUGAL, MYRES S.; LASSWELL, HAROLD D. and MILLER, JAMES C. **The Interpretation of Agreements and World Public Order (Principles of Content and Procedure).** New Haven: Yale University Press, 1967, 410 p.

No one serious about understanding international agreements, not to mention codes, constitutions and other legal instruments, can justifiably overlook this profound volume. A faithful application of the "configurative" and "policy-oriented" jurisprudence of Yale professors Lasswell and McDougal, it recommends an approach to interpretation that is revolutionary both in its emphasis upon contextuality rather than textuality as the irreducible concern of rational interpretation and in its demonstration of the procedures by which the context within which purported covenants are reached can be systematically weighed and weighted. Looking upon interpretation as a problem in communication, it stresses the "urgent need . . . to facilitate the making and application of agreements" in order to establish "a stability in peoples' expectations which lessens predispositions for arbitrary resort to violence;" and to this end, critically appraising past trends in interpretation in light of modern communication theory and other up-to-date behavioral science findings, it calls upon decision makers to give effect to the "genuine shared expectations" of contracting parties (in so far as such expectations comply with the basic constitutive policies of a "public order of human dignity") by referring to a host of highly sophisticated, non-hierarchical "principles of content and procedure." The function of these principles is to give disciplined guidance to the interpreter about what is important for him to look at and about how he can most effectively go about serving both individual and community goals. While the alert reader will be sensitive to the authors' insufficient treatment of the operational difficulties and competing sovereignty-oriented pressures that their proposals will encounter in unorganized arenas of decision, no one can avoid concluding that this volume constitutes one of the major creative achievements of international law scholarship in the last half century.

INTERNATIONAL ECONOMIC LAW

DELAUME, GEORGES R. **Legal Aspects of International Lending and Economic Development Financing.** Dobbs Ferry: Oceana (for the Parker School of Foreign and Comparative Law, Columbia University), 1967, 371 p.

This is the most detailed and the most comprehensive survey available on the legal problems involved in international lending. The author has examined and critically analyzed relevant provisions, clauses and findings from a great variety of sources, including international agreements, constitutional law, company law, civil law codes, decisional law emanating from international and domestic tribunals and the terms of bonds issued in connection with international loans. He thereby furnishes a systematic inventory of the substantive and procedural rules that have been devised to govern the legal relations between the parties to international lending and borrowing transactions.

As regards international law, those passages are of greatest interest in which the author expounds the thesis that "loans between international persons are normally governed by international law." This proposition is confirmed, in particular, in the treatment of loan agreements to which the World Bank is a party.

One of the special features of the book is the author's approach to choice-of-law problems. He insists that the distinction between private and public international law, though somewhat blurred by the necessity of modern international economic relations, has not become obsolete, and he explores meticulously legal situations in which the question of the determination of the "proper law" governing a particular type of loan transaction arises.

Procedures and techniques relating to the settlement of legal disputes arising out of international lending are treated in considerable detail in chapter 4 of the book with special reference to jurisdictional clauses, arbitration agreements and recognition and enforcement of creditor judgments and awards. The copious references to case law and the pertinent literature are carefully selected and expertly commented on.

Delaume's book is of interest as regards both contents and approach; it furnishes unique insights into the intricacies of the legal relations involved in international lending transactions as well as into the type of theoretical and practical questions with which the Legal Department of the World Bank is faced in its day-to-day operations.

METZGER, STANLEY D. **International Law, Trade and Finance: Realities and Prospects.** Dobbs Ferry: Oceana, 1963, 184 p.

A collection of essays on current problems of international law, with emphasis on their economic aspects, drawing on the author's experience as Assistant Legal Adviser for Economic Affairs at the Department of State for several years. His theoretical approach, indirectly expressed in most essays and explicitly stated in a few, is essentially pragmatic, marked by awareness of political and economic realities and by concern with the achievement of limited but feasible objectives. He views law as most effective when operating *in concreto* affirmatively to shape particular manifestations of major policies, to create channels and procedures for future interaction among states and to impose well-defined restraints on a limited scale and with respect to specific problems. He is skeptical of attempts to impart excessive precision and clarity in international legal relations and to exact open-ended commitments by means of formal statements of general principle (as in the proposed multilateral codes on the treatment of foreign investment). He favors instead narrower, less ambitious, but more effective instruments, such as bilateral commercial treaties, which codify "the pertinent legal, economic and political situations . . . in existence" while attempting few and minor innovations. Professor Metzger is at his best when describing specific cases in which legal skills and devices have been effectively used to construct flexible and workable structures and relationships in international agreements and organizations.

USE OF FORCE; NEUTRALITY

McNair, Lord and Watts, A. D. **The Legal Effects of War.** London: Cambridge University Press, 4th ed., 1966, 469 p.

Since 1920 this book, now in its fourth edition, has been practically unique in its field. It is the definitive study of the effects of war on the individual: his personal status, his business relationships and his property rights. In addition, and as essential corollaries, it contains studies in depth of such problems as the significance of the terms "war" and "other armed conflicts," the legal effects of belligerent occupation and the legal effects of the acts of a "government in exile."

While the authors emphasize that "the primary object of this book is to consider the legal effects in English municipal law of the existence of a war, whether the United Kingdom is belligerent or neutral," the discussion necessarily goes far beyond that, including numerous areas of international law, some of which have already been noted, and many rulings of non-English (and non-British) courts. Moreover, the authors are usually careful to point out whether a particular English practice, elaborated upon by them, is in accordance with the general practice of nations or is in any manner out of the ordinary. The book will, therefore, unquestionably continue to fill what would otherwise be a serious void for both the scholar and the practicing lawyer, no matter what his nationality and no matter what the national point of view from which a particular problem is approached.

Bowett, Derek William. **Self-Defense in International Law.** New York: Praeger, 1958, 294 p.

Traditional international law left to the states a large degree of discretion in the use of force. Reprisals against a wrong were an accepted method of self-help even if they involved the use of force. Self-defense was equally accepted as a reaction against an actual or anticipated attack. The Covenant of the League of Nations and the Kellogg-Briand Pact represent attempts to bring the use of force under legal control. The Charter of the United Nations and the London Charter of the International Military Tribunal (Nuremberg) are further stages in restricting the use of force.

Mr. Bowett subjects these developments to a searching analysis. Reprisals and intervention have become illegal. Self-defense, however, continues to be available to states, and even to members of the United Nations in spite of the text of Article 51 of the United Nations Charter which refers to self-defense, individual or collective, "if an armed attack occurs." Contrary to those who maintain that this proviso means what it says, Mr. Bowett considers first that self-defense is a lawful instrument for the protection of certain interests, economic and others (territorial integrity, political independence, rights of nationals), and secondly the lawfulness of measures short of or involving the use of force depends upon four conditions, namely: a delictual breach of a legal duty; absence of any alternative means of protection; the seriousness, imminence and actuality of the danger; and the reasonableness, limited scope and proportionality of the measures taken in self-defense. In this fashion the author succeeds in restoring not merely self-defense but also reprisals to their traditional position in the law. It should be noted, however, that contrary to the prevailing trend, Mr. Bowett takes a restrictive view of "collective self-defense": it creates no new rights. It merely means that members of the United Nations may exercise collectively their individual right. He thus appears as opposing the popular fiction that "an attack upon one is an attack upon all," unless there is a genuine interdependence of security.

STONE, JULIUS. **Aggression and World Order: A Critique of United Nations Theories of Aggression.** Berkeley: University of California Press, 1958, 226 p.

For about 50 years international lawyers and statesmen, the League of Nations and the United Nations have struggled with the concept of aggression: is it necessary, useful or feasible to define it? Since the application of collective security depended in the League on a prior finding of aggression, and the application of enforcement measures by the Security Council is predicated upon such a finding, the search for a definition is still on the agenda of a committee of the General Assembly. Professor Stone explores thoroughly both past and present attempts at defining this elusive notion. It should be said at the outset that he does not consider a definition essential for peace enforcement. Logically, a definition is certainly possible, but it is unlikely that it would be acceptable to a substantial number of states. Four definitions appear logically possible: (1) one that lists exhaustively the criminal (inculpating) acts and extenuating (exculpating) circumstances; (2) one that is open at the inculpating but closed at the exculpating end; (3) one that is closed at the inculpating but open at the exculpating end; and (4) one that is open at both ends.

None of these methods will yield a definition that is not open to manipulation by the aggressor or his victim. And none is likely to ensure that substantial justice be done, and justice is Stone's main concern. The application of the concept of aggression, an analogy to that of due process in constitutional cases in the United States, requires a careful and balanced consideration of the full "fact-value complex" of the case—that is, "a full assessment in the light of the whole course of the State relations concerned, of the merits of each side of the dispute to which the resort to arms is a climax, including the proportionality of the reaction to the wrong," the author says. This must be so in the present system of international law and the law of the United Nations Charter, neither of which can or does make resort to force illegal under all or any circumstances. A member of the United Nations is not "bound by law to wait for its own destruction."

While it must be conceded that a definition of aggression of and by itself will not ensure that justice be done, neither has its absence, in the light of the record of the United Nations, been conducive to that end. Stone's penetrating analysis is a contribution of the first order to a better understanding of the political and legal complexities of the problem.

BROWNLIE, IAN. **International Law and the Use of Force by States.** New York: Oxford University Press, 1963, 532 p.

Chapter 7 and Article 51 of the United Nations Charter, Korea, Suez, the Congo and the Six-Day War have forced writers to face the problems posed by the use of force by states. Dr. Brownlie divides his survey of this subject into four parts. His historical account goes back to pre-Christian times and finishes with coexistence. Part II deals with the delictual and criminal aspects of the illegal use of force, and the author accepts the contention that the Kellogg Pact outlawed and made war illegal and even criminal—an "emphatic prohibition" which was given effectiveness at Nuremberg and Tokyo, as well as in the Charter.

Part III of the book deals with legal justifications for the resort to force and is necessarily affected by the premises of part II. Thus, Dr. Brownlie is of the opinion that Article 51, despite its reference to an "inherent right," means that the customary right of self-defense has disappeared, and he tends to deny the legality of anticipatory self-defense. However, the launching of interceptive means against rockets would be permissible, and it is conceded that "the difference between attack and imminent attack may now be negligible."

Finally, Dr. Brownlie deals with a number of problems of a general nature, such as aggression, armed attack, responsibility, non-recognition and the like. Here the learned author's idealism and assertions of the supremacy of law over political reality become marked. Whether one accepts or questions the premises upon which Dr. Brownlie rests his interpretation in **International Law and the Use of Force by States,** it cannot be doubted that he has provided a useful and thought-provoking work on an important and complex topic.

COLOMBOS, CONSTANTINE JOHN. **A Treatise on the Law of Prize.** London: Longmans, Green, 3rd ed., 1949, 421 p.

This work started its life primarily as a compendium of the decisions of the prize courts of Austria-Hungary, Belgium, China, France, Germany, Italy, Japan, Portugal, Rumania, Russia, Siam and the United States, and the treatment laid emphasis on the decisions of the First World War (London: Sweet and Maxwell, 1926, 384 p.). The latest edition incorporates a great deal of material deriving from practice in the Second World War, although many of these decisions were still unobtainable when it was prepared. The work has survived as the only monograph on the law of prize in English to appear in half a century or more. It has been generally considered as readable and sound and, with less certainty, also as authoritative. At any rate it is a systematic exposition by a practitioner before prize courts.

The importance of the work is clear, but it has certain limitations. Thus the text contains only sparse reference to the literature and almost no use appears to have been made of literature in languages other than English. The author finds room for discussion of the principles, but there is no attempt to evaluate the materials in the general context of modern international relations. Most of the material dates from the First World War and, although old materials may represent existing rules quite well, there is a need for an examination of the possibility that changes have occurred in the basic assumptions underlying naval and economic warfare. In his last edition, Dr. Colombos did postulate the need for a revision of various parts of the law, including the law of contraband, but a lot has happened since he wrote. No doubt there is a need for a more definitive and modern work in English on the law of prize and one which is less exclusively British in outlook. The work of Colombos will remain of importance until such a book appears and, even after that, will remain as a classical exposition of the principles derived from the practice of the British prize courts.

CASTRÉN, ERIK. **The Present Law of War and Neutrality.** Helsinki: Finnish Academy of Science and Letters, 1954, 630 p.

In the aftermath of the Second World War and with the appearance of nuclear weapons, there was a falling away of interest in the law of war among writers on international law. At the most they indulged in apocalyptic forecasts about the whole body of the law of war and devoted little of their industry to the study of the particular rules and problems. This attitude has now changed to a great extent. The adoption of the Geneva Conventions of 1949 and the Hague Convention for the Protection of Cultural Property, and the persistence of conventional conflict in the Middle East, Korea and Southeast Asia, combined to produce a different perspective. The book by Professor Castrén thus has a particular value and is one of the relatively few major contributions in any language to the exposition of the modern law of war and neutrality. It is surely significant that in the two volumes (10 and 11, 1968) of Dr. Whiteman's "Digest of International Law" devoted to armed conflict, belligerency and neutrality, the three unofficial and non-judicial sources most frequently incorporated or cited are apparently Castrén's work, Greenspan, **The Modern Law of Land Warfare,** and Oppenheim, **International Law,** v. II, 7th ed., edited by Sir Hersch Lauterpacht.

Professor Castrén provides a very substantial account of the rules concerning neutrality, the conduct of hostilities, the beginning, suspension and termination of hostilities and belligerent occupation. The emphasis is on the laws of warfare although the question of the right to resort to force is not neglected. Considerable space is given to problems of naval warfare, blockade and neutrality. In general the text is well written, and the exposition rests on a wealth of material. This book was a valuable addition to the literature when it appeared, and it will long remain a standard work on a large and important area of international law.

TUCKER, ROBERT W. **The Law of War and Neutrality at Sea.** Washington: Government Printing Office (U.S. Naval War College International Law Studies), 1957, 448 p.

For nearly 70 years the Naval War College in Newport, Rhode Island, has been publishing its "Blue Books" of documents and text. The fiftieth volume is a treatise on the law governing warfare at sea written by Professor Tucker, at the time a consultant to the Naval War College and now of The Johns Hopkins University. A lengthy appendix contains the text of the official United States Navy manual, "Law of Naval Warfare," issued in 1955 by the Chief of Naval Operations.

This is the only recent treatise in English devoted exclusively to the law of naval warfare. It covers the general principles of the law of war, the rules governing the methods and weapons of warfare at sea, the law of neutrality in general and the relations between belligerent and neutral states in naval warfare (neutral rights and duties, contraband, blockade, unneutral service and visit, search and seizure). Total war, new weaponry and modern techniques of economic warfare, in which naval forces have a diminished role, make the law seem somewhat antiquated, and it is problematical how much effect it will have in future conflicts. But Professor Tucker has set it down, warts and all, in this highly authoritative and lucid book.

MCDOUGAL, MYRES SMITH and FELICIANO, FLORENTINO P. **Law and Minimum World Public Order: The Legal Regulation of International Coercion.** New Haven: Yale University Press, 1961, 872 p.

The legal philosophy—or what the authors modestly call "the framework of inquiry"—of two Yale professors is here given application to armed conflict between states. Garbed in somewhat daunting terminology are the familiar legal topics concerning resort to force and the conduct of hostilities—the legality of the use of force, aggression and self-defense, the initiation of warfare, neutrality, the conduct of hostilities, belligerent occupation and war crimes. But these topics are seen in the perspective of a value-oriented jurisprudence. The authors show the ways in which the world community attempts to give effect to a common interest in the prevention of the use of force and in minimum destruction of values when coercion is once employed. They identify the factors through an examination of which decision makers may arrive at rational decisions that will protect the values shared by mankind. This method of analysis is particularly appropriate to the difficult questions presented by the prohibition of the use of force, the authorization of the use of force in self-defense and the use of the term "aggression" in the United Nations Charter.

While the law has been put in this new framework, **Law and Minimum World Public Order** is not wholly theoretical. The existing law is set forth, and the work is heavily annotated with references to precedent and to the authorities. It is thus a work of reference as well as an analysis of the goals and workings of the law in light of the distinctive philosophy of law developed by Professors Lasswell and McDougal.

JESSUP, PHILIP CARYL, *ed.* **Neutrality: Its History, Economics and Law.** New York: Columbia University Press, 1935–1936, 4 v.

After the events of World War I, the adoption of the League of Nations Covenant and the signing of the Kellogg-Briand Pact, no one knew—and, for a time, few cared—where the traditional law of neutrality stood. But as the United States sensed the coming of another world war, it became a matter of great moment to determine what the policy of the United States should be toward hostilities elsewhere in the world. Should it maintain a policy of neutrality in order to preserve for itself the blessings of peace, or had the international system of the 1920s and 1930s made a policy of detachment and impartiality a legal and moral impossibility?

The answer of this compendious survey, which traced the history of the institution, came down on the side of neutrality. The United States should band together with other neutrals, as in the past, to protect neutral rights and should put peace above profits by refraining from the sale of essential military supplies to the belligerents.

In the event, history took a different course, and the United Nations Charter has drastically restricted the scope of operation of the law of neutrality (if indeed that institution survives at all). These four volumes are of interest today for their history of neutrality and of economic warfare at sea and for their framing of the problem faced by the United States as the war clouds gathered. The volumes are: Philip C. Jessup and Francis Deák, **The Origins** (v. I, 1935, 294 p.); W. Alison Phillips and Arthur H. Reade, **The Napoleonic Period** (v. II, 1936, 339 p.); Edgar Turlington, **The World War Period** (v. III, 1936, 267 p.); Philip C. Jessup, **Today and Tomorrow** (v. IV, 1936, 237 p.).

STONE, JULIUS. **Legal Controls of International Conflict: A Treatise on the Dynamics of Disputes- and War-Law.** London: Stevens, 2d rev. ed., 1959, 903 p.

Professor Julius Stone of the University of Sydney has made major contributions to both jurisprudence and international law. This great treatise on the law concerning disputes, peace enforcement, war and neutrality brings the perceptions of a legal philosopher to bear on that portion of international law which is subjected to the greatest pressures and strains.

Legal Controls of International Conflict is first a systematic survey of the law, heavily annotated with references to the practice of states and to treaties, cases and scholarly writings. But, in the words of the author, "it seeks to approach the full range of traditional materials in a manner which surveys concurrently both the materials *of the system,* and the materials *which challenge the system.*" The text is interrupted for 34 critical "Discourses," each considering and weighing the forces that threaten the existing system. These deal with such issues as "Radio Waves and Ideological Warfare," "Modern Problems of Unprivileged Belligerency: Guerrilla and Home Guard Formations, Spies and Saboteurs" and "The Problem of Definition of Aggression"—a question that Professor Stone took up in much greater depth in a subsequent volume, **Aggression and World Order: A Critique of United Nations Theories of Aggression.**

This novel scheme permits the author to pause on questions that particularly interest him without distorting the proportions of the book, but there are a number of points at which it seems unwise to separate the existing law from the forces that work upon it.

Although the title of the book might indicate otherwise, the various modes of the peaceful settlement of disputes are dealt with at some length. A particularly welcome change from past practice is that the law of naval warfare is now approached in the wider setting of economic warfare.

This is a highly reliable and informative work for reference purposes and a stimulating guide to areas of stress and change in the law.

GREENSPAN, MORRIS. **The Modern Law of Land Warfare.** Berkeley: University of California Press, 1959, 724 p.

There is no really good up-to-date treatise specifically on the law of land warfare. The most authoritative sources of guidance are the military manuals, especially "The Law of War on Land," part III of the British *Manual of Military Law* (the work of Judge Lauterpacht and Colonel Draper), and the four commentaries of the International Committee of the Red Cross on the Geneva Conventions of 1949.

Greenspan's book is heavily rule-oriented rather than problem-oriented. The orthodox topics are covered—the beginning of war, combatants, the victims of war (the wounded and sick, prisoners of war and civilians), belligerent occupation, conduct of hostilities, peaceful relations of belligerents, sanctions, neutrality, termination of war and civil wars—but in a bookish way and without any strong sense of the military and administrative problems that lie behind them. Much of the law is simply recited, and many pages are given over to quotations from or paraphrases of the governing treaties. This sort of treatment obscures the interesting problems of law and policy lying below the surface of such subjects as the selection and role of protecting powers, the persons entitled to be treated as prisoners of war, neutrality and control of economic life in occupied territories. And inevitably new problems about such matters as mixed international and civil war and United Nations forces have assumed major importance since the publication of this book.

In a small field of starters on the law of land warfare, Greenspan's book is out in front. But the race is not to the swift, and this work could be overtaken by a more perceptive and imaginative book on the subject.

THOMAS, ANN (VAN WYNEN) and THOMAS, A. J., JR. **Non-Intervention: The Law and Its Import in the Americas.** Dallas: Southern Methodist University Press, 1956, 476 p.

Non-intervention—the very word is a challenge to international law. It was one thing for President Monroe to tell a group of European powers in 1823 to keep on their side of the ocean, and it was still another thing for the Latin American states at Montevideo in 1933 to tell the United States not to interfere in their domestic affairs. For in both cases the principle of sovereignty was at issue. But that the cry of intervention should still be applied to the collective action of the whole community of states or a regional group of states calls for examination. Here we have a test whether international law can truly be called law.

The authors give us in this joint study a clear and detailed description of the successive phases through which the law has passed and how it now stands. The historical evolution of the doctrine is presented, and this is followed by an analysis of the conflict between the principle of non-intervention and the degree to which it has been set aside in favor of the collective action of the whole community in the interest of the maintenance of peace—the vital element of an effective system of international law. A final section deals with certain types of intervention, not always collective, which have taken place in areas of international relations where international law is still defective and inadequate.

The study is to be ranked among the leading histories of the relations of the United States with Latin America. It is a model of careful research and good judgment in handling controversial issues.

IX. INTERNATIONAL ORGANIZATION

GENERAL

See also Theory of International Relations; Methodology, p. 3.

MITRANY, DAVID. **A Working Peace System.** Chicago: Quadrangle Books, 1966, 221 p.

These essays, written between 1943 and 1965 by the leading exponent of functionalism as the means to world peace and order, systematically represent the functionalist doctrine. The volume takes its title from Mitrany's classic World War II statement of the case, reprinted here with a new introduction. Later essays reinforce the basic theme from several angles.

The argument is that working arrangements in which governments come together out of mutual interest are the best way to build a peaceful world community. Contemporary preoccupation with social rights and welfare while technology is shrinking the globe generates numerous needs for combination in the mutual interest. Functional arrangements, by linking authority to specific and limited tasks, evade traditional obstacles to the sharing of power by nation-states, accommodate demands for equality by smaller states and avoid the difficulties of federal schemes. Mitrany argues powerfully that plans for federal union encounter insuperable inherent dilemmas.

Mitrany's prophetic insights have influenced statesmen and governments. The European Common Market and functional institutions of the European Community and of the United Nations "family" are the most significant examples of functionalism in practice. Mitrany has also challenged scholars, especially the important contemporary school of neo-functionalist scholars who, in the light of recent experience, are examining critically Mitrany's beliefs that functional agencies can be essentially non-political and that the limits of their functions can be set by what he termed "technical self-determination."

CLAUDE, INIS LOTHAIR, JR. **Swords into Plowshares: The Problems and Progress of International Organization.** New York: Random House, 3rd ed., 1964, 458 p.

This is a revised and updated edition of Professor Claude's ambitious and successfully executed effort to analyze the main issues in the development, problems, progress and prospects of the most important multilateral international agencies, on which he brings to bear a penetrating critical intelligence coupled with a lucid and elegant style. The volume does not purport to be a compendium of all the facts about the multitude of agencies which dot the international landscape. It is, however, a helpful aid to thinking about and understanding many important issues of international organization, such as membership, voting, constitutional interpretation and development, international secretariats, peaceful settlement of disputes and collective security, disarmament and preventive diplomacy among others. In his final chapters, the author evaluates alternative approaches to peace such as federalism, functionalism, world government and international organization. Introductory chapters summarize the history of international organization from the nineteenth century on.

Claude's inclination is theoretical. His theory, however, has its feet on the ground, and this volume can best be described as a successful effort to confront abstract ideas with the realities of international processes. His realism leads him to emphasize the ambiguities in the contemporary role of international organizations, which he sees as both instruments of national purpose and potential supplanters of national functions. He remains an optimist and sees the historical process of international organization as "a secular trend which may yet effect a transformation of human relationships on this planet."

DEUTSCH, KARL WOLFGANG and OTHERS. **Political Community and the North Atlantic Area: International Organization in the Light of Historical Experience.** Princeton: Princeton University Press, 1957, 228 p.

In both the history and the scholarship of the era since World War II, a recurrent theme has been the effort to eliminate war by building community among nations. This collective study pioneers in that stream of scholarship. By comparative examination of a number of historical instances in which "security-communities" have existed, it seeks to derive lessons of relevance to the development of such a community in the North Atlantic area.

The result, the authors admit, is crude, in part because they sought generalizable insights from a broad comparison of disparate situations whose differences they did not examine in great detail. The resulting framework of hypotheses about background conditions and processes of integration has, however, stimulated much subsequent fruitful dialectic. Recent scholarship on integration, community formation and regionalism refers often to this study, if only to depart from it or take issue with it.

With respect to the North Atlantic area, the study concluded that a pluralistic route was more likely to produce the desired security community than a more direct attempt at amalgamation. The study seems to have relied too heavily on communication flows as an indicator of the potential for integration, with the misleading implication that the North Atlantic area as a whole held greater promise of progress in the desired direction than did its Western European component.

GARDNER, RICHARD N. **In Pursuit of World Order: U.S. Foreign Policy and International Organizations.** New York: Praeger, 1964, 263 p.

This book marks the high-water mark of United States commitment to the pursuit of national ends through the multilateral means of the United Nations and the related agencies. Its author was Deputy Assistant Secretary of State for International Organization Affairs at the time he wrote. That the work was "official" in character is confirmed by the fact that the foreword is by Harlan Cleveland, then the Assistant Secretary for International Organization Affairs.

The book argues unashamedly for the view that multilateral coöperation serves the national interest better than the available alternatives: "The central thesis of this book is that the pragmatic balancing of the advantages and disadvantages inherent in this system is yielding positive results over a widening range of subject matter." It pursues this thesis across much of the range of activities of the United Nations and the specialized agencies: peacekeeping, pacific settlement of disputes and promotion of legal order. There is a "ten-point program" for enhancing U.N. capabilities in the realms of economic and social development, world trade, the international monetary system, population, outer space and human rights.

The argument is eloquent and powerful, but it could not stem the tide which turned dramatically when the United States, not long after the book appeared, was forced to retreat from its position that General Assembly decisions to assess members for peacekeeping costs were binding. Gardner's book is a monument to the era whose passing it marked—an era when it could be argued that the international processes served national policy ends because the United States was able to dominate the processes.

GARDNER, RICHARD N. and MILLIKAN, MAX F., eds. **The Global Partnership: International Agencies and Economic Development.** New York: Praeger, 1968, 498 p.

As the late Max Millikan pointed out in his essay introducing this symposium, one of the important innovations in international behavior since World War II has been "the rapid growth of concern of the whole world community with the welfare of all its parts, and especially of its less advantaged members." This volume, which also appeared as a special issue of the journal *International Organization,* is a thorough, wide-ranging and deeply penetrating examination of the state of the effort with emphasis upon the economic aspects of the attempt to encourage development of the "less advantaged members."

An overall summary is to be found in Robert Asher's observation in the concluding essay of the volume that, while by historical standards "the progress of the less developed countries has been quite remarkable man does not live by historical standards alone." The contributions to this volume chronicle and examine the political, emotional, economic, institutional and technical sources of the "frustration and foreboding" to which Asher called attention in his conclusion.

No brief review can do justice to the range of analytical insight offered in this volume or to the competence of the roster of highly qualified authors. The symposium not only analyzes the programs and institutions for administering, regulating and advising on international aid, trade and finance—such as the U.N. Economic and Social Council, UNCTAD and GATT, the IMF and the World Bank group, and regional programs, including development banks—but also examines such crosscutting problems as education for development, population and the application of science and technology to development. While the purpose of the book is not to present information as such, the contents add up to the handiest available text for anyone interested in what may be the central international issue of the second half of the century and certainly must be included in any reckoning of the most important issues on the international agenda.

GOODRICH, LELAND MATTHEW; HAMBRO, EDVARD I. and SIMONS, ANNE PATRICIA. **Charter of the United Nations: Commentary and Documents.** New York: Columbia University Press, 3rd rev. ed., 1969, 732 p.

The Charter of the United Nations has been a living document. The meaning of any of its provisions at any given moment is a composite of the clear meaning of the text (although too often obscurity is the rule), what is known about the intentions of the drafters and the interpretations given to the provision in the practice of the organization. As the years have passed, the weight of practice on the meaning of the Charter has grown. The distance between the apparent meaning of the language itself when it could be ascertained and the cumulative meaning resulting from interpretation through practice has grown with it. No layman and few experts can understand the Charter without help.

That help is now at hand in the form of this massive, skillful and authoritative article-by-article analysis of the Charter as it has been shaped by practice. Ostensibly a third revised version of the volume of the same title first published in 1946 and in revised form in 1949, this is essentially a new book because of the vast body of experience in the intervening two decades. Unfortunately, the book carries the analysis only until 1966. For the period it covers, however, this work is to the U.N. Charter what the "Skeleton Key" is to "Finnegans Wake."

JAMES, ALAN. **The Politics of Peacekeeping.** New York: Praeger, 1969, 452 p.

The iconography of United Nations operations in the realm of peace and security has produced an awesome array of acronyms, from UNYOM and UNFICYP to the better known UNEF and ONUC. All the alphabetic mysteries are unravelled in this wide-ranging examination of "peacekeeping," prepared for the Institute for Strategic Studies series of "Studies in International Security."

The author has not confined himself to studying instances of United Nations field operations to which the description "peacekeeping" has commonly been applied—namely, those expressions of "preventive diplomacy" that have employed military units in non-coercive roles to stabilize tense situations with the consent of the principal parties—for example the United Nations Emergency Force (UNEF) in the Middle East. He has gone more deeply into history, seeking to organize information about all the interventions of both the League of Nations and the U.N. in the realm of peace and security, arranging them according to a scheme of purposes sought and of methods employed in each case. The result is an oddly organized encyclopedia of information covering disputes since 1919, from the Aaland Islands to the Yemen.

The approach is imaginative. The basic framework is threefold: "patching-up" or efforts to bring disputants to an agreement or assist in executing a settlement; "prophylaxis" or action to prevent a situation from deteriorating; "proselytism" or attempts to produce change in the existing order. But since the categories cannot be distinct, the result is no little confusion as to exactly where the lines are to be found with respect to this international action or that. Even so, it is a work that is rich in both facts and detailed insights.

SCHIFFER, WALTER. **The Legal Community of Mankind.** New York: Columbia University Press, 1954, 367 p.

This study is subtitled "A Critical Analysis of the Modern Concept of World Organization." In fact, it is both less and more than is implied by that description. It is less because to give meaning to the idea of "the modern concept of world organization" requires a broad-ranging examination of a variety of theories and much inference from a considerable body of practice, an examination the author did not undertake. Instead, he focused on what he took to be the central concept rooted in what he termed "progressive" thought—that the states of the world could be expected to behave with morality and reason to enforce universal law in behalf of the global community. The author was easily able to demolish this straw man. As so many have done before and after him, he shows that only because the conditions were absent were the League of Nations and the United Nations needed, and that the absence of the conditions assured that the concept could not be realized. The idea, he said, was "that everything could be obtained for nothing."

The work is more than the subtitle implies because of its examination of the history of legal ideas which he saw as underlying the world organizations of the twentieth century. In this exercise, Schiffer went back to Grotius and Pufendorf as the sources of the two main streams of international legal thought. He saw Pufendorf as the precursor of the positivist stream which, looking to the evidence of state behavior, emphasized the independence of states and their pursuit of self-interest. Grotius was the proponent of a natural law that emphasized the community of mankind, universal unity and solidarity. The World War I experience of a common effort against the Central Powers misled the victors to make Grotian assumptions about the bases for the world organization they created. Georges Scelle is the modern exponent of the monist doctrine that is the contemporary expression of Grotius' approach.

Schiffer's outreach is too narrow for this study to be satisfactory as an analysis of the ideas underlying contemporary world organization. As a work of legal intellectual history, however, it has both merit and interest.

LEAGUE OF NATIONS

General

CECIL OF CHELWOOD, EDGAR ALGERNON ROBERT CECIL, 1ST VISCOUNT. **A Great Experiment.** New York: Oxford University Press, 1941, 390 p.

Experiences in the First World War gave the author a lifelong hatred of war and led him to devote his life to doing what he could to prevent another. He helped in the writing of the League of Nations Covenant and tells here of the plans and discussions leading up to the proposal for the organization. He later served with the British and South African delegations to League Assemblies and as President of the

British League of Nations Union. His work for the League and his account of associations with Woodrow Wilson, General Smuts and with British leaders provide interesting and important insights into inter-war history. Cecil was aware of the weaknesses of the League but effectively demonstrates that too few wished to develop its strengths and that failures in British and Allied diplomacy after 1919 made the débâcle of Munich and its aftermath inevitable.

RAPPARD, WILLIAM EMMANUEL. **International Relations as Viewed from Geneva.** New Haven: Yale University Press, 1925, 238 p.

Writing from the viewpoint of a Swiss who had been a member of the League of Nations Secretariat for four years, Professor Rappard believed the League's "essential aim, the substitution of law and order for chaos in international relations, to be so absolutely beneficent and so clearly in the line of human evolution, that no one but a madman or a criminal can repudiate it." He saw the League as an organization to enforce the peace treaties, to promote international coöperation and to outlaw war. He realized, however, that states were not eager to use the Permanent Court of International Justice as much as necessary to fulfill the high purpose he had in mind for it and that they were already shying away from meaningful sanctions. He appealed to his American audience to see that the United States took its place in Geneva so that "without sacrificing either its full liberty, or endangering its internal peace, [it] could prevent injustice and thereby war. . . . [for] *ubi America, ibi jus, ibi pax.*" These lectures will charm all but the most hardened cynics, but their chief virtue is the light they cast upon a more innocent and optimistic age.

FLEMING, DENNA FRANK. **The United States and World Organization, 1920–1933.** New York: Columbia University Press, 1938, 569 p.

The author traces events from the "normalcy" of the 1920s to the crises of 1933, describing world politics as related to the League of Nations and the United States. He is particularly helpful in describing the role of Woodrow Wilson, the campaign of the League to Enforce Peace, the politics of the disarmament conferences and the varied activities of the League of Nations. He gives an extended account of the Manchurian "Incident" and surveys newspaper opinion about the League of Nations afterwards, concluding that events there had not completely undermined people's faith in the organization. The book ends with an essay confirming the author's belief in the values of the League.

VERMA, D. N. **India and the League of Nations.** Patna: Bharati Bhawan, 1968, 350 p.

India's ability to serve as spokesman for Asia in the United Nations in the years after Indian independence owes much, in the author's view, to its earlier membership in the League of Nations. The author analyzes India's anomalous place in the League—a member without independence and without full control over either its domestic or foreign policies. None the less, the League is shown to have helped Indian statesmen make the West appreciate the potential place Asia would occupy in world politics. The Indians used the League to prepare for their present role in international diplomacy, and the League proved an excellent training ground.

For an earlier account of India's role in the League, together with an appeal for larger Asian and African representation among its members, see Brij Mohan Sharma and Vangala Shiva Ram, **India and the League of Nations** (Lucknow: Upper India Publishing House, 1932, 239 p.).

AUFRICHT, HANS. **Guide to League of Nations Publications: A Bibliographical Survey of the Work of the League, 1920–1947.** New York: Columbia University Press, 1951, 682 p.

This volume is the absolutely indispensable companion for anyone doing research on the League of Nations who wishes to find his way around in the more than 100,000 documents the organization issued. It includes sales publications as well as documents and is arranged by subject matter, so that one can find in one place all the important documents on any subject the League of Nations dealt with. It also covers documents of the Permanent Court of International Justice, the International Labor Organization, the International Institute of Intellectual Coöperation, the International Cinematographic Institute and the International Institute for the Unification of Private Law. An appendix reproducing documents of the League, the ILO and the Court, and documents relating to the transfer of League assets to the United Nations, add to the value of this superb work.

Origins; History

DAVIS, HARRIET EAGER, ed. **Pioneers in World Order: An American Appraisal of the League of Nations.** New York: Columbia University Press, 1944, 272 p.

Sixteen Americans formerly associated with the work of the League of Nations contribute essays to this volume, which presents precisely what its subtitle promises. Each essay is an excellent introduction to its subject. Raymond B. Fosdick, sometime Under Secretary–General of the League, contributes the foreword. The other contributors and their subjects are: Arthur Sweetser, "The Framework of Peace;" James T. Shotwell, "Security;" Laura Puffer Morgan, "Disarmament;" Manley O. Hudson, "The World Court;" Frank G. Boudreau, "International Civil Service;" Carter Goodrich, "The International Labor Organization;" Sarah Wambaugh, "Control of Special Areas;" Huntington Gilchrist, "Dependent Peoples and Mandates;" Henry F. Grady, "World Economics;" Mitchell B. Carroll, "International Double Taxation;" E. Dana Durand, "Standardizing World Statistics;" Herbert L. May, "Dangerous Drugs;" Frank G. Boudreau, "International Health Work;" James G. McDonald, "Refugees;" Elsa Castendyck, "Social Problems;" and Malcolm W. Davis, "The League of Minds."

For an earlier, official assessment marking the League's tenth anniversary, see League of Nations—Secretariat, **Ten Years of World Co-operation** (Boston: World Peace Foundation, 1930, 467 p.). Another, unofficial study, comprising 20 essays by American and foreign experts, is **World Organization: A Balance Sheet of the First Great Experiment** (Washington: American Council on Public Affairs, 1942, 426 p.).

HOWARD-ELLIS, CHARLES. **The Origin, Structure and Working of the League of Nations.** London: Allen and Unwin, 1928, 528 p.

When Ellis wrote this book, there was no major treatise available about the League of Nations, and he wrote it as a textbook. It covers the story of the League's origins, structure, working and record as completely as could reasonably be expected, including an examination of its position and potential, as he saw them. The author traces the forces leading to World War I, showing the effects of the war on international relations, and then analyzes the Covenant and the organs, finances and diplomacy of the League. The book includes chapters on the International Labor Organization, International Law and the Permanent Court of International Justice.

MARBURG, THEODORE. **Development of the League of Nations Idea.** New York: Macmillan, 1932, 2 v.

The League to Enforce Peace was one of the earliest nongovernmental organizations in the United States to concern itself with international organization. The documents and correspondence presented here by the chairman of its Foreign Organization Committee give the inside picture of what was involved in the group's efforts to improve plans for a League of Nations in the four years before the Paris Peace Conference, to acquaint foreign governments with the group's purposes, to urge upon the Allies the importance of committing themselves during the war to the principle of a postwar international organization, to get neutral countries to make like commitments and to press governments to establish official committees to present official plans to the Peace Conference.

MILLER, DAVID HUNTER. **The Drafting of the Covenant.** New York: Putnam, 1928, 2 v.

Although "the history of the evolution of a document is of necessity a very weary tale," as Miller himself confesses, he does the job here for the League of Nations Covenant in a way that all concerned must approve. Volume II contains the 40 documents most relevant to the Covenant's history and two superb indices to both volumes (one to the Covenant by article numbers, the other by subject matter). Volume I gives the narrative story of the drafting and writing of the Covenant, drawing on knowledge and insights the author gained as a legal adviser to the American Commission. He tells us not just what the documents say but also what they were meant to say; what events lay behind the way specific articles, paragraphs and words were put on paper; and what the authors' intentions were. Miller believes "that if not written in 1919 as a party of the Treaty of Versailles, no Covenant would have been written at all, no League of Nations would have existed." He thus attests to the ephemeral opportunities for progress in international politics and shows us how men must go about seizing them. Nicholas Murray Butler, in his introduction, compares the work to Madison's Notes on the American Constitutional Convention.

For other commentaries on the Covenant, see Jean Ray, **Commentaire du Pacte de la Société des Nations** (Paris: Sirey, 1930, 717 p.), and Walther Schücking and Hans Wehberg, **Die Satzung des Völkerbundes** (Berlin: Vahlen, 1924, 794 p.). For documents dealing with Germany's entry into the League of Nations, see **Akten zur Deutschen Auswärtigen Politik 1918–1945, Series B: 1925–1933, Volume I, 2: August bis Dezember 1926** (Göttingen: Vandenhoeck and Ruprecht, 1969, 712 p.).

MORLEY, FELIX. **The Society of Nations.** Washington: Brookings Institution, 1932, 700 p.

Building on David Hunter Miller's history of the drafting of the League Covenant, Morley writes of the League's constitutional evolution. He tells the story not so much of what the League did as what it was becoming in 1932, before the Manchurian "Incident" started it on its downhill slide. Morley knew the League well, as a newspaperman and then as director of the Geneva office of the League of Nations Association of the United States. His contacts in the Secretariat and among the delegates were wide, and he used them well in portraying the relations among the League's technical committees, within the Secretariat, and the shifting balance of power and authority from the League Council to the Assembly. He shows the effects of the absence of the United States from the League's work but is hopeful still about the League's ability to organize the moral pressure of the world against Japan.

For a continental assessment of the League's past and prospects, which effectively captures the "spirit of Geneva," see Max Beer, **The League on Trial** (Boston: Houghton, 1933, 415 p.).

RANSHOFEN-WERTHEIMER, EGON FERDINAND. **The International Secretariat.** Washington: Carnegie Endowment, 1945, 500 p.

Of the organs of the League of Nations, the Secretariat was the newest in conception and its most distinguishing hallmark. The pressures upon an international civil service and the complexities of its administration are specialized subjects, but no one concerned with them can afford to miss this volume. Written by a former official who was a member of the League Secretariat for a decade, the book is the absolutely indispensable account of the League's internal administration. It is a model administrative study, filled with technical details, but readable all the same, and even supplying illustrative anecdotes. It covers basic concepts and problems of international administration, the scope and limits of international leadership, the machinery of the Secretariat and the way it adapted to circumstances, the qualifications international officials need and the pressures that operate upon them, personnel classification and salary administration. It concludes with useful appraisals and evaluations, appendices, a bibliography and an index.

For an earlier, less detailed study, but one which paints a broader canvas, see Norman L. Hill, **International Administration** (New York: McGraw-Hill, 1931, 292 p.).

WALTERS, FRANCIS PAUL. **A History of the League of Nations.** New York: Oxford University Press (for the Royal Institute of International Affairs), 1952, 2 v.

The author was personal assistant to Lord Robert Cecil during the Paris Peace Conference and served in the League of Nations Secretariat from 1919 to 1940 as personal assistant to its first Secretary-General, Sir Eric Drummond, and then as Under Secretary–General in charge of political activities. These volumes stand as the most comprehensive, authoritative and definitive history of the League of Nations to date, drawing on recollections and a close study of the record, although not supplying specific documentation for points made in the text. Walters traces the making of the League, the years of growth to 1923, the years of stability to the climactic Assembly of 1929, the beginning of the League's difficulties in 1931, the years of conflict to 1936 and then the final years of defeat. The second volume ends with the establishment of the United Nations in a chapter entitled "Death and Rebirth;" the title itself says much about the enduring faith the idea of international organization has inspired in its supporters.

For purely factual information about the League's organization and work up to 1935, see Denys Peter Myers, **Handbook of the League of Nations** (Boston: World Peace Foundation, 1935, 411 p.).

ZIMMERN, SIR ALFRED ECKHARD. **The League of Nations and the Rule of Law.** New York: Macmillan, 1936, 527 p.

Although some inter-war writers regarded the League of Nations as the zenith of international relations and as an entirely new way to conduct international affairs, Zimmern, though optimistic, is realistic enough to confess his doubts that the rule of law is at hand and even whether "in penning these pages . . . to employ the past or the present tense." This book looks at the League within the context of international relations as studied in the 1930s as part of a "new" diplomacy requiring skills in its practitioners that were different from their predecessors'. It devotes about one-quarter of its space to the period before World War I and shows how wartime ideas and practices influenced postwar organization. Zimmern is among the first to see that, whatever the fate of the League's political activities, its economic and social work effectively met the new demands placed upon the nation-states.

Peace and Security; Mandates

BARROS, JAMES. **The Aaland Islands Question: Its Settlement by the League of Nations.** New Haven: Yale University Press, 1968, 362 p.

Undoubtedly the definitive study of this subject, the volume is thorough in its research and broader in its scope than the title indicates. It draws on British, United States and League of Nations sources, as well as private papers, to show how the dispute was settled and how the League "was used or manipulated by all parties to assist them in attaining their domestic and international policy goals." The author describes the role of the Secretariat and Secretary-General, depicts the interplay between domestic and international politics, identifies all the international actors and assesses the values and limits of an international organization as a buffer, impartial third party or sounding board. The book has a theoretical value far beyond the analysis of the dispute which is its major focus.

DAVIES, DAVID. **The Problem of the Twentieth Century.** New York: Putnam, 1931, 795 p.

One of the most comprehensive discussions of sanctions and international police forces. It is a tribute to the author that the basic alternatives he develops for international police forces are still viable today and exhaust the theoretical possibilities—at least as they have manifested themselves in United Nations practice. The volume contains a historical survey of coöperative military efforts from the days of the Amphictyonic League; describes League of Nations planning to combat war; the development of sanctions; the practicality of an international peace force (whether contingent, truly international or composite); the economic implications of such forces; and their possible impact on the policies of the major powers of the 1930s: the British Empire, France, Germany, Japan and the United States. This study is the most important work on the subject to emerge during the League period.

Two sizable, competent and well-documented legal studies of the League's machinery for preventing war are Miroslas Gonsiorowski, **Société des Nations et Problème de la Paix** (Paris: Rousseau, 1927, 2 v.), and Charles Rousseau, **La Compétence de la Société des Nations dans le Règlement des Conflits Internationaux** (Paris: Imprimerie Administrative, 1927, 320 p.). Very brief case studies of actual League practice appear in James Thomson Shotwell and Marina Salvin, **Lessons on Security and Disarmament from the History of the League of Nations** (New York: King's Crown Press, Columbia University, for the Carnegie Endowment, 1949, 149 p.). Two special studies of a document some hoped would improve the League's capacity to deal with international conflict are David Hunter Miller, **The Geneva Protocol** (New York: Macmillan, 1925, 279 p.), and Philip John Noel-Baker, **The Geneva Protocol** (London: King, 1925, 228 p.).

ROUSSEAU, CHARLES. **Le Conflit Italo-Éthiopien devant le Droit International.** Paris: Pedone, 1938, 280 p.

This exhaustive and objective study by a French authority covers the background, outbreak and evolution of the Ethiopian conflict and its aftermath. Rousseau examines Ethiopia's status in international law and politics, the policies of the great powers in East Africa, the Wal-Wal affair, the League of Nations' handling of the dispute, the application of sanctions, the conquest of Ethiopia and its consequences, and the political and legal problems of recognition.

For a study focusing specifically on sanctions, see Albert Elmer Highley, **The Actions of the States Members of the League of Nations in Application of Sanctions against Italy, 1935–1936** (Geneva: Université de Genève, 1938, 251 p.). Highley discusses the League's theoretical studies of sanctions, the actions of states in applying sanctions in the Italo-Ethiopian war, the problems of coördinating sanctions and the ultimate lifting of sanctions. He advocates more preliminary planning to minimize political pressures and stresses the importance of great power commitments. He also demonstrates the need to make efforts at conciliation that will not neutralize the effects of sanctions.

A full and methodical account of the military and diplomatic aspects of the Ethiopian affair is George Martelli, **Italy against the World** (London: Chatto and Windus, 1938, 316 p.).

WILLOUGHBY, WESTEL WOODBURY. **The Sino-Japanese Controversy and the League of Nations.** Baltimore: Johns Hopkins Press, 1935, 733 p.

SMITH, SARA RECTOR. **The Manchurian Crisis, 1931–1932.** New York: Columbia University Press, 1948, 281 p.

We know now that the Manchurian "Incident" in 1931 was a turning point in the life of the League of Nations and indeed in world history. The most detailed and best documented history of the problem is that by W. W. Willoughby. He starts by analyzing and describing Japan's treaty rights in Manchuria, recounts the essential facts leading up to the Incident and then analyzes in great detail the legal and political issues before the League. The work considers the manner in which the League handled the controversy and examines the legal questions that arose in connection with it. The assessment shows how fragile the instruments of international coöperation are when some great powers are determined to ride roughshod over restraints of international law and organization and others are unwilling to take the risks of fulfilling their commitments.

The more recent and much briefer study by Sara Smith goes much further in assessing the actions of the principal powers and statesmen involved in the Incident itself. She condemns the United States for failing to realize the seriousness of the Mukden incident, for failing to coöperate sufficiently with the League and for neglecting to keep the American people adequately informed. She finds both the United States and Great Britain to blame for failing sufficiently to harmonize their policies; sees a lack of leadership in Geneva and poor timing and faulty judgment all around. She concludes with lessons the world still has to learn: that international organizations must be as nearly universal as possible, that it is important to stop wars before they begin and that, to be effective, international organizations must have power to act.

HALL, HESSEL DUNCAN. **Mandates, Dependencies and Trusteeship.** Washington: Carnegie Endowment, 1948, 429 p.
WRIGHT, QUINCY. **Mandates under the League of Nations.** Chicago: University of Chicago Press, 1930, 726 p.

In the long sweep of history, the League mandate system and the United Nations trusteeship system will occupy a short interval between 1919 and some time in the 1950s, when the move toward national independence in effect liquidated all but the last few trusteeships. Until someone evaluates the two systems definitively, these two volumes are the best starting points for anyone concerned with the experiment in international trusteeship, originally designed to help prevent war by administering internationally areas that had proved potential trouble spots.

Hall, of course, has the advantage of time and can compare and contrast the League and United Nations approaches to their responsibilities and place both in their different political settings. He evaluates mandates and trusteeships as phenomena on "the international frontier . . . formed by zones where great-power interests come together in conflict." He presents a general view of mandates and dependencies, describes the origin and working of the mandate system and introduces the start of the international trusteeship system.

Wright deals only with mandates and writes before the mandate system ended. He views the conception as a "notable triumph of statesmanship in solving perhaps the most difficult dilemma of the Peace Conference" and studies the system for the light it throws on problems of international administration. He explores the impact of the arrangements upon international law and assesses the significance of placing an area one-third the size of the United States and a group of people equal to one-sixth the population of the United States in a new category. Finally, he attempts the difficult task of assessing the merit of the system in terms of clashes of civilization. For another book, whose methodological concerns give considerable universality to its seemingly specialized subject, see John Alvin Decker, **Labor Problems in the Pacific Mandates** (New York: Oxford University Press, 1941, 246 p.).

Both Wright and Hall supply excellent appendices and bibliographies which confirm their value as starting points of investigation, either of the systems in general or of specific mandates or trusts. Three useful works not included in either bibliography are: Stephen Hemsley Longrigg, **Syria and Lebanon under French Mandate;** Elizabeth van Maanen-Helmer, **The Mandates System in Relation to Africa and the Pacific Islands** (London: King, 1929, 332 p.); Tadao Yanaihara, **Pacific Islands under Japanese Mandate** (New York: Institute of Pacific Relations, 1940, 312 p.).

Economic and Social Activities

SHOTWELL, JAMES THOMSON, *ed.* **The Origins of the International Labour Organization.** New York: Columbia University Press, 1934, 2 v.

LOWE, BOUTELLE ELLSWORTH. **The International Protection of Labor: International Labor Organization, History and Law.** New York: Macmillan, rev. and enl. ed., 1935, 594 p.

FOLLOWS, JOHN W. **Antecedents of the International Labour Organization.** Oxford: Clarendon Press, 1951, 234 p.

WILSON, FRANCIS GRAHAM. **Labor in the League System.** Stanford: Stanford University Press, 1934, 384 p.

PHELAN, EDWARD J. **Yes and Albert Thomas.** London: Cresset Press, 1936, 270 p.

Shotwell's work describes for us how the ILO came into being and accompanies the description with the texts of the relevant documents relating to the preliminaries of the Peace Conference, the negotiations at the conference, the first international labor conference and the United States connections with the ILO up to 1934. Lowe is more concerned to show how the United States, at the time of writing, lagged behind European states in developing labor legislation. His is a painstaking, detailed work, describing the origins of the labor movement in the early nineteenth century—he includes the international socialist and trade-union movements—and offers a supplement on the ILO, with a summary of its work and the texts of its draft conventions and recommendations up to 1934, when the United States joined the organization. The book is badly organized but brings together much material not otherwise easy to obtain.

Those interested in the intellectual origins of the ILO will find in the Follows volume short chapters on the major thinkers concerned with international labor problems, starting with Robert Owen. Follows also traces intellectual and organizational developments in the labor field, starting with the First International and ending with the establishment of the ILO itself. Wilson's book is a study of international administration. He looks at the major problems and challenges facing the labor movement, the nature and structure of the ILO, the work and organization of the Labor Conference and Office, and ILO activities in codifying labor standards, preparing and revising international labor conventions, enforcing labor standards and conducting research on labor problems. The book concludes with a chapter about the United States and its then new membership in the ILO. Analytical and descriptive, it gives a good inter-war view of what the ILO was then and what it was trying to do.

Wilson's work contains a glowing tribute to the first Director-General of the ILO, Albert Thomas. Those who would like a more personal view of what it was like to work with the ILO and to try to make it a meaningful international organization should see Edward Phelan's biographical work **Yes and Albert Thomas.** It makes the ILO come alive in a way that no less personalized a study can, and it is itself an exciting adventure in biography and international organization. Bearing in mind the spirit of the ILO as Phelan captured it, one might repair to the more somber works relating to the ILO and the labor movement with greater understanding, sympathy and perception. For a similar approach to the International Institute of Agriculture, forerunner of the Food and Agriculture Organization, see Olivia Rossetti Agresti, **David Lubin: A Study in Practical Idealism** (Berkeley: University of California Press, 2d ed., 1941, 372 p.). For an official, factual account of ILO activities, see World Peace Foundation, **The International Labour Organisation** (Boston: Author, 1931, 382 p.), which contains contributions by ILO officials.

DE AZCÁRATE Y FLÓREZ, PABLO. **League of Nations and National Minorities: An Experiment.** Washington: Carnegie Endowment, 1945, 209 p.

The author assesses attempts by the League to establish adequate juridical and political institutions to prevent the existence of minorities from becoming a threat

to the peace, international or national. Although he sees the issues as less international than national, he examines League experience as a possible precedent for
dealing with contemporary minorities problems. He considers the national minorities of Europe, their rights and duties and the League's role and machinery, paying
special attention to Upper Silesia where the most complete and elaborate experiment in administering minorities took place.

For earlier but excellent accounts, see Carlile Aylmer Macartney, **National
States and National Minorities** (London: Oxford University Press, 1934, 553 p.),
and Julius Stone, **International Guarantees of Minority Rights** (New York: Oxford
University Press, 1932, 288 p.). For a more recent account, with an excellent
annotated bibliography, that goes on to discuss United Nations work in the same
field, see Inis L. Claude, Jr., **National Minorities: An International Problem.** For
two continental commentaries, see Enrico Aci-Monfosca, **Le Minoranze Nazionali**
(Rome: Vallecchi, 1929, 2 v.), and Georg H. J. Erler, **Das Recht der Nationalen
Minderheiten** (Münster: Aschendorff, 1931, 530 p.).

RENBORG, BERTIL ARNE. **International Drug Control.** Washington: Carnegie Endowment, 1947, 276 p.

This monograph sets out in detail the administrative procedures and experience
growing out of the international control of drugs under the League of Nations, a
functioning system that operated during and survived the Second World War. It
describes the coördination between national and international authorities in limiting
production and controlling the manufacture, distribution and use of drugs. The
book analyzes the conventions on which League of Nations actions were based and
describes the organs involved, their terms of reference, the campaign against illicit
drug traffic, the limitations on producing raw materials and the results obtained.
Renborg elucidates the strengths and limitations of the League's work and suggests
that one may learn from them lessons useful in limiting armaments and establishing
other international regulatory processes.

For specific accounts of economic and social activities of the League of Nations
up to the dates of publication, see Harold Richard Goring Greaves, **The League
Committees and World Order** (New York: Oxford University Press, 1931, 266 p.);
Wallace Mitchell McClure, **World Prosperity as Sought through the Economic
Work of the League of Nations** (New York: Macmillan, 1933, 613 p.); Linden A.
Mander, **Foundations of Modern World Society** (Stanford: Stanford University
Press, rev. ed., 1947, 928 p.); and Royall Tyler, **The League of Nations Recon-
struction Schemes in the Inter-War Period** (Geneva: League of Nations, Secre-
tariat, Economic, Financial and Transit Department, 1945, 171 p.).

UNITED NATIONS
General

See also International Law: Sources; Codification, p. 135.

BLOOMFIELD, LINCOLN PALMER. **The United Nations and U.S. Foreign Policy.**
Boston: Little, Brown, rev. ed., 1967, 268 p.

Bloomfield's book is the outstanding example of a policy-oriented book about the
United Nations. One learns from it a great deal about the U.N. and about the
record of American performance in the organization, but the author keeps the
presentation of this material subservient to his central purpose: to develop a broad
conception, and to translate it into terms of concrete policy, as to the ways in
which and the means by which the United States should seek to use the United
Nations for the promotion of its interests and values.

This project requires the elaboration of carefully considered views concerning
the nature of the ends to be sought and of the instrumentality that is to be
employed, a task that Bloomfield undertakes with vigor and understanding. He

defines the basic national interest of the United States in terms of fostering the kind of world envisaged in the Charter of the United Nations, without indulging in the happy illusion that this definition eliminates the painful problem of reconciling conflicts between the national and global interest and without adopting the naïve assumption that the creation of that kind of world can simply be left to the United Nations.

In the final analysis, the book is not so much an argument for American pursuit of the goals stated by the author as a plea for the formulation of a coherent set of national objectives and the intelligent consideration of the potential utility of the United Nations for their realization. Bloomfield is a critic of our vagueness as to what we want to achieve—and of our tendency to expect too much of the United Nations while we devote too little effort and imagination to exploiting and increasing its usefulness. What he offers is not a formula but a challenge.

BOURQUIN, MAURICE. **L'État Souverain et l'Organisation Internationale.** New York: Manhattan Publishing Co. (for the Carnegie Endowment for International Peace), 1959, 237 p.

The intensive and systematic study of the United Nations has been all too nearly a monopoly of Americans, inclined, for understandable if not altogether good reasons, to treat general international organization as essentially a post–World War II phenomenon, and to consider the United Nations from the standpoint of American interests, concerns and values. Hence, it is a matter of particular importance to have available a first-rate work on the organization that is distinctly non-American in orientation. That is precisely what the late Professor Bourquin added to the literature. Accepting the responsibility of writing one of the volumes designed to synthesize the findings of the various national studies commissioned by the Carnegie Endowment for International Peace, he combined the reporting and interpretation of views expressed in those studies with the presentation of his own analysis of the United Nations—that of a distinguished European scholar whose intellectual roots were in Geneva and the League of Nations rather than in New York and the new world organization. His work contributes geographical breadth and historical depth to offset the "here and now" proclivities of American scholarship. Moreover, it provides a glimpse of the future as well as a link to the past. Considering that Bourquin completed his manuscript in early 1958, it is remarkable how well his assessment of the trends and possibilities of the United Nations stands up in 1970.

COHEN, BENJAMIN VICTOR. **The United Nations: Constitutional Developments, Growth, and Possibilities.** Cambridge: Harvard University Press, 1961, 106 p.

In this volume, the author applies to the United Nations the same combination of legal and political wisdom that characterized his contribution to American domestic affairs during the Roosevelt era. His treatment of major legal issues relating to the Charter is in the tradition of John Marshall; he conceives them as constitutional issues affecting the life and growth of a potentially dynamic institution. Cohen provides an excellent example of the imaginative and constructive approach to the United Nations that has marked Western statesmanship at its sporadic best. He sets out an ideal of constitutional interpretation that is infused with a political element, not in the sense of partisan bias toward narrow interests but in the sense of statesmanlike dedication to the general interest.

A substantial part of the value of Cohen's essays derives from their indication of the limitations of, and the difficulty of sustaining, the high-minded orientation toward the United Nations that he espouses. Cohen gives his blessing to the various devices by which the Soviet veto power has been overridden, but he generally advocates an emphasis upon consensus-building that comports poorly with a policy of circumventing the veto. He asserts that the United Nations must provide for peaceful redress of grievances if unilateral resort to force is to be effectively prevented, but insists that states should refrain from forcible action even though no system of peaceful change has been instituted. He takes a broad view of the capacity of the Secretary-General to act to carry out his responsibility when disagreement among member states paralyzes decision making, but he grants no similar latitude to states in meeting their vital responsibilities.

The ultimate virtue of this book is that, even when the answers may seem unsatisfactory, the questions are clearly of central importance. One learns more from disagreeing with Cohen than from agreeing with scholars whose vision of the law and politics of world order is less sweeping than his.

KAY, DAVID A. **The New Nations in the United Nations, 1960–1967.** New York: Columbia University Press, 1970, 254 p.

This book is important both for what it tells us about the development of the United Nations and for what it shows us about the development of scholarship in this field. It is a superb example of what can be accomplished by an able scholar who combines judicious and pragmatic use of modern quantitative techniques with hard and deep thinking about the facts of cases. It is an important study because it represents the intelligent utilization rather than the impressive documentation of skills in research and analysis. Kay keeps the methodological horse firmly hitched to the substantive cart.

His examination of the performance of new states in the United Nations since 1960 is designed to illuminate the changes to which they have contributed in the nature, tone and functional focus of the organization and, more precisely, to analyze the ways in which and the degree to which they have exercised influence within, upon and through the United Nations. The author never allows the urge to measure to blind him to the subtleties of the intangible elements of the political process. He recognizes that the new states have exerted influence not merely by what they have said and done but also by simply *being there,* gaining influence by being subject to influence.

Kay's political sophistication is particularly evident in his emphasis upon the distinctions among influence upon United Nations declarations and recommendations, influence upon United Nations actions and programs, and influence upon the attitudes and behavior of states in the external world. His assessment of the impact of new states upon the organization is disciplined by a shrewd awareness that domination of the politics of the United Nations is not the same as the domination of international politics.

NICHOLAS, HERBERT GEORGE. **The United Nations as a Political Institution.** New York: Oxford University Press, 3rd ed., 1967, 247 p.

For the reader who seeks, in one compact volume, an overview of the United Nations and its related institutions, Nicholas' book is to be highly recommended. The author presents an account of the formation of the United Nations, a description of its structure, procedures and functions, and a review of the highlights of its development—all enriched by his thoughtful interpretation and appraisal and enlivened by the wit and lucidity of his style. Nicholas approaches the world organization without sentimentality or cynicism but with a mature understanding of politics, which he brings to bear upon the United Nations with striking effectiveness. His commentary on the policies of the United States, the Soviet Union and his native Britain in and toward the United Nations is particularly valuable.

All in all, this book contributes measurably to the shaping of an intelligent conception of the organization and of educated expectations concerning how and to what extent it may be useful to governments in their handling of the complex business of international relations.

RUSSELL, RUTH B. and MUTHER, JEANNETTE E. **A History of the United Nations Charter: The Role of the United States.** Washington: Brookings Institution, 1958, 1,140 p.

"Definitive" is the word for this study, a clear presentation and intelligent analysis of the results of a truly monumental research effort. While new facts will undoubtedly be unearthed and revised interpretations of particular aspects of the origins of the United Nations will deserve consideration, it is most unlikely that anyone will ever think it necessary or find it possible to undertake a comparably thorough investigation of the process by which the foundations of the United Nations were laid.

The prominence of the United States in the shaping of plans for the United Nations was so great, and the significance of the United Nations in the conception of the postwar American approach to world affairs was so notable, that Miss Russell and her collaborator recognized and grasped the opportunity to make their scholarly enterprise a study of the transformation of American foreign policy as well as a history of the Charter. It is very nearly as valuable in the former sense as in the latter.

Both the United Nations and American foreign policy have changed and will change, in ways that violate the expectations generated in the period covered by this book. Nevertheless, this volume will remain the indispensable starting point for anyone who seriously wants to understand the continuing development of the United Nations and of the global role of the United States, and the linkage between these two centrally important phenomena.

Organs and Processes

BAILEY, SYDNEY D. **Voting in the Security Council.** Bloomington: Indiana University Press, 1969, 275 p.

This is a treasury of essential information about virtually every aspect of the procedure by which decisions are made in the Security Council, including such crucial matters as the veto, abstention and consensus procedure. It combines legal analysis of Charter provisions and rules of procedure with careful and detailed presentation of the actual record of the Council from its beginning to the end of 1967.

Invaluable as a reference work, this book is substantially more than that, for the author shows a fine capacity for spare but penetrating political analysis. His appraisal of the limited consequences of the use of the veto power and of the significance of the "hidden veto," which involves the defeat of proposals by amassing sufficient abstentions to deprive them of the required minimum of affirmative support, is a useful contribution to accurate and balanced understanding of the functioning of the Security Council. He places the voting process in political perspective, stressing the point that it should serve as a stimulus to negotiation among members of the Council rather than as a substitute for such diplomatic activity.

Bailey's study provides an indispensable basis for consideration of the role that the Security Council may play in the international politics of the future.

GORDENKER, LEON. **The UN Secretary-General and the Maintenance of Peace.** New York: Columbia University Press, 1967, 380 p.

The office of the Secretary-General of the United Nations not only has pivotal importance within the structure of the organization itself, but it is at least potentially a factor of considerable importance in the general realm of international relations. The notion that the invention of this post introduces the possibility of a distinctive type of international statesmanship that may complement and in some measure counteract national statesmanship has intrigued observers of the United Nations and challenged and inspired—and frustrated—those who have occupied the office.

What are, in fact, the opportunities open to the Secretary-General for influencing the course of world politics? What resources are available and what techniques may be useful to him in the development and performance of his role as global statesman? What brand of Secretary-Generalship is most likely to be effective in promoting the general interest in peace and order?

Gordenker's study of the office of the Secretary-General under Trygve Lie, Dag Hammarskjöld and U Thant is addressed to these questions. He develops a comparative analysis of the concepts of the office held and of the styles of operation employed by the three who have served in that position. His examination of their experience provides the basis for a sober and balanced appraisal of the potentialities and limitations of this unique position in international affairs.

HADWEN, JOHN GAYLORD and KAUFMANN, JOHAN. **How United Nations Decisions Are Made.** Leyden: Sijthoff, 1960, 144 p.

In this modest volume, two experienced and perceptive practitioners of United Nations diplomacy have given us an account and interpretation of the process by which decisions are made in the United Nations, using illustrative material relating primarily to activities in the field of economic development. The authors emphasize the informal, "behind the scenes," aspects of the process—the sources and methods of influence that all too often evade the grasp both of scholars who concentrate on legal and structural analysis and of those whose research deals with readily observable and quantifiable features.

This analysis provides the basis for suggestive comparisons between the political process of the United Nations and diplomacy, on the one hand, and parliamentary politics, on the other. It is particularly useful for the light that it sheds on the balance, and the connection, between the public and the private stages of negotiation and decision making within the United Nations, and for its demonstration of the impact that multilateral debate may sometimes have upon the policies of governments.

HOVET, THOMAS, JR. **Bloc Politics in the United Nations.** Cambridge: Harvard University Press, 1960, 197 p.

The stubborn individualism of states in their international relations is symbolized by their jealous insistence upon "sovereignty" and their dedication to "national interest." Recognition of this feature of state behavior should not blind us, however, to the important and persistent clustering tendency of states; one need only note the role of alliances in the history of international relations to become aware of the inadequacy of an approach to the subject that fails to treat states in molecular as well as in atomistic terms—that stresses the soloists to the exclusion of the choirs.

In the age of international organization, the tendency of states to combine in groups, typically in opposition to or rivalry with other such combinations, finds expression both in the tension between regional institutions and global ones and in the development of blocs within organizations of global scope. It should surprise no student of politics, national or international, that the decision-making process in the United Nations is to a great extent a matter of bloc politics.

Hovet's study is significant as an early and direction-setting contribution to the examination of the clustering phenomena in the United Nations, notable for its pioneering use of roll-call data as the basic material for analysis. The author's classification of groups functioning in the General Assembly, his appraisal of their cohesion and their interrelationships and his balanced evaluation of their effect upon the functioning of the organization make this book a landmark in the development of scholarly analysis of the quasi-parliamentary politics of the United Nations.

LIE, TRYGVE. **In the Cause of Peace: Seven Years with the United Nations.** New York: Macmillan, 1954, 473 p.

Almost by definition, the memoirs of a United Nations Secretary-General deserve serious attention from students of the organization, and this point applies with particular strength to those of the first holder of that office. Trygve Lie behaved in such a way as Secretary-General, and wrote his memoirs in such a way, as to guarantee the applicability of the point.

Lie's conception of the United Nations and of his office, and his emerging convictions as to the nature of the international problems that should rank high on the agenda of the organization, were decisive elements in the initial stages of the organization's development. His version of the events of his stormy career as Secretary-General and his reflections on the possibilities and limitations of the United Nations are important raw material for evaluation of his impact and for appraisal of the directions in which the fledgling organization moved.

Perhaps the most striking feature of the book is the degree to which it confirms the Soviet allegation that Lie approved and shared the anti-communist orientation that made the early United Nations essentially an instrument of Western policy. Even his dedication to international pioneering in the attack upon economic under-development is presented as a response to the danger of the expansion of a communist movement that menaces world peace.

Lie's book is important both as a source of information about the original character of the United Nations and as a backdrop that facilitates the appreciation of the extent to which that character has been altered since his term of office.

STOESSINGER, JOHN G. and OTHERS. **Financing the United Nations System.** Washington: Brookings Institution, 1964, 348 p.

The occasion for the research effort that culminated in this volume was the acute financial crisis that beset the United Nations in the early 1960s in consequence of political controversies aroused by the ambitious peacekeeping operations in the Middle East and the Congo. That crisis is at the center of the study, which is designed to explain its origins and implications and to explore possible means of surmounting it and preventing its recurrence. The book has more than transient value, as the critical budgetary problems have subsided without being in any real sense solved.

There are other bases, however, for the view that this work has lasting value. Its treatment of the financial emergency noted above is set in the context of a useful survey of the budgetary aspects of international organizations in general, including those that preceded the United Nations and those that exist alongside that organization. There is much to be learned about the bread-and-butter problems of the complex network of agencies and programs of contemporary international organization from this comprehensive study.

Ultimately, however, the importance of the book lies in the devotion of Stoessinger and his collaborators to the view that money matters are intimately related to political matters, in international organizations as in national governments. Budgets reflect policy choices, and quarrels over financial obligations reflect political differences. Adopting this premise, the authors make their examination of the problems of financing the United Nations system the basis for a perceptive analysis of the political struggle concerning what those institutions shall do and shall become.

Political and Security Activities

GOODRICH, LELAND MATTHEW. **Korea: A Study of U.S. Policy in the United Nations.** New York: Council on Foreign Relations, 1956, 235 p.

Despite the implication of its subtitle, this book is a comprehensive study of the involvement of the United Nations in the Korean problem, from its initial effort to foster a political approach to reunification, through its role in the military defense of South Korea and in the termination of the Korean War. The story of the United Nations and Korea is essentially the story of United States policy in using the United Nations to attempt to secure a solution of the Korean problem.

The sponsorship by the world organization of collective resistance to aggression against South Korea was an event of unique importance, though less because it set a precedent for future activities than because it seems likely to remain unique. Goodrich presents the Korean War not as a glorious demonstration of the potentiality of a collective security system, but as an incident replete with lessons for statesmen concerning the wisest and most practical ways of dealing with intractable problems and volatile situations. In a well-balanced critique that runs throughout the volume, he explores the mistakes and fallacies that marked American policy and the limits as well as the potentialities of resort to the United Nations as a means of coping with such problems and situations.

Herein lies the book's permanent value. Many of the issues raised by this case are central to the continuing problem of the management of international relations. The question of the wisdom of using international agencies to force issues that have not yielded to negotiation among interested parties, the question of when turning over important and weighty tasks to the United Nations is a responsible act of deference to the international community and when it is an irresponsible evasion of national obligations, the problem of how to exploit the value of international bodies as allies in the upholding of order without sacrificing their utility as mediatorial agencies in the quest for agreed solutions, and the numerous problems that arise in the delicate business of limited war—all these are issues of the present and the future. Goodrich's analysis presents judicious commentary and stimulates further thought on problems of this kind.

LEFEVER, ERNEST W. **Crisis in the Congo: A United Nations Force in Action.** Washington: Brookings Institution, 1965, 215 p.

The United Nations peacekeeping operation in the Congo, 1960–1964, was, in Lefever's words, "the most complex and protracted operation ever authorized, financed, and administered by an international organization." It involved the world organization in political confusion, complexity and controversy that overshadowed the legal, operational and financial difficulties of the enterprise. Both the Congo and the United Nations survived.

Lefever presents the main features of this story with admirable economy and clarity, and displays a fine analytical capacity in evaluating the successes and failures of the operation and examining the lessons and the warnings that it offers for the future. His sober and balanced judgment of the Congo operation is based not upon an ideal standard but upon a keen appreciation of the prevailing circumstances and the unforeseen complications, and a thoughtful assessment of the alternatives that might have been adopted. He regards its success as partial and costly, but impressive and significant.

ROSNER, GABRIELLA. **The United Nations Emergency Force.** New York: Columbia University Press, 1963, 294 p.

This study of the first United Nations peacekeeping force was written too soon to cover the withdrawal of that force from the Middle East and thus to offer a final appraisal of its contribution to peace and order in that troubled area, but late enough to enable the author to consider its significance as a precedent and model for the intervention organized by the United Nations in the Congo. In developing her informative treatment of the creation and utilization of the United Nations Emergency Force, and her examination of problems relating to its legal status, composition, direction and financing, Miss Rosner has given major attention to its innovative aspects and its value as an indicator of the possibilities and limitations of international peacekeeping operations.

The essential character and functions of UNEF and other forces subsequently organized and directed by the United Nations are difficult to ascertain and describe with clarity and precision. It is easier to say what UNEF was not and did not do than to say what it was and did or was intended to do. The author's efforts are more notable as evidence of the difficulty of these questions than as a display of capacity to answer them. Perhaps their most significant contribution is to suggest that these questions are not answerable in any general sense, and that they need not be answered. What emerges for this reviewer is the conviction that UNEF inaugurated a period of fruitful improvisation in the use of multilateral mechanisms to assist in the stabilization of international relations, involving the creation of instruments whose value may not be impaired, but may even be enhanced, by the facts that they fit neatly into no familiar category, that their functions are not reducible to a set formula, and that they represent experimentation rather than implementation of a well-defined doctrine. The pragmatic value of UNEF is effectively demonstrated in this careful study.

STEGENGA, JAMES A. **The United Nations Force in Cyprus.** Columbus: Ohio State University Press, 1968, 227 p.

Since World War II, unilateral and multilateral experiments in coping with threats to international order have had a disturbing tendency to produce horrible examples that discourage repetition rather than hopeful precedents that inspire emulation. One might have feared that the trauma of the Congo would have had the same negative effect upon prospects for United Nations peacekeeping that Korea had upon ambitions to institutionalize collective security or that Vietnam seems likely to have upon the American disposition to engage in limited war in support of order and stability. Yet, before the termination of the Congo operation and while the shattering effects of that affair were most painfully evident, the Security Council launched another peacekeeping effort, this time in Cyprus.

This case study of the force that has served in Cyprus since March 1964 makes it plain that this venture has been influenced by the urge to avoid the pitfalls as well as to exploit the possibilities revealed by previous experience. Provisions for periodic renewal of its mandate and for voluntary financial support indicate concern to avoid the perils of continuing the operation without adequate political consensus and of forcing the issue of collective financial responsibility. The decision to undertake a separate but coördinate effort at mediation reveals the recognition that peaceful settlement and peacekeeping are essentially different functions and the resolve to make the latter contribute more directly to the former. Stegenga's analysis shows that this resolve has been defeated, but that the major difficulties of the Congo case have been avoided and the positive lessons of previous experience have been successfully adapted to the circumstances of the Cyprus case.

The most heartening point of the story is the showing that, despite the discouragement and the disarray produced by earlier peacekeeping efforts, statesmen have found it possible and profitable to continue the development of this useful function of the United Nations.

TAYLOR, ALASTAIR MACDONALD. **Indonesian Independence and the United Nations.** Ithaca: Cornell University Press (for the Carnegie Endowment for International Peace), 1960, 503 p.

This book has permanent value both because it is a superb example of scholarly analysis of the handling of a political conflict within the framework of the United Nations and because the intrinsic importance of the Indonesian case was magnified by its significance as a precedent. The involvement of the world organization in the struggle concerning the political future of Indonesia, from the lodging of a complaint against Britain's military role in Indonesia by the Ukrainian S.S.R. in January 1946 to the admission of independent Indonesia to membership in September 1950, was a multifaceted "first" for the United Nations; it was the first major colonial case, it brought about the first effort of the organization to use a conciliation commission to promote the settlement of a dispute, and it resulted in what Taylor describes as the United Nations' "first definitive political achievement." The origins of much that has become familiar in the politics of the United Nations are traced with meticulous care and illuminated with admirable insight by the author of this monumental case study.

Above all, Taylor's analysis furnishes the basis for understanding how the United Nations has served to reverse the traditional expectation that the strong will triumph over the weak in diplomatic contests, where the dynamic of anticolonial nationalism is involved. This study reminds us that the most fruitful approach to the United Nations is not to ask what it can do but to examine what states attempt to do, and what they may succeed in doing, within the institutional context that the U.N. provides.

Economic and Social Activities

See also International Law: Human Rights, p. 141.

ASHER, ROBERT ELLER and OTHERS. **The United Nations and Promotion of the General Welfare.** Washington: Brookings Institution, 1957, 1,216 p.

This massive volume, produced by a team of specialists working under the auspices of the Brookings Institution, offers a comprehensive survey of the work undertaken through the organizations of the United Nations system during its first decade, in the field that may be roughly described as pertaining to the general welfare rather than to high politics and security. It presents more detail on some subjects than any particular reader will wish, or be able, to absorb, and its publication date implies that it includes facts that have faded into history and excludes developments of more lively current interest. The student who seeks to grasp the main outlines of United Nations activity in this field to date will be well advised to supplement his reading of this volume by turning to the less comprehensive but more recent study by Walter R. Sharp, **The United Nations Economic and Social Council.**

None the less, the work of Asher and his collaborators is by no means to be dismissed as an obsolete catalogue, or to be read in response to the scholar's routine sense of obligation to acquire "historical background." The major trends of development of United Nations activities in the area under consideration were discernible in the first decade of operation; what is more, the authors of this volume discerned them. To a remarkable degree, they gave analytical bite to a publication that might have been expected to be a dull compendium. The reader will find less reason to regard this book as out-of-date than to appreciate the contribution of the information and the interpretation contained within it to his understanding of present realities and future prospects.

JACOBSON, HAROLD KARAN. **The USSR and the UN's Economic and Social Activities.** Notre Dame: University of Notre Dame Press, 1963, 309 p.

This scholarly examination of the Soviet Union's attitude toward and involvement in the economic and social activities of the United Nations system focuses upon the reasons for and the consequences of the U.S.S.R.'s initial hostility or indifference and its shift, about 1953, to a fairly significant degree of participation. The author makes it clear that this change of Soviet policy, important as it was, did not inaugurate a period of intensive collaboration between the Soviet Union and the Western states in promoting the economic development of the underdeveloped areas or in achieving other values associated with international coöperation in "non-political" fields. As he puts it, the Soviet Union entered this sector of the organizational system less to coöperate than to compete, and the result has been primarily to make many of the organs and agencies arenas for East-West combat over economic and social issues.

Recognizing that this tends to invalidate rather than to confirm the functionalist expectation that joint effort in the economic and social sphere may prove an effective means of dulling the edges of political conflict, Jacobson nevertheless sees value in Soviet participation. He points out the importance of institutionalizing conflict, as distinguished from institutionalizing coöperation, in regard to economic and social matters, and stresses the role of the U.S.S.R. as gadfly and rival in stimulating other states to increase their commitment to constructive action within the context provided by the United Nations system.

SHARP, WALTER R. **The United Nations Economic and Social Council.** New York: Columbia University Press, 1969, 322 p.

The United Nations and the specialized agencies have devoted a major and steadily increasing proportion of their attention and resources to economic and social activities, particularly to programs related to the objective of promoting economic growth in the underdeveloped areas. In the scheme of things envisaged by the Charter, the central role in this sphere of international activity is assigned to the Economic and Social Council. How well has the Council played this role? To what extent, and for what reasons, has it been deprived of its central position? What might be done to enable the Council to reassert its position and to increase its effectiveness? Such questions as these provide the focus of this study.

Sharp presents a fascinating analysis of the troubles of the Economic and Social Council, which began with an ambiguous mandate, increased with the undisciplined proliferation of agencies and projects within the Council's purview, were complicated by the resistance of autonomous international bureaucracies and of national governments to efforts at coördination, and culminated in the bypassing and downgrading of the Council by the third world governments which, regarding that body as a "rich man's club," preferred to press their claims in the General Assembly and to pursue their interests in agencies more susceptible to their dominant influence.

Looking to the future, the author makes imaginative suggestions for the redefinition of the role of the Council, the provision of coherent leadership and the streamlining of its operations. If the development programs of the United Nations system are to avoid degeneration into utter confusion, conflict and chaos, the problems that Sharp identifies, if not the solutions that he proposes, must be given the closest attention.

X. WAR AND PEACE

GENERAL: POLITICAL AND MILITARY

See also International Law: Use of Force; Neutrality, p. 167.

FERRERO, GUGLIELMO. **The Principles of Power: The Great Political Crises of History.** New York: Putnam, 1942, 333 p.

This work is the final, most important volume in a remarkable trilogy concerning governments haunted by the specter of their own illegitimacy. Ferrero, who originally established his reputation as a historian of ancient Rome, uses the experiences of French governments between 1789 and 1814 as the main illustrative material. The initial volume, **The Gamble** (London: Bell, 1939, 305 p.), studies the Directory's first campaign abroad, arguing that domestic weakness led it to disregard conventions limiting the use of military force and the exploitation of victory. No party could place faith in the ensuing peace settlements. **The Reconstruction of Europe** (New York: Putnam, 1941, 351 p.) analyzes the success of the Congress of Vienna in mastering the issues which the French Revolution created for the international order. **The Principles of Power** is the most philosophic, far-reaching and useful volume in the trilogy, focusing directly on the ideas of legitimacy and illegitimacy.

The work may be the most rewarding modern study of legitimacy. It is more useful than Weber's familiar analysis because it focuses directly on politics, on how legitimacy is established, sustained and lost, and why legitimacy cannot be understood without considering its opposite—illegitimacy. Ferrero's discussions of the logical imperatives of particular legitimacy conventions, particularly as they relate to succession, and his analysis of the two major historical conventions, heredity and election, are especially interesting. The argument is that generally only countries of European civilization have been able to work out the implications of each convention, and hence free their governments from fear.

VAGTS, ALFRED. **Defense and Diplomacy: The Soldier and the Conduct of Foreign Relations.** New York: King's Crown Press, 1956, 547 p.

This massive work, printed in double columns, is the first detailed study of the soldier in foreign affairs. Treating all the major and many minor powers in five continents, the discussion moves from the eighteenth century to the mid-1950s. No subsequent study has demonstrated comparable scope or erudition.

The most important concerns are soldiers in diplomatic posts, military intelligence and espionage, the relations of foreign offices and general staffs, the influences of military decisions and advice on the determination to go to war and on the details of subsequent peace treaties, military training missions, the relations of armies during alliances, the diplomatic use of armed demonstrations and mobilizations and the organization of states during war. More theoretical discussions relate to the idea of preventive war since the Greeks and to the connections between strategic and diplomatic doctrines.

Although Vagts sees differences between the soldier's and diplomat's approach to foreign policy, readers familiar with his earlier, better known **A History of Militarism** will find much more cautious arguments advanced here. The soldier's inclination for adventure is conditioned by his view of the potential adversary's strength, while domestic political pressures and ignorance of military possibilities often make civilian leaders more adventuresome.

Readers will learn that predicaments we assume are peculiarly contemporary have in fact persisted since the eighteenth century. To cite four examples: (1) To make possible quick responses to foreign exigencies the executive has powers to move troops and has often employed them for purposes legislatures later found difficult to support. (2) War can be better justified when the enemy attacks and statesmen have manoeuvred to make their own countries victims of attack. (3) Imaginative impulses are thwarted by confusions about technological developments; between 1871–1914, for example, foreign and military policies lost their flexibility partly because everyone overestimated dependence upon railroads. (4) Military training missions have rarely created the desired capabilities in client states.

HUNTINGTON, SAMUEL PHILLIPS. **The Soldier and the State: The Theory and Politics of Civil-Military Relations.** Cambridge: Harvard University Press, 1957, 534 p.

The criticism that greeted Huntington's study when it was first published is testimony to the strength of the liberal tradition in academic circles. Huntington wrote as a political conservative, and his argument that national security should be the goal of policy, that the professionalism of the military—to which liberalism was opposed—was essential for security, and that Americans should therefore modify liberalism for the sake of security outraged many liberals.

Criticism of Huntington's conservative view of American society overlooked many of the virtues of his work. It is the first serious attempt to develop a theory of civil-military relations and to draw from it conclusions for American military policy. Huntington's model posits two types of civilian control—subjective and objective. In the first, the military shares the goals of the civilian and participates fully in political activities; in the second, the military is professionalized and becomes the tool of the state. Liberal democratic values have produced in the United States a subjective form of civilian control; objective control is best represented by Imperial Germany.

Huntington's model is based on a theoretical and historical analysis of the military profession in Western society and the United States. This analysis, which forms the larger part of the volume, is perhaps the most valuable part of the work. Whether or not one agrees with his thesis, one must admire the author's scholarship, perception and clarity. His treatment of the historical origins of the military profession and of the growth of military professionalism in the United States is original and suggestive, offering new insights for the student of military affairs.

VAGTS, ALFRED. **A History of Militarism: Civilian and Military.** New York: Meridian, rev. ed., 1959, 542 p.

The publication of **A History of Militarism** in 1937 was greeted with unqualified enthusiasm. It was a pioneer study of the military profession based on Vagts' experience as a Prussian officer in World War I and reflected the deep antipathy to war during that period. The scholarship of the volume was impressive, its range broad, offering a wealth of data drawn largely from European and German sources. Stressing the darker side of the military profession, Vagts' study constituted a powerful indictment of German militarism at a moment when a rearmed Germany under Hitler was setting out on the path of aggression.

Vagts defines militarism as an excessive preoccupation of the military with ceremony, customs and prestige. He criticizes the military for too often confusing its interests with the security of the state, and he tends to universalize the European, and particularly the German, experience. To him, all armies are the same. He concentrates throughout on the follies and excesses of the military, on its self-interest, its inefficiency, its preoccupation with tradition and honor. Though he recognizes that military forces serve a legitimate purpose in society, he virtually ignores this aspect of the subject.

The 1959 edition of the work adds two chapters covering the eventful years from 1937 to 1959, in which Vagts shifts his focus from the traditional militarism of the officer class to the growth of militarist values among political leaders—"civilian militarism," he calls it. Little of the vast amount of material that has come to light since the war and few of the many excellent studies of the prewar period written since 1937 have been used. The result is that much of the original work seems oddly out of date. Nevertheless, it remains an impressive study of the dangers of excessive concern with military values.

KNORR, KLAUS EUGEN. **The War Potential of Nations.** Princeton: Princeton University Press, 1956, 310 p.

One of the oldest and most persistent terms in the lexicon of international studies is the notion of "power." Knorr restricted himself to "military power" and then tried to differentiate between mobilized forces already in being as contrasted to a nation's capacity to add to these forces in case of hostilities. More importantly, he tried to differentiate between the basic physical elements entering into mobilizable military potential as contrasted to a wider array of political, economic, social and psychological elements that would determine what might be mobilized. Perhaps Knorr's uniquely different contribution within this overall effort was his special emphasis on the importance of a nation's administrative skills and its administrative-organizational arrangements viewed as critical elements in the nation's "war potential." Knorr's book remains a useful analysis of all those factors contributing to a nation's will and ability to exert military force at any level.

MONTROSS, LYNN. **War through the Ages.** New York: Harper, 3rd rev. ed., 1960, 1,063 p.

This story of war in all its phases from 490 BC to the present, written in a highly readable style for a broad lay audience, is perhaps popularized history at its best. Montross believed that "such timeless elements as preparedness, secrecy, deception and surprise"—in other words, the human factors in the combat zone—were more important than weapons technology, national political leadership and administrative skills. His history is therefore largely an account of battles and other engagements plus related strategies and tactics. Moreover, it is largely confined to wars within "Western Civilization," thus neglecting whatever significant contributions might have been made to the history of war by struggles indigenous to Africa, Asia and other non-Western areas. Still, with all its limitations, the work remains the most comprehensive and readable general survey of its kind in print today.

However, the book in no sense competed with Quincy Wright's monumental **A Study of War,** a pioneering effort to study war as a complex set of behavioral phenomena amenable to scientific inquiry, nor did Montross rival the work of his fellow historian Theodore Ropp's brilliant analytical focus on political and technological factors in the evolution of **War in the Modern World.**

SCOTT, ANDREW M. **The Revolution in Statecraft: Informal Penetration.** New York: Random House, 1965, 194 p.

Professor Scott's analysis of new factors in international politics assesses some of the actual and potential effects of increases in informal contacts between nation-states. Case studies (Nazi Germany, Soviet Union and United States) illustrate ways in which states can utilize informal access either to support or to attack other states. Because informal influence is an unavoidable consequence of power differential, this political scientist believes that nation-states should abandon the fiction of nonintervention and should develop international standards for peaceful interpenetration.

While stopping short of the assertion that all of the preconditions for lasting peace have been met, Scott concludes that "the decline of the impenetrable nation-state" (which his book describes in detail) "is a pre-requisite to the growth of world community."

Scott's chapter on treason and disloyalty (which, he points out, is "causally related to the growth of interpenetration") provides an able political-legal analysis which is missing in the more literary approach of Rebecca West's **The New Meaning of Treason**.

TURNEY-HIGH, HARRY HOLBERT. **Primitive War: Its Practice and Concepts.** Columbia: University of South Carolina Press, 1949, 277 p.

Primitive War is *the* classic study of violent strife among primitive or non-literate peoples. The author treats the technology, organization, justifications and motives of a vast array of peoples including, among others, the ancient Israelites, early Greeks and Romans, Celts and Germans, black peoples of sub-Saharan Africa and American Indians; and he shows how an analysis of their violent conflicts can be used as a prism to reflect their general capacities to coöperate for consciously formulated public purposes.

Violence is a universal phenomenon, but war develops late in human evolution, requiring a sophisticated level of conceptualization. Most primitive societies did not understand war: the organization necessary to defeat or conquer a neighbor was literally beyond their imagination. War and government generally emerge together in a people's history, both requiring a similar range of related concepts. Both imply among other things subordination and the distinction between public and private concerns. The movement to the military-political horizon signifies an irreversible revolutionary change in human consciousness potentially affecting every sphere of the society.

Military science, Turney-High contends, is the oldest social science, its basic principles understood for several thousand years. Its aim is to disarm the enemy, by finding his most vulnerable organizational point. The principal subjects, hence, are strategy and tactics. The author offers an impressive critique of academics for treating technology as the focal point of the military enterprise and obscuring the more fundamental human and organizational dimensions. In the process he introduces a view of the military activity which is traditional among the great military theorists and soldiers of the past but generally unfamiliar to contemporary academics.

COATS, WENDELL J. **Armed Force as Power: The Theory of War Reconsidered.** New York: Exposition Press, 1967, 432 p.

The concept of battle is the principal subject of this illuminating and erudite study. In successive chapters the author distinguishes the purpose of battle from that of war, discusses the history of battle, treats tactical and strategic components, relates battle to pertinent national aims, and finally shows how moral and legal considerations govern its conduct. Few books show a more profound grasp of the connecting points between military history, international relations and traditional political philosophy.

General Coats is particularly concerned with correcting Clausewitz, who argued that the purpose of war could not be achieved "with certainty until the adversary was disarmed." According to Clausewitz, in its pure form "war is the unlimited application of force." The doctrine exercised enormous pernicious influence on soldiers and politicians alike, encouraging them to think that there was "no substitute for victory," and that in war military considerations always governed. The impetus of the doctrine was to make wars more costly, more difficult to control, and peace harder to achieve.

Coats traces Clausewitz's difficulties to a failure to distinguish between war and battle. War, as Hobbes and Grotius knew, is a *condition* where battles or acts of force can be expected. Only in battle are military considerations paramount because only at that point is the primary aim to disarm an adversary. But the war itself must always be governed by political aims—that is, a peace treaty that both parties can accept. Important strategic consequences flow from this view which Coats illustrates by numerous historical instances.

STURZO, LUIGI. **The International Community and the Right of War.** London: Allen and Unwin, 1929, 249 p.

Don Luigi Sturzo was a priest-philosopher-politician who fled from Fascism in Italy to England where he completed this major treatise on war. It is a brilliant and scholarly work which, except for its brief historical sections, is as challenging and useful today as it was in the inter-war period. A quarter of a century before the UNESCO constitution was written Don Luigi concluded that "the fact of war . . . is necessarily linked with the will of man alone" and he argued that the end of war "can only be achieved in and by an interstatal organization."

While he was convinced that the facts of interdependence and man's need for sociability would lead to a natural development of "law" over "force" as the basis of power, Don Luigi's deep Christian faith was tempered by his realistic political understanding. He warned that conflict and struggle would always be facts of international life, and that war as a means of conflict resolution would be eliminated only when and where "the general conscience of the time and place" reflected the conviction that war is impractical and therefore wrong.

This timeless philosophical essay forms a natural trilogy with two more recent works, **War and the Minds of Men,** by Frederick Dunn, and Hadley Cantril, *ed.,* **Tensions That Cause Wars.** Together the three books provide an extremely stimulating analysis of the reasons for wars and the processes by which they may be eliminated.

CLARK, SIR GEORGE. **War and Society in the Seventeenth Century.** London: Cambridge University Press, 1958, 152 p.

The author, an eminent economic historian, examines the meaning of war in the social life of seventeenth century Europe. The period is important in the development of Western civilization because it gave birth to sovereign states, regular armies, total war and finally international law. Contemporaries will find the age especially interesting because it parallels our own in that no clear distinction between war and peace existed, and international struggles became domestic ones while domestic difficulties were transformed into international conflicts.

The violent strife seemed to have the qualities of a melee. Enthusiasms and resources flowed back and forth across borders to men and ideas. Wars could not be terminated, and their effects were unpredictable and uncontrollable. The polyglot armies could not be restrained and were often as dangerous to their employers as to their adversaries. War was not the instrument of policy so much as a condition which tore a people apart, constantly creating new predicaments for policy-makers.

Near the end of the period a reaction to mass enthusiasms set in. The state through its monarch became the major institutional focus of loyalty, able to place strict limits on international conflicts. Coterminous with this development, and perhaps necessary to it, was the revival of a sense of the European community with a set of common standards. Clark suggests that those common standards first emerged in the armies whose personnel had served a variety of foreign establishments.

FULLER, JOHN FREDERICK CHARLES. **A Military History of the Western World.** New York: Funk, 1954–1956, 3 v.

Major-General Fuller was a British staff college instructor during the period between the two world wars. His detailed treatment of hundreds of battles is an attempt to trace the influence of war on the history of the Western peoples. The first volume starts with the earliest recorded fighting and carries the story to the Battle of Lepanto (1571). The second, covering the development of the British Empire, runs from the defeat of the Spanish Armada in 1588 to Waterloo in 1815. The last, from the Seven Days Battle of 1862 to the Battle of Leyte Gulf in 1944, describes the wars which Western peoples have fought in a worldwide arena with results not yet measurable.

Fuller's style is interesting, puts military decisions in a full social, economic and political context, and is punctuated with diagrams, charts and tables. He does not hide his biases which reflect a clear longing for the fading days of empire. Bitterly anti-Churchill and anti-Roosevelt, he concludes that these Western leaders were inspired by "blind hatred" and, as a result of their unconditional surrender policy, the "Asiatic hordes are back in Germany."

NEF, JOHN ULRIC. **War and Human Progress: An Essay on the Rise of Industrial Civilization.** Cambridge: Harvard University Press, 1950, 464 p.

The author examines the relation between progress in science, in industrial production, in military technology and in the occurrence and conduct of war during three periods labelled "The new warfare and the genesis of industrialism" (1494–1640), "Limited warfare and humane civilization" (1640–1740) and "Industrialism and total war" (1740–1950). He finds that science, industrial technology and production advanced most in times of peace or of limited war. These advances created industrial civilization and higher levels of living but were utilized to make military technology more destructive, to produce, in the last period, an emphasis on material interests, a reduction of humane restraints on war, and eventually total war hostile to civilization.

Nef agrees with Norman Angell that war is not useful to achieve the interests men and nations seek in modern industrial civilization, but he does not believe that appeal to these interests can eliminate war. Governments and people must, he thinks, accept new values and build "a world totally different from the one which usually confronts them when they pick up the morning paper, switch on the radio, visit the cinema or the prize-fighting ring." To this end, there must be a changed direction in the "institutions of instruction, research, and worship as well as the governing institutions." The book is an original contribution to the study of war and peace.

HOWARD, MICHAEL, *ed.* **The Theory and Practice of War.** New York: Praeger, 1966, 376 p.

This collection of essays honoring the influential British military theorist Captain B. H. Liddell Hart is essentially a book on the history of Western military thought from the eighteenth century to the mid-1960s. From introductory essays on the influence of Jomini and Clausewitz, the contributions range over doctrinal development in particular countries (Britain, France, Austria, Germany, United States, Soviet Union and Israel), supplemented by summary treatments of European military thought from 1870 to 1914 and a review of NATO strategic doctrine. The contributors, most of them well-known authorities, are also drawn from several countries, about half from Britain.

This is a book in an older but still honorable tradition: how to organize, control and use military force (chiefly armies) in war. There is little about such latter-day concerns as deterrence, escalation or the "use of force in peace," and a good deal about such matters as battlefield tactics, the offense *vs.* the defense and command problems. Still, most of these writers are sophisticates in the modern mode of relating military force closely to its political context, and consequently the essays are generally less technical and broader in scope than the traditional military history. Between Gordon Craig on military-diplomatic relationships in Austria in the eighteenth and nineteenth centuries and Henry Kissinger on American strategic doctrine and diplomacy in the nuclear age the intellectual gap is small. The book provides a sense of continuity between military thinking of the past and present, although this element could have been highlighted by editorial comment.

MILLIS, WALTER. **Arms and Men: A Study in American Military History.** New York: Putnam, 1956, 382 p.

Unlike most books, **Arms and Men** delivers more than it promises in the title. Not only does Millis provide a survey of American military history, but he seeks also to integrate this history into the general development of warfare since the eighteenth century. According to Millis, the military experience of the United States, like that of other Western nations, has been shaped by four broad movements or revolutions. The first, the democratic revolution of the eighteenth century, democratized war and produced the nation-in-arms and the mass army. The supplies, weapons, transportation and communications required by the mass army were made possible by the industrial revolution. Just as the growth of government and industry had led to a managerial revolution in these areas, so did the necessity for mobilizing and directing the mass army lead to the development of general staffs and the bureaucratization of the upper echelons of the military—a military managerial revolution. The most recent revolution, Millis asserts, is the scientific revolution of the mid-twentieth century which has produced weapons of such destructive power as to make total war obsolete if it is to serve its historic role as an instrument of policy.

Millis' analysis of American military policy for the nineteenth century and for World War I is both cogent and persuasive. For World War II and the postwar period it is much less satisfactory. It fails to deal adequately with the problems of recruiting and training military leadership for a citizen army, with personnel procurement, and with the strategic problems of the cold war. Despite these few defects, **Arms and Men** fully deserves the success it has achieved. Strongly thematic, extremely readable, skillfully blending generalization and detail, it remains the best brief treatment of the American military experience down to World War II.

HOFFMANN, STANLEY. **The State of War: Essays on the Theory and Practice of International Politics.** New York: Praeger, 1965, 276 p.

Eight of the nine essays appeared in various places before being collected in this volume, but several were available only in French and most were expanded, some significantly, for publication here. They may be grouped under three major headings: a discussion of various theories of international politics since the seventeenth century; an attempt to bridge the gap between international law and politics; and a treatment of international politics since 1945 including a long critique of Herman Kahn and Thomas Schelling.

The unity of the volume derives from the author's disdain of contemporary academic passions for grand system building and inappropriate methodological precision which, he believes, invariably lead us to ignore the experience of statesmen and misconstrue their actual space for political manoeuvre. Only by immersion in history and in the works of great political philosophers will we grasp the peculiar features of the international world. The argument has been made often before, most notably by Raymond Aron, whose masterpiece **Peace and War** is the subject of one illuminating essay. But Hoffmann's choice of theorists, the particular historical incidents and his gift for striking metaphors and analogies make this volume worth reading. The principal drawback is the occasional predilection for scattering issues with a shotgun, which prevents the reader from concentrating on a target.

SPEIER, HANS. **Social Order and the Risks of War.** New York: Stewart, 1952, 497 p.

This is the first book by one of the earliest and most profound students of military sociology in America, who studied at Heidelberg when Max Weber dominated German social science and later became a guiding spirit at the RAND Corporation. Consisting of 32 pieces, including excellent reviews, written during a period of 20 years, the volume is divided into four loosely related parts. "Social Structure" treats class, risk and uncertainty, largely in civil society; "Social Theories" contains analyses of Shakespeare, Hegel, Marx, Mannheim, Sorokin, Tolstoy and Lasswell; "War and Militarism" shows how political purposes shape military conduct and problems; and "Political Warfare" is devoted to aspects of the theory and practice of psychological warfare.

The major theme which emerges in one way or another in most of the essays is the limits which moral, political and technological considerations place on the possibilities of action—an argument demonstrated most vividly in discussions of propaganda and war. War itself is treated as "a problem of social life rather than an aberration." In showing how institutions which guide them during peace influence the ways men fight, Speier feels justified in concluding that good books on war necessarily, though often unwittingly, reveal much about civil society which cannot be learned in any other way. A favorite method of argument in the essays is to analyze a contemporary predicament in the context of its historical roots and parallels in life and thought since the Greeks. The footnotes and bibliographical citations contain impressive sources of information and suggestions. None of the papers is trivial; all manifest an uncommon common sense.

MODERN WARFARE

General Treatments

ARON, RAYMOND. **The Century of Total War.** Garden City: Doubleday, 1954, 379 p.

Writing at the height of the cold war, Raymond Aron provocatively argued that the century's great watershed was 1914, the year when war became "hyperbolic," rather than 1945, when two atomic bombs were dropped on Japan. But the title of his book is misleading, since hyperbolic war is not total war so much as war waged without understanding that the object must be a durable and hence mutually acceptable peace.

Aron notes that hyperbolic war was responsible for the initial rise of Marxist-Leninism in 1917, and a second hyperbolic war fought with blind indifference to what might possibly follow brought Russian troops to the Elbe and created foreign bodies in most European states which could neither be assimilated nor rejected. In contrast to Marx's theory, the communist doctrine spreads not because of economic contradictions so much as by hyperbolic war and through subversion and force. To ask the communists to make peace is to ask them to "renounce the faith which justifies their rule." Visualizing the reaction to Stalinist excesses and the possible loosening of Moscow's influence over communist parties before the events occurred, Aron argued that the de-Stalinization program would have narrow limits and that the competition between communist parties might keep the militancy of the faith alive for generations.

The rationale of the cold war has nowhere been stated more eloquently than by Aron. He succinctly concluded: "The object of the West is and must be to win the limited war in order not to have to wage the total one."

TUCKER, ROBERT W. **The Just War: A Study in Contemporary American Doctrine.** Baltimore: Johns Hopkins Press, 1960, 207 p.

The post–World War II stress on "realism" turned most students of international relations away from serious moral discussions. But the domestic agonies over the Vietnam War, and the Korean War before it, indicate how naïve this approach to realism was. In an interesting, often incisive philosophic analysis of the contemporary American distinction between just and unjust wars, Tucker contributes one of the few useful attempts to remedy the gap. Written before Vietnam, it is quite revealing that he finds the remarks of statesmen and soldiers on the question worth discussing but never those of academics.

Tucker identifies three major elements in the "American doctrine": only defensive wars are just; the party striking first is the aggressor; the victim is entitled to do whatever necessary to secure victory. The logic of the doctrine suggests that moral considerations are only relevant during peace and has made the prevention rather than the limitation of war the great object of policy. The author notes that this doctrine draws our attention away from our belief that there are aggressive activities (*i.e.* subversion and satellitism) which may be as unjust and dangerous as armed attack. The difficulties of the doctrine become unmistakable in a nuclear age where states can be "destroyed" in the first blow.

A poverty of historical imagination mars this otherwise valuable work. The assumption seems to be that only nuclear wars breed immense moral anxieties for the defending party. Tucker fails to see that the just war described is only one of several doctrines that have dominated Western states since the French Revolution. A perversion of the much more subtle and acceptable Christian doctrine, it derives from the fact that conscription breeds an overwhelming domestic political necessity to find a clear test for aggression and to see the aggressor as beyond the moral pale. The definitive study of just war doctrines will have to relate them not simply to technology but to military recruitment.

GAVIN, JAMES MAURICE. **War and Peace in the Space Age.** New York: Harper, 1958, 304 p.

General Gavin is a thoroughly military man who, writing at the height of the cold war, believed that the "mortal danger" of communism could be overcome only by vast increases in military expenditures. Reflecting the post-sputnik concern about "missile lag," Gavin feared that his country might have "passed the high noon of military achievement" and entered "the long afternoon shadows of a deteriorating republic." He deplored American military weaknesses of the 1950s in Korea, Indochina and Hungary, and he was caustic in his criticism of civilian approaches to problems which "can only be solved by career officers of high intellectual attainment and dedication."

Gavin saw the earth shrinking to a single tactical theater requiring a variety of armaments, and he pled eloquently with his fellow officers to avoid the tendency to prepare "feverishly to fight the last war better." He implored his civilian counterparts to reorganize the Department of Defense by eliminating the Joint Chiefs of Staff and creating a military staff directly under the Assistant Secretaries.

A decade before he became a leading critic of the Vietnam War, Gavin warned that the media for victory in future wars would be outer space and the human mind. Urging greater reliance on the United Nations, James Gavin's "strategy for peace" would eliminate war by developing United Nations–controlled military space stations.

DE GAULLE, CHARLES ANDRÉ JOSEPH MARIE. **The Army of the Future.** Philadelphia: Lippincott, 1941, 179 p.

De Gaulle first published this elegant, admonitory essay in 1934 when he was a comparatively obscure colonel. His plea for a professional élite of some 100,000 troops and for the formation of armored divisions capable of taking the offensive was taken up by Paul Reynaud in the Chamber of Deputies but, unfortunately for France, met with a chilly reception both politically and militarily. Six years later De Gaulle's vision of armored divisions, closely supported by ground and air forces, exploiting surprise to thrust deep into the enemy's heartland, was realized— but by the Germans—and De Gaulle himself commanded an armored division in a vain attempt to stem the tide at the Somme.

Politically, De Gaulle's analysis was somewhat naïve. He believed, for example, that "the phobia of destruction, by which the nations were for such a long time tainted, has lost its virulence," and that defeat in war would not be pushed to the extreme of national dismemberment. Militarily, though not perhaps so original in his operational and technical ideas as Fuller, Liddell Hart or Guderian, he was nevertheless remarkably accurate in predicting the salient features of blitzkrieg. His description of the new kind of leader required in fluid, mechanized warfare fits Rommel perfectly; while his warning about the dangers of relying on short-service conscripts and fixed defenses was all too sadly borne out by the fate of the garrison of the Maginot Line.

Quite apart, then, from De Gaulle's subsequent fame, this book is historically important as unheeded prophecy. It also contains many stimulating reflections on the relationship between war, the military profession and society which have lost none of their relevance.

YOUNG, ORAN R. **The Politics of Force: Bargaining During International Crises.** Princeton: Princeton University Press (for the Center of International Studies), 1969, 438 p.

This is the first systematic attempt to develop and test theories of coercive bargaining through detailed case studies of international crises. Many of the concepts—"salience," "commitment," "manipulation of risk" and so on—are derived from the work of Thomas Schelling. The cases are the Berlin crisis of 1948–1949, the Taiwan Strait crisis of 1958, the Berlin crisis of 1961 and the Cuban missile crisis of 1962. Young's method is to begin each chapter with a particular bargaining hypothesis and then to present selected materials from each of the cases which presumably test the hypothesis.

Some of the findings are interesting and important. For example, parties to a crisis rarely use tactics of firm commitment or deliberate heightening of risks for coercion; such theoretical ideal types are drastically muted in practice by a desire to preserve freedom of action and to minimize dangers of the crisis getting out of control. Other findings—*e.g.* that crises are "politically fluid"—seem truistic. The book suffers from a rather pretentious style and a lack of theoretical coherence. The hypotheses are disconnected and unrelated to any overall theory; many of them seem to come from the case materials themselves, in which event they are not *a priori* hypotheses which are "tested" but just old-fashioned empirical "conclusions." Young deserves credit for taking some useful first steps down a path which badly needs exploring: confronting abstract theories of bargaining and coercion with the real behavior of statesmen. Also, the focus on interstate bargaining properly expands the conceptual and methodological scope of crisis studies beyond the "decision-making" and "content analysis" frameworks of most previous research.

HANCOCK, SIR WILLIAM KEITH. **Four Studies of War and Peace in This Century.** New York: Cambridge University Press, 1961, 129 p.

In four lectures at Queen's University in Belfast Sir Keith Hancock undertakes with grace and simplicity what he calls "a four-pronged reconnaissance of territory . . . in large measure unknown to me . . . that academic research should systematically explore and occupy." The first, "War in This Century," considers in the era of ICBM what guidance we may expect to find from "the bits and pieces of history" of pre-atomic wars. Adam Smith's contest between defense and opulence, Hancock finds, is still going on. The Boer War was a dress rehearsal for more recent "little wars." History may never repeat, but it is infinitely suggestive. Hancock's research on Jan Christiaan Smuts leads him to his second topic, "From War to Peace." Smuts believed in magnanimous settlements; he sought such a settlement both in defeat at Vereeniging in 1902 and in victory at Paris in 1919. The third lecture, "Nonviolence," builds on Gandhi's formative experiences in South Africa and his curious conflict with and victory over Smuts. In the fourth, "Civitas Maxima," it is Smuts and Lionel Curtis who are the protagonists with their very different visions of a "Commonwealth" of nations "engaged in the painful and difficult climb out of the Hobbist pit and up the rocky path that leads to international order." Together the four essays are much more than a recounting of Smuts' struggles with Kitchener and Milner, Lloyd George, Mahatma Gandhi and Lionel Curtis. The book is a temperate reassertion and demonstration of the social utility of rigorous scholarship in a world that often seems bent on destroying itself.

VON BERNHARDI, FRIEDRICH. **The War of the Future.** New York: Appleton, 1921, 310 p.

Probably the first published blueprint for Germany's participation in a second world war, this pre-**Mein Kampf** plan is explicit about its dedication to pure militarism as the only effective, and moral, way to ensure that "Germany will rise again." General von Bernhardi began his text during the First World War and completed it in the wake of a defeat which he bitterly blamed on the "so-called" people of Germany.

Von Bernhardi's detailed prescriptions of weapons and tactics are of little value except as illustration of the criticism that military planners may be more inclined to prepare for the last war than for the next one (*e.g.* he only grudgingly concedes that "air machines" may take over some of the cavalry's daytime reconnaissance functions). Germany should be dedicated, he says, to preparation for a two-front preventive war planned in secrecy by a government totally subservient to the military. "In the last resort, force is the foundation of all intellectual and moral progress. . . . The politician must unconditionally submit to the will of the soldier."

KECSKEMETI, PAUL. **Strategic Surrender: The Politics of Victory and Defeat.** Stanford: Stanford University Press, 1958, 287 p.

This pioneer study of the power of the apparently powerless tackles a theoretical problem: the general conditions determining whether or not cessation of hostilities will involve surrender. Fresh ideas on the strategic and political constraints shaping the decision to surrender and to accept surrender are developed from four cases during World War II: the French in 1940, the Italians in 1943, the Germans in 1945 and the Japanese in 1945. Kecskemeti stresses that surrender means that both victor and vanquished have chosen to avoid the last round of fighting; the agreement not only ends the fighting but starts a new political relationship. When the victor wishes to bring hostilities to an end sooner rather than later, the vanquished has some leverage, and the surrender agreement is in fact a political bargain. The author argues that the Allies' insistence on unconditional surrender did not prolong the war with Germany, the only truly unconditional case; for internal reasons not associated with what the Allies *said*, the Nazis were not prepared to give up until the final act of occupation. He examines other myths and fallacies entertained by the Allies and points out that adherence to the rule of "no-negotiation" permitted third parties to profit at Allied expense in the Italian and Japanese cases.

The way in which the author attempts to apply his ideas to the nuclear age reflects the fact that this RAND Corporation Research Study was written in the 1950s. Yet experience in the non-nuclear wars which have occurred since Hiroshima exemplifies many of the book's penetrating observations.

ROPP, THEODORE. **War in the Modern World.** Durham: Duke University Press, 1959, 400 p.

Social scientists will probably find this the most useful history of modern war in English. Its rivals (Oliver L. Spaulding, Jr. and Others, **Warfare,** New York: Harcourt, Brace, 1925, 601 p.; and John F. C. Fuller, **A Military History of the Western World**) focus on how battles are won and lost, while this volume concentrates more on using battles to illustrate trends in military thought and practices, relating those trends to possible political, technological and organizational transformations. No clear philosophical theme emerges, but the judgments concerning particular events, developments and problems are always apt and display enormous erudition. The footnotes have unusual merit; meant to form a bibliographical essay, they contain comments on items published in seven languages. The citations are discriminating yet thorough, and students will continue to find them extremely useful.

The text is divided into three periods: "The Age of the Great Captains" moves from the Renaissance to the overthrow of Napoleon; "The Industrial Revolution" carries us to World War I; and "The Age of Violence" ends with Korea. Ropp is concerned principally with major wars, the best section being on naval warfare, and while he neglects guerrilla and frontier clashes, his scattered remarks on them are worth reading. The discussion of military thinkers, including Machiavelli, Jomini,

Clausewitz, Mahan and Douhet among others, is valuable. Aside from a variety of factual errors which only specialists will see, the chief difficulties are that the treatment is not always systematic and the discussion of the political dimensions of war—its purposes, conditions and consequences—is thin.

RAMSEY, PAUL. **War and the Christian Conscience.** Durham: Duke University Press, 1961, 331 p.

When advocates of the balance-of-terror doctrine were in the ascendancy, Paul Ramsey (professor of religion at Princeton University) attacked their position, arguing both the moral and practical necessity of "recovering the just-war doctrine as the context of policy making." Christians originally formulated it as a single exception to the commandment against killing: attacking force could be repelled, and close coöperators in force directly repressed, to prevent many more people suffering unnecessary harm. Ramsey found the doctrine still valid against claims that the laws of war permit wholesale murder of persons not immediately involved in force that should justly be repelled. "Counter-force warfare is the modern term for the just conduct of war." The distinction between force and violence, between counter-force and counter-society warfare, must be made by moral will and political decision.

It is moral and political weakness not to see the "absurdity" of violence and the rational necessity of force for the purposes of politics, the author continued. We cannot deter by weapons we cannot use; and thermonuclear (or bacteriological, gaseous or radiological) weapons are beyond the scope of a minimally purposive national policy. A decision never to use an intrinsically unlimited weapon would be comparable to past-era decisions against using available weapons without limit. Ramsey saw the current determination of policy by technology continuing into the ICBM age, unless statesmen ceased yielding on policy to strategists and technologists. Arguing that the "aggressor-defender war concept" was almost worthless, he asked for courage to defy blackmail as the main ingredient needed to make the political choice of "a situation in which one people is destroyed . . . over a situation in which two peoples are destroyed by retaliatory and counter-retaliatory warfare."

Strategy

EARLE, EDWARD MEAD and OTHERS, *eds.* **Makers of Modern Strategy: Military Thought from Machiavelli to Hitler.** Princeton: Princeton University Press, 1943, 553 p.

The serious study of military strategy in the United States began with the late Professor Earle's **Makers of Modern Strategy,** the first comprehensive study of military thought in modern times. The volume consists of 21 chapters by 20 eminent scholars, each of whom discusses the work of a significant figure in the history of military thought from Machiavelli to Hitler. Published during World War II and foreshadowing the work of the postwar civilian strategists, the volume sought to provide a "broader comprehension of war" by relating the development of modern strategy to the political and social environment in which it originated. In Earle's view, war was an inherent part of the society at large and the proper study of strategy, therefore, should include not only the military factors but the economic, psychological, moral, political and technological ones as well.

Makers of Modern Strategy has stood the test of time well; the essays are authoritative and scholarly and the editing, including Professor Earle's introduction, admirable. The coverage is good, though more attention might have been paid to American military thought—only two Americans, Alfred Thayer Mahan and General "Billy" Mitchell, are included in the volume. Each of the essays is excellent, but, as one would expect, there are variations in scope and treatment. Some are based almost entirely on primary sources; some are analytical, and others are descriptive. Several, such as those on Machiavelli, Clausewitz and Adam Smith, probe deeply into the intellectual and social background of military thought; others, on Vauban, Jomini and Du Picq, are somewhat more technical in nature. But all are of uniformly high quality, combining sound scholarship with a deep understanding of the man and the period.

While the work is already a classic, it is also 27 years old and needs to be revised and brought up to date. Yet even in its present form, **Makers of Modern Strategy** is still the best survey of military thought.

LIDDELL HART, BASIL HENRY. **Strategy: The Indirect Approach.** New York: Praeger, 1954, 420 p.

Liddell Hart unfortunately left no single magnum opus on the theory of war on which he could be compared with Clausewitz. This volume, however, contains the fullest expression of his military philosophy embodied, with typical British empiricism, in a wide historical survey. It first appeared in 1929 as **The Decisive Wars of History** (London: Bell, 1929, 242 p.) and was subsequently expanded by the insertion of a brilliant section on Hitler's strategy. Later editions contain important appendices on the North African campaigns of 1940–1942 and the Arab-Israeli war of 1948–1949 by Generals Dorman-Smith and Yigael Yadin respectively.

Liddell Hart did not claim to have invented the concept of "indirect approach;" on the contrary, he recognized that its essential facet of psychological as well as physical deception—to put the enemy mentally as well as materially off balance—was as old as recorded military history. Rather Liddell Hart was inspired by the conviction that all the subtleties that had brought about meaningful victories in the past had been lost sight of in the nineteenth century under the influence of Clausewitz and his blinkered disciples with fatal results in the negation of strategy in the First World War.

As a historical study Liddell Hart's book was open to serious criticism. It was all too easy to read history backward and to assume that classical warriors were consciously practicing an indirect approach. Moreover, a thesis which could explain virtually every victory by indirectness at some level was in danger of becoming tautological. Insecure historical foundations, however, do not destroy the value of the theory. On the contrary, the general validity of most of Liddell Hart's views on contemporary strategy and policy have been widely recognized.

LIDDELL HART, BASIL HENRY. **The Remaking of Modern Armies.** Boston: Little, Brown, 1928, 327 p.

This is not one of Liddell Hart's best or best known books, but it gives a good idea of the scope of his reforming interests in the later 1920s. In 1927 he was military critic of *The Daily Telegraph* and one of a small band of writers who saw the urgent necessity to apply the lessons of 1914–1918 and prepare for the next war.

The keynote of this book is mobility—mobility of movement, action, organization and thought. Rebirth is the theme of the first part: the need to convert the classical mobile striking arm—the cavalry—into mechanized forces. "The result of the triumph of the machine-gun is to hasten the coming of tank armies. Improving upon the legendary phoenix, a newborn offensive power is rising from the ashes of the defensive overlord of the battle."

In the second part the emphasis is on the adaptation of infantry to the future style of mobile operations. An examination of postwar doctrines in France and Germany led Liddell Hart to the prophetic conclusion that the former were unduly influenced by the siege conditions of the Western Front, whereas the latter were paying more attention to principles of surprise, mobility and concentration through manoeuvre "which have ever been the instruments of the Great Captains." The final section consists of two retrospective essays on the First World War.

Despite the skillful juxtaposition of previously published articles with new material, this is a composite volume of uneven quality. Some of the chapters were of ephemeral interest, while others, such as that on "The Humanity of Gas," were to be amplified in Liddell Hart's later publications. Thus the chief value of this book today is probably for students of the evolution of the author's theories in the decade in which he established his reputation as a military critic.

MAURICE, SIR FREDERICK. **British Strategy.** London: Constable, 1929, 243 p.

This book was based on lectures given at London University and the Staff College in the late 1920s by one of the cleverest British officers of the First World War era. It was frequently reprinted until 1940.

General Maurice's objective was to lay bare the practical significance of the rather forbidding "principles of war"—which he preferred to call methods—and then to show their relevance to the peculiar needs of British strategy.

The study has two main merits: first, the lucidity with which historical principles are analyzed and related to recent developments; and secondly, the vivid use of historical examples—mainly from the American Civil War and the First World War—to bring abstract concepts to life. Despite the title, the author deals only very indirectly with contemporary British defense problems, and he is extremely cautious about future developments. For example, he is rather conservative in his view of the future role of the tank. The book's chief value now is for military historians, but its themes are of perennial interest to those concerned with the employment of military forces.

KINGSTON-MCCLOUGHRY, EDGAR JAMES. **The Direction of War.** New York: Praeger, 1956, 261 p.

This brief study of the problems of high command was one of the first to be attempted from an inter-service and inter-Allied approach. It is not a scholarly work, being somewhat untidy and repetitive and lacking either references or an index. Stereotyped accounts of British command problems from Cromwell to Haig are followed by more detailed analyses—often based on inside information—of episodes from the Second World War such as the Norwegian fiasco, Dunkirk and Normandy. The author is at his best in his frank analyses of the outstanding Allied leaders and how their personalities affected crucial decisions. Thus, for example, he describes how Montgomery's appointment had a galvanizing effect on the Eighth Army in August 1942, but also notes that an intolerable situation would have been created had the roles of Alexander and Montgomery been reversed. The author's personal involvement on the Air Staff adds spice to his discussion of the clash of personalities over the role of strategic bomber forces in Overlord, where his sympathies are clearly with Tedder and Leigh-Mallory rather than Harris and Spaatz.

Institutions such as the Ministry of Defense, the Defense Committee and the Chiefs of Staff Committee are subjected to critical scrutiny as well as individuals. The author skillfully exposes weaknesses—such as a deeply ingrained tendency to single-service thinking—but he proposes few specific remedies. Subsequent reforms have to some extent mitigated detailed criticisms raised by this well-informed authority, but the general problems with which he grapples remain as relevant as ever.

SCHELLING, THOMAS CROMBIE. **Arms and Influence.** New Haven: Yale University Press (for the Center for International Affairs, Harvard University), 1966, 293 p.

One of the most eminent strategic theorists of our time here further develops and enriches by illustration many of the seminal ideas which he advanced earlier, more abstractly, in his **The Strategy of Conflict.** The unifying theoretical focus is that of bargaining; Schelling pursues the bargaining motif along an ascending scale of conflict, from peacetime confrontation to limited war to general strategic war. Two masterly chapters elaborate various tactics of compellence and deterrence in situations when violence is mainly potential. But even when violence becomes actual, Schelling asserts, its primary function in the nuclear era is not so much to win in a pure contest of strength as to coerce the adversary by exploiting one's capacity to inflict damage. Modern wars are essentially bargaining affairs in which the sometimes contradictory objectives of preserving mutual restraints and getting one's way are both accomplished more by violence held in reserve than by violence used. This model is most plausibly associated with "limited war;" Schelling argues that it applies to general war as well, or could apply if the protagonists are rational. In concluding chapters he stresses that a disarmed world and a competitively arming world would not be so very different in their essential dynamics: a disarmed world would have its problems of "deterrence" and "stability" and an arming world has its intelligence and communication problems analogous to "inspection."

Schelling's purpose is to present the inherent *logic* of violence and potential violence in the nuclear age, and he accomplishes this brilliantly. It remains for others to explore the interaction of this logic with various non-logical aspects of human thinking and emotion in crisis and war.

BEAUFRE, ANDRÉ. **Strategy of Action.** New York: Praeger, 1967, 136 p.

This is one of a series of books in which General Beaufre implants a very characteristic style on strategic analysis. He is inclined to exaggerate the originality of his analysis and wavers between presenting it as a logical exercise and suggesting it as a practical panacea for immediate application to the cold war. Nevertheless, if some of his observations are commonplaces of modern strategic thought, the author's succinct and confident style has a clarifying impact after the ponderous and extended treatises all too often emanating from American sources.

In **Strategy of Action** Beaufre turns to policy intended to "make a gain" as distinct from the negative aims of deterrence. Given the difficulty of using overt force directly in the nuclear age, he believes that "indirect action" will increasingly dominate future strategy and that strategy must be conceived in a broad and political rather than narrowly military context. In one of his most useful passages, Beaufre suggests that particular levels of action have an inherent stability or in- stability in given technological and political circumstances. The task of statesman- ship is to see whether there is sufficient instability at any particular level to offer a prospect of gain. One of the gravest faults of statesmanship is to refuse to admit when action is impossible, and Beaufre particularly condemns the "strange reluc- tance to make unfavourable forecasts." He hopes the statesman of the future can accomplish, through indirect strategy, "manoeuvres made in good time while history is still pliable and malleable, thus . . . avoiding the necessity of recourse to major outbursts of the use of force."

HALPERIN, MORTON H. **Contemporary Military Strategy.** Boston: Little, Brown, 1967, 156 p.

The young author completed this little volume in May of 1966 just before he departed the Harvard campus to spend several years in Secretary McNamara's Pentagon and later in President Nixon's White House. The book is essentially an introductory primer, written in straightforward language, that sketches the major military policy and strategy options considered by the United States against the background of the evolving structure of international politics during the 20 years following World War II. But the author went beyond this analysis of strategic options and their implications within a historical narrative and time frame in order to discuss some of the research procedures used by military planners in reaching their decisions. Finally, he focused special attention on various strategic con- ceptualizations as they applied to specific geographic areas such as Europe and Asia. The book remains a useful short history and analysis of U.S. military strategy as it unfolded between the mid-1940s and the mid-1960s.

BRODIE, BERNARD, **Strategy in the Missile Age.** Princeton: Princeton University Press, 1959, 423 p.

Bernard Brodie's **Strategy in the Missile Age** was apparently intended to serve two purposes: first, it was a discussion of possible United States defense strategies during the early 1960s, a period in which manned bombers still constituted the backbone of U.S. strategic nuclear capability; second, it was a strongly argued effort to change the direction of those defense policies.

Writing in the final days of the Eisenhower Administration, Brodie argued, with other RAND strategists, that since the United States had renounced a first-strike strategy, it necessarily had to rely on a strategy of deterrence. In his view, there were three requirements for a sound deterrent strategy: measures for civil defense; security for the retaliatory forces; and a strong limited war capability. These arguments were apparently adopted by the Kennedy Administration and (except for civil defense) still provide the basis for much of American military policies.

With developments in nuclear technology (the ABM and MIRV), the value of Brodie's work has come to rest more heavily on its historical and theoretical aspects. The chapters on pre-nuclear strategy and the analysis of Douhet's theory of air power are still useful, and there is much of value in Brodie's discussion of credibility and intentions, intelligence, limited war, and the complexities and uncertainties of defense planning. It is still the best introduction to an understanding of the strategic problems of the nuclear age.

KAUFMANN, WILLIAM W., *ed.* **Military Policy and National Security.** Princeton: Princeton University Press, 1956, 274 p.

The four authors of this study, prepared under the auspices of the Princeton Center of International Studies, sought to link force and foreign policy at a time when nuclear duopoly was beginning to be significant and when the United States government seemed to be slow in adapting to new military conditions. (The other three writers were Gordon Craig, Roger Hilsman and Klaus Knorr, and all four were later to become associated with the federal government for a time either as consultants or as officials.) Believing that for an indefinitely long time the United States would need to guard against expansion by both the Soviet Union and Communist China, they examined the requirements for deterrence, discussed passive air defense and limited warfare, and evaluated the military potential of the United States (which looked relatively greater then than it did 15 years later). The continued usefulness of coalitions and alliances was accepted, with suggestions on how to make them even more effective, and the implications of the new German army for NATO were spelled out.

The general message was that the United States needed not just massive strategic air power (which as an all-purpose weapons system gave only limited freedom of action) but a large and diversified military establishment in a state of constant readiness, with mobility, adaptability and great power in all its members. This call was responded to by the Kennedy Administration later, and the policy of "flexible response" was a large part of its answer. In some other respects the book seems dated today, especially the authors' sanguine attitude toward both nuclear weapons and public acceptance of the sacrifices necessary to a huge military establishment. The lack of interest in questions of arms control in these essays is also striking.

SCHWARZ, URS. **American Strategy: A New Perspective.** Garden City: Doubleday, 1966, 178 p.

American strategic thinking after 1945 did not rise quite full-panoplied from the brow of Jove, but it must have looked that way to many Europeans. The Schwarz study, subtitled "The Growth of Politico-Military Thinking in the United States," was written for a European audience and very properly places the post–World War II strategic debate in its earlier twentieth-century American historical context.

This strategic debate was so long dominated by Americans and its terms set by decisions in prospect in American military policy that Schwarz's **American Strategy** was able to meet another important European need—to shorten the time lag between European and American discussions of strategy. If there are historical constants in American strategic thinking, there are also technological and world political variables so that bewilderingly rapid shifts occurred in the focus of the strategic debate.

That this book, first published in German, should also find a receptive audience in the United States is testimony to the virtue of viewing the American scene from afar in order to see it whole. Although based on a year's study in the United States and written at the Harvard Center of International Affairs, the objective viewpoint is sustained throughout. Schwarz made clear how the strategic debate has guided the United States along the path "from Zero to Leadership." In so doing, he contributed in an important way to the formation of what he calls an Atlantic community of thought.

SCHELLING, THOMAS CROMBIE. **The Strategy of Conflict.** Cambridge: Harvard University Press, 1960, 309 p.

Schelling's book does not deal with game theory, strictly speaking, but it develops ideas taken from game theory and carries them well beyond their original limits to important application in international relations. It has been the most influential single book in its area, and the discussion about his ideas still continues.

Schelling is the creator of the theory of threats. Every threat, he says, implies a tacit bargain. Carrying out the threat would be costly not only to the threatened party but also to the threatener himself. (If carrying out the threat against his adversary would cost him nothing, it would be in his interest not to threaten but to act.) Every threat, therefore, involves a mixed-motive situation. The threatener and the threatened party are adversaries because the threatened party seems intent on doing something which the threat is designed to forbid. Though in this respect their interests are opposed, however, the two parties also have a common interest: to prevent a threat from being carried out. It is not true, therefore, that what is good for one side in a deterrent situation must be bad for the other. There are courses of action, as Schelling shows, which are in the common interest of both. He then discusses the unresolved question as to which of the adversary interests ought to be sacrificed, and in what proportions the common benefits are to be shared.

Schelling applied his ideas to the topic of limited wars, both strategic and conventional, and to situations of arms control. His ideas are further described in his book **Arms and Influence.** They have been severely criticized, but they remain an indispensable contribution to the understanding of international politics in the age of deterrence.

Naval and Air Warfare

RICHMOND, SIR HERBERT WILLIAM. **Sea Power in the Modern World.** New York: Reynal, 1934, 323 p.

Most pre–World War II books on military subjects now seem to resemble quaint artifacts uncovered by some diligent archaeologist. Richmond's work, however, is quite a different matter. Although he remained a relatively obscure figure in the later American scholarly literature on military affairs, generally unrecognized even among professional officers of the post–World War II period, his own career in the Royal Navy was instructive of many lessons that later generations of officers had to learn, and his thoughts on warfare held up considerably better than the publications of more celebrated subsequent strategists.

Sea Power in the Modern World contained a number of ideas: for example, his opposition to the great emphasis on the strategy of fleet concentration that Mahan articulated and that was widely accepted in the British and American navies for half a century prior to World War II. Similarly, Richmond opposed the great emphasis on gigantic capital ships, an idea, incidentally, that began to receive increasingly favorable attention in the U.S. Navy in the early 1970s, although few American naval officers were aware of its origins. His heresies also included the conviction that ground, sea and aviation forces should be required to coöperate within combined command arrangements, and that civilian thinkers could often make more important contributions to military thought than professional military leaders. Later history did not vindicate every aspect of Richmond's thought and analyses, but his work still retained sufficiently significant validity and insight to be required reading for contemporary military and naval leaders.

SPROUT, HAROLD HANCE and SPROUT, MARGARET (TUTTLE). **Toward a New Order of Sea Power: American Naval Policy and the World Scene, 1918–1922.** Princeton: Princeton University Press, 2d ed., 1943, 336 p.

The "old order" of sea power implicit in the title was that of traditional British naval supremacy, which was analyzed and expounded as a politico-strategic doctrine by Admiral A. T. Mahan in the 1890s. The First World War underlined the continuing importance of sea power, but the employment of submarines and—to a lesser extent—aircraft raised profound questions about the primacy of capital ships. The danger of a renewed armaments race involving primarily the United States, Britain and Japan led to the Washington Conference of 1921–1922, which provides the core of this study.

The essential feature of the "new order" achieved by the Washington Treaties was the stabilization of political and naval relations by limitations on the strength —and indirectly on the use—of battle fleets. Although the size and armament of capital ships were limited, non-capital ships, aircraft and submarines were excluded from the agreement. A vital corollary was that there was to be no further development of insular naval bases and fortifications in the western Pacific. In effect the Treaties merely recognized and attempted to perpetuate the existing realities: the United States, for example, was assured of undisputed command of the sea approaches to North America and the Panama Canal, while Japan was confirmed in undisputed control of the western Pacific north of the equator. The moratorium on naval fortifications has sometimes been blamed for making possible the disaster at Pearl Harbor, but, as the authors point out, the attack was attempted only after considerable British and American naval strength had been diverted to the war against Germany.

Although the second edition of this elegant and lucid study of the interplay between sea power and diplomacy was published as long ago as 1943, it remains indispensable to students of the Washington Conference and of twentieth-century naval power generally.

BRODIE, BERNARD. **Sea Power in the Machine Age.** Princeton: Princeton University Press, 1941, 466 p.

The first book by Professor Brodie is an account of the influence of naval inventions on world politics from 1815 to 1941. It is also one of the last books of any consequence in which "seapower," including the naval air arm, is treated as if command of the seas in the classic sense was still a vital strategic objective and "airpower" is treated as a valuable but limited-purpose adjunct to sea power in the performance of its essential tasks.

Although the dynamic technology of air power, the lessons of World War II and the revolutionary advent of nuclear weapons have made Brodie's prescriptive conclusions obsolete, the book has enduring values. The careful account of successive technological advances—the steam warship; the iron-hulled warship; nickel-steel armor and the all big-gun battleship; the torpedo, the mine and the submarine; and naval aircraft and their strategic and political consequences—is a model for post–World War II students of science and technology as quasi-independent variables in the equations of world politics.

BRODIE, BERNARD. **A Guide to Naval Strategy.** Princeton: Princeton University Press, 3rd rev. ed., 1944, 313 p.

Brodie's **Guide,** originally written on the eve of American entry into World War II, reflected the ideas on strategy that were widely accepted in the U.S. Navy for at least half a century. Brodie himself described it as an "orthodox" treatment. The first edition therefore had a decidedly polemical tone, arguing for Mahan's doctrines—for example, in favor of fleet concentration—and against the claims of aviation enthusiasts both in and out of the Navy.

However, because the events of World War II rapidly demonstrated the limited relevance of the Mahan doctrines, Brodie's book was obsolete almost before it appeared in print. Brodie himself appeared to realize this because he noted in his preface to the 1944 edition that "the revolutionary events which have occurred since the last edition of this book was published have made necessary a further revision so thoroughgoing as to constitute almost a new book." Unfortunately, the revisions were not sufficiently thoroughgoing, and it remained essentially the same book. The main lesson of World War II from the naval point of view was that "sea power" is whatever capability that can be projected and sustained more advantageously by using seaborne vehicles than other devices, including attacks against land-based targets, in contrast to the simple and narrow Mahan vision of massed battleship actions to "command the sea" for the benefit of unfettered sea transport.

Unfortunately and ironically, by the late 1950s not even the Navy itself seemed to have recalled this lesson, because Brodie's book was reissued in generally unchanged revisions in 1958 and 1965.

MARTIN, L. W. **The Sea in Modern Strategy.** New York: Praeger, 1967, 190 p.

Although an avalanche of books on broad high-level military strategy appeared in the decades after World War II, the basic text on the naval dimensions of strategy continued to be Bernard Brodie's **Guide to Naval Strategy** dating from the outset of that war. L. W. Martin, an American-trained British scholar writing under the auspices of London's Institute for Strategic Studies, set out to correct this neglected gap in the literature, and endeavored to suggest how and why most of the influential ideas concerning naval forces during the first two-thirds of the twentieth century were probably of not much relevance for the remaining third. Martin tacitly rejected the categories of analysis used in much of the earlier writing—such as particular national threats, envisaged geographic theaters, ship types and other weapons systems—in favor of the terms of reference generally relating to kinds and levels of warfare that were in vogue in the strategy literature of the mid-1960s. Accordingly, his main substantive chapters dealt with the potentialities of naval forces in "general war," "limited war" and the like.

Martin was certainly correct that the lapse of almost 30 years since Brodie's work had generated a need for a new general commentary on naval strategy, and in some respects his relatively brief and readable book fulfilled the need.

MORGENSTERN, OSKAR. **The Question of National Defense.** New York: Random House, 1959, 306 p.

Morgenstern, a professor of economics at Princeton, was one of the "fathers" of game theory, helping to introduce this branch of mathematics into the array of social science research approaches to the study of conflict. **The Question of National Defense** was his only major foray into the popular unclassified literature on military strategy. Although Morgenstern wrote in an amiable, rambling style, he clearly intended the book as a serious discussion of many of the perplexing issues and dilemmas involved in adopting various strategies and weapons systems—issues and dilemmas such as nuclear stalemate or nuclear parity, the probabilities of long or short wars, whether and how wars could be limited and how limited wars could be settled by negotiation. The book also discussed some major economic and technological considerations, problems of intelligence-gathering and problems of communications between enemies. It will undoubtedly be best remembered, however, for its discussion of the various techniques for reducing the vulnerability of U.S. strategic nuclear retaliatory forces. Morgenstern believed that mobility and concealment were the two best and cheapest ways to gain this relative invulnerability for nuclear retaliatory forces, and that Polaris-type submarines were therefore the best solution. Furthermore, he also argued that the U.S. should use the seas as the main base for other kinds of military capability. The "Oceanic System" was his name for this overall strategic conceptualization.

Morgenstern's book (and most others of the same period) failed to analyze how the world might look in terms of other factors if nuclear deterrence could be made more reliable. On this point he was himself excessively sanguine.

MITCHELL, WILLIAM. **Winged Defense.** New York: Putnam, 1925, 261 p.

The dashing son of a U.S. Senator, "Billy" Mitchell served with distinction as a young army officer in many significant assignments from the Spanish-American War through World War I. While returning from Europe on board a troopship in 1919, he revealed his plans to lead a fight for a separate new federal air service embracing not only military aviation but also commercial aviation and all other conceivable applications of the airplane. Although he sought to make this idea more politically attractive by embodying it within a proposal for a new "Department of National Defense with sub-heads for the Air, Army and Navy," it was clear that he saw the separate new air force as dominant within any such tripartite arrangement because his version of military aviation reduced armies and navies to strictly secondary roles in all future wars. Mitchell was court-martialed for pursuing these goals somewhat too enthusiastically against the opposition of senior officers who did not fully share his vision of the airplane's future, but most of what he campaigned for was ultimately adopted.

Several wars later, some might wonder whether it was a good idea for the U.S. government to have accepted so many of his proposals.

DOUHET, GIULIO. **The Command of the Air.** New York: Coward-McCann, 1942, 394 p.

If General William Mitchell after World War I was the foremost American advocate of "air power" as the new all-purpose military weapons system, the Italian air general Giulio Douhet was certainly the foremost European strategic theorist in the same crusade. His book first appeared in 1921, and he added refinements in later editions and papers. The translated edition of his several collected writings was published in 1942.

The structure of all military forces prior to the invention of the airplane in the 1890s was based on one simple principle: if a military force fought on the land side of a coastline, it was called an army and was organized according to ancient traditional procedures; if it fought on the sea side of the coastline, it was called a navy and was organized according to another set of traditional procedures. But the invention of the airplane erased the longstanding use of the coastline as the basic organizing principle of armed forces. Douhet and his book are historically important because he was one of the most articulate spokesmen for one extreme and popular solution put forward in the effort to accommodate the airplane in military strategy. Of course, Douhet could hardly have been expected to foresee how even more advanced technology half a century after his earliest writings would alter the context and generally reduce sharply the significance of military aviation both offensively and defensively.

Atomic and Nuclear Warfare

SMYTH, HENRY DE WOLF. **Atomic Energy for Military Purposes.** Princeton: Princeton University Press, 1945, 264 p.

Given the extraordinary secrecy of the A-bomb project, even for wartime, the most interesting thing about this official report on the development of the atomic bomb is that it was published so soon after the project's successful end. Written at the request of Major-General Groves by a Princeton physicist and consultant to the project, the report gives a general account of the administrative history of the project since 1939 and the basic scientific knowledge on which it was based, subject to certain secrecy requirements still affecting the detailed content. The report's interest is now historical, not least in its reminder that: "Since there was always the chance that German scientists might be developing A-bombs sufficiently effective to alter the course of the war, there was, therefore, no choice but to work on them in this country."

The report is semitechnical, written for scientists and engineers who could understand the technical aspects of the bomb and could be expected to help educate their fellow citizens, on whom "the ultimate responsibility for our nation's policy rests." Because of the needs of military secrecy, it pointed out, there had been no chance for public debate on the many questions relating to future wars and international affairs raised by this "new tool" of "unimaginable destructive power." Those questions, it recognized, were not technical but political and social. The report did not attempt to indicate the nature of those political implications and questions.

The original text was completed in June 1945, just before the successful first test; the printed version also includes the War Department release on the test of July 10 in New Mexico—the one dramatic note in the volume.

BRODIE, BERNARD, *ed*. **The Absolute Weapon: Atomic Power and World Order.** New York: Harcourt, 1946, 214 p.

In the second year of the atomic era the collaboration of five political scientists at the Yale Institute of International Studies—Bernard Brodie, Frederick S. Dunn, Percy E. Corbett, William T. R. Fox and Arnold Wolfers—produced one of the first important analyses of the impact of atomic weapons on international relations. The insights into nuclear world politics contained in their essays on military implications, Soviet-American relations and arms control are especially noteworthy in view of the "impenetrable blank of the future" that faced all observers a quarter-century ago.

Several authors stressed that the American nuclear monopoly would be short-lived (unlike one prominent military figure who viewed the bomb as a "problem for our grandchildren"). In a bipolar world, peace and security would depend not on "permanent solutions" that risk atomic war to force world government, but on the capacities of the United States and Russia for atomic retaliation ("determent") and on controlling the levels of atomic weapons. A "policy of determent" by the United States, which would rely on forces in being, would not impute aggressive motives to the U.S.S.R.; indeed, the hope was expressed that friendly relations with the Soviets would be possible.

The absence of any cold-war ideological dimension in a book which accurately sketched some of the chief characteristics of world politics in the post-1946 decades—*e.g.* bipolarity, nuclear deterrence, arms control but not disarmament—suggests that the basic structure of the international system might not have been very different in the past 25 years had the "free world" versus "communist" division never occurred.

KISSINGER, HENRY ALFRED. **Nuclear Weapons and Foreign Policy.** New York: Harper (for the Council on Foreign Relations), 1957, 455 p.

Long before he became President Nixon's chief adviser on security affairs, Professor Kissinger had made a name for himself by his studies on the subject, including this attempt to assess the nuclear revolution in military technology which he made in the context of the Eisenhower-Bulganin-Khrushchev period of world politics. In this earliest of his strategic monographs he examined the impact of the nuclear revolution on traditional ideas of surprise attack, deterrence, all-out war and broad questions of coalition policy. He believed that for the first time in military history there was a prospect of stalemate, at least in the assessment of the risks of going to war, once the Soviet Union had also acquired nuclear weapons. Kissinger argued that the changed nature of deterrence pointed up the importance of determining intermediate objectives and of indicating to the Soviet Union the determination of the United States to achieve these if necessary by resisting Russian military moves with force. He sought to show the opportunities offered by forms of conflict short of all-out war. A chief task for the United States in NATO was to overcome the trauma attached to the use of "tactical nuclear weapons" and to quickly decentralize their possession; if the European allies had them this would help to dispel the air of mystery about nuclear weapons. Some of his ideas became United States government policy. However, by the 1970s others were calling for a radical reëvaluation of tactical nuclear weapons in the opposite direction, in view of further changes in technology and in public attitudes.

OSGOOD, ROBERT ENDICOTT. **Limited War: The Challenge to American Strategy.** Chicago: University of Chicago Press, 1957, 315 p.

Osgood's book was one of several responses made by scholar-strategists in the 1950s, mainly in reaction to the Korean War and the Soviet acquisition of nuclear weapons. He argued that deterrence capabilities probably would and certainly should be strengthened to work reliably at the level of major nuclear war, but that this increased the likelihood of smaller-scale localized wars. He believed that the United States greatly needed to increase its conventional capabilities to "contain Communist expansion" in the "gray areas" (*i.e.* everywhere but NATO-Europe) around the world. But he felt that longstanding American attitudes concerning international politics and the use of military force would make it very difficult for U.S. leaders to "utilize military power as a rational and effective instrument of policy." His chapter on the "American approach to war" summarized his analysis of these traditional attitudes, in terms similar to the more detailed presentation in George F. Kennan's **American Diplomacy 1900–1950;** and his chapters on "the decline of limited war" and "the advent of total war" in recent centuries were shorter versions of a historical interpretation more fully developed, for example, in Walter Millis's **Arms and Men** and Theodore Ropp's **War in the Modern World.**

Osgood's book seems an effort to figure out how the United States with its allegedly typical patterns of response could actually cope with what he saw as a persistently threatening communist menace but without blowing up the world. His answer was better American leadership to explain to the people why the nation could and should be ready and able to fight a number of limited wars around the world as an extension of the containment concept.

SNYDER, GLENN HERALD. **Deterrence and Defense: Toward a Theory of National Security.** Princeton: Princeton University Press, 1961, 294 p.

One of the first theoretical works on problems of military choice after the emergence of nuclear weapons, this book became quickly known for the systematic distinction it drew between deterrence and defense. By threatening an opponent with punishment, deterrence works on an opponent's intentions; it is coercive. Defense reduces the opponent's ability to effect damage and deprivation. Its main component is denial capacity—that is, the capacity to defend territory by sheer force. Defense may come into play when deterrence has failed, but is no substitute for it. Snyder also demonstrated how deterrence and defense require different types of military forces which can be combined in various ways depending on the nature of desired military choices. The book contains a theoretically interesting part which develops a mathematical model for relating the values of deterrence and defense, and the costs of relevant capabilities.

The conceptual framework developed by the author is applied in an analysis of the military security problems of Western Europe. There is also an interesting exploration of the relationships between the old balance of power and the balance of terror.

BLACKETT, PATRICK MAYNARD STUART. **Studies of War: Nuclear and Conventional.** New York: Hill and Wang, 1962, 242 p.

P. M. S. Blackett is a British physicist and operations researcher who has been a persistent gadfly on conventional Western strategic wisdom since the dawn of the nuclear age. This volume is a collection of his articles published between 1948 and 1962, most of them on policy matters, a few on technical problems of operations research. The policy essays attack successively such dogmas and theories as the early postwar belief in the quick decisiveness of atomic bombing in a war with Russia (1948), the massive retaliation policy (1954), Henry Kissinger's limited nuclear war thesis (1958) and Albert Wohlstetter's "delicate balance of terror" (1961), and conclude with a plea (1962) for a "drastic first step" toward disarmament by eliminating counterforce capabilities and accepting a posture of mutual "minimum deterrence."

While some of Blackett's views have been overtaken by technology and others have been absorbed into the conventional wisdom, some are still finding expression by the "left" opposition in 1970 debates. His emotional kinship with the contemporary left is evident, producing occasional distortions and errors, but his sophistication tends to highlight what is most valid in the left position. The incisive critique of Wohlstetter's 1959 warning about strategic instability could be directed, with considerable force, to current fears about a potential Soviet first-strike capability. Blackett's most telling thrust against Wohlstetter is that the presumed instability is based on an assumption of "moral asymmetry": that the Soviets will do their worst whenever their capabilities permit it, but that they know we will never strike first because of moral inhibitions, and will therefore not feel threatened by our measures to correct the "instability." Such an assumption that the opponent shares our self-image, Blackett suggests prophetically, "leads to an endless and increasing arms race." This position does not mesh easily with Blackett's repeated warnings against technological complacency, but it does point to a profound issue which has not yet been properly studied.

KAHN, HERMAN. **On Thermonuclear War.** Princeton: Princeton University Press, 1960, 651 p.

Partly because of some idiosyncrasies of style, but mainly because of the author's cool analytical posture in dealing with a terrible reality, the publication of **On Thermonuclear War** aroused a great deal of negative as well as positive response. Indeed, it presented the first comprehensive treatment of the subject in terms of relentless analysis. Today it is regarded as a classic in its field and remains valuable even though much of the context of nuclear deterrence has changed since the book was written.

Herman Kahn was an operations analyst and the use of quantitative data, whenever available, made his work one of systems analysis. Profiting from a great deal of research carried on at the RAND Corporation by himself and others, the book is highly original. Its broad subject is the impact of thermonuclear armaments on international conflict and human society. It deals with the nature and feasibility of nuclear war, including the characteristics that make such war different from war in the past, and the formulations of relevant military objectives and plans. Among the many interesting distinctions is that between Type I Deterrence (the deterrence of direct attack) and Type II Deterrence (the deterrence of other aggressive acts by an opponent), and that between the different strategic forces required by these two postures (second-strike versus first-strike capabilities). There are also interesting thoughts on various types of nuclear war, especially "spasmodic" and "controlled" retaliation.

KAHN, HERMAN. **Thinking about the Unthinkable.** New York: Horizon Press, 1962, 254 p.

The title of this book refers to the interesting fact that the author was sharply criticized, upon publication of **On Thermonuclear War,** for applying analytical thought to the awesome subject of nuclear war. This sequel is a collection of essays in which Kahn deepens the examination of many problems explored in his previous work. In the opening chapter, he demonstrates that only by hard thinking about nuclear war will it be possible to avoid it. Other chapters involve analyses of the rapidly changing character of nuclear technology, of different types of nuclear war, of different nuclear strategies and of civil defense. Of particular interest is the extensive use of the scenario as a technique of explaining sequentially how different conflicts and their results might come about. Chapter 6 contains provocative thoughts on crisis bargaining between nuclear powers. A final chapter identifies 14 alternative national policies open to nuclear superpowers—ranging from renunciation to preventive war.

KNORR, KLAUS EUGEN. **On the Uses of Military Power in the Nuclear Age.** Princeton: Princeton University Press, 1966, 185 p.

This is a thoughtful and well-informed essay by a distinguished scholar whose research has focused on the uses and limitations of various forms of military power within different configurations of the evolving international system. In this book Knorr modestly did not attempt to introduce or advocate any startling new ideas. However, what the book did achieve—and it is no small accomplishment—was to discuss the main dimensions of the problem in a calm, coherent and carefully reasoned manner. The basic problem, of course, is that the traditional international system continues to persist, and continues to encourage each nation to rely largely on traditional military means (including traditional diplomacy and alliances) to guarantee its security, but at a time when a wide variety of new factors are undermining the viability of this old system and thus producing less rather than more of a sense of security. Knorr proposed no easy or obvious solutions, but his book can be recommended to all interested in reading an excellent introductory analysis of the problem in most of its complex dimensions.

ARON, RAYMOND. **The Great Debate: Theories of Nuclear Strategy.** Garden City: Doubleday, 1965, 265 p.

Originally written for a European audience, this book presents a judicious synopsis of American modes and lines of analysis of nuclear deterrence and related subjects. In part because it pretends to no originality on these matters, the presentation is comprehensive, well ordered and lucid. As a result, a major part of this book is an admirable short introduction to a complex subject. In addition, Professor Aron not only explains American thinking to Europeans but also makes West European criticisms of United States policies, and particularly of the McNamara doctrine, intelligible to Americans. In this connection, the author examines the genesis and problems of an independent French nuclear force and offers a number of sharp observations on how the advent of nuclear arms affects the character of military alliances. Thus, he points to the strong desire of the big ally to control the behavior of smaller allies that may be in a position to precipitate extremely dangerous conflicts. Another notable conclusion suggests that nuclear opponents, who have every interest in avoiding nuclear war between themselves, should find even local hostilities an unacceptable risk.

QUESTER, GEORGE H. **Deterrence Before Hiroshima: The Airpower Background of Modern Strategy.** New York: Wiley, 1966, 196 p.

It is widely believed in 1970 that "strategic theory," with its awesome (or awful) battery of concepts such as deterrence, counterforce, countervalue, preëmption, stability and "balance of terror," is an intellectual product of the most recent decade or so of the nuclear era and relevant only to international politics since 1945. George Quester's fine book usefully corrects this error by demonstrating that most of these ideas were not only conceived in crude but essential form but also put into practice in air doctrine and strategy during and between World Wars I and II. The theory, in other words, dates from the introduction of aircraft, not nuclear weapons.

The book chiefly analyzes the bargaining aspects of strategic bombing in the two world wars. In both wars, statesmen and planners confronted the classical bargaining dilemma between preserving mutual restraints and coercing the opponent by the threat or infliction of punishment: concretely, the choice between counterforce and countervalue targeting. Initially, there was a mutual desire for restraints, but the restraints gradually collapsed and counterforce progressed to city-busting, not because of theoretical naïveté, but because of overoptimism concerning the discriminating capabilities of air bombing and miscalculation of the opponent's responses, and because of psychological factors which produced relative indifference to further damage after the shock of the first attack. This finding is significant for us today, for it suggests that theoretical sophistication is not enough to preserve restraints and points to a need for study of the psychological or nonlogical aspects of strategic interaction, research which had barely begun by 1970.

HEILBRUNN, OTTO. **Conventional Warfare in the Nuclear Age.** New York: Praeger, 1965, 164 p.

American, European and Soviet military planners generally agreed during most of the 1950s that any war in Western Europe would almost immediately become a general nuclear conflict. In the early 1960s, however, NATO planners gradually reversed their thinking and began to argue that NATO should be capable of deterring a conventional attack by a conventional defense or—if need be—meeting a conventional attack successfully without resort to nuclear weapons, although always remaining prepared for the introduction of nuclear weapons by the enemy. Heilbrunn's book was an effort to think through the implications of this problem in terms of NATO battlefield tactics, and contained his recommendations for a new NATO posture to meet any Soviet or Warsaw Pact conventional attack in Western Europe. He agreed that NATO needed a conventional force capability sufficient to avoid any automatic and immediate resort to nuclear weapons, but he concluded this would require new tactical doctrine for force deployment, rapid force mobility and operations in the enemy's rear within what he called the "concept of concentric dispersion."

It is probably fair to say that his recommendations were not precisely followed, but for reasons having little to do with the validity or invalidity of his case, given his assumptions. The world simply evolved somewhat differently than his assumptions anticipated.

GALLOIS, PIERRE. **The Balance of Terror: Strategy for the Nuclear Age.** Boston: Houghton, 1961, 234 p.

A French air force general presents in extreme form the familiar view that if thermonuclear weapons were used in war the degree of devastation would vitiate the very purpose of the conflict, but that none the less a policy of "dissuasion based on nuclear strength" is feasible and even desirable. He reasons that given certain precautions, ABMs make aggression "virtually impracticable," so it is better to prepare for "atomic war that cannot occur" than to accumulate weapons for a conflict that is possible precisely because waged by conventional means.

In his opinion, the United States failed to realize the diplomatic advantage of its original atomic monopoly ("to oblige the Communist menace to withdraw"); the West must therefore now maintain means of nuclear reprisal adequate to dissuade aggression. He would have the policy of reprisal reinforced by "a certain automatic quality," to overcome the "paralyzing influence of Western public opinion and its press." He believes that the American Secretary of State John Foster Dulles best understood the diplomatic requirements of the nuclear age, with his policy of "brinksmanship." Gallois follows his logic to the end, arguing that the study and conduct of public affairs in such circumstances are increasingly the task of the technician rather than of the politician or statesman: "It is therefore natural that the political context of world affairs be minimized and that the technocracy take over." Although maintaining that "the new weapons impose an equilibrium much more stable than yesterday's," Gallois notes that "tomorrow a new technological revolution could change everything."

SLESSOR, SIR JOHN COTESWORTH. **The Great Deterrent.** New York: Praeger, 1958, 321 p.

As Chief of the Air Staff in Britain Sir John Slessor presided over the Royal Air Force during a critical phase in the emergence of Britain's first strategic nuclear force. Moreover, during his tenure of that office, the effort by the British Chiefs of Staff to find a more economical way to wage the cold war than the massive conventional rearmament undertaken in the early months of the Korean War led them to lay heavy stress on nuclear deterrence. Their efforts apparently had some influence in encouraging the later evolution of the Eisenhower doctrine of massive retaliation.

The collection of articles that make up this volume, ranging in time from 1933 to 1957, offer an interesting study in the development of the concept of deterrence in the mind of a practical and unusually articulate airman. The book derives added interest from being coeval with the British defense policy announced by Duncan Sandys in 1957. That policy, with its heavy emphasis on nuclear war, forms the subject of Slessor's last chapter.

Whatever the influence of Slessor and his colleagues on the doctrine of massive retaliation, his book shows clearly that he did not regard strategic deterrence as a panacea. While he saw the bomber as, in the words of his title, "the great deterrent" that held out the best hope of keeping the cold war cold, he sharply repudiated the idea that this weapon was credible for any but the most major of issues. Thus, though air power had first call on Western resources, it was also necessary to deal with "the tactics of the termite, subversion, infiltration and the exploitation of factors like immature nationalism."

Political and Economic Warfare; Intelligence

*See also Communication: Propaganda; Public Opinion, p. 113;
East-West Relations: Cold War; Coexistence, p. 341.*

BARRETT, EDWARD WARE. **Truth Is Our Weapon.** New York: Funk, 1953, 355 p.

Edward Barrett believed that the main job of Americans in the second half of the twentieth century ought to be "waging the peace for a long period, intelligently and resolutely." He believed in a balanced peace offensive which gives recognition to the psychological as well as to the military, diplomatic and economic components. Writing in 1952, he hoped that his hindsight could "strengthen the foresight of others." Anyone interested in the early development of the U.S. approach to international information and persuasion will be well served to read carefully the final third of his book, a summary of practices, problems and prospects for an American psychological offensive. Barrett served for a decade, from Pearl Harbor through the Truman years, in various "sykewar" posts culminating in a two-year assignment as Assistant Secretary of State in charge of all international information and education exchange activities.

Truth Is Our Weapon is an accurate title for a partly autobiographical, largely anecdotal, but historically and analytically useful discussion of formal American governmental attempts at international persuasion. Although many of the examples are time-bound there is continuing value in the arguments which support Barrett's conclusion that "the real voice of America is the total impact abroad of our attitudes, our conduct, our press, our political figures, our business representatives, and our prominent private citizens."

CARROLL, WALLACE. **Persuade or Perish.** Boston: Houghton, 1948, 392 p.

This chronicle is the most complete and detailed history of American psychological warfare in the European theater during World War II. Carroll was in the

London office of OWI from the summer of 1942 until early 1944 and then returned to Washington as Deputy Director of the Overseas Branch for Europe. He writes an intimate account which not only covers the entire range of psychological warfare problems but is exciting reading as a battlefield history of the North African, Italian, French and German campaigns.

Convinced of the inseparability of military and psychological components in modern warfare, Carroll was distressed at the "fallacious concept of a military war" which often led to the "sacrifice of long-term political interests." While he describes many notable successes, particularly in working with General Eisenhower, he viewed the wartime development of propaganda skills as only a specialized military-related advance in a field where Americans "failed completely to develop the arts of persuasion as an instrument of foreign policy." He was dedicated to a "strategy of persuasion" which would "prolong the peace" even if, at times, it might mean prolonging a war. **Persuade or Perish** is a hopeful book which concludes that although much must be done before we learn to combine our policies, actions and words into a successful effort of persuasion, the opportunity is clear, and that "only America can defeat America, that only we ourselves can turn away the ready hands and eager hearts which will help us build the House of Peace."

DYER, MURRAY. **The Weapon on the Wall.** Baltimore: Johns Hopkins Press, 1959, 269 p.

Murray Dyer was one of several officers in World War II psychological warfare programs who later recorded their experiences at book length to encourage some basic reforms in the United States approach to informational activities. He was bitterly critical of the U.S. efforts ("predominant features are contradiction, conflict and wrangling") and argued repeatedly that the Russians were far ahead in every aspect except recognition of the persuasive value of truth. He is sure that we are innately superior to all potential enemies but that we undersell ourselves because "the weapon is on the wall when it should be in our hands."

Dyer's prescriptions for improvement are developed around a concept of "political communication" (rather than "psychological warfare") which he would promote to equal status with diplomatic, military and economic activities of the government. A "militant interpretation" of U.S. policies would be coördinated at the White House level, assisted by a Joint Congressional Committee and served by a National Information College for the study of the art of political communication.

For the most part the book is quite basic and often repetitive. It adds little to the work of Edward Barrett, **Truth Is Our Weapon,** on which it relies heavily, and its historical sections are very sketchy when compared to Wallace Carroll's **Persuade or Perish.**

PIGOU, ARTHUR CECIL. **The Political Economy of War.** New York: Macmillan, 1941, 169 p.

This short, admirably lucid book by a famous professor of economics at Cambridge is the revision of one published in 1921. It is an excellent introduction to the economics of the kind of conflict which the two world wars represented—prolonged wars of attrition between industrial powers. Since such wars are extremely unlikely in the nuclear age, the significance of this study is now limited to historical interest and to an understanding of protracted conventional wars between non-nuclear powers or between a great and a lesser power.

The book briefly discusses the economic war potential of states and then concerns itself mainly with the economic aspects of mobilizing such potential. A great deal of attention is paid to the finance of war by means of taxes, loans and inflation, and also rationing of producers and consumers. There is a chapter on the "Economic Causes of War" which is extraordinarily frank in analyzing the interest of business groups in empire and the disposition of governments to promote these interests. Pigou points out, however, that business profits derived from imperialist practices are of dubious net value to the nation, and that war itself can be a paying proposition only under improbable circumstances.

HITCH, CHARLES JOHNSTON and MCKEAN, ROLAND NEELY. **The Economics of Defense in the Nuclear Age.** Cambridge: Harvard University Press, 1960, 422 p.

This book by two distinguished former members of the RAND Corporation is a nonmathematical exercise in systems analysis or "operations research." Although it is concerned with a number of interesting substantive problems, the purpose is to teach a way of thinking about military problems. The chosen mode of thought is the economist's, which proves remarkably fruitful since all military problems essentially involve the efficient allocation and use of scarce resources. Part I analyzes the problem of resource limitation and presents a brief survey of the economic strength of the military powers. The second is a very original analysis of the efficiency problem in employing resources allocated to defense. Several of the techniques discussed here were subsequently introduced into the decision making of the Department of Defense when the author was appointed to a high executive position there. The third part deals, always interestingly, with such special problems as the management of military research and development, the economics of a military alliance (a contribution by Malcolm W. Hoag), economic warfare, mobilization and civil defense. At the end the choice of deterrence policies is explored in a succinct contribution by Albert Wohlstetter.

DULLES, ALLEN. **The Craft of Intelligence.** New York: Harper and Row, 1963, 277 p.

At his death in 1969, Allen W. Dulles had had more direct, practical experience in intelligence work than any other American. As a member of the diplomatic service in World War I, his job was to gather intelligence from the United States listening post in Switzerland. In World War II, he was chief of the OSS mission there. And beginning in 1950, he served 11 years with the CIA, almost nine of them as director.

The Craft of Intelligence is a description of the methods and techniques of modern intelligence, concentrating on the secret intelligence services of the United States and the Soviet Union—spiced with anecdotes, both personal and drawn from cases which have one way or another become public. Although the book reveals no new secrets, the result is interesting and informative.

The importance of the book, however, is the fact that it contains the personal, semiofficial testimony of a long-time director of the CIA on the issue of maintaining a secret service in a free society and on the rationale justifying a secret service engaged both in clandestine intelligence collection and in covert political action.

WEST, REBECCA. **The New Meaning of Treason.** New York: Viking, 1964, 374 p.

Detailed case studies of disloyalty in England are presented in support of Rebecca West's conclusions: that treason is costing taxpayers a lot of money; that it cannot be eliminated unilaterally; and that it has fallen from an act of idealism based on deep beliefs to the dishonorable profession of spying for profit. The fascist William Joyce (Lord Haw Haw) receives a kindlier treatment than that accorded the parade of communist traitors who carry the story up to the early 1960s. Probably most historians and political scientists would not share the author's conviction that Russian development of the H-bomb was made possible by a single traitorous act, or her conclusion that a United Nations victory in the Korean War was rendered impossible by a single spy's successes.

The literary style of the novelist makes the book highly readable. It lacks, however, the legal, political and psychological analysis which is so impressive in Andrew Scott's essay on treason, **The Revolution in Statecraft.** The author's right-of-center political sympathies and her biases against scientists (she believes that they are prone to disloyalty because they disapprove of capitalism) weaken her case. Much of the supporting material is admittedly conjecture (*e.g.* "there is no evidence of this but it could have happened").

Guerrilla Warfare

MAO, TSE-TUNG. **Basic Tactics.** New York: Praeger, 1966, 149 p.

"Wars of national liberation" have been advocated by both Moscow and Peking, but the major effort in developing the doctrine of "revolutionary warfare"—the blending of guerrilla tactics with political action—has been Chinese. And the principal theoretician has been Mao Tse-tung. Mao's ideas were developed over many years as he reflected on concrete experiences—his observation of the peasant uprising in Hunan in 1927, his attempt to develop a guerrilla base area in the Chingkang mountains and Kiangsi, and the struggle against the Japanese. In all, Mao wrote five major works on guerrilla warfare. Two came out of the early struggle with the Kuomintang; the other three, of which **Basic Tactics** is one, were all produced in 1938, in the midst of the war against Japan. Originally a series of lectures to men who were being trained as guerrilla leaders, the book deals with practical problems of guerrilla tactics and organization in very simple language. Devoid of any reference to the larger political and ideological questions contained in "On Protracted War" in volume II of **Selected Works, Basic Tactics** is a handbook for the men in the field. It is the last of Mao's known works on guerrilla warfare to be translated (this translation was made from a handwritten copy of the only known copy, which is in the Ministry of Justice Library near Taipei), and it is a valuable supplement to Mao's other works.

CHE GUEVARA. **Guerrilla Warfare.** New York: Monthly Review Press, 1961, 127 p.

A handbook on guerrilla warfare—strategy, tactics, organization, supply, training, intelligence and improvisation of weapons—by one of Fidel Castro's chief guerrilla leaders. The theoretical base of the book's treatment of guerrilla warfare follows the concepts of Mao Tse-tung, offering nothing new either in strategic concepts or ideology. The portions intended as a practical guide to tactics and techniques are standard, enlivened by illustrations drawn from the Cuban revolt against Batista. In part the book is an appeal and encouragement to other Latin American revolutionaries to follow the Cuban example, and it is principally because of this fact that the book is significant.

VO NGUYEN GIAP. **People's War, People's Army: The Viet Cong Insurrection Manual for Underdeveloped Countries.** New York: Praeger, 1962, 217 p.

General Vo Nguyen Giap, long-time Minister of Defense of North Vietnam, joined a nationalist revolutionary group while still a student. Later, after finishing his studies and embarking on a career as a history teacher, he joined the Communist Party. In 1941, he met Ho Chi Minh, who gave him the task of organizing a communist military force. He not only succeeded in this but in the process became a competent general—the architect of victory over the French at Dien Bien Phu and the commanding strategist in the struggle against South Vietnam and the United States that began in 1958–1959.

Giap's book, **People's War, People's Army,** is not an organized monograph with a central theme but a collection of speeches and essays prepared at different times for different purposes. Some are simply rhetorical exhortations, suitable for patriotic occasions. Others, however, are analyses of past battles and campaigns, presenting the rationale for the strategy adopted and giving Giap's explanation of the reasons for success or failure. Giap is not an original thinker or theorist of revolutionary and guerrilla warfare but a practicing revolutionary politician, military organizer and commander in chief. Thus his book is significant not so much for his own ideas as it is for his interpretation and application to concrete situations of the ideas of other men, notably Mao Tse-tung, whose theories have guided him.

THOMPSON, SIR ROBERT. **Defeating Communist Insurgency: The Lessons of Malaya and Vietnam.** New York: Praeger, 1966, 171 p.

R. K. G. Thompson was Deputy Secretary and Secretary for Defense in Malaya during the communist insurgency there. From 1961 to 1965, he was head of the

British Advisory Mission to South Vietnam, where he conceived the so-called "strategic hamlet" program, only to see it abandoned without ever being implemented. Subsequently, he attracted international attention as an occasional and unofficial adviser to Presidents Johnson and Nixon.

Thompson's book is flawed by a somewhat rigid and doctrinaire view of modern Asian communism and by an oversimplified analysis of the nature of the struggle in Vietnam. At the same time, it is based on a clear understanding of communist guerrilla strategy, and among the many writings on guerrilla warfare it is perhaps the closest yet to a theoretical doctrine of counterinsurgency.

Thompson's counterstrategy, like Mao's strategy, puts the political central. Thompson feels that military measures are essential, but that they are complementary to a political program and subordinate to it. Combining political appeals, such as national independence, with administrative efficiency, legal justice, various devices for maintaining law and order, and the shrewd use of such measures as land reform and pensions for workers in plantations and mines to obtain popular support, Thompson's program attempts to ensure that the guerrilla has no "sea of the people," to use Mao's phrase, in which to swim.

At the very least, **Defeating Communist Insurgency** is a handbook for an administrator forced to deal with an insurgency in an underdeveloped country, containing eminently sensible, even wise, advice on almost all the practical issues and problems—from rural administration to police operations, intelligence, and how to prevent military operations from being politically self-defeating.

PARET, PETER and SHY, JOHN W. **Guerrillas in the 1960's.** New York: Praeger (for the Princeton Center of International Studies), 1962, 82 p.

A very small book, Paret's and Shy's **Guerrillas in the 1960's** is nevertheless an important contribution to the literature on guerrilla warfare, representing one of the first scholarly attempts to put such warfare into a modern political and social setting. By and large accepting the doctrines of Mao Tse-tung as sound for the guerrilla, the book attempts to assess the potential of guerrilla warfare and to elucidate a doctrine for the counter-guerrilla. The authors argue not only that such warfare is far from being the invincible force it is sometimes claimed to be, but essentially that it is the tactic of the weak. Even so, defeating an insurgency is "neither simple to plan nor easy, cheap, and quick to carry out." The essence of a successful counter-guerrilla strategy is political rather than military—to isolate the guerrilla from the people and ultimately to persuade the people to defend themselves.

CAUSES OF WAR

See also Theory of International Relations; Methodology, p. 3.

WRIGHT, QUINCY. **A Study of War.** Chicago: University of Chicago Press, 2d rev. ed., 1965, 1,637 p.

Together with Lewis F. Richardson, Quincy Wright stands foremost among the founding fathers of modern peace research. Where Richardson relied on mathematics and statistics, Wright used history, law, political science and all the other social sciences for his monumental study of war. The one-volume equivalent of a library, Wright's book is the most informative single work on the role of war and on the role of international relations in giving rise to wars. Wright's approach is empirical rather than deductive. He looks for the interplay of many conditions rather than for a sweeping single cause. He emphasizes relationships such as that between technological change and social and psychological adjustment. Despite his large historical and humanistic knowledge, Wright's approach is that of a scientist. He insists on evidence and on verifiable cumulative knowledge. Like a good scientist he does not pretend to know more than he does or to be more certain than he is, but he sees himself as part of a search for knowledge and action that will never stop. His commitment to the scientific approach to international relations has been spelled out in greater detail in his later book, **The Study of International Relations.** But his study of war remains his outstanding achievement. For the understanding of a major part of international relations it remains indispensable.

DICKINSON, GOLDSWORTHY LOWES. **War: Its Nature, Causes and Cure.** New York: Macmillan, 1923, 155 p.

An impassioned plea for a wholehearted renunciation of war as the first step toward security. In curiously contemporary terms, Dickinson argued that, because of scientific developments, "If mankind does not end war, war will end mankind." War came from the policy of states "to keep what they have and to take more" and from the armaments produced by this situation. "The anticipation of war prompts policies that cause war" when suitable conditions arise.

International wars in turn engender civil wars by forcibly incorporating conquered peoples in the victor state. But this seldom results in "real acquiescence" by the conquered (*viz.* Ireland, Poland, Czechoslovakia). The same striving for freedom was beginning in India and Egypt; and with unusual prescience Dickinson foresaw "another proof," perhaps before long, by the "black races of Africa."

Versailles, in his view, was the predatory peace of the secret treaties, modified by Russian defection and camouflaged by the Covenant of the League of Nations. It perpetuated "fear, hatred and rage in Europe," which would lead to a new war and the destruction of mankind. Salvation could only come through a League with power to determine all issues between its members.

Although Dickinson prophesied Armageddon one war too soon, his fundamental perceptions are still relevant.

ANGELL, SIR NORMAN. **The Great Illusion, 1933.** New York: Putnam, 1933, 308 p.

This book, first published in 1910, was republished many times with additional comments by the author. It has had an enormous circulation and, together with Angell's other publications, won him the Nobel Peace Prize in 1933.

Its basic contention is that in the contemporary world war does not pay economically. Public opinion, which Angell believes controls policy in most states, now believes this, but it also believes that certain policies which induce war do pay. There is also a belief that war often has political and moral justifications, an argument which Angell refutes in later editions. Critics of the book often assumed that it argued that war could not occur. The author makes no such prediction although his critics implied that he did from his statement that war is not inevitable but, as a human creation, could be eliminated in large measure by rational human action.

Angell assumes that economic values pertain to individuals, not to states, and that since the industrial revolution, they have depended on the maintenance of a stable international structure of trade, credit, production and distribution. Transfers of territory or imposition of trade controls by war will break up this structure. Although a few individuals may profit from the sale of arms or from lucrative positions in conquered territories, they do so at the expense of the general public of both the victor and the vanquished.

The book is an important landmark in the peace movement. It changed the emphasis from the immorality and costliness of war itself to the disutility of its results even for the victor; from "moral exhortation to intellectual clarification."

CURTIS, LIONEL. **World War: Its Cause and Cure.** New York: Putnam, 2d rev. ed., 1946, 274 p.

A consolidated version of several pamphlets written during World War II by a well-known English publicist, arguing that anarchy among states inevitably breeds war and can be cured only by some surrender of absolute sovereignty. Curtis's plan differed, however, in crucial respects from conventional proposals for world federation.

It recognized that such merging of established sovereignties would have to be limited initially to a group of governments responsible to the will of their peoples, and would have to be restricted to the task of maintaining security, while powers to control their own composition and social structure would remain reserved to the national governments. The common fear that an international union would diminish the power of national governments to control their domestic affairs would thus be avoided. Curtis proposed specifically that the British Commonwealth governments take the first step, preferably with the Western European states. By thus merging for common defense, they would be strong enough to avert war in Europe for a generation and prepare public opinion in America for eventually joining the union, thus making it impregnable. The union would draw its authority directly from the citizens of its component nations and be entitled to make security a first charge on the resources of those nations.

With the announcement of the atomic bomb, Curtis considered that the creation of a world organization at San Francisco gave the democracies temporary breathing space to construct such an international union capable of controlling the bomb and responsible therefore to its citizens, not to their national governments.

CANTRIL, HADLEY, *ed.* **Tensions That Cause Wars.** Urbana: University of Illinois Press, 1950, 303 p.

This is a timeless book with a rare and precious quality: it practices what it preaches. The message, from a group of eight eminent social scientists representing different cultures and disciplines, is that the world would do well to compare its ideologies carefully and to build peace on similarities in ends rather than to fight wars over differences in means. The format illustrates the point. Brought together by UNESCO's "Tensions Project," the eight scholars met for two weeks of intensive discussion. Before the conference ended each was required to write his chapter for the book, and they reached agreement on a common statement. After the conference each read and made comments on the others' papers. These comments, interspersed throughout the text, give the book a flavor of scholarly conversation which is a marked improvement over a simple collection of monographs.

This diverse group of scholars argues in favor of joint research projects leading to an internationalized social science. Among other things they propose an international university where social scientists, teachers and students from the many nations could nurture the "tender seeds of critical attitude" and root out the "sturdy weeds of unquestioned ideological convictions." The results of their own brief efforts, still clearly valuable many years later, stand as both a model and a testament for anyone who sees hope in their common conclusion: "Effort in behalf of one's own group can become compatible with effort in behalf of humanity."

DUNN, FREDERICK SHERWOOD. **War and the Minds of Men.** New York: Harper (for the Council on Foreign Relations), 1950, 115 p.

Because it was written during one of the most strained periods of the cold war, in response to a specific policy decision by UNESCO, this book could well have been time-bound and of little use to readers of a later period. But Professor Dunn, reflecting the deep understanding of world politics which characterized his career as director of Yale's Institute of International Studies, wove contemporary concerns so carefully into the fabric of world political process that the essay will continue to be of basic value to students of international relations for a long time.

Having been an adviser to American delegations at several UNESCO conferences, Dunn knew well the arguments between those who wanted the organization to remain strictly "cultural" and those who favored political action. He saw the Korean War as an opportunity for UNESCO to give full support to the forces of freedom through a program of political education about the significance of the U.N. military action.

The timeless theme of the book, however, is the proposition that UNESCO—and everyone else—must utilize the developing science of human relations to stimulate "the infinitely slow building up of the connective tissues of world community." Dunn believed that the "minds of men" approach required simultaneous development of both interstate and interpersonal frameworks for understanding and influencing the course of world politics.

WALTZ, KENNETH NEAL. **Man, the State and War: A Theoretical Analysis.** New York: Columbia University Press, 1959, 263 p.

This book discusses three images of the cause of war—the nature of man, the nature of the state and the nature of international relations. Each of these images has had both a pessimistic and an optimistic interpretation. Human nature may be considered inherently self-centered and aggressive, or it may be considered social and rational, making the control of war feasible. States may be considered inherently warlike because of the claim to sovereignty, the need for adequate power to maintain security, or the need of an external enemy to maintain domestic unity. It may also be assumed that states are militant or peaceful according to their organization and traditions. The system of international relations may be considered inherently anarchic, requiring each state to depend on its power position for security, thus establishing a permanent condition of cold or hot war, or it may be considered capable of organization to maintain international peace and security.

After each chapter the author presents a critical analysis of proposals for peace based upon the image presented. In a final chapter he discusses the relations between the images with the conclusion that in an anarchic world, neither human rationality nor any form of national government can assure peace, and that world government "though it may be unassailable in logic is unattainable in practice." Opinions of numerous writers, ancient, medieval and modern, are classified in accord with their views of the three images. This approach to the study of the cause and control of war is interesting and useful, but it does not present the conditions of military technology and international relations under which the statements were made.

STALEY, EUGENE. **War and the Private Investor: A Study in the Relations of International Politics and International Private Investment.** New York: Doubleday, 1935, 562 p.

This book is not concerned with any systemic economic interpretation of foreign policy and imperialism but with the belief, widespread after World War I, that private economic interests are the most important immediate causes of international political friction. Inspired by Professor Jacob Viner, the author examined the scandal-case interpretation of imperialism in meticulous detail. The book is a still extremely valuable collection of case studies based on official records and secondary sources, mostly referring to the period from the 1880s to the 1920s. The reading of these studies still gives to the reader today a vivid impression of the unbelievable rapacity with which Western governments and business groups exploited the then undeveloped areas of the world. The author concludes that instances in which governments deliberately promoted private investments in many areas are as many as those in which business interests obtained government support for purposes of private gain. In many cases, these two initiatives are inseparably intertwined. Whenever a danger of military conflict with a major power loomed, governments protected investors only if considerations of power and prestige seemed to justify it. There is a painstaking analysis, based on numerous examples, of how business groups used governments as tools of private capital and of how governments used business enterprise abroad as an instrument of diplomacy.

ROBBINS, LIONEL CHARLES. **The Economic Causes of War.** New York: Macmillan, 1940, 124 p.

This slim volume of elegant prose offers what is probably still the best single analysis of the economic causation of war. It states the Marxian theories of imperialism (mainly Rosa Luxemburg's and Lenin's) and refutes them with references to the empirical historical work of Jacob Viner, Eugene Staley and others. Robbins does not deny that economic interests have pressed governments, often successfully, to support them in establishing profitable enterprises abroad by diplomacy, and by the acquisition of colonial dependencies—policies which not rarely led to serious international crises or war. He demonstrates, however, that it was often governments which induced bankers and businessmen to seek concessions abroad, and that, in any case, the business interests involved were only small sections of the capitalist class. The author admits that, especially between 1880 and 1914, the power diplomacy of governments was often partially motivated by economic considerations but finds the root cause of international conflict in a system constituted by the existence of independent sovereign powers. The ultimate remedy is federation, with a "United States of Europe" as a starter. Professor Robbins' theorizing is exceptionally subtle and judicious throughout. An appendix presents a penetrating examination of the meaning of economic causation.

HAWTREY, RALPH GEORGE. **Economic Aspects of Sovereignty.** New York: Longmans, 1930, 162 p.

The principal theme of Hawtrey's brief book, which attracted much attention in the 1930s, was a search for the motives for imperialism. Hawtrey found the profit motive of traders and settlers central, but noted that governments were moved to lend them support and develop "economic nationalism" essentially for the need of national military strength in an anarchical international system. Indeed, it is as a theory of international power that his book is still interesting—especially chapters 4 and 5, which are full of quotable phrases. Military power, the precondition of survival for states in such a system, rests primarily on the quantity and mobility of wealth: under modern conditions, "war is a highly capitalized industry." International prestige—the reputation for strength—also rests mainly on an economic basis. Thus the distinction between political and economic causes of war is unreal. "Every conflict is one of power, and power depends upon resources." The principal cause of war is war itself. In the final chapter, the author speculates on the possibility of abolishing war but concludes that the limitation of armaments and the strengthening of institutions for the peaceful settlement of conflicts will not remove war as long as the sanctity of the sovereign state prevails.

STRACHEY, JOHN. **On the Prevention of War.** New York: St. Martin's Press, 1963, 334 p.

Strachey's study emphasizes the political aspect of the problem, reflecting the late British socialist's experience as Secretary of State for War. He reasons that the existence of sovereign states makes war inevitable, while the threat of extinction in nuclear warfare makes it intolerable; its outbreak must therefore be staved off while concepts of the use of national force are drastically modified. Maintaining the stability of the Soviet-American balance of power is the only means of thus staving off catastrophe; and that can only be achieved through pooling U.S.-Soviet nuclear authority solely to prevent nuclear war—by enforcing nuclear disarmament on the rest of the world and by never making war on one another.

Once the two-power hegemony evaporates, "a concert of the world" managed through the United Nations by the then nuclear-power group might, with more difficulty, similarly make survival possible, Strachey notes. World peace so achieved, however, would prove neither just nor indefinitely stable but would provide a growth point from which "a real political world authority" might develop as a sole way to prevent nuclear war for the long run. He concludes that three social forces press us toward that world unification: dread of nuclear war; the convergence of industrial societies; and the increase in common features of a truly global society, despite the communist-noncommunist schism. That alone will "lead men to assent to true world government as they now assent to law within their own societies."

RICHARDSON, LEWIS FRY. **Arms and Insecurity: A Mathematical Study of the Causes and Origins of War.** Pittsburgh: Boxwood Press, 1960, 307 p.

————. **Statistics of Deadly Quarrels.** Pittsburgh: Boxwood Press, 1960, 373 p.

These two volumes bring together the remarkable papers, published first in the 1920s and 1930s, by the foremost pioneer of the mathematical theory of international conflict, the British scholar Lewis F. Richardson. Well edited by C. C. Lienau and Quincy Wright, these volumes show the remarkable power and relevance of Richardson's ideas. Richardson showed how rivalries among states, and particularly armament races, can assume the character of processes in nature, giving rise to an almost automatic conflict system which can no longer be controlled by any one of the participating states and which, on the contrary, imposes its own dynamic on their behavior. This model is then applied to the arms races that preceded World War I and World War II. As critics have pointed out, the results are not conclusive, but the predictions from his models often are so close to observed facts that they cannot be ignored. Richardson is one of the fathers of modern scientific research on international conflicts and on the conditions giving rise to war or peace, and one of the first analysts to use large amounts of quantitative data to test his theories. His influence on the later work of Anatol Rapoport and Kenneth E. Boulding is unmistakable.

BOULDING, KENNETH EWART. **Conflict and Defense: A General Theory.** New York: Harper, 1962, 349 p.

A prominent economist applies here the analytical tools of his craft to problems of international conflict, political and military power. Casting his analysis within a framework of general systems theory, Boulding also introduces considerations of sociology, psychology and the theory of organizations. His findings stress the importance of interaction effects in international conflicts which may produce outcomes unforeseen and undesired by the participants. He emphasizes the "declining gradient of power" with increasing geographic distance, and he suggests ingenious diagrams as aids in the identification and analysis of different types of cases. The author distinguishes international conflict processes that are self-aggravating in contrast to those which are self-limiting, or self-ameliorating. And he indicates analytic tests by which each of these different types can be identified. Knowledge of this kind, he suggests, may also help to limit or ameliorate actual international conflicts by means of appropriate policy measures. In a final chapter the author suggests possible applications of his ideas to a systematic program of research for peace. The book does not make easy reading, but its intellectual significance will repay the effort of serious study.

ARMS CONTROL

See also East-West Relations: Cold War; Coexistence, p. 341.

NOEL-BAKER, PHILIP JOHN. **The Arms Race.** New York: Oceana Publications, 1958, 579 p.

A British statesman, who played a leading part in the efforts to control and eventually to eliminate weapons of destruction under the League of Nations, has written a comprehensive account of the problems of the current arms race. The book is focused on the immediate postwar period, 1946–1957, although the author discusses important historical developments affecting disarmament prospects, particularly those between the two world wars. Drawing on his own experience, he gives particular attention to the problems faced by those who seek to negotiate agreements for disarmament.

Noel-Baker proposes banning the use of nuclear weapons in war, prohibitions against testing them, a cut-off of fissionable materials for weapons purposes and agreement not to stock nuclear weapons. Other chapters deal with such questions as the control and reduction of chemical and biological weapons and long-range missiles; ways to achieve disarmament of conventional weapons; limitations on military budgets; disengagement of warring forces and use of demilitarized zones; measures of inspection and control; and use of collective security arrangements to assist in the peaceful resolution of international disputes.

The author strongly opposes the use of armed force and believes that there are no insuperable obstacles to the achievement of the goal of comprehensive disarmament. With respect to his several suggestions, he writes: "The detailed technical provisions of a disarmament treaty will certainly be complex. . . . But the broad issues are quite simple; technical solutions will cause relatively little trouble when the political decisions have been made."

BULL, HEDLEY. **The Control of the Arms Race.** New York: Praeger (for the Institute for Strategic Studies), 1961, 215 p.

The author of this provocative discussion explicitly emphasizes the analysis of problems of the arms race, not solutions. He looks upon disarmament and arms control as functions of international stability and disclaims preconceived views as to goals to be sought. "Arms control" and "disarmament" are defined as quite distinct concepts: "Disarmament is the reduction or abolition of armaments. It may be unilateral or multilateral; general or local; comprehensive or partial; controlled or uncontrolled. Arms control is restraint internationally exercised upon armaments policy, whether in respect of the level of armaments, their character, deployment or use."

The author challenges many common assumptions, arguing, for example, that "arms races have not always led to war, but have sometimes come to an end." In his view the tendency to continuous innovation is the most distinctive feature of the modern armaments race, as well as the chief theme of strategic studies, and he asserts that there is not the slightest chance of a reversal of that tendency. The analysis, which all students of the subject will find worth reading, also challenges dissent.

MOCH, JULES. **Human Folly: To Disarm or Perish?** London: Gollancz, 1955, 222 p.

Moch's views are of special interest because of his position as a leading French Socialist deputy and a long-term delegate to the U.N. General Assembly and on the U.N. Disarmament Commission beginning in 1951. His argument is that there is no defense against the "atrocious" possibilities of thermonuclear weapons; therefore, the only solution is to end the cold war before it turns into a real war, which would now be one of total destruction. Progressive disarmament, under the necessary controls and guarantees, is thus imperative for all nations. "Security by disarming" is the only real security.

For the first time in history, in Moch's view, there is a thrust for which there is no parry. Any country may be ravaged and brought to capitulation by a surprise attack. Mutual distrust by the Soviet Union and the United States, based on a past of surprise aggression that each remembers and therefore fears, causes the present arms race: peace retreats in the face of war hysteria. Despite the lack of accomplishment in post–World War II disarmament efforts, which Moch summarizes, he finds that skepticism is on the wane, disarmament is making progress in the minds of men, and that "reason must and will triumph." Fifteen years later, the arms race continues and reason has succeeded only in warding off the feared surprise attack.

BEATON, LEONARD and MADDOX, JOHN ROYDEN. **The Spread of Nuclear Weapons.** New York: Praeger, 1962, 216 p.

One of the purposes of this book, sponsored by the Institute for Strategic Studies in London, was to estimate how far the spread of nuclear weapons is likely to go in the next decade. The book illuminates why states may or may not "go nuclear." Case-study chapters on Britain, France, Canada, Germany, China, India, Sweden, Switzerland and Israel are preceded by a general analysis of the process of developing a bomb and a delivery system—including acquisition from allies and the technical problems of going it alone—and followed by an assessment of present and future prospects (to about 1975).

Although the authors recognize the dangers of nuclear proliferation, they provide evidence for disputing the view that a rapid spread is inevitable. The spread of atomic capabilities is described as a consequence not of an inexorable law but of national choices which are affected by a variety of technical, military, political and economic considerations; for example, Beaton and Maddox wrote that China was not likely to explode her own nuclear bomb before 1964 (the first Chinese explosion occurred in October 1964); Canada has had the capability for some time but has chosen not to develop it. However, while many potential nuclear powers are content for the present with obtaining an option (a "hopeful and promising situation"), the authors conclude that there are no simple technical ways to stop the spread of nuclear weapons; ultimately, proliferation will depend on the degree of security the middle powers find in the international system.

SPANIER, JOHN WINSTON and NOGEE, JOSEPH LIPPMAN. **The Politics of Disarmament: A Study in Soviet-American Gamesmanship.** New York: Praeger, 1962, 226 p.

This analysis of Soviet-American disarmament discussions in the "diplomacy of the cold war" views these negotiations as diplomatic weapons which were utilized mainly to "weaken the political and military posture of the other side" rather than reduce or regulate armaments. In the disarmament "gamesmanship" of 1946–62, the positions of both sides concerning the Baruch Plan, nuclear weapons testing, surprise attack, etc., contained dual-purpose "jokers"—*i.e.* conditions which protected the security interests of the proponent while ensuring rejection of the plan by the opponent. For example, a frequent Soviet "joker" was its proposal to "ban the bomb;" the United States stressed "inspection and control," a well-known anathema to the Russians.

The authors regard quiet diplomacy as unlikely to resolve any of the fundamental political issues (due chiefly to the uncompromising, expansionistic and revolutionary nature of the U.S.S.R., which is "determined to destroy all states with different social and economic systems"). They recommend that the United States exploit the art of gamesmanship, essentially the shrewd use of propaganda and psychological warfare, particularly by using summit conferences. Due to the substantive failure of disarmament and arms control negotiations, "the best hope for arms control therefore remains in unilateral American and Soviet measures to provide invulnerable second strike forces. . . . At best, then, there will be a tacit, rather than formal, arms-control agreement."

While this pessimistic account is a corrective for readers of utopian tracts and is useful in explaining aspects of disarmament diplomacy during the period of greatest East-West hostility, its "zero-sum" gamesmanship needs reconsideration in light of what has become a "limited adversary relationship" of the two superpowers.

BRENNAN, DONALD G., *ed.* **Arms Control, Disarmament, and National Security.** New York: Braziller, 1961, 475 p.

This book, arising out of a series of papers published as a special issue of *Daedalus* in the fall of 1960, indicated that arms control and disarmament had arrived as a serious concern of the American academic and intellectual community.

The chapters cover a vast range of topics: the feasibility of control, limited war—conventional or nuclear, the role of small powers, the question of the inclusion of China in arms control agreements, the domestic implications of arms control, U.S. government organization for disarmament studies and policy, problems of enforcement, political and diplomatic prerequisites, the case for unilateral disarmament and many others. The range of viewpoint (from Edward Teller, Herman Kahn, Thomas Schelling and Henry Kissinger to Hubert Humphrey,

Jerome Wiesner, Erich Fromm and Kenneth Boulding) is one of the book's chief assets.

BECHHOEFER, BERNHARD G. **Postwar Negotiations for Arms Control.** Washington: Brookings Institution, 1961, 641 p.

This book presents the most detailed account of the vast array of international disarmament negotiations from 1946 to 1961. Any student of disarmament will find this treatise an important guide to an understanding of what took place among the major powers during this period. The author, who served in the U.S. Department of State in the early years of arms control talks, reveals insight about U.S. policy discussions and decisions. His evaluation of the positions of the countries involved—the United States, the Soviet Union, the United Kingdom, France and Canada—as well as those of other countries taking part in United Nations debates on the subject, are for the most part objective and thoughtful. Although he gives some personal judgments, the author tends to refrain from offering his own solution to the many problems still to be resolved if arms control is ever to become a viable basis for national security. In the end, however, there is a set of recommendations about how the U.S. government might strengthen itself organizationally to handle disarmament studies and negotiations for the future. In this respect the book constituted another voice urging the Executive branch to place more emphasis on disarmament.

BENOIT, EMILE and BOULDING, KENNETH E., *eds.* **Disarmament and the Economy.** New York: Harper and Row, 1963, 310 p.

This book is a symposium to which 11 experts contributed in addition to the editors. It is still the best analysis of the economic problems of disarmament—that is, of what these problems are (in terms of GNP, employment, research and development, and monetary, fiscal and balance-of-payments disturbances), what magnitude they are likely to assume, and how they can be solved or mitigated by appropriate government policy. The analysis is based on a disarmament model, designed by Professor Benoit, which assumes several stages of general and complete disarmament and spells out the probable consequences in terms of the American economy.

Among the chapters is one on input-output analysis by Wassily W. Leontief and Marvin Hoffenberg, and on adjustment problems for defense industries by Murray L. Weidenbaum. Professor Seymour Melman presents some interesting thoughts on the costs of inspections for disarmament. The conclusion by Professor Benoit is that the economic problems of disarmament are manageable provided the "politicians" (*i.e.* the President and Congress in the United States) introduce proper compensatory measures in time. Professor Boulding contributed an introductory chapter on "The World War Industry as an Economic Problem" which, though it has little to do with the rest of the volume, offers vintage Boulding: whimsical with quite a few provocative ideas.

BARNET, RICHARD J. and FALK, RICHARD A., *eds.* **Security in Disarmament.** Princeton: Princeton University Press (for the Princeton Center of International Studies), 1965, 441 p.

The post–World War II involvement of private and governmental institutions in national security research is reflected in the sources of support for this collection of essays: the U.S. Arms Control and Disarmament Agency, Institute for Defense Analyses, Peace Research Institute, Institute for Policy Studies as well as the Princeton Center for International Studies. Also reflecting the writing on arms control that began in the late 1950s, the 18 chapters by 11 scholars include theoretical, empirical and speculative analyses of the political and technical problems surrounding, for example, reduction of strategic delivery vehicles, a mixed national ("adversary") and international ("impartial") inspectorate, international police forces and security in total disarmament.

Nine chapters illuminate the function of inspection in initiating disarmament and protecting national security once it is underway. Rejecting certainty in verification techniques, various authors present alternative conceptions of inspection influenced by two basic models of general and complete disarmament (GCD). The "internationalist" viewpoint (*e.g.* Lincoln Bloomfield)—which holds that substantial disarmament is possible without the loss of national sovereignty—proposes "graduated levels of access," linking the inspection process closely to risks from possible violations at each disarmament stage. According to the "supranationalist" view (*e.g.* Richard Falk) inspection has been "greatly exaggerated" as a source of security; little formal inspection is necessary at the start of disarmament, whereas at the end of the process no inspection scheme can provide security since it cannot substitute for active distrust. Elimination of the latter and achievement of GCD necessitates world government and a redistribution of the world's wealth. An "intermediate" approach is offered by Klaus Knorr: lesser arms control agreements to mitigate the risks of the nuclear era without GCD, thereby gaining time for a "protracted learning process."

SINGER, JOEL DAVID. **Deterrence, Arms Control, and Disarmament.** Columbus: Ohio State University Press, 1962, 279 p.

Singer's concern is to analyze deterrence, arms control and disarmament within the single context of national security in the nuclear-missile age rather than to treat them as disparate if not conflicting sets of problems: "to pursue goals which are incompatible through strategies which are irreconcilable" courts disaster. Armament policy must therefore be designed to carry the nations through the dangerous transition from deterrence to disarmament, with arms control as the bridge. Singer sees deterrence as "surviving the environment;" arms control as stabilizing it; disarmament as modifying it.

The author argues that deterrent strategy must be only that; first-strike capabilities must be forgotten. Much can be done through arms control, either unilaterally or jointly with the adversary, to reduce reciprocal fears of sudden nuclear devastation, but that cannot eliminate the fear, since the weapons themselves are a major ingredient in the perceived threat. Both the tension-reduction and political-settlement approaches to disarmament also founder on the rock of perceived threat because the weapons remain in national arsenals. With a psychological significance of their own, they are more than mere manifestations of deeper conflicts and not susceptible to traditional disarmament techniques. Singer therefore proposes an ingenious disarm-by-disarming approach: a system of transferring initially conventional, then nuclear, weapons "on a phased, gradual and corroborated basis from national arsenals to international depots and bases," subject to easy access and repossession by the original owner until confidence developed. He hopes that the transferred conventional weapons would build up an international gendarmerie as national capability gradually diminished and the international system gradually transformed itself.

STONE, JEREMY J. **Containing the Arms Race.** Cambridge: M.I.T. Press, 1966, 252 p.

After a decade of continuous, rapid changes in weapons technology, and a concomitant increase in arms production, a plateau in both technology and strategic thinking appeared to have been reached by 1965. This, it was hoped, would increase the chances of reaching some significant arms control agreements between the United States and the Soviet Union, which had both engaged in the procurement of long-range strategic nuclear forces and a parallel attempt to procure strategic defenses against them: bomber, missile and submarine. Stone's study examined, from the technical and political point of view, two of the most important current arms control proposals: a freeze of strategic delivery systems and a Soviet-American undertaking not to deploy missile defense systems.

The importance of those objectives lay in the fact that a decision to embark on the deployment of full-scale ABM systems would signal a new round in the arms race that could destroy further prospects for arms reduction without increasing the security of either side. Stone proposed a "negotiator's pause," a five-year treaty limiting only numbers and freezing tacitly or formally the procurement of missile defenses, while intensive negotiations for more substantial agreement continued. Finding little that was hopeful in the long history of arms control efforts, he advocated settling for the possible rather than seeking the improbable. His proposals were to be considered "part of a process, rather than a series of ends in themselves."

This book should be read in conjunction with a companion study published by Stone the following year, **Strategic Persuasion: Arms Limitations through Dialogue** (New York: Columbia University Press, 1967, 176 p.).

XI. SCIENCE AND TECHNOLOGY

BERNAL, JOHN DESMOND. **The Social Function of Science.** New York: Macmillan, 1939, 482 p.

This profound discussion by a British scientist of the relationship of science to society and of its place and influence within society was published on the eve of the Second World War. It thus preceded the appearance of almost every major landmark in the modern history of scientific-social relationships in the United States upon which nearly all recent analyses of the relationships of science and society here have relied heavily, both for illustration and moral. It might, therefore, be expected that it would be notably dated.

The contrary is singularly true. In the light of 30 ensuing years of headlong evolution, parts of the treatment appear today somewhat limited and occasionally oversimplified. But the major virtues typical of a pioneering work of high quality are there in full measure: vitality, comprehensiveness, care in the marshalling of evidence, vigor in argument. Surely the strongest impression that a careful reading will leave is of the extraordinary ubiquity, and the durability, of the major questions with which we wrestle today. The sense almost of *déjà vu* that the book conveys is heightened by the fact that it was written in a period of disaffection for science, when its social purpose and social functions were being questioned in much the same fashion as they are at present.

One area in which the book clearly is dated is in its treatment of science and society in the Soviet Union. The author, pronouncedly socialist in view, looked to science in the Soviet Union with great hope and expectation. The nature of that hope, which is explicitly indicated, contrasts strongly with eventuality, and the contrast adds greatly to the interest of a contemporary reading of the book.

For the modern student of science and society, this book is a "must," not only for its historical connotations as ground-breaking work in its field but also for its current significance.

BERKNER, LLOYD V. **The Scientific Age: The Impact of Science on Society.** New Haven: Yale University Press, 1964, 137 p.

The author of this book has had a particularly rich life in science, engineering, education and public affairs. He was a crucial figure in the conception and organization of the International Geophysical Year, a guiding spirit in the formation of the Space Science Board of the National Academy of Sciences and for several years a member of the President's Science Advisory Committee. The entire thrust of the book, first presented as the 1964 Trumbull Lectures at Yale University, is the impact of science on society; and a number of the chapters are prophetic, particularly the opening one, "The Economy of Plenty," for the concerns of plenty and over-plenty are only now assailing us in full force. A section is devoted to the pros and cons of space exploration, in which the author has no hesitation in expressing his own keen advocacy of manned space ventures.

In the chapter "Advanced Education for a New Age," Berkner presents a detailed discussion of the state of and prospects for education for science in the United States, aided by an interesting set of statistics of training and degree-granting in the nation. "Science and Government" presents his philosophy for government support of science, a view deeply influenced by that of Vannevar Bush. "Science and Philosophy" is a particularly stimulating lecture, which takes off from

C. P. Snow's **The Two Cultures and the Scientific Revolution** and pursues that thesis critically. The final chapter of the book, "A Strategy of Maturity," includes further predictions, centering particularly about elementary and advanced educational opportunities, especially in the science-based professions and in scientific research. There is also a discussion of the evolving character of modern business as affected by these educational trends.

HASKINS, CARYL PARKER. **Of Societies and Men.** New York: Norton, 1951, 282 p.

This book seeks to elucidate some of the fundamentals of the human condition and of human prerequisites and requirements, both individual and social, against the broad canvas of individual and social evolution throughout living nature. One of the striking features of evolution, the author points out, is the phenomenon called "convergence": the extent to which many organisms of very different origins and distant relationships but living in similar environments tend to reflect those environments in the parallel courses of their evolution.

The author notes that these phenomena are purely analogous, and no significant conclusions related to evolutionary descent can or should be deduced from them. But he points out that it is possible to look at them in another way. As the convergent evolution of wings points to an environmental niche for flying creatures, for example, so the development of social life, and the form and mechanism of regulation of societies, among many organisms points to a common "social niche" or "social terrain" in the world. It is this terrain that the book seeks to examine. Since man, evolutionarily speaking, is by far the latest comer on this stage (and so, in some sense, the most evolutionarily "naïve"), it is the thesis of the book that some fundamental insights about human social organization and the human social environment can be suggested by a detailed examination of the modes of social evolution in other communal organisms such as the great insect societies.

The author distinguishes two general classes of social living in nature, the "associative" and the "integrative," and discusses the many distinguishing features between them (most important, perhaps, the fact that in "associative" societies individuals are still free to leave and rejoin the society at will and to live independently for a period). It is the conclusion of the book that human societies must remain as intimate mixtures of these two modes and that there is a delicate balance between the two which mankind has sought to achieve throughout history, with frequent lapses on both sides. Haskins believes that an optimal maintenance of this delicate equilibrium may be considered the highest achievement in human social evolution and social and political management, and may constitute our highest aspiration for the future.

WIENER, NORBERT. **The Human Use of Human Beings.** Boston: Houghton, 1950, 241 p.

In these essays the author traces the critical influence of Josiah Willard Gibbs in the United States and Boltzmann in Germany, who first introduced statistics, the science of distribution, into physics, adapting the method not only to natural systems of great complexity but also to systems as simple as that of the single particle in a field of force. Gibbs' use of probability in physics occurred well before an adequate general theory had been developed. Wiener underlines a striking parallel. He feels that Gibbs' concept of an element of incomplete determinism— almost of irrationality—operating in the world suggestively paralleled Freud's emphasis of a deeply irrational component in human behavior and thought. Gibbs theorized that a measure of probability, called entropy, tends naturally to increase as the world grows older. As entropy increases, the universe and all closed systems within it lose distinctiveness, moving from a state of organization and differentiation to one of chaos and uniformity.

But while the universe as a whole may be running down, Wiener reasons, there are particular enclaves, open systems, where the degree of organization tends to increase with time. One of these enclaves is life itself. The science of cybernetics, as conceived by Wiener, takes this point of view as its starting point. Cybernetics attempts to develop models for the understanding of communication and control. It is the contention of the author that the physical functioning of the living individual and the operation of some of the newer communication machines are analogous in their attempt to maintain organization and control through the operation of feedback mechanisms. An important practical, as well as theoretical, task of the scientist is therefore the discovery of such modes of organization in the universe.

The book ends with a statement of the author's personal faith: "Science is a way of life which can only flourish when men are free to have faith." These essays were first published in 1950, foreshadowing the whole developing science of how mind and brain work. Of great interest to the biologist, the student of communication and the political scientist, they are written in general terms and in a felicitous style.

EINSTEIN, ALBERT. **Out of My Later Years.** Totowa: Littlefield, Adams, 1967, 251 p.

Einstein writes in these essays about his philosophy and beliefs. Ranging through a wide variety of political, social, scientific and religious themes, they are gleaned from unpublished addresses, letters and miscellaneous papers. They indeed mirror a remarkable man.

Einstein was clearly dedicated to an abiding reverence for existence. In discussing the research life, his emphasis is everywhere that free research for the sake of pure knowledge should remain unfettered and unimpaired. In the same vein, in a tribute to his friend Max Planck, he writes that a man who blesses the world with a great creative idea has no need for the praise of posterity. His achievement itself confers a greater accolade.

The scientific essays trace generally the roots of complementarity, the development of the theory of relativity and the derivation of Einstein's law of the equivalence of mass and energy. The philosophical writing is even more striking. The author writes that a primary aim of science is a comprehension of the connection between sense experiences. Thus science, he believes, is above all an attempt to bring order to the chaotic diversity of our sense experiences, integrating them with a logical economy of thought.

What does science offer to mankind? Einstein believes that such a question basically inverts the real issue. For the goals and values of man, he contends, themselves determine what science does. The author is certain that the layman can rest confident that human thought is dependable and natural law universal. The author's humanity takes explicit form in his plan for a world government.

The essays offer to the student and the lay reader alike a glimpse of the working of one of the crucial minds of human history. They are of special value to the historian seeking source material to comprehend a critical period in the development of American understanding.

SNOW, CHARLES PERCY. **The Two Cultures and the Scientific Revolution.** New York: Cambridge University Press, 1959, 58 p.

Sir Charles Snow's famous thesis is that the intellectual life of the whole of Western society is increasingly dividing into two polar groups: literary intellectuals and scientists. Between the two, he says, is a widening gulf of mutual incomprehension and increasingly remote contact, and sometimes of hostility and dislike, for the unscientific is often incipiently antiscientific. In spite of the growth of science and technology, it is the traditional culture that "manages" the Western world, the author continues. The only way out is by "rethinking our education." Snow states that, in fact, two revolutions, the agricultural and the industrial-scientific, are the only qualitative changes in social living that men have ever known. He believes that industrialized countries characteristically get richer in time, while the nonindustrialized at best stand still.

In **Two Cultures? The Significance of C. P. Snow** (New York: Pantheon, 1963, 64 p.), F. R. Leavis published a critique of the concept of the two cultures. His thesis is diametrically opposite to that of Snow. He states that "mankind will need to be in full intelligent possession of its full humanity." It will need "a power—rooted strong in experience, and supremely human—of creative response to the new challenges of time; something that is alien to either of Snow's cultures."

The reader will find in the two books ample opportunity to form his own judgment about the two cultures and the art of politics.

BROOKS, HARVEY. **The Government of Science.** Cambridge: M.I.T. Press, 1968, 343 p.

Harvey Brooks, Gordon McKay Professor of Applied Physics and Dean of the Division of Applied Physics at Harvard University, here presents an edited group of papers, written between 1960 and 1967 for various particular occasions and, for the most part, published earlier in more specialized media. This exceedingly useful collection sets out the author's views on a wide range of subjects, all of which, however, concern the relationship between science and society, including such matters as the channels of penetration of modes of thought originating in science into the general culture, and the role and the promise of new technologies in meeting the needs of education in the future. A large share of the essays deal with the arena of science and public policy, a field in which the author has had long and wide-ranging personal experience. They embrace such subjects as the problem of federal support to research in universities; analyses of the thorny problems that surround attempts to determine priorities of federal support among widely differing major areas of technology (such as, for example, space research and research in atomic energy on the one hand and health or food production on the other); and the national allocation of scientific and technical resources between science and other publicly directed enterprises.

The decade of the 1960s was one of special conceptual ferment about the impact of science on society and was characterized by repeated attempts to visualize and to design coherent science policies for the nation. The problem has so far proved extraordinarily difficult and recalcitrant—a fact that lends added importance to this book.

DUPRÉ, JOSEPH STEFAN and LAKOFF, SANFORD ALLAN. **Science and the Nation: Policy and Politics.** Englewood Cliffs: Prentice-Hall, 1962, 181 p.

Among the aims of the authors of this book were a survey of the role of technology in industrial societies and the impact of science upon social thought, and, within this broader framework, a more specific consideration of the growth and formulation of science in the United States and the political activities of scientists.

Part I, entitled "Policy," focuses on the revolution in the growth of science, and most particularly its relation to government, which had occurred over the two decades preceding the appearance of the book, with an analysis of the nature and significance of that change. The initial approach is historical, beginning with an account of the relations of science and the American government from the very inception of the nation to the present. The book then turns to a detailed description of the growth of science in industry from the times of Thomas A. Edison, with special consideration given to questions of the relationships of industrial research to the military, to weapons-systems management in various situations and to new kinds of interactions between science and government. The authors also examine questions of the relation of government and university research, including such specific and thorny features as the issues of indirect costs and of loyalty-security requirements, and the question of financing capital facilities. The concluding chapter is devoted to an illuminating treatment of the modes of formulation of science policy and of the difficult questions comprehended under that rubric, including the still unsolved one of whether, in fact, a Department of Science should be formally constituted in the federal government.

Part II, "Politics," also approached in a historical vein, brings the analysis down to the urgent and controversial issues of the day in chapters entitled "Arms and the

Scientist," "The Politics of Decision," "Security in Science" and "Alienation and Responsibility." A reflective conclusion explores issues of the diplomacy of the scientific partnership, professional responsibility and the experience of the scientists, and the need for public understanding.

It is extraordinary that so slender a volume can comprehend such a thorough, detailed and thoughtful presentation of the multitudinous facets of the subjects addressed. Equally noteworthy are the clarity, the conciseness and the organizational balance of the work.

GILPIN, ROBERT and WRIGHT, CHRISTOPHER, *eds*. **Scientists and National Policy-Making.** New York: Columbia University Press, 1964, 307 p.

At the end of World War II, three issues particularly challenged American leadership in the field of government-scientific relations. As Robert Gilpin points out in this volume, the first was the need to determine the appropriate place of natural scientists in the formulation of national policy; the second, the need to develop a coherent policy toward the conduct of basic scientific research; and the and the national security. Gilpin notes that what were initially conceived as the third, the need to deal satisfactorily with the plethora of problems involving science main issues in all three of these categories have, in the years since 1950, been fairly well understood and to a considerable degree resolved. Even this degree of progress, however, may now seem less assured than it did in 1964. And, as the author points out, additional challenges have emerged in each of these areas in the years between, partly as a consequence of decisions already taken during the two fateful decades.

This important book is primarily devoted to a consideration of these newer and derivative issues. It is a compilation of nine essays by leading students in this arena. The first three essays, by Don K. Price, Robert C. Wood and Harvey Brooks, deal with various aspects of the place which natural scientists have come to occupy in American public life, and the reasons for this evolution. The following four essays, by Wallace S. Sayre, Robert N. Kreidler, Warner R. Schilling and Albert Wohlstetter, deal with the political activities of scientists in two major areas of policy: the support of science and the relation of science and scientific activities to questions of national security. In the two concluding essays, Bernard Brodie discusses the emergence on the American scene over the past few years of a newly budding profession which might be called that of the "scientific strategist," trained in areas both of the natural and the social sciences, and serving as a bridge between them, while Christopher Wright discusses and analyzes the nature and character of the many bridges which have been built between science and society in the postwar years.

PRICE, DON KRASHER. **Government and Science: Their Dynamic Relation in American Democracy.** New York: Oxford University Press, 2d ed., 1962, 203 p.

Don K. Price, Dean of the John F. Kennedy School of Public Administration at Harvard, is a leading pioneer of the post–World War II period in the exposition and analysis of the relationships between science and the American body politic. Though he has contributed much besides, his reputation can rest securely on two major works: the present one and the more recent **The Scientific Estate** (Cambridge: Harvard University Press, 1965, 323 p.). Both rank among the most important books in the field and are best read sequentially. If one is to be selected, **Government and Science** may present the wider view. First published in 1954, the work is in no sense dated.

The opening chapter explores the part that the philosophy and methodology of science had in modifying and broadening the American theory and practice of government through the years before World War II, a theme then developed in detail for the post–World War II period. Subsequent chapters deal with the establishment and evolution of the pioneering Office of Naval Research, direct predecessor of the National Science Foundation, with the history of the establishment of the National Science Foundation itself, the invention and design of the quasi-public corporations such as RAND, and of the Atomic Energy Commission.

There is a discussion of the problems involved in providing federal funds for research and development to private organizations, particularly the universities, and of the appropriate role of the National Science Foundation. There is also a thorough consideration of the benefits and the particular dangers of highly centralized as against more diversified patterns of grant distribution by government. Later portions of the book deal with such questions as the problems of security risk and publicity, and especially the modes through which continuing advice from capable individual and organizational sources in the private sector can most effectively be made available to government.

Our world is immensely more powerful and complex than it was in the decade when this book was written. Yet the great dominant tides govern us still. Nowhere are those that have dominated the relationships of science and policy been stated more clearly or examined more cogently.

ODISHAW, HUGH, *ed.* **The Challenges of Space.** Chicago: University of Chicago Press, 1962, 379 p.

Early in the era of America's most intensive interest and activity in space exploration, in May–June 1961, the *Bulletin of the Atomic Scientists* produced a special double edition wholly devoted to the scientific aspects of space exploration. The issue excited widespread interest and attention and was the genesis of the present volume. Hugh Odishaw has brought together a collection of articles which originally appeared in the *Bulletin,* expanded and brought them up to the date of publication of the book itself. Several new and significant ones were added. The volume is structured around three major themes of space activity as perceived by its editor—adventure and exploration, satellite applications, and research. A good balance has been maintained among these three major categories, and many leading pioneers are included among the authors.

Although—or perhaps because—the book is almost a decade old, it makes particularly valuable reading for the lay student who is anxious both to grasp the technical fundamentals of space exploration, and to gain some notion of the rapidly moving history of plans, dreams and priorities which characterized the time, some of which have since changed or evolved quite drastically. Across the web of specific and detailed discussions can be discerned a pattern of how the United States regarded the coming space age, and its own place and destiny within it, at the first flowering of that age. The work is as valuable a source-book of the social history of an era's beginning as it is of its scientific and technical background.

OSSENBECK, FREDERICK J. and KROECK, PATRICIA C., *eds.* **Open Space and Peace.** Stanford: Hoover Institution, 1964, 227 p.

In September 1963 a symposium on Open Space and Peace was held at Stanford University. The 19 papers in this book are the record of that conference. Inevitably, much of it is now history. But it is of special interest in its detailed presentation of much contemporary thinking on questions that are still open. The lay reader may be especially interested in the discussions of the implications of international surveillance raised by the general employment of satellites—for neutral nations, for assaying the situation and the objectives of "closed" states such as Communist China, for the U.S.S.R., and for United States policy. The comparisons of the possible consequences of unilateral satellite launchings as against bilateral and multilateral ones and launchings sponsored by the United Nations, as seen in that relatively simple day, will be found especially provocative. Two general addresses of particular interest, delivered at a special meeting open to the public, are included: the first, by Congressman George P. Miller, then Chairman of the House Committee on Science and Astronautics, "The Evolution of Space Science," and the second, by Edward Teller, on "Freedom of Space."

All the discussions are necessarily dated, but, in the context of the present, this may be a virtue. Not only do they illuminate the state of our thinking about the great problems of space at that relatively early point in its evolution, but, most importantly, they emphasize some of the invariants, underlying the grave issues that are still with us, more urgently in need of solution than when the book was written and, in many cases, hardly perceptibly nearer to it.

SCHWARTZ, MORTIMER D., *ed.* **Proceedings of the Conference on Space Science and Space Law.** South Hackensack: Rothman, 1964, 176 p.

The stated purpose of the conference, held at the University of Oklahoma in 1963, was "to close the gap between science and law." Eighteen papers related to this theme are presented in the volume. They are of varying quality. Taken together, however, they present an interesting panorama of the state of thinking—and perhaps even more importantly, of attitudes—in the nation in 1963, emphasizing significant, indeed almost historic, shifts that have since occurred. The first and last papers of the collection may be of particular interest to the reader primarily concerned with wider aspects of the history and impact of space concerns in that period. The opening address, by Lloyd V. Berkner, entitled "Science, the Scientist, and Space," is a comprehensive review of the growth of the space effort from its inception—a period in which its author played an especially active and significant part—and includes a contemporary appraisal and a strong argument for expanding national support. The closing paper, "Law and Public Order in Space," was delivered by Professor Myres S. McDougal of Yale University. It is a fascinating projection of legal contingencies of space exploration and legal challenges involved in space discoveries. Many of the contingencies discussed are still vital concerns.

This is a useful compilation of thoughtful source material, produced and articulated when the tide of anticipation, hope and imagination centering about space exploration was running at its fullest.

VAN DYKE, VERNON. **Pride and Power: The Rationale of the Space Program.** Urbana: University of Illinois Press, 1964, 285 p.

As the author emphasizes, this volume deals with the space effort primarily as a vivid test illustration of the motives that inspire political behavior, particularly in the field of international relations. In this context, the questions that he asks relate primarily to goals and national driving forces and less to the scientific, technological and economic aspects of the question. The treatment is especially significant because of the dating of the book. At that time challenging questions were being raised about the necessity of a trip to the moon—questions affecting every conceivable political as well as scientific and technological aspect.

Part I of the volume analyzes the rationality of the reasons commonly adduced for the space effort, examines how the decisions concerning it came to be made, and includes a significant history of the program during the Eisenhower presidency and the steps by which it enlarged and became accelerated in the Kennedy administration. There are revealing insights into Kennedy's own appraisals of the venture. Part II includes a fairly exhaustive examination of the various reasons then marshalled on behalf of the space program. Part III is devoted to the "shape" of organizations in the federal government designed to administer and to contain the space program. Part IV, the conclusion, deals with values and with decision making in the framework of the space effort.

Professor Van Dyke has produced a book with a breadth of emphasis on the philosophical, the social and the political aspects of American space development shared by few other contemporary works on the subject.

BUSH, VANNEVAR. **Pieces of the Action.** New York: Morrow, 1970, 366 p.

Future historians may well judge the era of World War II as a revolutionary period for American science and technology fully comparable in social depth and significance with the political revolutionary experience of the nation two centuries earlier. As that period demanded leaders in the mold of Jefferson and Franklin, so the middle years of the twentieth century called upon leadership of comparable stature in the fields of science and technology. Perhaps the greatest among that group of leaders to whom the nation owes so much is the author of this book.

It has been said, quite accurately, that the effectiveness and the dynamism and the morale of American science has never stood higher than in the concluding months of World War II, and that never have the American people been more vividly aware of its values. The period may truly be said to have marked the beginning of a major leap in the recognition and the service of national science, and in the relation of the federal government to its support. It is particularly valuable to have this intimate account of many salient features of that era by the author of the remarkable report of 1945 to President Franklin D. Roosevelt, **Science the Endless Frontier** (Washington: Government Printing Office, 1945, 184 p.), reprinted by the National Science Foundation in 1960, which did so much to determine the shape—and indeed the very existence—of the National Science Foundation. But the book is by no means confined to those years, any more than the versatile career of its author has been. An immensely personal book, it includes phases lived in other times and places: the years as a professor and later as Vice President of the Massachusetts Institute of Technology, the years as President of the Carnegie Institution of Washington and those years of struggle when so many significant battles were waged in many councils of the nation.

Perhaps the greatest contributions of the book inhere in its philosophy and apparently incidental observations, distilled from a long and immensely active and fruitful life cast predominantly at the interfaces between men and things: a territory sparsely occupied even today. Under the guise of what often appear as general and sometimes apparently unconnected accounts and observations there emerges a rich, many-faceted and profound, as well as a powerful, philosophy of thought and action, replete with wisdom yet light with humor.

HUXLEY, JULIAN SORELL. **Heredity East and West: Lysenko and World Science.** New York: Schuman, 1949, 246 p.

The Lysenko period in Soviet science is now, happily, a matter of history, and excellent recent discussions of it have appeared, notably in **Heredity, Evolution and Society** by I. Michael Lerner (San Francisco: Freeman, 1968, 307 p.) and by the eyewitness Zhores Medvedev, in **The Rise and Fall of T. D. Lysenko** (New York: Columbia University Press, 1969, 284 p.). The peculiar value of Julian Huxley's book is that it represents a balanced contemporary appraisal by a writer who is himself a world figure in genetics and who has made major contributions to the study of evolution. Now reprinted (New York: Kraus Reprint Company, 1969), it offers the opportunity to view that extraordinary era in its own time-frame and through the eyes of an expert and dispassionate judge.

Most interesting, perhaps, are the analyses by the author and by other contemporaries of the qualities of Lysenko himself. A quotation from Professor (now Sir Eric) Ashby, who had many occasions in the course of his official duties at that time to see Lysenko in action, is particularly striking and revealing: "He is not a charlatan. He is not a showman. He is not personally ambitious. He is extremely nervous and conveys the impression of being unhappy, unsure of himself, shy, and forced into the role of leader by a fire within him. . . . He is fired by his mission to scourge bourgeois genetics out of Russia, because he really believes it is harmful."

What is perhaps most extraordinary about the whole phenomenon is that, as the book points out, there was a long-standing and distinguished tradition of genuine genetics in Russia at the time, carried forward by many scientists of world eminence, to whom the pre-scientific and indeed rather medieval character of Lysenko's thought was perfectly obvious. Yet such was the nature of society at that time and place that for many years they were silenced, in an official climate more reminiscent than anything else of some pre-Newtonian eras in the West.

HASKINS, CARYL PARKER. **The Scientific Revolution and World Politics.** New York: Harper and Row (for the Council on Foreign Relations), 1964, 115 p.

This book, based on the text of the Elihu Root Lectures at the Council on Foreign Relations, deals with the impact of the scientific revolution on world developments, and particularly on those especially significant for American foreign policy. The first portion is primarily concerned with the growth of science and technology in the developing countries of the world and its significance for their future shaping and political autonomy. The author particularly emphasizes the historical separateness of the technological and the scientific revolutions in human history, and the significance of this circumstance in the context of the new nations. He stresses the importance to the new nations of developing a truly indigenous structure of science at the earliest opportunity.

Later portions of the book are concerned with the significance of world scientific events in nations at an intermediate stage of development and, finally, in the fully developed nations of the West and in the U.S.S.R. and China.

SKOLNIKOFF, EUGENE B. **Science, Technology, and American Foreign Policy.** Cambridge: M.I.T. Press, 1967, 330 p.

This may well be both the most thorough and comprehensive survey so far undertaken of the complex and far-ranging relationships of science to American foreign policy. The book emphasizes particularly the cardinal importance of a thorough integration of science and technology into the policy process—at the levels both of analysis and decision—for those issues where scientific and technological elements figure importantly. It is the author's feeling that the present mechanisms of government, particularly in the Department of State, are inadequate to ensure this sort of fusion or to discern areas in which science and technology can function as new avenues and new tools of foreign policy.

Against this background, the book gives detailed accounts of a number of sectors on which critical issues of foreign policy are arising or have arisen from scientific or technological developments: space and atomic energy, arms and arms control, and various international scientific and technological activities. There are good discussions of the problems of strengthening science and international policy, of the initiation and maintenance of international organizations and military alliances made against the background of scientific and technological developments, of the establishment and conduct of bilateral alliances with various nations in scientific and technological matters, including both developed and developing states, and of the problems of transfer of technology, investment in science and research.

The final section of this important book is addressed to a broad-scale discussion of technology and science in a world political setting.

GRUBER, RUTH, *ed.* **Science and the New Nations.** New York: Basic Books (for the International Conference on Science in the Advancement of New States), 1961, 314 p.

This book comprises the collected texts of speeches at the conference on the role of science in the advancement of new states, with 120 participants drawn from 40 countries, a very large proportion of them newly inaugurated states in the underdeveloped areas of the world. A wide range of subjects was covered, grouped under such topics as "Energy for Underdeveloped Countries;" "Radiation: Its Uses and Hazards;" "Food and Natural Resources;" "Water;" "Medicine and Health;" "The Population Explosion;" and "International Cooperation in Science."

This was the first congress of its kind, and it provided the model for later efforts, some more ambitious in size and scope, but almost certainly of less lasting impact. All the papers are worth reading. Some of the analyses, and particularly some of the proposed solutions, seem simplistic a decade later, though, in the main, the principles outlined and the general directions suggested are clear and forceful. In many respects the book is already history and as such is exceedingly valuable. The dominant impression that it leaves is of how much growth there has been in sophistication during the 1960s among the developed and underdeveloped countries alike—though in quite different ways—and how much respect and even awe for the magnitude of the difficulties have increased—to the point, sometimes, of defeatism.

The Rehovoth Declaration, which has since become famous, is included in an appendix.

PART TWO:

THE WORLD SINCE 1914

I. THE FIRST WORLD WAR

ORIGINS OF THE WAR

FAY, SIDNEY BRADSHAW. **The Origins of the World War.** New York: Macmillan, 1928, 2 v.

SCHMITT, BERNADOTTE EVERLY. **The Coming of the War: 1914.** New York: Scribner, 1930, 2 v.

ALBERTINI, LUIGI. **The Origins of the War of 1914.** New York: Oxford University Press, 1952–1957, 3 v.

The origins of the "Great War" have been studied more painstakingly than any other event in recent European history. Despite an avalanche of sources, however, there is still no consensus on how the war came about. No historian any longer puts the blame exclusively on Germany; that simplistic notion was discredited by "revisionist" historians long ago. But there has never emerged a generally accepted alternate interpretation. It is doubtful that there ever will.

The works cited above are a mere sampling, albeit a considered one, from an overwhelming bibliography. Professor Fay's book deserves first mention as a classic. Written in the aftermath of the war, it was the most influential non-German "revisionist" work. Since Germany at the time was the only nation that had fully documented its case, it is understandable that the Central Powers get a more than fair hearing. Despite its dated interpretation, Fay's judicious and readable account still deserves serious attention.

In contrast to Fay, half of whose work deals with the underlying causes of the war, Bernadotte Schmitt's two volumes concentrate on the immediate outbreak of the war. Using substantially the same sources, Schmitt's more exhaustive treatment of the July crisis of 1914 clearly favors the Allied side and as such presents an "anti-revisionist" counterpart to Fay.

Between Fay and Schmitt, both of them Americans, the issue of responsibility had been joined. Meanwhile European scholars had not been idle. As might be expected, the German historian Erich Brandenburg, in his **From Bismarck to the World War: A History of German Foreign Policy, 1870–1914** (New York: Oxford University Press, 1927, 556 p.), leaned toward the "revisionist" side; while France's Pierre Renouvin, in his **The Immediate Origins of the War** (New Haven: Yale University Press, 1928, 409 p.), pursued the opposite line. The last major study on the origins of World War I to appear before the outbreak of World War II came from Germany. Alfred von Wegerer's **Der Ausbruch des Weltkrieges, 1914** (Hamburg: Hanseatische Verlagsanstalt, 1939, 2 v.) is the fullest statement of the standard view then held by most Germans, that their country was totally innocent and the Allies wholly guilty.

The third of these featured works, by Luigi Albertini, a noted Italian journalist-turned-historian, first appeared in 1942–1943. Its first volume deals with European diplomacy from the Congress of Berlin in 1878 to Sarajevo; the other two are a detailed discussion of events from the assassination to the outbreak of war. Albertini was able to use the large quantity of new sources that had been published during the 1930s. These he supplemented by further archival research and by interviews with surviving figures of the pre-1914 era. The result is a well-balanced, judicious account which commands the respect of historians the world over. Albertini died in 1941, before he was able to summarize his findings in a concluding chapter. The tenor of the book, however, supports those historians who place the major responsibility for the war on the shoulders of the Central Powers rather than the Allies.

FISCHER, FRITZ. **Krieg der Illusionen: Die Deutsche Politik von 1911 bis 1914.** Düsseldorf: Droste, 1969, 805 p.

The debate on the origins of World War I was given fresh impetus in 1961 by the introductory chapters of Fritz Fischer's **Germany's Aims in the First World War.** The German historian's claim that his country bore the major responsibility for the war touched off a heated controversy among German historians which, in turn, led Fischer to enlarge his earlier assertions in this second massive book. According to Fischer, Germany's ruling classes, to perpetuate their power and to assure their nation's hegemony in Europe, had begun preparing for war long before 1914. Their belief in the inevitability of war, and their fear that Germany's chances for victory would diminish with time, made them force a showdown during the July crisis, even at the risk of its possible escalation into a world war.

Germany's expansionist *Weltpolitik,* according to Fischer, was more aggressive than the imperialism of the other powers, because Germany was a latecomer to the imperialist feast and because its rulers, through aggression abroad, hoped to divert attention from the growing clamor for political and social reform at home. While this interpretation is not new, it has never before been documented with such overwhelming evidence and stated in such dogmatic terms. Like Fischer's earlier book, this sequel has led to a lively debate among historians, some of whom reproach Fischer with trying to prove a preconceived thesis and with unfairly singling out Germany for censure.

DEDIJER, VLADIMIR. **The Road to Sarajevo.** New York: Simon and Schuster, 1966, 550 p.

Here is the latest, and perhaps last, word on the tragic events of June 28, 1914. The author, a biographer of Tito, argues that the Archduke's assassination at Sarajevo was the natural outcome of decades of Austrian tyranny and misrule. One need not agree with this indictment to appreciate the wealth of new material he has gathered from various national archives. Dedijer does not produce surprising new facts or conclusions about the nature of Austrian rule or about Austro-Serbian relations. In his use of Serbian documents, however, he throws much new light on the politics, philosophies and purposes of individuals and "subversive" organizations in Bosnia and Serbia. Dedijer concludes that the assassination was important only because of the use to which war-bent Austrian extremists put it. Whether or not the reader is convinced by this argument, he will recognize as valid the author's judgment that the conspirators did not intend to foment war through the assassination.

GENERAL TREATMENTS; HISTORICAL

RENOUVIN, PIERRE. **La Crise Européenne et la Grande Guerre, 1904–1918.** Paris: Alcan, 1934, 639 p.

This admirable book by one of France's leading diplomatic historians is still one of the best general histories of the prewar and war periods. It starts with the negotiations for the Anglo-French Entente in 1904 and ends with the armistice of Rethondes in 1918. About one-fourth is devoted to the prewar period. While the emphasis here is on foreign policy, Professor Renouvin does not neglect domestic, social, economic and cultural trends. As for the origins of the war, he holds the Central Powers mainly responsible. The war itself is treated in two parts, divided by America's entry, which the author considers crucial. In contrast to most books on the war, military events do not overshadow everything else. More attention is actually paid to the diplomatic than to the military fronts; and economic problems, political crises, civilian morale all get their due. The tone throughout is civilized and free from national bias. On the touchy issue of war aims, for instance, Renouvin admits that "in both [camps], policy was annexationist." A concluding chapter sums up the effects of the war on the belligerent peoples. Given the vast ground it covers, the book is remarkably free of errors.

KING, JERE CLEMENS. **Generals and Politicians: Conflict between France's High Command, Parliament and Government, 1914–1918.** Berkeley: University of California Press, 1951, 294 p.

This is a study of how France managed to emerge from the war with her domestic institutions intact. In the beginning of the war, expecting it to be brief, the politicians did not dare—or even want—to interfere with military operations. Once the stalemate at the front had been established, however, ministers and parliamentarians were emboldened to try their hand at reviewing military activities. The Briand government managed to ease out General Joffre, thus opening the door to even broader efforts to bring the generals under civilian control. Civilian supervision, however, was incapable of preventing the disastrous Nivelle offensive of 1917. The mutinies in the army and the scandals in high places of that year ultimately led to virtual civilian dictatorship under Clemenceau. The "Tiger," despite a desire to meddle, managed to devise a working relationship with General Foch and to save France from military rule. This is an excellently written and judiciously argued work. Wherever possible, Professor King allows the protagonists to speak their own briefs. To the reader he serves as a trusted guide through the labyrinth of French politics and the complicated relationship between civilians and soldiers.

WOODWARD, SIR ERNEST LLEWELLYN. **Great Britain and the War of 1914–1918.** New York: Barnes and Noble, 1967, 610 p.

In the words of the author, one of Britain's most distinguished historians, this is "a short account—the essential facts and a running commentary—of the part taken by Great Britain in the First World War." This is far too modest an assessment of so rich and comprehensive a work. To be sure, it does not add much to the mass of available information on the war. Professor Woodward's account is based on careful and critical reading of all the relevant printed sources; and his perceptive selection of facts and his often fresh judgment of men and events give flavor and excitement to a well-known story. The book deals primarily with military, political and economic events on the official level. It has little to say on the "home front" and on social and intellectual concerns. The author has certain prejudices, among them a suspicion of things German. This becomes most obvious in the concluding section on the peace settlement. But Professor Woodward's prejudices are hardly unique, and his judgments are stated with honesty and dispassion. The book is written with polish and a touch of irony, and it has a fine set of maps.

GUINN, PAUL. **British Strategy and Politics, 1914 to 1918.** New York: Oxford University Press, 1965, 359 p.

The squabbling between Britain's political and military leaders during the First World War has become proverbial. Professor Guinn has written the most scholarly and balanced account yet published. His study begins in the early months of 1915 when the debate between the "easterners" and the "westerners" developed in the wake of the stalemate on the Western Front. He covers the period of ministerial control over policy when the Balkan, Gallipoli and Mesopotamian fronts were opened; then the period of military control over policy when the appalling battles of the Somme were fought; and finally, the emergence of the Lloyd George coalition and the reinstitution of a "militarized" civilian control. The bulk of the book is devoted to this final phase. It traces the various bewildering combinations of political and military pressures which shaped grand strategy and determined the course of the argument between the "frocks" and the "brass hats." With unusual success the author manages to interpret military policy in the light of war aims, national politics and tactical developments. His research is impressive, and his style readable and clear.

MAY, ARTHUR J. **The Passing of the Hapsburg Monarchy 1914–1918.** Philadelphia: University of Pennsylvania Press, 1966, 2 v.

Professor May is a well-known authority on Austrian history. This book on the dissolution of Austria-Hungary is the sequel to his earlier work, **The Hapsburg Monarchy, 1867–1914** (Cambridge: Harvard University Press, 1951, 532 p.). Like its predecessor, it is scholarly, authoritative and based on extensive research in published and unpublished sources. But unlike the earlier book, this one is quite difficult to read. Its topical organization is confusing, and the treatment given to the various topics is quite uneven. The chapters on domestic conditions are excellent, as are those on foreign attitudes toward Austria-Hungary. Austro-German relations are treated less satisfactorily, and the Polish question is given far too much emphasis. May makes less of nationalism as a cause of Austria-Hungary's demise than do some other authors; instead he points to military defeat as the decisive factor. The fact that May's study, while excellent in detail, lacks coherence and sweep may make some readers want to turn to the shorter, less comprehensive, but more readable book by Z. A. B. Zeman, **The Break-up of the Habsburg Empire 1914–1918**.

PAXSON, FREDERIC LOGAN. **American Democracy and the World War.** Boston: Houghton Mifflin, 1936–1939, 2 v.

————. **American Democracy and the World War: Postwar Years, Normalcy, 1918–1923.** Berkeley: University of California Press, 1948, 401 p.

In the author's own words, his aim was "to reveal the more important of the stresses, and to describe the adaptability of the people and the Constitution of the United States that has made it possible for this country to stand, stronger than ever, in a world of upset." This statement at once reveals this study's unique contribution and its weakness. Paxson has undertaken a mammoth task—to assess the impact of the First World War on American national development in the broadest sense. Especially arresting is his first volume, "Prewar Years, 1913–1917," in which he treats the expanding war as only one, albeit an important one, of the influences on American development. (The second volume is titled "America at War, 1917–1918.") Paxson's statement of intent also hints at his study's regrettable lack of critical, sociological and economic rigor. His political assessments were not novel at the time, and he makes no attempt to analyze social and economic problems. Instead he describes them broadly and often vaguely. The chronological organization of this descriptive work leads the reader through so many sometimes trivial subject changes that reading often becomes a chore. Still, though outdated, this remains the only comprehensive work on the war and American society. Here is a topic that calls for fresh treatment.

DIPLOMATIC HISTORY; WAR AIMS

GOTTLIEB, WOLFRAM WILHELM. **Studies in Secret Diplomacy during the First World War.** London: Allen and Unwin, 1957, 430 p.

Few diplomatic problems were as acute after war had started as the status of Turkey and Italy. The negotiations which brought the two states into the war epitomized old-style "secret diplomacy" and power politics. Using Italian, Russian, German, Austrian and American documents, Gottlieb has written the most up-to-date study of these negotiations. Despite the inaccessibility of Turkish records, he has pieced together the best account to date of that state's entry into partnership with the Central Powers. Though less impressive than his treatment of Turkey, Gottlieb's discussion of Italy is sound, especially in assessing the interests, intentions and influence of various internal Italian political and social factions. The author has not attempted to deal with the later aspects of secret diplomacy as relating to war aims or a negotiated peace; nor does he discuss secret diplomacy as a catch-phrase for popular antipathy toward cabinet-style, "old" diplomacy. Within its limited framework, **Secret Diplomacy** is an important contribution to the study of World War I diplomacy.

FISCHER, FRITZ. **Germany's Aims in the First World War.** New York: Norton, 1967, 652 p.

This is not the only history of Germany's war aims, but it is the most comprehensive and most controversial. Its first appearance in 1961 gave rise to violent dispute among German historians, chiefly because of the introductory chapters on Germany's responsibility for the war—a controversy kept alive by Professor Fischer's subsequent work on the origins of the war. The main body of the present book tells the story of German war aims which, in sum, called for "an empire of grandiose dimensions." Had Germany gotten what she wanted, she would suddenly have risen to the ranks of a "world power"—hence the book's German title, "Griff nach der Weltmacht." Much of the debate over war aims has centered on Fischer's claim that the detailed annexationist program, worked out as early as September 1914, was stubbornly adhered to until the bitter end, despite the shifting fortunes of war. One of the main supporters of the program was Chancellor Bethmann-Hollweg, who thus emerges as a determined advocate of German national interests rather than the ineffectual man of good will as he had hitherto appeared. While most of Fischer's factual findings are now generally accepted, there is less agreement on his wider thesis that Germany's expansionist aims originated long before and continued long after the war, until they found temporary fulfillment under Hitler. It should be noted that the book exists in several revised German editions, of which the third, published in 1964, is the best for scholarly use.

BAUMGART, WINFRIED. **Deutsche Ostpolitik 1918: Von Brest-Litowsk bis zum Ende des Ersten Weltkrieges.** Munich: Oldenbourg, 1966, 462 p.

This impressive first book by a young German historian supplements and enlarges upon the earlier work by Fritz Fischer on German war aims. In meticulous detail it analyzes Germany's contradictory plans and policies for the occupied regions of eastern Europe. While the high command, under Ludendorff, tried to extend and perpetuate Germany's influence beyond the limits set at Brest-Litovsk, hoping at the same time to put an end to Bolshevism, the Foreign Office, under Kühlmann and Hintze, recognized the delusions inherent in such schemes and proposed instead to support the Bolsheviks, in order to keep Russia weak and to prevent the return to power of pro-Allied forces. German policy vacillated between these two alternatives, thus necessitating continued heavy involvement of men and material in the east, which in turn weakened Germany's position in the west. A clear-cut pursuit of Kühlmann's policy, Baumgart implies, might have brought the war to a different end. His findings rest on solid foundations of German and Austrian archival sources, and his book will remain a basic contribution to the history of the war's concluding phase. It has an impressive bibliography but, unfortunately, no maps.

SMITH, CLARENCE JAY, JR. **The Russian Struggle for Power, 1914–1917: A Study of Russian Foreign Policy during the First World War.** New York: Philosophical Library, 1956, 553 p.

Using the rich collections of documents from the Tsarist archives published by the Bolsheviks, Professor Smith's careful study is a significant contribution to the general history of pre-1917 Russian foreign policy. Much of it deals with war aims, among which the Straits and Constantinople stand out, although Russia's appetite for territory made her cast longing eyes at the Slavic regions of the disintegrating Hapsburg Empire as well. The author's approach is narrowly political and diplomatic. Attention to economic and social factors might have yielded more significant insights than the one conveyed in the obvious statement that there is "more than a passing resemblance between the Tsarist policies of 1914–1917 and those of Stalin between 1941 and 1948." Since the territorial deals between Russia and her allies involved regions of great ethnic complexity, a set of maps would have been helpful.

WHEELER-BENNETT, JOHN WHEELER. **The Forgotten Peace: Brest-Litovsk, March 1918.** New York: Morrow, 1939, 478 p.

The full history of the negotiations culminating in the abortive Russo-German Treaty of Brest-Litovsk still needs to be written. With complete German and at least partial Russian documentation available, this is now possible. The most recent account, based mostly on German sources, is in Wolfgang Steglich, **Die Friedens- politik der Mittelmächte 1917–18** (Wiesbaden: Steiner, 1964, 593 p.), one-third of which deals with Brest-Litovsk in the wider framework of Austro-German diplo- macy. The best treatment in English is still the book by Wheeler-Bennett. Its major contribution was to have rescued the "forgotten peace" from oblivion and to have assigned to it the important place it holds in world history. In many of its details new evidence clearly calls for expansion and emendation, but in its main outlines this most readable book will doubtless continue to hold its own.

MAY, ERNEST RICHARD. **The World War and American Isolation, 1914–1917.** Cam- bridge: Harvard University Press, 1959, 482 p.

Sound scholarship, good writing and meaningful scope make this the best single- volume study of American neutrality and the decision for war. The book is based on American, British and German archival sources. Expanding on Karl E. Birnbaum's **Peace Moves and U-Boat Warfare: A Study of Imperial Germany's Policy towards the United States, April 18, 1916–January 9, 1917** (Stockholm: Almqvist, 1958, 388 p.), Professor May has done much to elucidate further the position of the United States in German policy. It is the first American book that attempts to rehabilitate Bethmann-Hollweg. With a certain sympathy it describes the German Chancellor's efforts to limit military erosions of his power and his attempts to restrain military leaders from drawing the United States into war against Germany.

On the American side, May emphasizes that American neutrality was not de- liberately pro-Ally but reflected American views of international law and American trading interests. He shows how Wilson, Lansing and House conceived American national interests to include security, legal, economic and prestige considerations. American prestige and commitment to international law were most closely involved in Wilson's decision for war in response to unrestricted submarine warfare. May approves Wilson's realistic defense of endangered American trade and prestige, as well as Wilson's commitment to ideals of world peace.

BUEHRIG, EDWARD HENRY. **Woodrow Wilson and the Balance of Power.** Blooming- ton: Indiana University Press, 1955, 325 p.

The author, an expert on international organization, makes a notable contribu- tion to the historiography both of the American decision to enter the war and of American aims in World War I. He argues that Wilson had realistic perceptions of American national interests—short and long-term security; economic interests in freedom of the seas and partnership with Britain; and postwar peace through world law and organization. According to Buehrig, early pro-Allied neutrality reflected Wilson's appreciation of the world balance of power, a balance which Wilson desired to preserve as a basis for world order. When Britain appeared unwilling to negotiate peace, Wilson developed a concept of community of power, the result of peace without victory and the basis for a new order. In defense of American economic interests and security needs as he conceived them, Wilson turned first to Britain for help in realizing his aims, then attempted to mediate between Britain and Germany. When both countries had shown their extensive war aims, Wilson entered the war to secure American goals as best he could.

Professor Buehrig is one of the leading recent interpreters of the realistic aspects of Wilsonian diplomacy. His book remains one of the few not superseded by later work. He has used most printed and some manuscript sources to support his subtle and well-written study of Wilsonian aims and policies.

TRASK, DAVID F. **The United States in the Supreme War Council: American War Aims and Inter-Allied Strategy, 1917–1918.** Middletown: Wesleyan University Press, 1961, 244 p.

This book deals with a neglected phase in American diplomatic history—America's efforts to retain military and diplomatic independence in a coalition war. Given the usual patterns of compromise and mutual restriction prevalent in coalition politics, one would expect a story of failure; but Trask tells it differently. The United States hoped to work for a constructive peace settlement, from which a new order of right and justice could arise. The institution through which America and the Allied Powers linked political war aims with military strategy was the Supreme War Council. It was in this arena, therefore, that the United States had to carry its point. Yet to avoid endorsement of Allied war aims and retain freedom to formulate independent aims, Wilson and the United States steadfastly refrained from participating in the Council's political decisions. Thus we have the paradox of Woodrow Wilson, America's greatest internationalist, strongly expressing traditional American distrust of European political involvement. The author presents an interesting discussion of the Fourteen Points. With their qualified acceptance by all sides, Trask believes that Wilson triumphantly concluded American wartime diplomacy. The tragedy of Versailles could hardly have been foreseen at this point.

KENNAN, GEORGE FROST. **Soviet-American Relations, 1917–1920.** Princeton: Princeton University Press, 1956–1958, 2 v.

George Kennan, veteran United States diplomat, here presents himself in the role of historian. His experiences in the field give color and authority to his scholarship, and he is a superb writer. The first volume of this study—"Russia Leaves the War"—covers the period from the November Revolution of 1917 to Russia's final departure from the ranks of the belligerents in March 1918. The second volume—"The Decision to Intervene"—takes the story to the end of the war on the Western Front. By that time, American policy toward Russia had evolved from initial attempts to find a modus vivendi with the Bolshevik régime to one of armed intervention. Yet with the defeat of Germany, any possible justification for such intervention as ultimately aimed at the Central Powers had lost its meaning. By cutting off whatever slender threads for a viable relationship between the two countries existed at the time, America's futile intervention proved a costly mistake. "Never, surely, in the history of American diplomacy has so much been paid for so little."

Devoting two volumes to so short a period allows Mr. Kennan to paint with a fine brush. His is that rare work in diplomatic history—a true study in depth. Based on extensive new research in primary sources, interviews and a mass of published material, it is a wholly admirable book.

ULLMAN, RICHARD H. **Anglo-Soviet Relations, 1917–1921.** Princeton: Princeton University Press (for the Center of International Studies), 1961 and 1968, 2 v.

"The fact that Allied policy towards Russia . . . so largely *originated* in London, and not in Paris, Washington, or Tokyo, makes it important that there should appear a study devoted specifically to the formulation and conduct of British policy." Thus the author's justification for a work that in part runs parallel to Kennan's study. Professor Ullman first examines "London's initial, hesitant attempts to understand and to reach an accord with the Bolsheviks;" then he deals with British and Allied intervention; and in a projected third volume he will discuss Britain's efforts to reach accommodation with the Bolshevik government. The author sees Britain's response to Bolshevism as a far more haphazard and a far less deliberate effort to stifle the Bolshevik revolution than it has been described by Soviet historians. When the decision to intervene was made, it was not clear to the Allies that reopening an eastern front against Germany in fact entailed a commitment to overthrow Bolshevik rule in Russia. When it became certain that Britain could not decisively influence the Russian civil war without massive involvement, intervention gave way to conciliation. This is an important book, not least because of the relevance of its observations and conclusions on more recent international events.

RUDIN, HARRY RUDOLPH. **Armistice 1918.** New Haven: Yale University Press, 1944, 442 p.

RENOUVIN, PIERRE. **L'Armistice de Rethondes, 11 Novembre 1918.** Paris: Gallimard, 1968, 488 p.

Even though much new source material has become available since it was written, Professor Rudin's book remains the best study in English on the armistice of November 11, 1918. In the author's words, "it seeks to tell why the Germans wanted an armistice, how the Allies went about drafting one, and how the two armistice delegations came to find agreement in the forest of Compiègne."

Professor Renouvin, almost 25 years later, has covered much the same ground. Since he was able to use many fresh sources, especially from French archives, his is a richer book. Both authors concern themselves at length with the "stab-in-the-back legend" which Germany's military leaders propagated after the war to shift the responsibility for defeat on to civilian shoulders. Their conclusions agree that Germany was defeated from without, not from within. "Had the war gone on for several more weeks or months," Professor Renouvin adds, "Germany's defeat would have been still heavier." Both books cite relevant documents in an appendix, but Renouvin's collection is larger and more interesting. The latter also has an admirable bibliography and a set of fascinating pictures.

ECONOMIC AND SOCIAL ASPECTS

SHOTWELL, JAMES THOMSON, *ed.* **Economic and Social History of the World War.** New Haven: Yale University Press, 1924–1940.

This ambitiously conceived collection of monographs, sponsored by the Carnegie Endowment, set as its goal "to attempt to describe the displacement caused by the war in the processes of civilization." It was to cover "some sixteen European countries," each to be dealt with in a separate series, running in some cases to more than 30 volumes. In time the United States and Japan were added to the list. The project was never completed as planned, but by the late 1930s, more than 100 volumes of varying length, scope and importance had been published. Among the authors were noted scholars as well as government officials and experts. The emphasis throughout was on economics. Because of their narrow focus, most of the studies appeal only to specialists. To the historian they remain useful as introductions and sources for further research in areas where comprehensive studies are still very much needed.

CHAMBERS, FRANK PENTLAND. **The War behind the War, 1914–1918: A History of the Political and Civilian Fronts.** New York: Harcourt, 1939, 620 p.

To write a comprehensive history of the war and its many fronts—military and civilian, political and economic, social and ideological—requires a range of knowledge and a degree of impartiality possessed by few, if any, modern historians. These difficulties, to which should be added the lack of monographs on many important phases of the war, must be kept in mind when judging Chambers' book.

"The exacting standards of modern scholarship," he says in his preface, "are too often allowed to scare off attempts to see the bigger episodes of history as a whole." Fortunately, the author was not scared off. The book is an impressive performance, and though some of its details are by now outdated, it still presents an overview not found anywhere else. The emphasis is on the war's non-military aspects, but the most important military events are sketched in. The presentation is chronological and by country, which makes monotonous reading. Heavy emphasis on facts at the expense of analysis and interpretation is a further drawback. But the book is a mine of information; the treatment is always fair; and the bibliography and maps are very good.

MARWICK, ARTHUR. **The Deluge: British Society and the First World War.** Boston: Little, Brown, 1965, 336 p.

Professor Marwick tries to convey an impression of what it was like to live in Great Britain during the war and to draw some conclusions about the impact which this "deluge" had upon British society. He describes how the first flush of enthusiasm quickly yielded to a stubborn insistence upon "business as usual." This, in turn, gave way during 1915 to the early pressures for fundamental change: the need to conserve and allocate manpower; the rising affluence and recognition of labor; the first steps toward women's emancipation; and most important, the early, hesitant steps of the government to challenge the principle of a laissez-faire economy. Finally, the author shows how these trends gained momentum during 1917–1918, as disillusionment and shortages grew apace with control and regulation. He demonstrates how the war sped developments which had been noticeable before and which would, in any case, have come along later at a more leisurely pace. This is a remarkably fresh and sensitive book of admirably broad scope.

HURWITZ, SAMUEL JUSTIN. **State Intervention in Great Britain: A Study of Economic Control and Social Response, 1914–1919.** New York: Columbia University Press, 1949, 321 p.

During the First World War, the British government moved reluctantly from a policy of "business as usual" to one of extensive, if often haphazard, intervention into all major sectors of the economy. Professor Hurwitz traces the development of governmental controls in each of these sectors—munitions and other heavy industries, coal, leather goods, textiles, shipping and agriculture—paying particular attention throughout to the distribution of that most important scarce resource, "manpower," a term which, significantly, first gained currency during the war. Such action was of course contrary to the economic theories held by a majority of the British leaders, and in each case the author shows how persuasion and appeals to patriotism gave way to compulsion only slowly and under unremitting pressure for greater war productivity. This is a thoroughly researched and profusely documented book. In addition to his extensive use of official histories, reports and other documents, the author has taken special advantage of the British penchant for writing memoirs.

SINEY, MARION CELESTIA. **The Allied Blockade of Germany, 1914–1916.** Ann Arbor: University of Michigan Press, 1957, 339 p.

This is the first volume of a projected two-volume study of the diplomacy surrounding Allied attempts to prevent essential goods from reaching Germany during the First World War. It is based principally on unpublished sources from Great Britain, the Netherlands, the Scandinavian countries and the United States. More than a decade has passed since its publication without the appearance of the second volume. Thus, as it stands, the study is cut off in midstream and suffers accordingly. After presenting a summary of the prewar state of international law regarding "belligerent rights at sea and economic warfare," Professor Siney proceeds to discuss in detail the negotiations between the Allies, principally Britain, and the neutrals over measures by which the flow of goods to Germany was progressively diminished. The outcome of these negotiations depended on the strength of the relative bargaining positions of (usually) Britain and any particular neutral. Thus the British were more successful in dealing with the Norwegians, who depended on British coal, than they were with the Swedes, whose railway system was essential for transporting Allied goods to the Russian front. It is as a case study of bargaining in international politics that the book is most useful and interesting. The author has little to say about either the strategic importance of the blockade for the Allies or the economic impact of the blockade upon Germany.

READ, JAMES MORGAN. **Atrocity Propaganda, 1914–1919.** New Haven: Yale University Press, 1941, 319 p.

During World War I, the propagation of atrocity stories reached unprecedented proportions. Professor Read's study is a highly successful scholarly attempt to survey the atrocity literature and to reach some conclusions as to its veracity. He notes that atrocity propaganda served many purposes: instilling hatreds, stiffening the fighting spirit, stimulating war loans, encouraging enlistments and justifying breaches of international law. Generally the propaganda fell into five categories: exaggerated stories, flat prevarications, magnifications of the usual by-products of war, deprecation of new types of weapons and distortions of past history. In assessing truthfulness, Professor Read concludes that both sides committed excesses, but that there were not nearly as many atrocities as people believed. The British propaganda effort was the most successful, especially in influencing neutral opinion. The Germans were the least successful, because they wasted too much time refuting Allied charges and because tight control over the press set limits to journalistic flights of imagination. Professor Read has produced a valuable and highly readable introduction to a fascinating subject.

FELDMAN, GERALD D. **Army, Industry and Labor in Germany, 1914–1918.** Princeton: Princeton University Press, 1966, 572 p.

Except for the rather disappointing volume in the Carnegie Series by Albrecht Mendelssohn-Bartholdy, **The War and German Society: The Testament of a Liberal** (New Haven: Yale University Press, 1937, 300 p.), there are no general social and economic histories for Germany at war. Professor Feldman's monograph on the social and economic activities of the German army thus opens up a wide field in which much further work needs to be done. His subject is an intricate one, partly because of the triangular relationship between army, industry and labor; but also because the army itself was by no means monolithic in its policy, some factions favoring one, some the other of the two sectors of the economy at various times. By implication at least, the book is concerned with the phenomenon of "total war." In this connection it is worth noting that Feldman's picture of Ludendorff is far from the stereotype of a dictatorial practitioner of total mobilization. This is only one of many corrections of widely held assumptions about wartime Germany in this solid book. Its style is clear. One might have wished for a fuller bibliography; but even what little there is conveys an impression of careful research in a wide variety of sources.

PEACE SETTLEMENTS; PARIS CONFERENCE

TEMPERLEY, HAROLD WILLIAM VAZIELLE, *ed.* **A History of the Peace Conference of Paris.** London: Frowde, 1920–1924, 6 v.

Despite its age, this is still the standard work on the Peace Conference and the peace treaties. It was written for the most part by subordinate participants and edited by a noted British historian. The first three volumes cover the process of peacemaking, especially with Germany, beginning in 1916; the fourth and fifth describe the founding of new states on the ruins of the Hapsburg Empire; and the last volume deals with eastern Europe, as well as extra-European problems and the

League of Nations. Temperley admits to a certain Anglo-Saxon bias but points out that the study explicates the German position more fully than any other book at the time.

In his conclusions, the editor shares some of the disillusionment that had already grown around the peace treaties: "The aim of broad-visioned justice and mercy were too often defeated." But at the same time he took great comfort in the League of Nations: "The Peace Treaty will fade into merciful oblivion. . . . But the Covenant will stand as sure as fate." The disillusionment with the peace had found its most influential expression earlier in the notorious work of another participant in the Peace Conference, John Maynard Keynes. The youthful British economist's **The Economic Consequences of the Peace,** together with the belated rejoinder by a young French historian, Étienne Mantoux, **The Carthaginian Peace, or the Economic Consequences of Mr. Keynes** (New York: Oxford University Press, 1946, 203 p.), constitute the now classic debate over the alleged errors and injustices of the peace settlement.

NICOLSON, HAROLD GEORGE. **Peacemaking, 1919.** Boston: Houghton, 1933, 378 p.
BONSAL, STEPHEN. **Unfinished Business.** Garden City: Doubleday, 1944, 313 p.
————. **Suitors and Suppliants.** New York: Prentice-Hall, 1946, 301 p.

These books belong in the category of memoir-histories. Both authors took part in the Paris deliberations, and while they are writing long after the event, their accounts are based on diaries kept at the time. They both tell fascinating stories. Harold Nicolson, a junior member of the British peace delegation, is highly critical of much that went on in Paris, and his observations convey a vivid impression of the bewildered confusion that pervaded much of the Conference. Stephen Bonsal, a veteran American journalist, who served as aide to Colonel House and confidential interpreter for President Wilson, tells of his part in the deliberations leading to the League of Nations and of his involvement with the representatives of the smaller powers of Europe and Asia, the "suitors and suppliants" who came to Paris in pursuit of "self-determination."

The negotiations with the powers other than Germany have been the subject of detailed monographs. The most important of these special studies are: René Albrecht-Carrié, **Italy at the Paris Peace Conference** (New York: Columbia University Press, 1938, 575 p.), dealing with the plight of a power which, though nominally "great," felt that it received scant justice at Paris; Nina Almond and Ralph Haswell Lutz, *comps.* and *eds.,* **The Treaty of St. Germain** (Stanford: Stanford University Press, 1935, 712 p.); Francis Deák, **Hungary at the Paris Peace Conference** (New York: Columbia University Press, 1942, 594 p.), on the settlements with Austria and Hungary, including important documents; Ivo J. Lederer, **Yugoslavia at the Paris Peace Conference: A Study in Frontiermaking,** a scholarly account of the trials of the much-divided Jugoslav delegation; Sherman David Spector, **Rumania at the Paris Peace Conference: A Study of the Diplomacy of Ioan I. C. Brătianu** (New York: Bookman Associates, 1962, 368 p.), the story of the country that deserved least but got most at Paris; and Dagmar Perman, **The Shaping of the Czechoslovak State: Diplomatic History of the Boundaries of Czechoslovakia, 1914–1920,** which treats the issue of Czechoslovakia in the wider context of Allied diplomacy. Mention should also be made of the important study by Victor Samuel Mamatey, **The United States and East Central Europe, 1914–1918.**

MAYER, ARNO J. **Politics and Diplomacy of Peacemaking: Containment and Counterrevolution at Versailles, 1918–1919.** New York: Knopf, 1967, 918 p.

"Whereas in 1917–1918, in the heat of war, the Allied 'parties of movement' (predominantly of the Left) put their imprint on the diplomacy of the world crisis, in 1918–1919, while peace was being made, the 'parties of order' (predominantly the Right) reclaimed their primacy in the victor nations." Within this framework, Professor Mayer examines the domestic origins of peacemaking in the Allied nations, applying terms and concepts familiar to many readers from cold-war policy discussions. Mayer believes that the initial years of Soviet confrontation with the West elicited the hostile responses which after World War II would be called "containment" and "counterrevolution." To the author, these Western responses to the Soviet challenge dominated the Paris Peace Conference. Mayer is not alone in perceiving similarities between early and later responses to Bolshevik Russia. The question is whether the Russian problem loomed as large at Paris as he thinks, and whether he has not overweighted Russian concerns in relation to the main business at Paris—making peace with the Central Powers. The book is excessively long, but most of it makes rewarding reading. Like Professor Mayer's earlier work, **Political Origins of the New Diplomacy, 1917–1918** (New Haven: Yale University Press, 1959, 435 p.), it emphasizes the interaction of domestic and foreign policies. It is based on extensive archival research in the United States, Britain, France, Italy and the Netherlands, as well as on careful study of a broad range of secondary literature.

BIRDSALL, PAUL. **Versailles Twenty Years After.** New York: Reynal, 1941, 350 p.
　　Even though written long ago, this book remains one of the best discussions of the Paris Peace Conference. Birdsall refuses to blame the maladies of Europe between the wars on the Versailles Treaty. He contends that the territorial settlement was as judicious as any could have been. He takes issue with Keynes' assault upon the economic provisions of the treaty. But over all, his main aim is to demonstrate that Woodrow Wilson fought with great tenacity and considerable success for a treaty founded upon the principles which he had enunciated. He sees Wilson as one of the few true "internationalists" at the Peace Conference, a man who defended American interests where necessary but who, because the American stake was marginal and Wilson's principles were high, managed to approach the problems of the Conference with detachment and fairmindedness.
　　Devotees of Lloyd George will find Birdsall's treatment rather harsh. But it is the French, Wilson's principal antagonists, who provide the author with the juxtapositions he needs to place Wilson's accomplishments in relief. Although Birdsall's main intent is to describe Wilson's struggle with his European peers, the book is by no means a whitewash. The author is attuned to Wilson's failings and quite sensitive to French apprehensions. His remarks on the inter-war years are somewhat dated, but this in no way detracts from the value of this judicious and highly readable book.

TILLMAN, SETH P. **Anglo-American Relations at the Paris Peace Conference of 1919.** Princeton: Princeton University Press, 1961, 442 p.
　　At the Paris Peace Conference, Great Britain and the United States shared a fundamental community of purpose and followed parallel, often identical, policies. But Anglo-American harmony suffered frequent disruption—both as a result of direct clashes of interest and as a result of prior commitments to third parties. Anglo-American coöperation was at its worst in framing the economic provisions of the treaty; it was at its best in the drafting of the League Covenant and in making the territorial settlement. Over all, Professor Tillman argues, the two powers were never able to translate their unity of intent into a common strategy. Nevertheless, he concludes that Great Britain and the United States were responsible for the most humane and enlightened provisions of the treaty. That the democracies ultimately lost the opportunity of 1919 was, in Professor Tillman's view, not the fault of the peacemakers. Rather, it was due to the fact that the United States abandoned and Great Britain morally repudiated the treaties to which they had contributed so much.

NELSON, HAROLD I. **Land and Power: British and Allied Policy on Germany's Frontiers, 1916–19.** Toronto: University of Toronto Press, 1963, 402 p.
　　This well-written study treats the evolution of the territorial peace settlement with Germany, concentrating in the main upon British policy. Professor Nelson

demonstrates how the early British ideas for a postwar rearrangement, which emphasized the need for a balance between Russia and Germany, were affected by the Russian Revolution and the entry of the United States into the war. Not only did these developments alter the European balance, they also strengthened the movements for a negotiated peace based upon a "new diplomacy." The removal of Russia from the Allied ranks compelled the British to look to Poland as a necessary counter to German power in eastern Europe. But the British also recognized that France and the new "buffer states" of the east would not be able to stabilize the peace without extensive outside aid. British leaders, therefore, looked to the United States to take an active part in the policies of postwar Europe. Whereas American historians have emphasized the fact that Wilson was unable to exert decisive influence upon the French and the British at the Paris Peace Conference, Professor Nelson stresses the fact that Lloyd George and even Clemenceau looked upon close coöperation with the United States after the war as being important, if not essential, to European peace.

VAN DER SLICE, AUSTIN. **International Labor, Diplomacy, and Peace, 1914–1919.** Philadelphia: University of Pennsylvania Press, 1941, 408 p.

Organized labor was the only social group that was international in organization and activity at the time of the First World War. Not surprisingly, labor groups in the great Western states had aims and goals during the war which they tried to realize through pressures on public opinion and national governments. This interesting book tells of labor's early peace programs and their contributions to the ideas that went into the Fourteen Points. Labor was prevented from having maximum effect at Paris by secrecy of negotiations. And because labor was so closely allied with Wilson's program, when the Fourteen Points underwent emasculation, labor's aims and influence suffered accordingly. Unfortunately, Professor Van der Slice did not appreciate the comparative value of German labor to his study. But no other book deals comparatively with the labor movements in France, Great Britain and the United States in relation to war and peacetime policies. The author has used materials from most Western countries and has read widely in European and American newspapers and periodicals.

BAILEY, THOMAS ANDREW. **Woodrow Wilson and the Lost Peace.** New York: Macmillan, 1944, 381 p.

————. **Woodrow Wilson and the Great Betrayal.** New York: Macmillan, 1945, 429 p.

Professor Bailey wrote these books in the early 1940s, fearful lest Americans forget the lessons of World War I and the all-too-fragile Peace of Paris. The books were timely when they appeared, and they remain both thoughtful and stimulating. Bailey matches masterful and lively narration of events at Paris and Versailles (and later in the United States) with solid critical analysis to produce argumentative, but scarcely assailable, diplomatic history. He believes that the Allies lost the peace, or the chance for lasting peace, when they turned from pursuit of justice and a new beginning to wreaking vengeance and preserving the old order. American failure to adhere to the Versailles Treaty doomed a settlement already weakened by its harsh, almost unfulfillable terms. Pointing out Wilson's and the American people's errors in handling the peace settlement, Bailey implores his countrymen not to pass up the coming second chance to be a positive force for international peace and to accept international responsibilities.

THOMPSON, JOHN M. **Russia, Bolshevism, and the Versailles Peace.** Princeton: Princeton University Press, 1967, 429 p.

In editing his history of the Peace Conference, Professor Temperley omitted consideration of Russia. Thompson corrects this omission. The "specter" of Russia was ever present at Paris. There were the questions of boundaries, national claims and minorities, in many of which Russia was involved; and more important, there was the question of Russia's own future. Thompson sets out to discover how the peacemakers tried to cope with the challenge of Bolshevism and why they failed. He concludes that the statesmen at Paris were hardly aware of the true nature of Bolshevism and gave little thought to Russia. When they did, they hoped to solve the problem through traditional techniques of power and diplomacy. There were, interestingly enough, signs of "containment" and "roll-back" discernible in the policy preferences of Western leaders as early as 1919, but there was little realization of the ideological component of the Bolshevik danger. Nor was there much harmony among the powers when it came to dealing with the Russians. The main order of business, after all, was making peace with the Central Powers.

MEMOIRS AND BIOGRAPHIES

POINCARÉ, RAYMOND. **Au Service de la France.** Paris: Plon, 1926–1933, 10 v.

With very few exceptions, the writings of France's wartime leaders are too vindicative to be reliable and too bitterly vindictive to make enjoyable reading. Poincaré's memoirs, because of their size and the author's importance, hold a special place. Beginning with his premiership in 1912, they cover his presidency until the end of the war, in great detail for 1913–1915 and more sketchily thereafter. While dry and depressing in tone, the ten volumes do give an almost encyclopedic account of the war. Since Poincaré destroyed the papers on which his memoirs are based, they are an invaluable source.

A condensed English translation by Sir George Arthur, **The Memoirs of Raymond Poincaré** (New York: Doubleday, 1926–1930, 4 v.) only goes as far as 1915. Among several books on Poincaré, Gordon Wright, **Raymond Poincaré and the French Presidency** (Stanford: Stanford University Press, 1942, 271 p.), presents a balanced assessment of the man and the war. Pierre Miquel, **Poincaré** (Paris: Fayard, 1961, 636 p.), is a full-length portrait based on much fresh material, with emphasis on the war years. The rest of French memoir literature is disappointing. Among biographies of other leading figures, Geoffrey Bruun's sympathetic **Clemenceau** (Cambridge: Harvard University Press, 1943, 225 p.) and Basil H. Liddell Hart's **Foch: The Man of Orleans** deserve special mention.

LLOYD GEORGE, DAVID. **War Memoirs.** Boston: Little, Brown, 1933–1937, 6 v.

The list of memoirs and biographies of Britain's leaders during World War I is extraordinarily long and contains many outstanding works. Few are more interesting and readable than the record returned by Lloyd George. Although his self-defense is often unconvincing, the memoirs contain a wealth of firsthand information. Not unnaturally, the author believes that the civilians won the war in spite of the generals. He makes a good case, even though in the process he is too obviously self-serving and too often vindictive. The zest of these memoirs is maintained, but the reliability further weakened, in their sequel, **The Truth about the Peace Treaties: Memoirs of the Peace Conference** (New Haven: Yale University Press, 1939, 2 v.). Equally trenchant and often more exaggerated are Lord Beaverbrook's informative reminiscences, **Politicians and the War, 1916–1918** (London: Butterworth, 1928–1932, 2 v.) and **Men and Power, 1917–1918** (New York: Duell, 1957, 447 p.). The other prime minister of the war years, Herbert Asquith, has been the subject of a substantial, though rather defensive, biography: John A. Spender and Cyril Asquith, **The Life of Herbert Henry Asquith, Lord Oxford and Asquith** (London: Hutchinson, 1932, 2 v.). A very illuminating study of an important opposition leader and later War Cabinet member is A. M. Gollin's biography of Milner, **Proconsul in Politics: A Study of Lord Milner in Opposition and in Power** (New York: Macmillan, 1964, 627 p.). The useful, though excessively discreet reminiscences of Sir Maurice (Lord) Hankey, **The Supreme Command 1914–1918,** tell about the evolution of Britain's War Cabinet and defense organization.

CHURCHILL, WINSTON SPENCER. **The World Crisis, 1911–1918.** New York: Scribner, 1923–1927, 4 v.

The best known, if not the best, book on the war is the memoir-history of Winston Churchill. As always, Churchill is his own best chronicler. He recounts his experiences as First Sea Lord at the beginning of the war, as Minister of Munitions at the end, and as a gadfly politician and soldier in between. Mr. Churchill writes in his usual grand and rolling style. He argues terribly well in his own behalf—he is always plausible, not always convincing, seldom conclusive. The first two volumes cover his tenure at the Admiralty. The third and fourth, treating the years 1916–1918, are more in the nature of a general history and hence better. These four volumes have been condensed into an excellent single-volume abridgment (New York: Scribner, 1931, 866 p.). Whether taken in long or abbreviated doses, they remain a magisterial, winning study of the First World War, written by one of its most colorful participants.

VON VIETSCH, EBERHARD. **Bethmann Hollweg: Staatsmann zwischen Macht und Ethos.** Boppard: Boldt, 1969, 348 p.

The self-justifying strain, evident in most memoirs, is strongest among leaders of the defeated nations. Most of the prominent Germans, from William II on down, have told their story. Yet none of these apologias holds much value for the historian or much interest for the general reader. An exception is the posthumous edition of the papers of Admiral Georg Alexander von Müller, the Kaiser's chief naval aide: Walter Görlitz, ed., **The Kaiser and His Court: The Diaries, Note Books and Letters of Admiral Georg Alexander von Müller, Chief of the Naval Cabinet, 1914–1918** (New York: Harcourt, Brace, 1964, 430 p.), which provides fascinating glimpses into life at the top in wartime Germany. Among biographies, the harvest is equally slim. On William II the best, but by no means definitive, book is Michael L. G. Balfour, **The Kaiser and His Times** (Boston: Houghton Mifflin, 1964, 524 p.). Only Bethmann-Hollweg has thus far found a scholarly biographer. Eberhard von Vietsch's book is careful and dull. Given the subject and the fact that the Chancellor's papers were destroyed in World War II, this is understandable. Bethmann-Hollweg was an able bureaucrat, not a statesman. Until Fritz Fischer touched off the debate on German war aims, the Chancellor attracted little attention. The author never really takes issue with the questions raised by Fischer concerning Bethmann's character and motives. What emerges is the traditional picture of the well-meaning idealist, too small (and too good) for the rough-and-tumble world of *grosse Politik*.

LINK, ARTHUR STANLEY. **Wilson.** Princeton: Princeton University Press, 1947–, 5 v. to date.

Professor Link's work on Wilson, when completed, will not only be as nearly definitive a biography as possible, but it will also be a major contribution to the study of American diplomacy. It is based primarily on the wealth of information contained in Wilson's own papers, which Link has been editing simultaneously for separate publication. One may appreciate the maturity and insight of Link's judgment by comparing his **Wilson** with other studies he has written on special Wilsonian topics: **Woodrow Wilson and the Progressive Era, 1910–1917** (New York: Harper, 1954, 331 p.) and **Wilson the Diplomatist: A Look at His Major Foreign Policies** (Baltimore: Johns Hopkins Press, 1957, 165 p.). Such comparison will show a constant and open-minded reappraisal on the part of a self-critical scholar.

New Wilson scholarship increasingly concerns itself with the influence of the President's closest advisers. First among them was Colonel House, about whose activities one can still learn a great deal from Edward Mandell House, **The Intimate Papers of Colonel House** (arranged by Charles Seymour; Boston: Houghton Mifflin, 1926–1928, 4 v.). The Colonel was deep in Wilson's confidence until some time at the Peace Conference, and by all accounts he displayed considerable skill in handling Wilson. Secretary of State Lansing also learned to advance his ideas by couching suggestions in terms of Wilson's favorite language. His **The Peace Negotiations, a Personal Narrative** (Boston: Houghton Mifflin, 1921, 328 p.) is disappointing and shows Lansing some distance from the center of power. Because of Wilson's overpowering influence and America's late entry into the war, American military figures played a far lesser role than their British, French and German counterparts. General John J. Pershing's **My Experiences in the World War** is among the better world war memoirs by military leaders of the major powers.

CONDUCT OF THE WAR

General

BOURGET, JEAN MARIE. **Les Origines de la Victoire.** Paris: Renaissance du Livre, 1924, 582 p.

This lively, provocative and carefully reasoned study should not be retired because of old age. With an appreciation for sea power unusual in most European soldiers of the day, Bourget successfully integrates the war at sea with the campaigns on the Western and Eastern Fronts, at the same time considering the political and economic factors that helped to shape strategy in 1914–1918.

One paramount theme emerges—the failure of either side to achieve a unified command or even to coördinate strategy until the final campaign. France and Britain did not even synchronize military operations with the Russians or coördinate the campaigns in Egypt, the Dardanelles and Macedonia. This was especially tragic, Bourget contends, because only through the application of pressure at several points simultaneously could the Allies hope to defeat Germany. Even had the generals achieved a breakthrough on the Western Front after 1915, no strategic exploitation would have been possible without first having depleted the enemy's mobile reserves; and for this, war would have had to be waged aggressively on two or more fronts. This did not occur before the emergence of a unified command in 1918, when the United States provided the necessary reserve, enabling Foch to turn back the German attacks and launch massive offensives of his own.

Bourget blames the Allied leaders for not properly coördinating all efforts, whether in France or the eastern Mediterranean, against the Central Powers. He even insists that it was the final Allied advance in Macedonia, not the British, French and American attacks against the Hindenburg Line, that finally brought Germany to the peace table. This was so, he argues, because there were no reserves available to meet this threat to the rear.

FALLS, CYRIL BENTHAM. **The Great War.** New York: Putnam, 1959, 447 p.

The author's stated purposes are to convey what World War I meant to his generation and to "commemorate the spirit in which these men served and fought." He achieves these goals without chauvinistic overtones, and at the same time he manages to condense the history of the war into one tightly packed, remarkably balanced volume. To manage this feat, Falls slights social-political aspects and emphasizes military operations, without, however, doing a purely operational military history. He is obliged to treat minor operations hurriedly, and he also tells the reader less about administration and the home front than many will want to know. But if the student dismisses an occasional judgment, such as the statement that Allied success at Gallipoli might have "changed the fate of the world," there are other judgments he should weigh carefully (*e.g.* the contention that the Royal Navy was a crucial factor in the Allied victory formula).

Reflecting his grasp of the documents and his work on the official history, Falls argues that the military art did not lie stagnant everywhere and that generalship was not universally bankrupt. His succinct accounts of the key campaigns and thoughtful analyses of the character and performance of the principal commanders lend credence to his claims. Sir Basil Liddell Hart disagrees with this thesis in his **A**

History of the World War, 1914–1918 (Boston: Little, Brown, 1935, 635 p.). In this work, a revised version of **The Real War** (Boston: Little, Brown, 1930, 508 p.), Liddell Hart uses the account of the war to advance his theory of the indirect approach and probably underestimates the strategic value of Germany's central position. His book, though less well organized than Falls' work, admirably complements the latter.

A third work which is useful for its clear narrative and treatment of the war as a whole is Charles R. M. Cruttwell, **A History of the Great War** (Oxford: Clarendon Press, 2d ed., 1936, 655 p.). A veteran of the war and a trained historian, Cruttwell is least reliable in dealing with critical details of battles (*e.g.* the Marne and Jutland).

PIERI, PIERO. **La Prima Guerra Mondiale, 1914–1918.** Turin: Gheroni, 1947, 421 p.

More than a half-century after its end, there is no good narrative history of Italy in the First World War or of the Italian front in that war. Luigi Cadorna's **La Guerra alla Fronte Italiana** (Milan: Treves, 1921, 2 v.) is self-serving. An official history, **L'Esercito Italiano nella Grande Guerra (1915–1918)** (Rome: Istituto Poligrafico dello Stato, 1927–1939, 8 v.) bypassed Caporetto. That battle was studied in Giuseppe del Bianco, **La Guerra e il Friuli** (Udine: Del Bianco, 1937–1958, 4 v.), but Pieri's collection of short analytical studies is the best Italian work on the First World War since Giulio Douhet's classic and controversial **The Command of the Air.** A great military historian who had turned from the Renaissance to the Risorgimento, Pieri died before he could bring his full-scale analyses of modern Italy's military institutions and problems down to this century.

Direction of War

MAURICE, SIR FREDERICK BARTON. **Lessons of Allied Co-operation: Naval, Military and Air, 1914–1918.** New York: Oxford University Press (for the Royal Institute of International Affairs), 1942, 195 p.

From official histories, biographies and command papers, Sir Frederick Maurice traces the development of international coöperation during World War I. In 1914 the Admiralty and the War Office each had its own war plan, and neither was fully apprised of French intentions. By 1915, however, a rough formula had evolved enabling the French military command to determine the effectives, objectives and the dates for the commencement of each operation on the Western Front. Lloyd George took a devious step closer to a unified command when he tried to subordinate GHQ to the French command for the 1917 offensives, an "unpleasant intrigue" that set back the development of an Allied supreme command. The Italian disaster at Caporetto in October 1917 gave Lloyd George another opening, and with the subsequent establishment of the Supreme War Council the Allies finally established a political agency to undertake the unified direction of the war.

The need to coördinate the use of reserves to counter the German spring offensives in 1918 led to the appointment of Foch as commander in chief of the Allied forces in France. Under his direction the Allies conducted well-organized offensives that finally brought Germany to her knees. In a less spectacular manner the representatives of the Supreme War Council had also arranged to pool resources, but most of these measures "had hardly become effective when the war came to an end."

This book reveals the pitfalls one might expect in any wartime coalition. Half-measures, poor timing, political intrigue and the inevitable play of personalities marred most attempts to coördinate military operations, particularly at Gallipoli and Salonika, while even the tactical coöperation of armies on the Western Front "proved to be a . . . complicated and difficult business." With an anxious eye (in 1941) on the near future, General Maurice found a number of practical lessons that obviously had not yet outlived their usefulness.

A scholarly examination of the role of the United States in determining Allied military and political policies, which concentrates on the relationship between American military decisions and President Wilson's fundamental war aims, is to be found in David F. Trask, **The United States in the Supreme War Council.**

HANKEY, MAURICE PASCAL ALERS HANKEY, 1ST BARON. **The Supreme Command 1914–1918.** New York: Macmillan, 1961, 2 v.

From 1912, when he was appointed Secretary to the Committee of Imperial Defense, until his retirement in 1938, Lord Hankey served at the center of the control echelon in the British system of imperial defense. He has been characterized as its heart, even soul; in Churchill's words, "he knew everything." These two volumes, accordingly, are important because they reveal through expert testimony how the war was directed at state level and how the supreme command evolved under the pressure of war.

Hankey's work, based upon personal papers and his diary, is not a story of heroics and the trials of battlefield generalship but an account of the direction of the war through the cabinet system. Hankey holds that the supreme command, by its nature, is political—that statesmen and military men thresh out problems in committees which service it, the final decision always resting with the politician. His account clearly shows how the system worked—or failed to work. It is particularly revealing regarding the early growing pains exemplified by the utter chaos which existed in English councils at the time of the intervention in the Dardanelles and the Balkans.

Lord Hankey writes with humility and tries to be scrupulously fair. If occasionally he personally appears important, it is usually justified (*e.g.* his assisting in developing the tank and urging the use of the convoy system). And if he is overly complimentary to Lloyd George, he may be excused a personal bias. Few of his generalizations are glib, although the reader may quarrel with an occasional one; for example, that Russia's action in East Prussia saved France and made possible Allied victory on the Marne.

Two other works by thoughtful and careful historians augment Hankey's personal observations: Franklyn A. Johnson, **Defence by Committee: The British Committee of Imperial Defence, 1885–1959** (New York: Oxford University Press, 1960, 416 p.), and John Ehrman, **Cabinet Government and War: 1890–1940** (New York: Cambridge University Press, 1958, 137 p.).

ROBERTSON, SIR WILLIAM. **Soldiers and Statesmen, 1914–1918.** New York: Scribner, 1926, 2 v.

These memoirs of the wartime British Chief of the Imperial General Staff constitute one of the important contributions to the history of the conduct of the war. With moderation, restraint and minimal partisan argument Robertson discusses the development of British strategy and the problems attendant to civil-military relations in which he was involved. The CIGS must have been a difficult, but grudgingly admired, subordinate, and his advice frequently made his superiors impatient. But in his memoirs there are sobering judgments which future leaders will do well to consider; moreover, with his criticisms he includes alternative courses of action. Whether intentionally or not, Robertson shows the difficulty a nation can have in adapting its peacetime military planning and policy organization to cope with crisis-laden war situations—the strain of coalition efforts, for example.

Near the end of the war, Robertson was succeeded by a man who had served in France with the British army and had also been liaison officer to the French as well as a member of the Supreme War Council. Sir Henry Wilson was exasperated with politicians although it is doubtful that he understood the art of politics as practiced in a democracy. His insights into problems of coalition warfare and the forming of British policy complement Robertson's views. They are set forth in Charles E. Callwell, **Sir Henry Wilson: His Life and Diaries** (London: Cassell, 1927, 2 v.), in a caustic, sometimes impulsive, fashion.

LUDENDORFF, ERICH. **Ludendorff's Own Story, August 1914–November 1918.** New York: Harper, 1920, 2 v.

Before World War I ended, Ludendorff had become Germany's most influential military leader. The personality of this man, who was virtually the commander in chief of the armies of Germany and her allies in 1916–1918, emerges clearly in his writings; unswerving in his determination to win the war, he believed that the first requirement of a German is "a rigid self-discipline of the individual for the good of the whole."

Ludendorff was a brilliant technician, but he was less able in the important and delicate area of civil-military relations. Accordingly, his comments on the political and administrative side of the war as well as his views on motives and expectations of German officials are particularly significant. One can detect a degree of political naïveté and a failure to grasp the importance of international considerations. But if his interpretation of the ideas of Clausewitz was distorted, Ludendorff was a masterful battlefield strategist; in this respect, his account of operations in the east is very enlightening, although one must appreciate that he has often been too generously credited for the German success at Tannenberg. And his account of the 1918 German offensives contains a trace of self-vindication, a situation in which the critical question may be the manner in which Ludendorff related strategy to tactics.

Donald J. Goodspeed, **Ludendorff: Genius of World War I** (Boston: Houghton, 1966, 335 p.), is an impartial analysis which concentrates on Ludendorff's military contributions. It is valuable for insights into the inner thoughts of and motivating influences on the talented general who almost defeated the Allies.

VON TIRPITZ, ALFRED. **My Memoirs.** New York: Dodd, 1919, 2 v.

An important preliminary to World War I, both in the diplomatic and military spheres, was the German creation of a potent high seas fleet. Admiral Tirpitz was largely responsible for this achievement, and it is more for his account of how Germany became a naval power than for his discussion of wartime naval and political matters that his memoirs are important.

Once appointed secretary for naval affairs in 1897, Tirpitz gave up the opportunity for command and became the manager and technician par excellence. He believed in adapting arms for offensive purposes, although he opposed war, sought to strengthen the navy largely to secure German maritime interests, and wanted a rapprochement with England. Only reluctantly did he advance the "Risk Theory" which, while making the German navy second best, was aimed at tying England's hands.

As the builder of the fleet, Tirpitz played an active political role, but he exercised little influence on the naval staff or on war plans. When war came, his advice was neither solicited nor followed. Although he had initiated submarine construction in 1908, his objective had not been mercantile warfare; and he later opposed loosing the U-boats on merchant shipping until absolutely essential from a German viewpoint.

The egoism and unmistakable political overtone modified by special pleading which flavor the memoirs are detracting, and there are some generalizations and documentary notes which have been questioned. But if one reads the work recognizing that the author's avowed purpose was to prove "that the old structure of our state was not antiquated and rotten," there is still much valuable information to be gained.

Command and Strategy

TUCHMAN, BARBARA (WERTHEIM). **The Guns of August.** New York: Macmillan, 1962, 511 p.

The Guns of August is a brilliantly written popular account of both the inexorable movement of Europe toward war in 1914 and the first month of fighting in the west. The masterful character sketches of key military figures, although occasionally revealing a personal inappreciation of the cruelly subjective aspects of generalship, contribute greatly to the absorbing and fascinating story.

But if Mrs. Tuchman shows an acceptable grasp of the historical material and an excellent literary style, her account will leave many historians dissatisfied. Failure to consider carefully enough the research of such scholars as Albertini (**The Origins of the War of 1914**), Schmitt (**The Coming of the War: 1914**) and Fay (**The Origins of the World War**), coupled with an obvious prejudice against Germany, leads to a distorted account of the war preliminaries. Similarly, because she accepts atrocity tales now largely disproved, the author paints the German as an ogre all out of proportion. Finally, her discussions of strategy and campaigns would be more meaningful if some appreciation of the significance of tactics and technology had been shown.

The Guns of August rightfully dwells upon the well-known Schlieffen Plan in some detail. This critically important prewar German strategic concept has been analyzed by scores of critics and students, but few have done it more brilliantly than a great German historian, Gerhard Ritter, in **The Schlieffen Plan: Critique of a Myth** (New York: Praeger, 1958, 195 p.). Ritter, although basically hostile to Schlieffen and unwilling to concede how very nearly the plan succeeded, shows the critical inability of that individual to appreciate the vital impact of the political factor on his plan.

BARNETT, CORRELLI. **The Swordbearers: Studies in Supreme Command in the First World War.** London: Eyre and Spottiswoode, 1963, 386 p.

This book is more than a study of the characters and personalities of the four national military leaders selected for analysis—it is an examination of the societies which spawned them and the inexorable movement of events which they sought to regulate. Barnett's theme is "the decisive effect of individual human character on history," and his selection of swordbearers (Moltke, Jellicoe, Pétain and Ludendorff) allows him to weave his narrative admirably around this point.

The author's research is thorough, his use of sources excellent, and he writes with a freshness of approach which is stimulating. Some readers will object to several of his outspoken judgments (*e.g.* his reference to "the crude business of leadership in war") and his acknowledged use of hindsight. But all will profit from his penetrating analysis of campaign strategies and his critical examination of the tortuous and crucial tests of generalship to which not only his principal characters but many others are put in the course of Barnett's narrative.

HAIG, DOUGLAS HAIG, 1ST EARL. **The Private Papers of Douglas Haig, 1914–1919.** London: Eyre, 1952, 383 p.

Of all the leading military figures in the Great War, there is none around whom controversy has raged longer or so strongly as the commander of the British army in France. Douglas Haig has lacked neither partisans nor critics. He has been variously described as cold, ruthless, a squanderer of men's lives; as competent but unimaginative; as narrow, biased and rigid; as the embodiment of military stupidity; as an egotist; as a farsighted commander with real professional skills; as a leader with considerable intellectual equipment.

Robert Blake's careful and definitive selections from Haig's meticulously kept diary and personal papers make it possible for the reader to form tentative opinions on some of these assessments. Of almost equal value is his superbly written introduction which lends body to the diary selections and stresses the conflict trilogy which caught up Haig: an eastern *vs.* western strategy, disagreement between soldiers and politicians, and conflict between Liberal and Conservative. Haig's feelings about the Somme and Passchendaele, a unified command, his relationship with and apprehension about the French, his views on strategy and his feelings about Lloyd George ("astute and cunning . . . but I should think shifty and unreliable") are important revelations.

Favorable, and in some respects biased, views of Haig appear in the British official history, in John Terraine, **Ordeal of Victory** (Philadelphia: Lippincott, 1963, 508 p.) and in Alfred Duff Cooper, **Haig** (London: Faber and Faber, 1935–1936, 2 v.). The writings of Lloyd George and Liddell Hart present critical views, as does Leon Wolff, **In Flanders Fields: The 1917 Campaign** (New York: Viking, 1958, 308 p.). The latter work also captures vividly the atmosphere in which high-level command decisions were reached as well as the terrible loneliness of the battlefield.

WAVELL, ARCHIBALD PERCIVAL WAVELL, 1ST VISCOUNT. **Allenby: A Study in Greatness.** New York: Oxford University Press, 1941, 312 p.

Allenby is a carefully written study of generalship which is particularly instructive for military professionals but also valuable to the general reader for its insights into how one man exercised battlefield leadership during World War I.

Wavell, a competent leader in his own right in the Second World War, was well equipped to write this biography, having served in the areas where Allenby achieved his greatest triumphs. Unfortunately, the coming of World War II forced him to shorten the book and hastily add a summary chapter.

Wavell's account adds little material on campaigns which has not been presented elsewhere, but it does offer valuable assessments of Allenby as a soldier and commander. Along with Haig, this blunt cavalryman was in the forefront of England's soldiers during the war. Wavell shows how Allenby learned from his early experiences in France and argues that his rigid discipline and rages—he was non-affectionately known as "Bull"—were really caused by basic concern for his troops. He was not careless of men's lives. His brilliant achievements in Palestine, the author believes, should not have been unexpected, considering his prior experience. Wavell characterizes Allenby's mind as "powerful and weighty," noting that he was not a ready debater and in conferences with army commanders did not make the impression his abilities warranted. Intellectually he needed time and space to turn. T. E. Lawrence once said of him, "His mind is like the prow of the *Mauretania*."

LIDDELL HART, BASIL HENRY. **Foch: The Man of Orleans.** Boston: Little, Brown, 1932, 480 p.

Foch is a military study, not a conventional biography, and minimal attention is given to the private life of the man who led the Allied armies to victory in 1918. Tracing the growth of his military thought in the prewar years, Liddell Hart points to Foch's "innate tendency to confound the practicable with the desirable, the real with the ideal." (The English edition contains a lengthy appendix on "Foch's Theory of War.") He finds a similar rift between fact and theory in the early years of the war, and if he credits Foch with learning from his mistakes and ultimately adjusting his theories to fit the grim facts of trench warfare, he clearly believes that Foch should have mastered his lessons earlier.

This book is more than an analysis of the limitations under which the high command suffered as a result of the conditions of World War I. The author has achieved lasting fame for his own contributions to theory as well as for his writings on history and biography, and in this case the theorist often provides the standards by which the historian may judge his subject. Throughout his distinguished career Liddell Hart searched for the antidote to trench warfare. The reader should not be surprised therefore to see here the triumph of Liddell Hart's own theories, for while he always paid the strictest respect to historical facts, he also was mindful of the value of history in teaching the importance of mobility (and therefore of mechanized warfare) and the eternal validity of his "strategy of indirect approach."

His style, which always sparkles, is perhaps too highly seasoned with symbolic asides and suggestive metaphors, but the reader will have no difficulty in understanding Foch's influence upon the campaigns, and the role of these campaigns in the larger theater of the war.

PERSHING, JOHN JOSEPH. **My Experiences in the World War.** New York: Stokes, 1931, 2 v.

Although America's role in the Great War was brief, the contribution came at a crucial time, and the nation's experience with coalition warfare was instructive for future leaders. In the absence of an objective and analytical official history of the American participation, these memoirs by the commanding general of the American Expeditionary Force provide a valuable account of that overseas effort.

Writing in a straightforward, frank, but colorless manner which reflects his well-known personal characteristics, General Pershing describes America's contribution to the final victory. His account is particularly valuable for its discussion of the coalition arguments at the high command level and its treatment of the important areas of administration and training. Unfortunately, Pershing only briefly discusses campaign strategy, and he shows too little appreciation of those efforts to support the AEF which were mounted in America. One of Pershing's subordinates who was both a division commander and the chief of the Services of Supply probes more deeply into these efforts and also adds important material on the overall achievements of the AEF: James G. Harbord, **The American Army in France, 1917–1919** (Boston: Little, Brown, 1936, 632 p.).

A useful complementing treatment of the home front support function appears in Peyton C. March, **The Nation at War** (New York: Doubleday, 1932, 407 p.). March, the wartime Chief of Staff, is blunt, direct and polemic, and his writing reflects his strained relationship with Pershing; but his book, augmented by his biographer's admirable effort (Edward M. Coffman, **The Hilt of the Sword,** Madison: University of Wisconsin Press, 1966, 346 p.), covers the aspects of staff functioning, mobilization and logistics which were so important to the war effort.

VON FALKENHAYN, ERICH GEORG ANTON SEBASTIAN. **The German General Staff and Its Decisions, 1914–1916.** New York: Dodd, 1920, 332 p.

Along with Ludendorff's memoirs, this book provides the best account of the daily operations of the German high command. Relieving Moltke in 1914, Falkenhayn remained Chief of the General Staff until superseded by Hindenburg when Rumania entered the war in 1916. As such, he presided over the development of German strategy which led to the failure at Verdun for which he was severely blamed. Although opposed to seeking an early decision on the Eastern Front, Falkenhayn recognized the desirability of striking hard there in 1915. His book makes amply clear how much division of opinion there was on strategy, not only in the higher German circles but also between Germany and Austria, until Ludendorff gained almost dictatorial powers.

Although devoid of the normal historical documentation, Falkenhayn's work is notable for frankness and clarity, if also for a trace of apologia. His argument for the Verdun offensive is painstakingly traced, and the frustration inherent in coördinating strategy with Conrad (Austria) is sorrowfully evident. Although he does not discuss it, unlike several other deposed leaders, Falkenhayn accepted subordinate command after his relief and served loyally and generally competently to the end of the war.

Falkenhayn does not discuss details of how the general staff operated. For insights into this subject, if one makes allowances for a degree of special pleading, the reader will find useful a book by one of Germany's most talented staff officers, Hermann Joseph von Kuhl (**Der Deutsche Generalstab in Vorbereitung und Durchführung des Weltkrieges,** Berlin: Mittler, 2d ed., 1920, 218 p.).

HOFFMANN, MAX. **War Diaries and Other Papers.** London: Secker, 1929, 2 v.

General Max Hoffmann may well have been the greatest strategist of World War I and was probably Germany's most intellectually brilliant soldier. This is the more useful of the two books he wrote.

Hoffmann spent the war on the Eastern Front, much of it as chief of staff to Germany's commander there, but he understood clearly what was happening in the west. His diaries, recorded daily, show a sure grasp of fundamentals, a clear knowledge of events and a shrewd, if often cynical, appreciation of strategic developments. Disdainful of Falkenhayn, he also critically disagreed frequently with Ludendorff's methods. Moltke he blamed for losing the chance for early victory in the west; thereafter, he believed Germany could still have won if the major effort had been made in the east to drive Russia from the war in 1915 or 1916. Other German soldiers are not spared careful analysis in Hoffmann's diaries, their characters and qualifications being examined in a way which is revealing and instructive to readers today.

Military Operations

EDMONDS, SIR JAMES EDWARD; MILES, WILFRID and DAVIES, HENRY RODOLPH, *eds.* **History of the Great War: Military Operations.** London: H.M.S.O., 1927–1947, 45 v.

In spite of obvious shortcomings in any official history, the standard of the British history of World War I is excellent. The maps are particularly pertinent and useful. Covering British ground operations in all theaters, the series is not without critics; charges of bias in interpretation and use of documents have been leveled, particularly at volumes pertaining to the Western Front. Notwithstanding such possible shortcomings, the work is indispensable to the serious student and is clearly superior to its German **(Der Weltkrieg, 1914–1918,** Berlin: Mittler, 1925–1943, 14 v.) and French **(Les Armées Françaises dans la Grande Guerre,** Paris: Imprimerie Nationale, 1922–.) counterparts.

The latter works are based largely upon national documents whereas the British series makes considerable use of foreign sources. Moreover, in **Der Weltkrieg** one can detect something of a plaintive note, an occasional implication that the supreme command, not the army, failed. Oriented toward the military specialist, the French history is a mass of orders and data, with too little explanatory narrative which captures the spirit of the human drama.

A very useful, accurate and readable book which complements the British history is a summary of the Australian official account in Charles E. W. Bean, **Anzac to Amiens: A Shorter History of the Australian Fighting Services in the First World War** (Canberra: Australian War Memorial, 1961, 567 p.).

CHURCHILL, WINSTON SPENCER. **The Unknown War.** New York: Scribner, 1931, 411 p.

A half-century after the end of the Great War, Churchill's stirring and impartial account remains the best treatment of the Eastern Front. As in his other works, Sir Winston is at his best in masterfully depicting the strategic aspects of the largely unexplored gigantic struggle involving three empires. Emphasizing the vast area and fluidity of operations, his narrative treats skillfully of flexible strategies applied to a battlefront so extensive that trenches and firepower could not stifle mobility as they did in the west. Vivid characterizations portray leaders with both human strengths and frailties laid bare; German superiority in organization and technology stands in stark contrast to Russian ineptness, bolstered by magnificence in sacrifice and courage. For tactical analysis and perceptive coverage of underlying causes of the Russian collapse, however, the reader turns elsewhere.

The instructive opening campaign in East Prussia is accurately treated in operational detail in Sir Edmund Ironside, **Tannenberg. The First Thirty Days in East Prussia** (Edinburgh: Blackwood, 1933, 306 p.). Ironside's documented account of Russian errors and German efficiency furthered by opportunism is complemented by a similarly detailed Russian account by Nikolai N. Golovin, **The Russian Campaign of 1914** (Fort Leavenworth: General Staff Press, 1933, 410 p.). Sir Alfred Knox, linguist, prewar attaché and liaison officer with the Russian armies during the war, provides an intimate, dispassionate and fair description of Russian shortcomings in waging modern war. His keen analysis (**With the Russian Army,**

1914–1917, New York: Dutton, 1921, 2 v.) is borne out by telling evidence in the memoirs of Russia's most competent and courageous general, Alexei A. Brusilov, **A Soldier's Notebook, 1914–1918** (London: Macmillan, 1930, 340 p.).

TYNG, SEWELL T. **The Campaign of the Marne, 1914.** New York: Longmans, 1935, 413 p.

There are few battles in World War I which have attracted more attention from analysts than the climactic battle on the Marne which halted the German drive in 1914. Most of the key participants have expressed their views, and the official histories have examined the campaign in detail. Tyng has attempted to use all of this material to reconstruct, step by step, the chain of events which culminated in the Allied victory.

The book is a detailed military history of the campaign. There is much discussion of strategy, orders and key decisions but little about "friction in war" (heat, exhaustion, shortage of supplies, hunger, weather, etc.). Although the narrative is straightforward and factual, the author cannot conceal a slight French bias and a favoritism for Joffre. In spite of this shortcoming, Tyng's admirable work is important to any student of the Marne campaign.

Among the many personal accounts of the battle, several are useful to complement both Tyng and the British official history, which brilliantly presents the campaign as seen through British eyes. The most able of the German commanders of field armies in the campaign tells his story bluntly but with some partiality in a translated and annotated work: Alexander von Kluck, **The March on Paris and the Battle of the Marne, 1914** (New York: Longmans, 1920, 175 p.). Kluck's able chief of staff supplements his superior's account and deals at length with the famous Hentsch visit in Hermann Joseph von Kuhl, **Der Marnefeldzug** (Berlin: Mittler, 1921, 266 p.). Generals Joffre and Galliéni, two of the most important French participants, tell their respective stories in their memoirs (Joseph J. C. Joffre, **Personal Memoirs,** New York: Harper, 1932, 2 v.; Joseph S. Galliéni, **Les Carnets de Galliéni,** Paris: Michel, 1932, 320 p.), each claiming credit for the concept which led to victory—the massing and launching in counterattack of Maunory's army.

ASPINALL-OGLANDER, CECIL FABER, *comp.* **History of the Great War. Military Operations: Gallipoli.** London: Heinemann, 1929–1932, 2 v.

Few campaigns of the Great War have provoked more discussion and controversy, or, in the aftermath of failure, been advanced as holding more strategic promise, than the British invasion of Gallipoli in 1915. Between the world wars the operation was studied in light of its lessons on joint operations, and, in any era, it is instructive for the view it provides of the formulation and implementation of national policy.

Brigadier Aspinall-Oglander, a participant, has written the definitive work on that fateful campaign. In organization and scope of coverage, assembly and presentation of factual data and perspicacity in treatment of events his work is impressive; one may, nevertheless, disagree with his contention that success at Gallipoli would probably have saved a million lives and shortened the war by a year. He charges that initial incapacity in London in the higher control of naval and military operations and later vacillation in providing reinforcements doomed the campaign to failure. In dealing with the battlefield the author clearly captures the spirit of sacrifice and the heroism displayed by troops on both sides; and although he dutifully attempts to gauge impartially the performance of the commander, Sir Ian Hamilton, he is probably less critical than circumstances demand.

Hamilton has written a brilliant book on Gallipoli, but it leaves the reader wondering about his qualifications for command (**Gallipoli Diary,** London: Arnold, 1920, 2 v.). The Turkish side of the story emerges partially in Otto Liman von Sanders, **Five Years in Turkey** (Annapolis: U.S. Naval Institute, 1927, 325 p.). Sanders, head of the German mission in Turkey, commanded at Gallipoli and presents useful and frank information about his problems. A popular work which understandably stresses Australian contributions and captures not only the spirit of the private's war but also the crisis in London is Alan Moorehead, **Gallipoli** (New York: Harper, 1956, 384 p.).

HORNE, ALISTAIR. **The Price of Glory: Verdun, 1916.** London: Macmillan, 1962, 371 p.

In this brilliant book Horne reconstructs the personalities, the atmosphere and the tempestuous events that comprised "the worst battle in history." Using the views of Joffre and Falkenhayn to set the stage, he describes in detail the military scene as it existed in 1916 and the first terrible days at Verdun—the frightful bombardment, the probing German attacks, the crumbling French defenses and the drama of Fort Douaumont. The French response is forever associated with Pétain, and this book clearly demonstrates why he should be permitted one day to rest beside his old troops near the *Ossuaire*.

Falkenhayn's hopes to bleed France white miscarried because the means employed were unsuited to his strategy. As the German attack lost momentum and fresh French divisions arrived, the battle degenerated into a shapeless fight for possession of some advantageous section of the "catastrophic terrain." The highlights—Mort Homme and Hill 304, Forts Vaux and Souville, and the successful French counterstrokes—form convenient pegs upon which the author hangs his impressions of what happened. He shows what the battle meant to France at the time and the influence that it had upon both the army and French character.

The Price of Glory invites comparison with a popular French work on the subject that appeared about the same time: Georges Blond, **Verdun** (New York: Macmillan, 1964, 250 p.). Horne gives a better balanced and more intelligible history of the battle; Blond is impressionistic in his approach and involves the reader in the passions of the moment. Horne occasionally leaves the desolation of the battlefield to digress upon life in Paris during the war or to look at the great battles fought for control of the skies overhead while Blond never lets his reader escape from the battle. But the glimpses he gives of men in battle, particularly of Frenchmen in this battle, make this book nearly as valuable as **The Price of Glory.**

WAVELL, ARCHIBALD PERCIVAL. **The Palestine Campaigns.** London: Constable, 1928, 275 p.

Colonel Wavell's short but tightly packed and well-written book is an excellent campaign study. Detailed documentation and data of the type available in the official histories are lacking; but the narrative is clear, often sparkling, and the analysis of strategy and tactics is excellent.

The fighting in Palestine was indicative of the type of operation the "easterners" in the British higher councils advocated. Peripheral war, waged with minimum casualties, they believed, would sap German strength and avoid the slaughter on the Western Front. Wavell does not address this point, which is far less simple than thus outlined. But it is clear that he admired Allenby and believed that imagination, mobility, detailed preparation and deception combined to bring about victory with small losses; one might infer that Palestine was not the only locale in which this combination could have produced similar results, although the author would probably have admitted that the quality of the opposition in the west was a consideration.

Wavell served in one of Allenby's corps in 1917–1918 and writes with firsthand knowledge not only of the operations but of the difficulties of campaigning (climate, few roads, lack of water). Parenthetically, it seems no coincidence that Wavell, commanding in Egypt early in World War II, adapted so well to conditions in the area and conducted initially brilliant operations.

FROTHINGHAM, THOMAS GODDARD. **The Naval History of the World War.** Cambridge: Harvard University Press, 1924–1926, 3 v.

Captain Frothingham's work is the best naval history on the war as a whole. Relying upon documentation available in U.S. Navy files, the author, however, has been criticized for oversimplification of certain British problems, such as in the blockade of Germany. Unfortunately, there is no history of sea power in this war on the intellectual level of Sir Herbert Richmond, **Statesmen and Sea Power** (New York: Oxford University Press, 1947, 369 p.).

Sir Henry Newbolt's **A Naval History of the War, 1914–1918** (London: Hodder, n.d., 350 p.) is not a naval history of World War I but of the Royal Navy's operations in it. Essentially a popular work, its tone is nationalistic and apologetic: "Our late enemies were always determined to keep war wholly upon the professional plane, to emphasize the scientific and exclude the moral view." After the death of Sir Julian Corbett, Newbolt was chosen to finish the semi-official British **History of the Great War. Naval Operations** (New York: Longmans, 1920–1931, 5 v.). Arthur J. Marder, **From the Dreadnought to Scapa Flow,** is now the standard work.

Holloway H. Frost, **The Battle of Jutland** (Annapolis: U.S. Naval Institute, 1936, 571 p.); Donald Macintyre, **Jutland** (London: Evans, 1957, 210 p.); Geoffrey Bennett, **Coronel and the Falklands** (New York: Macmillan, 1962, 192 p.); and Oscar Parkes, **British Battleships, Warrior 1860 to Vanguard 1950: A History of Design, Construction, and Armament** (London: Seeley Service, 1957, 701 p.) are particularly useful or readable on specific topics. William Sowden Sims and Burton J. Hendrick, **The Victory at Sea** (New York: Doubleday, 1920, 410 p.), is the best account of American naval involvement. Reinhard Scheer, **Germany's High Sea Fleet in the World War** (London: Cassell, 1920, 375 p.) and Georg von Hase, **Kiel and Jutland** (London: Skeffington, 1921, 233 p.), are key German accounts.

MARDER, ARTHUR J. **From the Dreadnought to Scapa Flow: The Royal Navy in the Fisher Era, 1904–1919.** New York: Oxford University Press, 1961–1970, 5 v.

This definitive history really began with Marder's earlier works: **The Anatomy of British Sea Power: A History of British Naval Policy in the Pre-Dreadnought Era, 1880–1905** (New York: Knopf, 1940, 580 p.); **Portrait of an Admiral: The Life and Papers of Sir Herbert Richmond** (Cambridge: Harvard University Press, 1952, 407 p.); and **Fear God and Dread Nought: The Correspondence of Admiral of the Fleet Lord Fisher of Kilverstone** (London: Cape, 1952–1959, 3 v.), which Marder edited. Fisher was the organizer of a victory to which he contributed little after his recall to office in 1914. Concentration on battleships and fleet tactics had led to the neglect of amphibious planning and staff work, and an overcentralized command had failed to develop "a generally accepted, comprehensive, authoritative tactical doctrine." If Sir John Jellicoe was a naval Haig or Joffre, competent but unimaginative, the commanders' "belief in the superiority of their matériel" led to major reforms after the shock of Jutland. Jellicoe got the matériel for the battle against the submarine, but was hard to convince that convoy was necessary and had to be dismissed from the Admiralty. But the kindly, unselfish personality which had won the confidence of those under him can still be seen in his **The Grand Fleet, 1914–1916: Its Creation, Development and Work** (New York: Doran, 1919, 510 p.) and **The Crisis of the Naval War** (New York: Doran, 1920, 331 p.). Marder deals with these matters with rare insight into personalities and policies. Among historians of the First World War, his is a rare achievement.

Technology, Logistics and Soldier Life

HOLLEY, IRVING BRINTON, JR. **Ideas and Weapons.** New Haven: Yale University Press, 1953, 222 p.

This is the only book to deal meaningfully and in detail with the interrelationships between technology, weapons and military doctrine. Based on the United

States Army Air Service's experience in the First World War, it has been criticized as a study of intellectual and administrative problems which were not present in earlier periods and which have been solved by present bureaucratic methods of translating technological and military facts into new weapons and doctrines. But if Holley's theses on the importance of a continuous interaction between ideas and weapons are more easily documented for mechanized weapons for which incremental changes are both more critical and discernible, they remain the starting points for anyone dealing with this process. His later thoughts on these and related matters are in **Buying Aircraft: Matériel Procurement for the Army Air Forces** (Washington: Government Printing Office, 1964, 643 p.), a volume in the series "United States Army in World War II: Special Studies." The only other work on the same intellectual level is a short survey by Bernard and Fawn Brodie, **From Crossbow to H-Bomb** (New York: Dell, 1962, 288 p.), although there are good chapters on technology and warfare in Melvin Kranzberg and Carroll W. Pursell, Jr., *eds.,* **Technology in Western Civilization** (New York: Oxford University Press, 1967, 2 v.).

SWINTON, SIR ERNEST DUNLOP. **Eyewitness.** New York: Doubleday, 1933, 332 p.

The title of this book is misleading, in as much as the subject is the development of the tank, although the early chapters deal with the period when the author was the British official correspondent at the front. Colonel Swinton's observations of trench warfare convinced him that infantry assaults would not make progress unless a mechanical means was found to destroy machine guns and barbed wire. His slight knowledge of the caterpillar tractor led him to the idea of the tank.

Rather than a technological treatise, Swinton's work is an account of how salesmanship and management were used to bring tank units into being. His readable and forthright narrative, though caustic in places, shows how very difficult it can sometimes be to adapt an idea to practical use, even if there is no "rigid non-receptivity and complacent omniscience." Without help from the Committee of Imperial Defence, and particularly Churchill and the Admiralty, Swinton might well have failed to accomplish his goal.

The tank is the leading example of the technological attempt to break the trench deadlock, but there were also attempts to modify doctrine and tactics in search of the same objective. In this latter regard Germany led the way, both offensively and defensively. Although there is a dearth of factual coverage specifically on this important subject, there is useful material in both the British official history and Pascal Marie Henri Lucas, **L'Évolution des Idées Tactiques en France et en Allemagne pendant la Guerre de 1914–1918** (Paris: Berger-Levrault, 4th ed., 1932, 326 p.).

HAGOOD, JOHNSON. **The Services of Supply.** Boston: Houghton Mifflin, 1927, 420 p.

Written in response to an official request that he explain "the inner working of the operation as it shaped itself in the minds of the directing officers," General Hagood's memoirs are indispensable for an understanding of how the American Expeditionary Force was transported, supplied and fed. The most formidable problem appears to have been transportation, but even questions involving mail delivery and welfare services required careful supervision. The problems described are intricate, technical and usually not of general interest, but had they not been solved by Hagood and his competent associates, the story of the combat forces would make less exciting reading.

Perhaps the main value of the book is the light it casts upon the evolution of the Line of Communications (later known as the Services of Supply) in France from a handful of officers who would have preferred combat assignments to an efficient organization exceeding half a million men. From the included correspondence and memoranda we can detect the growing pains—the selection of personnel, an equitable system of promotion, inadequate planning and facilities and frequent conflicts of interest. General Hagood concludes his narrative with a plan to reorganize the War Department in accordance with the experience gained in France.

Readers of this lengthy and detailed work may question the aphorism "War makes rattling good history; but peace is poor reading." None, however, will question the vital importance of the work performed by the Services of Supply, nor the practical value of this kind of history.

EDMONDS, CHARLES, *pseud.* **A Subaltern's War.** London: Davies, 1929, 224 p.

A bibliography of World War I military history is not complete without some reference to works which depict war as it appeared to the soldier "on the line." Among the spate of books on this subject which emerged in the decade after the war this work, by the author who calls himself "Charles Edmonds," is among the best.

This is not an account of battles and tactics but rather a depiction of how ordinary men endured the hell of war in the trenches and survived mentally and physically after defeating Germany's best. There is also a moralistic essay on militarism which the author appears to have incorporated almost as an after-thought. Without making war out as a glorious adventure, Edmonds seems to be protesting against the flood of anti-war literature which often characterized the soldier as being driven by danger and suffering to deprecating self-pity and whining. A nobler, tougher—albeit frightened—and self-sacrificing man emerges as his model. All the while, in his first-rate narrative of two battles the author captures the never ending mental torture endured by the soldier and the contradictions posed by war. That great student of war psychology, Ardant du Picq, would have found this book immensely useful.

Among the many works in English similar to **A Subaltern's War,** two others are of significance for depiction of trench warfare and the spirit of the soldier: Edmund Charles Blunden, **Undertones of War** (London: Cobden-Sanderson, 1928, 317 p.), and Charles Douie, **The Weary Road: Recollections of a Subaltern of Infantry** (London: Murray, 1939, 226 p.).

II. THE INTER-WAR YEARS

GENERAL; HISTORICAL

BAUMONT, MAURICE. **La Faillite de la Paix (1918–1939).** Paris: Presses Universitaires, 5th rev. ed., 1967–1968, 2 v.

The first edition of this twentieth volume of **Peuples et Civilisations,** edited by Louis Halphen and Philippe Sagnac, appeared in 1945. The third edition of 1950 was revised and enlarged into two volumes. The fifth edition is substantially unchanged, except for the inclusion of some books which were published after 1950.

Where the factual base has been firmly laid since 1950, as in important parts of the Soviet story, Baumont's account is deficient. On the whole, however, his sober, detached narrative of events between 1919 and 1939 not only in Europe but also in other parts of the world, so far as these events directly affected the history of Europe, holds up remarkably well. Particularly impressive is his ability to present a multitude of facts without obscuring the main outlines of the story. This remains probably the best detailed account in any language.

CHURCHILL, WINSTON SPENCER. **The Aftermath.** New York: Scribner, 1929, 516 p.

Reading the concluding volume of Winston Churchill's **The World Crisis** is still, after 40 years, like listening to a great symphony. Age has not diminished the range or power of this tragic story. He saw much. He saw that, in the age of mass democracy, the freedom of action of the statesman was slight while the risk of impetuous action, or equally disastrous inaction, was great. He saw that the advances of science and technology had not merely ended the age of great military commanders but had made war "the potential destroyer of the human race." He saw that nationalism had become "the most powerful moulding instrument of mankind."

There were, of course, blind spots in Churchill's vision. For him, the rulers of the U.S.S.R., "mocked by natural and economic facts, are condemned by their creed to an indefinite process of self-impoverishment and self-torture." This judgment, written before the first Five Year Plan, is easy enough to understand. More remarkable is his blindness to what was going on in Italy. There is no evidence that for him Fascism was an important development; years after the revolutionary changes following the murder of Matteotti, Churchill was writing of Italy as a democracy, and of "the far-seeing realism of Mussolini."

Perhaps most instructive and most frightening is Churchill's optimism at the end of the 1920s. For him, Locarno and the Washington treaties of 1922 were "solid and unshakable" pillars of peace, the League of Nations "was set upon the living rock," while the greatest achievement of the First World War was probably to "make sure that the smallest state should have the power to assert its lawful rights against even the greatest." Churchill was one of the most perceptive and best informed observers of the international situation. If he could be so blind to dangers which became obvious only a few years later, then no one should be confident that he understands the drift of history.

CHURCHILL, WINSTON SPENCER. **The Gathering Storm.** Boston: Houghton, 1948, 784 p.

The concluding volume of Churchill's history of the First World War, **The Aftermath,** was published in 1929. Its robust optimism reflected the temper of the

Locarno years. **The Gathering Storm,** the first volume of the series **The Second World War,** reflects the fears of the terrible winter of 1946–1947, when the will to live faltered in Europe, and before the decisive shift in American policy, the Marshall Plan. The volume is a somber review of lost opportunities and a warning that Britain, France and the United States "have only to repeat the same well-meaning, short-sighted behaviour towards the new problems which in singular resemblance confront us today to bring about a third convulsion from which none may live to tell the tale."

As with all of Churchill's books, this is great history. His intimate involvement with the events he described, even in the years when he was at odds with the leadership of his own party, made possible the sustained vitality of the story. In fact, much can be learned from this volume about the workings of parliamentary government in Britain. Here was a master of unforgettable invective who mercilessly attacked the appeasement policy of Neville Chamberlain, but who worked loyally with Chamberlain when the war came, and under whom Chamberlain worked when the National Government was formed in May 1940. Churchill's diatribes against what he thought were Labor's "mistakes and dangerous pacifism" were even more cutting; indeed, when he spoke in the debate on Norway on May 8, 1940, and Labor members "broke in upon me I retorted upon them and defied them, and several times the clamour was such that I could not make myself heard;" two days later he sat down amicably with the Labor leaders and arranged the entrance of that party into the government he was forming.

Indeed, because this is history written with a purpose, the amazing resiliency of the British political system is obscured: in 1947 Churchill was conscious of the need for continued coöperation, not only among all parties in Britain, but among the British, the French and the American peoples; "therefore, in the after-light I have softened many of the severities of contemporary controversy." What he did not soften was his judgment on the results of appeasement: for him, as for Marc Bloch, the German victories in 1940 were victories of the mind and of the spirit; it was in these vital realms that Britain and France and the smaller nations of Western Europe had weakened.

WOLFERS, ARNOLD. **Britain and France between Two Wars.** New York: Harcourt, 1940, 467 p.

Wolfers wrote before most of the diplomatic documents and the memoirs became available and before the monographic studies had been made. But he possessed a knowledge of diplomatic practice, excellent judgment and a capacious memory. With this equipment he produced what may stand as a monument to the humanistic tradition in political science, probably still the best study of the conflicting policies of Britain and France, certainly one of the essential works on international relations in the inter-war years, and, possibly most important, a case-book on diplomatic thought and action, not just in these years but through modern European history. Even in the drastically altered world of our day, Wolfers' examination of concepts such as "the rule of law," "security," "peaceful change" and "balance of power" has relevance.

CRAIG, GORDON ALEXANDER and GILBERT, FELIX, eds. **The Diplomats, 1919–1939.** Princeton: Princeton University Press, 1953, 700 p.

A reading of **The Diplomats** is probably still the best way to study international relations from 1919 to 1939. A volume made up of essays by 17 authors is inevitably uneven, and much new evidence has appeared since the summer of 1952. Moreover, the biographical approach has obvious defects, particularly since the professional diplomat was, in most countries, held in low esteem. But the best of the essays go far beyond the diplomats and the foreign offices. Theodore von Laue uses Chicherin's career as a center for a subtle analysis of the changing fortunes and objectives of Soviet foreign policy from 1918 to 1930; Roderic Davison's center of attention is the Turkish nationalist movement, although his story comes to a climax in the fascinating duel between the soldier Ismet and the diplomat Curzon at Lausanne in 1923, in which the soldier appears much the better diplomat.

In such a dispersed account, the increasing horror of the international scene is not immediately apparent, but, on reflection, that horror emerges more powerfully than in more direct accounts.

TOYNBEE, ARNOLD JOSEPH. **Survey of International Affairs, 1920–1923.** New York: Oxford University Press, 1925, 526 p.

This first, like the succeeding volumes in the "Survey" series of the British (later the Royal) Institute of International Affairs, is no longer so important for its stated primary purpose: "to enable speakers and writers to gather . . . the factual material, carefully checked, upon which to base the advice which they offer to the public." Fortunately, the confident boast of G. M. Gathorne-Hardy in the preface to the series—"these volumes are confined to facts"—was never true: no volume by Arnold Toynbee could be confined to facts.

The view of the world which shaped the early "Survey" volumes was outlined in an extended essay by Toynbee, originally written as an introduction to the volume for 1920–1923 but published separately by the Institute as **The World after the Peace Conference** (New York: Oxford University Press, 1925, 91 p.). In this view, by 1920 the problem of nationalities was fairly well settled in Europe, and the victory of the national idea in Russia "might prove to be the one positive legacy of the Soviet regime." Now it seemed likely that the world would no longer be dominated by the great powers but rather by small and medium sized powers working through worldwide international organizations; the medium sized powers might be joined by France, Italy and Japan, which were not likely to be able to sustain their old role as great powers. The future of Germany and Russia was obscure, but they had been permanently weakened by the war and territorial losses.

In Toynbee's view, problems such as European land armaments were of relatively minor importance; the big issues of international politics were likely to center in the Pacific area. In that area, the hopeful factor was the success of the British Empire and the United States in adapting themselves to the changed world.

The **Survey** for 1920–1923 and the introductory **The World after the Peace Conference** are still indispensable, not as a collection of facts about 1920 to 1923, but for an understanding of much of British, and American, opinion in the hopeful years after 1923.

BARRACLOUGH, GEOFFREY. **An Introduction to Contemporary History.** New York: Basic Books, 1965, 272 p.

Barraclough argues that between the contemporary world and what is ordinarily called modern history "with its three familiar peaks, the Renaissance, the Enlightenment and the French Revolution," there is a transitional era, extending roughly from the fall of Bismarck in 1890 to the inauguration of President Kennedy in 1961. Barraclough has attempted to single out the main themes of these transitional years.

In his view the "solvent of the old order" and the "catalyst of the new" was scientific, technological and industrial change. In 1890 Europe was still the center of the world, and the world order "was securely anchored to two fixed points: the sovereign national state and a firmly established social order stabilized by a prosperous property-owning middle class." Already, however, these fixed points were being eroded. In the years which followed, Europe was dwarfed by the burgeoning population of the world outside Europe, made possible by the new science and technology; both within and without Europe, the older liberal individualism gave way to mass democracy. By the end of the Second World War it was evident that the old European balance-of-power politics had been replaced by a world politics within which the European powers occupied a subordinate position. Indeed, with the collapse of European imperialism, the new states of Asia and Africa were turning away from the older Western models and were following, at least for a time, the example of Soviet Russia. Some of the best parts of Barraclough's story pull together the research of scholars on the new states of Asia and Africa, and on the cultural shifts not only in these continents but within Europe and the Americas.

Barraclough admittedly writes with more assurance than our understanding of the cataclysmic shifts of recent generations warrants; he repeatedly warns of our ignorance and our lack of clear perception. It is good, however, to have this bold sketch of the origins of our obviously revolutionary age. At the very least, Barraclough compels a rethinking of received tradition.

HUIZINGA, JOHAN. **In the Shadow of Tomorrow.** New York: Norton, 1936, 239 p.
HALÉVY, ÉLIE. **The Era of Tyrannies: Essays on Socialism and War.** New York: New York University Press, 1966, 324 p.
ARMSTRONG, HAMILTON FISH. **"We or They": Two Worlds in Conflict.** New York: Macmillan, 1936, 106 p.

In the middle 1930s, when the drift toward a second world war was becoming obvious, there was a stocktaking among scholars in the West. Three works of these years can be taken as representative of powerful currents of thought. In 1935 the Dutch historian, J. Huizinga, published **In the Shadow of Tomorrow.** He began: "We are living in a demented world," and went on to detail evidence which suggested the abdication of reason and the triumph of feeling. From this upsurge of passion, he argued, had come the dictatorships and the praise of violence; Europe was being driven toward war, although it was easy for reasonable men to demonstrate that "the world can no longer bear modern war." Huizinga denied that he was a pessimist, but it was hard to draw hope from his pages.

The French historian, Élie Halévy, was frankly pessimistic in the report which he made to an assembly of intellectuals in November 1936 (**The Era of Tyrannies**). To Halévy, Soviet Russia was the "fraternal enemy" of Fascist Italy and Nazi Germany; all three had a common father—the nature of modern war. All were sworn enemies of Western democracy. If war came, to avert defeat the democracies must themselves become tyrannies, must resort to suicide.

In these years, there was plenty of such pessimism in Britain and the United States. But much more than on the Continent, there was robust optimism. For Britain, it is enough to cite the confidence of Keynes that courageous men, armed with knowledge, could win through to a better world. Armstrong's **"We or They"** has a similar fighting edge. For him, liberalism was very much alive and very much worth fighting for. Like Halévy, he saw the dictators as fraternal enemies, but he explained their origin only partly by the nature of modern war: the failure of liberals to fight effectively for social changes at home gave an opportunity for the enemies of liberalism to spread the doctrines of communism and fascism. He was, to be sure, pessimistic about the possibility of long-term "tolerably satisfactory relations" between the democracies and the dictators, and like Huizinga and Halévy he doubted whether liberalism could survive the rigors even of a victorious war. But he was confident that if the Western democracies made "energetic efforts at home to broaden the social and economic bases that sustain a solid political union," and if close coöperation was established between liberal states, then the spread of dictatorship would be halted, and the dictators would draw back from war.

It is as an aid to understanding the temper of the 1930s that Armstrong's vigorous plea, like the more despondent analyses of Huizinga and Halévy, richly repays study.

CROSSMAN, RICHARD HOWARD STAFFORD, *ed.* **The God That Failed.** New York: Harper, 1950, 273 p.

When it was published in 1950, **The God That Failed** was applauded largely because it explained why six writers, all well known and some among the greatest of their generation, lost faith in communism; the essays of Arthur Koestler, Ignazio Silone, Richard Wright, André Gide, Louis Fischer and Stephen Spender were prized as anti-communist tracts.

The essays are still valuable as aids to understanding why men who desperately wanted to believe in communism found that they could not; that is, the essays give clues to the failure of communism in the 1930s to advance the world revolution to which it was pledged.

More important, the essays give clues to an understanding of the failure of Western culture in the years between the two world wars. Why were so many sensitive and intelligent people, particularly young people, driven to rebellion, driven to work for the overthrow of that culture? The answers are inevitably different for the young American Negro, Richard Wright, and the aging French pagan moralist, André Gide. One important ingredient is found in all these answers —a conviction that middle-class liberalism was no longer capable of advancing the cause of human freedom, was not even capable of an effective defense of traditional middle-class values against fascism.

RAPPARD, WILLIAM EMMANUEL. **The Quest for Peace.** Cambridge: Harvard University Press, 1940, 516 p.

Much of the story which Rappard tells now seems boring and futile; it is difficult to believe that scholars and diplomats took seriously the many projects for ensuring peace through collective security, arbitration and disarmament which were furiously debated, and which all failed.

Rappard, who was Director of the Graduate Institute of International Studies in Geneva, was a scholar who devoted his life to the cause of peace. These Lowell Lectures were written during the summer, autumn and winter of 1939. He was, as he said in his preface, describing "the birth, the growth and the mournful destiny of the idea that lasting peace should result from the World War."

Rappard did not take the easy course of blaming the failure of the search for peace on individual or collective scapegoats, although "the dogma of national sovereignty" receives rough treatment and, less directly, there is a suggestion that the history of the inter-war years would have been very different if the United States had supported the settlement of 1919, in whose making Americans had played a decisive role. On the whole, however, Rappard was content to describe what happened, with the hope that peacemakers after the war of 1939 would do better than their predecessors. Whether that large purpose was attained is dubious, but the book has great value for an understanding of inter-war scholarly opinion on peace, security and disarmament.

CROUZET, MAURICE. **L'Époque Contemporaine: A la Recherche d'une Civilisation Nouvelle.** Paris: Presses Universitaires, 5th enl. ed., 1969, 944 p.

The first edition of this seventh volume of the "Histoire Générale des Civilisations," of which Maurice Crouzet is the general editor, appeared in 1957; in the fifth edition the story is continued to 1968. Crouzet begins with the years before 1914, when the whole globe seemed merely an extension of Europe, when liberal capitalism held unchallenged sway over European and therefore over world politics, society and culture, and when Europe and the world looked forward to a future which was confidently expected to be a richer, and therefore improved, model of what already existed. The few prophets who challenged this vision of the future were unheeded.

After this preliminary sketch, Crouzet centers his story around the series of shocks which destroyed this Europe-centered world. In a strict sense, what he presents is not a narrative history of Europe and the world since 1914 but a series of surveys built around this central theme. His discussions of the First and Second World Wars, the Russian Revolution and the spread of communism over a third of the globe, the impact of the Depression of 1929, the revolt of subject and dependent peoples, all are seen as stages in the demolition—or, better, the supplanting—of the dominant, confident Europe of 1914.

The demolition, of course, is easy to trace, and possibly this is as good a theme as any around which to center the story of Western civilization since 1914. Moreover, the volume contains a wealth of information useful in any understanding of the period, as well as an extensive and discriminating bibliography.

But by what has the liberal Europe of 1914 been supplanted? Here Crouzet, like most scholars, becomes vague: "A more or less clear consciousness of the profound transformations taking place in the world expressed itself in thought and art by a will to innovation." True enough; and possibly that, with the appended collection of evidence of "the veritable revolution which is taking place in all modes of expression," is as far as we can go. But that is not very far.

IKLÉ, FRANK WILLIAM. **German-Japanese Relations, 1936–1940.** New York: Bookman Associates, 1956, 243 p.

For an alliance that failed, the pre–World War II partnership of Germany and Japan has received surprisingly full scholarly attention. Frank Iklé's monograph traces the evolution of the alliance from the 1936 Anti-Comintern Pact to the conclusion of the Tripartite Pact in 1940. His treatment, which gives greater weight to the Tokyo end of the Axis, is complemented by Ernst L. Presseisen's broader study of **Germany and Japan: A Study in Totalitarian Diplomacy, 1933–1941** (The Hague: Nijhoff, 1958, 368 p.), which relies more on German sources. Both are neatly supplemented by Johanna M. Meskill's account of **Hitler and Japan: The Hollow Alliance,** which analyzes the failure of the wartime military partnership.

Professor Iklé describes the diplomacy of the two powers which led to the opportunistic alliance and reveals that it was not based on mutual needs nor did it produce coördinated policies. It did nothing to dispel mutual suspicion nor to prevent independent policies which were often at cross purposes. For example, German relations with China conflicted with Japan's continental policy, and the German-Russian Non-Aggression Pact contradicted Japan's policy toward the Soviet Union. The ineptness of Japanese military diplomacy was matched by Hitler's contempt for the Japanese. Undeniably, the two nations were thrown together by similar ambitions—the creation of their respective "New Orders." But Iklé shows convincingly how and why the alliance failed to achieve any real collaboration.

VON LAUE, THEODORE H. **The Global City: Freedom, Power and Necessity in the Age of World Revolutions.** Philadelphia: Lippincott, 1969, 302 p.

Theodore H. von Laue is a German by birth; his high-school years were spent in Nazi Germany. He came to the United States in 1937 as a college student and became an American citizen. His graduate studies at first centered on German history; his scholarly work has centered on Russia. Throughout, he has searched for an explanation of the great paradoxes of the twentieth century: the paradox of deepening divisions between states in an age when the world is being driven toward unity; the paradox of the appearance of the totalitarian state and the charismatic leader in an age of mass democracy; and the paradox of the alienated artist and intellectual in exactly those lands where science and technology were making world unity and mass democracy at least possible.

He finds the answer in the tension between old habits of thought, old values, old ways of defining the freedom of the individual and the group, and the swiftly changing and remorselessly disciplined thought and action imposed by the age of advanced technology. That technology has found a home, he maintains, in those countries where older traditions were less inhibiting or less deeply rooted—first in Britain and then in the United States. Because of the obvious superiority of high technology, not only in the material aspects of life but in everything which makes a decent life possible for the masses of mankind, countries on "the slope" are driven to imitation of "the metropolis;" in the language of the Soviet leaders, to attempt to "overtake and surpass" the United States.

This is a foreshortening of an argument which for knowledge and imagination, and above all for compassion, is one of the most important and rewarding of the many efforts to understand the developing world revolution which first became barely perceptible after the First World War and became an obvious fact after the Second.

RENOUVIN, PIERRE. **War and Aftermath: 1914–1929.** New York: Harper and Row, 1968, 369 p.
———. **World War II and Its Origins: International Relations, 1929–1945.** New York: Harper and Row, 1969, 402 p.

These volumes are a somewhat inadequate translation of the seventh and eighth volumes of the "Histoire des Relations Internationales," entitled **Les Crises du XXe Siècle, I: De 1914 à 1929; II: De 1929 à 1945** (Paris: Hachette, 1957–1958, 2 v.). The series was published under the direction of Pierre Renouvin, who is the author of the two volumes on the nineteenth century as well as of those on the twentieth century. The French edition, which is written in his characteristically clear and direct style, is much to be preferred. It has a good topical bibliography printed after each chapter, and a much too brief index for each volume.

For the student trying to find his way through the maze of events in international history since 1914, this is the best introduction. With skill sharpened by a lifetime of lecturing and writing, Renouvin marshals a multitude of facts into a coherent story. He repeatedly calls attention to gaps in the evidence, and protests that as yet it is possible to make only a sketch of the story, but he writes with firmness and brevity.

The story, of course, is a tragedy of unprecedented dimension, whether measured in human suffering, in territory involved, or in consequences for Western civilization. On the whole, the tone is restrained. There are harsh words, and some of the harshest are directed at the United States. In the first volume, the policy adopted by the American government and people in 1920 was the "determining factor" in the subsequent course of international relations, the underlying cause of the precarious character of the organization of peace. The second volume begins with an account of the economic crisis which forms the background for international politics in the 1930s; the crisis was, he says, an "American" fact. As a rule, however, even in speaking of Hitler the tone is restrained; and these volumes are, in effect, a deeply moving elegy for all that was lost, and all that might have been, in the generation between Sarajevo and Potsdam.

WATT, DONALD CAMERON, *ed.* **Contemporary History in Europe.** London: Allen and Unwin, 1969, 351 p.

This volume is made up almost entirely of working papers prepared for an international conference on contemporary history held in London in October 1966. Few of the papers have been revised to take account of developments or publications after 1966; and there is no index. These are defects. Inevitably, too, a volume with more than a score of contributors is of uneven quality.

Nevertheless, for anyone working in twentieth-century history, and particularly for a young scholar entering the field of the history of international relations between the two world wars, the book is invaluable. Nowhere else is there so much information not only about journals, collections of source materials and libraries, but about university offerings, schools of research and work in progress. The United States as well as Europe is included. Since no reports were received from the U.S.S.R., the excellent papers on current historical theory and on specific research activities in the Soviet Union were written by an American and a British scholar; there is also a note on Soviet archives.

Naturally, the fullest coverage is given to British teaching and research, but several of the other essays show an amazing breadth as well as depth of learning—for example, René Rémond's examination of "Work in Progress" in France.

POLITICAL AND ECONOMIC QUESTIONS

General

ARNDT, H. W. **The Economic Lessons of the Nineteen-Thirties.** New York: Oxford University Press, 1944, 314 p.

This wide-ranging report was prepared under the aegis of the Economic Group of the Chatham House Reconstruction Committee and issued under the auspices of the Royal Institute of International Affairs. Largely prepared in 1943, it examines the 1930s for economic lessons to guide the post–World War II world. The author sees little hope for an ordered world economy unless the major countries succeed in coping with their domestic economic problems. Thus he reasons that the costly disintegration of the international structure during the 1930s was in large part a reflection of the dominance of domestic unemployment problems. He attributes the growth of trade barriers to political insecurity, the trade cycle and the collapse of the gold standard, and finds the reduced international flow of labor and capital to have been another unfavorable factor. He concludes that the correction of maladjustments can no longer be left to market forces and that, in general, there must be new machinery for coördinating national economic policies as the gold standard did once upon a time.

CULBERTSON, WILLIAM SMITH. **International Economic Policies.** New York: Appleton, 1925, 593 p.

This book, by a former member of the United States Tariff Commission, is a general review of post–World War I economic policies. While it is somewhat more detailed with respect to those of the United States, it is in fact a world survey of treaties, tariffs, colonial treatment, raw materials, capital flows, cartels and shipping. It omits such temporary subjects as reparations. The emphasis is upon disputes and grounds for disputes arising from continuing economic causes. The author believes that, while international government may be a utopian ideal, much can be done by developing a series of institutions for the regulation of international economic relations. One of his suggestions which has been carried out far beyond any reasonable expectation at the time is that there should be general periodic international conferences which in turn would set up permanent bureaus, councils or commissions as appropriate to deal with various sectors of international affairs.

DELLE-DONNE, OTTAVIO. **European Tariff Policies since the World War.** New York: Adelphi, 1928, 288 p.

Professor Delle-Donne describes the protectionist wave which swept through England, France, Germany and Italy after World War I, explaining it in part by the creation of new national states which increased nationalist feelings in the old ones, the competitive threats which had been increased by the war, and the natural postwar objective of building self-sufficiency so far as possible. As a result, a state of economic warfare emerged, impeding trade, and the ideal of a "world economy" disappeared. The author offered a number of rationalizations for maintaining trade restrictions yet wishfully saw some signs of change, evidenced by the liberal recommendations of the Geneva World Economic Conference in May 1927 and the Stockholm Congress of the International Chamber of Commerce in June of the same year.

PAISH, SIR GEORGE. **The Road to Prosperity.** London: Benn, 1927, 154 p.

Sir George Paish's book is essentially a manifesto. With the treaties of Locarno and the entry of Germany into the League of Nations, he felt that it was time to set matters straight. He discussed very briefly the way in which each country was affected by the existing world disorganization, particularly by trade restrictions and reparations and debt payments. There must be a general restoration of confidence, he said, built on expanding investments and production, removal of handicaps to trade and some solution to the international financial tangle. He included the "Plea for the Removal of Restrictions upon European Trade" with the names of the financial and industrial leaders who signed it. Much the same position was taken by Sir Arthur Salter in **Recovery. The Second Effort,** although Salter considered political tensions a major contributor to the malaise.

PATTERSON, ERNEST MINOR. **The World's Economic Dilemma.** New York: McGraw-Hill, 1930, 330 p.

Ernest Minor Patterson, professor of economics at the University of Pennsylvania and long the moving force in the American Academy of Political and Social Science, saw the world economic dilemma as the conflict between universal economic interdependence and individual national interests. Since 1914, economic growth had demanded more coöperation, while excessive nationalism had developed. After discussing background factors—population, raw materials, technology and the like—he reviews the situation in six countries. His program is cautious: more and better commercial treaties, expansion of private international cartels and consortia, more active chambers of commerce, and more leadership by the League of Nations.

SALTER, SIR ARTHUR. **Recovery. The Second Effort.** New York: Century, 1932, 353 p.

Sir Arthur Salter was for many years economic and financial expert of the League of Nations and active participant at many of the postwar conferences. Regarding the 1920s as a period of instability ending in the world economic depression, he believed that the financial crisis was produced by deadweight debts, reckless lending and high tariffs. He laid out a program for correcting these conditions through increased national and international planning plus the reëstablishment of the gold standard with a higher gold price. On the political scene, he argued for the creation of a world system of law and order. It was a broad-brush pattern, leaving specific blueprints and operating details for others to fill in. Coming at a time when it was generally agreed that the world was out of joint, this book was widely read as an offering of solutions put forward by a wise and experienced man.

HANSEN, ALVIN HARVEY. **Economic Stabilization in an Unbalanced World.** New York: Harcourt, 1932, 384 p.

Professor Hansen describes in detail various aspects of worldwide economic maladjustment. It is not a balanced analysis; the indications are that the author put a number of separate studies within one set of covers. The worldwide depression was still developing so that it played only a limited part in his analysis. The trade payments area was dominated by reparations and debt payments, tariffs and Russian dumping, and a serious maldistribution of gold. There was worldwide unemployment with limited programs of unemployment insurance. As to population, he reflects the demographic estimates of the time that population growth was slowing down in Western Europe and the United States, and that the problem might become one of maintaining the optimum numbers. The final chapters deal briefly with a number of proposals for stabilizing capitalism, but they are not set within any broad framework.

HODSON, HENRY VINCENT. **Slump and Recovery, 1929–1937.** New York: Oxford University Press, 1938, 484 p.

For seven years, Hodson contributed to the annual "Survey of International Affairs" published by Chatham House. In this book, he has made his earlier writings into a continuous story, starting with a chapter dealing with 1920–1929 and then examining the period to 1937 in much more detail. The book portrays the international economic field with all its intricacy—country actions and country reactions, cumulative economic and political consequences, and numerous bilateral and multilateral conferences. In his analysis, commodity prices tend to be given unusual emphasis as an important carrier and cause of instability, although one is impressed by the number of short and long-run factors which entered into the fast-moving situation. The latest of these in the period covered was the stimulating effect by the armaments boom. This book is a record and interpretation of events rather than a theoretical analysis. The time span is longer and the coverage broader in his earlier **Economics of a Changing World** (New York: H. Smith, 1933, 260 p.).

BOWLEY, ARTHUR LYON. **Some Economic Consequences of the Great War.** London: Butterworth, 1930, 252 p.

This small volume in the Home University Library is almost a statistical hand-book of the postwar period to 1929, except that it also contains many cogent comments by its author, professor of statistics in the University of London. It deals primarily with the record of the United Kingdom but frequently includes data for other countries. While Professor Bowley warns about the accuracy of much of the statistics, he argues that they do indicate the direction and date of the principal recent economic changes.

STALEY, EUGENE. **World Economy in Transition.** New York: Council on Foreign Relations, 1939, 340 p.

Professor Staley prepared this basic analysis for submission to the International Studies Conference at Bergen, Norway in 1939. Among the conflicting forces which he noted are changing the world are technology with its push in the direction of a unified, worldwide economic system, set against the continuing importance of countries as political units and the increased role of individual governments in economic life. Staley pointed out the possibility of war between power economies and argued for a mixed system within countries and internationally with competitive laissez-faire and positive planning in combination, applying these ideas to various aspects of international economic life. Unfortunately, the chapters on the challenge of war were realized all too soon, but this book was clearly among those influencing postwar planning. In its basic analysis it parallels Patterson's **The World's Economic Dilemma,** though much more bold in its program.

MEADE, JAMES EDWARD. **The Economic Basis of a Durable Peace.** New York: Oxford University Press, 1940, 192 p.

Writing in the late 1930s, Professor Meade was concerned that no international regularization of economic affairs was possible without some form of international organization. Others had often reached that conclusion, but Meade moved on to the question of just what the structure and authority of the needed organization should be. Among his suggestions was an international currency issued by an international bank and backed by reserves in the various central banks. If this were not possible, he preferred variable exchange rates within limits. He believed that another international authority should endeavor gradually to reduce or eliminate trade barriers, that there might also be some supervision over capital movements directed at removing restrictions, and that obstacles to migration should be removed. It was a timely book, since the governments began to explore these same problems shortly after its publication.

CLARK, JOHN MAURICE. **The Costs of the World War to the American People.** New Haven: Yale University Press, 1931, 328 p.

This is one of the series of studies organized by the Carnegie Endowment for International Peace to build a complete record of World War I—without doubt, the greatest effort ever made in an organized examination and analysis of a world event. The volumes provide an invaluable background for any study of the war and postwar period. Cost studies parallel to the Clark volume were made for other countries, and special reports dealt with separate sectors of the various economies.

Professor Clark regarded his task of determining the cost of the war to the American people not as an accounting summation of fiscal payments but of the economic burdens on the whole economy—the destruction of goods, the diversion of productive power, the personal sacrifices made and the effect on attitudes toward government and law. Thus he faced the problem of how to measure the intangible. His final summary is qualitative rather than quantitative.

BASCH, ANTONÍN. **The Danube Basin and the German Economic Sphere.** New York: Columbia University Press, 1943, 275 p.

In some measure a sequel to Leo Pasvolsky, **Economic Nationalism of the Danubian States** (New York: Macmillan, 1929, 636 p.), which deals with the economic fragmentation of the Danube area in the 1920s following the dissolution of the Hapsburg Empire, this book treats the economic problems of the area in the 1930s. These were the years of depression and then of German ascendancy. A Czech economist with much practical experience in international economics, Basch was admirably equipped to undertake such a study, and his conclusions concerning the weaknesses of autarkic but backward economic units are sound and well documented. In retrospect one may feel—though it is certainly open to argument—that he placed perhaps too much emphasis on the German economic and commercial penetration of the region. It certainly took place, but the Danubian states' subsequent loss of independence seems to have resulted more from military and political factors than from economic pressures.

This is an informative and sympathetic study of the unsuccessful struggle of the Danubian states to meet a crisis quite beyond their powers. The future Basch hoped for bears little resemblance to what in fact occurred, economically and politically, in the years after 1945.

Reparations and War Debts

KEYNES, JOHN MAYNARD. **The Economic Consequences of the Peace.** New York: Harcourt, 1920, 298 p.

J. M. Keynes had spent six months in Paris after the Armistice, representing the British Treasury at the Paris Peace Conference and on the Supreme Economic Council. He viewed World War I as a European civil war and the postwar requirement as reconstruction and reintegration. To him the Conference was a "nightmare." He describes in bitter detail the personal characteristics and behavior of Clemenceau, Lloyd George, Woodrow Wilson and Orlando. In June 1919 Keynes resigned his government positions in protest against the draft terms of peace and returned to Cambridge where he published the grounds for his objection.

In general, he felt that the terms were political, dominated by revenge and the desire to enfeeble the Central Powers, and somehow envisaged as shifting financial burdens for rehabilitation onto them. As an economist, he saw no way of making the international payments required by a huge scale of indebtedness, a lesson finally taught by painful experience. He went beyond the reparations problem to propose that foreign purchasing credits of perhaps $1 billion should be extended to all the belligerent countries of continental Europe, Allied and ex-enemy alike. Keynes brought his discussion up to a slightly later date, but did not change his general position, in **A Revision of the Treaty** (New York: Harcourt, 1922, 242 p.).

The Economic Consequences quickly attracted public attention and undoubtedly contributed to a widespread disenchantment with the Versailles Treaty. To be sure, as Roy F. Harrod suggests in **The Life of John Maynard Keynes** (New York: Harcourt, 1951, 674 p.), the experiment of a more generous treaty might have failed, but it is farfetched to argue, as does Étienne Mantoux in his critical analysis of Keynes' position, **The Carthaginian Peace, or the Economic Consequences of Mr. Keynes** (New York: Oxford University Press, 1946, 203 p.), that this was what gradually came about in the 1920s and Hitler was the result. Harrod in his general review of the book follows Churchill in the view that the treaty should have been severe in dealing with German rearmament but lenient in economic matters.

Keynes' analysis concerning the difficulties of suddenly imposing large international payments on the economic system has had continuing influence. Thus the World War II Lend-Lease Act provided that no compensation would be due the United States for goods which it provided its allies during the war, and the later reparations programs were shaped with capacity to pay in mind. Étienne Mantoux has little support in arguing that Germany not only could have complied with the treaty terms, but that it would have kept her in her proper place.

MOULTON, HAROLD GLENN and MCGUIRE, CONSTANTINE EDWARD. **Germany's Capacity to Pay: A Study of the Reparations Problem.** New York: McGraw-Hill, 1923, 384 p.

MOULTON, HAROLD GLENN. **The Reparation Plan.** New York: McGraw-Hill, 1924, 325 p.

MOULTON, HAROLD GLENN and PASVOLSKY, LEO. **World War Debt Settlements.** New York: Macmillan, 1926, 460 p.

MOULTON, HAROLD GLENN and PASVOLSKY, LEO. **War Debts and World Prosperity.** Washington: Brookings Institution, 1932, 498 p.

These four books, plus a number of volumes relating to the debt situation in individual European countries, represent the work of the Institute for Economics (now the Brookings Institution) in the field of international economic reconstruction. They trace the record from the early punitive reparation concept through the breakdown of the payment programs to the onset of the Depression and the Lausanne settlement. The final conclusion as of the time of writing the last and virtually summary volume, **War Debts and World Prosperity** (1932), was that "a complete obliteration of all reparation and war debt obligations would promote, rather than retard, world economic prosperity." With elaborate statistical appendices, this last volume is an excellent summary of the problem and the record.

BERGMANN, KARL. **The History of Reparations.** Boston: Houghton Mifflin, 1927, 353 p.

This is a connected and detailed report on the early years of the reparations record, with particular reference to the efforts to carry out the provisions of the Treaty of Versailles. The author was one of the German financial experts throughout the entire negotiations, and his report of conference after conference is that of a participant with sufficient tenure to permit him to see the shifting positions. Writing two years after the Dawes Plan, he argued that its transfer requirements could not be met and proposed an entirely different formula which would limit the reparation debt to the total amount of loans which Germany might float in the world's capital markets. The author's official position made it possible for him to speak with authority concerning the German point of view. A later book by Jacques Seydoux, a parallel French participant, is a counterpart record with emphasis on French ideas, policies, hopes and fears: **De Versailles au Plan Young** (Paris: Plon, 1932, 332 p.).

Étienne Weill-Raynal's **Les Réparations Allemandes et la France** (Paris: Nouvelles Éditions Latines, 1947, 3 v.) is the most extensive history of the French aspects of the German reparations question. The first volume deals with the origins of the issue and the initial determination of the amount; the second with the events leading to the Ruhr occupation and the Dawes Plan; the third with the Young Plan and the final discontinuance of payments during the Depression. The author was formerly an official on the Reparations Commission.

PHILIPS, AUGUST. **Economic Aspects of Reparations and Interallied Debts.** Leyden: Van Doesburgh, 1930, 200 p.

This is one of the clearest descriptions of the postwar debt problem and its winding history, written strictly in economic terms. By 1930, the bibliography on this subject was extensive and controversial, and Philips took full advantage of it. He summarized the positions of various authors (mostly expressed in magazine articles) and then examined the basis of disagreement. His own position was that war destruction is a permanent loss and the problem is one of distributing the burden of rehabilitation. He made a clear distinction between reparations due from the vanquished and the inter-Allied debts relating to the cost of winning the war. He noted, however, that if they were put together, the result would be that reparations would flow largely to the ultimate creditor, the United States, and not remain in Europe for reconstruction of devastated regions. The Dawes Plan worked as long as it did because of the inflow of American capital. Unfortunately, in the author's eyes, this was not used to expand exports and thus ease the problem of international payments by Germany.

SCHACHT, HJALMAR. **The End of Reparations.** New York: Cape and Smith, 1931, 248 p.

Hjalmar Schacht, the "wizard," is perhaps the best known name in European finance because, as former president of the Reichsbank, he managed Germany's complicated financial affairs for many years. In this book, he considers the Versailles Treaty to be unjust, immoral and economically indefensible. He felt that the burden of international debts was an important contributing factor to the world depression and that unless something was done to eliminate it, only chaos lay ahead. He not only argued for the complete cancellation of reparations but for an economic union including Germany, particularly with its eastern neighbors, and for the return of the German colonies.

While the book is addressed to the reparations problem, Schacht used it as an instrument to castigate politicians, socialism and the failure of "capitalist leadership." He saw the major international problems as economic—debts, tariffs and economic barriers, and currency—and reasoned that these could best be solved by nonpolitical business-minded people. While Schacht, like Keynes, was right in arguing that reparations was an economic monstrosity, he went too far in implying that politicians are irresponsible or worse and that the hope of the future lay in their letting business alone.

BURNETT, PHILIP MASON. **Reparation at the Paris Peace Conference.** New York: Columbia University Press, 1940, 2 v.

This is primarily a collection of documents bearing on the drafting of the reparation clauses of the Treaty of Versailles. Most of the documents were obtained from the papers of members of the American delegation, and Burnett's extended introduction contains valuable information contributed by the members, notably Norman Davis.

Throughout, the viewpoint is that of the American delegation. In some ways this is an advantage, since the United States claimed no reparation, and therefore the American delegation did not work under the popular pressure to make Germany pay which weighed on other delegations. The unintended result is to make the American experts seem the most reasonable men working on the problem. But the introduction is not intended to be a history of the negotiations on reparation at Paris; it is a guide to a source indispensable to those who would study that history.

The ten-page foreword by John Foster Dulles, written in 1938, is an interesting footnote to later history. "The scope of what man can usefully attempt," Dulles concluded, "is constantly restricted by his lack of knowledge, and by moods which render unavailing that little knowledge which he does possess."

Disarmament

BUELL, RAYMOND LESLIE. **The Washington Conference.** New York: Appleton, 1922, 461 p.

The Washington Conference on the limitation of armaments in 1921–1922 appeared to check a ruinous competition in battleships and to bring some order into the complicated competition for concessions in China. Although initiated by Briand, it marked the appearance of the United States in a leadership role in world affairs for the first time since the Conference of Versailles. Professor Buell, then at Princeton and later research director for the Foreign Policy Association, gave a detailed picture of the Conference, including the national distrust and rivalries. One element that made agreement possible on the limitation of battleships was that some experts held that they were rapidly being made obsolete by the submarine and the airplane. No agreement was reached on either of these.

Buell was pessimistic concerning the Far Eastern aspects of the Conference. He regarded the imperialist rivalries in the Far East as largely evaded or dealt with in very general terms. All important territorial leaseholds and settlements were retained, as were the privileges of extraterritoriality and control of China's tariff. While it somewhat reduced the growing tension between the United States and Japan, he concluded that an outstanding danger remained in the possible growth of Japanese militarism and imperialism. While this forecast was to be proven right, he was less prescient concerning the continuing conflicts within and about China.

ICHIHASHI, YAMATO. **The Washington Conference and After.** Stanford: Stanford University Press, 1928, 455 p.

This is an important book about the Washington Conference, at which Professor Ichihashi was an insider as secretary to Viscount Kato, the senior Japanese delegate. He describes the event as though it were two conferences—one on the limitation of armaments and one on the Pacific and Far East, with each discussed in detail.

In his view, the main achievement of the armament discussions was the establishment of a capital-ship ratio of U.K. 5, U.S. 5, Japan 3, France 1.75 and Italy 1.75, along with agreed vacation periods on new construction. He reports that the experts of each country were dissatisfied, the British at the loss of naval supremacy, the Americans at the failure to deal with auxiliary craft and the Japanese at the check to their rapidly rising naval power. However, laymen were gratified by the formal association of the five powers to maintain peace, by the prospective reduction in armament expenditures and the establishment of more humane rules of war.

The Far East and Pacific conference centered on problems concerning China. It produced two treaties, one dealing with Chinese tariffs and the second establishing what was known as the open-door policy, described as an effort to provide equal opportunity in China for the trade and industry of all nations. Professor Ichihashi regarded these treaties as a great forward step in the history of Far Eastern diplomacy, though he found it hard to evaluate the overall situation because "in China chaos has continued to prevail," and American-Japanese relations were poisoned by the discriminatory exclusion of Japanese from the United States.

WHEELER-BENNETT, JOHN WHEELER. **Information on the Reduction of Armaments.** London: Allen and Unwin, 1925, 216 p.

An early review of the events of the first six years after World War I with respect to disarmament. The book covers the work of the Peace Conference of 1919–1920 and devotes most of its attention to the various efforts in this field by the League of Nations. As the title indicates, it is not an analysis but a series of relevant documents and quotations. An introduction by Major-General Sir Neil L. Malcolm does inject the idea that armaments are the result of "the wrong spirit" and a new moral code was needed. Somewhat later documents are to be found in John W. Wheeler-Bennett and Frederic E. Langermann, **Information on the Problem of Security, 1917–1926** (London: Allen and Unwin, 1927, 272 p.).

NOEL-BAKER, PHILIP JOHN. **Disarmament.** London: Hogarth, 1926, 366 p.

Based in part on his own experience in negotiations related to disarmament, Professor Noel-Baker of the University of London explored a wide variety of problems which emerge in any effort to achieve international agreement on the reduction of armaments and put forward specific suggestions for dealing with them. He examined past failures and successes, discussing land, maritime and air problems separately, noting particularly the difficult problem of reaching agreement on appropriate ratios of national arms. In particular, he suggested that military aircraft should not be permitted for bombardment but only for support purposes, to be determined on the basis of an identical proportional relation to permitted armies and navies. The book demonstrated the complexity of what to many people appeared to be a simple issue and, at the time, was generally recognized as the most comprehensive and technically competent publication in the field. It is marked by Noel-Baker's idealism and his belief that a reasonable answer can be found to every question.

FABRE-LUCE, ALFRED. **Locarno, the Reality.** New York: Knopf, 1928, 209 p.

Most observers at the time regarded the Pact of Locarno of 1925 as the turning point toward reconciliation among the former enemies of World War I, in that Germany, Belgium, France, Great Britain and Italy mutually agreed in a few words to guarantee the peace of Western Europe. Important problems were, however, unsettled. Though Germany agreed to accept its western boundaries in accordance with Versailles, it promised only to "arbitrate" eastern territorial disputes.

Fabre-Luce challenged the reality of the Locarno settlement, arguing that the assumed Franco-German reconciliation disregarded the causes of animosity in order to deal with the effect. The procedures for the prevention of aggression were focused on the violation of frontiers, but other acts of aggression were not considered. He noted that the Austrian-German problem remained unsolved, along with the dangerous question of the eastern frontiers. Surprisingly for a French source, he seemed to endorse a policy of general cancellation of war debts, perhaps because all-inclusive action might actually help France if its obligations to the United States exceeded the likely receipts of reparations. His hope for the future was a French alliance with Germany, the settlement of the issues still outstanding from the war, and Franco-German unity, based on the development of their common interests. Another world war was to intervene before that hope approached reality.

MILLER, DAVID HUNTER. **The Peace Pact of Paris.** New York: Putnam, 1928, 283 p.

A detailed record of the origins and events connected with the Kellogg-Briand Pact. Miller's work presents the written record in detail, particularly the American government's correspondence with other states, and nearly half the book consists of the various diplomatic notes involved. In his optimistic conclusion, the author felt that the treaty would be enforced—that "supine indifference to our own Treaty is unimaginable." Neutrality in case of war was no longer possible, he said, and the true sanction was the potential attitude of the United States toward a violator. He concluded that the new responsibility for maintaining the peace would facilitate and advance the date of American entry into the League of Nations.

SHOTWELL, JAMES THOMSON. **War as an Instrument of National Policy.** New York: Harcourt, 1929, 320 p.

War was officially "outlawed" in 1929. In 1918, the concept had been put forward by an American, S. O. Levinson, and had been actively publicized in the United States with particular support by Senator Borah. Suggested in April 1927 by Briand and followed up in December by Secretary of State Kellogg, 15 countries agreed in Paris in the following August that the settlement of disputes among them "shall never be sought except by pacific means." By the middle of 1929, practically every nation had declared its adherence.

In this book, which is somewhat misnamed, Professor Shotwell, an eminent American historian who was himself active during the period as a defender of the League of Nations and leading peace advocate, provides an analysis of the Pact of

Paris and its background. He was certain that the Pact established a new basis for international law and that it merely needed to be supplemented by "instruments of international justice." While much of the historical material in the book is documentary, the author believed that the signing of the Pact offered a clear case in which a rising tide of public opinion was responsible for action by the American government, and that the strength of the Pact lay in the popular will to peace. He supported the proposition that the basic causes of war could not be eliminated, but that law could be substituted for force as a means of settlement of international disputes, as in cases of private disagreement. What the supporters of the Pact did not fully appreciate was that law is effective only when it is enforceable and enforced.

O'CONNOR, RAYMOND GISH. **Perilous Equilibrium: The United States and the London Naval Conference of 1930.** Lawrence: University of Kansas Press, 1962, 188 p.

The London Naval Conference of 1930 was one more small step in the movement toward disarmament after the First World War. It dealt with the forms of naval expansion which had not been appropriately covered by the earlier Washington Conference. It temporarily stabilized conditions in the Pacific but did not resolve the problem of competitive arming in Europe, where security was not necessarily affected by sea power. The author picks up the naval limitation story in 1927 and carries it in detail through the London Conference. Once again, the difficulties, inadequacies and limited success of this approach to arms control are made evident.

DE MADARIAGA, SALVADOR. **Disarmament.** New York: Coward-McCann, 1929, 392 p.

The author, formerly chief of the disarmament section of the League of Nations, presented the record of disarmament efforts over the ten-year period after World War I less as a matter of historical detail than as an attempt to understand the record so that the obstacles could be faced effectively. His basic conclusion is that disarmament is not a separate problem but a subhead under the problem of "the world-community." He argued that armaments are significant as instruments of policy, except in a condition of international coöperation. Thus the Russian proposal for immediate disarmament and the Kellogg Pact were irrelevant. His discussion led inevitably to a demand for drastic strengthening of the League as an essential requirement for effective disarmament.

ENGELY, GIOVANNI. **The Politics of Naval Disarmament.** London: Williams and Norgate, 1932, 301 p.

Giovanni Engely of the University of Bologna gives a lucid and coherent account of the long train of negotiations which started with the Washington Conference in 1921. The bulk of the book is devoted to the London Naval Conference in 1930, in which Italy was a participant. As Engely sees it, this was essentially a European conference, with the objectives of fixing ratios among the British, French and Italian fleets and of lowering the overall level as much as possible. He describes the position of the five powers prior to the Conference, the diplomatic preparations, the Conference itself and certain subsequent naval negotiations. On its main objectives, the Conference was a failure, but the author looked forward to the General Disarmament Conference of 1932 for better results.

The Depression

ROBBINS, LIONEL CHARLES. **The Great Depression.** New York: Macmillan, 1934, 238 p.

An outstanding economist active far beyond his home territory of the University of London, Professor Robbins is here concerned with the unprecedented depression which began in 1929. He first clears away a number of misconceptions, suggesting that the fall of prices was a consequence, not a cause; it was the same for overproduction; deflation was no more a cause than the fall of prices; there was no shortage of gold, nor did the maldistribution of gold have opposite effects on the countries involved. Robbins' own theory involves excess anticipations, inflationary credit expansion and undue emphasis on capital goods. In considerable detail, he describes the steps which led to world boom and world collapse, enforced by restrictive commercial and financial policies. He saw the probability of recovery but did not think it would be enduring, fearing the possibility of war with Germany as well as profound internal tendencies making for instability.

BENNETT, EDWARD WELLS. **Germany and the Diplomacy of the Financial Crisis, 1931.** Cambridge: Harvard University Press, 1962, 342 p.

Edward W. Bennett has described the interplay of German, French, British and American diplomacy during the disastrous financial crisis of 1931. He explains that because the outstanding debts were so large, creditors and debtors were both endangered, and that despite the efforts of President Hoover to establish a procedure for approaching the problem of the revision of the existing arrangements with Germany, conflicting viewpoints permitted the financial crisis to get out of control. Meetings in Paris and London in July 1931 succeeded in taking a few ameliorating steps, but more important was the setting up of a committee by the Bank for International Settlements. This is a detailed study of a case in which international diplomacy failed miserably to deal with a situation of collapse, due in part to differing interests, partly to misunderstanding, and partly to antipathies and prejudices.

OHLIN, BERTIL. **The Course and Phases of the World Economic Depression.** Boston: World Peace Foundation, 1931, 355 p.

This report to the Assembly of the League of Nations is a classic in its field. Its comparisons among sectors and among countries were unique at the time. The report begins with the end of the First World War and traces changes in structural and financial conditions thereafter. However, its emphasis is on the boom, turn and decline. The rather pessimistic analysis is based on the proposition that a business-cycle recession occurred at a moment when structural changes and maladjustments had made the economic situation very unstable. While no recommendations for action were put forward, much can be read between the lines in the discussion of matters such as cost reduction, tariff restrictions and inflexible taxation. Not only is the report unusual in the volume of statistics presented, but in the extent to which it used the graphic form for presenting time series.

GOLDSTEIN, JOSEPH MARKOVICH. **The Agricultural Crisis.** New York: Day, 1935, 257 p.

One of the early students of the world agricultural situation, this eminent Russian economist, writing in New York, examined the agricultural record of the main wheat producers and concluded that the increase in wheat production was likely to produce a prolonged agricultural crisis. He had made such a prediction in a Russian volume in May 1914, but the war had delayed the appearance of surpluses. The economic crisis and trade restrictions of the early 1930s reduced consumer demand just as production reached new peaks, so there was an interacting downward spiral. In Professor Goldstein's judgment, too much attention was paid to price maintenance, since the basic requirements of improvement were restricted production and unrestricted international trade.

VARGA, EUGEN. **The Great Crisis and Its Political Consequences.** New York: International Publishers, 1935, 175 p.

The director of the Institute of World Economy and Politics in Moscow presents the official Marxist interpretation of the economic crisis of the 1930s. In general, Varga writes, overproduction leads to accumulation of inventory. Thus the postwar period saw an increase in productive power far beyond the capacity of markets under capitalism to absorb. In addition, the world experienced an agrarian crisis and a crisis in the colonies, all leading to the impoverishment of the proletariat. Moreover, because of the success of the Soviet Union, the ideological struggle was sharpened, and a new world war threatened. This book was followed several years later by a much more detailed study of earlier economic crises, edited by Varga, **Mirovoye Ekonomicheskie Krizisy, 1848–1935** (Moscow: Sotsekgiz, 1937–1939, 3 v.).

HANSEN, ALVIN HARVEY. **Full Recovery or Stagnation?** New York: Norton, 1938, 350 p.

Professor Hansen's book had a worldwide influence. It was taken in many circles as forecasting stagnation for the United States, and since it was one of the last economic books to reach foreign libraries before the war, it was literally the last word in American analysis for almost a decade. He outlined the possibility of an underemployment equilibrium which could not be improved by lowering wages. Full employment, he said, would depend upon getting new capital to flow into industry, a condition which was virtually absent in many countries during the 1930s. He suggested that the withdrawal of potential consumer purchasing power through such activities as social security has a deflationary aspect. Nor did he find much to be optimistic about in the international field.

VON HABERLER, GOTTFRIED. **Prosperity and Depression.** Geneva: League of Nations, 1938, 363 p.

As a result of a League of Nations Assembly resolution, Professor von Haberler, who had been on the League Secretariat but had just been given a professorship at Harvard, undertook the review and evaluation of existing theories of business cycles. While the volume is largely theoretical, it gives an excellent summary of the state of knowledge on the subject in the middle 1930s. After examining many theories, Von Haberler has very tentatively produced a general synthesis, pointing out the areas where substantial disagreement still existed. The longest chapter in the book discusses the international aspects of business cycles.

GALBRAITH, JOHN KENNETH. **The Great Crash, 1929.** Boston: Houghton, 1955, 212 p.

The author, an economist and diplomat, has discussed in his own special style the events leading up to and immediately following the New York stock market crash in the autumn of 1929. It was a drop heard around the world, but his analysis has little reference to any international aspect. He sees it as a speculative spree followed by the necessary collapse, happening at a time when the economy was weak in terms of distribution of income, corporate structure, banking structure, foreign balance and economic analysis. He believes that there has been some improvement in all these areas but that another period of excited speculation is still possible. A different approach is that of Milton Friedman and Anna J. Schwartz in **The Great Contraction 1929–1933** (Princeton: Princeton University Press, 1965, 150 p.). This is a reprint of a chapter in the authors' **A Monetary History of the United States, 1867–1960** (Princeton: Princeton University Press, 1963, 860 p.) and argues that the collapse was essentially the result of monetary forces.

Dawes and Young Plans; Bank for International Settlements

AULD, GEORGE PERCIVAL. **The Dawes Plan and the New Economics.** New York: Doubleday, 1927, 317 p.

This book, written by the former Accountant-General of the Reparations Commission, is probably the strongest defense of Allied demands for reparations available in English. Auld regarded such payments not merely as politically appropriate but as a proper economic program. Writing in 1927, he argued that there should be no voluntary cancellation, but that payments should be continued and that American aid and loans were making possible the necessary transfer payments. He insisted that France needed reparations and saw no reason why Germany could not pay; the Dawes Plan had worked for four years and should continue to work, provided its critics would not so undermine confidence in it as to interfere with the flow of capital into Germany. Without actually saying so, he was satisfied that reparations payments should be based on American capital flowing into Germany.

SERING, MAX. **Germany under the Dawes Plan.** London: King, 1929, 251 p.

Professor Sering of the University of Berlin devoted most of his discussion to the origins and execution of the Dawes Plan as seen from the German point of view. He criticized the Experts' Report underlying the Dawes Plan as failing to recognize the change in Germany's foreign investment position, the destructive effects of the inflation and the need for rehabilitation of industry. Sering places particular emphasis on the deterioration of agriculture. The working capital to be provided by the Dawes Plan would not suffice and would in fact create still another burden on the balance of payments. Therefore, he visualized Germany as being faced with increasing burdens and being steadily impoverished, and saw no prospect of the development of the necessary German export surplus. His solution was a new international committee to "redress the injustice done," based on an assessment of the remaining uncompensated losses of the civilian population in the occupied territories and a study of capacity to pay.

While this book does describe Germany's problems of the moment, its proposed formulation of a settlement could not possibly be quantified. The actual change from the picture which he presents to that of a rearming Germany demonstrates, in hindsight, quite different possibilities of economic productivity.

DAWES, CHARLES GATES. **A Journal of Reparations.** New York: Macmillan, 1939, 527 p.

Charles G. Dawes, later Vice President of the United States, was chairman of the experts' committee which drew up what came to be called the Dawes Plan. His diary, which includes not only political and economic discussion and related documents but incidents which were personal and irrelevant, is the record of the day-by-day steps as well as the dinners and other diversions. A supplement to the chairman's report is that by his brother, Rufus C. Dawes, **The Dawes Plan in the Making** (Indianapolis: Bobbs-Merrill, 1925, 525 p.). A successful businessman, he was chief of the staff of eight economic experts who accompanied Charles G. Dawes and Owen Young to Paris. Also largely in diary form, with working papers in the appendix, it portrays the gradual emergence of the final plan through fairly continuous negotiation over a period of three months.

DULLES, ELEANOR LANSING. **The Bank for International Settlements at Work.** New York: Macmillan, 1932, 631 p.

The Young Plan, signed June 7, 1929, not only established a reduced schedule of reparations payments to be made by Germany, but provided for the establishment of a new bank to supply the machinery for carrying out its provisions. Dr. Dulles had already written **The French Franc, 1914–1928** (New York: Macmillan, 1929, 570 p.), so it is not surprising that she became interested in the Bank for International Settlements being created in Basle. Her study thoroughly covers the very early period in its life from May 1930 to 1932—the period of organization and the development of procedures and policies. Concentration on this period also permitted the author to review the reparations situation and the financial crises of 1931–32. She concluded that, after two very successful years, the financial crisis greatly reduced the Bank's effectiveness. However, she suggested that the inevitable period of recovery might give the Bank for International Settlements an even more significant role along lines authorized in its charter, particularly in developing coöperation among national central banks. The Bank's monthly financial statements are included in an appendix. A much shorter monograph which brings the

Bank's story down to 1957 is that of Henry Hans Schloss, **The Bank for Inter-national Settlements** (Amsterdam: North-Holland Publishing Co., 1958, 184 p.).

PAPI, GIUSEPPE UGO. **The First Twenty Years of the Bank for International Settlements.** Rome: Bancaria, 1951, 270 p.

Professor Papi's book was published on the twentieth anniversary of the Bank for International Settlements. A professor of economics at the University of Rome, he worked closely with the BIS in preparing it and includes a 115-page bibliography "on the Bank and cognate subjects." While the Bank was established to handle certain post–World War I financial problems, its practical operations involved more than trustee functions. Originally founded to handle German reparations under the Young Plan, its functions had grown to include the holding of central bank reserves, acting as a clearing house between central banks, engaging in rediscounting, and encouraging coöperation between the central banks by bringing their officials together from time to time. After World War II, it was helpful in straightening out various financial tangles. One wishes that Professor Papi had given more detail about these operations, but he was undoubtedly limited by the built-in secrecy which seems to surround bankers.

Territorial Problems; Munich

GREER, GUY. **The Ruhr-Lorraine Industrial Problem.** New York: Macmillan, 1925, 348 p.

This economic study by the Institute of Economics (now the Brookings Institution) deals with the economic interdependence of Ruhr coal and Lorraine iron ore and their relation to the reparation question. The postwar arrangements changed and magnified the economic importance of the German-French boundaries. Not only were new barriers raised between the Ruhr and Lorraine, but the economic institutional structure within which they operated was destroyed. Since the European economy depended upon the regular functioning of this industrial complex, the requirements of reparations stood in the way of reconstruction. The author deplores the occupation of the Ruhr but recognizes it as a consequence of postwar arrangements. Greer analyzes the problem from the French and the German national points of view, and from the essentially economic point of view, and argues for a recognition of interdependence and a common effort to regain the efficient functioning of the Ruhr-Lorraine system.

In **Ruhrkampf** (Berlin: Hobbing, 1930–1932, 2 v.), Paul Wentzcke, a trained German historian, searched all available governmental records as well as the archives of many of the leading industrial concerns which were involved in the Ruhr crisis. The result is an elaborate two-volume history of the events relating to the Ruhr occupation as seen from the German side. It is well documented and objectively written.

POUNDS, NORMAN JOHN GREVILLE. **The Ruhr: A Study in Historical and Economic Geography.** Bloomington: Indiana University Press, 1953, 283 p.

A good background study of the history and recent developments in the Ruhr, by a professor of geography at Indiana University. One half of the book relates to the nineteenth century, but the remainder describes the coal and steel industries of the Ruhr, its elaborate system of transportation and various social aspects of the area. The final chapter points out its international importance, discussing very briefly its significance as the source of German armament, the Franco-Belgian occupation after the First World War up to the Dawes Plan, the period of dismantling physical equipment and subdividing cartels after the Second World War, and the new approach through the Schuman Plan.

WAMBAUGH, SARAH. **The Saar Plebiscite.** Cambridge: Harvard University Press, 1940, 489 p.

The definitive history of the Saar plebiscite by a member of the Saar Plebiscite Commission and the outstanding authority on plebiscites. Carried out 15 years after the war by the League of Nations according to peace treaty provisions, its procedures for obtaining a fair decision represented a new level in the use of neutrals. The book is much more than a technical report concerning the procedure followed, for it also describes the persistent problems of the Saar as a border land since the day of the Roman legions. Two interesting chapters describe the situation during the postwar period when the territory was governed by the League of Nations. Relevant documents are given in an appendix.

FREYMOND, JACQUES. **The Saar Conflict: 1945–1955.** New York: Praeger, 1960, 395 p.

Professor Freymond, Director of the Institut Universitaire de Hautes Études Internationales in Geneva, wrote this work as the first in a series of case studies sponsored by the European Center of the Carnegie Endowment for International Peace. After 200 pages describing the succession of events concerning the Saar between 1945 and 1956, the author shifts to the analysis of the controlling factors —individuals, political parties, other groups such as the clergy and the press, public opinion, international influences and the relative political and economic strength of the two countries involved. Professor Freymond concludes that these are all component parts influencing the course of events, although the unexpected outcome resulted from the will of the people of the Saar as shown through the plebiscite.

RUSSELL, FRANK MARION. **The Saar: Battleground and Pawn.** Stanford: Stanford University Press, 1951, 204 p.

One of the Stanford "Books on World Politics," this study is built upon the author's earlier **International Government of the Saar** (Berkeley: University of California Publications, Bureau of International Relations, 1926, v. I, number 2, pp. 113–249). It deals largely with the 15-year period during which the Saar was ruled under the aegis of the League of Nations. The author regards the international régime as having been efficient, economical and benevolent. Nevertheless, he sadly recognizes that the verdict of the plebiscite of 1935 demonstrated the power of nationalism over economics and internationalism—the totalitarian German régime with its emphasis on war preparation was clearly preferred over the proposed international statute, although as a public relations issue it was not debated in quite those terms.

ALLEN, HENRY TUREMAN. **The Rhineland Occupation.** Indianapolis: Bobbs-Merrill, 1927, 347 p.

In 1923, after nearly five years, General Allen, the American commander on the Rhine, returned to the United States. He described here in detail the problems faced during the Rhineland occupation—the conflicts between the participating governments, the military and civilian within the control structure and between the occupation authorities and the German officials. This volume can be supplemented by the author's widely read diary, giving much more detail concerning his personal involvements: **My Rhineland Journal** (Boston: Houghton Mifflin, 1923, 593 p.). The French point of view is presented by the French Commissioner, Paul Tirard, in **La France sur le Rhin** (Paris: Plon, 1930, 520 p.).

BURCKHARDT, CARL JACOB. **Meine Danziger Mission: 1937–1939.** Munich: Callwey, 1960, 366 p.

Though largely overlooked at the time, one of the focal points of Nazi German expansion before September 1939 was the Free City of Danzig, nominally international and supervised by the League of Nations, but increasingly, after the mid-1930s, controlled by Nazi or pro-Nazi elements. From February 1937 to September 1939, the League High Commissioner in Danzig was the Swiss historian Carl J. Burckhardt. In these important, if unintentionally self-revealing memoirs—which include, among other things, a substantial number of hitherto unpublished letters and reports of the author to his superiors at Geneva—Burckhardt, who was highly critical of the post-1919 Polish-German frontier settlement, leaves no doubt that he was well aware of the nature and objectives of Nazism and all it stood for at home and abroad. His memoirs contain, for instance, a shattering account of his visit in October 1935, as representative of the International Red Cross, to the notorious concentration camp at Esterwegen and of a brief meeting with the dying Carl von Ossietzky, who was incarcerated there. In Danzig Burckhardt fought at best a rearguard action. He seems to have had no faith that the Free City could be kept indefinitely out of Hitler's hands, and, like most of the appeasers of the 1930s, he was wracked by gnawing doubts about the righteousness of his own course. This intellectual-political defensiveness was, of course, at the heart of "appeasement." Like most neutrals or "neutralists" he seems to have trusted largely to luck to stem the totalitarian tide.

BRÜGEL, JOHANN WOLFGANG. **Tschechen und Deutsche: 1918–1938.** Munich: Nymphenburger Verlagshandlung, 1967, 662 p.

Because of the intensity of nationalist feelings on both sides, Czech-German relations have been an almost intractable subject of scholarly study. Neither most Czechs, nor most Germans, could be expected to write with the necessary detachment, and foreign analysts were hampered by linguistic and research difficulties. These handicaps are minimized in the person of J. W. Brügel, former secretary to the head of the Sudeten German Social Democratic Party—chief advocate of coöperation with the Czechs—who lived in Britain for more than 25 years before writing his book. He knows where the problems are and asks the right questions, using as sources the captured German documents and an impressive quantity of contemporary press and literature in both German and Czech. The analysis is both fair and exhaustive.

Brügel deflates most of the German nationalist myths. The Sudetenland, far from being saturated by the Czech bureaucracy, was governed by German officials. Czechoslovakia had more German schools per pupil than Germany itself. Judged by the accumulation of capital per person, the Sudeten Germans were economically the strongest ethnic group in Czechoslovakia. The Czech-sponsored land reform did not discriminate against them, although its gains—distributed as they were along party lines—benefited the Czechs more. During the Depression, the Sudetenland received in proportion more government aid than the Czech areas.

At the end of the 1930s, Hitler's aggressive policies rather than internal problems destroyed Czechoslovakia. But the easy susceptibility of the Sudeten Germans to Nazi propaganda casts doubts on Brügel's thesis that without Nazism democratic Czechoslovakia would have successfully integrated the German minority. Intent to show the strength of "coöperationism," he gives no satisfactory explanation of its catastrophic breakdown. His treatment of the late 1930s does not match the high level of competence characteristic of the analysis of the earlier periods. For the understanding of Hitler's policies toward Czechoslovakia, Boris Celovsky's **Das Münchener Abkommen, 1938** (Stuttgart: Deutsche Verlags-Anstalt, 1958, 518 p.) and Hans-Adolf Jacobsen's **Nationalsozialistische Aussenpolitik, 1933–1938** are superior. But such shortcomings do not significantly diminish the value of what is by far the best study of one of the most difficult nationality problems of modern times.

KALIJARVI, THORSTEN V. **The Memel Statute: Its Origin, Legal Nature, and Observation to the Present Day.** London: Hale, 1937, 256 p.

The literature on Lithuania's conflict with Germany over the Memel (Klaipeda in Lithuanian) region and its autonomy is even more numerous than on the Vilna question. Kalijarvi's monograph, though based primarily on German sources, is a factual study of the origin and growth of the Statute of 1924, according to which Memel was given autonomy under the sovereignty of Lithuania. Kalijarvi notes that the Lithuanians regarded the autonomy of Memel as a temporary solution until the region was fully integrated into Lithuania, while the Germans considered the Memel Statute as a guarantee of the German character of the province.

In March 1939 Hitler temporarily resolved the Memel problem by incorporating the disputed region into his Reich, and subsequent international developments have made the whole Memel question obsolete. Klaipeda today belongs to the Soviet Lithuanian Republic.

An attempt to review the Memel question in perspective was made by Ernst-Albrecht Plieg in his **Das Memelland, 1920–1939** (Würzburg: Holzner, 1962, 268 p.). The book is informative, but its purpose is to summarize the German arguments against the Lithuanian rule over the region. For the Lithuanian point of view one should consult the well-documented **Klaipėdos Problema,** by Rudolfas Valsonokas (Klaipeda: Rytas, 1932, 426 p.).

WHEELER-BENNETT, JOHN WHEELER. **Munich: Prologue to Tragedy.** London: Macmillan, 2d ed., 1963, 507 p.

Although much new evidence has appeared since 1948, when this book was first published, and the second edition is not revised substantively, Wheeler-Bennett's **Munich** remains the most vivid and thoughtful account of the crisis in English. The author was intimately involved with the men and the events of the 1930s, but he was not involved in the making of decisions; he was, therefore, able to recapture the intensity of thought and feeling of those years without being burdened by the necessity of defending his own actions. His point of view was strongly, but not blindly, anti-appeasement.

Of the many other accounts in English, possibly the most useful are R. G. D. Laffan, **The Crisis over Czechoslovakia** (v. II of the Royal Institute of International Affairs' "Survey of International Affairs" for 1938, London: Oxford University Press, 1951, 475 p.), and Donald Lammers, **Explaining Munich: The Search for Motive in British Policy** (Stanford: Hoover Institution, 1966, 73 p.). Laffan wrote a dispassionate, detailed account, using the documents published from the British and the captured German archives. Lammers also used documents published by the American and the Soviet governments for his brief interpretation and centers his discussion on Soviet policy in 1938 as well as on the "anti-Red" interpretation of British policy. Of the German accounts, the most useful are Johann Wolfgang Brügel, **Tschechen und Deutsche: 1918–1938;** Helmuth K. G. Rönnefarth, **Die Sudetenkrise in der Internationalen Politik** (Wiesbaden: Steiner, 1961, 2 v.); and Boris Celovsky, **Das Münchener Abkommen, 1938** (Stuttgart: Deutsche Verlags-Anstalt, 1958, 518 p.). Francis Loewenheim has edited a useful small volume, **Peace or Appeasement: Hitler, Chamberlain, and the Munich Crisis** (Boston: Houghton Mifflin, 1965, 204 p.), giving documents, selections from memoirs, contrasting interpretations by historians and a survey of scholarly writing on the Munich crisis.

It will be long before a "definitive" study of this or other episodes of the 1930s will be possible; for instance, the vast amount of evidence recently made available to historians by the opening of the British Foreign Office archives has not yet been incorporated in the story. But it is doubtful whether the main lines of the story will be changed by this, or other, evidence.

III. THE SECOND WORLD WAR

GENERAL; HISTORICAL

CHURCHILL, SIR WINSTON LEONARD SPENCER. **The Second World War.** Boston: Houghton, 1948–1953, 6 v.

Six volumes comprise this work: **The Gathering Storm** (1948, 784 p.), **Their Finest Hour** (1949, 751 p.), **The Grand Alliance** (1950, 903 p.), **The Hinge of Fate** (1950, 1,000 p.), **Closing the Ring** (1951, 749 p.) and **Triumph and Tragedy** (1953, 800 p.). They offer an exceptionally fine self-portrait of one of the greatest war leaders of this or any other century, so far surpassing other war memoirs in stylistic excellence and intrinsic interest as to stand alone in the foremost rank.

The method of their composition is to intermix narrative passages with either the complete texts of documents and speeches or longish extracts from them. (Appendices to each volume contain additional primary material.) The general effect on the reader is a lively impression of contemporaneity nicely tempered by the reflections of an ardent, generous mind. Subsequent publications and the gradual opening of governmental and private archives are permitting a rounder and more detached appraisal of the springs and limits of British wartime policy, but the judgments implicit in Churchill's selection and arrangement of his material will never lose their independent value and fascination.

The first volume begins, in essence, with the fall of the Lloyd George coalition and the emergence of Stanley Baldwin as the dominating figure in British politics. It closes with an account of Churchill's wartime service at the Admiralty, which ended with the political crisis that made him Prime Minister. This volume reveals, and its sequels amply confirm, Churchill's oft-remarked "romantic" conception of life: his knight-errantry, his view of foreign politics as a struggle between "good" and "evil" forces, his determination to treat all men and events in a historical perspective of really epic proportions. These qualities of mind and heart served the needs of embattled England very well, but at less heroic moments they led their possessor into errors of perception and judgment which left him isolated and impotent.

The remaining five volumes cover in rich detail the years of Churchill's greatest service to the state. In them the author has set down in ever-fresh language his impressions of the ebb and flow of battle; he has frankly and fair-mindedly chronicled the debates over grand strategy; he has taken the measure of the great politicians and commanders of the age; and he has given a particularly vivid accounting of the special strains which coalition warfare imposes on the parties to it. The result is often magnificent, but it is not, and never claimed to be, history in the ordinary meaning of the word. It is, rather, a massive contribution to history, a personal record of the higher direction of the war whose very strengths are also its limitations. Churchill judges military operations freely and confidently, as his experience entitles him to do, but his perception of events from a British angle of vision sometimes yields a distorted view of the American and Russian contributions to the defeat of the Axis powers. He consistently explains decisions, even political ones, by reference to the exigencies of war, and he understands—better than the Americans—that military and political purposes are not easily separable; yet he offers remarkably few general observations on the causes and nature of international tensions and war, and he refrains, no doubt wisely, from attempts to judge in the manner of history the political outcome of a struggle to which he is still much too close. He conveys very successfully the dramatic highlights of the crisis years but at the cost of neglecting the deeper changes quietly wrought on the peoples of England and the Empire by the experience of war. These are important qualifications which make a case for wider reading, but they leave undiminished the essential greatness of Churchill's achievement.

MICHEL, HENRI. **La Seconde Guerre Mondiale.** Paris: Presses Universitaires, 1968–1969, 2 v.

Henri Michel possesses singular credentials for undertaking a work of scholarly synthesis on the Second World War. As Director of the Comité d'Histoire de la Seconde Guerre Mondiale, editor of the *Revue d'Histoire de la Deuxième Guerre Mondiale* and author of several notable studies of French and European resistance movements, he has an almost unparalleled knowledge of (and access to) both primary and secondary materials on the subject. This book, which is described as "only a provisional stocktaking of knowledge" about the war, is consequently far more than another secondary survey. Michel has provided us with the most thorough, thoughtful and informed survey of the war in all of its theaters. The passages on European developments, reflecting Michel's grasp of the French and German sources, are especially impressive. Though containing no major revelations, and differing from Gordon Wright's **The Ordeal of Total War, 1939–1945** mainly in the amount of detail, the sections on Europe during the war summarize a considerable body of diffuse material and clarify many confused issues by authoritative exposition.

Where the sources yield no firm conclusions (as in the case of Stalin's early responses to the German invasion), Michel assesses the probabilities with sensitivity and common sense. The discussions of British and American experiences and policies, though not so detailed or subtle as those on continental affairs, are clear and reliable. Michel appears concerned to rebut the Gaullist tendency to downgrade the personal qualities and contributions of Roosevelt and Churchill, both of whom he treats very favorably; he also gives Stalin and De Gaulle their due, though with less enthusiasm. The sections on the war in the Far East are the most derivative, though distinguished by Michel's perceptive synthesizing. Beyond military considerations, Michel discusses the economic and social course and consequences of the war, technological and medical advances inspired by military needs, and the occupation policies of the Germans and Japanese, whose genocidal practices inspire a rather brooding quality in the narrative. The book ends with a survey of the material and moral damage inflicted on all sides. Specialists will regret that the series format precluded footnote references (short bibliographies are given at the beginning of chapters and some sections), but they are likely to agree that this *tour d'horizon* is indeed a tour de force.

FEIS, HERBERT. **Churchill—Roosevelt—Stalin: The War They Waged and the Peace They Sought.** Princeton: Princeton University Press, 1957, 692 p.
———. **Between War and Peace: The Potsdam Conference.** Princeton: Princeton University Press, 1960, 367 p.
———. **From Trust to Terror: The Onset of the Cold War, 1945–1950.** New York: Norton, 1970, 428 p.

In the first two of these books a distinguished historian describes the anxious beginning, perilous victory and fateful fracture of the grand alliance against the Axis powers. Drawing on his own experience as a close adviser to Secretary of State Hull, along with access to important papers of W. Averell Harriman and other officials as well as published documents, Feis is especially informative on the divergent war aims of the three great powers and the "political costs of coalition." In his view the Soviet Union held that if it could get what it wanted, the other two powers likewise could take what they wanted. "This was its rule, not the restraining precepts of the Atlantic Charter, to which the Soviet government had professed to adhere." By contrast the United States, "virtuous but ineffectual," talked of postponing major territorial settlements until after the war, while the British (less sanguine about proposed new international institutions) were more flexible, willing to concede some points and contest others.

The narrative of **From Trust to Terror** compasses the crucial situations and actions in "the swirling rapids" of the years from the Potsdam Conference to the autumn of 1949 and the Russian acquisition of atomic weapons. In outlining the interplay of aspiration, necessity and expediency, Feis presents what is still the most comprehensive coverage of Big Three relationships. Much of the strength of his books lies in the shrewd and balanced exposition of how the major Western leaders assessed and acted upon the choices open to them. Combining an insider's insight with a scholar's detachment, Feis is particularly successful in explaining large and complicated events and placing them in clear perspective. Like Churchill, he shows that the triumph over Hitler contained elements of tragedy.

MCNEILL, WILLIAM HARDY. **America, Britain, and Russia: Their Co-operation and Conflict, 1941–1946.** New York: Oxford University Press (for the Royal Institute of International Affairs), 1953, 819 p.

This volume of the "Survey of International Affairs" by a University of Chicago scholar closely parallels the two books by Herbert Feis noted first above. It was written a few years earlier and was based wholly upon published material, mostly American, but it retains permanent value for its systematic coverage of subjects and its thorough review of the pertinent literature. World War II was well and promptly recorded from almost every angle except that of the Soviet leadership, and on the basis of materials available in the early postwar years McNeill prepared an objective and illuminating review of the tense relationships among the Big Three. His explanations of Western policy are of course more cogent and persuasive than the more speculative and less documented sections on Russia. The theme of "coöperation and conflict" emerges with regard to military operations, production and transport, relief and rehabilitation, and especially political and economic manoeuvring for postwar power. McNeill sketched in the ideological factors influencing the three governments and then showed how the war against Hitler was gradually transformed into the cold war. Along the way he expressed provocative opinions on such subjects as the eclipse of the State Department, the waning influence of Chiang Kai-shek, the optimistic myth embodied in Roosevelt, Stalin's enigmatic ambivalence, Churchill's precarious balancing act and the cataclysmic effect upon Europe of two world wars.

LEAHY, WILLIAM DANIEL. **I Was There.** New York: Whittlesey House, 1950, 527 p.

As the title suggests, this is an eyewitness account of war at the top. Admiral Leahy, former Chief of Naval Operations and Governor of Puerto Rico, served as ambassador to France from January 1941 to May 1942 and then returned to Washington as Chief of Staff to the Commander in Chief of the United States Army and Navy, a post he held until 1949 under Presidents Roosevelt and Truman. Writing on the basis of notes prepared daily at such diverse stations as Vichy, Washington, Quebec, Cairo, Tehran, Yalta and Potsdam, Leahy conveys a lively sense of the pressures working on the Allied leadership. He was skeptical about nations and institutions and offered salty opinions about persons and policies, but he stoutly maintained that Roosevelt never made a military decision with any thought of his own political fortunes. While the book is more descriptive and anecdotal than analytical or interpretative, and rather unreliable in factual detail and chronology, it provides much solid information about the views and moods of the two Presidents and on the workings of the Joint and Combined Chiefs of Staff. Leahy, usually more an observer and intermediary than a protagonist, was alert and thoughtful, and he tells most convincingly how it was to be there.

DUCLOS, PAUL. **Le Vatican et la Seconde Guerre Mondiale.** Paris: Pedone, 1955, 254 p.

Scholarly investigation of Vatican policy during the Second World War remains in a provisional and controversial stage. Amidst an extensive literature, Duclos' book, though a good deal dated, still provides the most comprehensive coverage as well as a sustained defense of Vatican policy. The emphasis is legalistic. To Pius XII is admiringly attributed a balance of judgment and wisdom which, in Duclos' opinion, brought the Vatican enhanced prestige in the immediate postwar years. A much more critical view is presented in Saul Friedländer, **Pius XII and the Third Reich: A Documentation** (New York: Knopf, 1966, 238 p.). Although Friedländer's book is primarily a compilation of documents, most of them from the German Foreign Office archives, there is sufficient analytical comment to give it a narrative quality. Friedländer finds that Papal passivity and caution toward National Socialist actions reflected in substantial measure the Pontiff's predilection for Germans and fear of the bolshevization of Europe. Carlo Falconi, **The Silence of Pius XII** (Boston: Little, Brown, 1970, 430 p.), grounding his study on Polish and Jugoslavian sources, also comes to critical conclusions.

The Holy See is now bringing out a selection of its own documents of the years 1939–1945, "Actes et Documents du Saint Siège Relatifs à la Seconde Guerre Mondiale." So far, five volumes have been published, including one volume of letters from Pius XII to the German bishops. This documentation has not yet been fully assimilated into current research, though it has been drawn upon in the useful and up-to-date survey by F. L'Huillier, "La politique du Vatican dans la crise mondiale," *Revue d'Histoire de la Deuxième Guerre Mondiale,* v. XVI, 1966. A special study based on access to Vatican materials is that of Monsignor Alberto Giovannetti, **Il Vaticano e la Guerra (1939–1940)** (Città del Vaticano: Libreria Editrice Vaticana, 1960, 222 p.). A Soviet view is Mikhail Markovich Sheinmann, **Der Vatikan im Zweiten Weltkrieg** (Berlin: Dietz, for the Historisches Institut der Akademie der Wissenschaften der UdSSR, 1954, 500 p.).

FOX, ANNETTE (BAKER). **The Power of Small States.** Chicago: University of Chicago Press, 1959, 211 p.

This "inquiry into how the governments of small and militarily weak states can resist the strong pressure of great powers even in crisis periods" is an important contribution to the understanding of neutrality during the Second World War. The politics of Turkey, Finland, Norway, Sweden and Spain are subjected to a common analysis. Two of these states lost their struggle for neutrality, one became a co-belligerent, two remained neutral during the course of the war. Still, there were sufficient similarities in their individual attempts to stay out of the war to permit the author to draw some general conclusions. Turkey, Sweden and Spain succeeded not only because their strategic position and the existing power grouping favored them but also because they demonstrated convincingly that they were determined to defend themselves at all costs. In addition, each had important strategic raw materials to bargain with. "Where each belligerent believed that a small neutral can and will defend itself against sudden attack by the other, long enough for effective help to arrive, or at any rate long enough to inflict on the aggressor the loss of that which he most wants from the neutral, the small state is unlikely to lose its neutrality."

SCHMIDT, PAUL. **Statist auf Diplomatischer Bühne, 1923–45.** Bonn: Athenaeum, 1950, 606 p.

With the democratization of diplomacy after the First World War, French ceased to be the principal language of diplomacy because so few statesmen could speak it. The era of the interpreter as a key figure in international intercourse had begun. Dr. Paul Schmidt was one of the first products of a training program for interpreters initiated by the German Foreign Office in 1921. With his superb knowledge of French, English and Italian, he was also one of the most talented, and from 1923 to 1945 served regularly as interpreter to the highest officials of the Weimar and Nazi governments whenever the use of these languages was required. One of the techniques learned in the Foreign Office training program was the ability to take notes so as to have an accurate record from which to translate, and one of the prime duties of the interpreter after a conference was to transcribe his notes to provide his government with an accurate record of what had been said. Among the most valuable German documents captured by the Allies after the Second World War were the memoranda prepared by Dr. Schmidt on the basis of his translation notes.

His memoirs, appropriately called "mute on the diplomatic stage," are an account of his remarkable career and an attempt to correct "the partially mislead-ing impressions conveyed by the prosaic documents that have survived." The sur-viving Schmidt documents, certainly those of the Nazi period, can hardly be called prosaic, nor do his memoirs greatly alter the impressions they convey. But they do provide fascinating background material, and in reviewing the many international conferences at which their author was present, they are one of the most important sources for the study of German and diplomatic history during the Weimar and Nazi eras. The abridged English translation, **Hitler's Interpreter** (New York: Macmillan, 1951, 286 p.), covers only the Nazi period and contains numerous errors.

DIPLOMATIC ASPECTS; IMMEDIATE ORIGINS

TAYLOR, ALAN JOHN PERCIVALE. **The Origins of the Second World War.** New York: Fawcett, 2d ed., 1966, 304 p.

Writing expressly to controvert the Nuremberg verdict on Germany's sole re-sponsibility for causing the Second World War, Taylor has produced a book which purports to rest squarely on the documents and to eschew post facto moral judg-ments. Consistently absorbing, and frequently provoking, his account of the inter-national relations of the European powers proceeds from a short conspectus of the decade after Versailles to an increasingly detailed discussion of the crises which eventuated in the German invasion of Poland. Portions of the narrative contain keen and compelling if not invariably original insights: those dealing, for instance, with the political legacy of the First World War, with the fatal contradictions in French policy, with the course and broad implications of the Abyssinian crisis and with the moral and psychological elements of "appeasement."

Other portions, particularly those which treat the general and specific causes of war and the relationship between intention and action in statecraft, have given rise to serious objection. By showing that things rarely worked out in detail as Hitler expected them to (as with the famous "Hossbach Memorandum"), Taylor claims to have demonstrated that it was the blundering initiatives of others, not Hitler's lust for domination, which brought Europe to the point of war. But this view, while it usefully invites a reëxamination of the policy of Hitler's adversaries, seems gravely to underrate the typifying violence of Nazism and the possibilities for opportunistic behavior within a larger framework of stable purpose. This is an important book—epigrammatic, ironic, finely composed—but it should not be read in isolation from the commentary it continues to evoke.

HOFER, WALTHER. **War Premeditated—1939.** London: Thames, 1955, 227 p.

Although the coming of the Second World War was played out, almost entirely, for all the world to see, it was not until after 1945—when most of the German diplomatic records fell into Allied hands—that the inner history of Nazi planning for aggression and expansion became fully known. It was one of the great merits of Hofer's volume (first published in Germany in 1954) that it brought together, in interesting and readable form, the most important evidence on Hitler's "unleash-ing" of war in the summer of 1939. It should be noted that the latest and considerably expanded (fourth) German edition of Hofer's work, **Die Entfesselung des Zweiten Weltkrieges** (Frankfurt: Fischer Verlag, 1964, 518 p.), includes the texts of numerous important documents on the final crisis, as well as an extended discussion of A. J. P. Taylor's brilliantly perverse **Origins of the Second World War** and of David L. Hoggan's pro-German apologia, **Der Erzwungene Krieg** (Tübingen: Verlag der Deutschen Hochschullehrer-Zeitung, 4th ed., 1963, 893 p.). Hofer's general interpretation and conclusions, however, have remained unchanged. "If it is an indispensable historical fact that the war of 1939 was Hitler's war," he asks at the end, "the problem is, how was it possible that this fateful man was given the power to enforce his will against a whole world?" That still remains an unanswered question.

FEIS, HERBERT. **The Road to Pearl Harbor.** Princeton: Princeton University Press, 1950, 356 p.
————. **The China Tangle.** Princeton: Princeton University Press, 1953, 445 p.
————. **Japan Subdued: The Atomic Bomb and the End of the War in the Pacific.** Princeton: Princeton University Press, 1961, 199 p.

Herbert Feis focuses his attention on high-level decision making, deals meticulously with the issues and presents with fairness the various arguments. The scholarly excellence of these volumes is generally recognized, and they are unrivaled in the field of United States relations in Asia.

The Road to Pearl Harbor moves quickly to the two years preceding the Japanese attack. Beginning in the summer of 1939, both sides made fateful decisions. Japan acted with determination to make secure her position in Asia and to achieve an unchallengeable predominance. The United States, seeking to protect its own interests in the Pacific, doggedly opposed Japanese dominance. Ambassador Grew continued to believe that Japan might return to the moderate policies of Baron Shidehara. The author considers this a forlorn hope, finding a sounder appraisal of the realities in the sterner views of Henry Stimson. Feis shows in a lucid manner how time satisfied contestants on both sides that options had run out by the autumn of 1941.

The China Tangle is a study of relations with China during the war. American decision makers, faced by higher priorities and limited access to China, found it impossible to meet the Chinese need for supplies. The question of recapturing Burma, linked to the question of supplies, caused ill will and distrust among the Allies. By 1944 the rapid rise of the Communists and the weakness of the Kuomintang overshadowed all other questions. American efforts to promote coöperation failed. Although disillusioned with the Kuomintang, the United States adhered to the position that this party was the official government of China. A sharp division resulted among American officials on the proper role of the United States. Feis finds no easy answers to the problems confronted by both sides in the controversy.

Japan Subdued begins with a presentation of the options facing the new administration of Harry Truman. Whether to use the atom bomb and how to use it received agonizing analysis. Feis traces the development of each line of argument down to the making of the fatal decision. He is sympathetic with those who made the decision but believes that the war could have been ended shortly without using the bomb.

LU, DAVID J. **From the Marco Polo Bridge to Pearl Harbor: Japan's Entry into World War II.** Washington: Public Affairs Press, 1961, 274 p.

In his foreword to this book, Herbert Feis, the distinguished doyen of American diplomatic historians of the Second World War, takes exception to several aspects of Lu's frankly revisionist account of the road Japan traveled from the Marco Polo Bridge to Pearl Harbor. Lu contends, against considerable evidence to the contrary, that the main target of Japan's alliance with the Axis powers was the Soviet Union rather than the United States, and he therefore concludes that the alliance played an insignificant part in Japan's decision for war.

Lu also argues, despite the portrait that emerges from many primary sources of great authority, that Foreign Minister Yosuke Matsuoka, who aligned Japan with Hitler's Germany and then concluded a neutrality pact with Stalin, was more consistent and moderate than his colleagues in the cabinet. This extraordinary characterization of Matsuoka must be weighed against the incoherence and the lack of restraint that ran through his program as Foreign Minister.

From the Marco Polo Bridge to Pearl Harbor contains some interesting information but is marred by numerous typographical errors, by stylistic faults that should have been edited out of the text and by a rather haphazard approach to documentation. The shock effect of the opinions expressed by the author may stimulate other historians to strive toward an earlier broadening of truth than could perhaps be expected in the absence of such provocation, but the nonspecialist should reserve judgment until he has inquired further into the calamity of Japan's march toward war by reading broadly in the growing historical literature on Shōwa Japan.

BUTOW, ROBERT JOSEPH CHARLES. **Japan's Decision to Surrender.** Stanford: Stanford University Press (for the Hoover Institution on War, Revolution, and Peace), 1954, 259 p.

Professor Butow's two volumes on Japan's decisions for war and peace are distinguished by careful scholarship, mastery of Japanese sources and concern for detail, especially when dealing with nuances of the Japanese language.

In **Japan's Decision to Surrender,** the analysis of Japanese political institutions and behavior, particularly the respective roles and practices of the military and of the Emperor, is clear and perceptive. Butow is notably successful in portraying those features of the Japanese character which made it so difficult for leaders who knew they were defeated to reach the decision to surrender. His discussion of the concept of *haragei,* a method of communication in which the parties involved are presumed to understand the speaker's meaning intuitively, reveals that Japanese indirectness caused as much trouble for Japanese leaders as it did for foreigners seeking to understand their intentions. He also leaves no doubt as to the importance of the imperial system to the men responsible for Japanese policy—and of the costliness of Allied insistence upon unconditional surrender with its implicit threat to the Emperor. But he places principal responsibility for the delay in surrendering upon the Japanese military, their "police-state methods" and their fanaticism. The shadowy supreme command of the Japanese military is also held responsible for the coming of the war.

In Butow's second book, **Tojo and the Coming of the War,** Tojo is portrayed as a man who reflected rather than determined the views which prevailed within the Japanese military—particularly the conviction of Japan's imminent encirclement and the failure to conceive of the extent to which Japan's actions would make that fear a reality. Butow finds that Tojo as Premier was no less restricted by the prerogatives of the supreme command than were the civilian premiers who preceded him.

NAMIER, SIR LEWIS BERNSTEIN. **Diplomatic Prelude, 1938–1939.** New York: Macmillan, 1948, 502 p.

The first and most deliberately crafted of Namier's several volumes on pre–World War II diplomacy, this is a fine-grained account of the political manoeuvrings of the principal European powers between the Munich conference and the German invasion of Poland, with four supplementary essays on related topics. Subsequent publications reduce the book's authority in matters of fact, but it remains an exemplary demonstration of what can be achieved by close analysis of documentary collections (the "coloured books") and the newspaper press. Namier acknowledges the inevitability of a German recovery after 1918 and takes for granted the malevolence of Hitler and his movement. He locates the explanation of Hitler's successes in the weak and divided condition of postwar Europe and in a general failure of European statecraft and morality. Rebuking Anglo-French practitioners of "appeasement" for repeated deficiencies in perception and will, Namier also deals critically with Polish policy, some aspects of which he finds regrettably shortsighted and reprehensible. He considers the Anglo-Russian negotiations of 1939 to be the "tragic core" of prewar diplomacy and lays their failure to profound mutual suspicion, aggravated on crucial occasions by British ineptitude. What his treatment most obviously lacks, apart perhaps from a more imaginative effort to recreate the moral dilemmas facing the British and French leaders, is any sustained consideration of either the military-strategic situation or the complicating effects of important extra-European challenges and commitments on the European policies of the Western powers.

NAMIER, SIR LEWIS BERNSTEIN. **Europe in Decay.** New York: Macmillan, 1950, 329 p.

This is a collection of book-review essays of various lengths on political memoirs and documents published after Namier completed **Diplomatic Prelude,** supplemented by official correspondence furnished by Beneš and Lukasiewicz on, respectively, Czech-Polish and Franco-Polish relations. The longer essays, especially, show Namier at the top of his bent: acute and relentless in his handling of evidence, astringent in his judgment of responsible statesmen, comprehending in his general views of the condition of Europe. An understanding rather than a doctrinaire critic of "appeasement," he identifies as a prime source of Western weakness the great disparity between French policy in Central and Eastern Europe after 1919 and the material resources of France. He lays heavy stress, moreover, on the unfortunate effects of the subordination of French to British policy after the Rhineland crisis, showing how the French consistently sought advice which they knew would fit their own "unavowed inclinations" to acquiesce in the resurgence of Germany. His criticism of Flandin, Bonnet, Reynaud and Baudouin, while sometimes overbearing in manner, creates a vivid picture of moral confusion and faltering resolve among the leaders of the Third Republic; and his comments on Count Ciano and Sir Nevile Henderson show that the defects of superficial and impulsive judgment were very widespread. Subject now to some amendment in detail, Namier's accounts of the Anglo-Franco-Soviet negotiations of 1939 and of Nazi-Soviet relations, 1939–1941, remain impressive for their clear portrayal of the issues present and the motives operating in the last years of European hegemony. For further commentary, chiefly on German materials, see Namier's **In the Nazi Era** (London: Macmillan, 1952, 203 p.).

SCHROEDER, PAUL W. **The Axis Alliance and Japanese-American Relations 1941.** Ithaca: Cornell University Press (for the American Historical Association), 1958, 246 p.

The purpose of this study is not to trace the origins of the war in the Pacific but to examine the influence of the Tripartite Pact on Japanese-American relations in general and on the diplomatic negotiations in 1941 in particular.

In a careful and detailed analysis of the available German and English sources, the author attacks the conventional account of these negotiations. He shows that instead of the supposed undeviating aggressiveness of the Japanese and the persistent peacefulness of the Americans the attitudes of both countries underwent important changes. By July 1941, Japan was willing to retreat from southern Indochina and proceed independently of German foreign policy. Americans by about the same time, however, were no longer satisfied in holding a line against Japan but tried to compel her to withdraw from all her conquests and accept defeat in China.

Regarding the Tripartite Pact, Schroeder believes that Japan never intended to help her Axis partners but, on the contrary, hoped to stay out of the war, and that by entering into the Pact she assumed that she would have a free hand in Asia. But for American intransigence and hostility, the moderate forces under Prince Konoye would have prevailed. These latter aspects involve Japanese domestic policies and, in as much as no Japanese sources were used, are the weakest point in an otherwise excellent study.

TOGO, SHIGENORI. **The Cause of Japan.** New York: Simon and Schuster, 1956, 372 p.

When General Hideki Tojo acceded to the premiership in October 1941, he persuaded one of Japan's top diplomats, Shigenori Togo, to accept responsibility for foreign affairs. During the next six weeks Togo joined his civil and military colleagues in making decisions that brought disaster to their nation. Togo gave up his post in 1942, but three years later he returned to the Foreign Office where he soon began to work assiduously toward a termination of the war through diplomatic means, his object being to ward off an invasion of the homeland and unconditional surrender.

Togo's posthumously published memoirs—which originally appeared as **Jidai no Ichimen: Taisen Gaikō no Shuki** (Tokyo: Kaizō-sha, 1952)—were written while he was serving a 20-year sentence imposed by the International Military Tribunal for the Far East. They were subsequently translated in this condensed form by his adopted son, Fumihiko, and by Ben Bruce Blakeney, an American lawyer who had fought hard to win exoneration for his client.

The Cause of Japan, which touches only briefly on Togo's career prior to Pearl Harbor, is a revealing account of the decision-making process in His Majesty's Empire during periods of crisis in 1941 and in 1945. As an exposition of Japan's case with reference to the coming of the war, Togo's book is disappointing. It offers little more than the tiresome revisionist arguments of Charles A. Beard. Although Togo's efforts in behalf of a diplomatic settlement prior to Pearl Harbor should not be overlooked, his manoeuvring for peace in 1945, as Japan faced destruction, was far more courageous and astute than his handling of the situation in 1941, when his country was at the pinnacle of power.

SHIGEMITSU, MAMORU. **Japan and Her Destiny: My Struggle for Peace.** New York: Dutton, 1958, 392 p.

The years between the outbreak of the Manchurian Incident in 1931 and the termination of the war in the Pacific in 1945 were synonymous for the people of Japan with the word "upheaval." The period was one of successive crises at home and abroad, with ever greater power passing to the Japanese army and navy. It was a time of frustration for many of Japan's diplomats, including Mamoru Shigemitsu, whose career ran parallel to and sometimes crossed the events described in his book. After representing Japan in China as this turbulent era began, Shigemitsu took up the position of Vice-Minister for Foreign Affairs in Tokyo. He then moved on as ambassador to Moscow, London and Nanking. As Minister for Foreign Affairs from the spring of 1943 to the spring of 1945, he endeavored to find an effective way to extricate Japan from a war that threatened the destruction of the Japanese nation.

Shigemitsu is interesting when he writes about matters in which he was directly involved, but many of his pages cover developments that came to his attention second and thirdhand and in some instances not until the postwar Tokyo trial, at which he was a defendant, revealed a great deal that had previously been unknown. The episodic treatment throughout the book, with brevity a distinguishing characteristic, leaves much to be desired, but **Japan and Her Destiny** nevertheless contains valuable observations and insights. Readers with a knowledge of Japanese will want ultimately to turn, however, to the original, **Shōwa no Dōran** (Tokyo: Chūō Kōron-sha, 1952, 2 v.), from which this abridged translation was made.

DE LAUNAY, JACQUES. **Secret Diplomacy of World War II.** New York: Simmons-Boardman, 1963, 175 p.

Under the heading of "secret diplomacy" this book—in the French original, "Secrets Diplomatiques, 1939–1945" (Brussels: Brepols, 1963, 125 p.)—sets out to cover negotiations conducted through nonofficial or irregular channels, secret phases of official negotiations, amateur diplomacy and intelligence activities. It is not surprising, therefore, that this slim volume barely touches the surface of World War II developments as complex and heterogeneous as peace initiatives, relations between the Axis partners, the missions of Harry Hopkins and Myron Taylor, Vichy policies, OSS activities in Switzerland and the preparations for the Allied landings in North Africa. The book is based almost exclusively on memoirs and secondary works and makes no use of the collections of American, German and Italian diplomatic documents which have been available for many years. The author's failure to consult these documentary compilations is reflected in inaccurate statements concerning the lack of documentation on subjects such as the Hitler-Laval conversation of October 22, 1940, and Colonel William Donovan's visit to southeastern Europe in 1941. Yet the allegedly missing documents relating to these topics have been printed either in "Documents on German Foreign Policy, 1918–1945" or in "Foreign Relations of the United States."

The more limited subject of peace initiatives during World War II is treated by Maxime Mourin in **Les Tentatives de Paix dans la Seconde Guerre Mondiale (1939–1945)** (Paris: Payot, 1949, 221 p.). Drawing on published documentary sources of the early postwar period such as the Nuremberg records and the Ciano papers, the author gives an account of confidential peace feelers and public peace offers which is still useful even though it can now be supplemented and revised on the basis of more recent sources.

MESKILL, JOHANNA MENZEL. **Hitler and Japan: The Hollow Alliance.** New York: Atherton Press, 1966, 245 p.

This succinct story, based on the records of the Third Reich and the materials of the International Military Tribunal for the Far East, covers German-Japanese relations from the Tripartite Pact of 1940 to 1945. The author argues convincingly that the Berlin-Tokyo alliance was "hollow" because the two partners, united only by their common defiance of the existing international order, engaged in deceit and delusions regarding each other's political objectives. From the outset the automatic character of the Tripartite Pact was diluted by secret provisions. Subsequently, the divergent goals of the partners were reflected in German attempts to involve Japan in war, first against Britain, then against the Soviet Union, and in Japan's determination not to let the Tripartite Pact stand in the way of a settlement with the United States. Due to these divergent goals and to inadequate conceptions of global warfare the alliance did not achieve effective political and military coördination, although the two sides coöperated to some extent after Pearl Harbor with respect to military planning, exchange of strategic materials and propaganda.

The German-Japanese alliance prior to Pearl Harbor was first treated by Frank William Iklé in **German-Japanese Relations, 1936–1940.** Iklé's book, however, fails to emphasize the inherent weakness of the alliance. Ernst Presseisen's **Germany and Japan: A Study in Totalitarian Diplomacy, 1933–1941** (The Hague: Nijhoff, 1958, 368 p.), which covers the subject in more detail, also discusses the ideological background of German Far Eastern policy and the diplomatic antecedents prior to 1936. The study by Theo Sommer, **Deutschland und Japan zwischen den Mächten 1935–1940** (Tübingen: Mohr, 1962, 540 p.), making wide use of all available documentary sources, places the subject within the framework of international diplomacy and provides penetrating analyses of the Anti-Comintern Pact and the Tripartite Pact.

LUPKE, HUBERTUS. **Japans Russlandpolitik von 1939 bis 1941.** Frankfurt/Main: Metzner, 1962, 189 p.

"Until 1940, the power which Japan most expected to threaten its security and interfere with its plans was the Soviet Union, not the Western democracies." A year later, in April 1941, Japan and the Soviet Union had signed a nonaggression agreement in Moscow. How the change came about is here reconstructed from the archives of the Japanese Foreign Office. (As usual, few Russian documents were available.) Readers who expect an author to possess some minimal talent for narrative will have their patience tried, and so will those who like a certain amount of analysis with their facts; just what the motives of the two powers were, for instance, is hinted at, or guessed, rather than described. But patience will have its rewards. The outline of events emerges clearly enough, from the initial approach of trying to improve relations by a policy of small steps to the conclusion of the agreement with its secret addendum anticipating even wider coöperation. And future scholars will no doubt appreciate the guidance that the book provides through the Japanese archives.

HARADA, KUMAO. **Fragile Victory: Prince Saionji and the 1930 London Treaty Issue; From the Memoirs of Baron Harada Kumao.** Detroit: Wayne State University Press, 1968, 330 p.

During the decade prior to Pearl Harbor, Baron Harada was in a better position to observe the events of a period of turbulence for his nation than were many of the men who were directly involved in conducting the affairs of the Japanese government. As private secretary to Prince Kimmochi Saionji, the last of the "elder statesmen" who had achieved preëminence during the reign of the Emperor Meiji, Harada provided liaison between the old Prince and the civil-military officials who were responsible to Meiji's grandson.

While gathering political intelligence and performing the various tasks assigned to him, Harada jotted down notes for use in his weekly reports to Saionji. Later dictation produced transcripts that the Prince regularly read, making whatever emendations he considered necessary. These revised texts were eventually to total more than 10,000 pages and to figure prominently in the postwar Tokyo trial as the "Saionji-Harada Memoirs." The published version, which appeared under the title **Saionji-kō to Seikyoku,** ran to nine volumes (Tokyo: Iwanami Shoten, 1950–1952 and 1956). It is the first book of this series that Thomas Francis Mayer-Oakes has presented in a translation that is enhanced by copious explanatory notes and an excellent introduction of nearly 70 pages.

Harada's diary must be evaluated with care, for he was not an unbiased observer. Even so, his contemporary account of the power struggle within Japan over the London Naval Treaty provides material that is essential to an understanding of what transpired in His Majesty's Empire during the 1930s. One could hardly hope to find a primary source of greater value.

Correspondence between the Chairman of the Council of Ministers of the U.S.S.R. and the Presidents of the U.S.A. and the Prime Ministers of Great Britain during the Great Patriotic War of 1941–1945. Moscow: Foreign Languages Publishing House (for the Ministry of Foreign Affairs of the U.S.S.R.), 1957, 2 v.

One of the great problems of an alliance in wartime is the preservation of confidence among its members, for there is rarely a time when the partners in such an alliance do not have occasion to suspect one another of malingering, of conspiring to sell out to the enemy or of attempting to acquire advantages to improve their position in the postwar world. This was certainly true of the relationship among the major Allies during the Second World War. These volumes are primarily a record of the efforts of the American, British and Russian leaders to convince each other of their good faith, and of the steady erosion of that good faith, especially after victory over Germany appeared assured.

"Tendentiously selected parts of this correspondence were published outside the Soviet Union at different times," the Soviet editors state in their preface, "resulting in a distorted picture of the Soviet attitude during the war years." Unfortunately, so many important messages during these years appear to have been transmitted orally or through channels that did not ensure their deposit in official archives that it is often impossible to say with any certainty whether a particular document collection is tendentious or not. In this case the basic points of view of the three major Allies concerning the postwar treatment of their former enemies and the countries of Eastern Europe were so different that a distortion of evidence on either side is hardly necessary. As might be expected, there is nothing in this collection that Soviet historians think casts discredit on Stalin or the Soviet Union. Western historians, on the other hand, will find much of value here on the Soviet viewpoint and a useful check on their own document publications.

WEINBERG, GERHARD L. **Germany and the Soviet Union 1939–1941.** Leyden: Brill, 1954, 218 p.

On August 23, 1939, Stalin and Joachim von Ribbentrop signed, in the Kremlin, the Nazi-Soviet pact, a ten-year alliance that doubtless opened the door to the Second World War. Twenty-two months later, on June 22, 1941, on the pretext that the Soviet Union had repeatedly violated the treaty and was preparing for aggression against the Reich, Hitler declared war on Russia. Based largely on the vast collection of material made available at the Nuremberg war crimes trials and on other documents that fell into Western hands in 1945, Professor Weinberg has written an excellent, detailed account of this "strangest alliance." "We see," he concludes, "no Germany plotting anxiously from the very beginning to bring fire and destruction to the Soviet Union . . . nor do we see a Russia carefully searching for the most opportune moment to strike down the Nazi armies and state. . . . The impression we get is rather one of two great powers plodding fitfully along the path of expediency; one motivated by vast schemes of conquest, the other by the hope of protecting what it has and adding what can safely be picked up."

Despite the appearance of additional evidence since 1954, Weinberg's work has stood up well. This is especially true of his important finding that Hitler decided, as early as July 1940, to attack the Soviet Union—a view vigorously challenged by the detailed account of Philipp W. Fabry, **Der Hitler-Stalin-Pakt 1939–1941: Ein Beitrag zur Methode Sowjetischer Aussenpolitik** (Darmstadt: Fundus Verlag, 1962, 535 p.), who sees the unsuccessful Molotov visit to Berlin in November 1940 as the turning point in Nazi-Soviet relations. Fabry, moreover, views Hitler as a fairly conventional statesman who sought, in 1940, to divert Russia's attention southward into the Middle East against Britain's lifeline in that region. When Stalin persisted in moving into certain highly sensitive areas in the Baltic and the Balkans, Hitler—according to Fabry—had little choice but to attack while he still retained military superiority.

Although now somewhat dated, the readable narrative of Angelo Rossi, **The Russo-German Alliance: August 1939–June 1941** (Boston: Beacon Press, 1951, 218 p.), concludes that "it was Germany . . . who forced Russia into war and into an unwilling alliance with the Western democracies." Finally, it should be noted that although initially a critic of Weinberg's work, Andreas Hillgruber, in his important and massively documented **Hitlers Strategie: Politik und Kriegführung 1940–1941,** has now reached generally the same conclusions as Weinberg regarding the coming of Hitler's attack on Russia.

HILLGRUBER, ANDREAS. **Hitlers Strategie: Politik und Kriegführung 1940–1941.** Frankfurt/Main: Bernard und Graefe, 1965, 715 p.

With the fall of France in June 1940, Hitler appeared to be at the height of his power and his final military victory over Britain, his last opponent in the field, only a matter of time. Yet at this moment of triumph he was faced with the most difficult and dangerous decisions of his career. In this detailed and scholarly study, Professor Hillgruber examines Hitler's policy in the crucial 12 months between the fall of France and the attack on the Soviet Union within the framework of the world political situation, describing the rapidly changing developments in the situation itself and analyzing the various possibilities for continuing the war. The problem of the alternatives available to Hitler is particularly fascinating, since it raises the whole question of Hitler's war aims as opposed to tactics, opportunism and the necessities posed by the "realities" of world politics.

Hillgruber handles the vast complex of political, military and economic problems involving major and minor powers in masterful fashion. Inevitably he focuses at length on Hitler's policy toward Britain, his peace moves, the possibilities of economic warfare, invasion, "peripheral" strategy and the role of the United States and Japan in his calculations. He believes that Hitler temporarily abandoned all plans for a massive military campaign against Britain because of his fear of the strategic and economic threat posed by Russia, his belief that hope of Russia's intervention was a major reason for Britain's continued resistance and because the conquest of Russia was in itself his major war aim.

Hillgruber has also written an authoritative and valuable monograph on the critical problem of Hitler's relations with Rumania, the principal source of German oil during the Second World War, **Hitler, König Carol und Marschall Antonescu: Die Deutsch-Rumänischen Beziehungen, 1938–1944** (Wiesbaden: Steiner, 1954, 382 p.).

PEACE SETTLEMENTS

OPIE, REDVERS and OTHERS. **The Search for Peace Settlements.** Washington: Brookings Institution, 1951, 366 p.

It is hard to imagine a less tidy entity for historical treatment than the quest for a general settlement following the Second World War. In the case of Germany, after 25 years there is still merely a tangle of ad hoc arrangements, many of them of an ostensibly provisional character, which have been hammered out over the years. It is not surprising that no comprehensive scholarly account of the entire "peace settlement" as yet exists, though there are outstanding works on aspects of the subject. The need for a general treatment was, however, recognized early, and a first step was sponsored by the Brookings Institution. The resulting volume by Redvers Opie and several able associates, though written before the treaties with Japan and Austria had been completed, still retains value as a work of reference, particularly for its survey of the treaties with Italy, Hungary, Rumania, Bulgaria and Finland and the negotiations leading up to them. A useful supplement is the volume by Amelia Leiss in coöperation with Raymond Dennett, **European Peace Treaties after World War II** (Boston: World Peace Foundation, 1954, 341 p.), which contains the texts of the treaties with the above-named countries.

BYRNES, JAMES FRANCIS. **Speaking Frankly.** New York: Harper, 1947, 324 p.

The book is based primarily on Byrnes' experiences—mostly sad—in trying to reach agreements with the United States' wartime partners on terms of viable peace settlements following World War II. President Roosevelt took Byrnes (then War Stabilizer) to the Yalta Conference in February 1945, and President Truman appointed him Secretary of State and took him to the Potsdam Conference in July 1945. At those conferences Byrnes sensed the expansionist trend of Soviet ambitions but was hopeful of treaty agreements. Thereafter, he met frequently with other foreign ministers on problems of peace settlements. While noting limited success, he pulls no punches in describing the frustrations encountered in negotiations with the U.S.S.R. on major treaty terms. His previous experiences, he notes, had not prepared him "for negotiations with Mr. Molotov." He concluded that the United States must be prepared to take "measures of last resort" against the U.S.S.R. Byrnes wrote these memoirs after resigning in January 1947, owing largely to strained relations with Truman. They remain a valuable study on the development of the cold war.

CLAY, LUCIUS DUBIGNON. **Decision in Germany.** Garden City: Doubleday, 1950, 522 p.

The memoirs of General Clay, the American Deputy Military Governor in Germany from 1945 to 1947 and Military Governor from 1947 to 1949, constitute an indispensable source for the history of the American occupation. During these four years occurred the dramatic events which culminated in the Berlin blockade and airlift and the split of Germany and of Berlin. Within the U.S. Zone, where Clay served as a stern but fair, realistic but ideally committed proconsul, a punitive policy was at first carried out under the mandate of the central directive of the Joint Chiefs of Staff and the provisions of the Potsdam agreement. It was a policy characterized by the so-called "de's"—denazification, demilitarization, deindustrialization (shades of the Morgenthau Plan!), as well as democratization. Clay and his staff ran into difficulties almost from the start with the Soviets as well as with the French (the latter resolutely opposing any form of centralized German administration); impressed by the realities of the German situation and the breakdown of the economic provisions of Potsdam, he early saw the need for a rehabilitation of the German economy as quickly as possible. The new, cautiously modified policy which Clay had recommended to Washington did not become official until July 1947, long after the Stuttgart speech of Secretary of State Byrnes had signalled a turning point in U.S. occupation policy. The author tells the story in a calm, unpretentious manner, enriching his account with many personal observations and with lengthy excerpts from cables and telecommunications.

WILLIS, FRANK ROY. **The French in Germany, 1945–1949.** Stanford: Stanford University Press, 1962, 308 p.

This excellent monograph is a fair, dispassionate and copiously annotated analysis and evaluation of the French occupation in Germany. It is based on numerous interviews with French and German officials and on published materials, mostly official, of French, German and Allied origin—unpublished French documents being obviously not available. In meticulously tracing the political, economic and cultural occupation policies, the author pointed up some contradictions in French objectives in Germany, *i.e.* French security by the detachment of as much territory as possible from Western Germany, opposition to any form of centralized administration in Germany, economic exploitation in order to recoup the enormous losses suffered by France during the war, and—after a period of denazification and reëducation—the promotion of Franco-German rapprochement. Reëducation French style bore the peculiar stamp of the classic *mission civilisatrice,* yet denazification was less rigid than, for example, in the American Zone. All in all, it was a challenging, complex operation that was widely criticized, not only in German circles, and yet admittedly the French achieved some measure of success, particularly in the cultural field and in fostering a genuine Franco-German understanding.

NETTL, J. P. **The Eastern Zone and Soviet Policy in Germany, 1945–50.** New York: Oxford University Press, 1951, 324 p.

Although many special studies have been written on East Germany since this book appeared, it is still one of the best general introductions to the subject in English. The author concentrated on political, economic and administrative developments which he traced chronologically and topically in considerable detail, supported by copious statistical data. The statistics were largely derived from fairly reliable Western sources, though the provenance of many statistical tables is unfortunately not indicated.

Nettl leaned over backward in his effort to write an impartial work; in fact, his detachment is so great that the reader misses the human component in this account of the ruthless process of economic exploitation and political *Gleichschaltung.* The establishment of the government of the German Democratic Republic in October 1949 did not appreciably change the political realities but represented merely the logical continuation of the political and economic policies imposed by the Soviet occupiers and their henchmen, the SED—Socialist Unity Party—created by the forced merger of the Communist and Social Democrat Parties in April 1946.

In his conclusions, Nettl rightly pointed out the contradictions inherent in Soviet policies in Germany, *e.g.* economic exploitation and sovietization of East German society and culture, along with efforts to win German friendship and support for a reunited, centralized and—hopefully—communist Germany under Russian influence. Because of these diverse aims and because of the special situation obtaining in Germany, the process of sovietization was considerably delayed and modified so that, as the author notes, "Eastern Germany was in 1950 still a predominantly bourgeois country." It was not until 1961—with the building of the Berlin wall and the total collectivization of agriculture—that East Germany was to be completely converted to a Soviet-style "people's democracy."

DULLES, ALLEN. **The Secret Surrender.** New York: Harper and Row, 1966, 268 p.

As OSS representative in Switzerland, the author himself was one of the principal figures in the dramatic story of the secret negotiations leading to the surrender of the German forces in Italy in World War II. He tells an engrossing tale of tortuous negotiations with war-weary members of the top German command in Italy, including the SS leadership. The Germans, though anxious to end hostilities, hesitated to commit themselves to actions that might expose them to Hitler's wrath and the implacable hostility of rival Nazi cliques. The governments of the United States and Britain, on the other hand, had to take into account the ever-present Soviet suspicions of a secret Western understanding with the Nazis. The operation could not have succeeded without the resourcefulness and patience of the Allied negotiators or the coöperation of Swiss officials and individual Italians. Dulles also offers some general observations on the difficulties involved in ending a war when communications between the belligerents have ceased and when attempts to resume contact are branded as treasonable.

ZINK, HAROLD. **The United States in Germany, 1944–1955.** Princeton: Van Nostrand, 1957, 374 p.

Former Chief of the Historical Division of HICOG (the U.S. High Commission for Germany), an official of various military government organizations and a respected political scientist, Zink had practical as well as theoretical knowledge of military government and was uniquely qualified to write this book. It is a history of the American occupation from the preparatory efforts in 1944–1945 in England through the period of military government to the period of civilian control under HICOG, 1949–1955. His account is based on official American documents (mostly published), especially on the monographs written by specialists in the Historical Division of HICOG under his direction.

The book is more of a general description and, at times, a critical evaluation of the organization and functions of the U.S. occupation agencies than a detailed analysis of actual occupation operations and their impact on the German population. For, as Zink himself recognized, official documents alone cannot tell the whole story. In evaluating the American occupation efforts and achievements Zink, on the whole, took a positive view, but in certain areas—for example, education and denazification—he did not hesitate to express strong criticism. He also deplored the punitive policies of the earlier phases of the Occupation as well as the proliferation of channels and authority and the resulting confusion and delay in developing a constructive policy in Germany. These defects were to some extent mitigated, he felt, by the presence in Germany of a strong-willed, competent and rather independent American military governor, General Lucius D. Clay.

BALFOUR, MICHAEL and MAIR, JOHN. **Four-Power Control in Germany and Austria, 1945–1946.** New York: Oxford University Press (for the Royal Institute of International Affairs), 1956, 390 p.

This volume in the "Survey of International Affairs" series is one of the very few books which deal simultaneously with the occupation policies of the four powers in Germany and Austria. The authors, who are former officials of the British element of the Control Commissions, present the German and Austrian stories as separate entities, giving much more space to the former; but the two accounts shed light upon one another and thus contribute to a better understanding of the complex problems in these two occupied countries in the first two postwar years. This valuable work also points up the contrast between the occupation régimes in Germany and Austria. In the latter a democratic central government was established almost from the beginning under the redoubtable Socialist, Karl Renner, while in Germany the occupiers resisted the idea of centralization of government, fearing that it might revive aggressive tendencies. Moreover, Austria differed markedly from Germany both in dimensions and character. There was no "Austrian Question," as there always had been a seemingly insoluble "German Question," and therefore no need, for example, of reëducation. The objective was simply a restoration of an independent Austrian state. In theory, Austria was to be treated as a "liberated" country, but in practice it was treated, by the Russians at least, as a conquered territory.

Both accounts are based on published documents and secondary works since official government papers were not made accessible to the authors.

JONES, F. C.; BORTON, HUGH and PEARN, B. R. **The Far East, 1942–1946.** New York: Oxford University Press (for the Royal Institute of International Affairs), 1955, 589 p.

This volume in the Toynbee special series "Survey of International Affairs, 1939–1946" provides a detailed account of East and Southeast Asian events from Pearl Harbor into the postwar years of reconstruction and revolution. It is not a military history. Jones' portion mostly duplicates the latter part of his **Japan's New Order in East Asia: Its Rise and Fall, 1937–45,** still the best history of the subject. Working from Tokyo war crimes trials documents and Japanese Singapore newspapers, he describes the collapse of the white man's empires in Southeast Asia and the substitution of an even harsher Asian imperialism. The Japanese, he shows, only began taking their proclaimed ideal of Asian partnership seriously when their fortunes in the war declined. For the "Survey" Jones adds a section on China in wartime diplomacy and another, drawing heavily on the China White Paper, carrying the China story to the end of American mediation efforts in January 1947.

Pearn traces the tenuous reinstatement of Western rule in Southeast Asia after V-J Day. Borton, a veteran of the American occupation of Japan, contributes a judicious survey of MacArthur's proconsulship to 1948, with comprehensive treatment of reforms in Japanese government, economy and society. He is equally thorough in dealing with postwar Korea and concludes with a valuable chapter on American acquisition of Pacific Island trusteeships under the United Nations. Broadly conceived, authoritative and clearly written, this book remains the best introduction to a complex, obscure transitional period in Asian and Pacific history.

DUNN, FREDERICK S. **Peace-Making and the Settlement with Japan.** Princeton: Princeton University Press, 1963, 210 p.

For some time Dunn will remain the standard account of the origins of the Japanese peace settlement in 1951, if only because he had access to State Department records that are still closed. Further, it is a concise, illuminating case study in the metamorphosis of American policy in the postwar world and the international politics of the cold war. He begins with wartime planning for radical restructuring of Japan to prevent future aggression. He shows how the Wilsonian thought of Hull, postulating international harmony of interests, gave way to Realpolitik in 1947–1949. Containment strategy dictated a benign peace aiming at a thriving Japan closely aligned with the West, a Far Eastern bastion against Soviet expansion. Dunn describes the formation of consensus within the American government on a peace plan and then how Dulles, by tireless airplane diplomacy, overcame the objections of America's friends, particularly Britain, Australia and the Philippines, and secured an agreed draft treaty which Acheson rammed through the San Francisco Conference over Soviet objections. The key to agreement, Dunn makes clear, was a series of bilateral defense treaties between the United States and countries on the margins of Asia which laid the basis for a new Pacific security system.

TOYNBEE, ARNOLD JOSEPH and TOYNBEE, VERONICA MARJORIE, *eds.* **The Realignment of Europe.** New York: Oxford University Press (for the Royal Institute of International Affairs), 1955, 619 p.

This volume, the sixth in the "Survey of International Affairs, 1939–1946" series, deals with Europe in the years immediately following the breakup of Hitler's empire. The main themes of the period are discussed in Arnold Toynbee's introduction—the uprooting of the populations in the Soviet sphere, the frontier changes, the problem presented by the power vacuum in central and eastern Europe and the breach between the Western Allies and the Soviet Union. Part I, which includes a discussion of the economic consequences of the war, is devoted primarily to the history of the United Nations Relief and Rehabilitation Administration (UNRRA), its personnel, administration of supplies, operations in the field and an evaluation of its performance.

Otherwise the volume is organized along national lines. Part II is devoted to the countries of Eastern Europe, including Finland and the Balkan states, with a particularly extended treatment of Poland and the Polish problem in international relations; part III to Greece only; part IV to Italy only, with an extensive discussion of frontier problems; and part V to Western Europe, including France, Belgium, the Netherlands, Denmark and Norway, but not Germany or Austria, which are covered in another volume in this series.

The chapters by the various authors who contributed to this volume are uneven in coverage and quality, but on the whole this is a valuable survey of an extremely complicated period.

CONDUCT OF THE WAR

General; Historical

WRIGHT, GORDON. **The Ordeal of Total War, 1939–1945.** New York: Harper and Row, 1968, 315 p.

This is the best single history of an era of destruction "on the continent of Europe" which "probably exceeds that of any previous modern era." This was true of physical damage. Whether it was also true psychologically and politically depends on one's view of the whole age of violence, 1914–1945.

Wright's study, one in the series "The Rise of Modern Europe" edited by William L. Langer, is beautifully balanced. Chapters on "Europe on the Brink," the "Expansion of German Power" and three on the "Broadening Scope of War"— economic, psychological and scientific—lead to studies of "German Occupied Europe," the "Resistance Movements," the "Allied Resurgence," the "Dislocation of the Nazi Empire," "Preparation of the Postwar Era" and the "Impact of Total War." Military matters are well handled, though the common man appears more clearly as worker and victim than as soldier, and the story of the Russo-German war is so dispersed that its magnitude is not easily grasped. Wright's superb bibliography shows that the flood of Soviet works was still peaking while he was writing. His last chapter stands comparison with that of another masterpiece in this same series: Carlton J. H. Hayes, **A Generation of Materialism, 1871–1900** (New York: Harper and Row, 1941, 390 p.).

Wright's illustrations show that this war was too vast and mobile for still photography. They do not compare with the montages in Joel Colton's **Twentieth Century** (New York: Time-Life Books, 1968, 208 p.) or with Laurence Stalling's powerful collection on an essentially static war: **The First World War: A Photographic History** (New York: Simon and Schuster, 1933, 307 p.).

YOUNG, PETER. **World War 1939–45.** New York: Crowell, 1966, 447 p.

To write a short history of a major war calls for great skill in selection, compression and correlation. The achievement of an acceptable balance among the various theaters, alliances and services without the sacrifice of clarity or accuracy is no easy task. Brigadier Young's treatment is possibly the most useful short history for the average reader. His easy style makes for enjoyable reading, and his chronology at the start of each chapter helps orient the reader.

Inevitably, in such an all-embracing work there will be omissions and questionable interpretations. For instance, the air war receives less than its fair share of space, and the political and economic aspects of the struggle are often only hinted at. But Young clearly stresses the vital significance of the Eastern Front in achieving the ultimate defeat of Nazi Germany, a point that is sometimes slightly obscured by historians for reasons of political or national bias. On the other hand, the author does not minimize the scale or gravity of the United States' naval war in the Far East. Above all, we are reminded that "military history is about people" and also about the human spirit. No matter what radical changes occur in the weapons and techniques of warfare, that aspect will remain constant.

A number of similar works by distinguished authors have both preceded, and followed, this volume. Some that deserve mention are: Basil Collier, **Short History of the Second World War** (London: Collins, 1967, 638 p.); Helmuth G. Dahm, **Geschichte des Zweiten Weltkriegs** (Tubingen: Wunderlich, 1965, 918 p.); Cyril Falls, **The Second World War: A Short History** (London: Methuen, 1948, 312 p.); and J. F. C. Fuller, **The Second World War, 1939–45** (New York: Duell, 1949, 431 p.). Most recently there has been Sir Basil Liddell Hart's last work, **History of the Second World War** (London: Cassell, 1970, 768 p.). Each has particular virtues and shortcomings, but all share a single-volume format. Although some are twice as long as Young's volume, none of these works surpasses his achievement, and his book remains the best introduction and overall survey for the military events that transpired between 1939 and 1945.

VON TIPPELSKIRCH, KURT. **Geschichte des Zweiten Weltkriegs.** Bonn: Athenaeum, 1951, 731 p.

Written by a former German general officer and member of the famous General Staff, this broad survey presents a fine account of the Second World War. Relying upon his own extensive participatory knowledge, the aid of many former colleagues and a mastery of the then published materials, he has written a detailed military account of the conflict.

Given his own experience, Von Tippelskirch centers upon the European struggle, but he concentrates on balance and description rather than analysis or self-justification. His division of the struggle into an even dozen partitions set a pattern for most subsequent writers. The campaign descriptions are fair and honest although overly detailed for most readers. His sense of proportion and honesty earned this book an immediate place as the best general military study on the subject. While time and new scholarship have changed some details, they have not significantly eroded its reputation.

SCHRAMM, PERCY ERNST and OTHERS, *eds.* **Kriegstagebuch des Oberkommandos der Wehrmacht, 1940–1945.** Frankfurt/Main: Bernard und Graefe, 1961–1965, 4 v.

Among the published sources on the Second World War, these heavy volumes possess few rivals. The German high command during this conflict was an inter-service agency (the *Oberkommando der Wehrmacht*). Within its organizational scheme the *Wehrmachtführungsamt* (subsequently renamed *Wehrmachtführungsstab*) held both a coördinating and an operational authority. It provided Adolf Hitler's basic working staff for the conduct of military operations. In order to maintain a proper record of events, opinions and decisions, the governing authorities selected trained historians to keep a daily diary of events. These tomes represent those portions which the responsible men saved from destruction or reconstructed at a later date.

Together with numerous unpublished documents, explanatory notes and informational appendices, this publication—whose form varies from verbatim notes to individual studies—is a unique source. While the text excludes most issues other than military affairs, it does reveal a wealth of detail on military operations, leading personalities, satellite relations and organizational concerns. Above all, the materials offer an insight into the state of affairs in the totalitarian edifice created by Adolf Hitler. From the days of glory through the cataclysmic finish, this record provides an outstanding chronicle.

Direction of War; Strategy and Command

BRYANT, SIR ARTHUR. **A History of the War Years Based on the Diaries of Field-Marshal Lord Alanbrooke, Chief of the Imperial General Staff.** Garden City: Doubleday, 1957–1959, 2 v.

Lord Alanbrooke's **Diaries** form a major source for the British view of grand strategy during the Second World War. Sir Alan Brooke kept private records for his wife—and to relax from his daily tensions—and subsequently added a substantial commentary. Sir Arthur Bryant has performed a masterly feat in editing, expanding and, where propriety dictated, pruning this unique record of war seen from the top.

Brooke served as commander of II Corps in France in 1940, and it was largely due to his generalship that the BEF successfully reached Dunkirk. Returned to England, he became CIGS in 1941 and later chairman of the Chiefs of Staff Committee, posts he retained to the end of the war. His duties brought him into daily contact with Churchill. Their association, in Bryant's apt phrase, was "a partnership in genius." It was rarely an easy relationship, for Brooke found himself in continuous, usually amicable, conflict with the British premier, whose strategic concepts were often more brilliant than practicable and who reacted strongly to criticism. Brooke's overriding task was to temper Churchill's "great-hearted optimism," and he refused to be browbeaten. Fortunately Churchill respected a fighter and came to trust Brooke's advice implicitly. The picture of the great Prime Minister that emerges is one rewarding aspect of the work. In his official capacity, Brooke accompanied Churchill to the vital Allied conferences and also went with Atlee to Yalta. His recorded impressions of Roosevelt and Stalin, their entourages and commanders, are full of insight. He also had many encounters with De Gaulle, whose "unaccommodating patriotism" evoked the Churchillian comment that the Cross of Lorraine was not the least of his burdens. These books form a vital complement to Churchill's own great historical work, **The Second World War.**

Brooke was bitterly disappointed when the Churchill-promised supreme command in Europe eluded him. However, his proper place was at Churchill's side: the perfect foil, friend and adviser. As his master wrote, Brooke rendered "services of the highest order, not only to the British Empire, but also to the Allied cause."

POGUE, FORREST C. **George C. Marshall.** New York: Viking, 1963–1966, 2 v.

Although only two volumes of this projected four-volume biography of George Marshall have been published to date, the work has already taken its place as the definitive study of that great soldier-statesman. Unlike most other generals of the World War II period, Marshall never wrote his memoirs. He thought it unseemly. Instead, he turned over his papers to a research foundation established in his name at Virginia Military Institute and agreed to record on tape answers to questions about his career. As Director of the Foundation, Forrest C. Pogue, a World War II combat historian, is preparing the multi-volume biography.

The first volume, subtitled "Education of a General," traces Marshall's career from boyhood to his appointment as Chief of Staff in 1939, just as the war in

Europe began. Thoroughly researched, fully documented and objective, it provides a complete record of Marshall's life up to that point; but the general remains as distant and aloof a figure in the biography as he had in life.

The second volume, "Ordeal and Hope," takes the story down to the Allied landing in North Africa in November 1942, an operation that Marshall opposed bitterly. This volume is inherently more important and interesting than the first, covering in detail the way in which Marshall built and equipped the wartime army, developed a strategy for its employment and worked with his subordinates and superiors. It contains few surprises but provides a full account of the critical years 1939 to 1942 and presents the best account of the way the Army high command was organized in World War II and how Marshall managed the war from his desk in Washington. Marshall emerges clearly in this volume as a man of high character and immense integrity.

The third volume, dealing with Marshall's career down to the end of World War II, is scheduled for publication early in 1971.

GREENFIELD, KENT ROBERTS. **American Strategy in World War II: A Reconsideration.** Baltimore: Johns Hopkins Press, 1963, 145 p.

This little book of four essays, written by the former Chief Historian for the Office of the Chief of Military History, is a reappraisal of both American and Allied strategy. Greenfield begins by identifying the major strategic decisions of the war and, significantly, omits President Roosevelt's announcement of unconditional surrender at Casablanca. Instead, he includes the earlier agreement to defeat the Axis completely. Roosevelt in 1943 was simply expressing a long-standing policy, which made sense, Greenfield states, because it was the only possible cement for holding the coalition together.

The author then brings out how Allied strategy evolved from "Germany first" to the near-simultaneous victories over Germany and Japan. He gives primary credit for this evolution to Roosevelt, who overruled his military advisers not twice, as Robert Sherwood and others have stated, but twenty times. Greenfield couples this new look at FDR with near acceptance of Richard Leighton's interpretation of Anglo-American coalition problems. Greenfield notes that not only was Roosevelt dominant in the marriage of America's emphasis on concentration to Britain's concept of tightening the ring, but also that the union was acceptable to both. And both authors say that mutual, but primarily American, suspicions led to the false image of unwilling partners.

The Greenfield book gives a concise account of the LST problem, a balanced review of strategic bombing and a seldom found explanation of the army's difficulties in achieving air-ground coöperation for tactical operations. The author has written a rare book—one that draws heavily on the fine research of OCMH to update the early appraisals of Allied strategy. It deserves a niche in the historiography of World War II disproportionate to its size.

HALDER, FRANZ. **Kriegstagebuch des Generalobersten Franz Halder.** Stuttgart: Kohlhammer, 1962–1964, 3 v.

Virtually every serious publication devoted to the early history of World War II has drawn material from the private diary of General Franz Halder, Chief of the German General Staff, 1938–1942. At the end of each day Halder put down a few cryptic notes of his activities. They constitute a major contribution to military history.

Written without thought of publication, these jottings are the product of a superlative technical mind; there is no real gossip, no personal reflection, no moralizing. They do provide a remarkable insight into a busy man's schedule. Through them the reader may follow the German army in its victorious campaigns in Poland, Norway, France, the Balkans and Russia. Every major report, discussion, controversy and decision is at least mentioned by the highly placed Halder.

His notes also reflect the frustrations and difficulties of a military machine founded upon traditional ideas when confronted with a non-systemic leader like Adolf Hitler.

In view of the diary's economy of explanations on some points, the editor has provided copious explanatory and bibliographic suggestions. They provide useful references expanding Halder's notes and placing them in historical context.

GILBERT, FELIX, ed. **Hitler Directs His War.** New York: Oxford University Press, 1950, 187 p.

At the end of the Second World War Hitler ordered the mass destruction of all records. Fortunately, the implementation of his inclusive order failed of execution. Among the papers rescued from the fires were these shorthand transcriptions of Hitler's daily wartime conferences. While obviously only a minuscule portion of the totality (some 800 pages from 200,000), the fragments provide direct testimony of the German Führer, his views, his working methods and his human relations. It is a document of major historical value for the period between December 1942 and March 1945.

The editor has concentrated upon Hitler himself while eliminating or relegating technical issues to a brief appendix synopsis. The result is a verbatim report of Hitler's military thinking, his egomania and his singular approach to war. Any reader will be able to follow Hitler's military system and his conception of strategy and tactics in the most direct fashion.

For those readers able to use German, a more complete record may be found in Helmut Heiber, *ed.,* **Hitlers Lagebesprechungen. Die Protokollfragmente seiner Militärischen Konferenzen 1942–1945** (Stuttgart: Deutsche Verlags-Anstalt, 1962, 970 p.). Heiber found additional accounts which add substance to the Gilbert-edited version without changing its thrust.

Military Operations

General

GREENFIELD, KENT ROBERTS, ed. **Command Decisions.** New York: Harcourt, 1959, 481 p.

This volume consists of 20 essays, each of which analyzes critically a high-level decision of World War II. The decisions range in time and space from the basic Allied strategic decision to defeat Germany first and the Japanese decision for war to the German decision to fight on in Italy, the decisions to invade North Africa, land in southern France and the final decision to use the atomic bomb against Japan. The 16 authors who contributed to the volume have one thing in common: all worked at one time for the Army's Office of the Chief of Military History. The essays are fully researched and authoritative, but they are in no sense "official" and reflect no single line or position. In fact, several of the authors differ strongly in their interpretation of American and British strategy. The late Kent R. Greenfield did a superb job of editing, tying the separate essays together with a splendid introduction and setting a high standard of style and presentation.

Not all the important decisions of World War II are covered in **Command Decisions;** nor has the last word been said on them. Though a few Japanese and German decisions are included, the volume deals almost entirely with the American side of the war. Even on the American side there are a number of decisions omitted: to base the fleet at Pearl Harbor, to establish a base in Australia, to recall MacArthur to active duty and to evacuate him from Corregidor, to appoint Eisenhower supreme commander, to adopt the unconditional surrender formula. Despite these limitations, the volume is extremely useful as a study of the decision-making process in war and of the way in which the war was fought.

JACOBSEN, HANS-ADOLF and ROHWER, JURGEN, *eds.* **Decisive Battles of World War II: The German View.** New York: Putnam, 1965, 509 p.

Decisive Battles of World War II may prove to be one of the more enduring works in the vanguard of postwar writing. The editors have produced an excellent selection of essays on the turning points of the war from the German point of view. The subject matter is varied, ranging from technology and tactics in the air war over England to joint operations at Crete. The quality of writing is uneven: Warlimont's "Decision in the Mediterranean 1942," Görlitz's "The Battle for Stalingrad, 1942–43" and Rohwer's "The U-Boat War Against the Allied Supply Lines" are excellent; the others, fair. However, documentation is thorough and organization of the work is well thought out. Most of the authors focus on Hitler as the directing strategist and point out the growing conflict between the Führer and his army. The latter chapters trace the degeneration of Hitler's gift for sound decision.

Each author uses statistics extensively and quotes original sources at length; yet each still finds room for fascinating portraits of character: Dönitz shrewdly positioning U-boat "wolf packs," Rommel fighting for a realistic defense in Western Europe, Paulus fighting his conscience at Stalingrad. One should resist the temptation to read the book simply as individual essays and thus miss the development of an overriding and absorbing theme: how German military professionalism died as Hitler usurped command.

To supplement Jacobsen and Rohwer, the reader may refer to two other German writers: Heinz Guderian, **Panzer Leader** (New York: Dutton, 1952, 528 p.) and Erich von Manstein, **Lost Victories** (Chicago: Regnery, 1958, 574 p.). Both books are well written, and each contains a thought-provoking foreword by B. H. Liddell Hart. Both men were respected commanders whose thoughts on Germany's rise and fall deserve careful reading.

BUTLER, SIR JAMES, *ed.* **History of the Second World War: United Kingdom Military Series.** London: H.M.S.O., 1952–1969, 29 v.

The British "Military Series" is one of three major groups of histories dealing with World War II prepared during the past quarter-century under the auspices of the Cabinet Office. The complementary groups are a "Civil Series" of 29 and a "Medical Series" of 21 volumes. The "Military Series" itself has three divisions: six volumes on grand strategy, 23 on campaigns and four on civil affairs and military government. Still to be published are two of the strategy volumes and two on the war in the Mediterranean.

In the British tradition, officer historians have written most of the campaign volumes, civilian professionals those on strategy and civil affairs. All three types are notable for their readability and excellence of cartographic illustration. Little was done toward their preparation until after the war, and volumes dealing with the early war years were handicapped by inadequate and lost records typical of armies in retreat. The campaign volumes follow a multi-service approach, although for the European war their emphasis is on land combat because of the separate subseries on strategic air and war at sea. Also in the British tradition, authors have prepared fully documented confidential versions for governmental use and somewhat different texts for publication that are barren of reference to official records. Nevertheless, the knowledgeable reader can find ample assurance in the published works of definitive research in both British and enemy records, the British having generally shared with the American official historians on an equal basis the captured German and Japanese material. It is unlikely that the opening of the records will support allegations of distortion such as those that were levelled at the British official history of World War I.

United States Army in World War II. Washington: Government Printing Office (Department of the Army, Office of the Chief of Military History), 1947–1969, 70 v.

Plans in 1946 to write and publish a 99-volume narrative history of the United States Army's efforts in World War II, including those of its Air Forces, rested on a solid base of wartime historical activity at home and overseas which was launched in 1942 with the firm backing of President Roosevelt. For previous wars the Army had concentrated on publishing documents, but sheer volume was reason enough for turning to the narrative form. To write its World War II history, the Army depended primarily on civilian professional historians, attracted to the project by assurances of access to all relevant records and of fully accredited authorship responsibility. The works produced are official only in the sense that they have been prepared and published at public expense and are devoted to topics of value to the Army. They are not an official interpretation of the Army's role in the war.

Of 78 Army volumes published or in preparation, about half deal with the conduct and support of operations overseas, the rest with the strategic direction and support of the war on the home front. All but five are narrative in form, the exceptions being three combat pictorials, a chronology and a documentary treatment of civil affairs. Most are illustrated with pictures and maps, the latter of unusual excellence when compared to American works of similar character. These histories have been fully documented to provide students of the war with a guide to the records. Their citations of evidence lead to many sources which either security classifications might otherwise obscure or quantity of documents hide. Accordingly, they deserve to rank somewhere between primary historical sources and secondary works. For the European war, in particular, the authors have had almost as good documentation on the enemy as on American forces. Collectively these works represent the largest scholarly project of its kind ever undertaken in the United States.

MONTGOMERY, BERNARD LAW MONTGOMERY, 1ST VISCOUNT. **The Memoirs of Field-Marshal the Viscount Montgomery of Alamein, K.G.** Cleveland: World Publishing Co., 1958, 508 p.

Bernard Law Montgomery was not only one of the most successful British commanders of the Second World War but also one of its more contentious figures. After commanding a division in France (1940), he emerged two years later as the victorious leader of the British Eighth Army in North Africa, subsequently taking a major part in the conquest of Sicily and the invasion of Italy. Recalled to England and appointed to command the 21st Army Group, he ultimately received the surrender of the German army at Luneburg Heath. After the war he organized the British occupation zone, became Chief of the Imperial General Staff and completed his active career as Deputy Supreme Commander of SHAPE. The recording of these events makes up the bulk of this volume, but Montgomery's highly personal and usually incisive views of events and personalities appear on every page and give a sense of immediacy and deep conviction.

Montgomery's strong individuality and forthright views did not always make him the easiest of colleagues in the context of the Anglo-American alliance. It took all of Eisenhower's tact as Supreme Commander to avert major clashes of personality in the action-packed months that followed Operation Overlord. Omar Bradley in **A Soldier's Story** (New York: Holt, 1951, 618 p.) and George S. Patton in **War as I Knew It** (Boston: Houghton, 1947, 425 p.) reveal that their relationships with their British colleague were frequently acrimonious, particularly over the choice of the best strategy for the defeat of Germany. Whether the full adoption of Montgomery's concept would have materially shortened the war against Germany will always be debated; perhaps the failure of the Arnhem operation was due in no small measure to insufficient administrative backing for the 21st Army Group once Eisenhower had somewhat belatedly sanctioned Market Garden and accorded it a measure of priority over other major operations.

In battle, Montgomery preferred to build up a sufficiency of force before launching bold initiatives. He proved particularly adept at instilling confidence and a sense of purpose into the rank and file of the conscript armies of Great Britain and the Commonwealth. As Winston Churchill repeatedly reveals in his great history, **The**

Second World War, the Prime Minister had almost boundless faith in Montgomery's talents as both a field commander and administrator. The faith was not misplaced.

Air

CRAVEN, WESLEY FRANK and CATE, JAMES LEA, *eds.* **The Army Air Forces in World War II.** Chicago: University of Chicago Press, 1948–1958, 7 v.

In World War II, the United States Army wisely assigned many of the professional historians then in its uniform to document and begin to write the wartime history of the Army, including that of the Army Air Forces. Although the editors of these seven volumes and several of their principal colleagues quickly returned to academe after the war, they completed this work in coöperation with historians still in government, the University of Chicago and the new United States Air Force.

Every serious student of World War II aerial operations must consult these volumes. Their scope is so large and the sources on which they are based so enormous as to make it unlikely that any single effort ever will be made to cover again all the ground broken by them. Other historians, however, have already begun to modify or supplement portions of this work. For example, the more recent study of Sir Charles Webster and Noble Frankland, **The Strategic Air Offensive against Germany, 1939–1945** (London: H.M.S.O., 1961, 4 v.), in the United Kingdom Military Series, offers richer insights into the U.S.–British Combined Bomber Offensive than these volumes contain.

The authors of this work, ably guided by the editors, describe the operations of 16 wartime air forces and of the Air Transport Command. Five volumes deal with the combat history of the Army Air Forces, while a sixth covers organization, training and procurement in the United States and a seventh is devoted to worldwide support activities. Of continuing value are the editors' perceptive essays in volume I on the forerunners of the Army Air Forces.

United States Strategic Bombing Survey: European and Pacific Wars. Washington: Government Printing Office, 1945–1947, 319 Reports.

On November 3, 1944, President Franklin D. Roosevelt created the United States Strategic Bombing Survey to make "an impartial and expert study of the effects of our aerial attacks on Germany." The lessons derived were to be applied both in the ongoing air war against Japan and in postwar planning for national defense. On August 15, 1945, President Harry S. Truman expanded the survey to include newly defeated Japan. At its peak, the survey involved 1,500 civilian and military personnel, including such now familiar figures as Paul Nitze, John Kenneth Galbraith and George W. Ball.

Its 319 reports never received the attention justified by later combat experience. The key to this neglect probably was the persistent and widely held belief that the increasing availability of nuclear weapons after 1945 either had made another war unlikely or, in the event of war, had invalidated the bombing experience of World War II. Also, very few libraries have complete files on the survey's work. Most of its reports, however, are only supporting documents for the "Summary" and "Overall" reports on Europe (Washington: G.P.O., 1945) and the "Summary" report on the Pacific (Washington: G.P.O., 1946); and these three are more widely available. These key reports have contemporary significance, with their stress on the importance of control of the air, of proper target selection and of repeated sustained attacks against major targets as well as on the toughness of motivated civilian populations under bombardment.

WOOD, DEREK and DEMPSTER, DEREK DAVID. **The Narrow Margin.** New York: McGraw-Hill, 1961, 536 p.

Hermann Goering expected his Luftwaffe to knock England out of the war in 1940. Adolf Hitler would have settled for air superiority over the potential invasion beaches. The Royal Air Force denied them both objectives in the Battle of Britain.

Derek Wood and David Dempster have written the account most likely to satisfy the student of World War II aerial operations. They describe the battle largely as an institutional struggle between the British and German air forces. They emphasize their country's long-term organizational, scientific and technical preparations that preceded a seven-phase contest from July until October 1940. The handful of British airmen immortalized by Winston Churchill would have been powerless, in the authors' view, without radar and the Hurricane and Spitfire fighters, controlled by a then unique air defense system—all developed before the struggle began. German deficiencies receive considerable attention: a nightmarish air leadership, an incredibly poor use of scientific talent, faulty intelligence and, above all, the lack of a method whereby mistakes might be acknowledged and corrected.

This work could have been improved if its authors had given more attention to an analysis of the battle beyond that provided in their otherwise useful operational diary and to considerations such as the determination of the British government and people. The authors have improved the 1969 version by adding many well-chosen photographs from British and German sources along with a slightly expanded statistical appendix.

To view the battle in the context of the several German efforts to bring the British homeland to grief during World War II, the reader should consult Basil Collier, **The Defence of the United Kingdom** (London: H.M.S.O., 1957, 557 p.) in the United Kingdom Military Series.

RICHARDS, DENIS and SAUNDERS, HILARY AIDEN ST. GEORGE. **Royal Air Force, 1939–1945.** London: H.M.S.O., 1953–1954, 3 v.

This is the best overall account of Royal Air Force operations in World War II. Although not a part of the official British history, its authors were "officially commissioned" and apparently had access over a four-year period to considerable material in Air Ministry and higher level files, captured enemy documents and the personal records of RAF members.

The subtitles for each of the three volumes are well chosen: "The Fight at Odds," "The Fight Avails" and "The Fight Is Won." As they indicate, each volume covers a key phase of the RAF's struggle against Axis forces around the world. This is a detailed operational history, but the lively style of the authors holds the reader's attention, in spite of much detail. The major gap in this work, which the authors attribute primarily to space restrictions, is the absence of any coverage of the supporting services of the RAF.

A narrower subject, but probably the most controversial aspect of RAF (and U.S. Army Air Forces) operations, is the strategic bombardment campaign against Germany. While Richards and Saunders include five chapters on the RAF effort, the more complete account, which gives some attention to the Army Air Forces role, is in Sir Charles Webster and Noble Frankland, **The Strategic Air Offensive against Germany** (London: H.M.S.O., 1961, 4 v.). Perhaps their most impressive achievement is in conveying to the reader a sense of the operational problems encountered by Allied airmen.

LEE, ASHER. **The German Air Force.** New York: Harper, 1946, 310 p.

No fully satisfactory single account of the Luftwaffe in World War II is available. At a minimum, the reader must use several books to arrive at a reasonably comprehensive understanding of the subject.

Asher Lee won a reputation among Allied airmen during the war as one of the RAF's best informed officers on the German air force. His book is a shrewd outline of the work of a former enemy. A more authoritative account is the 1948 British Air Ministry study, recently republished and edited by W. H. Tantum, IV, and E. J. Hoffschmidt, **The Rise and Fall of the German Air Force, 1933–1945** (Old Greenwich: WE Press, 1969, 422 p.). Its unnamed authors in RAF Intelligence had access to Luftwaffe records in writing an operational history in the format of a military report, complete with numbered paragraphs, for use at the RAF Staff College and elsewhere.

Beginning in 1952, United States Air Force historians organized, translated and edited a series of monographs on the German air force, as part of "USAF Historical Studies." A group of Germans, mostly Luftwaffe veterans, either contributed information to supplement official records or wrote portions of the work. Twelve monographs of varying quality have appeared so far. Perhaps the most useful work for the reader interested in an overview is Richard Suchenwirth, **Historical Turning Points in the German Air Force War Effort** (Montgomery: USAF Historical Division, USAF Historical Studies no. 189, 1959, 143 p.). Suchenwirth, a German scholar, analyzes the key factors in the Luftwaffe's failure, including failures in leadership, doctrine and equipment.

DORNBERGER, WALTER. **V-2.** New York: Viking, 1954, 281 p.

This is more than the memoir of a defeated soldier. It is a continuing reminder of the fleeting nature of military superiority in World War II and thereafter. Dornberger was the military chief of the German scientists, including Wernher von Braun, who developed the V-2 rocket. Fortunately for the Allies, Dornberger and his group had to wait until July 1943 before they could persuade Hitler to give them a top priority. Even then, to bring the V-2 into full operation Dornberger and his colleagues had to fight the encroachments of the numerous empire builders in the Hitler régime.

Probably because Dornberger later entered the service of the U.S. missile and space program, he says very little about the potential significance of his work for the German war effort. For the most part, his account could erroneously be read as that of a group whose real interest was space exploration but who needed the stimulus of war to finance their work. What Dornberger chooses not to say is that if Hitler had fully supported him earlier in the war, Germany might well have been able to prevent the Allied build-up in England for D-Day. Also, through related rocket development, Germany might have made disastrous inroads on the U.S.–British air forces in the Combined Bomber Offensive.

For an account of Allied efforts to cope with the threat presented by Dornberger and his group, see the pertinent chapters in Basil Collier, **The Defence of the United Kingdom** (London: H.M.S.O., 1957, 557 p.), and in volume III of Craven and Cate, **The Army Air Forces in World War II.** An excellent account of the American role in the wartime struggle to achieve military superiority through new weaponry is in James P. Baxter, **Scientists against Time** (Boston: Atlantic, 1946, 473 p.).

OKUMIYA, MASATAKE and HORIKOSHI, JIRO with CAIDIN, MARTIN. **Zero!** New York: Dutton, 1956, 424 p.

Japan's crushing victories at Pearl Harbor and elsewhere in the Pacific in 1941–1942 implied a degree of aerial preparedness not borne out by later events. Unfortunately, students of aerial operations from the Japanese viewpoint will find only a limited bibliography in English. This book is the best available starting point. With the aid of aviation writer Martin Caidin, naval aviator Masatake Okumiya and aeronautical engineer Jiro Horikoshi have written a book that is at once a memoir and a piece of useful historical analysis.

The focus of their work is on the Japanese naval air arm which bore the brunt of the Pacific aerial fighting. The title of the book is somewhat misleading in that the role of the Zero is only one thread in the story. In two ways, though, the Zero explains the ultimate Japanese failure. That the Zero remained Japan's front-line fighter to the end of the war highlights the inability of the Japanese aircraft industry to stay ahead of the United States designers. Also, the crack pilots who first flew the Zero were replaced by relatively untrained men. Japanese planners simply had not taken into account the capabilities of an aroused American nation to destroy their initial superiority in aircraft and crews. Okumiya's personal account of his experiences in the face of growing American capabilities in the Southwest Pacific is arresting.

The failure of Japanese industry and training led directly to the Kamikaze program. This book has some insights into that suicidal effort, but for a fuller account, the reader should consult Rikihei Inoguchi and Tadashi Nakajima, with Roger Pineau, **The Divine Wind** (Annapolis: United States Naval Institute, 1958, 240 p.).

Naval

MORISON, SAMUEL ELIOT. **History of United States Naval Operations in World War II.** Boston: Atlantic (Little, Brown), 1947–1962, 15 v.

This 15-volume series is the bible for the United States naval historian of World War II. Professor Morison suggested to President Roosevelt in 1942 that such a series should be written and offered his services. The author was commissioned in the Naval Reserve and given the responsibility of producing this unofficial history. Morison used official records and all other records in possession of the Navy; he participated in naval actions afloat and in some amphibious operations, and he visited at one time or another in all theaters of the war.

The series begins with "The Battle of the Atlantic," moves to North Africa, then to the Pacific, comes back to Europe to win the Battle of the Atlantic and defeat Germany, then again to the Pacific to liberate the Philippines and defeat Japan. The last volume, the "Supplement and General Index," is divided into four parts: part I is the tale of the Navy's postwar operations in the Pacific; part II is a compilation of all named ships with their size and armament, all "lettered craft" and all airplanes in the Navy, 1941–1945; part III is errata in volumes I–XIV; part IV is the general index to the series. There have been no "revised editions," but each volume has had all known errors corrected before being reprinted. Volume I has had at least 15 reprintings, as has volume II.

Professor Morison did not complete this monumental task alone. His staff was large, and he gave credit where it was due. However, all opinions and conclusions are Morison's as is the style. This is no doubt the most official unofficial historical series ever produced.

CRESWELL, JOHN. **Sea Warfare 1939–1945.** Berkeley: University of California Press, rev. ed., 1967, 343 p.

This is as good a one-volume history of the maritime war of 1939–1945 as one can find. Captain Creswell's style is direct and substantial, displaying at times a pleasing salty flavor. The book contains the necessary maps and charts which allow even the layman to locate and follow closely all campaigns and actions of the war. The major campaigns and their attendant naval actions are placed in their proper perspective and adequately described. The author's description and critical analysis of the major naval battles of the war are worth the price of the book.

This is not a research vehicle for a student of naval warfare; but it is an overall, accurate and concise picture of the naval scene of World War II, although no claim is made by the author that his book is a comprehensive study of the war. The bibliography is highly selective, but it contains several major official British and American naval records plus authoritative works from the German, Italian, British and American points of view. The concluding chapter is a brief summary of the naval lessons learned and technological advances made during the war, the most important being radar, improved torpedoes and torpedo doctrine, aircraft and the fleet train.

ROSCOE, THEODORE. **United States Submarine Operations in World War II.** Annapolis: United States Naval Institute, 1949, 577 p.

This large and impressive volume has gone through eight printings, yet some errors still remain (for instance, the *Nautilus* still claims she sank *Soryu* at Midway, as illustrated by a full page painting). Regardless of these errors, this is a valuable study of the "Silent Service," its activities and its weapons. Especially good is the chapter on the United States torpedo, which was not truly an effective weapon until the end of 1943. The charts, maps, photographs and tables are priceless; this volume should be in all reference libraries.

Another excellent story of the United States submarine service is Vice Admiral Charles A. Lockwood, **Sink 'Em All** (New York: Dutton, 1951, 416 p.). Admiral Lockwood was Commander Submarines Pacific from 1943 to 1945, and his book reveals familiarity with his men, weapons and missions.

Both of these submarine volumes draw their material from diaries, interviews and official records, but they do not, of course, compromise official secrets of the naval service.

The submarine story of the Atlantic, from the British side, is ably presented in Donald G. F. W. Macintyre, **The Battle of the Atlantic** (New York: Macmillan, 1961, 208 p.), while a very useful and competent history of the submarine and its use—past, present and future—appears in Vice Admiral Sir Arthur Hezlet, **The Submarine and Sea Power** (New York: Stein and Day, 1967, 278 p.).

CONNERY, ROBERT HOUGH. **The Navy and the Industrial Mobilization in World War II.** Princeton: Princeton University Press, 1951, 527 p.

James Forrestal, Under Secretary of the Navy (1940–1945), was the originator of this volume in that he requested the Administrative Historian of the Navy, Professor Robert G. Albion, to undertake a study of the Office of the Under Secretary. Connery was assigned the task and spent three years consulting Navy personnel and records to "tell the story of the Navy's material program from the planning stages of 1920–1942 then through the war years to V-J Day and after." In this unofficial history he shows how the office of the Secretary expanded to meet the ever increasing needs of the Navy. However, there was initial resistance to these changes by reactionary chiefs of bureaus, resistance which slowly faded until by V-J Day the Navy had permanent administrative processes with which to cope with contemporary mobilization problems.

This is by far the best "administrative history" of the World War II Navy. The book's high watermark is its explanation of the Navy's connections with the other governmental agencies and the civilian-military rapport within the Navy itself. In his description of the "operations of the various agencies attached to the office of the Under Secretary, while James Forrestal held the post," Professor Connery has created a lasting memorial to the first Under Secretary of the Navy.

ROSKILL, S. W. **The War at Sea, 1939–1945.** London: H.M.S.O., 1954–1961, 3 v.

This volume, in the British Military Series, is concerned primarily "with events as they influenced decisions at the admiralty." All official British documents were accessible in writing these volumes. However, the footnotes refer only to sources made available to the public; a complete documentation has been made, but these references will be available only to future historians. Excellent appendices, maps, photographs, charts and tables are included.

Captain Roskill, RN, focuses his attention on the maritime events of the European theater but has adequate treatment and analysis of the Pacific events, with admitted advice from S. E. Morison. Roskill "set out to tell the story of the development of our maritime strategy from 1939–1945, and of its application to the unceasing struggle for the control of communications across the broad oceans and in the narrow coastal waters." He tells his story with the same courage that his countrymen displayed in living it. Roskill steps on some famous toes, and rightly so, in his critical analysis of several decisions which came from Whitehall and the Admiralty, but he is completely impartial in his treatment of men and events. **The War at Sea** is an excellent account of the Royal Navy's part in World War II.

A personal account of many campaigns described by Roskill may be found in Andrew B. Cunningham's autobiography, **A Sailor's Odyssey** (New York: Dutton, 1951, 715 p.). Admiral of the Fleet Sir Andrew B. Cunningham (later Viscount

Cunningham of Hyndhope) was Commander in Chief Mediterranean at the war's beginning, then First Sea Lord and Chief of Naval Staff in 1943. His style is plain and straightforward, interesting to the landlocked as well as the seafarer; his tale is for everyone interested in the British maritime situation of World War II.

RUGE, FRIEDRICH. **Der Seekrieg: The German Navy's Story, 1939–1945.** Annapolis: United States Naval Institute, 1957, 440 p.

The author states in his preface that his object "is to provide a general picture of naval warfare in the Second World War, to show the interaction of sea and land operations, the great effect of naval warfare on land campaigns, and the influence of naval strategy on the major decisions of politics and war." Vice Admiral Ruge certainly accomplishes his objective, but he deals mainly with Germany and the European theater.

After the surrender of Germany, Ruge, who had held several staff jobs (including one with Rommel) during the war, was one of a select group of prisoners chosen to collect information from German sources for Allied intelligence and historical use. Undoubtedly, **Der Seekrieg** is one result of his research. Ruge's sources are not mentioned; however, his critical analysis of the German strategy of the Mediterranean and Russian campaigns is reason enough to read the book.

To supplement **Der Seekrieg,** one should consult Anthony K. Martienssen, **Hitler and His Admirals** (New York: Dutton, 1949, 275 p.), and Karl Doenitz, **Memoirs: Ten Years and Twenty Days** (Cleveland: World Publishing Co., 1959, 500 p.). Martienssen has used the *Schloss Tambach* documents and evidence from the Nuremberg trials while Doenitz writes authoritatively from personal experience.

Since Ruge seldom describes tactics employed in naval actions, two sources are useful for this purpose: Dudley Pope, **The Battle of the River Plate** (London: Kimber, 1956, 223 p.), and David Woodward, **The Tirpitz and the Battle for the North Atlantic** (New York: Norton, 1954, 235 p.). Woodward describes the effect of the capital ships of the Kriegsmarine on the Royal Navy and the saga of the *Tirpitz,* while Pope gives an excellent account of the life and death of the *Graf Spee.*

Western Europe

HORNE, ALISTAIR. **To Lose a Battle: France, 1940.** Boston: Little, Brown, 1969, 647 p.

The collapse of a great power after a campaign of only a month and a half was so shocking and incredible an event that a full generation later the world still seems to be struggling to digest and comprehend the fall of France in 1940.

Naturally, the French themselves have probed the causes of their nation's débâcle. Efforts worth noting are General André Beaufre, **1940: The Fall of France** (New York: Knopf, 1968, 215 p.); Jacques Benoist-Méchin, **Sixty Days that Shook the West: The Fall of France: 1940** (New York: Putnam, 1963, 559 p.); and Colonel Adolphe Goutard, **The Battle of France, 1940** (New York: Ives Washburn, 1959, 280 p.). These books, especially Benoist-Méchin's, savor the old animosities of Frenchmen for fellow Frenchmen which do much to explain the defeat. So do the memoirs of more prominent participants, notably General Maurice Gamelin, **Servir** (Paris: Plon, 1946–1947, 3 v.), and the first volume of Charles de Gaulle's eloquent three-volume **Mémoires de Guerre.** The books by American and English writers, less flawed by innuendo than the French, include Telford Taylor, **The March of Conquest** (New York: Simon and Schuster, 1958, 460 p.); Guy Chapman, **Why France Fell** (New York: Holt, Rinehart and Winston, 1969, 403 p.), especially good on the internal politics and organization of the French army between the world wars; William L. Shirer, **The Collapse of the Third Republic: An Inquiry into the Fall of France in 1940** (New York: Simon and Schuster, 1969, 1,082 p.).

Horne's work, however, is probably the best single volume as historical literature and one of the best balanced. It includes enough of the history of France from 1919 to 1940 to set the stage, while concentrating on the military events of the 1940 campaign. It regards France as having been softened for defeat by political and social dissension, but it treats the defeat as finally a military one. Political and social decay had not gone so far that French soldiers could not fight bravely; but a command befuddled by the German blitzkrieg invoked their bravery only on occasions which were strategically and tactically hopeless. In both Horne's and Chapman's books, Charles de Gaulle himself, whatever claims to greatness he established later, appears less as the prophet of armored war and indeed much less as the competent battlefield leader than his own memoirs would have it.

ANSEL, WALTER. **Hitler Confronts England.** Durham: Duke University Press, 1960, 348 p.

This definitive study of Sea Lion—the German operation for an invasion of Britain—by an American amphibious warfare expert details Adolf Hitler's "struggle with a problem beyond him." Where other authors deal chiefly with high-level plans and inter-service bickering, Admiral Ansel goes into the composition, tactical training and movement of the forces assigned to carry them out. Interviews with many German officers show that preparations were quite advanced when Hitler called off the invasion on September 11, 1940, and turned his full attention to Russia. His failure to win the command of the air and the weakness of his improvised amphibious forces had left him no other short-term options. Ansel feels that a September 27 invasion would have ended in disaster, and that the Channel was Hitler's "Marne." The 1941 stalemate in front of Moscow did not cost him the strategic initiative against Russia, but he had already lost it against England.

MACDONALD, CHARLES B. **The Mighty Endeavor: American Armed Forces in the European Theater in World War II.** New York: Oxford University Press, 1969, 564 p.

This general history of the European theater during World War II is an American complement to Chester Wilmot's **The Struggle for Europe** (New York: Harper, 1952, 766 p.), which emphasizes British experience and presents a British view. But although MacDonald dwells on American participation, his interpretations are more balanced and less parochial. He takes a stand on all the critical issues, acute controversies and the important personalities of the war—and without hyperbole. He also presents an excellent mix of policy, strategy and tactics.

MacDonald addresses the major coalition disputes: a cross-Channel invasion was never a question of whether but of when; the Italian campaign was costly but was beneficial to Operation Overlord; Eisenhower's "broad front" strategy, a misnomer because it was a conventional combination of main and secondary efforts, was justified in light of logistical difficulties; and the decisions not to race to Berlin and Prague made sense because subsequent withdrawals had been agreed upon. He finds that, all told, the Allied politicians and generals compromised well in formulating the grand strategy and strategy for the European theater.

On the other hand, MacDonald is critical of the tactics of American and British generals alike—for Kasserine Pass, Sicily, Anzio, the Rapido, Valmontone-Rome, Argentan-Falaise, Antwerp, the Huertgen Forest and the Ardennes. His evaluations are both right and forthright, and not unexpected of one who fought at the company level in the European theater.

The author's experiences serve him well on two counts. MacDonald, the company commander, provides absorbing accounts of many World War II battles; MacDonald, the Deputy Chief Historian of the Office of the Chief of Military History, draws freely on the excellent research of that organization. Providing both readability and scholarship, he weaves the air and sea war into his narrative with succinct versions of the Strategic Bomber Offensive and the Battle of the Atlantic.

Overall, **The Mighty Endeavor** is the best one-volume history of the European theater in World War II.

RYAN, CORNELIUS. **The Longest Day.** New York: Simon and Schuster, 1959, 350 p.

An account of the Allied invasion of Normandy on D-Day, this relatively slim volume is the best known of the so-called "popular" histories that have emerged from World War II, based in large measure on extensive interviews with survivors well after the event.

The style is episodic, treating such diverse matters as Field Marshal Erwin Rommel's absence from his command, a Royal Navy lieutenant's thoughts as he views the invasion beach through a periscope, a German on horseback delivering morning coffee to gun crews in Atlantic Wall pillboxes, a French mayor's frantic efforts to put out invasion-set fires, a paratrooper dangling helpless from a church steeple, the vacillation of German generals wary of waking their sleeping Führer, a French resistance fighter jubilant to see a gun, whose location he had reported, blasted by Allied guns. Yet the overall effect, however kaleidoscopic, is comprehensive and rewarding, an intimate view of human beings caught up in one of history's more momentous events. In the process, the author developed interesting new material bearing on Allied success and German failure on D-Day, such as the negative reaction of German commanders to a staff officer's monitoring of Allied radio alerts to the French resistance.

EISENHOWER, JOHN S. D. **The Bitter Woods.** New York: Putnam, 1969, 506 p.

As the son of the Supreme Allied Commander in Europe, John Eisenhower was in a position to open a particularly illuminating window on the dramatic events of the German counteroffensive in the Ardennes in the winter of 1944–45 (the Battle of the Bulge), the greatest pitched battle American troops have ever fought. Having known most of the senior American commanders since childhood, having interviewed German generals extensively, and having drawn at length on his father's memory, the author affords rare insight into the workings of Allied and German command during this climactic engagement.

This is the author's first book, and he falls into some of the errors of the neophyte. He takes too long covering events preceding the counteroffensive and the final denouement after the bulge was eliminated. He also engages in a prolixity that his editors might have spared him; and for the general reader, as opposed to the military specialist, his narrative has too many geographical place names and numerical unit designations. Yet for all that, John Eisenhower has a talent for telling a story, and in addition to a facile recounting of the command role, he introduces exciting new material on small unit warfare.

Along with Hugh M. Cole, **The Ardennes: Battle of the Bulge** (Washington: G.P.O., 1965, 720 p.), a volume in the U.S. Army "European Theater of Operations" series on which the author has drawn extensively, **The Bitter Woods** provides a lucid view of Americans at war under extreme adversity, at command and fighting echelons alike.

POGUE, FORREST C. **The Supreme Command.** Washington: Government Printing Office, 1954, 607 p.

Written by one who subsequently became the official biographer of the wartime Chief of Staff, George C. Marshall, this volume is the official history of Supreme Headquarters, Allied Expeditionary Force (SHAEF) in Europe. As such, it is the capstone of the U.S. Army European theater subseries.

It is volumes such as this that have earned for the Army's official histories enthusiastic acceptance by academicians and others dedicated to objective history. The coöperation in the writing which Pogue enjoyed from all Allied commanders, including the Supreme Commander, General Dwight D. Eisenhower, and the author's unadorned presentation of the facts inspire further confidence.

The author begins the story with the selection of Eisenhower as the Supreme Commander and the evolvement of SHAEF as an instrument of command. He provides an overview of plans for the invasion of Normandy and subsequent operations, with particular attention to the Allied intelligence failure in the

Ardennes in the fall of 1944. An authoritative enemy story is based on captured records and postwar monographs by German commanders, while the superb maps which feature all the Army's World War II histories provide more than adequate geographical references. Detailed annotation affords a ready index to the official records.

Others writing later for more general audiences have provided additional anecdotes and human interest sidelights, but Pogue's official history remains a basic source—sober, authoritative and objective.

Eastern Europe

CLARK, ALAN. **Barbarossa: The Russian-German Conflict, 1941–45.** New York: Morrow, 1965, 522 p.

One of the most inconvenient legacies of World War II for historians has been the German generals' claim that Hitler lost the war singlehandedly. The similarity to the post-1918 stab in the back legend has seemed too pat. Alan Clark, who won his spurs jousting with the reputations of the British World War I commanders in **The Donkeys** (New York: Morrow, 1962, 216 p.), attempts the most radical refutation so far.

Barbarossa is a study of four phases in the war on the Eastern Front: the advance toward Moscow in 1941, the thrust to Stalingrad in the summer of 1942, the Battle of Kursk in 1943 and the last ditch defense of the Reich after January 1945. During the first two, according to Clark, Hitler's strategic thinking was clearly superior to that of the generals. In the great debate (July–August 1941) over whether to strike for Moscow or into the Ukraine, Hitler in choosing the Ukraine was the orthodox Clausewitzian, not the generals. In the summer of 1942, Hitler had "an absolutely clear idea of what he was going to do." The generals failed to understand him. The author notes that in the last two phases Hitler's powers declined, but suggests that one general, "the one whom Hitler respected most," Heinz Guderian, might have saved the day but for the backbiting egoism of his colleagues.

The Soviet generals are less in the foreground and come off better—except for the political types, such as Budënny and Voroshilov. They all would, no doubt, applaud the author's conclusion that the Soviet armies "could have won the war on their own, or at least fought the Germans to a standstill, without help from the West."

GOURÉ, LEON. **The Siege of Leningrad.** Stanford: Stanford University Press, 1962, 363 p.

In contemplating total war, of which World War II may have been only a sample, all governments must consider their own and their people's capacity for dealing with extreme stress. The siege of Leningrad may be history's most terrible example thus far of war-induced pressure. The city was under tight German envelopment from September 1941 to January 1943 and blockaded for another year after that. About a third of its three million inhabitants died from cold, hunger or sickness—or all three.

Leon Gouré, a RAND Corporation researcher, has written the history of the siege to January 1943 with emphasis on the "how" and the "why" of the survival of the city and its people. In doing so he has drawn on voluminous Soviet and German sources and conducted personal interviews with survivors.

As answers to the problem of future stress, Gouré's conclusions offer no encouragement for the U.S. government and, possibly, not very much for the Soviet Union. He attributes the resistance of Leningrad mainly to a cold-blooded totalitarian régime operating on a docile people already thoroughly inured to suffering and privation.

CHUIKOV, VASILI I. **The Battle for Stalingrad.** New York: Holt, Rinehart and Winston, 1964, 364 p.

A translation of the Russian title of this book, "Beginning of the Road" ("Nachalno Puti"), might fail to attract American readers not familiar with the name Chuikov, and probably few would be. Marshal Chuikov, in the 1960s Supreme Commander of Soviet Land Forces, was not one of the big names of World War II. But **The Battle for Stalingrad** is a somewhat misleading title, since the book barely touches on the main phase of Stalingrad, the great encirclement (November 1942–January 1943) in which the German Sixth Army was destroyed.

Chuikov commanded the Soviet 62nd Army, the army that held out in Stalingrad from September to November 1942, at the last by literally burrowing into the cliffs along the Volga. This was his and his army's "battle for Stalingrad." The 62nd Army stayed on in the city from November to January, but the main action then was elsewhere.

The book is a reasonably—by Soviet standards, surprisingly—forthright and dramatic account of the prologue to one of the decisive battles in world history. In the long run, however, it may be more significant as the opening verbal barrage in the "battle of memoirs" that had pretty well run its course in the West before it began in the Soviet Union. Chuikov gives more than ample credit to Khrushchev, in the war a "front" (army group) political commissar, and none or almost none to Zhukov, Vasilevskiy and Voronov, the real architects of Stalingrad. In his second book, **The Fall of Berlin** (New York: Holt, Rinehart and Winston, 1968, 261 p.), Chuikov brings his antipathy to Zhukov into the open. Zhukov has countered with memoirs of his own, published in part as Georgi K. Zhukov, **Marshal Zhukov's Greatest Battles** (New York: Harper and Row, 1969, 304 p.).

ZIEMKE, EARL F. **Stalingrad to Berlin: The German Defeat in the East.** Washington: Government Printing Office (United States Army Historical Series), 1968, 549 p.

Comparatively little has appeared so far in English on the four-year Soviet-German conflict in World War II—no more, perhaps, than has been written about Anzio or the Battle of the Bulge. Strangely enough, the campaigns of the last two and a half years, the ones in which the Soviet Union established its military reputation, have been the most neglected. Earl Ziemke has now closed the gap with this comprehensive account of the war in the east from the Stalingrad débâcle to the surrender.

The subject is total war at its worst to date, a clash of two utterly ruthless régimes on a front that for a time stretched from the Arctic Ocean to the Caucasus Mountains and by 1945 had rolled westward a distance of 1,500 miles. Eight to nine million troops, constantly engaged, spread death and destruction across Eastern Europe.

Ziemke shows how Hitler, having failed to defeat the Russians in a blitz in 1941 and faced with a second front in the west, was trapped into a war of manpower and matériel that Germany could not hope to win. The Soviet command could be more profligate of life and resources, but also became more skillful in these years. Ziemke considers their performances at Stalingrad, Kursk and against Army Group Center in 1944 equal to the Germans' best, but they were obviously not the complete masters of the art of war they have claimed to be. Their middle and lower command echelons remained weak, and they were capable of "comic opera" lapses right up to the battle for Berlin.

The Mediterranean

HOWARD, MICHAEL. **The Mediterranean Strategy in the Second World War.** New York: Praeger, 1968, 82 p.

Many histories depict the Western Allies' Mediterranean strategy as the product of a prolonged dispute between British and American planners, and postwar British and American historians have debated the merits of the strategy in a dispute probably more acrimonious than the debates of the planners. Michael Howard may have signalled a truce between the British and American historians and perhaps opened a period of less nationalistic and better balanced historical writing on the subject.

Howard does not attempt to paper over differences between British and American strategists. Unlike such fellow British historians as Chester Wilmot, in **The Struggle for Europe** (New York: Harper, 1952, 766 p.), G. A. Shepperd, in **The Italian Campaign, 1943–45: A Political and Military Re-assessment** (New York: Praeger, 1968, 450 p.), and John Ehrman, in **Grand Strategy. Volume V: August 1943–September 1944** in the British Military Series (London: H.M.S.O., 1956, 634 p.), Howard does not denigrate the American strategic planners as political blind men who sacrificed policy to strategy and especially ignored the Soviet menace. For that matter, Howard here differs also from such an American admirer of Winston Churchill as Hanson W. Baldwin, in his **Great Mistakes of the War** (New York: Harper, 1950, 114 p.). Howard approaches the conclusions of Maurice Matloff in the American official "War Department" series, **Strategic Planning for Coalition Warfare, 1943–1944** (Washington: G.P.O., 1960, 640 p.), and of Trumbull Higgins, **Soft Underbelly: The Anglo-American Controversy over the Italian Campaign 1939–1945** (New York: Macmillan, 1968, 275 p.): that policy shaped strategy for both partners of the Western alliance, but that there was much that was dubious both politically and strategically in British efforts to secure a continuing and even growing Allied commitment to offensives in Italy and the eastern Mediterranean. He is less confident, indeed, that the Italian campaign was ultimately worth its cost than is a recent official American historian, Martin Blumenson, in **Salerno to Cassino** (Washington: G.P.O., 1969, 491 p.), part of the U.S. Army "Mediterranean Theater of Operations" series.

JACKSON, WILLIAM GODFREY FOTHERGILL. **The Battle for Italy.** New York: Harper and Row, 1967, 372 p.

It is a principle of war that only minimum essential resources should be allocated to secondary efforts. In **The Battle for Italy,** W. G. F. Jackson illustrates the paradox attending every attempt to put principle into practice: how did the contestants in World War II draw the line between "minimum" and "essential" in their strategies for control of the Mediterranean? He never concludes that either side was wrong in its estimates but is content to show that the problem was bedevilling.

General Jackson's work is superior to most studies on the Mediterranean conflict because he traces the tactical consequences of strategic decisions from both Allied and Axis viewpoints. His exceptionally balanced effort should help to put the controversial Italian campaigns into their proper context. The author develops the origins of American and British strategic thought and outlines the military and political conditions governing each nation's outlook on the war. He then presents the key issues of each major strategic decision clearly and dispassionately and describes its effects on the fighting in Italy. He explains the interrelation between important operations, such as Cassino and Anzio. At the same time he does a masterful job of succinctly describing the heartbreaking battle for Cassino. He explains the importance of troop morale to overall strategy and does not shrink from criticizing individuals—especially Clark and Alexander.

This is an excellent historical study. Soldiers will find it valuable as an analysis in the laboratory of warfare; statesmen will appreciate its contribution to the continuing study of problems in integrating policy and strategy.

MAJDALANY, FREDERICK. **The Battle of Cassino.** Boston: Houghton, 1957, 309 p.

The controversial struggle for Cassino was the most protracted and costly of the World War II Italian campaign. The immense natural strength of Monte Cassino with its famous monastery made it the key sector of the German Gustav Line which stretched from the Mediterranean to the Adriatic. Majdalany's work is the definitive study.

Four months of the severest fighting and as many major battles were required to dislodge the German Tenth Army and thus open the way to the Anzio bridgehead and Rome. After American and New Zealand failures, the British Eighth Army strongly reinforced the U.S. Fifth Army for the final onslaught, Operation Diadem. The stalemate was broken by the great advance of General Juin's French corps through the Aurunci Mountains, supported by American and British attacks to left and right. General Anders' Polish corps captured the monastery. After six days of bitter fighting the victory was won, and the war in Italy again became mobile.

The Germans consider Cassino, despite its outcome, a considerable defensive strategic success. There is no question that it seriously delayed the Allied offensive. Both the employment of the U.S. 36th Division in the first battle and the bombing of the monastery on February 15, 1944, remain contentious subjects. From first to last Cassino was a struggle of attrition.

TRUSCOTT, LUCIAN KING. **Command Missions: A Personal Story.** New York: Dutton, 1954, 570 p.

Lucian K. Truscott first saw men die in battle 23 years after his graduation from West Point. Three years later he commanded a field army at grips with the Germans. In **Command Missions,** perhaps the best of many memoirs written by senior American commanders who served in World War II, Truscott explains how he made the transition from peacetime preparation to wartime payoff. In his judgment, the successful leader in combat must have "the ability to profit by the lessons of battle experience." It is evident that he was quick to learn.

His fighting career began at Dieppe, the first of a series of key wartime experiences. He observes that each added to his lore of combat wisdom and sharpened his judgment for high command. Analysis of combat actions also made him a remarkably perceptive and objective observer of people. He criticizes the personal and professional jealousies that diminished command effectiveness in Tunisia and sketches the personalities of leading figures in the Mediterranean—Patton and Alexander, whom he admired, and De Lattre, whom he mistrusted.

Not a few of today's senior commanders received their schooling in the élite 3d Infantry Division that Truscott led to fame through successive invasions at Sicily and Salerno. Anzio was their "postgraduate course." Anzio was also the climax of Truscott's accelerating career. His judgments on the strategies and decisions of senior commanders in this crisis makes firsthand history at its best. For this reason alone, **Command Missions** should be required reading for students of the Second World War.

LEWIN, RONALD. **Rommel as Military Commander.** Princeton: Van Nostrand, 1968, 262 p.

Erwin Rommel had few equals as a leader of troops. Originally a mountain warfare expert, he became a skilled tank commander in the western desert before being appointed to command army groups in Italy and northern France.

Undaunted by the arid regions of Libya and Egypt, he exploited speed and surprise and made use of the open desert flank to confound his earlier opponents, Generals Conningham and Ritchie. As Lewin makes clear, Rommel was a master of manoeuvre and of battle tactics. Undaunted by administrative problems, he developed a genius for opportunism and improvisation. The risks he accepted were often enormous—as at Gazala in May 1942—but until later that year his hunches normally came off.

Rommel's weakness was at the strategical level. From July to November 1942 he clung to an impossibly exposed position facing El Alamein, as Michael Carver expertly discusses in **El Alamein** (New York: Macmillan, 1962, 216 p.). Overextended communications and grave logistical problems, coupled with the Allied invasion of northwest Africa, foredoomed the Axis army to ultimate defeat by Generals Alexander and Montgomery, who refused to be forced into a premature counteroffensive until all was ripe. When Montgomery at last attacked, British material predominance was overwhelming, but it still required 11 days of bitter fighting, and three changes of plan, to overcome Rommel's defenses despite his initial absence in Germany. During the subsequent retreat to Tripoli and thence to Tunisia, Rommel's superb tactical skill was much in evidence; no general was ever more dangerous in defeat. Nevertheless, the British victory at El Alamein proved the final turning point of the Desert War.

The Pacific and East Asia

MORTON, LOUIS. **Strategy and Command: The First Two Years.** Washington: Department of the Army, Office of the Chief of Military History, 1962, 761 p.

The Army official histories must remain the first resort of any historian working in their field. Their field frequently includes diplomacy as well as the military art, as is evidenced by Louis Morton's **Strategy and Command**—a landmark in the still young American literature of strategy. Conceived, in Morton's words, as "more than a handmaiden of war, it is an inherent element of statecraft, akin to policy, and encompasses preparations for war as well as war itself."

More than any other volume, official history or otherwise, his **Strategy and Command** draws together the campaigns of Army, Navy and Army Air Force in the Pacific theater and links them with the diplomacy and war aims of the Grand Alliance. The coherence of Morton's account of Pacific strategy is the more noteworthy because the strategy itself usually lacked something in coherence, at first because after Pearl Harbor so much had to be improvised, then because the United States was never able to settle on a unified Pacific command. Morton sets his stage by presenting the best available succinct reviews of both American and Japanese strategic planning before 1941. His chapters on Japanese strategy during the war may still be the best English-language work on the subject. The arena of the book is "the council chamber rather than the coral atoll," but Morton writes with a constant regard for the immense sweep of Pacific geography and thus adds drama to the clarity of his narrative.

HAYASHI, SABURO with COOX, ALVIN D. **Kōgun: The Japanese Army in the Pacific War.** Quantico: Marine Corps Association, 1959, 249 p.

Kōgun is a high-level, insider's account of the Pacific war from Japanese high command perspective. Military secretary to Japan's last army minister, Colonel Hayashi served at the hub of decision making at the war's end. Never intended for foreign consumption, his unsparingly candid study was published in 1951 under the title of "Taiheiyō Sensō Rikusen Gaishi" ["Outline History of Pacific War Ground Battles"]. The translation, which follows the original faithfully, contains detailed new footnotes, photographs and a unique appendix of 91 biographical digests. After succinctly sketching the origins of the modern Japanese military system and of the war, Hayashi concentrates upon the period 1941–1945 in all theaters of Japanese operation. He provides penetrating insights into the weaknesses of Japan's technological and scientific infrastructure, the hidden workings of army factions and the private thoughts of the general staff regarding the feasibility of defending the homeland after the fall of Okinawa. Hayashi is more impressed by American firepower and logistics than by the intrinsic qualities of the American soldier.

Publication, starting in the 1960s, of the official Japanese war history—the "Senshi Sosho" ["Military History Series"] prepared by the Japan Defense Agency —does not detract from the importance of **Kōgun** for general reader or specialist. Conciseness and ready access are assets shared neither by "Senshi Sosho" nor by the work of another able Japanese colonel, Takushirō Hattori, **Daitōa Sensō Zenshi** [Complete History of the Greater East Asia War]. Unusual tribute to **Kōgun's** historical value and objectivity was rendered when the Russians brought out an unauthorized version titled "Yaponskaya Armiya v Voennykh Deistriyakh na Tikohom Okeane" (Moscow: Voenizdat, 1964). Low-keyed but encyclopedic, **Kōgun** remains the best, and indeed the only, single-volume Japanese military history of the entire Pacific war available in English.

WOHLSTETTER, ROBERTA. **Pearl Harbor: Warning and Decision.** Stanford: Stanford University Press, 1962, 426 p.

Heavily footnoted and dispassionate, **Pearl Harbor: Warning and Decision** was the product of five years of research by a highly professional clinician, not a popularizer. Thirty-nine volumes of Congressional hearings had been available to the public since 1946; the great service of Roberta Wohlstetter was to have read all of the oft-quoted, seldom examined transcript, from whose amorphous contents she rendered order. Her bibliography refers to dozens of other pertinent books, government documents and articles; Ladislas Farago's exciting **The Broken Seal** (New York: Random House, 1967, 439 p.) appeared afterward. Although interviews proved useful, they comprised no noticeable core element, perhaps because of their privileged nature. Mrs. Wohlstetter adequately recapitulated the Japanese story, but her sources were secondary and reflected no new findings.

The greatest value of this book is its remarkably clear and pioneering exposition of tangled American command and intelligence relationships and structures. On occasion the author seems naïve about the ways of the armed forces, particularly their systems of intelligence evaluation; but she is brilliant in her dissection of cryptoanalytic signals, noise, clutter, reception and interception. She places American war plans in perspective and, in the process, demolishes the myth that the Roosevelt administration, for occult reasons, concealed knowledge of specific Japanese strike intentions. Still not entirely laid to rest is the matter of the fiasco in the Philippines. The brief final sections on perspective and prospect are chilling in their emphasis upon the norm of uncertainty. The author's lessons from the case history of Pearl Harbor are apocalyptically relevant today, when the calculus of destruction is astronomic and the factor of strategic surprise is reckoned in minutes.

MORTON, LOUIS. **The Fall of the Philippines.** Washington: Department of the Army, Office of the Chief of Military History, 1953, 626 p.

Among the many carefully researched and ably written volumes in the Army's official history of the Second World War, this volume is one of the best. An unusual story of painful and depressing defeat for American-Filipino forces, it is at the same time a magnificent tribute to the men who bought precious time for a shocked United States in the first few months of the war.

In breadth of understanding, expert knowledge and familiarity with the material, Louis Morton is probably America's premier historian of the Pacific war. A combat historian there during the war, he later served for over a decade in the Office of the Chief of Military History where he headed the Pacific section and directed preparation of the "War in the Pacific" subseries.

Considering the dearth of official records normally associated with an army in defeat, Morton has expertly recounted the story of the first Philippine campaign. His development of Japanese strategy, plans and operations is superb and reveals not only a skillful foe but one with limited resources. Carefully and impartially, he traces the fluctuating American plans and unsuccessful efforts to piece together a strategy to succor the forces in the Philippines. At the same time, with scholarly attention to detail and fact and in a free-flowing prose, he addresses the key questions with skill, shrewdness and fairness: the loss of aircraft at Clark Field, the complicated retrograde movement to Bataan, the intricate command structure and MacArthur's appointment to command in Australia, the defense of Bataan, the naval role and the surrender. This work is an example of the best form of military history.

FUCHIDA, MITSUO and OKUMIYA, MASATAKE. **Midway, the Battle that Doomed Japan: The Japanese Navy's Story.** Annapolis: United States Naval Institute, 1955, 266 p.

This volume is one of the best naval histories on the war against Japan. The authors begin by deriving the Japanese naval strategy which led to Midway; as men who served in positions to know, they competently describe both men and matériel.

Neither the Doolittle raid nor the Battle of the Coral Sea could deter Admiral Yamamoto from his determination to attack Midway at the scheduled time.

The battle is vividly described from the Japanese point of view, with no punches pulled. The concluding chapter is an "Analysis of the Defeat" with several reasons, each well explained, being advanced. Not the least among these reasons are the lack of Japanese intelligence concerning American forces and Japanese "arrogance." The charts, photographs and appendices are invaluable.

To gain a more complete understanding of the naval war against Japan, one must consult the works of three of the four great American naval leaders in the war: Fleet Admiral Ernest J. King and Walter M. Whitehill, **Fleet Admiral King: A Naval Record** (New York: Norton, 1952, 674 p.); Fleet Admiral William F. Halsey and Joseph Bryan, **Admiral Halsey's Story** (New York: Whittlesey House, 1947, 310 p.); and Emmet Peter Forrestel, **Admiral Raymond A. Spruance, USN: A Study in Command** (Washington: G.P.O., 1966, 275 p.).

The Japanese version of some segments of the naval air war is presented in the autobiography of Saburo Saki, a former Imperial Japanese Navy pilot with 64 Allied planes to his credit (Saburo Saki with Martin Caidin, **Samurai,** New York: Dutton, 1957, 382 p.).

HOUGH, FRANK OLNEY. **The Island War: The United States Marine Corps in the Pacific.** Philadelphia: Lippincott, 1947, 413 p.

Only a year after the war's end, Major Hough completed his vivid account of the U.S. Marines' share of hell and glory in the Pacific. He made no claim to be official or definitive, but he drew heavily upon classified reports, reinforced by news dispatches and personal experience. The nature and recency of his main sources precluded any bibliography. Hough was remarkably skillful, however, at unraveling the complexities of amphibious operations, strategic planning, inter-service and inter-arm relations, while conveying the immediacy of jungle and atoll fighting, replete with gore and occasional humor. This consummate narrator sketched neither friend nor foe as pasteboard creatures. Of course, inconsistencies and errors crept in, and many points remained moot. The feeblest section was the "anticlimax" after Okinawa. Hough later helped to fill the lacunae by working on the official USMC histories, whose fifth and final volume appeared in 1968: **Victory and Occupation,** by Benis M. Frank and Henry I. Shaw, Jr. (Washington: United States Marine Corps, 1968, 945 p.), proceeding through the occupation of Japan and the expedition to North China.

Hough's pathbreaking work should also be supplemented by the 15 USMC historical monographs and by Jeter A. Isely and Philip A. Crowl, **The U.S. Marines and Amphibious War** (Princeton: Princeton University Press, 1951, 636 p.); Robert L. Sherrod, **History of Marine Corps Aviation in World War II** (Washington: Combat Forces Press, 1952, 496 p.); and the lives of selected wartime Marine commanders: **Once a Marine,** by A. A. Vandegrift (New York: Norton, 1964, 338 p.); **Coral and Brass,** by Holland M. Smith (New York: Scribner, 1949, 289 p.); **Marine! The Life of Chesty Puller,** by Burke Davis (Boston: Little, Brown, 1962, 403 p.).

In the main, Hough's exciting and conscientious narrative has withstood the test of time and fulfilled its purpose: to recount what the Marine comradeship accomplished, "how they did it, and what they went through in the process."

LONG, GAVIN M. **MacArthur as Military Commander.** London: Batsford, 1969, 243 p.

There is no shortage of biographies of Douglas MacArthur, but few if any of them can be considered impartial or objective. All his life MacArthur was a controversial figure. He was a man who inspired awe and veneration or deep distrust; no one was neutral about him. His talents were great, but his character was flawed by excessive egotism and his military career marred by thwarted political ambition. But most of MacArthur's fifty years as a soldier, though controversial, are open to inspection, and it is this aspect of the general's life that Gavin

Long deals with in his biography. A wartime correspondent and editor of the Australian official history of World War II, the author views his subject more dispassionately than most Americans. But Australians, too, are divided in their feelings about MacArthur; many felt then and still do that he never gave them sufficient credit for their contribution to the Allied victory.

Long does his best, usually successfully, to overcome any bias he might feel as an Australian toward MacArthur. He briefly describes MacArthur's early life and career through the First World War. From then on, MacArthur's rise was meteoric, culminating in his appointment as Chief of Staff of the U.S. Army in 1930, a post he held for five years. The next six years he spent in the Philippines as Military Adviser to the Commonwealth, only to be called back to active service as commander of U.S. forces in the Far East in July 1941. The book traces MacArthur's campaigns in World War II in some detail and is generous in praise of the general's qualities as a commander. Passing quickly over the Occupation period, Long reviews MacArthur's conduct of the Korean War, in which the high point was, perhaps, the Inchon invasion.

On the whole, the author treats MacArthur fairly, better than many of his critics but not as well as his admirers would like. He is not blind to MacArthur's weaknesses, but he gives him high marks for his generalship and rates him as one of the great captains of our time.

STILWELL, JOSEPH WARREN. **The Stilwell Papers.** New York: Sloane, 1948, 357 p.

Perceptively edited by Theodore H. White after Stilwell died, these are raw diary entries, notes and letters jotted down by the U.S. Army's stormy petrel. Although sometimes softened, and pared to less than half of the total collection, enough remains to demonstrate the pungency and fire of the feisty general known as "Vinegar Joe." His materials span the period from December 1941 to October 1944, when he was relieved of command in the China-Burma-India theater and departed in an "atmosphere of crime." At the heart of the complex tragedy was Stilwell's honest but acerbic obsession about extirpating Japanese by using Lend-Lease and renovated Chinese military manpower. He knew and loved China, but he reserved fierce private contempt for Chiang Kai-shek, with whom he claimed he always maintained impersonal relations. While Chiang seemed convinced that Stilwell was conspiring with the communists to overthrow the Nationalist régime, Stilwell insisted that his "crime" was that "I tried to stand on my feet instead of my knees."

The Stilwell Papers should be tempered by reference to the official U.S. Army histories by Charles F. Romanus and Riley Sunderland, **The China-Burma-India Theater** (Washington: Department of the Army, Office of the Chief of Military History, 1953–1959, 3 v.); the unfriendly evaluation found in the biography of the ambassador to China, **Patrick J. Hurley,** by Don Lohbeck (Chicago: Regnery, 1956, 513 p.); the magisterial **Wedemeyer Reports!** by Stilwell's replacement, Albert C. Wedemeyer (New York: Holt, 1958, 497 p.); and the sympathetic impressions of two senior Britons, Vice Admiral Louis Mountbatten, **Report to the Combined Chiefs of Staff by the Supreme Allied Commander South-East Asia, 1943–1945** (New York: Philosophical Library, 1951, 280 p.), and Field-Marshal Sir William Slim, **Defeat into Victory.** Despite their partiality, however, **The Stilwell Papers** constitute an indispensable resource for study of wartime Sino-American relations, the campaigns in the Far East and postwar repercussions.

SLIM, SIR WILLIAM. **Defeat into Victory.** New York: McKay, 1961, 576 p.

Sir William Slim proved one of the ablest army commanders of World War II. His greatest achievement was the transformation of the discouraged survivors of 1942 into the fine Fourteenth Army of 1944. It was an amazing accomplishment— a triumph over natural hazards as well as the Japanese. The reconstruction on the inhospitable Indo-Assamese frontier was complicated by rampant malaria, shocking roads, the monsoon and supply shortages. Only Dakotas and mules made the problems supportable. Slim's hybrid army comprised 500,000 men holding 500 miles of front; many had to be convinced they were not the "Forgotten Army."

Sir William's account of the Burma campaigns is distinguished by historical accuracy and literary quality. His modesty and sense of responsibility emerge clearly. Successes he attributes largely to his superiors (particularly Mountbatten) or to his subordinates (especially Scoones, Snelling and Baldwin, RAF); failures he blames on no one but himself. The book is a military classic.

Conflicting strategic priorities and clashes of personality further bedevilled Slim. To Roosevelt and Chiang Kai-shek, Burma was a sideshow, protecting the tenuous air link with China; to Churchill it was a major war front. Slim was caught in the cross fire. Problems of coördination and Allied coöperation were aggravated by such strong-willed and contentious commanders as Wingate and Stilwell, but Slim proved equal to the situation. He emerged to win the defensive victory of Kohima-Imphal in 1944 and thereafter crossed the Irrawaddy to win the double success of Mandalay-Meiktila, thus breaking the Japanese hold on Burma. A master of administrative improvisation, he demonstrated what could be achieved through the proper use of air supply (based on air superiority).

Atomic Bomb; the Resistance; War Economy

LAURENCE, WILLIAM LEONARD. **Dawn over Zero.** New York: Knopf, 1946, 274 p.

So apocalyptic a series of events as the development, first explosion and first use in war of the atomic bomb inevitably inspired the making of many books. One of the earliest, Laurence's book has held up remarkably well. As told by the science reporter of *The New York Times,* the story has an emotional immediacy and a sense of the awesome which tended to diminish in later works, to their detriment. Laurence combines excellent factual science journalism with some of the first appropriate and deeply emotional warnings of the perils which the bomb held over mankind. In sufficient and clear detail for the average reader, he traces the evolution of nuclear physics from Sir James Chadwick's discovery of the neutron to the trip to Nagasaki on August 10, 1945, on which he was a passenger. Laurence expertly reviews the organization and production as well as research achievements of "the battle of the laboratories" in which the United States and Great Britain mobilized their scientific resources against the conviction that they were running a perilous race with German atomic scientists. It is startling to be reminded how little American scientists at the beginning of World War II thought about coöperation with the military, and how even the government was so little prepared for such coöperation that the scientists at first had to improvise their own security precautions. The freedom and informality which in 1939 still surrounded the most portentous research has been not the least of the casualties of what Laurence called "the potentialities of atomic energy on the loose."

FEIS, HERBERT. **The Atomic Bomb and the End of World War II.** Princeton: Princeton University Press, 1966, 213 p.

In **Japan Subdued,** the fifth and final volume of his account of the wartime alliance against the Axis, Herbert Feis detailed the great events of the four months from May 1945, when the war in Europe ended, to September of that year when Japan surrendered. In that volume, published in 1961, Feis dealt at length with the decisions that led to the final defeat of Japan. The great problem facing the Allied planners in the spring of 1945, Feis then wrote, was how to bring about the unconditional surrender of Japan as quickly as possible and at the lowest possible cost. He concluded that the United States could not have done other than it did in making the decision to use the atomic bomb.

The present volume represents Feis's response to the criticism of his earlier work as well as a revision based on the appearance of new material. The volume covers the same period and events as **Japan Subdued,** but additional material has been added, notably that dealing with the efforts of the scientists to establish international control of the bomb. Feis has also tempered his earlier judgment on the use of the atomic bomb. A major issue in the criticism leveled against the use of the bomb was the charge that it was intended to coerce Russia and that its use was not necessary to bring about the defeat of Japan, which was already defeated militarily and was seeking a way out of the war. Feis concedes this point in part in this work, but he does not go as far as others in asserting that the decision was made solely or even mainly for this reason.

Though the controversy over the use of the bomb is central to the volume, there is much noncontroversial material of value in Feis's work. The book presents a vivid picture of the perplexities and problems of the time and the factors that shaped the momentous decisions in the final days of the war. And, as in all his work, Feis writes with facility and authority and a broad understanding of the conduct of international affairs.

GRANET, MARIE and MICHEL, HENRI. **Combat: Histoire d'un Mouvement de Résistance de Juillet 1940 à Juillet 1943.** Paris: Presses Universitaires, 1957, 330 p.

If much of the vast literature on World War II European resistance movements is biographical, anecdotal and partisan, northwestern Europeans (including the Swiss and Swedes) are producing good official or semi-official histories. That of Belgium, for example, under the Ministry of National Education, has related sections for deportees and concentration camp victims. Henri Michel, the joint author of this fine book on one of the major organizations of the Resistance, also wrote the best survey of **Les Mouvements Clandestins en Europe (1938–1945)** (Paris: Presses Universitaires, 1961, 127 p.) before producing his massive **Les Courants de Pensée de la Résistance** (Paris: Presses Universitaires, 1962, 844 p.).

In Eastern and Southern Europe the subject remains entangled with diverse ideas of guerrilla war and Marxist and nationalist claims and panaceas. There are few analyses of the military—as distinct from the economic, psychological and political—effectiveness of these movements. They gave the Allies much strategical information, but could not furnish timely tactical intelligence and aid in thickly settled areas with good communications; and German troop movements were seriously hampered only in the "natural" guerrilla areas of southern and central France, Greece, Jugoslavia and White Russia.

HANCOCK, WILLIAM KEITH and GOWING, M. M. **British War Economy.** London: H.M.S.O., 1949, 583 p.

Only the United Kingdom and Australia have produced civil histories of the Second World War which rank with the Carnegie Endowment **Economic and Social History of the World War,** edited by James T. Shotwell. Hancock and Gowing introduce the official British "Civil Series" which deals with "War Production, Civil Industry and Commerce, Financial Policy, Manpower, Shipping, Land Transport, Food Policy, Agriculture, Fuel and Power, Building, War-time Social Services (including Education), Civil Defence, Economic Warfare, [and] Colonial Policy." Most of the authors shift from the specific to the general with great skill; most of them also deal with Britain's partial dependence on American, Commonwealth and neutral resources. Hancock's and Gowing's volume is one of three "synoptic" treatments. The others, equally important for an understanding of Britain's war effort and the welfare state which developed from what was, in a very real sense, a people's war directed by a "Ministry of all the Talents," are M. M. Postan, **British War Production** (London: H.M.S.O. and Longmans, 1952, 512 p.), and Richard M. Titmuss, **Problems of Social Policy** (London: H.M.S.O. and Longmans, 1950, 596 p.). All of them begin with the heritage of the Great War, the long armistice and, for Britain, the long Depression. Titmuss ranges from the social services to families under strain in a classic social history. Hancock, who edited the series, has brilliantly summed up some of its "lessons" in "War in This Century" in his **Four Studies of War and Peace in This Century.**

IV. THE POSTWAR PERIOD

EAST-WEST RELATIONS

General

BALDWIN, HANSON WEIGHTMAN. **The Price of Power.** New York: Harper (for the Council on Foreign Relations), 1948, 361 p.

This book, of which Mr. Baldwin is the main author, was based on the discussions of a study group formed in the autumn of 1945 under the auspices of the Council on Foreign Relations, which met some 18 times before concluding its labors in the spring of 1947. The volume represents, therefore, an informed collective effort by a group of well-qualified people to think through the problems of American military policy as they presented themselves in the immediate aftermath of World War II and the inauguration of atomic weapons. A product of the pre-missile, pre-sputnik and even the pre-sonic barrier age, its reasonings and findings have been generally overtaken by the revolutionary advances in military technology that marked the 1950s and 1960s. It nevertheless foreshadowed many of the American and Western military responses of the immediate postwar years, some of which have endured to the 1970s; and it stands, in its capacity as a record of the way the world looked to American strategic thinkers just after the ending of the Second World War, as a historical document of considerable importance.

JACQUOT, P. E. **Essai de Stratégie Occidentale.** Paris: Gallimard, 1953, 202 p.

In this work, prefaced by an introduction from the pen of André Malraux, General Jacquot, a professional soldier and World War II *maquis* fighter, outlined a new strategy for the West. It was his view that—the apparent Soviet military preponderance notwithstanding—an autonomous defense of Western Europe, and of France in the first instance, could reasonably be envisaged and should be undertaken. Although the book was written before the emergence of the Chinese-Soviet schism, the assessment of the nature and limitations of Soviet power was based on a keen awareness of geographic factors and especially of the exposed nature of the far-flung Soviet borders in Asia; and it was, in this respect, in strong contrast to the thinking of many other Western commentators. Reflecting as it did a point of view soon to be generally accepted by the French military establishment, Jacquot's work not only helps to explain the later decision to develop an independent French atomic *force de frappe* but may well have had a considerable influence upon it. It remains, for this reason, a significant historical document.

LERNER, DANIEL and ARON, RAYMOND, eds. **France Defeats EDC.** New York: Praeger, 1957, 225 p.

This series of essays by a distinguished group of French and American authors constitutes a species of intellectual autopsy on the defunct European Defense Community. Some of the authors, for instance André Philip, had favored the proposed arrangement; others, such as Jacques Fauvet, had opposed it. The book constitutes, therefore, not only an interesting effort of introspection but also a useful tool of research into national and cultural attitudes, some temporary and specific but others of a permanent nature, the recognition of which is essential to an understanding of that phase of European and Atlantic history. The essays serve both to illustrate and to explain the paradox that an institution conceived as a means of preventing German rearmament should have been ultimately defeated in the name of a fear of German militarism and then replaced by arrangements involving the entry of the German Federal Republic into NATO with an army of its own. The authors correctly foresaw that the "quest for a common European policy and an acceptable institutional housing for that policy" would continue to occupy the Western powers for many years to come. Many of the great domestic and international issues that have agitated the political scene in the period following the conclusion of the Treaty of Rome can be traced back to those so competently analyzed in this book.

DULLES, JOHN FOSTER. **War or Peace.** New York: Macmillan, 1950, 274 p.

This book, written by the future Secretary of State of the Eisenhower administration, was completed less than three years before the triumph of the Republicans in the 1952 election and the author's appointment to that high position. It reflects his awareness of the possibility of such a turn of events, as well as his natural desire to promote its realization. Drafted, presumably, in late 1949 when the author was serving under an interim appointment as United States Senator from the state of New York, the book must be considered against the background of the Truman Doctrine, the Marshall Plan and the North Atlantic Treaty, all of which were then prominently in the public mind. It contains a detailed account of the author's participation, as a representative of the Republican opposition, in a number of the international conferences and encounters of the 1945–1950 period and in this way adds significantly to the record of the East-West exchanges of that period. In the second portion of the book, Mr. Dulles outlined his views as to the directions which American policy ought to take in the coming period, stressing the need for bipartisanship in American foreign policy, particularly in Asia, for modifications of the charter and procedures of the United Nations, for greater unity in Europe, for preparation of an anti-communist alliance in East Asia and the Pacific and for a more aggressive American policy on the ideological front of the cold war, designed to take advantage of the internal weaknesses of the leading communist powers.

BURNHAM, JAMES. **Containment or Liberation? An Inquiry into the Aims of United States Foreign Policy.** New York: Day, 1953, 256 p.

This was the best known and best written of the numerous attacks from the conservative anti-communist side on the so-called "doctrine of containment," believed in those quarters to constitute the basis of American policy toward Soviet Russia in the late 1940s and early 1950s. The author urged the replacement of this policy by one directed at the disruption of the Soviet system of power and the "liberation" of the subject nationalities of the satellite area and the Soviet Union proper. Written in 1952, shortly before Stalin's death, the argument was of course based on the image of Soviet power that prevailed toward the end of the Stalin era, and in this sense was bound to be partially overtaken by the changes shortly to occur in Russia and Eastern Europe in the period of the post-Stalin "thaw." Nevertheless, it stands as the clearest and most influential statement of rationale of the sharp attacks mounted from the conservative right from 1949 to 1952 on the Truman policy toward Russia; and it continued to have an effect on thinking through the 1950s and even into the 1960s.

TRUKHANOVSKII, VLADIMIR GRIGOR'EVICH, *ed.* **Istoriia Mezhdunarodnykh Otnoshenii i Vneshnei Politiki SSSR.** Moscow: Institut Mezhdunarodnykh Otnoshenii, 1963, 901 p.

This work consists of three volumes, only the last of which deals with the post-1945 period, the narration running up to 1963. It is the collective work of a group of some 20 Soviet scholars, working under the direction and editorship of the prominent Soviet historian Vladimir Grigor'evich Trukhanovskii, and is intended as a textbook for university students and others interested in the history of Soviet foreign policy. Prepared, as any such work would be, under the most careful control of the Communist Party, it should be taken not as an attempt at an objective view of the events of the period in question but rather as a description of these events as the Party would like them to be known and understood, both by Soviet students and by the world public generally. A measure of the degree of objectivity may be found in the fact that the authors contrive to discuss the Berlin crisis and blockade of 1948–1949 without ever mentioning the Western airlift. This is only one of several studies which could serve equally well as expression of the official Soviet version of the events of the period; but the differences between them, in content and treatment, are so slight that a single example will do.

ROBERTS, HENRY LITHGOW. **Russia and America: Dangers and Prospects.** New York: Harper (for the Council on Foreign Relations), 1956, 251 p.

This book had its origins in the discussions of a study group at the Council on Foreign Relations during the years 1953–1955. Addressed to the worldwide range of Soviet-American relations in the oncoming thermonuclear age, it attempts both assessment and broad policy recommendations.

In retrospect, perhaps the most interesting—illuminating as well as limiting—feature of the book lies in the particular period of time in which it was prepared: the uncertain years following Stalin's death but before Khrushchev's anti-Stalin speech, the 1956 upheavals in Eastern Europe and the subsequent rifts in the communist bloc. In consequence, the communist world is here seen as still a single, purposeful unit (the possibility of schisms is envisaged but prudence cautioned against counting on them), and the conclusions drawn with respect to American military, economic and regional policy tend to follow from this perception. Hence, the book serves as a reasonably coherent exposition of the American premises of what might be called phase two of the cold war, a phase that extended into the early 1960s.

Cold War; Coexistence

See also War and Peace: Arms Control, p. 228.

ARNOLD, G. L. **The Pattern of World Conflict.** New York: Dial Press, 1955, 250 p.

In this thoughtful and well-written work, the author considers the cold war primarily from the standpoint of the changing nature of the economic and political relationship between Britain and the other advanced Western countries on the one hand, and the underdeveloped world on the other. He believes that only with the acceptance of the principle of economic planning within a democratic context, as an alternative to the laissez-faire liberalism of the prewar decades, does the West have a chance of finding a new relationship to the underdeveloped countries sufficiently productive and hopeful to compete successfully with the political pressures being brought to bear on these countries from the communist side. The author's thinking, bearing the intellectual and semantic traces of a moderate-Marxist continental education, is impressive in its logic and lucidity of statement. Some of its premises have, however, been severely dealt with by the developments of subsequent years. The author was unable to foresee either the economic miracle that was shortly to overtake large parts of Western Europe, or the difficulties which the Soviet economy would suffer in the coming period, or indeed the general development of polycentrism within the circle of communist states. Much of the argument is thus historically dated; but such is the author's acumen that considerable parts of the treatise, particularly the historical observations and the passages dealing with the phenomenon of poverty versus affluence, still make interesting and impressive reading.

LUKACS, JOHN ADALBERT. **A History of the Cold War.** Garden City: Doubleday, 1961, 288 p.

This book was first published in 1961 and treated events only up to the U-2 episode in May 1960. A second (Anchor) edition, published in 1962 (Garden City: Doubleday, rev. ed., 1962, 348 p.), extended the scope through the year 1961. The author, who describes himself as "Catholic, a Westerner, European by birth, now a citizen of the United States," is by profession a teacher and by temperament and avocation an essayist and analytical historian of the first order. What he has produced here is, in its first part, a chronological narrative and discussion of Russian-American relations over the crucial years from 1945 to 1961 and, in its second part, a series of critical essays on the two contending powers, treating them successively as peoples, societies, states and nations. Drawn from a very broad though frankly Western historical perspective, this study constitutes one of the most thoughtful and penetrating of the contemporary examinations of the cold war.

HALLE, LOUIS J. **The Cold War as History.** New York: Harper and Row, 1967, 434 p.

The cold war is viewed in this work, to use the author's words, as a "spasm" in Russia's perennial conflict with the West, "brought on by a collapse of the Western power structure." The period of this spasm is seen as lasting from 1945 to 1962; and it is to the events of this period that the book is addressed. This is less a chronological account of the cold war than a highly thoughtful and even contemplative consideration of the impulses on both sides that inspired it and determined its course. The author distinguishes carefully between the elements of myth and rhetoric on the one hand, and preoccupation with problems of power on the other, as formative factors in the statesmanship of both sides. Drawn from the author's personal experience as an official in the State Department as well as from his many subsequent years of creative work as a historian, this treatise stands in point of balance, detachment and penetration in the first rank of studies of the cold war.

PERROUX, FRANÇOIS. **La Coexistence Pacifique.** Paris: Presses Universitaires, 1958, 3 v.

In these three solid volumes, written with a certain taste for original semantics but with marked scientific detachment, the distinguished French economist François Perroux tests his own economic theories against the general problem of competitive coexistence between East and West. The first volume is devoted to an analysis of the inner contradictions of capitalism and of communism; the second traces the interaction between the two systems; the third discusses their respective approaches to the needs of the less-developed world. Professor Perroux is unabashedly an economic determinist. In his view, the primary factor governing social and political development in both systems is not any independent political will but rather the lagging of "productive relations" behind "productive forces." His economics, despite this determinism, are not purely Marxist, nor do they amount simply to a cut-and-dried accounting of material resources; they embrace the full scope of human activity. Since man, as he sees it, is man everywhere, the two economic systems ought theoretically to converge; but self-created rigidities in the conduct of the superpowers interpose obstacles, just as mutual competition forces them to an economic expansion they might not otherwise choose. Brilliant and highly theoretical, these volumes will have enduring value as a superior and authoritative expression of a typical French-intellectual reaction to the cold war.

BARNET, RICHARD J. and RASKIN, MARCUS G. **After 20 Years: Alternatives to the Cold War in Europe.** New York: Random House, 1965, 243 p.

This thoughtful discussion, written jointly by two co-directors of the Institute for Policy Studies in Washington, both of whom had recently served as disarmament advisers to the Kennedy administration, constitutes primarily an attack on the political and strategic concepts that dominated America's policy during the first two postwar decades, and particularly on the commitment to NATO as the kingpin of that policy. It urges an effort to end, or at least greatly to moderate, the cold war by a process of deëmphasis on the nuclear weapon, disengagement in Europe, replacement of NATO by a European security pact, and a new and positive universalistic focus of American policy to replace the negative regional one which NATO, in the view of the authors, represented. Written on the eve of the great expansion of America's involvement in Vietnam, the positive aspects of this argument were destined to be largely vitiated shortly after the book's appearance by that development and by the growing American disillusionment with foreign aid and with universalistic developmental undertakings generally. But the book turns out to have had an almost prophetic relevance to the efforts by Chancellor Willy Brandt, at the beginning of the 1970s, to arrive at a modus vivendi with Germany's eastern neighbors, to the nuclear nonproliferation treaty and to the SALT talks. It constitutes excellent background reading with relation to all those developments.

DAVISON, WALTER PHILLIPS. **The Berlin Blockade: A Study in Cold War Politics.** Princeton: Princeton University Press, 1958, 423 p.

Of all the episodes in the early cold war, the Berlin blockade of 1948–1949 was the principal test of will between the West and the Soviet Union and was also the most dramatic instance of successful resistance to Stalinist force. The symbolic influence of the airlift, which sustained the life of the city for nearly a year, became so great that when it ended after the blockade was lifted, many Berliners became psychologically disoriented. Davison's study notes the strong interaction of many levels of the conflict; it was evidently the purpose of the Russians in 1948 to exploit the exposed and vulnerable Western forces in the city as leverage to prevent the establishment of a West German state; yet as the contest of wills developed, it would seem that their goal shifted to simply obtaining control of the whole city for themselves.

In this contest of wills it was the American command in Germany and West Berlin, coupled with the SPD leadership in the city, which played the crucial role in sustaining a will to survive. Even after the airlift was instituted in the summer of 1948, Washington officialdom regarded it skeptically as at best a holding operation, a device to gain time for diplomatic negotiations with the Russians; its potentiality for breaking the blockade was not recognized early enough. This accounts in part for the weak bargaining posture taken by the Americans in Moscow in late August which led to vague preliminary agreement on introducing Soviet-sponsored currency under four-power control in the city. The author is critical of what he sees as the overly legal attitude taken by the Americans toward the situation: seeing Soviet manoeuvres as violations of legal rights, they were only secondarily concerned with the power play. Yet it may have been precisely this rigidity which saved the situation. Had the stress been upon power, the Americans with misplaced prudence might have recognized their extraordinary inferiority in the local situation and withdrawn. The author does not address the question: If the airlift really did break the blockade, why did not Washington press its advantage to seek firm Soviet guarantees of further access?

SAKHAROV, ANDREI D. **Progress, Coexistence, and Intellectual Freedom.** New York: Norton, 1968, 158 p.

The appearance in the West of this brief monograph from the pen of a prominent member of the Soviet scientific intelligentsia was one of the sensations of the late 1960s. The author is a distinguished Soviet scientist—one of the creators of the Soviet technology of hydrogen fusion. The work is replete with views, such as the theory of "convergence" (of the socialist and capitalist systems), the rejection of the theory of inevitable conflict between the two systems, the equal condemnation of American policies in Indochina and Soviet policies in the Middle East, which are positively heretical in relation to the current Soviet party line. The author deplores the continued competition of the Soviet Union and the United States in the development of the weapons of mass destruction, sees in its continuation only an irreparable disaster for the entire world and urges that it be replaced by the collaboration of the two powers in the struggle against poverty and pollution on a worldwide scale. He sees the collaboration as leading ultimately to a form of world government. He emphatically rejects the harshness and rigidities of the Stalinist heritage in Russia and pleads for respect for human rights and particularly for freedom of information and expression. The competent introduction and annotations by Harrison Salisbury add materially to the intelligibility of the document from the standpoint of the unschooled American reader.

The Economics of Competitive Coexistence. Washington: National Planning Association, 1959–1961, 8 v.

In 1956 the International Committee of the National Planning Association, in Washington, stimulated by a growing awareness in the United States of the trade-and-aid drives then being developed by the Soviet Union and Communist China, put in hand a series of studies under the title of "The Economics of Competitive Coexistence." When completed in 1961, the series consisted of eight monographs by different authors. The first seven dealt, successively, with Soviet growth and capabilities and with Russia's role in east central Europe, with the position of Germany between East and West, with the political-economic strategy of the Chinese Communist régime, with Japan's position with relation to China and the West, and with the positions, respectively, of India and Afghanistan with relation to the East-West competition. In the last volume, **Coexistence: Economic Challenge and Response** (1961, 323 p.), the project director, Professor Henry G. Aubrey, conducted an imaginative and useful exploration of American reactions to the Sino-Soviet drive.

LINCOLN, GEORGE ARTHUR and OTHERS, *eds.* **Economics of National Security.** New York: Prentice-Hall, 2d ed., 1954, 643 p.

Professor Lincoln and seven of his associates at the United States Military Academy examined here the economic implications of efforts to achieve security in a threatening, non-war situation such as that of 1950. The threat, as defined, was Soviet communism—worldwide, total and of indefinite duration. The response required preparedness for the full mobilization of resources. The problem to which the authors addressed themselves centered in finance and the danger of upsetting economic equilibrium. The international aspects which are explored are economic warfare, collective security with its problems of programming and burden-sharing, and foreign mutual assistance for national security. It is the only book of its kind and fortunately is thorough and objective.

ADLER-KARLSSON, GUNNAR. **Western Economic Warfare 1947–1967: A Case Study in Foreign Economic Policy.** Stockholm: Almqvist, 1968, 319 p.

This is by far the most detailed account of the cold war as it was reflected in restrictions by the West on trade with the non-Asian communist countries. Although not sympathetic with the embargo, the Swedish author gives the history in detail, plus the viewpoints of the various countries involved. His interpretation of the American state of mind in the initiating stages does not quite catch the impact of a relatively sudden recognition of Soviet military capabilities. He does present clearly the extent of the pressure put on other countries. The Russians themselves contributed unwittingly to the maintenance of the embargo by taking some provocative action whenever the tension began to relax. While the embargo probably delayed the Soviet military build-up by only a few months, it showed up certain weak spots, *i.e.* ball bearings, and forced the bloc into a greater drive for self-sufficiency. The embargo policy began to crumble in 1953, although important traces still remain in 1970. The author has difficulty in measuring at all exactly the economic effects of the policy, since it was only one element in the complex economic life of all modern countries.

NORTH ATLANTIC TREATY (NATO);
ATLANTIC COMMUNITY

Atlantic Alliance: NATO's Role in the Free World. New York: Royal Institute of International Affairs, 1952, 172 p.

This book records the conclusions of a Chatham House study group which deliberated in 1951–1952, under the chairmanship of Lord Brand, and included a number of people experienced in foreign and military affairs. It was a follow-up study to **Defence in the Cold War: The Task for the Free World** (New York: Royal Institute of International Affairs, 1950, 123 p.), which had appeared in October 1950. Expressing the shock precipitated by the Korean War, this first study had emphasized the "real nature and extent of the dangers confronting the United Kingdom and its friends in the free world" and had concluded that peace could be preserved only if the free nations of the West formed a close and militarily powerful partnership. The second report—like the first, written by Donald McLachlan—assessed the work of the NATO alliance, made several concrete suggestions for improving its structure and military preparedness and advocated the inclusion of West Germany in the alliance. It examined the possibilities of a European Defense Community. Pointing to the need for more integration in the alliance, especially regarding foreign policy, the report clearly looked forward to the establishment of an "Atlantic Community" but also noted the reluctance of member governments to accept appropriate modifications of national sovereignty.

KNORR, KLAUS EUGEN, *ed.* **NATO and American Security.** Princeton: Princeton University Press, 1959, 342 p.

This volume of papers delivered by a number of experts at a conference held at Princeton University in January 1958 discussed primarily problems of military strategy and tactics at a time when a strategic nuclear deadlock, characterized by a balance of terror between the United States and the Soviet Union, was definitely in the making. Since the prevailing posture of massive reprisal for deterring Soviet aggression in Europe had by this time become obsolescent, the crucial question was whether the assumptions relating to the protection of Western Europe were in need of basic revision. Various papers examined the merits and demerits of independent European nuclear deterrent forces under national or collective control, various forms of "nuclear sharing" and limited rather than massive nuclear reprisal against aggression. Among the conclusions were that, despite changes in military technology, there was no viable alternative to NATO, that deterrence by means of controlled and limited escalation deserved serious consideration and that—despite European reluctance—limited war forces on the European continent, especially forces with conventional armament, had to play an increasing role in any arrangements for European security. The conference papers served as part of the background for the modification of the deterrence policy which was effected under the Kennedy administration.

MOORE, BEN TILLMAN. **NATO and the Future of Europe.** New York: Harper (for the Council on Foreign Relations), 1958, 263 p.

This book is the product of a study group organized by the Council on Foreign Relations in New York in 1955 under the chairmanship of William C. Foster. Written after the development of nuclear arms by the Soviet Union and, indeed, under the shadow of emerging "nuclear plenty," it was based on rather pessimistic premises about the viability of the existing NATO structure. It noted NATO's "strategic dilemma" posed by the dependence of the European NATO allies on American military power in the face of the fact that the U.S.S.R. was beginning to develop deterrent power vis-à-vis the United States. Convinced that the system of nation-states in Europe was "dying," and seeing Western Europe faced with the choice between an Atlantic federation and an economic and military union, the author concluded that European union was immediately more practicable. He defined the required kind of integration as a "common market" in economic terms and an "integrated nuclear force" in military terms, strong enough to deter Soviet aggression independently. Analyzing various problems of economic integration, the author hoped that an "Atlantic Community" devoted to various constructive tasks, rather than merely to defense, might be built on the foundation of a more equal military and economic partnership between a united Western Europe and the United States.

HINTERHOFF, EUGÈNE. **Disengagement.** London: Stevens, 1959, 445 p.

Captain Hinterhoff's book consists essentially of an exhaustive inventory of statements made, or positions taken, by private parties and governmental figures with respect to the possibility of a separation or thinning out of the NATO and Soviet forces in Central Europe. In conclusion, the author presents his own proposal for a gradual and controlled withdrawal of nonlocal forces from Germany, Poland, Czechoslovakia and Hungary, to be followed by German unification, initially on a federal basis. Its argument proceeding mainly from a rich collection of quoted excerpts from other sources, the work is uniquely valuable, if not invariably complete or wholly accurate, as a compendium of the various ideas and proposals that have been advanced in this connection and the international discussion they have evoked. Nine of the more important official documents are reproduced *in extenso* in the Annex to the work. For the rest, grateful as he will be to Captain Hinterhoff for this careful listing, the reader will in some instances wish to consult the original documents for a complete understanding of their tenor.

SCHMIDT, HELMUT. **Defense or Retaliation: A German View.** New York: Praeger, 1962, 264 p.

This work, first published in German in 1961, constituted without question—even at the time of its publication—one of the most important, if not the most important, of the continental contributions to the analytical literature on the problem of Western defense in the NATO era. But its importance became greatly heightened eight years later with the appointment of its author, in October 1969, to the position of Minister of Defense of the German Federal Republic. Taking emphatic objection to the concept of mingling nuclear and conventional weapons in a common deterrent force, insisting that strategic and tactical nuclear weapons constitute credible deterrents only to the use, in each case, of the same category of weapons by the other side, Herr Schmidt refused to accept any suggestion that the value of conventional weapons has been undermined by the existence of the nuclear ones, argued with great logic and effectiveness for the strengthening, qualitatively and quantitatively, of NATO's conventional forces, and advocated the strict separation of control and plans for employment of the tactical nuclear weapons from those of the conventional ones. It is clear that his views had, subsequently, a significant impact on NATO policy; and this book, in which they were first systematically set forth, acquires accordingly the importance of a basic text.

FOX, WILLIAM T. R. and FOX, ANNETTE B. **NATO and the Range of American Choice.** New York: Columbia University Press, 1967, 352 p.

Although defined by its authors as "a book about the United States government in NATO and not about NATO itself," this painstaking and comprehensive study, written by the Director and a research associate of the Columbia University Institute of War and Peace Studies, represents, particularly in the first six of its ten chapters, one of the most readable and generally useful descriptions of the alliance's origins as well as its evolution—in structure, policy and method of operation—over the years. That it does so is attributable partly to the predominant role of the United States in the alliance, which renders a history of American participation largely coincidental with the history of the organization itself, but also to the consistently high level of scholarly precision by which the study is marked. The careful comparisons of NATO with other alliances and international organizations lead the authors to certain general conclusions (set forth in an appendix) concerning the possibilities for "organized alliance" generally, and of the strictures and necessities that appear to rest upon this mode of dealing with international security problems.

CLEVELAND, HAROLD VAN B. **The Atlantic Idea and Its European Rivals.** New York: McGraw-Hill (for the Council on Foreign Relations), 1966, 186 p.

This volume was written by the Director of the Atlantic Policy Studies at the Council on Foreign Relations and constitutes the central item of the series of studies produced under that program. The questions with which the book deals are, in essence, those flowing from the dichotomy within the NATO community between the Atlantic concept of mutual relationships among the respective powers and the concept of European unity. Examining primarily the military and the economic (financial and commercial) aspects of these problems, the author comes to the conclusion that while there does exist a certain essential conflict between these two concepts, and while in the commercial field the tendency is toward a weakening of the Atlantic concept in favor of the European one, the most powerful determining factor in shaping the interrelationships of the members of the Western community is still to be found in their common security interests, and particularly in the need of the European partners for American nuclear protection in the face of Soviet military power—a need to which, in the author's view, no acceptable alternative has yet been found.

BELL, CORAL. **Negotiation from Strength.** New York: Knopf, 1963, 248 p.

Miss Bell is an Australian scholar who has studied extensively in both England and the United States and whose earlier experience includes both diplomatic and academic phases. In this volume, written in the early 1960s, she has taken as her point of departure the verbal commitments of a number of leading Western statesmen—Churchill, Acheson, Adenauer, Nixon, Rusk and John Kennedy—to the principle of "negotiation from strength" and, as a test of the effectiveness of that principle, has subjected the nature and course of NATO's military and diplomatic policies over the course of the decade of the 1950s to an extremely sharp and perceptive analysis. Her conclusion is that the policies in question led neither to strength nor to any significant negotiation. In summarizing the reasons for this failure, she argues that "the compounded pluralism of decision-making in an alliance of democracies vitiated the effort at strength" whereas "the chosen concept of strength" (outstandingly the incorporation of West Germany into the structure of NATO) "ruled out the one promising issue for negotiation."

BARCIA TRELLES, CAMILO. **El Pacto del Atlántico.** Madrid: Instituto de Estudios Políticos, 1950, 685 p.

This volume, written very shortly after conclusion of the North Atlantic Pact, is interesting and useful as a view of the cold war in its early phases from a Spanish perspective. The author points out that during the four hundred years of preëminence of Spain, Portugal, England, France and Holland, it was the maritime powers that were strong and expansionist. Now this role, as he sees it, has been transferred to Russia, outstandingly a land power. America, on the other hand, while actually a great maritime power, has been reduced to a defensive role. Confusion is further compounded, in his view, by the fact that while Russia is ostensibly and in the geographic sense a European power and the United States is not, the latter is actually more European than the former in point of ethnic origins and cultural orientation. The author, a protagonist of old-fashioned geopolitics and disinclined to give high importance to ideology, sees in this state of affairs a revolutionary reversal of traditional roles and functions in international life, in the face of which the future of world politics appears to him hopelessly obscure. The book includes not only an account of major postwar events in international politics but also summaries of certain of the major current theories of geopolitics.

BUCHAN, ALASTAIR and WINDSOR, PHILIP. **Arms and Stability in Europe.** New York: Praeger (for the Institute for Strategic Studies, London), 1963, 236 p.

This study, prepared by the Director and a research staff member of the London Institute for Strategic Studies, reflects the impressions of extensive discussions conducted in 1961 and 1962 between members of that organization and two eminent continental institutions of similar character: Le Centre d'Études de Politique Étrangère in Paris and Die Deutsche Gesellschaft für Auswärtige Politik in Bonn. It thus represents a uniquely authoritative view of the problems of Western defense as they appeared at that juncture to a group of highly qualified private European experts. Prepared under the impact of the Kennedy administration's new emphasis on the development of a wider and more flexible spectrum of deterrent capabilities than just the strategic nuclear one in which the Europeans had grown accustomed to seeing their safety, the study reflects the uneasiness which that shift of policy occasioned in Europe; and much of it was devoted, accordingly, to the thorny question of control over the use of nuclear weapons within the NATO community. The authors were at pains to see whether there could not be found an arms control policy which, while stabilizing the military situation in Europe and avoiding an escalation of the arms race, would not bar the way to political settlements. The most promising approach seemed to them to lie along the lines of a reorganization of NATO's central institutions, involving a separation of the strategic planning from the ownership of nuclear weapons, and the establishment within the NATO framework of a European defense authority to assume major responsibility for certain of the functions of the alliance theretofore performed only in consultations between the European members and the United States.

KISSINGER, HENRY A. **The Troubled Partnership: A Re-appraisal of the Atlantic Alliance.** New York: McGraw-Hill (for the Council on Foreign Relations), 1965, 266 p.

The enduring value of this work is of course enhanced by the fact of Professor Kissinger's later service as President Nixon's adviser on matters of foreign policy, but the author's brilliance and the profundity of his preoccupation with the problems involved would have assured it a prominent place in any listing of the pertinent literature of the period in any case. Based on lectures delivered at the Council on Foreign Relations in early 1964, shortly after De Gaulle's veto of British membership in the Common Market, it represents an exploration in great depth of the problems of defense and political relationships among the NATO powers, as they presented themselves at that troubled moment in the mid-1960s. The author favored, in preference to the multilateral-force concept then under discussion, the formation of an allied nuclear force, to be made up of American and British (and eventually French) nuclear weapons, and to be controlled by a six-member executive committee of the NATO Council. The book was predicated on the assumption of an unchallengeable Soviet superiority in conventional forces in the European theater—an assumption destined soon to be at least weakened by the further development of the Chinese-Soviet conflict. Also, it predated, and could not therefore take into account, the great distraction of American resources and attention which the Vietnam involvement was soon destined to produce.

BALL, MARY MARGARET. **NATO and the European Union Movement.** New York: Praeger (for the London Institute of World Affairs), 1959, 486 p.

For anyone desirous of unravelling the interrelationships among the main international organizations of the North Atlantic–Western European community, as these had developed down to 1958, Professor Ball's book will be an indispensable aid. In this volume, the author gives her attention to NATO, the Council of Europe, the Organization for European Economic Coöperation (OEEC), Benelux, the "Europe of the Six" as embodied in the European Coal and Steel Community, the Common Market and Euratom, and the "Europe of the Seven" as represented by the Western European Union. The United Nations Economic Commission for Europe (ECE) and the European Free Trade Area, established at a later date, are not specifically treated. In the final chapter, Miss Ball examines in detail the various proposals and possibilities for consolidation designed to reduce to a more rigorous order the existing bewildering bureaucratic profusion of these international bodies and traces the advantages and drawbacks of each. She comes to the conclusion that there is little that could be done in this direction that would not create more problems than it would solve, and that the best hopes for progress in the streamlining and coördination of these various activities lie in the realm of substance rather than of form.

Britain in Western Europe. New York: Royal Institute of International Affairs, 1956, 121 p.

This was the last of the three Chatham House study group reports produced in the period 1950–1955, the earlier two being **Defence in the Cold War** and **Atlantic Alliance: NATO's Role in the Free World.** Written by the rapporteur of the group, Charles Janson, this report deals primarily with the formation and significance of Western European Union, as recently constituted in the wake of the failure of the effort to form a European Defense Community. A large part of the paper is taken up with an excellent and highly useful summary of the various steps and negotiations that led, from the outbreak of the Korean War and the emergence of a more intensive demand for German contribution to Western defense, down through the failure of the EDC proposal and the acceptance of West Germany into NATO, to the constitution of the WEU. The group, in its conclusions, saw only a dim future for WEU so long as the United States continued to be actively and intimately involved in NATO but recognized, perceptively, that if there were ever to be a diminution of America's involvement in the problems of Western Europe's defense, then WEU might achieve a different order of significance. Had they been able to foresee the emergence, 15 years hence, of a serious possibility of Britain's adherence to the Common Market, they would no doubt have recognized in this development, too, the possibility of a new and heightened role for the organization in question.

VAN DER BEUGEL, ERNST H. **From Marshall Aid to Atlantic Partnership: European Integration as a Concern of American Foreign Policy.** New York: Elsevier, 1966, 480 p.

This lucid and well-documented account of United States European policy was written by a distinguished citizen of the Atlantic commonwealth, a former Minister of State for Foreign Affairs in the Netherlands and European Secretary for the Bilderberg meetings. It owes much of its value to the author's familiarity with the protagonists of the drama and to his perspicacity in analyzing American motives. Written under the shadow of De Tocqueville's awesome prophecy about "Russians and Americans swaying the destiny of half the globe," it retraces the main thrust of American policy in the cold war. After World War II, Van der Beugel asserts, isolationism was defunct. In the first phase of an active policy, the United States sought European integration principally through economic means; in a second, a broader Atlantic community. Both efforts were conceived as means of containing Soviet power. In the evolution of these efforts, military concerns progressively overtook and swallowed the economic ones. The study remains one-sided in so far as it fails to deal with the pull of extra-European concerns on great-power policy in the postwar era; but within its limits, it remains an outstanding contribution to the understanding of American policies, written with the insight of a statesman and the conscientiousness of an accomplished scholar.

RITCHIE, RONALD S. **NATO: The Economics of an Alliance.** Toronto: Ryerson (for the Canadian Institute of International Affairs), 1956, 147 p.

This little book discusses the seldom recognized economic aspects of NATO. The larger part is devoted to the central problem of burden-sharing in an alliance, made particularly difficult in that the economic burden on national budgets and on manpower was assumed reluctantly. The record clearly shows the difficulties in a procedure which consists in determining the total amount of the costs of a common policy and then dividing this sum among the member nations. The problem is well illustrated in a special chapter devoted to the Canadian share. The author also examines other economic facets of the alliance, such as the part played by military coöperation in standardizing equipment and allocating sources of supply. In some cases, the activity of NATO has helped to reduce foreign policy disagreements among its members and to encourage a common posture toward other countries, for example, in regard to trade.

WESTERN ECONOMIC COÖPERATION

See also European Integration, p. 454.

WOODBRIDGE, GEORGE, *comp.* **UNRRA.** New York: Columbia University Press, 1950, 3 v.

This is the only official history of any of the relief and recovery agencies. Short-lived as it was, the United Nations Relief and Rehabilitation Administration broke the ground for international coöperation in the organized international provision of economic assistance. The first volume deals with organization and administration, the second describes activities in the field country by country, and the third contains resolutions, country agreements, administrative orders and summary statistics. This is a study of the life of an organization prepared by its official historian. It covers UNRRA admirably, but there is only limited discussion of the related internal problems of either recipients or donors. Those were not part of the UNRRA record and thus not readily available to the team of experts who prepared the study.

CROWTHER, GEOFFREY. **The Economic Reconstruction of Europe.** Claremont: Claremont College, 1948, 79 p.

This slight volume contains three lectures given by the editor of *The Economist* at Claremont, California, before the takeover of Czechoslovakia and final action on the Marshall Plan. While Crowther recognized the economic and political difficulties and dislocations of the time, he nevertheless viewed the future with optimism. His chief uncertainty centered around the question of what would happen to the German economy. Arguing that a greater measure of government control of economic affairs in Western Europe was inevitable, he recognized the same trend in the United States and concluded that the differences in that respect were merely a matter of degree and not of kind. To avoid the extremes of nationalism and to deal with the German problem, he advocated a much closer union of the countries of Western Europe—a development which he thought might take 15 or 20 years. His final lecture, which was widely publicized at the time, emphasized the importance to Europe of American policy decisions.

WILLIAMS, JOHN HENRY. **Postwar Monetary Plans and Other Essays.** Oxford: Blackwell, 4th rev. ed., 1949, 395 p.

This collection of essays by an influential American economist, vice-president of the Federal Reserve Bank of New York, was first published in 1944. The fourth edition adds discussions of European recovery, the International Trade Organization Charter, Bretton Woods and the Employment Act of 1946. The author sees the crux of the postwar European problem as the external deficit, which can be met only by external aid and internal restraint. But he insists that since the old international economic structure has been destroyed, there is need of thinking in larger and long-run terms. Greater capital investment in Europe is one requirement, and revived intra-European trade is another. He is particularly disturbed by the popularity of Roy F. Harrod's thesis that capital expenditures in the United Kingdom should be reduced, thus reducing the foreign deficit (**Are These Hardships Necessary?**, London: Hart-Davis, 1947, 178 p.). The appendix includes Professor Williams' testimony before the Senate Committee on Banking and Currency on the Bretton Woods Agreements Act.

ELLIS, HOWARD SYLVESTER. **The Economics of Freedom.** New York: Harper (for the Council on Foreign Relations), 1950, 549 p.

An important report and analysis of postwar Europe. While Professor Ellis is the responsible author, he was assisted by a number of outstanding scholars and a Council on Foreign Relations study group. The economic records of the United Kingdom, Western Germany, France and Italy are examined in some detail. Though the Marshall Plan had been in operation for only two years, the advance in industrial production was striking, along with a substantial restoration of European trade and improvement in internal financial stability. The political achievements had also been noteworthy. While the book regards Europe as having scored a phenomenal success in comparison with the post–World War I period, the author reasons that its ultimate success would depend in large part on future American policy. In short, America must avoid depressions, increase imports, support moves toward freer trade (though not in the form of European integration), encourage currency convertibility on a multilateral basis and develop the backward areas as growing markets for the future. Similarly, European actions are called for, the main purpose of which would be "to make free institutions more attractive . . . than the desperate remedy of totalitarian government."

PRICE, HARRY BAYARD. **The Marshall Plan and Its Meaning.** Ithaca: Cornell University Press, 1955, 424 p.

This book, written for the informed layman, was prepared under the aegis of the Government Affairs Institute and with the coöperation and support of the successive recovery agencies. Though not definitive, it does give the background needed for considering the administrative problems of foreign aid programs and related foreign policy issues and is the most complete history of the Marshall Plan available. Both text and footnotes present a mass of detail. While the author regards the Marshall Plan as a great success in achieving various immediate objectives, he regards as unfinished the broader task of constructing an international system so productive of justice and opportunity that it can withstand internal strains and external threats.

BUCHANAN, NORMAN SHARPE and LUTZ, FRIEDRICH AUGUST. **Rebuilding the World Economy.** New York: Twentieth Century Fund, 1947, 434 p.

This timely study by the two economist authors is followed by a series of recommendations by a distinguished committee set up by the Twentieth Century Fund. It is essentially an argument for the reëstablishment of international trade on a multilateral basis, recognizing that rehabilitation must come first, that American imports must be expanded, and that a new framework of international agencies is required. The early chapters are well ahead of their time, with discussions such as those of the issue of industrialization of low-income areas, the acute problem of population and the danger of American overexporting.

BALOGH, THOMAS. **The Dollar Crisis: Causes and Cure.** New York: Macmillan, 1950, 269 p.

Professor Balogh of Oxford, writing for the Fabian Society, discussed in his usual forceful style the problems facing Great Britain and Europe in general, with particular reference to proposals for sterling devaluation, which he regarded as a "pseudo-solution." It is not a study of balance-of-payments detail, but of economic progress in general. In the author's view, the postwar policies, particularly of the United States, brought convalescence to Europe but did not go far enough in national planning or true coördination of European economic policies. He considered that the Marshall Plan was unfortunately based on present needs under present policies, and not aimed at a target related to a given and higher standard of life. Because of Soviet policy, the idea of Western union as an association of progressive European communities along the lines of the Council of Europe was transformed into a politico-military coalition. The International Monetary Fund should have been an international central bank, and the International Bank for Reconstruction and Development an international board for economic development. (These were partially achieved in the 1960s.) Balogh argued further that the dollar problem should not be solved by reduced European standards but through much more detailed planning, greatly increased investment and more effective price policies. In a postscript, he notes that in 1948 these policies demonstrated their effectiveness.

KINDLEBERGER, CHARLES POOR. **The Dollar Shortage.** New York: Wiley; Cambridge: Technology Press, 1950, 276 p.

In this book, Professor Kindleberger makes use of his exposure in the government to foreign economic problems, and particularly his experience in the early development of the Marshall Plan. He is concerned with postwar disequilibrium, summarized as the dollar shortage, and examines the economic elements of the problem in contrast with Balogh's interest in political factors. He finds various pressures which create tendencies in the United States to overexport, underimport and underinvest. Using this as a starting point, he discusses various steps in the monetary, trade, exchange and investment field which should be helpful, reasoning that success in a global sense will require a reconstituted international long-term capital market along with appropriate domestic policy positions. At a time when so much emphasis was on short-run deficits and surpluses, Kindleberger stressed the long-run structural elements in the balance-of-payments problem. This is a book for a reader who already has considerable background in the subject.

MACDOUGALL, SIR DONALD. **The World Dollar Problem: A Study in International Economics.** New York: St. Martin's Press, 1957, 622 p.

Sir Donald MacDougall argued that it was likely that the rest of the world would run a payments deficit with the United States for the next 10 or 20 years. He based this conclusion on considerations relating to periodic recessions in U.S. economic activity, expansion and inflation elsewhere, greater increases in American productivity, limited enthusiasm in the United States for foreign investment, and the proposition that exchange rate adjustment cannot provide long-run balance in payments.

The book not only represents an opinion that was then widespread, but an argument supported by masses of evidence. Nevertheless, a decade later the projected deficit was reversed, and the problem became one of a U.S. deficit with the rest of the world, thus demonstrating the difficulty of prediction. MacDougall's forecast probably contributed to its own failure because it clearly stated the problem and thus encouraged countervailing action in both the United States and the rest of the world.

BROWN, WILLIAM ADAMS, JR. and OPIE, REDVERS. **American Foreign Assistance.** Washington: Brookings Institution, 1953, 615 p.

Although this is a general study of American foreign assistance, the larger part is devoted to European economic recovery and to mutual security. Because of its scope, the discussion of individual programs is necessarily brief, but it still provides the best overall summary of American assistance between 1940 and 1952. The book both records and appraises policy and actions. Written at the time when the authors were able to get direct testimony from many of the individuals involved, there are many details bearing on attitudes and intentions. The authors conclude that the greatest contribution which the United States can make to reducing world disorder lies in the field of commercial policy.

MARJOLIN, ROBERT. **Europe and the United States in the World Economy.** Durham: Duke University Press, 1953, 105 p.

These five lectures were given at Duke University in 1951 by Robert Marjolin, the Secretary-General of the Organization for European Economic Coöperation, created early in 1948. While describing the economic and political successes of the Marshall Plan, he noted that there was still much to be done to strengthen the incentives to progress and to bring about a rapid increase in productivity. Though fearing that the rearmament then in progress might curtail consumption, he suggested that it could create useful new productive capacity and a greater sense of security. The book stresses American responsibility for the world's economy, but makes a special point of the joint responsibility of Europe and North America in the development of the backward areas. Arguing for speed, the author prophetically remarked that "the danger, I think, lies especially in Southeast Asia and the Middle East, where the situation is volcanic."

DIEBOLD, WILLIAM, JR. **Trade and Payments in Western Europe.** New York: Harper (for the Council on Foreign Relations), 1952, 488 p.

One is likely to think of the Marshall Plan as the key postwar improvisation. However, extraordinary new forms of economic coöperation were created during the period 1945–1951 within Western Europe itself for financing trade and removing trade barriers, in particular the European Payments Union and the Organization for European Economic Coöperation. Diebold has written an excellent history of the period, tracing the institutional developments in finance and trade in considerable detail. His thorough examination of Europe's problems and activities covers most clearly the shifting importance of nationalism and international coöperation. He places less value on Europe's technical and organizational achievements, considerable as they were, than on the atmosphere of common interest which was created, making the various countries more sensitive to the foreign impact of their domestic policies and vice versa. Twenty years later, these nations still review and comment on each other's economic policies regularly in the Organization for Economic Coöperation and Development.

LUNDBERG, ERIK with KNOX, A. D., eds. **The Business Cycle in the Post-War World.** New York: St. Martin's Press (for the International Economic Association), 1955, 366 p.

This is a report of a conference held by the International Economic Association at Oxford in 1952, edited by a professor at the University of Stockholm. There are excellent statements by leading authorities of the experience of eight countries in the field of business fluctuations, followed by more abstract papers on trends in cycle theory. The book contains a lengthy report on the subsequent debate, prepared by A. D. Knox. Much of this discussion deals with methodology, in particular the contribution to be made by model-building and econometric analysis. Another focal issue was the extent to which the war had caused such structural changes that much of the usual continuity in the process of action and reaction had been broken. Papers by J. J. Polak and N. Kaldor treat the international aspects of the business cycle.

AUBREY, HENRY G. **Atlantic Economic Cooperation: The Case of the OECD.** New York: Praeger (for the Council on Foreign Relations), 1967, 214 p.

Professor Aubrey reports on the Organization for Economic Coöperation and Development, the successor organization to the Marshall Plan's OEEC. It no longer has the integrating functions which gave life to the original organization by recommending the division of American aid and freeing trade from the then-dominant quota system. Aubrey regards the primary function of the OECD today as that of influencing national policies, though it is done by a process which he aptly calls "collective groping." He finds evidence of achievement elusive since governments do not often give outsiders credit for national action. However, the volume of intergovernmental discussions and the flow of documents cannot be without some impact. Aubrey concludes that the OECD is whatever the governments want to make it, though in turn it can be a valuable catalyst in the strengthening of political will. The author, an economist, writes much more about economic problems and policies than about the political and operating problems of an international organization.

McCreary, Edward A. **The Americanization of Europe: The Impact of Americans and American Business on the Uncommon Market.** Garden City: Doubleday, 1964, 295 p.

In 1964 more than 3,000 American business firms were active in Western Europe. McCreary finds that they have no common pattern of behavior but that they have contributed greatly to economic change. The book is based on interviews with 300 American businessmen, with case histories in fields such as marketing, service-to-industry industries and management. The author ranges broadly in his analyses, even discussing culture shock, the lonely and bored, and the joys of having servants. The main emphasis, however, is on the American contribution to the recognition of the consumer, and the importance of the international corporation as a new unifying force in the international field.

Coppock, John O. **Atlantic Agricultural Unity: Is It Possible?** New York: McGraw-Hill (for the Council on Foreign Relations in coöperation with the Food Research Institute, Stanford University), 1966, 238 p.

In this book, which examines the conflicts among the agricultural policies of the Atlantic countries, the author notes that the different approaches to the problem of surplus production and low farm incomes, usually requiring protection or subsidy, became an increasing irritant as price disparities widened. The Common Market solution has been to establish a highly protected area and to make adjustments among the countries within the area. Coppock feels that there can be no sudden change in the way farmers are treated under the various national farm policies and that there is no great need for immediate action. He believes, however, that national policies should be substantially modified over the next two decades and that if farmers must be subsidized, it should not be done through high prices, since this encourages production. Proper price policies should be directed not at raising income but at slightly increasing output, and be related to the most efficient producing areas. In Coppock's view the objective is not so much economic gains as the elimination of the manifold problems which result from conflicting national agricultural policies. For a slightly earlier analysis of the same problem, see the author's **North Atlantic Policy** (New York: Twentieth Century Fund, 1963, 270 p.).

Cooper, Richard N. **The Economics of Interdependence: Economic Policy in the Atlantic Community.** New York: McGraw-Hill (for the Council on Foreign Relations), 1968, 302 p.

Professor Cooper addresses himself to the policy problem of how to obtain the benefits of close international economic relations without giving up an unacceptable amount of national independence. The issue comes to a head in actions made necessary by balance-of-payments difficulties and in different national policies toward business and taxation. Half the book is historical, discussing financial, trade and factor movements with many pertinent illustrations, making a clear demonstration of the increased interrelation of the economic sectors in each country and the greater economic interdependence of the industrial countries. The author reasons that the successful pursuit of national economic objectives becomes increasingly difficult because of international constraints. The requirements for the future are, he says, political cohesion—in the sense that nations should not merely shift their problem to some other country—ample liquidity to provide time for adjustments, and agreed restraints on unilateral action.

The work is a brilliant exposition of the political problems involved in carrying out international economic policy within the Atlantic Community.

Partnership for Progress. New York: Harper and Row (for the Atlantic Institute), 1963, 126 p.

A report prepared by Pierre Uri, Director of Studies of the Atlantic Institute, on behalf of the Institute, suggests ways of creating a more workable Atlantic relationship. He deals with the chief economic areas of foreign policy—commercial policy, agricultural policy, foreign aid, fair competition, balance of payments and monetary arrangements. In each case, he makes specific proposals, generally aimed in the direction of totally free trade and free markets. The Schuman Plan is cited as demonstrating that economic progress can be made which by its own evolution becomes a political achievement and provides a step to further advances. He suggests, therefore, that we can best start by creating economic foundations for greater unity. He proposes a broader, flexible and more vigorous Organization for Economic Coöperation and Development. This volume is important not only because of its various concrete and practical proposals but because of the list of distinguished individuals associated with the Atlantic Institute who gave it their general approval.

SERVAN-SCHREIBER, JEAN-JACQUES. **The American Challenge.** New York: Atheneum, 1968, 291 p.

The author, editorial writer for *Le Monde,* founder of *L'Express* and political activist, examines the subtle but massive postwar influence of American investment and business performance on the European economy and on political and economic habits of thought. A best seller both in Europe (where it appeared as "Le Défi Américain") and the United States, it attributes American success to management, education and large-scale operation. The author would answer the challenge by prompt action to improve European educational systems, recognize management as a form of skill, and encourage consolidations. A number of other authors have written about American penetration in political terms as colonialism in a new guise. However, except for a few Canadian writers, much less has been said in such a readable way about the economic and social impact of American methods of production and distribution on the economic and social structures and habits of other industrial countries.

NEW NATIONS

See also Nationalism, p. 55; Colonialism, p. 59.

EMERSON, RUPERT. **From Empire to Nation.** Cambridge: Harvard University Press, 1960, 466 p.

The new states of Asia and Africa in the post–World War II period are commonly referred to as "new nations." Rupert Emerson of Harvard, the leading American scholar of his generation in the field of colonialism and post-colonial nationalism, examines the conditions which might give substance to that conventional euphemism. He rejects the claim that "imperialism was the ideal instrument for the spread of the civilization of Western Europe," yet doubts that in the real world of history it could have come about without compulsion on some such scale. The ingredients of nationhood are examined one by one—territory, language, culture, religion, economic development. The prospects of democracy in the new states are appraised with more skeptical realism than was customary among American scholars at the time, and the dilemma of national self-determination is clearly exposed: "the most intransigent of nationalisms must live in a world of which interdependence has become a central feature." The book combines a rich knowledge of detail with a broad, urbane perspective. Its careful judgments have stood the test of time better than have many others formulated during that period.

WRIGGINS, W. HOWARD. **The Ruler's Imperative: Strategies for Political Survival in Asia and Africa.** New York: Columbia University Press, 1969, 275 p.

An American political scientist and former State Department official analyzes the problems of foreign and domestic policy that beset the presidents, prime ministers and other political leaders of the post-colonial states of Asia and Africa. Unlike other writers on the subject who have piously imputed to them such goals as "modernization," "nation-building" or economic growth, Wriggins assumes, simply and plausibly, that before anything else they want to stay in power. Writing about several score states collectively, Wriggins can allow himself more critical judgments than do most authors of country monographs. The approach is reminiscent of Machiavelli's "The Prince"—and like the original Machiavelli, it is marked by skepticism and humanism rather than cynicism. The prose is fluent and commendably free of the tortured jargon that mars most recent writings of American sociologists and political scientists. The rulers' "strategies for aggregating power" are summed up in the following eight imperatives, representing as many chapter headings: "project the personality, build an organization, promote an ideology, reward the faithful and the susceptible, intimidate the opponent and the wavering ally, develop the economy, expand (or contract) political participation, use foreign policy." Four earlier chapters set the methodological and historical stage, and a concluding chapter discusses "Strategic Mixes, the Longer Run, and the Purposes of Power." Together with Emerson's **From Empire to Nation,** this is perhaps the best single introduction to Asian and African politics in the post-colonial era.

DEUTSCH, KARL WOLFGANG. **Nationalism and Social Communication: An Inquiry into the Foundations of Nationality.** New York: Wiley, 1953, 292 p.

An impressive and fruitful attempt to apply a sociological perspective to the study of nationalism and, by implication, of politics generally. Where earlier works on nationalism have derived perspective from geographical, historical, economic or political factors, or from such mythological entities as a general will or a collective soul, Deutsch stresses that national sentiments in each individual are an acquired— that is, a learned—characteristic, and that this process of learning takes place within a network of communications. The strands of that network include speech, reading, writing, education, intermarriage, employment and commerce as well as the growing activities of government, and the network as a whole takes very different forms in traditional villages and modern cities. "In the political and social struggles of the modern age, nationality . . . means an alignment of large numbers of individuals from the middle and lower classes linked to regional centers and leading social groups by channels of social communication and economic intercourse, both indirectly from link to link and directly with the center."

Specifically, Deutsch traces the emergence of Czech nationality in Bohemia and of Finnish nationality after centuries of Swedish (and later Russian) domination. In each case, it was an increase of migration from Czech or Finnish-speaking villages into towns where only German or Swedish used to be spoken that furnished the crucial impetus—the key variables being what Deutsch calls the rate of mobilization (*e.g.* from village to city) and of assimilation (to one or the other nationality). More broadly, Deutsch criticizes such traditional concepts as sovereignty and power, which assume one-sided domination, and instead emphasizes the ties of interaction and communication that connect rulers and ruled alike. On the basis of

detailed demographic data, moreover, the book furnishes one of the more successful applications of quantitative analysis to the study of politics.

BLACK, CYRIL E. **The Dynamics of Modernization: A Study in Comparative History.**
New York: Harper and Row, 1966, 207 p.

Modernization became something of a catchword among American political
scientists and sociologists in the 1960s. Cyril Black, a leading American historian
of Russia, develops the concept more lucidly and coherently than most of his social
science colleagues and uses it for a broad interpretation of world history since the
end of the Middle Ages. He examines in turn the intellectual, political, economic,
social and psychological aspects of this modern revolution. The advance of human
knowledge, its application in material technology and social organization, and its
transmission through education are of the very essence of modernization. But it is
the political order within any given country that provides the scope and sets the
pace for such application and transmission. And political relations among countries, particularly colonial conquest, resistance to it and liberation from it, have
supplied the chief dynamics that have made modernization worldwide. Within each
of these several patterns, Black distinguishes four successive phases—the first when
the modern impact challenges traditional forms of thought and of politics, the
second when modernizing leaders take the initiative, the third one of economic and
social transformation and the last one of "integration of society." A four-page table
that attempts to date these phases precisely for each of the 150 or so states and
territories of the present world introduces a touch of schematism, but Black's text is
far more subtle and perceptive than this exercise would indicate. The author is at
his best in interpreting the contest between the Western democracies and Soviet
Russia. Victory, he suggests, will go to that side which can muster the better
understanding of the forces of modernization.

APTER, DAVID E. **The Politics of Modernization.** Chicago: University of Chicago
Press, 1965, 481 p.

One of America's leading academic specialists on African and comparative
politics traces the political problems posed by economic growth and increasing
social mobility in new states such as those of western Africa. Apter brings to his
subject a keen sensitivity to the psychological and social dimensions of politics and
makes a number of fruitful theoretical suggestions. Instead of forcing the political
patterns of modernization into the stereotyped democratic-totalitarian mold, he
introduces new and more flexible categories, such as those of the "reconciliation
system" and the "mobilization system" (of which democracy and totalitarianism
appear to be special forms), the "neo-mercantilist system" (of which Bismarck's
and Atatürk's régimes are seen as prototypes) and "modernizing autocracy." One
of his most suggestive hypotheses is that of an inverse correlation, in any given
political system, between the amount of information available to rulers and subjects
and the degree of coercion applied in their mutual relations. Throughout the book,
Apter reminds the reader that choice—moral choice—is at the crux of politics. The
presentation is marred by a great deal of awkward jargon, but behind the turgidity
one discerns the author's valiant efforts to emancipate himself from the formalism
that he inherited from such sociologists as Talcott Parsons and Marion J. Levy,
Jr.

RUSTOW, DANKWART A. **A World of Nations: Problems of Political Modernization.**
Washington: Brookings Institution, 1967, 306 p.

The author stresses the integral connection between modernization ("rapidly
widening control over nature through closer cooperation among men") and
nationalism. Both earlier in the West and at present in Asia, Africa and Latin
America, the formation of modern nation-states depends on three political processes: the growth of governmental authority, the definition or redefinition of

national identity and the never-ending quest for political and social equality. Different sequences among these factors and survivals of historic traditions make for a rich variety that belies any notion of unilinear evolution. In examining the prevalent forms of leadership in late-modernizing societies, Rustow discusses in some detail the applicability of Weber's concept of charisma to state-founders, attributes the prevalence of coups to civilian weakness rather than military strength and traces the evolution of stable party systems in such countries as Turkey, India and Mexico. He holds that the pluralist-democratic and communist party patterns are less widely applicable than is commonly assumed and, following the Kennedy-Khrushchev period, he foresees a measure of disinvolvement by the superpowers. This may give late-modernizing countries a chance to learn from the more successful members of their own fraternity. "Where so many different paths" have been taken, "other paths as yet untried may promise equal success." Yet there remains an inherent contradiction between national claims of independence and the technological and military facts of interdependence. "Sometime in the nineteenth century . . . modernization was wedded to the nation-state . . . ; but unless the marriage contract is renegotiated . . . it may well turn into a suicide pact."

Tables in the appendix provide original data on such matters as language composition of the states of the world and the rate of alternation of party governments in democracies.

ALMOND, GABRIEL A. and COLEMAN, JAMES S., eds. **The Politics of the Developing Areas.** Princeton: Princeton University Press, 1960, 591 p.

This coöperative work of six American political scientists signalled a major shift in attention among students of comparative politics from the industrialized to the newly independent and economically underdeveloped countries. Professor Almond's theoretical framework explains political systems by the manner in which they perform seven basic functions: political socialization and recruitment, interest articulation, interest aggregation, political communication, rule making, rule application and rule adjudication. Secondarily, it emphasizes the role of groups such as bureaucracies, political parties, businessmen, landowners, ethnic minorities and the like. Five area specialists proceed to apply this functional and group perspective to the southerly regions of the globe: Lucian W. Pye to Southeast Asia, Myron Weiner to South Asia (India, Pakistan and Ceylon), Coleman to Africa south of the Sahara, Dankwart A. Rustow to the Middle East including North Africa and George I. Blanksten to Latin America. The conclusion, by Coleman, seeks to relate political development, and particularly the prospects of democracy, to economic growth and related social changes.

The functional perspective was originally developed by cultural anthropologists such as Radcliffe-Brown and Malinowski and adapted by sociologists such as Parsons and Merton. Applied to the study of politics it helped to overcome the earlier preoccupation with formal, legal institutions and hence encouraged a less parochial and more worldwide perspective—but it has also been criticized for its allegedly static or conservative bias. The regional chapters that constitute the bulk of the book contain much empirical information, the value of which is quite independent of such critiques.

MILLIKAN, MAX FRANKLIN and BLACKMER, DONALD L. M., eds. **The Emerging Nations: Their Growth and United States Policy.** Boston: Little, Brown, 1961, 171 p.

This book is the result of the collective endeavors of ten political scientists, economists and sociologists at the Center for International Studies at the Massachusetts Institute of Technology, several of whom later became prominent as advisers or government officials in the Kennedy and Johnson administrations. It reflects generally an optimistic view of the ability of American policy-makers, through economic, technical and military assistance, to promote progress and stability in Asia, Africa and Latin America—a view that inspired such programs as the Alliance for Progress. The forces of economic development, the authors hold, have disrupted the social fabric of traditional societies who consequently are faced with a threefold choice. They can either try to preserve their traditional social and political institutions or else risk "the radical destruction by extremist measures, probably involving violence, of the whole political, social, and economic fabric of the traditional society and its replacement by something entirely different"—something, presumably, close to the communist model. The first alternative is untenable and the second undesirable.

The authors themselves sketch a "third choice" which emphasizes the training of modern men and the growth of modern economies. This suggests four aims for United States policy toward the "emerging nations": to encourage their independence from communism, to guide them toward peaceful and moderate foreign policies, to help them maintain effective but non-totalitarian systems of government and to strengthen the development of open societies "which are willing to cooperate in international economic, political, and social control measures." "Evolutionary and balanced progress toward modernization," the MIT group concludes, will not assure behavior in the American interest, but it is a necessary condition for such behavior. The final chapters examine the instruments of "information policy," military assistance and economic aid available for such a program.

FINER, SAMUEL EDWARD. **The Man on Horseback: The Role of the Military in Politics.** New York: Praeger, 1962, 268 p.

The role of the military in the politics of the developing areas has become the subject of an extensive American literature. Professor Finer, a British political theorist, places it in a broader geographical, historical and theoretical perspective. Instead of asking what makes the military intervene, Finer turns the tables. As soon as the military become a professional organization separate from the rest of the public service—a separation that occurred in Europe in the eighteenth century and since then has become standard throughout the world—military seizures of power become an ever-present possibility. Since the military, *ex hypothesi*, control the means of coercion, the question is what stops them from seizing it everywhere and always? The answer, Finer suggests, is "political culture"—a deeply felt commitment to a set of understandings about how and by whom political power should be exercised. Empirical details are adduced from the history of Europe since the eighteenth, Latin America and the Middle East since the nineteenth and Asia and Africa in the twentieth centuries. Inevitably some of these will seem skewed or inaccurate to the scholar specializing in the history of any one country. But being mainly illustrative, they do not affect the soundness of the basic argument which is brilliantly and perceptively stated.

JOHNSON, JOHN J., *ed.* **The Role of the Military in Underdeveloped Countries.** Princeton: Princeton University Press, 1962, 427 p.

A dozen scholars, 11 of them Americans and most of them political scientists, sociologists or historians, examine the political role of the military in Latin America, Southeast Asia and the Middle East in the years following the Second World War. In an attempt at general orientation, Edward Shils provides little more than a hasty adaptation of his **Political Development in the New States,** whereas Lucian W. Pye writes on "Armies in the Process of Political Modernization," in which he sees them playing a crucial role. Similar themes are echoed by Manfred Halpern, who sees military officers in the Arab countries as the spearheads of a "new middle class," and by Guy J. Pauker, who (several years before the coup of 1965) foresees an irresistible drift toward militarism in Indonesia. The three Latin American specialists (Johnson himself, Edwin Lieuwen and Victor Alba, a Mexican historian) take a more skeptical view and recognize that military officers can take a number of ideological positions in various political and social settings.

The volume originated in a conference assembled by the RAND Corporation. It concentrates on areas that were of concern to American foreign and military policy in the 1950s and 1960s and by and large reflects the optimistic view of the subject matter then prevalent in American academic circles. Among subsequent treatments, two essays by Samuel P. Huntington and David C. Rapoport take a more skeptical and more richly historical perspective, in Samuel P. Huntington, *ed.*, **Changing Patterns of Military Politics** (New York: Free Press of Glencoe, 1962, 272 p.); and Morris Janowitz sketches in outline a sociological analysis of Asian and African civil-military relations in **The Military in the Political Development of New Nations: An Essay in Comparative Analysis** (Chicago: University of Chicago Press, 1964, 134 p.).

JENNINGS, SIR WILLIAM IVOR. **The Approach to Self-Government.** Boston: Beacon Press, 1963, 204 p.

A leading British political scientist, constitutional adviser to various Commonwealth countries and onetime chancellor of the University of Colombo, discusses the problems of transfer of political practices from Westminster to Asia and Africa. The outline reflects a classical view of the nature and setting of representative government. There are chapters on such things as elections, bills of rights, the legislature, the executive and education. The general tone is meliorist in the grand British tradition from Bentham to the Fabians: where there is good will, a clear grasp of the theoretical issues and an adequate understanding of the historic circumstances, human ingenuity can find at least proximate solutions to the most pressing problems. A polemical aside against Woodrow Wilson identifies the most intractable of the post-colonial problems: "On the surface it seemed reasonable: let the people decide. It was in fact ridiculous because the people cannot decide until somebody decides who are the people." Having observed the process of transition at first hand, Jennings refuses to "draw a sharp contrast between 'colonialism' on the one hand and 'self-government' or 'freedom' or 'independence' on the other." As the memory of colonialism recedes behind fresher memories of post-colonial tyranny or civil strife, this position is likely to appear increasingly reasonable.

SHILS, EDWARD. **Political Development in the New States.** The Hague: Mouton, 1962, 91 p.

One of America's leading sociologists undertakes an ambitious attempt to identify the sociological variables that would allow us to explain political realities in the post-colonial states of Asia and Africa. The "determinants of political development" are seen in the social structure of kinship, territory and community; in culture, which ranges from traditionalism and parochialism to nationalism and a widespread oppositional mentality; personality (which rates no more than a page of discussion); and in political structure in the narrower sense. In their various assortments, these lead to five "alternative courses of political development."

The first of these, political democracy resting on "civilian rule through representative institutions and public liberties," is rare and difficult, although the author expresses some hopes for Malaya and Nigeria. "Tutelary democracy" gives a temporary preponderance to the executive and ranges from the relatively mild form of Nehru's India to "more deliberate and more drastic" forms such as Sukarno's Indonesia or Ne Win's Burma. "Modernizing oligarchies" include various military régimes such as those in Pakistan and the Arab countries, whereas "traditional oligarchies" are presumably represented by such countries as Ethiopia and Saudi Arabia. Despite the high demands it makes on civility, tolerance and administrative competence, the author concludes that democracy, in either its full-fledged ("political") or "tutelary" form, may well have, "in the long run, the best chance to survive among the alternative models." Shils' approach is characteristic of the tendency toward broad generalization among American sociologists and political scientists. In a highly summary treatment his distinctions at times remain sketchy, and there is a shortage of concrete illustrations. The prose, however, is refreshingly clear.

HUNTINGTON, SAMUEL P. **Political Order in Changing Societies.** New Haven: Yale University Press, 1968, 488 p.

Professor Huntington's central theme is supplied by a quotation from De Tocqueville: "If men are to remain civilized or to become so, the art of associating together must grow and improve in the same ratio in which the equality of conditions is increased." Modernization, by which Huntington means chiefly economic growth and social mobility, results in vastly increased political participation. Only a corresponding increase in political institutionalization can save a "civic" political system from suffering political decay or sinking into a condition of "praetorianism" (a concept adapted from David C. Rapoport). The ratio of institutionalization to participation is favorable in traditional societies (where both are low) and in fully modern societies such as the United States and the Soviet Union (where both are high). It is reversed in most of the post-colonial and economically underdeveloped countries today.

After laying out his concepts and giving a somewhat strained application to American and European history, Huntington turns to these contemporary problems of political modernization and examines some of the instrumentalities available for the restoration or maintenance of order. Hereditary monarchs are likely to be swept away by the sequel of their reforms, but military officers can play a positive role at least in the early stages of modernization. Revolutions, in the rare situations where they are possible, can provide decisive breakthroughs but can succeed only if they result in tight party organizations on the Leninist pattern. Democratic reform is an alternative even more rarely applicable, and its success seems to hinge on pitting the conservative peasantry against the restless urban masses. Huntington is in frequent danger of advocating order and institutionalization as ends in themselves, ignoring the purposes for which men may be "associating together;" hence he can praise monarch, militarists, Leninists and conservative democrats with equal fervor. Yet his book is lucidly written and digests a wealth of factual detail on the current politics of Asia, Africa and Latin America.

TOYNBEE, ARNOLD JOSEPH. **The World and the West.** New York: Oxford University Press, 1953, 99 p.

This succinct and lucid essay sums up much of the theory of cultural contact that hides in the author's 12-volume **A Study of History.** The superior technology, organization and firepower of the modern West forced upon other cultures with which it came into contact a painful dilemma. The "Herodians," who seek to emulate the intrusive culture, choose one horn, the "Zealots," who insist on wholesale rejection, choose the other. The contrast is traced in the first four chapters in the light of the experience of Russia, the Muslim Middle East, India and the Far East. Yet the actual course of events cannot be fully controlled by such conscious choice; for "in the game of cultural intercourse . . . one thing leads to another." For example, a maternity hospital built in the Alexandria naval yard in 1839 for the benefit of the wives of British shipwrights leaves an indelible impact on Egyptian obstetrics and demography. In other instances, the repercussions are less beneficial. Here as elsewhere, Toynbee takes a dim view of the European aberration that seeks "the criterion of Nationality in the shibboleth of Language." This notion worked badly enough in Europe, but it proved downright disastrous when, as a "diffracted culture-ray," it was applied to the *macédoine* of peoples from Salonica to Singapore. The volume originated in a series of BBC lectures. Toynbee expresses himself forthrightly and, where we disagree, stimulates our thinking without, for once, overwhelming us with his erudition.

PART THREE:

THE WORLD BY REGIONS

I. THE WESTERN HEMISPHERE

INTER-AMERICAN RELATIONS

See also Latin America, p. 419.

General; Historical

PERKINS, DEXTER. **A History of the Monroe Doctrine.** Boston: Little, Brown, rev. ed., 1955, 462 p.

This admirable work holds a privileged place in the literature on United States foreign policy and inter-American relations. Impressive in scholarship, persuasive in argumentation, graceful in style, it is today what it was when it first appeared: the best introduction to the Monroe Doctrine we have seen or are likely to see.

Professor Perkins, to whom the Monroe Doctrine was a lifelong professional interest, published an earlier version of this book in 1941, **Hands Off** (Boston: Little, Brown, 1941, 455 p.), as his contribution to the sharp debate between "isolationists" and "interventionists." The version reviewed here appeared when the cold war in the hemisphere had become a dominant concern. It is, therefore, more than an exercise in pure scholarship. While both are history, they are history written to inform judgments and decisions that were to be made in the 1940s and 1950s.

We are told by the author that in part his purpose was to clear up some popular misconceptions: ". . . that the Monroe declaration prevented the reconquest of South America by a wicked combination of European powers; . . . that the Monroe Doctrine prescribes complete abstinence from participation in European affairs; . . . that Latin Americans have been, are, and ought to be grateful for the doctrine." If such notions are no longer widely held among us, Professor Perkins can be credited with having helped, to some extent at least, to dispel them.

What we have in the book is largely diplomatic history, written from the perspective of an informed and profoundly patriotic United States citizen. Perkins was no economic determinist, no dialectician, no legalist, no believer in conspiratorial theories. He saw and described the efforts of striving and fallible leaders who worked within the contexts of their times: presidents and politicians, emperors and kings, foreign ministers and military strategists, press lords and intellectuals. On balance, he concluded, the Monroe Doctrine as it had evolved over more than a century had been a constructive force, on balance the United States had played a positive role in the hemisphere and the world. If there were compelling reasons for allowing the *name* Monroe Doctrine to slip into desuetude, it was far from certain that the fundamental principle the doctrine expressed—that of preventing the expansion of European power and influence in the Americas—was outdated and should or could be abandoned. What was required was reinterpretation to take account of challenges and opportunities unforeseen and unimagined by Monroe, Polk, the Roosevelts and Wilson.

BEMIS, SAMUEL FLAGG. **The Latin American Policy of the United States: An Historical Interpretation.** New York: Harcourt, 1943, 470 p.

Professor Bemis for many years taught diplomatic history at Yale where undergraduates referred to him affectionately as American Flagg Bemis. Readers of this important book will understand why, for the book is an exuberant hymn to the United States and its hemispheric mission. Not all scholars have found Professor Bemis's thesis persuasive, but few have been offended by his presentation of it and all have been obliged to take it seriously.

The work is distinguished by scholarship of a very high order: Bemis's primary obligation was to the historical record, and he knew that record thoroughly, his account running from 1776 through 1942. Two other features, however, give the book its peculiar interest and value. First, there is the notion, often explicit, always implicit, that the United States was a providential agent of history. The second feature is the quality of supreme confidence that informs almost every page: confidence in the fundamental soundness and rightness of the United States, confidence in Bemis's own capacity to understand and interpret the grand design. Bemis does not do battle with those who would disagree with his interpretations; rather, he seems to assume that rational and dispassionate examination of the record will lead men to accept his conclusions. His book is probably best known for its stout defense of what Bemis calls "preventive imperialism," as practiced by the United States in the Caribbean during the first third of this century: It "was, if you will, an imperialism against imperialism. It did not last long and it was not really bad."

This book is of major significance.

HARING, CLARENCE HENRY. **South America Looks at the United States.** New York: Macmillan, 1928, 243 p.

Harvard historian Haring prepared this book at a time when inter-American relations were approaching one of their periodic low points: the inter-American system very nearly disintegrated in 1928 at the sixth Conference in Havana because of Latin American distrust of the United States and because of accumulated reciprocal misunderstandings between the two parts of the hemisphere. Haring's purpose was to make his North American readers sensitive to the causes of Latin American discontent; what he had to say is for the most part as apposite to today's situation as it was to the one he surveyed. "Anything like North American tutelage is more and more resented," he wrote, having in mind United States efforts to instill in Latin Americans the virtues of political stability, democratic government and sound financial and business practice. "Latin Americans hate, admire, envy and fear the United States at one and the same time," he said; and this, an accurate statement then, is fully as accurate now.

Many features of the inter-American scene, however, have changed dramatically since Haring's book appeared, and reading some of his pages today engenders nothing so much as nostalgia: "Today steamship lines have been established between New York . . . and all the principal ports . . . and the passenger schedule between New York and Buenos Aires has been lowered from 22 to 17 days. The effect of the opening of the Panama Canal need not be dwelt upon."

MUNRO, DANA GARDNER. **The United States and the Caribbean.** Boston: World Peace Foundation, 1934, 322 p.

Professor Munro prepared this tightly written book as the United States, through liquidation of its Nicaraguan intervention and abrogation of the Platt Amendment, was moving toward full implementation of the Good Neighbor Policy. What Munro did was relate, coolly and with clarity, the essential minimum of facts necessary to a knowledge of United States behavior in the Caribbean and Central America from the turn of the century until 1933. Munro was in a particularly good position to make this presentation because, in addition to his abilities as a scholar, he had had much firsthand experience in the area as an officer of the State Department. The book has a peculiarly bloodless quality, evidently accountable to Munro's wish to avoid ascription of motive to actors and to keep himself and his opinions altogether in the background.

As an example of Munro's terse style, here is what he had to say about the foreign debt of Honduras in his consideration of Dollar Diplomacy: "Honduras, whose total annual revenues did not exceed two or three million dollars, owed the stupendous sum of $124,000,000. Her government had issued bonds to a nominal value of more than $25,000,000 between 1867 and 1870 for the construction of an interoceanic railroad across her territory, but the portion of the proceeds which had reached the national treasury had sufficed only to build sixty miles of cheaply constructed line. Payment of interest had been suspended in 1872."

History—bizarre, lurid, melodramatic—lies behind every sentence in that paragraph; but it was not Munro's purpose in this volume to say any more than was absolutely necessary to his narrowly defined purpose. This is an excellent book.

PALMER, THOMAS WAVERLY, JR. **Search for a Latin American Policy.** Gainesville: University of Florida Press, 1957, 217 p.

Thomas Palmer, whose premature death deprived the United States of a promising interpreter of inter-American relations, wrote this book at a time of dangerously reduced United States interest in and concern for Latin America. Vice President Nixon had not yet encountered the hostile crowds of Lima and Caracas; Fidel Castro was not so much as a name to most North Americans. It was Palmer's purpose to sound the alert, in a way designed to engage the sympathetic attention of those informed citizens whose opinions were assumed to have some influence in determining United States policy.

His approach, therefore, is low-key and noncontroversial. He does not challenge the official version of the Guatemalan events of 1954, for example, accepting that Arbenz was irretrievably under the control of communists responsive to Moscow and that the United States was not directly involved in Arbenz's overthrow. The point he makes, however, is that if the United States does not wish to see additional Guatemalas, it had best align itself with the forces of change in the region.

Again, Palmer does not suggest that a program of massive public spending for Latin America be launched; in 1956–1957 such counsel would have been wasted. Instead, he says that in the next decade Latin Americans will no longer be satisfied with merely "good will" on the part of Yankees. They will want moral, political and economic guidance. "This the United States must give. Let some say that it is a new kind of 'imperialism'—they will say it no matter what the United States does."

WHITAKER, ARTHUR PRESTON. **The Western Hemisphere Idea: Its Rise and Decline.** Ithaca: Cornell University Press, 1954, 194 p.

"From its emergence in the late eighteenth and early nineteenth century to the present, the core of the Western Hemisphere idea has been the proposition that the peoples of this Hemisphere stand in a special relationship to one another that sets them apart from the rest of the world." In this scholarly, trenchant and highly readable book, Professor Whitaker recounted and interpreted the career of one of the most powerful ideas in the political history of modern times.

Writing during a period of severe cold-war tension and noting that the United States had increasingly oriented itself toward the Northern rather than the Western Hemisphere since World War II in matters strategic, economic and political, Whitaker was prepared to assert that the idea—which had manifested itself in the Monroe Doctrine and its corollaries, in the Drago Doctrine, in hemispheric isolationism—was in a condition of irreversible decline. He could not have foreseen the Alliance for Progress, but had he been able to do so he would presumably have discounted its relative importance as he did that of the Rio Treaty (1947) and of the OAS Charter of Bogota (1948). Events have vindicated Whitaker's judgment: the Western Hemisphere idea is moribund in both the United States and Latin America.

This book is essential reading for any serious student of inter-American affairs.

MATTHEWS, HERBERT L., *ed.* **The United States and Latin America.** Englewood Cliffs: Prentice-Hall (for the American Assembly), rev. ed., 1963, 179 p.

Originally prepared for an American Assembly conference in 1959 and subsequently revised, the four papers that make up this volume retain substantial value today. Frank Tannenbaum presents with brevity and grace the ideas that he elaborated more fully in **Ten Keys to Latin America** (New York: Knopf, 1962, 237 p.), and Reynold Carlson does an admirable job of describing and analyzing the economic problems and prospects of Latin America and of assessing the nature and adequacy of resources to meet Latin America's development challenge.

Kalman Silvert's essay on "Political Change in Latin America" has long since acquired the status of a minor classic. Not only does it provide enduring and enduringly useful theoretical insights into Latin American politics, but it also contains many provocative judgments and observations that challenge the accepted wisdom—for instance, this oft-quoted sentence: "If the normal way of rotating the executive in a given country is by revolution, and if there have been a hundred such changes in a century, then it is not being facetious to remark that revolutions are a sign of stability—that events are marching along as they always have."

Also outstanding is Herbert Matthews' historical account of United States–Latin American diplomatic relations. What Matthews has to say about the postwar Latin American policy of the United States is largely critical although, writing in 1962–1963, he sees reassuring signs of change, most particularly United States sponsorship of the Alliance for Progress. But the difficulties of inter-American understanding and coöperation to which Matthews alludes are today as evident as ever they were.

CONNELL-SMITH, GORDON. **The Inter-American System.** New York: Oxford University Press (for the Royal Institute of International Affairs), 1966, 376 p.

A perceptive and skeptical British scholar examines the history of inter-American relations from the early nineteenth century to the height of the 1965 Dominican crisis. In doing so, he abundantly confirms the thesis with which he begins, namely, that "the United States has viewed the Inter-American System as an instrument for reinforcing her own policies; the Latin American countries as a means of persuading the United States to modify those policies."

Connell-Smith's sympathies are quite consistently with the Latin Americans in their many confrontations with their powerful northern neighbor; and some features of his account are bound to be disconcerting to North American supporters of United States hemispheric policy. For instance, he is critical of the contention of the United States that the Organization of American States in this hemisphere is an effective substitute for the United Nations: while the contention may be valid from the standpoint of the United States, it cannot have been valid from that of Guatemalan President Arbenz in 1954. Nor, Connell-Smith asserts, was it valid for Premier Castro in 1962: "The United States was inviting Cuba . . . to exchange the role of plaintiff in the U.N. for that of defendant in the OAS; and Castro to deprive himself of the main source of support in his struggle against her."

EISENHOWER, MILTON S. **The Wine Is Bitter: The United States and Latin America.** Garden City: Doubleday, 1963, 342 p.

In 1953 Milton Eisenhower was asked by his brother the President to visit Latin America and to prepare a report on the situation in the region and the state of inter-American relations. That trip was followed by others during the next eight years, with the author making Latin America an area of his special interest and concern. This book is the product of those years of observation, study and reflection.

Asserting that "revolution is inevitable" in Latin America, he sets out to examine the causes of discontent and to explore for ways to ensure that the revolution be peaceful and democratic. He is intensely preoccupied with Cuba and what it represents: "If the intelligent leaders of the other American republics do not move swiftly to correct historic injustices and inequities and to bring about a social revolution by peaceful means, Castro-type revolutions may rock and wreck country after country south of the border." He calls for all-out support of the Alliance for Progress and its principles.

The book's major usefulness today lies perhaps in its accounts of the numerous events and decisions with which Dr. Eisenhower was himself associated.

WOOD, BRYCE. **The Making of the Good Neighbor Policy.** New York: Columbia University Press, 1961, 438 p.

Bryce Wood is a superb craftsman. Both his books, **The United States and Latin American Wars, 1932–1942** and **The Making of the Good Neighbor Policy,** are soundly conceived, thoroughly researched, and carefully and persuasively presented.

Wood's account of the Good Neighbor Policy begins effectively with the Nicaraguan intervention of 1927 whose unanticipated complications and indirect effects helped precipitate a major crisis in inter-American relations and a profound reëvaluation of the premises that underlay United States hemispheric behavior. The account ends in 1943 with most of the states of the hemisphere closing ranks in a shared wartime effort. Wood tells his story largely from the perspectives of official Washington: Stimson, Roosevelt, Hull, Welles and Duggan are principal among the actors.

The Good Neighbor Policy did not, of course, emerge full-blown, but rather piecemeal, erratically, in a process marked by false starts, constructive gropings, numerous misunderstandings and disappointed expectations. Chief among those expectations, Wood asserts, was that of reciprocity: "For nonintervention and noninterference, would not Latin American governments respond by 'equitable' treatment for the property of United States citizens and corporations? In general, the answer to this question was in the negative."

Eventually, however, reciprocity of a different and vitally important kind was evoked. "By renouncing domination the United States had won a sympathy that accorded it wartime leadership acknowledged by nearly all the Latin American states. . . . In its time [the Policy] provided a promising demonstration of the desire of Americans to strive in good will to forget an often bitter past and, with mutual respect, to find amicable ways both to adjust differences of interest and to unite in furthering common aims."

DOZER, DONALD MARQUAND. **Are We Good Neighbors? Three Decades of Inter-American Relations, 1930–1960.** Gainesville: University of Florida Press, 1959, 456 p.

Professor Dozer performed a prodigious feat of research in preparing this useful volume. His purpose was to assess the effect of the Good Neighbor Policy upon Latin American attitudes toward the United States, to examine the relationship between the two parts of the hemisphere during World War II, and to trace the evolution of Latin American opinion during the decade and a half following that war. While the book can be read simply as history—it is as comprehensive and thorough an account of the period as any that has appeared—its particular value lies in its wealth of references to and quotations from Latin American spokesmen, whether statesmen, editors, journalists, intellectuals or political activists.

The author's investigation confirms—or documents—the view widely held among North Americans that the enunciation and implementation of the Good Neighbor Policy did induce a radical shift in Latin American opinion, away from one characterized by suspicion, hostility and fear of the United States toward one marked by confidence and admiration. After the brief years of wartime coöperation, Latin American attitudes again assumed their negative cast because of betrayed expectations, United States preoccupation with other parts of the world, and what was believed to be a general lack of North American understanding and sympathy.

Dozer, not at all lacking in understanding and sympathy himself, called for "a constructive, imaginative and outreaching policy" which would "have to take the form of a revitalized Good Neighbor Policy." It was a forecast of the Alliance for Progress, which was announced two years later.

Organization of American States; Alliance for Progress

DREIER, JOHN C. **The Organization of American States and the Hemisphere Crisis.** New York: Harper and Row (for the Council on Foreign Relations), 1962, 147 p.

John Dreier served with distinction for ten years as United States representative and ambassador to the Council of the OAS. This lucid book reflects that experience. But Dreier is more than a professional diplomat. He is also a profound student of inter-American affairs, committed to reducing frictions, eliminating misunderstandings, facilitating coöperation between the Americas. His book, while pivoting on the OAS as an institution, is really directed toward broader hemispheric problems. The OAS is not an end in itself; indeed it is nothing more than its member governments allow it to be.

Dreier's concern is that the OAS has been and will continue to be assigned functions and responsibilities which neither its authority nor its resources allow it to fulfill adequately. He strongly approves of making increased use of the OAS but calls for action along three principal lines. The first is the extension by the governments of a more vigorous support for the Organization and the improvement of their procedures for dealing with it. The second is the improvement and modernization of the Organization itself. "Third, and most important, is the adoption by the United States and the Latin American nations, through the OAS, of policies that are realistically related to the problems of the day and that will adequately guide the agencies of the Inter-American system in dealing with those problems."

In his book Dreier has set out a number of specific recommendations. Since its publication significant steps have been taken in the directions he advocated.

SLATER, JEROME. **The OAS and United States Foreign Policy.** Columbus: Ohio State University Press, 1967, 315 p.

In this forcefully argued book, Professor Slater puts forward the thesis that "since the enunciation of the Monroe Doctrine, the primary political objective of the United States in its inter-American policy has been the maintenance or attainment of political stability in Latin America." It is to be understood that by stability Slater means: maintenance of order within individual Latin American states; maintenance of peace between Latin American states; and maintenance of hemispheric security against external threats. He contends that the primary function of the OAS has been "to cloak and thereby legitimize the predominant role of the United States in the settlement of most hemispheric conflicts."

Slater would like to see the United States use the OAS collective machinery "on behalf of democracy." He argues that the case for pro-democratic intervention should rest on "the conviction that although it may or may not prove to be good for the United States, it will almost surely be good for the long-repressed peoples of Latin America." His interpretations and recommendations may not elicit agreement, but they deserve attention.

MANGER, WILLIAM. **Pan America in Crisis: The Future of the OAS.** Washington: Public Affairs Press, 1961, 104 p.

William Manger, who at the time this book appeared had spent more than 40 years in responsible roles in the inter-American system, knew this system as intimately as anyone in the hemisphere. It is from a hemispheric perspective, seen by an international civil servant, that this honest and revealing book is written.

Manger's assessment of the inter-American system in late 1961 was not optimistic. "In recent years inter-American relations have deteriorated to one of the lowest levels in history," he said, his mind running back to the near-débâcle of the 1928 Havana Conference. "The sense of political solidarity so laboriously built up in the years from 1930 to 1950 has gradually but steadily evaporated. . . . The unity and solidarity of the American republics has been seriously undermined and the community of American states is rapidly becoming a fiction."

Would the Alliance for Progress—which was announced while the writing of this book was underway—make a difference? "It is understandable if the hope should be tinged with skepticism. And yet, if the OAS has a future it will be found only in the spirit of the *Alianza*."

GORDON, LINCOLN. **A New Deal for Latin America: The Alliance for Progress.** Cambridge: Harvard University Press, 1963, 146 p.

Lincoln Gordon was a member of President Kennedy's Latin American task force which prepared the report that underlay the announcement of the Alliance for Progress in March 1961. A political economist with a long-standing professional interest in foreign assistance and development matters, Gordon soon thereafter became U.S. ambassador to Brazil. This book is drawn from a number of lectures Gordon gave before Brazilian audiences, designed to inform them about the conception, machinery, program and prospects of the Alliance. It is an authoritative statement by an exceptionally qualified American.

"What is the Alliance for Progress? In a single sentence, it is a sustained and cooperative effort to accelerate economic growth and social progress throughout Latin America, working through democratic institutions based on respect for the individual." The book attempts to draw out the implications of that sentence, dealing successively with themes such as "Economic Aspects of the Alliance," "Development and the Democratic Revolution," "Rebuilding the Educational Foundations" and "Free Initiative and the Alliance for Progress."

Today's reader of this—and other—early books on the Alliance may be struck by their profound optimism: the challenge of Latin American development is formidable, but rational men can summon the will and capacity to meet it. Striking also, in light of the region's more recent history, is the recurrent emphasis upon both the possibility and the essentiality of accomplishing the transformation of Latin America through democratic means.

PERLOFF, HARVEY S. **Alliance for Progress: A Social Invention in the Making.** Baltimore: Johns Hopkins Press (for Resources for the Future), 1969, 253 p.

Harvey Perloff, one of the original "Nine Wise Men" who were to evaluate development plans and performance of Latin American governments participating in the Alliance for Progress, here gives an authoritative account of the early years of the Alliance from the standpoint of the "development expert" who, in his professional role, was expected to rise above the narrowly defined national interests of both the United States and the Latin American states. Varying and incompatible definitions of those national interests, however, explain many of the difficulties and frustrations of the Alliance; and Perloff, from his comparatively independent perspective, has much that is useful to say about them.

The author, however, wrote the book with his eye directed principally toward the future, not the past: his hope was that lessons drawn from Alliance successes and disappointments during the 1960s would lead to a major overhaul of Alliance machinery to enable it to deal more effectively with the development challenge of the 1970s. The volume, therefore, is studded with specific recommendations for improvements and innovations.

Skeptics, cynics and others disillusioned by trends observable in the hemisphere will profit from reading this fresh and affirmative statement.

ROGERS, WILLIAM D. **The Twilight Struggle: The Alliance for Progress and the Politics of Development in Latin America.** New York: Random House, 1967, 301 p.

During the early years of the 1960s William D. Rogers, who was Deputy U.S. Coördinator for the Alliance for Progress, bore major responsibilities for formulating, interpreting and implementing United States development assistance programs for Latin America. This well-written book reflects his experience.

Much of the book is devoted to a description of the Latin American and inter-American situation with which the Alliance for Progress was designed to deal. What gives the report special significance is the latter part, which focuses on the domestic and international politics of the Alliance. Here the author takes up such matters as obstacles to understanding between the Congress and the Agency for International Development, the critical importance of the President and the President's style, the inherently tense relationship between older career foreign service officers and development planners and technicians. He also analyzes the requirements that the new, developmental diplomacy imposes upon our ambassadors in the field, as well as the hazards to which their new role exposes them.

Neither a developmental economist nor a career technician, Rogers assigns primacy to the political dimension of development. Unabashedly and unequivocally committed to the political values embodied in the Charter of Punta del Este, he deplores the apparent erosion of overt, official U.S. support for those values after the assassination of President Kennedy. The late Robert F. Kennedy wrote the introduction to the volume.

DREIER, JOHN C., ed. **The Alliance for Progress: Problems and Perspectives.** Baltimore: Johns Hopkins Press, 1962, 146 p.

In the spring of 1962 five distinguished public figures, variously associated with the Alliance for Progress, gave their assessments of it in a series of lectures at the Pan American Union. This historically valuable book is a result.

Milton Eisenhower, instrumental in persuading members of his brother's administration to adopt a more affirmative and innovative Latin American policy, traces the history of the Alliance concept; José Figueres, Costa Rican champion of constitutional democracy, considers the political goals of the Alliance; Teodoro Moscoso, manager of Puerto Rico's successful Operation Bootstrap and first U.S. Coördinator of the Alliance, talks about the Alliance and social change; Raúl Prebisch, whose provocative theories and proposals have dominated Latin American economic thinking since the late 1940s, deals imaginatively with the challenge of economic development; and Dean Rusk, whose State Department destiny it became to focus on a region half a world away from Latin America, places the Alliance in the global context of U.S. foreign affairs.

Something was astir in the hemisphere in 1962: there was a vision, a commitment, a confidence. Here, for instance, is Secretary Rusk: "When we succeed in our Alliance, as we shall, then we will have created on this continent a society where people will be liberated from material bondage in order to pursue unhindered the ceaseless quests of the human mind and heart. . . . With this achievement, many will look back in later years and say with pride, 'I lived during the Alliance for Progress.'"

Hemisphere Security

DUGGAN, LAURENCE. **The Americas: The Search for Hemisphere Security.** New York: Holt, 1949, 242 p.

Laurence Duggan was one of the principal architects of the Good Neighbor Policy, the others being Sumner Welles, Cordell Hull and Franklin Roosevelt. This book, edited and published after his untimely death, makes an incisive analysis of the inter-American situation as he understood it and lays down a number of policy recommendations that he believed would make the postwar hemispheric environment more wholesome. The book early acquired a towering reputation and has maintained it.

Duggan anticipated the developmental philosophy of the Alliance for Progress by more than a decade. What he wrote on this matter is as fresh and pertinent today as it was when he set it down. History has dealt less kindly with two other thrusts of his thinking. First, Duggan was a fervent advocate of the United Nations and would have seen the regional organization, the OAS, effectively subordinated to the global one. Second, he warned against letting cold-war considerations come to dominate hemispheric policy-making. It would be a calamitous mistake, he believed, to "try to fortify the inter-American system by capitalizing on the fear of Soviet influence which possesses the Latin American oligarchies. . . . Since the atomic bomb and bacteriological warfare, any thought of building security on a regional basis is an obsolete delusion."

DE MADARIAGA, SALVADOR. **Latin America between the Eagle and the Bear.** New York: Praeger, 1962, 192 p.

A note of urgency informs this work by the great Spanish liberal. At home in the cultures of three continents, he wrote this book from a European perspective to tell North Americans about Latin Americans and their attitudes toward the United States. His concern was that the United States, because of its complacent acceptance of dictatorships of the right and its strident, indiscriminate and unimaginative response to challenges from the left, was running the risk of forfeiting its moral authority in Latin America. As fervently as any convinced cold warrior, Madariaga abhorred communism and feared Soviet pretensions; as much as any North American he saw the United States as mankind's last, best hope. But the United States could not play its essential role as defender of liberal, democratic philosophy and practice, in the hemisphere and the world, unless it mended its ways—U.S. accommodation with Franco was as much in Madariaga's mind as was accommodation with Pérez Jiménez, Somoza, Trujillo and the others. The United States must "purify herself." Madariaga expected much of President Kennedy who, at the time the book was being written, was defining the positions of his administration.

Characteristically, Madariaga lards his presentation with uncomfortable asides ("I only know two things about the Monroe Doctrine: one is that no American I have met knows what it is; the other is that no American I have met will consent to its being tampered with. . . .") and with wild flights of speculative fancy: "The discovery of America was a disaster for Spain. America should have been discovered by the English, which is what might have happened if Ferdinand and Isabel had locked up Columbus in a lunatic asylum where he belonged." Yet all in all it is a worthwhile book.

MECHAM, JOHN LLOYD. **The United States and Inter-American Security, 1889–1960.** Austin: University of Texas Press (for the Institute of Latin American Studies, University of Texas), 1961, 514 p.

This formidable volume provides a comprehensive and quite detailed history of inter-American relations, principally as reflected in efforts to institutionalize and codify them. Mecham's basic premise is that "the inter-American system exists because of United States membership. The fact that the Latin-American countries enjoy exceptional advantages through their formal association with the United States . . . is the cement of the Alliance. Given the true role of the United States in the inter-American system, it follows that the strength and effectiveness of that system are conditioned by the degree of solidarity that exists between this country and its Latin-American associates." Solidarity becomes, therefore, the key notion employed by Mecham as he evaluates the historical record.

But solidarity in respect of what? For what purpose? Mecham notes that while concern for security has undergirded hemispheric organization during much of the period he reviews, increasingly economic problems are coming in Latin American minds to transcend threats in the security sphere. If solidarity is to be maintained, then, it is essential that the United States accommodate itself to this shifting Latin American emphasis.

BERLE, ADOLF AUGUSTUS, JR. **Latin America—Diplomacy and Reality.** New York: Harper and Row (for the Council on Foreign Relations), 1962, 144 p.

Much of Adolf Berle's extraordinary career has been devoted to inter-American affairs, his official involvement beginning in the 1930s and culminating in 1960–

1961 when he chaired President Kennedy's Latin American task force and served as a special consultant to the Secretary of State. In this forceful book he presents a stark picture of the hemisphere that is calculated to shatter complacency and to provoke feelings of pressing concern, if not alarm.

As one of the architects of the Alliance for Progress, he handles the many complex dimensions of Latin America's development challenge with ease and skill. What principally preoccupies him, however, is the communist threat to Latin America and, through Latin America, to the United States. "The cold war has been declared. Overseas as well as hemispheric operations are now in full blast, including planning, preparing, mounting, and in some areas directing, active guerrilla warfare. These operations are designed to conquer and to keep. . . . Preparations for a major offensive in Latin America are, if anything, more complete in 1962 than were Soviet preparations for the capture of Western Europe in 1947." Berle's book was in press before the Cuban missile crisis occurred in October 1962. It is as powerful an expression of hemispheric cold-war thinking as has appeared. Therein lies its enduring value.

WOOD, BRYCE. **The United States and Latin American Wars, 1932–1942.** New York: Columbia University Press, 1966, 519 p.

Three ugly disputes erupted and festered in South America during the years between 1928 and 1942: the Chaco War between Bolivia and Paraguay, the Leticia dispute between Colombia and Peru, and the Marañón conflict between Ecuador and Peru. Bryce Wood's primary purpose in this excellent book is to examine the role played by noncontending American states—and particularly by the United States—in bringing these contests to a halt. Wood demonstrates that that role was not efficacious. Despite a long-standing commitment in the hemisphere to avoidance of armed conflict and to peaceful settlement, the other states found it impossible to impose effective sanctions against the warring parties or to employ military force to stop the struggles.

Wood's conclusion, however, is that hemispheric recognition of the failure of the inter-American system to perform effectively in these situations contributed importantly to the willingness of the American states to commit themselves to those procedures of peaceful settlement embodied in the Rio Treaty (1947) and the Charter of the OAS (1948). It was precisely the refusal of the United States to do more than show "solicitude in anarchy"—in an earlier era it might have used its immense power in coercive fashion to bring the parties to a settlement—that helped persuade the Latin Americans that the United States was indeed dedicated to the policy of the Good Neighbor and that the Latin Americans themselves, without collective and effective inter-American machinery, were powerless to curb interstate aggression.

Wood's style is a happy one: "In the Chaco conflict in 1935 Bolivia and Paraguay resembled two unhorsed and wounded warriors, capable of nothing more than feeble gestures of defiance. Quite ingeniously, the [Peace Conference] was able to assist the warriors back to their camps with their dignity nearly unimpaired, but the fighting had not been prevented by the American states."

BARBER, WILLARD F. and RONNING, C. NEALE. **Internal Security and Military Power: Counterinsurgency and Civic Action in Latin America.** Columbus: Ohio State University Press, 1966, 338 p.

Guerrilla insurgency emerged as a major problem in a number of Latin American countries in the aftermath of Castro's successful campaign against Batista. OAS treaties and existing bilateral military arrangements between the United States and Latin American states did not in themselves provide an effective response to that challenge. During the early 1960s, therefore, the United States undertook to train and equip Latin American armed forces for counterinsurgency. Moreover, recognizing that the image held by Latin Americans, especially rural peoples, of their own military establishments was not necessarily a positive one, the United

States urged Latin American armies to involve themselves in "civic action" projects—road-building, sanitation works, school construction—and provided much of the machinery and tools for such activity.

Barber and Ronning have written a comprehensive, penetrating and balanced review of this effort. They conclude that the training provided in the tactics of riot control and anti-guerrilla warfare proved useful. The civic action program, however, was much less successful. The authors note that the developmental infrastructure could have been provided as well or better by agencies other than the armed forces, who were not particularly successful in gaining the trust, affection and coöperation of the populations among which they worked, and that there was little to indicate that civic action had encouraged democratic attitudes or behavior on the part of the military.

NORTH AMERICA

THE UNITED STATES

General; Historical

HARTZ, LOUIS. **The Liberal Tradition in America: An Interpretation of American Political Thought since the Revolution.** New York: Harcourt, 1955, 329 p.

In the 1950s the shock of American involvement in the seemingly permanent cold war and the experience for the first time of pervasive military insecurity provoked a wide-ranging inquiry into the foundations of American political thought and behavior. Theologians, political scientists and historians all sought to explain why Americans seemed so ill prepared for the situation confronting them.

Louis Hartz's **The Liberal Tradition in America** employs the techniques of the comparative intellectual historian in a search for an answer. Americans, he finds, have never experienced a genuine domestic political conflict. Lacking a feudal past, they have always believed in Lockean liberalism. Their political arguments have been superficial debates over distinctions without differences. As a result they cannot comprehend real conflict in international affairs. Their tendency is to ignore conflict through isolationism, try to preach it away, or eliminate it through war.

The book provided an elegant intellectual rationale for the "consensus" historians who dominated American historical writing for two decades after the Second World War. These historians assumed that the American past was characterized by fundamental agreement and that the historian's task was to explicate areas of agreement rather than to emphasize alleged conflict. For a discussion of consensus history against the background of the history which it supplanted, see Richard Hofstadter, **The Progressive Histories** (New York: Knopf, 1968, 498 p.).

BEARD, CHARLES AUSTIN and BEARD, MARY (RITTER). **The Rise of American Civilization.** New York: Macmillan, 1927–1939, 3 v.

The first two volumes of this general history of the United States in its social and cultural aspects were hailed in superlative terms when they appeared in 1927. Beard, with the assistance of his wife, applied an economic interpretation of history to the American experience. The nation's economic collapse, which began two years after the publication of the volumes, seemed to confirm this analysis that crucial decisions in American life were too often made in the interests of a narrow economic élite. Beard became unquestionably the most influential American historian of the 1930s.

The third volume, **America in Midpassage** (1939, 977 p.), appeared on the eve of the Second World War. It applied the same theory of economic determinism to the threat of United States involvement in the war with Hitler and reasoned that the same interests were working toward American intervention. When the United States entered the war in 1941 Beard's influence rapidly waned. In the late 1950s and early 1960s, however, several historians, too young to have studied with Beard personally, began to resurrect his analysis. The most notable of this group was William Appleman Williams, author of **The Tragedy of American Diplomacy** (Cleveland: World Publishing Co., 1959, 219 p.) and **The Contours of American History** (Cleveland: World Publishing Co., 1961, 513 p.). Williams, in turn, inspired a score of still younger historians. Beard, himself an argumentative historian, would have been pleased with the ensuing controversy.

HOFSTADTER, RICHARD. **The Age of Reform: From Bryan to F.D.R.** New York: Knopf, 1955, 328 p.

The majority of American historians writing in mid-century about their nation considered themselves liberal and sided with reform. They admired the Populists, the Progressives, Bryan, Wilson and the two Roosevelts. They did not admire McKinley, Taft, Coolidge and Hoover. Sometimes admiration led to blindness toward flaws in American reformers and their reforms.

The Age of Reform provided a corrective, welcomed by some, denounced by others. Hofstadter gives full credit to the Populists for their serious attack on the problems of industrialism and for their insistence that the federal government assume responsibility for the common welfare, but he also points to the dark side: "The conspirational theory and the associated Anglophobic and Judophobic feelings were part of a larger complex of fear and suspicion of the stranger that haunted, and still tragically haunts, the nativist American mind." Hofstadter is also critical of the Progressives, whom he describes as predominantly middle-class men anxious over a perceived loss of status to "the trusts" and corrupt urban politicians.

For further discussion of some of these matters, see John Higham, **Strangers in the Land: Patterns of American Nativism, 1860–1925** (New Brunswick: Rutgers University Press, 1955, 431 p.).

NEUSTADT, RICHARD ELLIOTT. **Presidential Power: The Politics of Leadership.** New York: Wiley, 1960, 224 p.

Richard Neustadt recalls President Harry Truman's prediction of what incoming President Eisenhower would discover: "He'll sit here, and he'll say, 'Do this! Do that!' *And nothing will happen.* Poor Ike—it won't be a bit like the Army. He'll find it very frustrating." The anecdote sets the purpose of the book: an analysis of how the President can exercise power within the Executive branch.

Students of American government traditionally described the President's powers in relation to Congress. Neustadt, a political scientist who served on Truman's staff, shows how the President must employ sophisticated political skill in order to have his way within his own branch. The book reflects Neustadt's admiration for Presidents Franklin D. Roosevelt and Truman and his dissatisfaction with Eisenhower's passive style. His ideal president is an experienced politician, "an expert on the presidency," who plans every move in terms of power. The author assumes that presidential power is good, the more the better. He shows none of the qualms which became so evident among scholars a decade later.

The book contains five case studies illustrating success and failure of leadership. The successes are Truman's dismissal of General MacArthur in 1951 and his seizure of the steel mills in 1952, and Eisenhower's enforcement of desegregation in 1957. The failures are Truman's acceptance of the decision to send troops north to the Yalu in the Korean War and Eisenhower's inability to make his views on federal spending for socially useful purposes prevail over the obstruction of Secretary of the Treasury George Humphrey. Neustadt suggests that Eisenhower's uncritical respect for the opinions of businessmen was similar to Truman's excessive respect for generals. John F. Kennedy is said to have read this book carefully.

LEUCHTENBURG, WILLIAM E. **Franklin D. Roosevelt and the New Deal, 1932–1940.** New York: Harper and Row, 1963, 393 p.

This is perhaps the best single volume on the New Deal and one of the best contributions to the "New American Nation Series" under the general editorship of Henry Steele Commager and Richard B. Morris. The book is based on judicious use of the specialized studies and a wide range of manuscript sources. The style is lively and compact.

The book represents a third phase in a swinging pendulum of interpretation. Contemporary friends and critics of the Roosevelt administration stressed the New Deal's sharp departures from the past. The pendulum then moved to a set of interpretations which belittled change and stressed the continuity of New Deal measures with Populism, Progressivism and the wartime measures of 1917–1918. Leuchtenburg returns to an emphasis on the New Deal as a genuine revolution—in the agenda of American politics, in the character of the presidency, and in the direct impact of the federal government on the people—but a revolution which only went halfway because it excluded many Americans, "sharecroppers, slum dwellers, most Negroes."

SCHLESINGER, ARTHUR MEIER, JR. **The Age of Roosevelt.** Boston: Houghton, 1957–1960, 3 v.

These volumes—like Roosevelt's New Deal—are full of life, partisan vigor, some hasty judgments and occasional oversimplifications. The first volume, "The Crisis of the Old Order, 1919–1933," is a colorful if somewhat unfair history of the Republican era culminating in the Great Depression. Herbert Hoover's failure is heightened for dramatic contrast with what was to come. The second volume, best of the three, describes "the Hundred Days" with which the New Deal began and the remaining events of 1933–1934. The third volume describes the rise of native radicalism—both right and left—as a potential threat to Roosevelt, the attack on New Deal legislation by the Supreme Court, and the triumphant reëlection of 1936.

Schlesinger's enthusiasm makes these volumes lively reading; it also leads him to restrain his criticism. He does not deal adequately with the question of business domination of National Recovery Administration codes. He passes quickly over discrimination against the Negro, ignoring, for example, the exclusion of Negroes from jobs in the Civilian Conservation Corps in many states. He admits that sharecroppers suffered from the operation of the Agricultural Adjustment Administration, but he emphasizes that "out of despair, there began to rise further emotions: a sense of solidarity and a sense of militance."

In 1961 Schlesinger joined the administration of John F. Kennedy and became a participant in the high drama which he had experienced vicariously with the New Deal.

PHILLIPS, CABELL. **The Truman Presidency.** New York: Macmillan, 1966, 463 p.

Some presidencies, like those of Franklin Roosevelt and John F. Kennedy, create an instant spate of historical writing. Others, like that of Harry S. Truman, fail to attract immediate attention and fall quietly into the limbo of the middle distance— too recent for academic historians, too remote for journalists. Phillips' account, the only overall view of the subject, attempts to fill a void. Relying heavily on newspapers, interviews and Truman's **Memoirs,** Phillips grapples with the issue of how a very ordinary man became such an extraordinary president. He notes Truman's softness for old cronies who on occasion served him ill and admits that the President failed to prevent the brutalizing investigations of the "loyalty" of government employees. But on balance Truman appears a hero, especially for his courageous foreign policy. By 1970 a generation of young, critical historians of the Truman years had begun to write—for a sampling of their work see Barton J. Bernstein, *ed.,* **The Politics and Policies of the Truman Administration** (Chicago: Quadrangle

Books, 1970, 330 p.). However, a second comprehensive assessment, to compare and contrast with Phillips, had not yet appeared.

MANCHESTER, WILLIAM. **The Death of a President: November 20–November 25, 1963.** New York: Harper and Row, 1967, 710 p.

The irrationality of the assassination of President John F. Kennedy in Dallas, Texas, on November 22, 1963, disturbed the nation profoundly. Within weeks of the tragedy a flood of books—some sensible, others preposterous—began to appear. The appointment of an official commission of investigation headed by Earl Warren, Chief Justice of the Supreme Court, could not arrest the torrent of rumor, innuendo and speculation.

Such were the circumstances in which the dead President's widow asked William Manchester to write an account of the assassination. No man could control all the ramifications of that event in a single book. Manchester does not. His study relies heavily on the enormous quantity of evidence gathered by the Warren Commission, supplemented by hundreds of hours of interviewing. The style is breathless, at times more suited for a Hollywood press release than its sober subject. Trivia clutter every page. There is no depth of analysis. Nevertheless, the book stood out as the best available. Manchester believes, with the Warren Commission, that the President was killed by Lee Harvey Oswald acting alone and motivated by impulses arising from his unhappy life and damaged personality. The publication of the book was attended by an overblown controversy between Manchester and the Kennedy family, and some portions of the original manuscript were deleted at the family's request.

GOLDMAN, ERIC FREDERICK. **Rendezvous with Destiny.** New York: Knopf, 1952, 503 p.

Goldman's books are generally partisan, colorful, optimistic and enlivened with the telling anecdote. He personifies the historian as cheerleader for the men and ideas he finds appealing. **Rendezvous with Destiny** (the title is from Franklin D. Roosevelt's phrase used in 1936) surveys the development of American liberal thought from the gentility of the reformers of the Grant era to the "give-em-hell" tactics of Harry Truman. The heart of the book analyzes what the author terms the "steel chain" of conservative social Darwinism which prevented men from reforming social, legal and economic conditions and then describes how reform Darwinism "dissolved" that chain.

Goldman's somewhat uncritical optimism about American liberalism also infuses his popular history of the post–Second World War era, **The Crucial Decade and After: America, 1945–1960** (New York: Vintage Books, 2d enl. ed., 1961, 349 p.). In the mid-1960s he served President Lyndon B. Johnson in the White House as a special consultant-liaison man with the world of the arts and the universities. His account of the Johnson presidency, **The Tragedy of Lyndon Johnson** (New York: Knopf, 1969, 531 p.), indicates that his previous optimism was shaken.

CHAFEE, ZECHARIAH, JR. **Free Speech in the United States.** Cambridge: Harvard University Press, 1941, 634 p.

President Woodrow Wilson in theory grasped the meaning of free speech as well as any leader of the twentieth century. In practice, however, violations of the individual's right to free speech by the federal government during his administration were extensive. What the federal government began during the First World War, state and local governments tended to copy. Chafee, then a young professor at the Harvard Law School, published the first version of this classic and compassionate treatise in 1920, under the title "Freedom of Speech." Two decades later he brought his work up to date by tracing the history of free speech through a decade of repression in the 1920s into a period of relative vindication by the Supreme Court under Chief Justice Charles Evans Hughes in the 1930s.

Chafee's work is timeless. As the authority on the subject for many years, he taught a generation of lawyers who became judges in the 1950s and 1960s when so many of the statutory and administrative barriers which he described and deplored were removed from American life by judicial decisions. The book should be studied both for itself and for the influence which radiated from it.

MASON, ALPHEUS THOMAS. **The Supreme Court from Taft to Warren.** Baton Rouge: Louisiana State University Press, rev. ed., 1968, 293 p.

One of De Tocqueville's most frequently quoted observations is that "hardly any question arises in the United States that is not resolved sooner or later into a judicial question." Professor Mason illustrates this comment through his history of the Supreme Court from the installation of William Howard Taft as Chief Justice in 1921 to the last years of the Court under Chief Justice Earl Warren.

Mason makes plain where his sympathies lie. He finds the Court under Taft conservative and narrow and the approach of the Warren Court imaginative and liberal. He denies that the role of the Supreme Court judge is or ever can be beyond politics. He deplores the effect of the Court on the nation's efforts to regulate the economy in the mid-1930s and rejoices that the justices "almost overnight" confessed the error of their ways, exercised judicial self-restraint and accepted the will of Congress. The Warren Court's involvement in political issues, Mason argues, was quite different than that of the conservative Court before 1937, since it expanded the limits of freedom, buttressed the moral foundations of society, kept open constitutional alternatives to violent change, and brought the society closer to the ideals it long professed.

For brief biographies of all Supreme Court justices, together with a generous selection of their more important decisions, see Leon Friedman and Fred L. Israel, *eds.,* **The Justices of the United States Supreme Court, 1789–1969** (New York: Chelsea House in association with Bowker, 1969, 4 v.).

BERNSTEIN, IRVING. **The Lean Years: A History of the American Worker, 1920– 1933.** Boston: Houghton Mifflin, 1960, 577 p.
————. **Turbulent Years: A History of the American Worker, 1933–1941.** Boston: Houghton Mifflin, 1970, 873 p.

The historian of labor movements and the laboring man in America has a difficult task. He can trace the myriad shifts in union organization and reorganization and follow the sometimes arcane debates over doctrine, and risk being dreary. A very competent and informative example of this genre is Selig Perlman and Philip Taft, **Labor Movements** (New York: Macmillan, 1936, 683 p.), the fourth volume in John R. Commons' classic series "History of Labor in the United States." Or the historian can pick a topic because of its color and drama, with the knowledge that his subject is not representative of labor as a whole. A brilliant, fervent book of this type is Melvyn Dubofsky, **We Shall Be All: A History of the Industrial Workers of the World** (Chicago: Quadrangle Books, 1969, 557 p.).

Bernstein's two volumes are labor history at its best, combining drama with careful attention to changes of organization. The first volume describes a period of broken dreams and strikes, dwindling union membership and repression by the courts. It is a powerful antidote to the myth of the 1920s as the decade of prosperity. The second volume follows the rise of union membership under the encouragement of New Deal legislation and administration and concludes with the momentous battles within the labor movement, swirling around the central figure of John L. Lewis.

MYRDAL, GUNNAR and OTHERS. **An American Dilemma: The Negro Problem and Modern Democracy.** New York: McGraw-Hill, 1964, 2 v.

This searching and influential study of the problem of race relations in the United States was first published in 1944. A twentieth anniversary edition appeared in 1964 with an introductory essay by Arnold Rose—one of the original staff members of the study—on changes that had taken place over two decades.

The "dilemma" of the title is the conflict between the nation's egalitarian values and its pervasive exploitation of Negroes. Myrdal and his staff travelled the land, interviewed, observed, compiled statistics and probed the past. Never had such a thorough and devastating account of the injuries—social, economic, legal, political—inflicted by whites on blacks been compiled. The theme of the study is the "vicious circle" by which "white prejudice and discrimination keep the Negro low in standards of living, health, education, manners and morals. This, in turn, gives support to white prejudices."

An American Dilemma became a bench mark from which to measure progress. Myrdal originally was optimistic, and in some respects his optimism proved correct. A quarter-century after the book appeared black Americans were much closer to legal, political and economic equality, though a great gap remained, especially in health, education and opportunity for leadership in the nation.

STEARNS, HAROLD EDMUND, *ed.* **Civilization in the United States.** New York: Harcourt, 1922, 577 p.

Americans have a fondness for pessimistic self-appraisals of their civilization. This landmark collection of 33 essays, all but three by Americans, is a measure of the discontent of the "younger generation" intellectuals at the beginning of the 1920s. The essays deal with such topics as the city (Lewis Mumford), law (Zechariah Chafee, Jr.), radicalism (George Soule) and the literary life (Van Wyck Brooks). They are a window on the era that came to an end with the collapse of the stock market and the onset of the Depression. It is interesting to see how many of the issues discussed are lively problems half a century later—the city built for machines rather than people; racial prejudice woven into "the general economic, social, political, and intellectual system;" inequality of the sexes; contradictions between law and justice; the political weakness of the Left; the high cost of medicine; the commercialization of the arts. Other problems, however, have diminished or disappeared—for example, small town domination, the low pay of scientists, the mistreated immigrant and "Prohibition."

ALLEN, FREDERICK LEWIS. **Only Yesterday: An Informal History of the Nineteen-Twenties.** New York: Harper, 1931, 370 p.

With the publication of **Only Yesterday,** Frederick Lewis Allen became the most popular and widely read social historian in the United States in this century. His affectionate and nostalgic portrait of the 1920s—silly, fun-loving, irreverent, prosperous—appealed to a nation suffering in the Great Depression and did more than any other book to fix a distorted image of that decade which had not faded half a century later.

Allen's chief competitor as a social historian was Mark Sullivan, author—compiler would be a better word—of **Our Times: The United States, 1900–1925** (New York: Scribner, 1926–1935, 6 v.). Sullivan manufactured scrapbooks, full of pictures, cartoons and headlines, good for browsing, devoid of analysis; Allen relied on his beguiling skill as a writer of light prose. He had many imitators, including himself with **Since Yesterday** (New York: Harper, 1940, 362 p.) and **The Big Change: America Transforms Itself, 1900–1950** (New York: Harper, 1952, 308 p.). John N. Brooks' **The Great Leap: The Past Twenty-Five Years in America** (New York: Harper and Row, 1966, 382 p.) is a well-written attempt to carry on the Allen tradition. But no volume since 1931 has had the appeal of **Only Yesterday.** Perhaps the American reader had seen too much to be deeply interested any longer in the lighter and more innocent aspects of the nation's past.

LERNER, MAX. **America as a Civilization: Life and Thought in the U.S. Today.** New York: Simon and Schuster, 1957, 1,036 p.

This book is a bold effort to grasp "the pattern and inner meaning of contemporary American civilization and its relation to the world of today." The result is not the description of a coherent "inner meaning" but a broad set of stimulating observations on almost every phase of American life during the years between 1945 and 1957 when the book was being written. Lerner's career as columnist, teacher and editor was one of vigorous, constructive liberal criticism. There is ample criticism in this volume—of political intolerance, racial prejudice, rigid manners and morals—but from the vantage point of the 1970s the conclusions seem optimistic. Lerner's wide reading and wider circle of friends in the worlds of politics, the arts and letters enabled him to condense and transmit the prevailing attitudes of the time. Therein lies the volume's historical significance.

Foreign Policy

LEOPOLD, RICHARD WILLIAM. **The Growth of American Foreign Policy: A History.** New York: Knopf, 1962, 848 p.

The increasing student interest in foreign affairs in the generation after the end of the Second World War led to the appearance of many historical surveys. Some of the best were new editions of respected volumes that had appeared before the war—for example, Samuel Flagg Bemis, **A Diplomatic History of the United States** (New York: Holt, 1936, 881 p.), stressing the continuation and permutation of basic policies laid down in the eighteenth and nineteenth centuries; and Thomas A. Bailey, **A Diplomatic History of the American People** (New York: Crofts, 1940, 806 p.), stressing the role of public opinion.

Leopold's volume is outstanding among the completely new works. After a brief thematic review of the period to 1889, Leopold concentrates on the twentieth century. Half the book deals with the period since 1939. The author is particularly effective in his treatment of the "interwar compromise" between Wilsonian internationalism and traditional nonentanglement. Recognizing that foreign policy is not a game played by diplomats alone, he gives systematic attention to the role of institutions—the Congress, the military, the Secretaries of State and the Presidents. This is a serious book for serious students.

BEALE, HOWARD KENNEDY. **Theodore Roosevelt and the Rise of America to World Power.** Baltimore: Johns Hopkins Press, 1956, 600 p.

Howard K. Beale achieved his distinguished reputation as a historian from his balanced, compassionate studies of American domestic history—especially of Reconstruction. In the 1950s he became deeply disturbed as historian and moralist over what he considered the desperate situation in the world. To what extent, he asked, was the United States responsible for the international conflict of mid-century? He decided that a study of the role of Theodore Roosevelt in world affairs might provide some answers. Hence this book, the fullest, most detailed and scholarly treatment of the subject.

Beale, like many American liberals of his time, began with an oversimplified image of TR as a braggart and irresponsible militarist. After years of research into mountains of published and unpublished material, Beale concluded that TR was, after all, far more effective than most presidents. He was devoted to the national welfare as he understood it, he knew how to balance ends and means, he sought to encourage the balance of power as a means of preventing war, and he shaped but was respectful of public opinion. He also was sensitive to the point of view of antagonists and was careful to give an enemy a chance to save face. His flaws were the flaws of his time: insensitivity to the latent nationalism of the non-European world, especially China; ignorance of the destructive combination of war and modern technology; overestimation of the power of the British Empire; and a tragic reliance on imperialism as a technique of civilization.

LEVIN, N. GORDON, JR. **Woodrow Wilson and World Politics: America's Response to War and Revolution.** New York: Oxford University Press, 1968, 340 p.

Several generations of American historians have discovered in the protean ideas and policies of Woodrow Wilson the roots of all that they admired or deplored in

American foreign policy. Levin represents a view which became widely shared in the 1960s among American historians on the left—that Wilson had a coherent program "to construct a stable world order of liberal-capitalist internationalism, at the Center of the global ideological spectrum, safe from both the threat of imperialism on the Right and the danger of revolution on the Left." Levin argues that, although Wilson's program was not accepted in his own time, "later generations of American decision-makers would seek fully to realize Wilson's design during World War II and especially during the Cold War." The strength of Levin's book is its emphasis on Wilson's anti-Bolshevik strategy. Its weaknesses are turgid prose and a tendency to find more order and consistency in Wilson's thought than is perhaps warranted.

FERRELL, ROBERT HUGH. **American Diplomacy in the Great Depression: Hoover-Stimson Foreign Policy, 1929–1933.** New Haven: Yale University Press, 1957, 319 p.

This volume is a continuation, in time but not in content, of the author's **Peace in Their Time: The Origins of the Kellogg-Briand Pact** (New Haven: Yale University Press, 1952, 293 p.). Ferrell's first work concentrated on one issue and analyzed in detail the role of private organizations and individuals in originating and carrying out a policy. This study surveys all the important foreign policy issues of the Hoover administration, with the focus almost exclusively on the President and the Secretary of State and their immediate advisers. The sources are predominantly official government documents and the private papers of leaders. The role of opinion outside the government is slighted, unfortunately so for a book whose theme is that "the Great Depression had . . . a catastrophic effect upon the maintenance of world peace."

The book reflects prevailing assumptions about the inter-war years: militaristic Japan and Nazi Germany gained world power and caused the Second World War because the United States and other democracies were too preoccupied by the Depression to use force to stop them. Ferrell's treatment of familiar events—the Manchurian crisis and the London Economic Conference, for example—is sound although somewhat one-dimensional. However, the archives of other governments, especially the British, were not available when he wrote.

DUROSELLE, JEAN-BAPTISTE. **From Wilson to Roosevelt: Foreign Policy of the United States, 1913–1945.** Cambridge: Harvard University Press, 1963, 499 p.

Thousands of American historians have written about Europe. Duroselle stands out in a small group of Europeans who have written knowledgeably about American history. In addition to skill as a diplomatic historian, his great advantage is his detachment from the political controversies which affect all Americans, historians included. His analyses of Woodrow Wilson's fight for the League of Nations, the isolationism of the 1930s and Franklin D. Roosevelt's relations with the Soviet Union are cool and balanced. Duroselle pays close attention to the economic and military foundations of foreign policy and thus sets himself apart from the majority of American diplomatic historians who do not handle such matters adequately.

Duroselle argues that Wilson was a great strategist with a consistent doctrine for the reordering of international relations but a failure as a leader of the American people. He sees Roosevelt, on the other hand, as a great leader but a poor strategist. Duroselle concludes that if Roosevelt had a doctrine "it was uncertain, elusive, and that if it was consistent, the consistency was only in the secret of the man's mind—a mind which revealed everything but the most important matter."

This is a translation of "De Wilson à Roosevelt: Politique Extérieure des États-Unis, 1913–1945" (Paris: Colin, 1960, 494 p.).

DIVINE, ROBERT ALEXANDER. **The Illusion of Neutrality.** Chicago: University of Chicago Press, 1962, 370 p.

This is the best study of the dominant role of Congress in shaping American foreign policy during the early years of the New Deal. Divine achieves his purpose of redressing the overbalance of historical attention to the purely domestic aspects of the New Deal.

The central issue of the book is the question of a legislated arms embargo. Divine begins by analyzing the failure in 1933 of the movement for a discretionary arms embargo, which would have allowed the President to discriminate between aggressor and victim nations and to have coöperated tacitly with collective action by the League of Nations against an aggressor. "The strength of the Wilsonian tradition, embodied in the sincere efforts of men like Hull and Davis, could not dissolve the grip of isolation on the people, the Congress, and the President." Instead isolationism triumphed with the hearings of the Nye Committee and the passage of the Neutrality Acts. Divine's personal preference is clearly for the "internationalists." His portrait of President Franklin D. Roosevelt—inconsistent and ready to sacrifice his own beliefs to Congressional whim—is not flattering. Secretary of State Cordell Hull also receives failing marks.

Other significant books touching on neutrality and isolation in the 1930s are Selig Adler, **The Isolationist Impulse: Its Twentieth-Century Reaction** (New York: Abelard-Schuman, 1957, 538 p.); Wayne S. Cole, **Senator Gerald P. Nye and American Foreign Relations** (Minneapolis: University of Minnesota Press, 1962, 293 p.); and Manfred Jonas, **Isolationism in America, 1935–1941** (Ithaca: Cornell University Press, 1966, 315 p.).

TANSILL, CHARLES CALLAN. **Back Door to War: The Roosevelt Foreign Policy, 1933–1941.** Chicago: Regnery, 1952, 690 p.

American participation in the two world wars and the cold war has produced three waves of revisionist historiography characterized by rejection of the official explanation of why the United States became involved and a tendency to find more guilt in Washington than in the house of the enemy. Each wave overlaps the next in time and content.

Charles Callan Tansill holds a prominent place in this continuing cycle. His **America Goes to War** (Boston: Little, Brown, 1938, 731 p.) was the most scholarly of revisionist accounts of American entry into the First World War published during the 1930s. **Back Door to War** marks a sharp decline in scholarly objectivity but, like its predecessor, it had wide influence. The book is the prototype of dozens of attacks from the right on President Franklin D. Roosevelt's foreign policy. Tansill's thesis is that Roosevelt's main objective was to save the British Empire. To that end he sought war with Germany. When Hitler refused to be provoked, Roosevelt manoeuvred Japan into attacking Pearl Harbor, thus enabling the United States to enter the "back door to war." Tansill argues that Roosevelt was pulling Russian as well as British chestnuts out of the fire. Far better, he implies, to have stood aside and let Germany and Japan defend the world against communism. The argument is related to the contention that during the Second World War Roosevelt "sold out" to Russia. The book was roundly condemned by most professional historians, but its thesis became part of the folklore of a segment of the American public.

WILLKIE, WENDELL LEWIS. **One World.** New York: Simon and Schuster, 1943, 206 p.

The book was the result of Wendell Willkie's wartime trip to the Middle East, Russia and China. It is a passionate statement of liberal war aims and belief in "internationalism." The title is the theme: this is now one world. The small book received extraordinary circulation (more than one million copies sold within seven weeks of publication, more than two million by 1945, plus syndication in 107 newspapers). The particulars of Willkie's message were threefold: there must be coöperation between the United States and the Soviet Union if there is to be peace; colonialism is dead and nationalism is rising everywhere; and if the United States is to hold the respect of other peoples it must eradicate racial prejudice at home.

Willkie's political career was a rocket which descended as dramatically as it rose. Unsuccessful Republican candidate for president against Roosevelt in 1940, he was quickly eliminated as a candidate for a second nomination and died in October 1944. His book remains a monument to a moment of hope and optimism about the future.

JONES, JOSEPH MARION. **The Fifteen Weeks (February 21–June 5, 1947).** New York: Viking, 1955, 296 p.

It is one of the myths of recent American history that a sudden, revolutionary transformation in foreign policy took place in the winter and spring of 1947. In the space of a miraculous "fifteen weeks" the United States threw away all doubts, confusions and the last tattered remnants of isolationism and put on the mantle of world responsibility as the defender of democratic civilization against Soviet totalitarianism.

Joseph M. Jones' account of events in the State Department between the day the British announced they could no longer afford to pay for military aid to Greece and the day that Secretary of State George C. Marshall delivered the "Marshall Plan" address at Harvard has contributed substantially to the myth. Jones at the time was a public affairs officer in the State Department and was occupied primarily in drafting speeches. He was a direct observer and peripheral participant in the process by which the Truman Doctrine and the Marshall Plan were announced. He has a dramatist's skill in constructing a suspenseful story, and a brisk journalistic style. Such divergent characters as Dean Acheson and George F. Kennan, both of whom were there, agree that Jones' account is a superior one. It suffers, nevertheless, from a narrow perspective. Jones had no means of judging the accuracy of American perceptions of events in Greece or of Soviet behavior. He was unaware of much of the background and thus overestimated the suddenness of American decisions. Stephen G. Xydis' massive treatment of **Greece and the Great Powers 1944–1947** supplies some of that background.

GRAEBNER, NORMAN ARTHUR. **The New Isolationism: A Study in Politics and Foreign Policy since 1950.** New York: Ronald Press, 1956, 289 p.

The word "isolationism," like the words "appeasement" and "interventionism," became an all-purpose weapon in the verbal arsenal of American politics after 1941. Such words tended to lose meaning as their use became more popular. Graebner's book epitomizes the loose application of the "isolationist" epithet. A historian writing as journalist in the midst of the events he describes, his research is not especially deep, but his passion is.

Graebner argues that the important policies of the late 1940s—the Truman Doctrine, the Marshall Plan, NATO—were based on the recognition that foreign policy ought not to be an issue in partisan politics and maintains that the critics, mostly conservative and Republican, forced the Truman and Eisenhower administrations to adopt unwise policies—for example, toward China. By concentrating on domestic politics Graebner slights the objective international factors to which the administrations were responding. For a deeper but less lively analysis see H. Bradford Westerfield, **Foreign Policy and Party Politics: Pearl Harbor to Korea** (New Haven: Yale University Press, 1955, 448 p.).

HILSMAN, ROGER. **To Move a Nation: The Politics of Foreign Policy in the Administration of John F. Kennedy.** Garden City: Doubleday, 1967, 602 p.

Roger Hilsman is a West Point graduate who made his career as an academic political scientist. From 1961 to 1964 he served as Director of the Bureau of Intelligence and Research in the State Department and then as Assistant Secretary of State for Far Eastern Affairs. His book is a crisply written history and memoir with a bit of unobtrusive theorizing about the decision-making process. He concentrates on the events in which he participated—the neutralization of Laos, the Cuban missile crisis, the Congo crisis, the effort to develop a new and more accommodating policy toward Communist China, the confrontation between Indonesia and Malaysia and, above all, Vietnam.

Hilsman argues that the Vietnam conflict could have been won with the sophisticated application of "political, economic, and social action into which very carefully calibrated military measures were interwoven." An exponent of counterinsurgency against communist guerrilla warfare, he was defeated by—at least that is his perception—the Army's stubborn inability to abandon traditional military action. Hilsman's text—based on secret documentation not cited or quoted, but deposited for future release at the John F. Kennedy Library—was cleared by security officials in the government before publication.

BROWN, SEYOM. **The Faces of Power: Constancy and Change in United States Foreign Policy from Truman to Johnson.** New York: Columbia University Press, 1968, 397 p.

Feeling that much of the debate on United States foreign policy has been simply a "contest between rationalizing platitude and deprecating caricature," the author —a political analyst who took leave from the RAND Corporation to write "an idiosyncratic book free of the pressure of deadlines"—undertook to examine the operating theories prevailing, and yet changing, in the quarter-century after World War II.

While finding elements of constancy in the reliance on implicit or explicit physical power, preferably in association with allies, he also discerns a growing search in the Kennedy-Johnson years for nonmilitary instruments, especially in dealing with the growing role of third-world countries. This hope, "to substitute the housing development for the aircraft carrier," was flickering when the author completed the first edition in late 1967.

It is indicative of the jolting shifts in American attitudes and policy in the late 1960s that, in an epilogue to the second edition of the book, appearing in late 1969, the author finds that even the element of constancy—the use of power, in whatever form, to check communism—was under serious challenge: "The consensus underlying the constancy in foreign policy from Truman to Johnson was at an end." While we are still too close chronologically to this discontinuity to judge its full import, Brown's sense of a kind of terminus rings true.

HOFFMANN, STANLEY. **Gulliver's Troubles, or the Setting of American Foreign Policy.** New York: McGraw-Hill (for the Council on Foreign Relations), 1968, 556 p.

In an exceptionally fine introduction Stanley Hoffmann stresses that he is less concerned with policy recommendations than with understanding the setting within which germane and applicable American policies can be made. The book is a brilliant, intricate but never obfuscating pursuit of this goal. While ostensibly concerned with Atlantic policy, it is in fact global in its scope and implications.

The author begins with an analysis of the international scene: the troubled world of the 1960s which had become so disconcertingly different from that of the preceding decade and a half. He then turns to the problems of the American response to this environment—problems stemming from its national style and from deeply rooted qualities of its political system. In the final section he returns to foreign policy and suggests guidelines for feasible objectives and approaches, with some emphasis here on the Atlantic alliance.

Hoffmann has a subtle, richly furnished mind that is exceptionally well equipped to see the United States at close hand and yet with a sense of distance (he was largely European-trained). His critical analysis of the American style of politics and diplomacy is in some respects devastating, not because of a display of outrage but because he recognizes its profound sources in the national life. For the same reason his analysis is most salutary: few books dealing with the flux of recent events have shown this capacity to dig down to bedrock, to indicate the level at which foreign policy must be rethought and reconstructed.

ROSTOW, WALT WHITMAN. **The United States in the World Arena: An Essay in Recent History.** New York: Harper, 1960, 568 p.

This book is important both for its content and for the subsequent career of its author. In the Kennedy administration Rostow served as director of the Policy Planning Staff in the Department of State. In the Johnson administration he moved to the White House as the President's closest adviser on foreign affairs. What he wrote in the late 1950s became a blueprint for policy recommendations in the 1960s.

Rostow's prescription for the 1960s called for an effort "to make war, major or minor, irrational for Communist leadership;" for assistance to the new nations of Asia, the Middle East, Africa and Latin America in the tasks of modernization without recourse to communism or other totalitarianisms; and for "the bringing into effective and responsible partnership of Western Europe and Japan in both military and economic policy." If these policies failed, Rostow argued, the ideological balance of power would shift against the United States with "major adverse consequences for the quality of American society and for the viability of the humanistic principles which underlie it." The American sense of democratic mission to the world would be threatened, a mission "which has given to American life much of its moral worth, its distinction, and its forward momentum." All three Presidents elected in the 1960s accepted this reasoning.

KENNAN, GEORGE FROST. **American Diplomacy 1900–1950.** Chicago: University of Chicago Press, 1951, 146 p.

This little volume, perhaps the most widely read book on American diplomatic history, represents George F. Kennan's first effort to influence policy by shaping the nation's understanding of its history. Written with grace and disarming diffidence, it conditioned the thinking of an entire generation of students.

By 1949 Kennan had completed nearly a quarter-century as a career foreign service officer. As head of the State Department's Policy Planning Staff, he had reached a position of high responsibility. Mainly through his famous "X" article, "The Sources of Soviet Conduct," his ideas were beginning to reach a broad public. Yet Kennan remained dissatisfied at what he conceived to be the profound failure of the American people to understand the sources of their own conduct in world affairs. He asked and received a "sabbatical" from the Department in order to undertake the historical review which, he hoped, would help reform American foreign policy, and began his study a few weeks after the outbreak of the Korean War.

American Diplomacy examines the war with Spain, the Open Door, the sentimental attachment for China, involvement in two world wars, and concludes that too often American policy was erratic, emotional and naïvely uninformed about the real needs and conditions of other countries. Ends were utopian, means inadequate. The basic flaw was "the belief that it should be possible to suppress the chaotic and dangerous aspirations of governments in the international field by the acceptance of some system of legal rules and restraints." Kennan's remedy was patient and realistic maintenance of power, a conservative recognition of the fact that there are no perfect, permanent solutions to international problems, and a greater reliance on trained professional diplomats insulated from the vagaries of public opinion.

OSGOOD, ROBERT ENDICOTT. **Ideals and Self-Interest in America's Foreign Relations: The Great Transformation of the Twentieth Century.** Chicago: University of Chicago Press, 1953, 491 p.

The two decades between the end of the Second World War in 1945 and the escalation of the American war in Vietnam in 1965 were marked by a broad consensus among academic commentators on foreign policy. **Ideals and Self-Interest** both reflected this consensus and helped create it. Osgood indicts American foreign policy prior to 1939 for failing to appreciate that shifts in the international balance of power were a threat to the nation's security. Instead of building the permanent power to deal with a world of naturally self-serving and often aggressive nations, the United States luxuriated in isolationism except for brief, spasmodic crusades against Spain in 1898 and Germany in 1917. Woodrow Wilson is Osgood's principal target because of his alleged failure to understand the primacy of power. Osgood and many of his colleagues in the "realist" school misrepresented Wilson. They also displayed a faith in the efficacy of power—persistently, patiently applied over decades—which seemed less convincing after 1965 than it had in the heyday of national self-confidence.

SPYKMAN, NICHOLAS JOHN. **America's Strategy in World Politics.** New York: Harcourt, 1942, 500 p.

This is a classic statement of power politics and geopolitics as applied to the United States. The author, for many years a professor of international relations at Yale, has a cold approach that permits no sentimentality or idealism: "The statesman who conducts foreign policy can concern himself with values of justice, fairness, and tolerance only to the extent that they contribute to or do not interfere with the power objective. . . . The search for power is not made for the achievement of moral values; moral values are used to facilitate the attainment of power."

The book appeared at a time of utmost uncertainty: 1942, when the United States had entered the Second World War but when the outcome was far from sure. Partly for this reason Spykman devoted much attention, about half the book, to the Western Hemisphere and South America—Eurasia seemed likely to fall to hostile powers.

In retrospect, the limitations to Spykman's approach are only too evident, less in the tendency to underplay the intangible factors in international politics than in the inherent contradictions of power politics as such, contradictions which have been made manifest in the thermonuclear age. Still, while Spykman does not provide sufficient criteria for foreign policy decisions and strategies, it remains uncomfortably true that one cannot blithely disregard his hardheaded and well-formulated insights: they remain a part of the picture. The book, though dated, continues to be rewarding reading.

MORGENTHAU, HANS JOACHIM. **In Defense of the National Interest.** New York: Knopf, 1951, 283 p.

Hans Morgenthau, a professor at the University of Chicago, became in the 1950s and 1960s one of the nation's most influential commentators on foreign policy and a leading exponent, along with George F. Kennan, of the thesis that a strain of moralistic and legalistic thought has crippled American diplomacy.

In Defense of the National Interest appeared at a time of controversy over the aims of American foreign policy and fears of an "inevitable" war with the Soviet Union. Morgenthau argued that the confusion was largely the result of a tendency (which he blamed principally on the influence of Woodrow Wilson) to seek total, utopian, moral solutions to world problems. He wrote that "the appeal to moral principles in the international sphere has no concrete universal meaning," and that to pursue such principles is to leave no room for negotiation and to create a situation where total war seems the only answer. Morgenthau's denunciation of Wilson's "intoxication with moral abstractions" and his extravagant praise of eighteenth-century American "realists" distorted history, but he wrote not for historians but in an effort to influence current policy. He used the basic concepts of this book in developing his critique of American involvement in Vietnam, **Vietnam and the United States** (Washington: Public Affairs Press, 1965, 112 p.).

BARNET, RICHARD J. **Intervention and Revolution: The United States in the Third World.** Cleveland: World Publishing Co., 1968, 302 p.

The traditional view of postwar American foreign policy as a response to communist aggression, as the defense of freedom against tyranny, fell increasingly under attack during the 1960s by "revisionist" writers, most of whom were on the left of the American political spectrum. Some revisionists, such as Gabriel Kolko in **The Roots of American Foreign Policy** (Boston: Beacon Press, 1969, 166 p.), offered rather simplistic, economically deterministic explanations. Barnet's **Intervention and Revolution** is the most sophisticated of the new critiques. He stresses the power of ideas (the concept of the United States as "Guardian at the Gates" of the Free World) and the self-perpetuating momentum of a permanent bureaucracy of "national security managers." His general analysis of the role of the United States as the suppressor of insurgency in the "third world" is illustrated by case studies of the application of the Truman Doctrine to Greece, the Eisenhower Doctrine to Lebanon, the Johnson Doctrine to the Dominican Republic, and of the Vietnam War. Barnet shares a failing common to many of his generation of revisionists—he discounts the importance of mischance on policy.

PRATT, JULIUS WILLIAM. **America's Colonial Experiment.** New York: Prentice-Hall, 1950, 460 p.

The subtitle of this book is "how the United States gained, governed, and in part gave away a colonial empire." Professor Pratt, a diplomatic historian whose high reputation is founded on original studies of American expansionism at the beginning and end of the nineteenth century, provides a survey of a neglected aspect of American history. Many historians have dealt with the debates over the acquisition of the Philippines and other colonies, but information on colonial policies and practices is widely scattered. Pratt brings it together. By the 1960s the concept of American imperialism had become a subject of bitter controversy, as it had been at the time of the acquisition of the Philippines. This book, written when tempers were cool and the issue was out of the public eye, is quiet, dispassionate, even a little dull. But it provides facts, as opposed to opinion, about the political, economic and social governance of overseas territories during the first half of the twentieth century.

GRISWOLD, ALFRED WHITNEY. **The Far Eastern Policy of the United States.** New York: Harcourt, 1938, 530 p.

For many years this volume stood as the best analysis of its subject. The broad theme is that the United States from 1899 to the mid-1930s passed through a series of cycles—an intense level of verbal support for the Open Door in China followed by retreat. Griswold is highly critical of American policy. He believes that it was based on false assumptions, was ignorant of the bearing of European rivalry on Asian affairs, and failed to define objectives carefully or to match ends with means. He argues that John Hay's original Open Door notes, the foundation of U.S. Asian policy, resulted more from British manipulation of American thinking than from a realistic appraisal of American interests.

Griswold's research in American and European sources is extensive and his grasp of traditional European diplomacy firm. Like most American writers on Asia of his generation, he did not know the Chinese or Japanese languages. Like the diplomats about whom he is writing, he assumes that the Chinese are pawns of the imperial powers, incapable of developing or carrying out policies on their own.

BORG, DOROTHY. **American Policy and the Chinese Revolution, 1925–1928.** New York: Macmillan (for the Institute of Pacific Relations), 1947, 440 p.
———. **The United States and the Far Eastern Crisis of 1933–1938.** Cambridge: Harvard University Press, 1964, 674 p.

This study stands out in the field of Chinese-American relations for the 1920s, a decade in which historians have much hard work yet to do. Miss Borg describes the intermingling of various American attitudes on policy toward China in the throes of revolution, and shows that each category of Americans involved with China was divided within itself—some favoring conciliation, others punishment of China.

During this period, all Chinese desired the recovery of China's sovereign rights from unequal treaties imposing extraterritoriality, tariff limitations and the presence of foreign military forces. While the American government felt that China would have to put its house in order before regaining its rights, the Chinese felt that the lack of rights was the principal obstacle to achieving this result. A solution to this impasse in the 1920s might have saved China and the world much misery. Miss Borg concludes that Secretary of State Frank B. Kellogg's policy was "both bold and imaginative in intent and his ideas were considerably in advance of his time." But good intentions were not enough. The practical effect of American policy was in due course explosive.

The United States and the Far Eastern Crisis of 1933–1938 is a detailed and painstaking volume, indispensable for an understanding of American policy toward China and Japan during the early years of the Roosevelt administration. Its focus, like the vast quantity of published and unpublished sources on which it is based, is American. The description and analysis of Japanese and Chinese behavior depends heavily on the reports of American diplomats. Miss Borg's theme here is that the United States maintained a passive, timid policy toward Japanese expansion into China throughout this period. She confirms the familiar picture of Roosevelt as an improviser, and seeks to refute both the official claims of the American government after December 7, 1941, that it had consistently supported China throughout the 1930s and the charges that insensitive American opposition to Japan brought the war nearer.

STEIN, HAROLD, *ed.* **American Civil–Military Decisions: A Book of Case Studies.** University: University of Alabama Press (in coöperation with the Inter-University Case Program), 1963, 705 p.

Before the Second World War few American scholars studied or wrote about the military side of the nation's foreign affairs. Wartime and postwar events demonstrated, however, that detachment on either side of the civil-military equation was often a euphemism for ignorance and an invitation to folly. Military leaders perforce became students of international politics. Political leaders immersed themselves in military affairs. Scholars flocked to study the new subject.

This massive volume of double-column pages is one result—a collection of 11 case studies ranging in time from "The Far Eastern Crisis of 1931–1932: Stimson, Hoover and the Armed Services" to three decisions in 1950 concerning objectives in the Korean War, the rearmament of Germany and the establishment of bases in Spain. The most substantial study, a small book in itself, is Paul Y. Hammond's "Directives for the Occupation of Germany: The Washington Controversy."

A similar volume, containing three case studies, is Warner R. Schilling, Paul Y. Hammond and Glenn H. Snyder, **Strategy, Politics, and Defense Budgets** (New York: Columbia University Press, 1962, 532 p.). The studies in both volumes are important contributions to contemporary history, within the inevitable limitations on access to sources, especially on the military side.

HAMMOND, PAUL Y. **Organizing for Defense.** Princeton: Princeton University Press, 1961, 403 p.

Dean Acheson once commented on the absurdity of trying to put "political" and "military" considerations through the intellectual equivalent of a cream separator. Paul Y. Hammond's analysis of the American defense establishment from the close of the war with Spain through the Eisenhower administration is an extended commentary on Acheson's point. His prose is even more involuted than the controversies he describes, but the subject is important for an understanding of American foreign policy in the twentieth century.

Hammond begins with Elihu Root's reorganization of the Army in 1903, discusses the Navy's problems before and during World War I, and then proceeds to examine the experience of World War II in detail. The final half of the book discusses the unification controversy, the establishment of the Department of

Defense, and the unsolved "problem of achieving effective civilian control without jeopardizing the effectiveness of centralized military planning."

Economic Questions

General

MITCHELL, W. C.; KING, W. I.; MACAULAY, F. R. and KNAUTH, O. W. **Income in the United States.** New York: Harcourt, Brace, 1921, 2 v.

The first in a series of many studies of national income by the National Bureau of Economic Research. It covered the period 1909–1919, when the problem was complicated by price and wage fluctuations. Familiar problems noted were the proper treatment of corporate surplus, how to handle taxes and to value government services, what to do about depreciation and depletion, and how to treat housewives' services. Among the conclusions were that pre-World War I per capita income in the U.S. was $335, in Australia $263, in the United Kingdom $243 and in Germany $146; that the share received by employees averaged 53.5 percent and was surprisingly stable; and in 1918 about 86 percent of the gainfully employed had incomes of less than $2,000. This work was a most important step toward the quantitative approach to economics and, while important in its own right, the measurement of income flows was essential to the use of the theoretical framework put forward later by Lord Keynes. The basic statistical work on national income was taken over by the government in the early 1930s.

Out of this initial effort grew many studies of various phases of the American economy by the National Bureau, usually oriented toward statistical rather than policy issues. The following are a few of the more general ones. Simon Kuznets, with Elizabeth Jenks, **Capital in the American Economy: Its Formation and Financing** (Princeton: Princeton University Press, 1961, 664 p.) is the last in a series dealing with capital formation and its financing. Raymond W. Goldsmith, **The National Wealth of the United States in the Post-War Period** (Princeton: Princeton University Press, 1962, 434 p.), contains the only comprehensive, detailed estimates of U.S. national wealth, its components and how it grew. Morris Copeland, **A Study of Moneyflows in the United States** (New York: National Bureau of Economic Research, 1952, 579 p.), was the first effort to create a complete systematic record of the process of payments. Two volumes by Milton Friedman and Anna Jacobson Schwartz, **A Monetary History of the United States, 1867–1960** (Princeton: Princeton University Press, 1963, 860 p.) and **Monetary Statistics of the United States** (New York: National Bureau of Economic Research, 1970, 629 p.), had a great impact on the importance given to monetary factors in stabilization policy.

Recent Economic Changes in the United States. New York: McGraw-Hill, 1929, 2 v.

These two volumes, begun in January 1928 and completed in February 1929, describe post–World War I developments in American economic life. They consist of a report of the Committee on Recent Economic Changes (Herbert Hoover, and later A. W. Shaw, chairmen) and staff papers prepared for it, under the auspices of the National Bureau of Economic Research. The period is described as one of substantial economic progress and increased solidarity. While Wesley Mitchell's final chapter is mostly about the forces which support prosperity, he does close on a mild note of caution, this being the spring of 1929. The chapter "Foreign Markets and Foreign Credits" was written by Professor James Harvey Rogers. It provides detailed statistics on trade experience from 1922 to 1928. The growth in U.S. foreign investment is described and attributed to lower interest rates in New York, made possible by its attractiveness as a place for deposit and by the inflow of gold, and the extension of foreign credits is closely associated with increased exports.

DEWHURST, JAMES FREDERIC and OTHERS. **America's Needs and Resources.** New York: Twentieth Century Fund, 1947, 812 p.

Started by the Twentieth Century Fund before the end of World War II, this ambitious project reviews demands, needs and resources ranging from food, liquor and tobacco to recreation, religion and private welfare. It examines capital requirements including urban redevelopment and government costs. Figures for demand were based on the past with adjustments for wartime shortages, and needs were calculated according to standards representing adequate nutrition, housing, medical care and the like. On such a basis, actual consumer demand was estimated to fall short of "needs" by about 10 percent in 1950 and 7 percent in 1960. The largest gaps were in food, housing and medical care. However, taking public and private capital goods and government services also into account would have required a gross national product of $200 billion in 1950 as compared with the study's estimate of $177 billion. In 1960, the gap would be between $219 and $202 billion. Whether resources would be adequate to meet the higher figures for need depends on productivity. This large volume provides a remarkable description of the level of living at the beginning of the Second World War and the way in which the war changed the pattern, at least in the short run. It is an important forerunner of the later efforts in development analysis to broaden the measures of progress beyond the strictly economic.

DORFMAN, JOSEPH. **The Economic Mind in American Civilization.** New York: Viking, 1946–1959, 5 v.

With volumes IV and V (published in 1959), Professor Dorfman of Columbia concludes his massive five-volume history of economic thought and doctrine in America. While physically separate, the last two volumes constitute a single work, with all of volume IV and half of volume V relating to 1918–1929. The final section carries the story to the inauguration of the New Deal in 1933. Dorfman not only summarizes the economic contributions of dozens of economists but puts them in their various settings, thus explaining not only their particular interests but often their prejudices. He notes particularly the "institutionalist school" which he regards as supplying much of the stimulus for more objective and empirical discussion and determination of policies in the years that followed.

HICKMAN, BERT G. **Growth and Stability of the Postwar Economy.** Washington: Brookings Institution, 1960, 426 p.

This intensive study of the performance of the American economy from 1946 through 1958 centers on three questions: were the business cycles like those of prewar times; how important were abnormalities caused by war and the cold war; how important were permanent structural changes. Hickman's conclusion is that the postwar record differed from the prewar period in that three powerful autonomous forces—war, rapid population growth and accelerated technological change —did much to determine the course of aggregate economic activity. They made themselves felt through federal spending, consumer demand, growth industries, financial changes and creeping inflation. The absence of any major depression during the period is ascribed in large part to demand backlogs, plentiful liquidity and a large stock of investment opportunities in important growth industries. Structural changes have provided stronger economic defenses against depression, not only in the form of a stronger financial structure but also a reduction in the importance of residential construction in the economy.

LANDSBERG, HANS H. and OTHERS. **Resources in America's Future: Patterns of Requirements and Availabilities, 1960–2000.** Baltimore: Johns Hopkins Press, 1963, 1,017 p.

This mammoth study, under the auspices of Resources for the Future, Inc., first examines the resource requirements for living, the consequent demand for key materials and the adequacy of the resource base, all for the year 2000. It does not predict any general running out of resources. Lower grades and substitutes can be used; more intensive or multiple use is often possible; and some things can be imported. But there can be severe problems of shortage in regions or particular raw materials. The field needs long-term planning, better public policies and better private management. The authors flag the water pollution problem as one important problem of the eastern United States. As to the international aspects of the resource problem, the report emphasizes the importance of foreign sources for various minerals and some agricultural crops such as sugar and coffee. It sees the best answer to this requirement in a reasonably free world trading system with greater price stability. U.S. foreign trade is projected to multiply sixfold by the year 2000.

MIKESELL, RAYMOND FRECH. **United States Economic Policy and International Relations.** New York: McGraw-Hill, 1952, 341 p.

Professor Mikesell stands out for his various books relating to American foreign economic policy. This volume deals with the major issues between 1919 and 1950—namely, commercial, financial, investment and aid problems. He points out the domestic economic pressures and the political and security motives behind various policy decisions. For this purpose, his main point of reference is the conflict between political and economic nationalism (isolationism) and increased international integration. He sees the latter as inevitable.

The Political Economy of American Foreign Policy: Its Concepts, Strategy and Limits. New York: Holt, 1955, 414 p.

This is the report of a distinguished study group sponsored by the Woodrow Wilson Foundation and the National Planning Association, with Professor William Y. Elliott as chairman. It deals primarily with the question of overall economic planning for the free world in the cold war. Although it deals primarily with American policy, it considers it in relation to the economic problems of Western Europe, Japan and the less-developed countries. Thinking in terms of economic growth and economic health, the analysis marches to much greater involvement by the United States in European affairs, pointing toward an Atlantic union. So far as the less-developed countries are concerned, the report stresses the variety of changes needed and the marginal part which the economic policy of these outsiders can play in their transformation. However, these outlying areas are important as sources of supply and as potential markets. The unusual characteristic of this book is the extent to which it insists that economic behavior is not self-regulating and that economic policy is not an independent field but must be grounded in total policy.

GORDON, KERMIT, ed. **Agenda for the Nation.** Washington: Brookings Institution, 1968, 620 p.

This extraordinary summary of the state of the nation, prepared in 1968, brings together the views of 18 outstanding authorities concerning major domestic and foreign policy issues which would be faced by the new President and the new Congress. It was edited by Kermit Gordon, who was Director of the Budget before becoming head of the Brookings Institution. Eight of the 18 chapters deal with foreign policy problems, written by Francis Bator, Marshall Shulman, Edwin Reischauer, John Campbell, Richard Cooper, Max Millikan, Carl Kaysen; the last, by Henry A. Kissinger, is on "Central Issues of American Foreign Policy."

DENISON, EDWARD F. **The Sources of Economic Growth in the United States and the Alternatives before Us.** New York: Committee for Economic Development, 1962, 297 p.

An important attempt to measure in quantitative terms the sources of economic growth in the United States from 1909 to 1958, and to make projections (under high employment conditions) to 1980. In general, Denison finds that increase in the quantity and quality of inputs is responsible for 68 percent of total growth and increased productivity for 32 percent. Three-fifths of the increased contribution by labor is explained by changes in volume of employment corrected for reduced working hours, and two-fifths by quality improvement as the result of education. The increase in capital input contributed 15 percent of total growth, the advance of knowledge (technology in a broad sense) 20 percent, and economies of scale, 9 percent. Other lesser factors were offset by forces adverse to growth. The author uses his statistical conclusions as a basis for recommending 31 specific steps which are estimated to raise the growth in the United States by about $20 billion a year by 1980. However, the specific conclusions and the statistical apparatus used in this study are less important than the demonstration of a fruitful approach to historical analysis and policy evaluation.

LEONTIEF, WASSILY W. **The Structure of American Economy, 1919–1929.** Cambridge: Harvard University Press, 1941, 181 p.
————. **The Structure of American Economy, 1919–1939.** New York: Oxford University Press, 1951, 264 p.
  Generally known as the father of input-output analysis, Harvard Professor Leontief's work has provided a method for making a statistically complete and consistent picture of an economy at work. Its equations and technical coefficients represent measures of the immediate and ultimate adjustment resulting from any change in some variable. The text of the 1941 edition is reproduced in the later volume, with additional chapters which discuss how it is possible to extend the system beyond a single nation's boundaries. The concepts presented by Leontief have found active use in the recent efforts by many countries to formulate national plans. See also Raymond W. Goldsmith, *ed.,* **Input-Output Analysis: An Appraisal** (Princeton: Princeton University Press, 1955, 371 p.), which is the report of a National Bureau of Economic Research Conference, containing eight papers and discussion.

Trade and Payments

LEWIS, CLEONA. **America's Stake in International Investments.** Washington: Brookings Institution, 1938, 710 p.
————. **The United States and Foreign Investment Problems.** Washington: Brookings Institution, 1948, 359 p.
  Beginning with **Germany's Capacity to Pay** in 1923, the Brookings Institution published 16 studies in the field of international financial relations during the interwar period. Using these studies as background and filling in various lacunae, Dr. Lewis prepared a picture of the state of American international affairs as of 1936, plus comparable data for eight earlier dates beginning with 1869. While many text tables and statistical appendices give a somewhat greater impression of verity than the underlying data justify, one cannot quarrel with the conclusion that the United States ceased to be a net debtor to other countries by the end of World War I. At the time of the publication of this study, gold flows and U.S. loans had temporarily eased the payments problem. A more permanent solution to the threatening transfer problem suggested by Dr. Lewis included encouraging greater imports of commodities and the larger flow of invisible items such as shipping, tourism and other services.
  The author returned to the problem in 1948, at a time when World War II had not only put the United States in an even stronger creditor position but left it as the only significant international source of capital since the former great lending countries were all foreign borrowers. The problems discussed in this volume are essentially the same as in the earlier volume, but the magnitudes are much greater, and much more attention is paid to the various types of foreign investment, private,

governmental (including the Marshall Plan), and through international institutions such as the International Bank for Reconstruction and Development.

AUBREY, HENRY G. **United States Imports and World Trade.** New York: Oxford University Press, 1957, 169 p.

In this book, written when the Paley Report had concluded on the basis of volume data that the American demand for most raw materials would rise so rapidly as to require expanded imports, Aubrey puts values on the quantities and extends the analysis to all imports, forecasting a rate of increase in constant dollars from 1952 to 1975 of 2.75 to 3 percent a year. He regarded this as a startling increase, but in actuality it has been far exceeded. In considering the problem of the dollar gap, Aubrey correctly forecast a substantial increase in American investment abroad and saw its servicing as preventing much increase in foreign purchases of American merchandise and services. Furthermore, he saw the growth in American imports as not coming from the areas with serious dollar shortages, so that the development of triangular patterns of trade would be essential. This study, done with meticulous care, demonstrates the difficulties of long-term forecasting in the trade field. Trade is dependent on many variables, and the behavior of foreign investment and reserve currency balances is even less predictable. Nevertheless, Aubrey did call the turn on U.S. import expansion.

BIDWELL, PERCY WELLS. **The Invisible Tariff.** New York: Council on Foreign Relations, 1939, 286 p.

In the midst of great concern over tariffs, Professor Bidwell described the less-visible barriers to trade. These include not only administrative regulations but countervailing duties offsetting subsidies, anti-dumping legislation, sanitary embargoes and special controls over the imports of animals, animal products, plants and plant products. Appendices deal with the buy-American policy and state legislation. At the time of writing, tariffs and quotas seemed to be the major obstacles to trade, and were undoubtedly much the easiest to handle through trade agreements. However, with their gradual reduction, the problems discussed in this book have moved up near the top of the GATT agenda some 30 years later. Bidwell's later book, **What the Tariff Means to American Industries** (New York: Harper, for the Council on Foreign Relations, 1956, 304 p.), examines eight manufacturing industries where tariffs had been lowered, shows the variety of elements involved in any attempt to evaluate the consequences, and argues that national defense is a greatly overrated argument for protection.

HUMPHREY, DON DOUGAN. **American Imports.** New York: Twentieth Century Fund, 1955, 546 p.

In this important study, jointly sponsored by the Twentieth Century Fund and the National Planning Association, Professor Humphrey concludes that after 20 years of tariff reduction, both liberals and protectionists should be surprised at the small increase in imports and so little injury to import-competing industries. He notes that many factors hamper the potential growth of imports and discusses business cycles, the selective process of tariff negotiation, invisible barriers, agricultural support policies and the like. Facing the U.S. payments problem, he argues that while the expansion of imports may be more difficult to achieve and temporarily more painful, it would lead to greater benefits than adjustment through lowering exports. He minimizes justifying imports as an anti-inflation program because it would squeeze the wrong industries, since inflation is brought about by the growth industries. If writing 15 years later, Humphrey would have had to give more recognition to the strength of protectionist groups. The import problem was kept at low intensity by the unplanned protection provided by the Great Depression and the war and postwar shortages. It was not until the end of the 1960s that high consumer and industrial demand and the Kennedy round reductions led to widespread demands for renewed protection.

PIQUET, HOWARD SAMUEL. **Aid, Trade and the Tariff, Including a Handbook of Major Dutiable United States Imports.** New York: Crowell, 1953, 358 p.

While much material on tariffs and import competition has long been available, often prepared by interested parties, Piquet (head of the Legislative Reference Service of the Library of Congress) brings together in meaningful form data concerning the major dutiable United States imports, their importance relative to domestic production, and the value of exports of the same items. The author estimates the effect of lowering trade barriers on imports, both in contributing to foreign purchasing power and in affecting domestic producers. The general impression created by the book is that even a complete suspension of tariff and quota restrictions would create only a limited area of serious import competition. The author develops the approach—subsequently adopted—that tariffs should be lowered and that there should be government compensation for any injury resulting from increased imports through assistance in industrial adjustment or even liquidation indemnities.

LIPSEY, ROBERT E. **Price and Quantity Trends in the Foreign Trade of the United States.** Princeton: Princeton University Press, 1963, 487 p.

This is an elaborate statistical study in the National Bureau of Economic Research's studies in international economic relations. New quarterly indexes concerning commodity trade have been calculated for the years from 1880 to 1929 and more than 70 percent of the book is in the statistical appendices. For the later years, adjusted Department of Commerce indexes have been used. According to the new price indexes, the U.S. terms of trade reached a low point in 1894, a high point in 1921, a low point in 1926, its highest point in 1934, a low point in 1951 and has risen somewhat thereafter. The swings are so wide that any conclusion about the trend in the terms of trade depends largely on the period chosen. Over the 80 years, there may have been a slight upward drift. Compared with domestic prices, prices for both exports and imports fell sharply during the inter-war period and the shift in relationship has not been reversed. The indexes are given by commodity groups and point up the unexpected fact that over the period the purchasing power of U.S. manufactured goods fell with respect to both exports and imports of primary products.

SALANT, WALTER S. and VACCARA, BEATRICE N. **Import Liberalization and Employment.** Washington: Brookings Institution, 1961, 388 p.

To estimate the impact of lowering tariffs on employment requires not only an estimate of the elasticity of imports but the consequent effect on the work force in the short run. (Presumably it would set various adjustments in motion in the long run.) Except for a study made by the U.S. Bureau of Labor Statistics for the Randall Commission, included in its "Staff Papers" (February 1954), this is the first thorough study of this important problem and makes an important contribution to methodology, since the same technique might be applied to examine the effect of other economic changes. It examines 1953 data industry by industry using an input-output matrix for the secondary effects of specific industry reactions. Both the displacement of domestic output and increases in exports are examined. The decreases in employment resulting from an assumed unilateral tariff reduction are found to be considerably less than had previously been assumed, though varying widely from industry to industry. They would be only minutely disturbing as compared with cyclical or technological unemployment.

LARY, HAL B. **Problems of the United States as World Trader and Banker.** New York: National Bureau of Economic Research, 1963, 175 p.

In 1943, Hal Lary analyzed the United States balance-of-payments situation in **The United States in the World Economy,** published by the U.S. Department of Commerce (Washington: Government Printing Office, Economic Series 23, 1943,

216 p.). This book, published 20 years later, shows the great contrast between the earlier contracting economy with its need to increase the outflow of dollars and the new situation when the outflow appears to be too buoyant compared with U.S. receipts. The U.S. economy is more exposed than at any time in recent decades to influences from abroad, and domestic policy is more affected by the prolonged deficit in payments and reduction in reserves. After analyzing the strength and weakness in the American position, Lary examines ways of improving the situation. Somewhat unusual sections are those dealing with disruptive movements of liquid capital and the requirement for the United States to hold large reserves. An interesting appendix discusses alternative ways of presenting the balance of payments and suggests that emphasis be given less to liquidity and more to sensitivity to monetary policy.

SALANT, WALTER S. and OTHERS. **The United States Balance of Payments in 1968.** Washington: Brookings Institution, 1963, 298 p.

The Council of Economic Advisors requested the Brookings Institution to prepare this report at a time when the United States had run large deficits for several years in its balance of payments and there had been substantial outflows of gold. There was rising hysteria about the safety of the dollar within and outside the government. However, analyzing the problem in detail and looking five years ahead, the authors foresaw improvement in the U.S. competitive position, lower military expenditures abroad, increasing foreign aid in the form of American goods and services rather than gold, reduced net capital outflow and increased investment income. They concluded that these underlying forces would press toward a basic surplus on the part of the United States. Under much less favorable assumptions, they still saw a small improvement. Their best guess was that the basic deficit would be eliminated in the five-year period. They were more concerned about the absence of any satisfactory adjustment mechanism other than undesirable domestic action, and the diminishing liquidity provided by gold reserves. Although by 1968 the war in Vietnam upset the authors' forecasts, their calming voices helped quiet the excitement of the earlier period, and their comments undoubtedly contributed to the development of new sources of international liquidity.

Foreign Aid

See also Economic Factors: Planning; Foreign Aid, p. 82.

CURTI, MERLE EUGENE and BIRR, KENDALL. **Prelude to Point Four.** Madison: University of Wisconsin Press, 1954, 284 p.

When President Truman enunciated Point Four, emphasizing that American technical assistance could help to relieve suffering and reduce poverty, it was in accordance with a long tradition. Not only had foreign missions by churches used the word "missionary" to cover health, education and agricultural activity, but the expanding private capital flow often had to be accompanied by the relevant skills. Curti and Birr have reviewed the record of the American government and found an amazing number of scattered, unrelated and often unbudgeted cases of technical assistance ranging from library cataloging to customs collection and mosquito control. Usually the foreign government paid for the mission, though it was often initiated and usually manned by the United States. The main criticism by the authors is that those missions tended to be inadequately prepared, narrow in concept and without any proper control or guidance from some headquarters. Between 1938 when this study was ended and 1949, the number of projects increased enormously, particularly in Latin America, and many of them at least were brought together under a single direction. In 1949 the organizational pattern changed completely, in large part in an attempt to meet the weaknesses found by Curti and Birr.

ASHER, ROBERT E. **Development Assistance in the Seventies: Alternatives for the United States.** Washington: Brookings Institution, 1970, 248 p.

According to Asher, at the end of the 1960s the United States reached the end of an era with respect to foreign aid because of changes in the global political and military landscape, in the economic scene, in the domestic situation and in worldwide understanding of the nature of the development process. The author believes that the 1970s should include a sizable international development effort which could be made much more effective, focusing on economic, social and civic development of low-income countries. Specific needs are better country-programming arrangements, less burdensome debt service, high priority for the population problem, better opportunities for low-income nations to earn more from foreign trade and greater utilization of international machinery. An interesting section of the book deals with additional possible sources of aid—the new special drawing rights, seabeds and ocean floors, commodity agreements and the earmarking of customs revenues from the products of less-developed countries. Finally, permanent legislation is proposed which would integrate trade, aid and investment policies, would spin-off the effort to encourage private investment and would place official lending in a new development lending agency.

KAPLAN, JACOB J. **The Challenge of Foreign Aid: Policies, Problems, and Possibilities.** New York: Praeger, 1967, 405 p.

A thoughtful discussion of the American foreign aid program by a man who had more than 20 years in foreign-aid administration in the Department of State and in the Agency for International Development. Kaplan's chief concern is the loss of public support for the program, resulting from confusion as to its purpose, ignorance as to the complexity of the development process, and exaggerated expectations as to the short-run results. He feels that even for the operators, the learning process was much too slow. He also believes that the program has been concentrated too much on economic goals, whereas the major interest of the United States lies in helping the less-developed countries become really independent, with institutions and values which are congruous with those of the United States. In addition, he presents a fresh point of view on many of the problems of policy connected with foreign aid programs.

MONTGOMERY, JOHN D. **The Politics of Foreign Aid: American Experience in Southeast Asia.** New York: Praeger (for the Council on Foreign Relations), 1962, 336 p.

Defense, politics and foreign aid all operated in a unique way in Southeast Asia in the late 1960s, the usual rationale in each field being submerged in the requirements of the wartime situation. This study was one of the first to make clear that the usual simple objective of accelerating growth in an underdeveloped country disregards the politics of aid. In Southeast Asia the objective which controlled all activity was to repel communist aggression. Thus the author notes that the alleged scandal arising out of aid-financed imports to South Vietnam was in fact an effort to strengthen the government by reducing inflation and that, for this purpose, it did not matter greatly what channels of distribution were followed so long as purchasing power was mopped up. He points out that the program resulted in a rapid distribution of goods and even caused changes in industrial structure, though it was violently criticized, especially in Congress. On the whole, this book is critical but optimistic. It emphasizes the need for mutuality, more coördination and the country approach, and a clearer national mandate in the United States.

Special Problems

SCHULTZ, THEODORE WILLIAM. **Agriculture in an Unstable Economy.** New York: McGraw-Hill, 1945, 299 p.

Professor Schultz of the University of Chicago prepared this important report for the Committee for Economic Development in 1945. It breaks new ground in the application of economic analysis to the problems of agriculture, including its relation to industrial expansion, business fluctuations and foreign markets. The author is concerned with low earnings in agriculture and the instability of farm income. He has no panacea but offers a series of measures to improve the situation without gross measures of restrictions on output or price floors.

The same general framework appears in his **The Economic Organization of Agriculture** (New York: McGraw-Hill, 1953, 374 p.), which gives more emphasis to the special nature of the problem in very poor communities. Writing some 15 years later, in **Economic Growth and Agriculture** (New York: McGraw-Hill, 1968, 306 p.), Schultz has pieced together various papers written in the meantime, frequently broadening his discussion to a world basis. In particular, this volume reflects his increased interest in manpower and education, and while it is a much less unified discussion than the earlier books, it contains many useful insights.

BENEDICT, MURRAY REED and STINE, OSCAR CLEMEN. **The Agricultural Commodity Programs: Two Decades of Experience.** New York: Twentieth Century Fund, 1956, 510 p.

In a study undertaken for the Twentieth Century Fund, two leading authorities in the field of agricultural economics have studied the record of government support programs in the United States over two decades. In a sense, they regard the period as a grand experiment in widely different agricultural programs, and they seek to report on the experience in order to contribute to a more informed and logical approach to the farm problem in the future. The detailed studies on a commodity-by-commodity basis are a record of continuing attempts to adjust policy to the changing methods of farming, although the degree of government participation in the production and marketing processes varied widely among the commodities and over time. As of 1955, the authors feel that farm price policy is neither settled nor consistent except in the responsibility of the government to find ways of bringing a better balance between supply and demand. The book is intended to deal not only with economic programs and policies, but with procedures and administrative difficulties as well.

CLAWSON, MARION. **Policy Directions for U.S. Agriculture.** Baltimore: Johns Hopkins Press, 1968, 398 p.

Written by an agricultural economist under the auspices of Resources for the Future, Inc., this book is not a discussion of agriculture as a productive industry; its scope is suggested by the subtitle, "Long-Range Choices in Farming and Rural Living." Clawson devotes his first hundred pages to a description of rural America and then discusses farming as a business, moving easily from national and global forces to the operational problems of the farmer, his income and his relation to the government. The remainder of the book consists of peering into the crystal ball to envisage the state of affairs in the year 2000. It does not present any specific agricultural program, but it does indicate possible paths of change and the forces which bear upon them.

BREWSTER, KINGMAN, JR. **Antitrust and American Business Abroad.** New York: McGraw-Hill, 1958, 509 p.

Increasing American investment abroad has raised many questions as to how far American corporations should be restrained in their foreign behavior by American law and regulations. The problem is particularly troublesome in the antitrust field because of widely differing national policies. Professor Brewster, then of Harvard Law School and later President of Yale, has written the authoritative work in this field, summarizing the confused legal implications of various possible policy positions, and presenting his own recommendations. He endorses the general effort to enforce competition, but would introduce flexibility which would take into account the apparent purpose of the action which is challenged and the economic effect of restraints. He believes that coöperation among exporters should be permitted so long as it does not curtail exports or restrain domestic competition. This book is an outstanding illustration of a review of public policy as expressed in law in terms of its economic implications.

ROSTOW, EUGENE VICTOR. **Planning for Freedom: The Public Law of American Capitalism.** New Haven: Yale University Press, 1959, 437 p.

This book by Professor Rostow of the Yale Law School is based on the William W. Cook lectures given at the University of Michigan in March 1958. Concerned with both law and economics, Rostow has bridged the gap between specialized disciplines, pointing out to economists the part which is and can be played by the law. and to lawyers the nature of the economic problems with which the law must deal. The discussion is wide-ranging—the chapter explicitly on foreign policy discusses the problems of communism and of underdevelopment. Much of the book relates to business cycles. He feels that the government must seek high levels of employment and growth, control overall fluctuations in the level of demand, assure price stability and encourage investment, including that in foreign countries. These are economic goals, but government action should always be within a system of law. While the problem of the relation between law and economic life is common to most countries, Rostow's analysis and nearly all of his illustrative material relate to the unique American scene.

LAWRENCE, SAMUEL A. **United States Merchant Shipping Policies and Politics.** Washington: Brookings Institution, 1966, 405 p.

United States shipping has played a disproportionately large role in national and international affairs. While this Brookings study gives some of the early history, it deals primarily with the period after World War II. Although both construction and operating costs are higher than those of any other major national fleet, the persistent government program has been to strengthen the American merchant marine. The author accepts this objective and then discusses critically the U.S. maritime programs and the dissatisfaction with their operation on the part of the industry, the shippers and the public generally. He calls for basic changes to stem the drift toward increasing government involvement.

Memoirs and Biographies

JESSUP, PHILIP CARYL. **Elihu Root.** New York: Dodd, 1938, 2 v.

Not the least impressive feature of Elihu Root's career was its duration. Born in 1845, he was a successful attorney during the last third of the nineteenth century, served as Secretary of War from 1899 to 1904, Secretary of State from 1905 to 1909, United States Senator from 1909 to 1915, and was incredibly active and influential as an "elder statesman" from the onset of the First World War nearly to his death at 91 in 1937. Philip C. Jessup, an eminent student of international law and, in his later years, a judge on the International Court of Justice, knew Root during the last quarter of Root's life and was admirably situated, by training, temperament and personal connection, to write this authorized (though Root seemed little interested in biographies of himself) and authoritative biography.

A good part of Root's official activities lies in the period before 1920, though his role as Secretary of State in Theodore Roosevelt's second administration is certainly pertinent, as is Jessup's perception of Root's inability really to comprehend the impulses in the Progressive movement. But even after he left public office Root was, in his 1917 mission to Russia, in the negotiations concerning the League of Nations, the World Court and the Washington Conference, an influential, though by no means always successful, figure.

This biography was written in the 1930s and hence lacks the additional, usually harsh, light cast by the Second World War and its aftermath upon the leading figures of the preceding era. Still, the man, and this biography, have ample substance to stand on their own.

PUSEY, MERLO JOHN. **Charles Evans Hughes.** New York: Macmillan, 1951, 2 v.

Despite the fact that Charles Evans Hughes was in the public eye for nearly four decades—as Governor of New York, presidential candidate, Secretary of State and Chief Justice—he has been a remote figure. This is partly a consequence of his rather formidable presence and appearance, his quite undeserved reputation as a human icicle. But more significantly, major aspects of his career seemed to place him, in retrospect, on the side of lost or waning causes. He lost, by a narrow margin, to Woodrow Wilson in 1916. His remarkable achievements as Secretary of State in the Harding cabinet were subsequently blurred by the dim reputation of that administration, and by World War II skepticism regarding the merits of the Washington Naval Conference, the Dawes Plan and such international efforts in the 1920s. As Chief Justice he was caught up in the turmoil of the New Deal, including President Roosevelt's effort to alter the Supreme Court.

Happily, Merlo J. Pusey's book, an authoritative and carefully documented biography, gives a fully rounded, if admittedly favorable, picture of this exceptional man. Hughes had remarkable intelligence and integrity. While lapses in judgment are not concealed, the general picture is one of real consistency in the man and his beliefs. For the student of foreign affairs the extensive section on Hughes' role as Secretary of State is particularly valuable, and reaches a quite dramatic climax in his naval disarmament proposals in 1921.

It is rather striking that, from the troubled standpoint of the 1970s, this book, written two decades earlier and about a man who had retired a decade before that, should tell so much about the United States and the qualities of its leadership.

HOOVER, HERBERT CLARK. **Memoirs.** New York: Macmillan, 1951–1952, 3 v.

From time to time in the course of his extended career, President Hoover prepared extended accounts of his life and activities. These he subsequently assembled, with some revisions and amplifications, in this three-volume memoir. His recollections of his early life and career as an engineer were written in 1915–1916; his activities in World War I, especially in Belgian relief and the U.S. Food Administration, were written in 1920–1924; his relief work after the war, including assistance to Soviet Russia, in 1925–1926; his years as Secretary of Commerce and President were drafted in 1933–1936. An "Aftermath" was written in the early 1940s.

The tragedy of Hoover's career was, of course, the Great Depression; the entire third volume is devoted to that and to the 1932 presidential campaign. It is a bitter volume. Hoover was quite irresponsibly charged with all manner of sins of omission and commission. His view of his opponents and the New Deal is correspondingly harsh. But quite beyond the element of polemic, it is most important to have Hoover's own record of his administration, as a counter to the stereotypes that threatened to become a national myth.

Not surprisingly, in view of the long period of preparation, the style and flavor of the memoirs vary greatly from volume to volume. A certain geniality and middle-western openness have largely vanished in the later years.

STIMSON, HENRY LEWIS and BUNDY, MCGEORGE. **On Active Service in Peace and War.** New York: Harper, 1948, 698 p.

Henry L. Stimson served President Theodore Roosevelt as a district attorney in New York, Taft as Secretary of War, Wilson as an army colonel, Coolidge as a peacemaker in Nicaragua and Governor General in the Philippines, Hoover as Secretary of State, and Franklin Roosevelt as Secretary of War. Like Elihu Root before him and Dean Acheson afterward, Stimson exemplified the imposing tradition of the patrician, Eastern lawyer dividing his life between private practice and long periods of active duty with the government.

Stimson retired in 1945 at the age of 78. For the next two years he and McGeorge Bundy, then a young Harvard scholar, prepared **On Active Service,** a book unsurpassed in importance by any other memoir on American foreign and security policy.

The book, and Stimson's career, have three climaxes. In the futile effort to reverse Japanese aggression in Manchuria in 1930–1931, Stimson found himself armed with "spears of straw and swords of ice." Joining FDR's cabinet in 1940 "as a Republican doing nonpartisan work for a Democratic President," he was centrally involved in the crises leading to the outbreak of war with Japan and Germany in 1941. Finally, Stimson was intimately connected with the decision to drop the atomic bomb in 1945 and, as a last act of his public career, he sought the formulation of a policy of coöperation with the Soviet Union for the control of atomic weapons.

In many respects his concerns throughout these years sensitively reflect a continuing problem in American foreign policy: how to combine a recognition of force as a necessary element in international relations with a recognition of the dead end of brute power politics and the need to achieve mutual trust between nations. Stimson's views changed and matured over the years, but the memoirs are a splendid record of an effort to confront this dilemma.

McGeorge Bundy's role in this remarkable collaborative effort was simply to assist in presenting "Mr. Stimson's actions as he himself understands them." For an appraisal of Stimson's career see Richard N. Current, **Secretary Stimson: A Study in Statecraft** (New Brunswick: Rutgers University Press, 1954, 272 p.).

BURNS, JAMES MACGREGOR. **Roosevelt: The Lion and the Fox.** New York: Harcourt, 1956, 553 p.
————. **Roosevelt: The Soldier of Freedom.** New York: Harcourt, Brace and World, 1970, 722 p.

The complexity of Franklin D. Roosevelt's character and the momentous content of his career impose formidable challenges to the biographer. Frank B. Freidel published three volumes of a projected six-volume biography in the 1950s—**Franklin D. Roosevelt** (Boston: Little, Brown, 1952–1956, 3 v.)—carrying the narrative to 1932, and then stalled. Burns, concentrating on Roosevelt as president and political tactician, was the first scholar to complete a detailed study of the entire 12-year administration.

The first volume describes Roosevelt in terms of the famous quotation from Machiavelli: "A prince must imitate the fox and the lion, for the lion cannot protect himself from traps, and the fox cannot defend himself from wolves. One must therefore be a fox to recognize traps, and a lion to frighten wolves." No one has come up with a better short characterization of Roosevelt, but even so, the book fails to explain the most enigmatic of presidents.

Burns waited nearly 15 years before publishing the second volume on Roosevelt as a wartime leader, hoping to have access to most important sources and the benefit of detailed scholarship on the Second World War. **Soldier of Freedom,** however, contains no conclusions that probably could not have been reached in the 1950s. In fact, the tone is more reminiscent of the simple patriotic enthusiasms of the war years than of a later awareness of the complexities and ambiguities of the war. **Soldier of Freedom** is useful for the discussion of domestic politics during the war; it adds little to an understanding of diplomacy and strategy.

SHERWOOD, ROBERT EMMET. **Roosevelt and Hopkins: An Intimate History.** New York: Harper, rev. ed., 1950, 1,002 p.

Presidents Woodrow Wilson in the First World War and Franklin D. Roosevelt in the Second World War both relied to an extraordinary degree on a single, intimate foreign policy adviser and personal diplomatic agent—Colonel Edward M. House for Wilson and Harry Hopkins for Roosevelt. The reputations of both advisers were enhanced by the fact that they kept copious records which became the basis of important books published shortly after the end of each war. Robert E. Sherwood's **Roosevelt and Hopkins,** like Charles Seymour's arrangement of **The Intimate Papers of Colonel House** (Boston: Houghton Mifflin, 1926–1928, 4 v.), provided readers with the first detailed, lavishly documented account of secret wartime diplomacy.

The similarity between books and men ends at that point. Where House could be devious and condescending toward his chief, Hopkins was direct, loyal and selfless. Where Seymour edited and excised in order to defend his subject, Sherwood sought to present a full, though undocumented record. **Roosevelt and Hopkins** was eventually superseded by publication of new material and the opening of archives, but it remains an essential and superbly written first source for the student of American foreign policy during the Second World War. The bulk of the book deals with the years 1941–1943 when Hopkins expedited aid to Britain and Russia and provided a link between Roosevelt, Churchill and Stalin. After 1943 Hopkins was less active; his health had declined to the edge of death. However, he did manage to go to Yalta and to Moscow in May 1945 to see Stalin on behalf of the new President, Harry S. Truman.

Sherwood, the distinguished playwright, worked in the White House during the war and knew Hopkins well. He paints him warts and all: flippant, irreverent, careless of health, but heroic in his devotion to Roosevelt. At Yalta in February 1945 Hopkins believed that coöperation between the Soviet Union and the West was assured—if Stalin remained alive. Two months later Roosevelt, not Stalin, was dead, and a year later Hopkins too was gone. Sherwood concentrates on the Roosevelt-Hopkins relationship. He does not speculate on how, if at all, events might have been different had one or both lived on.

BLUM, JOHN MORTON. **From the Morgenthau Diaries: Years of Crisis, 1928–1938; Years of Urgency, 1938–1941; Years of War, 1941–1945.** Boston: Houghton, 1959–1967, 3 v.

Henry Morgenthau, Jr., friend and Hyde Park neighbor of Franklin D. Roosevelt and Secretary of the Treasury from 1934 to 1945, was intensely aware of the historical importance of his work. He preserved a voluminous record—loosely termed a "diary," more precisely a chronological file running to hundreds of volumes of correspondence, memoranda, minutes of meetings, transcripts of telephone conversations and random notes. Morgenthau invited the historian John Morton Blum, author of **Republican Roosevelt** (Cambridge: Harvard University Press, 1954, 170 p.) and **Woodrow Wilson and the Politics of Morality** (Boston: Little, Brown, 1956, 215 p.), to write a three-volume account based on the diaries.

Morgenthau and Blum were inspired by the method used by Henry L. Stimson and McGeorge Bundy in **On Active Service in Peace and War.** Blum wrote a first draft from the written record. Morgenthau added observations from memory, although his failing health meant that his contribution diminished with each successive volume. **From the Morgenthau Diaries** is indispensable for the student of the New Deal and the foreign policies of the Roosevelt administration, for Morgenthau and the Treasury frequently were as important on many issues as Cordell Hull and the State Department—for example, on aid to the Allies before the American entry into the Second World War, relations with China and postwar planning for Germany.

HULL, CORDELL. **The Memoirs of Cordell Hull.** New York: Macmillan, 1948, 2 v.

Cordell Hull held the office of Secretary of State longer than any other man. His **Memoirs** reflect his strengths and failings. In 1916 Hull, then a Congressman from Tennessee, reached the conclusion that "unhampered trade dovetailed with peace; high tariffs, trade barriers, and unfair economic competition with war." This Wilsonian conviction, to which he adhered more persistently than any American leader of his time, became the guiding principle of his diplomacy, an ever-present topic of his speeches and memoranda. Historians disagree over whether this obsession was a platitude of marginal significance, a lasting contribution to a better world or a façade concealing a form of economic imperialism. Hull himself shows no awareness of the ambiguities in his thought.

President Roosevelt did not allow Hull and the Department of State to play an important role in the major issues of the Second World War. Thus the **Memoirs** are not informative on that score. They are valuable, however, for their full treatment of secondary questions such as Hull's feud with Argentina, his embroilment with Vichy and De Gaulle, and his management of wartime planning for the United Nations.

Hull ignores or mutes the clash of personalities within the Department of State. The diaries and memoirs of some of his associates provide a fuller picture of life in the Department during his tenure, *e.g.* **The War Diary of Breckinridge Long,** edited by Fred L. Israel (Lincoln: University of Nebraska Press, 1966, 410 p.); Jay P. Moffat, **The Moffat Papers** (edited by Nancy Harvison Hooker; Cambridge: Harvard University Press, 1956, 408 p.); and Dean Acheson's **Present at the Creation.**

VANDENBERG, ARTHUR HENDRICK, JR., *ed.* **The Private Papers of Senator Vandenberg.** Boston: Houghton, 1952, 599 p.

Senator Arthur Vandenberg, Republican of Michigan, was acutely aware of the alleged lessons of history and eager to protect his own historical reputation. He came to believe during the Second World War that the failure of the United States to enter the League of Nations was a mistake (although he himself was an isolationist until Pearl Harbor). He vowed to use his power as Republican foreign policy leader in the Senate to redeem the errors of the past. During the war he facilitated legislative and popular acceptance of the United Nations. As chairman of the Foreign Relations Committee after the election of 1946, he occupied the position held in 1919–1920 by Henry Cabot Lodge. Instead of opposing the Administration, he coöperated in carrying through the great measures of the late 1940s: aid to Greece and Turkey under the Truman Doctrine, the Marshall Plan for the economic revival of Europe, and the establishment of the North Atlantic Treaty Organization.

Vandenberg died in 1951. His son quickly issued this volume: a collection of his personal letters, memoranda and speeches, a full record of what Vandenberg called "non-partisan" and everybody else called "bi-partisan" foreign policy. The Senator's view of the world was simple and righteous. The book is an authentic expression of the working agreement between Congress and the Executive on the policies of the Truman administration.

GREW, JOSEPH CLARK. **Turbulent Era: A Diplomatic Record of Forty Years, 1904–1945.** Boston: Houghton, 1952, 2 v.

Grew's importance rests chiefly on his great mission to Japan from 1932 to 1941, during which he worked tirelessly to prevent war. The second volume of these memoirs is devoted mostly to Japan, with selections from his letters and monumental diary as well as a retrospective view of his mission after Pearl Harbor, where he contends that a meeting between President Roosevelt and Premier Konoe might well have averted the tragedy. Selections also describe his efforts as Under Secretary of State in the spring of 1945 to bring about Japan's surrender before Hiroshima and Soviet entry into the war. **Turbulent Era** does not duplicate but supplements Grew's earlier **Ten Years in Japan** (New York: Simon and Schuster, 1944, 554 p.), a compendium of diary excerpts skillfully woven into the story of his mission.

For Grew, Japan was the culmination of a lifetime in diplomacy. He was the first American to manage a complete foreign service career. **Turbulent Era** shows him, a well-heeled youngster from Groton and Harvard, enjoying a fling at courtier diplomacy in prewar Europe, then sobering and maturing as counselor of embassy in Berlin, 1914–1917. As Under Secretary in the 1920s Grew labored to establish American diplomacy on a fully professional basis. He also played a significant role in the Lausanne Conference on Turkey, 1922–1923, and served with great success as ambassador to Turkey, 1927–1932. Under the craftsmanlike editorship of

Professor Walter Johnson, the Grew memoirs present an enduring record of American diplomacy from Theodore Roosevelt to Harry Truman.

TRUMAN, HARRY S. **Memoirs.** Garden City: Doubleday, 1955–1956, 2 v.

Recent American presidents who had the greatest talent with the pen—Theodore Roosevelt, Woodrow Wilson and John F. Kennedy—chose not to write memoirs or died before they had the chance. Those who survived and wrote them lacked inspiration. Truman's **Memoirs** are less organized than Hoover's but warmer than Eisenhower's. They reflect the man: no philosophical depth, grace or elegance; cocky and combative, especially about the prerogatives of the presidency; clipped, energetic, honest.

The **Memoirs** confirm the popular image of Truman as a simple man, the least mysterious of modern presidents. He was blessed with a talent for making decisions, but, as Herbert Feis has suggested, may have used speed to conceal an inner sense of insecurity. He had no sense of the ambiguity in all great problems. Once he had made up his mind he never looked back, never doubted.

The coverage is unbalanced. The first volume, "Year of Decisions," covers little more than the first year in office. The remaining seven years are crammed into the second, "Years of Trial and Hope." The result is full treatment of Vice President Truman's sudden elevation to office, the Potsdam Conference of July 1945, the decision to drop the atomic bomb, and the international situation in 1946. On the other hand, the treatment of the Truman Doctrine, the Marshall Plan, the creation of NATO, McCarthyism, some aspects of the Korean War, China and a score of other domestic and foreign problems from 1947 through 1952 is thin.

The extensive quotation from documents available nowhere else makes the **Memoirs** an essential historical source. The episodic, pedestrian style makes them unsuited, however, for sustained reading.

MILLIS, WALTER, *ed.* **The Forrestal Diaries.** New York: Viking, 1951, 581 p.

James Forrestal served as Secretary of the Navy (1944–1947) and was the nation's first Secretary of Defense (1947–1949). Between 1944 and 1949 he dictated diary notes which provide the basis for this book. The informal nature of the material, plus the fact of Forrestal's nervous breakdown and suicide in the spring of 1949, presented the editor, Walter Millis, and his collaborator, Eugene S. Duffield, with an exceptionally difficult task, and the book shows the scars. Forrestal touched on topics of the highest security; hence a problem of clearance. He frequently expressed off-the-cuff judgments of persons and situations; hence the need for considerable editorial explanation and amplification. Despite the conscientiousness, skill and credentials of the editors, the book does not make for easy consecutive reading and cannot provide a definitive history of those years.

Still, this is an indispensable source for the history of the second half of the 1940s, both because of the information it provides on many crucial policy decisions and because Forrestal himself occupied a position of real influence. Through his eyes we see, on the domestic front, the enormous task of unifying the armed services. Through his eyes, too, we see the opening rounds of the cold war. In this connection, of course, Forrestal has come to occupy an important symbolic role, either as the acute early perceiver of the postwar Soviet threat or as a key figure in setting the tone of the cold war.

A haunting feature of the book is the collection of pictures of Forrestal, the tight jaw and mouth growing progressively tighter. The troubling implications of the personal element have been presented in Arnold A. Rogow, **James Forrestal: A Study of Personality, Politics, and Policy** (New York: Macmillan, 1963, 397 p.), a book which indicates both the need for, and the perils of, the psychological dimension. In the text of the diaries, however, the general sense, which gives the book its continuing value, is that of a sharp, rather narrowly focused, tough intellect grappling with, and responding to, an oncoming crisis that has had the world in its grip in the ensuing quarter-century.

ACHESON, DEAN GOODERHAM. **Present at the Creation: My Ten Years in the State Department.** New York: Norton, 1969, 798 p.

Dean Acheson was a distinguished representative of a group of Americans prominent in the conduct of foreign policy who move alternately between government service and private careers, usually in law or banking. After leaving the State Department in 1953, Acheson returned to his first career, law, and began a third—letters—which has resulted in a series of brief books combining criticism, often more implied than direct, of Republican foreign policy with anecdotal tales of his own experience. Among them are **A Citizen Looks at Congress** (New York: Harper, 1957, 124 p.), **Power and Diplomacy** and the graceful, evocative, humorous memoir of his youth and early middle age, **Morning and Noon** (Boston: Houghton, 1965, 288 p.).

Present at the Creation is a major work. It is a crisp, meticulously accurate and vigorously opinionated account of what Acheson did and thought during his years as Assistant Secretary of State (1941–1945), Under Secretary (1945–1947) and Secretary of State (1949–1953). Acheson was the principal shaper of the policies which guided American foreign policy at the beginning of the cold war and which were still largely in force at the beginning of the 1970s. This is the fullest inside account of the foreign policies of the Truman administration by one of the two twentieth-century Secretaries of State (John Foster Dulles was the other) who were indisputably the architects of policy for the President.

Acheson as an author in 1969 was more outspoken and sarcastic than circumstances allowed him to be as Secretary of State, but the underlying attitudes of the earlier period were faithfully reproduced in the book—the emphasis on military power, the careful cultivation of the Western alliance, the sponsoring of West Germany's rearmament, the apathy toward what later was called "the Third World," the indifference toward the United Nations, and the inclination to be unimpressed by most Congressional and public opinion. Acheson respected ideals, but dreamers made him uneasy. He sought power first, primarily military power, without which, in his opinion, there could be no successful negotiation with an adversary and no fulfillment of ideals.

KENNAN, GEORGE FROST. **Memoirs: 1925–1950.** Boston: Atlantic (Little, Brown), 1967, 583 p.

The literary talent of American career diplomats tends generally to be of a low order. The typical memoir is part travelogue, part gossip and quite devoid of deep reflection or sustained discussion of policy. A shining exception is George Kennan's **Memoirs.**

The book can be read on several levels—as a poetic lament for the human suffering of the twentieth century, as a searching autobiography of a self-centered and often lonely man, as a running critique of the oversimplifications of American foreign policy, as a philosophical examination of the futility of violence, and as a comment on the seeds of freedom in the most totalitarian systems and the seeds of oppression in the freest.

Half the volume deals with the author's early years in the foreign service—his first post in Germany, his special training in Russian language and civilization, his exciting assignment to Moscow under Ambassador William C. Bullitt immediately after the recognition of the Soviet Union by the United States in 1933, and his return to Moscow in 1943 under Ambassador Averell Harriman. The second half deals with the author's role during the early years of the cold war. Kennan argues that his original idea of containment was misunderstood and misapplied. He describes his unavailing efforts to persuade the American government to seek political, rather than military, solutions to the problems arising between the Soviet Union and the West. The **Memoirs** end in 1950 when Kennan, despairing of winning support for his views by staying in the government, went on semipermanent leave from the Department of State in order to seek influence in a new role as historian.

LILIENTHAL, DAVID E. **The Journals of David E. Lilienthal.** New York: Harper and Row, 1964–1968, 4 v.

The appearance of the first two volumes of these journals brought David Lilienthal a deserved reputation as one of the truly significant diarists among twentieth-century American public figures. Lilienthal began keeping a journal intermittently as a freshman in college in 1917 and in 1939 began a full, almost daily record. The first volume contains selections from 1917 to 1939 and a full record for 1939 to 1945, the concluding years of the author's chairmanship of the Tennessee Valley Authority. The second volume covers 1945 to 1950 when Lilienthal was the first chairman of the Atomic Energy Commission. The third and fourth volumes carry the diary from 1950 to 1959 and record Lilienthal's busy second career as an idealistic but practical businessman engaged in economic development in Asia and Latin America.

Lilienthal provides full reports of his conversations, his observations and inner thoughts. He is as frank as Harold L. Ickes—in **The Secret Diary of Harold L. Ickes** (New York: Simon and Schuster, 1953–1954, 3 v.)—but far more temperate and balanced in his judgments. He is more candid with himself than Colonel Edward M. House and as informative as Henry L. Stimson. The volume on the atomic energy years has the greatest historical importance, although the two on his overseas business ventures are unique for their subject matter and intensely interesting. If there were more businessmen who could write as well and were willing to publish, historians of the private side of American foreign relations would have an easier task.

EISENHOWER, DWIGHT DAVID. **The White House Years: Mandate for Change, 1953–1956.** Garden City: Doubleday, 1963, 650 p.
————. **The White House Years: Waging Peace, 1956–1961.** Garden City: Doubleday, 1965, 741 p.

In the four years following his two terms in the White House, President Eisenhower, with the assistance of his son John and his brother Milton and the research labors of William Bragg Ewald, Jr., prepared these substantial volumes of memoirs of his incumbency. The view is a personal one, displaying Eisenhower's special combination of stiffness and amiability, authority and informality, with sharp perceptions periodically lighting up the rather flat horizon of his prose.

The work is obviously an important source for the history of American foreign and domestic affairs of the 1950s. These were the Eisenhower years, and there is little question of the importance of his role. He tends to be restrained, as he was at the time, on some of the more contentious domestic issues. In the area of foreign policy he clearly intends to offer no support to those interpretations suggesting a difference between his stance and that of his forceful Secretary of State, John Foster Dulles. At times, and especially in the volume dealing with his second term, one misses a sense for the depth and complexity of problems that were surfacing in those years. But surely one of Eisenhower's great qualities, reflected in this book, was his ability to achieve a temporary state of national equilibrium.

GERSON, LOUIS L. **John Foster Dulles.** New York: Cooper Square Publishers, 1968, 372 p.

Secretary of State John Foster Dulles attracted intense admiration and equally intense dislike. John Robinson Beal's early biography, **John Foster Dulles** (New York: Harper, 1957, 331 p.), is friendly and uncritical. Coral Bell's **Negotiation from Strength** links Dulles and Dean Acheson in an even-tempered but thorough dissection of their assumptions. Herman Finer's **Dulles over Suez: The Theory and Practice of His Diplomacy** (Chicago: Quadrangle Books, 1964, 538 p.) is a splenetic condemnation.

Gerson's study, a volume in "The American Secretaries of State and Their Diplomacy" series under the editorship of Robert H. Ferrell, is sympathetic but a bit bland. It is the first study to make extensive use of Dulles' unpublished papers and the interviews of the Dulles Oral History project at Princeton. Gerson also had access to some of President Eisenhower's records. Dulles appears less impulsive and ideological than his oft-quoted slogans about "massive retaliation," "the brink of war" and "liberation" led the public to believe during his lifetime. The most important contribution of Gerson's study is the treatment of President Eisenhower as an active participant in foreign policy decisions, showing that Dulles had considerable freedom but by no means a free hand.

SCHLESINGER, ARTHUR M., JR. **A Thousand Days: John F. Kennedy in the White House.** Boston: Houghton, 1965, 1,087 p.

President John F. Kennedy's popularity with intellectuals, his readiness to challenge accepted assumptions, and his tragic assassination combined to produce a greater number of books about his administration in a shorter time than had appeared after any other presidency. The first full account was this volume by Arthur M. Schlesinger, Jr., chronicler of the ages of Jackson, **The Age of Jackson** (Boston: Little, Brown, 1945, 577 p.), and Franklin D. Roosevelt, **The Age of Roosevelt,** a Harvard historian with a taste for political controversy and participation.

Schlesinger, who served Kennedy as a special assistant in the White House with a variety of special assignments, principally with questions involving Latin America and the "third world," admits that his account is not a "comprehensive history" but a "personal memoir." It is also largely about personalities and contains hundreds of short, often biting observations on the men around Kennedy. The book has a dramatic structure: Kennedy's imagination versus the leaden ways (as Schlesinger sees them) of the State Department; and a search for new ideas versus a stubborn refusal by bureaucrats to depart from ingrained tradition or abandon platitudes for original thought. John Kenneth Galbraith, Schlesinger's onetime Harvard colleague and Kennedy's ambassador to India, presents a confirming and similarly colored picture in his **Ambassador's Journal** (Boston: Houghton, 1969, 656 p.).

The main emphasis in **A Thousand Days** is on foreign affairs, and the account is especially useful for the student of the Alliance for Progress, the test ban treaty and the President's goal of a world "safe for diversity."

SORENSEN, THEODORE C. **Kennedy.** New York: Harper and Row, 1965, 783 p.

This volume supplements Arthur M. Schlesinger's **A Thousand Days** as one of the most important contributions to the huge literature on the Kennedy administration. Where Schlesinger is witty, anecdotal and personally at the center of the narrative, however, Sorensen is orderly, systematic and less obtrusive. He joined the staff of newly elected Senator John F. Kennedy and remained his close assistant until the end of the President's life. His account covers the senatorial years, devotes several chapters to the drive for the Democratic nomination in 1960 and the campaign against Richard M. Nixon. In the White House Sorensen held a position for domestic affairs comparable to that of McGeorge Bundy in foreign affairs. His treatment of politics, economics and civil rights is thus more full than Schlesinger's. But, even for Sorensen, foreign affairs filled most of the horizon. As a major participant in the 1962 crisis with the Soviet Union over missiles in Cuba his account is an essential source for that event, ranking with Robert F. Kennedy, **Thirteen Days** (New York: Norton, 1969, 224 p.).

CANADA

General

DAWSON, ROBERT MACGREGOR. **The Government of Canada.** Toronto: University of Toronto Press, 4th rev. ed., 1963, 610 p.

Dawson's book has been the standard text on Canadian government since it was first published in 1947. Its only rival to this claim is **Democratic Government and**

Politics (Toronto: University of Toronto Press, 3rd rev. ed., 1959, 691 p.) by James A. Corry and J. E. Hodgetts, who, however, have treated Canadian government comparatively, relating it to the British and American forms.

Dawson's work is a studious but lively analysis of the nature of the written and unwritten Canadian constitution, including the British North America Act, and the organs of the federal government: for example, the crown, the cabinet, Parliament (House of Commons and Senate), the public service, the judiciary and federal political parties. Although he deals with the distribution of powers between the federal and provincial governments, Dawson does not purport to examine in any detail the structure or functioning of provincial or municipal governments in Canada. He also approaches his subject in the traditional historical-legal fashion and pays little attention to the more modern behavioral or systems treatments of the field. But despite this dated approach, Dawson's book remains the most informative and most readable account of the nature of the Canadian federal government. Since Professor Dawson's death, Professor Norman Ward had been revising successive editions.

BREBNER, JOHN BARTLET. **North Atlantic Triangle: The Interplay of Canada, the United States and Great Britain.** New York: Columbia University Press, 1958, 385 p.

When originally published in 1945, this was the last of the 25 volumes in the series, "The Relations of Canada and the United States," sponsored by the Carnegie Endowment for International Peace. In discussing the relations of North America and Britain from the earliest explorers down to World War II, Brebner drew on the work of earlier authors in the series, but his book is no mere summary but rather a work of original and highly readable scholarship which has enjoyed an enduring influence.

Brebner knew that he gave Canada considerably more attention than her position in the triangle warranted and justified the emphasis on the grounds of ignorance of Canada among Britons and Americans. Curiously, publication of the book at the end of the war, when Canada briefly played a much larger part internationally than before, may have supported the ambitions of Canadians who wished their country to assume a larger role permanently. Twenty-five years later, when the growth of American power is so clearly perceived, the validity of the concept of the triangle appears more open to question, but that is not to say that the book is seriously dated, with the exception of the last chapter. One of its strengths is the attention given to geographical and economic factors in the development of North America, and the generous provision of good maps enhances that strength. As a work of synthesis and interpretation, Brebner's volume remains a source both of information and the provocative idea.

MACDONALD, RONALD ST. JOHN, *ed.* **The Arctic Frontier.** Toronto: University of Toronto Press (in association with the Canadian Institute of International Affairs and the Arctic Institute of North America), 1966, 311 p.

This book brings together the work of 11 authorities in essays that vary greatly in approach and scale, ranging from the general, impressionistic survey to the detailed article that tells more about its subject than any but the specialist might want to know. Some pieces deal with the Arctic region as a whole, and others with Alaska and with the Soviet north, which is treated in two long articles. The focus, however, is on the Canadian north, which figures prominently in most general pieces and also has three long articles, amounting to over one-third of the book, devoted to it. Relatively little attention is paid to the scientific and economic topics that are the customary staples of previous studies. Instead, the emphasis is on the social sciences—social and political organization, human relations, environmental problems. For instance, the native peoples in Alaska, Canada and the U.S.S.R. receive three articles, and the administrative systems of northern Canada and the Soviet north two more. Another two deal with international relations, specifically the backgrounds of those current problems, the sovereignty question and the military-strategic role of the Canadian Arctic. Thus **The Arctic Frontier** fills important gaps in the general field of northern studies and of Arctic Canada in particular. The expertise of the authors, the range of subjects and the quality of the individual presentations make this a useful, significant book.

Foreign Relations

GLAZEBROOK, GEORGE PARKIN DE TWENEBROKER. **A History of Canadian External Relations.** Toronto: McClelland, 3rd rev. ed., 1966, 2 v.

This is the third version of this useful book, the only single work giving a general and comprehensive account of Canadian external relations and policies. The first eight chapters (to 1914) were published in 1942; a new edition covering the whole period to 1939 appeared in 1950. The third edition is materially revised, and although the text still ends in 1939 an extended and valuable "bibliographical essay" lists and comments on writings relating to the period from 1939 to 1964. The author, a distinguished historical scholar, is also a former officer of the Canadian Department of External Affairs. In spite of the extensive revision, the book is now somewhat out of date; and because much of it was written close to the events it suffers from paying too little attention to the influence of individuals (both ministers and civil servants) on the making of policy. Nevertheless, it is still the best survey of the subject.

MACKAY, ROBERT ALEXANDER and ROGERS, E. B. **Canada Looks Abroad.** New York: Oxford University Press, 1938, 402 p.

This volume, published in 1938, was the first modern study of Canada's international relations. It came at a time when Canadians were beginning to realize that they had taken charge of their own external policy and needed to develop some positive principles. The authors, both academics who later became diplomats, analyzed the domestic bases, economic and social, for such a policy, described the history of foreign and defense policies and the ways in which external relations were conducted, and considered various alternatives. The book also includes a useful collection of documents. Its continuing importance is that it provides a unique and reliable picture of Canada's relations with other countries on the eve of the Second World War and at the end of its adolescence. For students of present Canadian foreign policy it offers a perspective, and evidence of themes which persist in spite of changed circumstances.

EAYRS, JAMES. **In Defence of Canada: From the Great War to the Great Depression.** Toronto: University of Toronto Press, 1964, 382 p.

————. **In Defence of Canada: Appeasement and Rearmament.** Toronto: University of Toronto Press, 1965, 261 p.

The scope of James Eayrs' work is somewhat wider than the titles suggest. He interprets the word "defence" very liberally and deals in fact with a wide range of Canadian Commonwealth and foreign policies. He gained access to a great number of official and unofficial civil and military sources, including the papers and diary of Mackenzie King, Prime Minister of Canada for most of his period; and he writes with notable grace and energy. The books are an important original contribution to history, which no student of the time and topic could neglect. The first volume is rather more thorough than the second. The latter, though it makes significant revelations concerning the early period of the Second World War, had to be based on a less complete examination of the records than was the case with the earlier work.

KEENLEYSIDE, HUGH LLEWELLYN. **Canada and the United States.** New York: Knopf, rev. and enl. ed., 1952, 406 p.

The most extensive studies of the relations between Canada and the United States were those produced before and during the Second World War under the auspices of the Carnegie Endowment for International Peace, covering not only political but economic and social aspects. Dr. Keenleyside's standard work was first published in 1929 before he became a distinguished diplomat, public servant and senior member of the U.N. Secretariat. In 1952 the book was considerably revised with the assistance of Gerald S. Brown of the University of Michigan to reflect the new lights cast by the Carnegie Endowment studies. It is essentially a history from the time of the American Revolution and the Loyalist immigration through the boundary and other disputes of the nineteenth century to the two world wars, ending with Lester B. Pearson's prediction in 1951 that the relationship was bound to be more complex and difficult. The present serious issues between the two countries over defense coöperation, foreign investment and control have their roots in this history but had not risen to the surface by the time this book was written. An excellent historical treatment of the subject written in the light of later events and including them in its scope is **The United States and Canada** by Gerald M. Craig (Cambridge: Harvard University Press, 1968, 376 p.).

SPENCER, ROBERT A. **Canada in World Affairs: From UN to NATO, 1946–1949.** New York: Oxford University Press, 1959, 447 p.

This volume, the fifth in the biennial series sponsored by the Canadian Institute of International Affairs, is one of the best. Lucid and balanced, it covers a uniquely creative period in Canada's external relations. Although Professor Spencer, like the other authors in the series, was obliged to rely largely upon public pronouncements and newspaper comment, his interpretation and assessment are standing up well. One might wish for more detail concerning Canada's ardent promotion of NATO, but its growing involvement in the United Nations is amply documented.

In 1946 Canada's foreign policy was still handicapped by the cautious, continentalist leadership of Mackenzie King. The more global approach of St. Laurent and Pearson was on the rise, however, and it was implemented by an exceptionally able foreign service. The temporary weakness of many of the established powers, and Canada's close relations with the Western superpower, provided the basis for disproportionate influence. The style of Canadian diplomacy, however, diligent, coöperative and modest, also contributed to the emergence of Canada as a leading middle power, especially effective in the establishment of international institutions.

Spencer prefaced his narrative with a thoughtful analysis of the principles of Canadian foreign policy, and he concluded with a brief study of its formulation. Unfortunately, his description of the leading role played by the Department of External Affairs is no longer applicable, and Prime Minister Trudeau, although Lester Pearson's preferred successor, appears to be addicted to the policies of Mackenzie King. The achievement documented in this volume seems therefore unlikely to be repeated.

LYON, PEYTON V. **Canada in World Affairs: 1961–1963.** New York: Oxford University Press, 1968, 555 p.

Like R. A. Spencer's book, this volume is one of a biennial series sponsored by the Canadian Institute of International Affairs. Since much of the best Canadian writing on foreign policy has appeared in this series, listing of these two titles is intended to draw attention to all of the dozen and more "Canada in World Affairs" volumes.

Mr. Lyon's book is also an outstanding example of the art of writing recent history. By making use of a vast amount of official and unofficial, and of written and oral materials, the author not only reconstructs the narrative of events but also recaptures the atmosphere of the time. More than that, he provides incisive analysis and sharp assessment. In writing of a period when passions ran high (especially relating to the nuclear arms issue in the election of 1963), he presents fairly the opposing points of view but leaves the reader in no doubt about his own position. In brief, this is that Canadian foreign affairs were poorly handled by the Diefenbaker government in 1961–1963, and that the best stance for Canada is to rely on "quiet diplomacy" and to be a faithful member of the Western alliance.

McLIN, JON. **Canada's Changing Defense Policy, 1957–1963: The Problems of a Middle Power in Alliance.** Baltimore: Johns Hopkins Press, 1967, 251 p.

During the years of the Diefenbaker administration Canada was faced, as a consequence of the escalation of military technology, with a series of basic issues of defense policy. These issues were whether a middle power could produce its own sophisticated weapons and whether it should have nuclear weapons. The basic assumptions of the alliance relationship were in dispute, and consequently there occurred the most serious dislocation of Canada–United States relations since the First World War. This critical period is closely analyzed by a young American scholar who, in so doing, reveals the persistent dilemmas of Canadian defense policy, the problems of the lesser ally in a continental partnership, and the pitfalls of Canadian-American politics and diplomacy. Although the perspective is American, the author shows a perceptive understanding of Canadian policy, and there is no equivalent treatment of the subject by a Canadian, except in the biennial surveys of the "Canada in World Affairs" series, particularly that of Peyton Lyon for the critical years 1961–1963.

REFORD, ROBERT W. **Canada and Three Crises.** Toronto: Canadian Institute of International Affairs, 1968, 246 p.

Middle power diplomacy has been the subject of persistent debate in Canada since the Second World War, and there have been many efforts by scholars and government spokesmen to define its principles, as, for example, in **Diplomacy in the Nuclear Age** by the Rt. Hon. L. B. Pearson; **Paul Martin Speaks for Canada: A Selection of Speeches on Foreign Policy 1964–1967** by Paul Martin (Toronto: McClelland, 1967, 158 p.); a collection of essays entitled **Canada's Role as a Middle Power** edited by J. King Gordon (Toronto: Canadian Institute of International Affairs, 1966, 209 p.); a series of critical essays in **An Independent Foreign Policy for Canada?** edited by Stephen Clarkson (Toronto: McClelland, 1968, 290 p.); and **The Better Part of Valour: Essays on Canadian Diplomacy** by John W. Holmes (Toronto: McClelland, 1970, 239 p.).

The virtue of Reford's study is that it is largely devoted to a close analysis of the way Canada responded to three specific situations: the Offshore Islands crisis of the 1950s when Canada detached itself from the United States; the Suez crisis when Canada played a resourceful role complementary to that of the United States; and the Cuban missiles affair when Canada, having differed with the United States over Cuba, somewhat reluctantly aligned itself in the crisis. These solidly based, factual accounts fill important gaps in the history of Canada's external relations and reveal the practical alternatives of the policies Canada faces.

ROUSSIN, MARCEL. **Le Canada et le Système Interaméricain.** Ottawa: Éditions de l'Université d'Ottawa, 1959, 285 p.

French Canadians in this century have always been more concerned with hemispheric relations than have their English-speaking compatriots. In part at least, this was because *Canadiens* saw in *Latinité* a possible counterweight to the ties of empire. Roussin realizes that the Empire is dead, but his volume is yet another indication of French Canada's continuing interest in Latin America.

The book is rather badly mistitled. Almost two-thirds of the text is devoted to a summary history of the evolution of hemispheric organization, tracing the story from Bolívar to the Bogota Conference of 1948 and beyond. The remaining pages examine the various Canadian half-steps toward membership and half-steps away from it and summarize the potential advantages and disadvantages of membership; clearly, the author feels that the advantages would be great. Despite a good bibliography, this work is little more than a survey, and it does not supersede the earlier study by John T. P. Humphrey, **The Inter-American System: A Canadian View** (Toronto: Macmillan, 1942, 329 p.).

SPICER, KEITH. **A Samaritan State? External Aid in Canada's Foreign Policy.** Toronto: University of Toronto Press, 1966, 272 p.

Canada has been a contributor of foreign aid since the early 1950s. Perhaps slightly less concerned with winning political advantages with aid than are the major powers, the Canadian government and people have always seen their contributions as selfless and altruistic. In fact the Canadian aid budget has always been small, smaller even than those of less populous and less wealthy nations.

Spicer's volume was the first study of the Canadian program. The book provides substantial detail on specific projects, both successes and failures, and among the useful case studies is an analysis of the Canadian part in the construction of Pakistan's Warshak Dam. Spicer also presents a series of recommendations on ways to make Canadian aid more effective (some of which have since been implemented), and there is a long philosophical justification for external aid. There have been many changes in Canada's aid program since Spicer's book appeared, but **A Samaritan State?** still remains the best single treatment of the subject.

Economic and Social Questions

INNIS, HAROLD ADAMS. **The Fur Trade in Canada.** New Haven: Yale University Press, 1930, 444 p.

Harold Innis, who died in 1952, had such widespread influence on the field of economic history in Canada that it is hard to single out a particular book of his for examination. Some of his major ideas took essential form in **The Fur Trade in Canada,** a meticulously researched study that was a bench mark in setting forth the conditions and consequences of a great staple export trade. It made clear how much of the history of Canada had been shaped by the development of the fur staple—the country's very future extent being staked out by the continental drive of the trade in furs. It dealt with the interplay of Indian and white cultures, imperial expansion and rivalry, commercial competition and monopoly, technology versus the high costs of transport imposed by geography, and the crucial role of the St. Lawrence water route in a vast trading system. His book was well subtitled "An Introduction to Canadian Economic History."

In this and several other books Innis developed a staples approach that offered a unifying theme for Canadian history, focusing it on the country's characteristic production and sale of certain basic commodities—whether fish, lumber, wheat, minerals or pulp and paper—each involving particular kinds of political, social, demographic and cultural circumstances, no less than economic. In another direction, it has invited theories of economic growth applicable to countries other than Canada.

Innis was not only an economic historian. He also wrote on the interrelations of politics and economics as well as on communications and the media, strongly influencing the subsequent work of Marshall McLuhan, such as **Understanding Media** (New York: McGraw-Hill, 1964, 359 p.). While Innis's style was often involved or cryptic, it is well worth bearing with for the content.

CAVES, RICHARD EARL and HOLTON, RICHARD HENRY. **The Canadian Economy: Prospect and Retrospect.** Cambridge: Harvard University Press, 1959, 676 p.

As its subtitle implies, this book is an exercise in "backwards history." The "Prospect" part of the volume originated in a study for the Canadian Pacific Railway Company, its goal being "to furnish guidance for the firm's investment decisions." (It is not every company that can become immortalized in the Harvard Economic Studies.) The "Retrospect" part was written after the Prospect had been established, "although we reached the conclusions set forth [in the historical analysis] in the early days of plotting our forecasting strategy."

As to Prospect, the authors predict trend values for 1970 and warn us that "predicting trend values rather than actual values for the economic variables in 1970 means that the accuracy of the estimates cannot be evaluated until well after 1970," so nothing on that score can be said for several years yet. Methodologically, apart from an early use of inter-industry analysis to check the consistency and plausibility of its estimates, Prospect is for the most part another of those dreary exercises in limning future economic growth with which we have been bombarded since the end of World War II.

Part I, Retrospect, occupies less than a third of the volume if we exclude its first chapter, which deals not with "retrospecting" but with the problem of long-range forecasting. This historical section of the book is a synopsis of past economic growth in Canada written by two urbane economic theorists who are at once faintly amused and faintly impressed by the writings of Canadian economic historians. A certain freshness was imparted to the work by using materials from the early Canadian Censuses of Manufacturing, a source previously neglected by Canada's economic historians, who had not been strongly oriented to quantitative materials, nor for that matter to the history of manufacturing.

The Canadian Economy was well worth reading when it was published. It is even now, perhaps, worth skimming. A couple of decades hence it may well be interesting as intellectual history, as an example of the great emphasis that both economists and Canadians in the mid-1950s placed on economic growth—both in retrospect and in prospect.

SAFARIAN, A. E. **Foreign Ownership of Canadian Industry.** Toronto: McGraw-Hill of Canada, 1967, 346 p.

For over a decade there has been persistent questioning by Canadians about the political and economic consequences of large-scale foreign ownership of Canadian industry. This has raised important issues in relations with the United States, the major source of outside capital and technology, and has led to a growing list of restrictions on foreign ownership of Canadian industry.

Professor Safarian attempted to analyze one set of questions about foreign ownership by a detailed quantitative assessment of the performance of United States and other foreign-owned firms in Canada, and by comparisons with the performance of resident-owned firms. He examined the nature of the relationship with the parent firm abroad, and the consequences for the subsidiaries and for the economy in such matters as the hiring of senior personnel, exports, imports, research and financing. The results were summarized and updated in shorter form in his **The Performance of Foreign-Owned Firms in Canada** (Montreal: Canadian-American Committee, 1969, 123 p.).

While he found a number of industrial problems arising from foreign ownership, his main conclusion was that inferior economic performance could more convincingly be related to inadequate industrial policies. Fear of the political effects associated with such investment has been strengthened by the attempts by agencies of the United States government to extend laws and regulations to subsidiaries outside the United States.

The study by Professor Safarian did not deal systematically with overall economic benefits and costs and broader political questions. These, along with industrial performance, are analyzed in a study prepared for the government of Canada by a special task force and entitled **Foreign Ownership and the Structure of Canadian Industry** (Ottawa: Privy Council Office, 1968, 427 p.).

WONNACOTT, RONALD J. and WONNACOTT, PAUL. **Free Trade between the United States and Canada: The Potential Economic Effects.** Cambridge: Harvard University Press, 1967, 430 p.

This book quantitatively and theoretically examines the likely economic effects of free trade between the United States and Canada. Because the largest effects will fall on Canada, and within Canada on manufacturing, the central focus of the study is upon the Canadian manufacturing sector. The evidence presented by the Wonnacotts suggests that free trade in manufactured goods would yield substantial economic gains to Canada (in the order of 10 percent of Gross National Product) and slight gains to the United States (in the order of 1 percent of GNP). Contrary to popular fears, there is little danger of Canadians becoming "hewers of wood and drawers of water," although Canadian manufacturing is likely to become much more specialized.

These conclusions are based upon a comprehensive analysis. The first part of the book projects and compares Canadian and American manufacturing costs under free trade (by analyzing 13 American and five Canadian regions) and concludes that Canadian locations would be potentially more competitive than under existing tariff structures. The second part explores the adjustments that would occur in the Canadian economy as a consequence of free trade (by examining 14 sample products) and predicts that the major adjustments would occur within the manufacturing sector rather than between manufacturing and nonmanufacturing sectors. The third part considers the extent to which the differential in existing Canadian-American costs can be attributed to North American protection and to what degree they are independent of tariffs, and therefore likely to persist under free trade. The fourth part discusses various policy issues such as the timing and degree of economic integration, the form of this integration and possible political implications.

In summary, the book makes an extremely worthwhile contribution to the debate over Canadian-American integration and provides the first comprehensive attempt to estimate quantitatively the implications of integration. Not surprisingly, some sections are less rigorous and more speculative than students of the subject might desire, but nevertheless the book is required reading for those interested in the question of economic integration.

AITKEN, HUGH GEORGE JEFFREY. **American Capital and Canadian Resources.** Cambridge: Harvard University Press, 1961, 217 p.

Professor Aitken, an economist who has written extensively on Canadian economic history, describes the course of American investments in Canada, emphasizing the historical and contemporary importance of foreign investment to Canadian development and the political difficulties Canada faces because of its dependence on American sources of capital. The author's thesis centers around the familiar Canadian "dilemma" that the country's relationship with the United States is economically essential and politically suicidal. Aitken accepts without questioning the two propositions on which the "dilemma" is based—the first that "a Canadian nationality . . . can be defined only in terms of the ways in which Canadians regard themselves as being different from Americans;" the second that the flows of capital and goods between the two countries reduces "Canada's freedom of action." The first proposition is a half-truth, founded in an assertion about the feelings of Canadians that is not generally valid. If Aitken wishes to base a Canadian "dilemma" on the desire of Canadians to be different than Americans, he must tell us what kind of differences Canadians wish to create. The second proposition is simply false. Voluntary exchanges of capital and goods between two countries do not reduce the opportunities available to either except in the trivial sense that opportunities for exchange raise the cost of choosing autarky.

American Capital and Canadian Resources does not enlighten the reader regarding the effects of the economic interdependence between Canada and the United States. The book does not convey new insights, its empirical content is familiar, and its principal thesis is not carefully argued. The best empirical study on this topic remains Herbert Marshall, F. Southard and K. Taylor's **Canadian-American Industry** (New Haven: Yale University Press, 1936, 360 p.); Jacob Viner's **Canada's Balance of International Indebtedness, 1900–1913** (Cambridge: Harvard University Press, 1924, 318 p.) is the standard source on this aspect of Canadian economic history.

CRISPO, JOHN. **International Unionism: A Study in Canadian-American Relations.**
Toronto: McGraw-Hill of Canada, 1967, 327 p.

Canadians have long been concerned about the threat to the nation's independence from the actions or influences of the United States. In the past quarter-
century the focus has shifted from fear of military conquest or peaceful annexation
to the risk of more subtle control arising from economic interdependence and
"cultural imperialism."

Surprisingly little has been done to document the impact on Canada of the close
economic ties to the United States. The overwhelming portion of Canadian foreign
trade (both imports and exports) is with the United States. No other nation in the
world has such a large portion of its manufacturing and primary resource sectors
owned and controlled by foreign (particularly American) corporations. In no other
industrialized nation does the majority of the organized labor force belong to
unions with headquarters in another country.

John Crispo has provided by far the most enlightening study of the impact on
Canada and on Canadian labor of the close ties to U.S.-based unions. Crispo is no
apologist for international unions. Indeed, he pulls no punches in criticizing and
condemning them. On balance, however, he finds that the international ties have
benefited rather than harmed Canadian workers and have had no significant impact
on the Canadian economy. The major adverse effect has been the proliferation of
small unions which could not exist except for the American tie. The major benefits
to Canadian workers arise from the technical services and strike funds that the
large U.S. unions can make available to the Canadian members.

Crispo is scrupulously honest in pointing out the weaknesses of his methodology
and the areas in which conclusions are based on hunches or opinions with little
solid factual support. These weaknesses are due to the lack of data rather than to
any deficiencies on the author's part. He has gone to great pains to collect, analyze
and evaluate the limited information that is available on the subject. The book is
well written and should be read by all interested in Canadian-American relations or
in the Canadian labor movement.

SIEGFRIED, ANDRÉ. **Canada: An International Power.** New York: Harcourt, 1937,
341 p.

André Siegfried was one of the twentieth century's most perceptive students of
national character, and like De Tocqueville before him, he strove to understand the
meaning of American civilization, especially in relation to Europe. He travelled
frequently in the Western Hemisphere, and one of the results of his visits and
studies was this book, a companion-piece to his books on the United States,
America Comes of Age (New York: Harcourt, 1927, 353 p.) and **America at Mid-
Century** (New York: Harcourt, 1955, 357 p.). As in all of his studies of national
character, Siegfried tried in his book on Canada to see how political and religious
factors interacted with the realities of geography and economics.

But this was not Siegfried's first book on Canada, nor his best on that subject. A
generation earlier he had written "Le Canada, les Deux Races" (1906), published
in translation the following year as **The Race Question in Canada.** In 1966 this
work appeared in a new edition, revised and with an introduction by Frank H.
Underhill (Toronto: McClelland, rev. ed., 1966, 252 p.). As Underhill notes,
"Almost every paragraph in it is exciting today" because of its profound treatment
"of the terms on which English Canadians and French Canadians are to live
together."

PORTER, JOHN. **The Vertical Mosaic: An Analysis of Social Class and Power in
Canada.** Toronto: University of Toronto Press, 1965, 626 p.

The publication of Professor Porter's investigation of the structure of Canadian
society was a milestone in Canadian social science, and it remains without any near
rivals in the field. That a large book by a professional sociologist should become a

national best seller suggests that Canadians were ready to have an unaccustomed look at themselves. A study focused on class is a departure from the emphasis on ethnic factors usually found in discussions of Canadian life, although the book shows a clear relationship between these factors, and class and status.

The period from which the author derives most of his data is the 1950s, with extensive use of 1951 and 1961 census data. But newspaper reports, biographies, membership lists, company reports and numerous other sources provide material for portraits of Canadian business, labor, bureaucratic, academic and religious élites, and for an account of the relationships among these groups within the Canadian power structure.

As was to be expected, it is demonstrated that members of the British "charter group" occupy positions of status and power in proportionately much larger numbers than French Canadians, and that citizens whose origins are in neither of the two "founding races" have little opportunity of entering the élites. In showing the measure in which the often lauded "Canadian mosaic," with its allegedly tolerant encouragement of the preservation of cultural plurality, has created a "vertical mosaic" which gives economic and social advantages to the Anglo-Saxons, the book destroys a mythology and suggests numerous questions for future investigation.

WADE, MASON. **The French Canadians, 1760–1945.** Toronto: Macmillan of Canada, rev. ed., 1968, 2 v.

This monumental study, first published in 1955 and translated as "Les Canadiens-Français de 1760 à Nos Jours" (Montreal: Le Cercle du Livre de France, 1963, 2 v.), is the standard textbook on the subject. It is a political narrative of French Canadian survival in North America, recounting the conflicts within French Canadian society and also the series of crises in French-English relations in British North America and later in the Canadian Confederation. Nor is politics narrowly defined; the nationalist ideas of men like Bishop Laflèche and Lionel Groulx are analyzed, and sections on French Canadian literature and architecture are also included. The author does not conceal his preference for men such as Henri Bourassa and Wilfrid Laurier who worked for accommodation between the two cultural groups, but he does give a good deal of space to the more exclusive schools of French Canadian nationalism.

The value of this survey has diminished over the years. The book appeared at the beginning of a creative period in French Canadian historiography and was itself one of the reasons for the new interest in this field. Since then Fernand Ouellet's analysis of the economic and social background in the post-conquest era has introduced new dimensions to the historiography of that period, and Ramsay Cook's studies in French Canadian intellectual history have thrown more light on French Canadian nationalism in the twentieth century. The results of recent research have not been incorporated in the second edition.

COOK, RAMSAY. **Canada and the French Canadian Question.** Toronto: Macmillan of Canada, 1966, 219 p.

This is a collection of essays, translated as "Le Sphinx Parle Français" (Montreal: HMH, 1968, 187 p.), inspired by the contemporary debate on French-English relations in Canada. The author is a committed critic of nationalism and an advocate of Actonian liberalism, but he writes as a historian rather than a polemicist, and his studies are a major contribution to the intellectual history of French Canada.

His primary interest is the interpretations of Canadian history. The essay on Michel Brunet as a nationalist historian is the most original, but his comments on Henri Bourassa, Lionel Groulx and André Laurendeau are significant contributions to the study of French Canada. Some of the essays also deal with the English Canadian attitudes toward French Canada, covering the period from Confederation to the present day. Here again the insights into the ideology of historians and public figures have added depth to the understanding of both past and present controversies.

The author's thesis is the conflict between the French Canadian commitment to *la survivance* as a cultural group in its various forms and the English Canadian commitment to the survival of Canada as a political unit, which again has taken different forms. His personal commitment to cultural duality adds vitality to the style without detracting from the sensitivity to the many ways of looking at the French Canadian question.

Memoirs and Biographies

CREIGHTON, DONALD GRANT. **John A. Macdonald.** Toronto: Macmillan of Canada, 1952, 1955, 2 v.

Donald Creighton's **John A. Macdonald** is a classic achievement in the writing of Canadian biography. Not only is it a comprehensive authoritative study of the life of the first Prime Minister and leading architect of the Canadian federal union, but it is also a literary masterpiece that vividly interweaves the personality of the man and the condition of Canada across much of the nineteenth century. Holding that "history's closest association is with literature," Creighton writes with a strong sense of style and a keen concern for dramatic narrative. Some, accordingly, have found his work too much concerned with colorful effect, more overmastering than judicious in appraisal. Yet there is no doubt of its marked impact in Canada, on both the professional historian and the reading public. And it would be absurd to undervalue Creighton's broadly based historical scholarship and penetrating insights simply because he writes with deliberate artistry and vigorous subjective engagement.

These two volumes are informed throughout by an assertive Canadian nationalism, a belief that Canada has had and should have a separate destiny on the North American continent. Macdonald serves both as symbol and champion of this belief, whether in contending with internal disunity and Anglo-French cultural division or with external British imperial assumptions and—most importantly—the ever-recurrent possibility of Canada's absorption into the United States. This view of Creighton's is not a passing emotional predilection or a device to dramatize his major biography. It is a basic finding of all his historical research and writings, from his first, and seminal, book, **The Commercial Empire of the St. Lawrence, 1760–1850** (Toronto: Ryerson Press, 1937, 441 p.), to his latest, **Canada's First Century** (Toronto: Macmillan, 1970, 372 p.), a somewhat mordant account of the increasing failure of Canadians to live up to their destiny, and to Macdonald's nation-building visions, since the erection of the modern Canadian state in 1867.

CARELESS, J. M. S. **Brown of the Globe.** Toronto: Macmillan of Canada, 1959, 1963, 2 v.

George Brown, a force in Canadian politics from his first appearance in the legislature in 1853 until his death in 1880, was the founder, editor and moving spirit behind one of the greatest of English Canadian newspapers, the Toronto *Globe*. Much of the explanation of his political dynamism, as well as his failure to fully realize his political potential, lies in this juxtaposition of newspapers and politics.

As shown in his first biography, "The Life and Speeches of George Brown," written by a colleague, Alexander Mackenzie, in 1882, Brown was a distant figure of dour aspect who had brooded earnestly but austerely over a generation of Canadian politics. While not without merit, that book reflected Mackenzie's view that one did not obtrude private life in public books, and since many of Brown's contemporaries were still alive, Mackenzie felt circumscribed in that direction as well.

Maurice Careless, however, had gone to the west coast of Scotland where Brown's descendants now lived, and located large amounts of Brown's correspondence, chiefly letters to his wife, whom Brown had married in 1863 when he was 45 years old, and with whom he was a prolific correspondent. Careless's biography does full justice to such a find, and Brown emerges as a different person from that portrayed by Mackenzie.

Brown of the Globe is at once sympathetic and detached, conspicuously fair to Brown's opponents as well as to Brown himself. It is a major biography that illuminates a vital period of Canadian history.

DAWSON, ROBERT MACGREGOR. **William Lyon Mackenzie King: A Political Biography, 1874–1923.** Toronto: University of Toronto Press, 1958, 532 p. (v. 1).

NEATBY, H. BLAIR. **William Lyon Mackenzie King: The Lonely Heights, 1924–1932.** Toronto: University of Toronto Press, 1963, 452 p. (v. 2).

William Lyon Mackenzie King was the most successful politician in Canadian history. As Leader of the Liberal Party, 1919–1926, and Prime Minister, 1921–1926, 1926–1930, 1935–1948, he exerted a powerful influence on the development of policies concerning every aspect of Canadian domestic and foreign policy for nearly three decades. Although little more than the first decade of his leadership is covered by the first two volumes of an official biography, these volumes are essential to an understanding of ideas and events in Canada during the period.

The literary executors gave the authors of these two volumes a free hand in writing the biography while expressing the hope that as far as possible King should be allowed to tell his own story. The result is a definitive and authoritative study, well written, moderate in tone, with a somewhat detached attitude toward King, containing liberal quotations from his remarkable diary and supported by evidence from all available sources, particularly private papers and interviews with his colleagues.

Two major themes are King's restoration of national unity after the disruption over the conscription crisis of 1917 and his advocacy of Canadian autonomy against the principle of a single Empire foreign policy. His decisive influence on the evolution of the modern Commonwealth is made clear, although this influence has been regretted by those who claim that when King cut the British anchor a Canadian drift to the shores of Americanization became inevitable.

PICKERSGILL, JOHN WHITNEY and FORSTER, D. F. **The Mackenzie King Record.** Toronto: University of Toronto Press, 1960, 1968, 2 v.

This book is based upon the remarkable diary of William Lyon Mackenzie King, Prime Minister of Canada, for the period of the Second World War, 1939–1945. Two more volumes will continue the book to King's retirement in 1948 and his death in 1950. The first volume was written entirely by Mr. Pickersgill, a former member of King's secretariat and later a cabinet minister; for the second he had the assistance of Mr. Forster, a political scientist at the University of Toronto. **The Mackenzie King Record** is not a biography; essentially it is a digest (with many direct quotations) of the King diary. Although exception might be and has been taken to the selection of extracts, and there are a few editorial errors, the book is a first-class source of information on Canadian politics and policies, including foreign policy. Few public men have kept so complete and, on the whole, so frank a diary; and until the entire diary is published or opened to scholars, the **Record** is an essential tool for historians of the period.

GRAHAM, ROGER. **Arthur Meighen.** Toronto: Clarke, 1960–1965, 3 v.

Conservative federal politicians in twentieth-century Canada have received little attention from biographers, perhaps because they have enjoyed limited political success and thus have not appealed to the Whig bias which dominated Canadian historical writing until recently. These three volumes may seem to provide excessively extended treatment of a Prime Minister who led the government only briefly, once for a year and a half, and later for less than three months, but they are so thoroughly researched and well written that the reader's interest is easily sustained throughout. As a controversialist and parliamentary debater, Meighen was probably without a superior in the history of Canadian politics, and this eminence is well demonstrated in the author's generous and skillful use of Meighen's own words. Of central interest is Meighen's role as the foremost Conservative, after Borden, in the Union Government of 1917–1921, when he played an originating or leading part in the institution of military conscription, passage of the War Time Elections Act, the establishment of the publicly owned Canadian National Railways, the suppression of the Winnipeg general strike and the nonrenewal of the Anglo-Japanese Alliance.

Since Meighen's career in the Conservative Party spanned more than three decades, from his first election to parliament in 1908 until his ill-fated and brief return to leadership during World War II, this work is an indispensable source for the history of the Conservative Party. Since the author is a committed biographer, both he and his subject also provide valuable insights into the Conservative cast of mind in the Canadian context.

SWETTENHAM, JOHN. **McNaughton.** Toronto: The Ryerson Press, 1968–1969, 3 v.
This is the authorized biography of the late General A. G. L. McNaughton, who had a distinguished career in the First World War and afterward was Chief of the General Staff, Canada, and President of the National Research Council of Canada. In the Second World War he commanded the First Canadian Army overseas and later was Minister of National Defense. After the war he represented Canada at the United Nations and was Chairman of the Canadian Section of the Permanent Joint Board on Defense, Canada–United States, and also of the Canadian section of the International Joint Commission. This remarkable career touched and affected Canadian external relations at many points. Swettenham's book, mainly based on McNaughton's voluminous papers, illuminates these matters considerably. Some of its judgments, which in general are highly favorable to its subject, may undergo a degree of modification when more sources of information become available, but **McNaughton** is likely to be a biography of permanent value.

THOMSON, DALE. **Louis St. Laurent, Canadian.** Toronto: Macmillan of Canada, 1967, 564 p.
Louis St. Laurent played a central role in Canadian politics from 1942 to 1957. In that period he was successively Justice Minister, Secretary of State for External Affairs and Prime Minister, and more than most leaders he shaped his nation. This was particularly so in foreign policy, for under St. Laurent's lead Canada played a major part in the creation of NATO, tied herself still closer to the United States in both economic and defense relationships, and turned decisively away from her British past during the Suez crisis of 1956. Quiet diplomacy and alliance-based internationalism, the two favorite targets of the new Canadian nationalism, were the creations of St. Laurent.

There should have been a story to tell here. But Professor Thomson, a onetime aide to the Prime Minister and an academic at the Université de Montréal and Johns Hopkins University, unfortunately adds very little to the existing view of his subject. Clearly he had no access to significant manuscript collections, and the extensive interviews he carried out seem to have provided little more than pleasant anecdotes. This is neither a revisionist history nor a definitive biography, and it can be considered as nothing more than an interim account.

LATIN AMERICA

See also Inter-American Relations, p. 365.

GENERAL; HISTORICAL

TANNENBAUM, FRANK. **Ten Keys to Latin America.** New York: Knopf, 1962, 237 p.
This has been the most popular of the many books written by the unforgettable founder and guiding spirit of the famous Latin American Seminar at Columbia

University. Professor Tannenbaum brought together here, in a kind of summing up, the experiences and insights into hemispheric life that he had accumulated over many years.

The "keys" are broad aspects of New World life whose understanding is necessary to the outsider intent upon reaching the essence of Latin American reality: the interplay of land and population; the complications that arise from race; the role of the Roman Catholic Church; regionalism; the function of the hacienda; the characteristics of education; leadership in its many variations and manifestations; the peculiarities of politics; the relationship between the United States and the southern countries; and the complex of issues posed by the Cuban Revolution and Castro.

What is notable in this, however, is the texture of the author's mind and personality. Although Tannenbaum was a well-recognized scholar, his writing has less to do with lamp and cloister than with travel by mule and sustained personal involvement in the life of provincial church and remote marketplace. Intimacy, empathy, intuition were his forte, imparting to his book unique human warmth and value.

ARCINIEGAS, GERMÁN. **The State of Latin America.** New York: Knopf, 1952, 416 p.

When this book, translated by Harriet de Onis, appeared in 1952, U.S. interest in Latin America was at its nadir: American policy was preoccupied with the communist threat in Asia and Europe. Arciniegas contributed importantly to reversing these trends. The impact of his message derived mainly from his status in the United States; he was a well-known Latin intellectual, then teaching at Columbia University, and his two earlier books (of much better quality) had been well received here. The book was welcomed by Latin Americanists in the U.S., for it echoed what many of them were saying. Arciniegas appeals to the United States to understand that "a vast conspiracy against democracy, liberty and respect for human rights" exists in Latin America. The U.S., he says, believes that Latin America will remain "subservient to the will of the United States" and that it can be ruled successfully only by dictators. He condemns efforts by the U.S. to strengthen the Latin American military and to get Latin American troops to Korea.

However, the book's message was blunted by its numerous defects, and it must now be regarded as a historical curiosity rather than a serious analysis. Its style is uneven; its content a superficial potpourri of anecdote, vignette and impassioned rhetoric. Arciniegas, writing as a Colombian Liberal, was especially simplistic in his explanation of the "violencia" in Colombia as the fault of the Conservatives. In general, he shows no understanding of basic social and economic problems, despite his many references to the unrest of the masses.

LIEUWEN, EDWIN. **Arms and Politics in Latin America.** New York: Praeger (for the Council on Foreign Relations), rev. ed., 1961, 335 p.

This pioneering work initiated serious scholarly research on the Latin American military. It was, moreover, the first effective critique of the rationale for U.S. military assistance programs. These merits overbalance the fact that some of Lieuwen's analysis has been seriously challenged and that some of his policy suggestions were not practical. He correctly describes the military assistance programs of the 1950s as designed to meet the political threat of communism and to ensure political stability in the region, as well as lesser objectives. He concludes that the policy had not been successful in achieving these goals. Indeed, military aid was shown to have various adverse effects on relations among Latin American states and on the internal political process. It also led democratic leaders in the region to conclude that the United States preferred to support military dictators. Lieuwen urged that the U.S. favor democratic governments and avoid a concept of stability that would hamper the social revolution already under way. The military could be used for civilian purposes, especially economic and social activities, and the impact of aid to them should be proportionately diminished by new U.S. economic and social programs. He was wrong in his prediction that growing professionalism would produce a decline of military activism and influence.

WEST, ROBERT C. and AUGELLI, JOHN P. **Middle America: Its Lands and Peoples.** Englewood Cliffs: Prentice-Hall, 1966, 482 p.

The physical and human geography of Mexico, Central America and the Caribbean islands are presented here with unusual depth and comprehension. The approach, in the words of the authors, is "strongly cultural and historical," with the result that the heritage of the pre-European, colonial and nineteenth century eras is fully delineated and integrated into the entire mosaic of land, culture and society.

Economic and agricultural aspects in each of the geographical areas and political entities, from the largest national units down to the smallest dependencies, are fully treated. Physical setting, climate, flora and fauna, soils and resources, population and settlement, and land systems are among the many topics that receive full exploration. There is a useful analysis of culture areas and a chapter delineating the nature and impact of the West Indian colonial plantation. Graphs, charts and illustrations are provided in abundance. The book is equally appropriate for instructional purposes, as a compendium of specific information for the generalist or specialist, and as a source of interesting and unexpected tidbits for the reader who browses at random.

MECHAM, JOHN LLOYD. **Church and State in Latin America.** Chapel Hill: University of North Carolina Press, rev. ed., 1966, 465 p.

This work first appeared in 1934 and rapidly established itself as a classic. Written in a sober and even dry style, this "discussion of politico-ecclesiastical relations" takes the deep historical perspective warranted by the subject—an ancient religious institution deeply rooted in a complex and long-lived culture. The volume begins with a consideration of Church and State during Latin America's colonial epoch and then proceeds to chapters dealing with the wars of independence. Thereafter, the author dedicates himself to tracing the histories of Church-State relations in all the individual republics. Because this revised edition adds 30 years of history to each national treatment, the reader may sometimes feel a sense of haste in the concluding pages of each chapter, as contrasted with the spacious treatments given earlier historical happenings.

Mecham indulges in no sociological or psychological fancies. His work is a straightforward presentation of political history as it revolves about the religious question. Matters of theology, too, are touched upon only as they are necessary to explain conflict and ideological differences. If he is sympathetic to the Church, he is not blind to the secular dogmatisms of either the clergy or the anticlericals. He is also fully aware that Latin American Catholicism is in large part an anomaly in that very few Latin Americans are practicing Catholics. A believer himself, Mecham sees the threat to Catholicism in Latin America coming not from any "Protestant peril" but from "secularism, religious apathy, and indifference." In his last sentence, he reveals his hope both as an individual and as a historian: "Whether an expanded and aggressive Protestantism and a socially-conscious and reinvigorated Roman Catholicism will succeed in their great task of re-Christianizing Latin America remains for history to reveal."

NEARING, SCOTT and FREEMAN, JOSEPH. **Dollar Diplomacy: A Study in American Imperialism.** New York: Huebsch, 1925, 353 p.

The long shadow cast by this study still plays over the hemispheric scene as observed from the orthodox liberal viewpoint. It was written in the afterglow of the Progressive and muckraking eras, and in opposition to the notions of hegemony and strategic interest that had been widely publicized in the works of Admiral Mahan and Stephen Bonsal. As a critique of American imperialism in every aspect, it established a mood and a framework of analysis that have served the liberal cause for almost half a century with only minor variations and improvements.

The fundamental thesis holds that there has been an intimate relationship between economic investment and the diplomatic policy of the United States, and particularly so in the Caribbean area, which receives a preponderant portion of the authors' attention. They warn that the stages of this relationship are "not inexorable," but it is clear that they deem them to be very nearly just that. The final paragraph of the volume summarizes the types of governmental coöperation with American finance in Latin America, a lengthy list ranging from "mere warnings to armed intervention and the establishment of protectorates." All the classic instances are marshalled for review.

The book is neither balanced nor free from pejorative rhetoric, and it suffers from important limitations. But its influence has been extraordinary.

HANSON, SIMON G. **Dollar Diplomacy Modern Style: Chapters in the Failure of the Alliance for Progress.** Washington: Inter-American Affairs Press, 1970, 189 p.

This book, by the editor of *Inter-American Economic Affairs,* makes a strong and well-informed attack on the Alliance for Progress and condemns it as a failure: "During the decade of the Alliance for Progress dollar diplomacy was revived with a scope that dwarfed the earlier episodes in the association between the American dollar and American diplomacy which had occasioned the odium attaching to the term 'dollar diplomacy.' "

There are, of course, other assessments of the Alliance for Progress, and this book should be read in conjunction with **Alliance for Progress: A Social Invention in the Making,** by Harvey S. Perloff, which is a strong defense of the Alliance. The two volumes set the stage for a lively controversy which we may expect to continue for decades. The authors of both works are eminently qualified to express judgments.

ARÉVALO, JUAN JOSÉ. **The Shark and the Sardines.** New York: Lyle Stuart, 1961, 256 p.

This doggedly anti–U.S. diatribe was a minor sensation when it appeared in translation in the United States where few such tracts by Latin Americans have been published or sold so widely. Arévalo, President of Guatemala from 1945 to 1951, is reputed to believe that the book led the United States to veto his return to the Guatemalan presidency in 1963. A self-styled spiritual socialist, the author perpetuates in its grossest form the myth of "Wall Street" domination of U.S. "imperialist" policy for Latin America and Rockefeller–House of Morgan-millionaire economic exploitation of the region. The result, he writes, is that "the United States became great, while progress in Latin America was ground to a halt." The U.S. is the shark; the Latin American countries, the sardines. The first Spanish-language edition, published in 1956, two years after CIA involvement in the overthrow of the Arbenz régime in Guatemala, sold more than a million copies in Latin America. The Spanish edition is a standard item in the intellectual diet of Latin American high school and university students. Therein lies the importance of this error-ridden, polemical tract.

PARRY, J. H. **The Spanish Seaborne Empire.** New York: Knopf, 1966, 416 p.

In the history of mankind there have been few political constructions whose fascination for posterity has been as dramatic and long-sustained as that of the Spanish empire in America, "the first in time of the great seaborne empires of Western Europe," as Professor Parry reminds us, and "for long the richest and most formidable, the focus of envy, fear and hatred." In this volume the immense achievement, so rapidly achieved and so tenaciously sustained, finds its most profound and skillful interpreter.

The treatment is encyclopedic, based upon the central theme of the interplay between conquest and empire. The maintenance of the empire, the quality of its society, its complicated relations with metropolitan Spain, the problems of administration, the functioning of social institutions and the wider field of the empire's relationship with the world beyond peninsular Spain are all related. The book is written in a vein of admirable impartiality which seeks neither to reinforce the *leyenda negra* nor to excuse every error and excess to which the empire gave rise. Its style and tone, moreover, are those of quiet elegance, so that art and craftsmanship reinforce intellectual content.

BELAÚNDE, VÍCTOR ANDRÉS. **Bolívar and the Political Thought of the Spanish American Revolution.** Baltimore: Johns Hopkins Press, 1938, 451 p.

This volume by a Peruvian scholar and diplomat contributed significantly at the time of its publication to the already rising level of scholarship on Latin America within the English-speaking world. It was at once a thoughtful synthesis of the ideological panorama of the era of the Spanish American wars of independence, excluding Mexico, and a detailed analysis of Bolivarian thought. Belaúnde was particularly concerned with the intellectual roots of early nineteenth century political ideas in Spanish South America and was circumspect in evaluating the contributions of the French Encyclopedists, French revolutionaries, Spanish liberals and United States constitutionalists to the body of political thought that prevailed when the colonials took the first steps toward separation from Spain.

Relying heavily upon primary documents from the independence period, Belaúnde largely avoided the prevailing tendency, particularly among Latin American intellectuals, to treat Bolívar in either adulatory or polemical terms. The author, like Bolívar himself, was both surer and more imaginative when treating political and diplomatic issues than when analyzing economic matters. Despite its shortcomings in the economic field, this volume remains an important source for those who would understand this period.

JANE, LIONEL CECIL. **Liberty and Despotism in Spanish America.** New York: Oxford University Press, 1929, 190 p.

This is strictly a period piece. When it appeared, it offered what were then considered stimulating insights into the contradictions between theory and practice in the political life of the Latin American republics. Its underlying spirit is Spanish. To be good is to be Spanish, with all that being Spanish implied for the author: idealism, pride, patriotism, conservatism, love of liberty, local freedom and efficiency, and being "intensely nationalistic." For Jane, the only relevant components of Spanish American societies were those of the "Spanish race" who fare better when they adhere to the values of their ancestors than when they borrow foreign ideologies.

Based, one suspects, more upon the author's intuition than upon extensive research, larded as it is with gratuitous assumptions and unsupported generalizations (which repetition does not obscure), and further weakened by occasional outright contradictions, the volume has at times been considered to be no more than a carryover from the pre-World War I genre of historical writing on Latin America. But for at least four reasons it may deserve a better fate: (1) the author's argument associates him with that gathering band of scholars who in the 1940s launched a full-scale attack upon the Black Legend; (2) Jane was one of a very few English-speaking scholars who as early as the 1920s sensed the intellectual pitfalls of judging Spanish America in "teutonic terms;" (3) in drawing, however unscientifically, upon the emerging field of psychology, the author displayed an awareness of the desirability of an interdisciplinary approach to Latin American studies; and (4) writing with great clarity and conciseness, Jane contributed measurably to the state of the art of historical presentation, as it related to Spanish America.

ECONOMIC, SOCIAL AND CULTURAL QUESTIONS

ANDERSON, CHARLES W. **Politics and Economic Change in Latin America: The Governing of Restless Nations.** Princeton: Van Nostrand, 1967, 388 p.

The political economy of development is the subject of this work, whose author places it in the same category as Albert O. Hirschman's **Journeys toward Progress** in emphasizing the links between political and economic development. Anderson advances the thesis that in recent years economic development in Latin America "became the standard against which the performance of the nation-state was to be measured, and on the basis of which the Western political system was to be justified." This view of the prime objective of post–World War II Latin American politics is a reasonable reflection of the temper of time immediately past. Until very recently most Latin American governments were emphasizing industrialization as the key to true national autonomy, the United States was becoming increasingly interested in developmental assistance, and the Alliance for Progress came to be promoted as the instrument to foment dynamic change without courting authoritarian rule. In seeking development, Anderson sees Latin America as generally pursuing pragmatic and experimental policies, not dogmatic and extremist ones. In proving the thesis, he examines Latin American political systems as a whole, focusing then on decision-making processes to clinch his case, and finally probing the ways in which ten republics in Central America and the Andean region have applied developmental strategies.

The author's premises do not permit him adequate bases for understanding Marxist-socialist models of political-economic relations. His book, then, is not useful for understanding contemporary Cuba and other such moves in that developmental direction. But the study does provide a sound and deeply informed understanding of reformist, economically mixed political strategies of development. Anderson's emphasis on nation-building will probably be his most lasting contribution to studies of Latin American politics, for forms of nationalism are certain to persist there for a long time.

HIRSCHMAN, ALBERT O. **Journeys toward Progress: Studies of Economic Policy-Making in Latin America.** New York: Twentieth Century Fund, 1963, 308 p.

This sophisticated study examines Brazil's efforts to improve the economic position of its northeastern states, Colombia's attempts to find better patterns of land use and tenure, and Chile's experience with inflation. The aims of these case studies are "to learn something about the problem-solving capabilities of public authorities in Latin America, about the conditions favorable to the emergence and growth of such capabilities and about characteristic ways and motions with which they assert themselves." Is there a Latin American style or strategy of problem solving?

Hirschman admits, without apologizing, that he is "trespassing" on the terrain of political science, and he notes that his basic hypothesis is that "the existence of defects in political structure does not constitute an absolute impediment to progress in dealing with economic policy problems; by the same token, it is likely that problem solving will under these conditions follow quite unfamiliar paths whose possible efficiency and hidden rationality we must try to appreciate."

On Chile: "Through the device of inflation society gains precious time for resolving social tensions that otherwise might reach the breaking point right away." It offers "an almost miraculous way of temporizing in a situation in which two or more parties who are psychologically not ready for peaceable compromise appear to be set on a collision course."

This is one of the few books of the past decade by a North American author that must be in the intellectual arsenal of serious students of the interplay of politics with economics in Latin America. The author's term "reformmongering" for "the contriving of reforms" is becoming a byword.

URQUIDI, VÍCTOR L. **The Challenge of Development in Latin America.** New York: Praeger, 1964, 209 p.

This informative survey of Latin America's economic situation originated as a series of lectures delivered in 1961 at El Colegio Nacional in Mexico City. The original Spanish version was published in Mexico in 1962; the graceful and accurate translation was prepared by the author's wife. Because of the volume's genesis, the book is a teaching instrument—clear, simply stated, always respectful of the reader who may be unfamiliar with professional terminology or the precise meanings economists attach to their concepts. The book is thus an excellent introduction to its subject for the layman. It will also be interesting to the professional as a concise and precise statement of the views of a Latin American "structuralist" economist, one who believes that economic development must be planned and seen clearly within the context of social, political, institutional and ideological factors.

Urquidi takes a pragmatic approach to the politics and sociology of economic analysis and development, as the late Frank Tannenbaum points out in his foreword. The author strongly favors state planning, seeing it as reinforcing democratic growth if that is the direction in which the polity applies its power. He also argues for the rationality inherent in attempting to revive the Bolivarian dream of a politically and economically integrated Latin America. Because the lectures from which the book comes were delivered before the formal enunciation of the Alliance for Progress, Urquidi discusses that policy only in his last chapter. He concludes by seeing the Alliance as "the only road open to Latin America that guarantees us democracy, liberty, and personal dignity."

JAGUARIBE, HELIO. **Economic and Political Development: A Theoretical Approach and a Brazilian Case Study.** Cambridge: Harvard University Press, 1968, 202 p.

Helio Jaguaribe, a Brazilian, is one of Latin America's foremost political theorists and nationalistic ideologists of development. This work combines two of his essays, originally published in Brazil in 1962 and revised for the English edition to update his examples and the Brazilian case study through 1966. The first half of the book is a theoretical essay, designed to explain various models of political and economic development, and to group the Latin American republics in categories so that the most appropriate developmental models can be found for each set of cases. The second part of the book is a historical interpretation of Brazilian development in terms of the theoretical section.

Jaguaribe defines development as a "historico-social process" through which countries move toward "growing rationalization." He sees the processes of spontaneous growth in Britain and the United States as unrepeatable; thereafter, all development took place under the auspices of state power. The ideological and organizational issues of development, therefore, do not revolve around whether the state should involve itself in economic processes but rather how it should do so. Jaguaribe advances three models of such intervention: "neo-Bismarckism," suitable for countries led by an entrepreneurial bourgeoisie who employ the government as an arbitrating mechanism; state capitalism, to be administered by a technocratic middle class; and developmental socialism, in radical form for certain cases and in reformist mode where state capitalism itself needs strengthening.

This book will be of interest to the scholar for its ordered speculation and sophisticated case study. It will also be useful to the more general reader concerned with important ideological currents in contemporary Latin America.

ALEXANDER, ROBERT JACKSON. **Labor Relations in Argentina, Brazil, and Chile.** New York: McGraw-Hill, 1962, 411 p.

From a wide experience in the field of Latin American labor relations, the author, one of the most prolific Latin Americanists, offers an unadorned, adequately documented account of the growth of trade unionism in the ABC countries. Students of labor problems have long felt that unionism developed in the emerging nations in patterns which are significantly different from those that evolved in the United States and in Western Europe. This book is part of a broader study, undertaken by the Inter-University Study of Labor Problems in Economic Development, whose aim was the examination of these differences.

The volume describes the background against which the industrialization process and labor-management-government relations are conducted. An accurate portrayal is given of the living conditions of workers. The author discusses such basic problems as the change of paternalistic attitudes and relations between rural workers and large landowners when workers migrate to an urban setting, and the multifaceted difficulties of recruiting and training an industrial labor force. The dominant role of politics in Latin American labor relations is aptly emphasized by analysis of the development of workers' organizations in Brazil under Vargas and in Argentina during the Perón era. While showing how labor relations have developed differently in each of these countries (each treated separately) the study clearly suggests that in the union system emerging in Latin America, state interventionism, guidance or control plays a much more significant role than in the labor systems of the highly industrialized nations of the Western world. Alexander's volume is an invaluable aid to all students of Latin America's labor movement.

JOHNSON, JOHN J. **Political Change in Latin America: The Emergence of the Middle Sectors.** Stanford: Stanford University Press, 1958, 272 p.

The date of this book's publication is important to its understanding. After World War II, when the concepts of underdevelopment, foreign aid and modernization became popular, it was common to see the rise of a middle class as one of the keys to development. The economic difficulties of Latin America were often explained as resulting from the bi-class structure of those republics: the rich at one end, the poor at the other, and no group in the middle to press for reform, national loyalty, social equity and the other hallmarks of industrial and democratic lands. In attacking this stereotype, Johnson says that "urban middle groups are vitally, if not decisively, important in an area where one still commonly hears and reads that there is 'no middle class to speak of'—a statement that is both partially true and dangerously misleading." He discards the term "middle class" because he does not wish to confuse "middleness" in Latin America with the ideas surrounding social class in Europe. But he sees his middle sectors as sharing critical traits no matter what their country. They live in cities, they are educated, they grow with industrialization and promote more of it, they are nationalistic, they approve of state intervention in the economy, and they are active in party politics. In support of these theses, the author examines the growth of middle social groups in Uruguay, Chile, Argentina, Mexico and Brazil, socially and economically the area's most developed countries at the time of writing.

Although Johnson expects much from his middle sectors, he is wary of his predictions in this regard. Indeed, many later authors have pointed out the obvious existence of masses of middle-class persons in many Latin American countries but have argued that they identify with upper groups and thus fail to discharge the nation-building function that is their ultimate social reason for being. However sound this argument may be, Johnson's innovative book was one of the first in English to recognize the complexity of Latin American social orders and to attempt a historical analysis of the growth of that complexity.

The bibliography is excellent and remains very useful.

VELIZ, CLAUDIO, *ed.* **Obstacles to Change in Latin America.** New York: Oxford University Press (for the Royal Institute of International Affairs), 1965, 263 p.

Bacon's excess of books has come to pass in recent years in the form of edited volumes of Latin American studies, too often characterized by paucity of theme and unevenness of scholarship and usefulness. One welcomes, therefore, this collection of studies marked by high quality and coherence of design.

The editor is the distinguished Director of the Institute of International Studies at the University of Chile. The theme, ably delineated in his introduction, is the pervasive and obstructive influence of "a resilient traditional structure of institutions, hierarchical arrangements, and attitudes which conditions every aspect of political behavior and which has survived centuries of colonial government, movements for independence, foreign wars and invasions, domestic revolutions, and a confusingly large number of lesser palace revolts. More recently it has not only successfully resisted the impact of technological innovations and industrialization, but appears to have been strengthened by it."

The manner in which the middle classes have lent themselves to "this situation of relative stagnation and stability," and the tracing of its origins in a "sophisticated pre-industrial urban civilization" and in a unique form of import-substitution industrialization, among other factors, are described either implicitly or explicitly by ten outstanding Latin American scholars and specialists, including Felipe Herrera, Celso Furtado and Helio Jaguaribe. Other themes, subsidiary to the one described above, are also considered, including foreign investment, land tenure and violence. Aspects of Chile, Brazil, Colombia and Mexico form the principal subject matter of four studies.

LAMBERT, JACQUES. **Latin America: Social Structure and Political Institutions.** Berkeley: University of California Press, 1967, 413 p.

Vast in scope and speculative in nature, this volume, first published in French in 1963, offers a clear and insightful synthesis of the literature treating "development" in Latin America within the established political systems. Although the approach is essentially descriptive, there is a good deal of stimulating political analysis. The author skillfully avoids the easy generalization as he works his way from his broad philosophical underpinnings through his mass of materials.

Latin America explores nearly the full range of social, economic and political problems faced by the 20 republics, but Lambert never wanders for long from his central concerns: the rural-urban dichotomy and the importance of the emergence of self-conscious urban middle classes. For him, rural society is archaic and reactionary. Urban societies, with their increasingly politicized popular elements, are modernizing and provide bases for the new national radical parties, labor union movements and student politics which at the proper moment, he believes, will help to produce national states.

If the author is to be faulted, it probably should be for his profound faith in economic development as a panacea and for his tendency to discuss Latin America in terms of European models well known to him.

ADAMS, RICHARD NEWBOLD and OTHERS. **Social Change in Latin America Today: Its Implications for United States Policy.** New York: Harper (for the Council on Foreign Relations), 1961, 353 p.

This collection of six articles by well-known anthropologists is designed to illuminate politics through the insights of persons professionally skilled in studying pre-industrial societies. No attempt is made to link the articles with a common theory, or even to draw a single set of conclusions. Instead, each author embarks on his own attempt to knit values and so-called traditional structures with national politics as he sees fit. If the results vary widely from article to article, and are sometimes more revelatory of the authors than of events, they still remain useful in analyzing the ties that bind local, national and international politics in Latin America.

The first article, by John P. Gillin, entitled "Some Signposts for Policy," reflects his long-standing interest in psychocultural factors as they play on political ideologies and styles. The late Allan R. Holmberg then presents an important case for applied social research, describing a famous experiment in planned rural development in the town of Vicos, Peru—an area since devastated by the earthquakes of 1970. Richard W. Patch follows with an examination of the effects of United States assistance in Bolivia, a historical account that remains a key source for understanding the contemporary history of that unhappy land. Charles Wagley writes of social change in Brazil since 1930, following Patch in providing an analysis still relevant to an understanding of Brazil under military rule. Richard N. Adams then returns to the theme of American policy, treating it broadly as it relates to Guatemala. A chapter by Oscar Lewis on Mexico completes the book. Interestingly, the Lewis contribution finds him attempting a general country survey that is the polar opposite of his famed personal histories, presented in such books as **Five Families** (New York: Basic Books, 1959, 351 p.) and **The Children of Sánchez.**

This book is fascinating in its presentation of the encapsulated views of six famed anthropologists. It is less successful in revealing the relation between anthropology and politics than it is in showing what good minds from any discipline can do with political questions.

SILVERT, KALMAN H. **The Conflict Society: Reaction and Revolution in Latin America.** New Orleans: The Hauser Press, rev. ed., 1966, 280 p.

First published in 1961, this collection is based upon reports written by Silvert for the American Universities Field Staff. A revised edition in 1966 contains new chapters in place of a few of the old ones. The essays in both editions are somewhat disparate in theme and approach, although the author has grouped them under several unifying headings. The approach of some of the essays is unconventional by traditional scholarly criteria—for example, the informal essay on experiences with Chilean customs which effectively makes its point on differences between the Chilean life style and our own. Other essays rank among the best early efforts at typologies and other political analysis. Perhaps the most important piece in the revised edition, at least for U.S.–Latin American academic relationships, is the one on the ill-famed, ill-fated Project Camelot. Silvert properly viewed the Camelot fiasco as raising serious problems of an ethical nature for United States social scientists working abroad (its impact was not confined to Latin America) and as a setback for future social science research in Latin America. This was the most sensible and perceptive of the many writings on the issue that appeared here and abroad. In general, this book demonstrates why the author's influence has spread widely beyond his own discipline of political science and beyond his own country to make him a towering figure among Latin Americanists. With scholarship in the best sense of the word and with a broad humanism, Silvert has written a book that will stand as a landmark for many years.

JOHNSON, JOHN J. **The Military and Society in Latin America.** Stanford: Stanford University Press, 1964, 308 p.

This book is grand in its theoretical, geographic and chronological sweep. Called by the author "not a narrative history, but an interpretation, necessarily generalized, of military-civilian relations," the study covers a century and a half of Latin American history and is based on interviews as well as documentary sources. Johnson argues that the fundamental reason for military intervention in Latin American politics is the inefficacy of civilian authority and rule. Once installed, however, the military in turn inhibit the healthful growth of civilian institutions.

The book has been adversely criticized because it appears to some readers to be overly sympathetic to military establishments. For example, Johnson argues that military leaders tend to be less corruptible than their civilian counterparts and more dedicated to patriotism, thus gaining genuine support from many sectors of the public. While this statement is debatable, Johnson takes a much more evenhanded approach than his critics suggest. Seeking a constructive role for the military in a Latin American modernization process he sees as inevitable, Johnson puts no blind trust in military ways. He says, "There is absolutely nothing in the evolution of the Latin American armed forces to suggest that they can any longer be trusted to be the stronghold of traditions or that they will for much longer 'hold off the mob power of the left.' "

The book contains a sweepingly synthetic statement of civil-military relations throughout the Hispanic part of Latin America, with a separate section on Brazil which the author sees as unique in the area. The work is valuable not only as it explains civil-military relations in Latin America but also as it suggests ways of understanding the same problem throughout the developing world.

LIPSET, SEYMOUR MARTIN and SOLARI, ALDO, *eds.* **Elites in Latin America.** New York: Oxford University Press, 1967, 531 p.

Latin Americans are prone to think in terms of social classes when they speak of power, of rulers and ruled, and of leaders and followers. North Americans are more accustomed to the idea of élites, of those persons who occupy leading positions in the many institutional structures characterizing a modern society. Thus the Latin emphasis is on the social origins and class identifications of leaders, while North American attention is given to the selection and functioning of leaders. The former approach emphasizes continuity; the latter, process. The book at hand is a virtuosic collection of essays turning élite analysis onto an area unaccustomed to the approach, yet susceptible to its precepts—for, of course, élite analysis and class analysis are not mutually exclusive.

The first portion of the book deals with economic development in terms of entrepreneurship, the middle-class role and industrial élites. The second section turns to functional élites of a noneconomic nature—in politics, the military, the Catholic Church, cultural life, labor and the peasantry. The remainder of the volume describes the higher and secondary educational experiences of persons who become members of the élite. That is, the book examines the role of education either as certifying class status in the training of leaders or as providing one of the bases for social mobility into the ranks of leadership.

The editors include one Latin and one North American, and the contributors are also evenly divided between the two areas. With only one or two exceptions, the authors are among the most prestigious scholars in their respective disciplines, in almost all cases either sociology or political science. Fully half the articles are staples in Latin American social science literature, and none is less than highly competent.

HAUSER, PHILIP M., *ed*. **Urbanization in Latin America.** New York: Columbia University Press, 1961, 331 p.

This collection presents condensed versions of 11 papers written for a conference on urbanization problems held in Santiago, Chile, in July 1959, with an introduction and conclusion discussing some policy implications of urbanization. Because the conference was sponsored by four dependencies of the United Nations as well as by the Organization of American States, the political dimensions of urbanization are entirely neglected, except for some technical discussion of problems of public administration. Most of the contributors are sociologists, as is the editor.

The papers concern demographic, economic, occupational, educational and administrative problems associated with rapid urbanization. Great attention is paid to lower social strata, the growth of slum areas and problems of lower-class migration. Because the conference was the first major venture of its kind on this subject in Latin America, taking place at a time when little empirical sociological research had yet been done, the findings are fragmentary, and such major problems as rapid population increase are not given the importance they later assumed. Still, the introductory sections are thorough and skilled within their limitations, while the contributory papers include some of the earliest modern social analysis done in Latin America.

This book should be read for its historical interest and for the perspective it throws on the rapidity with which the recognition of issues changes. It also serves as an excellent introduction to the work of a series of Latin American scholars who have, by and large, earned international reputations with their later contributions.

WHITEFORD, ANDREW H. **Two Cities of Latin America: A Comparative Description of Social Classes.** Garden City: Doubleday, 1964, 266 p.

This excellent comparison and contrast of the class systems of two small cities, Popayan in Colombia and Querétaro in Mexico, was originally published as "Bulletin No. 9" of the Logan Museum of Anthropology, Beloit College, Wisconsin. Popayan is the ancestral home of some of the most aristocratic and influential families of Colombia, whereas the national influences in Mexico of the "best" families of Querétaro has been much more limited. Assisted by his students, Whiteford gathered the data for his analyses of the class system of Popayan during the summers of 1949 and 1950 and the year 1951–1952; he was in Querétaro briefly in 1955 and for four months in 1958. The detailed factual materials secured during these periods of observation were organized according to a well-conceived frame of reference into one of the most significant studies of urban society ever done in Latin America. Indeed, the detailed presentations of the nature of the upper, middle and lower classes in these cities and the various concomitants of each of the various socioeconomic statuses help make this book one of the more important contributions to the scientific study of social stratification in general.

ARCINIEGAS, GERMÁN. **Latin America: A Cultural History.** New York: Knopf, 1967, 594 p.

Written by a well-known Colombian scholar, journalist, editor, educator and diplomat, this is a rambling tale; but the description carries no reproach, and the task is neatly accomplished. A few errors can be forgiven when the author writes with such authority, elegance and persuasion. He paints a gigantic panorama and at the same time tells an unusually good story which reads like a breathless suspense tale. Beginning in pre-Columbian times and moving with the Spanish explorations, conquest and colonization, Arciniegas lets his tale float on the wondrous stream of the old chronicles. His descriptions of the ancient Indian cities are superb. Then he vividly pictures the independence period with all its romantic liberalism and passes on to the rise of the great *caudillos*. The study continues with the development of Latin American ideas in the transition from utilitarianism to positivism and is brought down to present times. It even includes some treatment, if superficial, of such recent events as the Cuban Revolution. Passages from Latin American writings are reproduced, ranging from the ancient Mayan "Popul Vuh," the books of Chilam Balam and the early *cronistas* through Bolívar, Rubén Darío and Jose Martí to the writers of the Mexican Revolution and Fidel Castro.

In a final chapter, the author argues that the region has a predisposition toward the "black arts." According to Arciniegas, Latin American literature and art move forward partly through magic, which entwines the European culture with that of the Western Hemisphere. Even communism, he claims, has advanced not by its materialistic approach to history but by its mystique. The book can be earnestly recommended as a remarkably comprehensive and readable history of Latin American culture in which the student of political and social phenomena can find much to ponder.

ZEA, LEOPOLDO. **The Latin-American Mind.** Norman: University of Oklahoma Press, 1963, 308 p.

The purpose of the author, a distinguished Mexican teacher, intellectual and public official, is to trace, with insight and skill, the post-colonial intellectual and spiritual pilgrimage of Hispanic American man, "passing . . . from one mode of being imposed by three centuries of colonial rule, struggling to reach by more violent means another mode of being."

Colonial Hispanic America had found its concept of the world, and the framework of its thought, in scholasticism. Independence was followed by the movement that the author terms "romanticism," whose disciples in the generation of 1840–1860 included Domingo Sarmiento, José Victoriano Lastarria, Andrés Bello and José María Luis Mora. Romanticism, in conjunction with various European currents, prepared the way for positivism, a philosophical movement whose entrenchment in Hispanic America has been second only to that of historical scholasticism. Varying from country to country in response to indigenous needs and characteristics, drawing now upon Compte, now upon Spencer and the English school, positivism was regarded as a constructive instrument of order, the means by which full intellectual freedom and its consequences in social and political life could be attained. Positivism achieved its highest influence in Mexico, Argentina, Chile, Uruguay, Peru, Bolivia and Cuba, although it was present to a lesser degree as a form of liberal ideology in several other countries. Positivism has been deeply significant in Brazil as well, but the author has excluded that country from his study because of the different form and purpose that characterized the movement there.

CRAWFORD, WILLIAM REX. **A Century of Latin-American Thought.** New York: Praeger, rev. ed., 1966, 322 p.

If Latin America is famed for its crude *caudillos,* it also has a long tradition of intellectual statesmen who combine in their persons scholarly, diplomatic, political and military skills. The activist intellectuals, Latin America's philosophes (or *pensadores*), have only rarely been treated systematically in English. This volume is the initial study of its kind. First published in 1944, it remains a standard survey of Latin American social thinkers from independence in the 1820s to the 1930s.

Crawford deals with his subjects in short sections, interspersing biographical vignettes with syntheses of major writings and some attempt to analyze the world views of the 35 thinkers he has selected. Specifically, he places emphasis on Echeverría, Alberdi and Sarmiento as exemplars of the independence and early nation-building epoch and then proceeds to Bello, Lastarria, Bilbao and Letelier to cover the period of liberal-conservative disagreement and the rise of positivism lasting through the nineteenth century. Rodó and Vaz Ferreira are analyzed to exemplify ethnocentric reactions against the Europeanizing bias of the former group, after which Crawford turns to social theorists in the contexts of their own countries. His remaining chapters then deal with Argentine, Peruvian, Brazilian, Cuban and Mexican ideologists and philosophers.

Because Crawford is a sociologist, the reader will miss the considerations which would be brought to this subject by a professional philosopher. Also, as the author points out, many well-known *pensadores* have been omitted, as have persons from Colombia and the Central American republics. Still, Crawford has chosen his subjects of study well, and he provides a sympathetic and unpretentious survey of their thought which is highly useful for the general reader and beginning student.

ADAMS, RICHARD NEWBOLD. **Crucifixion by Power: Essays on Guatemalan National Social Structure, 1944–1966.** Austin: University of Texas Press, 1970, 553 p.

Specialists tend to stay at their chosen level of generalization. Anthropologists have traditionally concentrated on small communities; political scientists, by and large, deal with nations; and experts in international relations often lose their way when they study domestic politics. There are exceptions to this rule, of course, and the book at hand is a major one. Adams and his collaborators (two colleagues who contribute a chapter each, and a long list of graduate students) take the nation-state as their primary unit of analysis and then point downward in the power hierarchy to the local community, and outward and upward to place Guatemala in its international context. The volume is an important contribution to anthropology, social theory and to our general knowledge of Guatemala. In the latter category, it is certainly the most sophisticated study yet published of that tortured and intricately interesting country.

Adams argues that power relations are the nexus of social interaction. In pursuit of that concept, one must examine the principal loci of power—nations—for they are the only structures pretending to sovereignty. Adams, an anthropologist, extends the domain of his discipline by thus directing himself to such macrosocial questions. Because all sovereignty is limited, and because the sovereignty of small states is especially limited, the author pays careful attention to Guatemala's ability to create power as well as to the international power context in which it must perforce exist. The crucifixion of the title is the result of Guatemala's being prevented from settling her internal problems in the light of her own structures, beliefs and abilities. Caught in North America's back yard, Guatemala's domestic life is influenced and sometimes determined from abroad in such a way as to foment instability by preventing long-term solutions to national problems.

MEXICO

WILKIE, JAMES W. **The Mexican Revolution: Federal Expenditure and Social Change since 1910.** Berkeley: University of California Press, 1967, 337 p.

This is a pioneering effort in studies of Latin American countries to gauge post-revolutionary governmental performance through financial analysis. As the author states: "Through an examination of carefully delineated statistical data, it is possible to assess the Mexican Revolution in two new ways. The Mexican federal budget may be tested against actual expenditures in order to determine to what extent the official party of the Revolution has carried out its projections to raise the standard of living for the poverty-stricken masses. By investigating and organizing budgetary figures in relation to social, economic, and administrative expenditure, we may characterize varying presidential programs from 1910 to 1963 and concretely test the ideology of each leader's program as it works out in practice."

The author develops a "Poverty Index" as offering "a method of examination of social change in a developing area," and he hopes that this method may be used for comparative purposes by other scholars in studying growth in developing countries. Some observers have suggested that the Mexican Revolution lost its dynamism after 1940, but the author concludes that "social benefits for the masses as well as economic development came at a rapid rate only after 1940."

This major attempt at a "sophisticated analysis of quantification of ideology" is an ambitious enterprise, but all "three-week experts" on Mexico ought to take a hard look at Wilkie's hard text before writing off the Revolution as a failure.

CLINE, HOWARD FRANCIS. **Mexico: Revolution to Evolution, 1940–1960.** New York: Oxford University Press (for the Royal Institute of International Affairs), 1962, 375 p.

This is an unusual book. Howard Cline, Director of the Hispanic Foundation of the Library of Congress, is a well-known historian of Mexico, as well as a Mexico "buff." The combination of profession and hobby is evident in the treatment of his sweeping theme which enables him to say meaningful things in a few words. The description and analysis of the Mexican Revolution, covering 1910 to 1940, for example, occupies only ten pages, but it sets the scene for a series of equally short chapters discussing the years of dizzying change in Mexico from 1940 to 1960. Cline goes from a skillful statement of geography to regionalism and sectionalism, communications, transportation and irrigation before turning to the people in all their ethnic and class complexities. Further chapters accurately describe the political situation, along with the educational, agrarian and labor policies of the period. The concluding sections deal with Mexico in world economics, its relations to its neighbors, its role in the United Nations and the Organization of American States, and there is a summary and truncated comparison of the Mexican and Cuban Revolutions.

The work goes merrily along, knowledge and intelligence everywhere evident. Cline advances his own interpretations but knows when to acknowledge competing views. He chooses his data with a keen eye for the significant and the accurate and is not so rushed that he fails to indicate when dubiety is called for. In short, this is a book for all readers: the tourist needs it, the person of passing interest will find it useful and reliable, and the specialist will enjoy its expertness.

WOMACK, JOHN, JR. **Zapata and the Mexican Revolution.** New York: Knopf, 1969, 435 p.

This book may be recommended to anyone asking for an introduction to the Mexican Revolution. It is not comprehensive; it does not provide a chronology nor an orderly account of constitutional developments; it is not a general political history of the Mexican Revolution. It is, however, a social history of the Revolution in the State of Morelos that provides a detailed narration of the popular movement led by Emiliano Zapata.

As the author says, the book is about country folk who, in 1912, did not wish to change their ways of living and for this very reason made a revolution. Their movement took a long time to achieve success, but in 1935 President Lázaro Cárdenas visited the town of Anenecuilco in Morelos and recognized the local people's title to their land. The book admirably conveys the confusion of the revolutionary conflicts. The officiousness of the heirs of the Díaz régime is described in all its bureaucratic significance, and the frustrations of the rebels and the murder of Zapata are graphically portrayed.

This is a work in depth about the Mexican Revolution such as the Mexicans themselves have not undertaken to write. It has been voted a prize in Mexico, but political opposition there has prevented the tender of the award. There is now a Spanish translation that may help Mexicans to understand the greatness of their Revolution.

TANNENBAUM, FRANK. **Mexico: The Struggle for Peace and Bread.** New York: Knopf, 1950, 293 p.

This book was written to contribute to the better understanding of Mexican–United States relations through insight into the Mexican Revolution. Though of limited usefulness today, one aspect remains significant: Tannenbaum was the last prominent United States advocate of the agrarian path in Mexico. A good friend and admirer of the great reformer President Lázaro Cárdenas, he believed that the post-1940 revolutionary leadership had gone wrong in its decision to industrialize, and considered the Indian village superior to the large urban industrial complex. The rural community is "the best thing Mexico has," he wrote, because of its moral superiority and its "beautiful, strong, and serviceable" handicrafts. Mexico, Tannenbaum argued, was caught in an economic trap: an industrialization predestined to failure and an uncontrolled population growth which meant a tragic inability to achieve self-sufficiency in food production in the future. The solution was a Mexico of thousands of prospering small communities subsisting on cottage industries, similar to Switzerland and Denmark. He was wrong, of course, in that Mexico achieved self-sufficiency in food in 1958, but right, at least, on the need for more rural investment.

CRONON, EDMUND DAVID. **Josephus Daniels in Mexico.** Madison: University of Wisconsin Press, 1960, 369 p.

Both Mexico and the United States were fortunate when, shortly after the presidential election of 1932, Franklin D. Roosevelt asked his former chief in the Department of the Navy what appointment he would like. Josephus Daniels replied: "Mexico." He was appointed ambassador and, more surprisingly, was accepted in Mexico City despite his role in the occupation of Vera Cruz in 1914.

The intent of this book is "to show something of the complicated nature and problems of Good Neighbor diplomacy." Mexico, "through its defiant expropriation of American-owned oil and agricultural lands, gave the Good Neighbor Policy its severest trial in the 1930's," the author writes, and he believes that the settlement reached in late 1941 was "the high-water mark of Good Neighbor diplomacy, contributing substantially to that stock of goodwill in Latin America which Vice President Nixon found so depleted a decade-and-a-half later."

Cronon has made careful and exhaustive use of the Daniels papers in the Library of Congress and also of those of Donald R. Richberg and others; he has thus gone well beyond Daniels' own **Shirt-Sleeve Diplomat** (Chapel Hill: University of North Carolina Press, 1947, 547 p.) to reconstruct the intricate and delicate negotiations following the oil companies' expropriation by President Lázaro Cárdenas on March

18, 1938. Daniels' unorthodox disregard of instructions from the Department of State was facilitated by his intimate personal ties to Roosevelt.

VERNON, RAYMOND. **The Dilemma of Mexico's Development: The Roles of the Private and Public Sectors.** Cambridge: Harvard University Press, 1963, 226 p.

It used to be widely accepted that the Mexican president was truly sovereign, a temporary monarch. A similar dictum held that Mexico's dominant official party, the Institutional Revolutionary Party (together with the formal state apparatus) was the ultimate arbiter of that country's national fate. Vernon reëxamines these shibboleths and advances a contrary argument. He maintains that while a strong executive did indeed have much to do with Mexico's extraordinarily rapid rates of industrialization, commercialization, urbanization, population growth and so on, the very successes of development have changed the nature of state power and are threatening the effectiveness of the system. Vernon holds that, contrary to being able to guide the details as well as the policies of economic growth, the Mexican government has become but one in a number of competing interest groups. The relative strengths of the parties at issue are such that they often create stasis, prevent effective decision making and threaten Mexico with crises avoidable in more rational, organized and politically freer climates.

The first portion of the book comprises a historical section providing background for the thesis. The remainder of the volume is an analytical treatment of the organization and politics of the Mexican economy, with case studies. The work is closely reasoned, the data are persuasive, and the case generally supported by succeeding events even though disputable as to detail and shading. This book is an excellent corrective to much romanticized writing about Mexico and serves as a partial explanation of that country's recent disorders and policy uncertainties.

GLADE, WILLIAM P., JR. and ANDERSON, CHARLES W. **The Political Economy of Mexico: Two Studies.** Madison: University of Wisconsin Press, 1963, 242 p.

Two monographs comprise this political and economic study of Mexico. Glade, an economist, starts with the recent industrialization of Mexico and examines that phenomenon as it fits into general social and political conditions. His thesis is that Mexico's extremely rapid economic growth is a direct product of its Revolution, which began in 1910 and is usually held to have ended in 1940. Anderson, a political scientist, takes an opposite tack by examining governmentally controlled development banking activities; that is, he embarks from political premises to explore an economic institution. His thesis, too, is that the growth of Mexican capitalism occurred as a direct result of political decisions and effectively applied authority.

These two studies fit well together. Both are clearly and crisply written and add substantially to our understanding of the peculiarities of Mexican industrialization. The Anderson study forms part of a fairly large but usually esoteric body of writings on Chilean, Venezuelan, Argentine and other Latin American development banking mechanisms; it is one of the best of these studies, and its ready availability is most fortunate. Glade's contribution fits a more standard body of literature relating economic to other social conditions, but is unusual in that few contemporary North American economists take an institutional and historical approach to their subject matter.

Both authors are careful in seeing the Mexican Revolution as an indigenous phenomenon whose success lies in the creation of new political power and in the pursuit of ends defined as in the national interest. Their work will be of little help in understanding such other revolutions as the recent upheavals in Cuba, Bolivia and possibly Peru—a natural consequence of the legitimate emphasis the authors place on the autochthonous nature of Mexican events.

REDFIELD, ROBERT. **A Village That Chose Progress: Chan Kom Revisited.** Chicago: University of Chicago Press, 1950, 187 p.

In 1931 Robert Redfield, an anthropologist of the University of Chicago, collaborated with Mexican anthropologist Alfonso Villa Rojas in a meticulous study of one small Maya Indian village in Yucatan. The results were published by the Carnegie Institution under the title **Chan Kom: A Maya Village** (Washington: Carnegie Institution, 1934, 387 p.). In 1948 Redfield returned to the village for a six-week period to take stock of the sociocultural changes during the 17-year period. This little classic contains the carefully considered and lucidly presented results of that re-study. As described by its author, "the book is a part of the biography of a community, of a people who conceived a common purpose, and of what they did to realize it." Specifically, the people of Chan Kom decided to make their small village into the head town, or seat of government, of a new county-like *municipio*. The pursuit of this goal brought profound changes to the village, to its economic activities and institutions, the language used in the homes, the educational institutions, the religious beliefs and practices, family organization and domestic life, and the general ethos of their society in miniature. It also produced deep schisms and conflicts. In a masterful manner, Redfield has captured and pictured in stark reality the nature of these drastic changes.

LEWIS, OSCAR. **The Children of Sánchez.** New York: Random House, 1961, 499 p.

Anthropologist Oscar Lewis first examined the Sánchez family in a study of four Mexican slum families and one middle-class family which was published as **Five Families: Mexican Case Studies in the Culture of Poverty** (New York: Basic Books, 1959, 351 p.). This was followed by separate books on two of the families—the Martínez and the Sánchez—and the latter by a sequel, **A Death in the Sánchez Family** (New York: Random House, 1969, 119 p.). The research for these books was conducted through lengthy taped interviews. By selecting the family as the focus, in place of the usual broader study of a community, Lewis has documented in detail the "culture of poverty." He has, however, developed almost no theoretical interpretation of his results. His findings, he believes, are applicable to lower-class culture throughout the world, in that promotion of economic development and reform requires serious efforts to change lower-class attitudes. He balances the gains and failures of the Mexican Revolution of 1910 and finds it wanting. In his view, exploitation of the poor finances Mexican development, while political stability denies them redress. He suggests that social revolution may again result.

Lewis's influential books have reached a worldwide audience. In Mexico, the reaction has been mixed: efforts were made to prevent publication of one of his works, but Mexican critics of the Revolution have applauded them.

SCOTT, ROBERT EDWIN. **Mexican Government in Transition.** Urbana: University of Illinois Press, rev. ed., 1964, 345 p.

This study provides a basis for comparing Mexico's governmental system with those of other countries. "It considers the multifold social, psychological, and physical conditions which go to make up the Mexican political culture, but relates them to action within a political system by discussing them as factors in the group approach to the study of the political process." The author believes that this approach has universality "in that the decision making process and the interaction of the interest groups which participate in it are common to all political systems."

The key word here is "system." Scott states that "the principal difference between this and other studies of Mexican government . . . is that the data is presented within a particular frame of reference, based upon what is hoped to be an internally consistent and logical method."

This is the first book to give serious attention to Mexico by applying the modern concepts recently developed in the field of comparative politics. One of the sources of new ideas has been research on contrasts between "Western" and "non-Western" political phenomena. The latter are characterized by charismatic leadership, unclear and nonspecific roles of political actors, informal and weakly organized interest groups, and other features. Scott concludes that "Mexican politics has become more patterned, more inclusive, more continuous, perhaps more sophisticated. It has, in short, become systematized into a working political culture in the Western sense." His deep research aims at substantiating this view.

BRANDENBURG, FRANK. **The Making of Modern Mexico.** Englewood Cliffs: Prentice-Hall, 1964, 379 p.

This "interpretation of the causes and effects of the Mexican Revolution" is written by a political scientist who taught in universities in Mexico for a substantial period of time.

The author observes that Mexico is ruled by an élite and calls it "the Revolutionary Family," of which he distinguishes three elements or levels: (1) the President and about 20 persons in an informal "inner council;" (2) some 200 "spokesmen" of industry, agriculture, journalism, labor unions and other sectors of society; (3) the formal political apparatus, including parties and official governmental institutions.

A statement by a Mexican senator, Manuel Moreno Sánchez, that Mexico is run by an oligarchy is quoted with approval. The senator is also quoted as saying that "this revolutionary minority" thinks of transforming the Mexican people, unlike other oligarchies—military, clerical, plantation or industrial—that think only of properties and businesses. Brandenburg concludes that political power is becoming concentrated more and more in the President, who is head of the "Family," and that "Mexicans avoid personal dictatorship by retiring their dictators every six years."

This book should be viewed in contrast to Robert E. Scott's **Mexican Government in Transition.**

THE CARIBBEAN

General

GUERRA Y SÁNCHEZ, RAMIRO. **Sugar and Society in the Caribbean: An Economic History of Cuban Agriculture.** New Haven: Yale University Press, 1964, 218 p.

Few if any have understood more thoroughly than Dr. Guerra, and no one has been able to set forth more clearly and concisely, the debasing effects—socially, culturally, economically, politically and demographically—of the concentration of the ownership and control of the land and large-scale monoculture. This little volume, first published in Spanish in 1927, deserves to be read and reread by everyone who in any way helps shape the basic policies of any nation, large or small, in any part of the world. The scholarly author, in a dispassionate way and with the clearest of prose, sets forth in stark outline the role throughout the entire Caribbean area of the great sugar-cane plantation system (or what the author calls the sugar latifundium), from the time of its origin in Barbados about 1640 to the eve of the débâcle in Cuba under Castro. The author repeatedly identifies the factors (abundant capital made available from abroad by absentee owners to use in large-scale production of a single crop by means of the manual labor supplied by hosts of imported "cheap" labor) which time and again produced the dismal effects that were appearing before his own eyes in Cuba. "The rising tide of the latifundium irresistibly destroys—as demonstrated by the history of twenty [once] prosperous Antillean islands—everything that stands in the way of its final goal: to produce at minimum cost a basic commodity or luxury article for a distant market at a profit, even though that policy will in the long run ruin the producing country economically, socially, and politically."

HOETINK, H. **The Two Variants in Caribbean Race Relations: A Contribution to the Sociology of Segmented Societies.** New York: Oxford University Press, 1967, 207 p.

This volume is an important contribution in the continuing debate about the interrelationships between race (or color), class and culture in general, in the heterogeneous Caribbean area in particular. In the preface to the English edition Hoetink bluntly states as the main thesis of his study that "one and the same person may be considered white in the Dominican Republic or Puerto Rico, and 'coloured' in Jamaica, Martinique, or Curaçao; this difference must be explained in terms of socially determined somatic norms. The same person may be called a 'Negro' in Georgia; this must be explained by the historical evolution of social structure in the Southern United States." He further maintains "that it is not the denial of the significance of racial factors, but only a sociological analysis of the concepts of 'race,' as attempted in this study, which can help us to understand the causes of conflict and tension between different ethnic groups." All those who seek to know and understand the sharply contrasting patterns of race relations in areas originally colonized by people from the Iberian Peninsula and those settled by persons from northwestern Europe will find this book of exceptional interest and importance.

MUNRO, DANA G. **Intervention and Dollar Diplomacy in the Caribbean, 1900–1921.** Princeton: Princeton University Press, 1964, 553 p.

Dana G. Munro, formerly an officer of the Department of State, emphasizes that what the United States was trying to do throughout the period with which this study deals was "to put an end to conditions that threatened the independence of some of the Caribbean states and were consequently a potential danger to the security of the United States." He argues that "dollar diplomacy" under both Taft and Wilson was purely political: "Both administrations were interested in loans as a means of stabilizing Caribbean governments and bringing about the establishment of American customs collectorships, and as a way to provide funds for economic development."

The policy, defined in terms of the security of the United States, is here regarded as successful, since "there is little doubt that European interference would have taken forms unacceptable to the United States and possibly dangerous to the independence of the countries involved." In nonsecurity terms, however, the United States got little economic benefit, failed to implant democratic processes and caused bitter hostility in Latin America. How real was the European "menace"? Americans feared it, even in 1916, but one wishes that the author had had time for research in European, especially German, archives.

LEWIS, GORDON K. **The Growth of the Modern West Indies.** New York: Monthly Review Press, 1968, 506 p.

Professor Lewis has provided here a "description and interpretative analysis of the growth of the modern West Indian society, that is to say of the English speaking Antilles, over the last forty years or so." In so doing he has filled an important need, for first-rate scholarship directed to this area is scarce.

The Caribbean background is sketched, as is the era of British colonialism. Important chapters treat of the emergence of national societies in the four independent countries of the Commonwealth Caribbean, but the lesser territories such as British Honduras, Bermuda, the Bahamas and the tiny islands are not neglected. The unfortunate Federation that crashed in 1962 receives extended treatment. In all of this, Lewis's grasp and deployment of significant detail is almost incredible. He appears to have read, classified and remembered every pamphlet, play, parliamentary debate, song, literary allusion, commercial report, novel and newspaper article in any way germane to the West Indies that has ever appeared.

His prognosis as to future possibilities in the area is not encouraging. "Effective unification of the entire region within a system of democratic hemispheric security" offers perhaps the best hope, but the author is quite aware of the immense difficulties. His views and analyses in regard both to problems and to solutions are colored by his strong ideological leanings, as in his **Puerto Rico.**

O'LOUGHLIN, CARLEEN. **Economic and Political Change in the Leeward and Windward Islands.** New Haven: Yale University Press, 1968, 260 p.

The many problems of the Commonwealth Caribbean are exacerbated by a deficiency of the kind of analysis whose findings would command a wide audience abroad. Of no part of the region is this more true than of the Leeward and Windward Islands. It is therefore gratifying to record the contributions of this volume to an area of learning so generally neglected.

Almost all aspects of life in these islands, which comprise the Associated States, are considered. The author's investigations extend to issues of demography, agriculture, land problems, government and finance, industrial possibilities, trade and tourism, politics, the unfortunate West Indies Federation and the subsequent "Little Eight" and "Little Seven" negotiations, communications, education and much else.

Perhaps particular value attaches to the light these small territories throw upon problems elsewhere that are associated with economic, political and geographic fragmentation, and the diseconomies of scale. The sustained relevance of parochial and insular attitudes and rivalries, and of the significance and ambiguities of human motivation, also merit and receive the author's attention.

WILLIAMS, ERIC. **Capitalism and Slavery.** London: Deutsch, 1964, 285 p.

The Prime Minister of Trinidad and Tobago is a remarkable amalgam of scholar-pedagogue and statesman. The most valuable of the works he has written in the first of these capacities is this striking study of West Indian and Negro history, which is also a study of English economic development.

Eric Williams' basic thesis in this volume is the decisive function of economic forces in shaping West Indian life. "The commercial capitalism of the eighteenth century developed the wealth of Europe by means of slavery and monopoly. But in so doing it helped to create the industrial capitalism of the nineteenth century, which turned around and destroyed the power of commercial capitalism, slavery, and all its works." Since all else is subordinate, "politics and morals are to be examined in the very closest relation to the economic development."

Other notable insights accompany the master theme. It is clearly demonstrated that slavery had nothing to do with either climate or race; the conditions of New World production simply required hordes of cheap labor, for which Africa was the only source. The pervasive influence of the West Indian trade in all the ramifications of commerce, finance and industry is also uncontestably demonstrated, its wealth being one of the main sources of English industrial and agricultural expansion up to 1783. And the significance of American independence is likewise remarked; it destroyed the mercantile system and ushered in the new era whose requirements were ultimately fatal to slavery.

Cuba

SUÁREZ, ANDRÉS. **Cuba: Castroism and Communism, 1959–1966.** Cambridge: M.I.T. Press, 1967, 266 p.

Like many another analysis of revolutionary Cuba, this is a controversial book. Experts will wish to claim this error or that in the author's presentation of facts, and some will object to the central thesis, contending that it unduly personalizes the revolutionary process and fails to give sufficient recognition to social forces. But to many the merit of the work is that it stresses the personality of Castro, his ambitions and his unique abilities as the prime movers of events. In any Latin American country such an analysis is worth pondering.

The author's contention is that Cuba in 1959 was devoid of any revolutionary situation in the classical Leninist sense; that there was merely a generalized desire for wide reforms, together with unbounded trust in Castro's decisions, whatever they might be; that Castro utilized this rather fluid situation for his own purposes, which evolved by mid-1959 into a desire to retain total power through the only means available, all-out social revolution; that this desire, and his equally strong desire to eradicate all American influence in Cuba, were made feasible by the configuration of international forces, since he could invoke the power of Russia as a shield for domestic and hemispheric revolutionary moves and his anti-American crusade.

FAGEN, RICHARD R. **The Transformation of Political Culture in Cuba.** Stanford: Stanford University Press, 1969, 271 p.

The literature on the Cuban Revolution steadily increased during the decade of the 1960s, ranging unevenly from journalistic accounts to descriptive history and cold-war polemics. Few works, however, have contributed much to an understanding of what is unquestionably the major political event of twentieth century Latin America. This book by a political scientist is one of the exceptions. It is a serious, systematic and lucidly written attempt to shed light on the nature of some of the social, economic and political changes which Cuba has experienced since 1959. By way of examining the nature of these changes, the author analyzes three of the Revolution's most important programs: the literacy campaign of 1961, the Committees for Defense of the Revolution, and the Schools of Revolutionary Instruction. The three case studies have a common focus: the revolutionary experience of political socialization and cultural change. Without representing the entire experience, they at least touch on its most distinctive aspects. After reviewing some basic concepts of the literature on political socialization, Fagen argues that most of these are not applicable to the Cuban phenomenon. In Cuba political socialization "has been a directed learning process through which the elite seeks to create a new political culture." In other words, the author is chiefly concerned with the sustained drive of the Cuban revolutionaries to create a "new man," and a new society, and he skillfully and honestly assesses the progress made by the Cuban revolutionaries toward these goals.

Because of the difficulties of visiting Cuba, the book is based on data drawn principally from Cuban newspapers, periodicals and public documents. The author candidly recognizes this limitation. But there is more than mere library material in this book, for the author finally visited Cuba three times between 1966 and 1969 to fill in gaps and "to 'soak' in the *ambiente* of the revolution." The appendices include a report written from field notes on visits to rural settings as well as lengthy portions of Castro's speeches relevant to each of the case studies.

DRAPER, THEODORE. **Castro's Revolution: Myths and Realities.** New York: Praeger, 1962, 211 p.

Castro's coming to power in 1959 and his "leftward shift" thereafter were the source of a lasting debate in the United States on the origins and nature of the Revolution. The most articulate and influential commentator on Castroism has been Theodore Draper. His main targets in this book were the pro-Castro left and *The New York Times* editorial writer, Herbert Matthews. Draper's anti-Castro interpretation tended to reinforce the anti-Castro position of the United States. His books were translated and distributed in Latin America by USIA. In this collection of essays first published in journals, Draper essentially gives a negative portrayal of the Revolution and its leader. Castro, he writes, betrayed the Revolution and has converted Cuba into a totalitarian terror state. He is, however, equally critical of the Bay of Pigs invasion, which he calls "one of those rare politico-military events—a perfect failure." Draper's second book, **Castroism: Theory and Practice** (New York: Praeger, 1965, 263 p.), both builds on and revises the first one but is a more balanced and accurate analysis. He is at his best in assessing Castro's economic policies as misguided. Draper's work has been superseded in important essentials and has been seen with less favor by scholars. None the less, because of their cogency, Draper's books will always remain required reading for serious students of the Cuban Revolution.

NELSON, LOWRY. **Rural Cuba.** Minneapolis: University of Minnesota Press, 1950, 285 p.

The author, a noted sociologist and educational statesman, took leave from the University of Minnesota in September 1945 and spent a full year in Cuba on assignment by the U.S. Departments of State and Agriculture. His instructions were to study social life in the rural parts of the island, and this little gem of a book is the result of his efforts. He discovered Cuban society to be one of "rich land— poor people" and found the basic explanation of this in the high degree to which the ownership and control of the land had been concentrated in the hands of a few people and corporations. Detailed analyses are presented, supported by substantial amounts of concrete data, of the demographic aspects of Cuban society, the institutionalized relationships between man and the land, the class structure, the Cuban family, the levels of living and the educational institutions. Rarely have the basic social institutions of any country been analyzed more thoroughly, and the results presented with greater clarity, than was done by Nelson in this study. The record shows that when Fidel Castro appeared on television through the facilities of the Columbia Broadcasting Company he held up Nelson's book and indicated that much of his program came from it; and the record also shows that in 1970 Nelson's request for permission to revisit Cuba to determine and report upon changes since 1946 was denied.

Dominican Republic; Haiti

WELLES, SUMNER. **Naboth's Vineyard: The Dominican Republic, 1844–1924.** New York: Payson and Clarke, 1928, 2 v.

One of the ablest diplomats the United States has produced, the former Under Secretary of State wrote this classic of Dominican historiography relatively early in his career. Within the limits of time and subject matter that he selected, Welles' work has no rival even today. He was well equipped for his task; he had been instrumental in negotiating the termination of the first Marine occupation in 1924, and his personal contacts with President Vasquez and other Dominican leaders were intimate.

The study is limited to the recording of political history from the beginning of independence in 1844 to the Marine withdrawal in 1924. The treatment is complete and authoritative. International developments, such as the evolution of the Roosevelt Corollary to the Monroe Doctrine, are covered in depth. One regrets that Welles did not devote his attention to social and economic events as well; the long introduction, with its description of daily life at the time of independence, indicates how well he would have performed such a task.

The author's adoption of the Dominican view toward most things Haitian, and his exaggerated confidence in constitutions, will seem outdated. But his plea for more favorable trade access to American markets, his warning against economic imperialism and the evils of military interventions, his regard for joint hemispheric initiatives and his recognition of the need for a consistent American policy toward Latin America are all surprisingly contemporary.

CRASSWELLER, ROBERT D. **Trujillo: The Life and Times of a Caribbean Dictator.** New York: Macmillan, 1966, 468 p.

A major contribution to our understanding of the politics of Latin America, this book, written in a lucid and sprightly style, is the best work on the Dominican Republic for the period 1930–1961. It is also more than a biographical study of Trujillo. Using vast documentary material from United States and Dominican sources as well as personal interviews with most of the principal actors in Dominican affairs during the period, the author, a careful researcher and an accomplished writer, offers essentially a fascinating case history of the unrestrained use of power.

The demonic and monstrous traits of the Dominican dictator are vividly portrayed. His desire for wealth, his megalomania, his almost superhuman physical energy and capacity for work, his passion for a systematic and precise approach to problems, his passionate but rigidly disciplined temperament, his extraordinary magnetism, his deeply seated distrust of people, and his total lack of moral scruples were all, according to the author, related to an unrelenting drive for power. He describes how Trujillo, in common with other great tyrants of history, utilized secrecy, uncertainty and unpredictable behavior to strengthen his power by devaluing the dignity of those who surrounded him. Trujillo was convinced that "humiliation and mistreatment and bullying were among the necessary ingredients of prestige and authority." With keen insight the author describes how Trujillo, in his constant search for sources of political power, discovered that every economic facet of national life could be effectively subverted to political ends. Comparing Trujillo's power pattern to those of the classical Asiatic despots, he sees the structure developed by the Dominican dictator as one based on the principle of the honeycomb: every center of power, cell-like, was joined to and supported the others, thereby producing the balance and strength of the whole. The book can be read with pleasure and profit by any reader, but it is simply a must for students of Caribbean politics.

BOSCH, JUAN. **The Unfinished Experiment: Democracy in the Dominican Republic.** New York: Praeger, 1965, 239 p.

This book is vintage Bosch, the product of the liberally oriented, idealistic and optimistic Bosch who could still affirm that "the Dominican people are fertile ground for the seeds of democracy." Several years later another of the several personalities that cohabit in the individual named Juan Bosch would emerge, the personality that would renounce all the works of democracy in Latin America in favor of "popular dictatorships." But that is another story.

Here Bosch writes in the aftermath of his electoral triumph in 1962 and his fall from power in 1963 at the hands of the military and various of their civilian supporters. He writes, as he states, "in order to point out the intrinsic weaknesses of a society that has remained backward because of the organized efforts of forces opposed to its progress." His dissection of Dominican society embraces themes long familiar in his writings: the selfish venality of the insecure middle class and the outrageous upper class; the greed and corruption of the upper and middle strata of the military; the caste formations of society; the virtues of youth and the lower classes. The book is valuable not only for the opinions so passionately expressed and the facts cited in support of them (however controversial some of the opinions and facts may be) but also as a mirror of the curiosities of mind and temperament and personality that make this excellent writer and ill-starred statesman the unique being that he is.

MARTIN, JOHN BARTLOW. **Overtaken by Events: The Dominican Crisis from the Fall of Trujillo to the Civil War.** Garden City: Doubleday, 1966, 821 p.

In the long history of diplomacy there can have been few books comparable to this, just as its author himself must be judged almost unique among diplomats. The substance of the volume is not remarkable; in essence, it is the account of Martin's tour of duty as U.S. ambassador in the Dominican Republic in 1962–1963, encompassing the brief presidency of Juan Bosch, with a final section covering his role as adviser to the United States government following the outbreak of civil war in Santo Domingo in 1965. The theme is best stated in Martin's melancholy words: "Despite all effort, the mighty United States had been unable to save Bosch. Now we could not budge the men who overthrew him. . . . One by one we gave up our objectives, until we were left with almost nothing."

But the manner of the writing is extraordinary. Martin is an accomplished author, and sustains the reader's fascination with great skill through a long and colorful narrative. Rarely has a diplomat written with such candor. An immense cast of actors passes in review, displayed in almost primordial nakedness, the author sparing himself nothing in the way of uncalculated self-revelation. Everything comes out in this vast mass of recollections, and it is not surprising that the book has had a strong effect in official circles in Santo Domingo, inhibiting the unofficial discourse that once flowed freely. Again, the book is a monument to the techniques of activist intervention by a foreign ambassador in the life of a host country; the controversial United States representative took the broadest possible view of his function and often seemed indistinguishable from the Dominican government.

SLATER, JEROME. **Intervention and Negotiation: The United States and the Dominican Revolution.** New York: Harper and Row, 1970, 254 p.

This attempt at further analysis of the U.S. intervention in the Dominican Republic in 1965 goes beyond earlier works by Theodore Draper, **The Dominican Revolt: A Case Study in American Policy** (New York: Commentary, 1968, 208 p.), Dan Kurzman, **Santo Domingo: Revolt of the Damned** (New York: Putnam, 1965, 310 p.), Tad Szulc, **Dominican Diary** (New York: Delacorte Press, 1965, 306 p.), John Bartlow Martin and others. It is based upon research in United States and Dominican published sources, including Dominican newspapers; the complete United Nations and Organization of American States records; and some 80 interviews with Dominican, United States and OAS officials.

Slater concludes that the United States government made several errors in the pre-intervention period: (1) the failure to use its influence to aid the moderate, non-communist leadership within the constitutionalist movement against both the "rightist military" and the Castroite forces; (2) the failure to support the moderate constitutionalist "provisional government" of José Molina Ureña; (3) the failure to offer support to ex-President Juan Bosch before the intervention.

Further, it is his view that the "No Second Cuba" policy was an error, based on obsolescent premises, but that it is arguable that in the domestic political atmosphere in the United States in 1965, the government "had trapped itself into the necessity of intervening against a *genuine* Communist revolution." However, in the Dominican crisis "the evidence of Communist influence in the constitutionalist movement was insufficient to justify the predictable political and human costs of the intervention."

This is a balanced account worthy of study by all those who are interested in the Johnsonian termination of the Good Neighbor Policy.

LEYBURN, JAMES GRAHAM. **The Haitian People.** New Haven: Yale University Press, 1941, 342 p.

This superb piece of scholarship is characterized by its author as "a study of the growth of Haiti's social institutions out of the backgrounds of slavery and French colonial life, or of the shaping of these institutions throughout the nineteenth century." He says that whether the book be classified as social history or as sociology is largely a matter of indifference to him because "to view a people with understanding in the characteristic setting of their institutions—marriage, religion, property arrangements, and the rest—one needs not only a description of their ways, but also a knowledge of how they came to be what they are." The book was published while its author was an associate professor of the Science of Society at Yale University. It was based upon extended periods of observation and study in Haiti itself, meticulous use of bodies of original source material and an enviable knowledge of works in all fields that had been written about the island of Hispaniola and its peoples. Produced at a time when very few American scholars exhibited anything more than a cursory interest in Latin American societies, this volume is definitely one of the more important landmarks in the development of Latin American area studies. For anyone seeking to know the Haitian people and their social institutions it will long continue to be required reading.

HERSKOVITS, MELVILLE JEAN. **Life in a Haitian Valley.** New York: Knopf, 1937, 350 p.

Melville J. Herskovits early became dissatisfied with the image of the Haitian people and their society that prevailed in the United States and elsewhere. Particularly distorted, from his point of view, was the lurid picture of the "voodoo" cult, especially after Sir Spenser St. John published his tale of the "cannibalistic 'Congo bean stew'" in 1880. By applying the anthropologist's methods and frame of reference in a meticulous study of the way of life of Haitians in one specific locality, Herskovits sought to provide the basis for a more adequate knowledge of life and labor in Haiti. The results were eminently successful. His vignettes of "The Cultural Ancestry of the Haitian," "The Daily Round," the "Haitian Religion" and "Haiti: A Cultural Mosaic" retain great interest and value even 35 years after his field work was done.

Puerto Rico

LEWIS, GORDON K. **Puerto Rico: Freedom and Power in the Caribbean.** New York: Monthly Review Press, 1963, 626 p.

This is an examination, in great depth and on the broadest possible lines, of Puerto Rican life within a Caribbean framework. All aspects of Puerto Rican society are examined astutely and in the most minute detail, from remote heritage and recent history to the nuts and bolts of every political body, social movement and artistic creation. Nothing is exempted from the author's apparently total scrutiny.

The book is also a commentary on the connection between Puerto Rico and the United States, and a plea for insular independence. Lewis admits that Puerto Rico is not oppressed colonially in the classic manner, but he nevertheless argues that "even in those areas of Puerto Rican life where it seems most beneficent, [the American connection] continues to work its distorting influence upon the local life;" and he cites the contrast between private affluence and public squalor, between economic development and social welfare. The massive encroachment of values and culture patterns from the mainland alarms him.

The basis for Professor Lewis's opinions is to be found in his deep devotion to socialism, to collectivist planning and to a view of the Cuban Revolution that will seem perverse, naïve and erroneous to most Americans. He makes a serious effort at fair-mindedness, and he credits the United States with various positive qualities and achievements, but when all is said and done, he is viscerally unhappy with most aspects of American life.

WELLS, HENRY. **The Modernization of Puerto Rico: A Political Study of Changing Values and Institutions.** Cambridge: Harvard University Press, 1969, 440 p.

This is a soundly based analysis, rooted in extensive scholarship and documented with craftsmanlike skill and thoroughness. The theme stated by Professor Wells is the study of the modernization process in Puerto Rico, in its political aspect. This embraces two parallel lines of investigation. One includes in its broad view the entire panorama of society and seeks there the revisions of social values that occur over time, a search that is also applicable to the changing values of political leaders. The other, more limited, looks to the changes that may be discerned in political tactics and means.

Appropriate attention is directed to historical factors and the sociocultural background, as well as to the conflicts, difficulties and successes of the Americanization process. The central figure in the story of modernization is of course ex-Governor Luis Muñoz Marín, whose long domination of the public life of the island has so recently terminated. The career of Muñoz and the policies of renewal, industrialization and commonwealth status that he espoused receive favorable but fair treatment. The results of the surprising 1968 Commonwealth election are not included; the author's projections of future developments, although thus in a sense incomplete, are otherwise persuasive.

STEWARD, JULIAN HAYNES and OTHERS. **The People of Puerto Rico: A Study in Social Anthropology.** Urbana: University of Illinois Press (for the College of Social Sciences, University of Puerto Rico), 2d ed., 1966, 540 p.

Julian H. Steward, professor of anthropology at Columbia University when the book was written and director of the research on which it was based, succinctly stated the nature of this substantial work. "The present volume," he says, "reports a cultural historical study of the behavior patterns or lifeways of certain of the Puerto Rican people. The study undertook to analyze the contemporary culture and to explain it in terms of historical changes which have occurred on the island."

In addition to an analysis of the cultural background of contemporary Puerto Rico, including contributions by all of the co-authors, and lengthy summary and conclusions, the book embodies five monographs. Four of these are analyses and descriptions of subcultures in selected type-of-farming areas: one, by Robert A. Manners, is of a tobacco and mixed crops *municipio,* or county-like entity; another, by Eric R. Wolf, is of a "traditional" coffee *municipio;* the third, by Elena Padilla Seda, deals with workers on a government-owned sugar plantation; and the fourth, by Sidney W. Mintz, is a study of a rural sugar plantation proletariat. The fifth, by Raymond L. Scheele, is a historical study of the prominent families of Puerto Rico. The result of lengthy collaboration on the part of six highly qualified scholars is a comprehensive study of enduring value. First printed in 1956, it was fortunately reissued in 1966.

BRAZIL

WAGLEY, CHARLES. **An Introduction to Brazil.** New York: Columbia University Press, 1963, 322 p.

This book is exactly what the title claims it to be, an introduction to Brazilian society and culture. It also is a masterly piece of work, representing modern scientific study of peoples and cultures at its best. The book is deceptively easy to read. The simplicity involved, however, is of the enviable kind achieved only when a gifted scientist applies many years of painstaking, objective observation and analysis to a subject of great interest and importance, and an equally long period endeavoring to master the most effective means of communicating his thoughts to other people.

Wagley spent 20 years studying the grass roots of Brazil's various sociocultural systems. His vantage points included "relatively untouched tribes, acculturated Indians in touch with the Brazilian frontier, small peasant communities in northern Brazil, and small towns." Early in the course of his scientific endeavors, however, Wagley concluded that he must be able to fit the significant details acquired in the small communities into general pictures of the region and the nation, and that he also must attend to the complex problems of Brazil as a whole by familiarizing himself thoroughly with "Brazilian politics, history, economics, education, literature, sociology, and even philosophy." The result is a book of exceptional quality and enduring value. For anyone desiring a knowledge of the unity and diversity, class systems, community organization and life, family and domestic institutions, religious beliefs and practices, and political and administrative organizations and activities of half a continent, Wagley's **Introduction to Brazil** is the best place to start.

SMITH, THOMAS LYNN. **Brazil: People and Institutions.** Baton Rouge: Louisiana State University Press, 2d rev. ed., 1963, 667 p.

To a generation of social scientists whose interests have touched on Brazil, the outstanding attribute of Smith's **Brazil** has been its usefulness. Those who have used it once have found themselves returning again and again to "look something up" in its compendious tables and matter-of-fact text. For what Smith achieved with this book was a grand collection of "basic data"—from population size and densities to the geographical distribution of agricultural techniques and land tenure, to marriage patterns and religious practices—which social scientists generally consider preliminary to more specifically focused research. Like any book of such scope, it has a certain unevenness about it. At his best in the chapters on demography, where he so clearly is in command of his material and exercising his full critical powers, the author shows elsewhere an unfortunate tendency to accept the often biased opinions of his Brazilian sources. Thus in his treatment of race he greatly underemphasizes the degree of racial prejudice which pervades Brazilian life; his discussion of agriculture underrates the adaptiveness of Brazilian agricultural systems to tropical conditions; his general attitude toward the rural lower class as unintelligent and tradition-bound does not do justice to their creativity and open-ended pragmatism under harsh conditions.

Yet, despite disagreements with some specifics of the conventional wisdom distilled in Smith's **Brazil,** it is nearly as true today as when it was first published in 1946 that Smith's book is the only convenient source for much of the material it contains.

SKIDMORE, THOMAS E. **Politics in Brazil, 1930–1964: An Experiment in Democracy.** New York: Oxford University Press, 1967, 446 p.

In the author's words, this book is an "interpretation of what I regard as the most important factors determining the trend of Brazilian politics since the Revolution of 1930 . . . with much attention to the pressure felt by politicians to find a satisfactory strategy of economic development and to deal with the recurrent financial crisis." Of great importance here is dependence on policies of the United States government on aid, and on attitudes of the International Monetary Fund.

Convinced that "the overthrow of Goulart brought to an end the era of democratic politics that began in 1945," the author has written a lucid and enlightening analytical history of political movements and leaders from the first Vargas presidency to the beginning of the present military régime. Attention is also given to the electorate's expansion in numbers and political consciousness and to endeavors of new, "populist" politicians to mobilize and organize political recruits into an effective power base.

The book is a valuable introduction to Brazilian politics (perhaps even to many Brazilians, for it has been translated) and may also bring Brazil into the ken of students of the "matching" of political systems with stages of what used to be called, simply, "economic development."

FURTADO, CELSO. **The Economic Growth of Brazil.** Berkeley: University of California Press, 1963, 285 p.

Celso Furtado, one of Brazil's most distinguished economists, has served in high administrative as well as academic positions in his country. Now in self-exile, he has long been a proponent of development policies that accent the growth of strong and autonomous national economies and pay particular attention to distributional factors. A prolific author of respected scholarly works, he relaxes in this volume into the role of introductory teacher, calling the book a text "accessible to the reader without a technical background in economics . . . providing as broad a perspective as possible."

Furtado begins by taking the reader back to Europe to explain the economic purposes of and social bases for the territorial expansion not only of Spain and Portugal but, in admirable comparative terms, of England and the Netherlands as well. He then speaks of the slave economy and tropical agriculture in sixteenth and seventeenth century Brazil, retaining a comparative focus, and of slavery and the mining economy in the eighteenth century. The second third of the book is devoted to Brazil's transition to an economy of paid labor in the nineteenth century, and the last third to that country's transition toward an industrialized state. The emphasis throughout on aspects of labor reflects Furtado's concern with a social approach to economic analysis and with a political-economic approach to capital formation and investment.

Although the work is clumsily translated, the author presents his ideas with clarity and efficiency. This study is useful not only as a general introduction to Brazilian economics, but it also provides a valuable interpretation of Luso-Brazilian history and is suggestive for the study of Hispanic America as well.

STEIN, STANLEY J. **Vassouras: A Brazilian Coffee County, 1850–1900.** Cambridge: Harvard University Press, 1957, 316 p.

This is a pioneering study in Latin American economic history, at least for North American scholars. It combines keen perceptions of local social hierarchies, political pressures and economic activities in a sector of the Paraiba river valley, not far north of Rio de Janeiro, with an illuminating discussion of broad international movements such as the slave trade, worldwide coffee demand and development of alternative sources of supply. For "local," here, read "people's," for the book's substance is the colorfully told story of the sudden rise of coffee plantations after 1830 and their frantic exploitation through greatly expanded importation of African slaves and through immediately profitable but, within 30 years, disastrously destructive misuse of irreplaceable soil cover created by virgin forests. The account is colorful because it is based on local records; individuals come to life, and their physical and cultural contexts are portrayed in detail.

Stein notes that "Notarial offices in county seats are the richest and most neglected repositories for historians, economists, anthropologists and sociologists," and the book upholds his claim. Emulators, however, are few, for local history, in Latin America even more than in the United States, has low academic prestige.

Luis González, in his significant **Pueblo en Vilo: Microhistoria de San José de Gracia** (México, D.F.: El Colegio de México, 1968, 365 p.), says that "Among Mexican intellectuals local history is apparently totally disesteemed." Hopefully, González may do for Mexicans, at least, what Stein has done for North Americans in his volume.

FERNANDES, FLORESTAN. **The Negro in Brazilian Society.** New York: Columbia University Press, 1969, 489 p.

Fernandes, the brilliant son of a Portuguese immigrant, prepared this study as the thesis for his permanent chair at the University of São Paulo. Its major theme is that the Negro inherited from the period in which he was a slave several "burdens" which "created various forms of social prejudice and discrimination (based on color) that consequently forced the Negro and the mulatto into a marginal position in the competitive social order." Fernandes identifies these burdens as demands of competitive society, market economy, urban style of life, and limitations stemming from deeply restrictive or negative attitudes. As a result of these, and of the Negro's inability up to now to cope with them, Fernandes considers racial democracy in Brazil a myth. He likewise condemns the efficacy of most of the measures Negroes and mulattoes are taking in an endeavor to improve their lot. He maintains that in the struggle it is impossible for anyone to be "neutral," holding that "no neutrality is possible in the face of such reality." He does maintain, however, that his data are objective and that they may be checked.

FREYRE, GILBERTO. **The Masters and the Slaves: A Study in the Development of Brazilian Civilization.** New York: Knopf, 1946, 537 p.
————. **The Mansions and the Shanties: The Making of Modern Brazil.** New York: Knopf, 1963, 431 p.

As described by Freyre in his preface to the English edition and in that to the first Brazilian edition of **The Masters and the Slaves** ("Casa Grande e Senzala"), these monumental works contain a study of "the formation and disintegration of patriarchal society in Brazil." For him the now classic "Casa Grande" is "an essay in genetic sociology and social history, with the object of determining and at times interpreting some of the significant aspects of the formation of the Brazilian family."

As a young man, Freyre was imbued with an extreme zoological interpretation of history and preoccupied with the problem of miscegenation and "the fearfully mongrel aspect" of Brazil's population. While in this state of mind he came under the influence of anthropologist Franz Boas at Columbia University, from whom he learned to distinguish race from culture and to differentiate the influences of the one from those of the other. Shortly thereafter a trip through the "deep South" in the United States convinced him that "the same influences deriving from the technique of production and of labor—that is to say, the one-crop system and slavery—combined here in this English-settled portion of North America, as in the Antilles and Jamaica, to produce social results similar to those that are to be observed in our country." Freyre then threw himself into the task of producing the four lengthy essays that became the chapters in his great classic: "General Characteristics of the Portuguese Colonization of Brazil: Formation of an Agrarian, Slaveholding and Hybrid Society;" "The Native in the Formation of the Brazilian Family;" "The Portuguese Colonizer: Antecedents and Predispositions;" and "The Negro Slave in the Sexual and Family Life of the Brazilian." The English translation of Freyre's monumental study, by Samuel Putnam, was widely praised by members of the scholarly community of the United States. Time has not diminished the esteem in which it is held by those best acquainted with Latin American societies, cultures and civilizations.

The manuscript Freyre produced in his effort to interpret Brazilian patriarchal society and the great extended family or clan proved to be excessively long, as he says, "exceeding the reasonable limits of a one-volume book." The study of certain aspects of the subject accordingly had to be reserved for a second volume, eventually published under the title "Sobrados e Mucambos," **The Mansions and the Shanties.** The analyses and interpretations in it are similar to those in the book that made Freyre known throughout the world. However, in **The Masters and the Slaves** the theme was the development of patriarchal society and the great family, whereas in **The Mansions and the Shanties** the emphasis is upon the decadence, under the influences of town life, of these two dominant features of Brazilian society.

DA CUNHA, EUCLYDES. **Rebellion in the Backlands.** Chicago: University of Chicago Press, 1944, 526 p.

Euclydes da Cunha's treatise "Os Sertões: Campanha de Canudos" is generally recognized as the greatest work written in Brazil. It first appeared in 1902 and went through two revised editions before the death of its author in 1909. Subsequently, revisions he himself had made were discovered and were incorporated in the fifth and definitive edition of the classic which appeared in 1914.

The author was a military engineer who fought one campaign after another in Brazil's vast backlands (*sertões*) against the fanatical followers of Antonio Conselheiro. These were finally ended by the complete annihilation of that great charismatic leader, his followers (men, women and children) and the New Jerusalem (*Canudos*) they had built and defended in north central Bahia. The first part of the book deals with the environment, the people and the society of Brazil's vast, drought-stricken and problem-ridden northeast; the rest of the volume presents vivid descriptions, accounts and personal experiences of the author during the various expeditions sent by the national government to put down the rebellion of Conselheiro and the sect he headed. This was a group holding fanatically to the belief that they must prepare a New Jerusalem, partially through the shedding of untold amounts of blood, to which Portugal's famed King Sebastião would return to earth. Samuel Putnam, the translator, himself a noted man of letters, approvingly quotes Carleton Beals' evaluation of the book as "a thrilling, vividly told tale, a great document, which, though not a novel, reads like fiction."

CHILE

MCBRIDE, GEORGE MCCUTCHEN. **Chile: Land and Society.** New York: American Geographical Society, 1936, 408 p.

Timely when it was first published, this volume has survived to become timeless. In 1936 it was described as "the most complete study on the subject" of Chile's traditional land systems. Despite numerous more recent studies, many scholars continue to view McBride's effort as a valuable beginning in assessing the ecological background and historical evolution of *latifundismo* and its role in the stratification of Chilean society.

While showing some concern for other regions and other forms of land tenure, McBride's major focus is central Chile and the *hacienda*. Obviously, he views the *hacienda* as more than a simple economic arrangement for exploiting land and labor. He sees it as the primary instrument in the structuring of social classes and in defining the relationship between the *patrón* (whom he whimsically calls don Fulano) and the *inquilino* (Zutano); as the principal author of wealth and political power; as the chief obstacle to progress and the most convincing argument for agrarian reform.

Uninhibited by the paucity of hard data, McBride's work relied heavily on direct field observation, personal intuition and the author's warm admiration for Chile and its people. Some contemporary social scientists armed with more data and theory may deem his method "unscientific" and some of his conclusions naïve; others who are aware that McBride was a geographer may even question his training for the task; but none will deny that his study is at least provocative.

BURR, ROBERT N. **By Reason or Force: Chile and the Balancing of Power in South America, 1830–1905.** Berkeley: University of California Press, 1965, 322 p.

The unique contribution of this book lies in bringing nineteenth-century international politics in South America into intellectual relationship with international politics in Europe and elsewhere. It is the counterpart for South America in this period of Edward Vose Gulick's **Europe's Classical Balance of Power** (Ithaca: Cornell University Press, 1955, 337 p.). Burr views the South American countries, which fought frequent wars between 1830 and 1880, as forming a system of power politics, regional until about 1860 and continental thereafter: "South American statesmen early showed their acceptance of the axioms and techniques of European power politics. They used its jargon, and did not hesitate to employ its forms of coercion in dealing with problems of intra-South American relations."

The focus of the study is on Chilean foreign policy, which was "remarkably successful in securing and maintaining Chile's hegemony on the Pacific Coast, whether by reason or by force." Both were used. The author has taken diplomatic history beyond the episodic, and through a profound exploitation of the Chilean archives has given us an excellent introduction to an understanding of balance-of-power politics among states that, though weak by world standards, were no less ingenious than great powers in devising locally effective techniques of survival.

GIL, FEDERICO G. **The Political System of Chile.** Boston: Houghton, 1966, 323 p.

Chile is commonly recognized as unique among Latin American countries, in that it has "come to have a fairly mature political system with all its characteristics of respect for legality, free elections, high voter turnouts, and parties that constitute an integral and effective wheel of the political machinery." Thus Gil begins his book. He concludes it by referring optimistically to the attempts of the Christian Democrats, whose electoral victory in 1964 was the first for that party anywhere in Latin America, to work a thoroughgoing socioeconomic "revolution in liberty." In the body of his work, Gil builds a persuasive case for the view that the strength of Chile's political culture is what has persistently permitted governments to withstand recurrent economic crisis and the continuing profundity of the divisions among Chile's social classes. That is to say, he sees politics in Chile as somewhat independent of economic factors and not as a feather blown about as an entirely dependent variable. Although Gil eschews grand theoretical explanation, his analysis is sweeping and firmly rooted in historical research.

Since the completion of this book, the Chilean electorate has chosen a Marxist executive who proposes to create a fully socialistic state within a democratic political frame. If Chile has heretofore been unique among Latin American countries, success in its present political plans would also make it unique among the countries of the world. Gil's book, however, clearly reveals that current developments do not represent a sharp break with Chilean history. His analysis remains fresh and pertinent, required reading for those who would understand Chile's contemporary situation as a coherent product of its past.

STEVENSON, JOHN REESE. **The Chilean Popular Front.** Philadelphia: University of Pennsylvania Press, 1942, 155 p.

Reflecting European example as well as internal political forces, a popular front movement organized itself in Chile in 1936. Comprised of the then usual coalition of secular centrist parties with the Marxist left (including the communists), the Front won the presidency in the elections of 1938 and remained intact as the governing bloc until early 1941. At that time, the socialists split from the communists, charging the latter to be under the domination of the Soviet Union. As is evident from these dates, the Chilean Popular Front lasted longer than any other such group in the world.

Stevenson chronicles the rise and achievements and failures of this movement with immediacy, intellectual fairness and perspective. He interviewed most of the principal political actors of the time and brings a felicitous style to bear on an analysis of lasting prescience. Correctly pointing out that Chile has weathered the usual crises causing political instability in Latin America, he also correctly singles out the so-called "social crisis"—the division among classes, inequitable economic distribution and the like—as certain to be the *leitmotif* of Chilean public life for the foreseeable future. Those who would understand the Christian Democratic and Marxist movements in Chile will find this book required reading.

The volume is historical in approach, and given its early date of publication, it is innocent of social-psychological interpretations, data or theory. Beginning with Chile under colonial rule, the author rapidly surveys that country's national history, after which he slows down for six detailed chapters that combine the best of anecdotalism and the broadest of élite interviewing with sufficiently rigorous documentation to maintain academic credentials. The style is pleasing.

PIKE, FREDRICK B. **Chile and the United States, 1880–1962: The Emergence of Chile's Social Crisis and the Challenge to United States Diplomacy.** Notre Dame: University of Notre Dame Press, 1963, 466 p.

A carefully researched and reliable guide to modern Chilean history, this book is written by a concerned scholar of liberal persuasion. Despite the title, diplomatic history is not the work's principal burden. Instead, Pike is at pains to reveal the internal dynamics of Chilean society and politics, and to show how Chile's foreign relations are a natural outgrowth of those domestic arrangements. Thus, although the book is organized chronologically, the line of argument mingles political, social, cultural, psychological, economic and diplomatic events in weaving the intricacies of a total international relationship. Because Pike is a historian, however, he advances no formal hypothetical structure, approaching his subject as an intelligent essayist and not as an empirical social scientist.

Pike is sensitive to the unwittingly revolutionary role played by the United States in varying ways among the Latin American republics. While ideology and motivation may differ among the many types of North Americans involved, preachment and example combine to foment profound change in such countries as Chile.

Often, however, this general American effect, when translated by Chileans into specific moves for radical change, provokes the ire of the United States. Pike writes, "In its dealings with Chile, the United States appears to align itself unquestioningly with the traditional groups of privilege." Writing immediately before the Christian Democrats took power in Chile in 1964, and warmed by the idealism of the Alliance for Progress, Pike ends on a strong note of optimism. The reader using this excellent book is given ample information on which to base his own conclusions, proof of the validity of the research.

The bibliography is exhaustive, well organized and worth the price of the volume.

ARGENTINA

BURGIN, MIRON. **The Economic Aspects of Argentine Federalism: 1820–1852.** Cambridge: Harvard University Press, 1946, 304 p.

This study set a scholarly level and tone for post–World War II historical writing that few Latin Americanists have been able to maintain. The volume overflows with evidence of Burgin's training in law and economics as well as history, his careful conceptualization and research, and his caution in not demanding more of his data than they could reasonably provide. The product convincingly established—with the aid of 51 tables—how the conflict between those Argentines who advocated a strong central government and those who sought to safeguard local autonomy was rooted in the divergent trends latent in the Viceroyalty of La Plata and which independence failed to reconcile.

Important as was the volume's contribution to our understanding of Argentine federalism—the outlines of which already had been delineated—it stands as a historical masterpiece for other reasons. Through it, Burgin proved that data do exist from which meaningful economic history of nineteenth-century Latin America can be written and that economic history can add a very important dimension to the political history of the area. Finally, in adhering strictly to the highest academic tenets and letting his data speak for itself, the author established that economic historians need not ride intellectual and ideological hobbyhorses.

WHITAKER, ARTHUR PRESTON. **The United States and Argentina.** Cambridge: Harvard University Press, 1954, 272 p.

Like most books bearing analogous titles, this one speaks much of Argentina, quite a bit less of the relations between Argentina and the United States, and hardly at all about the United States per se. No matter. This volume is an elegant introduction to the eighth largest country in the world, one which some 40 years ago was one of the dozen most advanced countries on the globe by almost any standard indicator of economic and social development.

A long-time student of Argentine history, Whitaker here distills his knowledge and presents it in a graceful style accessible to a wide public. The organization of the book is standard: first, the land and the people are described, and then pre-Perón Argentina is treated in separate chapters devoted to economic, political and social history, each handled chronologically. After a transitional section outlining the history of U.S.–Argentine relations, the author dedicates four detailed chapters to the Perón era. The conclusion begins with the statement that Whitaker believed Perón to be so firmly entrenched that there could be no doubt of his completing his term. The fall of Perón and the appearance of the book were virtually simultaneous. But again, no matter. If the prediction is wrong, the analysis behind it is in large measure correct. Clearly recognizing the majoritarian popular sympathy that supported Perón, and just as clearly indicating the class antagonisms involved in support for and opposition to Perón, Whitaker's more important prediction that Peronism was not likely to disappear from Argentine political life has, of course, been amply borne out since 1954.

If someone with a casual interest in Argentina is to read a single book on that country, this one should be it.

POTASH, ROBERT A. **The Army and Politics in Argentina, 1928–1945: Yrigoyen to Perón.** Stanford: Stanford University Press, 1969, 314 p.

It is the author's express intent to take a step beyond the "cliché-ridden" literature on the military in Latin America and to focus "on the real-life figures who have led the armed forces, on the details of institutional development, and on a broader spectrum of political behavior than the occasional coup." This he has done in depth through documents and interviews, with a detailed analysis of the role of the military in recent Argentine political history, which saw the imposition by the military of an unconstitutionally chosen president in 1930 for the first time in 70 years. An understanding of this period is essential to an understanding of the sources of support for Argentina's present military régime.

The author reviews the course of events beginning with Yrigoyen's overthrow by the army, through General Justo's term as president, and gives special attention to the presidency of Roberto M. Ortíz, when, briefly, it seemed that civilian rule might be reëstablished. The origins of the GOU (*Grupo de Oficiales Unidos*) and its key role in ousting Ortíz's successor, Ramón Castillo, are given detailed description, as are the intra-military manoeuvrings down to the triumph of Colonel Perón.

This illuminating study, scheduled to be followed by a second volume dealing with the post-1945 period, concludes that the tripling in size of the rank and file of the Argentine army and the doubling of the officer corps between 1930 and 1945, plus the recourse to the army by leaders of the Conservative Party for help in ousting Yrigoyen in 1930 and efforts by Radical Party leaders to gain army support in stopping systematic electoral frauds by subsequent régimes, led army officers to conclude that "only a military government could meet the problems of the day." This book provides a fine start for comparative studies among Latin American countries.

COLOMBIA; PERU; ECUADOR

DIX, ROBERT H. **Colombia: The Political Dimensions of Change.** New Haven: Yale University Press, 1967, 452 p.

This book is an attempt to study a total political system as it is employed by an élite bent on modernization. In adopting this strategy, the author is enabled to describe a polity, to present a theory of development, and to employ the theory to relate politics to such other facts of social life as population composition and distribution, cultural reactions to geographical situation, and social class. This ambitious study presents sufficient historical and contemporary data, as well as explicit theorizing, to enable the reader to judge it fairly on internal evidence alone—no small feat for any book of analytical description.

After discussing the scope and purposes of his book, and setting up the ecological and social structural facts of the case as he sees them, Dix devotes three extensive chapters to recent political analysis. He then turns to the formal structure of government, discusses the party system *in extenso,* and analyzes the influence of the Catholic Church and the military, the role of interest groups and, finally, the peculiarities of the extensive civil violence that plagued Colombia between 1948 and 1960, which still has not entirely subsided.

He does not view the efforts of Colombia's élites with great optimism, for he sees little chance that traditional institutions will soon or easily become the vessels for a participant and progressive modern society. He posits the likely sequels of élitist development as being either institutional decay or else the creation of a broad-based coalition that will embrace modernizers "within a wide spectrum of groups and classes." Of the two alternatives, Dix sees the former as more likely, a prediction not as yet belied by events in Colombia.

FALS BORDA, ORLANDO. **Peasant Society in the Colombian Andes: A Sociological Study of Saucio.** Gainesville: University of Florida Press, 1955, 277 p.

Fals Borda's classic study of one small community in the Colombian Andes exemplifies rural sociological research at its best. The author focused his "sociological spectacles" upon a closely knit group of 74 farm families whose social activities were centered about a small open-country school and two little mercantile establishments whose sales consisted largely of beer drunk on the premises. For religious purposes, and to buy and sell at the weekly market, the people of Saucio resorted to the town of Chocontá, two miles from their school and seat of their county-like *municipio*. For two years Fals Borda spent his weekends in the community, gaining an intimate knowledge of its ways of life and securing the answers to the questions on a long and carefully prepared schedule designed for gathering comparable information about all the families in the area. These materials were supplemented by those gathered by a careful search of historical sources of all types.

The facts thus assembled and ideas generated were analyzed in great detail, and in his concise exposition of them Fals Borda wisely chose to focus special attention upon the following aspects of society: demographic characteristics and trends, the precise delineation of the limits of the group he studied, the relations of man to the land, agriculture and other economic activities in relation to the level of living, the class system, the basic nucleated social institutions, the role of religion in the lives of the small farmers and the ethos of the community. The excellent portrayal was done just as the people in this small community, and thousands of others closely similar to it throughout the Andean region, were on the eve of being swept into the maelstrom of modern life.

FORD, THOMAS R. **Man and Land in Peru.** Gainesville: University of Florida Press, 1955, 176 p.

In this book a brilliant young sociologist helped fill one of the great gaps in the knowledge about Latin American peoples and societies. He spent a year in Peru gathering the materials for the study which eventually was presented as a doctoral dissertation at Vanderbilt University. In this work, some years before issues involved in "agrarian reform" became the preoccupation of almost everyone in Latin America or elsewhere concerned about its problems, Ford was "primarily concerned with the social systems that develop around the utilization of agricultural lands." As a result of his years of conscientious attention to basic details of Peru's social organization, each of the chapters in this solid volume is of lasting value. Anyone interested in Peru in particular and Latin America in general can ill afford to ignore his cogent and concise analyses of Peru's land and people, the evolution of systems of man-land relationships, patterns of ownership and control of the land, land tenure systems and reform measures.

BLANKSTEN, GEORGE I. **Ecuador: Constitutions and Caudillos.** Berkeley: University of California Press, 1951, 196 p.

The epigraph to this book reads, simply, "Ecuador is a very difficult country to govern." The statement's particular significance is that it was made by José María Velasco Ibarra, four times President of the country and a man who had as yet to complete a single legally defined term of office. Blanksten's work is a neatly written and classical account of the Ecuadoran political system. He is not concerned with any explicit statement of theoretical approach, contenting himself rather with an analytical description of the totality of the formal polity. He starts, traditionally, with the land and society and proceeds to a discussion of the causes of chronic political instability in Ecuador, an analysis still valid for that country as well as for some of the smaller and less-developed republics of Central America.

Turning to the executive, Blanksten describes a caudillistic system resembling a monarchy clothed in republicanism or, better, a "democracy in the Greek sense." By that phrase, the author means that the political system is headed by a small group of culturally European persons who deal among themselves with some degree of mutual respect and freedom, maintaining the remainder of the population in bondage. The author traces the paths of this control through the legislative system, the parties and down through the levels of government to the rural village.

This book was one of the first of the formal so-called "country studies" of Latin America to be done in the United States. Valuable as a stepping-stone in the history of Latin American studies, it also retains worth as a historical study and a still partially accurate description of some contemporary situations.

II. EUROPE

WESTERN EUROPE

EUROPEAN INTEGRATION

The European Idea

MONNET, JEAN. **Les États-Unis d'Europe ont Commencé: La Communauté Européenne du Charbon et de l'Acier: Discours et Allocutions, 1952–1954.** Paris: Laffont, 1955, 171 p.

There is general agreement that Jean Monnet had more to do with the evolution of the distinctive functionalist-supranationalist approach of the European Communities than any other single individual. It was Monnet who, as head of the French *Commissariat au Plan,* in collaboration with Paul Reuter, Etienne Hirsch and Pierre Uri originally invented the scheme for the European Coal and Steel Community as a first concrete step toward the twin goals of Franco-German rapprochement and European unification. He worked closely with Foreign Minister Robert Schuman to win over the French cabinet to the plan, served as the chairman of the inter-governmental group that negotiated the ECSC Treaty, and became the first president of the High Authority of the ECSC, serving from 1952–1955.

This small book contains excerpts from speeches made by Monnet during his years as High Authority President. Several basic themes which have formed the basis of his political actions emerge in these selections. First among them is the importance he attributes to technology as the dominant dynamic of the postwar world. Technological development is the sine qua non of power and progress in the modern world, but modern technology requires large investments in research and capital goods that are feasible only if industry produces for unified markets of continental scale such as in the U.S. and U.S.S.R. If Europe wishes to participate in the future, a single European market will be "an essential condition." Permanent institutions are another prerequisite for political progress. Nothing will really change in the relations between nations, and the advantages of the single market will not be realized, unless "men enshrine in permanent institutions the common experience which makes continued common action possible." Such institutions must have the power to enforce common rules throughout the area, and this requires a partial fusion of sovereign powers and eventually federation. But the long-term goal must be sought by pragmatic steps that gradually transform the context of political action. Other themes developed in these speeches are his confidence that other European countries will inevitably be brought to join, and that the United States and Europe will be brought closer together by the dynamics of integration.

ALBONETTI, ACHILLE. **Préhistoire des États-Unis de l'Europe.** Paris: Sirey, 1963, 311 p.

ZURCHER, ARNOLD JOHN. **The Struggle to Unite Europe: 1940–1958.** New York: New York University Press, 1958, 254 p.

SCHMITT, HANS A. **The Path to European Union: From the Marshall Plan to the Common Market.** Baton Rouge: Louisiana State University Press, 1962, 272 p.

Though the definitive history of the European movement remains to be written, each of these volumes is useful in its own right. Albonetti's is at once the most exhaustive and the most limited. It consists of a detailed chronological account of the major diplomatic and political events of European integration beginning with the prewar proposals of Coudenhove-Kalergi and Briand and with the 1948 Congress of The Hague and extending through the failure of Britain's membership application in 1963. There are extensive accounts of the negotiations relating to the Organization for European Economic Coöperation, the Treaty of Brussels, the Council of Europe, ECSC, European Defense Community and European Political Community, the *relance* of 1955–1957, the free trade area, the Organization for Economic Coöperation and Development, the various successes and failures of the European Economic Community and Euratom. Albonetti does not give us a systematic historical interpretation of these events, nor does he seek to explain them or link them systematically to domestic political developments. Rather, he presents us with some valuable raw material: namely, a summary description of all the major diplomatic manoeuvres, notes, proposals and counterproposals that mark the history of these organizational efforts.

Zurcher covers much the same ground, in less detail but with more of a narrative and interpretative sense. He places more emphasis on the contribution made by Coudenhove-Kalergi and the European movement in the United States. Another major analytical point is his account of the changes that occurred over time in the ways in which European union was conceived by major European political actors. Schmitt also deals with prewar, wartime and immediate postwar events, but the bulk of his book is a political history of the European Coal and Steel Community from its origins to the late 1950s.

CORBETT, JOHN PATRICK. **Europe and the Social Order.** Leyden: Sijthoff, 1959, 188 p.

Corbett, operating from the perspective of the rationalist social philosopher, addresses himself to the normative considerations and priorities that he feels do and should underlie European unity (the continued progress of which he takes for granted) and specifically to "the principles of social order" that it must embody if it is to be an adequate response to the challenges of the second half of the twentieth century. He acknowledges that the desire to overcome Europe's errors of the past—isolation of its economies, overemphasis on national sovereignty, idolization of the cults of nationalism—are vital goals, but argues that preoccupation with these problems will not suffice to make European integration truly relevant for the problems of the present and the future. Nor can Europe be united by reference to "the erstwhile cultural unity" of the past, or to fear and suspicion of the superpowers. The success of the movement to 1958 and its prospects for the future are linked not to "traditional sentiment or external fear" but to "the demands for more intensive innovation" in scientific, technological, economic and political institutions and practices. It is remarkable that these points were made a good ten years before they became commonplace among young European intellectuals.

Corbett sees "rapid, extensive, accelerating and above all systematic change" as the fundamental phenomenon of the second half of the twentieth century. He sees the time coming when the old ideals of equality and social justice can at last be realized in human societies. But the enormous capabilities to be made available to man could also be misused in unprecedented ways if guided by the wrong principles and ideals. He thinks that Europe, via the integration movement, can play an indispensable role in charting the future.

FRIEDRICH, CARL J. **Europe: An Emergent Nation?** New York: Harper and Row, 1969, 269 p.

Friedrich sets out to describe the informal processes of socialization and learning among those brought into contact by the institutions and arenas of European integration. His underlying assumptions are that political order is based on community consensus and that consensus is increased through face-to-face contacts. On the basis of close studies of informal consensus formation resulting from business collaboration, the phenomenon of "guest workers," the activities of international trade unions, the emergence of transnational organization and action among farmers' organizations, the booming "sister city" programs and university exchanges, he concludes that although the idealistic support of the 1950s is largely gone, the "hard-headed . . . and rather humdrum" work of modifying traditional nation-state weaknesses through integration continues. The end result, he believes, will be a federal nation on the Indian model.

Friedrich criticizes the work of other scholars who argue that integration has slowed down or ended. However, his own evidence, although intrinsically interesting and given in fascinating detail, is not presented systematically enough to constitute a clear refutation of such theses. The precise relationships posited by Friedrich among interpersonal contacts, consensus formation and federation are insufficiently articulated, and data have been chosen selectively as they appear to fit the argument rather than on a clear theoretical rationale for inclusion or exclusion. Nevertheless, the book offers a useful in-depth look at some of the informal ways in which integration has become a fait accompli in Europe.

LISKA, GEORGE. **Europe Ascendant: The International Politics of Unification.** Baltimore: Johns Hopkins Press, 1964, 182 p.

George Liska is one of the few "general theorists" of international politics to analyze seriously the European integration phenomenon and to seek to incorporate it into his overall view of the historical processes whereby nations and powers rise and decline. He notes that "the drama [of international politics] is at its height during a period of major changes in the nature of international actors and relations among them. Such appears to be the present moment." Liska sets out to analyze the "means and forces" that are forging Europe's new unity, both those that are novel and those that are "informed by the perennial principles of statecraft." The former refers to functional integration through the European Communities, which he compares with the German federal constitutional design of 1848–1849; by the latter he means the great actions of "statecraft" which transcend "ordinary stakes and planning," and here De Gaulle is likened to Bismarck. The basic analytic tools brought to bear by Liska are the analysis of the designs and strategies of great men and a heavy reliance on sweeping historical analogy. He ranges in magisterial style across fifteen hundred years of European history, as he seeks to illuminate the prospects and perils of the future of unification.

His analysis of the shortcomings of functional strategies and his prescriptions for moving from functional to "political phases"—this latter seen as a problem in statecraft—are still relevant and provocative. In his view the major danger for European unity is to be found in the externally induced (*e.g.* by U.S.–Soviet confrontation) need for Europe to act as a unity toward the outside world, before she has constituted "an integrated unity within."

SPINELLI, ALTIERO. **The Eurocrats: Conflict and Crisis in the European Community.** Baltimore: Johns Hopkins Press, 1967, 229 p.

Spinelli sets out to describe the "centers of European action and construction" that constitute united Europe. Although most of the empirical material presented is not new, his observations are shrewd and insightful, and he pulls together useful summaries of the extent and importance of European-level bureaucratic and interest group interactions. However, the chief interest of the book is in his evaluation of the prevailing functionalist strategy of integration. This is especially true since he was appointed to the Commission of the European Community in 1970.

Spinelli's prime argument is that although the Commission has been highly skillful in weaving a "vast capillary net of European influence" consisting of "a growing and permanent coagulation of economic interdependencies," and "strong and continuous relations of the Community administrations with the national ones and with the professional associations representing economic society," these multiple centers of influence are ultimately dependent upon those who hold political power, for "influence is not government." The Commission's functionalist strategy of building this bureaucratic-technocratic "Europe of offices" cannot diminish this ultimate dependency; and thus unless new strategies are devised, united Europe will remain incomplete, precarious and readily reversible by any determined political leader. He argues that more active and systematic efforts must be made by the Commission to mobilize the strong latent support among heretofore neglected grass roots political forces such as the political groups in the European Parliament, national political parties and private European movements. As evidence that such support exists and that it can be made a powerful force for Europe, Spinelli cites the "spontaneous action" of French interests and of the French voters in the presidential elections of 1965 against De Gaulle's effort to dismantle the Community. He considers that but for this unsought and unexpected intervention the Community would not have survived the 1965–1966 crisis.

HALLSTEIN, WALTER. **United Europe: Challenge and Opportunity.** Cambridge: Harvard University Press, 1962, 109 p.

Walter Hallstein was President of the EEC Commission from 1958 to 1967 and as such was a principal architect of the dominant integration strategy pursued by the Commission in those years. In these lectures, originally given in 1962 at the Fletcher School of Law and Diplomacy, he sets forth succinctly his view of how and why the institutions of the European Community are *sui generis;* how the inexorable logic of economic integration can be turned to political ends ("the Community is not in business but in politics"); and how its political character is further evidenced by its "power of attraction" vis-à-vis European nonmembers and the necessity it imposes for a redefinition of U.S.–European economic, political and military relationships. The book is an important historical document, giving us insights into the perceptions, goals and strategies of a crucial political actor during a period when the institution he headed was at the apogee of its influence and power in the integration movement.

In a sense, Hallstein's personal ideology, and his strategy for realizing it, can be viewed as a perhaps exaggerated faith in, and an effort to implement, an automatic integration process. He appeared to hold the view that political union would evolve naturally out of economic integration by means of the gradual accumulation of pragmatic incentives, and that the existing institutions of the communities were themselves the chief "motor" and the "center piece" of this evolution; and hence they must always be strengthened.

WILLIS, F. ROY. **France, Germany, and the New Europe, 1945–1967.** New York: Oxford University Press, rev. ed., 1968, 431 p.

Willis traces the dramatic steps whereby the "hereditary enmity of the French and German peoples," which had troubled the peace of Europe for centuries, was transformed "to close collaboration and even to friendship" in the two short decades following the most bitter and bloody of those encounters. His analysis reveals that Franco-German rapprochement, although eagerly sought by many leaders in both countries, could not have succeeded à deux but owes its ultimate character and lasting quality to the fact that it was merged into the construction of the European Communities. Similarly, the evolution of these institutions cannot be understood apart from the substance of Franco-German relations. Willis presents us, then, with far and away the best history of the European Communities as seen from the perspective of the crucial Bonn-Paris axis. In addition to detailing each stage in inter-governmental negotiation and bargaining, he includes extensive detail on domestic determinants, such as parties and interest groups, strategies and policy positions, and the role played by private groups such as Jean Monnet's Action Committee for the United States of Europe.

Analytical Concepts and Empirical Studies

LERNER, DANIEL and GORDON, MORTON. **Euratlantica: Changing Perspectives of the European Elites.** Cambridge: M.I.T. Press, 1969, 447 p.

The aim of the authors of this book was "to learn how the elites of post-war Europe would face the reality of their diminished post-war power . . . and how they would go about the task of positive construction." The findings they report and interpret are based on 4,000 interviews carried out in five waves over a ten-year period (1955–1965) with the leaders of "the principal sectors of public life" in Britain, France and Germany. Although there are many problems associated with such élite surveys, these data are unique in that they permit a longitudinal analysis of attitude change on vital policy dimensions. The effort to explain attitude change in terms of a theory of "psychopolitical development" is also interesting and suggestive for integration theory.

The specific issue-areas examined are protection, prosperity and prestige. The principal finding is that "there *is* an emerging consensus, within, and a convergent consensus between, the elites of the European nations." The convergence of attitudes is based on "shared long-term expectations" that the values of protection, prosperity and prestige will be optimized via international and transnational strategies. Therefore, the authors are convinced that phenomena such as Gaullism represent "a transient phase" and that the basic trend is toward closer integration within Europe and extended international coöperation among the industrialized nations of the world, principally between the United States and Europe.

Lerner and Gorden's conclusions about the future of nationalism and internationalism stand in sharp contrast to those of Karl W. Deutsch and others in **France, Germany, and the Western Alliance,** also based on élite surveys. Furthermore, their data and research design seem better suited to answer such questions, since the data are longitudinal and the base point for comparison is more carefully chosen, and the existence of national differences is not equated with nationalism.

LINDBERG, LEON N. and SCHEINGOLD, STUART A. **Europe's Would-Be Polity: Patterns of Change in the European Community.** Englewood Cliffs: Prentice-Hall, 1970, 314 p.

In this volume the authors attempt an overall assessment of two decades of polity-building through the three European Communities and some forecasts as to the outlines of probable future developments. In measuring the extent to which a "polity" is emerging, the authors focus on the development of varieties of mass public and élite attitudinal and behavioral supports, and on the development of effective transnational political institutions. In the latter case, they seek to measure the "functional scope" of collective decision making within the European framework, and the "institutional capacities" of collective processes to resolve conflicts and produce mutually acceptable outcomes.

The authors then construct an analytical framework which is designed to contribute to the synthesis of the various competing theories and empirical findings about political integration. On the basis of this framework they posit several abstract models which they use to try to explain how and why growth, stabilization or decline in "scope" or "capacities" has taken place over time. These models are explored empirically in a series of case studies and the resulting hypotheses are used in the final chapters to make tentative projections about the future of the Community.

Perhaps the most distinctive theoretical contribution of the work is the authors' emphasis on the role in integration of four different coalition-formation mechanisms: functional spill-over, side-payments and logrolling, actor socialization and feedback. In this interpretation the authors attempt a revision and restatement of the general neo-functionalist approach to integration dynamics.

On the basis of their findings about the past determinants of growth (forward-linkage), stabilization (equilibrium) and decline (spill-back), and using admittedly scanty and incomplete information as to the values of the critical variables, the authors conclude that the most likely future for the European Community (among a variety of scenarios considered) is for a slowdown in the growth of scope and capacities and the achievement of a rather stable "equilibrium" state well short of anything that could be termed federal or quasi-federal. The resulting system will also be far different from one of autonomous nation-states, however, and the authors conclude by raising questions for future research into the "new kind of polity" that may be emerging.

LINDBERG, LEON N. **The Political Dynamics of European Economic Integration.** Stanford: Stanford University Press, 1963, 367 p.

This book provides a detailed analysis of the policy-making process in the European Economic Community between 1958 and 1962, a period when the "community method" and "community spirit" were at their apogee. Lindberg determines the contribution made by the EEC to joint decision making among governments and to the delegation of decision-making tasks to autonomous central institutions; and to the restructuring of the activities and aspirations of national political actors, primarily governmental policy-makers and interest group leaders.

He begins with a careful examination of the formal commitments entered into by the signatories to the Treaty of Rome which set up the EEC. The focus is chiefly on the roles and competencies assigned to the central institutions of the EEC: the Commission, Council, Economic and Social Committee, and European Parliament. He subsequently analyzes how these institutions have evolved over time in response to internal and external stimuli. Special attention is given to the high degree of "interpenetration of roles" between the Commission and the Council which has blurred the formal lines of division established in the EEC Treaty and produced a quite diffused system of decision making. Four case studies are examined in order to trace the roles played by the various institutions to determine the ways in which major conflicts of interests were resolved; and to relate the domestic pursuit of political and economic institutions to the specific conduct of groups, parties and governments. The case studies reveal clearly the importance of the Commission both in setting the negotiating agenda and in inducing the governments to reach agreement. The willingness of interest groups to respond to integration in terms of perceptions of self-interest and how this propensity can be utilized by a tactically astute Commission are also well documented. Finally, the case studies underscore the advantages of the multiple issue-area EEC approach, which permits trade-offs and bargains across the entire economy, as contrasted with the sector integration of ECSC and Euratom. In spite of having been written during the salad days of integration, Lindberg's analyses have stood the test of time relatively well.

LICHTHEIM, GEORGE. **The New Europe: Today—and Tomorrow.** New York: Praeger, 1963, 232 p.

The value of this book lies in the broad socioeconomic framework within which the author interprets the actual and potential significance of the postwar trends toward economic and political integration in Europe. Lichtheim sees European integration as part of two interrelated processes of change: the ending of the era of European world hegemony and the emergence of a new "post-bourgeois" social order based on democratic planning. He seeks clues to Western Europe's development in the 1970s and thereafter in terms of how it is likely to fit into an emerging Atlantic system, and in terms of its success in evolving new and innovative mutations of liberal capitalism and socialism.

It is the creative combination of these two themes into Lichtheim's version of the "end of ideology" argument that represents the major contribution of the book. Western Europe is seen as capable of working out a unique system of democratic planning on a continental scale which will be the culminating stage in the gradual evolution that has brought about the erosion of historical class conflicts and that has seen the appearance of the mixed economy and the welfare state.

Lichtheim does not see (nor does he favor) the emergence in Europe of a "cohesive industrial and military bloc strong enough to rival the super powers." The integration process may produce some variant of a federal or confederal structure but with considerable fragmentation and cultural diversity and in a position of relative military inferiority. But, he says, it is precisely these characteristics that are likely to give Europe the kind of capacity for bold experiments with "social forms, political patterns, and intellectual creeds" that the ideologically rigid superpowers seem unable to muster because of their doctrinal rivalries. Hence the treatment is quite consonant with Ralf Dahrendorf's theory of conflict (**Class and Class Conflict in Industrial Society,** London: Routledge and Paul, 1961, 336 p.) in highly industrialized-bureaucratized societies.

HAAS, ERNST BERNARD. **The Uniting of Europe: Political, Social, and Economic Forces, 1950–1957.** Stanford: Stanford University Press, rev. ed., 1968, 552 p.

The Uniting of Europe has been perhaps the most influential book written on European integration. It was a pioneering work in several ways. First published in 1958, it drew the attention of social scientists to the new phenomenon emerging in Europe. Furthermore, it presented a research paradigm for the systematic analysis of international integration (that of functionalism) which still animates research in that field and which has proved extraordinarily fruitful from the perspectives of both theory development and an empirical understanding of the Community and of integration processes within it.

Haas set out to "dissect" the integration process and "to develop propositions about its nature." He sees political integration as the process whereby certain crucial élites, those in government, interest groups and political parties, who habitually participate in public policy-making and who can act as important unifying agents in any society, "are persuaded to shift their loyalties, expectations, and political activities toward a new center, whose institutions possess or demand jurisdiction over the pre-existing national states." The central theoretical conclusion of the book is that "major interest groups, as well as politicians determine their support of, or opposition to, new central institutions and policies on the basis of calculations of advantage," and that integration is thus favored by societal circumstances (such as an industrialized economy, politically mobilized masses channeling participation through parties and interest groups and pluralist-democratic political régimes) that favor or permit key élites to refocus their activities and loyalties freely. In this process the leaders of central institutions can play a vital role in advancing integration through their ability to propose and pursue collective policies that increase élite expectations and demands.

The empirical analyses in the book offer a definitive treatment of the experience of the ECSC between 1952 and 1957, focusing in great detail upon the extent to which interest groups and parties at the national level came to endorse supranational action; interest groups and parties organized beyond the national level and began to coalesce on the basis of common interests and a common ideology; interest groups, parties and governments accepted and carried out supranational decisions; governments exhibited community sentiment in their negotiations with each other; and the contribution to these processes made by the ECSC High Authority and Council of Ministers, respectively.

ETZIONI, AMITAI. **Political Unification: A Comparative Study of Leaders and Forces.** New York: Holt, Rinehart and Winston, 1965, 346 p.

Etzioni sets out to construct a general theoretical framework, derived from Parsons' structural-functional systems theory, for the analysis of international integration processes. Integration is defined in terms of the extent to which the following are achieved: effective control over the use of the means of violence, central decision making that affects basic resource allocations, and the growth of mass identifications and loyalties with a new political unit. The author develops an elaborate paradigm of the processes whereby such conditions might be attained. It consists of several parts: a discussion of prerequisites for the initiation of integration; a specification of the integrating power assets or potentialities that would be required if the new unit were to succeed; and the various stages of growth of the scope of integration, analyzed in terms of the extent to which the new system is able to solve the functional imperatives of adaptation, pattern maintenance, goal attainment and sub-unit integration.

On the basis of his paradigm Etzioni posits a series of 22 propositions which he then sets out to test (illustrate) in case studies of the European Community, Nordic integration, West Indies Federation and the United Arab Republic. His interpretation of secondary materials on the EEC is interesting and provocative and makes a useful contribution especially in regard to the analysis of "integrative power" and of the role of external actors in the integration process. However, the analysis is only suggestive and illustrative, and the overall utility of Etzioni's scheme is not really put to the test.

GRAUBARD, STEPHEN R., *ed.* **A New Europe?** Boston: Houghton, 1964, 691 p.

This volume, the product of an outstanding group of scholars from both sides of the Atlantic, is still the most valuable source of general analyses of the various processes of political, social and intellectual change that are transforming the European continent. Most of the 26 essays are explicitly tentative and are intended to raise provocative issues and posit hypotheses. As such they present us with a weighty agenda for future research rather than with empirical analyses.

Four or five major themes are dealt with from several perspectives. The problems, prospects and societal determinants of European unification preoccupy a third of the contributors, with the essays by Aron and Haas making especially important substantive and theoretical contributions to that literature. Several authors (Grosser, Bracher, Frankel) analyze the secular trends toward the decline of parliaments and the growth of executive and bureaucratic institutions in postwar Europe. Dahrendorf, Lipset, Touraine, Pizzorno and Rossi-Doria deal with changes and continuities in social structure and introduce important arguments relative to *embourgeoisement,* depoliticization, the "end of ideology," the decline of class as the basis of political consciousness, the implications of urbanization and so forth. The implications of broader patterns of economic, political and societal change for European education, science and technology are discussed in four essays, which analyze the new tasks that must be accepted by education in the New Europe, the existing trends toward and potential resources for change and reform, and the types of policy and organizational initiatives needed to apply resources to priority needs. A final theme is concerned with current developments in theological, philosophical and political thinking as they reflect the responses of European intellectuals to changes in society and in their own roles.

DEUTSCH, KARL W. and OTHERS. **France, Germany and the Western Alliance: A Study of Elite Attitudes on European Integration and World Politics.** New York: Scribner, 1967, 324 p.

This volume contains a fairly full statement of Karl W. Deutsch's influential and controversial analysis of the present state and future prospects of European integration. There are also separate analyses, by Roy C. Macridis and Lewis J. Edinger respectively, of French and German élite opinion on general domestic and foreign policy questions. While these are of considerable substantive interest in themselves, they are only marginally related to questions of European integration.

Although the basic data base for all three parts was extensive structured interviews carried out in 1964 with 147 members of French élites and 173 West German leaders, Deutsch's section supplements and interprets these materials with evidence from mass opinion polls, content analysis of the press, a survey of arms control proposals, and aggregative statistics on trade, travel, migration, mail flow among European countries.

Deutsch argues that all the data considered point to the same conclusion, that "the movement toward structural European unification since 1957 has been largely halted or very much slowed down." This interpretation is based on Deutsch's basic assumption that "social community formation"—the development by élites and masses in different countries of strong communications links, identitive ties and social similarities—is both a necessary condition for and an adequate measure of political integration, and by his findings that measures of such ties and links have uniformly levelled off. Unfortunately, since Deutsch does not demonstrate how transaction indicators are themselves linked to the respective roles that national actors or supranational institutions might be expected to play in integration, it is very difficult to evaluate his basic conclusion that "the next decade of European politics is likely to be dominated by the politics of nation-states and not by any supranational European institutions." Indeed, it is clear that governments have always been in control, but that they have pursued different goals toward integration at different times. What remains unclear is how choices among such different goals are to be related to the variables measured by Deutsch. Recent events suggest that the relationship is at best imperfect.

ALTING VON GEUSAU, FRANS A. M. **Beyond the European Community.** Leyden: Sijthoff, 1969, 247 p.

This work challenges the adequacy of the European Community system to realize the political goals and strategies that have been adopted by its leaders and supporters. Von Geusau's principal argument is that while the European Community's unique combination of the functionalist approach with the federalist conception may have accounted for its early successes, it has also limited its capacity for further growth. This is because the two components are ultimately contradictory. It follows that integration in the 1970s depends on the development of new conceptions and strategies that are more consonant with social, international and technological developments.

Von Geusau's approach is to describe in detail the formal provisions for institutions and functions (*e.g.* economic; defense, security, arms control; relations with third states, "Kennedy Round," relations with Eastern Europe; political unification) in the Community, and then to discuss their modification in practice. He concludes that given the structure of the EEC's institutions, efforts to induce spillover from one function to another are bound to fail because of national resistances. Even though Von Geusau argues that the Community has become "disfunctional" to the search for rational solutions to the real problems of the 1970s (to restore NATO cohesion, to improve world trade, to increase aid to developing countries, and promote technological, educational, cultural coöperation), The Hague summit of 1969 with its agreements on monetary policy, strengthening the European Parliament and British entry would seem to cast some doubt on these forecasts, as on the analysis which produced them.

European Institutions and Law

ROBERTSON, ARTHUR HENRY. **The Council of Europe: Its Structure, Functions and Achievements.** New York: Praeger (for the London Institute of World Affairs), 2d ed., 1961, 288 p.

HAAS, ERNST B. **Consensus Formation in the Council of Europe.** Berkeley: University of California Press, 1960, 70 p.

The first of these volumes provides an exhaustive description of the structures and activities of the Council of Europe: the membership, functions, procedures of the chief institutions of the Council, and a detailed account of meetings held, resolutions and conventions passed, subjects studied and special conferences and committees formed in the various spheres of activity.

The general conclusion is that although the Council of Europe cannot be said to have contributed much to the political unity of Europe it has "a good record as an instrument of European cooperation in the social, cultural and legal fields." As a result of its inter-governmental Conventions, national practices and standards have been harmonized and the foundations of a corpus of European law has begun to emerge. Through the debates and resolutions of the Consultative Assembly communication has been promoted among parliamentarians of 18 countries on a broad range of political, economic and cultural topics. This forum is said to have been especially useful in smoothing relations between the six members of the European Community and the rest of Europe, which has often looked upon the Communities with mixed feelings of suspicion, envy and fear.

Unfortunately, there is no analysis of the political process within the institutions of the Council. Thus Robertson's work tells us relatively little about the dynamics and potentials of inter-governmental coöperation. Similarly, the assertions made about the Council's impact and influence must be treated as tentative, since they are not rigorously demonstrated.

The only systematic effort to study the political process in the Council remains Ernst B. Haas' **Consensus Formation in the Council of Europe.** On the basis of an analysis of ten years of roll-call voting in the Consultative Assembly, Haas sought to determine the extent to which a consensus on transnational political lines had emerged such that one could claim a contribution to the overall integration process. His chief findings were that such a consensus had not come into existence, that the debates in Strasbourg were rhetorical exercises quite disassociated from national politics, and that the political groups in the Assembly showed no signs of developing into all-European parties.

The European Free Trade Association and the Crisis of European Integration: An Aspect of the Atlantic Crisis? London: Michael Joseph (for the Graduate Institute of International Studies, Geneva), 1968, 323 p.

The European Free Trade Area, created in 1960 by the so-called "outer seven" countries (Britain, Norway, Sweden, Denmark, Austria, Portugal and Switzerland) as a kind of counterweight to the European Community, has not received the scholarly attention it would seem to warrant. Aside from one or two legal exegeses of the EFTA convention, its rules, exceptions, escape clauses, dispute settlement machinery and compatibility with the General Agreement on Tariffs and Trade, such as that by John S. Lambrinidis, **The Structure, Function, and Law of a Free Trade Area: The European Free Trade Association** (New York: Praeger, for the London Institute of World Affairs, 1965, 303 p.), and some efforts to measure EFTA's economic impact (see Lawrence B. Krause, **European Economic Integration and the United States,** Washington: Brookings Institution, 1968, 265 p.), this volume by a study group at the Graduate Institute of International Studies in Geneva stands alone as a serious and substantial analysis of the organization.

The book leaves much to be desired, however, for it is not a thorough study of the nature of EFTA's institutions, of decision-making processes within them, or of the policy consequences of actions taken pursuant to the EFTA convention. The bulk of the book consists of analyses of the positions of each EFTA member toward the organization: the general diplomatic context of that policy, perceived economic and political benefits and risks, domestic political debates relative to EFTA and to EEC, views of the long-range utility of the organization, etc., with but a single chapter devoted to a survey of EFTA's operations from 1960 to 1966—the implementation of the free-trade area, the conclusion of bilateral agreements, the development of rules of fair competition, the association of Finland, the creation of new institutions such as a Consultative Committee and an Economic Development Committee.

The study concludes that EFTA can claim certain concrete achievements. Its limited success has demonstrated that a free-trade area among very diverse types of systems (as to size, political and economic traditions) can be made to work. It has strengthened the hand of those member countries who seem likely to try to bargain their way into the EEC. And the organization holds promise as an "integrating" mechanism for those countries of Eastern and Western Europe who will remain outside an enlarged European Community.

IMBERT, ARMAND. **L'Union de l'Europe Occidentale.** Paris: Librairie Générale de Droit, 1968, 238 p.

The Western European Union, an inter-governmental organization (with some potentially "supranational" features) which groups Britain and the six European Community countries, was created in 1954 in the aftermath of the defeat of the EDC as a central framework for the rearmament of Germany. Besides having the character of a mutual military assistance treaty—a function taken over from the Brussels Treaty Organization—WEU was assigned tasks in the area of arms control (primarily to ensure that Germany did not produce atomic, biological, chemical or certain heavy weapons), as well as the general promotion of political, economic and social coöperation. Its successes and failures in achieving these tasks, and the processes whereby new tasks were assumed by its several institutions, are traced by Imbert in the only book-length study of WEU available.

The author documents the atrophy of tasks in the economic sphere, due to the more appropriate framework of the OEEC, and in the social and cultural spheres as a consequence of a transfer of function to the more inclusive Council of Europe. Similarly, little progress was made in the areas of arms standardization or arms control primarily because of institutional overlap with NATO. Imbert particularly emphasizes the failure of the WEU Council to perform its "real role," namely, that of becoming an effective center for intra-European coöperation as a counterweight to U.S. domination of NATO. Still the Council has performed useful service as an ongoing diplomatic forum, especially in periods of political conflict between Britain and the Six. The WEU Assembly, a consultative body of 89 parliamentarians organized along transnational political party lines, has, on the other hand, sought to assert a more active political role and has assumed a kind of quasi-parliamentary supervision over the work of NATO and over national defense policies generally.

Imbert argues, however, that WEU, which will remain in existence according to treaty until the end of the century, could well assume new important tasks as the foundation of a European pillar of a newly constituted Euratlantic alliance and as a framework for the extension of the scope of European integration when (and if) Britain joins the European Community.

PALMER, MICHAEL; LAMBERT, JOHN and OTHERS. **A Handbook of European Organizations.** New York: Praeger, 1968, 519 p.

This useful reference volume summarizes the origins, structures, working methods and procedures, successes and failures to 1967 and the reasons therefore, of ten main regional organizations "working in and centering on Europe." Included are chapters on the Economic Commission for Europe, the OEEC, the Council of Europe, the three European Communities, Western European Union, the European Free Trade Association, NATO and OECD. Although the treatment of each organization is almost entirely descriptive, it is in each case comprehensive, competent and accurate.

In a concluding chapter the authors seek to formulate some tentative generalizations about the factors that seem to determine the overall performance of European international organizations. These fall into two categories: the nature and political orientations of the member countries, and the institutional forms employed. As to the first, the authors find that even in technical domains "ideological and power conflicts among the members tend to hamstring an international organization." They also conclude that organizations based on hegemonial relationships, such as between Europe and the United States, can function quite effectively only as long as there is "on both sides a strong political motive for the relationship," and as long as the dominant member "promote[s] policies strong enough to fulfil the shared political objectives, while paying enough attention to the special interests and views of the weaker partners."

As far as institutions are concerned, the authors conclude that although inter-governmental forms are inherently limited in making new policy decisions and in responding to changing circumstances, there are certain conditions under which substantial achievements are possible: when strong and legitimate leadership is provided by a dominant hegemonial member, when there is a common perception of an external threat, and when suitable rules and procedures are developed. But only "supranational" forms as in the European Communities would seem to be capable of generating sustained collective action in important policy areas. Although all international organizations ultimately depend on the political will to unite, supranational forms are better suited for actively promoting political will and for surviving periods of internal tension.

HOUBEN, P.-H. J. M. **Les Conseils de Ministres des Communautés Européennes.** Leyden: Sijthoff, 1964, 259 p.

Although it only covers the period 1950 to 1963, and is quite limited in scope, this remains an indispensable source for an understanding of the changing role of the Council of Ministers, as an institution representing the governments of the member states, in the European Communities. By means of careful analysis of diplomatic documents, legal texts and official publications, Houben traces the steps whereby the role of the Council evolved from the early debates (when its creation had not even been envisaged) through the ECSC Treaty (where it was given the task of harmonizing the actions of the High Authority with those of the govern-ments) to the EEC and Euratom Treaties when this evolution was completed by the establishment of its legal primacy in final decision-making authority.

It is to the author's credit that he sees this development as inevitable and indispensable; after all, as he points out, one cannot bring about economic or political integration against or without the governments. The Council of Ministers and its subordinate committees and working groups have been the vital institutional arena through which this necessary involvement of the governments in the daily life of the Communities has been brought about.

The book is excellent as a formal legal analysis of the Council's developing powers, of its relationship to the European Parliament and to national parliaments, and to the European Court of Justice. However, it does not penetrate into the political processes that lie behind these developments, at either the national or Community levels, nor does it attempt to assess the relative roles of Council, Commission, Parliament and Court in determining actual Community decisions, or to extract broader theoretical meaning from the data presented.

POLACH, JAROSLAV G. **Euratom: Its Background, Issues and Economic Implications.** Dobbs Ferry: Oceana Publications, 1964, 232 p.

One of the few book-length studies of the European Atomic Energy Community, this volume remains a useful brief reference guide to the historical and technical background of integration in the atomic energy field, to the original purposes and institutional arrangements of Euratom, and to the ways in which practice fell short of aspiration over the first years of operation. The descriptive portions of the book indicate the major relevant topics and problem areas rather than constitute a definitive treatment of them. The analysis of the causes and consequences of failures and shortcomings and the interpretation of the impact and significance of the Euratom experience suffer from the absence of any well-articulated and rele-vant economic or political theory.

To supplement this book, the reader should consult Lawrence Scheinman's "Euratom: Nuclear Integration in Europe," in *International Conciliation* (May 1967). It is a well-focused political postmortem which seeks to isolate five factors that brought about the failure of Euratom within the context of integration theory: (1) the reduction in national incentives to coöperate in the energy field as a consequence of the development of alternative petroleum and natural gas supplies; (2) the disparity of national interests and capabilities in the nuclear field between France and her partners; (3) the reëmergence of economic-commercial nationalisms which substituted national for collective priorities; (4) the lack of active and dynamic leadership from the Euratom Commission; and (5) the single-area bargaining context which, like the ECSC and in contrast to the EEC, did not allow cross-sectional bargaining as a way of adjusting competing interests. Scheinman concludes that future efforts in the energy field or in scientific and technological integration must be consciously structured to overcome centrifugal forces such as these which are probably inherent in transnational integration efforts.

WIGHTMAN, DAVID. **Economic Co-operation in Europe.** New York: Praeger (for the Carnegie Endowment), 1957, 288 p.

This is a historical-descriptive account of the functioning of the United Nations Economic Commission for Europe up to 1954, seen within the larger context of the postwar search for European economic recovery and the growing East-West rift. The author describes the institutions of ECE in some detail. Of special interest are his case studies of the problems, methods of work and achievements of the individual technical committees in the fields of coal, steel, engineering and raw materials, timber, housing, agriculture, electric power, inland transport and trade. Intensive analysis is given to the committee on coal, whose distributive recommendations in a time of scarcity enjoyed a de facto authority despite a lack of sanctions, and to the Committee on East-West Trade and its problems in the face of Western security controls on strategic goods and Eastern uncoöperativeness and misplaced emphasis on industrial trade.

The case studies confirm that the largely private nature of committee meetings facilitated agreements and understandings that could not have been reached in a more public and therefore more political arena. As such they provide useful background material for anyone concerned with methods and problems of organizing transnational coöperation in functionally specific realms among countries that may be in strong disagreement in other areas. For the period covered, the analysis is quite complete and well documented. It suffers, however, from the lack of a theoretical framework which might help make clearer the underlying principles at work in ventures in economic coöperation.

BEBR, GERHARD. **Judicial Control of the European Communities.** New York: Praeger (for the London Institute of World Affairs), 1962, 268 p.

HAY, PETER. **Federalism and Supranational Organizations: Patterns for New Legal Structures.** Urbana: University of Illinois Press, 1966, 335 p.

Bebr provides a formal description of the legal-political role of the Court in the Community, and of the nature, composition and organization of the Court itself, followed by a detailed legal analysis of its case law—of vital importance because the wide jurisdiction of the Court makes it similar to a European supreme court. While the author's specific conclusions are primarily of interest to the lawyer, at a more general level he stresses the extent to which the Court's ability to develop a consistent body of law has been hampered by the "lack of strong political and economic solidarity" and by the centrality of "policy considerations" in the Community.

Hay is more concerned with the broader implications of the European Community for legal policy and legal theory, specifically "the role of so-called supranational organizations . . . in international law and the legal structure of the member states." His discussion of the impact of Community law on national law and legal practice is of great interest to the student of the integration process. Unfortunately, the detailed analysis is limited to Germany and is based almost entirely on constitutional law and theory rather than actual practice. He notes that German law "has not yet found satisfactory solutions to the problem of accommodating supranationalism and the national constitutional structure," although he does discern a tendency in favor of the principle of the supremacy of Community law.

SCHEINGOLD, STUART A. **The Rule of Law in European Integration: The Path of the Schuman Plan.** New Haven: Yale University Press, 1965, 331 p.

Scheingold's book offers a sophisticated political analysis of the Court of Justice of the European Community, based on a study of the hundred or more binding decisions made by the Court in the first ten years of its existence, and on extensive interviewing in Luxembourg and Brussels. He sees courts as political institutions playing special roles in the authoritative settlement of conflicting individual and group claims in a society—a part likely to be decisive in federal-type systems, which require arbitration of central-local government conflicts of jurisdiction and where the court is also the court of last resort for constitutional questions. He finds that the Court of Justice is much closer to this kind of court than a standard international tribunal, and that as part of a supranational system it is historically unique.

In supranational (and federal) systems courts play a vital stabilizing role, Scheingold notes, assuring equal administration of justice and the predictability of behavior. But he argues that in performing this role the Court of Justice encounters a crucial dilemma, for the integration process is fluid, dynamic and highly politicized; and if the Court is to avoid making that process rigid, or being pushed aside as irrelevant by political actors, it must assure stability and determinacy by developing a special set of judicial techniques.

The development of what Scheingold calls a "functional technique" of interpretation may enable the judges "to bridge the gap between the practical demands of the political world and the textual rigidity of the legal world;" but that does not mean that there are no limits on judicial activism. The Court respects its limited role whenever major political decisions have not yet been made by the governments, wherever the treaties clearly reserve powers to the constituent states and whenever the governments signal unambiguously that they prefer to solve certain questions by bargaining among themselves. Still, the Court, through its case law, has "leavened the fluid process of integration with a vital measure of stability" and, through the threat of judicial veto, has kept negotiated solutions within the strictures of the treaties.

MANZANARÈS, HENRI. **Le Parlement Européen.** Paris: Berger-Levrault, 1964, 321 p.
KAPTEYN, PAUL J. **L'Assemblée Commune de la Communauté Européenne du Charbon et de l'Acier.** Leyden: Sijthoff, 1962, 270 p.
FORSYTH, MURRAY. **The Parliament of the European Communities.** London: Political and Economic Planning, 1964, 119 p.

The European Parliament, consisting of 142 members of the national parliaments of the Six elected by each national legislature, plays a role in the Community's decision-making process somewhere between that of a conventional international parliamentary assembly and a "true" legislature. It commands the attention of the student of regional integration for a number of reasons. First, there is no precedent for the granting of even sharply circumscribed powers of legislative control to an international assembly. Secondly, it has actively sought in practice (to some degree successfully) to expand its role even more, and has come to resemble a national parliament in many procedural ways. Finally, many analysts of the integration process have suggested that the internal processes of such an institution might have positive consequences for integration through the development of procedural and substantive consensus among its members and the capacity of the institution or its members to influence the attitudes and behavior of national public opinion or national decision makers in governments, legislatures and political parties.

These three volumes have contributed substantially to our knowledge of several of the above dimensions, but each is limited, either temporally, substantively or in theoretical scope. Kapteyn's is the broadest in conception, the best developed in analytic and theoretical terms, and the most thoroughly documented, but covers only the period from 1952 to 1958. He tries to answer two analytic questions: Did the Assembly succeed in evolving some sense of the common good (as against national interests) or some set of general principles in its deliberations? Did the Assembly succeed in playing a significant role in the determination of the general policy of the Community? Manzanarès and Forsyth carry the analysis to 1964, but the former is preoccupied with organizational details and analysis of formal legal competencies, and the latter, although concerned with the actual political role in the decision-making process, is rather brief and based on incomplete documentation.

These authors share the general scholarly consensus that the European Parliament does not play a really central role in the policy-making process, in spite of the considerable efforts of its members. There are marginal differences in assessment of its informal influence, but these may be a function of the period studied. Each recognizes the progress made by its members in overcoming strictly national points of view and in promoting further institutional integration, but the effects of the Parliament's activities on behavior at the national level have not been systematically investigated, although Forsyth and others suggest that they have been very limited. An updated account of the activities of the Parliament and the parliamentarians is needed, plus closer attention to what their impact may be at the national level.

ZELLENTIN, GERDA, ed. **Formen der Willensbildung in den Europäischen Organisationen.** Frankfurt: Athenaeum Verlag, Kölner Schriften zur Politischen Wissenschaft, 1965, 132 p.

This volume contains two analytical studies by the editor, dealing with decision-making patterns in the European Parliament and the Economic and Social Committee, respectively, as well as four essays by European officials expounding aspects of decision making in organizations in which they had been active. In principle, the format used here is of pioneering importance because it juxtaposes the analytical interests of the scholar interested in political processes with the insider's expertise. Unfortunately, the results do not entirely live up to the potentiality.

Gerda Zellentin's quantitative study of the composition of the committees and party groupings in the European Parliament discloses that supranational party cohesion is increasing, that committees are increasingly being constituted on the basis of expertise and that the voting record of the Assembly is more consistently integration-oriented than that of the Council of Europe and Western European Union. Her unique quantitative study of the EEC Economic and Social Committee shows that the relative cohesion of the trade unions acted as a catalyst for growing internal unity within each of the other two groupings. Case studies suggest that the ESC had more effect on its members than on the Council and the Commission because, while legitimizing the idea of supranational interest representation, it is systematically sidestepped and ignored by the major EEC organs. Political process analysis—not often used in Europe—demonstrates that legitimacy and authority are far from being covariant.

The contributions of the four high officials are uniformly disappointing as contributions to focused decision-making analysis.

Politics and Issues in Economic Theory and Practice

MEADE, JAMES EDWARD and OTHERS. **Case Studies in European Economic Union: The Mechanics of Integration.** New York: Oxford University Press (for the Royal Institute of International Affairs), 1962, 424 p.

JENSEN, FINN B. and WALTER, INGO. **The Common Market: Economic Integration in Europe.** Philadelphia: Lippincott, 1965, 278 p.

McLachlan, D. L. and Swann, D. **Competition Policy in the European Community: The Rules in Theory and Practice.** New York: Oxford University Press, 1967, 482 p.

Most economic studies of European integration analyze its impact on growth rates, productivity, investment patterns and the transnational movement of economic factors. Leading examples of this approach include Ingo Walter, **The European Common Market: Growth and Patterns of Trade and Production** (New York: Praeger, 1967, 212 p.); Lawrence B. Krause, **European Economic Integration and the United States** (Washington: Brookings Institution, 1968, 265 p.); and A. Lamfalussy, **The United Kingdom and the Six** (Homewood: Irwin, 1963, 147 p.). However, there are also analyses which focus on the institutions and policies of regional integration, asking either what kinds of integrated institutions and policies are necessary if given levels of economic integration are to be achieved, or seeking to plot the economic consequences of institutions which have emerged. The three works under review fall into this category, important to students of collective decision making as the prime motor of political integration.

The volume by Meade and others contains detailed case studies of the Belgium-Luxembourg Economic Union, Benelux and the ECSC, focused on the "mechanical" question: "What economic arrangements must be made in an economic union in order to make it work efficiently?" The section on the ECSC does not go much beyond the studies by Louis Lister and William Diebold, Jr., but those on BLEU and Benelux, although they exclude consideration of political variables, are among the best descriptive accounts in the literature.

Jensen and Walter cast their net more widely in their useful general descriptive survey of economic policy-making in the European Community, providing succinct summaries of the policy and institutional problems that arose in various sectors or that were likely to arise in the future. Especially interesting are the chapters on regional problems, social policy, competition, the coördination of national taxation and counter-cyclical policies, and monetary integration.

McLachlan and Swann provide us with a systematic and exhaustive account of competition policy: the goals sought in the treaties, the problems encountered, the common policies developed and their effects. They conclude that the communities have contributed to movements of concentration and specialization that have increased efficiency, while at the same time increasing competition among firms.

Klaer, Werner. **Der Verkehr im Gemeinsamen Markt für Kohle und Stahl: Beiträge zur Europäischen Verkehrspolitik.** Baden-Baden: Lutzeyer, 1961, 386 p.

This work is the authoritative treatment of the technical and legal aspects of establishing a nondiscriminatory transport policy for the common market for coal and steel. It covers the successful efforts of the Coal and Steel Community to eliminate various hidden and overt discriminatory rate-setting practices of the state railway systems; it covers equally conscientiously the far less successful efforts to do the same for trucking and inland waterways. The author, who was a participant in the relevant studies and negotiations in his capacity as head of the High Authority's Transport Division, speaks authoritatively and frankly.

The conceptual framework guiding the presentation is provided by the theory of industrial location: Optimally, industries should be located where the transport costs of the necessary raw materials are lowest. Discriminatory rate-setting distorts the benefits which the consumer may derive from optimal plant location. It also distorts competition between enterprises and creates artificially protected markets even in the absence of tariffs or other taxes. Klaer therefore demonstrates where and how the provisions of the Coal and Steel Treaty governing subsidies and competition seem to impose a nondiscriminatory transport policy and where there remains ambiguity.

Railways, because of their rate policy and because of the structural features of centralized state ownership, yielded most easily to supranational reform. This was possible because the basic operations and structures of the state railway systems were only minimally affected by the changes; in short, the railways were able to balance losses and gains in revenue. This proved impossible in the case of inland waterways, especially with respect to traffic on the Rhine and the northern French canals and rivers. In the case of highway trucking no agreement could be reached because of the dispersed character of ownership. Moreover, the Community Court held that supranationally imposed regulation of the trucking industry was not warranted by the treaty.

LISTER, LOUIS. **Europe's Coal and Steel Community: An Experiment in Economic Union.** New York: Twentieth Century Fund, 1960, 495 p.

This detailed analysis of economic developments during the first years of the life of the ECSC focuses mainly on its contributions to efficiency of production via increased national specialization, and the reciprocal roles of transnational and national institutions in this process. A great deal of valuable detail is provided on the coal and steel industries in Europe prior to and since the beginning of the ECSC. This material is given sharp focus as a consequence of the author's incorporation of economic competition theory and functional integration theory.

Lister concluded that spontaneous methods of restriction and reorganization had been the norm in the steel industry, but that at least part of the progress made could be attributed to the Common Market. The free price mechanism which was to promote competition and greater efficiency in the steel industry was, however, not put into effect—evidence of both a divergence between theory and practice and the effects of a fragmentation of authority. Much the same dependence on private or inter-governmental agreement was also the case with regard to the coal and energy industries. The author's survey of national government policies and actual practice indicates that improvements in efficiency in coal production through regional specialization depended on administrative decision and coördination rather than on the price mechanism. The chief role of the High Authority of the ECSC was to induce governments to coöperate with policies beneficial to the Community as a whole. In this regard they were hampered on the one hand by division of authority between EEC and Euratom and the lack of regulation of petroleum and, on the other hand, by the tension between the short-term welfare considerations of individual nations and the long-range welfare of the Community as a whole.

DIEBOLD, WILLIAM, JR. **The Schuman Plan: A Study in Economic Cooperation, 1950–1959.** New York: Praeger (for the Council on Foreign Relations), 1959, 750 p.

William Diebold, Jr. offers a carefully researched, gracefully written and politically wise analysis of the first decade of "economic cooperation" in the ECSC. After a thorough account of the historical background of the Treaty, he devotes the bulk of his book to detailed accounts of the progress made to 1958–1959 in putting the Treaty obligations into effect and in giving life to the new organizational system it established. Separate chapters are devoted to trade barriers, transport rates, subsidies, taxes, prices, scrap, investment, cartels and concentrations, aid for adaptation and external relations. A final section seeks to assess the ECSC's economic impact, to discuss the problems and consequences of partial sector integration and to estimate future prospects.

The author's emphasis on substantive accounts of how specific Treaty provisions worked in practice makes the book an indispensable supplement to Louis Lister's account of the impact of the ECSC on Europe's coal and steel industries, and Ernst B. Haas' analysis of decision-making processes and of changes in the behavior and beliefs of political actors involved in or subject to those decisions. (The three volumes taken together are essential background for anyone concerned with the early years of European integration.) It is especially impressive how well Diebold's characterization of the basic nature of the Community and his estimates of its staying power have met the test of time, especially in the face of periods of strong opposition from governments or interest groups, and of economic recession.

The European Community and the World

FELD, WERNER. **The European Common Market and the World.** Englewood Cliffs:
Prentice-Hall, 1967, 184 p.

ALLEN, JAMES JAY. **The European Common Market and the GATT.** Washington:
University Press of Washington, D.C., 1960, 244 p.

Werner Feld's work is a competent short survey of the EEC's relations with the
rest of the world to 1967. After detailing the Community's legal competences in the
conduct of external affairs, Feld gives a brief account of the roles of Community
institutions, economic interest groups and member governments in the determination of Community policies in this area. He devotes the bulk of the book to a
historical description of the relations between the EEC and European nonmember
states, other industrialized countries, the developing world and Asian and European
communist countries. An important virtue of this analysis is the light it casts not
only on the substance of policies and the diplomatic stages through which they
evolve, but also on internal differences within the EEC (between Commission and
governments and among governments) and how they were and were not resolved.
In the process, we learn something fundamental about the EEC as a *partial* political system and about the internal factors that determine the way in which it is
likely to function in its relations with the outside world. Feld's focus is thus
primarily broadly political.

More limited in scope but at the same time more definitive is James J. Allen's
detailed legal analysis of the compatibility of the EEC Treaty and the policies
implied therein with the General Agreement on Tariffs and Trade and with United
States trading policies and interests. The author argues that in general the EEC
does not on its face pose serious questions of compatibility, but that there are
potential problems in regard to quantitative restrictions, especially as they may be
imposed by an EEC member in order to deal with the balance-of-payments difficulties, and with the price-maintenance systems envisaged by the common agricultural
policy.

PLESSOW, UTTA. **Neutralität und Assoziation mit der EWG.** Cologne: Carl Heymanns
Verlag, Kölner Schriften zum Europarecht, 1967, 238 p.

One in a series of important legal studies, Dr. Plessow's work examines the
compatibility of neutrality with associate membership in the EEC, as applied to
Switzerland, Austria and Sweden. She examines the general law of neutrality as
well as neutralization by treaty and by self-imposed custom, and comes to the
conclusion that there is no incompatibility between neutrality and associate
membership, provided that the form of the association does not go beyond a
customs union. There may be incompatibility if the bonds approach a political
union, as was the case with the putative customs union of 1931 between Germany
and Austria. This conclusion applies to the three countries under study irrespective
of the differing bases of their neutrality. Full membership, by contrast, is not
compatible with neutrality in any of the three cases.

The second part of the book is concerned with the particulars of the treaty of
association recommended by the author. She examines agriculture, factor mobility,
commercial policy, the European Investment Bank, competition, fiscal policy,
economic and monetary policy, social policy suspension and denunciation of
associate membership and participation in EEC institutions. Can the three neutrals
avoid enmeshment exceeding a classical customs union if they involve themselves
in all these policy domains? Invariably, the author answers with a qualified "yes,"
but her discussions lend themselves to the opposite conclusion. She finds no
overwhelming legal barriers to such involvement, but she does uncover several
economic and political problems—for instance, Swiss limitations on the number
of foreign workers, as well as Swiss and Swedish concern over their high agricultural
production costs. Therefore, only with very special treaty arrangements could

these nations become involved in many of the widespread operations of the EEC and survive as neutrals.

ZARING, J. L. **Decision for Europe: The Necessity of Britain's Engagement.** Baltimore: Johns Hopkins Press, 1969, 221 p.

Zaring's book is a polemic in the best sense of the term. By virtue of the clarity of argument and the empirical understanding of strengths and weaknesses of the existing Communities, it stands out from that large class of tracts which proclaim the transcendent virtues of the works of "good Europeans" like Monnet and decry the perfidies of De Gaulle and other shortsighted nationalists.

The author's thesis is that the real promise of the European Community lies in its progress toward a truly non-hegemonial relationship among the countries of Europe that can facilitate the pooling of their vast resources for their collective good and for the good of the rest of the world. He sees this as a necessary condition for assuring the still uncertain domestic and international stability of European countries, the resolution of the ever explosive German problem, the emergence of a new relationship between Western and Eastern Europe, and of a "third force capable of balancing the few superpowers and capable of sharing the burdens of preserving peace."

While this is the promise of a larger integrated Europe, Zaring sees the recent history of the EEC as a potentially fatal crisis of loss of momentum, hiding the reëmerging hegemony of France or Germany. He considers it the prime mission of Britain to rescue Europe from such a trend, to restore the integration movement to its original thrust. Hence, even in the 1970s, Britain is thought to be more important to Europe than Europe is to Britain.

COOMBES, DAVID. **Politics and Bureaucracy in the European Community: A Portrait of the Commission of the E.E.C.** London: Allen and Unwin, 1970, 343 p.

Coombes' study is the only recent full-scale analysis of the activities, internal organization and political role of the Commission of the European Community. The author does not provide a complete and definitive treatment (a herculean task for any single scholar), but he reports interesting and important findings on the Commission's organizational structure and personnel policies, on the internal strains created by trying to mix political and administrative roles, on the trends away from dynamic, innovative leadership and toward bureaucratization, and the consequences of these strains and trends for the process of political integration.

Coombes argues that the Commission has tried to play four different roles since its inception: initiative (providing policy impulsion), normative (defense of the Community interest and that of the integrative process), administrative (staff support and policy implementation) and mediative (facilitating inter-governmental bargaining). But these roles are incompatible—"even contradictory"—with each other, he says, in that they require different forms of organization and recruitment and different styles of leadership. He notes that the Commission has come more and more to play administrative roles at the expense of the innovative and normative, and concludes that if the goal is a federal Europe, new institutions and strategies will have to be devised.

A major purpose of the author is to contribute to theory by systematically comparing his findings with those of earlier students, primarily neo-functionalists. He argues that these students have underestimated the importance of national political leadership, and exaggerated the integrative role of the Commission specifically and of "engrenage" generally. This critique of neo-functionalism, while substantively well taken, does no more than air revisions and refinements the neo-functionalists themselves devised after 1965.

CAMPS, MIRIAM. **Britain and the European Community, 1955–1963.** Princeton: Princeton University Press, 1964, 547 p.

————. **European Unification in the Sixties: From the Veto to the Crisis.** New York: McGraw-Hill (for the Council on Foreign Relations), 1966, 273 p.

Miriam Camps is the best informed and the most balanced and generally perceptive historian of European integration. In **Britain and the European Community** she chronicles "the British search for accommodation with the EEC" from the Messina Conference in June 1955 to the breakdown in the negotiations for accession on January 29, 1963. Although the chief concern of the book is to describe British policy as it evolved in this series of negotiations, at the same time the author provides a full account of internal EEC developments. In general, the emphasis is on very detailed descriptions of the complex and technical issues of inter-governmental negotiations and on "the development of official views" rather than on the role that the public, press, interest groups, political parties, civil service or other élites might have played in the evolution of these policies. (See Robert J. Lieber and Michael J. Brenner for such materials.)

Two central themes are developed. First, that Britain's difficulties with the Continent in the late 1950s and early 1960s stemmed from persistent miscalculations of the strength of the integration movement which led to a series of missed opportunities that lost the initiative for Britain. As a consequence, they were always in the position of reacting to "European situations created by others"—usually by Frenchmen, either in Brussels or in Paris. Secondly, the longer Britain failed to make up its mind the more this became so, because as the Six negotiated with Britain they were impelled to make more and more policy decisions and to continue the willy-nilly creation of the Community, and the more the Community began to take form the more economically and politically complex became the problems of accession.

In **European Unification in the Sixties** Miriam Camps carries the story of the development of the Community and of Britain's relationship with it to the spring of 1966. In a concluding chapter she speculates about the "short-term outlook" for the Community in view of the 1965–1966 crisis and the prospects for a renewed British effort to join. In general, she predicts a continuation of economic integration, although at a slower pace, and with many doubts as to its military and political implications.

KAISER, KARL. **EWG und Freihandelszone.** Leyden: Sijthoff, 1963, 270 p.

One in a series of integration studies sponsored by the Council of Europe, Karl Kaiser's book is a chronological examination of the European negotiations from 1955 to 1959 which culminated in the formation of the EEC and EFTA. In assessing the limitation of the EEC to six members, and the failure to include the EEC in a comprehensive European free-trade zone, the author concentrates on the policies of France and Great Britain. The former was largely responsible for initiating proposals which the latter found unacceptable, thereby excluding England from the EEC and widening the gap between the Messina states and the rest of Europe. Britain, on the other hand, was guilty of political myopia and diplomatic bungling, both of which resulted from an incorrect assessment of her position in the postwar world.

The first part of the book deals with the negotiations between the members of the ECSC and Great Britain over the formation of a broader European community (June 1955 to May 1956). England withdrew, and the Six decided to carry on without her. The second part (July 1956 to summer 1957) covers the OEEC negotiations concerning the formation of a free-trade zone for all West European nations. In this period, it became apparent that the Six had made a political commitment to integration which was absent in the other participants, and which shaped the final outcome of the talks. The final part (summer 1957 to January 1959) examines the final fruitless attempts by England to submerge EEC in a larger grouping, the breakdown of these efforts and the subsequent formation of EFTA as an intentional counterbalance to the EEC. The successful, though somewhat unexpected, continuity of French policy from the Fourth to the Fifth Republic is explained in terms of De Gaulle's historical and philosophical commitment to a renewal of French grandeur.

CALLEO, DAVID P. **Europe's Future: The Grand Alternatives.** New York: Horizon Press, 1965, 192 p.

David P. Calleo seeks to describe each of the "grand alternatives" open to renascent Western Europe in the 1960s and after, and to analyze their relative strengths and weaknesses, both as ideals that can move men and as practical guides for the future. The alternative policy and institutional directions Western Europe can take are "Atlantic Europe" of NATO and the Multilateral Nuclear Force, "supranational Europe and the Common Market," and "the Europe of States of General de Gaulle." Calleo's method is that of "the historian of the present." Each system of ideas is analyzed via a careful perusal of both the writings of major protagonists (Monnet, Spaak, Hallstein, De Gaulle, McNamara, Kennedy) and the scholarly literature relevant to its practical application. The contribution of the book then is less in its originality and more in its useful synthesis of the ideological conflicts associated with the integration phenomenon.

Calleo sees no inevitable or even probable trend toward European union. He concludes that the American-sponsored schemes (such as MLF) have been counterproductive and that Europe cannot unite as a "pillar" in an American "grand design." And he sees the only real chance for self-directed unity as lying in some kind of rapprochement between "the fundamental nationalist insight into the problem of democratic consensus and leadership with the functionalist appreciation for the possibilities of bureaucratic planning and management on an international scale." The key conditions for such rapprochement are British membership ("Only British banking and technology might make Europe's economy the equal of America's. Only its oldest ally could reconcile the United States to a new Western superpower.") and the forging of a "close alliance between Britain and France," which means "accepting a Gaullist vision of a Europe that looks to itself first and is genuinely independent of America."

Political Behavior and Decision Making: Specific Cases

SILJ, ALESSANDRO. **Europe's Political Puzzle: A Study of the Fouchet Negotiations and the 1963 Veto.** Cambridge: Harvard University Press, 1967, 178 p.

For eight months in 1961–1962 representatives of the six member countries of the European Community met under the chairmanship of Christian Fouchet of France to try to negotiate agreement to a political union plan proposed by President de Gaulle. The negotiations finally failed, essentially because the Dutch and Belgian governments refused to go along, and the failure seems to have disappointed and offended De Gaulle and to have signaled the end of his positive interest in European union. Allessandro Silj suggests that the Fouchet negotiations were a direct prelude to, perhaps even the chief cause of the crises of 1963 (British entry) and 1965–1966 (French boycott).

Silj traces the course of the negotiations, suggests the fears, preoccupations and policy differences that accounted for the adamant position taken by the Dutch government and ultimately by Belgium's Paul-Henri Spaak, and gives special attention to the "British interference." He also analyzes the peculiar rigidities in the French negotiating style and the factors that seem to have determined the unwillingness of the other governments and of the "Europeans" to help bring about a rapprochement of views.

In assessing the consequences of the failure of the Fouchet negotiations, Silj argues that the "Europeans" underestimated the importance attributed by De Gaulle to his "first and only 'European' enterprise." Rebuffed, he turned away from European options and deepened his hostility toward the existing communities. Silj's position is that De Gaulle's plan could have been accepted in the same spirit as most other proposals, *i.e.* as another small step toward union short of what is desired but which "keeps things moving."

LIEBER, ROBERT J. **British Politics and European Unity: Parties, Elites, and Pressure Groups.** Berkeley: University of California Press, 1970, 317 p.

Lieber sets out to offer an explanation of why British policy-makers so conspicuously "failed to come to terms with successive European developments." He finds the explanation in the nature of "British collectivist politics" which permits interest groups a veto power in situations when the public or the parties are not actively mobilized. He provides a detailed analysis of the positions taken and influence exercised in the various phases of negotiation between 1956 and 1967 by economic interest groups. His general argument is that pressure groups have played a crucial restraining role in Britain's movement toward Europe and that "it was not until Wilson's re-application in 1966–67 that the political authority of the parties and the Prime Minister reasserted itself in the name of the general national interest and exercised responsibility for national policy."

Lieber's findings about the relative roles of interest groups and political leaders, and his effort to interpret these in the context of a theory of decision making in highly industrialized systems, are useful contributions to a literature that is still weak at the level of explaining and predicting domestic determinants of pro and anti-integration policies. In this context, Michael J. Brenner's **Technocratic Politics and the Functionalist Theory of European Integration** (Ithaca: Cornell University Press, 1969, 164 p.) should be mentioned. Brenner is also concerned with the domestic determinants of policy choice and with Britain and Europe. He seeks to explain policy formation in Britain (the application for membership) and in France (the veto) in terms of the respective roles played in each country by political and technocratic élites. The contrasts drawn between the two countries (*e.g.* in the number and influence of "technocrats") are quite interesting and well documented, as is Brenner's effort to interpret his findings in the form of a critique of the functionalist theory of integration. The main thrust of his critique is that functionalist theory is not sufficient in explaining decisions to join supranational ventures.

FRIEDRICH, CARL J., *ed*. **Politische Dimensionen der Europäischen Gemeinschafts-Bildung.** Cologne: Westdeutscher Verlag, 1968, 445 p.

Carl Friedrich introduces this collection of studies, based largely on questionnaires and interviews, as partial proof of the slow but sure formation of a genuine European community, particularly between France and Germany. Rolf-Richard Grauhan discovers a paradoxical significance in the relations between officially paired municipalities of Germany and France, in that they promote a politically relevant feeling of unity among participating populaces so long as these relations are not understood as intentional instruments for the inducement of this unity. In his unique study of the formation of a European academic community, Dusan Sidjanski finds the most frequent and effective relationships to exist between the paired universities of France and Germany. Henri Schwamm examines the progress of European business interpenetration in terms of direct investment by single firms, and of special functional agreements among several enterprises. Hans-Viktor Schiervater presents an inventory of labor movements within the Common Market.

In his examination of the roles of various non-labor economic associations, Karlheinz Neunreither finds that the influential international groupings did not originate in enchantment with integration as such but rather resulted from conclusions by national associations that integration was going to succeed, and that it was good business to participate in that success. There are essentially four elements behind participation in the EEC by these associations: economic opportunism, political reality, protection from outside competition and the existence of a new platform for ventures into the world market. Enterprises affect community policy mainly at two levels: the Council and the Commission. Neither the Economic and

Social Committee nor the Parliament is considered to be very significant. The case of agriculture is somewhat different because national associations have developed an especially intimate relationship with community organs.

ZELLENTIN, GERDA. **Budgetpolitik und Integration.** Cologne: Europa Union Verlag, Europäische Schriften des Bildungswerks Europäische Politik, 1965, 114 p.

In studying the financial conditions of the European Communities during the transitional period, Dr. Zellentin argues that the budgetary authority of the European Parliament failed to increase in proportion to the integrative destiny of the relevant treaties. In practice, the budget procedures of the EEC and Euratom went roughly as follows: the Commission submitted an overly high estimate of expenditures, which was subsequently slashed by the Council to placate demands for economy from the national legislatures. The necessary revenue was contributed by the member states on the basis of a constitutional formula. Zellentin finds that the budgetary process did not adequately reflect real policy needs, was not subject to effective supranational parliamentary control, and remained tied to an unsatisfactory revenue system which did not allow financial autonomy.

The author anticipated two potential means for self-support: first, the autonomous taxing power which the High Authority would bring into the fused executive; and second, the eventual common external tariff and certain agricultural charges. Dr. Zellentin sees the European Adjustment and Guarantee Fund for Agriculture as a new procedure tending toward financial autonomy. The European Parliament likewise noted its potential; vigorous efforts were made to achieve parliamentary control over the Fund's revenues. The debate grew particularly urgent in 1964, when it became obvious that France was profiting disproportionately from the Fund as a result of an enormous wheat surplus. Most of these demands and suggestions came to naught until the *relance* of 1970.

NEWHOUSE, JOHN. **Collision in Brussels: The Common Market Crisis of 30 June 1965.** New York: Norton, 1967, 195 p.

In June of 1965, in response to what has variously been described as an "audacious," "unwise," "illegal" proposal of the EEC Commission, the French government under De Gaulle precipitated a six-month crisis which seemed to threaten the very survival of the European Community. The central focus of the attack was the Commission, its procedures, powers, initiatives—in short, its capacity for autonomous political action.

John Newhouse, long an intimate observer of integration politics, gives the diplomatic background of the crisis, which he sees as the first fundamental test of the survival capacity of the Community, noting how the various actors perceived the stakes, the strategies that were devised, and the final denouement. The material he presents constitutes vital data for our understanding of European integration: the ways in which the Community affects the whole gamut of foreign and domestic political interests, the strengths and limitations of the Commission, the persistent strains among member governments as to conceptions of integration and as to broad foreign policy goals, and the fundamental, if often residual commitment to salvage the Community experiment among interest groups as among most governments. The author's analysis stresses "the little miracle of the Five," the cool and determined resistance of De Gaulle's partners to his attacks. He considers German and Italian leadership crucial in saving and probably expanding the Community.

BEEVER, R. COLIN. **European Unity and the Trade Union Movements.** Leyden: Sijthoff, 1960, 303 p.

This study is still the most comprehensive analysis of the role of trade unions in European integration, setting forth the reasons for their consistent support of integration (except for communist unions) and showing the impact that integration has had, and will have, on the trade-union movement and vice versa.

Beever finds that trade-union support for integration is essentially ideological;

that is, it is rooted in a general internationalism and in a belief that a more enlightened social policy, rather than immediate economic benefits, was likely to come from a supranational Europe. He points out that although European-level structures adequate for general policy coördination and representation have been created, the main emphasis of trade unions is, and is likely to remain for some time, the national level where the basic trade-union concerns of pay and working conditions are still centered. Hence, relatively little progress had been made in developing trade-union consensus on substantive issues of public policy beyond urging governments to greater activity.

Beever's analysis has stood the test of time well. Only the barest move in the direction of Community-wide collective bargaining has been made, European-level organizations remain weak, and trade unions and workers are still basically national in political orientation. This has not as yet meant a weakening of trade-union support, but one wonders if the argument—such as André Gorz's in **Strategy for Labor: A Radical Proposal** (Boston: Beacon Press, 1967, 199 p.)—that the Community's brand of welfare capitalism cannot cope with the problems of the disadvantaged because it can never produce real economic planning might not become more compelling in the future.

MEYNAUD, JEAN and SIDJANSKI, DUSAN. **L'Europe des Affaires: Rôle et Structure des Groupes.** Port Washington: Paris Publications, 1967, 247 p.

In this volume, the first of a series devoted to the socioeconomic and political groups that have been spawned by the integration process, the authors pose the following questions: What has been the response of European and non-European business firms? Has it led to "concentrations" among firms at the national level and across national boundaries? If so, what have been (or are likely to be) the consequences of these processes of concentration on the distribution of political power? Finally, what role has "Europe of the businessmen" played in promoting progress in integration? The authors are addressing a vital but ill-documented topic, but unfortunately their treatment is not systematic nor based on extensive primary research. In both these dimensions they are surpassed by the detailed and highly technical study by Jean-François Besson, **Les Groupes Industriels et l'Europe: L'Expérience de la C.E.C.A.** (Paris: Presses Universitaires, 1962, 642 p.), though he covers only the early years of the ECSC and does not place his analysis specifically in the context of integration theory.

Meynaud and Sidjanski find that "Europe of the businessman is neither as total, nor as coherent, nor as solid, as is sometimes thought." Although integration has probably accelerated the movement toward agreements and joint undertakings at the national level, this trend is less than was expected. They conclude that while business concentration has not really acted as a motor to integration, it might in the future act as a catalyst, either indirectly or directly. In this sense "the American menace is tending to become a new motor of European integration."

VAN OUDENHOVE, GUY. **The Political Parties in the European Parliament: The First Ten Years (September 1952–September 1962).** Leyden: Sijthoff, 1965, 268 p.

The development of rudimentary political parties in the Parliament of the European Community, and the extent to which these parties have increased their internal cohesiveness and their authority to control the work of the Parliament, represent one of the more interesting aspects of integration. Both phenomena are distinct departures from the typical international assembly where the national delegation remains the repository of loyalty and the center of activity, and they at least suggest movement in a federal or quasi-federal direction in which a directly elected European Parliament, organized along the lines of European political parties, would have become a meaningful participant in a European government.

Van Oudenhove's study covers the period from 1952 to 1962 and provides a good historical account of the steps by which the political party groupings in the Parliament emerged, gained political and legal recognition, extended their role in the management of activities, and sought to enter into contacts with national parties and international party groupings such as NEI (*Nouvelles Equipes Internationales*). The author also traces in detail the role played by the groups in debate and in committee and the efforts made to develop some kind of uniform, consistent and coherent European party programs.

His chief findings were that the Socialists had gone the farthest in developing a coherent program and had been most persistent in promoting integrative measures; that the Christian Democrats followed rather far behind in cohesiveness, reflecting the more diverse positions of the constituent national parties; and that the Liberals could not be associated with any consistent positions. He found also that there was no apparent trend in the direction of substantive European-level policy debates among the parties. Rather, the emphasis has been on moderation, compromise and coöperation among the groups.

BODENHEIMER, SUSANNE J. **Political Union: A Microcosm of European Politics, 1960–1966.** Leyden: Sijthoff, 1967, 229 p.

Susanne J. Bodenheimer has written a very competent analysis of intra-Six efforts to extend the scope of their collective decision making to include foreign and military policy questions. She uses the 1961–1962 Fouchet negotiations as the primary point of departure for an analysis of what she takes to be the internal and external factors that have determined, and will continue to determine, the outcome of efforts to extend integration to these fields. The major emphasis is given to the French and Dutch positions in the negotiations for political union, describing them as polar opposites which "establish the center limits of the debates within Europe and the range of the dissensus about foreign policy and defense."

The chief theoretical thrust of the book is the argument that "political union" cannot be achieved by the same strategies, or through the same institutional forms, as economic union. The author attributes to neo-functionalists (scholars and political actors alike) the faith that there is "no basic difference between economic sectors and foreign policy," that both are amenable to "spill-over," and that political union "will result from a natural evolution" from the existing economic communities. She argues that such a transition is not automatic or even likely, for neo-functionalists have overlooked basic and distinctive political dimensions and external policy constraints. She does not conclude, however, that political coöperation in the future is impossible, only that it will require different strategies and institutions.

GREAT BRITAIN

History

ELTON, G. R. **The Tudor Revolution in Government: Administrative Changes in the Reign of Henry VIII.** Cambridge: University Press, 1953, 465 p.

Elton's thesis is admirably clear: under Henry VIII English administration changed rapidly from the medieval, personal type of government through the household to a modern bureaucracy. England ceased to be the monarch's private estate; it became a nation-state. The beginning of this transformation can be pinpointed quite sharply to 1529, its instigation to Thomas Cromwell. Through his tireless, detailed supervision of administration, English central government became more remote from the person and household of the king, the duties of secretariats and courts became more precisely defined, their development more autonomous. Such changes were necessary not only to cope with the expanded business which resulted from the Reformation and the dissolution of the monasteries, but also to support Cromwell's concept of national sovereignty.

Much of Elton's work remains valuable. He revived interest in institutional history, previously a neglected field, and told us much that we did not know about the reign of Henry VIII. He provided a generally accepted correction of the earlier view of Cromwell as the sinister mastermind behind all the changes that took place in England between 1529 and 1536. However, he presses his thesis too far and leaves open a number of questions. If, as he suggests, Elizabeth bequeathed a country run by an efficient bureaucracy, why did the Queen herself have to rely so much upon the coöperation of private individuals and the greed of public servants to make the system work? Why was the reformed financial machinery so inadequate before and after 1603? Why was the administration of early Stuart England so markedly out of date in a country where every other aspect of life was becoming increasingly modern?

MacCaffrey, Wallace. **The Shaping of the Elizabethan Regime**. Princeton: Princeton University Press, 1968, 501 p.

The events of the reign of Elizabeth I may seem so well known as to need no retelling. But Wallace MacCaffrey persuasively justifies this detailed narrative of the first 13 years of the Queen's reign. As he sees it, these years were both an ending and a beginning. They saw the end of a 40-year period of disturbance in English life which had begun with the Reformation, a movement which had gone beyond what even the authoritarian Henry VIII could control, and which had been deepened by the coincidental succession first of a sickly child and then of a Catholic woman. Welcomed though the accession of Elizabeth was, the fears of contemporaries that a woman could not restore stability were not fully allayed until 1572, by which time the régime had survived both internal and external crises.

Equally the years 1559 to 1572 were a beginning. It became clear then that, despite the rule of a strong, popular monarch, the character of English political life had changed. What had happened since the break with Rome had shattered the medieval, paternalistic world order. Although Elizabeth might cling to the traditional view of herself as the sole head of the body politic, there now existed an articulate, irrepressible public opinion, not prepared to remain silent on key issues such as the succession, religion and foreign policy. The initiative had begun to shift away from the monarchy.

Hill, Christopher. **Puritanism and Revolution: Studies in Interpretation of the English Revolution of the Seventeenth Century.** London: Secker and Warburg, 1958, 402 p.

Christopher Hill's works on the English Revolution have been among the more controversial in a controversial field. But even Hill's strongest critics cannot ignore books such as his **Puritanism and Revolution,** nor deny the extraordinary breadth of his approach to understanding the Civil War.

This collection of essays, written over an 18-year period, reflects both the changing historiography of the seventeenth century and Hill's own move away from the orthodox Marxist interpretation of his early **The English Revolution 1640** (London: Lawrence, 1940, 136 p.). The essays are organized into two groups, the first primarily concerned with movements, the second with the ideas of a range of individuals—from puritan divines to cranks, from contemporary historians and political theorists to poets and novelists. A connecting thread throughout is the rise of "bourgeois" ideas on government, social justice, religion and property. Above all, Hill shows the centrality of property, which helped to keep England Protestant, lest the spoils of the monastic lands be lost. The sanctity of property was part of the Anglo-Saxon inheritance which Englishmen under the Norman yoke must struggle to preserve. Property to Thomas Hobbes and many others was the cause and justification of the state. Property was the issue which caused the English Revolution to turn conservative, which by the late 1650s united men who had been enemies ten years before, and which made them return to monarchy if that were the way to protect "law and order and property."

STONE, LAWRENCE. **The Crisis of the Aristocracy, 1558–1641.** Oxford: Clarendon Press, 1965, 841 p.

This volume must be understood in the context of the centuries-old debate over the causes and significance of the English Civil War of the seventeenth century, and more particularly of the famous debate between Professors Tawney and Trevor-Roper on the changing status of the early Stuart gentry. Stone has raised this entire set of problems to a new level of conceptualization and significance. The most important work in early Stuart history had hitherto centered on the proceedings of Parliament, ecclesiastical reform and puritanism and the machinery of government. Tawney and others in the Fabian or Marxist tradition had also given much attention to the significance of social change; but their research, however important, was conceptually deficient and their conclusions poorly integrated into a larger explanation of the turbulence and transformation of early modern English society. Stone's most lasting and important contribution will be in pointing the way toward an integrated explanation, in seeing social change as a fundamental—perhaps the fundamental—variable in the process of societal change, and in explicitly subordinating seventeenth-century turbulence to the larger problem of modernization. It now seems likely that the most important work in Stuart and Hanoverian history during the next decades will concern the changing structures and functional relations within all classes of British society and the contributions which such changes were making to every aspect of national life.

NAMIER, SIR LEWIS. **The Structure of Politics at the Accession of George III.** New York: Macmillan, 2d ed., 1957, 514 p.

More than 40 years after its first edition, this book is still exercising a pervasive methodological influence on all work in its field and on much outside it. Namier's principal contribution was to shift attention decisively away from an almost exclusive concern with the color of national political life as it centered in Westminster and strongly deëmphasize the role of ideology as a motivational factor in mid-eighteenth-century politics. Namier preferred to trust not what men said but what they did. But while he excelled at delineating political intrigue and negotiation, as in his **England in the Age of the American Revolution** (New York: St. Martin's Press, 2d ed., 1961, 450 p.), and was a pioneer in the application of psychology and psychoanalysis to history, as in Namier and John Brooke, **Charles Townshend** (New York: St. Martin's Press, 1964, 198 p.), he principally emphasized that political power at the national level was unintelligible unless one first understood the roots of that power as it was generated in the constituencies. This first work, **The Structure of Politics,** was thus a synchronic "structural analysis" of British constituency politics and elections. It established a method of approach to political analysis which will last for decades to come.

THOMPSON, EDWARD P. **The Making of the English Working Class.** New York: Vintage, 1966, 848 p.

This book, probably the most important work on its subject since the classic works of the Hammonds and Webbs, is a distinguished piece of Marxist historiography, profoundly polemical, engaging and lively, immensely learned and solid. The work falls into three sections, the first and last of which provide the fullest and most reliable account to date of English working-class radical movements and ideology during the later eighteenth and early nineteenth centuries. It is the middle section, however, which is the most imaginative and suggestive, and which will prove influential for years to come. Thompson sees class not "as a 'structure,' nor even as a 'category,' but as something which in fact happens (and can be shown to have happened) in human relationships. . . . it evades analysis if we attempt to stop it dead at any given moment and anatomise its structure." In his central chapters, then, Thompson tries to evoke the working-class world, to reconstitute its conditions of life. He sees the working class as having systematically related psychological perspectives and values which are discontinuous from those of members of higher social strata. In his most experimental chapters he subjects the symbolism of working-class religious literature to Freudian analysis. It is fair to say that the book has settled few questions; but along with the recent work of Rude and Hobsbawm it has effectively raised and reopened questions of the first magnitude, which will be the subject of much research in a field which has been neglected and quiescent for too long a time.

Political Questions

BEER, SAMUEL H. **Modern British Politics: A Study of Parties and Pressure Groups.** London: Faber, 1965, 390 p.

This is probably the most important single book on modern British politics, although its scope is narrower than that of Richard Rose's **Politics in England** (Boston: Little, Brown, 1964, 266 p.). Beer does not have a clearly delineated analytic framework, nor is he concerned to argue a single thesis. Instead he treats, in a fairly discursive way, three main themes. First, he maintains (as opposed to R. T. McKenzie) that the democratic foundations of the Labor Party's constitution have not been completely eroded, and that, especially in opposition, Labor leaders can neither flout the party's democratic norms and rules of procedure nor always be certain of getting their way. Second, he asserts that, although the policies of the Conservative and Labor parties resemble each other more now than they did a generation ago, the clash of ideas and ideologies remains important in British politics, both within the parties and between them. Third, he deals with the rise of what he calls "the new group politics" in Britain. With the expansion of the state's functions, governments are forced to rely heavily on the knowledge, the advice and even the active coöperation of organized interests. It was once believed that strong parties meant weak pressure groups. Beer insists that, given the close electoral balance in Britain and also the acceptance by both major parties of the welfare state and the managed economy, Britain's pressure groups are probably even more powerful than America's.

Reread today, **Modern British Politics** has a slightly period flavor. The ideological differences between the two parties were even more unreal by 1970; however, "the new group politics" continued to flourish. The identification and description of this quasi-corporatist form of government remains Beer's greatest contribution.

BUTLER, DAVID and STOKES, DONALD. **Political Change in Britain.** New York: St. Martin's Press, 1969, 516 p.

Political Change in Britain is a recently constructed landmark of prime significance in the study of British politics. When used in conjunction with the British data in Gabriel A. Almond and Sidney Verba's **The Civic Culture** (Boston: Little, Brown, 1965, 379 p.), the Butler and Stokes study provides us with a topography of political and social opinion perhaps unequaled in any Western country.

The dominant theme of the book, which is based upon three extensive interview surveys conducted in 1963, 1964 and 1966, is an attempt to delineate the various factors involved in shifts in the electorate in political beliefs, party alignment and electoral choice in both a long-term and a short-term sense. Some of the general findings—for example, the limited ideological development of the electorate—will come as no surprise to the student of British politics. However, other findings are rather more provocative and original. The authors challenge the idea of the deferential Conservative worker as depicted by Nordlinger; they consider Conservative voting in the working class to be generational rather than deferential in the sense that older workers are the Conservative voters and they were politically socialized during a time when the Labor Party was not a fully accepted political force in the country. Perhaps the most striking dimension of the data is the repeated emphasis upon fluidity in the electorate.

The book has its faults. According to the authors, practically all of the demographic changes point to an extended period of Labor Party dominance—an assertion that may bear reconsideration in the light of the Conservative victory in 1970. Finally, little effort was made to integrate the findings into a coherent pattern after the exhaustive and very able presentation of the data.

BLONDEL, JEAN. **Voters, Parties, and Leaders: The Social Fabric of British Politics.** Harmondsworth: Penguin Books, rev. ed., 1969, 271 p.

This book has been revised and reprinted frequently since it first appeared in 1963. Its structure, however, remains the same. Blondel's chief concern is to provide social and political profiles of the main sectors of British politics—voters, political parties, politicians, interest groups, the bureaucracy. His method is to synthesize the available evidence and to provide a running commentary on it. His descriptions are not purely demographic; he deals with attitudes and opinions and with such matters as the sources of working-class Conservatism and the career patterns of members of Parliament and ministers. Little in the book has been overtaken by new research, although the chapter on the electorate wants substantial revision in the light of Butler and Stokes, **Political Change in Britain.** In so far as Blondel has a theme, it has to do with the quality and intimacy of the relationship between governors and governed in Britain. He asks whether the country is governed by a power élite, a ruling class or an establishment and concludes that an establishment exists but that it is not the only—or even necessarily a major—repository of political power.

MCKENZIE, ROBERT TRELFORD. **British Political Parties: The Distribution of Power within the Conservative and Labour Parties.** London: Heinemann, 2d rev. ed., 1963, 694 p.

Fifteen years after its first appearance, McKenzie's study remains the major work in the field. Its thesis is simple. The Labor Party's institutional arrangements are intended to produce intra-party democracy, and there was a time (so McKenzie claims) when many observers believed that they had succeeded in doing so. Conversely, the Conservative Party's institutions provide for the dominance of the leader, and there was a time (so it is said) when many observers believed that the leader was indeed all-powerful. McKenzie argues that Labor's parliamentary leaders are in fact much more powerful than was once imagined and that Conservative leaders are much more dependent on the good will of their followers than was once supposed. He concludes that the distribution of power within the two parties is in fact very similar.

Events since 1955 (discussed in subsequent editions) have tended to bear out McKenzie's central thesis. The main weaknesses of McKenzie's analysis are its imprecision and its failure to take account of differences in the distribution of power that may arise, not as between the Labor and Conservative Parties as such, but as between the governing party (whichever it is) and the Opposition. As a description of the power structure of Britain's two major parties, McKenzie has dated very little. As an essay in analytic political science, it has dated noticeably.

MUIR, RAMSAY. **How Britain Is Governed.** London: Constable, 3rd rev. ed., 1933, 335 p.

Ramsay Muir first published **How Britain Is Governed** in 1930, in the wake of Lord Hewart's **The New Despotism** (New York: Cosmopolitan, 1929, 311 p.). Along with Hewart he complained of the untrammeled growth of the executive in British government at the expense of the Parliament, which, he alleged, had been "reduced to a mere intermediary like the Electoral College in America." He also complained of a "cabinet dictatorship" due to "the two party system" which, with its rigid party discipline, enabled any Cabinet with a clear majority "to wield all the powers of the House of Commons—as well as the powers of the Royal Prerogative." And he warned of organized interests, not recognized by the constitution, bringing direct pressure to bear upon, or even control over, the government. He concluded that representative government in Britain was on trial.

Muir prescribed cures for the ills he described, seeking first the introduction of proportional representation. He also saw scope for increasing the range and the functions of parliamentary committees—"such as they have in America and in France, concerned with each of the main departments." And he advocated the "devolution" of the powers of British government into seven provinces (including London), each capable of being administered from a convenient center, endowed with a subordinate legislature and with a group of departments of its own.

Muir's book was an early contribution to what was to become, in subsequent decades, a steady stream of literature pressing for the reform of the British Parliament. The literature (including Muir's work) has not been without its effect, but in most instances the changes have been so delayed that they can only be tenuously related to the literature which advocated them.

JENNINGS, SIR WILLIAM IVOR. **Cabinet Government.** Cambridge: University Press, 2d ed., 1959, 586 p.

This is perhaps the most widely used and firmly established text on the workings of British central government. Sir Ivor established his reputation in his **The Law and the Constitution** (London: University of London Press, 5th ed., 1959, 354 p.), in which he criticized the underestimation of political factors displayed by previous legally-oriented students of the British constitution. This work, together with **Parliament** (New York: Cambridge University Press, 2d ed., 1957, 573 p.) and **Party Politics** (New York: Cambridge University Press, 1960–1962, 3 v.), represents Sir Ivor's determination to extend his previous legal commentaries to the basic political structure of Britain. The departure from the legal approach, partly because of its subject matter, is less evident in **Cabinet Government** than in the other volumes.

The work begins with a restatement of Sir Ivor's opposition to legalism, but the classic chapters on the choice of Prime Minister, the formation of governments, the office of Prime Minister and the position of the Monarchy bear clear traces of the legal mind. The precedents are noted, constitutional debates are rigorously dissected, and the idea of government according to clear constitutional rules is firmly held. The remaining chapters are more overtly concerned with political factors. The basic theme of the work is the extent to which all the central institutions of British government work in accordance with the principles of democracy and popular sovereignty despite their formal appearances and links with a pre-democratic age. This work, and its associated volumes, are excellent examples of the character of British political science: eschewing an overly legal approach but determined to give history and structure an important place.

CARTER, BYRUM EARL. **The Office of Prime Minister.** Princeton: Princeton University Press, 1956, 362 p.

This book represents an attempt by an American scholar to analyze for the first time in any coherent fashion the real position of the British Prime Minister. The organization of the book is colored by the author's secondary intention of indicating the nature of prime ministerial rule by comparisons with the office of American President. A brief and somewhat superficial history of the prime ministership is followed by chapters analyzing the role of the Prime Minister from the standpoint of different particular functions or powers. The analysis proceeds through relations with the Monarch, public, party, Cabinet and Parliament to a consideration of the Prime Minister's role in the conduct of war and foreign affairs. The author concludes that the Prime Minister is no longer *primus inter pares,* and that the unique status of the office is to be explained mainly in terms of the Prime Minister's control of a highly disciplined party, his importance as an electoral symbol and the need for leadership consequent upon the great expansion of the functions of the modern British state. The book resembles the later work by John P. Mackintosh, **The British Cabinet,** in its structure and conclusions, although Mackintosh's book is both historically more detailed and reliable and more exhaustive and sophisticated in its analysis of prime ministerial functions. None the less, Professor Carter's book is scholarly and readable, and is of great interest and significance as the first coherent study of an institution which has been a focal point of British interest in recent years.

MACKINTOSH, JOHN P. **The British Cabinet.** London: Methuen, 2d ed., 1968, 657 p.

   This book represents the culmination of British interest in the role of the Prime Minister. In the course of his thesis that the office of British Prime Minister since 1914 has become the focal point of political power, Professor Mackintosh examines the relative roles of all other political institutions. The first parts contain an account of the historical development of the Cabinet from 1660 to 1914, and its place in the constitution as a whole. Based upon enormous and careful research, this historical section is not merely the best available account of the rise of the Cabinet but also the best general introduction to the history of British political institutions since 1660. The following parts proceed in an analytical rather than chronological form, and it is in this section that the thesis about the role of the Prime Minister is developed. Professor Mackintosh is aware that evidence is scarcer about contemporary politics than about the period before 1914, and his conclusion that the prime ministership is an institutionalized office, with powers and responsibilities independent of its holder's personality, is carefully qualified. He describes the government of Britain as not in any way a personal domination by the Prime Minister but rather as a pyramid, with the Prime Minister at the head and a complicated and heterogeneous universe of the Cabinet, Cabinet committees, ministers and civil servants beneath. In this second and revised edition, Professor Mackintosh takes issue with those of his critics who have rejected what they regard as his exaggeration of prime ministerial power.

MORRISON, HERBERT STANLEY. **Government and Parliament: A Survey from the Inside.** New York: Oxford University Press, 2d ed., 1959, 386 p.

   This work represents the reflections in retirement of a British Labor leader on the political institutions in which he worked. It is a work of justification in the sense that Lord Morrison reflects that aspect of the British socialist tradition which has always adhered firmly to the methods of parliamentary government, and which attaches great importance to a genuine understanding of how such a system works. The book covers the operation of the Cabinet and its committees, ministers and their civil servants, the Monarchy, the party system, Parliament, the nationalized industries and economic planning. The illustrations used to support the author's general defense of the British political system are taken, in the main, from his experiences as second-in-command during the Labor government of 1945–1951. The chapter on nationalization is of particular interest, since Lord Morrison was, from the late 1920s onward, one of the major architects of Labor's public ownership program and the most articulate exponent of the public corporation as the best form of organization for state industries. In a sense the book's subtitle is misleading. The author uses some examples from his own experience, but on the whole the book resembles a rather orthodox textbook. A little more "autobiographical" material would have enabled the book to convey more of the feel of politics "from the inside." Nevertheless, it can be strongly recommended as a guide to moderate views about the character of British politics, especially in the postwar years.

RANNEY, AUSTIN. **Pathways to Parliament: Candidate Selection in Britain.** Madison: University of Wisconsin Press, 1965, 298 p.

   Ranney writes primarily as a student of political parties, not of political recruitment. He is not concerned to distinguish between the bulk of the British population and the politically active minority, nor between the active minority and the even smaller group that seeks parliamentary candidatures. Rather, his main purpose is to examine the belief—widely held until recently—that the central party headquarters dominate the selection of candidates and that this dominance helps explain the British parties' cohesion and strong leadership. Ranney demonstrates that this belief is largely false. Constituency parties have the formal right to select candidates, and they guard this right jealously. The party headquarters, moreover, use their formal power of veto cautiously and seldom. The author concludes that, in so far as candidate selection contributes to party cohesion in Britain, it does so not via central control but because the local parties think in national terms and see it as their function to select candidates who will be loyal to the national party's policies and leadership. In addition, Ranney provides a body of more general data on the factors affecting the local parties' choice of candidates, and on the social and political backgrounds of Conservative, Labor and Liberal candidates. Michael Rush in **The Selection of Parliamentary Candidates** (London: Nelson, 1969, 307 p.) adds substantially to Ranney's data but disputes none of his major conclusions.

FINER, SAMUEL EDWARD and OTHERS. **Backbench Opinion in the House of Commons, 1955–1959.** New York: Pergamon Press, 1961, 219 p.

Backbench Opinion was the first attempt by political scientists to consider systematically the attitudinal topography of the political parties in the House of Commons, in the context of the 1955–1959 Parliament. The technique was the cross-tabulation of the signatures on Early Day Motions—petitions sponsored and signed by backbench MPs requesting debates on particular subjects. Although the request is not in fact serious, the motions themselves, according to the authors, amount to "spontaneous, un-whipped backbench manifestoes." The purpose of the study was to discover backbench opinion groupings and to relate certain background variables to opinions. The most striking result concerns the differences in the patterns between the Labor and Conservative Parties. In the Labor Party, opinion groupings are much more clearly defined, and a stronger relationship appears to exist between the background of an MP and his political opinions. The Conservatives, on the other hand, would seem to reshuffle themselves kaleidoscopically from issue to issue with fewer clearly defined attitudinal blocs.

Backbench Opinion received rather mixed notices upon publication. Nevertheless, the book is an accurate reflection of reality, although at times this may result more from the obvious political knowledge of the authors than from the data.

POTTER, ALLEN MEYERS. **Organized Groups in British National Politics.** London: Faber, 1961, 395 p.

This volume is less a monograph than an encyclopedia. As such it provides the most exhaustive single compilation available of evidence about British interest groups: their variety, their internal politics, their sources of finance, their relations with government, Parliament and the public. The book is based on prodigious research and, a decade after its first publication, remarkably little of it is out of date. What it lacks is an analytic framework. Fact is piled upon fact, and it is largely left to the reader to make sense of it all. The author, although an American, does not introduce a comparative perspective. A better introduction for the nonspecialist is probably Samuel Edward Finer, **Anonymous Empire** (London: Pall Mall Press, 2d rev. and enl. ed., 1966, 173 p.). Approaches to a theory of interest group politics in Britain can be found in Beer's **Modern British Politics** and also in Harry Eckstein, **Pressure Group Politics: The Case of the British Medical Association** (London: Allen and Unwin, 1960, 168 p.). Eckstein argues, among other things, that by observing the activities of interest groups in any political system the outsider is enabled to identify the system's critical decision-points. All of the writers on British interest groups agree that for most groups most of the time, the access they desire is to the government of the day and the civil servant and not to either Parliament or the general public.

BEALEY, FRANK; BLONDEL, J. and MCCANN, W. P. **Constituency Politics: A Study of Newcastle-under-Lyme.** London: Faber, 1965, 440 p.

In Britain, as in most other countries, less is known about the rank and file of political activists than about either the mass electorate or the political élite. This survey of politics in a Midlands industrial constituency deals with voting behavior, party organization and local politics. Its chief interest, however, lies in its findings about the memberships of the three main parties. Of the total Newcastle electorate, 3 percent belonged to a party; of this 3 percent, rather less than half were active. The Conservative members' opinions, contrary to widespread belief, were more moderate than the opinions of Conservative voters in the country as a whole. There was no clearly identifiable Conservative right wing. Opinion on the Labor side was somewhat more doctrinaire than among the national leadership, but, although Newcastle had a left-wing MP, few local party members exhibited a syndrome of left-wing attitudes. Unfortunately, although the data is suggestive, it is narrowly time-bound (it was gathered in 1960–1961 and relates closely to the controversies of that time), and it is not informed by any theory either of the causes and consequences of political activism or of the relationship between local politics and national. Almost all of the later work, however, suffers from the same limitations, and this book remains the most comprehensive single study.

BUTLER, D. E. and KING, ANTHONY. **The British General Election of 1966.** London: Macmillan, 1966, 338 p.

　　The British General Election of 1966 is the seventh in the series of the Nuffield College election studies. Like its predecessors, it provides much valuable information concerning the British political system and manages to present the general flavor of the campaign. It includes details of electioneering at both the national and local levels and outlines the major relevant events since the 1964 election. An excellent chapter on television and radio presents some of the problems associated with the trend away from the simple reporting of political events toward a mixture of news, analysis and discussion. A chapter on the press concludes that there is a great deal of evidence to suggest that editorial advocacy and scare techniques have no effect on the election result; however, it does say that the press has an important indirect influence by helping decide that which is actually communicated to the public and also in determining the issues of the campaign. The growing significance of opinion polling is outlined and discussed. The performance of the parties and their leaders in the campaign is the unifying theme; what emerges is the increasing "presidentialization" of the campaign.

　　Critics of previous books in the series have argued that one learns much of what happened and little concerning why it happened and that the basic questions are asked but not answered. Apparently in response to these criticisms, Butler and King note that "for the moment" only tentative conclusions are possible and that "detailed explanations" can only be obtained by extensive survey research. However, it would be unwise for any of us to expect too much; the authors themselves point out in their conclusion that an attitude or explanation as expressed to a poll taker may be no more than a "neat rationalization for some other, more diffuse sentiment."

MACKENZIE, W. J. M. and GROVE, J. W. **Central Administration in Britain.** London: Longmans, Green, 1957, 487 p.

　　In 1954 the British Civil Service celebrated the centenary of the famous Trevelyan-Northcote Report which laid down principles for the conduct of "the Permanent Civil Service of the country." Soon afterward, Professors Mackenzie and Grove published this book, in which they saw the British government as "a universe" comprising a number of worlds—"relatively independent—but linked to one another by constitutional theory and the practical needs of business," and explained the various organs of administration subordinate to them. Theirs is the first comprehensive survey of British government to be presented in this unified way.

　　In surveying the growth of the British Civil Service in modern times, the book stresses how, in spite of its numerical size, the Civil Service owes its existence not to statute but to the prerogative powers of the Crown; and that there is practically no "juridical interpretation" to direct it. It sums up the legal position of the Civil

Service in three propositions: its internal organization is not regulated by Parliament; it derives its legal unity from the unity of the Crown; and while the Crown has important privileges in law, its servants have not—the legal status of Civil Servants is inferior rather than superior to that of the ordinary citizen.

Throughout the book's 24 chapters, the "fusion of powers" in British government is made very clear. A useful bibliography follows each chapter.

Foreign Policy

TAYLOR, A. J. P. **English History 1914–1945.** New York: Oxford University Press, 1965, 708 p.

This volume is the fifteenth in the series, "The Oxford History of England," launched 30 years ago. To some extent the manner of the Oxford history—detailed, comprehensive, austere—has imposed itself upon Taylor's ebullient, irreverent style. This is especially evident in the first ten chapters dealing with the 1914–1931 period, when first the military and political history of the First World War and then domestic affairs in the 1920s are recounted in a detailed, though racy, manner. The author's treatment of British economic problems of the times has been criticized by specialists, but the main outline is accurate enough. The book gathers pace and interest in the chapters on the 1930s and the Second World War when foreign affairs dominated the scene. As Taylor writes, bipartisanship characterized British foreign policy during the quiescent 1920s. By 1934, however, "the parties divided deeply and bitterly over foreign affairs, as much as at any time in English history, and perhaps more so." It is curious that Taylor, noted for his view, expressed in **The Origins of the Second World War,** that the war was as much the result of blunders as of conscious intention, should write in this book that "both Hitler and Mussolini fixed on 1943 for the outbreak of the next great war." But the same Taylorian philosophy that politics are conducted haphazardly as much as by design permeates the present work. **English History** is especially valuable for its sparkling vignettes of politicians and party attitudes, its captivating footnotes and superb bibliography.

MEDLICOTT, WILLIAM NEWTON. **British Foreign Policy since Versailles, 1919–1963.** London: Methuen, 2d ed., 1968, 362 p.

This book is a revised and enlarged version of Medlicott's short survey of British foreign policy between the two world wars published in 1940. The postwar section, carrying the story up to the first British application to join the European Common Market, is highly compressed, filling only 56 pages, though dealing clearly with the main outline of developments. The book is straightforward, traditional diplomatic history; but it is at all times lucid, urbane and compassionate. The central theme is the vulnerability of Britain's worldwide international commitments and interests in the inter-war period, challenged first by Japan, then by the European dictators. This vulnerability and the impossibility of effective military action in more than one sphere at the same time were, according to Medlicott, the chief concerns of British governments in the 1930s, as evidence that has come to light since the first edition of this book has revealed. Hence Medlicott's distaste for the word "appeasement" to describe British policy in the 1930s, with its now pejorative overtones. The British stake in worldwide stability was too great for Britain to defend alone, with uncertain French assistance. Her efforts on behalf of coexistence between the superpowers which dominated the world since 1945 later blinded her to the new prospects opened up by West European integration until it was almost too late.

WOODWARD, SIR ERNEST LLEWELLYN. **British Foreign Policy in the Second World War.** London: H.M.S.O., 1962, 592 p.

This volume in the official British histories of the Second World War is an abridgment of a larger work written for official reference. The author was given access to all the Foreign Office archives, and hence it will be impossible for the ordinary academic to test Woodward's interpretations until the state papers become publicly available. But the tone of this book is balanced and cautious, and it is likely to stand the test of time. Naturally, the Foreign Office in wartime Britain has always been subordinated to the conduct of military operations and heads-of-government meetings, but in the Second World War, in contrast to the First, relations between Prime Minister Churchill and the Office as headed by Anthony Eden were peculiarly close. The interesting thing, however, is to note how Foreign Office views differed from Churchill's, with his immediate concern to win the war, and how often the Office's views proved right. Woodward shows, for example, how the Office was more realistic even than Churchill in recognizing De Gaulle as the true leader of French resistance, hard as he was to deal with; how the Office pressed on Churchill the importance of accepting Soviet territorial gains in Eastern Europe; how it suspected American plans for Germany's "pastoralization" lest they create a vacuum in the heart of Europe. Above all, the introduction, dealing with twentieth-century changes in the role of the Foreign Office in making British policy, would be hard to excel as a source for students.

WOODHOUSE, CHRISTOPHER MONTAGUE. **British Foreign Policy since the Second World War.** New York: Praeger, 1962, 255 p.

Among studies of British foreign policy after the Second World War, C. M. Woodhouse's book is notable for its comprehensiveness of scope and its conservative assumption that, even with its postwar economic problems, Britain could still remain, if not a power of the first rank, at least one with global interests. Woodhouse prefers the Commonwealth to Europe as the "vehicle on which Britain might rise to the new order of magnitude . . . which the USA and the USSR had established" and considers worldwide organizations such as the United Nations "expensive and time-consuming" ways of approaching specialized problems. His method is first to survey the course of international affairs from 1945 to 1959 with the emphasis rather on orthodox Western interpretations of the cold war and then to review "the British reaction" under the headings of defense policies, relations with allies, the national economy, relations with the United States, decolonization and the problems of dealing with the resulting small states and new nations in the extra-European world, the United Nations and British party politics. The third part, focusing on united Europe, the Commonwealth, the Atlantic community and the concept of interdependence, ends with the optimistic thought that the "volcano" of world affairs was, in 1959, cooling down and hence that no fundamental change in Britain's international position was called for. The book stops short of the 1960s, when Britain's world role had to be limited, but it is a characteristic exposition of those who clung to that role for so long.

Economic and Social Questions

CAVES, RICHARD E. and ASSOCIATES. **Britain's Economic Prospects.** Washington: Brookings Institution, 1968, 510 p.

This book, written by a group of American and Canadian economists and edited by the Harvard economist Richard E. Caves, has the merit of true academic detachment, being relatively free of the ideological undertones that often punctuate the writings of economists.

The approach of the authors is avowedly empirical, not theoretical. A vast storehouse of the most relevant and useful economic data on the British economy is assembled in 89 tables and eight figures, in many cases spanning a 15-year time period up to 1966. The chapters are grouped under three headings: Managing Aggregate Demand, International Trade and Payments, and Growth and Efficiency. While there is some inevitable unevenness in the quality of the chapters, it is more than compensated for by the common characteristic of excellent surveys of the literature, pinpointing the main problems and controversies about the British economy, presenting the main arguments and counterarguments, and the relevant data.

While there is complete consistency between the contributions of the different authors, there is not as much cross-referencing and coördination as might be desired. This is substantially compensated for by an introduction containing the main analytical conclusions of the authors and an epilogue setting out their policy recommendations. Altogether, this volume seems destined to be a principal reference manual on the British economy for the next five, possibly ten years. No serious student of the British economy can afford to be without it.

WORSWICK, G. D. N. and ADY, P. H., *eds*. **The British Economy in the Nineteen-Fifties.** New York: Oxford University Press, 1963, 564 p.

This volume of essays by 13 U. K. economists deals with the performance of various sectors of the British economy during the first decade following the postwar reconstruction and critically examines the role of public policy in this performance. The first and longest essay provides a useful summary and chronological discussion of the major economic issues and related policy measures. Six essays on various aspects of Britain's international trade and payments position of this period then examine in turn the major features of commercial policy, the evidence of slow growth in exports and the reasons for more rapid expansion of imports.

The third part analyzes various forms of public economic policy—fiscal, monetary, regulatory and public enterprise. An excellent essay on fiscal policy evaluates its adequacy in the face of the multiple objectives confronting the government—full employment and price stability, growth, balance of international payments, equitable income distribution—and concludes that fiscal instruments were not sufficiently or properly utilized. The erratic growth record is largely ascribed to the stop-go effects of public policy on investment.

The last section presents in more detail the performance of and trends in the consumer, capital and labor markets and the relationship of government to these markets. There is a useful annotated bibliography.

Dow, J. C. R. **The Management of the British Economy, 1945–60.** New York: Cambridge University Press, 1964, 443 p.

This book evaluates British fiscal and monetary policy as applied over the 15 years following World War II. In making this assessment the author not only describes the major economic events and issues which confronted the policy-makers and generated their responses but also delves into the underlying determinants of British economic behavior. For the latter purpose, considerable attention is given to the findings of recent research in this field.

The work begins with a historical narrative of economic policy as formulated first by Labor governments up to 1951 and by Conservative governments thereafter together with the economic setting to which such policy responded. Attention is given to both the political philosophy and the economic ideas which shaped the course of policy measures during the two phases of this period. The major policy instruments as they were employed for stabilization purposes are then analyzed in some detail, including an evaluation of forecasting methods.

The third part covers the general behavior of the economy and in particular the major determinants of aggregate demand in the private sector. A chapter is devoted to the monetary influences (money supply, interest rates, credit availability). Dow is in general rather skeptical of credit restraint as a short-term stabilization device. A further chapter covers empirical studies of demand and cost-push inflation in Britain, the author taking the view that a steadier and lower growth of demand would have produced a better productivity, price and output growth record.

In a summing-up, British economic policy is criticized for having increased rather than subdued fluctuations in the growth of aggregate demand. The author suggests that additional policy instruments are needed to improve growth performance—particularly that of productivity—and to restrain cost-push inflation under high employment conditions.

BECKERMAN, W. and ASSOCIATES. **The British Economy in 1975.** New York: Cambridge University Press, 1965, 631 p.

The main purpose of this study is to analyze the long-term growth prospects of the British economy. It does so by assembling and discussing the evidence on economic trends and resources as seen from the vantage of the early 1960s, by putting the British postwar record into the perspective of other comparable countries' experience and by quantifying the conclusions in terms of a forecast of the size and structure of the national product in 1975. Its value to students lies not in the numerical details of the forecast but in the systematic way it synthesizes recent research on British economic opportunities and problems.

Beckerman brought to the project a personal fund of experience on European postwar growth gained at the OECD national accounts unit. His associates were a team of experienced researchers at the National Institute of Economic and Social Research, and they drew imaginatively on a considerable volume of past and continuing research on short and long-term British economic growth at the Institute, the University of Cambridge Department of Applied Economics and other academic and governmental centers. The result is an authoritative and thoroughly documented study of the British postwar economy which tests a number of familiar hypotheses for its poor growth record and is supported by detailed statistical analyses of recent and prospective trends in the main components of national output and expenditure and in the nation's basic economic resources and needs.

GUTTSMAN, W. L. **The British Political Elite.** London: MacGibbon and Kee, 1963, 398 p.

The literature of British political science contains relatively few examples of the application of sociological approaches to political life. This book is one of the best examples of the genre, and takes the form of a historical and analytical study of the social composition of the British Cabinet, Parliament and parties since the 1830s. Guttsman shows the process by which the monopoly of political offices by the landed interests gave way to a middle-class élite as a result of the advent of democracy. He traces the connections between social status and political attitudes among members of this group and investigates the relationships between the political élite and other élites such as those in business. He concludes that although the rise of the Labor Party has made the social composition of the élite more representative of society as a whole than ever before, there is none the less no real equality of opportunity to enter the élite. He regards this degree of autonomy among the élite as dangerous, in that it makes communication between rulers and ruled difficult, and deprives the political leadership of the services of groups and individuals whose skills and attitudes are of increasing importance in the modern technological age. The historical evidence is marshalled in a scholarly way, but Guttsman devotes relatively little space to two factors which are central to his argument: the relationship between social class and political attitude, and the qualities appropriate to modern politicians.

NORDLINGER, ERIC A. **The Working-Class Tories.** Berkeley: University of California Press, 1967, 276 p.

One of the most distinctive legacies bequeathed to the modern social sciences by traditional Western political philosophy is the assumption that social classes do or at least should behave as united blocs in the political arena. As a result, when a section of a social class demonstrates insufficient solidarity, it becomes an anomaly and thus a subject worthy of inquiry. The section of the British working class that votes Conservative is a major anomaly in Western electoral behavior. In Britain approximately a third of the working class votes Conservative, providing half of the total Conservative vote. Without their numbers, the British Conservative Party would long ago have been relegated to a position of political impotence. However, on the basis of this increment of working-class votes, the Tories have operated as the normally governing party in Britain in the last 40 years.

According to Nordlinger's data the Conservative working class in Britain appears to be divided into two distinctive groupings. Conservative "deferentials," about a quarter of the total, are workers who genuinely accept and support a hierarchical society and who identify strongly with national symbols and traditions. All things equal, the cloth-cap-in-hand Conservatives honestly prefer to be governed by persons drawn from the traditional British élite. A second group—"pragmatists," according to Nordlinger—displays fewer deferential characteristics. Their support for the Tories is primarily based upon a belief in Conservative competence and Labor incompetence. In a general sense both groups of Conservatives do not look upon themselves as social deviants. Quite to the contrary, in many ways they are more comfortably integrated into British political culture and society as they presently exist than are their Labor bench-mates.

McKENZIE, ROBERT and SILVER, ALLAN. **Angels in Marble: Working Class Conservatives in Urban England.** Chicago: University of Chicago Press, 1968, 295 p.

McKenzie and Silver explore the same political phenomenon—the working-class Conservative vote in Britain—which also concerned Nordlinger. In some ways the conclusions of the two surveys are congruent; however, there are a number of strikingly important differences. In general, McKenzie and Silver also find the Conservative working class divided into two components—"seculars" who vote Tory on pragmatic grounds and "deferentials," whose support for the Tories is based upon what might be termed contented mysticism.

The differences between the two studies are partially related to the caveat on the subject which has been raised by Butler and Stokes, who indicate, in **Political Change in Britain,** that Conservative voting in the working class is based upon early socialization patterns found only among older workers. As such, it is a dying phenomenon. McKenzie and Silver's data also indicate that the proportion of deferential Tories is far greater among older workers. On the contrary, Nordlinger sees a continuous production of deferentials. The argument remains to be resolved. Although the number of deferentials may be declining, it is possible that the general weakening of class bonds in Britain may result in a compensatory increase in the proportion of Conservative pragmatics in the working class. The result would be the indefinite perpetuation of a vitally influential group of voters who, according to McKenzie and Silver, have been "the principal arbiters of modern electoral competition in Britain."

SMELSER, NEIL J. **Social Change in the Industrial Revolution: An Application of Theory to the British Cotton Industry.** Chicago: University of Chicago Press, 1959, 440 p.

This work marks the first attempt to apply the sociological theories of Talcott Parsons and his school—social systems analysis and the general theory of action—to a historical subject. Smelser is himself a leading sociological theorist, and for the purposes of this study he developed a highly articulated theory of structural differentiation and applied it to the cotton industry during the later eighteenth and early nineteenth centuries. His focus was upon the differentiation of functions both within the industry and within the family structures which were affected by the developing industry. The importance of the work lies in its demonstration of the applicability and usefulness of theory in historical subjects (his explanation is highly ordered, and his conclusions are markedly different from those of his predecessors), in its emphasis upon the interrelationships between various forms of social change (in this case family and industrial), and in riveting our attention upon the central role which the family plays within the social system and upon the fact that familial functions alter radically from time to time and area to area.

Unfortunately, Smelser neglected primary materials such as probate and tax returns, and the study has not yet been replicated in other industries. But it is certain that increasing attention will be given to the problems raised by this seminal work, especially now that they are reinforced by the rising flood of interest in historical demography.

ROSE, E. J. B. and ASSOCIATES. **Colour and Citizenship: A Report on British Race Relations.** New York: Oxford University Press (for the Institute of Race Relations), 1969, 815 p.

The most vexing social and political question in Britain in recent times has been the problem of immigration and race relations. Other difficulties pale in significance in comparison to the subject of race. It is a situation which gives every sign of persisting in the future. However, it was only in the mid-1960s, with the acts restricting immigration and the now famous speeches of Enoch Powell, that the seriousness of the situation became apparent. A number of studies of the problem have followed on the heels of this awareness.

Rose and his associates have made a conscious effort to do a study of Britain's racial problems analogous in scope and impact to Gunnar Myrdal's classic, **An American Dilemma.** It is certainly too early to say whether this ambitious goal has been reached; however, **Colour and Citizenship** is the most comprehensive single volume that has been published on British race relations. The book is a collection of 33 chapters on a variety of subjects including the background to the problem, housing, politics, economics, social relations and a concluding set of general recommendations. Much of the quantifiable data comes from the 1966 Sample Census which, despite its inaccuracies, is probably the best material available. Perhaps the single most provocative section in the book is Mark Abrams' chapter on the incidence of racial prejudice in Britain.

The book does have a few deficiencies. It tends to be a collection of vignettes on particular aspects of the situation without a coherent unity. Nevertheless, it is an impressive study and quite indispensable in the study of British race relations.

Empire and Commonwealth

See also Africa: General—Historical, p. 831.

KOEBNER, RICHARD and SCHMIDT, HELMUT DAN. **Imperialism: The Story and Significance of a Political Word, 1840–1960.** New York: Cambridge University Press, 1964, 432 p.

Imperialism is one of those words which scholars should use cautiously and sparingly, if indeed at all. Military conquest, territorial annexation, slavery, exploitative economic relationships, religious interference—all these have relatively precise meanings. Imperialism may mean all or none of them. As Koebner shows, the term has shifted in relation to its surrounding context, from its original use to characterize the régime of Louis Napoleon, till the Gladstonian Liberals attacked Disraeli with it, till it became the banner under which Rhodes, Milner and Cromer set out to conquer Africa. Hobson and his pupil Lenin saw it as the extension of bloated finance capitalism, and in modern communist terminology it has come to mean any activity of an "imperialist" (*i.e.* capitalist) country. With perhaps equal justification, but clearly without corresponding success, the West has attempted to throw the slogan back at her cold-war enemies. And so it goes. Koebner ends with a doubt, as of 1960, that the debate has ended or that semantic variations have ceased: a prediction that has been fully borne out. This book, itself an excellent guide to a complex subject, should be used with the more incisive interpretations of A. P. Thornton, **The Imperial Idea and Its Enemies: A Study in British Power** (New York: St. Martin's Press, 1959, 370 p.), and **Doctrines of Imperialism** (New York: Wiley, 1965, 246 p.).

HARLOW, VINCENT T. **The Founding of the Second British Empire, 1763–1793.** London: Longmans, 1952–1964, 2 v.

Harlow's attack on the sharp division between the first and second empires and his argument that the foundations of Britain's Eastern dominance began before (not as a result of) the American Revolution have been generally accepted, and constitute an important part of a decisive recent reinterpretation of the historiography of the British Empire. From Tudor beginnings until well into the twentieth century, the broad aims of British imperialism have come to be regarded as more continuous than shifting: the British were impelled throughout by the demands and energies of their expanding society to seek "informal empire" that would make and keep the oceans and rivers of the world a vast extension of the Thames. Yet, as in other eras, such factors as domestic politics, economic pressures, local events, diplomatic rivalries and the vagaries of communications often transformed the simple aim of commercial extension into political intervention or control. Facing simultaneous and interacting crises at home, in Ireland, in America, in India and in Europe, the British evolved a set of half-solutions and experiments that endured; for no set "character" emerged after 1793.

Harlow narrates and synthesizes rather than probes. He assumes but does not explain the drive for world dominance. For example, a crucial part of his thesis concerns the effects on ministers of mercantile pressure, but he does not analyze its dimensions. The central argument is at times all but lost in the maze of diplomatic negotiations and court intrigues that take up most of his two volumes. Yet the historian who tries seriously to correct the shortcomings in a new synthesis will probably fail to match the sweep of Harlow's grand narrative.

STRACHEY, EVELYN JOHN ST. LOE. **The End of Empire.** New York: Random House, 1960, 351 p.

Strachey's book will endure as a period piece, showing what a thoughtful British socialist who had held power was thinking near the end of the postwar decolonization of the British Empire. He asks the right questions. Why and how are empires built? What are they like? What are their effects on colonizer and colonized? Do they pay? What happens after they dissolve? But his answers and analyses are uneven. He not only accepts without much qualification the Hobson-Lenin interpretation that the "new imperialism" of the late nineteenth century was a necessary search for fields for investment by capitalism in a stage of underconsumption, but he extends that outworn thesis to cover the relaxation of control during the interwar period, despite the fact that tropical investment greatly increased when presumably it ought to have been diminishing as capitalism passed into the "post-imperialist" phase. In his case study of British India he overemphasizes the direct British role in the destruction of the Bengal economy and ignores completely what was usually the most crucial effect of colonial rule in any country: the rearrangement of wealth, power and status *within* the colonized society.

Yet Strachey's analysis of the effects of decolonization is still the best we have. As he argues, the European powers are demonstrably better off without their colonies, and, as Americans have belatedly begun to realize, there is more than enough at home to keep fully occupied the energy, idealism and resources that once were drained off into empire. But foreign aid and the Commonwealth still have their crucial roles to play.

DAWSON, ROBERT MACGREGOR, *ed.* **The Development of Dominion Status, 1900–1936.** New York: Oxford University Press, 1937, 466 p.

This book is an authoritative, succinct account, supported by selected documents, of the transitory political phenomenon peculiar to the British Commonwealth known as dominion status. Canada and the Australian colonies had enjoyed responsible self-government for domestic concerns since the middle of the nineteenth century; but it was not until some years after the creation of the Commonwealth of Australia, when Canada had already begun to reach out for a say in some aspects of external affairs, that the name "dominion" began to be used generically. Professor Dawson traced the development of the concept of dominion status through participation in war and peacemaking, the abandonment of the idea of joint responsibility for foreign policy as a result of Chanak and Locarno, and the definition of the status of free association and theoretical equality under the crown. He also showed the influence of Anglo-Irish relations on dominion status up to 1936 when De Valera took advantage of the abdication crisis to establish that Eire was sovereign in internal affairs and recognized the king only for purposes of association with Britain and other dominions, thus effectively challenging the "inter-se" doctrine of a common allegiance that had replaced the older concept of the diplomatic unity of the Empire. (See J. E. S. Fawcett, **The British Commonwealth in International Law,** London: Stevens, 1963, 243 p.)

WHEARE, KENNETH CLINTON. **The Statute of Westminster and Dominion Status.** London: Oxford University Press, 5th ed., 1953, 357 p.

The interest in and importance of this book, which was preceded by Professor Wheare's **The Statute of Westminster 1931** (New York: Oxford University Press, 1933, 128 p.), can be indicated in part by the fact that it went through five editions between 1938–1953.

In the evolution of dominion status in the British Empire-Commonwealth between World Wars I and II, two events stand out. The first was the report of the Inter-Imperial Relations Committee of the Imperial Conference in 1926, which placed a particular emphasis on the equal and free status of its members. The second was the enactment of the Statute of Westminster in 1931. Characterized by Lord Jowitt as an act of "transcendental constitutional importance," the Statute incorporated a main part of the legal and nonlegal constitutional rules which defined dominion status, its provisions largely representing a formalization of existing practices. In particular, the Statute nullified certain relationships and situations which violated the principle of equality. It also recognized that British parliamentary legislation applying to the dominions should be enacted only at the request and with the consent of the dominions. Thereafter, some of the main provisions of the Statute were either explicitly or implicitly embodied in several new constitutions—for example, those which recognized the independence and new legal status of India and Pakistan, and Ceylon in 1947.

Events since the publication of the fifth edition of this book have reduced much of its content to historical interest, but Professor Wheare's contribution has remained the standard volume on the Statute of Westminster. Serious students of Commonwealth constitutional and legal history continue to rely on it.

DEWEY, ALEXANDER GORDON. **The Dominions and Diplomacy.** New York: Longmans, 1929, 2 v.

Published at the time when the concept of equality of status for British dominions, as proclaimed in the Balfour Declaration of 1926, was being translated by negotiating committees into practical legal form for the Statute of Westminster of 1931, this book suggested that the British Commonwealth was still in a state of flux and faced enormous problems. Dewey, a Canadian political scientist, looked on the evolution of the Empire with more detachment than scholars like A. B. Keith, a former British Colonial Office civil servant who had preached dominion status since 1909 ("Responsible Government in the Dominions"), who believed that the war had brought the Commonwealth to full flower (**Dominion Home Rule in Practice,** London: Oxford University Press, 1921, 64 p.) and who was convinced that a stable equilibrium had now been reached in an ideal constitutional balance which provided for equality of status but not necessarily of function.

In **The Dominions and Diplomacy,** Dewey analyzed the forces which had fashioned the Commonwealth since the Second Colonial Conference in 1897. He argued that too much attention had hitherto been paid to intra-Commonwealth relations and not enough to the relations of the various parts of the Commonwealth with the rest of the world. Transactions in 1919 in Paris, and since 1919 in Geneva and elsewhere, had shown that international recognition was the clue to an understanding of the evolution of the dominions. Although avowedly not an imperialist, Dewey defended British and dominion imperialists against nationalist charges that they were attempting to reassert a colonial relationship of subordination. He saw imperialism as a "greater nationalism" hampered by differences of interest caused by geographical and other factors which would also trouble a coöperative Commonwealth without strong central governing organs.

CARTER, GWENDOLEN MARGARET. **The British Commonwealth and International Security: The Role of the Dominions, 1919–1939.** Toronto: Ryerson Press, 1947, 326 p.

After the First World War the chief problem facing the dominions as newly fledged states was the need to regain the degree of security which had permitted them to develop before 1914. But they found neither the old imperial relationship nor the new League structure satisfactory for this purpose. Professor Carter, examining the record of international affairs between the wars, showed that the difficulties were caused by the dominions' general lack of faith in Britain's direction of foreign policy and also in the League as an instrument of collective security. But she also showed that the dominions, especially Canada and Australia, contributed greatly to the weakening of the League by their internal divisions and by their failure to accept responsibilities. At the same time many of their people severely criticized British deviations from the standards set by League ideals. It was only because they believed that Britain was at last acting in conformity with the principles of collective security and because they were aware that they could not afford to see Britain defeated that the overseas dominions went unanimously into the war with Nazi Germany in 1939. But victory was achieved at the cost of Britain's prewar strength, and in future the dominions must rely on a recreated international security system, on Anglo-American coöperation and regional alliances.

BRADY, ALEXANDER. **Democracy in the Dominions: A Comparative Study in Institutions.** Toronto: University of Toronto Press, 3rd ed., 1958, 614 p.

This classic by a distinguished Canadian political scientist was originally published in 1947 and has been revised through the third edition of 1958. In his own critically observant and scholarly way, the author is seeking to describe and interpret comparatively political institutions in the light of their "political culture." In so doing, he is following more in the tradition of Lord Bryce's **Modern Democracies** (New York: Macmillan, 1921, 2 v.) than of Almond and Verba's **The Civic Culture** (Boston: Little, Brown, 1965, 379 p.). The orientation of the author is that of a pragmatic liberal whose sympathetic acceptance of democratic values is implicit throughout his work.

The four dominions treated are members of the "old Commonwealth," namely, Canada, Australia, New Zealand and South Africa. Emphasis is placed upon environmental and hereditary factors, with the influence of the receding frontier and the British parliamentary and legal heritage receiving special attention. Some similarities, *i.e.* sparse population scattered over wide areas in Canada and Australia, are noted alongside differences, *i.e.* ethnic and racial factors in Canada and South Africa. The concluding chapters provide some overall comparative generalizations about frontiers and collectivism, education, parliament and parties, and threats to democracy. In the last chapter, the author suggests that the major threats are the ideological ones of ultranationalism and Marxian communism, and the internal stresses which result from the various social and economic forces in the modern world.

Looking back from 1970, it is easy to note conspicuous omissions and changes—the exclusion of the new Commonwealth countries in Asia and Africa, South Africa's departure from the Commonwealth and the profound alterations in the four countries covered. Nevertheless, the mature and sophisticated insights of this volume still provide one of the most useful overviews of the political systems of these three present and one former Commonwealth members.

DE SMITH, S. A. **The New Commonwealth and Its Constitutions.** London: Stevens, 1964, 312 p.

During the inter-war period, the writings of A. B. Keith provided some excellent historical and legal treatments of the British dominions, as they acquired the status of "sovereign states." Shifting his interest from the "old" Commonwealth to the "new" Commonwealth, Professor de Smith has more recently provided a balanced comparative examination of the constitutions of the newer states in the Commonwealth, preceded by discussions of the features of the Commonwealth itself, and of the routes followed in the transition from dependent to independent status.

The comparative treatment of the constitutions of the members of the Commonwealth is placed on a background of Westminster "export models." The author's preference for legal entrenchment in the newer constitutions is evidenced. One obvious feature of the new Commonwealth has been the extent to which "federal, or marginally federal, constitutions have been associated with the Commonwealth." Whether one considers such loose interstate federations as the East African federation and the West Indian federation, older country federations such as Canada and Australia, or newer federations such as India and Nigeria, the panorama is marked by great diversity.

In looking back to 1963, one is struck by the enormity of the change which would have to be described and analyzed if the volume were revised. But even so, Professor de Smith's judicious book constitutes one of the most recent and significant comparative studies of constitutional development in the Commonwealth.

MILLER, JOHN DONALD BRUCE. **The Commonwealth in the World.** Cambridge: Harvard University Press, 3rd ed., 1965, 304 p.

In the first edition of this book, Professor Miller analyzed the relations of each part of the former British Empire with its fellow "members of the Commonwealth" and with the rest of the world now that independence, rather than dominion status, was the possible destiny of all parts, great and small. He said that the name "Empire" was no longer applicable and, except in unofficial use by a few people in Britain, Australia and New Zealand, the adjective "British" had also been dropped. He argued that the reason why the Commonwealth persisted was that each country exercised complete control of its own internal and external affairs, as a sovereign state, and continued association was a matter of self-interest. The Commonwealth was thus, in a phrase coined by Miller, "a concert of convenience."

The author showed that the effect of the Suez incident in 1956 (described by James George Eayrs, editor of **The Commonwealth and Suez: A Documentary Survey,** New York: Oxford University Press, 1964, 483 p.) had been disillusionment about consultation as a means of preserving Commonwealth unity. He dismissed the possibility of organizational development to restore unity of action; but he thought that British leadership and initiative, although challenged, would continue.

Miller saw that India's decision to remain within the Commonwealth after independence, and the prospect of independence for so many "colonies of administration" peopled by non-Europeans, had created the prospect of a multiracial commonwealth, a concept described by Professor Frank Underhill in **The British Commonwealth: An Experiment in Coöperation among Nations** (Durham: Duke University Press, 1956, 127 p.). In the first edition of his work (1958), Professor Miller minimized the possibility of a Commonwealth stand on this issue. He did not expect multiracialism to be adopted as basic Commonwealth principle. He later altered this view. What he did not anticipate was the possibility that Britain herself, by closing the door to Commonwealth immigrants, would further weaken multiracialism and therefore the Commonwealth.

Memoirs and Biographies

NICOLSON, HAROLD. **King George the Fifth: His Life and Reign.** Garden City: Doubleday, 1953, 570 p.

This is a fascinating account of the place of a twentieth-century king in the constitution of Great Britain and of what used to be known as the British Empire and Commonwealth. It is official in the sense that Nicolson was commissioned to write it, but fortunately it is official also in that he was given "unrestricted" access to the Royal Archives. Apparently, in spite of certain restraints he mentions elsewhere (see **Harold Nicolson: The Later Years, 1945–1962: Volume III of Diaries and Letters,** edited by Nigel Nicolson, New York: Atheneum, 1968, 448 p.), it represents the honest results of the research of a competent historian.

George V was given Walter Bagehot as the oracle on the "modern" constitution; he was tutored by the celebrated constitutional historian, J. R. Tanner; he was advised by Sir William Anson early in his reign; and he was guided by a very wise private secretary, Sir Arthur Bigge (later Lord Stamfordham). Not that the King needed much guidance (and certainly no restraint) except in the tricky spots, for his natural inclination was for unity, compromise, peace and restraint. Such aims were badly needed in his reign. He came to the throne in 1910 in the midst of constitutional crisis, force and violence in all classes of society, labor troubles and the penultimate crisis in Irish relations. The first German war broke into this scene and was succeeded by prolonged economic stress, plus rebellion and change in the Empire and the rise of the Labor Party. In the midst of all this, George conducted himself with propriety (public and private) and correctness, and a driving sense of duty not equalled since George III. He was an exemplary king.

AVON, ANTHONY EDEN, 1ST EARL OF. **Facing the Dictators: The Memoirs of Anthony Eden, Earl of Avon.** Boston: Houghton, 1962, 746 p.

This book is the second in the trilogy of memoirs of Anthony Eden, now the Earl of Avon. The first, **Full Circle** (Boston: Houghton, 1960, 676 p.), covers the period from his becoming Foreign Secretary in 1951 until his resignation as Prime Minister in January 1957 after the Suez crisis. The third, **The Reckoning** (Boston: Houghton, 1965, 716 p.), deals with his period of office as Foreign Secretary during the Second World War.

Facing the Dictators falls into two parts: Eden's role in the making of British foreign policy, first from 1934 until 1935 as Lord Privy Seal and later Minister for League of Nations Affairs, then as Foreign Secretary until his resignation from Neville Chamberlain's government in February 1938. Lord Avon had the ex-Minister's privilege of using official papers in writing his book, but he has added "my present reflections upon past events." Hence, the account of his role in the 1930s is colored by the statesman's natural wish to place his part in events in the best light. But A. J. P. Taylor's judgment on Eden—"he did not face the Dictators; he pulled faces at them"—is too harsh. Eden's resignation in 1938 shows that he wanted some tangible sign of good will from the dictators before carrying relations with them further. For all that, in the main Eden supported the general lines of government policy, as his attitude over the reoccupation of the Rhineland and the Spanish Civil War shows. This book remains an indispensable source of insight into the dilemmas of British policy during a time of vast commitments and stretched resources.

BULLOCK, ALAN LOUIS CHARLES. **The Life and Times of Ernest Bevin.** London: Heinemann, 1960, 1967, 2 v.

Political biographies and memoirs have long provided scholars with a host of worthwhile insights into the workings of the British political system. Nevertheless, a major drawback in this area has been the fact that most of the material is by or about former Conservative politicians. Alan Bullock's massive biography of Ernest

Bevin partially rectifies this imbalance. Bullock had intended to write a two-volume work on Bevin's career with 1945 as the dividing line, but he modified this conception to devote the entire second volume to Bevin's service in Churchill's wartime cabinet, reserving a forthcoming third volume for Bevin's role in the Attlee government.

Although Bullock's interest is primarily in Bevin the public figure, Bevin the man comes through indelibly, portrayed as a hardhanded working-class pragmatist with unshakable concern for "my people." Bevin was, in a sense, pre-ideological with a sneering contempt for "intellectuals," a term which included most of the Labor left wing. Indeed, as *The Times* noted, "Like Churchill, he seemed a visitor from the eighteenth century," albeit from a different social class. Bullock presents a carefully drawn picture of Bevin's rise to power in the trade-union hierarchy. This section of the work is particularly valuable, for the trade-union hierarchy has provided a vital, although little studied, preparatory experience for many Labor politicians rather analogous to the role of public schools, the universities and the armed services for Conservative leaders.

MACMILLAN, HAROLD. **Winds of Change, 1914–1939.** New York: Harper and Row, 1966, 584 p.
——. **The Blast of War, 1939–1945.** New York: Harper and Row, 1968, 623 p.
——. **Tides of Fortune, 1945–1955.** New York: Harper and Row, 1969, 729 p.

Like all British Prime Ministers, Macmillan was *sui generis,* fitting no pattern. A member of the great publishing family, he went to the proper schools, served in the Guards and married high in the old landed aristocracy, but he served his long House of Commons apprenticeship as a rebel against prevailing currents in the Conservative Party. He was a member of various groups interested in social justice and advocating the mixed economy which everyone now accepts, and when the Second World War broke out he was a Churchillian, still on the back benches.

Under Churchill, he served as junior in the Ministry of Supply and the Colonial Office and then, with ministerial rank, as British representative at Allied Headquarters in North Africa. When the Tories returned to office in 1951 Macmillan became Minister of Housing, probably his most successful stint as a member of the Cabinet.

There are long unrewarding stretches of history in his memoirs—a pity, because when he is writing about his own experiences he can be most enlightening and interesting, and he writes well. A few passages on the Young Turks of the 1930s, all the portions on the Ministry of Housing experience and the parts about his service at Eisenhower's headquarters in North Africa are rewarding. Furthermore, his vignettes of Churchill and his views of him in the days when the old man was staying too long are affectionate and delightful. Macmillan is charitable and has a kind word to say about everybody but John Foster Dulles, even Stanley Baldwin.

JONES, THOMAS. **Whitehall Diary, 1916–1930.** London: Oxford University Press, 1969, 2 v.
——. **A Diary with Letters: 1931–1950.** London: Oxford University Press, 1954, 582 p.

Coming in middle age from an academic career in Scotland and Ireland, Thomas Jones joined the new Cabinet Secretariat in 1916 and remained in it until 1930, when he became secretary of the Pilgrim Trust, maintaining his gossipy political contacts in clubs and elsewhere. In 1937 he had his diaries to that date privately printed in "twenty-two small unbound volumes." The **Whitehall Diary** is drawn from this source. The editing leaves something to be desired, however, and the constant use of initials makes the book difficult to use.

Jones' diary is of so unusual a man, in so unusual an office, that it is of some importance in constitutional history. A socialist, a lifelong member of the Labor Party, an active partisan of this or that leader (especially Lloyd George) he was about as "uncivil" a civil servant as could be found. He and the rest of the Secretariat served the Prime Minister, not the Cabinet, wrote speeches for him, advised him, revealed inner confidences and, in short, threw themselves into an active political life. In doing so, the Secretariat seems to have been partly responsible for the great modern growth in the power of the Prime Minister. Their minutes frequently shaped decisions of the Cabinet, especially when the latter were vague, and their private minutes frequently corrected the memories of the ministers.

A useful work, if received with caution.

IRELAND

O'SULLIVAN, DONAL. **The Irish Free State and Its Senate: A Study in Contemporary Politics.** London: Faber, 1940, 697 p.

For 30 years serious students of Irish twentieth-century history have been brought up on this book. The author, who was clerk of the Senate of the Irish Free State, explains, "When . . . both the original Senate and the Irish Free State were successively brought to an end, I decided to compile a record in which the history of the Second Chamber and of the State itself should be combined, to serve as a chronicle of the past." The result is a work of almost 700 pages of narrative, of which over half is a general history. Except for the specialist political scientist, it is this half—a respectable length book in its own right—that is of importance.

Until recently, few of those who wrote about the events in Ireland during the quarter century from 1916 avoided being partisan. The fullest account of "the troubles" and the civil war, Dorothy Macardle's **The Irish Republic** (New York: Farrar, Straus and Giroux, rev. ed., 1965, 1,045 p.), is explicitly "an account of the Irish Republican struggle from the viewpoint of an Irish Republican" (the term had at that time a very specific meaning in an Irish context). Only the chapters on Ireland in successive volumes of the Royal Institute of International Affairs, "Survey of British Commonwealth Affairs," achieved the clinical detachment of the uninvolved professional. O'Sullivan's book is strongly anti-De Valera, for it was De Valera who had destroyed his job and the Irish state he believed in. But O'Sullivan's scholarship never deserted him, and this remains the most reliable and vivid account of the Irish Free State.

O'FAOLÁIN, SEÁN. **The Irish.** Harmondsworth: Penguin Books, rev. ed., 1969, 173 p.

When Seán O'Faoláin wrote the first edition of this book in 1949, the quantitative methods of the social scientists, which have made possible systematic investigations of the social structure and culture of communities, were only in the course of development. Conrad Arensberg and Solon T. Kimball had come and gone, but their books, **The Irish Countryman** (London: Macmillan, 1937, 216 p.) and **Family and Community in Ireland** (Cambridge: Harvard University Press, 1940, 322 p.), made little impression on Irish scholars, and no one followed them. Nor were there any social histories of Ireland. Undaunted, O'Faoláin set out to write a short, impressionistic "history of a racial mind." The scholars and the journalists who have followed have not improved upon the insights of this sensitive, professional literary man.

O'Faoláin's sketches of six representative types—the peasantry, the Anglo-Irish, the rebels, the priests, the writers and the politicians—which comprise the second part of the book, are what the sociologists whom he preceded would call stereotypes. Since "the Irish people have entered into the last stage of that process of urbanization which began with the Normans," he foresees "another type which I have barely hinted at, the new middle class, or native bourgeoisie . . . they are the peasant in process of development or final decay, it is too soon to say which."

BARRITT, DENIS P. and CARTER, CHARLES F. **The Northern Ireland Problem: A Study in Group Relations.** New York: Oxford University Press, 1962, 163 p.

The "problem" of Northern Ireland is simply stated. "In all spheres of life a man still tends to be placed according to the Church with which he worships. A divided education and a divided social and political life deepen and confirm the funda-mental cleavage." The religious cleavage is reinforced by differences of race and historical origin. It is in turn exacerbated by a blatant discrimination which, though both sides practice it, works overwhelmingly to the disadvantage of the Catholic minority. It is not only condoned but operated by a dominant party largely con-trolled by a sectarian society, the Orange Order.

The alienation of the Catholic population and the irredentist chimera of a united Ireland have led to one great issue dominating Northern Ireland politics, "the issue of whether or not the state should exist at all." Thus the Catholic minority have always appeared "disloyal" to the majority.

The Northern Ireland Problem was sponsored by the Irish Association for Cultural, Economic and Social Relations, and its authors—one an English econo-mist, the other a Northern Ireland businessman—are both Quakers. In a scholarly and objective way, they document and attempt to quantify many features of the Protestant-Catholic cleavage and discrimination in both private and public sectors. To read this book is to understand a little better why people there feel so strongly about what happened as long ago as 1690.

COOGAN, TIMOTHY PATRICK. **Ireland since the Rising.** New York: Praeger, 1966, 355 p.
"To anyone born and reared in Ireland since 1916, analysis of the Easter Rising and its aftermath is like dissection of the Mass by a layman." But in the 1960s laymen began to do just this. So, too, in Ireland, the generation that grew up in and after the Second World War began to question the older orthodoxies. The author—at present editor of the *Irish Press,* a Dublin daily—belongs to this generation. His book is easy to read and entertaining. It is also a serious piece of analysis and the most successful of the crop of popular surveys of Ireland's recent history and the contemporary scene.

Ireland since the Rising combines the fruit of wide reading and sound judgment in its cool and occasionally astringent comments, and the art of the journalist with his private sources and reliance on the interview. After a 100-page historical survey and a quick glance at the social, economic, political and cultural state of the country in the middle 1960s, the author passes to the four aspects of Ireland which preoccupy the Irish themselves—the language, religion, the Irish Republican Army (on which he is an acknowledged authority) and the North. On Northern Ireland, he concludes: "The plain truth about the North today is that the secret wish of most Northern Catholics is not for union with the South (entailing a fall-off in social benefits) but for an end to discrimination, and a fairer share of the Northern spoils." Few recognized this at that time, and fewer had the courage to say it even if they did. The events of 1969 demonstrated how right he was.

DEVLIN, BERNADETTE. **The Price of My Soul.** New York: Knopf, 1969, 224 p.
This is a best-selling autobiography of a young Northern Ireland working-class Catholic. In April 1969, this courageous, rough-tongued university student, then aged 22 but already a veteran of street demonstrations and protest marches, won the Mid-Ulster seat in the British House of Commons from the Ulster Unionist Party. She entered a Parliament she despised on the votes of an electorate the vast majority of whom almost certainly did not share her republican socialist views, it being sufficient for them that she was a Catholic.

Although Miss Devlin is forthright and humorous, this is a spiky and prejudiced book. What makes it important is the vivid portrayal of the Northern Ireland Catholic working class, alienated by discrimination in housing and employment, at the point in the late 1960s when, at last, they began to recognize that salvation would never come from the Republic in the South and that they must solve their own problems in a Northern Ireland context.

In a setting of student politics, however, the intellectual development of the rambunctious Miss Devlin took her rapidly beyond this position and headlong into an all-Ireland republican socialism. Paradoxically, then, her aims and ideals are far removed from those of most of the people she portrays so well by writing about herself, and of whom she is in many other ways so typical.

THE NETHERLANDS; BELGIUM

VANDENBOSCH, AMRY. **Dutch Foreign Policy since 1815: A Study in Small Power Politics.** The Hague: Nijhoff, 1959, 318 p.

This book is the best introduction to the subject in English. It is organized on both topical and chronological principles, resulting at times in lack of coherence, but the topical approach has nevertheless produced useful chapters about the formulation and execution of policy. The peculiar features of Dutch foreign policy are generally well analyzed. The author points out that the Dutch mercantile tradition had always been one of neutrality, and an alliance policy considered dangerous and exceptional, though at the same time the position of the country in Europe and in Asia often required that the Netherlands play an active role. After the separation of Belgium in 1830–1839, the tendency to withdraw from international politics prevailed. The author explains how and why the Foreign Ministry became a technical and nonpartisan department headed by career diplomats.

There is no systematic investigation of the influences on the making of foreign policy outside the government and parliament, a lack that seems most apparent in the chapters on the period after 1900, when the industrialization and the new imperialism in the Netherlands Indies caused changes in the attitude toward the rest of the world, as well as toward the colonies. The chapters dealing with the "Great Netherlands" idea, the Hague Peace Conference and the colonies are rather superficial. The absence of an analysis of the Dutch fascination with international law must be considered a real shortcoming.

VAN CAMPEN, SAMUEL ISIDORE PAUL. **The Quest for Security.** The Hague: Nijhoff, 1958, 308 p.

For the Netherlands the German invasion of 1940 meant the bankruptcy of a century of neutral foreign policy. The alternative of collective security had been tried in the League of Nations, of which the Netherlands had been one of the most dedicated members, but that had failed as well. Indeed, to a large extent the Dutch devotion to the League of Nations had been just another form of the traditional neutralism, *i.e.* a policy based upon the invocation of international law against power politics.

After the Second World War the Netherlands joined the United Nations with the same postwar enthusiasm witnessed in other participants, and even during the war Dutch foreign policy had become involved in the planning of integration and pooling of resources within Europe. The final break with the centuries-old Dutch tradition in foreign politics came with the signing of the Treaty of Brussels in 1948 and of NATO in 1949.

This dramatic switch in the period 1945–1950 is the subject of Van Campen's book. It is carefully researched and well written, though there are some apparent drawbacks to his method, since he uses official governmental documents and parliamentary records almost exclusively. An additional boon to the English reader is an appendix of about 150 pages of translations of Dutch documents. Another special feature of this important book is its treatment of Dutch-German relations in separate chapters following each general chapter. The author justifies this by pointing to the extraordinary ambivalence of Dutch policy from 1945–1949 vis-à-vis Germany, who was simultaneously Holland's principal trade partner and her most suspected ally.

STIKKER, DIRK U. **Men of Responsibility.** New York: Harper and Row, 1966, 418 p.

The reorientation of Dutch foreign policy after World War II was focused on three problems: European integration, NATO and the Indonesian struggle for freedom. The Dutch contribution to the first two issues has remained largely unrecorded in Dutch or English. Given the lack of scholarly work in the field, the lively memoirs of Dirk Stikker are particularly welcome. The author began his career as a businessman and first came into contact with politics during the German occupation. After the war he became a member of parliament as the leader of a newly formed Liberal (*i.e.* center) Party and was Minister of Foreign Affairs from 1948 to 1952. After a stint as ambassador to London and NATO, he was the Secretary-General of NATO from 1961 to 1964.

Stikker was minister in a most crucial period, and he played a major part in the solution of the Indonesian problem. He is critical of Dutch policy, but, like many Dutch authors, he nevertheless blames much of the failure on American intervention. From his own report it becomes clear, however, that without American intervention the Dutch conservatives, many of them right-wing members of his own party, would never have come around to accepting Indonesian independence. In the end Stikker's ministerial career was almost destroyed as a result of his party's stand on the New Guinea issue.

The chapters on the Marshall Plan, European integration and NATO are all equally interesting. They are also striking because of their unconditional adherence to the cold-war line. It is also true, however, that as minister Stikker did not meet with principled opposition to or doubts about NATO, except from communist representatives. The only non-communist opposition to NATO came from politicians whose pride had been hurt by the American policy in Indonesia.

LIJPHART, AREND. **The Trauma of Decolonization: The Dutch and West New Guinea.** New Haven: Yale University Press, 1966, 303 p.
————. **The Politics of Accommodation: Pluralism and Democracy in the Netherlands.** Berkeley: University of California Press, 1968, 222 p.

With the failure to solve the problem of New Guinea, after the Dutch-Indonesian treaty of 1949, that question was—as the Dutch said—put in the refrigerator. There it remained until 1962 when an agreement was finally concluded for the transfer of the island to Indonesia. This drawn-out aftermath of Dutch decolonization has always remained somewhat of a mystery.

Professor Lijphart, a political scientist, has approached the problem by examining the obstacles to a realistic solution that he finds embedded in party politics. After a study of the interrelation between foreign and internal politics he concludes, surprisingly, that the motives of the Dutch were, in effect, irrational—the forced transfer of the sovereignty of the rest of Indonesia in 1949 having been too much for the "egocentric altruism" of most of the political leaders as well as of the rank and file, not only among conservatives but also among the socialists. His book is a major, though controversial, contribution to the psychology of international relations.

The Politics of Accommodation by the same author seeks to solve the paradox that Holland has, on the one hand, an extraordinary degree of religious and class divisions and, on the other, a successful democracy. The analysis indicates how intricate and subtle is the balance of powers on which Holland's democracy is built; it indicates also the strength of the traditionalist Catholic and Protestant parties.

The author was not able to include the developments of the last three years in his study. A second edition of the book, covering that period, would be a boon for students of Dutch internal and foreign politics alike.

MILLER, JANE KATHRYN. **Belgian Foreign Policy between Two Wars, 1919–1940.** New York: Bookman Associates, 1951, 337 p.

Literature on Belgian foreign policy in English is scarce. Jane Miller's book is a generally solid, though pedestrian, introduction to the Belgian foreign policy of the inter-war period. It is not, however, a satisfactory substitute for Belgian works such as Omer de Raeymaker, **België's Internationaal Beleid, 1919–1939** (Brussels:

Standaard-Boekhandel, 1945, 561 p.), or Pierre van Zuylen, **Les Mains Libres** (Paris: Desclée, 1950, 580 p.).

The interesting peculiarities of Belgian foreign politics resulted from the clash between the tradition of neutrality, from which it was rudely shaken in 1914, and the necessity of an alliance policy during and after the First World War. The author gives a useful survey of the ensuing ambiguities of Belgian policy. She perhaps overstates the degree to which the Belgians switched to an alliance policy during the First World War and the Paris Peace Conference. The treatment of constitutional and internal politics is weak.

The book has a good bibliography. Some of the important titles which have appeared after its publication, in addition to Spaak's memoirs, are Marcel Henri Jaspar, **Souvenirs sans Retouche** (Paris: Fayard, 1968, 493 p.) and C. de Visscher and F. Vanlangenhove, *eds.,* **Documents Diplomatiques Belges, 1920–1940** (Brussels: Academie Royale de Belgique, Commission Royale d'Histoire, 1956–1965, 4 v.).

SPAAK, PAUL-HENRI. **Combats Inachevés.** Paris: Fayard, 1969, 2 v.

These memoirs are a godsend for an understanding of Belgian foreign policy after 1940. Paul-Henri Spaak was Minister of Foreign Affairs for most of the period from 1936 to 1965 and presided over the dramatic reversals of Belgian diplomacy. The return of Belgium to a policy of neutrality, or *mains libres,* began under his first tenure of office in 1936, though Spaak plays down the radical character of this change by pointing out that a preference for diplomatic independence had also characterized the policy of his predecessors. His observations on the incompatibility of the policy of neutrality with his personal ideals are fascinating. Until shortly before 1936 he had been one of the leftist *enfants terribles* of the Belgian Socialist Party and the comrade of Henri Rolin, who was to cause his final downfall in 1966. He none the less defends his neutrality policy of 1936–1940 as the only one possible for Belgium, at the same time contending that his later policy of entry into Benelux, the United Nations and NATO was rooted in the idealism of his younger years, sharpened by the awareness that in the postwar circumstances the security of small nations could only be guaranteed by a unified Europe.

The chapters Spaak devotes to European and world politics often offer new material and fresh insights. His preoccupation with these subjects prevents him from discussing internal Belgian politics thoroughly, though there are interesting passages about the part played by King Leopold III in domestic politics. The slight attention given by Spaak to the issue of the Congo is rather astonishing. Perhaps the author ("Mr. Europe," he has been called) had by this time in his career outgrown Belgian politics. If so, it was ironic that it was a split in his Socialist Party which caused his retirement. But even the last painful episode is told with the equanimity and detachment that characterize the book. It is one more reason why Spaak's memoirs can temporarily fill the place of the as yet unwritten history of Belgian postwar diplomacy.

SWITZERLAND

BONJOUR, EDGAR. **Geschichte der Schweizerischen Neutralität: Vier Jahrhunderte Eidgenössischer Aussenpolitik.** Basel: Helbing and Lichtenhahn, 1946–1970, 6 v.

A professor at the University of Basel presents a documented and authoritative review of the foreign policy of the Swiss federation since the seventeenth century. The first three volumes, originally published from 1946 to 1967 and republished since then in revised editions, cover the story of Swiss neutrality up to the eve of the Second World War. The author was commissioned by the Swiss Federal Council to carry the history through the period of the Second World War, which has been done in the last three volumes. Professor Bonjour concludes that Swiss neutrality was preserved in that war when the country was completely surrounded by the Axis powers thanks to its possession of an army with real striking power and modern equipment, willingness to suffer hardships (which included tight rationing of insufficient food supplies), and tough bargaining which included some compromises. The railroad tracks through the Gotthard tunnel were open for the shipment of civil merchandise but not for the transport of arms. The Swiss made clear their readiness to blow up the tunnel in case of attack. Professor Bonjour's account of these years is objective and absorbing. This is an important series.

DE ROUGEMONT, DENIS. **La Suisse ou l'Histoire d'un Peuple Heureux.** Paris: Hachette, 1965, 305 p.

In this serious and delightful essay, subtitled "the history of a happy people," the author's purpose is to show how small states—some of them very small—can consolidate to defend themselves against foreign powers and preserve their diversities. The Swiss showed themselves capable of astonishing military achievements in the Renaissance, but after defeat at the battle of Marignano in the sixteenth century, they lost interest in foreign conquest and foreign quarrels. The form of union of the Swiss Confederation, with a high degree of autonomy for each of the 22 cantons and with a voluntary surrender of rights in some directions to the federal government, was not accomplished until 1848. De Rougemont tells how the federation was formed and amended and how it functions today. There is also a beautifully written and perceptive survey of Swiss culture, and a chapter pointing the moral that lies so close to the author's heart—Switzerland as an example of federation for Europe.

STUCKI, LORENZ. **Das Heimliche Imperium.** Bern: Scherz, 2d ed., 1968, 342 p.

This book tells of Switzerland's evolution from a poor, underdeveloped country into a highly industrialized "secret empire." The country possesses practically no raw materials except water power. The density of the population is seven times that of the United States, and the agricultural area under cultivation is far from sufficient to provide enough food for the population. However, measured by its gross national product, Switzerland today is one of the richest countries in the world. Its economy provides work not only for its own inhabitants but also for hundreds of thousands of foreign workers in the country and nearly as many in enterprises established with Swiss capital in other lands. Stucki bases his story on the histories of many pioneering Swiss firms which developed small industrial and commercial enterprises into worldwide organizations. A lively part of the story of development is the account of the "risk-happy" hotel men, above all Cäsar Ritz, the son of a peasant from the Valais, whom King Edward VII of England is said to have called "the hotelier of kings and the king of hoteliers."

IKLÉ, MAX. **Die Schweiz als Internationaler Bank-und Finanzplatz.** Zurich: Orell Füssli, 1970, 187 p.

As astonishing as the industrial growth of Switzerland is the fact that the country has become a center of international finance, a close third in importance to New York and London, both of which possess natural advantages missing in this small inland country. The author of this timely summary of Switzerland's development as a center of banking and finance ascribes Swiss eminence in the field primarily to its policy of neutrality, aided by the multilingual tradition of its inhabitants, the quiet political climate and the conscientiousness, experience and initiative of the Swiss bankers. He points out that the beginnings of the development, which has blossomed in the period since the Second World War, go back to the early eighteenth century, and he traces its history through varied crises and reverses to its present strong position. Dr. Iklé notes that though Switzerland is not a member of the International Monetary Fund and the World Bank, it works closely with these institutions and strongly supports international solidarity in monetary policy. The Swiss National Bank has played a leading role in the intensified coöperation among central banks that developed during the 1960s.

FRANCE

General; Historical

CURTIUS, ERNST ROBERT. **The Civilization of France.** New York: Vintage, 1962, 237 p.

This book was published in 1930 as the first volume of an interpretation of modern France for German readers (E. R. Curtius and A. Bergsträsser, **Frankreich,** Stuttgart: Deutsche Verlags-Anstalt, 1930, 2 v.). The author, then a renowned professor of French history and Romance philology at Heidelberg, sought to offer a structural analysis (in Max Scheler's sense) of French values and systems of ideology. Parts of the book read like a special and urgent plea for Franco-German reconciliation; others are slightly dated because writers discussed or institutions explained have fallen into oblivion.

But the main themes of the book—an interpretation of the French concept of *civilisation* throughout history, of the various strands of Gallican Catholicism and of the nature of French radicalism (that "blend of emotionalism and logic")—are so richly and brilliantly developed that the study offers time and again a key to the understanding of present-day France. The methodological approach which hides its rigor behind elegant exposition remains fresh and useful. There are profound observations on the conditions of French modernization even if the term was not invented when Professor Curtius wrote. Entire pages read like a running comment on General de Gaulle's wartime memoirs. But there are also realistic appraisals of the instincts and values of the "common Frenchman."

COBBAN, ALFRED. **A History of Modern France.** London: Jonathan Cape, 1962–1965, 3 v.

For those who seek a detailed history of France, there is no substitute for the kind of multivolume French works best typified by the two older series edited by Ernest Lavisse, the "Histoire de France" and the **Histoire de France Contemporaine depuis la Révolution jusqu'à la Paix de 1919** (Paris: Hachette, 1920–22, 10 v.), and the more recent one edited by Louis Halphen and Philippe Sagnac, **Peuples et Civilisations: Histoire Générale** (Paris: Presses Universitaires, 1926–69, 21 v.). For the reader who wants a shorter, more manageable history of France, the work by Alfred Cobban, which begins with the year 1715, has the advantage of being up-to-date in scholarship, balanced in presentation and written in a witty, urbane style that does credit to the English tradition of the historical essay. Professor Cobban has challenged the traditional, especially the Marxian, interpretation of the French Revolution as a triumph of the bourgeoisie over the old régime's feudal aristocracy. Cobban had the temerity to suggest that the Revolution was essentially conservative in character. What took the place of the old aristocracy, he argued, was not an industrial-commercial middle class but a new oligarchy of landowners that was to dominate French society for most of the nineteenth century.

Because Cobban knows a good deal more about the Catholic Church in France than most liberal writers, he is almost always successful in depicting the problems of the French Right. When he deals with the French Left, however, even his long experience as a social historian seems to fail him. He can quote figures accurately on the French economy, but it is evident that he cares little about economics.

If Cobban has his critics, there is no question of the importance of his influence on contemporary historians, and few have contributed more to the whole range of modern French studies.

BROGAN, DENIS WILLIAM. **The Development of Modern France, 1870–1939.** New York: Harper, rev. ed., 1966, 2 v.

This remains one of the standard works in English on the Third Republic.

Domestic politics hold the center of the stage, but economic and social questions also receive attention; there are chapters on foreign and colonial policy. Cultural developments are neglected, as Brogan disarmingly acknowledges. His erudition is immense but lightly worn: one of the chief delights of the book is its witty and graceful prose. Its allusiveness, however, can sometimes make arduous reading. (Who is the heroine of "Gentlemen Prefer Blondes" to whom he refers?) The first half is preoccupied with the great crises which shook the Republic before the First World War. In his lengthy section on the Dreyfus affair, Brogan is staunchly anti-revisionist: the affair *was* a profound crisis; it *was* about justice. A shadow falls over the last half of the book as Brogan takes up the First World War and the inter-war period. Some of his pessimism about the political capacities of the French may reflect its original publication date (**France Under the Republic,** New York: Harper, 1940, 744 p.), but he has not seen fit to revise his views. A great deal of monographic literature has been published since then, and it is nearly time for someone with Brogan's knowledge and literary talents to write a new synthesis, in which the insights of the social sciences would be taken into account, as in Stanley Hoffmann's brilliant contribution to **In Search of France.** Meant for the general reader, Brogan's book contains no footnote references or bibliography. A beginning student of the Third Republic might wish first to consult the relevant sections of David Thomson, **Democracy in France,** and Gordon Wright, **France in Modern Times** (Chicago: Rand McNally, 1960, 621 p.).

CHASTENET, JACQUES. **Histoire de la Troisième République.** Paris: Hachette, 1952–1963, 7 v.

It seems unlikely that anyone will seek to surpass Chastenet's seven-volume tour de force. This history of the Third Republic is somewhat isolated from recent trends in French historiography. Belletristic, preoccupied with the unfolding of events, it is a kind of monument to nineteenth-century historical scholarship. But it is no less valuable for that. Politics predominate, but Chastenet is interested in everything, and there is much to be learned here about intellectual, social and economic developments. The volumes are organized chronologically, and each can be read as a separate unit. Chastenet writes from a Right-Center or moderate conservative position. His favorite word is "prudent," and his heroes are the *hommes de gouvernement,* men such as Jules Ferry, the later Clemenceau and Poincaré, who understood that in a parliamentary régime the art of governing is the art of compromising, and who combined a concern for stability and efficient administration with a concern for reform.

Chastenet concurs in the judgment of the late André Siegfried that prior to 1914 France was, on the whole, a well-governed, prosperous and happy land. Only after the First World War did new problems arise for which traditional ruling groups had no solutions. The Third Republic's ignominious collapse has tempted many to emphasize its failings over its achievements. Chastenet concludes that the Republic deserves not only the indulgence of Frenchmen but their respect as well. These volumes contain extensive footnote references but no bibliography or subject index.

LÜTHY, HERBERT. **France Against Herself: A Perceptive Study of France's Past, Her Politics, and Her Unending Crises.** New York: Praeger, 1955, 476 p.

In one sense, Lüthy's witty, sardonic, eminently readable analysis of why Fourth Republic France was unable to cope with her social, economic and political difficulties became dated upon publication. Lüthy documents well the *immobilisme* caused by the ubiquitous and conservative bureaucracy, bottlenecks in French commerce, industry and agriculture, the prevalence of values impeding progress, and the historical legacy of wartime destruction and internecine strife. What he failed adequately to recognize were the "winds of change" that were already transforming France in the early 1950s; what he could not anticipate was the extent of change since then.

France's population boom, economic renaissance and the republic of Charles de

Gaulle produced another revolution. Later books provide better descriptions of political events during the Fourth Republic, *e.g.* Philip Williams' **Crisis and Compromise** and John Ardagh's **The New French Revolution** (New York: Harper and Row, 1969, 501 p.). But despite the fact that **France Against Herself** was published two decades ago, it remains the most penetrating analysis of that subtle French blend of erratic instability and deep-seated conservatism, of Cartesian logic producing patently absurd conclusions. As history, **France Against Herself** has become outmoded and superseded; as a political psychology of the French, it remains the best we have.

HOFFMANN, STANLEY and OTHERS. **In Search of France.** Cambridge: Harvard University Press, 1963, 443 p.

This collection—in some ways a successor to Edward Mead Earle, *ed.,* **Modern France: Problems of the Third and Fourth Republics** (Princeton: Princeton University Press, 1951, 522 p.)—consists of six extended essays, all by distinguished experts. The longest and perhaps most interesting chapter is the opening one by Stanley Hoffmann, in which he develops his influential idea of the "stalemate society" through a historical analysis of the social-political bases of successive republican régimes. The succeeding contributions, by Charles Kindleberger, Laurence Wylie, Jesse Pitts and J.-B. Duroselle, enlarge on various aspects of Hoffmann's introduction.

The final summing up is provided by François Goguel, Secretary-General of the French Senate and author of the best single book on prewar France, **La Politique des Partis sous la IIIᵉ République.** He casts a gently skeptical eye over the theories of his American colleagues and offers some rather more traditional political explanations of his own: a useful addition to a sophisticated book, rich in large sociopolitical hypotheses, but with less on more mundane institutional analysis.

DANSETTE, ADRIEN. **Histoire Religieuse de la France Contemporaine.** Paris: Flammarion, rev. ed., 1965, 892 p.

Adrien Dansette must be classed as a popular rather than an academic historian. His many books range over a variety of topics and periods from the eighteenth century to the present, and the present work, which first appeared in two volumes in 1948 and 1951, has already found a large audience. Dansette writes a graceful, lively prose, and he often matches the academic historian in the depth and thoroughness of his research. The book under review reflects a master craftsman at his best.

When a Frenchman deals with the subject of Catholicism, there is no middle position: one is either a Catholic and believer or one is an anticlerical and a skeptic. In the first chapter of his book Dansette offers such an informative and dispassionate review of the role of the Church in eighteenth-century society that the reader might well have doubts about the author's allegiances. When Dansette comes to the Revolution and the martyrdom of the French clergy in the period of the Terror, no reader can fail to detect his basic sympathy for the cause of Catholicism and the Church. The striking thing about the book is not its bias; it is the amount of solid information Dansette can pack into what is essentially a digest of the many multivolumed histories of religious affairs in France. The one thing lacking is a detailed review of the contemporary position of the Church. The bulk of the book is devoted to the years before 1914 with only relatively short chapters on the years before World War II and a postscript on postwar changes.

WERTH, ALEXANDER. **The Twilight of France, 1933–1940.** New York: Harper, 1942, 368 p.

Alexander Werth served as Paris correspondent of the Manchester *Guardian* in the 1930s, and his eyewitness account of the last years of the Third Republic blurs the line often drawn between history and journalism. It is first of all an absorbing narrative of the events through which France passed as she edged toward the abyss, from the riots of February 6, 1934, to Munich and beyond. But it is also a book with a thesis. Werth's main concern is the interplay between the increasing polarization of French politics and decision making in foreign policy. Fearful of communism abroad, alarmed by the successes of the Left at home, such politicians of the Right as Laval, Flandin and Bonnet, supported by vocal and influential groups outside government, became increasingly disinclined to take a firm stand against Hitler. Munich was the result. But all the responsibility for the policy of appeasement does not fall upon the Right. In the long run, Werth suggests, perhaps the primary cause of France's drift into defeat was the war-weary pacifism of the French people. The book is filled with vivid character sketches and vignettes of such episodes as the occupation of the factories in the summer of 1936.

More recent works, such as the life-and-times biographies of Blum (Joel Colton, **Léon Blum: Humanist in Politics**) and Laval (Geoffrey Warner, **Pierre Laval and the Eclipse of France,** New York: Macmillan, 1969, 461 p.) and Georges Lefranc's **Histoire du Front Populaire (1934–1938)** (Paris: Payot, 1965, 501 p.), have altered or retouched areas of Werth's broader canvas. But Werth was there when it all happened, and his book remains an indispensable starting point for a study of the question: Why did France collapse in 1940?

ARON, ROBERT. **Histoire de Vichy: 1940–1944.** Paris: Fayard, 1954, 766 p.

A detailed, vivid narrative of the Vichy years, this volume by an eminent journalist-scholar attempts a dispassionate appraisal of the régime and its leaders. In drawing up the balance sheet, the book is fair to the point of making the best possible case for Vichy, or at least of refusing harsh judgment. Each phase, from the military defeat and armistice in June 1940 to the arrest of Marshal Pétain in April 1945, is examined with careful attention to domestic developments and foreign relations. The published and unpublished sources used are summarized in an extensive bibliographical note, but there is no specific documentation in the text itself. The volume is also available in a somewhat abridged but generally faithful English translation, **The Vichy Regime, 1940–44** (New York: Macmillan, 1958, 536 p.).

Although the Aron study remains the most complete and authoritative account of Vichy, it was written before the German Foreign Office documents became available and should be supplemented by Henri Michel, **Vichy: Année 40** (Paris: Laffont, 1966, 463 p.), a meticulously documented, scholarly exploration in depth of the first six months of the régime, which also provides a more up-to-date summary of the sources and secondary literature now available.

Political Questions

SIEGFRIED, ANDRÉ. **Tableau des Partis en France.** Paris: Grasset, 1930, 245 p.

André Siegfried was the founder of the modern school of French political science, based on electoral geography. Trained in the French tradition of human geography, he adapted it to the study of politics in his seminal "Tableau Politique de la France de l'Ouest sous la Troisième République." It was a method peculiarly well suited to the study of French politics of the first half of this century, for beneath the apparent confusion of shifting alliances in parliament and ever-changing party labels in the constituencies lay the extraordinary stability of French society and a persistent pattern of politics, both the result of the great Revolution and of slow and delayed industrialization.

Siegfried identified clericalism as the watershed dividing Left from Right in the countryside, but noted that it was partially crosscut by the new economic and social issues thrown up by the industrial revolution. And he gave the classic account of the radicalism of the French village and market town. His little book is in fact an analysis of political culture and behavior written in the less misleading language of an earlier age.

A source for many of the concepts still used to analyze French political life,

Tableau des Partis is essential reading for anyone concerned with prewar France. A somewhat edited and less satisfactory English version (but with an index) was published as **France: A Study in Nationality** (New Haven: Yale University Press, 1930, 122 p.). Raymond Aron's **France: Steadfast and Changing: The Fourth to the Fifth Republic** (Cambridge: Harvard University Press, 1960, 201 p.) provides perhaps the best recent introduction to France in the same style.

BONNEFOUS, GEORGES and BONNEFOUS, ÉDOUARD. **Histoire Politique de la Troisième République.** Paris: Presses Universitaires, 1956–1967, 7 v.

For the student of the Fourth and the Fifth Republics the yearly "L'Année Politique" has become an indispensable source of factual information on all aspects of public life in France. A similar though far more modest publication had furnished an account of the years 1874 to 1906. After the Second World War, Georges Bonnefous, who as deputy from Versailles had been an active participant in the politics of the Third Republic, assumed the task of becoming the chronicler of that period not covered by either the earlier or the current yearbooks. At his death he had treated the eight years prior to and including the First World War; his son took over to furnish the documentary record for the inter-war period and leading up to the suicide of the Third Republic at Vichy.

The format is essentially that of "L'Année Politique": a strictly chronological monthly account, facts and figures and a useful, partly annotated bibliography contained in an appendix. A demonstrative effort at objectivity does not prevent the authors' bias (that of middle-of-the-road Radicals) from shining through in their brief comments and even more in their selection of quoted speeches and of significant episodes. Most remarkable is the fact that political life is recorded almost entirely through parliamentary debates. This is indeed French representative tradition at its purest: the weightiest of diplomatic developments, social crises, economic upheavals become political "facts" in the mirror of utterances by deputies and senators. The fresco is fascinating and rich in details. Throughout it facilitates orientation into the labyrinth of French prewar politics.

For the first two volumes André Siegfried has contributed a succinct analysis of major trends as he saw them developing once the Republic had moved into the twentieth century.

GOGUEL-NYEGAARD, FRANÇOIS. **La Politique des Partis sous la IIIᵉ République.** Paris: Éditions du Seuil, 1946, 2 v.

Goguel's magisterial study of political parties and conflicts in the Third Republic has been followed by lengthier and more comprehensive histories of the Third Republic, but the value of **La Politique des Partis** does not lie in its chronological account. Rather, Goguel, who has been Secretary-General of the French Senate and one of France's foremost political scientists, provides an analysis of underlying tendencies and conflicts in the French body politic. He observes a struggle originating in the Third Republic between the "party of movement" and the "party of established order": the former optimistic, confident about man's ability to guide himself and careless of tradition; the latter espousing an opposing mystique. The alternation in power of the two tendencies can be discerned beneath the strife of the multiplicity of parties in Third Republic France.

The interpretation, especially when generalized to other periods in French history, has been challenged by other French scholars. For example, Maurice Duverger has argued, in **La Démocratie sans le Peuple** (Paris: Éditions du Seuil, 1967, 251 p.), that the most noteworthy feature of French political history has not been a struggle between an uncompromising Left and Right but an enduring "centrism" in which a political class has governed France without regard for program or ideology. René Rémond, in **The Right Wing in France from 1815 to de Gaulle,** points to the enduring division of the exponents of order into three quite distinct "Rights."

Goguel himself both sees other kinds of conflict (*e.g.* class conflict and government versus opposition) and, with René Rémond, perceives internal divisions within the camps of movement and order. His reply to Duverger has been that each of them was focusing on a partial aspect of French politics. Goguel's argument was buttressed by his subsequent research in electoral geography, in which he demonstrated that different regions remained extraordinarily stable in their electoral allegiances to the tradition of movement or order through fully a century. **La Politique des Partis** has been a landmark in French self-examination.

WILLIAMS, PHILIP M. **Crisis and Compromise: Politics in the Fourth Republic.** New York: Anchor Books, rev. ed., 1966, 496 p.

Originally published in 1954 as **Politics in Post-War France** (London: Longmans, Green, 1954, 500 p.), the book has, according to its author, a large but limited theme: the political machinery of France between 1944 and 1958 and the combinations of men who operated or obstructed it. In neither French nor English is there a study equally rich in detailed analysis of parliamentary life. Carefully selected maps, charts, tables and documents complete the fascinating and highly original account.

The author argues throughout that the roots of political instability and of *immobilisme* in France lie less in the quality of her leaders or in the nature of constitutional provisions and of electoral systems than in the country's historical memories and her social structure. The multiple fractures of French opinion supported an obsolete party system which in turn made the parliamentary institutions unworkable. Williams' book was among the first intensive studies of interest group activities. The interaction of pressure politics and of the sophisticated élites in the bureaucracy is brilliantly described.

The author's explanation as to why the historical dilemma of French democracy remained unresolved in the Fourth Republic helps to explain the achievements and shortcomings of the régime that succeeded it.

EHRMANN, HENRY W. **Politics in France.** Boston: Little, Brown, 1968, 368 p.

Professor Ehrmann has written a very useful book concentrating on the political culture of the Fifth Republic. The book is the best in a series on different countries, meant to follow a common framework and "functional" approach. The themes of **Politics in France** are the impact of the tensions of modernization on an ancient civilization, an old state machine and a very conservative society, and the conflicts between administrative efficiency and representative traditions, governmental stability and a very imperfect party system. There is perhaps too much emphasis on "authority patterns," on which the author closely follows the analysis of Michel Crozier, **The Bureaucratic Phenomenon.** Although the book was finished before the May events of 1968 and De Gaulle's resignation in 1969, it is a tribute to Professor Ehrmann's acumen that its main lines require little revision.

The book is divided into 11 chapters with a postscript on "the events." The first two chapters give the historical and social-economic setting. There are chapters on the family, class, religion and education, the mass media, voting behavior, interest groups (on which the author is a particular authority), political parties, the "political class," bureaucracy and a brief section on General de Gaulle. Three chapters deal with the political system properly speaking, and the last with modernization and legitimacy. The book may be particularly recommended to students; footnote references provide a good guide to further detailed investigation.

THOMSON, DAVID. **Democracy in France since 1870.** New York: Oxford University Press (for the Royal Institute of International Affairs), 5th ed., 1969, 344 p.

First published in the infant days of the Fourth Republic, the fifth edition of this book covers a century of French developments and ends with a convincing account of the *événements* of 1968. Intended less as a history of three French Republics than as an inquiry into the workings of French ideals and institutions, the book, to be sure, reveals strong continuities and recurrent features. But it also shows that the whole trend of French developments since 1870 is misunderstood when it is assumed that each of the many crises is ultimately the same crisis.

How the conflict between the ideals of liberty and equality and how the gap between democracy and government have determined for each generation the operative ideals of the various Republics is the book's principal theme. Exceptionally rich bibliographical footnotes and excerpts from a wide range of contemporary sources exemplify and illustrate the changes which inherited traditions have undergone. The author's investigation reveals much not only about France but also about the nature of modern democracy.

The Fifth Republic and Gaullism are brought into sharp focus by the author's reflections on the régime's claim to be a modern synthesis of nationalism and of Republican democracy. Professor Thomson's untimely death in 1970 is an irreplaceable loss for all students of modern France who had become accustomed to the author's comments, which grew more perspicacious from one edition to the next, even when he had to offer them without the benefit of historical distance.

RÉMOND, RENÉ. **The Right Wing in France from 1815 to de Gaulle.** Philadelphia: University of Pennsylvania Press, 2d ed., 1969, 465 p.

Behind the Left-Right cleavage in French political history stand many Rights and many Lefts; differences within the two camps have often been as sharp as those between them. Rémond's essay in historical typology sets forth the characteristics of, and interactions between, three distinct traditions within the Right and emphasizes continuities which have persisted in each despite profound changes in government and society. Ultraism, the counterrevolutionary strain, opposed an emphasis on the natural order to the mechanistic rationalism of liberal political philosophy; regionalism to the centralizing tendencies of later Bourbons and Jacobins alike; family and hierarchy to the individualism and egalitarianism of the Revolution; throne and altar to the secular state. Orleanism, the second tradition, represented a kind of middle-of-the-road attitude. The third tradition, Bonapartism, has always been Janus-like. Setting itself up as the reconciler of Frenchmen, Bonapartism looked to the Left with a popular, democratic and anticlerical face; to the Right with an authoritarian, anti-red and conservative aspect. Despite the distinctiveness of these three traditions, interminglings have taken place among them, of which the Action Française was perhaps the most notorious hybrid.

The main defect of this book is a reflection of its virtues. Sometimes the analysis nearly fits Rémond's own remark that "political reality is richer and more varied than abstract classification would suggest."

WEBER, EUGEN JOSEPH. **Action Française: Royalism and Reaction in Twentieth-Century France.** Stanford: Stanford University Press, 1962, 594 p.

Published the same year as Edward Tannenbaum's **The Action Française** (New York: Wiley, 1962, 316 p.) and coming shortly on the heels of Samuel Osgood's **French Royalism under the Third and Fourth Republics** (The Hague: Nijhoff, 1961, 228 p.), Eugen Weber's history indicated a surge of renewed interest in the ideas and political impact of the extreme Right. Immensely detailed but written with such grace, wit and verve that the reader is carried along through the ups and downs of Maurras' movement with never-flagging interest, Weber's book is more than a history of the Action Française and an analysis of its adherents and its publications: it is a guide, and the best available, to the mentality of the French radical Right in the twentieth century, and it is incidentally a directory of those men (both French and non-French) who fell under the spell of Maurrassian ideas. Indeed, Weber's central theme is the extent to which Charles Maurras dominated the horizon of intellectuals in a country in which "literature . . . is a way of life" and politicians and generals dream of election to the Académie Française. Undeceived by the rhetoric of the Action Française's publicists (though not inclined to deëmphasize the role played by this rhetoric in poisoning the atmosphere of French political life), Weber traces the movement's evolution from a revolutionary gathering of royalist conspirators to a conservative organization whose members were mainly bound together by their distaste for the present and their even greater fear of what the future might bring.

The book unites in a rare and exciting way an original interpretation, remarkably extensive research and a deep understanding of French political life.

WOHL, ROBERT. **French Communism in the Making, 1914–1924.** Stanford: Stanford University Press, 1966, 530 p.

A painstaking, carefully documented and thoughtful analysis, this volume traces the origins of the French Communist Party and its evolution along Bolshevik lines in the first few years of its existence. The book explores the emergence of the party in 1920 against the background of the conflicting traditions of the French working class in the pre-1914 years, the profound disillusionment that developed over socialist collaboration in the war effort, and the intoxicating example of the Bolshevik triumph in 1917. Skillfully relating developments in France over the next few years to the personal and ideological struggles for power in Russia, the author examines the replacement of the original party leadership of left socialists and syndicalists, at Comintern dictation, by a new generation of leaders less wedded to the libertarianism of pre-1914 socialism, more willing to mold a highly disciplined party organization, and unqualifiedly agreeable to identifying the interests of the French working class and nation with the Comintern and the Soviet state.

A well-written, illuminating monograph, the volume merits favorable comparison with the massive study by Annie Kriegel of the schism in the French working-class movement, **Aux Origines du Communisme Français, 1914–1920** (Paris: Mouton, 1964, 2 v.), and is more analytical and provocative than Jacques Fauvet's somewhat factual and detailed narrative, **Histoire du Parti Communiste Français** (Paris: Fayard, 1964–1965, 2 v.).

Foreign Policy; Military Questions

GROSSER, ALFRED. **La IVᵉ République et Sa Politique Extérieure.** Paris: Colin, 1961, 438 p.

Well-read in the works of American students of foreign relations and highly conscious of the interrelationships between internal and external affairs, Grosser eschews diplomatic history of the traditional sort in favor of a study of "le comportement de la Quatrième République devant les problèmes de politique extérieure." His interest in "le comportement de la Quatrième République" leads Grosser to devote almost half his book to the "dynamic forces"—the institutions, parties, pressure groups, newspapers and ideologies—that shape French foreign policy. The preference of "politique extérieure" to "politique étrangère," the traditional term for foreign policy, reflects the author's conviction that, along with the question of Germany's future, the major problem faced by the Fourth Republic was that of relations between the metropole and the empire, particularly Indochina, Morocco and Tunisia.

Grosser's book is sympathetic to the obstacles faced by French foreign policymakers, while at the same time it argues that they did not make the best of the possibilities they had. The internal repercussions of the two major conflicts of the twentieth century—the ideological war between communism and anti-communism and the struggle between old states and new nations over decolonization—divided the national community and made a liberal policy almost impossible, Grosser concludes. It took General de Gaulle's charisma and never-failing confidence in the face of crisis to convince the French of the success of economic and diplomatic policies that had in fact been devised and initiated by the Fourth Republic.

On the De Gaulle era, Grosser has added a briefer sequel: **La Politique Extérieure de la Vᵉ République** (Paris: Éditions du Seuil, 1965, 189 p.), translated as "French Foreign Policy under De Gaulle" (Boston: Little, Brown, 1967, 175 p.). A more detailed account of postwar Franco-German relations may be found in F. Roy Willis, **France, Germany, and the New Europe, 1945–1967.**

WANDYCZ, PIOTR S. **France and Her Eastern Allies, 1919–1925: French-Czecho-slovak-Polish Relations from the Paris Peace Conference to Locarno.** Minneapolis: University of Minnesota Press, 1962, 454 p.

This is the first scholarly study of French diplomacy in Eastern Europe in the years just after World War I. Based on impressive research, especially in unpublished Polish, German and United States archives, this excellent book is essential reading not only for European diplomacy but also for understanding the causes of Hitler's success and French weakness in the 1930s. The author analyzes in significant detail the Slavic tragedy of Polish-Czech disunity and the inability of French leaders to do anything about it or even to decide how important Poland and Czechoslovakia were to France. French policy was fitfully distracted by the desire not to alienate England, the hope of reconstituting the Franco-Russian alliance and, under Briand, the dream of reconciliation with Germany. The short-term, almost accidental, origins of the Franco-Polish and Franco-Czech alliances will surprise even experts; so will the extent to which French policy favored Prague over Warsaw. The author's sympathy for Poland is evident at times, but he carefully and conclusively proves his interpretation that most Czech and French leaders "failed to appreciate the long-range community of interests with Poland."

This study should be compared with the analysis of French policy in Eastern Europe a decade later, by William E. Scott, **Alliance against Hitler: The Origins of the Franco-Soviet Pact** (Durham: Duke University Press, 1962, 296 p.).

MICAUD, CHARLES ANTOINE. **The French Right and Nazi Germany, 1933–1939.** Durham: Duke University Press, 1943, 255 p.

The French Right and Nazi Germany analyzes a historic reversal in the traditional foreign policy of French conservatives. Although they had long advocated a policy of unremitting opposition to Germany, by the 1930s French nationalists were becoming the advocates and, ultimately, the architects of appeasement. Charles Micaud's analysis, essentially a study in public opinion, broke new ground in the field of diplomatic history, for it was among the first to focus upon the role of domestic determinants in national foreign policy. It demonstrated how domestic considerations—the rise of the Popular Front with its attendant bourgeois fears of communism and social upheaval—led the French Right, in varying degrees, to interpret Hitler not as the enemy of the Third Republic but as a defender of the social order and a bulwark against the spread of communism.

Far better than any conventional study of the diplomatic documents of the Quai d'Orsay, the book explains why France became a declining force in international relations and the timid partner of British appeasement. It is now somewhat dated. Micaud did not quantify his data, and his "sample" was limited to the parliamentary spokesmen of the Right and their journals of opinion. His book, indeed, often reflects the uncritical sense of moral outrage which the word "appeasement" once provoked. Yet Micaud also anticipated issues that historians did not really begin to explore until the tensions of the cold war had started to wane.

CHALLENER, RICHARD DELO. **The French Theory of the Nation in Arms 1866–1939.** New York: Columbia University Press, 1955, 305 p.

Richard Challener has written a book admirably designed to instruct the average reader in the complexities of military forces and their relations to the body politic. In placing the term "nation in arms" in his title, he highlights one of the two basic approaches to the French army which have conditioned attitudes of Frenchmen from the time of the Revolution.

Against the revolutionary faith in a popular army in which all citizens would serve stood an older tradition of a professional army dominated by an aristocratic officer corps and made up of voluntary, long-term recruits. One of the anomalies of the nineteenth century was that France tried to revert to what was essentially a long-term, professional army, whereas Prussia, a country noted for its conservatism and aristocratic officer corps, chose to adopt the principles of a relatively short-service army in which reserves had to play a major role. When the Franco-Prussian War of 1870 proved the superiority of Prussian numbers over French élite troops, France, like other continental countries, perforce adopted the German system of short-term conscript armies.

The experience of World War I convinced the French that the doctrine of the offensive had been a disaster and that under the conditions of modern war the defense would always prove stronger than the offense. In the 1920s and 1930s France turned to a defensive strategy typified by the Maginot Line, whereas Germany, the defeated power, shifted in the Nazi years to the doctrine of the offensive. Just as the exaggerated offensive doctrines of 1914 cost France dearly, so the débâcle of 1940 proved that an outmoded defense was equally vulnerable.

Professor Challener's book is an instructive, clearly written and admirably balanced study, easily the most important one on the French army written in this century. For more background on the nineteenth century, there is the brilliant essay by Raoul Girardet, **La Société Militaire dans la France Contemporaine (1815–1939).** Of the many recent books perhaps the best are Paul-Marie de la Gorce's **The French Army: A Military-Political History** (New York: Braziller, 1963, 568 p.) and Philip Bankwitz's **Maxime Weygand and Civil-Military Relations in Modern France.**

GIRARDET, RAOUL. **La Société Militaire dans la France Contemporaine (1815–1939).** Paris: Plon, 1953, 329 p.

This is not a conventional military history dealing with battles, strategy or the mechanics of civil-military relationships but an interpretative essay, in which Girardet seeks to analyze the social composition of the French military establishment, to delineate its customs, values and codes of behavior and, above all, to determine the esteem in which it was held by the dominant elements of French society. Early chapters, for example, interpret the many and subtle ways in which the "old army" of the Restoration and July Monarchy was separated from the nation and the slow evolution of the doctrine that the mission of the army was to give obedience to constituted authority.

The analysis of the national army of the years from 1870 to 1914 is equally thorough and perceptive, treating such major issues as the effect of republicanism upon the social composition of the officer corps, the impact of a growing anti-militarism, the evolution of new concepts of the social and colonial roles of the officer and, above all, the extension of the tradition of the army as the *Grande Muette.* The volume ends, in essence, with 1914, and the entire inter-war period from 1918 to 1939 is sketchily treated in less than 20 pages of generalization. This is less than satisfactory because of Girardet's contention, doubtful at best, that these years were a mere continuation of previous military trends—a thesis appropriate for the pre-1914 era but which, as casually applied to the inter-war years, leads Girardet to overlook the growing malaise of the 1930s and to fail to ask questions about the forces that were leading French generals along the path toward disobedience.

BLOCH, MARC LÉOPOLD BENJAMIN. **L'Étrange Défaite.** Paris: Société des Éditions Franc-Tireur, 1946, 194 p.

During the past three decades there have been countless detailed and documented analyses of the French defeat of 1940. But **L'Étrange Défaite,** though impressionistic and written only weeks after the event, still retains its original force, still conveys the shock of that unexpected disaster. (An English translation appeared in 1949: **The Strange Defeat,** New York: Oxford University Press, 1949, 178 p.)

Properly speaking, it is not history but the personal testimony of a historian who was a participant—the anguished "cry of conscience" of a distinguished French medievalist, Marc Bloch, who was a soldier in both world wars and, in 1944, a martyr of the Resistance. To Bloch, who served on the staff of the First Army, the root cause of the military disaster was the "utter incompetence" of the high command, its intellectual failure to comprehend how technology had revolutionized the timetable of war. Since 1940 other critics have both modified and expanded his thesis, but Bloch, anticipating what has since become a commonplace of strategic thinking, was among the very first to understand the way in which modern military technology has compressed time and space and to emphasize the psychological dislocation of those who were intellectually unprepared for that change.

Marc Bloch was too well trained as a historian to believe that he had explained everything about the defeat by pinpointing its military origins. His final, and most moving, chapter is a sensitive critique of the values and mores of the dominant bourgeoisie of the Third Republic whose complacency led to the suicide of a nation.

Economic and Social Questions

GILPIN, ROBERT. **France in the Age of the Scientific State.** Princeton: Princeton University Press, 1968, 474 p.

Gilpin's book takes as its starting point a dilemma. During the past 20 years French leaders have become increasingly aware that national power and even national independence are related to scientific and technological preëminence. Yet, while they have coveted the resources of the scientific state and aspired to the military and industrial capabilities of the United States and the Soviet Union, they have been reluctant to initiate those changes in social attitudes and institutions that the scientific state requires. To paraphrase General de Gaulle, they have wanted to become modern without ceasing to be French. The question is not as simple and as clear-cut as American commentators have often made it seem, and it is to Gilpin's merit that he presents the French perception of the issue with sympathy and understanding, in addition to tracing with painstaking detail the obstacles to the creation of a scientific state and the measures the French have undertaken to overcome them. The transformation accomplished in the last ten years, the author concludes, has been truly remarkable. But Gilpin is pessimistic when it comes to assessing French chances for long-term success because of the French unwillingness to break with the notion of the traditional nation-state and participate in the creation of a united Europe that would include Great Britain.

Narrower in focus but more detailed is Lawrence Scheinman's careful study **Atomic Energy Policy in France under the Fourth Republic** (Princeton: Princeton University Press, 1965, 259 p.).

KINDLEBERGER, CHARLES P. **Economic Growth in France and Britain, 1851–1950.** Cambridge: Harvard University Press, 1964, 378 p.

The question of why France had slower economic growth than other major industrial powers in the nineteenth and early twentieth centuries has elicited a mass of books and articles. The best summary and critique of this literature is the work of Charles P. Kindleberger, an authority on international trade and economic development.

Disclaiming that he is an economic historian, Kindleberger goes through the vast literature to examine periods and problems of French and British economic growth and "economic aging." He passes in trenchant review the discussions of a series of the relevant factors: among them resources, capital, population, social structures and attitudes, entrepreneurship, technology, the role of government, urbanization and regional balance, and foreign trade. He emphasizes France rather than Britain.

He finds no theory or theories of economic growth which explain the differences between France and Britain. But that does not lessen the utility of his work. Despite some errors of fact which reviewers of Kindleberger have gleefully pointed out, his brisk and sophisticated two-country comparison is an excellent introduction to the problems of a century of French economic growth and stagnation.

French economic development is superbly set in the general European history of the industrial age by David Landes (a leading authority on France) in **The Unbound Prometheus** (Cambridge: Cambridge University Press, 1969, 566 p.). A rosy picture of French innovation and initiative on an international scale emerges from the excellent work of Rondo E. Cameron, **France and the Economic Development of Europe 1800–1914** (Princeton: Princeton University Press, 1961, 586 p.).

HACKETT, JOHN and HACKETT, ANNE-MARIE. **Economic Planning in France.** Cambridge: Harvard University Press, 1965, 418 p.

Early in the Marshall Plan days, American and English observers were almost unanimous in berating the French government for its interventions in the economy. But France has shown steadily higher growth rates than the United States or Britain in the 1950s and 1960s. How far has the remarkable economic growth, under both the Fourth and Fifth Republics, been due to the national economic planning which began when De Gaulle in 1946 set up the Planning Commission under Jean Monnet? Who has done the planning and how have they done it?

The Anglo-French husband-wife team of the Hacketts answers the second set of questions well, but does not attempt the first and crucial question. The authors bring out the eclectic and pragmatic nature of the process to which French planning owes much of its strength. They are impressed with the importance of the massive consultation of interest-group representatives and hopeful about the possibilities of regional decentralization of some of the planning function, although they do not do much to evaluate the social forces and political pressures at work.

For a lively evaluation of the economic consequences of planning in a number of key industrial sectors, one turns to John Sheahan's **Promotion and Control of Industry in Postwar France** (Cambridge: Harvard University Press, 1963, 301 p.), which includes comparisons with American experience, from the standpoint generally—but critically—in favor of competition and market forces. Warren C. Baum gives a gloomy picture of many forms of state intervention in **The French Economy and the State** (Princeton: Princeton University Press, 1958, 391 p.). Pierre Bauchet's **Economic Planning: The French Experience** (New York: Praeger, 1964, 299 p.) profits greatly by the author's experience in the Planning Commission. Claude Gruson begins his **Origines et Espoirs de la Planification Française** (Paris: Dunod, 1968, 438 p.) with a reminder of the decline of the market economy after 1929 and concludes with a discussion of the social and political perspectives of French planning on a national and international scale.

CROZIER, MICHEL. **The Bureaucratic Phenomenon.** Chicago: University of Chicago Press, 1964, 320 p.

Crozier is one of the ablest of the outstanding group of French students of the sociology of work. His book, whose influence has already been great in France and the United States, is first of all a meticulous, subtle and humane description and analysis of work organization, social relationships and patterns of authority in two French public administrations. They are presented pro forma anonymously: "the Parisian Clerical Agency" (the postal checks bureau) and the "Industrial Monopoly" (the state tobacco manufacture). Both are exceedingly "bureaucratic," in Crozier's sense of the word, which "evokes the slowness, the ponderousness, the routine." The pattern of authority he finds is based on the "horreur du face à face," the avoidance of face-to-face relationships between dependent strata of employees and their hierarchic superiors. So "authority is converted, as much as possible, into impersonal rules." The organization is so "deeply stabilized" that it cannot make needed changes until periodic crisis overtakes it, and even then change must come from the outside.

The author goes on to characterize all French public and private administration, despite differences he points out, in terms of this extreme bureaucratic model and to relate this model to the social system and culture of France, and then to the "over-all" development of industrial society. This leads him to suggest a general theory of organization and of action notable for its emphasis on power and the functions of conflict and uncertainty, and for its view of man in organizations, that man identified by one reviewer as *homo crozierus*.

How much of the impressive theoretical structure rests on evidence from two minor, backward French public agencies? They are atypical for many reasons. The chiefs of the bureau of postal checks can hold to an organization worthy of the pen of Balzac, but other high *fonctionnaires*—notably the *inspecteurs des finances* and the other *Grands Corps* of the state, as Crozier points out—have been innovators in crisis-blocked public organization and outlook.

EHRMANN, HENRY WALTER. **Organized Business in France.** Princeton: Princeton University Press, 1957, 514 p.

One of the most creative and forceful writers on comparative politics, notably on interest groups and on bureaucracy, Ehrmann has a long and deep acquaintance with almost all aspects of French life. He has produced here the best single study of any national employers' movement. (There is nothing comparable to it for the United States.) This work followed Ehrmann's study of **French Labor from Popular Front to Liberation** (New York: Oxford University Press, for the Institute of World Affairs, 1947, 329 p.), which is superb on the whole period before the collapse of France in 1940.

Organized Business in France is informed by a fine sense of the historical opportunities and the tragic constraints on the actions of employer and other groups in the Popular Front period. The chapter on Vichy clears up many of the obscurities about a shadowy period when employer representatives played major roles, and it sets the stage for analysis of continuities and changes in employer behavior after the liberation.

The various currents in employer thinking and action, including the interesting minority currents of avant-garde employers, all receive their due in the documented study of postwar organization and activities, attitudes and policies. Ehrmann explores the relationships of employers to their competitors, their employees, government and political parties, legislature and bureaucracy, and public opinion. The concluding chapter on organized business and the future of French democracy remains important because of the peculiar notions of authority still present in French industrial ownership and management, the lack of openness in the relations between organized business and the polity, and the ambiguity of employer ideas about the social bases of democracy.

WRIGHT, GORDON. **Rural Revolution in France: The Peasantry in the Twentieth Century.** Stanford: Stanford University Press, 1964, 271 p.

Gordon Wright's book traces the major changes that have occurred in French agriculture in this century, particularly in agricultural interest groups and government farm policy. The period on which he focuses—the inter-war years through the beginning of the Fifth Republic—witnessed the transformation of France from an agriculturally based to an industrial, urban economy. Wright studies the defensive reaction and mobilization of French agriculture, the development of a powerful farm lobby and the continuity in the policies of organized agriculture, which can be traced through changes of epoch and régime.

The major clash among farm interests developed in the late 1950s and pitted a rising generation of young farmers, grouped in the JAC (*Jeunesse Agricole Chrétienne*) and then in the CNJA (*Cercle National des Jeunes Agriculteurs*), against their elders, organized in the powerful FNSEA (*Fédération Nationale des Syndicats d'Exploitants Agricoles*). The generational and organizational conflict was reinforced by a conflict over farm policy. The older generation of farmers ran large profitable farms in the beet-growing and wheat-raising north and sought measures, such as price fixing based on flexible sliding scales, subsidies and tax privileges, designed to raise farm income. Younger farmers welcomed the structural transformation of agriculture and sought government measures, including coöperative production, processing and marketing arrangements, whose aim was not primarily to raise farm income but rather to ease the transition from individual to coöperative agriculture.

History was on the side of youth, as Wright predicted. Yet the problems and conflicts Wright analyzes are far from resolved, as agricultural demonstrations and riots in recent years testify, and the rural revolution he describes has yet to run its course. For recent trends, there are two excellent essays: François de Virieu, **La Fin d'une Agriculture** (Paris: Calmann-Lévy, 1967, 291 p.), and Henri Mendras, **La Fin des Paysans** (Paris: SEDEIS, 1967, 361 p.). Political life in rural France is admirably analyzed in Mark Kesselman's **The Ambiguous Consensus: A Study of Local Government in France** (New York: Knopf, 1967, 201 p.).

WYLIE, LAURENCE. **Village in the Vaucluse: An Account of Life in a French Village.** New York: Harper Colophon, rev. ed., 1964, 375 p.

Laurence Wylie's description of life in a southern French village is organized around the life cycle of the town's inhabitants, from childbirth and infancy, primary school and adolescence, through adult professional, social and family life. It concludes with analysis of the village as a social and political unit.

Because of rare insight and by expert focus on everyday phenomena, Wylie is able to discern details and inner patterns that elevate the mundane to the universal. Thus, to choose several examples, his description of a local café, a game of *boules,* a local election, an elementary school class and a firemen's banquet are masterpieces in their own right and illuminate the complexity of French life.

A theme running throughout the book is the *immobilisme* described (in other aspects of French life) by Herbert Lüthy in **France Against Herself.** The conservatism of rural France was evident in numerous ways and was most manifest in the defensive retrenchment of the village in face of "les ils" (the outsiders), represented quintessentially by the national government, which was regarded as "anonymous, intangible, and overpowering."

Written in the early 1950s, the book does not anticipate the vast changes occurring in France which originated at that time and deeply affected the little town of "Peyrane" (Roussillon). In his epilogue to the revised edition of **Village in the Vaucluse** and in his chapter entitled "Social Change at the Grass Roots" (in Stanley Hoffmann and others, **In Search of France),** Wylie describes the transformation of the village after several years. The focus of these later essays on the dynamics of change provides an excellent complement to the focus in **Village in the Vaucluse** at a single point in time. Students of rural change in France should also consult Wylie's more recent monograph, **Chanzeaux: A Village in Anjou** (Cambridge: Harvard University Press, 1966, 383 p.) and Edgar Morin's **Commune en France** (Paris: Fayard, 1967, 287 p.).

LORWIN, VAL ROGIN. **The French Labor Movement.** Cambridge: Harvard University Press, 1954, 346 p.

Written with profound sympathy and understanding, but without complacence, this is the best analysis of French labor in historical perspective in any language. The history of labor—and much else, for the author provides a running commentary on French economic and social history and on French socialism as well— is briefly traced from 1789 to the Depression. There are perceptive chapters on the Popular Front and on the effects of war and the Resistance. The Communists finally gained control after the Second World War, but Professor Lorwin shows how the development of the movement made it vulnerable once "revolution became the opium of the masses."

For the grim irony of French unionism is that the doctrine of syndicalism became a contributing factor to the continued feebleness of the movement. Its fear of the state, hostility to political parties and the myth of the great general strike did not save labor from dependence on governments for gains it was itself too weak to win and encouraged an almost unconscious politicization of the unions. The resulting difficulties are ably explained in chapters on the postwar structure and operations of the unions, the system (or rather, lack of it) of collective bargaining, industrial relations at plant level and the unions and politics. The appendices include a chronology of French labor and a variety of useful documents.

For an up-to-date account of both employer and union activities, readers should consult Jean-Daniel Reynaud, **Les Syndicats en France** (Paris: Colin, 2d ed., 1967, 292 p.).

Colonial Questions

HANOTAUX, GABRIEL and MARTINEAU, ALFRED, *eds.* **Histoire des Colonies Françaises et de l'Expansion de la France dans le Monde.** Paris: Plon, 1929–1933, 6 v.

This series of six volumes is the most authoritative and ambitious work on French colonial history yet published. Most of France's major and minor overseas endeavors, from implanting of colonies and creation of imperial bases and enclaves to geographic and scientific exploration and conquest of foreign peoples, are described by eminent specialists.

The essays in the volumes are of varying quality, but as a general introduction to French activity overseas before 1930 the series as a whole is still valuable. Especially outstanding are those by Maurice Delafosse, probably France's greatest Africanist scholar, who gives a masterful account of France's long relations with black Africa, but who should be updated by the Marxist historian Jean Suret-Canale's **L'Afrique Noire, Occidentale et Centrale: L'Ère Coloniale (1900–1945)** (Paris: Éditions Sociales, 3rd rev. ed., 1968, 386 p.); by Georges Hardy, an important colonial educator who knew Morocco and Tunisia from firsthand experience; and by Augustin Bernard, whose work on Algeria should be supplemented with Claude Martin's **Histoire de l'Algérie Française, 1830–1962** (Paris: Éditions des 4 fils Aymon, 1963, 508 p.). As a reference work, the series is useful for the casual reader but of limited value for the specialist since bibliographies, sources and footnotes were omitted. Hanotaux's introduction and conclusion provide a classic statement of French attitudes toward the colonies and a rationale for empire, written at the high point of colonial fortunes.

GANIAGE, JEAN. **L'Expansion Coloniale de la France sous la Troisième République, 1871–1914.** Paris: Payot, 1968, 434 p.

This book attempts to trace the course of empire followed by France's Third Republic from 1871 to 1914. The author divides the work into three parts. In the first, after surveying France's colonial domain in 1871, he discusses the difficulties of Jules Ferry and his associates during the early phase of expansion and then reviews in detail the establishment of the Tunisian protectorate, the Egyptian crisis of 1876–1882 and the Tonkin affair. In the second, the triumphant period of the conquest of the 1880s down to 1914 is reassessed: the formation of the colonial party, the partition of black Africa, the conquest of the Sahara and Madagascar, the Franco-British rapprochement of 1900–1914 and the Moroccan crises. In the last, Ganiage describes all of the French colonies as they had developed by 1914— their administration, the state of the indigenous populations and French economic interests.

Professor Ganiage, who is a specialist on North African history at the Sorbonne, wrote this survey of French expansion as a series of lectures for his students. It is a helpful volume for readers unable to consult the six volumes of Hanotaux and Martineau's **Histoire des Colonies Françaises.** However, Henri Brunschwig's **La Colonisation Française** (Paris: Calmann-Lévy, 1949, 297 p.) should be consulted for the 1914–1945 period.

ROBERTS, STEPHEN HENRY. **History of French Colonial Policy, 1870–1925.** London: King, 1929, 2 v.

French colonial policy has been studied by many British historians because of its obvious contrast with their own. Roberts, actually an Australian and a "colonial," brought great insight to this volume which attempts to analyze colonial policy and to present case studies of how that policy has been carried out in practice in France's colonies. The author is successful in his first aim and provides a clear discussion of the relationship between economic and political policy, how these policies were formulated in Paris, and an excellent analysis of the central organization of the former Ministry of Colonies. This analytical section on policy should be supplemented by the later work of Raymond Betts, **Assimilation and Association in French Colonial Theory, 1890–1914** (New York: Columbia University Press, 1961, 224 p.), and Hubert Deschamps, **Les Méthodes et les Doctrines Coloniales de la France** (Paris: Colin, 1953, 222 p.).

Roberts is less successful in the second part of the volume devoted to colonial policy in practice in the colonies. The sections on North Africa and Indochina are incisive, but the sections on black Africa are not as detailed or well researched; they should be supplemented with Raymond L. Buell, **The Native Problem in Africa.** Since Roberts' study, a number of works have appeared which examine the practice of colonial theory in the field. Michael Crowder's **Senegal: A Study in French Assimilation Policy** (New York: Oxford University Press, 1962, 104 p.) is a good example.

MORTIMER, EDWARD. **France and the Africans, 1944–1960: A Political History.** New York: Walker, 1969, 390 p.

The struggle of French-speaking black Africans to gain local self-rule and eventual independence is the subject of this narrative history of France's *Afrique Noire* during the postwar period. With the exception of Senegal's Four Communes, black Africans had no political rights until De Gaulle initiated colonial reforms at the Brazzaville conference of 1944. This set in motion basic changes in each colony of French West and Equatorial Africa, Togo and Cameroon which provided for election of deputies to the French parliament, territorial councils, colonial councils and municipal officials. These new political opportunities called for the creation of African political parties. Mortimer tells in detail how these parties were organized, what politicians led them, and how France tried to avoid another Indochina or Algeria by adopting a policy of gradual transfer of power to the African élite.

This descriptive account brings together for the first time a number of complex details on the political aspirations and activities of Africans from the 14 former colonies (Madagascar and Somaliland are omitted) and is most useful in clarifying a confusing but important period in French colonial history. The book concludes with the referendum of 1958 (which enabled Guinea to gain independence) and the creation of the short-lived French Community, which was destroyed by the surge to independence of the other colonies. Mortimer's work is strong on the French side but needs to be supplemented by Ruth Schachter Morgenthau's **Political Parties in French-Speaking West Africa** for a fuller picture of African motivation, and the two background volumes by Virginia Thompson and Richard Adloff, **French West Africa** and **The Emerging States of French Equatorial Africa** (Stanford: Stanford University Press, 1960, 595 p.).

Memoirs and Biographies

DE GAULLE, CHARLES ANDRÉ JOSEPH MARIE. **Mémoires de Guerre.** Paris: Plon, 1954–1959, 3 v.

A masterly work of epic quality, written in superb prose, these memoirs recount the exploits of Charles de Gaulle in the five and a half years from the disastrous defeat of June 1940 to the reëstablishment of France at the end of the war. As much a work of history as of autobiography, the memoirs represent a brilliantly written account of these years as well as an indispensable source for future historians. Scholars will find especially valuable the appended selection of documents (letters sent and received, speeches, proclamations, etc.) that comprise the latter half of each of the three volumes.

From the beginning of the first volume ("L'Appel, 1940–1942"), the author makes clear that there are two protagonists in his story, France and himself, and that his personal mission and destiny were to recall France to her greatness. In the dark days of 1940, after successfully commanding one of the nation's only too few armored divisions and serving briefly as undersecretary for war in Paul Reynaud's cabinet, he established himself in London and refused to accept defeat when Marshal Pétain prepared to sue for an armistice. From that moment the personification of France's resolve to fight on, De Gaulle considered himself the legitimate embodiment of France herself. With scant resources and few followers, and utterly dependent upon the British and Americans (the "Anglo-Saxons") for material support, he undertook the long, laborious task of creating French fighting forces capable of participating actively in the war and thereby ensuring France a role in the settlement of her future. He successively created a government in London (which was transferred in 1942 to Algiers), coördinated the Resistance movement in metropolitan France, and rallied almost all of overseas France to his cause. From the beginning he made clear his intention not only to play an active military role in the war but to defend French territorial rights and integrity wherever they were at stake.

Stubborn, intractable, convinced of his sacred mission, De Gaulle had more than his share of friction with Winston Churchill, who befriended and supported him but who was himself dependent on the vast resources of the United States. Franklin D. Roosevelt remained suspicious of his dictatorial propensities and, to his chagrin, maintained official relations with Vichy. American coöperation with the Vichy authorities in the landings in North Africa was a source of special exasperation and is detailed in volume II ("L'Unité, 1942–1944").

The final volume ("Le Salut, 1944–1946") ends on a note of new crisis. Once the final months of combat were over, victory achieved, France restored to its rightful rank as a great power, and the possibility of a communist triumph in France averted, he saw the nation as beginning to relax and to slide back into older easygoing ways ("la facilité"). Above all, he recognized that the country would not accept his constitutional prescriptions for a strong presidential system but was returning to the older system of party rule and party bickering. In January 1946, he dramatically resigned his office as President of the Provisional Government and withdrew to write these remarkable wartime memoirs, which were published in translation as "War Memoirs" (New York: Viking and Simon and Schuster, 1955–1960, 3 v.).

Readers who wish to examine De Gaulle's relations with Roosevelt and Churchill from a more detached point of view may profitably turn to two useful scholarly books: Arthur L. Funk, **De Gaulle: The Critical Years, 1942–1943** (Norman: University of Oklahoma Press, 1959, 356 p.) and Milton R. Viorst, **Hostile Allies: FDR and Charles de Gaulle** (New York: Macmillan, 1965, 280 p.).

COLTON, JOEL. **Léon Blum: Humanist in Politics.** New York: Knopf, 1966, 512 p.

The two socialists, Jean Jaurès and Léon Blum, were both intellectuals as well as politicians, Jaurès a historian, Blum an essayist and literary critic; for years both were the undisputed leaders of the French Socialist Party, and there was little to distinguish between their brands of parliamentary reformist socialism. Both were men of unchallenged integrity and devotion to the cause of world peace. Léon Blum had an even longer parliamentary career than Jaurès, stretching from the First World War to his death in 1950, but his fame (or infamy) rests almost entirely on the three short years between the beginning of the Popular Front in 1936 and the French defeat in 1940.

Joel Colton has made the choice of concentrating nearly all of his large volume on the period of the Popular Front, virtually ignoring the early years when Blum was making a reputation as a literary critic and serving as a lawyer in the prestigious *Conseil d'État*, or even the years of the 1920s when he was the leader of the Socialist Party in the Chamber. For all the courage with which he faced adversity, as Premier of France Blum betrayed all the weaknesses of the intellectual. It is to the credit of Colton that, despite his admiration for Blum the man, he could be pitiless in depicting the shortcomings of Blum the politician and political leader. By the end of the book, however, Colton almost manages to make the reader forget Blum's failures and recall only his virtues. The heavy concentration on the years of the Popular Front also has some advantages, for this book is not only an excellent biography but a sure guide to the intricacies of French politics and international diplomacy in a fateful period for Western Europe. No one has written a better account of the Popular Front and no one need write another biography of Léon Blum for those years.

GOLDBERG, HARVEY. **The Life of Jean Jaurès.** Madison: University of Wisconsin Press, 1962, 590 p.

In presenting his biography of Jean Jaurès, Harvey Goldberg has chosen to write a large book, one that places the man in the political setting of a career that spanned most of the period of the Third Republic down to his assassination at the outbreak of war in 1914. While it can hardly be said that Goldberg does for the period what one would find in a book like D. W. Brogan's **France Under the Republic,** Jaurès the politician was involved in so many social and political issues that to follow his life in the Goldberg manner is to deal with almost all aspects of French politics and society. While the focus throughout remains on Jaurès, one can turn to Goldberg for the basic information on elections, political scandals, the Dreyfus case, Millerandism, separation of Church and State, the unification of the Socialist Party, the issues of revanchism versus the peace movement to which Jaurès devoted so much of the last years of his life, and the diplomatic events that led to the outbreak of war. It is a solid, informative book that is likely to stand for many years as the best one-volume biography of one of the great political figures of this century.

Jaurès was a man capable of arousing intense devotion among his admirers, and Harvey Goldberg clearly belongs among the devotees. Although he recognizes that Jaurès was not infallible, his effort to maintain a critical balance breaks down. Too often the study leaves the reader with the impression that Jaurès, whatever the circumstances, had done all that was humanly possible.

At some time Jaurès will be accorded a multivolume biography comparable to the one done by Suarez on Briand. Goldberg stops his book with the assassination of Jaurès in 1914.

SUAREZ, GEORGES. **Briand.** Paris: Plon, 1938–1952, 6 v.

This massive work is a flawed monument, an irritating blend of biography, history and romanticized journalism, strongly peppered with the author's bias—*e.g.* Jean Jaurès and Léon Blum are savagely caricatured. Suarez frequently invents retrospective conversations and has no scruples about describing an episode or analyzing the secret emotions of his characters on the basis of little visible evidence beyond his own imagination. Yet these egregious faults are offset by certain undeniable virtues. Suarez is an unusually well-informed observer of the backstairs reality of French political life; in addition, he draws heavily on what he calls "the immense dossier" of Briand's personal papers (which no other author has used); and finally, the subject of his portrait is one of the most significant and representative figures in twentieth-century French politics. Suarez has given us not only a biography of this elusive and influential man, but a life-and-times treatment that will fascinate any student of the Parisian political scene from 1890 to 1930.

Aristide Briand, during his sinuous career, moved from the extreme left of anarcho-syndicalism through a Marxian socialist phase to a position in the fluid center of French political life. He was intimately involved in almost every important political episode of his time, from the emergence and unification of the Socialist Party to the attempt at Franco-German reconciliation in the Stresemann years. An early protagonist of the general strike, he did not hesitate as Premier in 1910 to break a national railway strike by mobilizing the strikers into the army. An "areligious" man, he was named minister of cults during the touchy period just after Church and State were separated, and through his moderation helped to avert open conflict. A pacifist by temperament, he favored preparedness in the tense pre-1914 years and served for a time as wartime Premier. But he reached the apex of his career in 1925–1932, when he became an irreplaceable foreign minister in every successive cabinet, the embodiment of the Locarno policy and the apostle of reconciliation and peace in Europe. Not every Frenchman today would regard that policy as successful, or even wise; nevertheless, it is Briand alone among France's foreign ministers whose memory has been consecrated by a monument at the entrance to the Quai d'Orsay.

Briand, though no doubt a flawed human being and political leader, deserves better than a flawed biography. But until one is written, that of Suarez offers us the fullest portrait of a remarkable man.

BANKWITZ, PHILIP. **Maxime Weygand and Civil-Military Relations in Modern France.** Cambridge: Harvard University Press, 1967, 445 p.

Maxime Weygand was supposed to carry the secrets of Foch in his baton. Called to command the French armies after the first disasters of the spring of 1940, he failed to stem the German tide and almost immediately began to call for an armistice. His subsequent acts of disobedience to civil authorities culminated in the death of the Third Republic. Weygand, without question, was one of the principal gravediggers.

Philip Bankwitz's biography, which rests upon distinguished scholarship, is sympathetic yet critical, a book which seeks to explain rather than merely condemn the general and his limited perceptions. His thesis, cogently argued though occasionally tendentious, presents Weygand as a complex personality with a "narrow, traditionalist-legalist" conception of the relationship between the soldier and the state but, above all, as a man who had by 1940 come to regard himself as the guardian and conscience of the nation and a soldier-patriot who intervened to save nation and army from the failures of the régime.

The principal contribution of this study, however, is its careful delineation of the military issues and political events, especially the crisis of February 1934, which began to alienate members of the high command from the régimes they served. Bankwitz presents impressive evidence in support of the thesis that the ultimate disobedience was rooted in the growing malaise and politicization of the high command in the 1930s. His book thus transcends biography and raises issues which go far beyond the personal history of a particular general: the loyalty of the soldier to the state and the motives which may impel him to political activism and even disobedience.

ITALY

General; Historical

CROCE, BENEDETTO. **A History of Italy, 1871–1915.** New York: Oxford University Press, 1929, 333 p.

By 1925 Mussolini's Fascist dictatorship controlled Italy. Internal opposition to the régime became increasingly difficult as the government silenced its opponents or forced them into exile. Fascist censorship curtailed freedom of the press. Thus subtler ways of manifesting opposition to authoritarianism had to be devised. It was then that Benedetto Croce, long an important figure in the intellectual life of twentieth-century Italy, emerged as the leader of a small, dedicated group of anti-Fascists who remained in the country. Between 1928 and 1938 he wrote three books, all of which went through numerous editions, inspired by the conviction that liberty remained the ultimate goal of mankind and was necessary for the continuation of culture and civilization. In addition to the book here reviewed, which was first published in 1928, the books were **A History of Europe in the Nineteenth Century** (New York: Harcourt, 1933, 375 p.), which followed in 1933, and **History as the Story of Liberty** (New York: Norton, 1941, 324 p.), in 1938.

Croce himself explains in the preface to **A History of Italy** that the book is "a sketch of Italian history after the establishment of political unity," "an attempt to present events as an objective whole." Noting that the book covers the so-called "years of peace," he points out that these years "present movement and dramatic interest to all those who recognize that such features are not solely to be found in noisy struggles and spectacular achievements."

Croce was too honest a historian to ignore the shortcomings and deficiencies of liberal Italy, but since his book was written to counter Fascist denigration his account tends to emphasize the positive achievements during Italy's first half century of existence as a national state. Despite this bias, understandable if one is aware of the circumstances that inspired it, Croce's summary of this period of Italian history remains an important source for any student of Italian affairs, for it tells us much about the outlook of Italy's ruling class to which Croce belonged both by birth and education, and indirectly illumines the reasons for its failure to understand the new social and political forces of the twentieth century. It was this failure that led to the demise of liberal Italy after the First World War.

MACK SMITH, DENIS. **Italy: A Modern History.** Ann Arbor: University of Michigan Press, rev. ed., 1969, 542 p.

Brilliantly written and thoroughly researched, Mack Smith's book stands alone as the best political history in English of Italy from unification to 1968. Covering over one hundred years of Italy's existence as a united nation, Mack Smith attempts to clarify and place in historical perspective Italy's shortcomings and achievements. Liberalism, nationalism and totalitarianism all molded Italy's history, and Mack Smith's interpretation rests on the thesis that the success achieved by unification in the nineteenth century was followed by collapse and defeat in the twentieth century because of mistakes in foreign policy linked to constitutional weaknesses in domestic politics. Constitutional defects, more than any other factor, he believes, prevented the evolution of Italy into the modern and liberal nation *Risorgimento* leaders had envisioned. Thus his views on pre-Fascist Italy tend to be negative, and he concludes that liberal Italy committed suicide. The book has been translated into Italian, widely read in Italy, commented upon and criticized by Italian historians who feel that Mack Smith's judgment is too severe, but the author, when he presented the book, was aware that its thesis might be challenged and wrote "he is a coward and a dullard who does not risk some interim judgment on the course of history." Mack Smith is neither a coward nor a dullard, and his book upholds the high standards set by English historical scholarship.

SETON-WATSON, CHRISTOPHER. **Italy from Liberalism to Fascism, 1870–1925.** London: Methuen, 1967, 772 p.

The result of some 20 years of work, Seton-Watson's book has only one shortcoming: it stops at 1925. Not a book to be read easily or quickly, it is a detailed political history. However, the author is too modest when he writes that his book was intended for the enterprising undergraduate who had no knowledge of the Italian language. That may have been his intention when he began to work on the book, but the final result is a scholarly, informed and informative work that synthesizes the wealth of material available, especially in Italian, on Italy's domestic and foreign affairs from 1870 to 1925. Seton-Watson neglects no aspect of Italy's political activity at home and abroad, and judiciously discusses Italian developments in four chronological parts: 1870–1887, the years of consolidation for the new state; 1887–1901, the period of stresses and strains; 1901–1914, the age of expansion; 1914–1925, the crisis and downfall of liberalism. The result is a book that should be read in its entirety to get a panoramic, yet detailed, account of pre-Fascist Italy and referred to from time to time for information on some particular issue in Italian political life. No serious student of modern Italy should neglect it.

HUGHES, H. STUART. **The United States and Italy.** New York: Norton, rev. ed., 1968, 297 p.

First published in 1953 as one of the volumes in the Harvard Foreign Policy Library, Hughes' book tells us a great deal about modern Italy and very little about relations between the United States and Italy. However, as a study of Italy and the Italians the book is probably the best introduction to an understanding of this complex people described by one scholar as "a tragic country—with a smiling face." Hughes surveys the past and focuses on the present. The last half of this revised edition has been rewritten and brought up to date, and the bibliography includes many important works published since 1953. Well-versed on Italian political, economic, social and cultural developments after the Second World War, Hughes presents a balanced and highly informative account that can be read with profit by anyone with an interest in Italian affairs. Moreover, the book is not only knowledgeable but also elegantly written, which should recommend it especially to the general reader wishing to learn about contemporary Italy.

Fascist Era

General; Mussolini

MEGARO, GAUDENS. **Mussolini in the Making.** Boston: Houghton, 1938, 347 p.

The most important critical biography of Mussolini to be written before World War II was this book by the late Gaudens Megaro. This American scholar carefully explored the Duce's career prior to the autumn of 1914 when he rejected the Socialist Party line and urged Italian intervention in the war. At considerable risk, Megaro conducted an on-the-spot investigation in the places where Mussolini had spent his early manhood. He was able to demolish the myth that Mussolini had engaged in irredentist agitation in the Austrian province of Trent in 1909. He also took a hard and skeptical look at the assertions that the development of Mussolini's mind was profoundly influenced by Georges Sorel. Although Mussolini admired Sorel for a time, finding in the French writer a brilliant rationalization of his own political sentiments that came out of his native Romagna, his enthusiasm for Sorel was short-lived. A model of what such a field study should be, Megaro's book was to be warmly acclaimed in Italy after the overthrow of the dictatorship.

KIRKPATRICK, IVONE. **Mussolini: A Study in Power.** New York: Hawthorn Books, 1964, 726 p.

Thus far the best biography of Benito Mussolini in English is by the late Sir Ivone Kirkpatrick, who was commissioned to write a companion volume to Alan Bullock's **Hitler.** Though it falls short of the Bullock model, Kirkpatrick's book is of high quality and very readable. A career diplomat, Kirkpatrick served in the British embassies in Rome and Berlin from 1930 to 1938 and thus had opportunities to observe the Duce in person. The author's experience of the realities of power politics has enabled him to present an incisive analysis of Mussolini's political and diplomatic moves. At the same time he probes deeply into the psychological aspects of Mussolini's complex personality; in this regard, his analytical chapter, "The Duce," is particularly revealing

The book has four parts. The first covers the years through the March on Rome.

The author describes Mussolini's career prior to 1919 as that of a "revolutionary" and says that the ensuing four years saw his "tactical skill, which was almost political genius," at its best. The second takes up the period from 1922 to the Ethiopian War; and the third, the decline that continued almost imperceptibly until the coup d'état of July 25, 1943. The final section describes the anticlimactic months of the German-controlled Italian Social Republic from the autumn of 1943 until Mussolini's execution at the hands of Italian partisans in April 1945.

Whereas the first and final parts of the book rely heavily on Gaudens Megaro's **Mussolini in the Making** and on F. W. Deakin's **The Brutal Friendship,** the two middle sections are based on much original research. Also good are the chapters on the Lateran pacts and the diplomacy of the 1930s. The author stresses that the conquest of Ethiopia proved more damaging than any other enterprise in contributing to Mussolini's decline, for "he became convinced of his own infallibility and was no longer prepared to listen to the voice of reason." A serious deficiency in Sir Ivone's book is the complete neglect of domestic history during the 1930s and a far too cursory explanation of the corporative state. One looks in vain for a discussion of how the different social and economic classes viewed Fascism and how Fascism affected their well-being.

DE FELICE, RENZO. **Mussolini il Rivoluzionario, 1883–1920.** Turin: Einaudi, 1965, 773 p.
———. **Mussolini il Fascista: La Conquista del Potere, 1921–1925.** Turin: Einaudi, 1966, 806 p.
———. **Mussolini il Fascista: L'Organizzazione dello Stato Fascista, 1925–1929.** Turin: Einaudi, 1968, 600 p.

Three volumes have now appeared in Renzo de Felice's massive "political biography" of Mussolini. The author's periodization of Mussolini's life is revealed in the subtitles: "the Revolutionary" (1883–1920); "the Fascist" (1921–1929); "the Duce" (1929–1939) and "the Ally" (1939–1945), not yet published. De Felice, a professor of history at the University of Salerno, based his work on intensive research in the Archivio Centrale dello Stato and the archives of the Foreign Ministry. Appendices to each volume present considerable hitherto unfamiliar documentary material.

The author declares he is trying to write a "new" kind of biography that fuses political, sociological and psychological interpretations. Much of the time, however, it would seem that he is writing a history of Italian Fascism rather than a biography of Mussolini. He says almost nothing about Mussolini's personal life. Indeed, the protagonist often gets lost from view for pages at a time; the author's exposition in this estimable study is far from lucid.

According to De Felice, Mussolini's youthful socialism was a "state of mind" to which Marxism was substantially extraneous. For Mussolini socialism was action; he was distrustful of theories. The Romagna was not as influential as Milan in shaping his political outlook. De Felice finds no fault with Mussolini for accepting French money in 1914–1915, since he had already changed his attitude toward the war; what was bad was that he turned ever more toward class discrimination instead of socialism. From 1914 to Caporetto, Mussolini was a "sleeping socialist;" Caporetto shocked him and he began to move toward the right. Nevertheless, the early Fascism of 1919, despite its nationalist and anti-socialist slant, was still predominantly a left-wing movement (an assertion which many historians would debate). After the failure of the sit-in strikes of mid-1920, Mussolini became more conservative. At this juncture "true," "mass" Fascism (squadrism) emerged in the countryside; without this agrarian Fascism Mussolini could not have achieved power, De Felice declares.

In his second volume De Felice stresses the lack of vision of Giovanni Giolitti and other liberals who erroneously calculated between 1920 and 1922 that at the proper moment they could "tame" the Fascists into yet another variant of the political game of *trasformismo*. Neither does the House of Savoy fare well in De

Felice's judgment. It was the decision of Victor Emmanuel III alone on the morning of October 28, 1922, that prevented the Italian army from moving against the Blackshirts. The author also takes the King to task for not dismissing Mussolini during the prolonged crisis that followed the murder of Matteotti in 1924. One of the best sections in this volume is an excursus in chapter 5 wherein De Felice analyzes the personality of Mussolini at the time he took office and before he became a victim of his own myth, contending that he fell short of genuine leadership because he was only a brilliant tactician with no fixed goals, was too distrustful of his countrymen both individually and collectively and was unable either to select or retain good lieutenants.

The third volume begins with the coup d'état of January 3, 1925, the start of a two-year process in riveting down the police state. Though Mussolini coined the term "totalitarian," his régime was far less total than that of Stalin or Hitler. For a while in the late 1920s Mussolini actually played down the Fascist Party in favor of the State.

The penultimate chapter is devoted to the Lateran pacts with the Church—"the truest and most important success in [Mussolini's] entire political career."

SCHNEIDER, HERBERT WALLACE. **Making the Fascist State.** New York: Oxford University Press, 1928, 403 p.

This is a vivid and perspicacious, if sometimes impressionistic, account of the events and, more particularly, of the ideas that were involved in the origin of the Italian Fascist movement and the setting up of its régime. Writing before the consensus among liberal-minded or left-wing intellectuals as to the moral horror of "totalitarianism," at least of the non-communist variety, Schneider treats the events recounted in fairly evenhanded fashion and, indeed, on occasion shows what (in a nonpreferential sense) might be called a sympathy for the Fascists as they faced largely unforeseen political and governmental problems. Moreover, he showed much trust in the real effectiveness of the incipient syndical system and hoped that it would represent a democratic and working-class leaven preventing the consolidation of the tendencies that ultimately culminated in an ungenerous, oppressive and illiberal dictatorship. These hopes and errors of prophecy probably lowered the repute of this work in the period shortly after its composition, but this absence of political tendentiousness is somewhat of a recommendation for the work today. We want to know what early Fascism was actually like (and not merely what it became), and this work shows that at the level of leadership it has as many roots in personal experience and in intellectual influence from the left as from the right.

Schneider is a philosopher of repute. His basic interest was in the coming together of currents of thought to create what he recognized as a rather new and unprecedented political position. He shows well something that in the light of subsequent events may readily be overlooked—that a coming together in the 1920s of various established Italian intellectual trends in some relation of at least tentative sympathy with the new régime gave Fascism a certain intellectual respectability in that period.

FINER, HERMAN. **Mussolini's Italy.** New York: The Universal Library, Grosset and Dunlap, 1965, 564 p.

First published in London in 1935, this is essentially a commentary on and a restrained argument against the political claims of the Italian Fascist movement and its leader, Benito Mussolini. The approach is thus dated. It obviously addresses those Anglo-Saxons of the time who were inclined to treat Mussolini as the author of brilliant political innovations very likely valid, at least for his own countrymen. The argument rejects this assessment on the basis of liberal and democratic values while nevertheless treating the régime, its leader and its ideas with some respect. For present purposes the book contains a still valuable account of the political and social background out of which the régime arose and a summary of its institutions and policies, the latter rather more deeply embedded in critical evaluation than the present historic repute of the subject will seem to most readers to warrant.

EBENSTEIN, WILLIAM. **Fascist Italy.** New York: American Book Co., 1939, 310 p.

This is a moderately detailed account of the institutions and practices of the Italian Fascist régime in what may be called its "fully developed" period shortly before World War II. Most useful for reference are perhaps the two chapters evaluating the results of Fascist economic policy. Possibly because we are today much more familiar with the idea of dictatorial rule in fairly developed countries, readability of the earlier political chapters is impaired by a sort of open-mouthed amazement with which the violent or merely undemocratic tricks and devices of the Fascists are recorded. The account of the origin of the régime is insufficiently digested and analyzed. Particularly, the impression—hardly credible in view of the extreme social disorders after World War I and the basic division between socialist and bourgeois views—is conveyed that with a bit of courage (or perhaps heroism) on the part of Italian democrats a workable democratic régime could easily have been preserved in the 1920s, or even restored at the time of the Matteotti crisis.

VIVARELLI, ROBERTO. **Il Dopoguerra in Italia e l'Avvento del Fascismo (1918–1922). Volume I: Dalla Fine della Guerra all'Impresa di Fiume.** Naples: Istituto Italiano per gli Studi Storici, 1967, 620 p.

Frustrated nationalism, political polarization and the paralysis of the parliamentary system account for the deterioration of the liberal state and the rise of Fascism in postwar Italy. Conforming to a generally accepted practice among scholars, Vivarelli takes the First World War as his starting point. The Italian government's decision to enter the conflict was not only a major turning in Italian foreign policy but also a watershed in domestic affairs. By deciding to go to war in spite of the opposition of the parliamentary majority, the government set a precedent for the subsequent Fascist challenge to the liberal order.

Vivarelli gives great relevance to questions of foreign policy. He argues that Fascism arose from the fusion of those groups demanding expansion abroad and an anti-socialist course at home. Fascism is seen largely as a projection of Mussolini's irrepressible will to power, an approach that leads the author to gloss over the heterogeneity of early Fascism and to suggest by implication that the movement was much more monolithic than it really was. Rejecting some recent interpretations which suggest a principle of continuity in Mussolini's conduct, the author falls back on the traditional view of Mussolini as an opportunistic agitator.

Political personalities receive special attention, and many of the author's biographical sketches are models of conciseness and perception. He has drawn extensively both from the recent scholarly literature on Fascism and from the resources of the Archivio Centrale dello Stato in Rome. Unfortunately, there is no bibliography to guide the reader through the extensive documentation cited in the footnotes. Documents, many of archival origin, appear in the appendix.

TASCA, ANGELO. **Nascita e Avvento del Fascismo: L'Italia dal 1918 al 1922.** Bari: Laterza, 1965, 2 v.

This controversial book holds a most distinguished place in the historiography of Italian Fascism. First published in English and French in 1938 under the author's pseudonym "Angelo Rossi" as **The Rise of Italian Fascism** (London: Methuen, 1938, 376 p.), the book has been translated into many languages and has gone through several editions. As an anti-Fascist exile and a founding member of the Italian Communist Party (expelled in 1929 for right-wing deviationism), the author conceived the work in a frankly polemical spirit. But in spite of its obvious ideological slant, the book has withstood the test of time and criticism with remarkable success. The present edition features Tasca's extensive footnotes, missing in most of the others. An appendix of supplementary notes and documents which Tasca intended to publish as a separate volume has never appeared in print.

Although Tasca presents Fascism as a counterrevolutionary movement, he does recognize that the Fascist appeal cut across class lines and that Fascism reflected many conflicting aspirations, some of which were not inherently conservative. This awareness of the complexity of Italian Fascism is probably Tasca's most lasting contribution to an understanding of the Fascist phenomenon. He points to the socialist failure to form a united front against Fascism as a primary reason for Mussolini's success. This criticism of socialist tactics indicates that the book should also be read as a contribution to the socialist-communist debate on how to deal with Fascist movements.

AQUARONE, ALBERTO. **L'Organizzazione dello Stato Totalitario.** Turin: Einaudi, 1965, 620 p.

The first in the series "Storia e Documenti del Fascismo," this study combines an analysis of the structure of the Fascist state with a judicious selection of documents illustrating the 20 years of Fascism. In some 300 pages of text, Alberto Aquarone, one of Italy's abler young historians, reviews the way the Fascist state was organized and illustrates its ultimate failure to become a truly totalitarian régime. This failure may be attributed both to the numerous unresolved contradictions arising from the continual intra-party dissensions and to the structural and ideological deficiencies of Fascism itself. Aquarone concludes that Fascism remained in power for two decades not so much because it effectively controlled almost all sectors of Italian life, but because the majority of Italians, while not enthusiastic supporters of the régime, did not consider it a mortal enemy to be overthrown at any cost. Thus militant anti-Fascists included only an embattled minority periodically raided by an efficient police apparatus. It took a war and defeat to bring about the repudiation of the system by the Italian people. While Aquarone refuses to speculate whether the inner weakness of Fascism might perhaps not have led to its downfall even without the war, his analysis indicates that it never truly regimented Italy and that its structure remained a paper façade behind which Italian life went on with few fundamental changes. The 66 documents assembled by Aquarone from archives, newspapers, speeches, letters and other sources reinforce the text.

DEAKIN, FREDERICK WILLIAM. **The Brutal Friendship: Mussolini, Hitler and the Fall of Italian Fascism.** New York: Harper and Row, 1962, 896 p.

This massive volume is centered on the last three years of Italian Fascism, when the fatal bond with Germany doomed Mussolini and his régime to the final catastrophe that enveloped the Axis partners in 1945. Overshadowing all other themes is the effect of the special tie between the two dictators, a personal attachment neither man ever renounced but which, in the last weeks of his life, Hitler wished had not prevented him from assuming a more "brutal friendship in regard to Italy."

Deakin is unquestionably successful in proving the importance of this friendship as a determinant in Italo-German relations; but as a whole his account remains a disappointment, all the greater because a masterly achievement seemed to be within his grasp and yet eluded him. There is much promise in the opportunity given the author to be the first to exploit a uniquely rich mass of documentary material. But he proved not completely equal to the occasion, above all because he was unable wholly to master this material. Indeed, it mastered him to the point that he could not resist reproducing it in countless and lengthy quotations. The very volume of these quoted passages is detrimental to narrative clarity; it also works against that acute analysis which, evident in brilliant flashes throughout the book, would have resulted in a superlative account had interpretation dominated the work instead of being submerged by raw data. But if Deakin's effort is a partial failure, it is a noble one of grand proportions.

DELZELL, CHARLES F. **Mussolini's Enemies.** Princeton: Princeton University Press, 1961, 620 p.

Professor Delzell's large and extensively documented work incorporates a wealth of primary sources and virtually all existing monographic studies dealing with the resistance against Mussolini's régime. Somewhat less than half the coverage is devoted to the clandestine opposition up to 1943; the balance of the book deals with the armed Resistance during the last two years of Fascist rule. This proportion is essentially justified by the fact—one of the work's themes—that the efforts of the opposition before 1943, however heroic, never seriously endangered Fascism's hold on the country. But 20 years of such efforts prepared the cadres for the successful culmination of the armed Resistance, thus assuring to the parties in the Resistance a prominent role in Italy's postwar life.

Although an impressive achievement, Delzell's account has some imperfections. His sharp criticism of the Fascist régime is easily justified, but his caustic views on pre-Fascist Italy's liberal leaders are more controversial and less well substantiated. The endeavor to mention every person and organization playing some role in anti-Fascist activity is commendable, but it makes the book something of an encyclopedia of the Resistance movement. The style inevitably suffers from the multitude of names and is not improved by an overabundance of adjectives and frequent use of Italianisms. Finally, the decision not to include a bibliography listing all sources cited seems unfortunate. But the foregoing criticism does not alter the fact that Delzell's book occupies a position of preëminence over all other relevant works in the English language.

SALVATORELLI, LUIGI and MIRA, GIOVANNI. **Storia d'Italia nel Periodo Fascista.** Turin: Einaudi, 5th ed., 1964, 1,192 p.

That a work of this length should appear in a fifth edition is a tribute to the authors' capacity to combine sound scholarship with readable style. Both Salvatorelli and Mira were active participants in the anti-Fascist Resistance; and although their sympathies are obvious, they have succeeded in presenting as objective an account of the Fascist period as is yet possible. Regrettably, sources are not cited; there is no bibliography; and the detailed table of contents does not wholly repair the limitations of an index that lists only names. But these mechanical weaknesses, which somewhat reduce the book's otherwise considerable usefulness as a work of reference, do not affect its merit as an excellent synthesis of the voluminous documentary and interpretative literature on the Fascist era. The many judiciously brief and apt quotations, woven into the narrative with telling effect, are but one of the various indirect signs of the authors' confident acquaintance with this literature. The new edition is especially noteworthy for its incorporation of recently published documents and analysis regarding the formative years of the Fascist movement and the period of its disintegration after 1942.

SALVEMINI, GAETANO. **Under the Axe of Fascism.** New York: Viking, 1936, 402 p.

This is one of the earliest and most effective works in English attempting a systematic refutation of the claim that Fascist corporativism had solved the labor and social questions in Italy on a basis equitable to both workers and capitalists. The evidence presented by the author is so voluminous and detailed that at times it may appear redundant. But, up to 1935, the claims made on behalf of Fascism were so uncritically accepted and disseminated by academics and popular writers alike, particularly in the English-speaking world, that only an impressive array of incontrovertible evidence (gathered primarily by a meticulous culling of Fascist publications) would suffice to cast strong doubts on Fascism's alleged economic and social achievements.

The first part of the work proves beyond question that Italian labor had no effective rights and say in the so-called corporative state. The second part sets out to show that, in consequence, the interests of the workers were sacrificed to the benefit of their employers and to what the régime deemed to be the nation's superior interests.

It is ironic that in proving so decisively how Fascism's many "innovations" in social welfare were in fact but a continuation—rarely for the better—of programs introduced by the pre-Fascist liberal governments, Salvemini, who had been a severe critic of these governments, demonstrates how superior they were to the régime that replaced them.

CHABOD, FEDERICO. **A History of Italian Fascism.** London: Weidenfeld, 1963, 192 p.

Modest in proportions and almost colloquial in style, this work by a participant in the anti-Fascist Resistance in Piedmont is superior to many lengthier accounts of the Fascist era by virtue of its calm and perceptive assessment of why Italians accepted and tolerated Fascism for more than 20 years. The style, derived from the book's original form as a series of 12 lectures delivered at the University of Paris in 1950, is deceptive in its simplicity. The author is most effective in tracing the reasons for the socioeconomic disorientation after 1918, the consequent fragmentation and paralysis of parliamentary politics, the nature of the appeal that brought Fascism to power, and the basis for its endurance until it collapsed with defeat in war.

The book does not pretend to extensive original research; it is not a major reassessment of current historiography; and it is least impressive in the comparatively lengthy treatment of the post-Fascist years between 1945 and 1948. In fact, this latter coverage makes the title of the English translation somewhat misleading. But as a thoughtful survey of the more balanced judgments on Fascism and its effects, this brief work reflects the qualities which made the late Professor Chabod one of contemporary Italy's most distinguished historians.

Foreign Policy

BAER, GEORGE W. **The Coming of the Italian-Ethiopian War.** Cambridge: Harvard University Press, 1967, 404 p.

Beginning with an introductory survey of the Ethiopian question back to 1869, Baer concentrates on the period between spring 1934, when Mussolini resolved to attack Ethiopia, and October 3, 1935, when the invasion was launched. Little archival material from the major powers involved was available when Baer wrote; in compensation, he has supplied a formidable bibliography in which memoirs and monographs abound (whether all are directly pertinent may be questioned), and his footnotes are very thorough. This is certainly an authoritative work if not perhaps definitive.

To some extent Baer discusses the motives and preparations for war; he ascribes Mussolini's belligerence to the internal needs of Fascist Italy. But the main concern of the book with the international background distinguishes it from such studies emphasizing the military side of the war itself as A. J. Barker, **The Civilizing Mission: A History of the Italo-Ethiopian War, 1935–36** (London: Cassell, 1968, 354 p.), and Angelo Del Boca, **The Ethiopian War, 1935–1941** (Chicago: University of Chicago Press, 1969, 289 p.). Baer comes to no startling conclusions about the diplomatic prelude to the Italo-Ethiopian War; the British and French were hellbent on appeasement all along without any regard for the League of Nations. However, the conventional wisdom is presented here with greater exactitude than anywhere else.

DI NOLFO, ENNIO. **Mussolini e la Politica Estera Italiana, 1919–1933.** Padua: C.E.D.A.M., 1960, 315 p.

This book covers essentially the same area as Gaetano Salvemini's **Mussolini Diplomatico (1922–1932)** (Bari: Laterza, 1952, 536 p.), although in a more scholarly and dispassionate manner. Like Salvemini, Di Nolfo challenges the notion that in foreign affairs Mussolini's first ten years in office constituted a decade of good behavior.

There is an excellent introductory chapter chronicling Mussolini's inconsistent pronouncements on international affairs before taking office. Di Nolfo's chronological survey of Fascist Italy's early diplomacy illustrates Mussolini's predilection for international revisionism, although not for its practical application (in the Alto Adige, for example). Di Nolfo also demonstrates Mussolini's interpretation of foreign policy as a branch of propaganda, and he emphasizes the relative lack of control that Italy's career diplomats were able to exercise over the Duce.

When Di Nolfo wrote, the published "I Documenti Diplomatici Italiani" covered only the years 1922–1925. Consequently, the latter part of his book is based mainly on memoirs and press material. Unfortunately, too, Di Nolfo has used no German sources. Another shortcoming is that there is little discussion of the vital nexus between Fascist policies at home and abroad. Nevertheless, this book stands as a reliable survey, although usefully supplemented by such later publications as Alan Cassels, **Mussolini's Early Diplomacy** (Princeton: Princeton University Press, 1970, 425 p.), and Giampiero Carocci, **La Politica Estera dell'Italia Fascista (1925–1928)** (Bari: Laterza, 1969, 391 p.).

TOSCANO, MARIO. **The Origins of the Pact of Steel.** Baltimore: Johns Hopkins University Press, 1967, 417 p.

Mario Toscano's **Le Origini Diplomatiche del Patto d'Acciaio** (Florence: Sansoni, 1948, 414 p.) was first published in 1948. A second edition, revised in the light of new material, appeared in 1956. **The Origins of the Pact of Steel** is a slightly updated version, translated anonymously into English.

This is traditional diplomatic history, sticking close to the documentary sources. Toscano has used all the available published documents from the archives of Italy, Germany, Japan and Great Britain. As editor of Series 8 and 9 of "I Documenti Diplomatici Italiani," he also had access to unpublished material in the Italian Foreign Ministry files.

Two features stand out in his narrative. First, from 1937 Berlin hoped for a tripartite accord embracing Germany, Italy and Japan. It was only in the spring of 1939, when Japan grew suspicious of Germany's growing rapprochement with Soviet Russia, that a bilateral Italo-German pact emerged as a substitute. Second, Fascist Italy accepted the German draft for an offensive alliance, which became the Pact of Steel on May 22, 1939, with incredible insouciance. Mussolini and Ciano took at face value the Nazi promise that war would not come for three years.

Toscano's book is not speculative diplomatic history. For instance, there is little consideration of the long-term objectives of the Nazi and Fascist régimes, nor of the influence of ideology. It is a classic, but of a limited genre.

SIEBERT, FERDINAND. **Italiens Weg in den Zweiten Weltkrieg.** Frankfurt/Main: Athenaeum, 1962, 460 p.

This book is a diplomatic history of Fascist Italy from the Munich Conference in September 1938 to the Italian entry into World War II on June 10, 1940. It is based on published sources, principally the series of Italian, German and British diplomatic documents. In dealing with Italo-German relations up to May 22, 1939, Siebert follows in the steps of Mario Toscano, **The Origins of the Pact of Steel,** and also covers some of the same ground as Elizabeth Wiskemann's **The Rome-Berlin Axis** (London: Collins, rev. ed., 1966, 446 p.).

However, the chief merit of this work is that it places Italian foreign policy in a wider context than the Axis. Its *leitmotif* is Italy's vacillation between Nazi Germany on the one side and Britain and France on the other, ending in March 1940 when, so Siebert contends, Mussolini made his irrevocable decision to join Hitler in the war at the first propitious moment. The author offers few surprises about either the nature of Fascist Italian foreign policy or its emergence from the interplay of forces and personalities within Italy, but his book is detailed, thorough and reliable.

MACARTNEY, MAXWELL HENRY HAYES and CREMONA, PAUL. **Italy's Foreign and Colonial Policy, 1914–1937.** New York: Oxford University Press, 1938, 353 p.

Both Macartney and Cremona were for many years newspaper correspondents in Rome, and their book was written out of that experience. In consequence, it is not deeply researched—there is no bibliography, for instance. None the less, within limits, it is a perceptive and well-balanced work, reflecting some influence of the inter-war geopolitical school.

Without being pro-Fascist (indeed, Cremona was expelled by Mussolini's government), the book is sympathetic to some Italian nationalist claims in the Mediterranean and Africa, especially in the light of traditional Anglo-French disparagement of Italy. It also rightly emphasizes the continuity of Italian nationalist ambitions from the liberal years to the Fascist era. Though actually a series of essays on central themes, the essays mesh together so well that the whole constitutes a comprehensive survey. There is still no comparable overview of this quarter century of Italian overseas policy in the English language.

After 1943

General; Political

GALLI, GIORGIO and FACCHI, PAOLO. **La Sinistra Democristiana: Storia e Ideologia.** Milan: Feltrinelli, 1962, 470 p.

This is an invaluable analysis of the history of the various left-wing factions in the Italian Christian Democratic Party during the period 1943–1960. The book is divided into two parts—one dealing with the factional conflicts within the Christian Democratic Party, the second examining in considerable depth the ideological norms of the left-wing factions. The authors show that while ideological considerations have a good deal of influence on factional behavior in Italy, the desire for patronage and power is also a highly significant factor. For instance, such ostensibly progressive leaders as Gronchi have been willing to reverse their field and flirt with the extreme right when circumstances so dictated. And on a number of occasions, left-wing factions have accepted incongruous alliances with conservative forces, with the result that their policy goals have had to be temporarily abandoned.

But this is more than a mere chronicle of factional wheeling and dealing. There are two central themes: a steady movement toward the shifting of control over some key levers of economic power from private enterprise to the public sector, and a painfully gradual process of acceptance of the need for an alliance with the Italian Socialist Party: the famous "opening to the Left." The authors also offer some intriguing generalizations regarding the instrumental character of certain ideological postures, which are actually designed to serve the pragmatic interests of the faction which assumes them.

BLACKMER, DONALD L. M. **Unity in Diversity: Italian Communism and the Communist World.** Cambridge: M.I.T. Press, 1968, 434 p.

The author is primarily concerned with the relationship between the Italian Communist Party (PCI) and the international communist movement, but he also sheds much light on the purely domestic problems confronted by the PCI and on the factional divisions within the Party.

This is an unusually balanced and insightful treatment of Italian communism in the post-Stalin period. The careful interweaving of motivational and environmental factors does a great deal to explain the sometimes seemingly erratic behavior of the Party. For the Italian Communists are concerned not only with maintaining the unity and strength of the international communist movement but also with demonstrating their autonomy and their preference for democratic methods for the benefit of Italian public opinion.

However, the increasingly independent line assumed by the PCI cannot be dismissed as being only a tactical response to domestic political necessities. An increasing number of Italian Communist leaders have become convinced that the problems faced by the proletariat in a highly industrialized neo-capitalist society require some rethinking and adaptation of Marxist doctrine. There is also a growing tendency to see Western European economic developments as posing certain special problems which must be dealt with on a Western European regional basis. As a result of these trends, the PCI has come to assume the role of a loyal opposition within the international communist movement and has taken on a rather revisionist coloration. But this bare summary fails to do justice to the richness and complexity of Blackmer's analysis or to the intricate interplay of countervailing factors which he describes.

GALLI, GIORGIO. **La Sinistra Italiana nel Dopoguerra.** Bologna: Il Mulino, 1958, 287 p.

While the title of this book implies that it deals with the history of the Italian left during the post–World War II period, the author actually focuses his attention on the years 1948–1949 when it became evident that the Italian Communist Party could neither seize power by force nor win a free election.

Galli's thesis is that the Italian Communist Party is essentially a conservative organization, interested in preserving its acquired position as a powerful opposition party with widespread influence in local and provincial governments. Much evidence is mustered to show that Italian Communist leaders have been anxious (as during the riots following the attempted assassination of Togliatti) to avoid any real showdown with the Italian economic and political establishment. The split in the trade-union movement and the victory of the leftist faction in the Italian Socialist Party are also discussed at some length. Again, the emphasis is on leadership which is radical in language and style, conservative in basic strategy.

While Galli's effort to depict the leadership of the PCI as a group of tired opportunists is partly convincing, one feels that insufficient weight is assigned to possible empirical justifications for the Party's policies, and that Blackmer's multifaceted analysis gives a somewhat more balanced picture of a complex reality. Nevertheless, this is a well-documented and powerful treatment of a crucial period in Italian political history.

KOGAN, NORMAN. **The Government of Italy.** New York: Crowell, 1962, 225 p.

Dr. Kogan, a professor of political science at the University of Connecticut, here provides a most useful account of Italy's postwar institutions and political system. The book describes in detail Italy's electoral and political systems, executive and legislative machinery, the operation of local government, and gives a brief account of the country's foreign policy and trade relations. It is useful to find here the English text of the Republican Constitution of 1948, from which many of Italy's present institutions spring. At the same time the author's historical sense prompts him to set present-day developments in perspective, and his sidelights on the line of descent from Italy's past, traceable in so many of those institutions today, give his book a value far beyond that of a student handbook or work of reference.

KOGAN, NORMAN. **Italy and the Allies.** Cambridge: Harvard University Press, 1956, 246 p.

In this earlier work, Norman Kogan deals with the period of the war following the fall of Fascism in 1943, and subsequent postwar developments to the conclusion of the peace treaty in 1946. During this period Italy's fate was in a sense subservient to outside considerations—first to the broader strategy of the war as a whole and then to the interplay of tactics between the Allies in the negotiations for an Italian peace treaty. The author notes that in the process of reaching a modus vivendi between the Eastern and Western powers, "Italian interests were usually sacrificed," and that the resulting bitterness was the greater because of the struggle that had gone before, when Italy rid herself of Fascism and, in Churchill's words, sought to "work her passage home." In the author's view, the United States showed greater sympathy than the other Allies for Italy's difficulties, including the institutional question of whether the state was to be a monarchy or a republic, which loomed large at home during 1945 and 1946 while the Allies were arguing over Italy's fate in Paris. The bibliography, though to some extent now outdated, is nevertheless still valuable as a pointer to most of the main works covering the period.

Economic and Social Questions

GRINDROD, MURIEL. **The Rebuilding of Italy: Politics and Economics, 1945–1955.** New York: Royal Institute of International Affairs, 1956, 269 p.

This survey of Italy's postwar recovery, like most scholarly surveys, is more useful for the information and impressions it imparts than for any strikingly novel political insights. But the author is an acute and knowledgeable observer of the Italian scene and has produced a useful and solid piece of work. In addition to a chronological treatment of Italian political developments, there is a section devoted to problems of Italian foreign policy and another dealing with such various social and economic questions as emigration, housing, industry and the south.

In general, the author is quite sanguine (justifiably so, hindsight reveals) regarding the prospects for Italian democracy and the ability of Italian society to cope with its economic and social problems. At the same time, there is awareness of the fact that earlier hopes for a thoroughgoing renovation of the Italian state have not been realized. Students of Italian political history will find a good deal of valuable descriptive data intelligently discussed in this volume.

ROSSI-DORIA, MANLIO. **Dieci Anni di Politica Agraria nel Mezzogiorno.** Bari: Laterza, 1958, 412 p.

Manlio Rossi-Doria is the dean of the Italian agronomists and *meridionalisti* who believe in southern Italy's renaissance, and his writings cover agricultural economics and polemical partisan politics. This volume includes lectures given to professional and political organizations between 1948 and 1958, all of which have one theme: the revitalization of the Italian south must be based on sound agrarian policies consisting of rational land reform, reorganization of farm tenure and government-directed financial and technical aid. Rossi-Doria criticizes the Italian land reform legislation of the 1950s as being politically rather than economically inspired. This legislation encouraged land fractionalization and did not substantially modify the status of the sharecropper or encourage coöperative farming.

Rossi-Doria emphasized in the 1950s those elements of economic development which economists have only recently realized are essential—political will and the desire for social change. He pleaded for coördination among various branches of the government and various development policies on behalf of the south, and his persistence proved invaluable to southern development. It is evident from first page to last that the author not only thought but "felt" the difficult problems he discussed. Although some of the lectures included in this volume are 20 years old, they are still fresh and relevant.

VÖCHTING, FRIEDRICH. **Die Italienische Südfrage.** Berlin: Duncker, 1951, 680 p.

Southern Italian problems have been debated by economists and policy-makers since national unification, a century ago. Around the turn of this century, F. Nitti, P. Villari and G. Salvemini attempted to arouse the nation to halt the decline in the south. Between the wars, Fascist totalitarianism muted the discussion but could not silence it.

This "Southern Question" is the title of Friedrich Vöchting's volume published in Germany in 1951, one of the most comprehensive studies of southern Italian development problems. The early 1950s marked a change from a century of public neglect to the beginning of direct public intervention in the south, whose problems as seen by Vöchting arise from overpopulation and a lack of industrial infrastructure. About half the volume is dedicated to the historical causes of backwardness, while the rest of the book discusses the problems of and possible solutions for the agricultural sector.

Vöchting believes, with many other development economists today, that the sociocultural environment is paramount to economic development, *i.e.* social change precedes economic change. Still, he concludes that the Italian south needs: (1) a policy of industrialization; (2) better terms of trade for southern agricultural products; (3) encouragement of emigration; (4) getting back the colony of Libya [*sic*]; (5) birth control. All these points (excluding, of course, the fourth) have been partially fulfilled over the last two decades.

This volume made history at the time of its publication and is still often quoted by economists. The style is prolix, but the comprehensiveness and scholarship of the book are undeniable.

CLOUGH, SHEPARD B. **The Economic History of Modern Italy.** New York: Columbia University Press, 1964, 458 p.

Until recently the economic history of modern Italy has not been given much attention by either historians or economists. Professor Clough's broad investigation of this subject examines the process of the economic development of Italy in its political and social context, thus reflecting the sensitivity of a historian. Yet he does not go far back in searching for the foundation of the economic resurgence of Italy. In his view, the new Italian state was emerging from its traditional agricultural basis at the end of the nineteenth century, after taking advantage of certain infrastructures laid after the unification. The book analyzes all the sectors of the economy in detail and with abundant documentation. The reader gains a clear impression of the contrasts and obstacles which hampered the development of a country poor in natural resources and rich in people. The gravity of that problem is rightly recognized by the author who, unlike many economists, sees this imbalance as a serious disequilibrium in the economic structure of Italy. Clough notes that, in spite of many hindrances, Italy achieved a remarkable economic expansion for which there is no "monocausal" explanation. The growth is the result of a great many factors—a conclusion which certainly reflects a very complicated reality. Although sometimes descriptive and not very penetrating, the author has rendered good service to all scholars interested in the new economic experience of this old country.

HILDEBRAND, GEORGE H. **Growth and Structure in the Economy of Modern Italy.** Cambridge: Harvard University Press, 1965, 475 p.

This stimulating work by Professor Hildebrand is one of the most detailed analyses of the economic development of Italy after World War II. In the author's view, the monetary and economic policy adopted by Alcide de Gasperi and Luigi Einaudi was the foundation stone of the reconstruction of the country, stopping inflation by 1947 and stabilizing prices, thus favoring the formation of new saving for investments. Under these favorable conditions, industry grew quickly through the expansion of fixed capital and output, though employment did not keep pace with the growth of industrial output. To a certain extent, labor unions were partially responsible for the lag in employment, since they tended to favor the requests of those workers employed in the most efficient sectors. Thus large and efficient industry was capable of paying higher wages and still making substantial profits through high productivity. This situation represented one of those bottlenecks or disequilibria which characterize the Italian economy.

The author points out that other structural imbalances, such as agriculture and the south, also accounted for the unbalanced growth. Some of these disequilibria, he suggests, might have been eliminated by a higher degree of competition and mobility—a judgment that is far from a practical conclusion in the Italian context, as the author acknowledges.

LUTZ, VERA C. **Italy: A Study in Economic Development.** New York: Oxford University Press (for the Royal Institute of International Affairs), 1962, 342 p.

This is an interesting and balanced study of the impact of "economic dualism"— a system of dual wage levels in industry—on economic development, focusing on the experience of the Italian economy in the 1950s. Under the circumstances of dualism there are high-capital intensive industries which can afford to pay high wages, and units of restricted size that tend to employ less fixed capital and pay lower wages. This, broadly, is the pattern of the Italian economy, where different income levels correspond to a geographical split between north and south. In spite of a remarkable growth of industry throughout the 1950s this gap between the two labor groups was not eliminated, and the north and south remained divided in terms of per capita income, even though some improvements were registered. As the author points out, the lack of capital and natural resources are major factors in the persistence of that division. The study does not, however, make evident the degree to which the persistence of this system is due to a high degree of monopoly in Italian industry.

Mrs. Lutz reasons that internal migrations are a possible solution to the problem of dual wages. The migrations that took place in the late 1950s relieved pressure in the south, though creating new social problems in the cities of the north. Migration to the north relates to the expansion of industry in this area, particularly to the growth of large concerns which eliminate small units. The author notes that a continuation of this tendency requires a process of private accumulation which fosters the growth of industry; but this policy also has its shortcomings. Certainly there is no single cure for all these complex problems, given the economic and political context in which they are located. The author concludes that it will take some time before the problem of underemployment—the essence of economic dualism—can be solved.

HOROWITZ, DANIEL L. **The Italian Labor Movement.** Cambridge: Harvard University Press, 1963, 356 p.

The communist domination of the Italian labor movement and its consequences for the stability of Italian society have aroused much interest among American scholars. Professor Horowitz has faced this problem in broad perspective, seeking to analyze and understand the nature of trade unions in their historical development, thus departing from the traditional American method of analyzing union movements and industrial relations. Through a balanced and impartial story of the evolution of trade unions from 1860 to 1960 and their relations with political parties, the author sets forth his interpretation: "The nature of political forces and political problems, the urge for—and resistance to—social transformation, the rigidity of the society's structure, the incomplete economic-industrial transformation, combined to determine the essential nature of the trade-union movement. The trade-union movement pressed hard to become a movement oriented toward industrial relations. It remained a movement in which, or over which, political forces influenced and at times held sway in determining the direction and the nature of its activities."

This evaluation also explains the relative lack of congruence in the social and economic structure of the society. The Italian Communist and Socialist Parties were the most active organizations in exerting political influence. Catholic movements, on the other hand, never had significant influence on the working class until 1948. Yet the economic progress of Italy may have its impact upon the social structure of the country, and the democratic trade unions may contribute to a political, economic and social congruence. This final prediction by Horowitz was partially confirmed by the behavior of the unions during the 1960s.

Church-State Relations

BINCHY, DANIEL A. **Church and State in Fascist Italy.** New York: Oxford University Press (for the Royal Institute of International Affairs), 1942, 774 p.

Though written 30 years ago, when the pertinent archival sources were unavailable, Binchy's book on Church-State relations in Fascist Italy is a remarkably accurate study of the subject. Even its prophecies have come to pass.

Starting with the premise that both history and geography have intertwined the fortunes of the Holy See and the Italian Church so closely as to make them almost inseparable, Binchy shows that the Roman Question was not merely a political question but also a religious dispute which had far-reaching repercussions on the organization and influence of the Catholic Church in Italy. After a brief survey of the origins of the *dissidio*, the author makes the Lateran Settlement of 1929 the focal point of his book. He analyzes exhaustively and perceptively Fascist relations—political, cultural, legal and administrative—with the Papacy and the Italian Church during the period 1922–1939. He concludes that Catholicism and Fascism were essentially incompatible; where their doctrines coincided, such convergences were fortuitous, deriving from different assumptions and sometimes leading to different conclusions.

Although the author makes no effort to conceal his personal abhorrence for Fascism and his sympathy for the Catholic Church, and especially for Pope Pius XI, he has written an objective and highly readable account of Church-State relations during the Mussolini era. The bibliography is selective, consisting of the best printed sources in English, Italian, French and German available when the book was being composed.

GORRESIO, VITTORIO, *ed.* **Stato e Chiesa.** Bari: Laterza, 1957, 268 p.

The first part of this book is a collection of papers read at meetings held in Rome and Florence in 1957 by the friends ("Amici") of *Il Mondo*. The common theme of the papers was that Italy had become clericalized, and the tone was generally polemical.

Luigi Salvatorelli (the most balanced in his presentation) spoke on "La Politica della Chiesa in Italia" and showed that historically the Church had always claimed a sovereignty higher than that of any state. In Italy, the Church sought the maximum of influence in society. Raffaele Pettazzoni, discussing "La Chiesa e la vita religiosa in Italia," contended that the Church's totalitarianism embraced the political as well as the religious sphere of life: the Church was an anti-democratic institution *per eccellenza*. In "Costituzione e Concordato" Paolo Barile brought out the basic incompatibility of the Concordat with many of the principles of the Italian Constitution. Carlo Falconi's "L'Azione della Chiesa nella vita pubblica italiana" detailed in a variety of ways (some rather trivial) the Church's interference in Italian life in 1955–1956 and concluded that Italy had become a barren ecclesiastical province. Lamberto Borghi's "Scuola e Chiesa in Italia" had as its theme the Church's domination of elementary education.

The second part of the volume contains four documents (including a hitherto unpublished letter by Garibaldi) relating to the theme of the meetings, and also includes discussions from the floor. The last part reproduces the motion adopted at the conclusion of the meeting in Rome calling for the separation of Church and State and the abrogation of the Concordat.

Documentation is sparse and there is no bibliography. The volume is useful as a reflection of the climate of opinion in many intellectual circles in Italy in 1957.

JEMOLO, ARTURO CARLO. **Church and State in Italy, 1850–1950.** Oxford: Basil Blackwell, rev. ed., 1960, 340 p.

This is an objective, interpretive survey of Church-State relations in Italy. Despite the title, this edition carries the story from the *Risorgimento* to the beginning of the pontificate of John XXIII in 1958. The author considers it necessary to provide the political background of these relations, no matter how well known it may be to the average reader, and at times he strays too far from his main topic. His own personal reflections and observations—philosophical and theological—are also somewhat of a distraction.

The longest and most valuable part of the book deals with the period from 1850 to 1918. From Jemolo's analysis of the major personalities and trends of this period, the conclusion is inescapable that there was less animosity between Italian Catholics and the Italian state than is generally supposed. The character sketches of the leading figures in the book are very valuable and instructive. In discussing the post-Fascist era, Jemolo is critical of the inclusion of the Concordat in the Constitution. Though personally sympathetic to Catholicism he is opposed to confessionalism, which was assured by this inclusion.

The book contains no general bibliography, but each chapter ends with a very useful bibliographical note. The readability of the book would have been enhanced by a less literal translation.

SPAIN

General; Historical

CARR, RAYMOND. **Spain 1808–1939.** New York: Oxford University Press, 1966, 766 p.
In an effort to provide a theoretical framework for what some have called the quagmire of modern Spanish history, often seen as nothing more than a series of guerrilla wars and palace coups staged by army generals, Carr has couched his history in the form of a Manichaean struggle between liberalism and traditionalism. To say, as the author does, that liberalism failed in Spain says nothing about the social, economic and intellectual developments which militated against its success.

The principal achievement of the book is its articulation of the political history of Spain, a task which it performs better than any other general history of the period now in print. But the book includes very little social history. This is especially true in its consideration of the Spanish Civil War. Since many nonspecialists who come to the book will be looking specifically for information on the Civil War, the sparseness of its treatment of organizational structure of the Nationalist and Republican sides, the paucity of information about reforms carried out by anarcho-syndicalists and by Carlists, and the slight discussion of economic effects of the war are disappointing. In the last section of the book, Professor Carr's historical method, with its almost total disregard for Spanish working-class history and its devotion to high politics, is most noticeable. However, until another comprehensive book of equal or greater insight is published, the work remains a starting point for anyone interested in modern Spain.

FERNÁNDEZ ALMAGRO, MELCHOR. **Historia del Reinado de Don Alfonso XIII.** Barcelona: Montaner y Simón, 1933, 611 p.
The late Melchor Fernández Almagro was dean of the narrative political historians of modern Spain. He was not an academic but was a member of the Spanish Royal Academy of History and was extensively employed in newspaper writing as well. This book still stands as the leading political narrative of the troubled reign of Alfonso XIII (1902–1931), though it was written only a few years after the final events that it chronicled. Typical of the author's work, it is a factual, narrative history in the old style that provides detailed chronological treatment of royal, parliamentary and party politics on the national level. There is little or no discussion of the cultural, economic and social forces that played such a major role in shaping public affairs in Spain during this period, nor is there any notable attempt to place the political problems of the time in analytical perspective or to compare them with the general framework of European politics. For such considerations, the reader is best advised to turn to the relevant chapters in Raymond Carr's **Spain 1808–1939.** Nevertheless, the book remains useful as a descriptive account of formal politics because of the wealth of fact and detail it contains. While Fernández Almagro wrote from the viewpoint of moderate conservatism, he held to firm professional standards of objectivity and accuracy;

consequently, his work has not been replaced or surpassed in this genre of historical writing despite the passage of nearly four decades.

ULLMAN, JOAN CONNELLY. **The Tragic Week: A Study of Anticlericalism in Spain, 1875–1912.** Cambridge: Harvard University Press, 1968, 441 p.

Approximately half of Professor Ullman's 312 pages of text are devoted to a detailed reconstruction of the "Tragic Week" of Barcelona in July 1909. They are of interest to a wide audience. Except for the Russian Revolution of 1905, the *semana trágica* was probably the most powerful popular upheaval in Europe between the end of one revolutionary cycle in the 1870s and the start of another after the First World War. Moreover, a variety of influences—socialist, anarchist, bourgeois radical, regionalist—were operative. Finally, the week provides an interesting case study of the interaction between antiwar feeling and social protest. In describing the conflict with objectivity and precision, Professor Ullman makes a valuable contribution to the literature on the dynamics of working-class revolt. Her study not only introduces the subject to the non-Spanish world of scholarship but supersedes the Spanish treatments as well. A better narrative account can scarcely be expected in the near future.

The rest of the text is divided between 126 pages on the national and regional background to the rising and some 30 pages on its long-range effects. Although these sections (particularly the first) contain many data of interest, they are considerably less successful than the core of Professor Ullman's work. There is excessive emphasis on anticlericalism as a key to understanding the entire 1875–1912 era. Her conclusion that the Tragic Week ended the chances for peaceful reform involves an exaggeration of the relevance of Maura's program and an underestimation of the crushing economic and social realities that confronted him and all subsequent Spanish leaders.

RAMA, CARLOS M. **La Crisis Española del Siglo XX.** Mexico City: Fondo de Cultura Económica, 1960, 373 p.

The relationship between the individual and the state in modern Spain is the central theme of this comprehensive political history of Spain to the end of the Civil War. Never overly obtrusive, Rama's thesis is that Spain remained an authoritarian state until the creation of the Second Republic in 1931, and that for five brief years a liberal democratic state was established, only to be torn asunder during the Civil War by a combination of regionalism, libertarianism and religious conflict which led to the emergence of two new authoritarian forces: communism and fascism.

According to Rama, modern Spain has been struggling to resolve the issue of centralization under an authoritarian régime which would try to quash separatism and unify the country, and a federal structure which would allow the maximum of local initiative and control with the minimum of repression from the central government. What resulted was widespread division about the function of the state. In the author's view, Spain at the end of the Civil War was approximately where it had been in 1900 with regard to the unresolved question of the nature of the state and the relationship between it and the individual.

In the course of elaborating his theory, Rama provides concise and varied discussions of the rise of Basque and Catalan regionalism, based on previously unused manuscripts and materials from private collections in France. He also provides detailed information on the Spanish left. One might have wished for more material on the conservative and rightist factions and on each side's syndical organizations, but, all in all, Rama's work is one of the best single volumes dealing with twentieth-century Spain.

TREND, JOHN BRANDE. **The Origins of Modern Spain.** New York: Macmillan, 1934, 220 p.

Although misleading in title and superseded by several French and Spanish works on many aspects of its specific theme, J. B. Trend's work remains the best introduction in the English language to the Krausist-*Institución Libre de Enseñanza* intellectual current. Its approach is largely biographical; about a third of the book is devoted to Giner de los Ríos, founder of the *Institución,* and there are shorter sketches of such figures as Sanz del Río, Cossío and Azcárate. Trend attempts some analysis of the intellectual development of each of his subjects, but fails to tie them as closely as he might to each other and to other intellectual figures of the time. Since the author himself is not really interested in politics as such, there is almost nothing on the political activities of his protagonists.

Aside from its monopoly of its theme in the English language, Trend's short work is well worth reading for its epigrams, its flashes of insight, and, above all, the grace and pleasure of its writing. Moreover, because **The Origins of Modern Spain** is distinguished by the same humaneness that characterized several of the founders of the Second Republic, it gives some of the flavor of the initial stages of that régime. The pity was that humaneness proved not to be enough, thus preventing the Republic from developing into "modern Spain," as Trend envisaged.

GARCÍA VENERO, MAXIMIANO. **Historia de las Internacionales en España.** Madrid: Ediciones del Movimiento, 1956–1957, 3 v.

García Venero's three volumes collectively run to about 1,400 pages. Their publication in Spain in the mid-1950s constituted a cultural event of importance since they were the first serious analysis of the Spanish left to appear after the Civil War. Although obviously biased, they are not the work of a propagandist but of a cultivated man concerned with finding his particular version of the truth. The first volume covers the period from 1868 to 1914, the second 1914 to 1936, and the third the Civil War itself. All working-class movements are included, with the socialists receiving the most extensive treatment.

The work is not well organized or consistent in emphasis. Important events are passed over with scarcely a word while others of lesser significance are given many pages. The whole of the Second Republic, for example, is brushed aside in only 54 pages, and many of these deal with bourgeois rather than working-class politics. There also seems an excess of attention devoted to discussing the congresses and other activities of the various international organizations of the proletarian groups, as well as the general political and diplomatic context of Europe in different periods.

Nevertheless, this is a work of monumental scope which contains much valuable information that does not appear elsewhere. As such, it is indispensable for scholars of Spanish political and social history. Nonspecialists are fortunate to have a good substitute available in English—Stanley Payne's **The Spanish Revolution** (New York: Norton, 1970, 398 p.), which incorporates many of García Venero's most important findings and at the same time transcends him for many periods.

The Civil War

ZUGAZAGOITÍA, JULIÁN. **Guerra y Vicisitudes de los Españoles.** Paris: Librería Española, 1968, 2 v.

This is a second edition, without any change of text, of the author's "Historia de la Guerra de España," originally published in Buenos Aires in 1940. It is uniquely valuable as an eyewitness account of the Civil War. Zugazagoitía was an excellent journalist, famous before 1936 for his powerful memory and his fairmindedness. For some years he was the editor of *El Socialista,* official daily of Spain's largest political party, and also a deputy in the Cortes. Under Juan Negrín he served as Minister of the Interior, 1937–1938. The book narrates in detail the political and military history of the period from July 1936 to April 1939 as experienced in the Republican zone. It is particularly strong concerning the defense of Madrid, the internal quarrels and changes of the wartime cabinets, the relations among the successive governments and the anarchists, communists and Catalan autonomists. There are no scholarly footnotes and bibliography, but the memoirs of hundreds of other participants and the verbal references of many persons still living today both in Spain and in exile testify to the overall accuracy of the author's account.

Later books on the Civil War are more complete in their statistical information and in their documentation, but none can rival Zugazagoitía's knowledge of persons. He knew, observed and described the interaction among such leading civilian figures as Azaña, Prieto, Largo Caballero, Negrín and Luis Companys, and among such leading military figures as Generals Miaja, Hernandez Sarabia and Vicente Rojo. Although he was a socialist, his judgments of the various parties and factions are almost entirely free of partisan bias, with the exception of his evidently very low opinion of the anarchists. For deep personal insight his work is comparable to George Orwell's **Homage to Catalonia** (London: Secker and Warburg, 1938, 313 p.), with the significant difference that he knew Spanish politics far more thoroughly than did Orwell or any other foreign observer of the Civil War.

BRENAN, GERALD. **The Spanish Labyrinth: An Account of the Social and Political Background of the Civil War.** New York: Cambridge University Press, 2d ed., 1950, 384 p.

Few works have been more successful in grasping the labyrinthine character of Spanish history than Gerald Brenan's book on the six decades preceding the Civil War. Recent historiography has discovered new data, correcting some of Brenan's factual information, but the overall analysis and interpretation remain as pertinent as ever.

Today we can no longer accept the notion that during the first few years of the anarchist movement "one can scarcely find the name of a single laborer or factory hand." A quick glance at the statistical material recently compiled by Renée Lamberet (in Max Nettlau, **La Première Internationale en Espagne, 1868–1888,** Dordrecht: Reidel, 1969, 684 p.) makes one realize the extent and popularity of anarchism among the Spanish laboring masses of town and country. Similar criticism may be directed toward the chapter on Carlism, where Brenan underlines the dynastic and religious causes of this century-long struggle. A study of the economic structures of Spain's diversified countryside as well as its relationship to urban centers and markets would shed some decisive light on the problem.

None the less, Brenan's book resists such partial criticism. His was the first successful attempt to integrate social and political history into a balanced study of Spain. The precision in the analysis, together with the multiplicity of questions raised at every point, contributes to making **The Spanish Labyrinth** one of the most challenging and stimulating books for students of contemporary Iberian history.

JACKSON, GABRIEL. **The Spanish Republic and the Civil War, 1931–1939.** Princeton: Princeton University Press, 1965, 578 p.

This is the only scholarly study of the entire eight-year period of the Second Republic and Civil War in Spain. As such it achieves a perspective superior to the numerous volumes devoted exclusively to the three years of the Civil War. A general account, it synthesizes social and economic as well as political history and attempts to weave in cultural developments to some extent as well. The work is somewhat partial to the moderate middle-class Republican left and is at its best in dealing with the first Republican reformist biennium of 1931–1933. The treatment of the Civil War itself is more political and social than military, and includes a noteworthy chapter on "Efforts to Limit Suffering and Destruction," thus drawing attention to the kind of efforts normally overlooked in histories of wars foreign or civil. One of the book's major achievements has been to place the struggle clearly in its Spanish dimensions instead of providing the exaggerated coverage of foreign volunteers and aesthetes that has distorted other accounts. Jackson's study is somewhat less impartial than Hugh Thomas's **The Spanish Civil War** but is superior in lucidity, organization and literary style. Its structure is well controlled and provides a comparatively clear interpretive framework, making it the most readable of major scholarly books on Spain in the 1930s.

THOMAS, HUGH. **The Spanish Civil War.** London: Penguin, 2d ed., 1965, 911 p.

This was the first serious, scholarly study ever made of the Spanish Civil War and was received with great praise in several countries when it first appeared in 1961. Like most non-Spanish scholars studying Spanish affairs at that time, Thomas had no previous training in the field. The achievement of this book was to have assimilated material from a great variety of sources and to have presented a relatively unbiased account; indeed, a decade later, this still remains the most impartial of the general histories of the Spanish Civil War. Thomas cut through a great many of the myths surrounding the conflict and for the first time reduced it to credible empirical proportions.

On the other hand, the book lacks a clear perspective of Spanish history and politics and consists of an enormous amount of narrative material that is not well organized for the comprehension of the ordinary reader. The author was not able to resist throwing in numerous facts and anecdotes that often impede rather than clarify the explanation of events. He has also been charged by critics with excessive credulity in accepting doubtful accounts from other sources, though many of these deficiencies have been corrected in the second edition. Despite limitations of conception and organization, this remains the principal detailed narrative of the Spanish Civil War in English.

BROUÉ, PIERRE and TÉMIME, ÉMILE. **La Révolution et la Guerre d'Espagne.** Paris: Les Éditions de Minuit, 1961, 542 p.

No other general history of the Civil War has analyzed in such detail the internal political conflicts within both the Republican and the Nationalist zones, and very few books have dealt as precisely with the specific effects of foreign intervention on the course of both the war and internal developments. The book is divided into two almost equal halves. Broué, whose sympathies lie with the anarchists and anti-Stalinite communists, writes of the Popular Front parties, of proletarian and peasant revolutionary activities, and of the eventual suppression of those activities by the Negrín government. Témime, whose sympathies are with the parliamentary socialists, treats the diplomatic history, the main course of the war and the evolution of the Franco government. Broué's chapters are particularly valuable concerning the first days of the war, the moment at which the populace of the main cities prevented the Insurgent generals from obtaining a quick victory, and likewise concerning the anarchist revolution in Catalonia and parts of Aragon. Témime's chapters place the war in its full international context, analyzing the distinct ambitions of Italy, Portugal and Germany in aiding the Nationalists, the effects of Soviet intervention and the attitudes of both governments and populations in the Western democratic countries. The authors provide an extensive critical bibliography. They have made especially effective use of the French press and of the written and oral memoirs of both Spanish and foreign combatants.

A translation in English is scheduled for early publication.

COLODNY, ROBERT GARLAND. **The Struggle for Madrid: The Central Epic of the Spanish Conflict (1936–37).** New York: Paine-Whitman, 1958, 256 p.

This book deals with the siege of Madrid from late October 1936, when the Nationalist columns converged on Madrid from the west, to late March 1937 when General Franco turned his attention to other fronts after the defeat of the Italians in the battle of Guadalajara. It is an excellent military and political history, with strong background on the international diplomatic and interventionist activities as well. The author provides clear definitions of military units, much order of battle information, explanations of supply problems and evaluation of weapons and tactics. He also characterizes succinctly the political factions and the leading personalities on both sides. Colodny fought in the International Brigade. His account is based upon experience, the world press (particularly French and Russian), memoir literature and numerous interviews. The footnotes and bibliography are excellent; the maps are poor. The detailed narrative makes the following principal interpretive points: that the Nationalist columns were better trained and equipped than the Republican militia but were spread too thin to capture the capital in a first assault; that the geography of the western approaches to Madrid and the upsurge of popular resistance slowed the advance in the first week of November; that Soviet arms and the arrival of the first International Brigade units saved Madrid in the ten days from November 8 to 18; and that General Franco, for prestige reasons, continued the all-out effort to capture the capital until late March.

BOLLOTEN, BURNETT. **The Grand Camouflage: The Communist Conspiracy in the Spanish Civil War.** New York: Praeger, 1961, 350 p.

This book studies in detail the influence of the Communist Party between the outbreak of the Civil War in July 1936 and the fall of the Largo Caballero government in May 1937. According to Bolloten there were two main aspects to the "grand camouflage." First the Party struggled mightily to deny that a social revolution was occurring in the Republican zone, and then it minimized its own influence over an army and a government which it came to dominate once it had engineered the overthrow of Caballero. The Party pursued the following objectives simultaneously: to fight the Trotskyites, to undermine the anarchists and revolutionary socialists, to attract the middle classes by insisting that Spain was a "bourgeois" republic and by offering protection against the leftist "uncontrollables," and to occupy the highest military and political posts in the Republican army created from October 1936 on. In the international arena, it also sought to develop an anti-fascist alliance of the Soviet Union and the Western democracies to defeat world fascism on the battlefields of Spain. Among all writers on the Civil War Bolloten has an unrivalled coverage of the wartime press. His accounts of anarchist power in the Levante, and of the infighting among socialist, communist and anarchist factions, are based upon local newspapers and on interviews and correspondence conducted over some 15 years with important personalities in Spain and among the emigrés. His footnotes weigh the value of sources in a fashion that permits the reader to follow the author's full reasoning on controversial items.

Franco Régime

MATTHEWS, HERBERT LIONEL. **The Yoke and the Arrows: A Report on Spain.** New York: Braziller, rev. ed., 1961, 258 p.

Written in 1956, the twentieth anniversary of the Franco régime, this report was extended to 1960 in a second edition which includes corrections as well as additions. The book offers valuable insights: *e.g.* that the significance of the base agreement is that Rota established the United States as a Mediterranean naval power for the first time. But its real value is in the clear expression of the concepts employed by a writer who has played a major role in the formation of American public opinion on Spain, both as a correspondent for *The New York Times* and later as a member of its editorial board. Matthews contends that Franco has consistently considered liberals, not communists, his primary enemy. But Matthews' liberalism is exceedingly traditional. He describes Franco's allies as landowners, generals, priests; only in the 1961 edition does he add "big business and banking." He defines the "people" as "intellectuals, peasants, workers," and asserts that a democracy can provide both social justice and personal liberty, yet he never confronts the dilemma they pose in an underdeveloped country as poor as Spain. Another limitation is his treatment of the Franco régime as an interim one, reflected in his repeated image of Franco "sitting on a lid," clamped down in 1939, to be blown off at his death. This concern with political immobility causes him to neglect socioeconomic and cultural changes; he cannot therefore explain the longevity of the régime.

PAYNE, STANLEY G. **Politics and the Military in Modern Spain.** Stanford: Stanford University Press, 1967, 574 p.

As in most underdeveloped countries, the army in Spain is one of the most important social institutions and has often provided the determining force in political changes. Stanley G. Payne's book was greatly needed for any understanding of contemporary Spanish history. Through his meticulous scholarship and his good fortune in being permitted to draw on military archives never before utilized by historians, the author has begun to piece together the facts about the structure of the Spanish army and its role in political events in the nineteenth and twentieth centuries.

By thus accumulating new data and restructuring old information, Payne has helped provide a quantitative view of the internal dynamics of the armed forces. Although one might have wished for more sociological treatment of the class structure of the army itself and how it was used as a means of social mobility, the data give ample material from which other scholars can work. The study is particularly informative on the importance of the Moroccan wars for the later developments of the politicized army and on the machinations of the army under the Primo de Rivera dictatorship. It also adds valuable information on the organization and structure of the Carlist army and of the communist forces during the Civil War. In this work, Professor Payne has once again displayed the skill, intellectual agility and precision which make him one of the leading contemporary historians of Spain.

CLEUGH, JAMES. **Spain in the Modern World.** New York: Knopf, 1953, 339 p.

Writing in 1952, during the negotiation of the Spanish-American defense pact, Cleugh attempts to remove the Franco régime from the emotive context of the Civil War and to situate it in the postwar world as a potential "keystone" of Western defense, not by dint of her economic and military prowess but of her strategic and moral importance. In defending this assertion, Cleugh does not factually describe personalities and forces but instead offers a rather awkwardly organized *catalogue raisonné* of the geographic and sociohistoric factors that led some Spaniards to support the National cause in 1936 and the Franco régime since then. He posits a national psychology guided since the Middle Ages by ideals unpopular today (he readily admits) among both Western humanists and democrats, and communists—ideals of national unity and order that "must override all secondary considerations concerned with privilege, or individual or corporate liberties." Only a professional army can defend these ideals, only the Catholic Church (in Spain at least) can provide the needed complement of a "generally recognized moral imperative," and until the psychology changes, unity must be interpreted as rule by one man. This rationale is not accepted by "most" Spaniards, as Cleugh claims, but simply by one sector of the governing élite. The ideals themselves, however, have a real and wide appeal in Spain and thus constitute a factor too often ignored by critics who ascribe Franco's triumph in the war and continuation in power as due exclusively to the use of force.

WHITAKER, ARTHUR PRESTON. **Spain and Defense of the West: Ally and Liability.** New York: Harper (for the Council on Foreign Relations), 1961, 408 p.

This is an unexcelled, objective study of the dynamics of the foreign policy of the Franco régime. Although focused on negotiation and implementation of the Pact of Madrid from 1950 to 1960, it goes back through the era of postwar isolation to 1942 when military considerations dictated American overtures to Franco, as they did again in 1953. Whitaker also looked ahead, predicting accurately that successful economic planning (forced on the régime by foreign policy considerations), coupled with Franco's continued refusal to name a successor, would secure him a new lease on power. In a context of national self-interest, requiring that a small power like Spain maintain open options, Whitaker describes the shifts in Franco's policy. His "bridge to Islam" (1950–1957), as a way out of postwar isolation and later as an alternative to dependence upon the United States, ended primarily because of the Russian presence in the Mediterranean in the wake of the Suez crisis. Recognizing also that American aid was of only short-range value to the economy, while long-term expansion required closer ties with Europe, Spain tried various approaches: directly to NATO, indirectly through a Mediterranean pact with France and Britain, and successfully through the OEEC. Whitaker analyzes the economy, politics and the Church as strategic factors. And he defines the key problem for American policy-makers: the evolution by 1960 of the Pact of Madrid from a limited military agreement to a quasi-alliance because of the loss of Moroccan bases and reliance on Polaris missiles. Whitaker notes yet does not synthesize these factors in terms of a major shift of power in the Mediterranean during this decade.

Political and Economic Questions

RAMOS OLIVEIRA, ANTONIO. **Politics, Economics and Men of Modern Spain, 1808–1946.** New York: Crown Publishers, 1948, 720 p.

It is the author's thesis that the history of Spain since the Napoleonic invasion has been one continuous civil war during which the *pronunciamientos,* the Carlist wars, the peasant and proletarian risings, and the Civil War of 1936–1939 have been only the most dramatic, overt symptoms. He divides the entire era into alternating periods of revolution or reform, and counterrevolution or conservatism. The Cortes of Cadiz, the governments of Mendizabal, Espartero and Prim, the First and Second Republics are treated as periods of reform. The governments of Ferdinand VII, of Narvaez, of the Restoration, of Primo de Rivera and of Franco are seen as deeply conservative. The author is not a trained historian, and apparently without realizing his own shifting perspectives, he alternates between economic and political-personal explanations for events. Thus he offers rich information on such questions as land ownership, financial and industrial development, the economic power of the Church and its orders, the weakness of the middle classes, and the militancy of the working class. At the same time, he attributes critical importance to such things as the poor health of the great reformer Joaquín Costa and the artistic temperament of the Republican Prime Minister Manuel Azaña.

About one-third of the text deals with the period 1808–1931, and two-thirds with the era of the Second Republic and the Civil War, 1931–1939. As a socialist, a journalist and a recent exile, Ramos writes with great fluency and conviction. His schematic representation of reformist versus conservative periods is oversimplified, particularly in respect to the Restoration era, 1876–1923. But it is an intelligent, coherent, defensible interpretation of events which earlier historians have treated as a mere accidental sequence of comic opera intrigues. The book is in no sense definitive, but it offers an interestingly written, generally accurate and thought-challenging introduction to the history of nineteenth and twentieth-century Spain.

MALEFAKIS, EDWARD E. **Agrarian Reform and Peasant Revolution in Spain.** New Haven: Yale University Press, 1970, 469 p.

This is without doubt the most detailed and scientific study in any language of Spanish agrarian problems. It covers all questions of climate and technology, productivity and profits, historical development of land tenure in the several regions, and social struggles of the late nineteenth and twentieth centuries. The *latifundio* problem is seen as dating from the thirteenth century Reconquest, at which time war captains and military orders received their huge estates from the crown. The *desamortización* of 1837 practically expropriated the Church as a landowner and greatly reduced the proportion of noble landowners, but it simultaneously aggravated the general problem because land sales of the ensuing decade, mostly to wealthy bourgeois, concentrated land ownership in southern Spain even more highly than during the previous five hundred years. Republican efforts of the 1930s met the following obstacles. No arable state or municipal land was available. There were no Church lands, as in the French Revolution, and no significant foreign-owned estates, as in Rumania in 1918 or Algeria in 1963. Any Spanish land reform was thus bound to injure the native bourgeoisie. In discussing peasant revolutionary impulses in southern Spain, Malefakis points out that the thirst to own land was the great motivating factor. Northern peasants might have just as low a standard of living, but the possession of a bit of land, or of a secure lease, kept them from following revolutionary leadership. All interpretations are buttressed by massive historical and sociological data, and all statistics are handled critically.

TAMAMES, RAMÓN. **Estructura Económica de España.** Madrid: Sociedad de Estudios y Publicaciones, 1960, 677 p.

Scientific studies of the Spanish economy have been difficult to make in the past. Statistics were most unreliable, and few men were trained in the analysis of economic data. The situation has improved markedly since about 1950, and the present work is the best comprehensive treatment so far of the Spanish economy. Besides dealing with climate, natural resources, agriculture and industry, the author devotes substantial chapters to transport, foreign commerce, monetary and banking problems, and to economic factors which have been particularly important in Spanish development such as irrigation, reforestation and tourism. With each topic he gives the reader historical background at least to the mid-nineteenth century and compares Spain with its Mediterranean neighbors in regard to technology and productivity.

The interpretations are eclectic, owing much to such different figures as Marx, Keynes, Myrdal and Einaudi, and the author combines factual description with a concern for Spain's ability to achieve integration with the general European and world economy. In this connection he notes that Spain is an underdeveloped country living next to a Europe in which both technological levels and international commerce have been highly developed since the eighteenth century. Over the past century Spanish tax returns have been insufficient for governmental development projects, and this fact has hampered the internal diversification of the national economy. Since 1892 protective tariffs have been even higher for industry than for agriculture, and both main sectors of the economy are inefficient and uncompetitive by European standards. The book is not a jeremiad, however, but a highly competent, cogently reasoned survey.

VICENS VIVES, JAIME and NADAL OLLER, JORGE. **An Economic History of Spain.** Princeton: Princeton University Press, 1969, 825 p.

One of the outstanding contributions to recent Spanish historiography has been the "Manual de Historia Económica de España," prepared by the late Jaime Vicens Vives in collaboration with Jorge Nadal Oller. In contrast to unsuccessful previous attempts by other writers to interpret Peninsular history by reference to economic data, this book marked a revolution in Spanish historiography: for the first time the study of population trends, subsistence crises, price and trade curves were made essential to the understanding of the entire history of Spain.

This comprehensive study, translated by Frances M. López-Morillas, is a careful synthesis of the material that had thus far been published, and its extensive bibliography is an indication of the magnitude of this enterprise. The book abounds in challenging working hypotheses which emphasize the significance of such questions as fiscal policies, markets and tariffs, property distribution and economic development, and their impact on social and political crises.

Yet we must regret that no attempt was made to define such concepts as class, feudalism, peasantry, bourgeoisie and capitalism more rigorously, despite the general awareness among modern historians of the danger of applying these terms too loosely. Also, one must regret the fact that this study is essentially Catalonia-oriented, thus particularly concerned with urban and industrial problems. The economy of rural Spain has remained somewhat marginal to the purpose of this work despite its decisive presence in any overall picture of Spain.

Research published in the last decade has somewhat altered these findings and has filled some of the gaps. Even so, this is so far the single most important work devoted to Spanish economic history.

PORTUGAL

LIVERMORE, HAROLD V. **A New History of Portugal.** New York: Cambridge University Press, 1966, 365 p.

This is an abridgment and revision of Professor Livermore's earlier **A History of Portugal** (New York: Macmillan, 1948, 502 p.), which has generally been recognized as the leading one-volume history of Portugal available in English. The original work was based to a large extent on the **História de Portugal** edited by Damião Peres (Barcelos: Portucalense Editoria, 1928–1935, 7 v.). The new edition has been reduced by approximately one-third but devotes proportionately more attention to the nineteenth and twentieth centuries. Unfortunately, the small amount of material on social and economic matters that appeared in the first edition has been even further reduced in the new book. Nevertheless, greater attention to recent Portuguese history is helpful to general readers, even though the treatment of the Salazar régime is largely restricted to diplomatic affairs. Though limited in perspective and detail, this narrative political history remains the principal account of the Portuguese past, medieval or modern, that is currently obtainable in English.

DE CAMPOS, EZEQUIEL. **O Enquadramento Geo-económico da Populaçao Portuguesa Através dos Séculos.** Lisbon: Revista Ocidente, 1943, 305 p.

Though the title would indicate a general geoeconomic history, two-thirds of this volume is devoted to an analysis of Portuguese economic structure and problems in the 1930s and 1940s. Its greatest merit is that it is the only work on the mid-twentieth century Portuguese economy that places the latter in historical perspective. The first hundred pages provide brief, clear analyses of the principal phases of historical evolution of the society and economy of Portugal. The main part of the book treats the problems of land, commerce, finance and electric power. Great care is taken throughout, in both the historical and contemporary sections, to differentiate economic problems by geographic region. The author, a leading Portuguese economist, supplemented his treatment of contemporary problems with a subsequent work, **Problemas Fundamentais Portugueses** (Lisbon: Revista Ocidente, 1946, 228 p.).

PASQUIER, ALBERT. **L'Économie du Portugal: Données et Problèmes de Son Expansion.** Paris: Librairie Générale de Droit, 1961, 234 p.

This work by a leading French specialist in Portuguese social and economic problems is the best study that has been published on the structure of the Portuguese economy in the 1950s and early 1960s. It is concise and nontechnical in language, and thus can easily be used by general readers. The book offers an overall description of the Portuguese economy, including helpful statistical data. There is considerable attention to the larger agrarian sector, but also treatment of demography, industry and commerce. Space is devoted to analysis of government policy and the state regulatory agencies. Pasquier provides a clear discussion of structural weaknesses and imbalances and gives a lucid evaluation of the first development programs of the 1950s. Though the book does not have a major comparative dimension, occasional contrasts between French and Portuguese economic indices provide some comparison with a developed economy. A consideration of the

Portuguese system in comparison with those of other less-developed south European countries is, however, not attempted.

PABÓN, JESÚS. **La Revolución Portuguesa.** Madrid: Espasa-Calpe, 1941, 1944, 2 v.

This work by a leading contemporary Spanish historian is the principal narrative of Portuguese politics from 1908 to 1926. A work of "old-fashioned" political history that concentrates on prominent personalities and the details of official politics, the study relies heavily on published memoirs. It is relentlessly critical of Portuguese radicalism, and liberal commentators have stringently criticized its evident bias. Those who are interested in the social and economic dimensions of Portuguese affairs in this period, or even in the broader infrastructure of Portuguese politics, will find such aspects completely ignored. Despite these severe limitations, Pabón's two-volume work remains the only detailed study of high politics in Lisbon under the parliamentary régime. It won the Camoens Prize in 1942 and has also been published in a Portuguese translation.

NOGUEIRA, FRANCO. **The United Nations and Portugal: A Study of Anti-Colonialism.** London: Sidgwick and Jackson, 1963, 188 p.

As a defense and explanation of the Portuguese government's diplomatic position in the face of the anti-colonial campaign, this slender volume makes the best case that has thus far been published in English. Dr. Nogueira, who at the time of the book's publication was Portuguese Foreign Minister, does not pretend to an impartial analysis but rather provides a critique of the international anti-colonialist posture from the Portuguese viewpoint. His approach is temperate, analytical and well controlled, making the book an indispensable document for the understanding of the thinking and the position of the Portuguese government vis-à-vis the United Nations and the African world.

PLONCARD D'ASSAC, JACQUES. **Salazar.** Paris: La Table Ronde, 1967, 350 p.

Antonio de Oliveira Salazar, Prime Minister and ruler of Portugal from 1933 to 1968, was one of the unique heads of government in contemporary Europe. Though numerous books have been written about him, there is no adequate biography. Ploncard d'Assac's volume is perhaps less incomplete and unsatisfactory than the others, but it makes no pretense of being an objective or critical biography and is in many ways a eulogy. Its principal merit is that it provides a rough chronicle of Salazar's career and government down to the last years of his rule, and it gives a fairly clear exposition of his theories of society and politics. In this enterprise the author relies greatly on Salazar's public utterances and includes numerous long quotations from his speeches. The book thus becomes a personal sketch, doctrinal anthology and to some extent a thumbnail outline of the formal political history of Salazar's régime. Though inadequate in each of these aspects, it is none the less the most useful single volume on Salazar currently in print.

SALAZAR, ANTONIO DE OLIVEIRA. **Doctrine and Action: Internal and Foreign Policy of the New Portugal, 1928–1939.** London: Faber, 1939, 399 p.

Volumes of selected speeches by government leaders do not always merit particular attention, but the public addresses of Dr. Salazar, Prime Minister and virtual dictator of Portugal for 35 years, are indispensable to an understanding of the attitudes and policies of the Portuguese régime. As an intellectual, scholar and former professor of law, Salazar was more careful than many authoritarian leaders to exercise precision in his formal policy utterances. The speeches in this volume deal with the formative period of the Portuguese New State, from Salazar's entry into the government as Finance Minister in 1928 through his virtual takeover of state policy in the years from 1930 to 1933 to the eve of the Second World War in Europe. In these statements Salazar explained his notions of fiscal integrity, his doctrine of conservative anti-statist authoritarianism, his concept of the relationship between Portugal and its colonies and his policy of relative neutrality in Europe while upholding the alliance with Britain.

GERMANY

General; Historical

HOLBORN, HAJO. **A History of Modern Germany. Volume III: 1840–1945.** New York: Knopf, 1969, 818 p.

As a scholar and teacher Hajo Holborn was one of the most influential of that eminent group of Germans who came to the United States from the wreckage of Weimar Germany. The present book, the third and final volume of his magisterial history of Germany since the Reformation, was completed only shortly before his death. It is a fitting monument to his vast range of knowledge and his profound sense of humanity. In many respects (organization, scope, topics) a conventional general history, it is informed by the author's deep familiarity with political and diplomatic history and by his intimate sense of German *Geistesgeschichte*. Moreover, since Germany came to play such a central role in international and intellectual affairs in the years under consideration, Holborn affords many important insights into the general climate of ideas and politics in the last hundred years.

WEBER, MAX. **Gesammelte Politische Schriften.** Tübingen: Mohr, 1958, 593 p.

This is the enlarged edition of a book which first appeared in 1920. Its 28 lectures and articles, most of them originally published in newspapers, touch upon such disparate subjects as European foreign policy, the Russian Revolution of 1905, German party politics, the war guilt question and constitutional reform in Germany. However, certain themes recur and give the book not only unity but an interest far beyond its somewhat ephemeral subject matter. All the articles reveal a striking mixture of democratic and nationalistic ideas which go far to explain the future fate of the Weimar Republic. In its entirety the collection is a remarkable example of good contemporary history; by placing the happenings of the day in the framework of sociological categories Max Weber succeeded in gaining distance from the events and in discovering those factors that would have lasting effect. Finally, because Weber's sociological categories are steadily applied to the analysis of political events, the book becomes a convenient and useful introduction to Weber's sociological thought.

RITTER, GERHARD. **Staatskunst und Kriegshandwerk. V. 3: Die Tragödie der Staatskunst. Bethmann Hollweg als Kriegskanzler (1914–1917).** Munich: Oldenbourg, 1964, 707 p.

The dispute between Professors Gerhard Ritter and Fritz Fischer (as in **Germany's Aims in the First World War**) has aroused contemporary German scholars perhaps more than any other single historical issue. Both dealing with Germany's political aims in World War I, each in his way dealt with the matter of German "guilt"—Fischer, for instance, asserting that the outrageous German territorial annexational demands during the war were already widely advocated in military, industrial and intellectual circles long before 1914. Ritter's more temperate analysis would see the principal sources of this fateful policy to lie more in acute strategic dilemmas of German statecraft and in the profound popular messianism which total war aroused in Germany, as in all other European belligerent states.

From a rational-strategic viewpoint (not unlike that of Israelis after the Six Day War), a well-grounded neurotic fear of a two-front war inspired the German wish for annexations as buffers against recurrences, while the terrible sacrifices exacted from ordinary Germans by the futile tragedy of 1914 found no effective sublimation save in dreams of a grand, national mission. So also, the author sees the motives of German civilian policy in July 1914 as inspired by defensive, not aggressive, motives; if the civilian leaders such as Bethmann-Hollweg then found themselves haplessly committed to the General Staff's contingency plans, this was less a consequence of their relative political inferiority than of the deadly strategic situation which had been built up over the previous decade, of which the Schlieffen Plan was an absolute component. To Ritter the historian, as to Bethmann-Hollweg the statesman, the war was to be seen as a consequence of conflict among the power and prestige requirements of all the European powers; that German war aims became "idealized" turned out in practice to have catastrophic consequences; yet in the author's view, "without the attempt at self-justification and spiritual self-defense, a modern nation cannot bear the heavy burden of war."

CRAIG, GORDON ALEXANDER. **The Politics of the Prussian Army, 1640–1945.** New York: Oxford University Press, rev. ed., 1964, 538 p.

This is the most comprehensive and significant one-volume study of the political role of the Prussian army in either German or English, here republished with corrections. Its only rivals are Walter Görlitz's apologetic and unreliable **History of the German General Staff** (New York: Praeger, 1953, 508 p.) and Gerhard Ritter's four-volume **Staatskunst und Kriegshandwerk.** The latter work is less well balanced than Craig's, but it is more thorough and it corrects Craig in points of detail. A valuable addition to Craig's study on the sociological side is Karl Demeter, **The German Officer-Corps in Society and State, 1650–1945** (New York: Praeger, 1965, 414 p.).

The particular value of this study lies in the way it combines a highly judicious presentation of the fruits of previous scholarship with findings based on original research by the author. The work, for example, incorporates material and ideas from Friedrich Meinecke's studies of Generals Boyen and Radowitz. At the same time, however, it presents important new material based on the author's research in the papers of Generals Edwin von Manteuffel, Albrecht von Roon, Wilhelm Groener and Kurt von Schleicher, as well as Craig's investigation of the military attachés under William II. The author is highly critical of the role played by the Prussian-German army. He suggestively views modern German history as a series of constitutional crises in which one of the key issues was civilian control over the army. Above all, he convincingly charts the degeneration of the officer corps' moral fiber from its high point under Scharnhorst and Gneisenau to its collapse under Keitl and Jodl. This degeneration, which the author consistently relates to the officer corps' peculiar brand of politics, culminated in the army's succumbing to Hitler's domination and its betrayal of the responsibility it had to the German people.

RITTER, GERHARD. **Staatskunst und Kriegshandwerk. V. 4: Die Herrschaft des Deutschen Militarismus und die Katastrophe von 1918.** Munich: Oldenbourg, 1968, 586 p.

This last volume of Ritter's great study of German statecraft and military power, finished shortly before his death, brings the story through the last terrible months of the First World War. The account of these years shows how delicate was the balance, inside all of the exhausted warring states, among force, diplomacy and domestic social stability. All of them feared the miscarriage of peace overtures might lead to an unravelling of domestic support for the war and internal collapse. Yet each knew that persistence in the war would test their strength to the breaking point. The Germans, divided between parliamentary reformers on the one hand and the OHL on the other, solved the dilemma temporarily by accepting the dictatorship of Ludendorff and his rigid policy of force and annexationism. His iron resolve to risk everything on a battlefield decision was coupled with an astonishing and foolhardy diplomacy. In the end, his gamble quickly failed, and the entire Hohenzollern system crashed. As the Weimar period began, in conditions of revolutionary collapse, the new socialist leaders of the republic—themselves fearful of major revolution—ironically found themselves dependent upon the very military institutions which had brought about the disaster.

NETTL, J. P. **Rosa Luxemburg.** New York: Oxford University Press, 1966, 2 v.

This lengthy biography of an almost legendary figure of the revolutionary left provides the evidence for a new and perhaps definitive assessment of the place of Rosa Luxemburg in the history of the European working-class movement and of socialist thought. Rosa Luxemburg is important less for her revolutionary achieve-ments—she failed to make the revolution in Germany for which she had worked for much of her life, and she was murdered in January 1919 as a result of her revolutionary activities—than for her theories about revolutionary spontaneity, about the effects of imperialism on all aspects of society and about the links between capitalism, militarism and imperialism.

J. P. Nettl's book, though it does not wholly replace Paul Frölich's earlier work, **Rosa Luxemburg** (English translation, London: Gollancz, 1940, 336 p.)—a more personal study based on close friendship—is the result of wide and deep research in the German and Polish sources. Nettl combines biographical with sociological techniques, focusing, for example, on Rosa Luxemburg's relations with her "peer group," the Polish revolutionaries with whom she was linked all her life. He provides a clear account of her theoretical work and deals imaginatively and sensitively with her passionate personality and her intense private life. J. P. Nettl, a British historian and sociologist from the Universities of Oxford and Leeds, has removed the figure of Rosa Luxemburg from the realm of myth to that of reality in a work which makes one regret all the more his untimely death.

STERN, FRITZ RICHARD. **The Politics of Cultural Despair: A Study in the Rise of the Germanic Ideology.** Berkeley: University of California Press, 1961, 367 p.

The lives of the three figures studied in this book—Paul de Lagarde (1827–1891), Julius Langbehn (1851–1907) and Arthur Moeller van den Bruck (1876–1924)—span a century of German history. Their thought and careers provide a most significant insight into the evolution of that spiritual malaise which was to prove so devastating to Germany and the world in the 1930s. Haters of modernity and liberalism, their "leap from despair to utopia" provided many of the com-ponents of the "conservative revolutionism" which helped pave the way to National Socialism (though the two are by no means identical). The title of Moeller's major work, **Das Dritte Reich** (Berlin: Ring-Verlag, 1923, 261 p.), suggests both the final thrust of his thought and its ominous implications.

This is an admirable piece of intellectual history, of real diagnostic value.

KRIEGER, LEONARD. **The German Idea of Freedom: History of a Political Tradition.** Boston: Beacon Press, 1957, 540 p.

As the author of this important, and quite difficult, book observes, it "is not designed to cover a section of history. It is designed, rather, to provide answers to a definite set of historical questions arising out of the 'German problem.' " The "problem," as Krieger defines it, is the failure of the Germans "to achieve, under their own power, a liberal democracy in the western sense."

The sources of the problem are seen to lie in the evolution of a very particular conception of liberty (and of its relation to the state) which was largely developed before Germany had become a unified nation-state. Hence the bulk of the author's study has to do with the crucial years between 1789 and 1870. It is, nevertheless, of real value for the student of twentieth-century Germany.

Krieger's work (like that of Fritz Stern) is important in providing a historical setting that enables us to escape the shortsighted fallacy of regarding the advent of Hitler as simply a consequence of a lost war and a depression without falling into the opposite fallacy of regarding Hitlerism in terms of innate national qualities rooted in the depths of the *Teutoburger Wald.*

Weimar Republic

General

ROSENBERG, ARTHUR. **The Birth of the German Republic.** New York: Oxford University Press, 1931, 294 p.

Rosenberg's study, first published in 1931, remains the classic presentation of the internal conflicts which racked the Second German Empire and brought about its collapse and the founding of the Weimar Republic. Despite the vast amount of new material discovered since 1945 and the large number of new publications covering the 1871–1918 period, this book remains quite reliable in its factual presentation of domestic politics, resting as it does on material gathered during Rosenberg's membership on the Reichstag committee investigating the causes of the 1918 collapse. The book is much less satisfactory by contemporary standards in its discussion of foreign affairs, and it is quite unreliable on military matters, where Rosenberg defends the military judgment and tactics of Germany's military leaders in a manner most surprising for a historian of his left-wing inclinations.

Although only the first two of its seven chapters are devoted to the 1871–1914 period, they constitute a masterful description of the basic political constellations of the prewar years and a powerful argument for the contention that "the Bismarckian Empire was mortally ill from the day of its birth" and that by 1914 Germany had undergone crises "typical of a pre-revolutionary period." The war, which receives the bulk of Rosenberg's attention, only temporarily suspended the internal conflict, and the collapse of the Kaiser's authority was already evident in the creation of a virtual Ludendorff dictatorship in 1917–1918 on the one hand, and in the establishment of an oppositional Reichstag majority on the other. The failure on the field of battle led to the abdication of the army and the "revolution from above" which placed the Reichstag majority in power in October 1918. The November 1918 Revolution merely completed the creation of the middle-class parliamentary régime of which Bismarck had cheated German liberalism. For all intents and purposes, according to Rosenberg, the basic purposes of the revolution had been achieved in October 1918.

ROSENBERG, ARTHUR. **History of the German Republic.** London: Methuen, 1936, 350 p.

Written in exile by a refugee professor of ancient history and apostate communist, this is still an essential book in its field. Although it has been superseded in terms of data by numerous subsequent studies, it remains important for its seminal interpretation of the formative stages of the first German republic. Nearly half the book is devoted to the revolution of 1918–1919 and its aftermath. Writing as a left-wing democratic socialist, Rosenberg viewed the revolution as a failure, finding the cause in a tragically fortuitous misalignment of forces and personalities in the faction-riven socialist movement. He saw the result as a triumph of the most conservative elements of the Social Democratic Party and the creation under working-class auspices of a bourgeois state that was, as a consequence of its origins, despised by the middle classes. In Rosenberg's view, the republic was thus crippled at the outset by a fundamental birth defect. The second half of the book, dealing with the period from 1920 to 1930, is, by comparison with the first half, a superficial and conventional narrative political history. The terminal date is 1930, Rosenberg's judgment being that the republic died with the Reichstag's acquiescence at that time to Chancellor Heinrich Brüning's use of presidential emergency powers to circumvent the parliament. The book contains no footnotes or references to specific documents but instead has notes at the end on the sources used for each chapter.

TROELTSCH, ERNST. **Spektator-Briefe.** Tübingen: Mohr, 1924, 321 p.

Like Max Weber's **Gesammelte Politische Schriften,** the **Spektator-Briefe** of his friend, Ernst Troeltsch, arouses ambiguous feelings in today's reader. These letters were comments on political events which Troeltsch published monthly from 1918 until his death in 1923 in the *Kunstwart,* a well-known German periodical. During these years Troeltsch was not only one of the most famous teachers at Berlin University but also a deputy in the Prussian parliament and, for some time, Under-Secretary in the Prussian Ministry of Education. His political observations were based on a good amount of inside information. Indeed, as a chronicle of events and life in these revolutionary years the letters are invaluable.

Troeltsch's descriptions of the shabbiness of Berlin streets, full of poorly dressed, hungry-looking people, and covered with loud, badly tattered political posters, or of the difficulties of traveling in unheated, overfilled trains, catch the German atmosphere of these years brilliantly. He also gives a penetrating analysis of the nature and the dangers of German militarism; clearly, he already saw things then which we now believe only the experiences of the Nazi régime have revealed to us. But in Troeltsch's mind penetration and shortsightedness are strangely blended. Although he was a democrat and approved of the Weimar Republic, he was full of the prejudices of the academic classes. The letters show contempt for the lack of education of the new German rulers. Troeltsch is very much a man of "order," which for him has priority over social changes. He is inclined to ascribe responsibility for all that goes wrong to the Treaty of Versailles, and his speculations about the international situation are naïve. These letters demonstrate how heavily the legacy of the Empire hung over the Weimar Republic—and that perhaps is their greatest value.

PRELLER, LUDWIG. **Sozialpolitik in der Weimarer Republik.** Stuttgart: Mittelbach, 1949, 560 p.

This remains the fundamental study of the social legislation of the first German republic. Placing the subject in the widest possible context, the author devoted the first half of the volume to a review of the political and economic position of the German working classes in the early twentieth century, the impact of the First World War on social legislation, and the political and economic organizations concerned with the problem. The second half consists of a detailed chronicle of the social legislation adopted during the republic and an analysis of its implementation. In the opinion of Preller, who was closely associated with the socialist trade-union movement, the republic's social legislation was of crucial political importance. It represented an attempt, following the failure to effect thoroughgoing socialism after the revolution, to reform and democratize Germany's capitalist economy gradually through democratic methods. In his judgment this attempt was a qualified success. For nearly ten years the economic conflicts that had come to the boiling point during the revolution were held in check by a complex system of measures whereby the state intervened to protect the worker and regulate his relations with his employer. When this system collapsed under the strains of the Depression, the explosive issues of economic policy were thrown back into the political arena, paralyzing the parliamentary system and setting off the fatal crisis of the republic.

Writing under adverse circumstances during the Third Reich, Preller was forced to rely on very limited source materials, mainly trade-union publications of the Weimar period. Consequently, his book is more valuable as a record of what happened in the field of social legislation than as an analysis of why it happened. It is particularly weak on the politics of the republic, for which Preller frequently relied on simplistic Marxist interpretations.

CARSTEN, FRANCIS LUDWIG. **The Reichswehr and Politics, 1918–1933.** Oxford: Clarendon, 1966, 427 p.

First published in German in 1964, this is the most comprehensive study to date of the role of the military in the first German republic. Utilizing a vast range of source materials, the author recounts the successful efforts of the imperial officer corps to achieve for the Reichswehr, the army of the republic, the position of a state within the state, an autonomous status beyond the surveillance or control of the democratically elected government. Refuting efforts by other writers to extenuate the conduct of the military leaders, he marshals an impressive array of evidence indicating that they frequently put themselves above the law and were motivated by reactionary views as well as selfish class interest. Carefully tracing the military's increasingly massive intrusion into the political life of the republic during its final crisis-torn years, Carsten places upon the generals a heavy share of responsibility for the developments that destroyed the democratic order and ultimately brought Adolf Hitler to power. The chief weakness of the book lies in its tendency to exaggerate the importance of the army and to relegate to the background the many other factors in the political life of the republic. Also, no effort is made to explain why the leaders of the republic were unable or unwilling to challenge the autonomy of the military.

BRACHER, KARL DIETRICH. **Die Auflösung der Weimarer Republik: Eine Studie zum Problem des Machtverfalls in der Demokratie.** Villingen/Schwarzwald: Ring Verlag, 4th ed., 1964, 809 p.

Of the younger generation of German historians determined to analyze fearlessly and dispassionately the origins and nature of National Socialism and to enable Germans to look at their recent past sanely and responsibly, Professor Bracher, now professor of political science in the University of Bonn, has made the most original and substantial contribution. This is his earliest major work, and first appeared in 1955. The third edition (1960) was revised and enlarged; this edition is unchanged.

Bracher combines the approaches of a political scientist with those of a historian. He is concerned to analyze the political power structure of Germany and to study the reasons for its collapse as well as to give a very detailed narrative of the actual sequence of events.

While there are moments in which the author seems rather overwhelmed by the weight of his own knowledge, so that the style is sometimes hard to follow (Bracher has overcome these stylistic defects in his later works), the book is an indispensable account of the fall of the Weimar Republic, based on very extensive original research. It is unlikely to be superseded in its general lines, though other detailed monographs such as F. L. Carsten, **The Reichswehr and Politics, 1918–1933,** will add to our knowledge. The subject is still controversial, as Bracher himself scrupulously points out, but his book inaugurated a new phase of informed discussion of it.

CLARK, ROBERT THOMSON. **The Fall of the German Republic.** New York: Macmillan, 1935, 494 p.

R. T. Clark was a British journalist who worked in Germany for some 12 years. His book was one of the first serious attempts to analyze the reasons for the failure of the Weimar Republic, and, although there are inaccuracies here and there and although we know more now about the details of many of the events Clark discusses, this is a book which remains well worth reading. The author's personal contacts with political leaders in Berlin were excellent, and he gives vivid descriptions of their personalities. He was remarkably well informed about political events, so that many of his surmises about what went on behind the scenes have been confirmed by later research. Above all, he understood the workings of the German constitutional system extremely well, and his account of the functioning of the parties under the system of proportional representation, and of their relationship to parliament, government and electorate, gives one of the best pictures available of the political situation in the Weimar Republic.

This is a political narrative by a highly intelligent, perceptive, literate and well-informed journalist. It makes no claim to examine the deeper social, economic and intellectual causes for the collapse of the German republic, and the result is that the author perhaps overestimates the possibility of purely political solutions in 1931–1933. Nevertheless, as a piece of firsthand interpretative analysis of political events it is still hard to beat.

JORDAN, W. M. **Great Britain, France, and the German Problem, 1918–1939: A Study of Anglo-French Relations in the Making and Maintaining of the Versailles Settlement.** New York: Oxford University Press (for the Royal Institute of International Affairs), 1943, 235 p.

This slender volume is best described by its subtitle. Clearly and dispassionately, Jordan traces the divergence of British and French policy toward Germany from 1919 to 1936. To this divergence he attributes the breakdown of the European order established at Versailles. Jordan describes in detail how the disagreement influenced the postwar summit conferences and the functioning of the various inter-allied agencies set up to supervise the execution of the peace treaty. He shows how the conflict between Britain's hope to appease Germany and France's wish to coerce her affected the fundamental issues of reparations and disarmament and broke down the security which France desired from the settlement. Carefully he follows the evolution of these two policies and points out their nuances. Many of Jordan's conclusions, formulated some 30 years ago, are still historical orthodoxy.

By the author's own admission the focus of the book is narrow. Jordan omits all aspects of British and French diplomacy which do not bear directly on the German problem. He ignores the two powers' relations with the League and with the Soviet Union. More seriously, he excludes disputes in other areas which clouded the Anglo-French friendship and thus impinged indirectly upon policy toward Germany. Nor does Jordan attempt to correlate domestic politics and foreign policy; he is not concerned with what he calls "social forces." The book should be read in conjunction with Arnold Wolfers, **Britain and France between Two Wars.**

EYCK, ERICH. **A History of the Weimar Republic.** Cambridge: Harvard University Press, 1962–1963, 2 v.

During the Weimar years, Eyck was a lawyer and journalist in Berlin. His history of the republic is based upon personal recollections, conversations with contemporaries and a careful study of the records. Eyck is interested primarily in the politics of the period, and here he excels. He reconstructs the crises of the republic in scrupulous detail, and his characterization of the political figures—minor and major—is masterly. Eyck's sympathy for the liberal cause is never in doubt, but this sympathy does not cloud his awareness also of political failures on the left. The narrative is graceful and fluent, the tone urbane and detached.

Eyck is a historian of the old school. He believes that history is made by men, and that the historian's task is met in recording the activities of these men. The approach has obvious charm—and obvious limitations. Eyck neglects the social and economic forces at work during the Weimar era. He does not understand the implications of the abortive revolution; he says nothing of the cultural brilliance and malaise of these years; and he takes little account of the traditionally and enduringly hostile environment in which the republic attempted to survive. Hitler's assumption of power, like many other political crises in the book, appears as a series of moves upon a chessboard. As a serious history of the republic, the book is largely superseded. It is, however, still the most comprehensive single study of the Weimar years, and thus the most useful introduction to the period.

FISCHER, RUTH. **Stalin and German Communism.** Cambridge: Harvard University Press, 1948, 687 p.

Ruth Fischer was a founding member of the Austrian Communist Party but soon transferred her activities to the German Party. She was a prominent member of its left wing and served for some time as a member of the Comintern Presidium. Thus she was well situated to observe the Stalinization of the Communist Party of the Soviet Union and its corresponding effects in the Comintern and especially in Germany, a crucial area of communist strategies and hopes in the 1920s. Her book, which appeared in the early years of the cold war and occasioned a good deal of controversy, continues to be a rewarding source of information for the first decade of communism. Parts of her story have been amplified or corrected by others, a polemical and partisan tone often obtrudes, and her personal judgments must be approached cautiously. Still, this is a major work and is particularly successful in recapturing the political temper of the radical left in the years after 1918.

Memoirs and Biographies

SUTTON, ERIC, *ed.* **Gustav Stresemann: His Diaries, Letters, and Papers.** New York: Macmillan, 1935–1940, 3 v.

Consisting of an abridged translation of the German edition of the papers of Stresemann, the former Chancellor and Foreign Minister of the first German republic (**Vermächtnis,** Berlin: Ullstein, 1932–1933, 3 v.), these volumes are at most of very limited value. Research made possible by the Allied capture of the Stresemann papers at the close of the Second World War revealed that the German edition itself represented only a fraction of the total collection. Moreover, documents that cast doubt on Stresemann's public stance as a champion of European coöperation and the League of Nations were systematically excluded. In many cases, even those documents that were included were edited to omit passages considered potentially damaging to Stresemann's reputation. As a consequence, the English edition, which represents only a partial version of the German, must be used with considerable caution. For reliable documentation on Stresemann's career, one should consult the original papers, which are available in a microfilm publication of the U.S. National Archives. An informative guide to the microfilms is the article by Hans W. Gatzke, "The Stresemann Papers," *Journal of Modern History,* v. 26 (1954).

VON KESSLER, HARRY, GRAF. **Tagebücher, 1918–1937.** Frankfurt/Main: Insel-Verlag, 2d ed., 1961, 799 p.

In **Gesichter und Zeiten: Erinnerungen** (Berlin: Fischer, 1935, 257 p.; reissued in 1962), Kessler composed a poignant (and never indiscreet) memoir of a childhood and adolescence spent in French and English schools and among the haute bourgeoisie in Germany. These diaries were to serve as source material for this volume of further recollections. They are the record of a German aristocrat of democratic sympathies, a man of leisure at home in the society and culture of Germany, Britain and France. Kessler cultivated friendships—with conservative diplomats and republican politicians, with cloistered scientists and left-wing journalists. He sought the company of artists and of men of letters. His government used him for diplomatic missions, official and unofficial; on his own he propagated pacifist causes and championed Germany's entry into the League of Nations. He saw Berlin during the revolution and in the last year of the republic, London during the crisis over the Ruhr invasion, Paris when Stresemann died and at Briand's death, and Rome during the election of Pius XI. All this he recorded, often minutely. What emerges is another dimension to the history we know—the personal encounter, with its gossip and insights, its prejudices and obligations. Kessler also comments: his often acerbic thumbnail sketches of contemporaries are finely wrought. Because of the breadth of his interests and of his personal contacts, Kessler is unique among the Germans who have left us their journals. His records afford an unequalled portrait of Weimar society.

VON KESSLER, HARRY, GRAF. **Walther Rathenau.** New York: Harcourt, 1930, 379 p.

This is still the best biography of Rathenau, one of the most successful industrial magnates of imperial Germany, author of popular quasi-philosophical works and controversial Foreign Minister during the Weimar Republic. His name is associated most readily with Weimar's "policy of compliance," aimed at fulfilling the terms of the peace treaty while demonstrating the practical impossibility of doing so, and with the Treaty of Rapallo, which he concluded with the Russians in 1922. Always the target of chauvinist and anti-Semitic criticism, he was assassinated by young nationalists who deemed him a traitor to his country.

Kessler is not primarily interested in Rathenau the magnate or the statesman. There is little on Germany's prewar industrialization, in which the Rathenaus (father and son) played a prominent part. Of the postwar summit conferences Rathenau attended, Genoa alone, which Kessler himself witnessed, is treated in detail. Kessler's principal purpose is to portray, sympathetically though not uncritically, the unresolved contest between reason and emotion that shaped Rathenau's life. For Kessler, Rathenau's often conflicting allegiances are the manifestations of this contest. It explains his idealization of a German nation of blond and blue-eyed Teutons, his admiration for the traditional Prussian virtues from which he, as a Jew too proud to convert, was excluded. Thus his efforts to integrate himself into the nation were vitiated at the outset. Drawing freely upon Rathenau's letters and books, Kessler casts the biography as a tragedy in which Rathenau, always the "outsider," moves inexorably to his doom.

Nazi Era

See also International Law: International Criminal Law, p. 162.

General

RAUSCHNING, HERMANN. **The Revolution of Nihilism: Warning to the West.** New York: Alliance, 1939, 300 p.

This book is a prime example of the literature of disenchantment with National Socialism. The author, a Prussian conservative, joined the Nazi movement in the expectation of a national revival and became president of the Danzig Senate. But when he became aware of the rampant nihilism of National Socialism, he broke with the party and dedicated himself to sounding a "warning to the West."

However, the main value of the book does not lie in its personal accent. It is one of the earliest attempts at an analytical interpretation of National Socialism, and as such it has become a classic. Brushing aside the assumption that National Socialism was an intensification either of the nationalist-conservative position or of monopoly capitalism, Rauschning addresses himself to the question of the "suicide of the old order." If National Socialism had any parentage, it was liberalism. Liberalism, the "destroyer of all standards," created a vacuum which was filled and exploited by the nihilism of National Socialism. This relationship between liberalism and National Socialism has been demonstrated by analyses of the voting records of Germany in the early 1930s. Rauschning further points to the altogether novel and revolutionary features of National Socialism. Its irrationality was actually its source of strength; it was "action pure and simple" and "dynamics *in vacuo;*" its "philosophy," in so far as it existed, was carefully designed to sway the masses. National Socialism, as Rauschning sees it, aimed not at crushing the "mass revolt" but at carrying it to completion.

The Revolution of Nihilism holds up strikingly well after more than 30 years. Its main weakness is the author's excessive tendency to make excuses for the part which the Germans played in the Third Reich, in arguing that they were "involuntarily" and "in good faith" involved in a "tragic entanglement."

TOYNBEE, ARNOLD JOSEPH and TOYNBEE, VERONICA MARJORIE, *eds.* **Hitler's Europe.** New York: Oxford University Press (for the Royal Institute of International Affairs), 1954, 730 p.

This book (volume IV of the "Survey of International Affairs, 1939–1946") deals not only with Germany, the German-occupied countries and Germany's satellites (including Italy), but with the resistance movements, the governments in exile and the Free French (including the differences of the Free French with the British and Americans) during the years 1939–1945. Coverage is very uneven, as is the quality of the various chapters of this multi-authored work. The longest and most useful sections are those devoted to Germany, Italy and France, which cover political developments, administration, law and the economy. So many sources have become available since this book's publication that it is now somewhat out of date, but it remains a useful reference.

NEUMANN, FRANZ LEOPOLD. **Behemoth: The Structure and Practice of National Socialism, 1933–1944.** New York: Oxford University Press, new enl. ed., 1944, 649 p.

Despite the passage of more than a quarter-century since its first appearance in 1942, this book remains singularly difficult to appraise, by reason of its virtues rather than its faults. At the time of its publication it was recognized as the most weighty and serious interpretation of National Socialism. Passing years both highlighted the contemporary features of the book (it was written when Hitler was at his height) and brought into dispute the author's heavily argued thesis that the Nazi system is best described as "Totalitarian Monopoly Capitalism." Moreover, the research of the last 25 years, the availability of vast bodies of information on the Hitler years and the workings of the system, have necessarily brought about numerous revisions, refutations and amplifications.

Still, the work is a classic in at least three ways. First, it is a major study by a supremely penetrating intellect that is at once hardheaded and humane. It is no disrespect to Marx to say that Neumann was a thinker who had absorbed and comprehended Marxism and yet, with his own creative impulse, was pressing beyond Marx—a strenuous effort that was to engage Neumann until his death in 1954. Second, whatever the revisions, Neumann took the Nazi phenomenon seriously and tried to relate it to the broader issues of German and Western history. The range of reading and knowledge, from the classics to the present, is tremendous, and Neumann is really at his best in his analysis of ideas. Finally, scattered liberally throughout the book are perceptions about human and social behavior, the nature of society, the quality of law, that are a contribution to the grand tradition of political philosophy and provide—as indeed they have provided—starting points for numerous books and monographs by those who have followed. A rereading of the book in 1970 clearly reveals the distinction between the ephemeral husk and the lasting kernel.

MEINECKE, FRIEDRICH. **The German Catastrophe.** Cambridge: Harvard University Press, 1950, 121 p.

This is a very minor, one might say weak, work of the great German historian who was in his eighties when he wrote it. In it Meinecke tries to explain the developments leading to the rule of the Nazis in Germany. His explanations are brief and general, but they show that Meinecke has not only turned away from power politics and militarism but is also abandoning the idea of national sovereignty. Because his earlier writings have always expressed a strong belief in the value of the national state, this small book is of great interest to students of his thought. But it has a higher significance. It is a document which indicates the extent to which the defeat of 1945 shook and upset all the deeply rooted traditions and convictions in Germany.

BRACHER, KARL DIETRICH. **Die Deutsche Diktatur.** Cologne: Kiepenheuer, 1969, 580 p.

In this volume Bracher has used his own earlier researches and those of other scholars to produce the most ambitious and most up-to-date account of the Third Reich yet to appear. While it contains a mass of detailed information and a useful bibliography, it is notable for its attempt, largely successful, to analyze the nature of Hitler's dictatorship, to relate it to German history and thought before 1933, and to discuss the possibility of a revival of Nazi ideas in Germany today. It demonstrates clearly the consistency of Hitler's thought and action, and is particularly valuable for its discussion of the actual working of Nazi government and of the relation between the party and the state.

The book should be widely used as a student's textbook for many years, but it is much more than this in its interpretative analysis of twentieth-century German history and in its unflinching determination to explain the atrocities for which the Hitler régime was responsible. Bracher, by refusing to regard Hitler as an accident to which the German people fell victim in a moment of aberration, and, equally, by his insistence on National Socialism as a specifically German phenomenon and not just as one aspect of an experience common to all Europe, is able to give a detailed and convincing account of National Socialism and at the same time to convey a warning of the dangers of irrational extremism of all kinds in a society in which democratic government has perhaps not yet taken firm root.

HEIDEN, KONRAD. **Geschichte des Nationalsozialismus.** Berlin: Rowolt, 1932, 304 p.
————. **Geburt des Dritten Reiches.** Zurich: Europa Verlag, 1934, 267 p.
————. **Der Fuehrer.** Boston: Houghton, 1944, 788 p.

Heiden was a political correspondent for the liberal *Frankfurter Zeitung* and the first serious student of National Socialism. His **Geschichte des Nationalsozialismus** and **Geburt des Dritten Reiches** still rank among the best studies of German fascism. These books offer an elaborate picture of the internal history of the party between 1920 and 1934 and abundant information on the political intrigues which brought Hitler to power. We learn much of the personal rivalries within the party, the never-ending disputes with the SA, the opportunistic vacillations of the party line, propaganda tactics and the details of organization. The description of the consolidation of power after January 1933 is extensive. From the short range of his immediate observation, Heiden makes no attempt to throw Nazism into a broader context. His reportage, however, is acute, minute and invaluable. There is an English-language condensation of these two books, **A History of National Socialism** (New York: Knopf, 1935, 430 p.), but it is poorly done and badly translated; the material is truncated and the shortcomings of the original—the absence of analysis, the lack of pattern and order—stand out unjustly.

Der Fuehrer, a sophisticated biography superbly translated, supplements the earlier works and overcomes their failings. Heiden traces Hitler's career until the blood purge of 1934, studying him not only as a person but also as a personification of the Nazi movement. He enlarges upon firsthand information to analyze the social forces that contributed to the rise of National Socialism and the motives and personal backgrounds of Hitler's early followers. The book is still of interest, even though Alan Bullock's **Hitler: A Study in Tyranny** is more recent and more authoritative.

BRACHER, KARL DIETRICH; SAUER, WOLFGANG and SCHULZ, GERHARD. **Die National-sozialistische Machtergreifung.** Cologne: Westdeutscher Verlag, rev. ed., 1962, 1,034 p.

This book is in effect a sequel to Bracher's **Auflösung der Weimarer Republik** and analyzes the stages by which Hitler took over the German state after coming to power and the way in which he established his total dictatorship. Bracher has written the introduction and the account of the consolidation of Hitler's political power. Schulz deals with the Nazi domination of the various branches of the administration and the economy, while Sauer, who had collaborated with Bracher in the section on the army in the earlier volume, has contributed the chapters on the army, the SA and the first preparations for rearmament and war.

Read in conjunction with another major piece of German collective research, Erich Matthias and Rudolf Morsey, *eds.,* **Das Ende der Parteien, 1933** (Düsseldorf: Droste, 1960, 816 p.), it provides an excellent account of the process of

Gleichschaltung by which the Nazis won control over all aspects of German life. The book ends with the purge of June 1934, which, as Bracher points out here and elsewhere, revealed the ruthlessness of Hitler's methods and his total breach with the notion of the *Rechtstaat* and the rule of law. It is a major contribution to twentieth-century German history and a frightening political case study in the methods by which a dictatorship can succeed in establishing itself.

LOCHNER, LOUIS P., *ed.* **The Goebbels Diaries, 1942–1943.** Garden City: Doubleday, 1948, 566 p.

Of all the top Nazi leaders, only Goebbels, apparently, kept a personal diary. The remains of it, found in the ruins of the Propaganda Ministry after the capture of Berlin, amounted to some 7,100 pages; yet these cover only the period January 1942 through December 1943. In this carefully edited edition, Lochner nevertheless manages to present an intimate glimpse into the state of Nazi leadership and thought at the height of the war, when its fortunes were decisively turning against Hitler.

These daily accounts, filled with gossip and commentary on the current situation, display a strange combination of clarity and realism with strategic myopia. Goebbels' fanatic faithfulness to Hitler, whom he genuinely adored, did not blind him to the many foibles of his other peers. But it did impair his perception of the utterly impossible strategic situation in which Germany found itself after Pearl Harbor. Temperamentally a "radical" in the movement, Goebbels had a contempt for capitalist "plutocracy" which outweighed his hatred for Bolshevism; and so, while the diary displays an acute, realistic assessment of the terrifying conditions on the Eastern front, it consistently downgrades the capacities of the Western democracies. Only once, in these pages, did Goebbels permit himself to touch on the possibility of a negotiated peace. In September 1943 he wrote: "If we actually had a choice [of peace with either England or Russia] it would naturally be much more pleasant to start talks with London than with Moscow. One can always make a better deal with a democratic state, and once peace has been concluded, such a state will not seize the sword for at least twenty years. . . . It is different with the Bolsheviks."

HOFFMANN, PETER. **Widerstand—Staatsstreich—Attentat.** Munich: Piper, 1969, 988 p.

Had Stauffenberg, the designated assassin of Hitler, managed to stuff his briefcase with the prescribed dosage of explosives (he was accidentally surprised in his room while packing), the "July 20th Conspiracy" would certainly have turned out differently. The poignancy of the plot, meticulously planned, lay in the fact that it so nearly did succeed. Hoffmann's study, meticulous and exhaustive, shows it to be far more than the putsch of disillusioned German generals belatedly convinced that the war was lost. The origins of the plot reach far back before 1939.

After Hitler's seizure of power in 1933, there seems never to have been a prospect for a successful German opposition to Nazism except one in which the Reichswehr would play the central role. This in turn, especially after the outbreak of war, meant that the German resistance, unlike that elsewhere in continental Europe, was far from being a romantic guerrilla movement; it was necessarily non-populist and élitist. Doubtless this was a key reason why such Westerners as Eden and Sumner Welles, who were sporadically informed of it, viewed it with skepticism. One might even say, on reading this book, that the plot was essentially the uprising of a decent Prussian conservatism against a perverted populism.

Hoffmann's book raises once more the interesting question: What might have happened had America and Britain both abandoned the 1942 Casablanca unconditional surrender formula and publicly advocated a self-governing, unitary, constitutional German state? Hoffmann is realistic enough to see the hazards: on the one hand, the risk of a separate peace on the Eastern front between Hitler and Stalin; on the other, the possibility of alienating vast numbers of non-German Europeans, victims of an evil which to them was both Nazi *and* German—a mood which communist undergrounds could mercilessly have exploited. The admirable courage of the German resistance lay in its resolve to persist without any external encouragement and with no certainty of domestic popular support. This book, in its author's words, is dedicated to the *Opfern der Tyrannei*—which in this instance honors men who proved to be far more than mere victims.

Political and Military Policy

See also Inter-War Years: Territorial Problems; Munich, p. 294.

KOGON, EUGEN. **Der SS-Staat: Das System der Deutschen Konzentrationslager.** Frankfurt/Main: Verlag der Frankfurter Hefte, 1946, 339 p.

Concentration camps—devices of authoritarian and totalitarian régimes—were neither the invention of Nazis nor were they abolished when the Nazi régime was defeated. They have since performed functions of political repression for Stalin, Chinese Communists, Castro and others. They probably will be around for some time to come. Yet memories of Nazi camps still inspire a special horror. Soviet slave camps, Hitler's best competitors for mass extermination, had their special deadliness, but even these lack the unique features of the KZ.

Kogon's study of the German camps—the first authoritative one by a survivor—shows the essential differences. These were accounted for by the qualities of Nazi ideology and by their characteristics as organizational polities. Far from being mere systems of political repression and extermination, they were instruments by which an ethnic-biological utopia could be achieved. In them, all of Nazism's chosen enemies were represented: racial enemies, the Jews especially and gypsies; communists; socialists; other German political opponents; antisocial types; homosexuals; Jehovah's Witnesses; ordinary criminals and, after the war began, political opponents captured outside the Reich. Thus the camps came to embody all the irreconcilable counter-values to Nazism; the camp administrators cherished their functions, not as simple brutal jailers and murderers, but as authorized consummators of a future Reich. What is essential to see in these camps is not only their extralegality (they existed outside the legal system) but their perverse constructive functions. Without them, Nazi goals could not have been attempted. That the brief golden age of the camps only began after Hitler had seized most of Europe shows that the Nazis' purpose was not simply to cleanse Germany but to purge an entire continent of human impurities.

The book has been translated and published as "The Theory and Practice of Hell" (New York: Farrar, Straus, 1950, 307 p.).

BRAMSTED, ERNEST K. **Goebbels and National Socialist Propaganda, 1925–1945.** East Lansing: Michigan State University Press, 1965, 488 p.

In the author's view, Goebbels and Lord Northcliffe were the first twentieth century masters of mass-opinion manipulation. The systematic art of it developed, he argues, in England in World War I. But Northcliffe was an amateur stunt flier in comparison with Goebbels. The English newspaperman's object had been to affect enemy-country public opinion in order to get a war won—nothing more than that. Goebbels' objects were: to recruit and animate party members and storm troopers to an ideological party; to facilitate a "legal" Nazi electoral victory in Germany; then to manipulate German opinion so that it would support or tolerate Hitler's permanent revolution; finally, strategically to intimidate or cajole foreign opinion into accepting Nazi will and supremacy. Northcliffe's propaganda was a temporary expedient; Goebbels', a strategic system of manipulation. In the early years of the NSDAP, Goebbels belonged to the radical "northern" wing of the party, along with the Strassers, and it seems from this account that for him, the socialism in National Socialism was more pronounced than its racism. Aside from the Jewish question, racist claptrap does not seem to have interested him very much. "Finance capitalism" to him was a more important enemy, as was England, than Bolshevism. In power, Goebbels as Propaganda Minister synchronized party and state propaganda systems in accordance with political strategy. Bramsted's exhaustive study portrays the power of simple thematic repetitions, the psychological advantages of constant attack, the uses of hate-objects and the immense importance of constant movement toward goals. Thus, Nazi propaganda never was that of a static Orwellian "1984" but of a dynamic, purposive movement which managed to hijack an entire nation.

FRANÇOIS-PONCET, ANDRÉ. **The Fateful Years.** New York: Harcourt, 1949, 295 p.

These are the memories of the French ambassador to Berlin from 1931 to 1939. Oddly enough, during the 1930s he and the American ambassador, William Dodd, were the only Western diplomats able to converse fluently with Hitler and his monolingual followers; Dodd, outraged by them, finally refused to speak at all, and so that left François-Poncet. Stationed in Berlin from the twilight of Weimar until a few months after Munich, he thus had a more sustained intimacy with the Third Reich than any other foreign diplomat. Less a biography than a narrative of Hitler's actions, his book displays the consistent inability of Hitler's victims to comprehend his intentions until too late. The same style of action—sequential spasms of violent willfulness and of seeming benign complacence—was first used by Hitler to overwhelm his domestic victims and was later used against his foreign adversaries. That style seems not so much a rational contrivance as it was the essence of Hitler's personality. What is disturbing in this terrifying but lucid story is that in its cast of actors, no one adversary seemed endowed with a contrary will equal to his. The author sees Munich, in calm retrospect, as a necessary stage in Western strategy. Without this last pacific gesture and its subsequent betrayal by Hitler, that contrary will might never have effectively appeared.

JACOBSEN, HANS-ADOLF. **Nationalsozialistische Aussenpolitik, 1933–1938.** Frankfurt/Main: Metzner, 1968, 944 p.

It was fashionable for Nazi officials and German diplomats in the mid-1930s to reassure anxious foreigners that **Mein Kampf** was a book for the 1920s, a product of Hitler's early political career and of the bitter postwar situation, essentially irrelevant to current conditions and to Hitler's intentions for the future. Jacobsen's study of Nazi foreign policy through 1938 clearly shows that this was not the case: a continuity of purpose on Hitler's part permeated all parts of Germany's foreign policy apparatus. That it was not more clearly perceived was due not simply to deception, but to the fact that before 1938 Hitler of necessity had to rely upon the traditional-conservative instruments of state, which were themselves cautious and "revisionist" in their own assessment of the nation's goals. At no time before 1938 were the authentically revolutionary elements of the party in any position to assume central decision-making roles; and so the Foreign Office and the Reichswehr retained their official supremacy, while party organs, such as Bohle's *Auslandsorganisation* and Rosenberg's *Aussenpolitisches Amt,* havens for amateur ideologues, remained on the sidelines performing minor tasks. Yet given Hitler's intentions, this situation simply could not continue. The direction of Hitler's policy—namely, a revolutionary, racial reshaping of the entire European continent—could not be achieved by diplomats and generals: these could only create the power conditions within which the basic policy could be applied. *The* consummating agency, Himmler's SS, thus lay concealed behind a façade of plausible conventionality. Hitler had made such a fundamental break with all traditions of German foreign policy that it was simply incomprehensible to the German public. Jacobsen's book—meticulous and much too detailed—is a useful antidote to William Shirer, **The Rise and Fall of the Third Reich** (New York: Simon and Schuster, 1960, 1,245 p.), and to A. J. P. Taylor, **The Origins of the Second World War.**

ROBERTSON, E. M. **Hitler's Pre-War Policy and Military Plans 1933–1939.** New York: Citadel Press, 1967, 207 p.

Bearing a misleading title, this volume consists mainly of an interpretive survey of the diplomatic developments that led to the outbreak of war in Europe in 1939. The emphasis is on Germany, but there is no systematic effort to isolate Hitler's part in the formulation of the Reich's foreign policy. In so far as Hitler's role is scrutinized, the focus is on his diplomatic strategy and tactics rather than on his fundamental policy aims. Regarding the latter, the author vacillates irresolutely between the two polar schools of interpretation which have portrayed Hitler on the one hand as a fanatical ideologue committed to the conquest of vast territories in eastern Europe and, on the other, as an opportunistic nationalist seeking merely a favorable revision of the 1919 settlement. Although the book was published well after the appearance of A. J. P. Taylor's controversial treatment of the same subject (**The Origins of the Second World War**), no attempt was made to relate the findings to Taylor's thesis or to the controversy it generated. The chief contribution of the book lies in its attention to the limitations imposed upon Hitler's actions by military considerations, a factor often insufficiently treated in other studies. Originally written as an internal monograph for the British Cabinet Office Historical Section, it displays many of the characteristics of bureaucratic scholarship: excessive and often irrelevant detail, inadequate identification of persons and cryptic, sometimes erroneous, references to documents. Unpublished documents are expressly left unidentified "in accordance with official practice," greatly diminishing the scholarly value of the work.

Hitler; Anti-Semitism

HITLER, ADOLF. **Mein Kampf.** New York: Reynal, 1939, 994 p.

It is surprising, given the extraordinary importance of this work, that it did not appear in full English translation until 1939—15 years after its appearance in Germany. Hastily assembled, this particular edition has the unique merit of footnoted commentaries written by its American editorial sponsors, including Alvin Johnson, Carlton Hayes and William Langer. Equally astonishing is the extraordinary correspondence between Hitler's thoughts and his (much later) attempt to impose them forcefully upon the German nation and upon Europe. What is equally interesting, in retrospect, is to recognize what some contemporaries of Hitler failed to see: namely, that for all its literary incoherence, this rambling book did contain a logically consistent ideology. What to some must certainly seem a colossal egotism in demanding cultural reality to be forced into a procrustean bed can equally well be seen as an immense act of will. For Hitler the act of will was the essence of politics; his will was to be placed at the disposal of the subjective needs of an "ethnic people." A total rejection of any universal judgmental criteria of national excellence can be seen in Hitler's turgid formulation: "The quality of a State cannot be evaluated according to [its] cultural height in the frame of the rest of the world, but exclusively according to the . . . quality of this institution with regard to the nationality involved in that particular case."

HITLER, ADOLF. **Hitler's Secret Book.** New York: Grove Press, 1962, 230 p.

A toned-down sequel to **Mein Kampf,** this short "revised standard" work never saw the light of day until discovered in manuscript form in the mid-1950s. Far less fantastic, and less turgid than the first, it was probably written for a different audience than was the original. Yet in no way is there a basic deviance of theme. Hitler still asserts his basic "line" with all its inherent contradictions. Territorial expansion and conquest are necessary for a people's growth; no one owns any part of the world—the nation must therefore be perpetually defended and extended. Germany's territorial task should not be the mere alteration of boundaries, but dynamic expansion. The case again is made for a Rome-Berlin-London axis, and

Hitler again fails to perceive the fundamental antagonism between his goal of continental domination and his wish for a partnership with England. Here again we see Hitler's obsession with the need for definite decisions—and his rejection of "game theory rationality." "Only one question is to be examined: whether a situation demands a definite decision or not. If such a decision is established and recognized as incontestably necessary, then its execution must be carried out with the most brutal ruthlessness . . . even if the ultimate result will be a thousand times unsatisfactory . . . or will meet with only a small percentage of probability of success." What title Hitler might have chosen for this book in published form we cannot know, nor do we know why it was never published. Perhaps this was not expedient: in 1928, when he finished it, the NSDAP was committed to a "legal" course of action. His basic contempt for bourgeois values, majoritarianism, capitalism and for the party system is as clearly shown as is his hatred for Jews and Bolshevism. Hardly an ingratiating, vote-catching tract.

BULLOCK, ALAN LOUIS CHARLES. **Hitler: A Study in Tyranny.** New York: Harper, rev. ed., 1964, 848 p.

Alan Bullock, Master of St. Catherine's College, Oxford, and Vice-Chancellor of Oxford University, is one of the most distinguished contemporary historians in Britain, and his biography of Hitler was the first major work to make his reputation. It was first published in 1952 and has subsequently been extensively revised to take into account the mass of new primary and secondary material which has since appeared. It still holds its own as the most balanced and perceptive study of Hitler's life and personality, and of his impact on Germany and Europe. The book has a high reputation in Germany as well as in the English-speaking world and will remain an important element in any reinterpretation of the history of the Nazi régime.

The book concentrates on the personality of Hitler, the way he achieved dictatorial power and how he used that power. This involves a discussion of Hitler's political role in Weimar Germany, and the author makes the important point that Hitler's success in 1932–1933 was due to the skill with which he manipulated the existing constitutional system so as to achieve his ends without a formal breach of legality. The account of Hitler's years in power concentrates largely on his foreign policy and on his conduct of the Second World War, and Alan Bullock deliberately says little about the actual working of the Nazi system inside Germany—a topic which social and economic historians are now beginning to investigate.

Bullock's picture of Hitler's consistent and determined attempt to extend German power and achieve something like world dominion has subsequently been challenged by some historians, notably by Bullock's Oxford colleague, A. J. P. Taylor, in his **The Origins of the Second World War.** This influential and controversial book, by studying Hitler's foreign policy up to 1939 in isolation from what followed, presents a picture of Hitler as a much more opportunistic figure than Bullock portrays—a man making major decisions at the last minute and unwilling to make long-term strategic or economic plans. Alan Bullock in his revised edition has reaffirmed his belief in his original interpretation, though expressing appreciation of the stimulus he has received from Taylor's work. There are signs, however, that Bullock has since accepted some at least of Taylor's points, and his analysis of Hitler's prewar policy in his 1967 Raleigh Lecture to the British Academy, "Hitler and the Origins of the Second World War," suggests that, as far as the period between 1933 and 1939 is concerned, there is less difference between the two points of view than at first appeared.

However, where Bullock's interpretation remains most convincing is in his overall picture of Hitler's personality and aims, and in the relation of the visionary ideas of **Mein Kampf** to Hitler's actual career. Bullock is especially successful in providing in clear English prose a consistent account of Hitler's turgidly Germanic system of belief. He brings out well the insane racialism which was the main motive of very many of Hitler's actions, and he successfully performs the feat of compressing the irrational within the framework of a tough and lucid intellectual analysis. Although there is still work to be done on the functioning of the Nazi party and on the working of German administration and society under National Socialism, the general lines of Bullock's picture of Hitler are unlikely to be seriously challenged.

TREVOR-ROPER, HUGH REDWALD. **The Last Days of Hitler.** New York: Macmillan, 1947, 254 p.

At the end of the Second World War, H. R. Trevor-Roper, a British historian serving as an intelligence officer, was given the task of reconstructing as accurately as possible the events of the last few weeks of Hitler's life. This was done in part "to establish the facts of Hitler's end, and thereby to prevent the growth of a myth." Although no major Hitler myth emerged in the succeeding quarter-century, the whole question of the actuality of the death, how it came about if it did, and what became of the body, remained a subject of speculation, some fantasy and occasional new bits of information. Nevertheless, Trevor-Roper largely succeeded in his task, and his account of the flickering last hours of the Third Reich and its Führer seems substantially correct.

It is a story well researched and well told, with the Nazi entourage faltering or disobeying as the Allied armies press toward the heart of Germany until the scene is finally reduced to the narrow confines of the underground bunker.

This is, however, a picture of Hitler at the very end, when he was physically and spiritually a broken man; in some measure this affects Trevor-Roper's general view of the man and his purposes: perhaps too great emphasis on the nihilism, the passion for *Götterdämmerung*.

ARENDT, HANNAH. **Eichmann in Jerusalem: A Report on the Banality of Evil.** New York: Viking, 1963, 275 p.

The highly controversial trial (beginning in April 1961) in Jerusalem of Adolf Eichmann, who had played a central role in the transportation of European Jewry to the Nazi extermination camps, may be looked at from a number of angles, all of them involving some excruciatingly difficult and painful issues. In her extended commentary on the trial and its implications, Miss Arendt acted in part as an observer and reporter, in part as a critic of some of the legal and political procedures. (She was quite critical of the case presented by the Israeli prosecution and found in the trial as a whole many of the stumbling blocks encountered in the earlier Nuremberg trials of Nazi leaders.)

But the central theme of her book, which renders it particularly noteworthy, is her profound analysis of the circumstances which could lead such a man as Eichmann, and many others, to participation in such horrible acts. She finds Eichmann not to have been a perverted sadist; much more terrifying was his "normalcy," his all-too-human foibles and shallownesses: the incredible "banality of evil," which is upsetting to both our sense of justice and our sense of drama, and yet clearly figures as a major component in the atrocities of the Nazi régime.

Many of her principal insights are prefigured in her earlier **Origins of Totalitarianism,** but here they are developed through the career of a Nazi official who, with no particular anti-Semitic feelings or passions, functioned most effectively and efficiently, from the expropriations, to the expulsions, to the herding into camps and ultimately to the gas chambers of the "final solution."

A good part of the impact of the book lies in the power with which it conveys this sense of the averageness of the participants: Everyman becomes monstrous without even being aware of the fact. There are no easy answers to the dark problems Miss Arendt poses, but from the actions of a few courageous individuals and of some courageous people (notably the Danes in their effective refusal to coöperate with their German masters) she does draw one important conclusion: resistance in the face of evil is not fruitless; the "holes of oblivion" are but part of the totalitarian myth; the human instruments of genocide are subject to doubts, even remorse, when confronted by moral opposition, by a voice that breaks through the closed, self-reinforcing circle of their system.

HILBERG, RAUL. **The Destruction of the European Jews.** Chicago: Quadrangle Books, 1961, 788 p.

Of the many works dealing with this tragic subject, Hilberg's is the best from the point of view of both accuracy and comprehensiveness. It is based almost entirely on the documentary and oral evidence assembled for the war crimes trials held in almost all countries formerly in the Nazi orbit and on the testimony of survivors of ghettos or concentration camps. At many points in his book Hilberg may be charged with accepting too much of this evidence at face value, and throughout he shows little sympathy or understanding for the dilemmas of non-Jews caught in the Nazi network. The nature of his evidence is always clearly indicated, however, and his mastery of this vast amount of material is impressive.

The book opens with a discussion of precedents and antecedents, the scope and organization of the destruction. Two major sections follow on the process itself. The first of these deals with the problem of defining Jews, a major difficulty for officials in Germany and the occupied territories; the methods of economic expropriation (outright confiscations of property, "Aryanization," special taxes, blocked currency, forced labor, wage and food controls); and the concentration of Jews in ghettos and concentration camps. The second section describes the deportations of Jews and the actual killing procedures. In conclusion there are reflections on the perpetrators and victims, the consequences and implications of the destruction process.

Concerned as he is with the destruction of Jews throughout Europe, Hilberg does not confine himself to a discussion of Germany but deals with all European countries where such annihilation took place. His analysis of the administrative apparatus in these countries, although at times somewhat schematic and over-simplified, nevertheless constitutes one of the best surveys of German occupation administrations and satellite governments to be found in a single volume.

War Economy

KLEIN, BURTON H. **Germany's Economic Preparations for War.** Cambridge: Harvard University Press, 1959, 272 p.

The investigations of the United States Strategic Bombing Survey and the testimony of Nazi officials at the Nuremberg trials revealed a German war economy far different from that which the victors thought they had confronted. The rearmament of the 1930s absorbed about 10 percent of the gross national product, and until well into the war the conflict between guns or butter was not sharp, no matter what the Nazi leaders said. Until at least 1943 the German economy was not fully mobilized, the level of arms production was well below what it could have been, and the system of guiding the war economy rather inefficient.

Klein's book marshals the evidence on these points and provides a set of explanations for them. At the core lies the doctrine of blitzkrieg; Hitler did not need total mobilization of the economy for the kinds of wars he planned to fight. Other major factors, according to Klein, were the fear of inflation which limited government spending and deficit financing; an unwillingness to cut into civilian living standards or give up government spending on nonessentials; a lack of rational planning of the war economy and the division of authority among competing groups.

Most of Klein's research was done in 1946–1948. Some of his sources are not above suspicion; there are moments when one feels that Dr. Schacht, General Thomas and Albert Speer are almost coauthors. Like most bringers of news, Klein sometimes overstates some points, but the main features of his analysis have stood the test of time and new material. The significance of the changed picture is emphasized by what Lord Dalton said (in a review in *The Economic Journal*): "If these conclusions had come to me [when he was Minister of Economic Warfare] I should have disbelieved most of them."

MILWARD, ALAN S. **The German Economy at War.** New York: Oxford University Press, 1965, 214 p.

Essentially an account of production with little said about finance or other aspects of Germany's war economy, this book contains a remarkable amount of information, much of it quite detailed. It is much fuller than Burton H. Klein's book on the later years of the war and the collapse of the German economy. A key point of the analysis is that Germany's initial emphasis on current war production instead of the expansion of capacity created a major obstacle to the full mobilization of the economy when that became necessary. Britain and the United States, in contrast, were forced from the first to think in terms of a long war and so rather quickly achieved a higher level of mobilization than Germany. Bad handling of manpower was a major German weakness, particularly in the latter part of the war. Milward shows, too, that the Germans failed to make full use of the economic resources of occupied Europe, concentrating on booty, slave labor and ready sources of certain raw materials.

Working at a later period and with fuller material, including additional German and British sources, the British author does not challenge the fundamentals of Klein's analysis. He allows somewhat greater rationality to the early strategy of limited mobilization for blitzkrieg and believes that the method of running the war economy worked quite well so long as full mobilization was not called for. He thinks the shift in approach, forced by the heavy loss of equipment on the Russian front, was well underway before Stalingrad (which Klein calls the turning point). Consonant with this chronology, Milward gives Todt more credit for the change but, like Klein, finds Speer's role of major importance.

SPEER, ALBERT. **Inside the Third Reich: Memoirs.** New York: Macmillan, 1970, 596 p.

Of all the Nazi protagonists in Hitler's entourage, Albert Speer was least a politician. This was a blessing for his career, making him relatively immune to intrigue. For the reader of the memoirs, however, Speer's unpolitical disposition is a disappointment; his writing is shallow wherever he deals with political issues. The author is much more at home when it comes to the personalities of the Nazi leaders whom he knew so intimately. His characterizations are factual, clear, free from psychoanalytical clichés, yet subtle and fair. The "élite" of the Third Reich emerges from Speer's account in all its evil humanity.

Speer himself, a bright young man from a respectable middle-class family, differed from the Nazi hard core. But he, too, was attracted to Nazism as a movement of "action" without unduly worrying about its direction. Driven by an overriding ambition to "accomplish things," he was ready—as he admits—to sell his soul. The architectural monstrosities prepared on his drawing board would not have ensured his fame or notoriety—except as illustrations of the plight of the arts under Nazism. He began to make history only after he was put in charge of Germany's economic mobilization for war in 1942.

The story of Speer's achievement in bringing Germany's military production to the highest wartime level of output and efficiency in 1944 despite formidable obstacles from the feuding Nazi leaders has been told in excellent studies by American and British economists and historians—Klein, Milward, Trevor-Roper— who had used both Speer's earlier testimony and the records of his ministry. In that respect, the memoirs offer little new information of any substance, but they add the personal touch. They are not great memoirs in the style of Churchill or De Gaulle, for their author is too seriously deficient in depth of intellect, breadth of vision and, above all, moral stature, to achieve that. But they are nevertheless honest, lucid and informative.

German Federal Republic

ADENAUER, KONRAD. **Erinnerungen.** Stuttgart: Deutsche Verlags-Anstalt, 1965–1968, 4 v.

These memoirs of West Germany's first Chancellor are confined to the last 17 years of a very long political career, and they fade off in a final volume of notes and documentary fragments which his devoted family assembled after his death in 1967. The first volume has been published in an English translation, **Memoirs 1945–53** (Chicago: Regnery, 1966, 477 p.).

The first three volumes are a spare and unsentimental account of the author's role as obstinate pilot of Germany's arrival as an authentic sovereign nation in Western Europe. Had Adenauer had his way (and of course he did not) Western European political integration would have been a far more profound cultural transformation. Adenauer displays in these memoirs a stubbornly held conception of a new Europe which for him seems always to have had a traditional potentiality: a pluralist, moderate civic polity, devoutly Christian and supranational. Such a view was never popular either in Imperial or Nazi Germany, of course; but neither was it viable during the Weimar years, although as mayor of Cologne Adenauer had then sought to advance it. That it became attractive as a European idea after 1945 under his leadership in Germany is at first glance paradoxical, since its special character was so deeply rooted in Rhenish civic traditions. That his stubborn pursuit of this provincial aspiration met with the success that it did can be explained largely by the power realities of postwar Europe. But within a continental framework, what made it politically viable was the fact that, aside from Communist Party strength, the only foci of popular loyalty which remained in the ruins of the war were Catholic universalism and Social Democracy. These alone could not long have survived the pressure of Soviet expansion, and thus throughout his memoirs two key conceptions stand out, distinguishing Adenauer from most of his Western colleagues in France and England: a conviction that an American military presence in Europe was necessary; and that the Soviet threat was both a real military and ideological threat which had to be met on both levels simultaneously if it was to be met at all.

His stubbornness an aspect of his steadiness, and his steadiness an aspect of his simplicity, Adenauer as Chancellor achieved what previous German statesmen failed at: a German reputation for stability and for becoming a normal part of a normal Europe. These laconic memoirs display a steady ability to harness German emotions and aspirations to civic goals which only a few years before had seemed utterly alien to German style.

SCHWARZ, HANS-PETER. **Vom Reich zur Bundesrepublik: Deutschland im Widerstreiy der Aussenpolitischen Konzeptionen in den Jahren der Besatzungsherrschaft 1945–1949.** Berlin: Luchterhand, 1966, 884 p.

This study of Germany's political transformation from its 1945 condition of *debellatio* into the two now-familiar state entities of Bundesrepublik and D.D.R. very likely is the most rigorous analysis of its subject yet to appear. Schwarz's work is distinguished by its multifaceted perspectives and by his acute discernment of the many strands of national policies and actions, options and necessities, which contributed to the final outcome. For cold-war scholars, his analysis of the uncertain, dragging development of American policies is especially interesting. While many historians now would date the cold war's outbreak to early 1947 at the latest, Schwarz indicates that strong elements of Roosevelt's conciliatory policy toward Russia persisted in Germany well beyond the Berlin blockade of 1948–1949. As late as then, influential U.S. policy-makers continued to argue for a "policy of postponement" of final decisions, or for reciprocated troop withdrawals from central Germany accompanied by efforts to establish an all-German state. That the "hard line" (West German state plus West German integration into West Europe plus rearmament) prevailed was due as much to harsh objective realities as it was to conscious planning. As for premeditated plan, there was none.

BARING, ARNULF. **Aussenpolitik in Adenauers Kanzlerdemokratie.** Munich: Olden-bourg, 1969, 492 p.

A young German political scientist's evaluation of Adenauer's achievements as Chancellor. As Bismarck's policies could only be understood when seen as the work of a Prussian, so (the author argues) Adenauer's achievements and failures must be seen as those of a Rhinelander and a lifelong citizen of Cologne. Adenauer believed his own province to be the very heart of Western Europe. As the West German republic grew, he saw the possibility of locking its destiny to its Western neighbors. This personal conviction—already to be seen in Adenauer's activities as *Buergermeister* of Cologne during the Weimar period—was not, as some critics portrayed it, a cover-up for black clericalism, treasonous Francophilia or crude provincialism. His instincts rather than his reason bred in him a conviction that the cultural properties of his regional homeland provided an ideal proportional balance to politics—of Catholicism and liberalism, North and South Europe, French culture and Prussian virtue. For this reason, despite all of his successes as statesman, Adenauer (in the author's view) failed to obtain his one central strategic objective: that of tieing West Germany irrevocably to its other Western neighbors by strategic integration. The crisis of the European Defense Community in 1954 thus marks both the high point and the point of failure of Adenauer's policy. After this, his statesmanship shrank into improvisation, and his improvisations became increasingly dominated by conventional German national goals. The author happily confines his strictures on social science methodology to an appendix.

DAHRENDORF, RALF. **Society and Democracy in Germany.** Garden City: Doubleday, 1967, 482 p.

In the preface Dahrendorf directs attention to the astonishing fact that no attempts have been made "to describe the 'whole' of our society;" his book is meant to fill this gap. Its pioneering character is noticeable throughout. Dahrendorf discusses and evaluates the opinions which sociologists and political scientists such as Max Weber, Schelsky and Franz Neumann have expressed on problems such as the character of the German ruling group, the weaknesses of the labor movement or the role of the family in German society; and he gives a very convincing criticism of the explanations of the German developments which historians have offered. On issues such as social stratification and the composition of the German élite, Dahrendorf presents brief, scholarly investigations based on most interesting statistical material. He is inclined to measure the German situation against an ideal of liberal democracy which he has taken from the Anglo-Saxon world. And since he ascribes the past failures of German democracy to the delayed and then over-rapid industrialization, he also provides a historical sketch of German developments since the foundation of the Reich. The book is rich, almost over-rich, in facts, in analyses, in theories and suggestions. And because it tries to cover an immensely wide field the presentation is somewhat breathless. Yet it is the most informative, the best treatment of the German situation after the Second World War.

WALLICH, HENRY CHRISTOPHER. **Mainsprings of the German Revival.** New Haven: Yale University Press, 1955, 401 p.

If a miracle can be explained, it is no longer a miracle, but then credit may be given where credit is due. Quite a few Germans resented having the label *Wirtschaftswunder* put on the rapid recovery of their country which they thought was the product of their own hard work. In what is still the best book on the German economy from 1948 to 1954, Henry Wallich, an American economist born in Berlin, did not deny the importance of hard work—though statistics did not show German performance to be extraordinary in that respect—but rested most of his explanation on other factors, notably German and Allied policies.

The *Sozialemarktwirschaft* of Dr. Erhard and his colleagues turned out to be "not . . . altogether free nor especially outstanding for its social consciousness." It did, however, produce "great social results. By rapidly lifting total income, however ill distributed, it eventually raised everybody's income." Though "freedom for the strong" was a key element, Wallich shows clearly how the government guided the economy in the direction of high investment and—at least at the time he was writing—relatively low consumption. Labor was very restrained in its demands, and the refugees, usually thought of as a burden on the economy, were absorbed in ways that made them an asset. As usual in Germany, fear of inflation made conservative financial and monetary policies popularly acceptable. A comprehensive social security system set a floor below which the poorest could not fall. The contribution of the Allies, as Wallich sees it, came not only in the crucial form of aid for the balance of payments but in policy measures as well, notably the drastic currency reform and setting Germany on the course of trade liberalization.

By giving primacy to external considerations instead of to domestic full employment, the Germans developed a strong balance-of-payments position in advance of other European countries. At the time Wallich was writing, however, they had not caught up with others in production and living standards and had a good bit of unemployment. The miracle came in the recovery from their own bad starting position. Looking ahead the author saw problems, some of which have appeared and others not. His remarkably comprehensive book remains valuable not only for its assessment of a key period but as a safeguard against oversimplified memories or the interpretation of Germany only in terms of the 1960s. Full weight is given to noneconomic factors and, though highly professional, the book can easily be read by those who are not economists.

German Democratic Republic

STERN, CAROLA. **Ulbricht: A Political Biography.** New York: Praeger, 1965, 231 p.

Twentieth-century Germany has shown an extraordinary propensity for producing dangerous mediocrities in politics. It is the common denominator of the otherwise incongruous group which includes William II, the majority of the Nazi protagonists and—as the greatest nonentity of all—Walter Ulbricht. Anti-heroes do not lend themselves easily to biographical treatment, unless it can be shown that their very dullness is of supreme interest and importance. In that respect, Carola Stern has succeeded admirably; her account is lucid, judicious and dramatic—a model political biography. The story of Walter Ulbricht is, in fact, that of the many failures and few accomplishments of German communism.

Ulbricht's adaptability was not a result of pure opportunism or a lack of convictions. He is a supreme example of a party bureaucrat who combines genuine belief in the basic Marxist formulas—the source of simple certainties but not of critical doubts—with devotion to the party as an apparatus, divorced from any particular policy. Despite his loyalty to the Soviet Union, his interests and Moscow's have not always been identical, especially after he had become the chief of the East German state. Whereas for the Russians the D.D.R. was a pawn, possibly expendable, in international politics, for Ulbricht it was the justification of his existence. Intense and artificially fomented hostility to West Germany shaped his role as the chief defender of "Socialism" along the hottest lines of the cold war and determined his rigid domestic politics—congenial, to be sure, to his personality.

The author is right in viewing the record of her dubious hero as overwhelmingly negative. Yet her conclusion that Ulbricht, "next to Stalin, has done the most to discredit Communism in Germany," is debatable. East Germany of the 1970s, though in poor shape compared with the western part of the country, is better off than ever before. Although the majority of East Germans detest communism, they respect many social and economic achievements of the régime. These may have been achieved despite rather than because of Ulbricht. But undoubtedly there are hopeful features in the edifice to whose building he so decisively contributed.

LUDZ, PETER CHRISTIAN. **Parteielite in Wandel.** Opladen: Westdeutscher Verlag, 1968, 438 p.

The recruitment of élites and the change of generations present especially severe problems in the communist countries of East Central Europe, where no established mechanisms exist to assure smooth transition.

Ludz presents a thorough empirical analysis of the East German governing stratum in the period from 1954 to 1967, noting the tensions generated within the ruling party by the pressures of industrialization. The party coöpts and tries to absorb increasing numbers of the experts who alone are capable of coping with the growing complexity of modern society. Thus "consultative authoritarianism" replaces the earlier "totalitarianism" characterized by the effort to regiment the nation in conformity with the narrow tenets of the Marxist dogma.

The author points out that the old élite is, however, reluctant to permit enough democratic participation to transform the régime into "participatory authoritarianism." Yet the trend toward government separation of the state and the party—the latter's role to be limited to the "commanding heights"—is unmistakable. The new "anti-élite" of experts is becoming institutionalized and concentrated in the bodies linked especially closely with the technological transformation: the Council of Ministers, State Planning Commission, Research Council. New mobility threatens the entrenched interests of the Old Guard, and revisionism is the ideology of the "anti-élite." It considers Marx's concept of alienation the clue to the adaptation of his teachings to the dynamic of modern industrial society. Respect for technological and economic progress, for social differentiation and dynamism, and for efficiency give the new élite "an element of rationality which may facilitate a dialogue with it."

RICHERT, ERNST. **Das Zweite Deutschland: Ein Staat, der Nicht Sein Darf.** Gütersloh: Mohn, 1964, 341 p.

Despite his antipathy for the East German "state which should not exist," Richert explains rather than condemns the reality of its existence, and his conclusions follow from a balanced critical analysis of the party and governmental system, indoctrination and culture, industry and agriculture. Although no footnote references to sources are given in the book, its extensive bibliography leaves no doubt that this is a serious and exhaustive treatment of the subject.

The author maintains that the creation of a communist state in East Germany, though intensely desired by Ulbricht and his associates, was not part of the Soviet design before 1953 or perhaps even 1955. The D.D.R. was less a result of premeditation than a by-product of the cold war. Adenauer's and Dulles' insistence on the unacceptable demand for free elections in East Germany, along with the Soviet bloc's critical need for manpower and resources during the period of rapid economic growth in the mid-1950s, led Moscow to consolidate and intensify its control over East Germany. Although the initial "great leap forward" failed, the building of the Berlin Wall facilitated internal stabilization. Ulbricht the revolutionary and "cold warrior" adjusted with considerable skill to his new role as the chief technocrat. By communist standards, his government offers the people fairly decent working and living conditions and even encourages their initiative by a well-conceived system of incentives and rewards. The survival of political and ideological rigidity in East Germany is a result partly of the régime's ability to satisfy the swelling ranks of the technocrats, partly of the lack of national consciousness which is prerequisite to the more relaxed "National Communism."

The author maintains that the West's best hope of closing the growing gap between the two German states is to encourage accommodation between the two parts of the divided country by promoting their mutual contacts and aiming at loose confederation, reasoning that for the majority of East Germans such a policy, likely to promote tangible "small freedoms," holds more attraction than the unrealistic prospect of complete liberation.

AUSTRIA

Hapsburg Empire

MACARTNEY, C. A. **The Habsburg Empire, 1790–1918.** London: Weidenfeld and Nicolson, 1968, 886 p.

This work, formidable in its learning and wisdom, will long be the standard book on the Hapsburg monarchy. It has been said (by Mr. Grant Duff) that Austria is "a science in itself, nay . . . half a dozen sciences." Macartney is a master of them all. He traces the history of that unique monarchy, "sprawling clean across Central Europe," in a magisterial fashion, encompassing each individual nationality but pleading the cause of none. The author's concentration on political, social, economic and national developments and his calculated neglect of cultural history and foreign affairs do not in any way detract from the book's distinction.

Hapsburg history has been "a success story which no other European dynasty could rival." Macartney's work, however, beginning with the reign of Joseph II, is essentially the history of retreat. The success of the dynasty had been achieved at the expense of homogeneity, and the awakening of national spirit among the peoples of the monarchy—even if, as Macartney stresses, it did not necessarily add up to irredentism—constituted a hard test to the supranational structure.

There are magnificent thumbnail sketches of the main personages of more recent Hapsburg history: Joseph II was "a terrible genius" and the Archduke Francis Ferdinand "a very nasty man." There are also learned passages on the problems of the peasantry. Dealing with the history of retreat, Macartney cannot avoid coming to terms with the question, fiercely debated by all historians in the field, of the causes for the collapse of the monarchy in 1918. If its death sentence was pronounced by the foreign powers, he argues convincingly, the future of the monarchy had been "at best" problematic prior to the war. Francis Joseph had failed to make his peoples forget their national loyalties. Macartney's magnum opus thus ends with neither a sentimental evocation nor a moral verdict but with a sober and judicious summary that manifests his mastery of and respect for the complexity of his subject.

TAYLOR, ALAN JOHN PERCIVALE. **The Habsburg Monarchy, 1809–1918.** New York: Macmillan, rev. ed., 1949, 279 p.

Like all other works by A. J. P. Taylor, this book is as thought-provoking as it is irritating. Taylor belongs to the tradition of "Whig" historiography, but he has also overcome it. While the first edition of his work, published in 1941, was still dominated by the "liberal illusion" lamenting "lost opportunities," this one is marked by a harsh verdict concerning the incompatibility of the supranational state with the national principle; the conflict between the two had to be "fought to the finish."

In contrast to Macartney, Taylor emphasizes foreign affairs. "The Habsburg Monarchy, more than most Great Powers, was an organization for conducting foreign policy." The author is as fascinated by as he is hostile to the concept of the "Austrian mission," which he attributes to "clever writers in Vienna." While maintaining that "the truly great do not need to justify their existence," he argues that the mission of the Hapsburg monarchy in the nineteenth century was to function as a barrier against a Great German national state. But under Francis Joseph the monarchy became a device by which Hungarian landowners and German capitalists grew rich from the labor of the lesser peoples. Francis Joseph finally ended his reign as a German auxiliary.

In the end, however, Taylor admits that the Hapsburgs left their people with two problems: the internal problem of authority and the external one of security. His suggestion that Marshal Tito is after all "the last of the Habsburgs" is moving but also pathetic from the pen of a man who prides himself on his grasp of political realities.

JÁSZI, OSZKÁR. **The Dissolution of the Habsburg Monarchy.** Chicago: University of Chicago Press, 1929, 512 p.

Starting from quite different premises than Taylor, Oszkár Jászi, minister of nationalities in the ill-fated Károlyi cabinet of 1918–1919, was of the rare breed of bona fide Hungarian liberals who devoted their political and scholarly efforts to achieving equity among the nationalities in Hungary. The book is part of a series undertaking to investigate the state of civil education in various countries in the world. Jászi's conclusions, however, are that civic consciousness is dependent on a basic political and social cohesion which was absent in the Hapsburg monarchy. The dissolution was not a "mechanical" but an "organic" process, centrifugal forces were stronger than centripetal ones, and ironically the difficulty of the national problem increased to exactly the same extent to which the various nations grew in economic strength and in political and cultural rights. It took a great deal of independence for a Hungarian to focus his chief criticism not on Germanization in the Austrian half of the monarchy but on Magyarization in the Hungarian half. In fact, one of his main targets is the Compromise of 1867, essentially an agreement between the Emperor and the Magyar ruling classes which the German bourgeoisie accepted, at the expense of the Slavic population.

The Dissolution of the Habsburg Monarchy has become a classic: a pioneering work in political science as well as a monument to humanitarianism.

KANN, ROBERT ADOLF. **The Habsburg Empire.** New York: Praeger, 1957, 227 p.

Robert A. Kann is one of the foremost authorities on the Hapsburg monarchy and on the nationality problem. The above volume, a sequel to his monumental work, **The Multinational Empire** (New York: Columbia University Press, 1950, 2 v.), is quite explicitly a case study of political integration. Unlike most other works on the subject, its emphasis is not on dissolution. "The chief cause for wonderment regarding the Monarchy is not the fact of its dissolution after four centuries, but the remarkable . . . fact of its preservation throughout four centuries." Kann sees the problem of the Hapsburg monarchy essentially as "not the reverse of that found in the integration process of other states," but "simply different in degree." This thesis may hold for the sixteenth century but hardly for the nineteenth century, when the "separatist" tendencies clearly outweighed the "consolidating" ones; certainly the effect of the 1867 Compromise was fatal in this respect. The great distinction of Kann's analysis of the forces of integration and disintegration lies in his careful classification of nationalities, both those with and those without history, and also in his convincing correlation of the various national aspirations with economic and social power.

As for the inevitable question of the final dissolution, Kann stresses that the Dual Monarchy was in need of some sort of federal reform. If the "non-inevitable" World War had not come about, such a reform might have been successful. But under the material and ideological impact of the war the monarchy could not endure a major structural change.

This book constitutes an exemplary blending of history and political science.

REDLICH, JOSEF. **Emperor Francis Joseph of Austria.** New York: Macmillan, 1929, 547 p.

The life of Francis Joseph is inseparable from the history of his time and his country, and this book is at once a fine character study and a searching analysis of the whole Austro-Hungarian problem. It is based partly (for the period up to 1867) on Redlich's monumental **Das Österreichische Staats- und Reichsproblem** (Leipzig: Reinhold, 1920–1926, 3 v.) and partly (for the period from 1867) on

Redlich's lifetime observations. Josef Redlich, both a distinguished political scientist and an influential political figure in Vienna, was one of an unusual breed: an Austrian liberal. He portrays Francis Joseph, the self-styled "last European monarch of the old school," as dedicated to one aim: the maintenance of the Hapsburg rule. This monarch's concessions to political progress constituted at best rearguard actions in defense of his royal and imperial prerogatives. Seen in this light the life of Francis Joseph was a tragic one.

This work, informed by an unequaled mastery of the constitutional complexities of the Dual Monarchy and also by a subtle feeling for the realities of foreign affairs, is marked by the distinctly impatient liberal bias of the author; it remains to this day, however, the best biography of the long-lived emperor.

BROOK-SHEPHERD, GORDON. **The Last Hapsburg.** New York: Weybright and Talley, 1968, 358 p.

Few historians doubt that when Charles succeeded Francis Joseph the fate of the monarchy was already sealed. As related by Gordon Brook-Shepherd, the story of his life is all the more a melancholy one. Brook-Shepherd is an English journalist who has done a great deal of interesting work in modern Austrian history. He does not belong to the "Whig" tradition; if anything, he writes "Tory" history of a slightly sentimental variety. This particular volume is based in part on the Hapsburg family papers, put at the author's disposal by the Archduke Otto, and in part on interviews with the Empress Zita. The book no doubt has her imprimatur.

The tragedy of Charles' life and reign is heightened by the fact that this monarch who took over in the middle of the terrible war was pacific and conciliatory by temperament. He was deeply religious, opposed the alliance with the Germans and surrounded himself, much to the annoyance of the Kaiser's ambassador, increasingly with pacifists like Heinrich Lammasch, who was his last Prime Minister. Brook-Shepherd writes good biography, taking us down the thorny path through the last war years (highlighting the "Sixtus Affair") into exile in Switzerland. Twice in 1921 the former Emperor attempted to reclaim his Hungarian throne before dying a lonely death on the island of Madeira in 1922. He was not the strongest of personalities and not always well advised, but with his "mildness" and aversion to violence he was not unworthy of having been the last of the Hapsburgs.

ZEMAN, ZBYNEK A. B. **The Break-up of the Habsburg Empire 1914–1918: A Study in National and Social Revolution.** New York: Oxford University Press, 1961, 274 p.

This is a distinctly revisionist work by a Czech scholar living in England. Based on archival studies in the Austrian archives as well as in the records of the German Foreign Office, it sets out to challenge the "national" schools of historians focusing on the "organic" decay and also the communist historians attributing the downfall of the Hapsburg monarchy to the Bolshevik revolution and its aftermath. While Zeman argues that "the ultimate responsibility for the disappearance of the Habsburg Monarchy rests squarely on the shoulders of its rulers," and while he does not altogether discount the role of the Entente powers, his focus lies on the interaction during the war years between the radicals inside the monarchy and the exile groups abroad. His findings are striking. While there was considerable anti-dynastic subversion at the start of the war, the bulk of the population in the monarchy did not consider its dissolution. There is little connection between the radical anti-Hapsburg movements among the Austro-Hungarian peoples and those of the last two years of the war; the former did fizzle out in the course of the war years. In fact, Zeman argues that as late as the spring of 1917 "energetic and resolute action" on the part of the government could have saved the monarchy and that mistakes on the part of the government, the impact of the "hot-house conditions generated by the war," played into the hands of the radicals at home and ensured "the triumph of the exiles."

Republic of Austria

General

BENEDIKT, HEINRICH, *ed.* **Geschichte der Republik Österreich.** Munich: Oldenbourg, 1954, 632 p.

The historiography of republican Austria has for a long time been lagging behind that of Weimar Germany. This volume constitutes the first and altogether successful attempt to draw even with the German scholars and furnish a scholarly and possibly objective introduction to Austria between the wars. Of the four parts of this coöperative work, that by Walter Goldinger, "Der Geschichtliche Ablauf der Ereignisse in Österreich von 1918 bis 1945" (see also Walter Goldinger, **Geschichte der Republik Österreich,** Vienna: Verlag für Geschichte und Politik, 1962, 311 p.), and that by Adam Wandruszka, "Österreichs Politische Struktur," are particularly important. Goldinger, one of Austria's distinguished archivists, has produced an almost impeccable narrative based on his intimate knowledge of archival materials. Wandruszka, now professor of history at the University of Vienna, has come up with an exemplary analysis of political parties and movements. His emphasis on the common origins, going back to the so-called Linz Program of 1882, of the three political "camps"—the Christian Socialists, the Pan-Germans and the Social Democrats—has been generally accepted by subsequent historical writing. The third part, by Friedrich Thalmann, deals with the economy of Austria and the fourth, by Stephan Verosta, with the all too fuzzy concept of Austria's European function.

The volume, with an excellent bibliography, has become a standard work.

GULICK, CHARLES ADAMS. **Austria from Habsburg to Hitler.** Berkeley: University of California Press, 1948, 2 v.

This is a massive work. Charles Gulick, an expert on labor relations and labor history, has done extensive documentary research to produce his two volumes which are an almost inexhaustible source of information. Gulick is a committed historian. He belongs to the left, and he writes leftist history. However, his painstaking documentation enables the reader to separate the copious information from the heavy bias and, indeed, to come away from the book with conclusions different from those intended by the author. The chapters in the first volume are particularly informative, recalling the unusual accomplishments of the little Alpine republic which was struggling for its very existence. The very fact that the Constitution of 1920 was the result of a broad consensus was in itself an achievement. The story of social and labor legislation, trade unionism, coöperatives, municipal housing, welfare work and education does much to honor Austria, and in particular its Social Democrats.

For the rest, Gulick attributes the demise of democracy in Austria to a concerted plot on the part of "Clerical fascism." The validity of the concept is not questioned; the motivations of the arch-villain, Prelate Ignaz Seipel, are not sufficiently scrutinized; and, last but not least, the role which the Austro-Marxists themselves played in undermining parliamentary democracy is not investigated.

This is nevertheless a great book. It has set the tone for much subsequent historiography on Austria.

MACDONALD, MARY. **The Republic of Austria 1918–1934.** New York: Oxford University Press (for the Royal Institute of International Affairs), 1946, 165 p.

This is an excellent, concise study of "the failure of democratic government" in Austria (though for the broader aspects of the problem the reader may wish to turn to Werner Conze, "Die Strukturkrise des Östlichen Mitteleuropas vor und nach 1919," *Vierteljahrshefte für Zeitgeschichte,* v. I, October 1953). Here the story is told *sans phrase,* but with admirable competence.

Austrian democracy in 1918 was a result partly of pressure from outside and partly of exhaustion. And while at the outset all parties and all shades of opinion were agreed that the state and the constitution were to be democratic, by 1920 the country had become a house divided, split into two main camps of the Social Democrats and the Christian Socialists (with whom the Pan-Germans soon entered into a "bourgeois" coalition), represented by their respective leaders, Otto Bauer and Ignaz Seipel. Miss Macdonald carefully examines the weaknesses of the 1920 Constitution (in particular the excessive weakness of the executive and proportional representation), the attempts at constitutional reform, the impact of the party structure on the failure of the democratic process (the ascendancy of extremism in each party, the leanings in both parties—in particular the Social Democrats—toward a "party totalitarianism") and finally the influence of foreign policy on the domestic scene (the outlawed Anschluss, the failure of the 1931 Customs Union). If a criticism is in order, it is that the volume is too one-sidedly concerned with the political factor and too little with psychological, social and economic considerations.

DIAMANT, ALFRED. **Austrian Catholics and the First Republic: Democracy, Capitalism, and the Social Order, 1918–1934.** Princeton: Princeton University Press, 1960, 325 p.

Alfred Diamant's book offers a badly needed discussion of Catholic conservative social theory of the nineteenth and twentieth centuries and of Catholic criticism of democracy and capitalism. The thoughts and policies of men such as Karl von Vogelsang, Karl Lueger, the sociologist Othmar Spann and the eminent conservative statesman Ignaz Seipel are analyzed. The two competing courses of Catholics in modern society—namely *Sozialreform* (restoration of the old ideal, organic order) and *Sozialpolitik* (gradual reforms within the existing order)—are traced. The author argues that whereas the German Catholics were forced to make their peace with the new society because of the rapid industrialization in Germany, Catholics in Austria, where industrialization proceeded at a slower pace, inclined more toward *Sozialreform*.

Though Diamant's liberal point of view disposes him to be basically critical of the Catholic position, he sees its strength in its criticism of the ills of a society in transition. It is interesting that Adam B. Ulam, in an essay on the "Sources of Influence of Marxism and Communism" in **The Unfinished Revolution** (New York: Random House, 1960, 307 p.), should have stressed the similar appeal of Marxism upon societies in transition from a traditional phase to industrialization. Since most of twentieth-century Europe is in one or another stage of this transition, the Catholic as well as the Marxist position has a great deal of relevance. Otherwise, Diamant argues, the former has no future because of its essentially backward-looking, agrarian, pre-industrial outlook: according to Ulam, even the latter ceases to be attractive to a society which has achieved an advanced industrial level.

LESER, NORBERT. **Zwischen Reformismus und Bolschewismus: Der Austromarxismus als Theorie und Praxis.** Vienna: Europa, 1968, 600 p.

Leser has written a penetrating analysis of Austro-Marxism, that unique breed of European Marxist socialism. The party of Viktor Adler was distinguished among the socialist parties of Europe not only for its theoretical creativeness but also for its pragmatic leadership. Leser therefore is justified in setting out to measure the relationship and the tensions between theory and practice. The conflict between the two becomes particularly apparent during the first republic when the Austrian Social Democracy was under the frequently conflicting influence of Otto Bauer and Karl Renner (and, as Leser reminds us, also of Max Adler, the "philosopher of Austro-Marxism") and when it persisted in adhering to the course, originally set by Viktor Adler, of "unity at all cost."

Belonging to the younger generation of Austrian Socialists, the author rips into many of the legends surrounding Austro-Marxism (see the Gulick school) and presents a harsh self-criticism of the party's past. The dissonance between revolutionary phraseology and reformist practice produced a "passive radicalism" that was disastrous to the fate of the party and democracy in Austria. These "Girondists in the garbs of Jacobins" condemned themselves to a continuous "attentism." Otto Bauer is not, then, the hero in Leser's eyes. In the drama that led to the destruction of democracy in Austria, he played into the hands of his adversary Seipel (*Ergänzung zum Unheil*) and furthered the cause of "Austro-fascism."

This challenging book successfully combines scholarship and political engagement.

BROOK-SHEPHERD, GORDON. **Dollfuss.** New York: St. Martin's Press, 1961, 296 p.

Gordon Brook-Shepherd does not mind supporting unpopular causes. Engelbert Dollfuss, whom he calls "the most maligned" of twentieth-century statesmen, appears in most history books as the destroyer of Austrian democracy and also as the stooge of Mussolini. The author has set out to set this picture straight, and he has succeeded in neutralizing at least some of the bias of the "left-wing" historians.

He reminds us that Dollfuss "faced the most impossible odds with the greatest of courage." At home he fought the Social Democrats, who advocated democracy as an instrument of socialism but cared little for Austria, and the Nazis, who respected neither. Dollfuss' cause was that of Austria which, the author concedes, was not at that time that of democracy. In search of security for his little country he managed to keep Hitler and Mussolini apart in the mid-thirties; indeed, Dollfuss was "the first challenger of Hitler anywhere on the European continent," and also his first victim.

No doubt the Austrian situation in the early thirties was much too complex to be explained in terms of a plot theory like that of Gulick, who comes down hard on the Seipel-Dollfuss tradition. But Brook-Shepherd in his apology of Dollfuss is much too lenient in his handling of what he calls the racist and fascist "fringe" of the Christian Socialists and indeed in his handling of the *Heimwehr* itself. The distinctions among authoritarianism, dictatorship and fascism remain to be sharpened. "Hitler's dynamism could only be checked by echoing it." Was this really the case? Brook-Shepherd goes into elaborate detail to relate the negotiations between Dollfuss and the Social Democrats preceding the February events of 1934—but the fact is that they failed. Dollfuss' tie with Mussolini had no small connection with this failure. "The beginnings of 'Austro-fascism' were rooted not in ideology but in desperate patriotism." But fascism it was.

Anschluss

BALL, MARY MARGARET. **Post-War German-Austrian Relations.** Stanford: Stanford University Press, 1937, 304 p.

The Anschluss problem, a unique one in modern history, involves diplomatic relations between two sibling states—Germany and Austria after 1918. But the "prehistory" of the Anschluss movement goes back to Austria's defeat by Germany in the battle of Königgrätz, to the expulsion of Austria from Germany, which many German-Austrians, in particular the Pan-Germans, could never bring themselves to accept. Its history of course goes back to 1918–1919, to defeat and "revolution" in both Germany and Austria. But while the secret "protocol," signed between the German and Austrian Foreign Ministers in March 1919, gave detailed prescriptions for an Anschluss, the Treaties of Versailles and Saint Germain both contained a ban on the union of the two German states. The Anschluss movement in every phase of its existence has embodied a policy motivated by ethnic considerations and aimed at overcoming the hard and fast realities of the European state system as established by the treaties.

Not only the European powers identified with the treaty system opposed it. Both Stresemann and Seipel, who shaped Germany's and Austria's foreign policies between the wars, were, to say the least, skeptical about the Anschluss, and Seipel in particular incurred much hostility at home for his foreign policy. In the early 1930s, as the political situation in both states deteriorated, Anschluss agitation became more active, partly (in Germany) out of hopes of scoring for the republic and thus preventing the rise of National Socialism, partly (in Austria) out of sheer despair. The failure of the Customs Union in 1931 put an end to the attempts of the two German republics to join forces. It is a deep irony that the European powers finally allowed Adolf Hitler to consummate the Anschluss on his own terms. It has been said that the triumph of the Austrian Hitler constituted Austria's revenge for Königgrätz.

Miss Ball's monograph is a well-researched and well-documented work. It should perhaps be read together with more recent works such as Gordon Brook-Shepherd, **The Anschluss** (Philadelphia: Lippincott, 1963, 222 p.), Ulrich Eichstädt, **Von Dollfuss zu Hitler: Geschichte des Anschlusses Österreichs, 1933–1938** (Wiesbaden: Steiner, 1955, 558 p.), and Jürgen Gehl, **Austria, Germany, and the Anschluss, 1931–1938** (New York: Oxford University Press, 1963, 212 p.).

KRULIS-RANDA, JAN. **Das Deutsch-Österreichische Zollunionsprojekt von 1931.** Zurich: Europa, 1955, 211 p.

The Customs Union project of 1931 between Germany and Austria, one of the focal episodes in European diplomacy before the advent of Nazism in Germany, still awaits comprehensive treatment. Meanwhile Krulis-Randa's book serves as an able summary of the political, legal and economic aspects of the affair.

The historical background for the Customs Union lies in the failure of all efforts during the nineteenth and twentieth centuries to bring about a Central European economic unit, and particularly in the unsettled conditions of Central Europe after the First World War. While it is pertinent to rehearse the background of political and economic relations between Germany and Austria-Hungary, as the author does, it is still more important to focus on the discontents of Germany and Austria after 1918. In fact, Germany and not Austria was the agent pushing for a Customs Union. Austria, hemmed in by the Treaty of St. Germain and the Geneva Protocol of 1922, was in no position to envisage an active role in European politics. It was the German Foreign Minister Julius Curtius who was the father of the project, departing from Stresemann's Locarno policy. Germany's claim that she was implementing Briand's Pan-Europe plan was merely a way of dressing up a bold venture into a new diplomatic offensive. A triumph for Brüning's government, this would have taken the wind out of the Nazis' sails, but it would have also meant a new step by Germany toward the economic domination of Central Europe. This aspect of the Customs Union project has been convincingly documented by F. G. Stambrook in "The German-Austrian Customs Union Project of 1931: A Study of German Methods and Motives" (*Journal of Central European Affairs*, v. XXI, 1961).

The final decision of the International Court of The Hague against the Customs Union was determined, as the author argues, by the judges' disagreement as to whether the case under consideration was an abstract or a concrete one. If the majority did in fact address itself to the concrete German-Austrian case, it nevertheless cannot be charged with having been guided by primarily political considerations.

VON SCHUSCHNIGG, KURT. **Im Kampf gegen Hitler: Die Überwindung der Anschlussidee.** Vienna: Molden, 1969, 472 p.

"In March 1938," writes Kurt Schuschnigg, "the grandchildren of Königgrätz confronted one another," but this time they did not fight. As the frontier barriers went up, a population exhausted by years of civil strife gave a frenzied welcome to Adolf Hitler.

Schuschnigg has already related the ordeal of Austria in two books, **My Austria** (New York: Knopf, 1938, 308 p.) and **Austrian Requiem** (New York: Putnam, 1946, 322 p.), with rather strong emotional overtones. But now the statesman has had the time and leisure to turn scholar. **Im Kampf gegen Hitler** is a thoroughly documented as well as an absorbing work, incorporating much interesting material from Austrian and German archives.

The ordeal of Austria goes back of course to 1918. Republican Austria, as has harshly but rightly been said, was a "state against its own volition," and the Anschluss was prevented only by the terms of the treaty system and by the vigilance of the European powers. Schuschnigg is correct therefore in stating that international guarantees were essential to the maintenance of Austrian independence. Once the European powers, in particular Italy, had lost their interest in this, the road to the Anschluss was cleared.

If the fate of Austria was decided in Abyssinia, this should nevertheless not mean that happenings in Austria were immaterial to its political future. Schuschnigg's argument, justifying an authoritarian course since 1933 in terms of the foreign political situation, in particular the pressure from Italy, is altogether too fatalistic. As a historian, he explores insufficiently, as he did as a statesman, the avenues that might have led to a democratic anti-Nazi front among the Austrians.

For the rest, Schuschnigg has outlined with exemplary clarity the alternatives open to Austria in choosing the mode of its death and the main phases of the agony, and has told the story with restraint and dignity.

KEREKES, LAJOS. **Abenddämmerung einer Demokratie: Mussolini, Gömbös und die Heimwehr.** Vienna: Europa, 1966, 235 p.

The scholarly literature on the history of the first Austrian republic and the memoirs of contemporaries contain many indications that the paramilitary *Heimwehr* was backed up in its policy by the Italian and Hungarian governments. The originator and driving force in this coöperation was, as we now know, the Hungarian Prime Minister Count Bethlen. The Hungarian historian Lajos Kerekes has used materials from the Hungarian Foreign Ministry—memoranda by the *Heimwehr* leaders, financial statements, plans for secret transfers of weapons, correspondence between the Foreign Offices—to bring the extent and the objectives of the "plot" into the open. On the Austrian domestic scene, it contributed much to the radicalization of the right, the "settling of accounts" with the Social Democrats in February 1934 and the establishment of the corporative state. Here is a concrete instance of the shift in loyalties on the part of a fascist group from traditional national concerns to ideological ones. The South Tyrolean issue, in which the *Heimwehr* had a stake, receded behind the prospect of a rightist coup in Austria supported by Hungary and Italy and the vision of a solidarity of fascist powers. The latter was realized in the Rome Protocols of 1934, creating an "ideological bloc" among the three states, which, however, was not enough to protect Austrian independence against Nazi Germany.

After 1945

HISCOCKS, RICHARD. **The Rebirth of Austria.** New York: Oxford University Press, 1953, 263 p.

The author, British Council representative in Vienna from 1946 to 1949, has produced a work on postwar Austria that shows considerable understanding and insight. The frontispiece shows Karl Renner, whose designation by the Russians as chancellor of the second republic (Stalin: "What, that old traitor is still alive? He is exactly what we need.") turned out to be a blessing for the country. Renner, who looked back upon a distinguished political career in the old monarchy and the first republic, was far from being a mere figurehead and set the tone for an Austrian policy of caution but also of firmness and perseverance. Above all, having always been an advocate of the Red-Black coalition, he was the right man to heal the deep political divisions of the twenties and thirties and to cement the new coalition which carried the republic successfully through the first two decades of its second incarnation. There was one new factor, of course, on the domestic scene—the

Communist Party, an aggressive, Moscow-trained and well-organized group, but consistently rejected at the polls. Decisive in this respect were the election of November 1945 and the failure of the Putsch in 1950.

Among the fine chapters are those on Marshall aid and foreign relief, currency, prices and wages, social change, cultural revival, negotiations for a treaty, Russian obstruction and the communist challenge. Though published two years before the signing of the State Treaty, the book contains the following prediction: "Austria is a region where the two sides could come to an agreement without sacrificing any major interest or principle. It may be, therefore, that the Austrian genius for conciliation, which has always been favored by geography, has its greatest victory ahead." This is slightly on the sentimental side, but accurate after all.

BADER, WILLIAM B. **Austria between East and West, 1945–1955.** Stanford: Stanford University Press, 1966, 250 p.

The challenging problem taken up in this learned and lucid study is that of explaining the "lingering enigma": Why did the Soviet leaders, in the spring of 1945 in sole control of Austria, withdraw their troops from that country some ten years later? The temptation, of course, is to compare Austria with Germany which, by contrast, emerged from the four-power occupation divided. But the German situation, the author wisely stresses, was different; the stakes were much higher. No less important was the fact that in the Moscow Declaration of November 1943 the Foreign Ministers of the United States, the United Kingdom and the U.S.S.R. had agreed that Austria, "the first country to fall victim of Hitlerite aggression," should be "liberated from German domination."

The pieces in the elaborate game between the Western powers, which supported the government, and Russia, which supported the Communists, were, apart from the loyalty of the population, the control of the security forces, the trade unions and the so-called "German assets." After the final failure of the Communists in the unsuccessful domestic Putsch of 1950, Austria remained an object of the external shifting East-West power struggle.

Generally there are not many concrete, immediate lessons to be learned from history. But it is impressive to register that there have been instances when the Soviet leadership could be outwitted (the abandonment of the veto in the Second Control Agreement of 1946) and defied (Austria's joining the Marshall Plan in 1947). There were also important instances of the Russians' restraint—for example, in the spring of 1948 when they refrained from duplicating the Berlin blockade by one of Vienna, or at the time of the abortive Communist coup.

Finally, Bader carefully accounts for the lingering enigma of 1955. The Warsaw Pact now gave the U.S.S.R. sufficient military strength. At the same time, the neutralization of Austria, besides imposing military and political restrictions upon the country, disrupted the logistics between the NATO powers, West Germany and Italy. Furthermore, the Russians speculated that Austria's neutrality might serve as a tempting model for both West Germany and Italy.

While it is fair to state that Austria's own role in the game of high diplomacy was minor, the evidence assembled in this fine volume shows that the valiant rejection of communism by both the conservative and the socialist camps has had its share in the achievement of Austrian independence.

SHEPHERD, GORDON. **The Austrian Odyssey.** New York: St. Martin's Press, 1957, 302 p.

The dust jacket of this book shows the Hapsburg double eagle, the red, white and red colors of the "reluctant Republic," the three arrows of the Socialists, Dollfuss' *Krukenkreuz* and Hitler's swastika. It thus symbolically recaptures the "odyssey" of Austrian history. The author's theme is the lack of continuity between these different historical periods, and he has produced an exemplary essay, marked by intimate familiarity with the subject and by a lucid and elegant style.

Mr. Brook-Shepherd, whose first book was on **Russia's Danubian Empire** (London: Heinemann, 1954, 262 p.), is here chiefly concerned with the future of the Danubian Basin. A key chapter in **The Austrian Odyssey** is devoted to the resistance movement in Austria which kept alive the "blurred vision of Austrian independence." In Austria's regained sense of national identity after the Second World War and in her neutrality the author sees a guarantee against union with Germany as well as the promise of a renewed role for Austria in East Central Europe. But here a challenging and beautiful review of Austria's discontinuous history turns into daydreaming.

GREECE

CAMPBELL, JOHN and SHERRARD, PHILIP. **Modern Greece.** New York: Praeger, 1968, 426 p.

To date, this is the best introduction to modern Greece. It is a remarkable synthesis of all notable scholarly research in modern Greek studies and reflects its authors' firsthand knowledge of Greek life. It treats, as related aspects of one underlying cultural configuration, social values and institutional arrangements, as well as political, economic, social and intellectual developments. Though the history of modern Hellenism is admirably reconstructed from its origins in the late Byzantine period, the bulk of the book deals with the last 50 years, especially the post–World War II period. The most rewarding chapters, apart from one on the Greek church and another on modern Greek literature, are the last three, dealing with economic dilemmas, the countryside, and city and state, respectively.

An unfortunate by-product of the book's objective, matter-of-fact approach is a tendency to obscure the fact that the set of historical events which it reconstructs is susceptible to alternative or varying interpretations. It should therefore be read in conjunction with Constantine Tsoucalas' suggestive but inadequately documented **The Greek Tragedy** (Baltimore: Penguin, 1969, 207 p.), which is revisionist regarding the civil war and foreign intervention in Greece during and after World War II and more sensitive to the role of economic factors and social class in political development. An older work of continuing value is Nicolas Svoronos' **Histoire de la Grèce Moderne** (Paris: Presses Universitaires, 1953, 126 p.).

LEGG, KEITH R. **Politics in Modern Greece.** Stanford: Stanford University Press, 1969, 367 p.

This is the first systematic investigation of Greek politics to appear in any language. Published as a case study of a category of nations falling somewhere between developed and underdeveloped, it describes and analyzes the Greek political system by utilizing those features of recent political science conceptual models which its author considered applicable to Greece. Based on field research conducted during the year 1964–1965 and involving interviews with members of parliament and other Greek notables, its chief focus is the manner in which political change is reflected in patterns of socialization and political recruitment. But it also analyzes the social, historical and international determinants of political behavior, interest groups such as the military, the structure of political parties and the political process at both the parliamentary and extraparliamentary levels. Legg includes a valuable chapter on the role of the international factor in Greek political life. The chief shortcoming of the book is the author's lack of access to Greek sources because of the language barrier, but his study is far richer, both descriptively and analytically, than the slightly earlier publication by Jane Perry Clark Carey and Andrew Galbraith Carey, **The Web of Modern Greek Politics** (New York: Columbia University Press, 1968, 240 p.).

DRIAULT, ÉDOUARD and LHÉRITIER, MICHEL. **Histoire Diplomatique de la Grèce de 1821 à Nos Jours.** Paris: Presses Universitaires, 1925–1926, 5 v.

For Greek foreign affairs during the period 1920–1970, there is nothing to compare with this authoritative and indispensable five-volume diplomatic history of the first century of Greek independence. There are two major works in Greek covering shorter periods: Panagiotes Pipineles, **Historia tes Exoterikes Politikes tes Hellados 1923–1941** [History of the Foreign Policy of Greece 1923–1941] (Athens: Saliveros, 1948, 374 p.) and B. P. Papadakes, **Diplomatike Historia tou Hellenikou Polemou, 1940–1945** [Diplomatic History of the Greek War, 1940–1945] (Athens, 1956, 510 p.).

Apart from the excellent short monograph on the Greek-Turkish settlement of 1923 as a part of the Treaty of Lausanne by Harry J. Psomiades, **The Eastern Question: The Last Phase. A Study in Greek-Turkish Diplomacy** (Thessaloniki: Institute for Balkan Studies, 1968, 145 p.), there are three important works in English, also of more limited chronological scope, reviewed below.

KOUSOULAS, DIMITRIOS G. **The Price of Freedom.** Syracuse: Syracuse University Press, 1953, 210 p.

As an account of Greece's role in world affairs and the impact of international events on Greece, this book is as valuable for international and Balkan regional politics as it is for Greek political affairs. An "examination of international rivalry over the Balkans as reflected by the political developments in Greece," it utilizes Greek, Western and international publications available by the end of the period covered, such as memoirs, League of Nations and United Nations documents, official state records and newspaper accounts. Preceding in time a specialized monograph by the same author on communism in Greece, **Revolution and Defeat: The Story of the Communist Party** (New York: Oxford University Press, 1965, 306 p.), it provides the contextual background for the detailed analysis of the latter book. Though lucid, judicious and comprehensive, it fails to deal adequately with Greek internal politics and reflects the cold-war outlook of the West and the Greek right on the Greek civil war and Soviet global strategy during the early 1950s. For a different approach to the same subject, one should read Tsoucalas' **The Greek Tragedy** (Baltimore: Penguin, 1969, 207 p.), which is revisionist in its interpretation of the cold war and better on the interaction between internal Greek affairs and international events.

XYDIS, STEPHEN G. **Greece and the Great Powers 1944–1947: Prelude to the "Truman Doctrine."** Thessaloniki: Institute for Balkan Studies, 1963, 758 p.

A detailed, microscopic, exhaustive "record of communications between political elites," this bulky volume is a conventional diplomatic history constituting a mine of valuable information. Like Kousoulas' more general survey, it describes international politics with Greece as a nexus, but it is basically a history of Greek diplomacy. Though it utilizes all pertinent published sources, many of which were not yet in print when Kousoulas wrote his book ten years before, the core of this story is drawn from unpublished archival material, especially the records of the Greek Foreign Ministry and the Greek Embassy in Washington, as well as the valuable personal archives of Emmanuel Tsouderos, Premier of the Greek government-in-exile during part of World War II, and of Philip S. Dragoumes, Under-Secretary of Foreign Affairs in 1944 and 1946. Its title notwithstanding, this study also covers the period 1941–1943 by way of introduction. A major concern is "the dramatic swing of U.S. interest in Greek affairs from its nadir in 1944 to its zenith in March 1947, with the 'Truman Doctrine.'" More than a hundred pages of footnotes provide valuable background information and interpretive comments. The bibliography, though not annotated, is exhaustive. The major shortcoming of the book is the relative sparseness of broad interpretation and analysis, which may leave the nonspecialist bewildered in the midst of such rich and valuable detail.

COULOUMBIS, THEODORE A. **Greek Political Reaction to American and NATO Influences.** New Haven: Yale University Press, 1966, 250 p.

This lucid and judicious book deals with Greek foreign policy and world politics in the post–World War II period as they relate to Greek domestic politics. It is essentially a study of foreign policy attitudes and orientations which characterized the major Greek political movements during the period 1952–1963 and focuses on the effects of Greek foreign policy on inter-party struggles and polemics. It is based primarily on Greek newspaper sources as well as on interviews with representative political figures in Greece through the use of a structured questionnaire. The causes and more general effects of Greek foreign policy, whose two major features were active membership in the North Atlantic Treaty Organization and close association with the United States, are treated only incidentally. Nevertheless, the author shows that defense against Slavic neighboring states was a major cause of Greece's international orientation, analyzes the disintegrating effects of heavy military expenditure and the Cyprus issue on Greek foreign policy, and points up some major byproducts of the Greek-American association, such as the strengthening of conservatism in Greece, coöperation with Turkey and limited flexibility in foreign policy. Couloumbis has demonstrated the fruitfulness of studying the domestic politics of a state in terms of the international factor and reveals both the extent and limits of that factor's impact.

NORTHERN EUROPE

SCANDINAVIAN STATES

General

Scandinavia Past and Present. Copenhagen: Arnkrone, 1960, 3 v.

No finer introduction to the experiences and achievements of the five nations of the Scandinavian north exists than this luxurious work. The result of the combined efforts of many editors and a large number of expert authors, these volumes take the reader on a magnificent tour of Scandinavia in all its aspects from the time of the Vikings to the present age. The first two volumes are largely historical in their approach and carry the story to the present, while the massive third volume offers a panoramic view of Scandinavian conditions today: law and government, the welfare systems, the educational systems, mass communications, cultural affairs, economic conditions in all their aspects, and so on. Although this work might well be called a labor of love and an obvious attempt to put Scandinavia's best foot forward in the English-speaking world, the qualifications and reputations of the authors of the various special articles cannot be questioned. The volumes must be viewed as a general introduction on a high level, an appetizer designed to whet the reader's taste for more serious study, and as such it is unequalled.

CONNERY, DONALD S. **The Scandinavians.** New York: Simon and Schuster, 1966, 590 p.

In this weighty but entertainingly written tome an American journalist deals with all aspects of life in Denmark, Norway, Sweden, Finland and (in an appendix) Iceland. Love and sex, suicide, educational and social advances are closely scrutinized as are also many other aspects of what the author calls the "Nanny State." The material, interestingly and authoritatively presented, is divided into five sections dealing, respectively, with the "new Vikings" (*i.e.* Scandinavians in general), the "cosy country" (Denmark), Norway's "rugged individualists," Sweden's "perfectionists," Finland's "fatalists" and Iceland's "ultimate Vikings."

Having studied the northern countries for some 20 years, Connery has amassed a wealth of information and makes the reader aware how life is lived in a society which, if it has no social classes, does have many levels. The differences that set the five nations apart and the factors that set them apart from the rest of Europe emerge clearly. Each chapter contains a brief treatment of that particular country's stormy past, but one might well wish that international relations and inter-Scandinavian coöperation both yesterday and today had received more emphasis.

SVARLIEN, OSCAR. **The Eastern Greenland Case in Historical Perspective.** Gainesville: University of Florida Press, 1964, 74 p.

The Eastern Greenland Case, settled by the Permanent Court of International Justice at The Hague in 1933, involved a dispute of many years' standing between Denmark and Norway. It is the only dispute over Arctic territory settled by an international tribunal and as such remains of especial significance today. The author of this booklet, a model of its kind, sets the stage with an account of the discovery and early settlement of Greenland in the tenth century, the decline of the Norse colony, the effect of the union of Denmark and Norway, the Treaty of Kiel (1814), the Norwegian economic interests in eastern Greenland, the Danish activities in the island, the Convention of 1924 and the Norwegian occupation in 1931 of what Norway claimed was *terra nullius*.

Professor Svarlien deals in some detail with the proceedings and the judgments and offers a brief appraisal of the award. It is his opinion that the Danish case was rather shaky as far as international law was concerned, while Norway's case was even less firmly buttressed, resting as it did on an uncertain and wavering attitude toward the area in contention.

JONES, SAMUEL SHEPARD. **The Scandinavian States and the League of Nations.** Princeton: Princeton University Press (for the American-Scandinavian Foundation), 1939, 298 p.

After five decades of virtual retirement from European politics, Denmark, Norway and Sweden reappeared on the international scene after World War I when they joined the League of Nations. In a sense, however, they "accepted only *limited* membership in the post-War international system": they refused to participate in the game of power politics, although they appointed themselves to serve "as an ever-alert conscience to the Great Powers." They concentrated their efforts within the League on the promotion of international peace and justice through disarmament and arbitration of disputes, and their influence was also felt in the League's humanitarian endeavors and in the realm of international economic coöperation. According to Jones, no secondary powers took a more prominent part in the League's work, and few were more influential. Their influence was enhanced by their ability to work together for their common aims and by the fact that no suspicion of political ambition could be directed against them.

ZIEMKE, EARL F. **The German Northern Theater of Operations, 1940–1945.** Washington: Government Printing Office, 1960, 342 p.

During World War II, Germany's northern theater of operations was essentially a backwater, although Hitler always assigned a high priority to it. He kept two armies of more than a half-million men there after 1941, one of them awaiting the expected British invasion along the vast coastline of Norway, the other conducting a futile campaign against Murmansk. This volume, the first major work on this topic based extensively on captured German military and naval records, details the planning, the active campaigns and the ultimate defeat and surrender in this theater of war. About one-third of the book deals with the invasion of Denmark and Norway, and the remainder covers the operations in Finland in 1941–1945. Although it is above all a campaign history, it is also a valuable contribution to the political history of the Nordic countries during the period.

SCOTT, FRANKLIN DANIEL. **The United States and Scandinavia.** Cambridge: Harvard University Press, 1950, 359 p.

A volume in "The American Foreign Policy Library" (edited by Sumner Welles), this book by the dean of American historians of Scandinavia is much more than a treatment of an aspect of American foreign policy; in fact, it is much more an introduction to Scandinavia than it is a study in American-Scandinavian relations. Professor Scott introduces the reader to the lands and peoples of Scandinavia, their heritage, their successful experiment in social democracy, their economy and their foreign relations from 1600 to the aftermath of World War II. Into this presentation he weaves an excellent discussion of "Scandinavian-American crosscurrents," including the impact of Scandinavian immigrants on America and the impact of America on Scandinavia. He concludes, fittingly, with a perceptive analysis of the nature of American-Scandinavian relations in the postwar world, noting that the "common ideals and interests which bind the Scandinavians together link these peoples intimately with the United States": in cultural tradition, economy, political institutions and blood relationship, "the tie with America is exceptionally potent."

FRIIS, HENNING KRISTIAN, *ed.* **Scandinavia: Between East and West.** Ithaca: Cornell University Press (for the New School for Social Research), 1950, 388 p.

This useful volume resulted from a series of lectures on postwar developments in Scandinavia given by a number of American and Scandinavian scholars at the New School for Social Research in 1948. The lectures as well as the book helped to explain to puzzled Americans the many ramifications of social democracy and also why in 1949 there suddenly appeared a fork in the Middle Way, when efforts to create a regional military alliance failed, and Denmark and Norway joined NATO while Sweden chose to rely on her traditional neutrality. The editor, who also arranged the series of lectures, limited their scope to Denmark, Norway and Sweden and mainly to social, political and economic affairs.

Still to be read with much profit are the chapters on Scandinavian democracy (Henning Friis), the Scandinavian countries in a changing world economy (Svend Laursen), government economic planning and control (Jakob Bjerve), the labor movement and industrial relations (Walter Galenson), social welfare (Henning Friis), housing (Charles Abrams), producer and consumer coöperatives (Edith J. Hirsch), adult education (Per G. Stensland), Scandinavian foreign policy, past and present (Brita Skottsberg Åhman), coöperation among the Scandinavian countries (Gunnar Leistikow) and Americans and Scandinavians (Bryn Hovde). There is also a useful appendix containing statistical tables and a selected bibliography.

ANDRÉN, NILS. **Government and Politics in the Nordic Countries: Denmark, Finland, Iceland, Norway, Sweden.** Stockholm: Almqvist, 1964, 241 p.

This is the only available survey in a major language of the political systems of all the five Nordic countries. The core of the book consists of five chapters in which the system of each country receives separate treatment. Although this approach makes for a certain degree of superficiality, the essential features are all adequately and accurately covered. These five chapters are bracketed, however, by introductory and concluding chapters in which each national political system is placed in its appropriate Nordic context. Professor Andrén describes the accumulated heritage of many centuries which all the Nordic states share, the interlocking influences which have made their present political systems and attitudes so similar to one another. He discusses the impact of economic and social change on political reforms and innovations in the twentieth century and concludes, appropriately as well as symptomatically, with a description of recent developments in Nordic coöperation.

ANDERSON, STANLEY V. **The Nordic Council: A Study of Scandinavian Regionalism.** Seattle: University of Washington Press (for the American-Scandinavian Foundation), 1967, 194 p.

This book seeks to "describe and explain Scandinavian regionalism by illuminating its most prominent organ, the Nordic Council." It succeeds well. On the basis of massive empirical data, the author demonstrates that Nordic coöperation is not an exercise in supranationality. It is a pragmatic effort to solve international problems within a region, but it does not aim at regional integration. "Regional harmonization" is what the Nordic states seek, according to Professor Anderson, and it is what they have achieved. He debunks the notion that homogeneity promotes integration: the Nordic states, in spite of their historic homogeneity, do not want integration. They want coöperation. They are experimenting with "novel and effective techniques of accomplishing peaceful change within the nation-state system," and their "primary loyalty is firmly lodged in the nation-state."

Denmark

SJØQVIST, VIGGO. **Danmarks Udenrigspolitik 1933–1940.** Copenhagen: Gyldendal, 1966, 417 p.

The years from Hitler's rise to power in Germany to the German invasion of Denmark were anxious ones for the Danes. Sjøqvist, the chief archivist of the Danish Foreign Ministry, has written the first serious scholarly account of the formation and conduct of Denmark's foreign policy during those years, and his book is likely to remain the standard work on the subject for a long time. It deserves to be translated into English.

Based chiefly on a wealth of unpublished Danish and German diplomatic and military records as well as the private papers of a number of prominently involved persons, the book's main emphasis is on Danish-German relations and the growing Danish fear of a possible threat from the south. It was assumed in Copenhagen that a German invasion of Denmark would come only in the event of a general European war, except that a German demand for the restoration of its pre-1920 border with Denmark might be presented under any circumstances. It was also assumed that Denmark could in no event repulse a German attack. Accordingly, Denmark in 1933 was the only Scandinavian state which accepted a German offer of a nonaggression pact.

OUTZE, BØRGE. **Denmark During the German Occupation.** Copenhagen: Scandinavian Publishing Company, 1946, 155 p.

The Danes have been remarkably prolific in committing their experiences under World War II German occupation to print. Every act of heroism, hardship and atrocity seems to have been made a matter of published record, a fact which probably reflects the relative impact of five precarious years in Denmark's otherwise peculiarly tranquil modern history rather than the actual harshness of an occupation which could not compare with the terrors visited upon most of the nations occupied by Germany. Fortunately, most of this massive occupation literature remains safely untranslated. On the other hand, it is regrettable that the very few scholarly Danish accounts of the occupation period as a whole have not been translated into major languages, although a handful of monographic and more popular studies of special aspects have appeared in English.

Børge Outze, a prominent journalist with impeccable credentials for writing about the occupation of his country, published his brief general account immediately after the war, but it remains the only recommendable English-language account. For a far more detailed and objective account, based on prodigious research, the reader is referred to Outze's impressive **Danmark under den Anden Verdenskrig** (Copenhagen: Hasselbalch, 1968, 4 v.).

SØRENSEN, MAX and HAAGERUP, NIELS J. **Denmark and the United Nations.** New York: Manhattan Publishing Company, 1956, 154 p.

This volume, prepared for the Carnegie Endowment for International Peace and published in the "National Studies on International Organization" series, was produced as a collaborative effort by a group of Danish professors and students. Its emphasis is on Denmark's attitude toward the United Nations as a universal organization, and even the treatment of Danish attitudes toward regional organizations such as NATO is handled with that overriding consideration in mind. As a small country with much to lose in some future European war, Denmark's fate depends on the preservation of peace. Hence Denmark sees the United Nations as its main hope and believes that "the primary objective of the Organization is to adjust conflicting interests among groups of powers and, in so doing, bring about the *detente* which is the direct prerequisite of the safeguarding of peace." In line with this belief, Denmark, though allied with the United States in NATO, has regularly differed with the United States in the United Nations on a number of political questions, such as the representation of China.

Dansk Sikkerhedspolitik 1948–1966. Copenhagen: Udenrigsministeriet, 1968, 2 v.

This is an official account of Danish security policy in the years since World War II, prepared by the Foreign Ministry for the information of parliament. The hefty second volume consists of documentation, a total of 238 diplomatic telegrams and memoranda, excerpts from speeches, letters, announcements, communiqués, press releases and treaties. Together these volumes provide a comprehensive and authoritative survey of every important aspect of Denmark's defense and security policy in the postwar world. Not surprisingly, the emphasis has been placed on Denmark's participation in NATO, starting with the abortive attempt to establish a Scandinavian defense alliance in 1948–1949 and the eventual decision to join the Atlantic alliance. The Danish reluctance to go along with the proposed entry into NATO of Turkey, Greece and West Germany in the early 1950s is given due attention, as is Denmark's refusal to permit NATO bases on its territory except on Greenland. The treatment of the negotiations leading up to the establishment of the joint Danish-German NATO Baltic Approaches Command in 1961, a development which precipitated an international crisis, is particularly interesting. Denmark's defense establishment, its nuclear policy, its efforts to promote disarmament and reduced international tension and its participation in United Nations peacekeeping operations also receive coverage.

Norway

STORING, JAMES A. **Norwegian Democracy.** Boston: Houghton Mifflin, 1963, 246 p.

The first significant survey of Norway's present political system, this book covers the executive, legislative and judicial branches of government on all levels, national and local. The chapters on political parties, nominations, elections, the social security system and the role of government in the economy are first-rate. Regarding Norway's particular brand of "welfare state," Storing notes that it "has long since passed the stage of political conflict;" only the method of implementation remains an issue. Norway today has a "mixed system operating with certain socialistic principles and at the same time allowing a significant degree of free enterprise." Above all, it is thoroughly democratic.

MATHISEN, TRYGVE. **Svalbard in International Politics 1871–1925.** Oslo: Brøggers Boktrykkeris Forlag, 1954, 211 p.

Subtitled "Solution of a Unique International Problem," this volume by a Norwegian international relations scholar fills a void in the English-language literature on the Arctic archipelago better known as Spitsbergen. Judicious, well balanced and sufficiently detailed, the work places the rivalries and conflicting interests involved in the context of European diplomatic history and unravels the many strands that made up the tangled international Spitsbergen question.

By way of preface, Mathisen deals with the islands' early discovery and virtual status as *terra nullius.* He describes the activities of British, Dutch, French, Russian and Scandinavian whalers and hunters and the rivalry between the Norwegians and the Swedes during the nineteenth century which preceded the new era that came with the opening up of coal mines by companies from several countries, among them the United States. Turning to his main topic, Mathisen surveys the last three decades of the nineteenth century during which these conflicts were exacerbated. He discusses the numerous diplomatic exchanges and the serious attempts made immediately before World War I to settle what was indeed a very fluid situation. The treaty signed in Paris in 1920, by which Norway obtained sovereignty over the area while acceding certain rights to other nations, and the actual establishment of a Norwegian administration in 1925 are also fully dealt with.

RISTE, OLAV. **The Neutral Ally: Norway's Relations with Belligerent Powers in the First World War.** Oslo: Universitetsforlaget, 1965, 295 p.

The concept of neutrality underwent great changes during World War I, and the experiences of Norway present a case in point. As a maritime power heavily dependent on foreign trade and the earnings of its merchant marine, Norway was extremely vulnerable to pressure from the Allied powers. The British navy ruled the waters plied by Norwegian vessels, which meant that Norway's economy could in large measure be manipulated by the Allies. As a result, Norway's neutrality grew increasingly pro-Entente out of sheer necessity. Eventually, as German submarines took a heavy toll of Norwegian ships and seamen, the pro-Entente orientation became a popularly endorsed policy as well. Based on much new research into unpublished Norwegian, British, American and German sources, Riste traces and analyzes the underlying conditions and the evolution of Norway's wartime policy. He shows that the danger of a more overt Allied violation of Norway's neutrality was always real, while the fear of more serious German intervention was probably exaggerated. Through it all, he points out, the major and overriding principle of Norway's neutrality was "simply to stay clear of the conflict."

ØRVIK, NILS. **Sikkerhetspolitikken 1920–1939.** Oslo: Tanum, 1960–1961, 2 v.

Nils Ørvik, the leading scholar in the field of Norwegian foreign policy, is the author of a number of books and numerous articles on Norway's defense and foreign policies during and after World War II. In these two volumes, the standard work on their subject, he examines his country's security policy between the two world wars. His examination focuses on the reaction in Norway to the great international events and issues of the inter-war period as reflected in the deliberations of the governments of that era, in the debates of the Norwegian parliament and in the press. The primary question for the Norwegians was not so much the continued maintenance of the country's traditional neutrality as what kind of neutrality to observe and how to defend it. Neutrality within the League of Nations system seemed a viable policy in the 1920s, but the gradual collapse of that system under the stresses of the 1930s called for a reëxamination of the policy. Norway opted for continued emphasis on its social and economic reform programs at the expense of its defense establishment, leaving itself open to aggression in 1940. It would be most valuable if Ørvik would publish a one-volume edition of this study in English.

ANDENAES, JOHANNES; RISTE, OLAV and SKODVIN, MAGNE. **Norway and the Second World War.** Oslo: Tanum, 1966, 167 p.

Three eminent Norwegian scholars—two historians and a jurist—combined their talents to produce this book, prodded by the Press Department of the Norwegian Foreign Ministry. What triggered the prodding was the publication in England of a book which attempted to rehabilitate Vidkun Quisling, the Norwegian traitor who was executed after World War II. The primary purpose of the three Norwegian authors was to correct the "sometimes distorting" accounts published abroad, and their book consequently emphasizes those aspects of Norway's wartime history which best serve to justify the punishment meted out after the war to Quisling and other collaborators with the enemy. The book's title is therefore somewhat misleading, and an English-language history of Norway in World War II remains to be written. Nevertheless, this book is a good, if rather unbalanced, introduction to the subject, and it is the only worthwhile account of the entire five-year experience available in English. Riste writes well about Norway in Allied and German military plans up to the German invasion and about the activities of the Norwegian government-in-exile in London; Skodvin does the same for the occupation years;

and Andenaes explains the postwar proceedings against Norway's Nazi collaborators.

BURGESS, PHILIP M. **Elite Images and Foreign Policy Outcomes: A Study of Norway.** Columbus: Ohio State University Press, 1968, 179 p.

The German attack and occupation triggered a significant rethinking of Norway's foreign policy, a process started during the war years when the Norwegian government was in exile in London and continued after the liberation in 1945. The outcome of the process was that Norway abandoned its traditional neutrality and opted for a policy of solving its security problem in collaboration with the Western powers. In the first postwar years this meant collaboration with these powers within the framework of the United Nations. The emerging cold war posed new problems, however, and Norway opted for alliance with the Western powers in preference to a "neutral" Scandinavian defense alliance. Burgess focuses his study on these crucial years between 1940 and 1949 and seeks to discover how the "authoritative elite," *i.e.* the prime ministers, foreign ministers and defense ministers of the period, perceived the potential threats to Norway's security and the policy options available to meet those threats. The result of his labors is the best study yet produced of Norwegian foreign politics in the years since 1940.

Sweden

ANDRÉN, NILS BERTEL EINAR. **Modern Swedish Government.** Stockholm: Almqvist, 1961, 252 p.

This well-written manual on Swedish constitutional organization and practice can serve as a survey for the general reader, a reference work for the semi-specialist and a university textbook. Although it has been rendered partially obsolete by the constitutional reform of 1970 which changed Sweden's parliament from a bicameral to a unicameral assembly, it remains relevant and up to date in most aspects. After a brief introduction to the historical background, legal framework and economic and social conditions which form the setting for modern Swedish politics, Andrén describes and analyzes his country's party system, its direct and representative democracy, its parliamentary organization and procedure, the organization and functions of its executive power, its administrative organization, the method of budget making and budget control and its system of local self-government. The chapter on constitutional reform is especially interesting, since it deals with the problems which subsequently led to the adoption of a unicameral parliament.

TINGSTEN, HERBERT LARS GUSTAF. **The Debate on the Foreign Policy of Sweden, 1918–1939.** New York: Oxford University Press, 1949, 324 p.

Tingsten had a brilliant career as a political scientist, writer and editor of one of Scandinavia's largest newspapers. The present work, which appeared in Swedish in 1944, is fundamental and standard. The chief sources are newspapers, used in an exemplary fashion, periodicals and parliamentary debates.

Swedish neutrality during World War I led to active discussion of participation in the League of Nations. Once the decision was made, Sweden became an effective member. Tingsten's account of the Åland question—involving the islands between Sweden and Finland whose inhabitants sought to exchange Finnish sovereignty for Swedish—is the best in English. The same applies to his account of the second Åland question when, on the eve of World War II, Sweden and Finland proposed jointly to fortify the islands. Sweden's close relations with the other Scandinavian states are well outlined in two chapters on Scandinavian coöperation where the difficulties involved become clear. In the background is always Sweden's special relationship with Finland. Hopes for disarmament in the 1920s were replaced by arguments for rearmament in the 1930s. In all of this Tingsten is a dispassionate observer but, in his conclusion, he admits that public interest in the foreign policy debate was relatively limited. He briefly explains and criticizes a certain Swedish tendency to indulge in feelings of moral superiority.

BOHEMAN, ERIK C. **På Vakt: Kabinettssekreterare under Andra Världskriget.** Stockholm: Norstedt, 1964, 316 p.

HÄGGLÖF, GUNNAR. **Svensk Krigshandelspolitik under Andra Världskriget.** Stockholm: Norstedt, 1958, 317 p.

WIGFORSS, ERNST JOHANNES. **Minnen. Vol. III. 1932–1949.** Stockholm: Tiden, 1954, 455 p.

These three volumes are important contributions to an understanding of Swedish foreign policy during World War II. Boheman was Undersecretary of State for Foreign Affairs (1938–45), and Hägglöf was in charge of commercial affairs in the same ministry (1939–44). Wigforss was Minister of Finance (1932–49), a pillar of the Social Democratic Party and an architect of Sweden's "New Deal." Together these books provide explanations of how Sweden managed to stay out of the war. Partly it was luck, partly natural caution—a foundation stone of Swedish foreign policy since the nineteenth century—and partly intelligence and skill on the part of men such as these.

The fundamental decision was taken in March 1940 when Sweden, along with Norway, refused the British and French request to send troops across Scandinavia to aid the Finns against the Soviet Union. For the Swedes it was a decision based in part on a knowledge of the weakness of the Western countries. Sweden's escape from the fate of Norway and Denmark in April 1940 can be explained in geographical terms, as the German leadership realized that nothing was to be gained by an invasion of Sweden. Subsequent Swedish concessions in the form of the transfer of German troops and matériel across Swedish territory were violations of Sweden's neutrality. Boheman argues that Swedish policy should properly be described as nonbelligerent rather than neutral.

The books, based on both published and unpublished official materials as well as private notes, demonstrate that the men involved in Swedish decision making during World War II acted with intelligence and ingenuity as well as patience.

Sweden and the United Nations. New York: Manhattan Publishing Company, 1956, 315 p.

Prepared for the Carnegie Endowment for International Peace and published in the "National Studies on International Organization" series, this volume was written by a special study group of the Swedish Institute on International Affairs. Its three main subdivisions deal with Sweden's attitude toward the United Nations, its policy in the United Nations and its attitude toward international organizations in the economic field.

The members of the study group conclude that Sweden during the first postwar decade regarded the United Nations as an organization which, "in spite of its shortcomings, is indispensable for the world." Hence Sweden sought to utilize every opportunity "to promote, step by step, the effectiveness of the work of the United Nations and a higher degree of respect for its decisions." As a nonaligned neutral, Sweden tended to welcome the efforts of the great powers to solve their security problems through regional alliances, reasoning that this increased the significance of the United Nations as an essentially universal organization. Sweden also regarded the work of the specialized agencies as very valuable, and it supported proposals to extend the compulsory jurisdiction of the International Court.

ANDRÉN, NILS. **Power-Balance and Non-Alignment: A Perspective on Swedish Foreign Policy.** Stockholm: Almqvist, 1967, 212 p.

Sweden's foreign policy since World War II has been described officially as one of "non-alignment in peace in order to make neutrality possible in war." Professor Andrén sets this policy in its historical perspective and traces it through the first two postwar decades as it changed from a reactive to an active policy. The basic principle has been noninvolvement in the cold-war rivalries among the great powers, balanced by Sweden's active interest in promoting international peace and conciliation through the United Nations, Nordic coöperation, European integration, disarmament and support for developing countries. The author concludes that Sweden has been able "to vindicate the primacy of its non-aligned position in all major crises in which the country has been forced or called upon to participate," and that the best-foreign-policy-is-no-foreign-policy attitude of the past is now "definitely and absolutely obsolete." Professor Andrén draws heavily on public documents, 29 of which are reproduced in his book. Unfortunately, the excellent bibliography contained in the original Swedish-language edition has been drastically reduced in the English version.

Finland

MEAD, W. R. **Finland.** New York: Praeger, 1968, 256 p.
KALLAS, HILLAR and NICKELS, SYLVIE, *eds.* **Finland: Creation and Construction.** New York: Praeger, 1968, 366 p.

For the general reader who wishes to learn something about Finland's civilization and its past, these books are useful in different ways. Professor Mead's work is primarily historical in approach; and, although Mead is a geographer, this is probably the best short history of Finland in any language. Mead gives an admirably rounded account of the course of Finnish development in its political, economic, social and cultural aspects. He displays an intimate acquaintance with the literature of and about Finland in the Finnish and Swedish languages and preserves a praiseworthy balance in treating controversial questions.

The book edited by Kallas and Nickels, on the other hand, lacks a unifying thread. It consists of 32 brief contributions by more than 20 British and Finnish writers concerning history, politics, geography and various aspects of social and cultural life. No subject is treated in depth, but the reader has many doors opened for him through which he glimpses interesting vistas he may explore if he cares to.

WUORINEN, JOHN H. **A History of Finland.** New York: Columbia University Press (for the American-Scandinavian Foundation), 1965, 548 p.

Professor Wuorinen's book is essentially a history of modern Finland: 80 percent of the coverage deals with the post-1809 period, and more than 60 percent deals with the post-1917 period. This stands in sharp contrast to Professor Eino Jutikkala's rival volume, **A History of Finland** (New York: Praeger, 1962, 291 p.), which emphasized the pre-1809 period and barely managed to get beyond 1917 at all. The volumes should be read together.

The Wuorinen volume is a labor of love, an emigré historian's ode to his native land. It is also a professional job of historical writing, solidly researched in most instances, admirably organized, lucidly written and delightfully candid on controversial issues. One does not have to agree with all of the author's interpretations to say that this is the standard history of Finland in any major language. The emphases in the book are on political and economic developments almost to the exclusion of other aspects, it should be pointed out. Social and cultural coverage is provided only to illuminate political events. The nine documents reproduced in the appendices are all political, and practically all of the very useful tables serve to illustrate political and economic aspects.

PAASIVIRTA, JUHANI. **Suomi Vuonna 1918.** Helsinki: Söderström, 1957, 383 p.
SMITH, CLARENCE JAY, JR. **Finland and the Russian Revolution, 1917–1922.** Athens: University of Georgia Press, 1958, 251 p.

Paasivirta is the first reputable Finnish historian to surmount the psychic polarization of Finland after the civil war and to present, *sine ira ad studio,* a fair and unemotional picture of the events in Finland in the disturbed years from 1917 to approximately 1921. In view of the predominantly rightist-nationalist bias of the historical profession in Finland for about four decades after the civil war, Professor Paasivirta's earlier work did little to help his status among his peers; but the mellower climate since about 1960 has allowed him to gain some of the prestige he well merits. This book is a careful study of the various factors, recent and more remote, domestic and foreign, ideological and economic, that led to the bloody confrontation of 1918.

Professor Smith, on the basis primarily of Russian sources, explores thoroughly the complex relationship between the Russian revolutions, the achievement of Finnish independence and the Finnish civil war. Although he cites no Finnish-language or Swedish-language materials, he has succeeded to a remarkable extent in understanding the aspirations and concerns of the Finnish Reds who were later to become communists.

PAASIVIRTA, JUHANI. **The Victors in World War I and Finland.** Helsinki: Finnish Historical Society, 1965, 198 p.

Based on extensive archival research both in Finland and abroad, this book explores thoroughly the complex of problems, hopes, calculations, fears, errors, pressures, misinformation and prejudices that led the victorious Allies, interested more in the future of Russia than the future of Finland, to pursue a policy—or confusion of policies—toward the smaller country that deferred for some time the necessary rational decisions.

MANNERHEIM, CARL GUSTAV EMIL, FRIHERRE. **The Memoirs of Marshal Mannerheim.** New York: Dutton, 1954, 540 p.
PAASIKIVI, JUHO KUSTI. [**Reminiscences**]. Helsinki: Söderström.
TANNER, VÄINÖ ALFRED. [**Reminiscences**]. Helsinki: Tammi.

The authors of these volumes of memoirs were contemporaries whose impressive careers in the public life of Finland spanned the first half of the twentieth century. Paasikivi's earlier volumes, **Paasikiven Muistelmia Sortovuosilta** (Helsinki: Söderström, 1957, 2 v.), deal with the period of Russification at the turn of the century, an aspect treated perfunctorily by Mannerheim who writes instead about his career in the Russian army, while Tanner, in **Näin Helsingin Kasvavan** (Helsinki: Tammi, 1947, 343 p.) and **Nuorukainen Etsii Sijaansa Yhteiskunnassa** (Helsinki: Tammi, 1948, 469 p.), focuses on his work in the labor and coöperative movements. For the civil war period of 1918, Paasikivi left no memoirs; Mannerheim, who commanded the White forces, concentrates on the military aspect; and Tanner, a half-hearted adherent of the Red cause, deals primarily with political and social matters, **Kuinka Se Oikein Tapahtui?** (Helsinki: Tammi, 1948, 499 p.).

For the World War II period, Mannerheim's memoirs are the most stirring, Tanner's the liveliest, and Paasikivi's **Toimintani Moskovassa ja Suomessa 1939–41** (Helsinki: Söderström, 1958, 2 v.) the most thoughtful and, probably, reliable. All three agree that the prewar Finnish government bungled by its intransigence in the negotiations preceding the Soviet attack in 1939. During the Winter War, Tanner was Foreign Minister. He described the war experience in **Olin Ulkoministerinä Talvisodan Aikana** (Helsinki: Tammi, 1950, 437 p.), translated as **The Winter War: Finland against Russia** (Stanford: Stanford University Press, 1957, 274 p.). Paasikivi was minister without portfolio, and Mannerheim was commander in chief. Their memoirs give full accounts of the necessity for making peace and the problems of obtaining it. Tanner, **Suomen Tie Rauhaan 1943–1944** (Helsinki: Tammi, 1952, 416 p.), and Mannerheim give full, if often conflicting, accounts of the 1941–1944 Continuation War. Paasikivi did not write about it: he was in retirement, from which he emerged after the war to help his shattered country rebuild itself.

For perceptive essays on these three men, the reader is referred to Marvin

Rintala's **Four Finns: Political Profiles** (Berkeley: University of California Press, 1969, 120 p.).

WUORINEN, JOHN H., *ed.* **Finland and World War II, 1939–1944.** New York: Ronald, 1948, 228 p.

LUNDIN, CHARLES LEONARD. **Finland in the Second World War.** Bloomington: Indiana University Press, 1957, 303 p.

Finland's situation during World War II was an unenviable one; trapped in the struggle among the great powers, it was caught up in the fighting on three separate occasions: alone against Russia during the Winter War of 1939–1940, against Russia on the side of Germany in 1941–1944 and alone against Germany in 1944–1945. In the end it emerged mutilated, staggering under an enormous war reparations obligation to the Soviet Union, but still independent.

Professors Wuorinen and Lundin have given the only accounts available in English of all of these events. The Wuorinen volume, which was translated and edited by him from an anonymously written Finnish manuscript (apparently from the pen of the late Finnish historian Arvi Korhonen), must be regarded as a court historian's version of the events as Finland's wartime authorities would like posterity to see them. Lundin's study, on the other hand, is the critical analysis of those events as perceived by a liberal historian to whom Finland's wartime association with Germany was not entirely accidental. For all their deficiencies, however, these two volumes, if read together and judiciously, will provide the reader with fairly accurate impressions of the great problems that confronted Finland and its leaders during World War II.

JAKOBSON, MAX. **The Diplomacy of the Winter War.** Cambridge: Harvard University Press, 1961, 281 p.

A translation and thoroughly revised edition of a volume originally published in Finnish as **Diplomaattien Talvisota: Suomi Maailmanpolitiikassa 1938–40** (Helsinki: Söderström, 1956, 399 p.), this book remains the classic study of the Winter War as an issue in international politics. Written by a brilliant young journalist who shortly thereafter embarked on an equally outstanding career in Finland's foreign service, this is the story of a brief war on the periphery of World War II. But it was a war which captured the imagination of the world, moved the League of Nations to expel the Soviet Union from membership, and nearly unhinged the power alignments of World War II when the Anglo-French allies tried to use it as an excuse to open a second front against Germany in Scandinavia. It ended with Finland's defeat after one hundred days of gallant resistance, but Finland survived with its sovereignty and institutions intact. Given the great odds against such an achievement, says Jakobson, there was "victory in defeat."

UPTON, ANTHONY F. **Finland in Crisis, 1940–1941: A Study in Small-Power Politics.** Ithaca: Cornell University Press, 1965, 318 p.

KORHONEN, ARVI. **Barbarossa Suunnitelma ja Suomi: Jatkosodan Synty.** Helsinki: Söderström, 1961, 340 p.

KROSBY, H. PETER. **Finland, Germany, and the Soviet Union, 1940–1941: The Petsamo Dispute.** Madison: University of Wisconsin Press, 1968, 276 p.

————. **Suomen Valinta 1941.** Helsinki: Kirjayhtymä, 1967, 411 p.

No aspect of Finland's involvement in World War II has become more controversial than the origins of its participation with Germany in the attack on the Soviet Union in 1941. The "official" Finnish position, namely, that Finland was an innocent bystander drawn into the conflict by an unprovoked Soviet attack three days after the German invasion of the Soviet Union began, was given its first scholarly underpinnings by Professor Korhonen. A restatement of Korhonen's version was later published by Dr. Heikki Jalanti in his book, **La Finlande dans l'Étau Germano-Soviétique, 1940–41** (Neuchâtel: Éditions de la Baconnière, 1966, 380 p.).

The "official" Finnish version had already been challenged, however, by Professors Lundin **(Finland in the Second World War)** and Ziemke **(The German Northern Theater of Operations, 1940–1945),** and it was given a still more telling blow by Upton's carefully objective study. While Lundin's and Upton's studies were based largely on published sources, Ziemke's was based almost exclusively on wartime German military and diplomatic records. Professor Krosby's two studies, one dealing with the special problem of the diplomacy surrounding the Petsamo question and the other specifically with the origins of the Finnish-German alliance, confirmed Ziemke's findings. Based primarily on unpublished German records and interviews with top-echelon German and Finnish generals, Krosby's **Suomen Valinta 1941** documented extensive collusion between the German and Finnish military authorities during the winter of 1940–1941, culminating in a political understanding and full-fledged general staff planning sessions in May–June 1941. Out of these sessions came a coördinated plan for a joint attack on the Soviet Union.

All of these authors agree that Finnish policy-makers faced a terrible dilemma in 1940–1941. But while Korhonen and Krosby hold that Finland had no viable alternative to the alliance with Germany, Upton (and Lundin) suggest that neutrality in collaboration with Sweden might have proved a successful option.

Finnish Foreign Policy: Studies in Foreign Politics. Helsinki: Finnish Political Science Association, 1963, 232 p.

This collection of essays by 14 Finnish scholars covers the range of Finland's foreign policy concerns and attitudes from the declaration of independence in 1917 to the early 1960s. Two introductory essays provide the background history of Finnish foreign policy attitudes under Swedish and Russian rule, and Max Jakobson sets the stage for the remaining essays with a summary of Finland's foreign policy since 1917. Of particular interest to foreign readers are Risto Hyvärinen's essay on foreign policy decision making and administration, Nils Meinander's essay on Finland's commercial policy and Jaakko Nousiainen's essay on the attitudes of Finland's political parties to foreign policy. Other essays deal with Finnish attitudes to the League of Nations and the United Nations, Finland's foreign treaties and other agreements, the problem of the post-World War II reparations deliveries to the Soviet Union, the press and foreign policy, Finnish societies for international contacts, and the evolution of the concept of neutrality in Finnish policy. Although these essays are somewhat uneven in quality, together they serve as a useful and at times excellent introduction to Finland's international involvement.

JAKOBSON, MAX. **Finnish Neutrality: A Study of Finnish Foreign Policy since the Second World War.** New York: Praeger, 1969, 116 p.

Max Jakobson, Finland's ambassador to the United Nations, has given a clear and authoritative description and explanation of Finland's postwar foreign policy in this brief volume. Written by a foreign service officer on active duty, it carries, of course, an invisible imprimatur, and as such it is somewhat vulnerable. Nevertheless, it is the best available summary source of information on how Finland has survived and prospered since the war in the shadow of its wartime enemy, the Soviet Union. Finland's postwar foreign policy has been conditioned by its wartime experiences. Jakobson points out that a policy of passive neutrality failed to save Finland from involvement in World War II because the Soviet Union did not believe that the Finns were able to maintain it. Therefore, the primary task of Finnish foreign policy after the war was to create a new relationship with the Soviet Union. The basic assumption of the so-called Paasikivi-Kekkonen foreign policy line was that Finland could enjoy considerable freedom of action so long as its policy did not conflict with basic Soviet interests. Jakobson shows how this policy has been applied successfully by examining a number of important crises and issues.

Iceland

GRIFFITHS, JOHN C. **Modern Iceland.** New York: Praeger, 1969, 226 p.

Although this volume is a somewhat uncritical as well as unabashedly admiring treatment of Iceland and the Icelanders, past and present, it is nevertheless the most useful and up-to-date introduction to this little insular nation in the middle of the north Atlantic Ocean. Iceland's geographical isolation, according to Griffiths, is both its problem and its strength: its problem, because it is hard to make ends meet on a not very fertile island, dependent largely on the fish in the sea around it (there is a chapter ominously titled, "If the Fish Should Swim Away . . ."); and its strength, because it makes possible the continued preservation of what the Icelanders—and Griffiths—regard as a unique civilization (hence the concern about the "pernicious" cultural impact of American troops). The book deals very well with Iceland's postwar search for economic security. It gives a clear view of both the political and social institutions of the country, a brief survey of its foreign relations and an excellent account of the Anglo-Icelandic "Cod War" of the early 1960s. The introductory historical chapter is probably the best mini-sized summary of Iceland's history in the English language.

NUECHTERLEIN, DONALD EDWIN. **Iceland, Reluctant Ally.** Ithaca: Cornell University Press, 1961, 213 p.

This is a study of Icelandic foreign policy in the period from 1939 to 1960, a period during which Iceland was forced out of its sleepy isolation into alliance with the United States and NATO. As the book's title implies, Iceland was a reluctant partner in these developments, an innocent bystander, as it were, caught up in conflicts which refused to leave it alone. The author, who was attached to the United States Embassy in Reykjavik briefly in the mid-1950s, traces the story from the Anglo-American occupation of Iceland in 1940–1941 through the American-Icelandic Defense Agreement of 1941, the so-called Keflavik Agreement of 1946, Iceland's decision to join NATO in 1949, its attempt in 1956 to remove all American forces from the island, and the change of heart following the Hungarian Revolution and the resultant intensification of the cold war. These events stirred powerful emotions among the Icelanders, and the author's focus is on the domestic political repercussions.

BALTIC STATES

General

VON RAUCH, GEORG. **Geschichte der Baltischen Staaten.** Stuttgart: Kohlhammer Verlag, 1970, 224 p.

A solid history of the Baltic States, from the establishment of their independence in the last phase of World War I to their occupation by the Soviets in May 1940, based on a thorough study of most of the published sources. The author, a Baltic German by birth and a professor of East European history at the University of Kiel, Germany, emphasizes the diplomatic relations among these states and discusses their international politics, especially in connection with the Polish-Lithuanian differences over Vilna, the German-Lithuanian conflict over Memel and the great power talks in 1939. Von Rauch also surveys the political changes in the individual countries and favorably reviews the treatment of national minorities in Latvia and Estonia. He concludes that in 1939 there were no alternatives for the Baltic States that would have prevented a Soviet takeover, and that only a more thorough coördination of the foreign policies of Latvia, Lithuania and Estonia with those of Finland and Poland, as initiated by the Latvian Foreign Minister Meierovics in the early 1920s, would have given more weight to their international role. There is a valuable, though selective, bibliography.

Somewhat outdated, but still a useful general survey of the history in the inter-war period is: **The Baltic States: A Survey of the Political and Economic Structure and the Foreign Relations of Estonia, Latvia, and Lithuania,** prepared by the Information Department of the Royal Institute of International Affairs (New York: Oxford University Press, 1938, 194 p.).

MANN, BERNHARD. **Die Baltischen Länder in der Deutschen Kriegszielpublizistik, 1914–1918.** Tübingen: Mohr, 1965, 161 p.

A discussion of the immense German literature published from 1914 to 1918 on the German plans for the Baltic provinces, including Lithuania, after the expected victory in World War I.

The author demonstrates that the majority of the leading German publicists and politicians, no matter whether reactionary *Alldeutsche,* liberals of various shades, Social Democrats or members of the Center Party, favored the separation of the Baltic provinces from Russia. At the same time, the author shows the unbelievable diversity of the various conceptions for dealing with the future of these provinces. The more conservative and reactionary groups, abetted by many leaders of the German minorities in Estonia and Latvia, asked for the incorporation of the Baltic provinces in the German Reich, and their views to a large extent determined the policies of the German military governors of the occupied Baltic territories. After the Treaty of Brest-Litovsk in March 1918, when Lenin was obliged to cede Russia's claim to the Baltic provinces, the German military governors of the occupied territories, supported by the Baltic Germans and some conservatives in Germany, went ahead with their plans for bringing the Baltic provinces into close union with the German Reich. These plans, however, did not win the support of the indigenous populations, and, after the 1918 November Revolution in Germany, a completely new situation emerged which was seized by the democratic leaders of the Baltic peoples who had demanded complete independence.

Mann's thorough and methodical study throws new light on the relationship between official German policies and the views expressed during the war by leading German publicists on the Baltic problem. There is a comprehensive bibliography.

GRIMM, CLAUS. **Vor den Toren Europas, 1918–1920: Geschichte der Baltischen Landeswehr.** Hamburg: August Friedrich Velmede Verlag, 1963, 312 p.

This history of the Baltic German military forces (the *Baltische Landeswehr* in Latvia and the *Baltenregiment* in Estonia), formed in November 1919 to oppose the advancing Bolshevik armed forces, also contains information on the very complicated political situation in the Baltic countries at that time and on the ambitions of the small but very influential German minorities who had lived in Latvia and Estonia for centuries.

The emphasis is on the events in Latvia where, in 1919, troops of the German army, with the consent of the Western Allies, were still present, along with the small military forces of the young Latvian state. Since the new pro-Western Latvian government was still rather weak, the Baltic Germans, with tacit support from various groups in Germany, tried to overthrow the Ulmanis cabinet and to establish a pro-German Latvian government. The military and political ambitions of the Baltic Germans came to an end in June 1919 when their troops were defeated by the Estonians and Latvians in northern Latvia. After this defeat, the Baltic German forces were incorporated into the Latvian army and fought the Bolsheviks in eastern Latvia, while other Latvian troops defeated the Russian-German adventurer army under Bermondt-Avalov at Riga.

Grimm's book is not the definitive history of this period—the author is openly pro-Baltic German—but he nevertheless provides an outline of the chaotic military operations in 1919 that were watched with concern by the American, British and French military observers.

A Soviet account of the military operations in Latvia in 1919 in which Soviet forces were involved is: **Latviešu Strēlnieki Cīņā par Padomju Latviju 1919. Gadā** [Latvian Rifles in Fight for a Soviet Latvia], by V. Bērziņš (Riga: Izdevniecība "Zinātne," 1969, 263 p.).

TARULIS, ALBERT N. **American-Baltic Relations 1918–1922: The Struggle over Recognition.** Washington: Catholic University of America Press, 1965, 386 p.

A well-documented study, based on published sources and the documents in the National Archives in Washington, of the efforts of the Baltic diplomats and the representatives of various Baltic organizations all over the Western world to gain recognition for their newly won independence. The bulk of this monograph deals with the reasons for the reluctance of the United States government to recognize the Baltic States. According to the author, a Lithuanian-born historian, the United States was the last of the great powers to grant recognition (on July 25, 1922) because it placed Russia's interests above the Baltic peoples' right of self-determination and hoped that the confusing Bolshevik interlude in Russia would eventually end with the establishment of a pro-Western Russian government that would need the Baltic ports and industries. Tarulis claims that the attitude of the State Department toward the Baltic States was strongly influenced by various Great Russian advisers, particularly by Boris A. Bakhmetev, whom Kerensky had appointed ambassador in Washington. Tarulis also describes the activities of the various American, British and French observers and representatives in the Baltic States during this period.

In the conclusion the author contrasts the United States reluctance to recognize the Baltic States after World War I with its reluctance to recognize their incorporation into the Soviet Union after World War II.

A useful documented survey, also dealing with the recognition question, is **The Diplomatic Recognition of the Border States,** by Malbone W. Graham (Berkeley: University of California Press, 1936–41, 3 v.).

MEISSNER, BORIS. **Die Sowjetunion, die Baltischen Staaten und das Völkerrecht.** Cologne: Verlag für Politik und Wirtschaft, 1956, 377 p.

This is a thorough historical and legal examination of the incorporation of the Baltic States into the Soviet Union. The author, a well-known German expert in East European law, gives a resumé of the diplomatic aspects of the history of these states in the inter-war period, especially during the French-English-Russian and Russian-German negotiations in 1939, and describes in detail the nonaggression pacts that the Baltic countries were forced to sign with the Soviet Union in 1939 and the subsequent incorporation of these states.

Meissner also deals with the attitudes of the great powers, especially the United States, toward the recognition of the incorporation, discusses its aspects in international law and analyzes the Soviet efforts to justify the annexations. Since in Meissner's opinion the problem of the incorporation of the Baltic States into the Soviet Union is still relevant to the establishment of a stable European comity of states, he thinks, perhaps erroneously, that a time might come when the Soviet Union would be willing in its own interest to find a solution for this region in accord with the norms of international law. The work has a comprehensive bibliography.

For additional information on the incorporation of the Baltic States into the Soviet Union, and for a review of Soviet-Baltic relations since 1918, consult **Soviet Policy toward the Baltic States, 1918–1940,** by Albert N. Tarulis (Notre Dame: University of Notre Dame Press, 1959, 276 p.).

Estonia

UUSTALU, EVALD. **The History of Estonian People.** London: Boreas, 1952, 261 p.

This monograph, the most useful introductory survey of Estonian history in English, is part of the "nationalist" interpretation. The three periods best covered are the national awakening of the nineteenth century, the coming of Estonian independence and the interval of independence between the world wars. The author sketches the major events of the Second World War and ends his study with 1945. He devotes little attention to the economic aspects of Estonian history but treats the cultural achievements of independent Estonia at great length.

A Soviet survey of Estonian history is **Eesti NSV Ajalugu** [History of the Estonian SSR], edited by Gustav Naan (Tallinn: Eesti Riiklik Kirjastus, rev. ed., 1957, 650 p.), of which there is a Russian translation.

LAAMAN, EDUARD. **Eesti Iseseisvuse Sünd** [The Birth of Estonian Independence]. Tartu: Loodus, 1936, 748 p.

This is the best political study of a particular period in Estonian history, February 1917 until the beginning of 1920. The author, a moderate socialist, participated in the political events at this time, and the descriptions of the activities of Estonia's political leaders, many of whom the author knew personally, are especially valuable.

Beginning with an introduction on the Estonian national awakening, the 1905 Revolution and conditions in Estonia during World War I, the study covers the 1917 February Revolution in Estonia, the movement toward autonomy and the repercussions of the Bolshevik October Revolution. Laaman also discusses the decision to declare Estonia independent and the German occupation in 1918. The concluding chapters treat the Estonian War of Independence and internal political developments until the signing of the Peace Treaty of Tartu in February 1920, in which Soviet Russia recognized the independence of Estonia.

An excellent account of the beginning of Estonian diplomacy are the memoirs of Ants Piip, a leading diplomat and subsequently Estonia's Foreign Minister, **Tormine Aasta: Ülevaade Eesti Välispoliitika Esiajast 1917–1918. Aastal Dokumentides ja Mälestusis** [The Stormy Year: A Survey of the Beginnings of Estonian Foreign Policy in 1917–1918 in Documents and Memoirs] (Tartu: Akadeemilise Kooperatiivi Kirjastus, 1934, 400 p.).

The memoirs of the leader of the German nobility in Estonia, Freiherr Eduard A. J. von Dellingshausen, are also indispensable for the study of history of this period in Estonia: **Im Dienste der Heimat** (Stuttgart: Ausland und Heimat Verlags-Aktiengesellschaft, 1930, 362 p.).

A collection of documents presenting the Soviet interpretation of Estonian history at the time is **Suur Sotsialistlik Oktoobrirevolutsioon Eestis: Dokumentide ja Materjalide Kogumik** [The Great October Revolution in Estonia: Collection of Documents and Materials] (Tallinn: Eesti Riiklik Kirjastus, 1957, 842 p.). There is an abridged Russian translation of this collection.

Eesti Vabadussõda 1918–1920 [The Estonian War of Independence, 1918–1920]. Tallinn: Vabadussõja Ajaloo Komitee, 1937–1939, 2 v.

This is a thorough and competent military history of the Estonian War of Independence, 1918–1920. The work was the result of almost two decades of research by the Estonian National Historical Committee, based on documents in the Estonian War Archives. The first volume deals with the formation of Estonian national military units in 1917 and 1918, the German occupation of 1918 and the first half of the War of Independence from November 1918 to May 1919, during which the initial Soviet attack was repulsed and Estonian territory cleared of Soviet forces. The second volume deals with the initial Estonian support of Yudenich in his attack on Petrograd, the clash between Estonians and the Baltic German *Landeswehr* and the German Iron Division, and the final battles of the war, which ended with the signing of the peace treaty between the Estonians and Soviet Russia. The Estonian success in organizing a strong army was a major factor in advancing the cause of the independence of the Baltic States and in convincing the Western Allies of the seriousness of their claims for independence.

A reprint of the English summary of this military history appeared as **Estonian War of Independence, 1918–1920** (New York: Eesti Vabadusvõitlejate Liit, 1968, 47 p.).

MÄGI, ARTUR. **Das Staatsleben Estlands während seiner Selbstständigkeit. I: Das Regierungssystem.** Uppsala: Almqvist and Wiksells, 1967, 327 p.

A solid history of the development of the parliament in Estonia during its independence, with an introduction on the working of the Estonian Diet in 1917. The author devotes considerable attention to the debates in the Estonian Constituent Assembly of 1919 and to the formulation of the constitution. Critical of the constitution because it made provisions for an all-powerful parliament and for a weak executive, Mägi describes the functioning of the parliamentary system which produced 21 governments in Estonia from 1919 to 1934. There is also a discussion of the constitutions of 1933 and 1937 and of the crisis of parliamentarism from 1934 to 1940.

The parliamentary period in Estonian history ended in 1934 as the last Premier, K. Päts, established an authoritarian régime which lasted until 1940. A highly sympathetic account of the life and politics of Päts is **Konstantin Päts, Poliitika— Ja Riigimees** [Konstantin Päts: Politician and Statesman], by Eduard Laaman (Stockholm: Vaba Eesti Kirjastus, new enl. ed., 1949, 338 p.). An interesting and very critical account of Päts' seizure of power has been written by William Tomingas, a member of the extreme rightist movement VABS which was suppressed by Päts, **Vaikiv Ajastu Eestis** [The Silent Era in Estonia] (New York: Eesti Ajaloo Instituut, 1961, 554 p.).

MAASING, RICHARD and OTHERS, *eds.* **Eesti Riik ja Rahvas Teises Maailmasõjas** [The Estonian State and People in the Second World War]. Stockholm: Kirjastus EMP, 1954–1962, 10 v.

More than a hundred authors contributed to this ten-volume work on Estonia during the Second World War, many with personal recollections, others in chapters analyzing these events in historical perspective. Among the subjects covered are relations with the Soviet Union, fighting on Estonian territory and German wartime policy toward Estonia. The quality of the articles is uneven, but the work as a whole is indispensable for anyone seeking to understand the conditions in Estonia during the war.

MAASING, RICHARD and OTHERS, *eds.* **Eesti Saatusaastad 1945–1960** [The Fateful Years in Estonia, 1945–1960]. Stockholm: Kirjastus EMP, 1963–1968, 5 v.

A five-volume account of the sovietization of Estonia since 1945. Despite the title, the most recent volumes cover developments until 1965. Though very useful and informative, the work is sometimes marred by an anti-Soviet tendentiousness. Some of the volumes also describe the activities of the Estonian refugees in Germany from 1944 to 1950 and the fate of the Estonian soldiers who fought the Soviets in the ranks of the German army. A sixth volume is being prepared.

A brief but factual survey of the Soviet period in Estonia from 1945 to 1957, covering the whole gamut of political, economic, social and cultural developments, has been written by Aleksander Kaelas: **Das Sowjetisch Besetzte Estland** (Stockholm: Eesti Rahvusfond, 1958, 134 p.). The political aspects receive the best coverage. The sections on the Communist Party and the administration are particularly useful.

KAUR, UNO. **Wirtschaftsstruktur und Wirtschaftspolitik des Freistaates Estland 1918– 1940.** Bonn: Baltisches Forschungsinstitut, 1962, 174 p.

This monograph is a useful introduction to the Estonian economy. After a summary of economic developments before independence, the author discusses the structure of the economy and the problem of development during the period of independence from 1918 to 1940. Kaur argues that government investment in industry (state capitalism) was necessary because of the shortage of native private capital.

A Soviet account of Estonian economic history has been written by Arnold Veimer, the former head of the Soviet Estonian *Sovnarkhoz:* **Kompleksnoe Razvitie i Spetsializatsiia Promyshlennosti Estonskogo Ekonomicheskogo Administrativnogo Raiona** [General Development and Specialization of Industry in the Estonian Economic Administrative Region] (Tallinn: Estonskoe Gos. Izd-vo, 1961, 347 p.). Veimer is extremely critical of the economic policies of independent Estonia and contrasts the rate of industrial growth with the higher rate achieved during the Soviet period.

Latvia

ŠVĀBE, ARVEDS, *ed*. **Latvju Enciklopēdija** [Latvian Encyclopedia]. Stockholm: Trīs Zvaigznes, 1950–1955, 3 v.

An encyclopedia on Latvian history, politics, economics, social conditions and culture, which contains detailed descriptions of the foreign policies of Latvia since World War I, the conditions in Latvia during both world wars, the sovietization of the country since 1940, the various Latvian political parties and groups, the considerable demographic changes since World War II and the Latvian communities in the Western world. The biographical entries are of particular interest. The encyclopedia bears the strong imprint of its editor, a leading Latvian historian and an active participant in Latvian politics in the early 1920s, who wrote many of the articles. A supplementary volume, **Latvju Enciklopēdija: Papildinājumi,** was edited by Lidija Švābe in 1962 (Stockholm: Trīs Zvaigznes, 214 p.).

A one-volume reference work on Latvia in English, which has particularly useful chapters on government, administration, population and geography, is **Latvia: Country and People,** edited by J. Rutkis (Stockholm: Latvian National Foundation, 1967, 681 p.).

ANDERSONS, EDGARS. **Latvijas Vēsture 1914–1920** [History of Latvia, 1914–1920]. Stockholm: Daugava, 1967, 754 p.

This work describes the political and military events in Latvia during and immediately after World War I that culminated in the establishment of an independent Latvia. Particularly valuable are the detailed references to the sources that should be used for the study of this period. The author, a professor at San Jose State College in California, discusses how the plans of the various Latvian political factions for autonomy and independence were influenced by an extraordinarily complicated set of circumstances: the German occupation of Courland at the beginning of the war, the 1917 revolutions, the German occupation of Latvia in 1918, the establishment of the Soviet régime in 1919 and its collapse, the War of Liberation against the German-Russian adventurers in 1919, Estonian aid to Latvia and the reluctance of the Western Allies to support the cause of independence of the Baltic States. In the author's opinion the idea of the Latvian independent state started to gain ground chiefly after the Treaty of Brest-Litovsk, when Lenin officially foreswore Russia's claim to the Baltic provinces and the Germans went ahead with their plans for bringing this region under their tutelage.

A most useful memoir, with a collection of documents, dealing with the contacts of the author and other Latvian statesmen with the representatives of the Western Allies in the years from 1914 to 1921, both in Russia and in Western Europe, is **Latvijas Valsts Izcelšanās Pasaules Kara Notikumu Norisē: Atmiņas un Apcerējumi, 1914–1921** [The Birth of the Latvian State on the Background of the Events of World War I, 1914–1921], by J. Seskis (Riga: Valters un Rapa, 1938, 427 p.). There is an introduction by J. Noulens, the French ambassador to Russia from 1917 to 1919.

Important information on this period is also provided by Ādolfs Klīve, a member of the Peasant Union and a leading participant in the struggle for Latvian independence, in **Brīvā Latvija; Latvijas Tapšana: Atmiņas, Vērojumi un Atzinumi** [Free Latvia; the Birth of Latvia: Recollections, Observations and Conclusions] (New York: Grāmatu Draugs, 1969, 493 p.).

For a Soviet view of the military and diplomatic activities in Latvia during the last phase of World War I, see **Die Ausländische Intervention in Lettland, 1918–1920,** by Vilnis Sīpols (Berlin: Rütten, 1961, 248 p.).

VĀCIETIS, JUKUMS. **Pa Aizputinātām Pēdām: Pulkveža J. Vācieša Apcerējums Latviešu Strēlnieku Vēsturiskā Nozīme; U. Ģermaņa raksti par Latviešu Strēlniekiem un Pulkvedi J. Vācieti** [On Snow-Covered Tracks: Col. J. Vācietis' Study "The Historical Significance of the Latvian Rifles;" U. Ģermanis' Essays on Latvian Rifles and Col. Vācietis]. Stockholm: Daugava, 1956, 360 p.

The memoirs of Jukums Vācietis, first commander in chief of Lenin's Red Army from September 1918 to July 1919. Before the 1917 February Revolution Colonel Vācietis was commander of one of the Latvian Rifle regiments of the Russian army that fought against the Germans at Riga. After the February Revolution, and after the German occupation of Latvia, a substantial part of the Latvian Rifles supported Lenin and for a considerable time were the backbone of the new Red Army. Vācietis was liquidated by Stalin in the 1930s, and for many years his name was not to be found in any Soviet publications. His memoirs, a little known but important source for Latvian and Russian history, were originally published in Pskov in Latvian in 1922–1924.

Uldis Ģermanis, the editor who prepared the new edition of the memoirs, has supplemented the text with two essays dealing with Vācietis' military career and political views. According to Ģermanis, for Lenin Vācietis and the Latvian Rifles were a means for strengthening the Bolsheviks' hand in Russia, whereas for Vācietis Lenin was a means for defeating the reactionary forces in Russia that were against the establishment of an independent Latvia.

Documentation on the German government's interest in having the Latvian Rifles fight on Lenin's side in 1918 (because only Lenin among the important Russian leaders was for unconditional peace with Germany) has been published in **Deutsche Ostpolitik 1918: Von Brest-Litowsk bis zum Ende des Ersten Weltkrieges,** by Winfried Baumgart. For a Soviet account of the role of the Latvian Rifles in the Russian Civil War see **Latviešu Strēlnieki Cīņā par Oktobra Revolūcijas Uzvaru, 1917–1918** [Latvian Rifles in the Fight for the Victory of the October Revolution, 1917–1918], by J. Kaimiņš (Riga: Latvijas Valsts Izdevniecība, 1957, 415 p.).

CIELĒNS, FĒLIKSS. **Laikmetu Maiņā** [In the Change of Epochs]. Lidingö: Memento, 1961–1964, 3 v.

These are the memoirs of the Latvian statesman, diplomat and writer, Fēlikss Cielēns (1888–1962). A prominent Social Democrat both before and after World War I, Cielēns participated in the formation of the independent Latvian state, was a member of the Latvian delegation in Paris during the 1919 Peace Conference and belonged to all Latvian parliaments. From 1926 to 1928 he was Foreign Minister of Latvia and from 1933 to 1934 its minister in Paris. He opposed the establishment of the authoritarian régime of Kārlis Ulmanis (1934–1940) and the subsequent Soviet rule. His very forthright and subjective reminiscences, interspersed with many documents, are an important though one-sided source for the study of Latvian politics and foreign relations.

A useful study of the foreign policies of Latvia during the time when Cielēns played an important role in its politics is **Slepenā Diplomātija: Buržuāziskās Latvijas Ārpolitika 1919.–1932. Gadā** [The Secret Diplomacy: The Foreign Policy of the Bourgeois Latvia from 1919 to 1932], by Vilnis Sīpols (Riga: Liesma, 1965, 255 p.)—especially since its author had access to the archives of the Latvian

Ministry of Foreign Affairs. It is written from a communist point of view and is very selective in its use of sources.

VON HEHN, JÜRGEN. **Lettland zwischen Demokratie und Diktatur: Zur Geschichte des Lettländischen Staatsstreichs vom 15. Mai 1934.** Munich: Isar Verlag, 1957, 76 p.

A brief but well-documented study of the establishment of the authoritarian régime in Latvia in 1934, when Kārlis Ulmanis, the American-educated first Prime Minister of Latvia and leader of its Peasant Union, abolished all political parties, suspended the constitution and (with a rather widespread popular support) governed Latvia until the incorporation of the Baltic States into the Soviet Union in 1940, when he was deported to Russia. Von Hehn argues that Ulmanis' takeover was caused by the inability of the Latvian parliament to create stable governments and to reform the electoral laws that permitted the many splinter parties to play a role out of all proportion to their size. In the author's opinion, Ulmanis' takeover did not change the course of Latvia's foreign policy, which remained neutralist and considered both Hitler's Germany and Stalin's Russia the chief menaces.

For an insider's view of the Ulmanis régime, the memoirs of Ulmanis' Minister for Public Affairs, Alfreds Bērziņš, **Labie Gadi: Pirms un pēc 15. Maija** [The Good Years: Before and After May 15] (New York: Grāmatu Draugs, 1963, 414 p.), may be consulted.

Ulmanis' takeover as seen by a strong defender of the Latvian democracy is described by the Social Democrat and former Finance Minister, Voldemārs Bastjānis, in **Gala Sākums** [The Beginning of the End] (Lidingö: Memento, 1964, 175 p.).

The Soviet view of Ulmanis' foreign policies is presented in **Dzimtenes Nodevība: Buržuāziskās Latvijas Ārpolitika no 1933. līdz 1940. Gadam** [The Betrayal of the Fatherland: The Foreign Policy of Bourgeois Latvia from 1933 to 1940] (Riga: Latvijas Valsts Izdevniecība, 1963, 259 p.).

AIZSILNIEKS, ARNOLDS. **Latvijas Saimniecības Vēsture: 1914–1945** [Economic History of Latvia, 1914–1945]. Stockholm: Daugava, 1968, 983 p.

This is a thorough, comprehensive and well-documented study of economic conditions in Latvia from 1914 to 1945. The first part deals with the extremely chaotic conditions during World War I, from the beginning of the war—when Latvia was part of the Tsarist empire—through the events caused by the German occupation of Courland to the revolutions of 1917, the German occupation of the whole of Latvia in 1918, the Bolshevik interlude in 1919 and the War of Liberation. Subsequent parts deal with the reconstruction of the Latvian economy in the early 1920s, the Depression, the remodelling of the national economy in the years from 1934 to 1940 and, finally, with the Soviet and German occupations during World War II. The author has sought to describe the political factors, institutions and laws that determined the economic processes at each specific period and to describe the various economic activities themselves, for the purpose of finding out how political and economic doctrines and philosophies influenced the economic developments. The comprehensive bibliography is of particular importance.

ŠILDE, ADOLFS. **Bez Tiesībām un Brīvības: Latvijas Sovjetizācija 1944–1965** [Without Rights and Freedom: The Sovietization of Latvia from 1944 to 1965]. Copenhagen: Imanta, 1965, 436 p.

An informative, though not definitive, study of the sovietization of Latvia from 1944 to 1965. The author, a Latvian publicist living in Germany, reviews the political, social, economic and cultural developments during this period. Particularly useful are the chapters on the Latvian Communist Party and its leaders, the administrative changes, the Soviet fight against the "remnants of bourgeois nationalism," the mass deportations and the widespread resistance against the Soviets in the years immediately after World War II.

For economic policies during this period consult **Economic Policies in Occupied Latvia,** by Gundar Julian King (Tacoma: Pacific Lutheran University Press, 1965, 304 p.).

Lithuania

Encyclopedia Lituanica. Boston: J. Kapočius, 1970–.

There are few reference works on Lithuania, and the **Encyclopedia Lituanica,** now being issued in English in six volumes, is a useful compendium on the geography, history, literature and arts of Lithuania. It is satisfactory on the politics of independent Lithuania but inadequate on the Soviet period. This reference work is a distillation of **Lietuvių Enciklopedija,** published in Lithuanian and edited by Professors V. Biržiška, J. Girnius, P. Čepenas and J. Puzinas (Boston: Lietuvių Enciklopedijos Leidykla, 1953–1969, 36 v.). Both the Lithuanian and the English versions were written by Lithuanian scholars in the West and contain a wealth of information on Lithuania from ancient to modern times.

In Soviet Lithuania two of the three planned volumes of a Lithuanian encyclopedia have appeared since 1966: **Mažoji Lietuviškoji Tarybinė Enciklopedija** [The Small Soviet Lithuanian Encyclopedia] (Vilnius: Mintis, 1966–1968, 2 v.). This much more modest work adequately covers medieval Lithuanian history and describes the Soviet period in great detail but is very weak on the period of independence between the world wars.

SENN, ALFRED ERICH. **The Emergence of Modern Lithuania.** New York: Columbia University Press, 1959, 272 p.

Professor Senn's book on the creation of the Lithuanian state during World War I and its early political life is a pioneering work and has no rival. Senn's thesis is that "in the final analysis, the decisive factor in the establishment of the Lithuanian national state was the existence of a titanic power struggle in Eastern Europe in 1918–20." The author neither overlooks nor overemphasizes the Lithuanians' contribution to the creation of their own state and shows that their efforts were successful because the disintegration of the Russian and German empires had created favorable circumstances for Lithuanian self-assertion and defense against the successors of the two empires and Poland. There is a useful bibliography.

For the study of German policies toward Lithuania during World War I, when Lithuania was under German occupation, consult **Die Beziehungen zwischen Litauen und Deutschland während der Okkupation 1915–18,** by Börje Colliander (Åbo: The Author, 1935, 241 p.) and **Die Deutsche Politik in Litauen im Ersten Weltkrieg,** by Gerd Linde (Wiesbaden: Otto Harrassowitz, 1965, 265 p.).

RŪKAS, ANTANAS, ed. **Mykolas Šleževičius.** Chicago: Terra, 1954, 343 p.

A volume of essays on Mykolas Šleževičius, Prime Minister of Lithuania in 1918, 1919 and 1926, and a Populist leader who played an important role in Lithuanian politics in the 1920s. Since the political developments in Lithuania between the world wars still await scholarly attention, this volume on Mykolas Šleževičius can serve as a useful introduction to the politics of the parliamentarian period of independent Lithuania.

For the political developments of the 1920s another important work is **Pirmasis Nepriklausomos Lietuvos Dešimtmetis, 1918–28** [The First Decade of Lithuanian Independence, 1918–28] (Kaunas: Išleido Vyriausias Lietuvos Nepriklausomybės 10 Metų Sukaktuvėms Ruošti Komitetas, 1930, 404 p.), by J. Barkauskas, P. Klimas and others, who were all active in Lithuanian politics at that time.

Indispensable for the study of Lithuania in the inter-war period is **Antanas Smetona,** by Alexandras Merkelis (New York: Amerikos Lietuviu Tautinė Sąjunga, 1964, 740 p.). Antanas Smetona was the first and last President of Lithuania who abolished the parliamentarian system and established an authoritarian rule in 1926.

The Soviet interpretation of Lithuanian politics from 1917 to 1940 is presented in **Lietuvos TSR Istorija** [History of the Lithuanian SSR], Volume III, edited by Juozas Žiugžda (Vilnius: Mintis, 1965, 406 p.).

SENN, ALFRED ERICH. **The Great Powers, Lithuania, and the Vilna Question, 1920–28.** Leiden: Brill, 1966, 239 p.

The literature on the Polish-Lithuanian conflict over the city of Vilna, the ancient and present Lithuanian capital, which after World War I was a multi-national city and was finally incorporated in Poland, is rather sizable. It includes various collections of diplomatic documents issued by both the Polish and the Lithuanian foreign ministries, commentaries by experts, much propagandistic material, pamphlets and a few scholarly monographs in English, Italian, French, Lithuanian and other languages—among which Senn's work takes a central place. Senn studies the conflict from its origins and traces its development through the conference of Königsberg in 1927–1928. In analyzing the conflict, the author pays close attention to domestic politics, especially in Lithuania, and emphasizes that "the Vilna question drew its character more from the Lithuanians than from the Poles." He concludes that "in the long run, the resolution of the Vilna question was in the hands of neither the Poles nor the Lithuanians."

Of the earlier writings, a study by Ladas Natkevičius, a Lithuanian diplomat and his country's last minister in Moscow, remains of considerable value for its frank examination of the conflict and the statement of the issue from the Lithuanian side: **Aspect Politique et Juridique du Différend Polono-Lithuanien** (Paris: Édouard Duchemin, 1930, 355 p.).

VARDYS, V. STANLEY, ed. **Lithuania under the Soviets: Portrait of a Nation, 1940–65.** New York: Praeger, 1965, 299 p.

The purpose of this collection of essays is to examine the sovietization of Lithuania "from the destruction of Lithuania's independence and the 'bourgeois' order to its complete integration into the Soviet State and society." The book contains useful data on the Communist Party and government of Soviet Lithuania and concisely reviews the economic, cultural, religious and social developments. Special attention has been devoted to the Lithuanian attempts to assert their national interests. Little-known information has been presented in the chapters dealing with the widespread Lithuanian resistance movements against the Germans during World War II and against the Soviets during the same time and afterward. Four of the essays, including a profile of independent Lithuania and a description of the Soviet takeover in 1939–1940, were written by Professor Vardys.

SIMUTIS, ANICETAS. **The Economic Reconstruction of Lithuania after 1918.** New York: Columbia University Press, 1942, 148 p.

Books on economic conditions in Lithuania are rare. Simutis' brief survey is a useful introduction to economic developments in the inter-war period.

For an examination of independent Lithuania's agricultural resources, organization of production, economic policies and the land reform, one should consult **Agriculture in Lithuania,** by Jurgis Krikščiūnas (Kaunas: The Lithuanian Chamber of Agriculture, 1938, 155 p.). For the Soviet period Lithuanian agricultural problems have been examined by Pranas Zundė in **Die Landwirtschaft Sowjetlitauens** (Marburg/Lahn: Herder Institut, 1962, 153 p.) and by Marijonas Gregorauskas in **Tarybų Lietuvos Žemės Ūkis, 1940–60** (Vilnius: Valstybinė Politinės ir Mokslinės Literatūros Leidykla, 1960, 464 p.). The last book, written by a Soviet Lithuanian scholar and government official, is especially valuable for data on the collectivization and the establishment of the *kolkhozes.*

The industrialization of Soviet Lithuania is competently described by Kazys Meškauskas, the director of the Economics Institute of the Academy of Sciences of Soviet Lithuania, in **Tarybų Lietuvos Industrializavimas** [Industrialization of Soviet Lithuania] (Vilnius: Valstybinė Politinės ir Mokslinės Literatūros Leidykla, 1960, 261 p.).

EASTERN EUROPE

GENERAL; HISTORICAL

PALMER, ALAN. **The Lands Between: A History of East-Central Europe since the Congress of Vienna.** New York: Macmillan, 1970, 405 p.

This is probably the most satisfactory and up-to-date general historical survey of the entire area lying between Germany and Italy on the west and Russia on the east. The author, an able British specialist, begins his narrative with the reorganization of Europe at the Congress of Vienna and follows the developing national movements through the nineteenth century. About two-thirds of the book, however, is devoted to the years since the outbreak of the First World War; it provides a very thoughtful review of the foreign and domestic vicissitudes of the subsequent half-century. Conventional enough in its approach and treatment, it is judicious and balanced in its appraisals and does not carry the banner for any one cause or nationality.

GRAHAM, MALBONE WATSON. **New Governments of Central Europe.** New York: Holt, 1924, 683 p.
————. **New Governments of Eastern Europe.** New York: Holt, 1927, 835 p.

These two volumes, designed as companion pieces, are the somewhat pedestrian result of a conscientious effort to portray "concretely, scientifically, and entirely dispassionately" the political systems that emerged from the wreckage of the Hohenzollern, Hapsburg and Romanov Empires, *i.e.* Germany, Austria, Hungary, the U.S.S.R.; the successor states, Czechoslovakia, Jugoslavia, Poland, Finland and the Baltic States.

The coverage extends only to the early or mid-1920s, but a great deal of information has been assembled. Among the more interesting items are graphic presentations of the evolution of party politics in each of the countries. The Polish chart, of incredible complexity, is particularly intriguing, with Piłsudski as a kind of brutal QED at its end.

KOHN, HANS. **Pan-Slavism: Its History and Ideology.** Notre Dame: University of Notre Dame Press, 2d rev. ed., 1960, 468 p.

Pan-Slavism is a peculiarly elusive historical entity; at times it has seemed to be a force of great power, looming large (as a promise or a danger) on the eastern horizon, only to evaporate or to become a tool of national interests with no real life of its own. And yet the history of Eastern Europe is hardly to be understood without reference to Pan-Slavism.

Professor Kohn, an influential student of nationalism, a native of Prague who came to the United States in the 1930s, has provided an admirable and concise guide. With critical sympathy he leads the reader from the Herderian and Romantic origins among the Czechs and Slovaks to the messianism of the Poles, the Illyrian movement among the South Slavs, and to the Prague Congress of 1848. The scene then shifts eastward to the slavophiles and Pan-Slavs of Imperial Russia and to the mounting German-Russian estrangement of the late nineteenth century. The final section is devoted to the abortive phenomenon of neo-Pan-Slavism before the First World War, to the shifting balance between West and East Slavs between 1920 and 1950, and finally the engulfment of the Slavic world, and of Pan-Slav ideology, by the Stalinist imperium after 1945.

SETON-WATSON, HUGH. **Eastern Europe between the Wars, 1918–1941.** New York: Cambridge University Press, 2d ed., 1946, 445 p.

Although subsequent scholarship has provided numerous amplifications and modifications, and although the author himself changed his views on some major questions, this book remains an extraordinarily valuable inter-war survey of the whole area lying between Germany and Russia, from the Baltic to Greece. The son of R. W. Seton-Watson, one of the pioneers of East European studies in Britain, Hugh Seton-Watson came to the subject with an intimate familiarity with the region and its many languages. His book is personal—"my sources have mainly been people"—and yet informed with a marked comprehension of the salient economic, political and social issues. Organized topically, it is a striking example of comparative study at its most complex. Even the book's weakest point (as the author later and emphatically recognized)—its failure to size up the Russian presence to the east and to gauge the nature of the communist impact that was to dominate the following decades—is usefully revealing of the initial stance from which much of the serious study of postwar Eastern Europe took off.

Hugh Seton-Watson's **The East European Revolution** (New York: Praeger, 1951, 406 p.) is in some respects a less striking work, partly because by the early 1950s the world's attention had been directed toward Eastern Europe and the sovietization of the area was in the daily headlines. Nevertheless, it is a valuable book—essentially an account of the revolution, "imposed from outside and from above," from the latter years of the Second World War to the end of the Stalin era. The organization of the book, which is topical and comparative rather than by countries, is useful in highlighting the successive stages in the communization of Eastern Europe but tends to obscure the very important emergence of Titoism in Jugoslavia.

MACHRAY, ROBERT. **The Little Entente.** New York: R. R. Smith, 1929, 394 p.

The melancholy nature of the demise of the Little Entente may account in part for the fact that no one, apparently, has felt inclined in recent years to write a full-dress history of it making use of the materials that have become available since 1945. Machray's book, written in 1928, is suffused with the belief that Europe was on the brink of achieving a new "normalization" of its affairs, an achievement in which the Little Entente was seen as playing a very constructive role. If the reader can clear his head of the wraiths of the 1930s and 1940s, he will find a good deal of information on the formation, organization and modest early achievements of the Entente through the 1920s. A more detailed monographic treatment, but covering roughly the same span of years, is Florin Codresco, **La Petite Entente** (Paris: Les Presses Modernes, 1930, 710 p.).

MAMATEY, VICTOR SAMUEL. **The United States and East Central Europe, 1914–1918: A Study in Wilsonian Diplomacy and Propaganda.** Princeton: Princeton University Press, 1957, 431 p.

The author's stated purpose is to reconstruct "the United States attitude toward the break-up of the old Habsburg Empire and the creation of Czechoslovakia and Yugoslavia, the unification of Rumania, and the completion of the unification of Italy." The narrative centers on the two years prior to the Paris Peace Conference; by 1919, in the author's considered judgment, the new dispensation was largely a fait accompli. Greatest emphasis is placed on Czechoslovak affairs, but justifiably so, as the disposition of this traditionally pivotal area was crucial to the whole question of the continued existence of the Dual Monarchy. More extensive treatments of Jugoslav and Rumanian issues are now available, and the theme of Wilsonian diplomacy seems subject to endless exploration and refinement. Still, this is a major work in examining the origins of American policy toward an area previously quite beyond its ken.

DZIEWANOWSKI, M. K. **Joseph Piłsudski: A European Federalist, 1918–1922.** Stanford: Hoover Institution Press, 1969, 379 p.

The author was certainly correct in his observation that it was important "to rescue Piłsudski from his admirers as well as from his enemies." Few modern figures have been the object of such uncritical veneration and of such unbridled abuse. But behind this cloud of opposing views there is clearly a significant histori-cal figure.

Dziewanowski is concerned with but one phase of Piłsudski's career, a most important one. He undertakes to analyze Piłsudski's efforts to achieve a "federalist" organization in Eastern Europe out of the chaos accompanying the Russian Revo-lution and the defeat of Germany. Was this simply a device for achieving Polish hegemony through subtle mastery of Lithuania, Belorussia and the Ukraine? Or was it a serious effort to transcend the evident contradictions of the nation-state principle in that part of Europe? If so, did it have any hopes for success?

Dziewanowski is a sympathetic, though not uncritical, appraiser of Piłsudski's aims and policies, and his judgments are based on extensive research. One may still have doubts, but it is a value of this book that the author presents the picture in such a way that the reader may disagree precisely because of the clarity with which the evidence has been presented.

NAGY-TALAVERA, NICHOLAS M. **The Green Shirts and the Others: A History of Fascism in Hungary and Rumania.** Stanford: Hoover Institution Press, 1970, 427 p.

The author of this enlightening, if at times unbridled, comparative study of inter-war Hungarian and Rumanian fascism was himself as a young Jew familiar with both Hungary and Transylvania, in immediate contact with these movements and with the societies that produced them. The subject has absorbed him, he has read much, and he writes with considerable fire and passion, but his outlook is the opposite of stereotyped. Indeed, in such apparently jolting statements as that Iuliu Maniu, Ion Antonescu and Corneliu Codreanu were the only three "incorruptibles" in Rumanian politics, he is unmistakably seeking an explanation for Danubian fascism that goes beyond the simplistic formulas of hooliganism, anti-Semitism or hyperthyroid nationalism to the ills and discontents that made a Szalasi or a Codreanu appear to many simple, desperate folk as the bearer of salvation, horrible though the consequences may have been.

MORGAN, ORA SHERMAN, _ed._ **Agricultural Systems of Middle Europe.** New York: Macmillan, 1933, 405 p.

This extensive source book on the state of agriculture and agrarian policies in Austria, Bulgaria, Czechoslovakia, Greece, Hungary, Poland, Rumania and Jugo-slavia was prepared by agricultural experts and officials of the countries involved. In consequence some of the sections are a bit apologetic and at times evasive about the seamier side of the peasant's life. Still, it remains a useful collection of informa-tion for the inter-war years before the Depression had its full impact.

Briefer, more sharply focused and certainly more readable is Doreen Warriner, **Economics of Peasant Farming** (New York: Oxford University Press, 1939, 210 p.). This pioneering investigation, based on considerable field work in the mid-1930s, emphasizes the problem of efficiency in peasant agriculture, the prevalence of overpopulation and the depressed standard of living. Feeling that the Soviet pattern was unsuitable for these land-hungry nations, her pessimistic conclusion was that only a quite extensive redistribution of the farm population to regions outside Europe could provide any promise of economic progress and political stability.

MOORE, WILBERT ELLIS. **Economic Demography of Eastern and Southern Europe.** New York: Columbia University Press (for the League of Nations), 1946, 299 p.

There is some poignancy in the fact that at a time when the League of Nations was leading a shadow existence, having long since ceased to be a factor in the preservation of a vanished peace, it should have supported a quite remarkable flowering of scholarly works, chiefly under the auspices of the Economic, Financial and Transit Department.

This study is an outstanding example, and it has proved to be an important basic work for students of Eastern and Southern Europe. Essentially, it is a statistical study, with interpretation, of the region's demographic position, agricultural production, agricultural overpopulation and the implications of all this for economic development. It is particularly helpful in providing, in its tables and maps, the material for comparative and regional study. It is most useful as a starting point for explaining many of the social and economic ills of this area in the inter-war years; it is a pioneering work for the subsequently expanding interest in underdeveloped economies. An extensive appendix provides a most helpful country-by-country survey of land tenure and agricultural labor systems from the Baltic to the Aegean.

MEYER, PETER and OTHERS. **The Jews in the Soviet Satellites.** Syracuse: Syracuse University Press, 1953, 637 p.

This volume, together with Solomon M. Schwarz's **The Jews in the Soviet Union,** was sponsored by the American Jewish Committee in the hope of assembling an organized body of knowledge "on the Communist attitude towards Jewish problems and the effect of the Soviet system on Jewish life." It comprises essays on the situation of the Jews on the eve of, during and immediately after the Second World War in Czechoslovakia, Poland, Hungary, Rumania and Bulgaria. Prewar and wartime conditions differed markedly from country to country, and the fact that the essays were prepared during the agonizing last years of the Stalin era, when a pall of terrified uniformity seemed to have descended on all of Eastern Europe, served to dim the continuing differences of the postwar era. The essays add up to an exceedingly painful and disheartening story.

LUKACS, JOHN A. **The Great Powers and Eastern Europe.** New York: American Book, 1953, 878 p.

This is a book that has weathered far better than the time and circumstances of its appearance might suggest. Written by a young scholar only recently come to the United States from Hungary, it was published in the midst of the first wave of angry debate over the origins of the cold war. And yet it is far more than a reflection of early postwar polemics or the anguish of an East European over the communization of his native land. It is a remarkably sensitive and penetrating study of diplomatic relations within, and relating to, Eastern Europe between 1917 and the end of 1945, when Soviet hegemony was well assured. Writing as a Catholic conservative who believes that his grandfather's was a better age, Lukacs is able to give a consistent and remarkably broad interpretation of the vicissitudes of the Eastern European states during their period of brief independence and of subsequent Nazi and Soviet domination. This interpretation may be debatable—in its view of Russia and in its ideological stance—but it is solid, informative, grounded in the sources then available and very stimulating.

WISKEMANN, ELIZABETH. **Germany's Eastern Neighbours: Problems Relating to the Oder-Neisse Line and the Czech Frontier Regions.** New York: Oxford University Press (for the Royal Institute of International Affairs), 1956, 309 p.

It is understandable that Miss Wiskemann, an old hand in the study of German-Slav relations, should have found that this book "presented more difficulties than any work of the kind which I had previously attempted." The difficulties ranged from disputes over nomenclature to the collection of essential economic data. Ultimately, of course, the problem lay in the intense and prolonged thorniness of German-Polish and German-Czech relations, a problem involving frontiers, territories and persons.

After reviewing concisely the historical background of the areas of German-Polish and German-Czech dispute, and the experience of the inter-war years and of German wartime hegemony over Eastern Europe, she turns to a consideration of the origins of the Oder-Neisse Line and the massive expulsion of German populations from the east. In the aftermath of this upheaval Germany had the task of settling and integrating the refugee population; the Czechs and Poles the job of settling, organizing and integrating the territories gained or reclaimed.

It may be said, however, that the principal value of the book is as a review of the past. The sections on the mid-1950s—written before the events of 1956 in Poland and Hungary—are dated. Such is often the fate of the contemporary historian.

POUNDS, NORMAN J. G. **Eastern Europe.** Chicago: Aldine Publishing Co., 1969, 912 p.

This volume in the series, "Geographies for Advanced Study," edited by S. H. Beaver, was prepared by a leading expert on Eastern Europe. While the book is essentially a substantial work of reference—the bulk of it comprising a country-by-country survey from East Germany to Albania—it can be dipped into with pleasure and has an extended introductory section treating the physical geography, the historical peoples and states, and the resources and economy of the entire region. A concluding chapter deals with boundary and frontier problems after World War II. An appendix contains a convenient listing of the multiple forms of place-names. Probably the most satisfactory and up-to-date survey of the entire region.

EASTERN EUROPE AND THE SOVIET BLOC

See also Germany: German Democratic Republic, p. 571.

BRZEZINSKI, ZBIGNIEW K. **The Soviet Bloc: Unity and Conflict.** Cambridge: Harvard University Press, 1967, 599 p.

As the subtitle suggests, this is an inquiry into the opposing centrifugal and centripetal impulses within the constellation of communist states that emerged in the wake of the Second World War. The author is certainly one of the most brilliant of that group of young scholars of East European background and American training who played such a signal role in postwar research and writing. Brzezinski, whose studies have ranged from the Soviet purges to explorations of the future, here provides a particularly fine example of his analytic powers. While his treatment of the subject is chronological—a sequence of phases from enforced unity to diversity, and back to a mode of uniformity—his way of thought is essentially analytical, a persistent search for the structure of a problem in its temporal unfolding. Lest this praise sound too Hegelian, it should be stressed that Brzezinski has a comfortable mastery of, and respect for, the facts. His efforts to penetrate into the heart of the issues that have led to rifts in the seamless fabric of the communist world are persuasive and even of predictive value.

BURKS, RICHARD VOYLES. **The Dynamics of Communism in Eastern Europe.** Princeton: Princeton University Press, 1961, 244 p.

This book is ostensibly directed to the question whether communism in Eastern Europe has been predominantly proletarian in character. The answer is obviously "no," and to this extent the author is overreacting to the dogmas of the faithful. But if Eastern European communism has not been a reflection of the "distress of the proletariat," what are its sources? Here Burks has much of interest to offer. With admirable energy and imagination he sought the answers through such means as interviewing so-called "repentant" communist prisoners in Greece in the early 1950s, and in making quite refined statistical analyses of East European elections, demonstrating that even dubious elections can provide exceptionally informative data. His conclusions stress the importance of ethnic tensions, of uprooting and of the dislocative impact of Western influences in providing the impulse toward communism. It is a somewhat uneven book but with really original components.

BROWN, J. F. **The New Eastern Europe: The Khrushchev Era and After.** New York: Praeger, 1966, 306 p.

The uncertain but growing diversity among the communist states of Eastern Europe in the decade or so following Stalin's death is reflected in a number of able studies that sought, through various approaches, to take the measure of that change. Brown's study is centrally an informal, intelligent account of the principal political, economic and cultural developments in the area but also includes the external relations with the Soviet Union and the Western powers. H. Gordon Skilling, **The Governments of Communist East Europe** (New York: Crowell, 1966, 256 p.), a work by an experienced and very well-informed student of East Central Europe, is essentially a serious study in comparative government: an inquiry into the patterns of power, the holders of power, the process of governing and the carrying out of decisions. Ghita Ionescu, **The Politics of the European Communist States** (New York: Praeger, 1967, 303 p.), explores the theme of the developing relations between state and society and is particularly concerned with the obstacles to the unfettered exercise of power by the communist "apparat": counterforces within the system and the manifestations of opposition and dissent from without.

KERTESZ, STEPHEN DENIS, *ed.* **The Fate of East Central Europe: Hopes and Failures of American Foreign Policy.** Notre Dame: University of Notre Dame Press, 1956, 463 p.

This symposium by 16 distinguished authorities was prepared during that uncertain period when most of East Central Europe had been subjected to a decade of Stalinist control but before the perturbations of the post-Stalin adjustment (especially the tremors of 1956) were fully manifest. The first part of the book comprises reflections on what was essentially the wreckage of U.S. hopes for the area and on the ensuing debate over containment, liberation or coexistence. The core of the book, however, is a country-by-country account of the establishment of the Soviet imperium, though chapters are also devoted to Finland, Austria and Jugoslavia.

A sequel, taking account of developments in the next half-decade, is Stephen Denis Kertesz, *ed.,* **East Central Europe and the World: Developments in the Post-Stalin Era** (Notre Dame: University of Notre Dame Press, 1962, 386 p.).

SPULBER, NICOLAS. **The Economics of Communist Eastern Europe.** Cambridge: Technology Press; and New York: Wiley, 1957, 525 p.

This book was prepared under a twofold set of difficulties: the uncertain and fragmentary nature of the economic data in the decade after 1945 and the thaw that came on fitfully in the three years after Stalin's death. Still, it retains its value as an interim assessment of the early evolution of the communist-directed economies of Eastern Europe. Beyond that it is a good source of factual information. painstakingly and carefully assembled, on the nationalization of the economies, the first phases of the economic plans and development programs, the creation of "joint" companies, which worked to the inordinate advantage of the Soviet Union, the successive stages in the redistribution and collectivization of agriculture. Whatever the subsequent changes, these years were instrumental in setting the pattern and premises of Eastern European economic life for years to come.

ZAUBERMAN, ALFRED. **Industrial Progress in Poland, Czechoslovakia, and East Germany, 1937–1962.** New York: Oxford University Press (for the Royal Institute of International Affairs), 1964, 338 p.

This work for the general reader by a Polish-trained economist focuses on the most highly industrialized zone of East Central Europe, with particular attention to the principal "growth" industries: energy, metal and chemical. Consequently, the question of central concern is how a collectivist, centrally planned economic system is able to deal, not with backwardness or underdevelopment, but with a mature industrial system pointing toward higher and more sophisticated levels. This is a thoughtful study, with a wealth of useful statistical data, including Eastern and Western figures for industrial expansion over the extended period from 1937 to 1962.

KASER, MICHAEL. **Comecon: Integration Problems of the Planned Economies.** New York: Oxford University Press (for the Royal Institute of International Affairs), 2d ed., 1967, 279 p.

This is the best single work on the Council for Mutual Economic Assistance of the communist countries (Comecon and CMEA being variant acronyms). The author, an Oxford economist who previously served on the U.N. Economic Commission for Europe, quite usefully divided his study into two sections—historical and functional.

As a historical phenomenon, Comecon reflected the peculiar circumstances of its founding in 1949, under undisputed Soviet hegemony and as a response to the Marshall Plan and associated Western coöperative activities. Actually, it seems to have meant little in the last Stalin years, but it gained a new lease on life in the middle and late 1950s. These years, however, revealed a number of divergent interests, most evidently in the case of Rumania, that were to erupt in the 1960s.

Kaser considered its role as a functional entity in the fields of trade, technical coöperation, pricing and economic integration. It obviously did not perform as hoped, in good part because the growing plurality of communist sovereignties, of effective centers for decision, was accompanied by a growing diversity of economic interests and purposes.

PRYOR, FREDERIC L. **The Communist Foreign Trade System.** Cambridge: M.I.T. Press, 1963, 296 p.

This is a close analysis of the foreign trade system in the European communist nations as it had evolved through the 1950s. Given the nature of their economies, the author was obliged to pay considerable attention to matters of organization, price-setting and decision making. The East German experience in this regard is used as a salient example.

A detailed review of Soviet trade with the East European states is provided in Miklós Vásárhelyi, **Die Entwicklung des Sowjetischen Aussenhandels mit den Europäischen Ostblockstaaten seit der Gründung des Comecon (1949–1963)** (Aarau: Keller, 1967, 221 p.). The Soviet view may be found in M. F. Kovrizhnykh and S. M. Stepanov, *eds.,* **Vneshniaia Torgovlia Stran Narodnoi Demokratii** (Moscow: Vneshtorgizdat, 1961, 286 p.).

MARCZEWSKI, JAN. **Planification et Croissance Économique des Démocraties Populaires.** Paris: Presses Universitaires, 1956, 2 v.

This is an ambitious effort to place the planned economies of the Eastern European "people's democracies" in the historical setting of an effort to overcome economic backwardness. The first part of the book examines the situation in the inter-war years, especially the endemic problem of agricultural overpopulation. The second part deals with the economic growth of the area for the years 1945–1954. The third part looks into the mechanisms introduced for achieving this growth, chiefly the instrument of central planning. The author finds mixed results, with agriculture still at the short end of the stick, receiving less than its needed share of investment and obliged to suffer unnecessary dislocations of collectivization. The principal merit of the book is its effort to present in one picture both the prewar and the postwar economies of East Central Europe.

POLAND

ROOS, HANS. **A History of Modern Poland.** New York: Knopf, 1966, 303 p.

This is a thoroughly competent, concise history of Poland from the establishment of the republic at the end of the First World War up to the mid-1960s. The author, a prominent German historian, displays warmth and understanding for his subject and considerable admiration for the dominant figure of Piłsudski, "the last great ruler of the epoch of the Jagellonians." Stress is chiefly upon politics and foreign affairs but with an eye to Poland's serious economic and social difficulties; somewhat less is said on cultural and intellectual developments. Certain topics are treated more exhaustively in other works (for example, Piotr S. Wandycz, **Soviet-Polish Relations, 1917–1921,** and Joseph Rothschild, **Piłsudski's Coup d'Etat),** and the handling of Gomulka's rule after 1956 is necessarily rather tentative. Still, this is perhaps the best introduction to this period of Poland's history.

BROMKE, ADAM. **Poland's Politics: Idealism vs. Realism.** Cambridge: Harvard University Press, 1967, 316 p.

The basic premise of this book is that Poland, because of its geographic location, has suffered more than most nations from a "security dilemma": anxiety and uncertainty about its neighbors' intentions. In consequence, there has persisted, at least since the partitions of the eighteenth century, a polarity between political idealism—a "romantic" effort to remold reality, often by insurrection—and political realism—a pragmatic inclination to adapt to the existing circumstances.

Bromke traces the fluctuating course of this polarity through the nineteenth century, where the picture is relatively clear, but devotes most of his attention to Poland since 1945, when the situation became far more complex. His particular concern is Polish foreign and domestic policy under Gomulka.

There is obviously a methodological danger in setting up such a perennial dualism; the course of history may come to be seen as simply swings of the pendulum, all new stages only reiterations, and no forward movement. In some measure Bromke's scheme does thus restrict him. Still, on the whole, and especially in the Polish case, the approach is fruitful for analyzing the various strands of thought and action that have come to the fore in recent decades.

KOMARNICKI, TITUS. **The Rebirth of the Polish Republic: A Study in the Diplomatic History of Europe, 1914–1920.** London: Heinemann, 1957, 776 p.

The explicit purpose of this book is "to ascertain the role played by Polish problems in world policy" from the outbreak of the First World War to the conclusion of the Polish-Soviet War of 1919–1920. While the familiar note of polonocentrism can be a bit wearing, there is no doubt that the "Polish Question" has been a remarkably significant barometer of world politics in modern history, and not least in these years.

It is an unduly lengthy book, somewhat heavily laden with extended quotations from other writers. Still, it is a basic study for this period, though the important theme of Soviet-Polish relations is now more satisfactorily handled in the work by Piotr Wandycz **(Soviet-Polish Relations, 1917–1921).**

Perhaps Komarnicki's central intellectual target is those historians, such as E. H. Carr, who have argued that the statesmen at Versailles unduly favored the small states at the expense of Germany and Russia and of a rational organization for a postwar Europe. The author finds little such favoritism and a lot of indifference and ignorance.

ROTHSCHILD, JOSEPH. **Piłsudski's Coup d'Etat.** New York: Columbia University Press, 1966, 435 p.

This book is an admirable example of the way in which a particular event or episode, if examined carefully and with imagination, can illuminate a whole historical period or a major complex of issues. In May 1926 Józef Piłsudski staged a successful coup against the faltering Polish parliamentary system. As Rothschild observes, the coup adumbrated "the failure of parliamentary democracy throughout East Central Europe . . . it aggravated within the Polish nation a rift which was not to be healed during the lifetime of the interwar republic, and its division runs deep within Polish political memories to this day."

The book is indispensable for an understanding of Polish politics in the 1920s and 1930s; by inference it tells much of the tribulations attendant upon "state-creation." But beyond that the narrative has moments of high drama and pathos:

one really becomes involved in the hopes and quandaries of Piłsudski's forces (and of their opponents) as they crossed the Kierbedź bridge in the early evening of May 12.

WANDYCZ, PIOTR S. **Soviet-Polish Relations, 1917–1921.** Cambridge: Harvard University Press, 1969, 403 p.

During the years from the Russian October Revolution to the Treaty of Riga, Soviet-Polish relations were most complex, and a multitude of strands entered into the web. In effect, two new states were in the process of creation, and yet the long history of rivalry, conflict and partition was ever present. Conflicting revolutionary and nationalistic ideologies hovered over the scene. Other nationalities—Lithuanians, Ukrainians and Belorussians—were intimately involved in the struggle for the "borderlands." Not far offstage were other great powers, also locked in conflict.

Professor Wandycz, a historian of Polish birth, has done an admirable job in threading his way through this difficult but important terrain. Carefully documented, remarkably dispassionate, his book is most valuable in providing a coherent picture and interpretation of events that were to set the stage for much that happened in the years to follow. Of particular interest is his tracing of the intermittent, abortive and yet revealing efforts at Polish-Soviet negotiations in the period preceding the outbreak of full-scale warfare in 1920.

CIENCIALA, ANNA M. **Poland and the Western Powers, 1938–1939: A Study in the Interdependence of Eastern and Western Europe.** Toronto: University of Toronto Press, 1968, 310 p.

Poland's role and fate between the two world wars was not a happy one, and there have been few useful, and reasonably balanced, studies of Polish domestic and foreign policy during those troubled decades. This work is a notable exception. Based on a large amount of printed, but hitherto little used, material, as well as on personal interviews and on the important collection of prewar Polish diplomatic documents in the General Sikorski Historical Institute in London, Dr. Cienciala has written a sympathetic but not uncritical account of Polish diplomacy, with special emphasis on the period between the German annexation of Austria (March 1938) and the British guarantee to Poland (March 1939) and on the role of Colonel Józef Beck, the Polish Foreign Minister from 1932 to 1939. "The diplomacy of Col. Beck," she concludes, "was not a factor in the disintegration of the peace settlement but a reflection of this process. . . . The containment of Germany, and thus commitment to the support of Eastern Europe, was as alien to the tradition of British foreign policy as to British public opinion. France, with a very different tradition of interest in the area, subordinated herself to Great Britain. These factors, whether inevitable or not, were decisive not only for the fate of Poland but, with it, for the fate of Europe."

ROZEK, EDWARD J. **Allied Wartime Diplomacy: A Pattern in Poland.** New York: Wiley, 1958, 481 p.

The Polish question was one of the most contentious diplomatic issues in World War II, and the outcome in 1945–1947, involving both a loss of eastern territories and the destruction of domestic independence, left a very bitter aftertaste for many participants and observers. Rozek's book, while showing this bitterness and sharply critical of Western policy vis-à-vis Poland, is a richly documented work of scholarship that makes good use of the abundance of materials, including the Mikołajczyk files.

Stanisław Mikołajczyk's own story of these unhappy years when he tried, unsuccessfully, to bridge an impassable abyss is told in his **The Rape of Poland** (New York: Whittlesey House, 1948, 309 p.); Jan Ciechanowski, the Polish government-in-exile's wartime ambassador in Washington, tells of his fruitless negotiations with the Western powers in **Defeat in Victory** (Garden City: Doubleday, 1947, 397 p.). A picture of the disaster of Polish-Soviet relations is provided by the Polish ambassador to the U.S.S.R. in 1941–1943: Stanisław Kot, **Conversations with the Kremlin and Dispatches from Russia** (New York: Oxford University Press, 1963, 285 p.), which is a condensed translation of two books in Polish, **Listy z Rosji do Gen. Sikorskiego** (London: Jutro Polski, 1955, 576 p.) and **Rozmowy z Kremlem** (London: Jutro Polski, 1959, 336 p.). A very angry American report on the immediate aftermath of the wartime settlements is given by the American ambassador to Poland in 1945–1947: Arthur Bliss Lane, **I Saw Poland Betrayed** (Indianapolis: Bobbs-Merrill, 1948, 344 p.). None of these works rises above the fray; each is important for an understanding of it.

ZAWODNY, JANUSZ KAZIMIERZ. **Death in the Forest: The Story of the Katyn Forest Massacre.** Notre Dame: University of Notre Dame Press, 1962, 235 p.

The German discovery in 1943 of the bodies of thousands of Polish officers in mass graves in the Katyn Forest, slightly west of Smolensk, caused a wartime controversy of major proportions. The Nazi and Soviet governments each charged the other with the murders; Polish-Soviet relations never recovered from the event. During the war, and for some time thereafter, the picture remained murky, and a good deal of evidence was withheld from the public. Of the efforts at reconstruction, Zawodny's is the most effective and thorough. His conclusions leave little doubt that it was a Soviet act, despite the fact that the bullets used were of German origin. The reasons for the executions are less certain. The possibility of an error, a misunderstood directive, is not to be excluded, but the author's preferred explanation appears most plausible: Polish officers were, almost by definition, "enemies of the Soviet Union," were hardly to be converted, and their physical destruction would eliminate an important element of the Polish élite—as indeed it did.

DZIEWANOWSKI, M. K. **The Communist Party of Poland: An Outline of History.** Cambridge: Harvard University Press, 1959, 369 p.

As the author suggests in his subtitle and stresses in his preface, this book is a beginning, "a preliminary sketch that can serve as a point of departure for further investigation." Still, Dziewanowski, despite the incompleteness of the sources and no very warm sentiments for his protagonists, has provided a serious and scholarly review of the exceptionally tangled history of Polish communism. In some respects his treatment of the pre-1918 period is the most interesting, when Poland was still partitioned and when Polish socialists—including such notable figures as Rosa Luxemburg, Radek, Marchlewski and Dzierżynski—were important in the international movement. The inter-war years were disastrous: the party was outflanked by Piłsudski and eventually liquidated by Stalin. The years after 1939 and the advent of the Communists to state power are treated conscientiously but with evident distaste. The victory of Gomulka in 1956 and its aftermath have been treated more extensively in subsequent works such as Adam Bromke, **Poland's Politics: Idealism vs. Realism,** and Richard Hiscocks, **Poland: Bridge for the Abyss?** (New York: Oxford University Press, 1963, 359 p.).

MONTIAS, JOHN MICHAEL. **Central Planning in Poland.** New Haven: Yale University Press, 1962, 410 p.

This is a substantial analysis of the theory and practice of central economic planning in Poland in the years from 1945 to 1961, though rather formidable for the noneconomist. The Polish case is of considerable interest both because of the generally sophisticated quality of Polish economic thought, communist and noncommunist, and because of the emergence of a rather special Polish model after 1956.

The focus of the book is upon the activities of the Central Planning Commission in Warsaw. After sketching the political background and the economic problems confronting the planners, Montias turns to a close examination of the issues of short-term and long-term planning as they evolved from 1949 to 1956, with special reference to the operation of the socialized enterprises, the functioning of the price system and the pricing of producers' goods. The latter part of the book deals with the first half-decade of the Gomulka régime: the reforms introduced and the practical—*i.e.* ultimately political—limitations to experiments with decentralization.

KORBONSKI, ANDRZEJ. **Politics of Socialist Agriculture in Poland: 1945–1960.** New York: Columbia University Press, 1965, 330 p.

This is one of those permanently useful books which, while strictly monographic in character, have the advantage of casting light in several directions and hence of being useful for a variety of interests. As Korbonski himself points out, three considerations led him to the topic: 1, the agrarian problem has been, and remains, a major hurdle for the countries of Eastern Europe; 2, the interplay of politics and economics in communist countries is of central importance and requires close analysis; and 3, the quite specific evolution of communist policies in Poland with respect to agriculture warrants particular attention. The third of these considerations provides, appropriately enough, the main thread of the narrative, which culminates in the collapse of collectivization after October 1956.

MILOSZ, CZESLAW. **The Captive Mind.** New York: Knopf, 1955, 251 p.

These essays by a Polish writer and poet who fled his country in the late Stalin years had quite an impact at the time of their appearance as a firsthand insight into the plight of intellectuals trying to make do in a communist-ruled society; a good part of the book deals with case studies of writers trying vainly to function in a society being progressively sovietized. In the years of "thaw" that followed the death of Stalin it appeared that minds were not so "captive" as Milosz had portrayed them, that accommodation was more superficial, internal integrity stronger and more resistant. Indeed the cosmos of Diamat, Socialist Realism and the Communist Party is now far less awesome. But the abiding virtue of Milosz's book lies in the continuing pertinence of the struggle for intellectual, moral and esthetic integrity under the pressures of our century.

CZECHOSLOVAKIA

MASARYK, TOMÁŠ GARRIGUE. **The Making of a State.** New York: Stokes, 1927, 538 p.

Many years ago Henry Wickham Steed ventured the prediction that the man who would stand out as the most creative statesman of the First World War was Thomas Garrigue Masaryk. There seems to be little reason to question the soundness of that prediction; only the fact that the stage Masaryk trod was relatively small has obscured the dimensions of the man. A scholar and philosopher, a sober-minded revolutionary, a most effective diplomat and the founding father of his country—Masaryk possessed an extraordinary combination of talents.

This book records his "memories and observations" for the crucial years 1914–1918. Important as a source for the student of the breakdown of the Hapsburg monarchy and the origins of the Czechoslovak state, it is also of great interest for Masaryk's reflections on the crisis that led to the war and on the multiple holocausts that ensued. In these years Masaryk was all over the world, promoting the Czech cause: in Rome, Geneva, Western Europe, revolutionary Russia and Wilson's America. One can only be astonished by the breadth and humane cosmopolitanism of this ardent nationalist.

Among the dividends of the book are his asides, from suicide as a social barometer (an early scholarly interest) to Dostoevsky, to the evolution of German thought, to observations on William and Henry James and the "Spoon River Anthology." This is a translation of "Světová Revoluce za Války a ve Válce, 1914–1918" (Prague: Čin a Orbis, 1925, 650 p.).

There is no satisfactory biography covering the whole of Masaryk's lengthy career. Useful are two translations of his conversations with Karel Čapek: **President Masaryk Tells His Story,** by Karel Čapek (New York: Putnam, 1935, 302 p.), and Tomáš G. Masaryk, **Masaryk on Thought and Life: Conversations with Karel Čapek** (New York: Macmillan, 1938, 214 p.).

PERMAN, DAGMAR. **The Shaping of the Czechoslovak State: Diplomatic History of the Boundaries of Czechoslovakia, 1914–1920.** Leyden: Brill, 1962, 339 p.

This admirable monograph serves as a companion to the studies by Francis Deák **(Hungary at the Paris Peace Conference,** New York: Columbia University Press, 1942, 594 p.), Ivo Lederer **(Yugoslavia at the Paris Peace Conference)** and Sherman Spector **(Rumania at the Paris Peace Conference,** New York: Bookman Associates, 1962, 368 p.) in augmenting and rounding out our picture of the Paris Peace Conference as it bore upon the fortunes of the smaller states of Central and Eastern Europe. Miss Perman makes extensive use of the existing published literature plus a great deal of significant documentation made available only after the Second World War, especially the rich holdings of the Hoover Library.

Her exposition of some extremely complex and controversial issues—notably the sorry Teschen dispute—is lucid and illuminating. Her narrative amply supports her general observation: "Above all he [Masaryk] sought to avoid the creation of an 'independent, *isolated* state.' It is the tragic irony of his life that while every minute detail of his territorial blueprint was implemented, this basic premise of his Central European universe was never achieved."

BENEŠ, EDUARD. **Memoirs: From Munich to New War and New Victory.** Boston: Houghton, 1954, 346 p.

A figure who was subject to both uncritical praise and venomous obloquy, Beneš played a central role in the foreign and domestic history of the Czechoslovak republic up to his death in 1948. This volume of his uncompleted memoirs (a translation of **Paměti: Od Mnichova k Nové Válce a k Novému Vítežství,** Prague: Orbis, 1947, 518 p.) gives a brief sketch of the events leading up to (but not including) the Munich Conference and then deals with his wartime activities, in the East and the West, to reëstablish Czech independence.

His very comprehensive and important memoirs dealing with the initial struggle for Czech independence in the First World War appear as **Světová Válka a Naše Revolucie** (Prague: Orbis, 1927–1928, 3 v.); a considerably abridged English translation is **My War Memoirs** (London: Allen and Unwin, 1928, 512 p.).

There is no adequate appraisal of Beneš' entire career. Probably the most satisfactory single book is Sir Compton Mackenzie, **Dr. Beneš** (London: Harrap, 1946, 356 p.).

SETON-WATSON, ROBERT WILLIAM. **A History of the Czechs and Slovaks.** London: Hutchinson, 1943, 413 p.

The author, a pioneer for East Central European studies in the English-speaking world, wrote a number of major books on the nations and peoples of the Danubian and Balkan regions. One of his later writings was this general history of the Czechs and Slovaks. Appearing in the anguish of the post-Munich world, and not a particularly tightly knit work, it remains a most valuable and illuminating general historical survey, with about a third of the volume devoted to the years after 1918. Seton-Watson's sympathies were strongly pro-Czech and pro-Masaryk, and he himself played a not unimportant role at several points; the book, however, is the work of a learned, humane and democratic spirit.

Paralleling this book but carrying the narrative through the war years and up to the communist coup of 1948 is the survey by an American pioneer in Czech studies: S. Harrison Thomson, **Czechoslovakia in European History** (Princeton: Princeton University Press, 2d rev. ed., 1953, 485 p.).

LETTRICH, JOZEF. **History of Modern Slovakia.** New York: Praeger, 1955, 329 p.

Slovakia has been a particularly neuralgic point in a particularly sensitive area of Europe. Slovak-Hungarian relations before 1918, Slovak-Czech friction during the inter-war years, the role of the Slovak state in the Hitlerian empire, and the postwar position of Slovakia both before and after the 1948 communist seizure of power—all these issues make it highly unlikely that there can be any consensus as to the best history of Slovakia. Lettrich's book, however, provides a solid review of events from 1918 to the end of World War II, with particular emphasis upon the questions of autonomy, separatism and the wartime resistance against Germany. His own position is reflected in a concluding sentence: "The future of the Slovaks is at the side of the Czechs in Czechoslovakia [no hyphen]." The Slovak separatist position may be found in Joseph A. Mikus, **La Slovaquie dans le Drame de l'Europe: Histoire Politique de 1918 à 1950** (Paris: Les Îles d'Or, 1955, 475 p.).

KERNER, ROBERT JOSEPH, *ed.* **Czechoslovakia: Twenty Years of Independence.** Berkeley: University of California Press, 1940, 504 p.

This volume of generally quite able essays appeared in the immediate aftermath of Hitler's destruction of the Czechoslovak republic. Opening with a poetic lament by Edna St. Vincent Millay and closing with a prayer by Karel Čapek, it is evidently and explicitly a partisan piece. Still, the discussions of Czech history, of inter-war political, constitutional, economic, social and cultural developments, by such writers as the editor, Hans Kohn, Malbone W. Graham, Oszkár Jászi, Matthew Spinka, Harry N. Howard, Wickham Steed and Bernadotte E. Schmitt, are valuable in themselves. Whatever blemishes one may find in the Masaryk-Beneš years, the record, by the measures of our disastrous century, is a good one.

WISKEMANN, ELIZABETH. **Czechs and Germans.** New York: Oxford University Press, 1938, 299 p.

This book, by a leading British authority, went to press in the spring of 1938 just as Hitler and the Henleinists were beginning to mount their fatal assault on Czechoslovakia. This fact of timing may be fortunate, as the author was not under the enormous emotional pressure of the Munich crisis and its disastrous denouement.

The work is an excellent historical account of Czech-German relations since the Battle of White Mountain in 1620. The greater part, however, treats the period after World War I and the position of the German minority in Czechoslovakia, though Miss Wiskemann stresses the continuity of the conflict from earlier times. While granting the mistakes that the Czechs made in dealing with their difficult minorities question, she is clear that the Sudeten German Party was hardly a body with which they could come to reasonable terms.

Miss Wiskemann's book may be profitably supplemented by a very good and more recent work on inter-war relations between Czechs and Germans that makes use of the German diplomatic documents that became available after World War II: Johann W. Brügel, **Tschechen und Deutsche: 1918–1938.**

BUŠEK, VRATISLAV and SPULBER, NICOLAS, *eds.* **Czechoslovakia.** New York: Praeger, 1957, 520 p.

This volume, one of the series "East Central Europe under the Communists," was organized under the auspices of the Free Europe Committee. Prepared by a competent group of American specialists and Czech and Slovak exiles against the harsh cold-war background of the mid-1950s and forced to contend with uncertain and unreliable information, it remains a useful compendium on all aspects of Czechoslovak life in the postwar years. In some respects it amounts to a sequel to the volume edited by Robert J. Kerner, **Czechoslovakia: Twenty Years of Independence.** For information on the 1960s the reader may consult Heinrich Kuhn, **Handbuch der Tschechoslowakei** (Munich: Robert Lerche, 1967, 1,021 p.), and Václav Brož, *ed.,* **Hospodářskopolitická Rukověť** (Prague: Československá Tisková Kancelář, 1968, 2 v.).

TÁBORSKÝ, EDWARD. **Communism in Czechoslovakia 1948–1960.** Princeton: Princeton University Press, 1961, 628 p.

The author of an able study of the institutions of inter-war Czechoslovakia, **Czechoslovak Democracy at Work** (London: Allen and Unwin, 1945, 159 p.), provides in this book the most comprehensive account in English of the first 12 years of communist rule in that country. Táborský served in the Czech Foreign Ministry before the Second World War, was Beneš' personal aide during the war, and was Czechoslovak envoy to Sweden in 1945–1948. It is understandable that his "interim evaluation" of the communist endeavor is somewhat unfriendly. The book, however, presents a great deal of information about Czechoslovakia in those years: the ruling party, the organization of government, the industrial and agrarian policies. Curiously, while the author felt that the Communist Party had not achieved its goals and had not won the confidence of the people, there is little in his conclusions that would point toward the agitated course of events in the 1960s, which marked a striking shift from the "overcautious, strictly realistic" mentality which he thought would perpetuate a sort of *immobilisme* for the future.

ZINNER, PAUL E. **Communist Strategy and Tactics in Czechoslovakia, 1918–1948.** New York: Praeger, 1963, 264 p.

The object of this study is quite sharply defined: the communist seizure of power in Czechoslovakia in February 1948. But in seeking to comprehend this dramatic event, Paul Zinner achieves an admirably knowledgeable and penetrating synthesis of historical narrative and political analysis. He convincingly demonstrates that the nature and strategies of Czech communism must be sought in the extended history of the Czechoslovak Communist Party in the particular setting of Czechoslovak politics during the inter-war and wartime years. He also shows how the specific circumstances surrounding the reëmergence of Czechoslovakia from occupation and dismemberment provided the Communists with a solid stage for their subsequent victory. His general thesis places less emphasis upon such external factors as "Soviet power" and more on the fact that from 1945 on the Communists were in a very advantageous position for a drive to power. While the Czech case resembles in a number of respects corresponding events elsewhere in Eastern Europe, a great virtue of Zinner's book lies in its display of the elements of distinctiveness that marked the takeover in Czechoslovakia.

MICHAL, JAN M. **Central Planning in Czechoslovakia: Organization for Growth in a Mature Economy.** Stanford: Stanford University Press, 1960, 274 p.

In 1938, 1948 and again in 1968 Czechoslovakia played a peculiarly poignant role in international affairs. In each instance the internal development of the nation was abruptly, and externally, set on a course not of its own choosing. One consequence of 1948 was to make Czechoslovakia become, perforce, a test case for the working of comprehensive central planning in an already industrialized society. Michal's book is a detailed and technical examination of this experience for the decade 1948–1958. While cautious in his conclusions he does not find the results particularly impressive.

A later and highly critical inside view is provided by Ota Šik, **Plan and Market under Socialism** (White Plains: International Arts and Sciences Press, 1968, 382 p.). This work by a Czech economist prominent in the brief, and harshly interrupted, thaw of 1967–1968, sharply criticizes the whole pattern of administrative planning and management in his country and argues for the need for certain kinds of market relations in such an economy.

HUNGARY

See also Austria: Hapsburg Empire, p. 573.

MACARTNEY, CARLILE AYLMER. **October Fifteenth: A History of Modern Hungary, 1929–1945.** Edinburgh: Edinburgh University Press, 1957, 2 v.

For reasons that are not altogether clear, Hungarian historians appear to have turned less to contemporary history than have their colleagues in some other East

European nations. Consequently, it was particularly fortunate that the leading Western authority on Hungary should have addressed himself to fairly recent events. This massive work recounts the domestic and foreign vicissitudes of Trianon Hungary from the onset of the Depression to the day in 1944 when the Nazis abducted Regent Horthy. It is an invaluable work for the period, based as it is both upon extensive study of the sources and upon Macartney's numerous personal contacts.

The book has definite political leanings; the Regent and the traditional conservative order appear in a quite favorable though not uncritical light. But like any really substantial historical interpretation, the work provides a wealth of information for those inclined to view the story from a somewhat different angle. Particularly good are Macartney's depictions of the wide array of right-wing movements as they emerged and competed in the deteriorating political climate of the 1930s.

An American edition appeared under the title "A History of Hungary, 1929–1945" (New York: Praeger, 1957, 2 v.); a second edition was published as "October Fifteenth: A History of Modern Hungary, 1929–1945" (Chicago: Aldine Publishing Company, 1962, 2 v.).

TÖKÉS, RUDOLF L. **Béla Kun and the Hungarian Soviet Republic: The Origins and Role of the Communist Party of Hungary in the Revolutions of 1918–1919.** New York: Praeger (for the Hoover Institution on War, Revolution, and Peace), 1967, 292 p.

Although the Hungarian Soviet Republic had only an ephemeral existence in 1919 and although its leader, Béla Kun, was hardly a titanic figure in the roster of early communists, the close examination of the man and the movement which Tökés provides certainly warrants the effort. For one thing, the Kun régime tells us much about the early history, expectations and frustrations of communism: "Next to the establishment of the Communist International, the creation of the Hungarian Soviet Republic represented the most significant, and for some time the only, solid achievement of Bolshevik designs for world revolution." Moreover, the brief but hectic passage of the Kun régime across the Hungarian scene had important effects on subsequent Hungarian history, both in giving precise form and substance to the "Red scare" and in providing cautionary lessons to the Hungarian Communists when they again strove for power after 1945. In this latter respect Tökés' careful study, making extensive use of Hungarian materials, provides a most useful background for the works by Zinner, Váli and Kecskemeti, mentioned elsewhere.

MACARTNEY, CARLILE AYLMER. **Hungary and Her Successors: The Treaty of Trianon and Its Consequences, 1919–1937.** New York: Oxford University Press, 1937, 504 p.

Although this book was written as part of a series dealing with the problems of treaty revision, its permanent value far transcends the now remote issue of an adjustment of the Treaty of Trianon. As treated in this book, the subject of Hungary's lost territories proved to be a remarkably effective means to an understanding of the whole complex of national and territorial controversies in East Central Europe that followed upon the collapse of the Hapsburg Empire. What could have been a technical exercise or a piece of special pleading became in Professor Macartney's hands a major historical work.

His treatment is simple and straightforward: after a brief introduction covering the history of the nationality question in Hungary and the terms of the treaty after World War I (not a mutilation but a dismemberment), he turns directly to the territories involved: the Burgenland, Slovakia, Ruthenia, Transylvania, Croatia, the Voivodina and Fiume. But by the time one has completed Macartney's scholarly and informed tour of the shorn territories one has learned a great deal about the past history and contemporary crises of the entire region. That the author's sympathies lie with the Hungarians in no way detracts from the utility of the book.

ZINNER, PAUL E. **Revolution in Hungary.** New York: Columbia University Press, 1962, 380 p.

The Hungarian Revolution of October 1956 was notable in the vast volume of information which became available after the event. This included radio broadcasts, press reports and most importantly hundreds of eyewitness accounts by the flood of people that fled the country after the Revolution was suppressed. It is probably one of the best documented upheavals in history. A valuable bibliography of the materials is provided in **A Bibliography of the Hungarian Revolution 1956,** compiled by I. L. Halasz de Beky (Toronto: University of Toronto Press, for the Canadian Institute of International Affairs, 1963, 179 p.). In addition to the numerous personal accounts and reports by journalists, two works besides Zinner's stand out as efforts to provide a general analysis of this extraordinary occurrence— the first revolution within a communist-controlled society: Paul Kecskemeti, **The Unexpected Revolution: Social Forces in the Hungarian Uprising** (Stanford: Stanford University Press, 1961, 178 p.), and Ferenc Albert Váli, **Rift and Revolt in Hungary: Nationalism versus Communism** (Cambridge: Harvard University Press, 1961, 590 p.).

Together these books offer the reader an exceptional body of scholarly thought on a contemporary event. Kecskemeti's is the most purely analytical; in substance it is an inquiry into the genesis of a revolutionary situation—why an explosion should have occurred when and where it did. Váli, who escaped from Hungary in November 1956, gives a more extensive historical narrative, extending from the early postwar years, through the Revolution, to the bleak aftermath up to 1961. As the subtitle suggests, his principal theme is the conflict between nationalism and communism. This is certainly a pervasive feature of the years 1945–1956 and was undoubtedly an important factor in the Revolution. It is not, however, altogether satisfactory as the main key to the Revolution itself, which seems to have had its direct source within the communist structure. Zinner's study is particularly valuable in this connection for its portrayal of schisms within the party, and the conflicts among the intellectuals and the cadre élite. Zinner's close familiarity with corresponding events in Czechoslovakia and Poland assists him in drawing out the special features in the Hungarian situation. Any student of the Hungarian Revolution would do well to start from these three books.

JÁSZI, OSZKÁR. **Revolution and Counter-Revolution in Hungary.** London: King, 1924, 236 p.

Oszkár Jászi was an eminent example of a notable cluster of figures who emerged in East Central Europe in the early years of this century—highly educated, humane, democratic, socialist in a non-dogmatic way and largely free of reactionary or integral nationalism. Some entered briefly onto the political scene in the immediate aftermath of the First World War, but nearly all were swept aside— nowhere more than in Hungary—and history has suffered dearly for their defeat.

In this book, an informal and personal analysis, Jászi undertakes to show "the main forces which led Hungary into the two revolutions and the counter-revolution" of 1918–1919. This is not scholarly history at a distance, but it is saved from being the fulminations of an embittered exile by the qualities of Jászi's mind and character. Nearly half the book is devoted to the short-lived Károlyi government (October 1918–March 1919), in which Jászi assumed the thankless post of minister of nationalities. This is the most impressive part and is tantalizing in its picture of a Hungary that might have been, though Jászi was certainly not blind to the enormous foreign and domestic odds against Károlyi's political survival. The months of the Béla Kun régime and of the white terror of the early Horthy régime which followed on its heels were observed from exile and are more definitively treated elsewhere.

Despite the personal nature of this work, it makes for remarkably pertinent reading half a century later.

ACZÉL, TAMÁS and MÉRAY, TIBOR. **The Revolt of the Mind: A Case History of Intellectual Resistance behind the Iron Curtain.** New York: Praeger, 1960, 449 p.

The two authors of this book were highly successful communist writers at the peak of the Stalinist era in Hungary. Ultimately they swung to the anti-Rakosi, pro-Imre Nagy camp, participated in the events of 1956, and were obliged to flee after the suppression of the Revolution in that year. Thus they were in an excellent position to describe the grubby and corrupting intellectual climate of the years after 1945, the dominating figures of the Rakosi régime, the growing crisis within the ranks of the party intellectuals after 1953, and the very important role of the intellectuals in preparing the way for the explosion of 1956. The narrative ends with the famous pulling down of the Stalin statue in Budapest.

KÁROLYI, MIHÁLY, GRÓF. **Memoirs of Michael Karolyi: Faith without Illusion.** New York: Dutton, 1957, 392 p.

The value of memoirs of figures associated with post-1918 Hungary seem somehow to be in inverse ratio to the political success of their authors. Count Károlyi was spectacularly unsuccessful in 1919 and also failed in his effort to work with the Hungarian communist régime after 1945. Yet these recollections of an aristocrat turned radical are eminently worthwhile, and his observations about Hungary and inter-war Europe, where he spent much of his long exile, afford many vivid pictures and insights.

Miklós Kállay, **Hungarian Premier: A Personal Account of a Nation's Struggle in the Second World War** (New York: Columbia University Press, 1954, 518 p.) is narrower in focus and perception but provides a useful, though undocumented, source for Hungary's vicissitudes between 1942 and 1944 as the increasingly unhappy ally of Hitler.

In contrast, Admiral Miklós Horthy had (until the end) a remarkably successful career as Regent from 1920 to 1944. Unfortunately, his **Memoirs** (New York: Speller, 1957, 268 p.) are quite disappointing and far less informative than they could have been.

KERTESZ, STEPHEN DENIS. **Diplomacy in a Whirlpool: Hungary between Nazi Germany and Soviet Russia.** Notre Dame: University of Notre Dame Press, 1953, 273 p.

This book is made up of three rather distinct parts. The first is a concise, somewhat defensive review of Hungarian foreign policy in the inter-war and wartime years. The second deals with the period of utter confusion accompanying the collapse of Nazi power and the coming of the Russians; here the emphasis is chiefly on domestic matters, especially the beginnings of Soviet domination. The third and most valuable part deals with Hungary's efforts at the end of the war to reëstablish itself diplomatically and to defend itself at the forthcoming peace conference (not really covered in this book). Here Kertesz, who was then serving in the Foreign Ministry, is able to give a firsthand picture of the utter hopelessness of the Hungarian bargaining position.

RUMANIA

MITRANY, DAVID. **The Land and the Peasant in Rumania.** New Haven: Yale University Press, 1930, 627 p.

The many volumes of the **Economic and Social History of the World War,** edited by James T. Shotwell, are a surprisingly little-used source. Among the outstanding contributions to the series is this work by David Mitrany. The focus of the study is the important and extensive Rumanian agrarian reforms immediately following the First World War—the nature of the provisions and the effects, so far as they could be measured, of the extensive redistribution of large estates. But the book extends much beyond these years. Mitrany reviews from a "peasantist" perspective the whole sad history of the Rumanian agrarian problem. The book is a major source for the problems and literature of the crisis of peasant agriculture in the developing economies of the Balkans. Although one may worry about some of the statistics (a difficulty in any study of Eastern European agriculture) and query some of the premises, the work is prodigiously full of information and sustained by a real feeling for the long-suffering Rumanian peasant.

ROBERTS, HENRY LITHGOW. **Rumania: Political Problems of an Agrarian State.** New Haven: Yale University Press, 1951, 414 p.

In a sense this is a sequel to Mitrany's study, in tracing the implications for the Rumanian agrarian problem from the promising years of reform through the difficulties and disappointments of the inter-war years and into the catastrophes of the Second World War and its immediate aftermath. The picture the author presents of a crisis-ridden agricultural system, a variety of abortive political approaches to it and the destructive interplay of widespread poverty and an unstable political life is somber. The concluding chapters deal with the first half-decade of communist rule and the redefinition, but not eradication, of old problems under the new dispensation.

FISCHER-GALAŢI, STEPHEN. **Twentieth Century Rumania.** New York: Columbia University Press, 1970, 248 p.

This thoughtful and stimulating survey of contemporary Rumanian history is centrally directed to the question whether the relationship of communist Rumania to the country's "historic legacy" (itself a rather mixed bag of positive and negative elements) had, by the late 1960s, undergone significant transformation. The author presents a generally persuasive picture of a cyclical movement: first, a break with and departure from the past in the initial years of communist rule (1945–1948); then a wholesale move to Stalinism and satellite status; then, increasingly, a stress on "socialist-patriotism," greater domestic autonomy vis-à-vis the Soviet Union, in the last years of Gheorghiu-Dej; and subsequently an effort—symbolized by Ceausescu's attack on Gheorghiu-Dej's own domestic Stalinism—to restate the national legacy within the frame of the "Socialist Republic of Rumania." A work of synthesis, with useful notes and leads for more intensive study of the various themes and topics.

SETON-WATSON, ROBERT WILLIAM. **A History of the Roumanians.** New York: Macmillan, 1934, 596 p.

This is certainly the basic general history of Rumania in English and is probably the best single work by the eminent British student of Eastern Europe. On the whole it is quite sympathetic toward the national aspirations of the Rumanians, though Seton-Watson does not flinch from depicting the "corroding effects of foreign rule" upon public life and politics.

The narrative, which is chiefly political and diplomatic though with some attention to cultural and social questions, carries the story only to the achievement of "Greater Rumania" at the conclusion of the First World War. A more recent and detailed treatment of Rumania's wartime diplomacy is provided by Sherman David Spector, **Rumania at the Paris Peace Conference: A Study of the Diplomacy of Ioan I. C. Brătianu** (New York: Bookman Associates, 1962, 368 p.).

IONESCU, GHITA. **Communism in Rumania, 1944–1962.** New York: Oxford University Press (for the Royal Institute of International Affairs), 1964, 378 p.

This book by a Rumanian-born scholar who has spent the post-1945 years in the West is of importance both for those interested in the tangled course of recent Rumanian history and for those concerned with the comparative study of communism. As a historical work it in effect picks up the narrative from Henry L. Roberts' history of inter-war Rumania, **Rumania: Political Problems of an Agrarian State,** and traces the story through the Stalinist years to the beginnings, in the early 1960s, of Rumania's cautious but very real search for a new relationship with the Soviet Union. Though completed before the death of the Rumanian Communist leader, Gheorghiu-Dej, it well adumbrates developments under his successor Ceausescu.

For the student of communist movements the book offers a valuable analysis of the peculiar features of the Rumanian party since its origins after World War I: the highly unpromising beginnings, the murky history of factionalism, infighting and constant Soviet intervention over the next three decades, the mortal conflict between the "Muscovites" and the local comrades within the party, and the eventual victory of that generally underestimated figure, Gheorghiu-Dej.

MONTIAS, JOHN MICHAEL. **Economic Development in Communist Rumania.** Cambridge: M.I.T. Press, 1967, 327 p.

This book is a singularly gratifying demonstration of a real advance in scholarship on Eastern Europe. John M. Montias, a sophisticated economist who also took the pains to learn Rumanian (and several neighboring languages), here applies the tools of economic analysis and data collection to an appraisal of the Rumanian economy under communist auspices.

After tracing the principal stages of development (reconstruction from 1944 to 1948; the Stalinist industrial drive, 1948–1953; the shifting course of the mid-1950s; and the gathering momentum after 1958) he discusses the agricultural sector, the very important field of foreign trade and finally Rumania's contentious relations with Comecon in the 1960s in the matter of regional integration.

After discounting all the propaganda and recognizing the human and social costs involved, his is a "generally positive appraisal." In the latter years industrial output was growing very rapidly, health conditions were vastly improved, education had spread—all this in a system that, up to 1967, had retained a system of highly centralized economic planning.

CRETZIANU, ALEXANDRE, *ed.* **Captive Rumania: A Decade of Soviet Rule.** New York: Praeger, 1956, 424 p.

In many respects this book is dated, and, as one can surmise from the title, it is hardly dispassionate. Still, this collaborative effort by a number of prominent Rumanians in exile succeeds in giving a picture of the "impact of Communism" on their country that is difficult to find in any one work. Somehow, their combination of fury, sorrow and contempt in commenting upon the economy, cultural and religious life, politics and law in Rumania during the sorry decade after 1945 is a triumph of expressionist portrayal.

Siebenbürgen. Bucharest: Institutul de Istorie Naţională, 1943, 2 v.

Important though Transylvania has been in Rumanian history and in setting much of the tone of Rumanian-Hungarian relations, there is no major, dispassionate study of this beautiful, ethnically diverse land "beyond the forest."

This massive work, with articles by many authors, contains a good bit of information and a good bit of special pleading. It appeared at the time Rumania had lost northern Transylvania to Hungary under the so-called Vienna Award. It can serve as a counterweight to a similar but opposing Hungarian compilation which had appeared somewhat earlier: **Siebenbürgen** (Budapest: Magyar Történelmi Társulat, 1940, 309 p.).

A recent and valuable book on the earlier history of Rumanian nationalism is Keith Kitchins, **The Rumanian National Movement in Transylvania, 1780–1849** (Cambridge: Harvard University Press, 1969, 316 p.).

BULGARIA

ROTHSCHILD, JOSEPH. **The Communist Party of Bulgaria.** New York: Columbia University Press, 1959, 354 p.

This book has proven doubly valuable: first, in adding very substantially to the rather sparse body of serious Western scholarship on Bulgarian history and politics;

second, in its contribution to the comparative study of communism and communist parties. Such works as this, Dziewanowski on the Polish Communist Party; Kousoulas on the Greek party; Ionescu on the Rumanian; Tökés on Béla Kun and Zinner on the Czechs and Hungarians—all reviewed elsewhere—provide a most useful array of serious works on communism in East Central Europe.

Starting with the interesting observation that in 1910 "with but two exceptions, every minister in King Ferdinand's cabinet had only a few years before been a zealous Socialist," Rothschild traces the unique yet highly revealing course of Bulgarian Marxism: the rivalry between Blagoev and Sakazov, the split between "Broads" and "Narrows" (resembling yet differing from the Russian Menshevik-Bolshevik schism of the same years) and the crisis of the First World War. Then came the mutually ruinous conflict with the agrarian Stamboliski, the disastrous September 1923 insurrection and the lean years that followed, with the Bulgarian Communists helpless in their homeland but playing a signal role in Comintern.

One's only regret in regard to the book is that the narrative stops with 1936.

BROWN, J. F. **Bulgaria under Communist Rule.** New York: Praeger, 1970, 339 p.

On the whole Bulgaria was the least noticed and commented upon of the European communist states in the 1950s and 1960s, partly because of its relative remoteness but chiefly because it witnessed no spectacular changes or upheavals, domestically or in its foreign relations. It seemed to proceed along its own unrevisionist course and in harmony with the Soviet Union.

In this concise, well-informed and informative work, J. F. Brown demonstrates the reality of Bulgarian change and ferment—within the party leadership, in agricultural and economic policy, in education and culture. While politics were not as murderous as they had been in the recent (and remote) Bulgarian past, there were real struggles. In the agrarian field Bulgaria was proving to be a genuine experimenter within the framework of collectivization.

One could wish there were more such books for other areas and other periods: unpretentious, thoughtful and to the point.

DELLIN, L. A. D., _ed._ **Bulgaria.** New York: Praeger (for the Mid-European Studies Center of the Free Europe Committee), 1957, 457 p.

This substantial handbook, in the series "East Central Europe under the Communists" prepared under the auspices of the Free Europe Committee, provides a number of useful essays on various facets of Bulgarian life in the first decade of communist rule. Of particular interest are the chapters written by the editor, on politics, political organization, labor and social security, and those by Nicolas Spulber on the economy.

More recent information may be found in Christo Ognjanoff, **Bulgarien** (Nuremberg: Glock and Lutz Verlag, 1967, 496 p.).

JUGOSLAVIA

WEST, REBECCA. **Black Lamb and Grey Falcon.** New York: Viking, 1941, 2 v.

This is a travel book, but it is much more than that. Indeed, it may be, and deservedly, considered the most important single book on Jugoslavia to have been written in English. Miss West did make a journey in the late 1930s, from Slovenia in the north to Old Serbia and Macedonia in the south, and she did write an account of her travels; but she brought to them an incredibly well-stocked mind, a sense of history, exceptional powers of description, great skill as a writer and, most important, an almost alarming and, if one may use the term, feminine perception.

The book is on the grand scale, in its faults as well as its virtues. The diplomatic historian will be worried by some of her reconstruction of the Sarajevo assassination; the student of Jugoslav nationalities may well protest at her treatment of the Serb-Croat conflict. But as one specialist has observed, whatever the flaws, one gains from this book more of a feeling for the country and its people than from many, many monographs. Some passages remain long in one's memory: the ritual slaying of a black lamb in Macedonia leads her to a passionate assault on the doctrine of atonement and on Saints Paul and Augustine.

HALPERN, JOEL MARTIN. **A Serbian Village.** New York: Columbia University Press, 1958, 325 p.

Such books as this and Irwin Taylor Sanders' **Balkan Village** are all too rare in Western literature on Eastern Europe. In 1953–1954 the author, then a young anthropologist, and his wife spent a year in the village of Orašac, in Serbia. The village has historical roots as the locale of the beginning of the Serbian uprising in 1804, but the burden of the book is neither historical nor explicitly political. It achieves rather an intimate picture of the lives of the inhabitants—their work, their way of living, eating and dying, their religion and folk beliefs, their local social organization. The sense of life at this level is indispensable for any real comprehension of higher politics in Jugoslavia or the Balkans. An admirable ethnographic study.

LEDERER, IVO J. **Yugoslavia at the Paris Peace Conference: A Study in Frontier-making.** New Haven: Yale University Press, 1963, 351 p.

The author of this excellent study conscientiously warns the reader that he will not be dealing with reparations, economic clauses, war guilt and such sundry issues at the Paris Peace Conference—only with frontier-making. In all conscience this is subject enough: Jugoslavia was bordered by eight states and had territorial disputes with all but one. While these disputes have been treated in various contexts, the signal advantage of this book is that it brings the whole range of problems within a single frame and shows their important connections with the confused and inchoate Jugoslav domestic politics of the period. Lederer is able to do this in part through his profitable use of Jugoslav sources, most particularly the unpublished minutes of the Jugoslav delegation to the Peace Conference and the Trumbić Papers, housed in Zagreb.

HOPTNER, JACOB B. **Yugoslavia in Crisis, 1934–1941.** New York: Columbia University Press, 1962, 328 p.

On March 27, 1941, a group of army officers overthrew the regency of Prince Paul, then in the course of crucial negotiations with the Third Reich. A fortnight later German bombers attacked Belgrade. This book is a scholarly effort to get at the background, foreign and domestic, of these climactic events in Jugoslav history. Following the assassination of King Alexander in 1934, Jugoslavia faced a monstrous double crisis: the evident collapse of the Versailles system and its corollary, the Little Entente; and the ferocious domestic Serb-Croat antagonism. On the basis of much original material, a good feel for Balkan politics and a humane regard for the losers in this disastrous situation, Hoptner wrote a most valuable analysis that has, inevitably, stirred up controversy but has significantly cleared away some misconceptions, especially with respect to the role of Prince Paul and the import of the fateful Simović coup d'état.

TOMAŠEVIĆ, JOZO. **Peasants, Politics, and Economic Change in Yugoslavia.** Stanford: Stanford University Press, 1955, 743 p.

This book is the happy product of a trained economist with a real sense of history. It is an enormously rewarding portrait of the social and economic problems that confounded Jugoslav politics in the inter-war years. After a very substantial review of the pre-1914 political, social and economic development of the territorial components—Serbia, Croatia-Slavonia, Bosnia and Herzegovina, Dalmatia, Macedonia, Montenegro, Slovenia and Voivodina—it turns to the staggering problem of state construction and consolidation that faced the Jugoslavs after the First World War.

While recognizing the destructive importance of the national issue (especially the Serb-Croat conflict) and the continuing tension between centralist and federalist impulses, the author's attention is focused on the underlying social layer, the peasantry—"an object of politics"—and the core of the book is devoted to the question of agrarian productivity, overpopulation and the generally sick state of farming. Although the agrarian sector may have appeared to be a relatively passive one, Tomašević has identified a crucial theme in Jugoslav, and Balkan, history: the impossibility of creating a healthy political superstructure upon such a depressed base.

This is probably the best single survey of inter-war Jugoslavia as it moved to the crisis of 1941, the terminal point of the book.

ARMSTRONG, HAMILTON FISH. **Tito and Goliath.** New York: Macmillan, 1951, 312 p.

Although this is one of the earlier serious efforts to take the measure of the Stalin-Tito rupture, it remains a notable contribution, chiefly because of the particular qualities Armstrong brought to bear on the subject. For many years editor of *Foreign Affairs,* widely read and widely travelled and with a long-standing interest in Balkan affairs, he had a remarkably sharp eye for the pertinent features of the conflict and for its implications in the communist world and in international affairs.

Armstrong had no particular affection for the Titoist régime or its manner of gaining and using power—except for the central fact that Tito's willingness and ability to thwart Stalin destroyed the myth of the unshakable unity of the communist cosmos. After relating the course of the controversy up to 1950, he examines the repercussions in other communist states. While later books follow the experiences of Gomulka in Poland, of Rajk in Hungary and of Kostov in Bulgaria at greater length and in greater detail, the unravelling effect that would appear dramatically in 1956 is clearly adumbrated in this work.

Readers interested in the documentation of the 1948 schism and its later manifestations should consult: **The Soviet-Yugoslav Dispute: Text of the Published Correspondence** (London: Royal Institute of International Affairs, 1948, 79 p.); Robert Bass and Elizabeth Marbury, *eds.,* **The Soviet-Yugoslav Controversy, 1948–58: A Documentary Record** (New York: Prospect Books, for the East Europe Institute, 1959, 225 p.); and Václav L. Beneš and others, *eds.,* **The Second Soviet-Yugoslav Dispute** (Bloomington: Indiana University Publications, 1959, 272 p.).

ULAM, ADAM BRUNO. **Titoism and the Cominform.** Cambridge: Harvard University Press, 1952, 243 p.

Although this book was prepared shortly after the Tito-Stalin break of 1948 and prior to Stalin's death in 1953, it remains a very useful and perceptive study of the advent of Titoism. Admittedly, a good deal of pertinent information has appeared subsequently, the sources of Soviet policy now seem more complex (as Ulam himself demonstrated in his later work on Soviet foreign policy), and perhaps too much emphasis was placed on the Cominform, a rather shadowy organization as it turned out. Nevertheless, Ulam has an extremely keen eye for the significant questions, an intimate feeling for East European politics, and much salutary hardheadedness. Above all, his emphasis upon the terrible preoccupation with power that lay at the heart of Stalinist communism is indispensable for any understanding of the relations between Stalin and Tito. Also perceptive is his observation that Titoism was a heresy before it became an ideology.

SHOUP, PAUL. **Communism and the Yugoslav National Question.** New York: Columbia University Press, 1968, 308 p.

A perennial but probably unanswerable question has been whether the Jugoslav communist régime can finally put to rest the national animosities which so divided the country in the inter-war years. Thwarted national aspirations and grievances appear to have an almost spore-like quality of remaining latent for long periods and then unexpectedly coming to life. Perhaps more significantly, current dissatisfactions can take on the coloration of old national issues, though the actual stimuli may be quite novel.

In this thoughtful study of the efforts of the Jugoslav Communists, before and after gaining power, to grapple with the national question the emphasis is upon the way in which the Tito régime's own programs have, against all intentions, been productive of regional conflicts not identical with those of the past but gaining from them some of their refractoriness. In consequence the author of this critical but not unsympathetic inquiry is doubtful of the ability of the Communists to tap a real pro-Jugoslav sentiment.

DEDIJER, VLADIMIR. **Tito.** New York: Simon and Schuster, 1953, 443 p.

Vladimir Dedijer, the author of this approved biography of Tito, was himself something of a legendary figure: a journalist and quite sensitive writer, a great bear of a man physically, and a close comrade of Tito in the fiercest fighting of the Partisan struggle against the Germans.

This book, though passionate in its devotion to Tito and Jugoslavia, is a most important source in part because, as Dedijer observes, "to the extent it has been possible, I have told it in Tito's own words." Hence a real sense of the man comes through; the book is particularly valuable in tracing the sources and the course of the Tito-Stalin break. Obviously, many things are not said, but clearly this is an important contribution to the biography of this leading figure of the mid-twentieth century.

There is, of course, a certain irony in the appearance of this book. Written in the full heat of the Soviet-Jugoslav rift (before Stalin's death but when it was evident that the Jugoslavs were holding their own), it stresses the comradely unity of the Jugoslav Communist Party. Very shortly thereafter came the Djilas affair, and Dedijer, one of very few to stand up for Djilas, also fell from favor. Even these events, however, do not diminish the stature of the protagonists: the same qualities of toughness, principle, pride and recklessness that led to defiance of the Soviet Union also and, perhaps, inevitably came to play within the party.

MACLEAN, SIR FITZROY, BART. **The Heretic: The Life and Times of Josip Broz-Tito.** New York: Harper, 1957, 436 p.

The author of this biography was chief of the wartime British Military Mission to the Jugoslav Partisans; he maintained his contacts with Tito over the ensuing years. In consequence this book is written with an intimate knowledge of the climactic period of Tito's resistance to the Germans and with a real and sympathetic appreciation for Tito's dimensions as a political figure and person.

After treating the early career of Josip Broz, his entry into the Communist Party and his rise in the ranks, Maclean turns with evident pleasure to the drama of the years of guerrilla operations (Maclean's own experiences in Jugoslavia have been recounted in **Escape to Adventure,** Boston: Little, Brown, 1950, 419 p.). The second half of the book is devoted to Tito as leader of the Jugoslav People's Republic, his conflict with Stalin and the embarking on the uncharted course of Titoism.

This book is, by necessity, an interim biography, especially as it appeared shortly after the crisis of the Hungarian Revolution and the unhappy Djilas affair. As Tito himself remarked to Maclean, "Remember, there may be more to come." Still, it stands as a solid contribution, British in style and vantage point, to our picture of an extraordinary figure in the twentieth century, whether he is seen as traitor, heretic or father of a new nation.

HAMILTON, F. E. IAN. **Yugoslavia: Patterns of Economic Activity.** New York: Praeger, 1968, 384 p.

For the noneconomist this survey in economic geography is perhaps the best introduction to the economic evolution of Tito's Jugoslavia. After presenting the historical and environmental background, the author in turn discusses the changes in economic policy since 1945, the various sectors of the economy and the highly variegated economic regions of the country. More technical studies, centering on the Jugoslav experiments with planning, are: George Macesich, **Yugoslavia: The Theory and Practice of Development Planning** (Charlottesville: University Press of Virginia, 1964, 227 p.), and Svetozar Pejovich, **The Market-Planned Economy of Yugoslavia** (Minneapolis: University of Minnesota Press, 1966, 160 p.). An extensive and up-to-date Jugoslav text is Jakov Sirotković and Vladimir Stipetić, **Ekonomika Jugoslavije** (Zagreb: Informator, 1967–1968, 2 v.).

HOFFMAN, GEORGE WALTER and NEAL, FRED WARNER. **Yugoslavia and the New Communism.** New York: Twentieth Century Fund, 1962, 546 p.

This is a substantial and comprehensive survey of Titoist Jugoslavia as of the beginning of the 1960s. The two authors, one a geographer, the other a political scientist, have no particular thesis to prove: while they are favorably impressed with some of the achievements of the régime, they are not uncritical with respect to the limits of political tolerance or the effectiveness of the economic experiments. They do feel, however, that Titoism is well on its way to becoming a system on its own, not simply a no-man's-land between East and West.

Also of value as general references for the postwar period are: Robert Joseph Kerner, *ed.*, **Yugoslavia** (Berkeley: University of California Press, 1949, 558 p.), Werner Markert, *ed.*, **Jugoslawien** (Cologne: Böhlau, 1954, 400 p.), and **Yugoslavia** (New York: Praeger, for the Mid-European Studies Center of the Free Europe Committee, 1957, 488 p.).

CAMPBELL, JOHN C. **Tito's Separate Road: America and Yugoslavia in World Politics.** New York: Harper and Row (for the Council on Foreign Relations), 1967, 180 p.

It is the usual and not surprising fate of most "policy" books to look forlornly dated after the passage of a very few years. There are, however, occasional exceptions.

This modest, low-keyed essay on Jugoslavia's foreign policy and on the U.S. stance toward the Tito régime has the flavor of the mid-1960s and is addressed to some issues that have since receded from prominence or been significantly altered. Still, the book remains fresh and pertinent, chiefly because of the qualities of the author. A longtime student of Balkan and Middle Eastern affairs, Campbell has read much, seen much, reflected much and is notably unflappable. His quiet, often wry, observations on the whole history of American-Jugoslav relations are balanced, perceptive and mature. His chapter on Jugoslavia and the "third world" is particularly interesting.

ALBANIA

SKENDI, STAVRO, *ed.* **Albania.** New York: Praeger (for the Mid-European Studies Center), 1956, 389 p.

Albania is the smallest, least well known and least studied of the Balkan states. Scholarly access to the country has been extremely limited in recent years. This handbook, while suffering the inevitable difficulties of the paucity or nonexistence of sources, does provide a solid survey of the nation in the first decade of communist rule, 1945–1955, as well as offering important background information on Albania's history, culture and economy. Organized topically, it is hardly to be read as a unit; an important reference, with a helpful bibliography.

GRIFFITH, WILLIAM E. **Albania and the Sino-Soviet Rift.** Cambridge: M.I.T. Press, 1963, 423 p.

This volume, one in a series on international communism sponsored by the Center for International Studies at the Massachusetts Institute of Technology, is of principal value in carefully tracing the origins and course of the Soviet-Albanian conflict in 1960–1961, a conflict that gains considerable significance through the interesting role it played in the much more portentous schism between the U.S.S.R. and Communist China. More than half the volume comprises a useful selection of pertinent documents. Domestic developments in Albania serve chiefly as background; emphasis is upon international and inter-party affairs.

SWIRE, JOSEPH. **Albania: The Rise of a Kingdom.** New York: R. R. Smith, 1930, 560 p.

This is not a distinguished book. The style is plodding (the author, quite properly, claimed for it "no literary merit whatever"), and the reader may well lose sight of the forest *and* the trees because of the underbrush. Still, it helps fill a gap in our quite unsatisfactory knowledge of Albanian history. A far more scholarly and satisfactory work has superseded Swire's treatment of the pre-1914 years: Stavro Skendi, **The Albanian National Awakening, 1878–1912** (Princeton: Princeton University Press, 1967, 490 p.), but Swire's book is important for the years from the exceedingly brief reign of Prince William of Wied, through the confusion of the First World War and the establishment of the republic, to the rise of Ahmed Zogu and his proclamation as Zog I, King of the Albanians, in 1928.

BALKAN AREA

KERNER, ROBERT JOSEPH and HOWARD, HARRY NICHOLAS. **The Balkan Conferences and the Balkan Entente, 1930–1935.** Berkeley: University of California Press, 1936, 271 p.

This book makes for melancholy reading, as indeed it must have very shortly after its appearance. It is a conscientious and well-documented study by two highly competent American scholars of an abortive effort to achieve some manner of unity and harmony in the Balkans. Unfortunately, as the map in the frontispiece indicates only too clearly, the Balkan Entente encircled Bulgaria; and no way was found to square this circle. Presently each nation was driven into the *sauve qui peut* stance that marked the descent into the Second World War. The work remains of significance, however, both as an able contribution to a facet of recent history and as a reminder of creative, if unrealized, aspirations.

STAVRIANOS, LEFTEN STAVROS. **The Balkans since 1453.** New York: Rinehart, 1958, 970 p.

This is an exceptionally able and readable history of the Balkan peoples, including the Greeks, from the beginnings of Ottoman rule to the peace settlements following the Second World War. Largely superseding Ferdinand Schevill, **A History of the Balkan Peninsula from the Earliest Times to the Present Day** (New York: Harcourt, 1922, 558 p.), about one-third of the text is devoted to the period since 1914. Of particular value is its attention to and understanding of the changing Turkish role in the area. The author is concerned equally with international affairs and with the tangled course of domestic political and social history. Its extensive annotated bibliography should be of great assistance to both scholars and teachers. Together with Robert Lee Wolff's book, **The Balkans in Our Time,** it provides an excellent introduction to the area. One could wish for equally good surveys of other regions, in East Europe and elsewhere.

WOLFF, ROBERT LEE. **The Balkans in Our Time.** Cambridge: Harvard University Press, 1956, 618 p.

Through his professional training as a Byzantinist and his wartime experience as head of the Balkan Section in the Office of Strategic Services, the author was exceptionally well equipped to face the strenuous challenge of writing contemporary history with a sense of historical perspective. While a third of the volume is devoted to a concise but very meaty review of the Balkan peoples from the origins to the outbreak of the Second World War, the central theme is the vicissitudes of the area in the decade that witnessed Hitlerian control, the unhappy and confused dealings of the "Big Three," the communist ascendancy after 1945 and the sovietization that followed. The book is an admirable complement to Stavrianos, **The Balkans since 1453.** Despite the domestic and international changes that took place after the mid-1950s, the book retains a clear focus and a warmth that derives from Wolff's own enthusiasm for the subject. One's only regret is that the book is limited to Rumania, Jugoslavia, Bulgaria and Albania.

LENDVAI, PAUL. **Eagles in Cobwebs: Nationalism and Communism in the Balkans.** Garden City: Doubleday, 1969, 396 p.

The student of the contemporary history of the Balkans encounters a problem when dealing with the period following the crucial years immediately after the Second World War, years well covered by Seton-Watson, Wolff and Stavrianos. Fortunately, a Hungarian-born correspondent, writing in the best tradition of serious Central European political journalism, has provided a knowledgeable account of developments through most of the 1960s in Jugoslavia, Albania, Bulgaria and Rumania. Lendvai obviously has a feel for the area, was able to make regular visits to all the Balkan countries (except Albania) and has done the requisite amount of homework in the monographs, journals and newspapers. He has his preferences and prejudices, but his book serves as a welcome guide through that most uncertain of terrains—the recent but not immediate past.

LADAS, STEPHEN PERICLES. **The Exchange of Minorities.** New York: Macmillan, 1932, 847 p.

This book is one of those that are the delight of the working scholar though its virtues may be excessive for the casual reader. Ladas undertook "to describe and appraise the exchange of minority populations which has taken place from 1920 to 1930 in Bulgaria, Greece, and Turkey." In so doing he carefully followed such tiresome but indispensable details as those involving the disposal of movable and immovable property, the vexing problem of appraisals, the protracted negotiations on debts, indemnities and taxes.

In general, the legal and diplomatic measures represented efforts to catch up with, give sanction to and if possible ameliorate, a vast process of uprooting that was set in motion as a consequence of the First World War. One's conclusion must be that while such exchanges of minorities may indeed permanently resolve past discords, it would be a rash, or callous, statesman who would urge population transfers as a solution: the human costs were tremendous. (A more recent study, emphasizing the Greek side of the picture is Dimitri Pentzopoulos, **The Balkan Exchange of Minorities and Its Impact upon Greece,** Paris: Mouton, 1962, 293 p.)

SWIRE, JOSEPH. **Bulgarian Conspiracy.** London: Hale, 1939, 356 p.

The Internal Macedonian Revolutionary Organization (IMRO) has become an epitome for one's picture of Balkan intrigue, violence and terror. This is the most complete Western account of the movement, its origins, its intricate role in Bulgarian politics and its increasingly hooligan degeneration in the years after 1918. The author, a well-informed British journalist who lived in Bulgaria from 1932 to 1935, writes with a good deal of firsthand knowledge and considerable feeling. He is very critical of Bulgaria as against Serbia and is no friend of Tsar Boris. His particular hero is Damian Veltchev, who was instrumental in putting down IMRO in the mid-1930s.

The organization of the book is a bit awkward, and it is not always easy to thread one's way through the labyrinth of plots and schemes in the 1920s and 1930s, but the study certainly captures the flavor of the seamy side of inter-war politics south of the Danube.

BARKER, ELISABETH. **Macedonia: Its Place in Balkan Power Politics.** New York: Royal Institute of International Affairs, 1950, 129 p.

This little book has the special merit of bringing a quite unmanageable historical issue within reasonably manageable limits. Admirable in the amount of balanced information it presents in small compass, it traces the vexed Macedonian problem from its origins in the 1870s through the inter-war years to its reëmergence during the Second World War and through the 1940s. Despite changes of Greek, Jugoslav and Bulgarian régimes, the Macedonian question proved to be a hardy, and thorny, perennial in their relations.

One can proceed from this study to much more detailed, and usually highly partisan, books reflecting the Greek, Bulgarian, Jugoslav or Macedonian autonomist points of view. But before doing so the reader might well consult Henry R. Wilkinson, **Maps and Politics: A Review of the Ethnographic Cartography of Macedonia** (Liverpool: University Press of Liverpool, 1952, 366 p.). The book may utterly shatter one's faith in the objectivity of maps and cartographers, but it is a brilliantly conceived demonstration of the impact of politics upon scholarship.

SANDERS, IRWIN TAYLOR. **Balkan Village.** Lexington: University of Kentucky Press, 1949, 291 p.

This is an exceptionally rewarding book, the product of extended experience and deep sympathy for the subject. For a number of years in the 1930s the author, an American sociologist, taught at the American College in Sofia. During that time he made an intimate study of Dragalevtsy, a village of some 1,600 inhabitants living not far from the capital but very conservative in their ways (and reputedly of Pecheneg descent). Here, then, was a Balkan peasant community largely unchanged (though it had electric power by then), and Sanders carefully and appreciatively traced in it the cycle of the seasons and the cycle of life. He departed in 1937 but returned to the Balkans at the end of the Second World War, as agricultural attaché at the American Embassy in Belgrade, and was able to revisit Dragalevtsy briefly in 1945. The final three chapters are a poignant account of the impact of vastly accelerated change, including the coming of communism, upon this village.

The book is marvelously evocative and is one of all too few books to provide a real sense of peasant folkways, deep-rooted but ultimately uprooted.

MITRANY, DAVID. **The Effect of the War in Southeastern Europe.** New Haven: Yale University Press, 1936, 282 p.

This book concludes, and in some measure summarizes, the series of volumes on Southeastern Europe in the monumental, if infrequently consulted, **Economic and Social History of the World War,** sponsored by the Carnegie Endowment for International Peace. Subsequent catastrophes and other preoccupations have attracted attention from the quite specific and important theme of this study. Just what was the immediate impact of the First World War upon government, society and economic life of the areas within and adjacent to the Hapsburg monarchy that were subsequently redistributed under the Treaties of St. Germain, Trianon, Neuilly and Sèvres? In the aftermath it was all too easy to dismiss the wartime political and economic changes as "temporary," something to be bracketed. But some very significant and revealing events took place in the war years, whatever the outcome. Mitrany is particularly effective in pointing up the fact that brotherhood-in-arms was far easier to achieve than brotherhood-in-money.

HELMREICH, ERNST CHRISTIAN. **The Diplomacy of the Balkan Wars, 1912–1913.** Cambridge: Harvard University Press, 1938, 523 p.

The Balkan Wars, though of enormous importance, have tended to be overshadowed in interest and in research by the First World War that followed on their heels. And yet the 1913 Treaty of Bucharest, largely the work of the Balkan states themselves, turned out to have established, with only few modifications, the frontiers for the area in the succeeding half-century. Happily, we have in Helmreich's book a solid, well-documented and satisfactory account of these crucial years. It includes a substantial review of intra-Balkan relations in the preceding decade, a substantial account of both wars, the bitter rivalries that emerged among the Balkan states, the contradictions and confusions that beset the great powers in their last, and faltering, effort to operate as the European Concert.

UNION OF SOVIET SOCIALIST REPUBLICS

History: Russia and the U.S.S.R.

FLORINSKY, MICHAEL T. **Russia: A History and an Interpretation.** New York: Macmillan, 1953, 2 v.

Florinsky's two-volume survey of Russian history from the founding of the Kievan state to the Bolshevik victory in 1917 is still the most detailed and reliable textbook available in English. It is divided into three parts, representing the Kievan-Mongol period, the Moscow period and the St. Petersburg period, but in effect four-fifths of the work is devoted to the last period, the eighteenth, nineteenth and early twentieth centuries. Although the early period is treated much too lightly, topics and materials are selected and arranged very carefully within each subdivision corresponding to a reign, and no important aspect of Russian life is neglected.

The author recognizes in history "the play of the contingent and the unforeseen," and themes such as the conflict between social classes or the interplay between the steppe and forest regions—favorite preoccupations of other Russian historians—are avoided in Florinsky's presentation. Instead, much attention is devoted to the sketch of historical personalities, and events are narrated in great detail. A reader being introduced to Russian history might find the reading tedious in places, but intertwined with the factual information are outspoken judgments of a revisionist historian. The conventionally maligned rulers such as Peter III and Paul receive sympathetic reassessment while the achievements of the "great" rulers, Peter I and Catherine II, or even of Stolypin, are seriously disputed.

ROBINSON, GEROID TANQUARY. **Rural Russia under the Old Régime.** New York: Longmans, 1932, 342 p.

A "classic," first published almost 40 years ago, this still remains the most serious and thorough analysis in the English language of the agrarian problem in Russia before the Revolution. The first chapters relate the history of the peasantry before the Emancipation, and the remaining chapters offer a detailed analysis of the terms and consequences of the Emancipation and an assessment of the rural situation on the eve of the Revolution.

It is not quite clear from Robinson's detailed analysis and strictly impartial tone whether the peasants were better or worse off economically after the Emancipation than before, so serious did the agrarian situation remain even after 1861. In spite of his great sympathy for the peasants struggling against both the government and landlords to break out of their impossible situation, Robinson also gives due credit to the government for making some serious and sincere attempts to tackle the peasant problem. Stolypin's agrarian reforms, Robinson shows, did result in some serious changes in the agrarian order and, had the First World War not intervened, a peaceful solution to the agrarian problem might have been worked out.

For a background on peasants up to Emancipation, see Jerome Blum, **Lord and Peasant in Russia: From the Ninth to the Nineteenth Century** (Princeton: Princeton University Press, 1961, 656 p.).

SUMNER, BENEDICT HUMPHREY. **A Short History of Russia.** New York: Reynal, 1943, 469 p.

This survey of Russian history reads like an essay, and not simply because it is "short." Dispensing with the usual chronological outline, the author delves into the

Russian past by discussing seven basic themes that run through it—the frontier, the form of the state, the land, the Church, the Slavic peoples, the sea and the relationship with the West. In each of the seven chapters of the book in which these themes or "influences" are examined, the present situation is described first, then the reader is introduced to the immediate past, and then to the remote historical background. Sumner's style is racy; quick judgments intertwine with frequent quotations from contemporary documents. In spite of the eclectic approach, the book meets the highest standards of scholarship.

Written at a time when the Soviet Union was drawing new attention as Britain's ally against Nazi Germany, Sumner's **Short History** was clearly designed to explain the enigmatic present in terms of the past. The book now appears unmistakably dated, not so much because Sumner's historical knowledge and observation of events in the past have been surpassed as because the perspective from which his history was viewed—the Stalinist Russia of the early war years—has now changed, and much that the great historian was unaware of or only vaguely suspected has now been revealed.

SETON-WATSON, HUGH. **The Russian Empire 1801–1917.** New York: Oxford University Press, 1967, 813 p.

The third volume in the "Oxford History of Modern Europe," this was written primarily as "the history of institutions, classes, political movements and individuals," intended for the English-speaking reader interested in general history, not for specialists in Russian history. "My aim," the author further explains in the preface, "has been to see the period as it was, rather than in terms of what happened after it."

Following the conventional chronological scheme, Seton-Watson has divided the space almost equally among the five reigns under consideration, and the overall impression is that the pre-Emancipation period is treated in greater detail than the ensuing, certainly more crucial and eventful, decades. Foreign policy receives greater attention than is usual in the general surveys of this nature, but there is no serious omission in the selection of other materials and topics. A few errors in judgments and facts, some obvious, are inevitably there, but they are not serious enough to impair the general reliability. The book is impartial and moderate in judgment and notable for its rich store of factual material and extensive bibliography, rather than for any originality of interpretation or colorful style.

BILLINGTON, JAMES H. **The Icon and the Axe.** New York: Knopf, 1966, 786 p.

This attractive book is the most ambitious attempt by a Western scholar to provide a comprehensive history of Russian culture. It is a pioneering work of synthesis, covering the whole modern period from the seventeenth century to the present, with a formidable scholarly apparatus that testifies to the author's industry and erudition. Above all, it is Billington's capacity to draw stimulating comparisons that makes his book so absorbing. Yet this can be a drawback, for the comparisons are occasionally strained or idiosyncratic. Moreover, the author's penchant for symbols leads to a good deal of unfounded conjecture. Indeed, the key symbol of the book, the icon and the axe, is based dubiously on the peasant "custom" of hanging the two objects together on the wall of their huts. Nor is this an isolated example. There is a disturbing number of errors of both fact and interpretation. Cultural matters, moreover, are seldom related to the economic and social conditions from which they at least in part derive. Yet, in spite of these shortcomings, the book is a remarkable achievement. It is an essentially personal work, highly informative, frequently provocative, and written with a liveliness of style and of imagination that will hold the reader's attention from beginning to end.

KIM, M. P., *ed.* **Istoriia SSSR: Epokha Sotsializma (1917–1957 gg.).** Moscow: Gos. Izd-vo Polit. Lit-ry, 1957, 771 p.

———. **Istoriia SSSR: Epokha Sotsializma (1917–1961 gg.).** Moscow: Izd-vo Polit. Lit-ry, 1964, 646 p.

TREADGOLD, DONALD W. **Twentieth Century Russia.** Chicago: Rand McNally, 1959, 550 p.

The two histories of the Soviet period edited by M. P. Kim carry the central theme that since 1917 the "popular masses" have been the "free creators of their own lives." Detailed but tendentious, the books cite as major achievements of the period the replacement of capitalism with socialism and the initiation of the transition to communism.

A few examples will suffice to illustrate the authors' simplistic interpretations and exclusion of important facts and, significantly, how they present the Soviet past to their students. In discussions of foreign policy Russia is at all times depicted as a peace-loving state and the United States generally as the leader of "reactionary imperialist powers." Leon Trotsky and his decisive role in the Revolution of 1917 are virtually ignored. The only reference to his activities of that year is contained in the accusation that he aided the Bolsheviks' enemies by divulging the date of the coup. The 1964 edition also grudgingly concedes that he did not oppose the action.

In both volumes Stalin is briefly chided for his "defects" and for having introduced "illegal repression," although the criticism is more strongly phrased in the second than in the first. But both emphasize that the negative features of Stalin's rule do not detract from the essential virtues of the Soviet system. In the 1957 edition, one year after the inauguration of de-Stalinization, Khrushchev is commended for his campaign against the cult of personality. In 1964, however, when Khrushchev's ouster took place, the author mentions the campaign but deletes the name of its principal architect. (The most exhaustive discussion of the twists and turns of Soviet historical writing can be found in Cyril E. Black, *ed.,* **Rewriting Russian History,** New York: Praeger, 1956, 413 p.)

Donald W. Treadgold has written a comprehensive and balanced account of the same period, although he does not conceal his distaste for Bolshevism. He considers the victory of the Bolsheviks in 1917 to have been a defeat for Russian democracy and the introduction of the First Five-Year Plan in 1928 a "decisive step in the building of Soviet totalitarianism." Unlike the Russian authors, Treadgold views the historical process not as an inevitable unfolding of necessary stages but rather as a complicated series of events at least partially subject to human control. Organized around the "chief threads of political change," the book also devotes adequate space to economic and cultural developments.

MOSELY, PHILIP EDWARD, *ed.* **The Soviet Union, 1922–1962: A Foreign Affairs Reader.** New York: Praeger (for the Council on Foreign Relations), 1963, 495 p.

Diversity is the most arresting feature of this collection of 30 articles on the Soviet Union. All the writings initially appeared in *Foreign Affairs,* and the contributors range from leading scholars in several disciplines to Soviet and United States government officials.

In one of the most intriguing articles, Nikolai Bukharin, a major communist ideologist, earnestly argues that "A phrase like 'the imperialism of the U.S.S.R.' is a contradiction in terms, like 'dry water' or 'square circles.' " In addition, he contends that it is "logically" impossible for a "clash of real interests between proletarian states . . . [to occur]; on the contrary, their real interest is in maximum cooperation." It is hard to take such assertions seriously, but Bukharin's piece serves to remind us that many people find them persuasive. Thus, when a basic conflict does arise between communist countries, the statesmen of each accuse the other of having abandoned the faith.

The volume also contains the famous 1947 article by George F. Kennan, then chief of the Policy Planning Staff of the State Department. Well-informed, judicious and penetrating, Kennan's analysis of the Kremlin's foreign policy under Stalin remains one of the finest examples of official American thinking. Among the outstanding contributions by professional Sovietologists are Bertram Wolfe's study of how Russian historians adjust their views to changes in the political line of the

Communist leadership, Philip Mosely's timely analysis of the forces and factors making for stability in Soviet Russia and Isaiah Berlin's discussion of Soviet cultural trends and their implications for the future. Its catholicity and the high quality of its articles make this a valuable anthology.

Revolution; Lenin Era

AVRICH, PAUL. **The Russian Anarchists.** Princeton: Princeton University Press, 1967, 303 p.

This book, one of the studies of the Russian Institute at Columbia University, helps fill the gap in scholarship on the internal history of the non-communist political parties in revolutionary Russia. It provides a painstakingly detailed survey of the anarchist movement and its various factions from the time of Bakunin to Stalin's purges. The author, a historian at Queen's College, New York, stresses the distinctive strands in the movement, particularly the "Anarchist-Communists" (with violent and idealist tendencies stemming from Bakunin and Kropotkin) and the Anarcho-Syndicalists. He interprets this split as a parallel with the cleavage among the socialists between the peasant-oriented Populists and the industry-oriented Marxists. The Anarcho-Syndicalists saw much of their program and their following captured by the Bolsheviks in 1917, and many of them were absorbed by the Communist Party despite Lenin's eventual repudiation of their decentralist philosophy.

Professor Avrich emphasizes the anti-intellectual bias of Russian anarchism and its prophetic repudiation of the philosophy of Marxism as a rationale for the rule of intellectuals and officials—foreshadowing the theory of the "New Class." The author does not explicitly mention it, but the book is replete with parallels with the European and American student movements of the 1960s, in terms of the emotional rejection of reasoned analysis and the lack of organization and coherent goals.

AVRICH, PAUL. **Kronstadt 1921.** Princeton: Princeton University Press, 1970, 271 p.

This is the first non-Soviet book devoted to the history of the uprising at the Soviet naval base of Kronstadt in 1921. With objectivity and extensive documentation Professor Avrich recounts the background and course of this tragic attempt to defy the communist régime in the name of the Revolution itself.

The book is particularly useful on the social conditions of war communism leading to the revolt and on the involvement of anti-communist emigrés (they hoped for revolt and attempted to aid it but actually contributed nothing). The military events of the uprising are recounted in extensive detail.

Professor Avrich sees the significance of the Kronstadt revolt and its suppression less as the reason for the New Economic Policy than as a landmark in the realization of the totalitarian potential of Leninism.

CARR, EDWARD HALLETT. **A History of Soviet Russia.** New York: Macmillan, 1951–.

This multivolume history is the crowning achievement of an already prolific student of revolution and international relations, well known for such major works as **The Twenty Years' Crisis, 1919–1939** (New York: Macmillan, 1939, 313 p.). No one interested in Soviet policy up to 1929, in the antecedents of Stalin's "great break," can afford to miss the series.

Despite its great length, this is not panoramic history. Thus **The Bolshevik Revolution, 1917–1923** (1951–1953, 3 v.) gives much space to analysis of Bolshevik strategy and tactics, little to the march of events, which are covered more successfully and graphically by such chroniclers as Chamberlin and Trotsky, Sukhanov or Reed. Also, Carr slights the opposition. In fact, his tendency to imply an inner logic of Bolshevik takeover and subsequent policy is controversial all the way through.

Time divisions of the books already in print are apparent from the titles—for example, the fourth volume, **The Interregnum 1923–1924** (1954). For each period politics, economics and international relations are treated in painstaking detail within the limits of Carr's approach. Foreign relations receive a particularly brilliant illumination. The first volume of **Socialism in One Country, 1924–1926** (1958–1964, 3 v. in 4 pts.) contains a description of the social, legal, cultural and religious policy in Soviet Russia and sketches of the leaders locked in the post-Lenin power struggle. Volume one of **Foundations of a Planned Economy, 1926–1929,** written with R. W. Davies (1969, in 2 pts.), treats the economic genesis of the First Five-Year Plan in great depth. Carr's chosen end point is the formal adoption of that plan in May 1929. Two companion volumes, on politics and international relations, are to complete this last installment of Carr's monumental enterprise.

CHAMBERLIN, WILLIAM HENRY. **The Russian Revolution.** New York: Macmillan, 1935, 2 v.

Chamberlin's monumental history of the Russian Revolution is the product of a dozen years of research, largely carried out in the Soviet Union, where the author was an American newspaper correspondent during the 1920s and 1930s. Based on a wide range of sources, it accomplishes the difficult task of providing a comprehensive narrative of the Revolution and Civil War with admirable clarity and scholarly detachment. Its value, moreover, is enhanced by translations of key documents and by an extensive bibliography. One might regret its occasional lack of depth or of imaginative insight, but this is more than outweighed by its reliability, fair-mindedness and objectivity. What is perhaps most remarkable about this work is that, despite the advances in Western scholarship during the 35 years since its original publication, its value remains undiminished. It is still the best general history of the Revolution, indispensable for laymen and specialists alike.

DANIELS, ROBERT VINCENT. **The Conscience of the Revolution.** Cambridge: Harvard University Press, 1960, 526 p.

The focus of this meticulously researched book is the period 1917–1929, in which the leadership of the Soviet Communist Party faced a continuous succession of oppositional groups. Some of these stood to the "right" of the Central Committee leadership, some to the "left"—slippery terms that Daniels elucidates in an original graphic appendix. There was no durable organization of the opposition and many "consciences," including those of Trotsky, Zinoviev, Kamenev and Bukharin. Daniels carefully describes the changing ideas and feeble tactics of these and numerous others, all of whom he finds greatly inferior to Lenin and Stalin as political leaders. Above all, he argues that they were unable to disenchant themselves with Lenin's ideal of the monolithic party, and this paralyzed their resistance to the leadership at crucial junctures. The book is an essential complement to works dealing with the mainstream of the history of the CPSU rather than the opposition.

Studies in depth of Russia's largest party, the Socialist Revolutionaries, are Oliver Radkey's **The Agrarian Foes of Bolshevism** (New York: Columbia University Press, 1958, 521 p.) and his **The Sickle under the Hammer** (New York: Columbia University Press, 1963, 525 p.).

FISCHER, LOUIS. **The Life of Lenin.** New York: Harper and Row, 1964, 703 p.

This is the most ambitious and substantial biography of Lenin in English. Based on prodigious research, it has been further enriched by the firsthand observations of the author, a distinguished American journalist who spent 14 years in the Soviet Union and was personally acquainted with many of the figures—Bukharin and Radek, Chicherin and Litvinov—about whom he writes. Yet on several counts it is a disappointing book. Rambling and unsystematic, it does not present a clear and connected account of Lenin's life. Rather, the story is broken up into a series of essays of varying length and quality in which the reader may easily lose his bearings. Disproportionate space—more than three-quarters of the book—is allotted to the post-revolutionary period, which for all its importance occupied only a half-dozen years of Lenin's life. The emphasis is heavily on narrative and anecdote at the expense of sustained analysis, and the author includes a good deal of trivial information while leaving many larger questions—political, economic and social— unanswered. Moreover, for a writer of Fischer's reputation, the style is surprisingly undistinguished and at times even irritating. As a result, Lenin remains an elusive figure who still awaits a definitive biography.

DEUTSCHER, ISAAC. **Trotsky.** New York: Oxford University Press, 1954–1963, 3 v.

Leon Trotsky has found in Isaac Deutscher a worthy biographer. Only a man of Deutscher's literary gifts could convey to us the life of Trotsky in all its complexity, colorfulness and tragedy. This is not, however, a critical biography in the true sense of the word. Although the author recognizes that Trotsky is not without "blemish or blur," he has immense admiration for him. Moreover, the biographer's political and moral judgments are those of a Marxian for whom Bolshevism before Stalin was at once an irresistible wave of history and the most virtuous régime Russia could have had during that period. His hero's fall from power marks for Deutscher the beginning of the swift decline of the Soviet Union into Stalin's totalitarian horrors.

The first volume traces Trotsky's career until 1921. Here Trotsky is represented as a man of unrivalled intellect among Russian revolutionaries and as a sovereign figure on the revolutionary stage of 1917, towering at times even above Lenin. In the second and third volumes the scene grows more somber with every page. Trotsky is exiled, hounded from country to country and finally assassinated. During the last, most tragic phase of his life, the revolutionary Titan had been reduced to political impotence, a faintly quixotic figure presiding over a loose congregation of intellectuals, GPU agents disguised as his followers and posturing revolutionaries—all of which he called the Fourth International, challenging Stalin's communist empire.

KATKOV, GEORGE. **Russia 1917: The February Revolution.** New York: Harper and Row, 1967, 489 p.

Of the many books which appeared on the fiftieth anniversary of the Russian Revolution this is perhaps the most controversial. The author, bent on dispelling the "myth" that the February Revolution was a spontaneous explosion of mass discontent, merely creates a new myth: that behind a movement of such proportions there had to be some "directing power." On slender evidence he attributes the uprising to various groups of political conspirators, in particular Russian Freemasons who undermined the government from within and German agents who did the same from without. But the fact that several leaders of the Duma opposition were Masons scarcely warrants the conclusion that a "widespread net" of conspirators worked in concert to overthrow the autocracy. Nor can one agree that German agents masterminded the Revolution when one does not know how much "German gold" actually reached Russia or how it was put to use and with what effects. Few scholars, moreover, will share Katkov's unrelieved contempt for Guchkov and Rodzianko, the arch-villains of his drama, and fewer still will accept his portrait of their alleged victim, Nicholas II, as a ruler of serene intelligence and patient dignity. Yet, whatever its defects, his narrative skillfully evokes the mood of intrigue and confusion which surrounded the Winter Palace on the eve of the uprising. This is an intensely personal book, absorbing for all its eccentricity and of more than passing significance.

RUSSELL, BERTRAND RUSSELL, EARL. **Bolshevism: Practice and Theory.** New York: Harcourt, 1920, 192 p.

This book was written in 1920 after Bertrand Russell's return from a visit to the Soviet Union where he had gone at the invitation of the Bolshevik government. It consists of two overlapping parts—an account of his travels within Russia written in the manner of a travelogue, and an analytical appraisal of the new communist society being born and of the Marxian creed of its leaders. He had known that the new régime was harsh and dictatorial, but he had thought these features to be the transient concomitants of the state of siege imposed upon the Bolsheviks by their enemies who had converged to destroy them. Upon closer inspection, however, Russell discovered the dictatorship to have deeper roots independent of the circumstances of siege and war, and that chief among these roots was the fanaticism engendered in the rulers by their belief in the Marxian dogma. He foresaw that the road upon which the Bolsheviks were travelling would not lead to the society of the free and the equal but to one resembling an oriental despotism. With uncanny clairvoyance, and in a luminous, epigrammatic style, he foretells the emergence of a privileged ruling class, the regimentation of the arts, the extinction of intellectual freedom, the revival of an imperial foreign policy.

SCHAPIRO, LEONARD BERTRAM. **The Origin of the Communist Autocracy: Political Opposition in the Soviet State—First Phase, 1917–1922.** Cambridge: Harvard University Press, 1955, 397 p.

The losers of history seldom receive the attention they deserve. This is unfortunate, for political success is by no means the only measure of the worth of a movement, and the belief that triumphant causes alone should interest the historian narrows our view of the past. It is good, therefore, to have this scholarly examination of political opposition to the Bolshevik dictatorship from the Revolution of 1917 to the end of Lenin's active participation in government in 1922. It is the only systematic history of the various revolutionary groups, both inside the Communist Party (Left Communists, Workers' Opposition, Democratic Centralists) and outside (Mensheviks, Socialist Revolutionaries, Anarchists), which rivalled Lenin for power. The story of their struggle and defeat is told with clarity, insight and literary distinction. Schapiro has examined an immense quantity of material, and his analysis is both accurate and penetrating. This is an outstanding and original work, essential for all students of the Russian Revolution and the early years of the Soviet régime.

SHUB, DAVID. **Lenin.** Baltimore: Penguin Books, rev. ed., 1966, 496 p.

This book, by a well-known student of the Russian revolutionary movement, is much more than a biography of Lenin. It is also a history of the Bolshevik Party, of the Revolution of 1917 and of the first five years of the Soviet régime. The author, himself a participant in the Revolution of 1905, was personally acquainted with his subject and therefore writes with the authority of an eyewitness, if not always with the detachment of a professional historian. His uncritical use of sources occasionally leads him to indulge in imaginative excesses about Lenin's private life, notably the fictitious love affair with "Elizabeth K" during the years between 1905 and the First World War. Moreover, while the force of Lenin's personality is amply demonstrated, there is no serious analysis of his revolutionary theories or of his economic policies after the Bolshevik seizure of power. Furthermore, the book is marred by questionable interpretations and occasional errors of fact. Yet, for all its limitations, it has not been superseded by more recent works. It remains a readable and informative study, perhaps the best biography of Lenin in English.

SUKHANOV, NIKOLAI NIKOLAEVICH. **The Russian Revolution 1917: A Personal Record.** New York: Oxford University Press, 1955, 691 p.

Sukhanov is the chronicler par excellence of the Russian revolutions of 1917. Few momentous events in modern history have had as enthusiastic, perceptive and honest a Boswell. His tale, more than a memoir, less than a history, is not as partisan as that of Trotsky and is more balanced and vivid than the eyewitness accounts of Chernov and Kerensky.

This book, skillfully translated and abridged from the original Russian work,

Zapiski o Revoliutsii (Berlin: Grschebin, 1922–1923, 7 v.), by Joel Carmichael, is colorful and important both because of the man himself and because it was written shortly after the event, well before Sukhanov became a servitor of the Soviet state and then, in 1931, an early victim of the Stalinist purges. The author (whose real name was Himmer) was a talented journalist, a non-party Marxian socialist and an inveterate busybody, who was present in Petrograd throughout 1917, from the collapse of Tsardom to the Bolshevik seizure of power.

Though he was sympathetic to the socialist revolution and suspicious of the "bourgeois" parties, Sukhanov judges critically friends and foes alike, concluding that the Bolsheviks, though "champions of democracy," were too dictatorial and should not have taken power alone. His evaluations of leading revolutionaries are perceptive and judicious. His near-hero, Martov, fails because of an ingrained inability to act. Lenin is keen and decisive but sacrifices Marxism to expediency. Above all, Sukhanov catches the mood and excitement of the Revolution and provides an engrossing and invaluable account of this turning point of the twentieth century.

TROTSKY, LEON. **The History of the Russian Revolution.** New York: Simon and Schuster, 1932, 3 v.

An indispensable source for study of the Russian revolutions of 1917, Trotsky's account, despite its title, is not a history. Rather, it is a fascinating memoir, a personal justification and a brilliant Bolshevik interpretation of the event. In his preface Trotsky, an active participant in the Revolution and a major architect of the Bolshevik victory, claims the mantle of "historic objectivism," but his partisanship is clear on almost every page. He glorifies Lenin and the party, castigates and defames Stalin, and ignores or scorns non-Bolshevik parties and leaders.

Yet the challenge of Trotsky's biting analysis cannot be denied. Covering in colorful detail and with a dramatic and dynamic style the full sweep of the Revolution from the fall of the Tsar to the triumph of the Bolsheviks, Trotsky forces the reader to puzzle over new questions, to see familiar events in a fresh light, and to ponder the larger meanings of the momentous upheaval in Russia. Not always factually reliable, Trotsky's narrative nevertheless provides a sense of historical grandeur and a contagious excitement about the Revolution that intrigues and captivates the reader. The dazzling power of his story makes subsequent Soviet accounts schematic and lifeless. This book remains essential to an understanding of the spirit and driving force behind the Revolution and is still the best Bolshevik view of 1917.

ULAM, ADAM B. **The Bolsheviks.** New York: Macmillan, 1965, 598 p.

The title is plural but the subject of this book is not. It is a biography of V. I. Lenin, whom Ulam regards as a singular political genius. This appreciation, which is presented with urbanity and wit, is a notable achievement for the author because he does not conceal his distaste for leftist ideologists and ideologies. But Lenin emerges from the book as one whose native political insight and toughness enabled him to rise above the creed he espoused and did so much to shape. The emphasis is therefore much more on Lenin's active political manoeuvres than on his famous theoretical writings.

Ulam provides an excellent picture of the changing historical environment from which Lenin emerged and in which he functioned. Readers particularly concerned with Lenin's career after the seizure of power will, however, be better advised to read Louis Fischer's **The Life of Lenin.** Ulam's coverage of this crowded era is acute, especially with respect to the dying leader's quarrels with his heirs apparent, but Lenin's last years are treated in relatively brief scope.

WOLFE, BERTRAM DAVID. **Three Who Made a Revolution.** New York: Dial Press, 4th rev. ed., 1964, 659 p.

Through a biographical study of the three outstanding Bolshevik leaders—Lenin, Trotsky and Stalin—Bertram Wolfe provides a detailed and absorbing history of

Russian Marxism from the late nineteenth century to the outbreak of the First World War. It is a pioneering work, based on exhaustive research, which retains much of its value nearly a quarter-century after its original publication. If the portraits of Trotsky and Stalin have been partly superseded by the extensive biographies of Isaac Deutscher, the treatment of Lenin, who occupies a central place in the book, is yet to be surpassed. The author is at special pains to disentangle the numerous inter-party disputes which plagued the Social Democrats from the turn of the century onward. Yet his account is always easy to follow and often brilliantly written. The chief failing of the book is the absence of a proper bibliography and of reference notes, which leaves some of its facts and conjectures open to doubt. Nevertheless, owing to its rich and fascinating story and its elegance of presentation, it has deservedly become a classic.

Stalin Era

DEUTSCHER, ISAAC. **Stalin: A Political Biography.** New York: Oxford University Press, rev. ed., 1967, 661 p.

The most widely read biography of Stalin and one of the most influential books on Soviet Russia, **Stalin: A Political Biography** performs an outstanding interpretative feat: it justifies the rise and reign of Stalin within a Trotskyist world view. In this work Deutscher, who is the distinguished and admiring biographer of Trotsky, in a sense completes the work that was interrupted by Trotsky's assassin—Leon Trotsky, **Stalin: An Appraisal of the Man and His Influence** (New York: Harper, 1946, 516 p.). It also carries on the study of the French supporter of Trotsky, Boris Souvarine, whose pioneering work ends just as Stalin's career as dictator is well started (**Stalin: A Critical Survey of Bolshevism,** New York: Alliance, 1939, 690 p.). Trotsky himself laid the foundations for Deutscher's perspective on Stalin by positing a Thermidorean-bureaucratic reaction to the Russian Revolution in the absence of a continuing, international upheaval. But Deutscher goes farther, seeing in Stalin something more than a contemptible nonentity and even offering a kind of apologia for the purges. Nor does Deutscher regard the Nazi-Soviet Pact of 1939 as a betrayal. In fact, Soviet foreign policy throughout Stalin's lifetime is sympathetically appraised. Although Deutscher added a chapter to the revised edition of the book, subsequent to Khrushchev's attack on Stalin, he did not attempt the kind of thorough revision necessary to encompass the post-Stalin disclosures in Russia.

CONQUEST, ROBERT. **The Great Terror: Stalin's Purge of the Thirties.** New York: Macmillan, 1968, 633 p.

————. **Power and Policy in the U.S.S.R.** New York: St. Martin's Press, 1961, 485 p.

An important theme of **The Great Terror** is party opposition to the creation of Stalin's personal dictatorship. Emphasizing the 1932 "Ryutin Platform" and the "moderating" influence of Kirov, Kuibyshev, Ordzhonikidze and others, Conquest concludes that Stalin did not achieve "absolute autocracy" until February-March 1937 (see Boris I. Nicolaevsky, **Power and the Soviet Elite**). Stalin then proceeded to annihilate many of his own supporters, altering even more radically the composition and functions of the party.

Conquest devotes more attention to the impact of the purges—especially on the upper levels of the party—than to the agonizing question, "Why?" The author believes that Stalin's ruthless desire for "unchallenged power" and his skillful centralized planning and execution of the purges are the crucial explanatory factors. Analyzing important contextual conditions, such as the public confessions of Stalin's chief opponents and their "almost total failure to oppose him *after* his aims and methods had declared themselves," Conquest places heavy emphasis on the authoritarian attitudes and psychological makeup of all Bolshevik leaders, particularly their reification and deification of the party. The author concludes that more than 20 million people perished between 1930 and 1953 as a direct result of Stalinist terror, not including war casualties.

Conquest draws information from a wide range of communist and non-communist sources, published and unpublished. Particularly important are recent Soviet accounts prior to 1965, "official" materials not intended for publication, and information from defectors who had access to political and police evidence or actual experience in Soviet labor camps. A valuable source on the purge instrument is Simon Wolin and Robert M. Slusser, *eds.*, **The Soviet Secret Police** (New York: Praeger, for the Research Program on the U.S.S.R., 1957, 408 p.); on the camp system, see David Y. Dallin and Boris I. Nicolaevsky, **Forced Labor in Soviet Russia** (New Haven: Yale University Press, 1947, 331 p.).

Robert Conquest's **Power and Policy in the U.S.S.R.** is a sequel to **The Great Terror** and in a sense also to Boris Nicolaevsky's **Power and the Soviet Elite.** It is particularly valuable for its coverage of the period before 1953, for it provides a detailed analysis of the Leningrad affair, the obscure events in Georgia and the "doctors' plot." The departure of Stalin is put into proper perspective as we read a continuous account of political trends.

FAINSOD, MERLE. **Smolensk under Soviet Rule.** Cambridge: Harvard University Press, 1958, 484 p.

The data base of this book is unparalleled in Soviet studies. It consists of countless documents contained in the private party files of the Smolensk *obkom* which were captured by the Germans and eventually turned over to the Americans during World War II. These intra-party and interorganizational communications—including hundreds of letters from private citizens—provide a view of Soviet history through the eyes of actual participants in a primarily agricultural province of 6,500,000 people.

Fainsod's analysis of these data is judicious and restrained. His frame of reference is presented, explicitly and implicitly, in **How Russia Is Ruled.** Frequently, however, the author simply describes and synthesizes the contents of the Smolensk archive, letting the documents speak for themselves—especially on questions and time periods for which data are thin and one's inferences necessarily tentative.

To a considerable extent, this technique successfully accomplishes Fainsod's two major goals: to describe the activities of regional and party organs during the 1930s and to analyze the impact of official policies on different groups of the Soviet population (and vice versa). The Smolensk *obkom* bureau is in a sense the central figure in this "biography," illuminating many aspects of Soviet life. Although no subject is examined in exhaustive detail, Fainsod's findings—and above all his documentation—are lasting contributions to Soviet studies. Particularly important are his descriptions of collectivization, of weak discipline in the lower party organs and Komsomol during the early 1930s, and of a wide range of administrative practices and problems. Important topics on which the Smolensk archive sheds relatively little light include national policy-making processes, budgeting and resource allocation at the provincial level, and the staffing of local party committees.

KRAVCHENKO, VIKTOR ANDREEVICH. **I Chose Freedom.** New York: Scribner, 1946, 496 p.

Kravchenko's autobiography is a moving, insightful and exceedingly well-informed document. The author, a Communist Party member from 1929 until his defection in 1944, was a rising young engineer in the Soviet industrial élite. Because of his wide-ranging experience as a party brigade leader during collectivization, a factory manager and division chief in various regions of the U.S.S.R., and eventually a high-ranking official in the R.S.F.S.R. *Sovnarkom,* Kravchenko provides firsthand information about numerous aspects of life in Stalinist Russia: technical education, collectivization, famine, purges, production accomplishments and problems, NKVD harassment, forced labor camps, national defense, Lend-Lease aid and others. In short, Kravchenko's is a perceptive insider's view of Stalinist policy-making and implementation as seen from various middle and top-level managerial and governmental positions during peacetime, the blood purges and wartime. Without embellishments his book traces his responses and growing doubts.

Above all, Kravchenko's book is an indictment—of personal and party dictatorship, of the exploitation and terrorization of the Russian people, of bureaucratic privilege, inefficiency and aloofness, of the perversion of socialist humanitarian ideals. In light of subsequent disclosures, Soviet and non-Soviet, Kravchenko's assertions in this and in his later work, **I Chose Justice** (New York: Scribner, 1950, 458 p.), have borne the test of time exceptionally well. See especially Merle Fainsod, **Smolensk under Soviet Rule,** which gives support to Kravchenko's account, and Bertram David Wolfe, **Khrushchev and Stalin's Ghost** (New York: Praeger, 1956, 322 p.).

Both Kravchenko books respond "no" to the proverbial but important question: "Was Stalin, or Stalinism, an integral, unavoidable, 'necessary' part of the achievements of the period?"

LEWIN, MOSHE. **Russian Peasants and Soviet Power: A Study of Collectivization.** Evanston: Northwestern University Press, 1968, 539 p.

One of the principal tasks of Soviet studies in our time is to reopen some basic problems of Soviet historical development in the light not only of the older known sources but of the wealth of fresh material that has appeared in Russia since Stalin's death. Professor Lewin's work is an impressive example of what can be done along this line. Making full use of the new data contained in the "revisionist" Soviet history of collectivization that emerged during the Khrushchev years, he has reëxamined the complex historical prelude to the Soviet decision to collectivize.

He begins by describing the situation in the Soviet countryside at the end of the NEP period and then launches into a detailed reconstruction of the economic and political developments of 1928–1929 that led to the rural revolution from above at the end of 1929 and after. The argument, in brief, is that the "great turn" came as the culmination of a "chain-reaction" set off by the procurement crisis of 1928, and that the latter in turn resulted from the interaction of three major factors: the overthrow of NEP, the structure of the Soviet state and the personality of Stalin. Although the contribution of the third of these factors remains insufficiently disclosed, this is the deepest and most illuminating account yet produced by a Western scholar of the background to Soviet collectivization, and a work that belongs on the small shelf of classics in Soviet studies. See also Alexander Erlich, **The Soviet Industrialization Debate, 1924–1928.**

MOORE, BARRINGTON, JR. **Soviet Politics—The Dilemma of Power.** Cambridge: Harvard University Press, 1950, 503 p.

Professor Moore's analysis is particularly strong because he does not merely describe, juxtapose or compare similarities and differences between Marxist theory and Soviet practice; nor does he overgeneralize about their influence on one another. Instead, he analyzes intensively the interrelationships and reciprocal effects of these and other factors in numerous different situations and contexts. The result is an important study of the mutual impact of ideas and social change.

Another distinguishing characteristic is Moore's analysis of the changing functions of Soviet ideas and beliefs under situational pressures. Many of "the democratic and populist aspects of Communist ideology" that in the early pre- and post-revolutionary years competed for recognition and adoption as party policy were later used to help create and legitimize highly authoritarian forms of government. A *leitmotif* of Moore's book is that the Bolshevik ideology of means "have swallowed up and distorted the original ends."

Moore consistently emphasizes the adaptive, responsive, flexible nature of Soviet domestic and foreign policy-making. Subsequently he correctly observed that the study's major weakness was its deëmphasis of Stalinist terror, and that its most incisive analysis was of the adaptations in theory and practice "that the Bolsheviks made in response to the dilemmas of political responsibility." Moore reflects on dynamics and prospects in **Terror and Progress, USSR: Some Sources of Change and Stability in the Soviet Dictatorship** (Cambridge: Harvard University Press, 1954, 261 p.).

SCOTT, JOHN. **Behind the Urals.** Boston: Houghton, 1942, 279 p.

Unlike many foreigners who have published their observations of Soviet Russia on the basis of a short trip, John Scott lived for five years (1932–1937) as an ordinary worker in the new steel complex of Magnitogorsk. His perspective on Soviet industrialization in the early five-year plans is sympathetic and even enthusiastic, but he retained his critical balance and records both achievements and failures in Stalin's drive to establish a major industrial base beyond the reach of potential European enemies. Scott considers the patriotism and toughness of the ordinary Russian (and also of members of the minority nationalities that were absorbed in the new labor force) to be the most imposing Soviet asset. He makes it clear that in this period, at least, strong popular support for the régime's economic goals should not be underrated by foreign observers.

Against this, he witnessed enormous wastage and inefficiency under the guise of economic planning, as well as corruption of administrators, hardships for the worker and, finally, arbitrary terror inflicted by the secret police. Scott's interpretation of Stalin's motivation in this, or any matter of high policy, is superficial, but his record of the life and work at the open-hearth level is a valuable contribution.

The best in the literature of disillusion and second thoughts includes André Gide, **Back from the U.S.S.R.** (London: Secker and Warburg, 1937, 121 p.); William Henry Chamberlin, **Russia's Iron Age** (Boston: Little, Brown, 1934, 400 p.); and Eugene Lyons, **Assignment in Utopia** (New York: Harcourt, 1937, 658 p.).

TIMASHEFF, NICHOLAS SERGEYEVITCH. **The Great Retreat.** New York: Dutton, 1946, 470 p.

The author was a young liberal Russian lawyer in 1917 and emigrated in 1921. The book was one of the most thoughtful and important analyses of Russia to appear just after World War II. Timasheff believed that late Tsarist Russia was moving dynamically toward industrial development and constitutional democracy before World War I. He saw the Revolution as an immense shock which stopped the country in its tracks and forced it into new, peculiar and unnatural paths for 15 years. Inevitably, he thought, the nation would reassert itself, producing the "Great Retreat," predominant under Stalin from 1934 on. This involved reëmergent Russian nationalism as opposed to internationalist rhetoric, national minorities and foreign powers, a revival of economic and class distinctions, a return to a highly structured legal system, a strong family ethic and so on. He judged World War II to be the victory not of communism but of the Russian people. In spite of many arguable points, so much of this analysis is now accepted without debate that this once controversial book is now rarely read. The great retreat in history is ably sketched in Klaus Mehnert's **Stalin versus Marx: The Stalinist Historical Doctrine** (New York: Macmillan, 1953, 128 p.).

ZAGORIA, JANET D., *ed.* **Power and the Soviet Elite: "The Letter of an Old Bolshevik" and Other Essays by Boris I. Nicolaevsky.** New York: Praeger (for the Hoover Institution on War, Revolution, and Peace), 1965, 275 p.

Nicolaevsky was a Menshevik before the Revolution and throughout decades of emigration, during which he was a leading archivist and analyst of Soviet affairs. The "Letter" was his retelling of information and views received from Bukharin in Paris in early 1936 on the life and struggles of the Soviet élites since 1932. It is the most important source for those who believe that Stalin's power was really threatened by moderates led by Kirov before and during the Seventeenth Communist Party Congress in 1934, and an early source for the now accepted belief that Stalin arranged the ensuing murder of Kirov. The other essays, from the 1950s and early 1960s, support the theses of the "Letter," analyze struggles in the Kremlin from Stalin's death through Khrushchev's "Secret Speech," and supply political biographies of Bulganin, Konev and Suslov. Nicolaevsky's contacts with Russia continued throughout the Stalin era, his information was astonishingly correct, and his interpretations were anti-Stalinist but always intelligent, complex and interesting.

SALISBURY, HARRISON E. **The 900 Days: The Siege of Leningrad.** New York: Harper and Row, 1969, 635 p.

The outstanding book on the Second World War in Russia is Harrison E. Salisbury's account of the siege of Leningrad. While Alexander Werth's **Russia at War, 1941–1945** (New York: Dutton, 1964, 1,100 p.) provides a popular history of the entire war, Salisbury deserves preëminence on the basis of his remarkably evocative description and his careful consideration of a wide range of Soviet works. His admiration for the ordinary Leningrader is immense and well documented. Many of the military leaders, too, receive full credit for steadfastness and intelligence. Even A. A. Zhdanov, the Politburo member who was the supreme commander of the besieged city, emerges as a sympathetic figure, relentlessly striving to save the city from the Germans and himself from the hazards of Kremlin politics. Stalin's failure at the opening of the war has received no better presentation, and the subsequent story of the siege reveals much of the centralized, brutal and conspiratorial character of his wartime leadership.

While providing a close-range picture of both civil and military society in besieged Leningrad, Salisbury has curiously little to say about the role of the Communist Party, either on the level of command or in the life of the ordinary citizen. It is debatable whether this is an accurate assessment of the importance of the party in this situation or a reflection of Soviet reticence in this matter. In any case Salisbury's work will endure as an impartial monument to the suffering of thousands of Leningraders.

Khrushchev and After

CRANKSHAW, EDWARD. **Khrushchev: A Career.** New York: Viking, 1966, 311 p.

Khrushchev was one of those politicians who look better in retrospect than in power. The reader of this book cannot but wonder if Crankshaw would have been as critical of his subject if he had been writing five years later. His description of Khrushchev's period of power—"dictator by consent"—is essentially accurate. He does not, however, analyze the costs Khrushchev had to pay to obtain his colleagues' consent. There was an unhappy logic about Khrushchev's career which does not quite come through in this biography. Khrushchev did give a high priority to improving the Soviet standard of living. (This is the argument of Mark Frankland's more favorable account, in **Khrushchev,** New York: Stein and Day, 1967, 213 p.) To accomplish this aim he needed a reduction in arms expenditures and détente with the United States—even if this had to be purchased at the cost of Chinese hostility.

Though one may disagree with the point of view, this book is a readable and well-documented account of Khrushchev's career which is especially good (given the paucity of data) on the prewar period and which aids understanding of developments Crankshaw treats skillfully in **Khrushchev's Russia** (Baltimore: Penguin, rev. ed., 1962, 178 p.).

Khrushchev Remembers. Boston: Little, Brown, 1970, 639 p.

The publishers explain that these purported words of Khrushchev are put together from "various sources." Strobe Talbott has translated the text, and edited it, but we do not know in what respects. A long-time specialist on Khrushchev and Russia, Edward Crankshaw, has provided commentary and notes. There is an earthy, "authentic tone" to the book as Crankshaw states, but it is not present everywhere, and inaccuracies and omissions abound. Some discrepancies, such as in dates, can be attributed to the fact that these words are not Khrushchev's finished, re-thought memoirs. Probably they originate at least partly in tapes of ex-promptu remarks. Until more is known about their sources and editing, judgment must be reserved on the completeness of their authenticity and the reasons for their being leaked into capitalist book covers.

Khrushchev's avowed purpose in the recollections, if they are his, is to rebut military memoirs praising Stalin, to warn against repeating mistakes committed by Stalin and in his name, and to assist party "self-purification." The book has a rudimentary reform platform: rehabilitate all purged leaders, cut arms spending, lift restrictions on travel and culture (but with "no peaceful coexistence in ideology"), and put leaders "under popular control."

The text is contradictory, the apologia of a former Stalinist condemning Stalinism. There are no smashing revelations for those who have read descriptions of Stalin and his court in Svetlana Alliluyeva's **Twenty Letters to a Friend** (New York: Harper and Row, 1967, 246 p.), Milovan Djilas' **Conversations with Stalin** (New York: Harcourt, Brace and World, 1962, 211 p.), Viktor Kravchenko's **I Chose Freedom,** in the Kremlinology of Conquest and Nicolaevsky, and in Khrushchev's secret speech—reproduced in this book, along with a Khrushchev chronology, sketches of fellow leaders, good photographs and useful index.

Khrushchev's reminiscences on foreign affairs, if genuine, provide some insights (however mendacious or incomplete) into how international crises looked from the Soviet side and furnish a key to the ideologically based drives and suspicions in Soviet foreign policy. Stances such as "no peaceful coexistence in ideology" and goals such as "the complete domination of the socialist, communist system throughout the world" not only will not guarantee peace but would rule out the very reforms Khrushchev advocates. Sakharov's goals in **Progress, Coexistence and Intellectual Freedom** provide a more consistent and viable alternative.

LEONHARD, WOLFGANG. **The Kremlin since Stalin.** New York: Praeger, 1962, 403 p.

The theme of this book is that the Soviet Union is no longer a riddle, that it was (and is) possible to do intelligible political analysis about the Soviet system. The author was among the first to challenge the well-established view that the Soviet system was a totalitarian dictatorship whose real character had not been changed by the death of the dictator.

Leonhard had an inside knowledge of the Soviet system unparalleled among Western writers. All of his experience, however, was acquired during the Stalin period. It is all the more surprising, therefore, that Leonhard did not share in the consensus. He was the first to apply the "interest-group" approach to the study of Soviet society. He described the system as consisting of five "pillars": the party, the economic administration, the state bureaucracy, the army and the police. The leaders of these groups made up a "new elite" of a system evolving toward oligarchic rule. Today we might disagree with some of Leonhard's analysis; for example, he probably should have included the scientists and intellectuals as a separate interest group. It may be that he granted too much independent power to the police. These comments should not, however, detract from the value of a book which genuinely broke new ground in the analysis of Soviet society.

This is a revised version of a work, "Kreml ohne Stalin," first published in 1959, with the English translation by Elizabeth Wiskemann and Marian Jackson. Another distinguished study by a German observer is Boris Meissner, **Russland unter Chruschtschow** (Munich: Oldenbourg, 1960, 699 p.).

LINDEN, CARL A. **Khrushchev and the Soviet Leadership: 1957–1964.** Baltimore: Johns Hopkins Press (in coöperation with the Institute for Sino-Soviet Studies, George Washington University), 1966, 270 p.

This study of power and policy and "the combustion produced by their interaction" in the Soviet leadership is written by one of the few specialists in Soviet politics who was aware of Khrushchev's precarious position before the Soviet leader's abrupt dismissal in 1964. The book emphasizes the "conflict model" of politics within the top party leadership. According to this approach, the leaders formulate policies in the course of continuous struggles, form opposing factions on particular issues, win limited victories and suffer temporary setbacks—all described by Professor Linden in suitably military terms.

Using published sources, primarily the Soviet press and periodicals, the author portrays Khrushchev as a "leader of reform," and an "iconoclast" whose career as Party First Secretary was largely devoted to dynamic innovation and a break with the Stalinist legacy. Khrushchev's antagonists are generally described as "conservatives" whose views are "orthodox," whether the debate concerns steel *vs.* chemicals production, or questions of ideology. Finally, Khrushchev's downfall is attributed to a growing unfavorable reaction to his "radicalism" on the part of the conservatives, joined by the "more cautious reformers." The entire work can be recommended as a highly competent, informative account of factional disputes within the Soviet leadership during the Khrushchev years, and the final chapter provides a particularly commendable summary of Khrushchev's political legacy and the major attributes of this important transitional period in Soviet political history.

RUSH, MYRON. **Political Succession in the USSR.** New York: Columbia University Press, 1965, 223 p.

The more enduring sections of Professor Rush's book describe, with considerable insight and thoroughness, the process by which Lenin, Stalin and Khrushchev emerged into positions of predominant leadership in the Soviet Communist Party. To some extent, this portion of the book is drawn from the author's earlier work on the subject, particularly **The Rise of Khrushchev** (Washington: Public Affairs Press, 1958, 116 p.) and **Khrushchev and the Stalin Succession** (Santa Monica: RAND Corporation, 1957, 224 p.).

The less enduring aspect of the book consists of an attempt to formulate a general theory of Soviet succession crises, based on the material from the Stalin and Khrushchev cases. According to this theory, upon the "physical or political demise" of the primary leader, a succession crisis is "inevitable" due to the failure of the Soviet system to provide a legitimate process for leadership succession. According to Rush's "cyclical theory of Soviet politics," "a stable phase of personal rule" is followed by "an unstable phase of succession crisis," and then by a "final phase" in which the crisis is resolved.

While the theory is still of considerable interest as an interpretation of the events and historical period from which it was drawn, the author's insistence on the inherently unstable and transitory nature of the collective leadership pattern has apparently fallen victim to the remarkably durable relationships in the group of leaders who have populated the Kremlin since the removal of Khrushchev in 1964.

A second edition, which includes two additional chapters on the post-Khrushchev leadership, appeared in 1968. This edition retains the cyclical theory, but somewhat inconsistently concludes that "prolonged oligarchical rule [which] would change the character of the Soviet regime" is now a possibility.

TATU, MICHEL. **Power in the Kremlin: From Khrushchev to Kosygin.** New York: Viking, 1969, 570 p.

This is a remarkably detailed account of the political history of the Soviet Union from 1960 until early 1966. The emphasis is on the period up to the retirement of Khrushchev (October 1964), when Tatu was resident in Moscow as correspondent for *Le Monde.*

Tatu has not solved the more intriguing mysteries about the Soviet leadership such as sudden demotions or Khrushchev's part in the Soviet response during the U-2 affair. He does offer some interesting guesses, even if they are often based on rumor or other unpublished sources. The virtue of this book is that, despite the author's frequent Kremlinological excursions into the darker reaches of Soviet politics, he does provide a very solid analysis of the system and the conflicting styles of the leadership, before and after Khrushchev. Tatu also points out (and we need to be reminded of this) that October 1964 was a supremely important turning point in the evolution of Soviet politics. Stalin's associates were intimidated, and prevented from taking action against the dictator, not only by fear for their own lives but by a genuine concern for the stability of the régime itself. Now, however, the leader *has* been overthrown without serious disruption to the system. This fact alone changes the nature of political leadership in the U.S.S.R. and provides some guarantee against a return to simple autocracy.

This is a valuable book, and until the Kremlin archives are opened to scholarly inspection it will undoubtedly be a standard work.

Foreign Policy; International Communism

RUBINSTEIN, NIKOLAI LEONIDOVICH. **Vneshniaia Politika Sovetskogo Gosudarstva v 1921–1925 Godakh.** Moscow: Gos. Izd-vo Polit. Lit-ry, 1953, 566 p.

A rewritten and enlarged version of the author's **Sovetskaia Rossiia i Kapitalisticheskie Gosudarstva v Gody Perekhoda ot Voiny k Miru, 1921–1922 gg.** (Moscow: Gos. Izd-vo Polit. Lit-ry, 1948, 461 p.), this is one of the most impressive efforts by a leading Soviet historian to provide a scholarly study of the foreign relations of Soviet Russia in its first years of peace and coexistence. Both the 1948 volume and this expanded version seek to portray Soviet diplomacy as victorious in overcoming repeated efforts by the major capitalist countries to isolate or exploit the new Soviet state, and thus to demonstrate the success of the "Leninist-Stalinist" policy of coexistence of the two world systems for a prolonged period. Carefully avoiding any attempt to analyze or criticize Soviet policy and largely ignoring international communism and revolutionary movements, Rubinstein directs his efforts mainly at describing Soviet relations with the Western powers, tracing those relations particularly through detailed accounts of the Genoa, Hague and Lausanne Conferences.

A professor of the Party Academy of Social Sciences at the time of his death in 1952, Rubinstein established his reputation with his work on Russian historiography in the early 1940s. Although attacked in 1948 for being "objective and academic," his work found more favor with the party after his death, and his reworked manuscript was published shortly after the passing of Stalin in 1953. He has made use of Western sources as well as Soviet works and archives (especially some new material on the famine relief of 1921–1922), but both the source notes and bibliography found in the earlier volume were omitted from this edition.

MINTS, ISAAK IZRAILEVICH and OTHERS, *eds.* **Sovetskaia Rossiia i Kapitalisticheskii Mir v 1917–1923 gg.** Moscow: Gos. Izd-vo Polit. Lit-ry, 1957, 694 p.

A collective work of 23 authors, edited by the distinguished Soviet historian, I. I. Mints, from material prepared for the Institute of History of the Soviet Academy of Sciences, this volume brings together some of the best Soviet accounts of the important 1917–1923 period. One of the most inclusive and complete histories of its kind ever published in the Soviet Union, it is further distinguished by the extraordinary amount of attention devoted to revolutionary activities and movements not only in Eastern and Western Europe but also in the Near and Middle East, the Far East and Latin America. The persistence and universality of struggle, on the part of the "proletariat" in the West and the national liberation movements in the colonial and "semi-colonial" countries, emerges as the salient feature of the "new era" begun by the Bolshevik Revolution.

Although dealing more openly with their main theme than most Soviet works, the authors preserve the usual dichotomy between Soviet relations and party-revolutionary activities and thus obscure if not completely hide any connection between the two. Accounts of the Comintern and revolutionary movements in

Germany, China, India and elsewhere ignore leading figures such as Zinoviev, Trotsky, Radek, Borodin and Roy. A notable feature, however, is the treatment of the difficulties experienced by foreign communists, particularly those caught in the contradiction between Soviet support for national leaders in countries such as Egypt, Turkey and India and the anti-communist policies of such leaders at home. The only sources cited in this hefty volume with no bibliography are Lenin, Stalin and resolutions of the Soviet Communist Party.

FISCHER, LOUIS. **The Soviets in World Affairs.** New York: Cape and Smith, 1930, 2 v.
Fischer's work on Soviet foreign policy in 1917–1929 is a classic, one of very few books on Soviet affairs deserving this title. A sympathetic and readable account, the study derived its lasting significance from the sources used rather than from the interpretation presented. As a foreign correspondent in Moscow from 1922, Fischer followed developments on a day-by-day basis. Moreover, he knew many of the top officials, including the People's Commissar for Foreign Affairs, Chicherin, and his eventual successor, Litvinov. His friendship with them and with others such as Rakovsky, Karakhan and Borodin enabled him to draw not only upon their reminiscences but also on their archives. Fischer did not neglect other sources of information, however, including documents published abroad as well as in the U.S.S.R. and reminiscences of foreigners involved in relations with the Soviet Union.
The basic organization of the book is chronological, each of 31 chapters treating a successive headline episode in Soviet international relations. The structure makes it difficult to follow a single topic over the entire period, but a good index alleviates the problem.
Fischer's own postwar abridgment of the work (Princeton: Princeton University Press, 1951, 617 p.) reduced its volume by about one-sixth. The revision occurred after Fischer's change from sympathy to antipathy regarding the Soviet Union, and therefore involved not only tense changes and elimination of detail but also a perceptible shift in passages considered by the disillusioned Fischer of the 1950s too friendly to the U.S.S.R. or too hostile to Western opponents of Soviet policy. For the original flavor of the book it is necessary to use the 1930 edition.

FISCHER, LOUIS. **Russia's Road from Peace to War: Soviet Foreign Relations, 1917–1941.** New York: Harper and Row, 1969, 499 p.
The late Louis Fischer initially intended this book to be a history of Soviet foreign policy superseding his 1930 work, **The Soviets in World Affairs,** and extending the coverage to the present. Instead, he cut the work off with Hitler's invasion of the U.S.S.R. For the 1920s Fischer had access to unique sources. These advantages did not exist for the following decade, though Fischer found some new material throwing light on events leading to World War II in archives at Bonn, London and Paris, in the Trotsky papers at Harvard, and in interviews with survivors.
His earlier sympathy for Soviet foreign policy is, of course, no longer present in this work. Fischer assigns major blame for the events leading to the war to Russian policy and portrays the Nazi attack on the Soviet Union as an understandable, if aggressive, response to major Soviet provocation. There are unresolved contradictions in the presentation. For example, Fischer seems to have believed that the Soviet Union could have, and should have, stayed out of war with Germany. He also suggests, however, that the U.S.S.R. should have bolstered an incipient anti-Nazi coalition.

ZORIN, V. A. **Osnovy Diplomaticheskoi Sluzhby.** Moscow: Izd-vo "Mezhdunarodnye Otnosheniia," 1964, 352 p.
A Soviet Deputy Foreign Minister (1956–1965) with extensive experience in the diplomatic service here presents a textbook designed primarily for the training of future Soviet diplomats. In addition to providing information on such matters as

the structure and functions of the organs which formulate and execute foreign policy in the Soviet Union and other countries, Zorin has given the book a personal stamp by basing his analysis in considerable part on his own experience and by offering shrewd observations concerning the rules of the diplomatic game as he has observed it. He avoids politically controversial subjects—for example, Khrushchev's name occurs nowhere in the book, even though the doctrine it professes is largely the Khrushchevan brand of peaceful coexistence, and even though it was sent to the press a full month before his overthrow. Similarly, Communist China is generally passed over in silence, although on occasion, for example with regard to Chinese opposition to the 1963 test ban treaty, Zorin's reticence breaks down momentarily. The book's continuing value lies in the insights it provides into the mental world of a successful Soviet diplomat and into the kind of basic training undergone by Soviet diplomats in the making.

LEDERER, IVO J., *ed.* **Russian Foreign Policy: Essays in Historical Perspective.** New Haven: Yale University Press, 1962, 620 p.

The participants in a conference of specialists in Russian-Soviet foreign relations were asked to look for elements of continuity and change in Tsarist and Soviet foreign policies. The results were presented under five headings: contexts, formation, instruments, action and prospects. Most of the essays stressed the Russian aspect of their topic, but those dealing with propaganda and international organizations were obliged to concentrate on Soviet phenomena, and only one, that on domestic politics, made effective use of the experiences of the Provisional Government.

One might maintain that the broader the perspective taken by an expert, the more likely he was to find elements of continuity between Russian and Soviet behavior—a generalization particularly supported by the pieces on objectives, "isms," modernization, Russia and America, and contemporary perspectives. The functional and area specialists, on the other hand, tended to see greater differences, but this may have been due to their greater emphasis on historical description than on comparative conceptualization. No matter what the approach, the depth of knowledge of the authors is impressive, and therefore the reader, especially one informed on Soviet foreign policy, can make his own comparisons based on the historical narrative. There is certainly much food for thought in this volume.

DALLIN, ALEXANDER, *ed.* **Soviet Conduct in World Affairs.** New York: Columbia University Press, 1960, 318 p.

This volume reprints 15 important articles on Soviet foreign policy originally published in various years from 1947 to 1958. One of the articles included is unique in that it had a major impact on American public attitudes toward the U.S.S.R. after World War II—George F. Kennan's "X" article on containment, "The Sources of Soviet Conduct." Other essays in the collection, such as Daniel Bell's "Ten Theories in Search of Reality," were influential in academic circles. A symposium on ideology and power politics to which R. N. Carew Hunt, Samuel L. Sharp and Richard Lowenthal contributed stands out from most of the material in the collection by providing a direct clash of opposed views, in this case on the priority of Marxism-Leninism or of "national interest" in determining the external behavior of the Soviet Union.

None of the selections presents a defense of Soviet foreign policy, and there is no Soviet material included. Most of the essays deal with broad questions on a fairly high level of abstraction. Except for Philip E. Mosely's discussion of Soviet negotiating techniques, based on his experiences opposite Soviet representatives in wartime negotiations, there is not much here for readers interested in detailed analysis of Soviet foreign activities at particular times and places. Despite these qualities, and the dated character of some of the material, Dallin's collection is still useful as a book of readings on international relations and Soviet foreign policy.

BARGHOORN, FREDERICK CHARLES. **The Soviet Cultural Offensive.** Princeton: Princeton University Press, 1960, 353 p.

Barghoorn's account of Soviet cultural relations with the United States and other countries, although somewhat out of date, remains useful as a mine of detailed information on the subject, especially for the period 1945–1960. The author, a professor of political science at Yale, has had many years' experience both as a government and an academic specialist on Soviet affairs. Frequent trips to the U.S.S.R. provided him with personal impressions to supplement his mastery of documents. The book antedates, however, Barghoorn's arrest in the Soviet Union in 1963 on espionage charges, from which he was freed after President Kennedy's intervention.

The study describes the organizations involved in Soviet foreign relations outside the politico-economic field, considers the objectives and practices of Kremlin policy in this area, and devotes separate chapters to relations with developing countries, Western Europe and the United States. Unfortunately, the material is rather haphazardly organized and includes an excessive amount of trivia. While Barghoorn offers opinions freely, the analysis is less rigorous than impressionistic and subjective. The final chapter offers some "conclusions" which, however, are not conclusions on the determinants of Soviet cultural policy but recommendations to Americans on managing contacts with Soviet officials and citizens.

ULAM, ADAM B. **Expansion and Coexistence: The History of Soviet Foreign Policy, 1917–67.** New York: Praeger, 1968, 775 p.

This brilliant synthesis from Western and Soviet sources by the author of **The Bolsheviks** and **The Unfinished Revolution** (New York: Random House, 1960, 307 p.) is an unsurpassed history of Soviet foreign policy.

In its coverage of Soviet diplomacy up to the Six Day War, the most important and controversial portion of the book concerns the cold war. The author's analysis of its causes will comfort neither hardliners blaming it on Western concessions nor revisionists blaming it on Western threats and hard line. Ulam sees it as the virtually inevitable outcome of "internal" causes on both sides. Basic differences in the Soviet and U.S. systems resulted in unreconcilable differences in the psychology of their diplomacy, in U.S. immaturity and Soviet suspicion. A mercurial Western public opinion confronted a felt Soviet need for isolation in which to lick wounds, catch up in production and weaponry and conceal weaknesses. The West overestimated Soviet capacity and desire to aggress. The skillful diplomatist, Stalin, underrated American staying power and readiness to intervene, misled by his ideology and our waverings. Then there were Stalin's "irrational quirks." That this irrationality "did not preclude a degree of calculation and caution when it comes to foreign affairs" is a point Marshall D. Shulman also made well in **Stalin's Foreign Policy Reappraised** (Cambridge: Harvard University Press, 1963, 320 p.). One might wish for some more explicit summary of "lessons learned," specifically abjured by Ulam, and for a bibliography or discussion of sources.

Ulam attributes continued U.S.-Soviet tensions to "anachronistic assumptions" on both sides and emphasizes the persistent force of a pre-revolutionary Russian credo: "That which stops growing begins to rot." His analysis of internal, systemic causes of East-West conflict may be compared with the sociology of the Institute of Philosophy, U.S.S.R. Academy of Sciences, **Sotsiologicheskie Problemy Mezhdunarodnykh Otnoshenii** (Moscow: Izd. "Nauka," 1970, 328 p.).

TRISKA, JAN F. and FINLEY, DAVID D. **Soviet Foreign Policy.** New York: Macmillan, 1968, 518 p.

This textbook is unconventional. Unlike Adam Ulam's **Expansion and Coexistence,** it has no summary of the development of Soviet foreign relations. Nor is there a systematic coverage of current policies. Triska and Finley address themselves to "how" and "why" questions. They provide a series of essays on selected aspects of such topics as the making of foreign policy in the U.S.S.R., the role of ideology, Soviet relations with other communist parties and states, with developing countries and Western states, and with Soviet use of international organizations and international law.

Probably the two chapters of most interest consider Soviet-Western relations and the extent of risk-taking in Soviet behavior. The authors advance a "multiple symmetry model" to explain Soviet-American relations in terms of stimuli and responses which repeatedly disrupt or seek to restore the equilibrium. The chapter on risk-taking presents a rather elaborate treatment "testing" various hypotheses about Soviet propensity to take risks, but emerges with unexciting conclusions.

This study is strong on statistics, charts, graphs and sweeping generalizations. Its novelty lies in the emphasis on methodology, however, rather than in the discovery of fresh material or the advancement of unorthodox viewpoints.

DALLIN, ALEXANDER and OTHERS. **The Soviet Union and Disarmament: An Appraisal of Soviet Attitudes and Intentions.** New York: Praeger (for the School of International Affairs, Columbia University), 1964, 282 p.

The outgrowth of a conference organized by Columbia University in 1963, this book is one of two studies on Soviet arms control policy during the Khrushchev decade sponsored by the U.S. Arms Control and Disarmament Agency, the other being **Khrushchev and the Arms Race: Soviet Interests in Arms Control and Disarmament, 1954–1964,** by Lincoln P. Bloomfield, Walter C. Clemens, Jr. and Franklyn Griffiths (Cambridge: M.I.T. Press, 1966, 338 p.). The Dallin book focuses more on arms control issues and policy implications than **Khrushchev and the Arms Race,** which is more historical in character. Dallin considers the uncertain balance of "pro" and "con" factors affecting Soviet interests in arms control matters. His work is one of the first to evaluate the range of economic, societal and military considerations conditioning the Kremlin's position on arms control.

The book analyzes a series of measures, extending from general and complete disarmament to limited confidence-building gestures, noting both their origins and their prospects. A chapter is given over to issues of secrecy and inspection, matters of great concern in the early 1960s. Written in the year following the 1963 test ban and other accords, the book has a more optimistic and even-minded orientation than most earlier Western writings on these themes. It also benefits from the revelations of the 1962–1964 Sino-Soviet polemics and contains an appendix on the disarmament issue in the dispute between Moscow and Peking.

LARSON, THOMAS B. **Disarmament and Soviet Policy, 1964–1968.** Englewood Cliffs: Prentice-Hall, 1969, 280 p.

Written under the auspices of Columbia University's Russian Institute, this book is one of several studies on Soviet arms control policy carried out by university research centers under contract to the U.S. Arms Control and Disarmament Agency. Larson's book is one of two works that focus on the period between Khrushchev's ouster and the Warsaw Pact intervention in Czechoslovakia, the other being **The Arms Race and Sino-Soviet Relations,** by Walter C. Clemens, Jr. (Stanford: Hoover Institution, 1968, 335 p.). Larson's study and a companion volume, **Soviet Politics since Khrushchev,** edited by Alexander Dallin and Thomas B. Larson (Englewood Cliffs: Prentice-Hall, 1968, 181 p.), place Moscow's arms control policy squarely in the context of political and economic developments within the U.S.S.R. and key changes in military technology. The book's tenor is sober and somewhat skeptical, emphasizing that the arms control accords of the period occurred mainly in peripheral domains of limited strategic interest to either superpower. The tone minimizes the significance of the nonproliferation treaty and suggests that the U.S.S.R. and the United States will continue a quest for nuclear dominance, despite doubts about the value or feasibility of strategic superiority.

Comprehensive in scope yet succinct, the brief argument leaves some of the author's interpretations not fully explained. The book contains a useful selective bibliography, a chronology of events, 1964–1967, and an analysis by Kenneth

Liberthal of the impact on the Soviet Union of Chinese disarmament policies, 1964–1967.

RA'ANAN, URI. **The USSR Arms the Third World: Case Studies in Soviet Foreign Policy.** Cambridge: M.I.T. Press, 1969, 256 p.

Contrary to what the main title might suggest, this book is not a full study of Soviet military aid to the developing countries; the subtitle is a more accurate description of its contents. Ra'anan offers two very detailed case studies—the Soviet arms deals with Egypt and Indonesia. Both are minutely analyzed in the multidimensional context of factional struggle in Moscow, the Sino-Soviet rivalry, domestic politics in Cairo and Djakarta, and the manipulations of the two recipients to take advantage of great power competition.

A wealth of data has been amassed, though not always effectively marshalled. The book nevertheless leads to several substantial factual revisions, the most important of which is dating the initial sales of communist arms to Egypt in February 1955, not in the following September as is generally accepted. Its revisions are an important contribution to the study of the origins of the post-Stalin involvement of the Soviet Union in the third world, treatment of which in diplomatic studies often abounds in schematic and therefore incorrect generalizations.

Moreover, the author pioneers in analyzing in depth the process of Soviet policy-making for the developing countries. Given the lack of open sources for a straight-forward diplomatic history, Ra'anan succeeds very well with the available published materials and with circumstantial evidence in suggesting the multitude of domestic and foreign pressures that shape decisions. Although the book does sketch the general evolution of Soviet relations with the developing countries, Western literature still lacks a comprehensive study of Soviet policy toward the newly independent states.

MIRSKII, G. I. **Armiia i Politika v Stranakh Azii i Afriki** [Army and Politics in the Asian and African Countries]. Moscow: Akademiya Nauk, 1970, 348 p.

This is the first book on the role of the military in the developing countries to appear in the Soviet Union. It is a wide-ranging study by a scholar who, since 1962, has been prominent among the advocates of a fresh analysis of social structure in the newly independent countries free of the rigid Marxist stereotypes.

Mirskii considers it impossible to classify schematically all the policies that the military in the nonindustrial world are likely to pursue. In looking for possible clues to the officers' political role, he does not examine the structure or level of economic development of the society in which a coup takes place as thoroughly as does J. C. Hurewitz, for example, in **Middle East Politics: The Military Dimension.** Mirskii's analysis focuses more on the army itself as the matrix of an independent sociopolitical institution with its own corporate interests to uphold. Like Morris Janowitz in **The Military in the Political Development of New Nations** (Chicago: University of Chicago Press, 1964, 134 p.), he recognizes that the organizational qualities that make it possible, and tempting, for the military to intervene are the obverse of the characteristics that limit their ability to bring about social and economic change. But he goes beyond this observation to stress the danger that officers will act as a military bureaucracy intent on safeguarding its own status and interests instead of effecting change on behalf of other social groups or the entire nation. Western military aid is briefly discussed, but the goals and effects of Soviet arms sales are not mentioned. (See Uri Ra'anan, **The USSR Arms the Third World.**)

Despite its occasional deference to a political line—*e.g.* Soviet allies are found more "progressive" than other régimes—it is a scholarly inquiry, free from the usual oversimplifications in Soviet studies which have pigeonholed the military as the instrument either of progress or of reaction, depending on the class interests it presumably served.

GOLDMAN, MARSHALL I. **Soviet Foreign Aid.** New York: Praeger, 1967, 265 p.

One of the most important changes in Soviet foreign policy following Stalin's death was the launching of a major program of economic assistance to developing countries. Goldman's book is a readable, detailed and dispassionate account of these Soviet activities in foreign economic and military assistance, though the scope and significance of military aid receive somewhat skimpy treatment. The author, a professor of economics at Wellesley College, uses both Soviet and other sources for his data, which are profitably supplemented by material from on-the-spot visits in recipient countries and the Soviet Union. Comparisons with American experience enrich the treatment. Working on a subject burdened by fragmentary and contradictory "facts" and figures, Goldman provides numerous statistical tables on commitments, deliveries and repayments, almost all well documented.

The book is valuable both for readers seeking a general appraisal of Soviet programs, difficulties and accomplishments in the foreign aid field, and for students requiring a base for further research on the subject.

Joseph S. Berliner's **Soviet Economic Aid: The New Aid and Trade Policy in Underdeveloped Countries** (New York: Praeger, for the Council on Foreign Relations, 1958, 232 p.) is an earlier book that makes statistics of Soviet aid to underdeveloped countries meaningful by comparing them with the free world's aid and trade, with the underdeveloped countries' growth and with Soviet production.

ZIMMERMAN, WILLIAM. **Soviet Perspectives on International Relations, 1956–1967.** Princeton: Princeton University Press, 1969, 336 p.

The author notes that prior to Stalin's death in 1953 there was little if any original thinking or writing in the Soviet Union about the theory of international relations (aside, that is, from the basic writings of Lenin in this field). Soviet writings on international relations tended to be a derivative and secondary branch of social and political studies, being based on the allegedly immutable foundations laid down by Marx, Engels, Lenin and (at least until his death) Stalin.

Zimmerman points out that it was primarily the Soviets' perception of the revolutionary effects of atomic weapons in international relations which led to a sharp break with this tradition and to the rapid development, from 1956 on, of a new and flourishing body of doctrinal writings on the theory and practice of international relations. He traces the lines of this development, as the political climate of the Khrushchev era fostered more speculative views and the work of Soviet specialists in this field gained in range, depth and methodological sophistication. Acutely aware of the concurrent growth of international relations theory in the West, the Soviet specialists made a valiant and partially successful effort to elaborate an independent Soviet theory which would combine fidelity to observed fact with continued reliance on the Marxist-Leninist theoretical base, and which would serve as a reliable ideological shield against the insidious and potentially disruptive effects of the rival theories being developed in the West.

Tracing in detail the development of this new field of Soviet scholarship, Zimmerman shows that it can serve as a valuable guide to understanding the shifting influences, aspirations and goals of Soviet foreign policy. An effort, somewhat labored, to convey and evaluate the reverse perspectives has been made by William Welch in **American Images of Soviet Foreign Policy** (New Haven: Yale University Press, 1970, 316 p.).

BORKENAU, FRANZ. **World Communism: A History of the Communist International.** New York: Norton, 1939, 442 p.

This book, written in the very exceptional circumstances of the eve of the outbreak of the Second World War, retains its value as a key history of the Comintern during the major phases of its existence. Actually, the bulk of the work is devoted to the hectic days of the 1920s, years of considerable spontaneous action, zigzags in the tactics, but of increasing control by Moscow. By the time

Stalin was firmly in power in the Soviet Union, the Comintern had become little more than one of his instruments of foreign policy.

Borkenau had been a member of the German Communist Party through most of the 1920s and had worked for the Comintern in a technical capacity. By the time of writing, however, he was definitely out of the movement and in opposition. Despite charges of "renegacy," this book is an example of the advantages that may be gained through the combination of initial intimacy and involvement followed by subsequent increasing distance. Borkenau was a formidable and penetrating student of contemporary politics (George Lichtheim felicitously refers to his being "daring or even reckless in the discovery of new territory"); this book probably presents his skills at their best and most disciplined. His later work, **European Communism** (New York: Harper, 1953, 564 p.), while abounding in striking perceptions, inclines to run roughshod over the facts and must be used with caution.

MEYER, ALFRED GEORGE. **Communism.** New York: Random House, 3rd ed., 1967, 241 p.

Responding to a widely felt need for a knowledgeable and thorough yet succinct and readable introduction to the subject of communism, Professor Meyer of the University of Michigan has drawn upon his several specialized studies on Marxism, Leninism and the Soviet political system to produce one of the best summary treatments. While acknowledging that communism has become an elusive term meaning many different things, he has achieved a notably comprehensive coverage of the various aspects and forms which it has assumed, including its theoretical foundations, the structure and evolution of the Soviet state, and the organization, international activities and recent problems of the communist movement around the world.

Meyer avoids being either superficial or tendentious. With a gift for meaningful generalization, he approaches his task with the competence of a leading specialist and one who recognizes and seeks to neutralize his own biases. His effort to illuminate the character of the modern Soviet system by a comparison with a giant American corporation remains controversial, but his analysis never fails to be thought-provoking, and it is not likely to be surpassed in its happy combination of breadth of coverage with disciplined brevity of presentation. On the Soviet system alone, see **The Soviet Political System: An Interpretation** (New York: Random House, 1965, 494 p.), by this same author.

MOSELY, PHILIP EDWARD. **The Kremlin and World Politics.** New York: Vintage, 1960, 557 p.

More than 20 years of the author's expertise in domestic and foreign policies of the U.S.S.R. are covered in these articles. The essays are loosely grouped into chronological parts covering World War II diplomacy, early postwar problems, the cold war and the post-Stalin era. Articles written during Stalin's time are usually supplemented by an introduction or footnotes which place them in context and update factual information. Opinions have bravely been left unaltered for all to see.

Professor Mosely combines research and journalism in those articles dealing with the purges, intellectual freedom and travel. In one of the most enlightening pieces, that on the Berlin settlement, he draws on his own participation in negotiations with the Soviets. The essays fuse the academic researcher's thoroughness with the insights of an experienced observer. Several deal with the challenge of Soviet foreign policy and its implications for the United States.

MORRIS, BERNARD S. **International Communism and American Policy.** New York: Atherton Press, 1966, 179 p.

The main thesis of this thoughtful book is that American policy, blinded by a powerful hatred of communism, has been grossly insensitive to tensions and conflicts within the communist world. In the first part of his study, Professor

Morris gives a brief but sound analysis of the changing character of the communist movement. He succinctly assesses the importance of the drift toward polycentrism while at the same time underlining the continuing influence of the idea of world revolution. Thus, though communism as an organized unitary movement has ceased to exist, he sees it as remaining strongly internationalist in outlook.

In the second, more provocative section, Morris seeks to demonstrate that its quasi-paranoid hostility has dulled the reactions of the United States to the disintegrating tendencies at work in the communist world. This ideological animus, he argues, has led to numerous policy weaknesses and errors. In particular, the United States, in his judgment, has been slow to realize the significance and implications of the Sino-Soviet schism, less than creative in its response to Moscow's policy of peaceful coexistence, blindly and unnecessarily hostile to all radical nationalist movements (which Washington tends automatically to identify as communist) and all too ready to use force to repress revolutionary activity, a policy which led to the U.S. involvement in Vietnam. Though in places overdrawn and rather generous in its assessment of Soviet purposes, the argument presented by this former State Department official is challenging.

NOLLAU, GÜNTHER. **International Communism and World Revolution: History and Methods.** New York: Praeger, 1961, 357 p.

Günther Nollau is a West German lawyer, and he approaches the history of European communism almost as an attorney. His work is a careful summation of the history of the movement with copious references to sources and secondary materials. While he lacks the immediacy, cogency and certainly the intenseness of earlier works such as Franz Borkenau's **World Communism,** he is free of the need of political catharsis often evinced in the works of former Comintern functionaries.

Nollau's work professes to be an examination of international communism; in fact, his exclusive concern is really with Europe, Chinese communism being dismissed in pitifully few pages and other non-European movements being ignored. The book is really a history of the Comintern, the Cominform and de-Stalinization in Europe, and on these subjects Nollau offers useful, reasonably reliable and lucid analyses. He breaks no new ground and has no new theories or hypotheses to offer. Yet he is in control of his biases (although one might wonder if Wilhelm Pieck's moment of cowardice in 1919 is really worth a separate appendix) and as such offers his reader an honest, if dated, history of European communism; no more and no less.

ROMANOVSKII, SERGEI K. **Mezhdunarodnye Kul'turnye i Nauchnye Sviazi SSSR** [International Cultural and Scientific Relations of the U.S.S.R.]. Moscow: Izd-vo "Mezhdunarodnye Otnosheniia," 1966, 240 p.

The author has good qualifications for writing this book, having been for a number of years the chairman of the U.S.S.R.'s Committee for Cultural Relations with Foreign Countries, a government agency under the Council of Ministers. Romanovskii includes no inside information, however, and the work has value only as a chronicle of Soviet participation in cultural and scientific relations with other countries. Most of the material concerns the decade 1956–1965, though foreign cultural relations under Tsarism and in earlier Soviet periods are briefly reviewed. Following the short narrative are appendices printing texts of Soviet exchange agreements with some countries, plus lists of other countries having Soviet exchange agreements, and of international scientific and cultural organizations in which there is Soviet participation.

Except for some overly kind words on Intourist, there is no discussion of how the Soviet Union organizes its exchange activities. Also missing is any analysis of the purposes underlying Soviet programs of international exchange, any allusion to changes in Soviet policy in this area, and any admission that other countries might have encountered difficulties stemming from that policy, particularly during the Stalin era. In sum, this book assembles some facts and figures which may be useful for scholars but offers no contribution to understanding, either individual or international.

LEONHARD, WOLFGANG. **Child of the Revolution.** Chicago: Regnery, 1958, 447 p.

A fascinating political biography of a young German communist who, after ten years' residence and political training in the Soviet Union, became a member of the "Ulbricht group," which in 1945 established the foundations of communist rule in Soviet-occupied East Germany. In 1949, after four years as an official in the central apparat of the ruling Socialist Unity Party, Leonhard fled to Jugoslavia.

This well-written volume, one of the most revealing of the "literature of defection," has two outstanding merits. First, it vividly describes life among European communists living in the Soviet Union before and during the Second World War. His account of the Comintern school, where children of revolutionaries from all over the world were admitted for training as Soviet political agents, is especially revealing. Second, the book portrays the slow but certain intellectual alienation of a gifted young communist who sacrificed a promising career as an East German party functionary for the sake of his socialist principles. As Edward Crankshaw observes in his introduction, Leonhard writes not as a lapsed communist or a refugee from the harshness of the Soviet system (which, as he stresses, treats its political servants only too well) but "as a convinced Marxist who thought he was a better socialist than his Soviet foster-parents." One of the West's most eminent Soviet specialists, Leonhard has also written **The Kremlin since Stalin** and has contributed to many publications from West Germany where he now lives.

FONTAINE, ANDRÉ. **History of the Cold War.** New York: Pantheon Books, 1968–1969, 2 v.

This massive history of the cold war claims to be revisionist but, by recent American standards, is only mildly so. The author's perspective as a seasoned French journalist helps him thread his way through the mass of events he deals with and imparts a welcome detachment from conventional American biases. At the same time, these volumes exhibit none of the naïveté about Stalin's intentions which have marred some other revisionist accounts.

Largely descriptive, lively and (in the best sense) journalistic, this study covers the entire period from 1917 to 1963, with a tentative epilogue on the subsequent years. The first part, carrying the story to 1945, while sensible enough, is essentially unoriginal and perhaps superfluous. The later years are dealt with in greater detail and with greater insight.

Fontaine sees the cold war not as a struggle between good and evil but essentially as the duel between "two states with differing universalist ideologies, each with sufficient strength to make it a candidate for world leadership." Its outcome he depicts as a draw—"an armistice without victor or vanquished." He finds it miraculous that a sort of coexistence was indeed established, with rules of the game, some mutual comprehension and even interpenetration on the increase (as of 1963).

Any thoughtful reader will find both a wealth of information and opinions to quarrel with—beginning with the assertion that the essence of the conflict was "the antagonism between socialism and capitalism." Considering the vast scope of the study, the factual errors are minor. The sources used are solid though far from exhaustive, with perhaps excessive reliance placed on French accounts.

Military Policy

GARTHOFF, RAYMOND L. **Soviet Military Policy: A Historical Analysis.** New York: Praeger, 1966, 276 p.

This study by one of the West's best-informed students of Soviet politico-military affairs offers a discerning analysis of the role and influence of military power in Soviet foreign and internal policy, as conditioned over the past few decades by the interplay between communist goals and theory on the one hand, and the operative politics and interests of the Soviet state on the other. Beginning with a survey of the uses of military power in pre-Soviet Russia, Garthoff's book points out both similarities and differences in the politico-military methods of Tsarist Russia and the Soviet Union. The study also gives close attention to the evolving role of the military as a sociopolitical group in Soviet society, finding that a new military class has emerged in the Soviet era, essentially apolitical as was the military élite in Tsarist times, though for somewhat different reasons. The author believes that only in the rather unlikely event of a collapse of party rule is there much prospect that the military would try to assume a leading role in the political realm.

A major portion of this work is devoted to appraisal of the place of war in the outlook of the Soviet leadership, as affected by changes in the political, strategic and technological environment of the nuclear age. Briefly summarized, the main argument is that the old doctrinal relationship between war and revolution has undergone revision to accord with the power realities of modern times. While military-technical advances have greatly increased Soviet power, at the same time they have served to rule out nuclear war as an instrument of political choice, except as an ultimate defensive recourse. This does not mean, however, that the Soviet leaders have not set great store on the possession of modern military power, which remains of positive value in their eyes—both as a deterrent to possible Western attack and as a "counter-deterrent" to discourage Western military resistance to communist pressures.

While recognizing that possible developments may "radically change means of waging war," Garthoff takes the conservative position that technological and geostrategic changes do not offer any prospect to the Soviet Union "of gaining 'military superiority' or of offsetting the continuing assured American retaliatory deterrent capability." Although the book was written before the Soviet missile build-up of the late 1960s had greatly narrowed the margin of strategic power between the U.S.S.R. and the United States, its thesis that the Soviet Union is unlikely to acquire meaningful superiority has not been disproved by events.

SOKOLOVSKII, VASILII DANILOVICH. **Voennaia Strategiia** [Military Strategy]. Moscow: Voen. Izd-vo, 3rd rev. ed., 1968, 464 p.

When the first edition of this book was published in 1962, it was described in the Soviet press as the first comprehensive work on the subject to appear in the Soviet Union since 1926. Prepared by a collective group of authors headed by Marshal Sokolovskii, the book also immediately attracted wide notice in the West, where it was regarded as a significant landmark in post-Stalin Soviet thinking on strategy and war in the nuclear-missile age. Basically, the work marked a broad shift from past Soviet preoccupation with continental land warfare toward greater focus on the problems of global strategic war, paralleling in a sense Khrushchev's "new strategy" statement of January 1960. At the same time, however, the book also reflected internal debate over many aspects of doctrine and strategy, as attested by the authors themselves when a second revised edition was brought out in 1963. Among debated issues explored further in the revised volume were: the possibility of limited wars without "inevitable" escalation to nuclear war; the wider role opening up for naval forces; the feasibility of attaining effective defenses against missiles; and the proper relationship between civilian authority and the military leadership in planning the country's defense posture.

The third edition, published in 1968 shortly before Marshal Sokolovskii's death and well after Khrushchev's political demise, has been cosmetically revised to expunge references to Khrushchev, but otherwise little in the way of fresh substantive material has been added, suggesting that Soviet authorities may no longer regard the volume as a suitable forum for airing current strategic issues and exploring new concepts. Despite the somewhat dated character of the third edition, however, the Sokolovskii work as a whole still stands as the single most informative document on Soviet strategic thought in the open literature. Moreover, part of its value to students of the subject lies in the comparison that can be made between the successive editions.

Two English-language versions of the first edition have been published: **Soviet Military Strategy,** analyzed and annotated by Herbert S. Dinerstein, Leon Gouré and Thomas W. Wolfe of the RAND Corporation (Englewood Cliffs: Prentice-Hall, 1963, 544 p.), and **Military Strategy: Soviet Doctrine and Concepts,** with an introduction by Raymond L. Garthoff (New York: Praeger, 1963, 396 p.). Neither the second nor the third editions have been published commercially in English, but a noncommercial translation showing changes in all three editions has been prepared by Harriet Fast Scott.

KOLKOWICZ, ROMAN. **The Soviet Military and the Communist Party.** Princeton: Princeton University Press, 1967, 429 p.

The competition and coöperation between two of the dominant institutions in the U.S.S.R. is the central theme of this work, based in part on research carried out at the RAND Corporation. The relationships between the military and the Soviet Communist Party are traced from 1917 through the mid-1960s, with particular emphasis on the post-Stalin years. Kolkowicz studies the cyclical movements implicit in the rise of military "professionalism" under Marshal Zhukov; the ascendance of the party apparat in the military and the Khrushchev reforms, 1957–1960; and, later, the reassertion of military claims after Khrushchev's fall. The author outlines in fascinating detail his thesis about the importance of World War II battlefield associations (*e.g.* the "Stalingrad group") in affecting career patterns in the 1950s and 1960s.

Kolkowicz goes beyond his historical survey to consider the fundamental dilemmas posed for the party leadership by the growing complexity of military technology and the party's dependence upon military technocrats. His research combines solid historical investigation with imaginative methods designed to maximize the insights obtainable from the available data.

This book provides insights not only in the realm of interest groups in the U.S.S.R. but also regarding the prospects of Soviet society generally and the opportunities for superpower coöperation.

WOLFE, THOMAS W. **Soviet Strategy at the Crossroads.** Cambridge: Harvard University Press, 1964, 342 p.

This study, part of research conducted by the RAND Corporation for the U.S. Air Force, focuses on the dilemmas facing Soviet strategists in the aftermath of the Cuban missile crisis and the détente symbolized by the 1963 Moscow treaty on nuclear testing. The works of Soviet military writers are studied on a variety of themes—the question of war as an instrument of policy; the debates between "modernists" and "traditionalists;" the character of Soviet military relations with the Warsaw Pact countries and with China. But Wolfe's underlying concern is whether Moscow would rest with a position of minimum deterrence (confronted, however, with U.S. strategic advantages in some domains) or pursue a posture of equality or perhaps superiority vis-à-vis the United States. This scholarly and balanced analysis provides important background for understanding the competing impulses of later years, such as the mass deployment of SS-9 missiles and the SALT negotiations.

Wolfe's essay may be read profitably in conjunction with such works as **Soviet Military Strategy,** edited by V. D. Sokolovskii (Englewood Cliffs: Prentice-Hall, 1963, 544 p.), and earlier Western writings such as Herbert S. Dinerstein, **War and the Soviet Union** (New York: Praeger, rev. ed., 1962, 268 p.), and Raymond L. Garthoff, **Soviet Strategy in the Nuclear Age** (New York: Praeger, rev. ed., 1962, 301 p.). The Wolfe book also forms part of an international dialogue reflected, for example, in later editions of Sokolovskii's compilation.

ZHUKOV, GEORGI K. **Vospominanie i Rasmyshlenie** [Reminiscences and Reflections]. Moscow: Novosti Press Agency, 1969, 736 p.

Many Soviet military men have committed their reminiscences of World War II to print, but none has had the stature of Marshal Zhukov, who was not only a leading wartime figure but the only military professional to be admitted later—if but briefly—into the select circle of top political leaders in the Party Presidium. His memoirs, therefore, even though affording scant insight into his personal life, are of signal interest in historical terms.

The principal thrust of the Zhukov account is its defense of the way the war was run by Stalin and the general headquarters group (Stavka), of which Zhukov himself, as Stalin's first deputy and chief of the general staff, was a key member. Among controversial issues treated at length are the criticism by some Soviet historians that proper prewar preparations were not carried out in the time "bought" by the 1939 Nazi-Soviet Pact; the charge of failure to avoid being caught by surprise by the Nazi attack of June 21, 1941; and the assertion, made by Marshal Chuikov, that Berlin could have been taken in February 1945 by the Red Army and the war ended sooner but for errors of judgment by Zhukov and Stalin.

With respect to relations with the West, Zhukov seconds the customary Soviet argument that Lend-Lease help to Russia was greatly exaggerated and, apart from a ritual nod to the valor of Western troops, takes a generally deprecatory view of the Allied contribution to victory over Germany. A number of interesting sidelights emerge, however, such as Zhukov's comment on the Potsdam Conference: he notes that Stalin did indeed appreciate the significance of Truman's Potsdam revelation about the American atomic bomb, and that Stalin remarked to Molotov that evening that he was going to tell Kurchatov (the physicist in charge of Russia's atomic program) "to step things up."

Throughout the Zhukov memoirs, there are also some notable omissions. In describing the initial formation of the Red Army, for example, Trotsky's contribution is omitted. Nothing is said about the curious period of Soviet-German military-industrial collaboration from Rapallo to Hitler's rise, although the West is blamed for helping to rebuild German industry. Another subject studiously skirted, except for one noncommittal paragraph, is Stalin's purge of the military command in 1937. In the wartime portion of the memoirs, Khrushchev's role is deflated and Stalin's portrayed rather sympathetically.

Portions of the Zhukov memoirs appeared in English just prior to publication of this work under the title **Marshal Zhukov's Greatest Battles** (New York: Harper and Row, 1969, 304 p.).

ERICKSON, JOHN. **The Soviet High Command: A Military-Political History.** New York: St. Martin's Press, 1962, 889 p.

Much information not only about the high command but also about the entire Soviet military establishment emerges in this major study of Russian sources. No other single book contains as much material on this subject; however, Erickson's work stops with the battle of Moscow in 1941, somewhat in midstream. Although the Red Army was subject to more deliberate and thorough political controls than any other in previous history, Erickson makes it clear that it had its own politics, which were continuously embroiled with the politics of party and state. Such captains as Voroshilov, Frunze and Tukhachevsky are shown to have been major political figures within the armed establishment, while Trotsky, Stalin and lesser lights from civilian politics took a direct hand in military affairs.

The first part of this work, dealing with the creation of the Red Army during the Russian Civil War, digests an especially large volume of material and constitutes one of the basic works on that period of Soviet history. Subsequent sections deal with debates on military doctrine, industrialization, foreign connections (especially German), small wars, the massacre of the high command in 1937 and finally the German onslaught.

BIALER, SEWERYN, *ed*. **Stalin and His Generals: Soviet Military Memoirs of World War II.** New York: Pegasus, 1969, 644 p.

The editor is a Polish political scientist who emigrated in 1956. The book consists of 86 excerpts (of one to 20-odd pages) from the memoirs and other writings of Soviet generals on World War II, plus the editor's explanatory material and interpretations. These Soviet reminiscences, appearing under Khrushchev and Brezhnev, have much modified the Western view of the Eastern Front hitherto based on German sources. The purges, insufficient preparedness and Stalin's refusal to heed warnings of Hitler's attack were military disasters, but when war came, Stalin was neither a genius nor an idiot. He retained all political power, effectively marshalled supplies and chose, not wisely at first, among military strategies developed by his generals. He listened to Zhukov during the battle of Moscow, so the Red Army could use its still superior forces skillfully and decide the war in December 1941. This book contains the best selection in English of these materials on the coming of the war, the initial disasters, the Moscow campaign, political-military relations and (skipping Stalingrad and 1943–1944) the fall of Berlin. Professor Bialer's interpretive essays carry conviction.

Soviet Marxism

MEYER, ALFRED GEORGE. **Leninism.** Cambridge: Harvard University Press, 1957, 324 p.

What is Leninism? For Stalin, "Lenin was, and remains, the most loyal and consistent pupil of Marx and Engels," whose doctrines he developed "in accordance with the new conditions of development, with the new phase of capitalism, with imperialism." For Sidney Hook, Lenin's teachings "constituted a far greater deviation from the traditions of orthodox Marxism than the Revisionism he so scathingly excoriated." Meyer chooses neither view, insisting that Leninism is indefinable—a grab bag of Lenin's contradictory and frequently ambiguous writings, pronouncements and political decisions. Meyer carefully gathers, organizes and painstakingly sifts through a vast amount of this material to document Lenin's vacillations and the growth of his ambiguous views of the party, the Russian Revolution, the doctrine of socialism in one country and the theory of imperialism.

Purposefully uncritical, the author meticulously catalogues the many texts which later Marxist-Leninists exploit on particular topics. The scholarship is sound and thorough. The final portion of the book—where we finally get a feeling of excitement at dealing with new ideas and some insight into how such an unsystematic corpus could have so strong an intellectual appeal for so many followers and interpreters—is particularly good. The book is an analytical companion-piece to Adam Ulam, **The Bolsheviks,** Bertram Wolfe, **Three Who Made a Revolution,** and Louis Fischer, **The Life of Lenin.**

HAIMSON, LEOPOLD HENRI. **The Russian Marxists and the Origins of Bolshevism.** Cambridge: Harvard University Press, 1955, 246 p.

This book deals with the difficulties and controversies engendered in the attempt to apply Marxist doctrines to Tsarist Russia and create a viable Russian Marxist movement. It is therefore concerned with the origins of Menshevism as much as with those of Bolshevism. Its focus is the age-old problem of the Russian social movement, the dialectic of consciousness and spontaneity, or the problematic relationship between the leaders and the masses. Haimson traces the divergent views on this and related problems of four outstanding leaders of Russian Marxism, Plekhanov, Akselrod, Martov and Lenin, especially during their formative years. He also discusses the intelligentsia culture to which all of them belonged, personality differences notwithstanding. A highly readable book by an erudite cultural historian whose method is enlivened by Freudian theories.

A stimulating support for the thesis of the Russianness of Bolshevism is Nikolai

A. Berdyayev, **The Origin of Russian Communism** (New York: Scribner, 1938, 239 p.).

BUKHARIN, NIKOLAI IVANOVICH and PREOBRAZHENSKII, EVGENII ALEKSIEEVICH. **The A.B.C. of Communism.** Baltimore: Penguin Books, 1969, 481 p.
BUKHARIN, NIKOLAI IVANOVICH. **Historical Materialism: A System of Sociology.** Ann Arbor: University of Michigan Press, 1969, 320 p.

Until his political defeat by Stalin in 1928–1929, Nikolai Bukharin was regarded as the official theorist of Russian Bolshevism, and thus of the international communist movement. Equally important, he was a "seeking Marxist" and the most interesting thinker among the original Bolshevik leaders. Although neither of these two books truly reflects the nature of his theoretical or programmatic ideas, they were his most widely read works. Together they formed the doctrinal education of a whole generation of Soviet and foreign communists and were largely responsible for Bukharin's fame as the ideological spokesman of the Bolshevik Revolution.

The A.B.C. of Communism was written in 1919 with Evgenii Preobrazhenskii, another young Bolshevik leader and later Bukharin's chief theoretical opponent in the factional debates of the 1920s. Designed as a popular exposition of the party's recently adopted program, the book was not meant to be an original contribution to Marxist thought but "an elementary textbook of communist knowledge." It quickly became a party canon and the most famous handbook of pre-Stalinist Bolshevism. What gave **The A.B.C.** its appeal, and recommends it today, is its detailed chronicling of the party's utopianism and militant optimism that invigorated the Bolshevik movement during the heady civil war years.

Historical Materialism, published in 1921, also became a widely used textbook, but it was a much more ambitious undertaking than **The A.B.C.** In addition to providing a systematic exposition of Marxist social theory, Bukharin sought to answer Marx's most formidable critics, especially those representing the emerging schools of modern sociology, and to make his own contribution to Marxist thought. As a result, **Historical Materialism** was a highly influential and controversial book, which played a major role in Soviet intellectual life of the 1920s.

That both these works are still frequently reprinted in translation after 50 years is testimony to their importance as historical documents and chapters in the history of Marxist ideas. That they are still proscribed in the Soviet Union is further evidence of the present leadership's disdain for its own revolutionary and intellectual heritage.

JORAVSKY, DAVID. **Soviet Marxism and Natural Science, 1917–1932.** New York: Columbia University Press, 1961, 433 p.

In this scholarly and carefully documented study David Joravsky has analyzed the seminal period in the formation of official Soviet attitudes toward dialectical materialism as a philosophy of nature. Two different currents—"mechanism" and "Deborinism"—developed among Soviet philosophers in these early years. The members of the first faction tended toward positivism and reductionism; they saw the natural sciences as the determining elements of the philosophy of science. The supporters of Deborinism (named after A. M. Deborin) emphasized the Hegelian dialectic, the non-reductive element in scientific theory and the utility of philosophy as a guide for scientific research. Joravsky describes in great detail the predominance, first of the mechanists, then of Deborinists, and, finally, the emergence of Stalinist philosophers who triumph over both, demanding political loyalty above all things.

The great virtue of this work is its attention to historical detail and its criticism of earlier superficial generalizations, such as the alleged link between Bukharin and the mechanists, on the one hand, and that between Trotsky and the Deborinists on the other. Blemishes contained in the study are the relative lack of generalizations or conclusions to replace those which the author criticizes and a certain obscurity in style. The virtues clearly outweigh the blemishes. Specialists in Soviet intellectual history will find the book rewarding.

The organization of Soviet science is described in Loren R. Graham, **The Soviet Academy of Sciences and the Communist Party, 1927–1932** (Princeton: Princeton University Press, 1967, 255 p.); Alexander S. Vucinich, **The Soviet Academy of Sciences** (Stanford: Stanford University Press, 1956, 157 p.); Eugene Zaleski and others, **Science Policy in the U.S.S.R.;** and Alexander G. Korol, **Soviet Research and Development: Its Organization, Personnel, and Funds** (Cambridge: M.I.T. Press, 1965, 375 p.).

KUUSINEN, OTTO V., *ed.* **Fundamentals of Marxism-Leninism.** Moscow: Foreign Languages Publishing House, 2d rev. ed., 1963, 734 p.

The communist movement has trained its followers with a succession of official textbooks: Engels' "Anti-Dühring," Bukharin's **The A.B.C. of Communism,** and then the Stalinist "Short Course" of the **History of the Communist Party of the Soviet Union (Bolsheviks).** When the last of these was withdrawn after Stalin's death, the party was for some years without an ideological text. **Fundamentals of Marxism-Leninism,** written by a large group of authors at the Institute of Marxism-Leninism, now fills this gap. It is a comprehensive, quite sophisticated work, introducing the reader to all major questions of Soviet ideology under the customary five principal headings—philosophy, historical materialism, the nature of capitalist society, the history of the communist movement, and "scientific communism," *i.e.* the tasks of communist parties after attaining power. Specialists must carefully comb successive editions of this work for subtle changes which always have political significance.

MARCUSE, HERBERT. **Soviet Marxism: A Critical Analysis.** New York: Columbia University Press, 1958, 271 p.

Despite changes in Soviet theory and practice since this book was first written, it is still a penetrating and pertinent discussion of Soviet Marxism. Marcuse shows the continuity in basic Marxist categories which develop through Lenin to Stalin and into the post-Stalinist era. He emphasizes that since the key propositions of Soviet Marxism are pragmatic, ideological, ritualized, quasi-magical directives for action, they are not invalidated by their falsity. The doctrine of socialism in one country forms the nucleus for much of the first part of the work. From this vantage point Marcuse develops and analyzes some major developments of Soviet society and their interrelation with Marxist theory. The accuracy of his analysis is borne out by the fact that both the promulgation of the party program of 1961 and the 1968 invasion of Czechoslovakia fit easily into his framework.

To his credit Marcuse was one of the first in the West to take seriously the development of Soviet ethical theory, to which he devotes the second part of this book. Though Soviet ethical writings flowered several years after Marcuse wrote this work, he perceptively characterized on the basis of a remarkably small number of writings the externalization of values which they would promote and the competitive work-morality which they would preach. See also Richard T. De-George, **Soviet Ethics and Morality** (Ann Arbor: University of Michigan Press, 1969, 184 p.).

LEITES, NATHAN CONSTANTIN. **A Study of Bolshevism.** Glencoe: Free Press, 1953, 639 p.

An ambitious attempt to describe the state of mind of communist leaders, their way of viewing reality and their manner of coping with it ("operational code"). The author's generalizations are supported by copious quotes from communist ideological writings and from nineteenth and twentieth-century Russian fiction, materials which are then integrated with the help of bold Freudian interpretations. The resulting image of the communist leader which apparently applies to all of them unvaryingly portrays them as shrewd Machiavellians with paranoid delusions.

For them the world is full of mighty and cunning enemies that cannot be placated but must be killed when possible, avoided when necessary. The communist leadership emerges as a group of dangerous madmen, who will be rendered more innocuous only if the United States prepares its defenses and talks to the communists bluntly. Written for the U.S. Air Force, this book was one of the principal theoretical justifications for a tough American attitude in the cold war.

HUNT, ROBERT NIGEL CAREW. **The Theory and Practice of Communism.** Baltimore: Penguin Books, 5th rev. ed., 1963, 315 p.

This is the work of a British Foreign Office official who for many years specialized in the study of international communism. Assuming that theory was the single most important key to an understanding of Soviet behavior, he was baffled by a doctrine so totally alien to his own upbringing. Carew Hunt wrote a clear style and tried to be fair as well as dispassionate; but the book still turned into a cold-war tract. He was not sufficiently familiar with the intricacies of Marxism and with works about it, and cites minor secondary sources rather indiscriminately. Nor was he capable of seeing far beyond his own liberal and empirical assumptions. As a consequence, his summary of Marxism tends to be as dry and mechanical as Stalinist catechisms, despite some happy phrases. Indeed, much of it might be based on Stalinist textbooks, because—and this is the major fault of the book—its author has generally identified the thoughts of Marx with those of Engels, Lenin and Stalin. Since its publication it has been a very popular book.

Communist Party; Soviet Politics

PONOMAREV, BORIS NIKOLAEVICH and OTHERS. **History of the Communist Party of the Soviet Union.** Moscow: Foreign Languages Publishing House, 1960, 765 p.; 2d rev. ed. (n.d.), 763 p.

The publication of **History of the Communist Party of the Soviet Union (Bolsheviks)** (New York: International Publishers, 1939, 364 p.) in 1938, known as the "Short Course," established party history as the most important guide to the self-image of the Stalinist élite and the basis of the entire Soviet system of political indoctrination. This pattern was continued after the opening of Khrushchev's critique of Stalin with the publication in 1959 of a new text, which brought the narrative up to date and castigated "the cult of personality." A second edition of this work, published in 1964, had to be hastily replaced because it bore the marks of the emergence of Khrushchev's own cult, just at the end of his active career. A more thoroughly revised and updated third edition appeared in 1969, placing Stalin in a more favorable perspective and substantially revising the interpretation of the post-Stalin years.

All editions of the official party history share an intense concern for struggle with deviation from the one truth, represented by Lenin in his time and the party as a corporate successor since his death. The life of the party in the past, and probably the indefinite future, is perceived as a struggle with class enemies without and within. The argumentation is tendentious and must be compared with non-Soviet writings, but the text amply fills its role as an essential introduction to Soviet political culture.

SCHAPIRO, LEONARD BERTRAM. **The Communist Party of the Soviet Union.** New York: Random House, 1960, 631 p.

Before Schapiro's study all communist party histories were authorized, and they varied with each change in the party line. This work is a pioneering effort to determine the truth. Using much material excluded from previous official histories the author attempts to disclose the plausible choices presented at each turn of party history by various party theorists and to speculate on the causes of Stalin's assumption of dictatorial powers over his party.

Schapiro tries to overcome the Stalin-sponsored myth that objective factors compelled adoption of the party line first developed by Lenin, later evolved by the interregnum between Lenin and Stalin, and finally dictated by Stalin during his nearly 30 years of rule. Ample documentation for the years before 1930 makes possible the study's most enduring section. Speculation increases, of necessity, as the purges silenced potential authors and reduced publication of opposition views.

Schapiro's general theme is that subjective factors have been as important as objective ones in determining the course of party history. Consequently, he emphasizes personalities and intrigue in the historical process. This makes for difficult reading for neophytes because of the steady progression of names. Little use is made of statistics and none of élite studies designed to determine trends in party composition and function. A second edition is scheduled.

A bibliographical note provides a basis for extended research by readers knowing Russian. For an intensive study of relations between Bolsheviks and other political groups, see Schapiro's **The Origin of the Communist Autocracy** and John S. Reshetar, Jr., **A Concise History of the Communist Party of the Soviet Union** (New York: Praeger, 1960, 331 p.).

FAINSOD, MERLE. **How Russia Is Ruled.** Cambridge: Harvard University Press, rev. ed., 1963, 684 p.

Merle Fainsod's study of Soviet political institutions is perhaps the single most influential book that has been written on the subject in the United States. It is a major building block for understanding the Soviet political system, and since its publication (the first edition appeared in 1953), most Western political studies of the U.S.S.R. have both drawn from and tried to add to its findings. Hence the great impact on American political scientists teaching in the Soviet area and on their students.

Fainsod's achievement is that his study has almost everything for the serious student of Soviet politics. It is a reference work that is incisive, analytical and interesting. His work details the history of Bolshevism, analyzes the institutions of the Communist Party and of the Soviet government from 1917 to 1962 (using élite analysis and organizational theory known at that time) and examines how the party leadership manages conflict between itself and the parochial interests of the military and of those working in industry and agriculture.

If the work has any weakness it is that time has somewhat dated it. Its focus is less on post-Stalinist developments than on Stalinism. And it differs from more recent studies such as Zbigniew Brzezinski and Samuel P. Huntington, **Political Power: USA/USSR,** and Peter H. Juviler and Henry W. Morton, *eds.,* **Soviet Policy-Making: Studies of Communism in Transition** (New York: Praeger, 1967, 274 p.), by stressing institutional analysis rather than issues and policy-making.

BARGHOORN, FREDERICK CHARLES. **Politics in the U.S.S.R.** Boston: Little, Brown, 1966, 418 p.

Frederick Barghoorn, well known to students of Soviet affairs for his **The Soviet Image of the United States** (New York: Harcourt, 1950, 297 p.) and **The Soviet Cultural Offensive,** has written an imaginative and useful text. It is a pioneering attempt to apply Gabriel Almond's structural-functional schema of comparative politics to the Soviet polity.

Barghoorn is most successful in his lucidly descriptive analysis of Soviet political behavior. His chapter on "Implementing Public Policy," a process ignored by most texts, goes far in explaining what happens to policy when it is filtered through the labyrinthine channels of a highly bureaucratic system. In "Soviet Justice" Barghoorn's own encounter with the KGB (he was arrested by Soviet security agents in the autumn of 1963 and released only after President Kennedy's personal intervention) highlights an excellent treatment of a complex subject. The author has difficulties, however, in joining Almond's concepts to the study of Soviet politics. Terms such as "political culture" and "system adaptability," employed in the first part of the book, are not fully explained or integrated into the mainstream of the subject matter. Thus those who look for new conceptual comparative insights may be disappointed; they will, however, gain from the author's sound analysis of Soviet political behavior. Methodological problems and applications are pursued in Frederic J. Fleron, Jr., *ed.,* **Communist Studies and the Social Sciences: Essays on Methodology and Empirical Theory** (Chicago: Rand McNally, 1969, 481 p.).

BRZEZINSKI, ZBIGNIEW and HUNTINGTON, SAMUEL P. **Political Power: USA/USSR.** New York: Viking, 1964, 461 p.

Two well-known American political scientists have made an original and stimulating comparison of the American and Soviet political systems. It is an ambitious yet concisely written book, studded with thought-provoking generalizations about the Soviet and American political processes which force the reader either to accept them or prove them wrong. Hence the challenge and stimulation of the work to the general reader, who believes he knows at least how the American system works, and to the specialist who thinks he knows both.

The study contrasts a whole range of political activities including, among others, the political styles of the two societies, leadership recruitment and the role of political élites, the policy process from initiation to execution of decisions, the handling of alienation and dissent, and the possibilities of convergence of the two systems.

The book can be criticized for certain questionable conclusions. For example, the authors at the time of writing overemphasized the importance of ideology in determining Soviet decisions and underestimated the force of ideology in American society. But because it is constantly challenging, the study has retained its value.

ARMSTRONG, JOHN ALEXANDER. **The Soviet Bureaucratic Elite: A Case Study of the Ukrainian Apparatus.** New York: Praeger, 1959, 174 p.

Armstrong was among the first to study biographical material on Soviet leaders to determine the nature of the Soviet élite. Believing that generalized studies of Soviet institutions needed to be supplemented to reveal the nature of the Soviet political process, he examined unpublished doctoral theses deposited in Soviet libraries as well as conventional sources to find out who rules. His conclusions were that top party positions were held by generalists schooled in practice, while lower level functionaries were well educated in specialties. The generalists still held power when he wrote, and prevented the emergence of a technocracy, but he foresaw a conflict of generations as the generalists aged. In his view a humanistically minded leadership might emerge in time to replace the case-hardened seniors as they retired.

A pattern of rotation among party secretaries was discovered. Those who proved to be ineffective leaders were returned to the ranks, thus purging the leadership élite of incompetents. Friendships with generalists did not save failures at leadership, but friendships gave competent men and women a chance to show their skills when promoted. The prime example of this process was Khrushchev's selection of colleagues whom he came to know while working as wartime leader in the Ukraine for promotion to the national level. One result may have been development of collegial leadership at the top level under Khrushchev to replace one-man dictatorship, because this method had been developed successfully in the Ukraine.

HOUGH, JERRY F. **The Soviet Prefects: The Local Party Organs in Industrial Decision-Making.** Cambridge: Harvard University Press, 1969, 416 p.

This is the most informative study written so far on regional government in the U.S.S.R. It is a specialist's book and is overstuffed with detailed facts and repetitious examples. Yet if the general reader will persevere, he will have gained a much better understanding through these concrete instances of how the Soviet system works, what the duties of party and government officials are, how they differ and where they overlap, than he would be likely to have gained from a general analysis of the subject.

The book focuses on industrial decision making in the provinces, a vital concern of the party leadership which rewards or punishes sub-leaders primarily on the basis of their area's economic performance. The First Party Secretary of the province is supreme coördinator, with primary responsibility for the economic development of his area. His two most difficult tasks are to allocate scarce resources within his province, and to assist directors of large plants in securing chronically undelivered goods and materials needed to fulfill monthly and yearly plans by lobbying for their delivery before higher party and ministerial officials.

Hough performs a valuable service in showing how the system operates. By stressing its functional aspect, however, he passes too lightly over its many defects, thereby blunting the critical edge of his analysis.

Law

KELSEN, HANS. **The Communist Theory of Law.** New York: Praeger, 1955, 203 p.

The distinguished legal theorist, Hans Kelsen, leading proponent of legal positivism, has written a serious and trenchant critique of Marxist and of Soviet jurisprudence up to Stalin's death. The book includes analysis of the legal thinking of Marx and Engels, Lenin, Stuchka, Reisner, Pashukanis, Vyshinskii and early Strogovich.

Kelsen finds serious flaws both in the early Soviet legal theory of the 1920s and in that of the Stalinist period. The earlier Marxian jurisprudence of Pashukanis and Stuchka suffered from its denial of the normative content of law (these theorists treated law variously as a form of social relations and as ideology). In fact, Stalin rejected this jurisprudence because it tended to weaken the law as an instrument of social control. Later Soviet legal theorists, led by Vyshinskii, restored the primacy of normative law for Stalin. But Kelsen strongly objects to the fact that Vyshinskii derives Soviet law from what amount to natural law sources, rather than from human and social acts (as the positivist would have it).

Kelsen's analysis of Soviet legal theory is based primarily on the selections translated in John N. Hazard and Hugh W. Babb, **Soviet Legal Philosophy** (Cambridge: Harvard University Press, 1951, 465 p.). For translations of further materials on Soviet legal theory, including some more recent, see **Soviet Political Thought: An Anthology,** selected, translated and edited by Michael Jaworskyj (Baltimore: Johns Hopkins Press, 1968, 621 p.).

VYSHINSKII, ANDREI IANUAR'EVICH. **The Law of the Soviet State.** New York: Macmillan, 1948, 749 p.

Published in 1938, this textbook for Soviet law students represents a major turning point in the transition from a sociological to a positivist approach to Marxist jurisprudence in the U.S.S.R. Led by E. B. Pashukanis, the Marxist sociologists of law dominated the 1920s with their assumptions that law originates in the marketplace as the legal expression of commodity exchange and that the state is derivative from law primarily for sanctioning these legal relationships. Law and the state were considered peculiar to capitalism and were expected to "wither away" during socialism, or a society based on public property and a planned economy.

In the 1930s Pashukanis' legal theory came into conflict with the needs of the Soviet Union as a developing country. He was purged, and Vyshinskii then undertook the formulation of a positivist approach to Marxist jurisprudence in conjunction with a detailed exposition of the "Stalin" Constitution of 1936. Castigating Pashukanis' group as traitors, spies and "wreckers" for their "perversions . . . of the Marxist-Leninist theory of law," the textbook's author outlined the new assumptions, including the primacy of the state as a source of legal norms, the significance of the "socialist" state and law for Soviet development, and the necessity of strengthening the Soviet state and law before it could wither away. Although changes have occurred in Soviet jurisprudence since 1938, this volume published by the authoritative Institute of Law of the Soviet Academy of Sciences still has value as an introduction to contemporary Soviet legal positivism. The translation is by Hugh W. Babb, and there is an introduction by John N. Hazard.

KARPETS, I. I.; KUDRIAVTSEV, V. N. and GERTSENZON, A. A., eds. **Kriminologiia** [Criminology]. Moscow: Iuridicheskaia Literatura, 1969, 471 p.

An important consequence of de-Stalinization was the revival of sociology, including sociology of crime and criminal law. During the 1960s young Soviet lawyers, under the guidance of criminologists who had survived since the 1920s, once again took up questions of the cause and prevention of crime. Since the establishment in 1963 of a criminology institute under the Soviet Procuracy and Supreme Court, the impact of criminology has been keenly felt both in criminal policy-making and in the administration of justice.

This book is the second official textbook of criminology published in the post-Stalin period. It is designed for a course in criminology, required for law students since 1964. The text gives a good summary of the history of Soviet criminology and of the accepted Soviet theory of causation of crime (a blend of Karl Marx and Edwin Sutherland). Most useful of all is a series of chapters on the dynamics and causes of particular crimes (hooliganism, theft, murder) and on juvenile delinquency and recidivism. It also discusses methods of research and ways of organizing activities in communities to prevent crime.

From the viewpoint of the West, the main achievement of Soviet criminology lies in study of the effectiveness of Soviet legal institutions (*e.g.* parole, short-term sentences, custodial régimes, recidivism laws) in preventing recidivist crime. A major research report on this subject is B. S. Nikiforov, *ed.*, **Effektivnost Ugolovnopravovykh Mer Borby s Prestupnostiiu** (Moscow: Iuridicheskaia Literatura, 1968, 255 p.).

BERMAN, HAROLD J. **Justice in the U.S.S.R.: An Interpretation of Soviet Law.** New York: Vintage Books, rev. and enl. ed., 1963, 450 p.

This is a major study of Soviet law and legal institutions. In his analysis of the sources of Soviet law, Professor Berman considers the roles of Marxism, Soviet social institutions and Russian and Western legal traditions in the shaping of the Soviet legal system. As part of his discussion, the author outlines Soviet legal history and the reforms after Stalin. In addition, he describes the main features of Soviet economic law (property, contract and arbitration) and discusses briefly Soviet criminal law, family law and labor law, as well as forensic psychiatry in the U.S.S.R.

Berman believes that the unique and defining aspect of Soviet law is neither its institutions nor its letter, but the intent and spirit behind it. In his view, Soviet law is "paternal" and is imbued with positive purpose—to educate or guide Soviet citizens toward a moral (read "socialist") habit of social relations. With the decline of terror, Berman believes, the strong social dynamic of Soviet justice has become more prominent.

Berman's other contributions to the study of Soviet law include a long essay on the history and development of Soviet criminal law (see the extended introduction to his **Soviet Criminal Law and Procedure,** Cambridge: Harvard University Press, 1966, 501 p.) and, with Miroslav Kerner, **Soviet Military Law and Administration** (Cambridge: Harvard University Press, 1955, 208 p.).

FEIFER, GEORGE. **Justice in Moscow.** New York: Simon and Schuster, 1964, 353 p.

This is a popular, lively, even racy account by a graduate student turned journalist of what happens inside Moscow criminal courts. The author spent the better part of a year sitting in Moscow courtrooms listening to trials. Much of his account consists of reconstructions of actual proceedings complete with dialogue.

Feifer's book communicates the informality of Soviet court practice, and in addition gives much support for Professor Berman's thesis about the educative purpose of Soviet law. In his enthusiasm and in an attempt to present Soviet legality in its best light, Feifer may occasionally judge Western justice too harshly. This in no way spoils the impact of his account. His is a book, above all, for the reader who would feel, as well as understand, Soviet justice in everyday cases.

CHKHIKVADZE, VIKTOR MIKHAILOVICH, ed. **The Soviet State and Law.** Moscow: Progress Publishers, 1969, 333 p.

Continuity and change in Soviet jurisprudence since the 1930s are the underlying themes of this volume written by a group of prominent jurists headed by the Director of the Institute of State and Law of the Soviet Academy of Sciences. Soviet legal positivism continues as the basic theoretical orientation and the Constitution of 1936 remains the "triumph of socialism," but there are also significant changes in emphasis and style. The educational role of Soviet law is stressed, "socialist legality" for the individual as well as the state is emphasized, greater attention is given to public participation in administration and law enforcement, and the authors even cautiously speculate on the shape of Soviet society after the "withering away" of the state and law. Similarly, the "cult of personality" in jurisprudence is criticized, but Vyshinskii is not branded a criminal; there are a few positive references to the Marxist sociology of law of the 1920s; and the traditional question about the independence of the Soviet judiciary is treated with refreshing candor.

Nevertheless, continuity is the dominant theme. The Communist Party is still the "directing and guiding force" of the Soviet system, economic development continues to have the highest priority, the state remains the primary source of legal norms, and law is still regarded as "a most important lever" in the ongoing modernization of the Soviet Union.

HAZARD, JOHN NEWBOLD. **Communists and Their Law.** Chicago: University of Chicago Press, 1969, 560 p.

In the 1930s, John N. Hazard was a pioneer in the study of Soviet law in the United States. In recent years he has turned increasingly to the comparative study of law in communist countries and in the socialist-oriented countries of Africa. This book attempts to define what is common and unique to the socialist family of law, as opposed to the Romanist and common law traditions. After systematically comparing the main features of the legal systems of the U.S.S.R., Jugoslavia and other East European countries and China, Professor Hazard concludes that socialist law is original and distinctive neither in its methods (which are Romanist) nor in its attitudes toward legal sources. Instead, socialist law is distinguished from other law by its "conscious and purposeful involvement with politics, economics, and social organization." In short, communists everywhere view the law as an instrument to be used for the achievement of social goals and values—including a public economy, a directed polity and a society marked by a high level of social involvement.

Apart from its theme and purpose, Hazard's book is useful as a source for general descriptions of Soviet and East European land law, property law, inheritance, copyright and patent law, contracts and torts. The sections dealing with the U.S.S.R. are always the strongest. The sections on Eastern Europe are useful, and those on China and Africa are suggestive rather than complete.

Among Hazard's other important books on the Soviet legal system are **Law and Social Change in the U.S.S.R.** (London: Stevens, for the London Institute of World Affairs, 1953, 310 p.) and **Settling Disputes in Soviet Society** (New York: Columbia University Press, 1960, 534 p.).

Economic Questions

SCHWARTZ, HARRY. **Russia's Soviet Economy.** New York: Prentice-Hall, 2d ed., 1954, 682 p.

A generation of students of the Soviet economy, now teaching the same subject in numerous American universities, cut their professional teeth on this first American textbook, written in 1950 by an economist who later became a member of the editorial board of *The New York Times*. Hence the great impact of this volume on Soviet studies in the United States.

One of the distinguishing virtues of this book, giving it enduring value, is the sense of continuity and completeness provided by the first three chapters dealing respectively with the resources, the historical and the ideological background of Soviet economic development. Even the 1958 printing of this second edition is factually out of date, partly because of the many changes which occurred in the Soviet economy after the death of Stalin, and partly because of considerable progress in Western research on the Soviet economy. On the other hand, those who wish to acquire a detailed view of Soviet economic institutions under Stalin will still be richly rewarded if they consult Schwartz.

In a display of courage unusual for academicians writing texts, Schwartz discussed in some detail the prospects for future economic development in the U.S.S.R. He correctly predicted rising capital requirements (in housing, among others), the need for the post-Stalin leadership to raise living standards, manpower shortages and the need to raise productivity. He did not quite predict the reform of industrial management, but neither did anyone else at that time, nor is the Soviet version of this reform (introduced in 1965) a radical one. He erred in thinking that grain output could not be doubled in two decades, but no one else had the inkling that a New Lands program (first resorted to by Stalin in the early 1930s) would again be introduced by Khrushchev. As a prophet, therefore, the author's record is considerably above par.

NOVE, ALEC. **The Soviet Economy: An Introduction.** New York: Praeger, 2d rev. ed., 1969, 373 p.

This is a textbook by one of the most prominent and knowledgeable economists in the field of Soviet studies, fully reflecting the great analytical abilities, the sure grasp of detail and the verve of its author. It fulfills its promise of making at every step the necessary distinction between what "ought to be" (and is found largely in official directives) and what actually occurs (and can be glimpsed only through a patient and extensive perusal of Soviet scholarly journals, of the daily press and of Soviet belles lettres).

Nove deals first with institutions and then examines in great detail the issues arising at the enterprise level as well as problems of investment, supply and output planning, and of factor pricing. The last part of the book is devoted to basic concepts, including those of measurement of economic activity, to Soviet economic "laws," and concludes with an interesting assessment which views the Soviet case within the broader concept of economic development in general.

One disappointing feature is the failure to use more extensively the results of accumulated Western research on the Soviet economy. Abram Bergson, for example, is mentioned only once. It is perhaps because of this feature that important quantitative aspects of Soviet growth are neglected in this otherwise excellent, well-written book which has been translated into several languages and is widely used, with full justification, as an undergraduate text.

CAMPBELL, ROBERT WELLINGTON. **Soviet Economic Power: Its Organization, Growth, and Challenge.** Boston: Houghton, 2d ed., 1966, 184 p.

By the beginning of the 1960s, the prodigious effort mounted by American and other Western scholars to understand the working of the Soviet economy and to measure its performance had already borne considerable fruit, despite Soviet secretiveness. When Campbell's excellent little book first appeared in 1960, it represented in a sense a concise and coherent summary of the main results of these researches (including, of course, the author's own). Written with care and precision but on a plane of considerable sophistication and in a lucid and readable style, the book quickly gained acceptance in American colleges and universities as a standard brief introduction to the Soviet economy. Now in its second edition,

Campbell's book remains as good an introduction to the subject as any of similar compass.

Although published very shortly after the so-called economic reform of 1965, the second edition correctly appraises the impact of that measure as minimal. The concluding chapter, which discusses the problems and choices before the Soviet economy, remains as relevant today as when it was written.

ERLICH, ALEXANDER. **The Soviet Industrialization Debate, 1924–1928.** Cambridge: Harvard University Press, 1960, 214 p.

The book is a path-breaking inquiry into the exceedingly interesting debate conducted during the 1920s within the Soviet Communist Party on the nature and the rate of the economic development program which ultimately assumed the shape of the famous five-year plans. No such public debate, even within the narrow confines of an "establishment," had been conducted anywhere else. As Professor Erlich shows, Soviet economists often anticipated many developmental views and theories, worked out subsequently in the West with a greater (and necessary) theoretical rigor.

The author translates views, which the protagonists such as Bukharin, Preobrazhenskii and Stalin expressed in Marxist jargon, into modern economic terminology and guides the reader gently through the debate. The latter was accompanied by a bitter power struggle within the top echelons of the party, the results of which are well known: they led to the establishment of Stalin's dictatorship and ultimately to the emergence of the Soviet-type economy—which continues to operate today.

A reader in the 1970s should note that Evgenii Preobrazhenskii's **The New Economics** has recently been translated into English (Oxford: Clarendon Press, 1965, 310 p.). A very useful compendium of translated Russian texts of the debate was edited by Nicolas Spulber (**Foundations of Soviet Strategy for Economic Growth,** Bloomington: Indiana University Press, 1964, 530 p.). The economist will wish to consult Evsey Domar's **Essays in the Theory of Economic Growth** (New York: Oxford University Press, 1957, 272 p.) for an early Marxist version of a two-sector growth model elaborated by G. A. Feldman.

Professor Erlich concludes that there was nothing inevitable about Stalinist development and terror, that a feasible alternative program (*e.g.* as advocated by Bazarov) was possible. This view has since been strengthened by further theoretical and empirical studies.

JASNY, NAUM. **The Socialized Agriculture of the USSR: Plans and Performance.** Stanford: Stanford University Press, 2d ed., 1967, 837 p.

A second edition of a monograph in the field of Soviet and East European studies is a rare phenomenon. A second printing of a book, undertaken by the original publisher 18 years after the first and without any corrections by the author, is unique.

But Jasny's massive work is indeed unique. His was the first monographic study of Soviet agriculture in English and, except for Otto Schiller's **Die Landwirtschaftpolitik der Sowjets und ihre Ergebnisse** (Berlin: Reichsnährstandsverlag, 1943, 192 p.), the first larger monograph on the subject in the West. It was written in that remote period when no statistical handbooks were available to assist the analyst, and when every researcher was forced to resort all too frequently to the technique of piecing together scattered bits of information, supplied by sources of varying reliability.

Jasny's underlying general thesis has also withstood well the acid test of time: that collectivization dealt nearly a death blow to that important sector of the Soviet economy (a blow from which Soviet agriculture has by no means fully recovered). This is also true of the implied thesis that there were alternative ways of extracting from agriculture a substantial contribution to assure a rapid growth of the economy as a whole. In addition, it was in this book that Jasny skillfully presented his phenomenally accurate estimates—often 100 percent accurate—of the actual barn outputs of grain for the years 1933–1939 and contrasted them with the inflated figures, published (until 1953) by official Soviet statistical agencies, which reflected the infamous "biological," or "on the root," yields.

By now, much new information on the 1930s and 1940s has been published in various Soviet sources, and it would be possible to close many of the inevitable gaps that Jasny could not fill in 1948–1949. Some of this information has been used by various Western specialists on Soviet agriculture, but there is as yet no substitute for Jasny's volume in English. The writer of that future substitute will owe a huge debt to Jasny, however he may disagree with some of his conclusions.

BERGSON, ABRAM and KUZNETS, SIMON, *eds.* **Economic Trends in the Soviet Union.** Cambridge: Harvard University Press, 1963, 392 p.

This volume of seven essays by Abram Bergson and his colleagues invites favorable comparison with an earlier volume edited by Bergson, **Soviet Economic Growth: Conditions and Perspectives** (Evanston: Row-Peterson, 1953, 376 p.). In the intervening decade Soviet authorities relaxed their strict censorship of statistical materials, especially after 1956, and each of the scholarly contributors conducted painstaking research in his particular area of specialization. In contrast to the earlier volume, the contributors also made meaningful comparisons with United States developmental experience. Each essay is the finished product of perhaps the leading specialist in the field: national income—Abram Bergson; labor—Warren Eason; capital—Norman Kaplan; industrial production—Raymond Powell; agriculture—Gale Johnson; consumption—Janet Chapman; and foreign trade—Franklyn Holzman. The period studied generally refers to the years 1928 to 1959 so that unfortunately little evidence is presented documenting the slowdown in Soviet growth in the early 1960s.

In his summary, Professor Kuznets raised some interesting broader questions involved, such as the noneconomic costs of Soviet economic growth (to human life and happiness, for example), and concluded that Soviet growth "is a case of high rates of growth, with large inputs of resources and heavy human costs; of rapid shifts in industrial structure, away from agriculture and with emphasis on the industrial sector . . . that differed in its speed and concentration from other countries." Kuznets also emphasized the qualitative differences between the results of Soviet planning before and after the war, specifically the postwar rise in consumption and generally greater efficiency.

GRANICK, DAVID. **The Red Executive.** Garden City: Doubleday, 1960, 334 p.

This widely read volume exemplifies the evolution of a Sovietologist into a comparative economist. Granick's earlier volume, **Management of the Industrial Firm in the USSR** (New York: Columbia University Press, 1954, 346 p.), was the product of the author's graduate work under Professor Bergson at the Russian Institute. Building on this, as well as on Professor Berliner's valuable contribution to Western knowledge of Soviet management practices (**Factory and Manager in the USSR,** Cambridge: Harvard University Press, 1957, 386 p.), Granick was then able to make meaningful comparisons with the United States "organization man."

Although the Soviet managerial practices are primarily shaped by material shortages, in contrast to the United States manager's concern with sales, Granick shows that hired managers in the United States and plant managers of the Soviet Union both operate in bureaucracies. Granick does not limit himself to typical economic comparisons but attempts to compare things normally assigned to sociologists: mobility, family life, job security, housing, educational background, as well as management's relationship to the Communist Party in the U.S.S.R. and to the corporate shareholders in the United States. Granick's unfootnoted work reflects a nice combination of the results of a scholarly background and field research.

Subsequently, Granick's comparative studies produced **The European Executive** (Garden City: Doubleday, 1962, 390 p.). A later comparative study of Soviet management by a Canadian expert, Barry M. Richman (**Soviet Management: With**

Significant American Comparisons, Englewood Cliffs: Prentice-Hall, 1965, 279 p.), proved to be something of a disappointment compared with the earlier studies. Mention should also be made of Jeremy R. Azrael's study of the political role of Soviet managers (**Managerial Power and Soviet Politics,** Cambridge: Harvard University Press, 1966, 258 p.).

PISAR, SAMUEL. **Coexistence and Commerce: Guidelines for Transactions between East and West.** New York: McGraw-Hill, 1970, 558 p.

Samuel Pisar's landmark volume offers the first comprehensive analysis of the framework within which economic dealings between the communist world and the rest of the international community are conducted. Cautiously optimistic about the value of trade to each partner both in purely economic terms and as a means of building political bridges, the author surveys the record of past performance in the realm of commerce and suggests how previous practices and existing mechanisms can be improved to maximize the utility of business transactions to all concerned.

The book is not a starry-eyed plea for more Western trade with the communist states for the sake of establishing common bonds, converting local régimes to recognizing the superiority of the capitalist system or subverting their traditional hostility through the lure of material incentives. Indeed, the author openly admits that the impact of East-West trade on the inner core of the economic structures erected by the Soviet, East European and Asian communist leaderships is marginal at best and that the attraction of commercial relations with the West, while not negligible, does not lend itself to exploitation as an effective lever to alter the political or ideological complexion or aims of the members of the "socialist Commonwealth."

Nevertheless, within these limits, both sides stand to gain considerable advantage from expanding inter-bloc trade contacts, with ensuing economic and political benefits for mankind at large. The great merit of the book lies in its sober and sensible appraisal of the obstacles which hinder East-West economic bargaining, how they can be most readily overcome, the objective parameters of such economic coöperation posed by the divergent ethical commitments of "Western" versus "Eastern" social models, the inherent competitiveness which marks the division of the world into rival political teams and, finally, the residue of cold-war mentality and the power of bureaucratic inertia.

PROKHOROV, G. M., ed. **Problemy Sotrudnichestva Sotsialisticheskikh i Razvivaiush-chikhsia Stran** [Problems of Coöperation between the Socialist and the Developing Countries]. Moscow: Akademiya Nauk, 1966, 255 p.

This innovating and informative work offers a forthright analysis of the problems and prospects facing Soviet aid and trade with the developing countries. Its appearance marked a refreshing departure from the customary practice in the U.S.S.R. of describing Soviet foreign economic policies in terms of factual listings and claims of unfailing successes beneficial to both sides.

The book suggests several new policies to stabilize relations and transform them into a source of economic gain. One proposal is to take advantage of the international division of labor through the construction of assembly plants abroad, the joint exploitation of natural resources and specialization in production. Another is to make aid and trade more advantageous through greater correlation of planning in the communist bloc with the development plans of the recipient nations and a much more thorough examination of the indexes of comparative advantage.

These arguments indicate that there is now a trend in the Soviet Union to consider the pursuit of economic advantage as an important policy consideration in expanding economic ties with the third world. Interestingly, in 1958 Joseph S. Berliner saw this as the logical but politically disregarded motivation for the Soviet aid and trade offensive: **Soviet Economic Aid: The New Aid and Trade Policy in Underdeveloped Countries** (New York: Praeger, for the Council on Foreign Relations, 1958, 232 p.).

Social, Cultural and Scientific Questions

INKELES, ALEX. **Social Change in Soviet Russia.** Cambridge: Harvard University Press, 1968, 475 p.

This collection of essays written over a 20-year period reveals how much the sociologist can offer to our understanding of Soviet reality. The essays here cover a wide range of topics, such as social stratification, mass communications, the family and ethnic groups. Particular essays focus on the problem of continuity and change in Soviet society and on the models which can be used for studying the Soviet social system. On the whole, the essays remain as significant today as when they were written, especially those on social change, social stratification and models for Soviet society.

Professor Inkeles' theme over the years has been that politics has shaped Soviet society far less than Western analysts generally acknowledge. Instead, the social consequences of modernization account for the nature of many central institutions in the Soviet social system—such as the stratification system, family and education.

Some of the essays are based on materials from the Harvard Project on the Soviet Social System, which involved interviews of a large number of Soviet refugees in Germany in 1950–1951. The results of this important sociological study appear in Alex Inkeles and Raymond A. Bauer, **The Soviet Citizen,** and more briefly in Raymond Bauer, Alex Inkeles and Clyde Kluckhohn, **How the Soviet System Works** (Cambridge: Harvard University Press, 1956, 274 p.).

Cyril Black, *ed.,* **The Transformation of Russian Society** (Cambridge: Harvard University Press, 1960, 695 p.), and Allen Kassof, **Prospects for Soviet Society** (New York: Praeger, for the Council on Foreign Relations, 1968, 586 p.), are also outstanding studies of Soviet society.

INKELES, ALEX and BAUER, RAYMOND AUGUSTINE. **The Soviet Citizen.** Cambridge: Harvard University Press, 1959, 533 p.

This is a unique study of Soviet society, indispensable for its understanding, especially of the Stalin period. It is equally valuable for the sociologist, political scientist and historian for its wealth of detailed information on such major topics as social classes and mobility, standard of living, social-political controls, family life, education, attitudes toward the Soviet system, communications, nationalities and others. Of particular significance is the fact that it is the only comprehensive study of Soviet society based primarily on a large sample of former Soviet citizens whose personal experiences and attitudes are utilized, together with other relevant historical and sociological data; 764 long interviews and 3,000 questionnaires were used, most of them in the years 1950–1951. The majority of the respondents left the U.S.S.R. between 1943–1946, but in spite of this the book is hardly dated.

The authors presented a realistic picture of the durability and adaptability of the social order created under Stalin and of the modest desires of most Soviet citizens in regard to greater freedom, self-determination and a more meaningful participation in public life. Along with the sheer quantity of information and its careful and insightful interpretation, the book makes a significant theoretical contribution.

H. Kent Geiger, **The Family in Soviet Russia** (Cambridge: Harvard University Press, 1968, 381 p.), dips into materials from the same interview project, and is an important study within the limits of the urban Russian context and up to the 1950s. Two valuable journalistic accounts are Klaus Mehnert, **Soviet Man and His World** (New York: Praeger, 1962, 310 p.), and Maurice Hindus, **The Kremlin's Human Dilemma: Russia after Half a Century of Revolution** (Garden City: Doubleday, 1967, 395 p.).

OSBORN, ROBERT J. **Soviet Social Policies: Welfare, Equality, and Community.** Homewood: The Dorsey Press, 1970, 294 p.

Robert J. Osborn examines Soviet efforts to motivate its urban population "to fill useful roles in modern society" and Soviet responses to questions of equality and opportunity. Welfare, career and work choices and urban planning are the major policy areas investigated. Important subtopics include national manpower policy, "social wage" benefits (*obshchestvennye fondy potrebleniya*), nonindustrial investment allocation among regions and cities, educational opportunities, material incentives and labor turnover.

These topics are not analyzed in detail, nor are they linked by a central theme, argument or focus of analysis. The author is more successful at describing the impact of selected social policies on the everyday life of Soviet citizens than in systematically analyzing the intentions, values and goals of Soviet leaders. Indeed, one of the more interesting implications of this study is that Soviet party and government officials, social scientists, urban planners, economists and educators will have to do considerably more thinking about the social goals they desire and possible ways of achieving these goals. The nature of social organization in the future communist society is unclear, even in theory.

OSIPOV, G. V. and SHCHEPANSKII, IA., *eds.* **Sotsial'nye Problemy Truda i Proizvodstva: Sovetsko-pol'skoe Sravnitel'noe Issledovanie.** Moscow: Izd-vo "Mysl'," 1969, 489 p.

By the early 1960s the new sociology in the Soviet Union was ready to take its first steps in empirical research. Industrial sociology was a natural starting point for the new Marxist-Leninist discipline, and the decade saw a plethora of studies in this and related subfields. The present volume provides an excellent overview of Soviet industrial sociology as well as a sampling of Polish work in the field.

Primarily a compilation of Soviet and Polish research on similar problems, the book includes several instances of Soviet-Polish collaboration on surveys. The opening selection is a summary of the first major sociological survey in the U.S.S.R., V. N. Shubkin's 1962–1966 Novosibirsk investigation of occupational choice among secondary school students. Other authors then discuss labor turnover, management, workers' use of leisure time and the relation of job content to the cultural level of the worker. Included is a summary of findings of the most methodologically sophisticated Soviet survey to date, the so-called Leningrad study of 1967 (A. G. Zdravomyslov, V. P. Rozhin and V. A. Yadov; translated by Murray Yanowitch; **Man and His Work,** White Plains: International Arts and Sciences Press, 1970, 398 p.). The closing section of the book turns the reader's attention to problems of working women and includes an article by A. G. Kharchev, the leading Soviet expert on the family.

The volume gives proof that by the end of the 1960s Soviet use of sociological methods had reached the level of Polish standards. The Polish selections do give finer breakdowns of variables, however, and one senses in them less reluctance to discuss income levels or worker-management relations. Significantly absent in both the Soviet and Polish articles is any discussion of workers' control.

BRONFENBRENNER, URIE. **Two Worlds of Childhood: U.S. and U.S.S.R.** New York: Russell Sage Foundation, 1970, 190 p.

The central thesis of Bronfenbrenner's provocative analysis of youth in the United States and the Soviet Union is that the force of the peer group, which is considerable in both places, intensifies antisocial tendencies in the West but reinforces adult and conformist values in the East. He attributes the former to the intensive age segregation in the United States, which results in children being brought up not by their parents but by their age group. He believes that this pattern has developed not because it has been deliberately sought by parents or children but chiefly as a result of the urban-suburban pattern of living which reduces the number of persons with whom one is acquainted. The rhetorical commitment to individualism in the West has prevented interposing adult standards upon children, particularly adolescents, but has not prevented the tyranny of the peer group.

Bronfenbrenner finds the pull of the peer group also powerful in the Soviet Union, but there collective responsibility is forced upon exacting conduct of children consistent with the values of the adult society. He believes that this influence will result in children who are more conformist but less anti-adult, rebellious, aggressive and delinquent.

The book is based upon research Bronfenbrenner did in the U.S.S.R., the United States and four other Western nations. The data come largely from young adolescents, and one hopes that Bronfenbrenner's next book will deal with studies of late adolescents, the group in both the East and West which tends most to defy the established values.

DeWitt, Nicholas. **Education and Professional Employment in the U.S.S.R.** Washington: National Science Foundation, 1962, 856 p.

Drawing on a wide range of Soviet sources (the bibliography lists about 1,100 items, including the 1959 census reports), DeWitt and his colleagues offer a massive compendium of information about Soviet education and professional employment. Although more than ten years old, their study retains its usefulness. The descriptions of institutions and organizations are extremely detailed for the periods covered. The researcher requiring more current data on most of these questions would have to consult Soviet sources; and he would have no easy time replicating the painstaking work of DeWitt (for example, in compiling tables from multiple sources).

Some of the areas covered include: distribution of student population by sex, social and economic origin; enrollment and success rates; and educational policy and institutions. Material is presented on schools ranging from nursery and kindergarten through graduate professional education; vocational training is included as well. Separate chapters describe the Soviet system of higher education and graduate training, and the system of occupational placement of graduates of higher educational institutions.

George Sylvester Counts reported well on Soviet education before the attempted Khrushchev reforms in **The Challenge of Soviet Education** (New York: McGraw-Hill, 1957, 330 p.).

Harris, Chauncy D. **Cities of the Soviet Union.** Chicago: Rand McNally (for the Association of American Geographers), 1970, 484 p.

With this book Professor Harris has made a major contribution to our knowledge of the urban geography of the U.S.S.R. Essentially what he has done is to compile a wide array of urban data going back to the middle of the nineteenth century and to analyze these data by drawing on such concepts in urban geography as central-place hierarchies, population potential, urban systems analysis and functional classification. In short, he has related urban development in the Soviet Union to recent theoretical work in the West, combining in an original and imaginative way traditional and recent approaches to urban geography. Two introductory chapters are devoted to a survey of the Soviet study of the geography of cities in the U.S.S.R. and a functional classification of Soviet cities. There is also a 56-page selected bibliography, primarily of works in Russian and English. The book is well written and well illustrated (96 maps and graphs and 34 tables) and should be of great value to a wide range of students of the U.S.S.R. and urbanism.

For an authoritative and documented survey of Soviet geography, see Chauncy D. Harris, *ed.,* **Soviet Geography: Accomplishments and Tasks,** translated from the Russian edition sponsored by the Geography Society of the U.S.S.R. under the Academy of Sciences of the U.S.S.R. (New York: American Geographical Society, 1962, 409 p.). See also Theodore Shabad, **Basic Industrial Resources of the U.S.S.R.** (New York: Columbia University Press, 1969, 393 p.).

Hollander, Paul, *ed.* **American and Soviet Society: A Reader in Comparative Sociology and Perception.** Englewood Cliffs: Prentice-Hall, 1969, 589 p.

Amid all the heat generated by the theory of the convergence of industrial societies, surprisingly little attention has been paid to the light that comparative sociology can shed on the subject. This book helps to fill the gap by placing

American and Soviet societal studies side by side. The readings deal with social values and beliefs, the polity, social stratification, the family, crime, ethnic discrimination, leisure, alcoholism, mass culture, youth, old age, rural and urban problems, population movement and religion; appraisals of sociology and a brief discussion of convergence are appended.

Since the factory is a focus of Soviet life, it is unfortunate that the industrial sphere was slighted. Education is dealt with only cursorily. But on the whole the selections are judicious, and the editor's comments provide the necessary minimum of objective interpretation. The differences apparent between the sociology of the two countries are at least as illuminating as the similarities and differences between the two societies.

STRUVE, GLEB. **Soviet Russian Literature, 1917–1950.** Norman: University of Oklahoma Press, 1951, 414 p.

Even in the perspective of 20 years, Struve's book continues to be a very valuable staple in the critical diet of students of Soviet Russian literature. The passage of time, however, has made it possible to identify areas in which other works by scholars in the field have filled gaps in his coverage. In a balanced and sensitive manner Struve competently covered the entire Soviet literary production known up to 1950. (A 1957 German edition published in Munich by Isar Verlag brought it somewhat further up to date.)

This comprehensiveness is not altogether a blessing, for it means that the reader must wade through the discussion of many works and writers of limited literary value. In compensation, however, Struve offers an analysis—valid to this day—of schools and controversies. His vast familiarity with his field determines the book's wide focus—in terms of quality, number of authors and variety of genres. No one else has such erudition and scholarship in this area or has written as thorough a treatment of it in any Western language. What we now need is a comprehensive work which would include not only Soviet literature since 1950 but works from earlier periods which have only recently come to light (albeit Struve should be given credit for making some shrewd speculations about them).

An essential companion to Struve's book is **Political Control of Literature in the USSR, 1946–1959** by Harold Swayze (Cambridge: Harvard University Press, 1962, 301 p.), which captures the political atmosphere and social ecology in which this creativity struggled to perform.

PIPES, RICHARD, *ed.* **The Russian Intelligentsia.** New York: Columbia University Press, 1961, 234 p.

These 12 essays, originally published as the Summer 1960 issue of *Daedalus,* are only variously useful or appropriate in studying the Russian intelligentsia. Martin Malia's attempt at a "dynamic" definition deserves attention for its reconciliation of many different points of view. Leonard Schapiro reiterates in detail the known fact that the Russian intelligentsia was not "liberal" and cared little for Western legal procedures. Boris Elkin competently describes the vicissitudes of the group on the eve of the Revolution. The transition from the Russian to the Soviet intelligentsia is provocatively discussed by Richard Pipes: he argues that unlike the engagé Russian intellectual with his plans to transform society, the Soviet intellectual resembles his dégagé Western counterpart. Leopold Labedz, studying the structure of the Soviet intelligentsia, cites useful statistics and makes clear the distinction between the worker who has technical knowledge and the party bureaucrat who has power; despite the increased need for "knowledge," the intellectual remains powerless. David Burg's article on Soviet students—with its characterization of three different types of student opinion as neo-Bolshevik, liberal socialist and anti-socialist—is the most informative in the book.

Two documents are appended: a published account of a conference on science and Marxist philosophy as well as *Novy Mir's* official rejection of "Dr. Zhivago" sent to Boris Pasternak.

MORTON, HENRY W. **Soviet Sport: Mirror of Soviet Society.** New York: Collier, 1963, 221 p.

Organized sports after the Russian Revolution provided healthful exercise, cheap entertainment and emotional release, increased factory efficiency, and a handy network of local and regional clubs for the dissemination of communist thought. In recent years, as Soviet athletes starred in the international arena, sport has become an important tool of external propaganda as well. While Soviet sports are rarely as grim as critics claim, they are always serious and scientific and, most significantly, an integral aspect of the life of the country.

Morton's work is invaluable in its documentation of the roles of the Communist Youth apparatus, the secret police, the trade societies and the party itself in the growth of sport; the "turning inward" of Soviet sport during the U.S.S.R.'s pre-World War II cultural isolation; and the current organization that allows for the relatively simple selection, training and maintenance of national teams under conditions that Western countries attack and envy. That poor facilities, bureaucratic conflict and frequent policy reversals caused by extreme self-examination sometimes stymie the system is yet another fascinating aspect of this unique study of a nation whose pragmatic play is deeply revealing of its structure, its needs and its goals.

KOLARZ, WALTER. **Religion in the Soviet Union.** New York: St. Martin's Press, 1961, 518 p.

Scholarly study of religion in the Soviet Union has gone through three phases, each initiated by a historic rupture of consequence to the whole of Russian life: the revolutions of 1917, the inauguration of a five-year economic plan in 1928, the outbreak of world war in 1939.

Walter Kolarz completed his book just as the third phase came to a close. It is the best and most comprehensive work in the field. To a judicious use of earlier works the author has added careful research in primary materials as well as relevant data culled from ethnographers and demographers. The first and last chapters consider the fundamental issues—the survival and future of religion within the framework of an atheistic state; the middle chapters offer detailed surveys of all the major and many of the minor religious groups in the U.S.S.R. Kolarz lays stress on the postwar period but includes ample sketches of the history of each community beginning with the Revolution.

This book will be the definitive study for some time to come. In the wake of a fresh attack on religion launched by Khrushchev and continued in abated form by his successors, a fourth phase of scholarly activity in the Soviet religious field has begun. More disciplines have embraced the subject than ever before, and with greater intensity. The regnant imperative is now monographic research of narrow focus. Until the contemporary trend has matured, no new synthesis will be possible. And until its appearance, Walter Kolarz's study will remain the indispensable background for lay readers and specialists alike.

George L. Kline has written a good short study of the philosophy of religion and anti-religious thought: **Religious and Anti-Religious Thought in Russia** (Chicago: University of Chicago Press, 1968, 179 p.). Valuable background on the standing of the Orthodox Church is in John Shelton Curtiss, **The Russian Church and the Soviet State, 1917–1950** (Boston: Little, Brown, 1953, 387 p.).

JOHNSON, PRISCILLA and LABEDZ, LEOPOLD, *eds.* **Khrushchev and the Arts: The Politics of Soviet Culture, 1962–1964.** Cambridge: M.I.T. Press, 1965, 300 p.

This collection of documents serves to illustrate the rapidity with which events continue to unfold in the U.S.S.R. and also, in retrospect, to remind us that the change has, unfortunately, not been for the better. In the early 1960s the issue at hand was whether Soviet culture, and Soviet society generally, would proceed with the process of de-Stalinization that set in following Khrushchev's attack on the dead dictator at the Twentieth Party Congress in 1956. At the time, the outcome was quite uncertain. Today the situation is far less promising, and in retrospect even the "conservatives" of 1962–1964 appear surprisingly moderate.

Much of the volume is taken up by the attacks on several nonconformist Soviet writers, artists and painters, and by the equally impassioned rejoinders of those under attack and their liberal friends. It is sad to ponder that such clashes are unlikely to occur today, simply because the "provocations"—*i.e.* unorthodox literary and artistic productions—would not be allowed to see the light of day. Ilya Ehrenburg's iconoclastic memoirs, which inspired much of the heated discussion, would not be published in 1970. Yevgeni Yevtushenko's "Babi Yar," the famous poetic indictment of all anti-Semitism, would be considered dangerously subversive in 1970, at a time when Soviet newspapers grind out massive amounts of anti-"Zionist" propaganda, and when blatantly racist attacks on the Jews such as Ivan Shevtsov's two novels, "In the Name of the Father and the Son" and "Love and Hate," are printed by Soviet publishers. The novelist Alexander Solzhenitsyn ("One Day in the Life of Ivan Denisovich"), hailed by many as the great hope of Soviet literature, has since been expelled from the Union of Soviet Writers. Two later novels, "The First Circle" and "Cancer Ward," had to be printed abroad.

EHRENBURG, ILYA. **Memoirs: 1921–1941.** Cleveland: World Publishing Co., 1964, 543 p.
————. **The War: 1941–1945.** Cleveland: World Publishing Co., 1965, 198 p.

The author of one brilliantly iconoclastic novel, "The Extraordinary Adventures of Julio Jurenito," first published over half a century ago, and of scores of dull, didactic tomes of orthodox Stalinist prose, Ehrenburg can hardly aspire to lasting fame on literary merit alone. Yet there can be little doubt that his reputation will survive long after his more gifted colleagues are forgotten, just as he has miraculously succeeded in surviving most of his friends and associates who disappeared in Stalin's prison camps. At least two generations of Soviet citizenry will long remember him: those who read his sarcastic and impassioned attacks on Nazi barbarism in wartime Soviet newspapers, and their sons and daughters whose first acquaintance with Ehrenburg was through his memoirs, completed before his death in 1967, and serialized in the liberal Soviet monthly *Novy Mir* in the early 1960s.

Of all the memoirs that were published after the long silence under Stalin, Ehrenburg's were far and away the most important. Their evasions and distortions notwithstanding, they were, in many respects, the closest thing to a reasonably accurate account of Soviet Russia's intellectual history. Ehrenburg was no martyr or hero, as his biography amply demonstrates. His writings and speeches include much that is obnoxious, much that was written to ingratiate himself with Stalin and his henchmen. Yet there is no questioning the fact that of all of Ehrenburg's many enthusiasms, his love for West Europe and her culture is most genuine, just as the second volume of his memoirs, covering the period from 1941 to 1945, reveals the honesty of his implacable hatred for the Nazis. His memoirs of the wartime period of initial defeats are outspoken enough but often maintain a discreet silence when the subjects become too delicate, *e.g.* about the extent of Soviet defections to the Nazi side, or civilian populations' collaboration with the Germans. Ehrenburg was equally reticent earlier in his account of the Great Purges of the 1930s.

It is a pity that there is no English translation of the concluding parts of Ehrenburg's memoirs, those covering the postwar years which saw not only a disappointment of the great expectations of 1941–1945 but brought about a period of terror, including the anti-Semitic purges of "cosmopolitans" which had nearly claimed Ehrenburg as a victim.

INKELES, ALEX. **Public Opinion in Soviet Russia: A Study in Mass Persuasion.** Cambridge: Harvard University Press, enl. ed., 1958, 393 p.

This pioneering depiction of mass communication also affords valuable insights into the operation and spirit of the Soviet system as a whole. Chapters on the Soviet press, domestic broadcasting and the Soviet film industry are preceded by extended discussions of the Bolshevik "theory of public opinion," fashioned largely after the ideas of Lenin, and the practice of personal oral agitation. The treatment is both historical and analytic, with a good number of tables and charts. Much attention is given to the interrelations among the party leadership, the Soviet masses and the mass media. The central thesis is that the party, eschewing spontaneity, has the mission of leading and teaching the masses, and that the mass media have a central part to play in achieving that goal. Many of their distinctive features can be traced to that assignment.

The second part, "Personal Oral Agitation and Opinion Leaders," contains an especially valuable discussion of the organization of personal influence in the form of face-to-face contact between representatives of the Communist Party and the Soviet masses, which serves as an important supplement in Soviet theory and practice to the influence of the mass media themselves. An indispensable publication for those seeking the underlying "logic" as well as the basic patterns of Soviet mass communication.

HOPKINS, MARK W. **Mass Media in the Soviet Union.** New York: Pegasus, 1970, 384 p.

Hopkins has been writing on Soviet affairs for *The Milwaukee Journal* since 1964 and has lived and travelled in the U.S.S.R. His book concentrates on the Soviet press, although one chapter deals with radio and TV, characterized for their lack of development as the "stepchildren" of the Soviet mass media. Sources include discussions with Soviet journalists, personal observation of Soviet practice, and reliable Western writing as well as a rich and well-exploited variety of Soviet publications. His book is a sequel to the treatment of the press in Alex Inkeles, **Public Opinion in Soviet Russia,** and to the treatment of TASS in Theodore Edward Kruglak, **The Two Faces of TASS** (Minneapolis: University of Minnesota Press, 1962, 263 p.).

Topics covered include the historical development and functions of the press in Soviet society; censorship and other forms of control, and evasion of them; the educational and career patterns of journalists; political and administrative aspects of news gathering and publishing; the different types, circulation, content and audience response to newspapers and magazines; the Soviet news agencies TASS and Novosti; and the role played in all this by the Soviet people. Maps, tables and illustrations are of excellent quality, and the discussion is enlivened with references to specific, often colorful, experiences.

Hopkins traces the steady growth in the quantity of information processed and disseminated, the limits on independence of the press and its unique tasks set by the Communist Party, the heritage of Stalinism and a continuing "credibility gap" on the part of the people, and the recent signs of flexibility and openness to innovation. This is a definitive scholarly work, encyclopedic in coverage, well written and containing judicious analogies and personal opinions, the latter always identified as such.

ZALESKI, EUGENE and OTHERS. **Science Policy in the U.S.S.R.** Paris: Organization for Economic Coöperation and Development, 1969, 615 p.

Written by a team of European and American specialists, this new OECD study has become the basic reference volume on Soviet scientific organization and problems of science policy. It contains five research essays, dealing respectively with the role of research and development in central planning (including the institutions which plan and finance scientific research); with scientific manpower resources; with the organization of the Soviet Academy of Sciences, including an interesting section on the Research Councils—a new Soviet institution designed to help coördinate scientific research; with research in higher educational institutions; and with the relationship of science to industry. The focus of the book is on the years 1955–1965. It covers in detail the reforms of the Academy of Sciences and of the industrial research institutes in 1961 and 1963.

The authors stress that Soviet science policy faces its most serious challenge in the area of development rather than research. The physical and bureaucratic distance between researchers in Academy institutes and engineers in plant design bureaus has provided real obstacles to the successful transfer of research results into practical applications. The party edict of September 24, 1968 (no. 760) was designed to correct these difficulties.

Nationalities; Minorities

See also Baltic States, p. 596.

PIPES, RICHARD. **The Formation of the Soviet Union: Communism and Nationalism, 1917–1923.** Cambridge: Harvard University Press, 1954, 355 p.

However critically the Soviet state might have been viewed abroad before the Second World War, few challenged its claim to success in the nationality question. Yet the wartime collaboration with the enemy by large numbers of the non-Russian agrarian population and intelligentsia, followed during and after the war by deportations of certain of the smaller nationalities and by the launching of the twin campaigns of Russification and of the repression of "rootless cosmopolitans" (chiefly of members of the Jewish intelligentsia), induced a reappraisal of Soviet policies toward the national minorities. Professor Pipes has exposed the basic Bolshevik dilemma in the nationality question: in order for an essentially working-class and Russian-oriented party to establish and maintain centralized power, it needed to make concessions to particularist, non-Russian, chiefly agrarian interests. According to the author, the resulting contradictions explain not only the vacillations in Soviet nationality policy but also the persistence of national antagonisms in Soviet society.

In the course of his study Pipes has shed new light on many aspects of the nationality question: the growth of a secular nationalism among the Turkic peoples of the Russian Empire, the emergence of national Bolshevism as a challenge to the Great Russian, centralizing mentality of the Bolsheviks and the development of the Commissariat of Nationalities under Stalin into a quasi-state. The author includes the complete text of Lenin's memorandum "Concerning the Question of Nationalities or About Autonomization," by which Lenin laid to rest one of the Soviet Union's most carefully cultivated myths, that of Stalin as the chief architect of the state structure of the U.S.S.R.

Firuz Kazemzadeh, **The Struggle for Transcaucasia (1917–1921)** (New York: Philosophical Library, 1951, 356 p.), is a useful supplementary study.

GOLDHAGEN, ERICH, ed. **Ethnic Minorities in the Soviet Union.** New York: Praeger (for the Institute of East European Jewish Studies of the Philip W. Lown School of Near Eastern and Judaic Studies, Brandeis University), 1968, 351 p.

While much of the literature on Soviet nationalities is polemical and tendentious, this collection of essays is one of the better scholarly works on that complex subject. John Armstrong's attempt to categorize Soviet nationalities as "internal proletariats," "mobilized diasporas," "younger brothers," "state nations" and "colonials" affords a suggestive approach to official policy as well as a potential integrating perspective for the other essays in the volume. These deal with several nationalities—Ukrainians, Armenians, Balts, Turkic peoples, Jews and Belorussians —as well as with more general questions. Vsevolod Holubychny tackles the extremely difficult but important problem of the economic relations among Soviet republics; Jacob Ornstein discusses the evolution of Soviet language policy; and Edward Allworth examines the history of the nationality idea in pre-revolutionary Central Asia. The two essays on aspects of Soviet Jewish life are somewhat more narrow in focus than the rest, one being a close analysis of the content of *Sovetish Heymland,* the other a discussion of the legal position of the Soviet Jewish community. Regrettably, the editor has not synthesized the rich factual material in the volume in an integrating essay which could have provided a more comprehensive overview of ethnic minorities in the U.S.S.R.

KOSVEN, M. O. and OTHERS, *eds.* **Narody Kavkaza I.** 1960, 612 p.
GARDANOV, V. K. and OTHERS, *eds.* **Narody Kavkaza II.** 1962, 683 p.
TOLSTOV, S. P. and OTHERS, *eds.* **Narody Srednei Azii i Kazakhstana I.** 1962, 767 p. **II.** 1963, 778 p.
    Moscow: Izd-vo AN SSSR.
ALEKSANDROV, V. A. and OTHERS, *eds.* **Narody Evropeiskoi chasti SSSR I.** 1964, 984 p.
BELITSER, V. N. and OTHERS, *eds.* **Narody Evropeiskoi chasti SSSR II.** 1964, 918 p.
    Moscow: Nauka.

These volumes, together with "Narody Sibirii" (which has already appeared in English translation as **The Peoples of Siberia,** Chicago: University of Chicago Press, 1964, 948 p.), make up that part of the "Narody Mira" series which deals with the peoples of the Soviet Union. Unlike other volumes in the series, dealing with North America, Africa, non-Soviet Asia, etc., they are based to a significant extent on original ethnographic research and on material collected especially for them. Taken as a whole, these volumes set a high standard for completeness and accuracy of coverage, and for clarity of organization, despite certain features which limit their usefulness for particular purposes. Their scope is encyclopedic, including not only the traditional material culture and social organization of peasant and tribal (or formerly tribal) populations, but also matters such as city planning, architecture, industry, home furnishings and the costume and diet of the working class and the urban population generally, which Western practice—not necessarily to its credit—usually omits from ethnographic discussions.

The drawbacks of these volumes are due either to this same breadth of scope or to the inevitable effects of committee authorship. In the first place, there is no documentation of individual points, except for references to the Marxist classics, to modern political documents and to a very few other sources, most of them pre-revolutionary. This makes the volumes difficult to use for purposes of detailed ethnographic reporting. Secondly, the ideological theoretical passages tend to represent Soviet Marxism in a particularly hidebound form which is not characteristic of later publications or even of articles that appeared in journals contemporaneously with the "Narody Mira" volumes. The non-Soviet reader will no doubt feel a certain impatience with the obligatory ideological statements and the obligatory and monotonous photographs of factories, public buildings and farm machinery which accompany them. However, he would be well advised to overcome this impatience and take advantage of the opportunity to look closely at what for most Westerners is still another world.

The first volume of each set contains general information on the history, archaeology and demography of the area dealt with. Following this, the various peoples are discussed separately, with the pre-revolutionary culture being set apart into special sections in each case. A valuable feature of all of the sets is the multilingual glossaries which cover all aspects of material culture and many social phenomena. No comparable source of information on these peoples exists in English (or perhaps any other language except Russian). No time should be lost in translating these volumes into English in abridged and edited form.

For an introduction to the ethnography of the Russians, see Stephen P. Dunn and Ethel Dunn, **The Peasants of Central Russia** (New York: Holt, Rinehart and Winston, 1967, 139 p.).

HRUSHEVSKY, MIKHAILO SERGEYEVICH. **A History of the Ukraine.** New Haven: Yale University Press, 1941, 629 p.

Michael Hrushevsky is unquestionably the most authoritative Ukrainian historian of the late nineteenth and early twentieth centuries. He was also one of the principal leaders of the Ukrainian national movement and served as the first president of the non-communist Central Rada government in the Ukraine in 1917–1918.

A History of the Ukraine is based on the author's earlier one-volume work entitled "Illustrated History of the Ukraine," which was published in 1911. The history faithfully presents Hrushevsky's general views and interpretations of Ukrainian history—with their emphasis on the separateness and distinctiveness of the Ukraine's historical development—but it does not contain the carefully developed arguments and solidly documented materials that one finds in his major ten-volume study, which is still regarded as the standard scholarly work.

This volume is well balanced with good treatment of all the periods of Ukrainian history. Hrushevsky, however, is at his best in the discussion of the Kievan state and the Cossack period, on which he published many specialized studies. The book closes with a chapter on the Ukrainian national revolution, a process in which Hrushevsky himself played a significant part, and a brief chapter, written by the editor of this volume, O. J. Fredericksen, introducing the reader to the Ukrainian political developments in the inter-war period.

Despite its shortcomings, Hrushevsky's **A History of the Ukraine** must be regarded as the best English-language work on the subject. Robert Scott Sullivant has continued the story, with a political focus, in **Soviet Politics and the Ukraine, 1917–1957** (New York: Columbia University Press, 1962, 438 p.).

RESHETAR, JOHN STEPHEN, JR. **The Ukrainian Revolution, 1917–1920.** Princeton: Princeton University Press, 1952, 363 p.

The Ukrainian Revolution, for many years the standard work on the subject, is still the most reliable and readable study of the Ukrainian efforts to regain independence in the wake of the collapse of the empires during and after World War I. It is without doubt the best English-language work on the Ukrainian national movement of that period. While not as comprehensive as some Ukrainian studies, it is an impressively documented and objectively presented account of a national movement in an area that must still be regarded as one of the most neglected fields in European history and politics.

The author's sympathy with the Ukrainian efforts to recover national independence is apparent throughout the work; but he also made a consistent effort to present the views and attitudes of those who opposed the Ukrainian movement, and nowhere can he be accused of deliberate bias or distortion. After a brief but reliable chapter on the rise of Ukrainian nationalism in the period prior to the outbreak of World War I, Reshetar traces the Ukrainian efforts to regain national statehood, in the broad context of the war, the Russian Revolution and the Civil War. The author also maintains at all times a good balance between local Ukrainian developments and the plans and policies of the great powers that played an active role in the affairs of the East during this period.

The work, which has been widely used by scholars and students of Soviet and East European affairs in the United States and abroad, is an indispensable volume for the study of the modern Ukraine and will have an important place in the literature on this subject for many years to come.

MAZLAKH, SERHII and SHAKHRAI, VASYL'. **On the Current Situation in the Ukraine.** Ann Arbor: University of Michigan Press, 1970, 220 p.

On the Current Situation in the Ukraine is unquestionably the most daring of all the studies of Soviet nationalities policy to appear legally under the Soviet régime. It was written in Ukrainian and was published in Saratov in January 1919. At the time, the Bolshevik policies were still in the making, and not only the authors but many other Ukrainian patriots of socialist persuasion hoped that the Bolshevik approach could furnish a good working formula for the solution of the nationalities problem in Russia and simultaneously provide a solid basis for the development of genuine communist internationalism.

The two knowledgeable authors were both old Bolsheviks. Serhii Mazlakh

(Robsman) was a Ukrainian Jew, and Vasyl' Shakhrai a Ukrainian from the Poltava district. Addressed above all to Lenin, the work is obviously polemical, but it is also carefully documented. It is not only the earliest and the most eloquent statement of Ukrainian national Bolsheviks on the question of self-determination of peoples, but a thoughtful study of the Ukrainian independence movement of the 1917–1918 period as well; it is also the first comprehensive statement of the national communist credo to appear in print anywhere. The freshness and relevance of this impassioned early critique of the Leninist nationalities policy, still suppressed in the Soviet Union, are truly remarkable; they fully justify the appearance of this work in English.

The work has been carefully annotated by its editor, Peter J. Potichnyj, and is preceded by an excellent introductory essay by Michael M. Luther on the background of the events discussed in the book.

ARMSTRONG, JOHN ALEXANDER. **Ukrainian Nationalism, 1939–1945.** New York: Columbia University Press, 2d rev. ed., 1963, 361 p.

This volume is the most comprehensive and objective study in any language of Ukrainian nationalism during the World War II period. It also throws new light on the Soviet nationalities policy of this period as well as on the struggle of other non-Russian peoples of the U.S.S.R. for national independence, in the context of the Russo-German rivalry for domination over Eastern Europe.

The bulk of the book, however, is devoted to aspects of Ukrainian nationalism: preparations made by Ukrainian nationalist forces, especially in the western Ukraine and abroad, for an all-out liberation effort in the event of the outbreak of another world war; intensified struggle of Ukrainian nationalists against the Kremlin following the extension of its control to the western Ukraine; closer coöperation and then conflict with the Germans, followed by a renewed struggle against the return of Soviet rule in the Ukraine mainly through the intensification of an underground guerrilla movement that had its origin in the period of the German occupation.

The book is thoroughly researched and carefully documented. The enlarged and updated edition contains a useful chapter on Ukrainian nationalism in the period after the Second World War.

DZYUBA, IVAN. **Internationalism or Russification? A Study in the Soviet Nationalities Problem.** London: Weidenfeld, 1968, 240 p.

This volume is one of the most important works to come out of the Soviet Union in recent years. It was written in the early 1960s by one of the leading younger Ukrainian literary critics, Ivan Dzyuba, a native of the Donbas, ethnically the weakest, *i.e.* the most Russified, of all the Ukrainian regions. It is a sophisticated and scholarly study of the Soviet nationalities policy of the post-Stalin period which was presented in December 1965 in the form of a detailed memorandum to the party and government leaders of the Ukrainian SSR, with a letter containing an ardent plea for the restoration of the old Leninist norms in the field of Soviet national relations.

At first the origin and authenticity of this well-documented study were questioned by Western scholars—the language in the book was daringly sharp and the author continued his professional activities undisturbed—but published attacks on Dzyuba in the Soviet Ukrainian press confirmed the identity of the author and the authenticity of his work.

It is written entirely from the Marxian point of view, by an erudite Marxist who is both a good internationalist and a devoted son of the Ukrainian people. Dzyuba relies almost exclusively on published Soviet sources, placing especially heavy emphasis on Lenin's writings and specific recommendations for the treatment of the non-Russian peoples of the U.S.S.R., who now constitute more than 50 percent of that state's population. The central theme of the book is his plea for true equality among and justice for all the peoples of the Soviet Union, which in his view can be achieved only through the restoration of Leninist norms regardless of the difficulties that the long overdue implementation of such a policy would entail.

Dzyuba's analysis draws heavily on the Ukrainian experience, but he also makes a serious effort to treat the problem of Soviet nationalities in the broad all-Union context within the framework of Soviet laws and constitutional guarantees.

PIERCE, RICHARD A. **Russian Central Asia, 1867–1917: A Study in Colonial Rule.** Berkeley: University of California Press, 1960, 359 p.

The author conceives his main task here to be the refuting of Soviet historians who have not faithfully represented the half-century of Russian experience in Central Asia preceding the 1917 Revolutions. This choice has put him in the position of delivering an apologia for Tsarist aims and procedures in the area. He agrees with most major Russian contentions about the Central Asian conquest advanced by Tsarist and Soviet Russian historians: that Russia's invasion of Central Asia was provoked and therefore justifiable, that the conquest brought great advantages to the region, and that achievement of law and order under a foreign (Russian) tyranny was preferable to slower indigenous processes, often bloody and chaotic, of settling internal political differences.

The book is divided into five nearly parallel parts, developed chronologically: conquest and administration; colonization; economic development; cultural conflict; fall of the Tsarist régime. Since it intentionally adheres to the Imperial Russian viewpoint, **Russian Central Asia** may be consulted most profitably as a detailing of Tsarist colonial measures and their chronology from 1867 to around 1900. It is weaker in its analysis of the Tsarist government's later treatment of the Central Asian people and their behavior under provocation.

PARK, ALEXANDER GARLAND. **Bolshevism in Turkestan, 1917–1927.** New York: Columbia University Press, 1957, 428 p.

This well-written book is one of the earliest American political-historical inquiries into aspects of the Soviet nationality question as it was posed in Soviet Central Asia, including Kazakhstan, during Soviet Russia's first decade. Possibly because the work employs no Central-Asian language sources, it exhibits two characteristics of pioneering American scholarship in this field: perhaps unconscious acceptance of the Soviet idiom concerning nationality problems, as well as sharing some Russian attitudes toward the Central Asians that are being questioned today in informed Western research.

The author approaches the nationality question through a study of official nationality doctrine and policy. He examines mainly political organization and control but also looks at application of policy in supposed drives for economic equality, in agricultural development and land reform, culture and religion. This survey leads him to conclude that *Sovnatspol* up to 1927 failed because it had been actuated by a leadership which distrusted the public will. Such policy never achieved "tolerance and respect for human dignity and regional aspirations," something the author apparently believes certain Soviet politicians aspired to. Basic inequality between the Russian center and all the outlying regions, however, had been bred into the system of relationships before 1917, he says, and was reconfirmed no later than 1923 by the primacy granted openly to the proletarian heartland of the U.S.S.R. at the expense of the periphery.

Central Asia: A Century of Russian Rule, edited by Edward Allworth (New York: Columbia University Press, 1967, 552 p.), is a solid work on the land and peoples of Central Asia, showing especially the effects of Russian influence on its development since the fall of Tashkent in 1865.

SCHWARZ, SOLOMON M. **The Jews in the Soviet Union.** Syracuse: Syracuse University Press, 1951, 380 p.

For all the polemical and journalistic literature on the Jews in the Soviet Union, there are few scholarly works on the subject. Twenty years after its publication,

Solomon Schwarz's pioneering effort remains the definitive scholarly study of Soviet Jewry. The major strengths of the study are its reliance on statistical and demographic materials in discussing such questions as assimilation and economic transformation, the absence of polemical and subjective rhetoric and, perhaps most important, Schwarz's ability to place the Jewish situation in the broader context of the evolution of Soviet nationality policy. His discussion of communist doctrine on the nationality question remains one of the best summaries of that complicated topic.

The first part is a survey of Soviet Jewish history, with emphasis on the interaction between the régime and the Jewish community, from the Revolution until 1950. The second half is a thorough study of anti-Semitism in the U.S.S.R. from the 1920s through the Second World War. Unfortunately, Schwarz has not followed up this volume with a study of Soviet Jews in the late Stalinist and post-Stalinist eras, though he has published a less satisfactory monograph, in Russian, on the Jews in the U.S.S.R. from 1939 to 1965.

Although he did not use the Soviet Yiddish press extensively, the author took full advantage of Russian-language material on Soviet Jewry and made profitable use of Soviet Jewish scholarship of the 1920s and thereafter. His reliance on official sources and Russian-language materials prevents him from plumbing the depths of internal developments in the Soviet Jewish community but also enables him to approach his subject in a dispassionate manner. This book remains the basic work on the history of the Jews in the U.S.S.R.

For a useful survey of journalistic literature on Soviet Jewry see Ronald I. Rubin, *ed.,* **The Unredeemed: Anti-Semitism in the Soviet Union** (Chicago: Quadrangle Books, 1968, 316 p.).

KOCHAN, LIONEL, *ed.* **The Jews in Soviet Russia since 1917.** New York: Oxford University Press (for the Institute of Jewish Affairs, London), 1970, 357 p.

Not since Solomon Schwarz's **The Jews in the Soviet Union,** published two years before Stalin's death, has there been as good a scholarly work in English on the complex subject of Soviet Jewry as this one. Despite the apparent irrelevance of two or three of the contributions, this anthology manages to touch on all the important issues and aspects of Soviet Jewry. S. Ettinger's discussion of Russian Jewry's renaissance in 1917 vividly brings home the potential for cultural, economic and political development that existed immediately after the fall of the *ancien régime* and provides the background necessary to the understanding of later developments. J. Miller's explication of Soviet theory on the Jews from Lenin's time to the present and William Korey's treatment of the legal position of Soviet Jewry provide a description of the context in which Soviet Jewry must operate.

One of the most informative articles is the sober, cautious and objective discussion of demographic and occupational trends among Soviet Jews, by J. A. Newth and Alec Nove. They conclude that it is impossible to deduce a policy of conscious socioeconomic discrimination against Jews from available statistics, though they admit that Jews are barred from responsible positions. Chone Shmeruk pays Soviet Yiddish literature the respect due it by refraining from maudlin lamentations and concentrating on a scholarly analysis, while Yehoshua Gilboa relates the fascinating and tragic story of Hebrew literature—illegal since the 1920s—in the Soviet Union. Religion, Zionism, the Birobidzhan project and the Second World War are other areas competently discussed. All in all, this volume, though not a systematic treatment, offers a solid, scholarly overview of the tangled question of contemporary Soviet Jewry.

III. THE MIDDLE EAST

GENERAL

LAWRENCE, T. E. **Seven Pillars of Wisdom.** New York: Doubleday, 1935, 672 p.

The Arab revolt against the Turks in World War I could have no more brilliant exposition than is provided by **Seven Pillars of Wisdom.** Since then the worshippers and debunkers of the Lawrence legend have been using it as a source for their varying interpretations of the author's conduct and character. And perhaps his own book does tell more about Lawrence himself than about the war seen in its broad perspective. Indeed, he set out to write a personal narrative pieced out of memory, not based on "proper notes" and not impartial. Let it be conceded that he has exaggerated his own role. The book remains a classic with all the flavor of war in the desert and finely done portraits of individual Arabs great and small. If it is not history, it is in many respects a truer picture than one would get from professionally written history. The Arab revolt, the capture of Aqaba and the Arab campaign on the right wing of Allenby's offensive in Palestine and Syria may not have been decisive in the total picture of the war. They did have military significance and even greater political significance, and Lawrence's contribution on both counts was substantial.

The narrative ends with the entry into Damascus. Lawrence then began his experience in the entanglements of peacemaking which were to test his British and Arab loyalties and his faith in himself. Of this experience he gives some prior indications in this book, as when he refers to the lack of support from his own government, "whose action and silence were at once an example, a spur and a licence to me to do the like."

KEDOURIE, ELIE. **England and the Middle East: The Destruction of the Ottoman Empire, 1914–1921.** London: Bowes and Bowes, 1956, 236 p.

At the close of World War I Britain and France seized from the Ottoman Empire the "Fertile Crescent" of mostly Arab territory between Anatolia and the Arabian Peninsula, and divided it into five states which they governed as League of Nations mandates. There are still five states in the Fertile Crescent, and except for the mutations of the Palestine-Transjordan complex and the transfer of the Alexandretta *sanjaq* (renamed the Vilayet of Hatay) from Syria to Turkey, the imposed territorial divisions proved remarkably durable.

The blueprints for the statemaking by the imperial powers were drawn in the heat of World War I. The principal agreement embodying the results of their diplomatic and cartographic exercises immortalized the names of Sir Mark Sykes and Charles François Georges-Picot, who negotiated the several instruments that made up the agreement which Russia also originally signed. British negotiations with Arab and Zionist leaders complicated an already complex pattern. The truth of allied wartime diplomacy has been blurred by the massive partisan literature of the Bolsheviks, who repudiated and selectively publicized the Sykes-Picot and related secret agreements, and by that of the Arab nationalists and Zionists and their supporters who have devoted more effort to repudiating each other's charges than to clarifying the meaning of the allied secret undertakings. Though writing before he could consult the pertinent classified files in the Public Record Office, Kedourie produced a work that nevertheless remains invaluable because of his thorough study of the Arabic as well as the available European materials. So, too, is W. W. Gottlieb's **Studies in Secret Diplomacy during the First World War,** though the analysis is limited to European diplomacy. Writing in the late 1960s, Jukka Nevakivi in **Britain, France, and the Arab Middle East, 1914–1920** (London: Athlone, 1970, 284 p.) deepened the European analysis by thorough examination of the unpublished materials in the Public Record Office in London, the National Archives in Washington and a wide assortment of private papers in England, the United States and Canada. Still awaited are the release of the French archives and the historian who will blend the European and Middle East sources into an integrated narrative.

TRUMPENER, ULRICH. **Germany and the Ottoman Empire, 1914–1918.** Princeton: Princeton University Press, 1968, 433 p.

The German-Ottoman alliance of 1914–1918 significantly influenced the war if not the settlement which followed. The closing of the Straits weakened the Tsarist military effort and the Entente coördination, and the thrusts toward Suez tied British troops down in the eastern Mediterranean. For far too long this alliance has received only marginal attention. Ulrich Trumpener has gone some distance toward satisfying the need for an authoritative analysis. The value of his work lies in meticulous scholarship resting on a systematic and comprehensive search of the German Foreign Office files, and on use of the standard published works in Western languages as well as several Turkish books. Unfortunately, the author was denied access to the Turkish State Archives. Thus, while German policy is vividly presented, we get only an impressionist view of the Sublime Porte, reconstructed from chance reports in the German records.

Rather than evaluating the fighting itself, the author concentrates on the central issues of the wartime alliance: the conversion of the formal alliance into a real one in the autumn of 1914, an assessment of the top German officers assigned to Ottoman duty, the tough bargaining of Ottoman politicians and diplomats, the German quest for postwar economic preference in the Ottoman Empire, German failure to moderate the brutal Ottoman policies toward the Armenians, and German muddling on the Baghdad Railway. All these topics, including the collapse of the alliance in 1918, are examined on the whole with mature judgment and convincing argument.

TOYNBEE, ARNOLD J. **The Islamic World since the Peace Settlement.** New York: Oxford University Press (for the Royal Institute of International Affairs), 1927, 611 p.

Consideration of the Islamic world, omitted from the first two volumes of the annual "Survey of International Affairs" because of lack of space, required book-length treatment when it was finally taken up for review. This was a happy accident, for the volume remains one of Toynbee's memorable and durable works. In examining the effects of the First World War on Islamic society, he took as his central theme the conflict between European imperialism and regional nationalisms and the search for accommodation between them. He found that nationalism among Muslims, as "among almost all other non-Western peoples who had come into contact with Western civilization," was propelled by "a negative impulse . . . to throw off the ascendency of the Western powers" and by "a positive impulse . . . to adopt the military technique, the political institutions, the economic organization and the spiritual culture of the West." Through its organization of a mass of otherwise diffuse and bewildering historical events around that theme, the book gives unity to the period and illuminates the years which followed. Hailed as a classic on appearance, it has lost little of its value as a reference work on the political transformation of Islamic states and societies.

In a sense Toynbee promised more than he delivered. There is a presumption that he is examining the zone of Islam from Morocco to the Dutch East Indies and

China, a zone which he vividly notes acquires geopolitical importance because it lies athwart the main constriction points on the busiest sea-lane in the world. The real focus, however, from the opening assessment of the contest of religion and secularism in Islamic society sharpened by the abolition of the Ottoman Caliphate, is on the Middle East and North Africa.

GIANNINI, AMEDEO. **L'Ultima Fase della Questione Orientale 1913–1939.** Milan: Istituto per gli Studi di Politica Internazionale, 2d ed., 1941, 428 p.

A distinguished diplomatic historian who has published many volumes of treaties and other documents, Giannini in this important work established himself as a pioneer in the diplomatic history of the Near East. The first edition covered the 1920s in some detail, while the second added material from 1932 to the outbreak of war in 1939 which is somewhat more sketchy. The book begins with the Treaty of Sèvres and its aftermath in Turkey's relations with the powers, covers the negotiations at Lausanne, and then goes into a series of separate studies on the Armenian and Kurdish questions, the individual Arab states and territories (including Palestine), Egypt and the Suez Canal, the Dodecanese and Cyprus.

Looked at in retrospect, Giannini's work appears superficial in spots, too much tied to documentary texts and short on the explanation of policies. It is obviously out of date. Yet the range of historical and contemporary sources is extraordinarily wide. Like the Middle East chapters of the annual surveys put out by the Royal Institute of International Affairs in London, this book served for years as a valuable guide and reference work to all interested in this fascinating but unfortunately not final phase of the Eastern Question, and it is still useful today.

The diplomacy of the First World War is not really dealt with, despite the 1913 date in the title. Harry N. Howard's **The Partition of Turkey, 1913–1923** (Norman: University of Oklahoma Press, 1931, 486 p.) is much better for that period.

STORRS, SIR RONALD. **The Memoirs of Sir Ronald Storrs.** New York: Putnam, 1937, 563 p.

The author's career in the Middle East spanned 28 years (1904–1932) and three countries (Egypt, Palestine and Cyprus). Of these, the middle years, from 1914 to 1920, were the most important. Storrs started out as a functionary in the office of the British Financial Adviser to the Egyptian government, later becoming Oriental Secretary or top aide on Egyptian affairs to the British Agent and Consul General in Cairo. During World War I Sir Ronald served as a troubleshooter on Arab affairs for the High Commissioner in Egypt. As such he took part, in 1915–1916, in the exchanges between High Commissioner Sir Henry McMahon and Sharif Husayn of Mecca, later king of the Hejaz, in negotiating the terms of an accord for an Arab revolt against Ottoman rule; and in 1917 in Baghdad in trying to mediate the conflicting Arab policies framed by the Foreign Office, which he represented in the Hejazi negotiations, and the India Office, which handled wartime arrangements in the rest of the Arabian Peninsula and Mesopotamia. Immediately after the British conquest of Jerusalem in December 1917, Storrs became military governor of the city and its surrounding district where he remained for eight years, also serving the civil administration under the mandate. On the Arab-Zionist dispute he managed to be sympathetic to both Zionism and Arab nationalism, and as a dedicated town planner he created a "pro-Jerusalem society" that brought together the leaders of all religious communities and made them jointly responsible for preserving the architectural beauty of the city. He ended his Middle East career as Governor of Cyprus.

At the time of the book's appearance, it was invaluable for the background it provided on the Anglo-Egyptian dispute, the British organization of the Arab revolt in 1915–1917 and the British military administration in Palestine as seen from Jerusalem in 1918–1920. The memoirs were drawn largely from the author's letters to his mother; retrospective analysis provided the connective tissue. With the opening of the pertinent classified archives at the Public Record Office in London, the book lost its importance as a primary source of information but is still useful as a contemporary chronicle.

MONROE, ELIZABETH. **The Mediterranean in Politics.** New York: Oxford University Press, 1938, 259 p.

The settlement after World War I placed the Mediterranean essentially under Anglo-French hegemony, with marginal influence on the European and North African shores exercised by Italy in the center and Spain in the west. Once again Russia, preoccupied elsewhere, was denied a Mediterranean and Middle Eastern role by the other great powers, and the challenge in the Mediterranean during the inter-war period came more from the Axis powers than from the Soviet Union.

Elizabeth Monroe, writing in the late 1930s, examined the Italian threat to Anglo-French supremacy in Mussolini's *mare nostrum* doctrine, a blueprint for the attempted creation of a new Roman Empire. With a sure eye for pertinent detail and an uncommon skill for explaining complex problems in simple terms, she produced an essay of more than historical value. A comparable volume, Margret Boveri's **Mediterranean Cross-Currents** (New York: Oxford University Press, 1938, 451 p.), appeared at about the same time. Despite occasional lapses into racism and sympathy for Italian expansionism, Miss Boveri, a German observer, wrote with commendable detachment. Her book admirably blends geography and history, though at the expense of analysis.

World War II eliminated Italian Fascism but so weakened France and Britain as to require growing American participation in support of the Western strategy of containing Soviet pressures to become a Mediterranean power. Although the Mediterranean area as such never had much reality in American strategic thought or policy, there was no doubt of its importance in a global strategy which included the defense of Western Europe and of the Middle East. William Reitzel's **The Mediterranean: Its Role in America's Foreign Policy** (New York: Harcourt, 1948, 195 p.) examined the cold war in the Mediterranean as it was starting to take shape. His brief but incisive book showed how American resources propped up the faltering British system, and he accurately predicted that, despite Western success, "there is no reason to expect a reduction of . . . [Soviet] pressures." On the British side, a Chatham House report, **British Interests in the Mediterranean and Middle East** (New York: Oxford University Press, for the Royal Institute of International Affairs, 1958, 123 p.), assessed the consequences for Britain of the replacement of the Anglo-French system by one with America in the leading role after the Suez crisis of 1956.

KIRK, GEORGE E. **The Middle East in the War.** New York: Oxford University Press (for the Royal Institute of International Affairs), 1953, 511 p.

A volume in the wartime series of the "Survey of International Affairs, 1939–1946," George Kirk's study is indispensable to all concerned with the Middle East, whether with military operations, the policies of the powers or political developments on the local scene. He performed a remarkable job of coverage, using a variety of contemporary sources plus material which came to light in the immediate postwar years. The book has the special virtues, and the inevitable shortcomings, of the Chatham House "Surveys." It comes as close to dependable history as is possible when written so close to the events it describes; yet it makes no claims to disembodied objectivity, for George Kirk is interpreter rather than chronicler of what has happened. Wisely, he decided to give major attention to the political aspects of the war; more specifically, to the bids for independence which it spurred: by nationalists in Egypt and the Fertile Crescent, by Jews in Palestine and the world Zionist movement, by Ethiopians and by the peoples of the Maghrib.

The successor volume by the same author, **The Middle East 1945–1950** (New York: Oxford University Press, for the Royal Institute of International Affairs, 1954, 338 p.), has the same theme of the interplay between the policies of the major powers and the various movements for national independence. In these years the decline of Britain's authority in the Middle East, described by Kirk as "inherent in her post-war position," was marked by a relatively smooth transfer of responsibility to the United States in the countries of the northern tier and also by sharp differences with the United States on Palestine. His concern with Palestine is manifest in the detailed account in which he gave the evidence as much coherence as it permitted and did not shirk the controversial issues, allowing conclusions and judgments on British and American policies and on the conduct of Arab and Zionist leaders to emerge from the coldly recounted facts. In general, the book is of high quality but is not quite the tour de force that its predecessor was, and in many respects has been superseded by later studies.

DeNovo, John A. **American Interests and Policies in the Middle East 1900–1939.**
Minneapolis: University of Minnesota Press, 1963, 447 p.

America's role in the international politics of the Middle East during the first four decades of the twentieth century was primarily that of a spectator. Its interests were not vital, and its policies were largely the traditional ones of protecting the rights of American citizens and institutions, defending the principles of equal opportunity and the open door, standing for peace and humanitarianism, and giving advice to others. Yet if in the larger sense this was much ado about relatively little, it is none the less a story to be told. John DeNovo, using official U.S. diplomatic documents and many other sources, has told it competently and in detail. Except for monographic treatment of certain phases, subsequent scholars need not bother to tell it again.

Highlights of the book are the temporary American involvement in the peace settlement in the Near East after World War I, the story of the Chester concession and the Anglo-American disputes over oil rights, and such individual episodes as the Shuster and Millspaugh missions in Iran. The author's general theme is that the cultivation of economic and cultural ties could hardly be adequately protected without political involvement, a price the American nation, despite the brief flurry of Wilsonian peacemaking, was not prepared to pay. He found the interests and policies of those years, however, to be essential background for understanding the problems to be faced after World War II. What lessons were learned and by whom is another question.

A more detailed and intensive study of one part of this period, the years of the war and the peace settlement, is Laurence Evans' **United States Policy and the Partition of Turkey, 1914–1924** (Baltimore: Johns Hopkins Press, 1965, 437 p.), an excellent monograph which traces the course of American policy from non-involvement to involvement and back again.

CAMPBELL, John Coert. **Defense of the Middle East: Problems of American Policy.**
New York: Harper (for the Council on Foreign Relations), rev. ed., 1960, 400 p.

This was the first major dissection of the postwar American role of leadership and responsibility in the Middle East, a role that the United States accepted step by step and only reluctantly. Campbell evaluated in depth the nature and the scope of the Soviet threat in the Middle East to the security of the United States and its Western allies in the late 1950s. "So long as we have no assurance of a workable system of global arms limitation or a fundamental change in the aims and character of the Soviet regime," he observed, "we must keep in the forefront of all our calculations and decisions the deadly thrust of Soviet power at the service of Soviet policies fundamentally hostile to this country." In that sense the book reflected the cold-war atmosphere of the time. But for the author the concept of defense was much wider than the demands of military strategy imposed on American policymakers by an expansive Soviet Union. He investigated the whole range of problems arising from the urgency to find a fresh basis for bringing into a new equilibrium the relations between the West and the Middle East at a time of Western European withdrawal and of social and economic revolution in the region. In his view, the establishment of conditions of mutual respect among the region's plural societies and between them and the outside world is essential to such an equilibrium.

In the decade since the appearance of this book many of the problems have become more critical. Their shape has changed, owing to events both inside and outside the region. Soviet-American rivalry has sharpened in the Middle East at a time when the domestic American repercussions of Vietnam have compelled the United States to reappraise its role the world over. In the circumstances, American perceptions of the Soviet challenge and the future role of the United States in that explosive strategic region are bound to be different from those of the 1950s. Despite these changes, the book provides a useful analysis of the American response to the earlier challenge.

SPEISER, EPHRAIM AVIGDOR. **The United States and the Near East.** Cambridge: Harvard University Press, rev. ed., 1950, 283 p.

For the author, a lifelong archaeologist converted by wartime service in Washington into a contemporary analyst, the Near East represented what later scholars have generally designated the Arab East, that is, Arab Asia and Egypt. This was one of the earliest and best analyses of the problems that beset the volatile region and its interested extra-regional powers at the close of World War II, and the only one devoted specifically to American interests and concerns. Of modest dimensions, the book manages to convey a sense of authoritative yet felicitous interpretation, for the author seems as familiar with the ancient and medieval past as with developments of the nineteenth and twentieth centuries and contrives to tell his story painlessly. In one chapter which is a brilliant synthesis of the region's vital legacy, entitled "The Enduring Cultural Factor," Speiser provides a perspective of four thousand years of history. In another outstanding chapter he examines the interplay of Zionism, Arab nationalism and British imperialism which then made up the problem of Palestine, "a land haunted by history . . . [and] the victim of geography." The problems which Speiser investigated immediately after the war later changed character, as British power dissolved, to be replaced by Soviet-American rivalry. He overestimated Britain's staying power, as did many others, and he overplayed Anglo-American rivalry as a postwar theme. But the historical interpretation leading up to World War II has, despite its brevity, passed the test of time.

MONROE, ELIZABETH. **Britain's Moment in the Middle East, 1914–1956.** Baltimore: Johns Hopkins Press, 1963, 254 p.

Here is an urbane inquiry into the four decades of Britain's paramountcy in the Middle East from the seizure of Baghdad and Jerusalem in 1917 to the Suez crisis of 1956. The sparse annotation and the lively style tend to conceal the soundness and originality of the work. An old Middle East hand, the author infused new light into accustomed themes relating to the consolidation and decline of British power in the region by drawing upon a wide range of evidence—personal observation, unpublished official and private papers (some not previously used by scholars) and published works. Miss Monroe found the British legacy in the Islamic states less impressive than elsewhere in Asia and Africa and attributed it to the fact that Britain's presence in the Middle East was designed to serve primarily extra-regional goals. Nevertheless, "Britain, in its forty years of dominance in the Middle East earned enough acquiescence and at times admiration to save the British skin in two world wars. It also afforded the local peoples a life-giving interlude of freedom from the disagreement and upheaval that was bound to follow the break-up of the Ottoman Empire."

Any definitive study of so vast a subject as British supremacy in the Middle East must await the many monographs that are certain to appear as the Public Record Office progressively opens to scholars the records of the 1940s and 1950s. Until then, this essay which judges so well that 40-year "moment" will continue to serve as a useful introduction.

LAQUEUR, WALTER Z. **The Soviet Union and the Middle East.** New York: Praeger, 1959, 366 p.

Among the handful of scholars well grounded both in the history of communism and in the affairs of the Middle East, Walter Laqueur is probably the most competent. He has surely been the most productive in writing on the subject of Soviet policy in that region, with **The Soviet Union and the Middle East** standing as his best work. It is a carefully done survey, year by year and country by country, from the First World War to the late 1950s. Because few relevant Soviet documents are available, Laqueur relied heavily on the specialized periodicals and, for the earlier period, the material of the Comintern in addition to the Soviet press. He used the "scholarly" articles wisely, not assuming that every Soviet author wrote with the authority of Lenin or Stalin.

In his treatment of the interplay between Soviet policy, Middle Eastern communism and the various types of nationalism Laqueur built on his earlier **Communism and Nationalism in the Middle East** (New York: Praeger, 1956, 362 p.), which contains a good deal of information on local communist parties and on Middle East politics but is a rather disjointed and less than satisfactory book. **The Soviet Union and the Middle East** is much more solid.

A later work by the same author, **The Struggle for the Middle East: The Soviet Union in the Mediterranean, 1958–1968** (New York: Macmillan, 1969, 360 p.), serves as a sequel, bringing the story through the Six Day War and its aftermath. Although it does not bear the marks of the extended research that went into its predecessors, the author in this instance had over ten years of active and largely successful Soviet policy to write about, with diminished need to interpret esoteric emanations from the Soviet academic institutes. He is not loath to give his own views and speculations on Soviet and Western policies, but those personal passages, like the rest of the book, are well worth the attention of both expert and general reader.

KOHN, HANS. **A History of Nationalism in the East.** New York: Harcourt, 1929, 476 p.

A prolific historian who often wrote about contemporary problems and a profound scholar of historical and contemporary nationalism, Hans Kohn was among the first to consider for popular consumption the interplay of nationalism and imperialism in the inter-war Middle East. In **A History of Nationalism in the East,** which encompasses the Caucasus and Central Asia as well as the non-Soviet Asian countries to the south (including India but excluding the Fertile Crescent) and Egypt, the author explores the results of the policies of Britain and of Tsarist and Soviet Russia toward the peoples under their rule or influence. His contention that the contest of "white" imperialism and "Oriental" nationalism "has given an impetus to the unification of mankind" seems hard to justify in the 40 years that have since passed. It probably continued to appeal to expectant observers of the 1950s, many of whom, however, began to grow disillusioned by the 1960s. Kohn also exaggerated the then "solidarity of the white race" as much as the anticipated "corresponding solidarity . . . among the Oriental Peoples."

Kohn's later **Nationalism and Imperialism in the Hither East** (New York: Harcourt, 1932, 347 p.) focused on political developments in the Arab East in the 1920s, with a brief historical retrospect going back to ancient times. The author assessed the search for consolidation and independence of the states emerging from World War I and the peace settlement. Basically, it is a study of Arab nationalism, the influence of Cairo as the center of the nationalist movement and the hardening quarrel in Palestine with Zionism. In general, the two volumes are still valuable, not so much for the substantive information which now has been overtaken by more comprehensive research, but as a reflection of the type of contemporary history that helped mold the judgments of scholars, officials and interested laymen in the inter-war years.

LOVE, KENNETH. **Suez: The Twice-Fought War: A History.** New York: McGraw-Hill, 1969, 767 p.

Of all the books on the Suez crisis of 1956 this is the longest and heaviest, the fruit of many years of research in the documents and published memoirs, plus interviews with many of the principals. The result is a wealth of detail, including many interesting points not previously known, all brought together in a colorful running narrative which is occasionally held up for extensive excursions into the past to provide background. Despite the subtitle, the book is about the first Suez war; a chapter on the second is merely tacked on.

No "definitive" history of the Suez affair and the related phase of the Arab-Israel conflict is possible at this stage, if ever, but Love's book is the nearest we have some 15 years after the events. It is surely the best on the subject of American policy, thanks to the use of the Dulles papers and to direct testimony from President Eisenhower. Yet the broad view is hard to find, and the interpretation of Arab and Israeli concerns and policies is definitely partial to the former. The story has a hero, Gamal Abdel Nasser, who is presented as a man of peace forced reluctantly into conflict by those who were bent on war to destroy him long before the crisis of 1956. Many of the author's interpretations are based on what Nasser told him in many interviews over the years, all of it taken at face value.

Herman Finer, in a book nearly as large and similarly supported by many footnotes, came to quite contrary conclusions. His **Dulles over Suez: The Theory and Practice of His Diplomacy** (Chicago: Quadrangle Books, 1964, 538 p.) is an unrelenting attack on the American Secretary of State for high-handed treatment of allies and of Israel, rejection of their legitimate demands and actions to obtain justice, misunderstanding of Nasser, mistaken morality and lack of courage. The book contains much that illuminates the story of the crisis and is worth a careful reading. It was too bad that Finer, an eminent scholar, allowed himself to be so carried away by his personal feelings.

THOMAS, HUGH. **Suez.** New York: Harper and Row, 1967, 261 p.

So much has been written on the Suez crisis of 1956, especially the British side of the story, that it is difficult to select a single book or even a half-dozen as the best. Hugh Thomas does not claim to have written a definitive history, but perhaps no one ever will, for the documentary record which historians consult in the future may be as full of holes as the "interim report" he has pieced together ten years after the event. He used the published apologiae and memoirs of the principal actors (Eden, Eisenhower, Pineau, Dayan, et al.) as well as other published material, but the book rests mainly on his search for oral testimony from ministers, advisers, military officers and others in a position to know this or that fact. The totality of that evidence permitted the author to write a carefully footnoted and convincing account. The great frustration for the reader, anxious to know and judge the evidence, lies in the anonymity of the sources.

The almost day-by-day narration, covering the three months of crisis, sheds a great deal of light on the often obscured main questions of policy, decision and responsibility, as well as clarifying who said—or failed to say—what to whom on a particular occasion. The failings and the personal tragedy of Anthony Eden, the single-minded toughness of French and Israeli leadership, the fact of collusion with Israel despite official denials, and the grave miscalculations about the United States (which, in Macmillan's words, the British leaders expected to "lie doggo")—all come through clearly. So also does the illusion of past imperial power that swept away from the realities of the 1950s not only the Prime Minister and his cabinet but the Conservative Party and a majority of the British public.

Much of Thomas's account is corroborated by Anthony Nutting's **No End of a Lesson** (New York: Potter, 1967, 205 p.) which appeared soon after it. Nutting, though a junior minister, was in a special position by virtue of his personal participation in Britain's policy in the Middle East prior to the crisis. Though left out of the most secret top-level conversations prior to the attack on Egypt, he knew a great deal, and his revelations are devastating, especially when compared to Eden's own story in **Full Circle** (Boston: Houghton, 1960, 676 p.). Additional revelations appear in Terence Robertson's **Crisis: The Inside Story of the Suez Conspiracy** (New York: Atheneum, 1965, 349 p.), which is especially good on Anglo-French relations and on Canada's role.

LERNER, DANIEL. **The Passing of Traditional Society: Modernizing the Middle East.** Glencoe: Free Press, 1958, 466 p.

The purpose of this book was to apply modern methods of the behavioral sciences to a study of six Middle Eastern societies that were in the process of transition from old to new attitudes and institutions—Turkey, Iran, Lebanon, Syria, Jordan and Egypt. In method it is a survey through interviews with individuals, some 300 in each country, carried out by native interviewers; the results were then collated, analyzed and reanalyzed by staff members at Columbia University's Bureau of Applied Social Research and by the author. The whole undertaking took nearly a decade. The result is a book with numerous interesting statistics, useful comparisons among the six countries, some probing into matters of indi·vidual and social psychology and occasional flashes of insight from individual interviews.

As a pioneering work it has the expected strengths and weaknesses. The questionnaire method of research always has its hazards. Reducing to percentages and statistical tables the responses of assorted denizens of the Middle East to a series of questions is no assured foundation for broad conclusions. Fortunately, the author based his narrative also on a wide reading of historical and contemporary material. He has provided a sense of how the modernization process shows itself in the lives and outlooks of people in different sectors of society. But the general approach and method, applied to so large and diverse a subject, have not wholly proved themselves in this book.

HALPERN, MANFRED. **The Politics of Social Change in the Middle East and North Africa.** Princeton: Princeton University Press, 1963, 431 p.

To draw patterns of social and political development in the heterogeneous area from Morocco to Pakistan (but not including Israel) is a most difficult task which has nevertheless held great attraction for Western scholars and observers. Manfred Halpern's study, based on a wealth of available literature in many languages and on his own deep knowledge of the area, has many merits. The most stimulating part of the book deals with "the range of political choices," in which he takes up a series of ideologies, assesses their actual and potential influence, and relates them to each other and to the overall trend toward modernization. In discussing reformist Islam, neo-Islamic totalitarianism, communism, nationalism, democracy and socialism, he concedes that his analysis goes beyond any attempted by Middle Eastern intellectuals or leaders; but it is based on their words and their actions.

The interpretations at times seem too precise, and the patterns too neat, for the diversity of the facts. The principal themes are revolution from the top and the rise of the "new middle class," with the military as its principal instrument for the modernization of society. Yet even at the time of writing Halpern found conflicting evidence, and the years since publication of his book have shown how difficult it is to find uniform patterns among Turks, Persians, Pakistanis and the many kinds of Arabs. Again and again one is driven back to explaining differences, or explaining them away. The book is none the less a most important synthesis which brings method and order to developments often misunderstood both in the West and in the Middle East itself.

HUREWITZ, J. C. **Middle East Politics: The Military Dimension.** New York: Praeger (for the Council on Foreign Relations), 1969, 553 p.

The spate of military coups in Asia, Africa and Latin America after World War II has set scholars to studying the patterns of this phenomenon and the nature of the régimes it has produced. Much of the writing has tended to generalities insufficiently supported by knowledge of the politics of individual countries. J. C. Hurewitz, in contrast, made the effort to give his overall analysis a solid foundation in separate studies of the role of the military in 18 states from Morocco to Afghanistan. It makes for a big book, but his conclusions become of greater interest, and some are original. Inevitably, such a book could not satisfy all the specialists on the individual states, nor were the categories in which the author classified them likely to go without challenge. But as a large-scale pioneer work in a difficult field the book has succeeded in its purpose. Its only close rival is Eliezer Be'eri's **Army Officers in Arab Politics and Society,** which is confined to the Arab East and so differs in its approach as to make the two books hardly comparable.

Hurewitz's volume is really several books in one, for in addition to the country studies he has a set of chapters on the history of the military institution in the Ottoman Empire and other Islamic states, an analysis of the role of the military in modernization and development (in which he takes issue with generally accepted theories) and some well-grounded and penetrating concluding chapters on the arms races and the policies of the outside powers, especially the United States.

In addition to general works, several books and many articles have been written on individual military establishments in the Middle East. Worthy of particular mention are P. J. Vatikiotis, **The Egyptian Army in Politics** (Bloomington: Indiana University Press, 1961, 300 p.), and Amos Perlmutter, **Military and Politics in Israel: Nation-Building and Role Expansion** (New York: Praeger, 1969, 161 p.).

ECONOMIC PROBLEMS

HERSHLAG, Z. Y. **Introduction to the Modern Economic History of the Middle East.** Leyden: Brill, 1964, 419 p.

This is the only systematic economic history of the modern Middle East and, indeed, the only attempt—other than Charles Issawi's **The Economic History of the Middle East, 1800–1914: A Book of Readings** (Chicago: University of Chicago Press, 1966, 543 p.)—to study this subject. In time it covers the period from 1800 to 1939, and in area Turkey, Iran, Egypt and the Fertile Crescent. The first part tends to concentrate on diplomatic and political history rather than description and analysis of the changes that took place in the economic structure of the various Middle Eastern countries, but is worth consulting. The second half of the book, which deals with the inter-war years, forms an interesting introduction to current economic problems and contains much useful information.

BONNÉ, ALFRED. **The Economic Development of the Middle East.** New York: Oxford University Press, 1945, 164 p.
———. **State and Economics in the Middle East.** London: Routledge, 1948, 427 p.

Alfred Bonné was a pioneer in the study of the Middle East as an economic region. The first of these two books, subtitled "An Outline of Planned Reconstruction after the War," traces the population trends of the area (Turkey, Egypt and the Fertile Crescent), discusses the available data on size, composition and distribution of national incomes, estimates productivity in agriculture and industry in comparable units and calculates the agricultural absorptive capacity of the various countries. It also investigates possible lines of development, with special attention to the financial and political aspects of economic growth.

State and Economics is a socioeconomic analysis of the region and is divided into four parts. The first, "The Middle Eastern State in Transition," describes the evolution of the Ottoman government and its successor states and discusses such matters as public finance, administration and local government. The second part, "The Agrarian Society," describes the climatic, technical and institutional factors affecting agriculture. The third, "The Industrial Revolution," gives a lengthy account of nineteenth-century attempts at industrialization and the more successful ones carried out in the inter-war period and during the Second World War. The last part, "Problems and Prospects of a Changing Society," is mainly sociological in its approach and, as it is based on scant available research and information, tends to overgeneralize and schematize. Both books, however, still contain much that is useful to students of the economic and social evolution of the Middle East.

WARRINER, DOREEN. **Land and Poverty in the Middle East.** New York: Royal Institute of International Affairs, 1948, 148 p.
————. **Land Reform and Development in the Middle East.** New York: Oxford University Press (for the Royal Institute of International Affairs), 2d ed., 1962, 238 p.

Doreen Warriner is one of the most distinguished students of current agrarian questions and perhaps the most perceptive. Her recent **Land Reform in Principle and Practice** (New York: Oxford University Press, 1969, 457 p.) is a masterly survey of the field and includes valuable chapters on Iran and Iraq. **Land and Poverty,** her earliest work on the Middle East, is a succinct but meaty study of the interactions of land tenure and economic conditions in Egypt and the Fertile Crescent. It is still worth reading as a general introduction to the agrarian problems of the region.

Land Reform and Development discusses developments in the 1950s, including the Egyptian land reform of 1952 and the Syrian and Iraqi reforms of 1958. Particularly valuable, in the light of subsequent events, is her account of the expansion of Syrian agriculture under the leadership of merchants and progressive landlords and of the achievements and shortcomings of Iraq's development program, which was designed mainly by engineers and financed by oil revenues. Her account of the reforms themselves has, however, been largely superseded by subsequent research, including her own.

Both books are written with a crispness and clarity extremely rare among social scientists.

LONGRIGG, STEPHEN HEMSLEY. **Oil in the Middle East.** New York: Oxford University Press (for the Royal Institute of International Affairs), 3rd ed., 1968, 519 p.

Brigadier Longrigg, who played an important part in the development of the Middle Eastern oil industry, has written the most authoritative account of its historical evolution. Particularly valuable are the chapters dealing with the beginnings and early years of the industry. Another very useful feature is the relatively lengthy treatment of operations in the Levant countries, southwestern Arabia, Egypt and the Sudan, which usually receive little attention in studies of Middle Eastern oil. On the more recent controversies between companies and governments, however, his account must be supplemented by other sources giving the Arab or Iranian point of view. For the former, see, for example, Muhammad Jawad Al-Abusy, **Al-betrol fil bilad al Arabiyya** (Cairo: Institute for Higher Arab Studies, 1956); for the latter, Laurence Paul Elwell-Sutton, **Persian Oil: A Study in Power Politics** (London: Lawrence and Wishart, 1955, 343 p.). The third edition of the Longrigg book carries the narrative through the mid-1960s and assays the prospects for the future.

ISSAWI, CHARLES and YEGANEH, MOHAMMED. **The Economics of Middle Eastern Oil.** New York: Praeger, 1963, 230 p.

Most economic studies of Middle Eastern oil are primarily concerned with its place in the world market. The focus of this book is on study of the economics of the Middle Eastern oil industry itself. In it, the authors analyze such matters as the factors determining the price of Middle East oil, its cost of production, the amount of capital invested in its various branches and areas (with a breakdown by country of origin), the returns on this investment, the share accruing to the governments of the region and various other related questions. The center of attention is 1948–1960, but earlier developments are also discussed. The final chapter describes the changes that began to make themselves felt in the late 1950s, including the growth of exports from North Africa and the Soviet Union, the increasing activity of independent oil companies, the consequent pressure on prices, the formation of the Organization of Petroleum Exporting Countries and the conclusion of new types of agreements between the companies and most of the producing countries.

SHWADRAN, BENJAMIN. **The Middle East, Oil and the Great Powers, 1959.** New York: Council for Middle Eastern Affairs Press, 2d rev. ed., 1959, 529 p.

The main emphasis of this book is on the diplomatic and political struggles for Middle Eastern oil, but it is also concerned with the impact of the industry on the political and economic development of the producing countries. Drawing on a very wide range of sources, it gives a clear yet detailed account of the international rivalries, the political, military, economic and financial forces at work, and the ensuing conflicts, compromises, arrangements, deals and recriminations. Perhaps the most exciting part is that concerned with the struggle for the Mesopotamian oil fields, which was ultimately resolved by the Red Line Agreement of 1928. But the accounts of the clashes between the companies and the governments of the producing countries are also interesting, as are those dealing with the crisis resulting from the Arab-Israeli war of 1956. Most of the book is naturally devoted to Iran, Iraq and Saudi Arabia, but the other Arabian Peninsula producers, as well as those of the Levant, Egypt and Turkey, also receive attention.

LENCZOWSKI, GEORGE. **Oil and State in the Middle East.** Ithaca: Cornell University Press, 1960, 379 p.

As its title suggests, Lenczowski's study is political and is focused on the relations between the oil companies and the governments and peoples of the producing countries. Part I puts the industry in its historical, regional and world setting. Part II examines a variety of legal aspects arising out of the peculiar pattern of oil concessions in the Middle East—where huge areas were assigned, for long periods, to one company. Part III studies the political, economic and other grievances of nationalist circles against the companies and the latter's response—in the form of both changed business methods and greater stress on public relations. Part IV is concerned with the huge labor force employed in oil, its wages and level of living, the services provided to it by the companies, the industrial legislation within which it operates and the trade unions which it has organized. The last part is devoted to the repercussions of the Suez crisis of 1956. In conclusion, the author discusses the challenges posed to the companies by the change in their political environment and points to the need for increased flexibility and responsiveness on their part to local nationalist demands.

TURKEY

LEWIS, BERNARD. **The Emergence of Modern Turkey.** New York: Oxford University Press (for the Royal Institute of International Affairs), 1961, 518 p.

The leading Western historian of Turkey furnishes us with a thoughtful, authoritative and superbly written account that offers the best single introduction to modern Turkey for the layman, yet includes a wealth of detail and careful interpretation that commands the respect of the specialist. The first half of the work traces Western political and cultural impact period by period from the decline of the Ottoman Empire in the eighteenth century, through the reform movement of the *Tanzimat* and the Young Turk (or Union and Progress) period, to the Kemalist Republic and subsequent developments up to the opposition victory in the elections of 1950. The second half assesses the resulting changes in Turkish styles of thought and of life under the headings of "community and nation," "state and government," "religion and culture" and "élite and class." Professor Lewis' erudition is solid, but it is leavened with a subtle sense of humor. An extensive bibliography of works in Turkish and in Western languages adds to the usefulness of the volume.

EARLE, EDWARD MEAD. **Turkey, the Great Powers, and the Bagdad Railway: A Study in Imperialism.** New York: Macmillan, 1923, 364 p.

The dream of a continuous rail link from Berlin to Baghdad served as the focus of the most promising imperialist venture of Imperial Germany—its mounting search for influence throughout the Ottoman Empire. But Great Britain, Russia and other powers pursued competing interests, and Turkey underwent a succession of political régimes, some of which were tempted to play off one foreign interest against the other. German influence reached its peak during the First World War, when a joint Turkish-German command structure reached from supreme head-quarters at Istanbul down to division or regiment level—but whereas Turkey quickly recovered from defeat, Germany's imperial role was ended. Professor Earle, one of the leading American diplomatic historians of his generation, weaves from these strands a classic account of imperialism, thoroughly researched and compactly told.

For a more recent and more detailed account of the last phase of German-Ottoman coöperation, see Ulrich Trumpener, **Germany and the Ottoman Empire, 1914–1918,** as well as the memoirs of Otto Liman von Sanders, the head of the German military mission of 1913 and later commander at the Dardanelles and Syrian fronts, translated as **Five Years in Turkey** (Annapolis: U. S. Naval Institute, 1927, 325 p.).

ATATÜRK, MUSTAFA KEMAL. **Nutuk.** Ankara: 1927, 543 p. (Romanized Turkish version: "Nutuk, Gazi Mustafa Kemal Tarafindan." Istanbul: Devlet Matbaası, 1934, 3 v.)

In this original version of his "six-day speech," the founder of modern Turkey reviews his leadership from the time he took up the cause of national resistance in 1919 to the appearance of the first open divisions in his movement in 1924. The emphasis is on the consolidation of civilian and military organization in Anatolia in 1919–1920. Kemal's goal was full independence, but he was ready to seize upon any available means to that end and he kept in touch with the shifting situation throughout Turkey by means of an enormous flow of telegrams, many of which are reprinted in the body of the six-day speech or in the appendix. Certain embarrass-ing subjects are glossed over, *e.g.* his early efforts at accommodation with the Sultan, his temporizing on the question of an American mandate, and the support that his movement obtained from exiled Young Turks and from the Soviets. Some later quarrels with close associates are projected back into an earlier period. Yet, such minor flaws aside, this remains the most important and most authoritative source on the formation of the Turkish Republic.

The English translation, **A Speech Delivered by Ghazi Mustapha Kemal, Presi-dent of the Turkish Republic, October 1927** (Leipzig: Koehler, 1929, 724 p.), is awkward and often inaccurate and omits the appendix. An even richer selection of documents relating to the Turkish War of Independence will be found in facsimile and romanized transcription in a quarterly journal edited by the War History Division of the General Staff: *Harp Tarihi Vesikaları Dergisi* (Ankara: E. U. Basımevi, 1952–).

KINROSS, JOHN PATRICK DOUGLAS BALFOUR, BARON. **Atatürk, the Rebirth of a Nation.** London: Weidenfeld and Nicolson, 1964, 615 p.

Lord Kinross, previously known for his sensitive travelogues of the Near East, here rises to the challenge of heroic biography. He has produced the most authori-tative single account of his subject, based on available Turkish and foreign materials, including some archival documents. The narrative dwells on the forma-tive years in Salonica and in the conspiracy-ridden army of the Young Turk period, on the defense of the Gallipoli peninsula in 1915 and the Syrian front in 1918, and above all the War of Independence (1919–1922). The development of Atatürk's aims and ideals is traced against a realistic appraisal of the political and military situation in and around Turkey. Delicate subjects, such as Atatürk's relations with women, are treated forthrightly and without sensationalism. The somewhat anti-climactic last decade (1928–1938) is appropriately foreshortened. For a more detailed examination of Atatürk's political principles and methods in the light of Max Weber's sociological and Erik Erikson's psychoanalytic theories, see the essay by Dankwart A. Rustow, "Atatürk as Founder of a State," in the volume edited by him entitled **Philosophers and Kings: Studies in Leadership** (New York: George Braziller, 1970, 526 p.).

CEBESOY, ALI FUAT. **Millî Mücadele Hâtıraları.** Istanbul: Vatan Neşriyatı, 1953, 528 p.
————. **Moskova Hâtıraları.** Istanbul: Vatan Neşriyatı, 1955, 348 p.
————. **Siyasî Hâtıralar.** Istanbul: Vatan Neşriyatı, and Doğan Kardeş Yayınları, 1957–1960, 2 v.
General Cebesoy was a childhood friend and classmate of Kemal Atatürk but had a long and illustrious career in Turkish politics in his own right. These four volumes of memoirs cover the years from 1919 to 1926 when he was successively commander of the western front in the early phases of the War of Independence, Kemalist Turkey's first ambassador to Moscow, and a parliamentary leader of Kemal's more moderate supporters who in 1924 formed the Progressive Republican Party. The narrative is supported by numerous verbatim documents that interlard the text.
The first volume goes into considerable detail on the support among Turkish nationalists for the idea of an American mandate and on the Kemalists' bold attempt to beat the communists at their own game of infiltration and front organi-zation. The second volume reviews the complex relations among exiled Young Turks, Kemalists and Bolsheviks, and is the best single source on this phase of Russo-Turkish relations. See also George S. Harris, **The Origins of Communism in Turkey** (Stanford: Hoover Institution, 1967, 215 p.). The third volume goes into some detail about the tug-of-war within the Turkish government at the time of the Lausanne negotiations between Prime Minister Rauf Orbay and Foreign Minister Ismet İnönü, with Cebesoy espousing the former's point of view. The last volume recounts the formation and dissolution, at Kemal's behest, of the Progressive Party.
Cebesoy is generous in his retrospective judgments. "I am still convinced," he says, that Atatürk in the early 1920s "would have administered the revolutionary program better by remaining an impartial head of state. Who knows, perhaps I am mistaken." How rare such restraint has been in Turkish memoir literature may be appreciated by referring to Atatürk's comments in his **Nutuk** about Orbay, and to the sharp polemical asides in the long-suppressed memoirs of Kâzım Karabekir, commander of the Kemalist eastern front: **Istiklâl Harbimiz** (Istanbul: Türkiye Yayınevi, 1960, 1,171 p.).

EDIB, HALIDE. **Memoirs.** New York: Century, 1926, 471 p.
————. **The Turkish Ordeal, Being the Further Memoirs of Halide Edib.** New York: Century, 1928, 407 p.
Halide Edib (1885–1964) was the outstanding Turkish novelist of her genera-tion, and her works were translated into many foreign languages. In 1901 she became the first Muslim to graduate from the American College for Girls in Istanbul. Her husband was Dr. Abdülhak Adnan, a physician, political figure and orientalist. The two volumes of memoirs weave personal reminiscence and con-temporary history into an impassioned, vivid and fair-minded narrative. In the months after the armistice of 1918, Halide became one of the most effective nationalist orators in Istanbul, and when the British reinforced their occupation in 1920, she and Adnan fled to Anatolia. She insisted on enlisting in the army, where she advanced to top sergeant, while her husband served in parliament and as

Minister of Health. In 1924 he joined the opposition against Mustafa Kemal, and in 1926 Adnan and Halide began 13 years of political exile. But she leaves such political quarrels at the water's edge as she conveys the daily life and the political aspirations of Turkey during its period of most intensive change. The second volume includes some vivid portraits of Mustafa Kemal and other leading figures.

TOYNBEE, ARNOLD JOSEPH. **The Western Question in Greece and Turkey**. Boston: Houghton Mifflin, 2d ed., 1923, 408 p.

During the First World War, Arnold Toynbee edited the Asquith government's Blue Book on the "Treatment of Armenians in the Ottoman Empire" and in that connection "learnt, I believe, nearly all there is to be learnt to the discredit of the Turkish nation and of their rule over other peoples" (preface to the first edition of the book here reviewed). After the war, he travelled to Greece and Turkey on behalf of the Manchester *Guardian* at a time when Greek armies were undertaking their farthest advance into Turkish Anatolia; he returned converted to the Turkish cause and became an impassioned critic of the Lloyd George government's philhellene policy. Toynbee has a sharp eye for the vivid contemporary and historical detail, and here is his first foray into the analysis of the world's political scene such as he was to undertake for many years in the Royal Institute's "Survey of International Affairs." There are also premonitions of his later theories of "the contact of civilizations" as spelled out in his magisterial **A Study of History,** where the Islamic Near East forms one of the more massive bodies of evidence.

ZIEMKE, KURT. **Die Neue Türkei.** Berlin: Deutsche Verlagsanstalt, 1930, 550 p.

A German lawyer and diplomat treats the foreign and domestic policy of Turkey during the crucial period of the collapse of the Ottoman Empire and the formation of the Turkish Republic. Although many new sources are now available for the domestic developments, the general perspective in this part of the book remains valid. The first four parts, dealing with German-Turkish relations in the World War, postwar diplomacy from San Remo and Sèvres to Mudanya and Lausanne and the questions left for later settlement, such as Mosul, remain the best single account of these complex events.

For a more detailed (semiofficial Turkish) point of view on the Lausanne conference see Ali Naci Karacan, **Lozan Konferansı ve Ismet Paşa** (Istanbul: Maarif Matbaası, 1943, 488 p.). For the results of more recent scholarship on the diplomatic history of the 1918–1923 period see Roderic H. Davison, "Turkish Diplomacy from Mudros to Lausanne," in **The Diplomats,** edited by Gordon A. Craig and Felix Gilbert; and Gotthard Jäschke, "Beiträge zur Geschichte des Kampfes der Türkei um ihre Unabhängigkeit," *Welt des Islams* (New Series, v. 5, 1957, pp. 1–64).

ANCHIERI, ETTORE. **Costantinopoli e gli Stretti nella Politica Russa ed Europea.** Milan: Giuffrè, 1948, 268 p.

A review of the Straits question from 1774 to 1937 based mainly on published diplomatic documents of Russia and other major powers. The account begins with the Treaty of Küçük Kaynarca, at the end of the Russo-Turkish war of 1768–1774, when Catherine II dispatched the first Russian naval force to the Mediterranean. Chapter 1 carries the account to the 1830s when Ottoman Turkey was in danger of becoming a Russian protectorate. Chapters 2 and 3 review all the major European diplomatic conferences and initiatives from 1840 to the turn of the century. Chapters 4 and 5 return to the evolution of the Russian position to the fall of the Tsars, and chapter 6 fills in the Allied policies of the First World War period. The concluding chapter deals with the postwar developments—above all, Lausanne and Montreux. The only natural waterway that connects two international seas while passing through the territory of a single state, the Turkish straits fully reflect the shifting international and diplomatic balance of each period.

KARPAT, KEMAL H. **Turkey's Politics: The Transition to a Multi-Party System.** Princeton: Princeton University Press, 1959, 522 p.

Professor Karpat, a political scientist and historian raised in Turkey and trained in the United States, provides a lucid and coherent account of the intricate political manoeuvres and debates of the period from 1946 to 1950. This was the time when the government of the Republican People's Party under Ismet Inönü encouraged the formation of opposition groups and at length surrendered power in a free, honest and orderly election to the Democrats under Bayar and Menderes. The narrative is based on a thorough examination of the vast primary source material available: newspapers, parliamentary debates, pamphlets, periodicals. The central chronological portion (part II) is followed by an examination of the changes in ideology and political behavior that democracy brought in its train. Part I, which attempts to trace the antecedents of the transformation in Kemalist and late Ottoman history, is marred by a tendency to a somewhat schematic class analysis of politics. Karpat's sympathies are with the Democratic Party, but his account is fair and balanced. His analysis may be supplemented by reference to Tarık Z. Tunaya, **Türkiyede Siyasî Partiler, 1859–1952** (Istanbul: Doğan Kardeş Yayınları, 1952, 799 p.)—a rich compilation of party programs and related documents, with connecting narrative, which is particularly extensive for this period and that following the armistice of 1918.

FREY, FREDERICK W. **The Turkish Political Elite.** Cambridge: M.I.T. Press, 1965, 483 p.

An examination of the social and political structure of Republican Turkey in the light of the composition of its parliament and cabinet in the period from 1920 to 1957. Professor Frey is an American political scientist equally versed in statistical method, sociological theory and Turkish contemporary history. He finds that Atatürk, instead of deploring "the basic bifurcation in Turkish society between the educated elite and uneducated masses," exploited it by "solidifying his hold over the dominant intellectual group" and using that group as his instrument for change. Party competition since the 1940s has replaced the soldier and the bureaucrat with the lawyer, the merchant and the landowner. Religious officials, who formed a sizable contingent in the legislatures of the early 1920s, disappeared almost completely in the 1930s—and for good. During the one-party régime, the average age of deputies rose from 43 to 53, but the multi-party régime has brought a new infusion of youth. Local ties are once again important, as they also were in the early 1920s. The author throughout compares the results of his tabulations with what is known about Turkish ideals and social patterns from works of literature, travelogues and other sources. The result is a successful and well-written blend of "behavioral science" with cultural-historical study.

BERKES, NIYAZI. **The Development of Secularism in Turkey.** Montreal: McGill University Press, 1964, 537 p.

Din-u-devlet, "faith and dynasty," were the principles of the Ottoman Empire, and Islam promised to the believers power and prosperity on earth as well as bliss in the hereafter. Hence the military defeats that the Ottomans kept suffering at the hands of Christian powers from the eighteenth century onward were bound to shake the Empire's spiritual as well as material foundations. The early reforming sultans, such as Selim III and Mahmud II, were concerned to strengthen their tottering state by borrowing military techniques and educational principles from the West. The Muslim *ulema* resisted and thus contributed first to a bifurcation between traditional and secular institutions and finally to the withering of their branch of the fork.

Professor Berkes, a Turkish-born professor of Islamic studies at McGill, takes up this theme of growing secularism to write what amounts to an intellectual history of Turkey in the nineteenth and twentieth centuries. Berkes also has translated and edited selections from the writings of Ziya Gökalp (1876–1924), who was the leading theorist on secularization and modernization during the Young Turk and early Kemalist periods: **Turkish Nationalism and Western Civilization, Selected Essays of Ziya Gökalp** (New York: Columbia University Press, 1959, 336 p.).

HERSHLAG, Z. Y. **Turkey: The Challenge of Growth.** Leyden: Brill, 1968, 406 p.

This is a comprehensive and thoughtful economic history of Turkey from the beginnings of the Republic to the mid-1960s. An earlier edition appeared in 1958 with the title **Turkey: An Economy in Transition** (The Hague: Van Keulen, 1958, 340 p.). The core of the book is three sections on "The Étatist Period" (1931–1945), the postwar period ("From Liberalism to Interventionism") and the most recent period ("The Seven Percent Growth Target of the Nineteen Sixties"). They are preceded by two summary sections reviewing the 1920s and two concluding parts on the social implications of economic growth and on manpower problems. Professor Hershlag, of the Hebrew University, has researched his subject thoroughly, mastered the economic and statistical detail and is modest and responsible in his conclusions. The political rationale behind the successive government policies and the tenor of the later debate on free enterprise versus planning are fully reported. The charts in the text are well chosen to present the major aspects of growth, and there is an extensive statistical appendix and a map.

For a much more summary and less technical discussion of economic developments in their political and international context see **The First Turkish Republic: A Case Study in National Development** (Cambridge: Harvard University Press, 1963, 367 p.), by Richard D. Robinson, a M.I.T. professor of business with many years experience in Turkey; however, the historical details on the origins of the Republic are not always accurate.

The Economy of Turkey. Washington: International Bank, 1951, 276 p.

In 1949, the Republican People's Party government invited a survey mission from the World Bank, in part to strengthen the case for economic liberalization against the party's old-time étatists. The mission, headed by James M. Barker, arrived after the Democratic Party's election victory of 1950, and its comments on étatism were far more charitable than those in an earlier unofficial report to the Twentieth Century Fund, directed by an American petroleum economist—see Max Weston Thornburg and others, **Turkey: An Economic Appraisal** (New York: Twentieth Century Fund, 1949, 324 p.).

In its formal conclusions, the Barker mission recommended for the 1952–1956 period an emphasis on transport (highways, not railroads), agricultural development, electric power, communications and training programs. The body of the report contained many other constructive criticisms and suggestions—from the need for a simple metal plow to replace the prevalent wooden stick to streamlining cumbersome bureaucratic practices. It also gave an early warning of future population problems.

RAMSAUR, ERNEST EDMONDSON, JR. **The Young Turks: Prelude to the Revolution of 1908.** Princeton: Princeton University Press, 1957, 180 p.

An American historian and foreign service officer here offers a succinct and competent history of the Committee of Union and Progress, from its inception until 1908, that manages to clear up much previous confusion. The Committee began as a conspiracy of a handful of students at the Military Medical School and continued in exile in Paris and other capitals until infiltration by Abdülhamid's agents and defections all but destroyed it by 1897. The struggle was resumed by a new wave of exiles at the turn of the century and by military conspirators in Salonica and other cities of the Empire. The squabbles among the exiles foreshadowed the bitter nationality conflicts of the next decade. But it was the internal conspirators who by their telegraphic threats in 1908 frightened the Sultan into reproclaiming the parliamentary constitution. The further history of the Union and Progress movement in and out of power, down to the outbreak of the World War, may be followed in Feroz Ahmad, **The Young Turks** (Oxford: Clarendon Press, 1969, 248 p.).

DAVISON, RODERIC H. **Reform in the Ottoman Empire, 1856–1876.** Princeton: Princeton University Press, 1963, 479 p.

Professor Davison of George Washington University takes up the second half of the Ottoman reform period known as the *Tanzimat,* from the *Hatt-i Hümayun* of 1856 to the Constitution of 1876. The *Hatt* of 1856 was suggested by the British ambassador, Stratford Canning, as a means of ensuring further European support for Turkey at the peace negotiations that were to end the Crimean War. It elaborated ideals of civic equality and common Ottoman loyalty that the Sultan had proclaimed since 1839 and his European-trained bureaucrats had championed for decades. In contrast to the numerous recitals of the "Eastern Question," which somehow present the Turks as supernumeraries in the wings of a European drama, Davison's sympathetic and critical account places the reforming Ottomans at center stage. He has mastered not only the European diplomatic and American missionary archives but also the burgeoning Turkish literature on the period. One of the most original chapters traces the influence of the constitutional reforms among the Armenians and other non-Muslim *millets* on the reform of 1876. The intellectual ideas and social antecedents of the New Ottomans of 1865—the most colorful and influential group within the reformist opposition of the period—are treated in fuller detail in Serif Mardin, **The Genesis of Young Ottoman Thought: A Study in the Modernization of Turkish Political Ideas** (Princeton: Princeton University Press, 1962, 456 p.).

IRAN

AVERY, PETER. **Modern Iran.** New York: Praeger, 1965, 527 p.

Avery's work is one of the best of an increasing number of books on modern Iran to have appeared in the English language and the only good one written primarily for the general reader. Though the author does not approach his subject as a social scientist, his treatment of it is comprehensive, and he has been able to utilize many Persian sources. The general thrust of the work allows him to treat intrigues, episodes and rumors as well as social, political, cultural, economic and historical developments. Modern Iran is treated chronologically, beginning with the rather arbitrary date of 1813 when Russia forced Iran to conclude the Treaty of Gulistan. While the specialist may suffer from the book's verbosity, inadequate organization and occasional printing mistakes, he will profit from insightful interpretations scattered throughout. The general reader, however, to whom it is addressed, will find it a good introduction to modern Iran, rich in detail and useful information, and broad in understanding.

RAMAZANI, ROUHOLLAH K. **The Foreign Policy of Iran: A Developing Nation in World Affairs, 1500–1941.** Charlottesville: University Press of Virginia, 1966, 330 p.

While Iran has a long history as an independent state, there have been few periods in modern times when it has in fact been able to act independently in international affairs. During World War I and its aftermath "Iranian foreign policy" was a misnomer, so little did Iran control its own destiny. In the two decades of Reza Shah's rule, however, the country acquired an unprecedented degree of political and economic independence which found its reflection in foreign policy; indeed it was the main purpose of Reza's foreign policy to consolidate and strengthen that independence. R. K. Ramazani's book is the only work in any language which gives an objective and detailed account of Iran's international role during this entire period. Beginning the main part of the story with the revolution of 1905, he carries it up to the abdication of Reza Shah in World War II. He has fully used the published works in Persian and in the Western languages. Since he has not explored archival material, some of his statements and conclusions must remain subject to later confirmation or dispute when additional information becomes available.

Ramazani provides a pattern as well as a chronological account, although the book does not really live up to the promise of wider significance for other developing nations. He skillfully draws a picture of the traditional elements in Iranian policy and notes how Reza clung to some of them and discarded others, doing some clever and effective balancing in his country's interest. His strong anti-Russian views and his fear of British encroachments, however, finally brought him to a policy which was beyond the reach of his country, leading first to excessive reliance on Germany and then to invasion by Germany's enemies. The author covers this final period well and draws some interesting parallels between Iran's policies in the two world wars.

VON BLÜCHER, WIPERT. **Zeitenwende in Iran: Erlebnisse und Beobachten.** Biberach a. d. Riss: Koehler, 1949, 337 p.

Ordinarily a diplomat's memoirs would not merit mention as a major work on Iran's foreign relations, but in the absence of more fundamental studies covering the ebb and flow of its relations with Germany, this book must be recognized as an important source. Wipert von Blücher served as an officer in the German army in the Near East in the First World War, handled Iranian affairs in the German Foreign Office during the 1920s and was German ambassador in Tehran from 1931 to 1935.

Not a systematic history or a detailed account of specific international issues, the narrative nevertheless ranges over a variety of subjects from protocol to petroleum. It contains some interesting observations on the internal Iranian scene, especially on the personality and policies of Reza Shah. Von Blücher's diplomatic career in Iran, a country he considered his second home, was cut short by the Shah himself, who took offense at some of the ambassador's remarks and insisted on his recall.

One phase of Iranian foreign relations in the period encompassed by Von Blücher's memoirs, that of the aftermath of the First World War, is well covered in a thorough, scholarly work by Nasrollah Fatemi, **Diplomatic History of Persia, 1917–1923: Anglo-Russian Power Politics in Iran** (New York: Moore, 1952, 331 p.).

LENCZOWSKI, GEORGE. **Russia and the West in Iran, 1918–1948.** Ithaca: Cornell University Press, 1949, 383 p.

For nearly 30 years prior to publication of this study, no single work on Iran concerned itself primarily with political developments during the all-important period 1918–1948. The 1950s and particularly the 1960s witnessed the appearance of an unprecedented number of scholarly books on Iranian politics and foreign policy, but none of these works could have escaped the influence of Professor Lenczowski's book.

Although the author pays detailed attention to the internal political developments of Iran, particularly during the period 1941–1948, the real contribution of his work lies in its treatment of the great-power rivalry in Iran. The material is based not only on documentary and press sources but also on the author's own keen field observations during 1942–1945. In spite of the rather categorical assertion of former ambassador George V. Allen in the foreword that the major problem in Iran today "results from two different ideologies, not from conflicting national interests," the author's own emphasis on the role of ideology in Soviet policy in Iran is tempered by his realistic appraisal of the element of power.

The newer trends in political science emphasize cultural, sociological and psychological contributions to the understanding of politics and international relations. They also stress the need for better understanding of the perspectives of small states in domestic politics and foreign policy. But the author's emphasis on the historical factors and the role of great powers is understandable in light of the state of political science in the 1940s. All students of Iran will still profit from this pioneering work.

BANANI, AMIN. **The Modernization of Iran, 1921–1941.** Stanford: Stanford University Press, 1961, 191 p.

This study was a bold undertaking at a time when reliable information on the rule of Reza Shah was scanty (as indeed it still is) but the author drew upon Persian sources previously seldom utilized in his examination of the social and institutional reforms of the Shah. The strength of the study derives from its overall success in describing these reforms from within, as contrasted with an earlier book by Laurence Paul Elwell-Sutton, **Modern Iran** (London: Routledge, 1941, 234 p.). Banani's work, however, takes little account of the vast literature on the problems of acculturation and modernization, makes no attempt at providing a theoretical framework and indulges in simplistic and sweeping generalizations about the interaction of Eastern and Western civilizations. Students of social sciences in general and Iran in particular still await publication of a satisfactory work on the crucially important 1921–1941 period. This study, meanwhile, is useful for its contribution to the understanding of Reza Shah's institutional and legal reforms.

BINDER, LEONARD. **Iran: Political Development in a Changing Society.** Berkeley: University of California Press, 1962, 362 p.

This study of the Iranian political system is based on the author's field research in Iran during 1958–1959. The bulk of the work describes Iran's political system by characterizing it as "a rational-traditional system" and by examining what the author terms the "machinery of rationalization," the "structures of social power," the "political functions," "the politics of economic development" and "external pressures." The work stands out as the first rigorous analysis of Iran's contemporary political system. The theoretical framework of the study is general, but most of the descriptive material bears the imprint of the contemporary period. The author's own firsthand observations are marked by rare perception, accuracy and acuteness.

This study is outstanding in still another sense. It is among those in contemporary political science which have increasingly marked the emergence of an unprecedented trend in the general field, especially in the study of "political development," in spite of continuing conceptual ambiguities. The author, like Almond, Apter and others, draws upon structural-functionalism but pleads for the study of "a whole political system" and suggests imaginative typologies of his own. The increasing literature on political development in general and Iran in particular since the publication of this work includes corrective as well as complementary materials.

COTTAM, RICHARD W. **Nationalism in Iran.** Pittsburgh: University of Pittsburgh Press, 1964, 332 p.

This is the first systematic and comprehensive study of Iranian nationalism. It purports to explode clichés about that subject by attempting to lift it out of the cold-war context in general and the alleged American romanticism and intuition of the "Dulles years" in particular. It seeks to provide better understanding of Iranian nationalism by examining its cultural, historical and social bases, and by pointing out its racial, linguistic, religious and regional problems. The book also aspires to furnish a case study of nationalism as a major key in understanding political behavior.

The author's strictures of the United States policy toward Iran in 1953 may be open to question in light of both the situation in Iran itself and the broader context of conditions in the Middle East, but this does not diminish the value of his contribution. The study of Iranian nationalism, like any other nationalism, requires more than the usual bag of tools and skills of political science; it demands sensitivity to intricate, complex and often intangible cultural and historical factors. This study reflects such a sensitivity, is clearly written and is commended to both students of political development and area specialists and to the general reader.

ZABIH, SEPEHR. **The Communist Movement in Iran.** Berkeley: University of California Press, 1966, 279 p.

Given the publication of a number of general works on Iranian politics and foreign policy during the 1960s, the appearance of this specific study on the communist movement in Iran significantly complements the studies by Binder, Cottam and Ramazani. The author himself shows awareness of the relevance of his analysis of the appeal of communism in Iran to Binder's discussion of political alienation. His discussions of the relationship of nationalism and communism, and communism and Soviet policy tie in with the works of the other authors as well.

The significance of the work, however, extends beyond the ways in which it complements the more general works on Iranian politics and foreign policy. Following in the path of Professor Lenczowski, the author concerns himself simultaneously with the evolution of the communist doctrine in the East in general and the movement in Iran in particular. The strength of the book derives from its study of the sociocultural and socioeconomic bases of the appeal of communism in Iran, the composition of the leadership and rank and file, and the relationship of communism to nationalism and to Islam. The author's ability to draw on Persian and Russian sources adds to the value of the work, which is free from both jargon and rhetorical flourish. His readable style should please both the specialist and the general reader.

MILLSPAUGH, ARTHUR CHESTER. **Americans in Persia.** Washington: Brookings Institution, 1946, 293 p.

The author headed two private American economic missions in Iran, first from 1922 to 1927 and again from 1943 to 1945. Both were periods of crucial importance in Iran's modern history, and this work, like its antecedent **The American Task in Persia** (New York: Century, 1925, 336 p.), stands out by reason of the author's firsthand experience as Administrator General of the Finances of Persia.

An air of pessimism, verging at times on cynicism, permeates this study. There seemed to be little hope for Iran in 1946, except perhaps for the establishment of some kind of a benevolent American-Russian-British condominium over the country. That was a prescription which even the author himself did not find plausible, but it reflects both the era of belief in great-power coöperation and the pathetic conditions of Iran at the end of World War II. Reza Shah emerges as a dictatorial giant in this study; whereas he had been admired by the author in his first book, in which he appeared as an effective, dedicated and patriotic statesman and even a man of the people. That earlier book was published before Reza Shah terminated the Millspaugh mission, but the author's different attitude toward him must also be explained by the lapse of some 20 years and the changes in both the ruler of Iran and the author.

The value of this study at the time of its publication lay in its plea for a more positive American role in Iran and its critique of the administration of United States foreign policy. Today it provides firsthand information on some of the origins of the cold war in general and of the Soviet-American rivalry in Iran in particular.

EAGLETON, WILLIAM, JR. **The Kurdish Republic of 1946.** New York: Oxford University Press (for the Royal Institute of International Affairs), 1963, 142 p.

In spite of the pioneering article by Archie Roosevelt, Jr., on the Mahabad Republic published in the *Middle East Journal* in July 1947 and the recent book by Hassan Arfa, **The Kurds** (London: Oxford University Press, 1966, 178 p.), this study, though slender, is still the most detailed standard work on the Kurdish Republic of Mahabad. A comprehensive study would still seem impossible because of the Kurdish destruction of records of their involvement and the unavailability of Russian and of reliable Persian written materials.

This book is an account of the Kurdish Republic based primarily on interviews and field observations made by the author, a United States foreign service officer, over a number of years. He is a careful and meticulous reporter and is also aware of the broader significance of the rise and fall of the Kurdish Republic, pinpointing the role of the Soviet Union, relating the episode to the larger problem of Kurdish nationalism and noting its implications for both Iran and Iraq. The study is indispensable for the student concerned with the history, politics or foreign policy of Iran and is also important for better understanding of the continuing Kurdish problem in the Middle East.

ISRAEL

HALPERN, BEN. **The Idea of the Jewish State.** Cambridge: Harvard University Press, 1961, 492 p.

This book is divided into two parts. The first, which analyzes the difference between Zionism and other nationalist movements, examines the origins of the idea of the Jewish state up to the nineteenth century and traces the subsequent evolution of that idea in the context of three sets of problematic relationships: between Jews and Gentiles as both were affected by the changes in historical circumstances since the dawn of the Enlightenment; between Zionist and non-Zionist Jews as they responded differently to the problems raised by the change in traditional Jewish-Gentile relations; and among various Zionist groups as they developed different conceptions of the specific problems that Zionism was intended to resolve. The incredibly complex interplay among these three sets of relationships and how it resulted in the emergence of an idea of the state that eventually commanded the support of the bulk of world Jewry is elucidated through masterly organization, impressive scholarship and penetrating insight. This part of the book is absolutely indispensable for anyone who would understand the origins and dynamics of Jewish nationalism and the ideological foundations of Israel. It is also very useful for anyone interested in the relationship between ideology and social forces in general.

The second part of the volume deals with the Jewish state as a sovereign entity interacting with other states. The author tries to apply to his material the overall theoretical concept of the work, but the attempt yields no new insight and ends by being essentially a repetition of a previously known and far from uncontroversial story. The bibliography and documentation, however, are excellent.

WEIZMANN, CHAIM. **Trial and Error: The Autobiography of Chaim Weizmann.** New York: Harper, 1949, 498 p.

More than 20 years after publication, Chaim Weizmann's memoirs remain a major historical and human document. While the history of the Zionist movement seen through the life of the man who led it for nearly three decades may well be corrected when his own papers, now in the course of publication, are available, Weizmann's own retrospective perception of that history as presented in his autobiography will remain of historical interest in itself. It is surely significant, for example, that throughout this volume the supreme commander of Zionism makes only scant references, almost afterthoughts, to Ben Gurion, the field commander of the forces of Zionism in Palestine, who had both clashed and coöperated with him since 1930. Moreover, one cannot fail to be struck by the difference in the tenor and texture of Zionist pleading as voiced by Weizmann before the establishment of the state and subsequent pleading voiced by others. De Gaulle once said of his *Résistance* years that as long as he lacked power he could only inflict moral arguments upon the British and the Americans. Similarly, the Zionist movement found in Weizmann a man who was ideally suited to impress others with moral power when it lacked strength of other kinds.

As a human document, Weizmann's memoirs will stand as a fascinating record of a man who combined to a very high degree not only C. P. Snow's two cultures but also a whole gamut of opposite characteristics that are seldom united in one person. In the Weizmann of these memoirs one alternately catches glimpses of the scientist and the humanist, the statesman and the ward politician, the proud Jew and the *shtadlan* (implorer), the zealot and the man of infinite warmth, the adoptive English aristocrat and the native Jew from Motele.

STEIN, LEONARD. **The Balfour Declaration.** New York: Simon and Schuster, 1961, 681 p.

The author, who worked closely with Chaim Weizmann as political secretary of the World Zionist Organization, has written probably the closest thing to a definitive study of the background and origins of the Balfour Declaration. The book not only marshals a massive amount of directly relevant evidence but also provides sketches of British and Jewish organizations and personalities involved in promoting or opposing the idea—significant historical contributions in themselves. This is a study in "decision making," and its lesson is rather ironic: although broad considerations of strategy, personality and altruistic vision were presented in the course of the long discussions and debates that preceded the British Cabinet's resolve to issue the Balfour Declaration, the decision itself when it finally came was made on very narrow and fleeting tactical grounds. What bearing, if any, the broad factors had on the final decision, the author does not venture to say.

EYTAN, WALTER. **The First Ten Years: A Diplomatic History of Israel.** New York: Simon and Schuster, 1958, 239 p.

This story of Israel's diplomatic ventures in the first decade of its existence carries the authority of its author, the Director General of its Foreign Ministry during that period. He does not pretend to write an objective history, nor does he reveal any important secrets. He simply presents in an orderly fashion and easy style the problems Israel faced and the case for—not the causes of—Israel's actions and reactions. For example, Israel's 1956 campaign in Sinai is treated as a totally independent event springing from purely local causes and having no connection with the Franco-British action against Egypt. This may be true as far as the inner intent of Israel's decision makers goes and may be an understandable approach for an Israeli diplomat to take. But it is not history.

From the perspective of 1970, the value of the book is chiefly as a document of the history of Israeli diplomatic argumentation. As such, its value is enhanced rather than lessened by the fact that the Israeli case has been presented quite differently in later years. Eytan unwittingly conveys the psychological mood of Israeli diplomacy, which has had more than a touch of a persecution complex whose roots are not hard to find.

BAR-ZOHAR, MICHEL. **Ben Gourion: Le Prophète Armé.** Paris: Fayard, 1966, 412 p.

This book must be mentioned in the absence of a really first-rate biography of the man who, more than any other single person, shaped the destiny of Israel in the last years of its gestation and the first 15 years of its existence; and indeed it has some usefulness. Ben Gurion permitted the author to examine large masses of his private papers and gave him apparently unlimited opportunity for observation and discussions with him. Although the material placed at the author's disposal was more than ample for a truly significant biographical and political study, however, it was used instead to produce what is primarily an adulatory and unfortunately careless work, even though it contains valuable bits of information and conveys much of the general flavor of its chief character.

The author focuses his beam so sharply on his hero that he obscures, and sometimes distorts, other persons and events. We get no idea how Ben Gurion came to occupy the center of the stage, no inkling of the environment in which he had to act, no idea why he behaved the way he did toward some other important characters on the same stage. All we have is the incarnation of a pure will, a great fighting leader prevailing against terrible odds over less worthy or evil people.

The errors and inaccuracies are often elementary, and the judgments of such personalities as Lavon and Weizmann are caricatures; but there are also the revelations and the direct citations from unpublished papers. So, there is something of value here, but *caveat lector*.

FEIN, LEONARD J. **Israel: Politics and People.** Boston: Little, Brown, 1968, 338 p.

This is an excellent survey of Israeli politics by an American political scientist, fully versed in his material, which he presents with much empathy and perceptiveness. It complements the systematic treatment of the domestic politics of Israel's earlier years presented in Marver H. Bernstein's **The Politics of Israel: The First Decade of Statehood** (Princeton: Princeton University Press, 1957, 360 p.).

A great merit of Fein's book is that while the analysis is cast in a framework of systematic political science, the argument is presented in flowing, idiomatic English. Since the scope of the book is extraordinarily broad—it describes Israel's political system, parties, coöperative institutions, the West-East gap, the generational gap and the nature of the "establishment"—inevitably the treatment runs at a very swift pace, giving only glimpses of some important subjects and leaving only a hazy impression of their relative importance. It is particularly regrettable that the author did not apply his talent as a scholar and his obviously profound knowledge of Israel to a more substantial analysis of the role of the military, a subject which is admirably covered in Amos Perlmutter's **Military and Politics in Israel: Nation-Building and Role Expansion** (New York: Praeger, 1969, 161 p.). Israel's economy and the domestic sources of its foreign policy also cry out for more adequate treatment. But let us be grateful for what we have.

SAFRAN, NADAV. **The United States and Israel.** Cambridge: Harvard University Press, 1963, 341 p.

The great merit of this work lies in its exposition and analysis of the political system of Israel as the background and explanation for its policies. Thus it serves simultaneously as a reference book for such subjects as political parties and institutions (as of the time of writing) and as a key to the understanding of such complex matters as the different strands of Zionism, the nature of the Histadrut and the relations between religion and state. Economic factors receive only cursory treatment, and the author deliberately omits discussion of the place of the Arab minority in the society on the ground that it would lead him inevitably into the entire Palestine issue and thus into writing a different book. The Arab minority, fortunately, is the subject of a later detailed work by another author, **The Arabs in Israel: A Political Study,** by Jacob M. Landau (New York: Oxford, 1969, 300 p.).

Safran describes the policies of the United States toward Israel both in their historical context, leading to the American role in the birth of Israel, and in the pattern of the cold war of the 1950s and early 1960s. He does not hesitate to give his judgment on such delicate questions as "Jewish political pressure" and "oil diplomacy" in a balanced survey of the component elements of United States policy. While the narrative necessarily stops short of the cataclysmic events of 1967 in Arab-Israeli relations, the book's basic analysis is by no means outdated by those events, and the conclusions retain their perspective.

ARAB WORLD

GENERAL

LEWIS, BERNARD. **The Arabs in History.** London: Hutchinson's University Library, 2d ed., 1954, 196 p.

This outstanding volume is a model of what short histories ought to be. It is clear and concise, perceptive and well written. It begins with a description of Arabia before Islam and ends by discussing the impact of the West in a short chapter that could serve as introduction to a fine later work by the same author, **The Middle East and the West** (Bloomington: Indiana University Press, 1964, 160 p.). Both books throw light on the present by their treatment of the past. Such a treatment is bound to be selective, but here the basis of selection rests on the author's honesty and his ability to distinguish forest from trees.

The book's very virtues, however, lead to its faults; for example, its conciseness at times borders on risky simplification. Yet few will complain about Mr. Lewis' risk-taking; he not only sketches history's sweep, he helps us understand its mechanics. Those who seek ungeneralized detail will find it in Philip K. Hitti's standard **History of the Arabs: From the Earliest Times to the Present** (New York: St. Martin's Press, 6th ed., 1956, 822 p.).

HOURANI, ALBERT. **Arabic Thought in the Liberal Age, 1798–1939.** New York: Oxford University Press (for the Royal Institute of International Affairs), 1962, 403 p.

Albert Hourani's writings stamp him as one of the most thoughtful, sensitive and well-informed scholars on the modern history and contemporary politics of the Arab world. This work of synthesis is the product of mature reflection. With breadth and balance of historical judgment, it covers the course of Arab political and social thought from the nineteenth century up to World War II. It should be considered not only for its own merits but also as an organizing framework for other reading on the period.

Hourani's account of increasing contacts between Arabs and the West, the responses engendered, and the intellectual syntheses produced among Arabs, is told in the finest prose. By virtue of its attention to the totality of Arab society, the account provides a multidimensional, realistic portrayal of an age only recently departed. The central story of the relationship between Islam and Arab national-ism, each evolving and reacting in its own way over the last century, constitutes basic material for the ponderings of specialists and an important backdrop for all students of modern Arab politics.

ANTONIUS, GEORGE. **The Arab Awakening: The Story of the Arab National Move-ment.** Philadelphia: Lippincott, 1939, 471 p.

The Arab Awakening, while mixing history with advocacy, has nevertheless attained the status of a classic. It was the first book on the rise of Arab nationalism to set forth for the Western reader in a comprehensive and comprehensible way the story of the movement and the international developments which marked its progress and its defeats.

There is heavy emphasis on foreign missionary influence and the role of Chris-tian Arabs, especially that of American Protestants and French Catholics, who became "the foster-parents of the Arab resurrection." Tracing the story of intellec-tual ferment and organizing activity, centered in Syria during the nineteenth century, the author paid relatively little attention to trends within Islam and widespread efforts at reform to enable the Muslim and Arab peoples to find answers to the impact of the West. The second half of the book, covering the years since the First World War, is devoted largely to a history of the policies and diplomacy of the great powers and the ways in which they helped, betrayed or ignored Arab rights and interests. The record of pledges and counter-pledges, Anglo-French rivalry, the series of Allied decisions from Sykes-Picot to the Paris Peace Conference to San Remo, and the Arab reaction to them, is described with general accuracy and understandable bitterness. On Palestine, Antonius concluded his book with the statement that the logic of facts was inexorable: "It shows that no room can be made . . . . for a second nation except by dislodging or exterminat-ing the nation in possession."

Later publications have provided more detailed and accurate accounts. Zeine N. Zeine's **The Emergence of Arab Nationalism** (Beirut: Khayats, 1958, 205 p.) is excellent on the early period. Jon Kimche's **The Second Arab Awakening** (New

York: Holt, Rinehart and Winston, 1970, 288 p.), with apologies to Antonius, is especially enlightening on the policies of the powers. Yet the Antonius book remains a landmark.

NUSEIBEH, HAZEM ZAKI. **The Ideas of Arab Nationalism.** Ithaca: Cornell University Press, 1956, 227 p.

Supplementing but not duplicating the earlier work of George Antonius **(The Arab Awakening),** Nuseibeh delves into some of Arab nationalism's environmental and religious antecedents but spends most of his time analyzing the ideological and political content of nationalist and other writing up to the mid-1950s.

One of the book's assets is that it recreates a historical period—not really so long ago as it might seem—in which Arab thinking about nationalism was more formative and adventurous. Written by a member of a noted Palestinian Arab family who later held high office in Jordan and who does not disguise his yearning for Arab unity, it flavors scholarship with valuable intuitions that Westerners do not ordinarily possess, although it does not reach the standard of the best Western works on nationalism. Since publication of the book, moreover, the ideas of Arab nationalists have evolved in many ways. What is needed now is not only an updating of the story told by Antonius and Nuseibeh but a thoroughgoing reassessment in the light of later thinking and of later events. Much has been published in the press and in books, but there has been no new Antonius to answer such questions as what happened among politically oriented Arab intellectuals after the emergence of Nasser's Pan-Arab interests and whether and why the concept of unity has been abandoned as the major solution for Arab problems.

SETON-WILLIAMS, M. V. **Britain and the Arab States: A Survey of Anglo-Arab Relations, 1920–1948.** London: Luzac, 1948, 330 p.

This volume, written just after World War II, is an introduction to an era in which the British—despite French rivalry—were the dominant force in the Arab East. Seton-Williams surveyed the area and wondered how long British influence and aid would retain its crucial importance. In short chapters he took a careful, sometimes pedestrian, look at each country and at the Arab League. It is not a work of great distinction but served its purpose as a useful general survey at a critical time.

Two other books carry the story forward and document the end of Britain's role as the preëminent outside power in the Arab East. John Marlowe's **Arab Nationalism and British Imperialism** (New York: Praeger, 1961, 236 p.) looks at the Arab world through British eyes more than it looks at Britain's role introspectively; it documents the Egyptian failure to establish hegemony and, in passing, the British failure to act wisely at the twilight of empire. More a conventional narrative of events than a study of either nationalism or imperialism, it nevertheless contains some shrewd judgments on both. Elizabeth Monroe's **Britain's Moment in the Middle East, 1914–1956** should be mentioned here because the major portion of it has to do with Britain and the Arabs. Miss Monroe, linking past and present, has related in brilliant fashion the events leading to the Suez climax and the sudden change in Britain's status.

POLK, WILLIAM R. **The United States and the Arab World.** Cambridge: Harvard University Press, 2d rev. ed., 1969, 377 p.

The bulk of William Polk's book is historical. It serves as an introduction to the Arabs, beginning with the land and the people and running briefly through the centuries until the time of the impact of the West on the Ottoman Empire and its subject peoples, the effects of the First World War and its revolutionary aftermath, and finally the fortunes of the individual Arab successor states. Particular attention is given to Palestine, the one mandated territory that did not make the transition to independence as the others did. Throughout this part of the book Polk showed his surefootedness and powers of selection within his limitations of space. It is still rather conventional summary history, yet he can hardly be faulted for not doing the impossible.

In the latter part of the book, the author made good use of his analytical talent in describing what he called "the matrix of the new Arab." Discussing the social revolution and the economic prospects, he stressed the role of the "new men." These are not the men of the traditional society, nor are they necessarily representatives of the middle class. Drawn from all classes, they are the men who are in fact leading the search for discipline, efficiency, economic growth, and for dignity and nationhood. It is a thesis worth further debate, definition and testing.

In the first edition of the book (1965), Polk had comparatively little to say on international relations and on American policy. In the second he added several chapters on American interests and policies, which show a sound knowledge of the facts (the author served in the Department of State in the early 1960s) and a willingness to point specifically to misjudgments on both the American and the Arab side.

BADEAU, JOHN S. **The American Approach to the Arab World.** New York: Harper and Row (for the Council on Foreign Relations), 1968, 209 p.

This book stands out among the many dealing with American policy in the Middle East by virtue of Ambassador Badeau's special knowledge of the Arabs. Through long experience as an educator, foundation executive and diplomat in Arab lands, he acquired an understanding which enabled him to make shrewd and almost intuitive judgments about the attitudes of peoples and the policies of governments. It is not surprising that his book turned out to be critical of certain American policies, especially when they lacked consistency or steadiness, nor that it also found much to commend. Above all, in an exposition of views which deserve a hearing whether or not they elicit agreement, the author attempted to show clearly what American interests are and what policies and instruments are best suited to protect and to advance them in relations with Arab countries. Devoting much of his attention to the United States–Egyptian relationship, he saw no inevitable conflict between the bedrock interests of the United States and those of Egypt and the Arab world, despite American frustrations in dealing with Abdel Nasser and the violent anti-American rhetoric of Arab nationalism.

Badeau did not dodge the question of Israel and its special place in U.S. policy, describing forthrightly how it has become and will remain a formidable obstacle to better American relations with the Arab world. But his book cannot be dismissed as a pro-Arab or anti-Israel discussion of American policy. It shows a balance and an awareness of realities which demand thoughtful attention. Wisely the author attempted no set of precise recommendations for the future but did call for a new approach and a change of mood. He remained optimistic that even Americans could learn from experience.

KHĀLID, KHĀLID MUHAMMAD. **From Here We Start.** Washington: American Council of Learned Societies, 1953, 165 p.

This has been a widely read and much discussed book in the Arab world, for it posed the fundamental question why the Arabs were lagging behind other peoples, and it reached some radical conclusions. If the basic cleavage in Arab society is between a secular modernism and a traditionalism imbued with the spirit of Islam, such a book by a member of the religious establishment is—and was so considered when it was published—disloyal, unorthodox and decidedly controversial. Khālid Muhammad Khālid was, in fact, tried (but acquitted) on charges of anti-religious agitation. His real crime was to break the unwritten law that religious traditionalism should not be openly attacked by anyone—and especially by one of the *ulema*.

After vigorously assailing the inequalities of society and the part played by the *ulema* themselves in maintaining them, Sheikh Khālid defined and pleaded for social justice, arguing the case for the secularization of government and the complete emancipation of women. In the context of the Egypt of 1950, beset as it was by royalty and Muslim Brethren, the book was courageously relevant. Its impact continues to be felt wherever the Islamic tradition confronts with uncertainty the impact of new ideas.

MACDONALD, ROBERT W. **The League of Arab States: A Study in the Dynamics of Regional Organizations.** Princeton: Princeton University Press, 1965, 407 p.

As indicated by its subtitle, this useful book is written by a scholar concerned with describing and analyzing the Arab League as a regional organization. Set in this mold, the text misses some of the meaning and flavor of inter-Arab relations. On the other hand, references to other regional organizations and their relationships to the United Nations add a valuable dimension to the discussion of the functions the Arab League performs and ought to perform. In this sense the book is a good antidote to oft-heard opinions concerning the League's inadequacy. Inadequate for what? Macdonald points out that by its nature the League cannot be a launching pad for Arab unity nor a regional defense organization associated with a great power; what it can be—and is in significant measure—is an organization that provides a way for Arab states to coöperate when they choose to coöperate.

Although the book suffers somewhat from the author's academic prose and his tendency to say everything with painstaking care, he has done a thorough study that reveals important and often unconsidered facets of Arab policies and postures in international life.

BERGER, MORROE. **The Arab World Today.** Garden City: Doubleday, 1962, 480 p.

In this general overview, a sociologist whose horizons are not limited by his discipline not only analyzes Arab social institutions and their history but also makes important and carefully qualified comments on the Arab psyche. Then he devotes the latter portion of his book to the political implications of the diverse social and psychological situation he earlier describes. The treatment of ideologies, national and international, draws comparatively little on the earlier social analysis, but it does include a lucid discussion of the interrelationship of nationalism, Islam and socialism. The book is enlivened by the author's own observation of Arab life, in addition to his mastery of the existing literature. Not everyone who knows Arabs will agree with his views on Arab psychology and its relation to political life, but all will be grateful for his willingness to discuss in a straightforward way matters that have received too little attention.

Another book of comparable excellence, **The Arabs, Their History and Future,** by Jacques Berque (London: Faber, 1964, 310 p.), covers the same general ground; but its author, who is also a broad-gauge sociologist, is more daring in his attempt at what might be called ethnic psychoanalysis and brings such dimensions as language and the arts into his picture with considerable success.

BE'ERI, ELIEZER. **Army Officers in Arab Politics and Society.** New York: Praeger, 1970, 514 p.

While this useful and perceptive book focuses on army officer politics in the eastern Arab states (excluding Libya but including Sudan), it covers a great deal more. It could almost be considered a general history of the two decades preceding the Arab-Israeli war of June 1967. In describing the role of the military, Be'eri takes up the development of the officer corps in each country and recounts with clarity the confrontations and attempts at coöperation between various military rulers. Where necessary, he probes into trends and episodes of earlier history, such as the military traditions arising from nineteenth-century Egypt and, more immediately relevant, the Iraqi military coup of 1936. The book's second half seeks to generalize about Arab officers and their place in government and society with more success than one might expect. Criticizing other writers who have extolled military rule as the answer to the Arabs' problems, he finds their supposed efficiency a myth and certainly not worth the sacrifice of democratic institutions.

The author admits his biases—he is an Israeli—and the reader will discern their presence from time to time. Yet he also shows insight and balance in his political judgments, particularly in the complicated and central story of the relationships among Iraq, Syria and Egypt. Not so well done is the treatment of Sudan, a territory less familiar culturally to Be'eri than the Arab heartland.

ARABIAN PENINSULA; PERSIAN GULF

HOWARTH, DAVID. **The Desert King: Ibn Saud and His Arabia.** New York: McGraw-Hill, 1964, 307 p.

David Howarth has produced an informative and readable portrait of the unifier of modern Arabia, King Abd al-Aziz ibn Saud. Few such works have appeared in recent years, except those published by or with the concurrence of the Saudi Arabian government, and these generally lack the spark of good writing. While Howarth's account is that of a journalist rather than a scholar, it fills a gap since H. C. Armstrong's **Lord of Arabia** (London: Barker, 1934, 306 p.) drew a vivid picture of the warrior-king some 30 years before. Howarth carries the story from Ibn Saud's boyhood through the Second World War to his death in late 1953 and draws in the major local reverberations which resulted from his decision to open the country to change. Like the Imams of Yemen, Ibn Saud faced the dilemma of modernization: whether to face the profound reactions it would summon from the ultraconservatives who had won him his kingdom or to bolt the doors against change and progress. Unlike the Yemeni Imams, he made a clear and decisive choice for a foreign partnership and in 1931 admitted an American oil company to concessionary exploration and development. He introduced gradual social change into his Wahhabi society by a pragmatic application of religious (Shari'a) law.

Much of the book traces his early struggles for tribal unity before oil was discovered; his conquest of the vast Arabian interior against rival forces, especially the Rashidis; his troubles with the fanatical forces of his own *Ikhwan;* and his long friendship with H. St. John B. Philby, British-born royal counselor who documented the King's life and the kingdom itself. The latter half deals with the stabilized period of Ibn Saud's reign and the substitution of the American for the British factor in the Western spectrum of his relationships, the wealth that came too quickly from oil and the deep problems that ensued.

PHILBY, HARRY ST. JOHN BRIDGER. **Sa'udi Arabia.** New York: Praeger, 1955, 393 p.

Acquaintance with Philby's many works is indispensable to a knowledge of the Arabian Peninsula. This great explorer, who after many years of British service in the Gulf region took his pension, turned Muslim and started a second family in Arabia (setting the example of a double life for his son Kim), was an extraordinary trailblazer of Western contact with a land always difficult of access. His knowledge of Arabic was deep and his observations meticulously accurate (his coördinates were verified in later years by surveyors of ARAMCO). He was less a writer than a recorder, faithful in detail, wholly wrapped up in his subject, but turgid and monotonous in his Victorian style. As a member of the council of advisers of King Ibn Saud he saw the emergence of modern Arabia and probed the Peninsula's deep and little understood past.

Philby traces the progenitors of the Saud clan from the fifteenth century through centuries of tribal warfare, the nineteenth-century clashes with the Ottoman Turks and the forces of Muhammad 'Ali of Egypt acting for the Sultan at Istanbul, to Ibn Saud's final consolidation of rule from the Persian Gulf to the Red Sea. Particularly illuminating—since he was a close observer—is the account of relationships with Great Britain in the closing days of the Ottoman Empire and how Ibn Saud obtained recognition for his primacy, then his independence as sovereign of Nejd, the Hejaz and its dependencies. The story of the 1934 clash with Yemen is very useful. Contributing less than has been published elsewhere are Philby's references to the discovery of oil, the Buraimi and other boundary disputes and the solidifying of Ibn Saud's relationship with America.

Of all Philby's books, which include **The Heart of Arabia** (New York: Putnam, 1923, 2 v.), **Arabia of the Wahhabis** (London: Constable, 1928, 438 p.), and **Arabian Jubilee** (London: Hale, 1952, 280 p.), this history is basic, if difficult reading.

KELLY, J. B. **Eastern Arabian Frontiers.** New York: Praeger, 1964, 319 p.

This book is a significant and in many ways unique summary of the background and denouement of the Buraimi dispute, which for the period of a decade after 1949 became the central element of Saudi territorial claims against British-protected states and helped to preserve if not cause a six-year break in relations between Saudi Arabia and the United Kingdom. It is an important book despite its wholly pro-British standpoint, its primary dependence upon Foreign Office sources and its burden of lengthy quotations at the expense of analysis.

Its central object is to cite and rebut (with ridicule) all Saudi claims to tribal allegiances which could have affected the arbitral award and especially to disprove the Saudi Memorial of 1955. It charges the Saudi government with bad faith and responsibility for the collapse of the international arbitration tribunal of that year, to which its memorial was presented. It inadequately explains the walkout from the tribunal of Sir Reader Bullard, the British member. It does, however, cite extensive captured correspondence to prove Saudi subornation of tribes.

Regardless of the merits of the British case on Buraimi, the book is source material of real importance in Peninsula history, especially for the period in which frontier claims and disputes became acute as the result of oil exploration and development. Prior to that time, territorial questions in bedouin life were incidental to the shifting spectrum of tribal loyalties and were expressed primarily in contests over range lands and water wells. Ultimately the very abundance of oil in the region plus the pressures of revolutionary Arab youth against traditional régimes rendered less urgent the final settlement of the boundaries of these old and still conservative societies, whose leaders became concerned with unity against radical currents in the Arab world. Read today, the book therefore has somewhat the flavor of *temps passé,* but it remains a useful reference.

DICKSON, HAROLD RICHARD PATRICK. **Kuwait and Her Neighbours.** New York: Macmillan, 1956, 627 p.

This book, along with the author's earlier work, **The Arab of the Desert** (New York: Macmillan, 1950, 648 p.), constitutes a unique documentary, both historical and descriptive, of the fading age of tribal Arabia by a remarkably qualified observer. Colonel Harold Dickson spent most of his life among the tribes of southern Iraq and the northern Arabian Peninsula. Born in Jerusalem in 1881, his bedouin Arabic included mastery of dialectal differences of peoples who could make no concession to the foreigner's ear. Dickson's service in the British army and Persian Gulf political service started with the Indian 29th Lancers in 1908 but quickly focused on Mesopotamia and those Gulf states in special treaty relationship with Britain. He continued in this service until his retirement in 1936, then remained in Kuwait as chief local representative for Arab relations of the Kuwait Oil Company until his death.

Dickson's span of Arab history thus began with the closing days of the Ottoman Empire and continued through the transformation from ancient patterns of desert life to the present urban-centered detribalization and oil economy. While the book takes Kuwait as its point of departure, the most significant of its historical and long descriptive chapters center on the emergence of a unified Arabia through the genius of Ibn Saud. Dickson had repeated contacts with the rising monarch during the fanatical *Ikhwan* movement, on the wave of which Ibn Saud achieved power. Dickson knew the *Ikhwan* and other tribal leaders personally, understood their motivations, documented their relationships and shifting loyalties and recorded their traditions and anecdotes. His description covers the thousand miles of eastern Arabia from inner Oman north to the Euphrates. The only important deficiencies are maps inadequate to the text and an incomplete index.

WENNER, MANFRED W. **Modern Yemen: 1918–1966.** Baltimore: Johns Hopkins Press, 1967, 257 p.

So few books in English have focused upon the recent history of turbulent and little-understood Yemen that Professor Wenner's study helps to fill a great void. It is a readable, short account, painstakingly researched from a considerable bibliography of works in Arabic and the Western languages and from travellers and students of the area. The author has not visited the area himself, and as maps of the Yemen are generally inadequate, his geography is understandably vague and his knowledge of leading Yemeni personalities is second or thirdhand. He also stretches points, as when he says that the aloof, isolationist policy of the Yemeni Imams gained for them "considerable stature among the other Arab states" during the period after World War I. Unfortunately for its people, the Yemen has enjoyed very little stature of any kind in recent centuries among any communities, Arab or other, because it has been so little known.

The book concentrates on the period from the beginning of Yemeni independence to the unresolved civil war as seen in mid-1966. The policies of Imam Yahya and his successor son Ahmad are interestingly but briefly outlined. Stress is given to the dilemma the Imams faced in seeking to preserve the fragile tribal and religious balance by resisting foreign influences while invoking great-power and U.A.R. assistance to assert territorial claims against the British Protectorates surrounding Aden. The story of the collapse of the Imamate and the ensuing civil war is marked by important omissions concerning inter-Arab mediation, the Bunker Mission of 1963 and United States support to Saudi Arabia's independence, and there are a few misstatements of fact. Most of the defects of this final section, however, are the result of sparsity of firsthand information and an excessive dependence on Western news reports. Much additional research is needed on the Yemen civil war and its international implications.

None the less, the book is a real contribution and well worth reading, particularly in conjunction with Harold Ingrams' **The Yemen: Imams, Rulers, and Revolutions** (New York: Praeger, 1964, 164 p.).

INGRAMS, HAROLD. **Arabia and the Isles.** New York: Praeger, 3rd ed., 1966, 386 p.

As an account of British rule in the South Arabia of the 1930s Ingrams' book is important primarily for its final chapters which concern his remarkable success as a colonial administrator in establishing tribal peace during that period in the hitherto little known Hadhramawt. Ingrams' *solh* (peace) became legendary in an area long rendered anarchical by tribal warfare and raiding. He was indeed one of the finest of British pioneers in far-flung responsibilities, a one-man development assistance program in an area of hardship and backwardness, ably assisted by a plucky and resourceful wife. With minimum resources he taught a retarded people to govern itself. His book reflects love of the population, whether of the town or desert, and its reciprocation in terms of trust and support of his program. Peace was accomplished mainly by patient and indefatigable discussion but at a few critical points required the use of force against recalcitrant raiders: the controversial Royal Air Force bombardment of forts and dwellings vacated after due warning.

The book's style is that of a diary of treasured impressions, but analysis is provided in a 102-page introduction to this latest edition. It is a documentary of unique historical value.

MARLOWE, JOHN, *pseud.* **The Persian Gulf in the Twentieth Century.** New York: Praeger, 1962, 280 p.

There has been no book on the Persian Gulf in recent times comparable to Sir Arnold Wilson's classic **The Persian Gulf** (New York: Oxford University Press,

1928, 344 p.), which carried the story to the end of the nineteenth century. Marlowe's survey history of the area since the First World War, however, is a competent and workmanlike job which properly puts its emphasis on the one factor which brought the Gulf area into a new prominence—oil. At times he is diverted into rather standard accounts of political affairs in Iran or Iraq, but fortunately the issues revolving about oil and the policies of the powers sooner or later bring the narrative back into focus on the importance of the region as a whole. From the geopolitical standpoint the author concludes that the Gulf area represents a power vacuum—even though at the time of writing the British were still physically present. Since outside states will not allow each other to fill the vacuum and cannot agree to guarantee the neutralization of the region, he argues that it therefore must be filled by the growth and development of the Gulf states themselves.

Jean-Jacques Berreby's **Le Golfe Persique** (Paris: Payot, 1959, 228 p.) covers much the same ground as Marlowe's work, is based on a close knowledge of the region and of the oil industry, and has the merit of representing a French viewpoint. Written with a light touch, it unfortunately offers also a rather light treatment of important issues which should have been probed more deeply.

IRAQ

IRELAND, PHILIP WILLARD. **Iraq: A Study in Political Development.** New York: Macmillan, 1938, 510 p.

The emergence of Iraq from dependent to full international status, following a transitional period of tutelage under the guidance of Great Britain and the League of Nations, is treated in considerable detail by Philip W. Ireland. His work deals almost exclusively with internal forces and events and gives a straightforward account of the origin and development of nationalism culminating in Iraq's independence in 1932, when Great Britain relinquished its task as guardian, although remaining in treaty relations with Iraq for another quarter of a century. Ireland also provides a brief account of development after independence and the events leading up to the first military coup of 1936. The most important parts of the book are those devoted to the nationalist movement, the establishment of the Iraqi government and the role of King Faisal. These are based on researches done in Iraq and England, partly derived from then unpublished documents (now available to scholars), and on personal interviews with British and Iraqi personages.

Ireland's work admirably complements the earlier study of Charles A. Hooper, **L'Iraq et la Société des Nations** (Paris: Pedone, 1928, 108 p.), which discusses the principles of the mandates system and their application to Iraq. Hooper, a former British adviser to Iraq during the mandate period and the author of **The Constitutional Law of Iraq** (Baghdad: MacKenzie, 1928, 277 p.), deals with the subject from both the legal and diplomatic aspects and explains how the machinery of government operated under the mandates system.

WILSON, SIR ARNOLD TALBOT. **Loyalties: Mesopotamia 1914–1917.** London: Humphrey Milford, 1930, 340 p.
————. **Mesopotamia 1917–1920: A Clash of Loyalties.** London: Humphrey Milford, 1931, 420 p.

The "personal and historical record" contained in these two volumes is an essential source for the Mesopotamian campaign and the unfolding of British policy in what was to become Iraq. Much of the first volume is devoted to the details of military operations, but since Wilson had the task of creating a civil administration behind the lines he provides a wealth of material on dealing with the local Arabs and on a variety of problems from currency and trade to public health and human turpitude. The second volume covers the completion of the military campaign to the armistice, further development of a civil administration and the diplomacy which eventually brought Iraq under British mandate. The author's central role in dealing with Arab nationalists who opposed the mandate and in the installation of Emir Faisal as head of state gives his story a unique value.

The **Letters** of Gertrude Bell (New York: Boni and Liveright, 1927, 2 v.) admirably supplement Sir Arnold Wilson's memoirs. Her knowledge of Arab matters was so valuable that she made herself indispensable to the British military command in Mesopotamia and later served as Oriental Secretary in Baghdad, serving both the British and Iraqi governments until her death in 1926. Many of the letters deal with personal rather than political matters, but the political affairs of the time and her part in them come through to the reader. The second volume contains two historical essays, by Sir Percy Cox and Sir Henry Dobbs respectively, on the events of the time.

LONGRIGG, STEPHEN HEMSLEY. **Iraq, 1900 to 1950: A Political, Social and Economic History.** New York: Oxford University Press (for the Royal Institute of International Affairs), 1953, 436 p.

In 1925 Longrigg published **Four Centuries of Modern Iraq** (Oxford: Clarendon, 1925, 378 p.), based on original sources in Middle Eastern and Western languages, which covered the history of Iraq under Ottoman rule from the sixteenth to the nineteenth centuries. In this second volume he continues the modern history of Iraq to the mid-twentieth century. In addition to published material, he draws on his own experiences as a former official first in the Iraqi government and then in the Iraq Petroleum Company. After his retirement, he kept in touch with Iraq and followed its domestic politics with a keen eye.

Longrigg's book is essentially a precise and meticulous narrative of events; each chapter gives an average of five years of Iraqi history. The author also discusses the social and economic development of Iraq and provides valuable information on changes in the urban and the rural areas of the country. However, he makes no attempt to interpret political events nor to discern any trends or patterns in the country's social and economic development. Along with his detailed account of Iraq's internal politics, Longrigg discusses Britain's formal relations with Iraq and provides the names of almost all important British officials, civil and military, who served during the period under discussion. No attempt is made to discuss broader matters of policy in this respect; the author's principal aim is to record with pride the achievements of compatriots who contributed in no small measure to the rise of a former Ottoman province from dependent to full international status under British guidance.

KHADDURI, MAJID. **Independent Iraq, 1932–1958: A Study in Iraqi Politics.** New York: Oxford University Press (for the Royal Institute of International Affairs), 2d ed., 1960, 398 p.

No book in any language can compare with this detailed study of Iraq's internal and international politics from the end of the British mandate to the end of the Hashemite dynasty. Khadduri, born and educated in Iraq, has had a long and distinguished career as an American scholar of Arab law and politics. He made full use of his unique qualifications to penetrate the jungle of Iraqi politics and come out with this balanced and lucid account which combines painstaking detail with informed interpretation. His personal knowledge of and acquaintance with many of the leading actors enabled him to supplement, and sometimes correct, the evidence gleaned from documents and from the press, for Iraqi political life is the politics of personalities rather than that of laws and constitutions. At the same time he is fully aware of the social forces and the international currents which give some pattern to the moves and countermoves of the various political and military leaders. Here, for example, is a portrait of Nuri as-Said superior to those one will find in the biographies devoted to that doughty warrior and master politician.

The sequel, Khadduri's **Republican 'Iraq: A Study in 'Iraqi Politics since the Revolution of 1958** (New York: Oxford University Press, for the Royal Institute of International Affairs, 1969, 318 p.), is cast in the same mold, and if it does not penetrate quite so deeply it is nevertheless by far the best available account of the first decade of the republic. The latter half of the book dissects the concept of Arab socialism in its Nasserist and Baathist forms, showing the interaction between ideology and the fierce factional struggles among army officers and politicians which have marked every step of Iraq's road. The author is basically sympathetic to the revolution of 1958, which he regards not as a mere coup d'état but as the expression of the three fundamental forces of nationalism, social modernization and Pan-Arabism. His final word on "the unfinished revolution," after his chronicle of ten years of government by violence, is most charitable: that the process is long and slow and that "Iraq's choice of a revolutionary procedure may be justified on the ground that any political system which may ultimately emerge would be derived from tested principles of government."

BIRDWOOD, CHRISTOPHER BROMHEAD BIRDWOOD, 2d BARON. **Nuri As-Said: A Study in Arab Leadership.** London: Cassell, 1959, 306 p.

Before General Nuri was assassinated in 1958, Lord Birdwood started to write his biography, based on oral material given to him by Nuri himself during his occasional visits to London. At Nuri's death, Lord Birdwood had scarcely completed the story of the early years following World War I and had to rely on published works for the remaining chapters. A great admirer of Nuri, Birdwood published the biography a year after Nuri's death, in memory of one of Britain's greatest friends in the Arab world. Though well written, the book is very sketchy on Nuri's later career, especially after World War II.

Another admirer of General Nuri, Waldemar J. Gallman, American ambassador to Iraq from 1954 to 1958, gives a full account of Nuri's later years, and of his achievements, personality and character, in **Iraq under General Nuri** (Baltimore: Johns Hopkins Press, 1964, 241 p.). Gallman had known Nuri intimately, seeing him almost daily, and was deeply impressed by him. The book focuses on Nuri's foreign policy, with an account of the origins of the Baghdad Pact, the implementation of its program in Iraq and a candid discussion of his difficulties in trying to obtain Western support against Iraq's potential enemies.

DANN, URIEL. **Iraq under Qassem: A Political History, 1958–1963.** New York: Praeger, 1969, 405 p.

This monograph, the first in a series published under the Reuven Shiloah Research Center of Tel Aviv University, covers the years of Iraq's history under Qasim's rule. It is based essentially on the Iraqi press, radio and periodical publications, and the picture that emerges is one rather favorable to Qasim, who is viewed primarily as an Iraqi nationalist. This picture may, however, be open to some question, since the author unfortunately had no opportunity to check these sources by interviews in Iraq with persons who had been close to Qasim. The author notes Qasim's opposition to Nasser, but his view of Qasim as an Iraqi rather than a Pan-Arab nationalist is not wholly shared by many Iraqis. Qasim had great sympathy with the poor, improving their housing and social conditions, opening new streets and constructing bridges, schools and hospitals. Because of the almost total halt in reconstruction later, Qasim accomplished more than his successors; but, in fact, he did not launch any program of reconstruction which his predecessors had not laid down. Despite these reservations, Dann's book can be recommended for its detailed account and analysis of the internal political events, especially the struggle for power among competing leaders and groups, both civil and military.

EDMONDS, CECIL JOHN. **Kurds, Turks and Arabs: Politics, Travel and Research in North-Eastern Iraq.** New York: Oxford University Press, 1957, 457 p.

This work, covering only the period from 1919 to 1925, may be regarded as the first installment of memoirs of the author's long service as a British political officer in Iraq. It is unique, however, for no comparable work on the subject exists. More than a mere record of Edmonds' experiences in Iraqi Kurdistan, it combines a study of the geography of the region, its recent history and its social and economic conditions. The core of the historical part is a detailed account of the Mosul dispute between Great Britain, then the mandatory power over Iraq, and Turkey. The author, who served in Kurdistan during the period covered in the book, writes from an intimate knowledge of the contested territory.

Although Edmonds writes with sympathy about the Kurds, he makes no apology for his opposition to Sheikh Mahmud, the most eminent tribal leader, who once aspired to be the ruler of Kurdistan. His opposition to Sheikh Mahmud's drive for independence was instrumental in carrying out Britain's policy of integrating Kurdistan within Iraq's political and administrative system.

QUBAIN, FAHIM I. **The Reconstruction of Iraq: 1950–1957.** New York: Praeger, 1959, 277 p.

This is a survey of the reconstruction schemes induced by the sudden increase of Iraq's oil revenues after World War II, designed to raise the standard of living of a people, the majority of whom had long lived at the subsistence level. General Nuri, founder of the Iraq Development Board, hoped that within ten years of the launching of these schemes, Iraq would have become a model welfare state in the Arab world. Unfortunately for him, the young leaders, civil and military, did not wait for the promised millennium and precipitated the revolution of 1958, hoping to achieve overnight what Nuri promised in a decade. The revolution did not even complete the big projects that had already been started by the Development Board. Qubain provides a highly useful study of the reconstruction schemes during the formative period, 1950–1957. It is not merely a statistical abstract; it discusses the implementation of the schemes and points out the human obstacles to development.

SYRIA; LEBANON

DE GONTAUT-BIRON, ROGER, COMTE. **Comment la France S'Est Installée en Syrie, 1918–1919.** Paris: Plon, 1922, 354 p.

The author was a French official during the early years of the French mandate over Syria and Lebanon, and his objective in writing this work was to set forth the French position with regard to the mandate and refute prevalent British and American interpretations of French actions.

De Gontaut-Biron viewed British and American actions and attitudes in the Levant as an Anglo-Saxon conspiracy conceived to deprive France of its just rights in the Middle East. The faculty of the American University of Beirut and the American Red Cross are particularly singled out for allegedly carrying out a scurrilous campaign against the French. While these charges might seem absurd to American readers today, their presentation in this work gives a valuable insight into the atmosphere of the period and goes a long way toward explaining French feelings and actions. In addition, this work gives a detailed description and analysis of the problems the French faced at the time and how they attempted to solve them.

HOURANI, ALBERT HABIB. **Syria and Lebanon: A Political Essay.** New York: Oxford University Press (for the Royal Institute of International Affairs), 1946, 402 p.

As its title indicates, this is not only an essay but a history of the two countries under French mandate—and certainly an outstanding one. Professor Hourani wrote this work during the Second World War, and it has stood the test of time well. His objective was to explain the peculiar influences which had come to make up these two former French mandates and why they were governed separately. After a brief introductory history of geographical Syria to the end of the First World War, he discusses the influence of westernization upon the area and how it interacted with the native Arab culture. Out of this came the dual problem of creating a unity of the two civilizations and of Syria's relationship with the West. He shows that Arab nationalism was a political response to these problems, aimed at preserving the Arab people against a disruptive force and, hence, at controlling and directing it to the Arabs' benefit on their own terms.

The author then considers how this interaction of cultures has affected political life by change in the spiritual, intellectual and social conditions brought about by the westernization process and the rise of Arab nationalism. Another subject of particular interest in the book is the thorough description of the minorities and their influence.

LONGRIGG, STEPHEN HEMSLEY. **Syria and Lebanon under French Mandate.** New York: Oxford University Press (for the Royal Institute of International Affairs), 1958, 404 p.

With his long experience as a British official in the Middle East, Brigadier Longrigg was especially qualified to write on this subject. His work is the most comprehensive and unbiased on Syria from mandate to independence.

The first two chapters give a short background on Syria under Ottoman rule and during the First World War. The description of the Arab Kingdom and Faisal's problems with the victorious Allies are treated in detail, as well as the complexities of establishing and maintaining the French mandate. Certainly no pro-British bias is discernible, and the author fully outlines the French point of view. The influence of domestic French politics on French policy in Syria is well brought out, as is the French infatuation with their "civilizing" mission in a land of proud people with a long history. Longrigg, however, does point out the benefits that the mandate brought, along with its shortcomings.

Covering both political and economic developments, the book aptly delineates the vicissitudes of Syrian national politics and the shaping of the Syrian state prior to full independence at the end of the Second World War. The account of the Druze rebellion of 1925–1926 is of particular interest, especially the explanation as to why it was not a national uprising, although a number of Syrian nationalists took part. The efforts to draft the Syrian constitution are treated at length, and both the French and the Syrian viewpoints are well explained. This background makes it much easier to understand the reasons for the failure of parliamentary democracy in Syria and the period of xenophobia and military coups that followed. Especially valuable are the appendices which include a list of administrative units, the text of the mandate for Syria and a bibliographical note.

SEALE, PATRICK. **The Struggle for Syria: A Study of Post-War Arab Politics 1945– 1958.** New York: Oxford University Press (for the Royal Institute of International Affairs), 1965, 344 p.

The thesis of this work by a journalist well acquainted with Arab affairs is that Syria is the cockpit in which its neighbors' rivalries are projected onto the local political scene; thus, whoever desires to dominate the Middle East must control Syria. It is in Damascus that the elements of Arab nationalism—language, culture, historical experience and aspirations—have been most cogently drawn together and given force by the Baath movement.

The book opens with a short resumé of the conflicting forces present on the Syrian scene and the events which led to the first army coup in 1949. It then proceeds to discuss Syria's various political problems until the union with Egypt in 1958, placing special emphasis on the influence that foreign relations played, an emphasis that appears strained at times.

The author consulted numerous participants in the events recounted and explored all shades of opinion; however, critical judgments on the statements quoted would have been of considerable assistance to the reader. Despite this criticism, this is a first-rate work and an education in inter-Arab relations as well as in Syrian politics of the period.

TORREY, GORDON H. **Syrian Politics and the Military, 1945–1958.** Columbus: Ohio State University Press, 1964, 438 p.

The Republic of Syria in the first decade of its independence became known as an ungoverned and ungovernable state, a classic case of political instability and chaos. For readers interested in the details, this book provides a month-by-month and cabinet-by-cabinet account of how it all happened, from the early disintegration of the parliamentary system in the 1940s through the three successive military régimes of 1949–1954 and the period of political shifts and combinations which finally led to the union with Egypt in 1958. By extensive use of the contemporary press the author manages to make his way through the infinitely complex ups and downs of parties and politicians without getting lost. Nor does he lose sight of the tie between Syrian politics and the broader questions of Syria's relations with other Arab states, especially the two which were competing for influence or control in Syria: Iraq and Egypt.

The disappointment of the book, aside from the obvious limitations on source material, lies in the author's modesty in not matching his chronicle of events with more interpretative analysis. For example, the narrative bears out the prominence of the military in Syrian politics pointed up by the title, but the absence of a deeper inquiry into the politics of army officers and into civil-military relations is all the more noticeable. Similarly, more probing thoughts on the effects of the interaction between political ideas and personal politics (particularly in the light of the overlapping concepts of Arabism and Syrian nationalism mentioned by the author) remain relatively unexplored and unexplained.

QUBAIN, FAHIM ISSA. **Crisis in Lebanon.** Washington: Middle East Institute, 1961, 243 p.

Dr. Qubain's work is the most comprehensive on this critical period in contemporary Lebanese history. Following a short historical background, the work details the underlying causes of the crisis of 1958 and how the civil war developed. The roles played by President Camille Chamoun, the various political leaders and General Shihab, commander of the Lebanese army, are described as they developed. Likewise, the actions of the various outside powers on the scene—especially the United States, the United Arab Republic and Iraq—are delineated in detail and assessed. There is an extensive treatment of the crisis in the United Nations' context, both in New York and on the scene in Lebanon. The author is eminently fair in his judgments, and the work shows extensive use of all types of sources—documents, the press and interviews with participants themselves. The summary and conclusions carefully assess the implications of the crisis for Lebanon and the Arab world and delineate the lessons learned from it.

TRANSJORDAN AND JORDAN

ABDULLAH I, KING OF JORDAN. **Memoirs of King Abdullah of Transjordan.** New York: Philosophical Library, 1950, 278 p.

Ottoman and Arabian politics, the Hejaz and Istanbul, dominate this first installment of the King's reminiscences. The Arab revolt of 1916–1918 is the high point, and the establishment of the Emirate of Transjordan in the early 1920s concludes the detailed narrative. Later events are dealt with sketchily, but Abdullah's quest for the throne of greater Syria during World War II is represented by several contemporary official documents. This translation significantly modifies the Arabic first edition by omission and rearrangement, frequently very seriously in passages which set forth the King's reflections on history, Arabism and Islam, but in only a minor way in the passages which narrate events. No fault can be found with the translation of the concluding installment, **King 'Abdallah of Jordan: My Memoirs Completed** (Washington: American Council of Learned Societies, 1954, 121 p.). The random recollections here assembled mostly recall the King's difficulties with other Arab governments after 1945, chiefly over Palestine and greater Syria, but some memoranda concerning Palestine written in the 1930s are included.

GLUBB, SIR JOHN BAGOT. **A Soldier with the Arabs.** New York: Harper, 1958, 458 p.

Sir John Glubb took command of the Arab Legion just when World War II prompted the creation of the first military formation within what had been a police force. He commanded the Legion in its first, and longest, true military operation, the Palestine War of 1948–1949. When he was relieved of command in 1956, he left an organization which included a combat-ready division. These developments, as Sir John's account implies, took place as a result of British policy; although the longest step in the transformation of the Legion into a military force was stimulated by the Palestine War, Britain in the end provided the means. Nevertheless, except for a few highly illuminating passages, British thinking and plans are slighted. Sir John spent his years in Jordan in the service of the Jordanian, not the British government, and his book is about Jordanian politics and policies.

The military operations of 1948–1949 receive the most detailed treatment, but Jordan's relations with the other Arab states, friction with Israel after 1949 and Jordanian internal politics are also depicted in considerable depth. General Glubb obviously writes with much greater sympathy for the Jordanian and British points of view than for the Israeli and Egyptian, but he writes as an informed and rational partisan. His book is thus a highly useful general treatment of Jordanian politics and foreign relations as well as an indispensable source by a major participant.

Politics and diplomacy are far from the center of the stage in the memoirs of Britain's official representative in Jordan, Sir Alec Seath Kirkbride, **A Crackle of Thorns: Experiences in the Middle East** (London: Murray, 1956, 201 p.). The author, whose service in the country began in 1918, was British resident (1939–1946) and minister (1946–1951). He relates in general terms the major political developments, but more of his book is given over to charming and brilliantly evocative sketches of the geographical, cultural and human setting.

VATIKIOTIS, P. J. **Politics and the Military in Jordan: A Study of the Arab Legion, 1921–1957.** New York: Praeger, 1967, 169 p.

Civil-military relations, as conceptualized by recent political science theory, are the starting point and main focus of this monograph, but in pursuing his analysis the author has written an excellent brief history of the formation of the Emirate of Transjordan and its evolution into the Hashemite Kingdom of Jordan. The period 1948–1957 receives most attention, with the most thorough analysis devoted to the attempted coup of Abdullah al-Tel in 1949 and the more serious crisis in 1957. Remarks on the Samu incident in 1966 and on the 1967 war are appended. The author credits King Hussein with a great deal of political acumen and sagacity and concludes that the existence of the Jordanian state depends on the presence of a *corps d'élite* of ground forces supporting a monarch with extensive powers of rule. In his careful consideration of the state's capacity to survive in the face of Pan-Arab nationalism, Jordanian social change and the alleged progressive nature of other Arab régimes (*i.e.* Egypt, Syria and Iraq), he very convincingly questions the widely held opinion that these forces portend the necessary extinction of the Jordanian anachronism. The need still exists for studies which probe much more deeply into the factual reality of governance in Jordan—indeed, in all the Arab states. Vatikiotis, however, has delved more deeply than most who have written about the Arab countries. Above all, he has handled his material with imagination and intellectual discipline.

PALESTINE; ARAB-ISRAELI CONFLICT

HYAMSON, ALBERT MONTEFIORE. **Palestine under the Mandate, 1920–1948.** London: Methuen, 1950, 210 p.

Mr. Hyamson served as head of the Department of Immigration in the Palestine mandate government for a period of 14 years. He has written a conscientious and honest account of the British administration during the mandate period, albeit from the viewpoint of a hard-pressed British official. Mr. Hyamson was quite aware at the time of writing that a "definitive" story could not be written until the British archives made the basic materials available, and his work has a perspective sometimes lacking in memoirs of this type. The story begins with an account of early British and Jewish interest in Palestine, the British government and the Jews, and the Balfour Declaration and the mandate. The rest of the book provides a detailed story of the British administration in Palestine, immigration, citizenship and employment, the land problem, self-government, the mandate during the inter-war period, World War II, industry and finance, social and cultural services, and the Holy Places.

Mr. Hyamson, who wrote his book immediately after establishment of the state of Israel, rightly observes that Great Britain faced an insoluble problem in the mandate, which involved establishment of "a national homeland" for the Jews, while safeguarding the rights of the very large Arab majority, and that it failed, therefore, to meet the basic problems. He believes that, while the British inevitably made mistakes, any nation would have failed in the same task, granted the nature of the problem. Whatever the criticisms, it was the British administration during the mandate which made possible the homeland and the state of Israel. The book will continue to be read and studied, not only because of the data which the author provides concerning the mandate, but because the material is presented in a fair-minded and balanced manner by one who had direct and long experience in the mandate government. Of Jewish origin, Mr. Hyamson has not hesitated to call a spade a spade in this book.

BENTWICH, NORMAN DEMATTOS. **England in Palestine.** London: Kegan Paul, 1932, 358 p.

This is an account of the British stewardship in Palestine during the first decade of the mandate period. It is written by a distinguished Anglo-Zionist who came into Palestine with British forces, served as attorney-general in the civil government, 1920–1931, and then occupied the chair of international relations at the Hebrew University. The volume is divided essentially into two basic parts, with the first treating the historical background and the second the government of Palestine. Historical research and publication have now gone much beyond what Mr. Bentwich was able to write; nevertheless, his book is of special importance both because of its treatment of the early mandate period and because it is based on the author's very extensive experience in dealing with the problems which arose during that period, when Sir Herbert Samuel, Field Marshal Lord Plumer and Sir John Chancelor served as High Commissioners. There are detailed discussions of the executive, legislative and judicial branches of government and very interesting characterizations of the people with whom the author served. The volume should be read along with a number of other books by Mr. Bentwich, including his **Palestine** (London: Benn, 1947, 302 p.), **Israel Resurgent** (New York: Praeger, 1960, 255 p.) and, with his wife, Helen Bentwich, **Mandate Memories, 1918–1948** (New York: Schocken, 1965, 231 p.).

JEFFRIES, JOSEPH MARY NAGLE. **Palestine: The Reality.** New York: Longmans, 1939, 728 p.

This is the most comprehensive statement of the Arab viewpoint on the Palestine problem prior to World War II. It is a frank polemic from start to finish, *ex parte* pleading, a massive indictment of British and Zionist policy and action, often discursive, repetitive and sometimes confusing. A British journalist who was associated with the Arab Center in London, Mr. Jeffries is utterly unsparing of British statesmen and Zionists, whom he regarded as responsible for the sorry plight of the Holy Land. Like others who have dealt with the problem of Palestine, the author goes back to early history, traces something of both the Arab and Jewish connection with the land, and then plunges into the controversies relative to political Zionism and Arab nationalism, the conflicting promises made to Zionists and

Arabs during World War I, the establishment of the mandate and its development to the book's publication in 1939. He charges that the British government had no right to make its promises under the Balfour Declaration and observes that in any case it ignored the restrictive clause against prejudicing the "civil and religious rights of existing non-Jewish communities in Palestine." He also contends that establishment of the mandate was illegal, and that British and Zionist actions thereunder denied the basic rights of the Palestinian Arabs—nine-tenths of the population in 1917—to self-determination in their own country and could only lead to moral and political disaster.

To be more helpful, the author's annotations should have been more precise, and his bibliography should have been more carefully prepared. While Mr. Jeffries' work is obviously based on very extensive research into the documentation of the period, it remains an indictment, not a balanced, scholarly approach to the subject. But it must be read and pondered, balanced with other works, if one is to understand the depth of Arab anger concerning Palestine and the policies which were pursued in connection with it. What's past is prologue.

HUREWITZ, JACOB COLEMAN. **The Struggle for Palestine.** New York: Norton, 1950, 404 p.

Now one of the "earlier" treatments of the Arab-Israeli conflict, this is a detailed study of the political history of the problem during 1936–1949, based on thorough study of the available published documents of the period. Granted the vast polemic literature and outright propaganda of the era, Professor Hurewitz has examined his material with calm and dispassionate consideration and produced the best general history of the Palestine conflict at the time, and his book remains of enduring value. It begins with the struggle for ascendancy between Arabs and Jews, especially during the latter period of the mandate, considers the issues confronting the British government and the pressures which were brought to bear on it by both Arabs and Zionists. He also treats the period immediately prior to and during World War II, when Nazi totalitarianism increased the Jewish pressure upon Palestine; and the Arab-Israeli conflict of 1948–1949 is well covered. The volume contains a very useful bibliography. Professor Hurewitz's book now becomes part of the history of the history of the Palestine problem and should be supplemented by other works which have since appeared.

SYKES, CHRISTOPHER. **Cross Roads to Israel.** Cleveland: World, 1965, 404 p.

As Mr. Sykes tells us, there are literally hundreds of books on Zionism and the historical background of the state of Israel. His own reason for writing an additional volume was twofold. On the one hand, he felt that the younger generation was growing up entirely ignorant of the history of a problem which had engaged much attention on the part of their fathers. Secondly, he wanted to write a new account as free of bias as J. C. Hurewitz's earlier study, **The Struggle for Palestine.** Mr. Sykes has consulted the basic published works, documentary and other, and has used much archival material, including that in the Zionist and Israel State Archives in Jerusalem. The result is another masterly and penetrating volume on the very complicated problem of Palestine, with all its ramifications, covering the early history of the Zionist movement and moving in a broad sweep through the development of the mandate to the establishment of the independent state of Israel on May 15, 1948.

The volume will not tell the specialized student much in detail which he does not know, but it is especially valuable because of the thoroughness of the author's research, the intelligence and reflection with which he has written, and the genuine perception and balance with which he has approached his problem. His characterizations of the primary actors on the scene are well rounded; his judgments of men and events are seldom harsh or sharp. While very sympathetic with Zionism, Mr. Sykes is often critical of the pressures and propaganda which were brought into play and seems somewhat disturbed that achievement of a state did not fulfill the dream or ideal. This is a penetrating volume, which should be read by all students of the Palestine problem.

POLK, WILLIAM ROE; STAMLER, DAVID M. and ASFOUR, EDMUND. **Backdrop to Tragedy: The Struggle for Palestine.** Boston: Beacon Press, 1957, 399 p.

The purpose of this study is to dig deeply into the emotional and psychological elements, the historical, political, social and economic forces, which provide the framework of the Palestine problem. The book is divided basically into four sections. The first, which deals with the historical antecedents, was jointly written, and tells the essential story to the establishment of the state of Israel. Part II, written by David M. Stamler, an Anglo-Jewish student of modern Hebrew literature, deals with Jewish interests in Palestine. William R. Polk, an American specialist, is the author of the third part, dealing with the Arabs and Palestine. Edmund Asfour, a Lebanese economist, author of part IV, has devoted his section to the economic framework of the Palestine problem, and his section is noteworthy for its treatment of landholdings and Arab refugee abandoned property. Despite the different viewpoints of the authors, the book is a unified whole, and it is well written, well balanced and well documented—the kind of work which should be studied and considered by all interested in the problem. Writing in 1957, the authors make the basic point that the problem of Palestine is so intricately interwoven into our very lives "as probably to be incapable of *solution*," and they observe that "our real solution is only in learning how to live with and control the situation as we now see it." While they hoped for "a period of cooling off," they added: "But time which is measured in units and decades of raids, counter-raids, threats and fear counts for naught." As there has been no "cooling off," so there are, as yet, no durable solutions. It is still necessary, however, if we are to have any understanding of the issues, to consider the backdrop. There is an excellent, selected bibliography.

BURNS, EEDSON LOUIS MILLARD. **Between Arab and Israeli.** New York: Obolensky, 1963, 336 p.

This is an altogether excellent memoir of General Burns' experience as Chief of Staff of the United Nations Truce Supervision Organization and commander of the United Nations Emergency Force during the years 1954–1956 and 1956–1957. Confining himself largely to matters of which he had firsthand knowledge, he has written a factual account which must be read by all students of peacekeeping activities in the Middle East. General Burns knows whereof he writes, and he writes without fear or favor. His memoir is especially valuable for the light which it sheds both on the operations of UNTSO and of UNEF. His discussion of the difficult problems, involving incidents along the Egyptian-Israeli, Syrian-Israeli and Jordan-Israeli demarcation lines, is informed and objective; and in particular his observations on the Israeli attack on Syria in December 1955 and of the background of the Suez conflict are illuminating.

The final portion of the memoir deals with the Israeli attack on Egypt at the end of October 1956 and the origins and establishment of UNEF, of which General Burns became commanding officer. His conclusions are of much interest, for he considered both UNTSO and UNEF essential elements of the U.N. peacekeeping machinery in the Middle East, and he concluded in 1962 that no peaceful solution of the Palestine conflict was in sight and that there was always a possibility of another conflict. Written with candor and objectivity, General Burns' story will remain as a very important contribution to the history of the Palestine problem. It should now be supplemented with the later book by his successor as Chief of Staff of UNTSO, Major General Carl von Horn, **Soldiering for Peace** (New York: McKay, 1967, 402 p.).

PERETZ, DON. **Israel and the Palestine Arabs.** Washington: Middle East Institute, 1958, 264 p.

This is an able, pioneering study of the development of Israel's policy toward the Palestine Arabs—both the refugees and those who stayed—written some ten years after the beginnings of the problem. It describes in objective detail the ways in which the government of Israel dealt with the problem of the Palestine Arabs during the first decade after 1948 and is especially helpful in delineating the internal political and military factors which determined Israeli policy. One of the distinctive features of the book lies in its treatment of Israeli policy toward the Arab minority, which then numbered something more than 200,000. The story of military and police restrictions and of the sequestration of Arab refugee abandoned property in Israel is well told and well documented. There is also treatment of the UNRWA effort in attempting to meet the problem of those Arabs, then numbering some 900,000, who became refugees as a result of the 1948 conflict and the establishment of the state of Israel.

Professor Peretz's book has stood the test of time, although its statistical data and some of the observations now require updating as a consequence of the passage of time. A later book by Jacob M. Landau, **The Arabs in Israel: A Political Study** (New York: Oxford University Press, for the Royal Institute of International Affairs, 1969, 300 p.), has much more up-to-date and detailed data on the Arabs of Israel.

GABBAY, RONY E. **A Political Study of the Arab-Jewish Conflict: The Arab Refugee Problem (A Case Study).** Geneva: Droz, 1959, 611 p.

Mr. Gabbay discusses the refugee problem in practically all its aspects and properly begins his study with the origins—the Arabs of Palestine prior to 1948. A second chapter takes up the causes of the Arab flight from Palestine and notes that, whatever the specific responsibilities, the fact of the conflict itself in 1948 was the basic cause. Another chapter treats the work of Count Bernadotte, the U.N. mediator, in connection with the refugee problem and the broader issues which he had to meet during 1948. While Mr. Gabbay treats political issues and the attempts, especially through the U.N. Conciliation Commission for Palestine, to achieve a solution of the Arab-Israeli conflict, the bulk of the volume is concerned with the refugee problem as such. He discusses the problem of numbers of refugees, how they live, their status in the Arab host countries, the issues of repatriation and compensation, along with that of resettlement, abandoned Arab properties and the work of UNRWA in behalf of the refugees. There are brief reflections on the Suez campaign of 1956 and some interesting conclusions. The work closes with an excellent bibliography of pertinent source materials and other works which should serve as a guide for further study.

It is not necessary to agree with all that Mr. Gabbay writes in order to appreciate his work and to commend it as a welcome addition to a growing library of books on the subject. His book is written with perception and balance and without undue bias. While it is marred by typographical errors and could have been compressed, it is basically a very useful contribution to consideration of problems which continue to baffle statesmen.

KHOURI, FRED J. **The Arab-Israeli Dilemma.** Syracuse: Syracuse University Press, 1968, 436 p.

This is probably the most comprehensive single volume devoted to the Arab-Israeli conflict, bringing the story up to the date of publication in 1968. It is objective, well balanced and based on a thorough command of the documentation and pertinent secondary literature. The work covers the Palestine problem to 1948, the conflicts of 1948–1949 and 1956–1957, the war of June 1967 and then the separate problems of Jerusalem, the Arab refugees and the attempts since 1949 to achieve a peaceful adjustment. An appendix includes selections from the McMahon-Hussein correspondence (1915) and other pertinent documents. There is also a helpful bibliography.

No apologist for the Arabs, the Israelis or the great powers, the author has criticism for all concerned in the story—although many critics of the book, especially those generally favorable to Israel, have not accepted it as impartial. Writing in 1968, he finds Arab-Israeli hatred, fear and distrust as acute as ever. He holds that by denying the elementary right of the Arab refugees to national self-determination and establishing an "alien" state in their midst the Zionists and the West committed a grave injustice in the Arab world. While the hour is very late, Professor Khouri, who adheres to Matthew Arnold's "sweet reason and the will of God," urges active U.N. involvement in the continuing controversy, abandonment of American partisanship of Israel and a more objective Soviet approach to the problem. Peace, in his view, remains a forlorn hope unless the Arab states move toward a less hostile attitude toward Israel and Israel moves toward mutual concessions in the interest of a peaceful solution. The book is likely to remain a lasting contribution to scholarship relative to this complicated dilemma.

RODINSON, MAXIME. **Israel and the Arabs.** New York: Pantheon, 1969, 239 p.

This is a brilliant and profound analysis, written by a French Marxist sociologist of Jewish origin, who has had much experience in the Middle East. It is without doubt one of the best books dealing not with the day-to-day aspects of the Arab-Israeli conflict but with its deeper backgrounds and the imponderables. Professor Rodinson, a distinguished Orientalist, understands both sides of the conflict, and he is fair and balanced in his judgments. He discusses Jewish nationalism (political Zionism) and Arab nationalism, the first decade in the history of Israel, the development of Arab socialism, the Arabs and the world at large, and the continuing Arab-Israeli conflict. He argues that Western views of the conflict are oversimplified because we tend to be interested intermittently, during periods of crisis, are ignorant of Arab politics and unaware of the pressures involved, and start from a position of basic sympathy with Israel which inevitably colors our attitudes and appraisals. M. Rodinson holds that the central Arab problem is that of achievement of economic progress, while hostility toward Israel is diversionary to the extent that Israel acts as a counterrevolutionary force in the Middle East. On the other hand, the long-term Israeli problem is how to reconcile the more aggressively Zionist and expansionist views of Israel with the more moderate and integrationist position. The shifting attitudes and policies of the superpowers, the Soviet Union and the United States, continue to be important factors. For those who seek something more than a fly-by-night account of contemporary events and desire to plunge more deeply into the problem, this will remain an analysis which should be given serious consideration.

LAQUEUR, WALTER. **The Road to Jerusalem: The Origins of the Arab-Israeli Conflict, 1967.** New York: Macmillan, 1968, 368 p.

This book, by a well-known Israeli writer, deals with the origins and immediate antecedents of the war of June 1967. Its account of the crisis which preceded the June conflict is based largely on the contemporary press, and may not be up to the author's best, but it is none the less revealing as to Israeli attitudes, politics and policies. The author himself tells us at the outset that he does not pretend to "objectivity," since he has a point of view, but he holds that he has presented the evidence fairly and believes that when archival material becomes available the essence of his story will remain intact. The book opens with a brief history of the development of political Zionism and Arab nationalism, treats Israel and the Arab world during 1948–1966, and then plunges into the immediate background of the June conflict and carries through to its aftermath.

Mr. Laqueur believes, as others have stated, that both the U.A.R. and Israel stumbled into a conflict which neither had planned. Perhaps the best two chapters in the book are those dealing with public opinion and the aftermath, with the latter embodying the basic reflections of the author, who thinks that fundamental changes are occurring in the Middle East and that the Zionist phase of Israel's development has passed. While points of view of course will differ much, and a more basic assessment must await the passage of time, Mr. Laqueur's brief treatment is certainly one of the better accounts. It is superior to Theodore Draper's

Israel and World Politics: Roots of the Third Arab-Israeli War (New York: Viking, 1968, 278 p.), which barely digs at the roots, or the many examples of instant history which followed immediately in the wake of the June 1967 conflict. But it should be balanced with study of "the other side."

SAFRAN, NADAV. **From War to War: The Arab-Israeli Confrontation, 1948–1967.** New York: Pegasus, 1969, 464 p.

Professor Safran places the Arab-Israeli confrontation within the context of competition and conflict among the Arab states and the cold war among the greater powers, especially the United States and the Soviet Union. More specifically, he treats the evolution of the conflict, the pattern of Israeli-Arab relations, the interests and policies of the great powers in the Middle East, the dynamics and development of the arms build-up, the crisis during May–June 1967 and the Six Day War, and the war and the future.

While Safran deals with both the regional and the world patterns, along with the basic origins of the Arab-Israeli conflict, he appears at his best in analyzing the arms race, the military aspects of the 1967 crisis and in describing the campaigns, although not really hiding his enthusiasm over the Israeli military victory. He seems both "certain" and "uncertain" as to the prospects of "peace," and he certainly has no prescription for it. Repeatedly, the text refers to American "commitments" to Israel, but the author does not tell his readers their source, their nature or their quality. He also observes that Israel was the first to strike or attack on June 5, 1967, but makes a distinction between "attack" and "aggression," which he regards as two entirely different concepts. These are not major defects. As a whole the book remains a valuable contribution, especially for its military analysis.

EGYPT

VATIKIOTIS, P. J. **The Modern History of Egypt.** New York: Praeger, 1969, 512 p.

Among the virtues of this book is that it manages to cover the main political events without becoming a lifeless chronology and at the same time achieves real distinction in probing the intellectual and cultural currents which explain so much about the independent and revolutionary Egypt of the 1950s and 1960s. The author is particularly good in describing the failure of European liberalism in the period after the First World War and the strong reaction to it in the form of the Muslim Brotherhood and the fascist-type Young Egypt movement. At a time when surface politics were dominated by the Palace, the Wafd and the British, radicalism of the right exercised a potent influence on professional men, students and the lower classes of cities and towns.

The military régime of 1952 and the subsequent "Arab socialism" are seen to rest on established trends in Egyptian society. On the other hand, as the study is primarily a history, it does not present more than a summary treatment of the record of that régime.

As the author intended, the emphasis throughout the book is on internal affairs. He does not tarry long with the history and diplomacy of the Eastern Question, which is dealt with in so many other books. Yet he does see very clearly the interaction between internal and international developments, especially important in Egypt's case since the country did not have a truly independent foreign policy from 1882 to 1954.

LLOYD OF DOLOBRAN, GEORGE AMBROSE LLOYD, 1ST BARON. **Egypt since Cromer.** New York: Macmillan, 1933–1934, 2 v.

Lord Lloyd served as British High Commissioner in Egypt from 1925 to 1929. These were difficult years in Anglo-Egyptian relations, crowded with such crises as the control of the Egyptian army, the Nile Waters Agreement, treaty negotiations and the Sudan. The first volume is a provocative and highly controversial interpretation of the record of British indirect rule in Egypt from the end of Cromer's proconsulship in 1907 to the end of the First World War and the rise of the Zaghlul nationalist movement. Lloyd's assessment of that policy amounted to an indictment of the British government for failing to follow a firm policy. He argued that by 1919 Britain should either have permitted Egypt complete independence or, if that were not considered opportune, governed the country more directly and firmly. Hesitation was disastrous. He also vehemently criticized the introduction of Western political ideas into Egypt even though he was aware that they came largely from the French. Yet it is difficult to reject his argument that "the clash between the two ideas of benevolent administration and the development of autonomy has been the cause of many of our difficulties."

The second volume is an interpretative study of Britain in Egypt from 1922 to 1929, the year Lloyd was recalled from his post by the Labor government. In contrast to the previous period, he describes this as one of drifting, and the volume on the whole constitutes an attack on British policy. More important, however, are Lloyd's general remarks about British imperial policy, his thesis that the main task of government is to provide good administration from which constitutional and other ideas and institutions of self-government can emerge, and what he deplores as "the dangerous illusion that we can achieve anything by promises, however liberal—to be redeemed in the distant future."

Like Lord Cromer in his "Modern Egypt," Lloyd set down the record of British rule in Egypt as he saw it. But he did more than Cromer: he attacked British hesitation over policy and especially Liberal and Labor Party ideas of government.

COLOMBE, MARCEL. **L'Évolution de l'Égypte, 1924–1950.** Paris: Maisonneuve, 1951, 361 p.

Until a few years ago this was the only available survey in a European language of the political history of Egypt from independence to the end of the Second World War. Since its publication in 1951, however, several monographs and books have appeared, based on research made possible by newly available archival material in Egypt and England. Thus parts I and II, dealing with the political evolution of Egypt from 1924 to 1945, are mainly a political narrative of men and events at the formal, or official, level, written without the benefit of the British records dealing with the period 1920–1940 which are now open to students. Moreover, in dealing with the Wafd party and the so-called minority governments of that period which were drawn from the Liberal Constitutionalist, the National, the Saadist and the Palace parties such as the Ittihad, the author does not consider the social and economic background of and ideological influences on the leaders of these groups. Similarly, in part III on the evolution of ideas and society in the same period, many of the author's general formulations—for example, on Islamic reform and the political conflicts over the role and control of religious institutions—have been superseded by the findings of later research, especially the work of Abdel-Malek, Elie Kedourie and Malcolm Kerr. Although the last part, "Egypt after the End of the War (1945–50)," is mainly a discussion of the problems of Anglo-Egyptian relations, Colombe also dealt with the domestic scene, seeing the ominous prospects that could emerge from the dissipation of the parliamentary system after the Palestine War of 1948–1949 and the heightened activities of such radical organizations as the Muslim Brotherhood.

A more recent, more ambitious and less conventional work is Jacques Berque's **L'Égypte: Imperialisme et Révolution** (Paris: Gallimard, 1967, 746 p.). Berque takes a broad social view of Egyptian history on the general theme of decolonization, which in his belief provides an approach rich in facts and theory. His book certainly does that, for he has been assiduous in his research and provocative in his thinking. The narrative leads up to the revolution but stops with "Black Saturday" in January 1952.

LACOUTURE, JEAN and LACOUTURE, SIMONNE. **Egypt in Transition.** New York: Criterion Books, 1958, 532 p.

This book by two French journalists first appeared in French as **L'Égypte en Mouvement** (Paris: Éditions du Seuil, 1956, 480 p.) about the time of the Suez crisis. The expanded English translation was published two years later when President Nasser was at the height of his "Arab political career."

The authors view the condition of Egypt not simply as a transient phase but in permanent transition; thus they allude to the difficulty in really solving any of its permanent problems, such as overpopulation, and depict the stubborn continuity in Egyptian life despite what appear as revolutionary breaks in its history.

The best part of the book deals with the Free Officers, especially the authors' description of the junta and its members. It is unfair to criticize the third part, which deals with agrarian reform and economic development plans, as it was too early to assess results or difficulties in 1958. And, in any case, other students of modern Egypt have written specifically about these matters since then. Equally imaginative and flavorful is the authors' discussion of the tensions present in Egyptian society as regards religion, politics and culture in their excellent section, "Forging a Society." Finally, the chapter entitled "Nasser as He Really Is," gives one of the earliest indications by any European writer on Egypt of Nasser's consuming interest in power.

The intelligent skepticism of the authors comes through in discussing the events after Suez and particularly the Syrian-Egyptian union in 1958. It was "too mythical," in their view, to last—a most accurate prognosis in 1958. This is perhaps one of the most excitingly readable general introductions to modern Egypt for the lay reader to have appeared in the last 20 years.

NASSER, GAMAL ABDEL. **The Philosophy of the Revolution.** Buffalo: Smith, Keynes and Marshall, 1959, 102 p.

First published in Cairo in 1953 as a pamphlet sponsored by the Revolutionary Command Council, this volume (though abridged) is the best of the translations in English. A personal statement by the Egyptian President written in connection with the army coup of July 1952, it will remain an important though curious document. The controversy, or mystery, surrounding its true authorship will not be cleared up, if at all, for many years to come. Cynics might aver that Nasser, or one of his aides, wrote the piece at a time when his political future was uncertain—actually, dangerously in the balance—and suggest that he had it published in order to attract his fellow countrymen to his cause.

To say that the 1952 military coup was the culmination of Egypt's long struggle for national liberation is an assertion on which many Egyptians will argue and differ. Similarly, to identify the three concentric circles within which Egypt, according to its President, has a leading, heroic role to play is also now a matter of bitter historical record for many Egyptians. Thus one picks one's way through the shambles of Egypt's Arab policy (1957–1967), African policy (1958–1963) and her frankly nonexistent Muslim policy. All of that, one could argue, may not be relevant. What is interesting about this document is what it says about its author in his instinctive groping for a Machiavellian understanding of history and power— perhaps more than he intended.

Free of the pseudo-philosophical and racist rantings of Hitler's **Mein Kampf,** this document clearly tells us that Nasser's basic political attitudes, perceptions and beliefs were essentially formed in the years of mounting radical activity in Egypt from 1933 to 1948, on the periphery or outside the framework of the then constituted parliamentary political parties. It was in such extremist groups as the Young Egypt Association and the Muslim Brotherhood, including perhaps their paramilitary organizations, that President Nasser and his closest associates seemed to have developed their political consciousness. The conservative Muslim ethos in their upbringing was fused with the "modernity" of a power-oriented nationalism.

WHEELOCK, KEITH. **Nasser's New Egypt: A Critical Analysis.** New York: Praeger, 1960, 326 p.

This was the first major study of the Nasser military régime in Egypt, supplementing and in some ways supplanting Tom Little's **Egypt** (New York: Praeger, 1959, 334 p.). Without lengthy preliminaries Wheelock considers realistically the way the Free Officer junta consolidated its power. The chapters on agricultural, social and economic problems and policies are the most complete for that time (1958). The author's discussion of "Nasserism," a term used to describe Egypt's policy after 1954, is balanced and critical. He clearly assessed its purely Egyptian motives in terms of Egyptian state interests, as distinguished from any commitment on the part of the new military régime in Egypt to an Arab ideology.

Given the author's generally balanced views, one or two assertions in his final chapter are surprising. Posing the question whether rapid development required an authoritarian government or a "single leader with dictatorial powers," he concluded that "monarchy" (in its classical theoretical sense) might be the only suitable form of government in Egypt. After all, it was the acceptable common form of government in Europe for nearly 2,000 years. It was also perhaps a pure guess on the author's part when he opined that Nasser's failures in Syria and Iraq in 1958–1959 suggested he would "hesitate in the future before committing himself heavily to Communist support." That aspect of Egypt's status as a client state of a major power turned out to be not simply a function, or the result, of inter-Arab conflict but of wider regional conflict.

ABDEL-MALEK, ANOUAR. **Egypt: Military Society: The Army Régime, the Left, and Social Change under Nasser.** New York: Random House, 1968, 458 p.

This translation of the author's "Égypte, Société Militaire" (Paris: Éditions du Seuil, 1962, 379 p.) is as remarkable for its erudition, imaginative analysis and passionate conviction as it is sweeping in its obscurantist and polemical Marxian interpretations of modern Egyptian political history. A teacher and journalist in Egypt before he went into exile in Paris in 1959, the author was involved in the Egyptian Marxist movement in the immediate postwar years. His marshalling of detailed information, especially in the notes, is impressive and will remain a service to all students of modern Egypt. Moreover, his political assessment of the Nasser régime does not differ in substance from that of Western writers whom the author accuses of being motivated by feelings of enmity toward Nasser himself.

It is his analysis which raises serious questions about the application of Marxian and other sociological theories to the study of Egyptian politics. Understandably, the author has a burning desire to see in the sporadic, spasmodic upheavals of recent Egyptian history a progressive politicization of his country's masses. But he fails to convince the reader that this in fact has occurred; he only promises that it will occur. Thus he concedes that revolutionary political activity in Egypt had been brought to a standstill by the Free Officer autocracy. To argue in Marxian fashion that the emergence of certain social and economic structures produces new conditions of political behavior may satisfy one's theoretical preference to explain politics in economic terms and vice versa. It does not, however, tell us whether these new structures change the ways in which state power is exercised and policies determined. Unfortunately, the author cannot describe or explain the objectives of the revolution that he argues will or must occur in the country.

MITCHELL, RICHARD P. **The Society of the Muslim Brothers.** New York: Oxford University Press, 1969, 349 p.

The story of the Muslim Brotherhood, long clouded by partisanship and ignorance, is told with clarity and balance by Richard Mitchell. He gathered his material—press stories, ephemeral pamphlets and other sources—during a two-year stay in Cairo in the early 1950s, the time of the running struggle between the Brotherhood and the military régime. His book covers the early history of the Society; the crisis with the old régime, which finally dissolved it and arranged the murder of its leader, Hasan al-Banna; the later revival of the Society under Hasan Hudaybi; its brief honeymoon with the military régime after the revolution of 1952; and finally its anti-régime activity and the attempt on the life of Abdel Nasser; and the Society's final decapitation at the hands of Nasser and his colleagues, whose program and whose concern for their own security could not tolerate any independent movement or party.

Mitchell brought to light much fascinating detail about the Society itself. He also performed a service in his effort to describe and explain the movement's ideology, especially the way in which a puritan view of Islam was combined with practical political action including violence. The trend of the times was and probably will continue to be secular, yet there is no doubt that the Muslim Brothers made an impact on Egyptian politics with their "back-to-religion" ideals and evoked a deep response in Egyptian society.

Christina Phelps Harris has written on the same subject, but despite the subtitle of her **Nationalism and Revolution in Egypt: The Role of the Muslim Brotherhood** (The Hague: Mouton, 1964, 276 p.), much more attention is given to the Islamic reform movement which preceded the foundation of the Society, and little effort is made to answer some of the major questions concerning the Society's place in Egyptian politics.

Issawi, Charles. **Egypt in Revolution: An Economic Analysis.** New York: Oxford University Press (for the Royal Institute of International Affairs), 1963, 343 p.

Professor Issawi has spent 25 years studying the economic problems of Egypt. His first study, **Egypt: An Economic and Social Analysis** (New York: Oxford University Press, for the Royal Institute of International Affairs, 1947, 219 p.), was published in 1947, a second revised edition of which **(Egypt at Mid-Century,** New York: Oxford University Press, for the Royal Institute of International Affairs, 2d rev. ed., 1954, 289 p.) appeared in 1954. His **Egypt in Revolution,** appearing nearly ten years later, is still the best study in English of Egypt's economic problems. A rich source of economic information, it is organized imaginatively and also serves as an excellent social history of modern Egypt.

On the whole, Professor Issawi's own definition and listing of the problems of development, which encompass economic, social, cultural and political dimensions, are still valid: *e.g.* the rate of population growth in relation to the rate of economic growth; the problems of urbanization; high expenditure on arms; relations with the great powers; poverty and overpopulation.

Issawi's suggestion that "the second Egyptian revolution, of 1960–1" introduced an ideological polarity in the Arab Middle East is debatable. Even now it is not clear whether this cleavage goes beyond that which divided Arab states in their conflicts before 1961. Equally debatable is his consideration of Western dilemmas regarding the establishment of a new basis for relations with the Arab states generally and Egypt particularly. Singling out the prime Western interests in the region as keeping it from being absorbed in the Soviet bloc and safeguarding the flow of oil, he suggested that that could best be done under the circumstances by generous aid. Such may have been the case until the mid-1960s—but it still did not produce the desired results. The belief that economic measures can have definite or preconceived political results, especially in the relations between states, represents a weakness in an otherwise masterful volume.

O'Brien, Patrick. **The Revolution in Egypt's Economic System: From Private Enterprise to Socialism, 1952–1965.** New York: Oxford University Press (for the Royal Institute of International Affairs), 1966, 354 p.

In this monograph Patrick O'Brien describes and evaluates the institutional changes which were introduced by the Nasser régime for the organization of the economy. The author, a brilliant economic historian, examines the new economic institutions created by the state in order to provide a basis for explaining changes in economic policy as well as the transformation of the economic system itself. He finds that the basic economic problems of Egypt imposed a policy of encouraging free enterprise on its military rulers in the first years of their rule. The failure of the private sector to respond to such state encouragement largely forced the government into the next phase of more rigorous planning and a centrally controlled economy after 1957. Although he calls the third phase in the 1960s "the Socialist Economic System," the author inquires intelligently into its ideological premises and finds them meagre. He also finds that the nationalization of property and redistribution of income made too slight an impact on the mass of Egyptian peasants for the system to warrant the title "socialist." Instead, more pragmatically, the demise of private enterprise was the culmination of a process whereby government control extended over the whole economy. This the author finds more in keeping with Egypt's highly centralized and autocratic political system. The connection between the state and economy in Egypt dates back to Muhammad Ali the Great, and laissez-faire policies have been the exception rather than the rule in recent Egyptian economic history. Thus, the author concludes, the system is not quite socialist and its transformation into a command economy "can be adequately explained without recourse to ideology."

KERR, MALCOLM. **The Arab Cold War, 1958–1964: A Study of Ideology in Politics.** New York: Oxford University Press (for the Royal Institute of International Affairs), 1965, 139 p.

This "interpretative essay," as the author calls it, is the best study of an important segment of Egypt's foreign policy: its relations with the other Arab states. Unfortunately limited both in time and scope, it none the less captures the essence of Egyptian policy at a critical period. The old issue of Arab unity, whether slogan or reality, and by whom it might be used, provides the thread by which to draw together many of the political moves and tortuous negotiations of those years. The Cairo negotiations of early 1963 (whose text was later published by decision of the Egyptian government) provide a fascinating story.

Kerr's study can be supplemented by a chapter which he contributed to **Egypt since the Revolution,** a collaborative volume edited by P. J. Vatikiotis (New York: Praeger, 1968, 195 p.), where he discusses the relative weight of ideology and Egyptian national interest in Nasser's foreign policy. Charles D. Cremeans' **The Arabs and the World: Nasser's Arab Nationalist Policy** (New York: Praeger, for the Council on Foreign Relations, 1963, 338 p.) deals at greater length with Egyptian foreign policy during the first decade of the Nasser régime. His book tends to exaggerate "Arab nationalist foreign policy" and reflects a spirit of optimism for better U.S.–Arab relations, characteristic of the Kennedy years, which was not borne out by later developments. The author's main purpose was to draw up policy choices for the United States, and this he has done with commendable clarity.

SCHONFIELD, HUGH J. **The Suez Canal in Peace and War, 1869–1969.** Coral Gables: University of Miami Press, rev. ed., 1969, 214 p.

More popular than scholarly, Hugh Schonfield's book is the only one which covers the history of the Suez Canal from its beginning in the days of De Lesseps and the Khedive Ismail to its forcible closing in the Arab-Israeli war of 1967. Unfortunately there is no treatment on the period of the past half-century comparable to Sir Arnold Wilson's indispensable **The Suez Canal** (New York: Oxford University Press, 1933, 224 p.) on the earlier years. Schonfield's book gives the bare bones of the story of the Canal's importance in World War I, the Italian-Ethiopian war, World War II, the Anglo-Egyptian disputes in the early 1950s and the crisis of 1956. In the revised edition of the book he added a brief discussion of the Canal's "golden decade," when the Egyptians proved beyond doubt that they could run it, and its status since the Six Day War.

The Canal still awaits a study going deeply into the legal and commercial aspects of its role in world affairs, which get inadequate treatment here. Much more could be said, moreover, at this time, in answer to the author's final question: "Does the world need the Canal?" His own conclusion is in the affirmative: that although it has seen its greatest days it "still has tremendous relevance to us in this troubled age" as part of a permanent pattern of communication and a potential bridge between men and nations.

SUDAN

HOLT, PETER MALCOLM. **A Modern History of the Sudan.** New York: Grove Press, 1961, 241 p.

Because of the long British connection with the Sudan it is no surprise that Britons who served there provide most of the studies of its history and politics, and if the point of view tends to be British and Western, most of the books are none the less informative. The best modern history is the comprehensive and balanced account of P. M. Holt, for many years the archivist of the Sudan government, who goes out of his way not to take a British view. Most authoritative on the period of the Mahdist state, he carries his narrative on into the era following Kitchener's reconquest, an era marked by great confidence on the part of the British in the early years and then by the hesitancies of the inter-war period.

Writing with sympathy toward Sudanese nationalism, Holt traces its rise, its challenge both to Britain and to Egypt, and the events leading to the granting of self-government. His treatment of the experiments with parliamentary government and of the military coup of 1958 is brief, but here he is the historian writing very close to contemporary events and obviously aware of the dangers of inadequate perspective.

The coverage of the period of the Anglo-Egyptian Sudan up to the early 1930s may be supplemented by Sir Harold MacMichael's **The Anglo-Egyptian Sudan** (London: Faber, 1934, 288 p.). Sir Harold devoted a large part of his career to service in the Sudan, finally serving as Governor General. His account is descriptive and official rather than personal in tone and content. For the more recent period the best and most comprehensive book is **Sudan Republic** by K. D. D. Henderson (New York: Praeger, 1965, 256 p.).

ABBAS, MEKKI. **The Sudan Question.** New York: Praeger, 1952, 201 p.

Although the Sudan during the first half of the twentieth century was in theory a joint Anglo-Egyptian responsibility, in fact it was ruled by the British alone. The Egyptians continued to covet it but were frustrated first by the efforts of British officials, whose long-range goal was an independent Sudan, and later by Sudanese nationalism.

Mekki Abbas is one of the most able and respected Sudanese who have explored the central role of the Sudan in the relationships between Britain and Egypt. In a well-documented and well-written analysis, critical of both the British and the Egyptians, he brings a Sudanese point of view to this complex question. He regards the country as having served as a negotiable item between the two powers in their struggle for hegemony in the Middle East and control of the Suez Canal. At the same time he shows how the Sudanese themselves were seriously torn between admiration for Egypt in the north and their own sense of identity as an independent territory on the middle Nile. His account ends in the early 1950s, and some of his predictions of a more prosperous future have not been borne out by present events. Nevertheless, as an attempt to outline the international relations between Britain and Egypt in the Sudan, this is a milestone of Sudanese scholarship and a respected contribution to the literature.

A different view is that of L. A. Fabunmi, who argues the case for the unity of the Nile valley in **The Sudan in Anglo-Egyptian Relations** (New York: Longmans, 1960, 466 p.). It is by no means a polemic but a detailed study full of useful information.

BESHIR, MOHAMED OMER. **The Southern Sudan: Background to Conflict.** New York: Praeger, 1968, 192 p.

Relations between north and south in the Sudan are a domestic matter, but they have had international repercussions and significance because Sudan's civil conflict provides a limited and violent version of the wider problem of the interaction of race and culture between Arab and Negro Africa. Moreover, some of the leaders of southern Sudan have tried, though without success, to make their cause an international one by formally bringing the United Nations into their dispute with the Sudan government.

Unfortunately, though there are scholarly historical studies on earlier periods, there is no outstanding book on the north-south relationship in this century and especially the critical years since Sudan gained independence. Beshir's book, as he himself says, has no claim to originality. It was intended to provide background for those keen to learn about a problem which, largely because of failures in education, has been shrouded in ignorance on both sides, even in the Sudan itself. He follows the story chronologically from the differing origins and history of the two groups of peoples through the record of the British administration during the Condominium, the first years of Sudanese independence, military rule under the Abboud régime, the Juba conference of 1965 and more recent events. The author is a frank advocate of national unity of the Sudan and an opponent of southern separatism. A second study, by Beshir Mohammed Said, **The Sudan: Crossroads of Africa** (Chester Springs: Dufour, 1966, 238 p.), covers much the same ground. The other side is presented in a frankly political pamphlet written by a southern leader in exile, **The Sudan: A Southern Viewpoint,** by Oliver Albino (New York: Oxford University Press, for the Institute of Race Relations, London, 1970, 132 p.). These three works represent an introduction, albeit an inadequate one, to a subject deserving of fuller inquiry.

IV. ASIA

SOUTH ASIA

GENERAL TREATMENTS

BROWN, WILLIAM NORMAN. **The United States and India and Pakistan.** Cambridge: Harvard University Press, rev. and enl. ed., 1963, 444 p.

Students of South Asia continue to refer to this standard introduction to India and Pakistan because of the richness of the humanistic learning that has been poured into it. The author, for many years professor of Sanskrit at the University of Pennsylvania, shares his interests between classical and modern studies; it thus is understandable that his interpretation of India and Pakistan links the persistence of ancient tradition to the changing circumstances of modern times.

The first eight chapters, concluding the background to independence in 1947, have the most lasting value. The chapters on contemporary events, even in the revised edition of 1963, are dated and have been superseded by a specialized monographic literature of greater detail and accuracy. References to Islam and to Pakistan, unfortunately, do not reflect the same sympathy and insight that accompany the author's treatments of Hinduism and India.

Other introductions to South Asia have appeared since Norman Brown's pioneering work. However, the wisdom and balance in **The United States and India and Pakistan** lead many teachers to advise students new to the field to "go back to Brown" for an initial understanding of how old civilizations are creating new societies on the subcontinent.

SPATE, O. H. K. and LEARMONTH, A. T. A. **India and Pakistan: A General and Regional Geography.** London: Methuen, 3rd rev. ed., 1967, 877 p.

In what will probably long remain the standard geographic text on South Asia, Spate and Learmonth (Spate alone in the first two editions) have blended erudition, perspicacity and painstaking scholarship with graceful prose to fashion a monumental synthesis of the diverse but interrelated factors which impart distinctive regional character to the area. The work is evenly balanced between topical and regional coverage. The former considers South Asia as a whole in respect to "Land" (structure and relief, climate, vegetation and soils), "People" (demography, social groups, historical outlines and settlement) and "Economy" (agriculture, industrial resources, industrial evolution and planning). The latter is organized within a detailed, hierarchically ordered spatial framework. Though regions are delimited mainly in terms of physical features, their descriptions relate largely to settlements, land use and historical development. Nepal, Sikkim and Bhutan are treated briefly in the sections on the Himalayas, while Ceylon is discussed in detail in a subjoined chapter by B. H. Farmer.

Throughout the text the physical and biogeographic exposition is too technical for non-geographers—the chapters on South Asia by John Brush in Norton Ginsburg's **The Pattern of Asia** (Englewood Cliffs: Prentice-Hall, 1958, 929 p.) provide more digestible fare—otherwise lay readers will find the going smooth enough. Certain chapters (*e.g.* "Historical Outlines") flash with brilliant insights, and some of the regional vignettes are literary gems. But the section on the economy suffers a bit from disjointedness stemming from insufficient revision since the first edition in 1951. If the book has any serious shortcoming, it is the relative inattention paid to community and caste in the regional descriptions.

DAVIS, KINGSLEY. **The Population of India and Pakistan.** Princeton: Princeton University Press, 1951, 263 p.

Kingsley Davis' book comprises a panoramic overview of the demography of India and Pakistan. Although issued in 1951, and therefore largely dependent upon the 1931 and 1941 censuses for pre-partition India, it still stands as the only overall survey—aside from the censuses themselves—of the full range of demographic interests as they relate to South Asia. Even on many of the subtopics covered— distribution and density; fertility, mortality and natural increase; immigration, emigration and internal migration; urbanization and numerical aspects of education, caste and religion—his work has rarely been surpassed by the monographic literature that followed. Since the book was written before Davis spent much time in India, his section on social structure and social change is accordingly the weakest; moreover, most of the research on these subjects was yet to come when this book was written. It is also interesting to read the debate pro and con the adoption of a government policy to limit population growth. How quickly the problematical becomes the assumed. Also missing is the apocalyptic sense of disaster in the face of swelling numbers, a mood typical of most of the later literature. The many tables, charts and graphics are abundant, well produced and clear. It would be an extremely useful exercise merely to take this book and update it.

COALE, ANSLEY J. and HOOVER, EDGAR M. **Population Growth and Economic Development in Low-Income Countries: A Case Study of India's Prospects.** Princeton: Princeton University Press, 1958, 389 p.

Coale and Hoover's book comes seven years later than Davis', but from the same Princeton Office of Population Research. The contrast with Davis' volume reflects a more general shift of American research on India from descriptive survey to more focused, more problem-oriented monograph. Davis' general survey style has now given way to an essay pointed to those aspects of population increase and its control which are related to economic development. The authors make three projections of the size of the total population at five-year intervals in the future based upon three different assumptions of accelerating, stable and decelerating rates of growth fitted to the 1891–1951 experience curve. The aggregate growth estimates are refined by taking into account probable component changes such as the sex ratio, age groups distribution, public health campaign and infant mortality. The various population projections are then considered both in terms of their dependence on and, more fully, their influence on economic development. Prospects for development and the impact of population growth on them are considered in terms of: crop acreage and output; livestock supply; the availability and use of fertilizer; agricultural manpower and mechanization; natural and personal income, savings and investment; the general labor force; urban growth; social service and educational outlays; and income-expenditure ratios.

A final chapter attempts to show a wider relevance of the analysis beyond India. In general, the book argues that a lower fertility rate would lead not only to a higher per capita income but to a more rapid growth in aggregate output. The book was written before the so-called "green revolution" of improved seeds made a sudden jump in agricultural productivity possible.

FISHER, MARGARET W.; ROSE, LEO E. and HUTTENBACK, ROBERT A. **Himalayan Battleground: Sino-Indian Rivalry in Ladakh.** New York: Praeger, 1963, 205 p.

The authors evaluate Chinese and Indian claims to Aksai Chin ("white stone desert"), the disputed and sparsely populated area where the borders of Tibet, Sinkiang and Kashmiri Ladakh converge. The first nine chapters are a scholarly review of fifteen hundred years of Ladakh's history, showing that while Ladakh, including Aksai Chin, was sometimes of strategic concern to neighboring political powers, it was often autonomous. Since the fourteenth century, Ladakh's main cultural ties have been to Tibet through the Lamaist monastic and commercial system. But the Moghul and British empires claimed suzerainty over Ladakh, and these claims were recognized in treaties and diplomatic negotiations between Tibet, Kashmir and the British Government of India.

In the last three chapters, the authors assess the strategic implications and the merits of the conflicting border claims advanced during the 1960 discussions between Chinese and Indian officials which were held after India discovered that the Chinese had opened a road across Aksai Chin, linking western Tibet with Sinkiang, and before the Chinese drove Indian troops from the contested areas. The authors argue that while the Indians presented thorough, well-documented claims to Aksai Chin, the Chinese were careless, inconsistent and contemptuous of these claims, some of which relied on British "imperialist" maps, surveys and treaties. They conclude that "the Chinese had no genuine interest in negotiating" and that the Chinese used "Hitlerian" methods to obtain access to Tibet from the west when the eastern routes were endangered by Tibetan rebellion.

INDIA

General; Historical

THOMPSON, EDWARD JOHN and GARRATT, GEOFFREY THEODORE. **Rise and Fulfilment of British Rule in India.** New York: Macmillan, 1934, 690 p.

Edward Thompson, a former missionary, and G. T. Garratt, a retired member of the Indian civil service, combined their Indian experience and historical talents to produce the first frankly critical, truly "modern" cultural history of the British Raj to be written by Englishmen. Though first published in 1934, **Rise and Fulfilment of British Rule in India** was reprinted in Allahabad as recently as 1966, attesting to its singular ability to transcend temporal as well as geographic limits. Some of the chapter titles reflect the range of subject matter and modernity of focus of this admirable work, *e.g.* "Racial Estrangement and Changing Hindu Outlook," "Decline of Paternalism," "Bureaucracy on the Defensive" and "Repression and Conciliation." The authors rely upon primary sources in reconstructing John Company's transition from commerce to conquest and paramountcy over India. For current students of India too much attention is devoted to details of mid-nineteenth-century Anglo-Indian military conflict and too little to the more important early twentieth-century political controversy; but Thompson and Garratt are sensitive to and sympathetic toward Indian national aspirations, and their book remains a valuable general survey of British Indian history.

STOKES, ERIC. **The English Utilitarians and India.** New York: Oxford University Press, 1959, 350 p.

This is a study in applied philosophy. As the Indian subcontinent was consolidated under British rule in the early nineteenth century, the English utilitarians were presented with an extraordinary opportunity to apply their doctrines to the construction of a system of government, and the lessons they and others learned from their efforts in India were to influence the history of British political thought. Eric Stokes considers it remarkable "how many of the movements of English life tested their strength and fought their early battles upon the Indian question," and he regrets the tendency of historians of Britain to disregard this segment of British experience. A review of the past decade's literature in Victorian studies suggests that Stokes' work, at least, has not suffered this neglect.

As a contribution to modern South Asian history, this brilliant book can fairly be considered the most distinguished work published in either the 1950s or 1960s. Its core is a careful exposition of the utilitarian influence on reforms in the executive and judicial branches of government, and in the land revenue systems in the 1820s and 1830s. It is the concluding section on the utilitarian legacy, however, which has excited most interest, with its striking demonstration that John Hobbes was a legitimate ancestor of utilitarianism. "It was India," Stokes asserts, "which most clearly exposed the paradox in utilitarianism between the principle of liberty and the principle of authority," and it was "in the realm of authority and not liberty that the utilitarian work was done."

Eric Stokes does not explore the influence of utilitarianism on Indian thought. To complain of this is to criticize him unfairly for not writing someone else's book, but it is not impertinent to observe that the mainstream of South Asian historical writing in the 1960s shifted away from British activities in India to the Indian experience itself. As a result Stokes' work has not been seminal.

COUPLAND, SIR REGINALD. **The Indian Problem.** New York: Oxford University Press, 1944, 711 p.

Written to provide background material for the transfer of political power in India, Coupland's massive study has a quasi-official tone, but this adds to its value for understanding both how the British understood the situation in India in the 1940s and what the political realities actually were. The book is divided into three parts (originally published as separate volumes), each serving a different purpose within the general scheme. The first is a lucid survey of constitutional developments from the Charter Act of 1833 to the India Act of 1935. The main theme is the orderly growth of autonomous institutions, with the implication that if Muslim-Hindu tensions had not been generated by the nationalists, a smooth transition could have been made to dominion status. The author shows little awareness that by 1935 this status was no longer of much interest either to the Congress or the League.

Part II remains one of the best accounts of the working of the new constitution, based, presumably, partly on information to which the author had access as an unofficial adviser to the Cripps mission. The third part is a detailed analysis of that and other schemes put forward to enable the transfer of power to take place with a minimum of dislocation to the old system. Coupland's account has a lofty tone of moral superiority as he bids the Indians show themselves worthy of responsibility; but rereading it now one is aware, as he was not, that by 1943 the British were no longer able to direct the course of development in Indian politics. Useful appendices include statistics and selections from relevant documents.

SEAL, ANIL. **The Emergence of Indian Nationalism: Competition and Collaboration in the Later Nineteenth Century.** Cambridge: Cambridge University Press, 1968, 416 p.

This volume is in a number of respects comprehensive, containing ample materials, voluminous data, many tables, statistics, maps and appendices. Not all of the accumulation of data and information is, however, particularly relevant to the proclaimed subject of the book. The author stipulates that the study is based upon certain hypotheses concerning the operational role of collaboration (with the alien rulers) and competition (among Indian élites and counter-élites) in the growth of Indian nationalism. But these interesting hypotheses get lost in a welter of ofttimes poorly digested facts. By and large the book follows the by now well-worn path in recounting the development of political life and activity in Calcutta, Madras and Bombay.

The author has put together some valuable and cogent material on the situation of the Muslims in India and the development of communal politics out of their situation. Similarly, he has dealt effectively with the tangled story of Hume and Lord Dufferin and the origins of the Congress. The volume is handy in the sense that it brings together, between two covers, so much information, so many tables and such potentially useful statistical evidence. If only this plethora of data had been put to more effective use by rigorous selection.

TALBOT, PHILLIPS and POPLAI, SUNDAR LAL. **India and America: A Study of Their Relations**. New York: Harper (for the Council on Foreign Relations), 1958, 200 p.

In some respects this brief volume is unique. It is a real collaborative enterprise, the joint product of an Indian and an American scholar, based on some two years of study during 1954–1956 by two groups, one organized by the Indian Council of World Affairs in New Delhi, the other by the Council on Foreign Relations in New York.

In spite of an obvious desire to accentuate the positive, most of the volume is devoted to differences between India and the United States. Although published at the height of the Nehru era, its general theme has a timely ring. India and the United States differ on many general and specific issues, but they "have much in common" and they should be able to work "in closer cooperation in the future than they have in the past." Nearly a decade and a half later the differences still exist, and the hopes for closer coöperation are still largely unrealized, in spite of generally satisfactory official relations and growing, though still limited, contacts between Indians and Americans.

BUCHANAN, DANIEL HOUSTON. **The Development of Capitalistic Enterprise in India**. London: Cass, 1966, 497 p.

Buchanan's study of India's industrial development, first published in 1934, is one of the best known and least influential works in the field of Indian economic history. Its "failure" is perhaps partly ascribable to the fact that it was long out of print. A certain naïveté of approach—to wit, the lengthy discussion on the relative merits of industrial and pre-industrial economies—and a heavy emphasis on description to the almost total neglect of analysis are the more serious defects which have detracted from its value. Characteristically, Buchanan nowhere referred to the two works bearing on his subject which provided at least some analysis of the dynamics of India's industrialization—Dhananjaya Gadgil's **The Industrial Evolution of India in Recent Times** (London: Oxford University Press, 4th ed., 1959, 317 p.) and Parimal Ray's **India's Foreign Trade since 1870** (London: Routledge, 1934, 300 p.). For an explanation of India's industrial weakness, he fell back primarily on impressionistic sociology.

Yet Buchanan first perceived some of the commonplaces of academic thinking on the subject today. He was the first to notice that despite the impressive record of industrial development in absolute terms, the Indian economy was structurally stagnant. The evidence on which he based his conclusion that the proportion of the working force in agriculture was on the increase has, however, been questioned. His work first emphasized the preponderance of handicrafts in modern Indian industry. The implications of this fact for the conventional wisdom on the subject are only beginning to be appreciated. Above all, one is grateful to Buchanan for his detailed description of how it all worked in real life. As the trend of analytical research is in a very different direction, it is unlikely that this lifelike reconstruction of early Indian capitalism at work will ever be replaced.

SMITH, WILFRED CANTWELL. **Modern Islam in India**. London: Gollancz, rev. ed., 1947, 344 p.

Smith's work was the pioneer social science analysis of Islam and Muslims in modern South Asia. Although he occasionally slips into historical narrative, the book was organized loosely into the various types of intellectual movements (part I), political movements (part II) and theological groups (part III). However, his mode of analysis was naïve Marxism. It abounds with pseudo-scientific but normatively intended appellations such as "reactionary" and "progressive." Part I especially is largely textual commentary, devoid of the kind of empirical data now considered necessary to substantiate the existence in a given context of class categories such as "feudal," "bourgeois" and "proletarian." An example of his terminological confusion is his characterization of one sect as "conservative" but "not advanced enough to be termed reactionary."

Part II is the more concrete and useful of the two main sections. Smith's delineation of the Muslim movements and parties which arose in this century—the Muslim League, Khilafat, Nationalists, Jamiat-ul-Ulema, Ahrars, Khudai Khidmatgars, Khaksars, Ahmadiyas—has provided subsequent scholars with the building blocks for understanding the structure of much of Muslim politics in both India and Pakistan in the succeeding generation. The particular juncture at which he wrote, just before partition, left his limited predictions vulnerable to falsification by events, but his psychological insights into the functions of religion and religious reform for different segments of the population during the process of modernization are of permanent value, once the pervasive ideological bias is discounted.

BROOMFIELD, JOHN H. **Elite Conflict in a Plural Society: Twentieth-Century Bengal.** Berkeley: University of California Press, 1968, 349 p.

Presented as a historical analysis of the period between the first and second partitions of Bengal (1905–1947), this volume describes the complex of tensions that animated the various political actors who laid the basis for the post-independence political situation in the two Bengals: West Bengal and East Pakistan. The text is preceded by a most perceptive description of the political goals of Bengali élite groups (the *bhadralok*) in this century, based on an analysis of the various socioeconomic factors underlying the factional groupings within *bhadralok* society. This opening section sets the stage for the main narrative, which traces the entry of the *bhadralok* into agitational and electoral politics, the factional conflicts that arose among the Bengali political élite as a result of differences in interests and conceptions of strategic gain, and finally, the split between Hindu and Muslim élites that resulted in partition.

This volume fills a great gap in our knowledge of the history of India in this century, since it is the first authoritative volume to deal with Bengal in this period. It is important to scholars of India not only because it deals with one of the two areas most severely affected by the partition of the subcontinent but also because it explains so well the decline of Bengal relative to other parts of India in this century. Because of its intrinsic importance, its author's appealing style, flair for capturing the subtleties of human interaction and command of a wealth of archival and interview data based on many years of research, this book shared the Watamall Prize of the American Historical Association for the year 1968.

MAYO, KATHERINE. **Mother India.** New York: Harcourt, 1927, 454 p.

Katherine Mayo's **Mother India** appeared in 1927 and quickly became the most widely circulated and most notorious book about India in this century. Its author, a spinster lady writer of strong reforming energies, spent six months in India, and in what obviously struck her there as fetid sexuality on a vast scale, she found the most congenial and successful subject of her writing career. Her book is an Anglophilic Hinduphobic recital of examples of child marriage, caste practices, the plight of the untouchables, backward conditions of health and sanitation. Written on a single plane of total revulsion and narrowly focused bias, it carefully avoided anything resembling qualifications or other sides of any parts of the story. The most salient point made by more thoughtful Western and Indian critics was that while the book did not falsify many of its particulars, it was monumentally false as a whole. Gandhi called it "a drainpipe study," although he advised Indian readers to take some of its facts seriously into account.

The book became a sensation in the United States, Great Britain and in India. It was the center of a storm that raged on for half a dozen years in the newspapers, periodical press and on the lecture platforms in all three countries. It provoked some ten books in reply by Indian authors who tried, with varying success, to turn Mayo's technique on the United States, focusing exclusively on some of the more grisly features of American life and making the most sweeping possible generalizations from the selected facts. In self-defense, Miss Mayo went through the nine volumes of testimony taken by a commission of inquiry on child marriage which sat in India following the furore raised by her book. In 1931 she published another book, called **Volume Two** (New York: Harcourt, 1931, 313 p.), devoted mainly to excerpts of testimony by Indians saying in their way many of the things she had been attacked for saying in her way. She never did understand the difference. **Mother India** was gradually forgotten everywhere but in India, where its name became and remains a shorthand epithet for whatever Indians regard as Western slander and dishonesty about Indian life and culture.

Political Questions

MORRIS-JONES, W. H. **The Government and Politics of India.** New York: Hillary House, 1964, 236 p.

Morris-Jones deals with what has recently been called political culture in terms of languages of politics or political idioms. He finds three in India: the modern, the traditional and the saintly. "The contrast between modern and traditional languages," he writes, "is a contrast between the political institutions of a nation state and the structure of an ancient society. . . . the key to Indian politics today [1964] is the meeting of these two strangers." The third language, the language of saintly politics, is "at the margin" of Indian politics. Spoken by a few but understood by many, it has something of the meaning that "margin" suggests in economics, "a kind of reference mark."

By putting his discussion of the languages of politics in the context of society, history and ideas—as well as politics—he is able to get at dimensions of reality and to provide explanations that analyses of political culture have slighted or ignored. One of the most impressive chapters is the second, dealing with society and politics. Other chapters deal with such subjects as "legacies," a masterful synthesis of historical forces that affect contemporary political life; events from 1947 through 1963; governance, a behavioral analysis of such political institutions as the senior civil service, the planning commission, the states in the context of "bargaining federalism," and the contributions of local government to rural modernization and political participation; and political forces in India.

This is a book for all seasons among those with an interest in India and in comparative politics. Those with little or no knowledge of one or both subjects can be sure that the many syntheses, generalizations and judgments are both authoritative and wise. Those who are knowledgeable in one or both will be challenged and stimulated by the sophistication of Morris-Jones' conceptual and interpretative simplicity.

HARRISON, SELIG S. **India: The Most Dangerous Decades.** Princeton: Princeton University Press, 1960, 350 p.

Selig Harrison's book was the first major study of Indian politics in the post-independence period to give due attention to the importance of regional, language and caste loyalties for the future unity and political stability of India. Based on a truly massive collection of published and unpublished documents, books and pamphlets concerning regional movements in all parts of the country, and on personal interviews with important regional political leaders, the book is full of insights, some prophetic, on the character of Indian federalism, on the difficulties of sustaining all-India political activity and on the inevitable regionalization of Indian politics. Harrison's major argument, that political organizations in India must identify with regional and local sentiments to survive and to capture power and that all-India political activity is, therefore, significantly limited, remains valid.

The book suffers from having been written in the anti-communist vein fashionable during the 1950s and 1960s and from an apocalyptic tone which conjured up images of impending Balkanization or "totalitarianism" or communization of particular regions of the country. Moreover, the case for the dangerous congruence of regional, linguistic and caste boundaries and for the emergence of cohesive regional political forces based on them was overstated and the importance of intra-regional divisions and fragmentation not sufficiently stressed. Finally, Harrison's use of his remarkable collection of documents and pamphlets was sometimes undiscriminating, treating with equal respect the fantasies of a lone pamphleteer of an obscure regional movement and the flood of literature from the major regional movements of the country.

WEINER, MYRON. **The Politics of Scarcity: Public Pressure and Political Response in India.** Chicago: University of Chicago Press, 1962, 251 p.

This book has had an important influence on political theorists, policy-makers and students of Indian politics. It was the first attempt to analyze the way in which interest groups operate in a non-Western electoral system, and it develops in considerable detail the relationships between India's democratic institutions and the bargaining cultures that have evolved in India during the past few centuries. With this volume Professor Weiner initiated systematic debate concerning the problems confronting Indian governmental and bureaucratic élites in their attempts to promote a democratic cultural infrastructure while at the same time engineering a program of economic development.

Theorists have used this book to help identify critical stages in the process of political development, to learn more about the nature of interest groups (both in developing and developed political systems), to formulate general theory and to sharpen conceptual ideas about the processes of political and economic change. Policy-makers, both in India and abroad, have used the book to pinpoint key areas for investments or inputs into India, and students have made wide use of the book in their attempts to understand the dynamics of India's complex political system. One measure of the objectivity and persuasiveness of the book is the fact that it has been praised by Indian intellectuals and party and governmental leaders holding diverse and often contradictory ideological positions, while being widely read and quoted.

MENON, VAPAL PANGUNNI. **The Story of the Integration of the Indian States.** New York: Macmillan, 1956, 511 p.

There is no more literal example of nation building than the joining of 550 princely states to the Indian Union in 1947–1949. These states varied greatly in size and development, from a few square miles of farmland to the massive Hyderabad, from progressive Mysore to the backward central Indian feudalities. Some had their own armies, substantial revenue and a sense of independence and identity. Today they are almost entirely absorbed into the Indian democracy (Kashmir remains a partial exception) and reveal few traces of their origins.

The "story" of this integrative process is aptly told by V. P. Menon, the distinguished civil servant directly responsible for enticing, cajoling and—when required —forcing these states into the Indian Union. His account is marked by a centrist perspective and is laden with bureaucratic prose but provides a detailed description of his own efforts and those of Sardar Patel, the conservative Congress politician who shared Menon's labors.

Their first step was to cut the legal ties of the princely states to Britain. The princes were then offered union with India if they surrendered three powers: defense (which included internal security), communications and foreign relations. This accession provided the legal basis for further integration and eventual Union military intervention in several states. The states' rulers were at the mercy of the Union authorities, and most of them quietly yielded up their powers in exchange for ceremonial positions and liberal privy purses.

Menon's own account has not been surpassed; perhaps such bureaucratic successes do not attract their fair share of scholarly attention. It shows, however, that major structural and social disparities can be neutralized, if not eliminated, by clarity of purpose and direction. Menon's book stands today as both a guide and a monument to his and Patel's work.

BRASS, PAUL R. **Factional Politics in an Indian State: The Congress Party in Uttar Pradesh.** Berkeley: University of California Press, 1965, 262 p.

Largely through interviews, Brass examines the working of the dominant Congress Party in five districts of India's largest state. He contends that because of the size and diversity of Uttar Pradesh, the hegemony of Congress in the state, the considerable ideological agreement in the party and lack of strong leadership, the key element in political dynamics is the faction: a non-ideological, non-communal, non-caste-based, highly personalized grouping built around local notables and political entrepreneurs who seek group advantage by complex, shifting alliances within the Congress and with factions outside it. Among other important contributions, he indicates how local, district and state-wide factions are related, often in bewildering fashion; how factional competition helps to politicize the citizenry; and more briefly at the end, how the UP picture seems similar to and different from patterns prevailing elsewhere in India and in other countries.

There are certain weaknesses—for example, the term "faction" remains rather a vague, catchall phrase; ideological and caste factors are generally underemphasized; and there are a number of loose ends, as Brass himself tacitly admits when in certain cases factional strife persists to the detriment of Congress electoral success, even in the face of strong local competition. But despite many changes in UP and in India, this book remains a most valuable source of information on party building and politics generally, not only for an understanding of India but also for comparison with political activity in other relatively open political systems.

WEINER, MYRON. **Party Building in a New Nation: The Indian National Congress.** Chicago: University of Chicago Press, 1967, 509 p.

Professor Weiner's third and most detailed study of political participation in contemporary Indian democracy is as crowded with facts and teeming with ideas as the reality it portrays. The study seeks both to enrich and to confirm political development theories through the use of five microcosmic case studies, three from the countryside and two from cities. There is no better portrayal of Congress Party life in the literature nor of the immense complexity and frequently confusing arabesques of idiom that characterize India's continental diversity.

"Congress is primarily concerned with recruiting members and winning support," the author writes. "It does not mobilize; it aggregates. It does not seek to innovate; it seeks to adapt." In adapting, it comes to reflect the social diversity of its host society rather than New Delhi's plan for the new India. Thus, India's parties are given to factionalism, and responsible governments are more and more characterized by working coalitions composed of parties with distinctive factional constituencies.

This process is general in India, but its specific attributes require the depth and detail lacking in almost all broad "political systems" surveys. Weiner's study argues for a patient mapping of Indian political diversity, and for a clear differentiation between the agents of change under the direction of government and the agents of representation which compel public policy to meet the realities of local political behavior.

OVERSTREET, GENE DONALD and WINDMILLER, MARSHALL. **Communism in India.** Berkeley: University of California Press, 1959, 603 p.

More than ten years after publication this book is still almost universally considered to be the standard scholarly reference on the nature of the communist movement in India. As testimony to its objectivity, it has been quoted as an authority on a number of topics by leaders of both the major communist factions in India and is a standard reference work for both Soviet and American scholars. The founder of the communist movement in India, Muzaffar Ahmad, has stated publicly that he has since regretted his unwillingness to talk with Windmiller and Overstreet when they were compiling data for the book, since he now feels that he could have added even more to what he considers to be the only authoritative party history.

The strength of this volume is its objectivity, general accuracy and painstaking attention to the detailed ideological and organizational twists of Indian communism, based on party documents, newspapers, private papers and interviews. Its weaknesses have been identified as an overemphasis on the role of M. N. Roy during the years of party formation (Roy dominates the first quarter of the volume); as insufficient attention to the diverse regional strands of the Indian communist movement; and as a style of writing that makes for accuracy but is often tedious to read. In addition, the book has frequently been criticized for its "historicist" and "institutional" conceptual framework, despite occasional attempts on the part of the authors to articulate their thoughts in terms of "process" and "structural-functional" categories.

RUDOLPH, LLOYD I. and RUDOLPH, SUSANNE HOEBER. **The Modernity of Tradition: Political Development in India.** Chicago: University of Chicago Press, 1967, 306 p.

This is a book of three essays—on caste associations, on Gandhi and on legal institutions in India. The main theme—that it is not desirable to continue to view modernity and tradition as polar concepts, but rather to see them as "continuous" and "dialectically related," to recognize that certain traditional sectors of Indian society are capable of modernizing change and to observe the development of new forms of modernity drawing on both traditional and modern notions and structures—is best developed in the first essay on caste associations, which takes up more than half the book. The essay on Gandhi emphasizes his effort to give precedence to public values over private obligations, his search for a personal and a national identity through the development of courage and self-respect based on nonviolent political action and inspired by indigenous values and his professional approach to political organization. The essay on the development of legal norms and institutions in India stresses the imperfect interaction among three sets of structures and laws—the parochial customary law, the written Brahmanic law and the universalistic legal codes introduced by the British.

All three are creative essays, based on wide reading of contemporary and historical materials. The tendency of the authors to overgeneralize on the basis of scattered bits of data is a defect somewhat overcome by the basic soundness of the main argument, with which most students of Indian society and politics now agree.

Economic and Social Questions

BLYN, GEORGE. **Agricultural Trends in India, 1891–1947: Output, Availability, and Productivity.** Philadelphia: University of Pennsylvania Press, 1966, 370 p.

This is one of the most important empirical contributions to our knowledge of the economic history of South Asia. The title precisely identifies the subject matter. Already a classic, Blyn's work has served to underpin discussions of Indian agricultural performance past and future and has been used as a fundamental building block in all recent attempts to construct a national income series for India. It is a work that is not likely to be supplanted in the foreseeable future.

The author has worked out long-run trends in agricultural output and per-acre productivity by crop and groups of crops, by region as well as for all British India (excluding Baluchistan and Burma) for the period 1891–1947. The time series reproduced in extensive appendices are carefully constructed, and the qualifications to and limitations of the data have been explicitly identified. Blyn's data show that during the half century before independence, agricultural output per capita remained essentially unchanged. When examined in detail, the all-crop output rates suggest grimmer Malthusian tendencies. Prior to World War I (the period 1891¬

1916), the average rate of growth of all-crop output exceeded the average rate of population growth. After World War I (1921–1946) the average rate of growth of all-crop output was less than the population growth rate.

What emerges from Blyn's work is evidence of the complexity of agricultural performance. The overall stagnation did not imply a lack of change in the Indian agricultural sector but represented the sum resultant of growth and retardative forces. Since the study is essentially descriptive, it explores only tentatively a few of the many factors which contributed to the distressingly unsatisfactory overall performance. Possibly, despite the care with which the data were constructed, the results for the later period may be downward biased and imply too grim a tale. But whatever the limitations, Professor Blyn's study tells us more about the performance of Indian agriculture than we were ever able to know in the past. It is the necessary starting point for any serious work on modern Indian agriculture.

HANSON, A. H. **The Process of Planning: A Study of India's Five-Year Plans, 1950–1964.** New York: Oxford University Press (for the Royal Institute of International Affairs), 1966, 560 p.

A. H. Hanson supplies more detail on the organization and sequencing of India's first, second and third five-year planning exercises than most readers will want, and his long book is notably dated. In 1964, when he finished his research, it was still easy to take the then Planning Commission and its influence too seriously, to misjudge the declining power of the Congress Party, particularly for mediating federal-state issues, and to miss the coming reforms in development policy, especially in agricultural production, that brightened the later 1960s. Economists (of whom the author emphasizes he is not one) are likely to detect inadequate appreciation of the difference between the market and the private sector or of the former's potentialities as an organizing mechanism, little attention to either the savings or foreign exchange constraints on growth, and some insecurity in the handling of industrialization issues.

Despite some gaps, such as the interaction between planning and annual Government of India budgeting, Hanson does indeed make good his comparative advantage as a political scientist, especially in chapters on planning's social and political background, on center-state fiscal sharing and on grass roots organization. Yet the weakness of the book's grasp of such underlying substantive issues as agricultural strategy, population control, spatial strategy and the role of foreign aid and exports leaves the focus of its knowledgeable, often insightful, politico-administrative analysis rather blurred.

GADGIL, DHANANJAYA RAMCHANDRA. **Economic Policy and Development (A Collection of Writings).** New York: Institute of Pacific Relations, 1955, 248 p.

Written by one of India's most eminent economists and chairman of the Planning Commission, these papers, selected from articles and speeches prepared between 1940 and 1954, are a valuable source book on the assumptions underlying economic development strategy and policy in the post-independence period. Stressing the fundamental importance of the social and political environment in determining economic policy, the author argues that laissez-faire concepts formulated on the basis of experience in Europe cannot be applied in former colonial territories where the constellation of factors constituting underdevelopment are qualitatively different from those of late-industrializing countries in the West. He advocates an approach based on state intervention, economic planning, controls, fiscal devices and restrictions on private property, both to build up a large central pool of savings for investments in modern business and industry, and to accomplish a redistribution of income in favor of the majority of people and make acceptable the sacrifices associated with development. The later essays are also notable for their critique of the First Five-Year Plan which examines the political constraints confronting the Indian government in effectively implementing the development strategy and helps explain some of the contradictions in policy that subsequently weakened the planning effort.

KIDRON, MICHAEL. **Foreign Investments in India.** New York: Oxford University Press, 1965, 368 p.

This is the best available analytical study of the process of Indian government decision making relating to private foreign investment. It paints a detailed picture of the evolution of governmental attitudes and policies through 1962.

Beginning with a brief history of the position of foreign investments during the colonial period, Kidron then describes the evolution of the policies of the independent Indian government toward old and new investment. He traces with great skill the panoply of intricate political and economic factors underlying the evolving policies and makes intelligible the environment in which bargaining among foreign and local private investors, the Indian government and, at times, the government of the foreign investor takes place. The experimental and pragmatic nature of the government's policy is illustrated by many instances.

The book examines in detail the motivations and amount of foreign investment, its sectoral allocations and the nature and form of its collaboration with Indian capital and the cost of foreign investment to India. The author points up the need for foreign capital and "know-how" but believes that India is paying a high price to satisfy these needs.

While there is no conclusion and no policy recommendations, Kidron's book provides a careful analysis of past policies. Knowledge of these policies and how they were arrived at should be helpful for anyone wanting to speculate about the future.

LEWIS, JOHN PRIOR. **Quiet Crisis in India: Economic Development and American Policy.** Washington: Brookings Institution, 1962, 350 p.

This is a perceptive, well-reasoned and intelligent policy-oriented analysis of some of the principal assumptions and policies in the Indian Third Five-Year Plan (1961–1966). Emphasis is placed on basic development strategy, mobilizing idle manpower, planning and plan implementation, agriculture, industrial location, private enterprise and exports.

In general the author, who later became Director of the AID Mission in India (1964–1969), is favorably impressed with the Plan. He rejects the anxieties of many about India's shortage of internal savings and argues that the foreign exchange gap is the "pivotal scarcity." He supports a strategy of balanced growth with strong inputs both in heavy industry and agriculture. The greatest weaknesses that he sees are the neglect of the problem of underemployment and unemployment, *i.e.* the failure of the Plan to develop a strategy to mobilize idle manpower, and the expansion of agriculture which, in his opinion, is the "most problematical element in the nation's whole near term development prospect." To overcome problems in agriculture he proposes a comprehensive organizational and communication reform which would replace the village-centered approach and include rural public works, a system of markets, non-farm opportunities and development bloc coöperatives. Perhaps the most innovative of his ideas is a proposal that industry be excluded from India's 12 largest cities and their environs and developed instead in cities of less than 300,000 population. He finds the conflict between public and private investment overplayed. Among his more controversial proposals is that of nonreciprocal preferences for Indian exports, an idea which has received substantial support from the less-developed countries at the U.N. Conference on Trade and Development meetings in 1964 and 1968.

EPSTEIN, TRUDE SCARLETT. **Economic Development and Social Change in South India.** Manchester: Manchester University Press, 1962, 353 p.

The title of this book is somewhat misleading; it is a comparative study of two villages in Mandya district of Mysore State. The author says of her field work:

"My own studies do not enable me to regard the development of the two villages as necessarily representative of the region." Within the limitations that the author is careful to specify, this is a valuable analysis of the relationships among technological, economic and social change and an excellent example of the fruits of carefully controlled comparative research. Moreover, although this is primarily a monograph in social anthropology, as the economist W. A. Lewis testifies in his foreword to the book, the author is also thoroughly trained in economics.

Canal irrigation was brought into the Mandya region, which is located in the *maidan* or plains portion of the southern Deccan, between 1936 and 1942. One of the villages under study, which is called Wangala (for "wet"), received water in this development; the other, Dalena ("dry"), did not. Dr. Epstein analyzes organization and change in the economic, political and social life of each village separately before comparing them in a detailed concluding chapter. She says that "before the advent of irrigation . . . the two villages were almost identical in all aspects of their economic and social life."

Irrigation made possible an intensification of agricultural production in Wangala, reinforcing patterns of economic, political and social organization that had existed prior to the coming of the canal. Lacking irrigation, however, Dalena villagers have continuously diversified their economic activities, with many new opportunities having been created by the increased productivity of the irrigated villages in the area. Changes in economic roles and relations in Dalena have resulted in changes in the village social system that the author describes as "radical."

BAILEY, FREDERICK GEORGE. **Caste and the Economic Frontier: A Village in Highland Orissa.** New York: Oxford University Press, 1958, 292 p.

The author is an anthropologist who has presented a well-documented, lucid and admirably organized study of socioeconomic change in highland Orissa, one of India's eastern and least developed states. The only comparable anthropological study of equal distinction is T. Scarlett Epstein's **Economic Development and Social Change in South India,** which deals with a more technically elaborate phase of socioeconomic change in the plains of Mysore.

Bailey's study presents us with a nexus of interacting factors: the alienation of land through debt and its parcelling through population growth; the attendant decline of clientship which has traditionally been one of the strongest forces for caste and village cohesion in India with an attendant increase in agricultural "wage" labor; the rise of low caste and foreign "mercantile" groups which raised their social status through the acquisition of alienated lands, the assumption of higher caste ritual procedures and the exploitation of new legal and political institutions.

Since Bailey published **Caste and the Economic Frontier,** this story has become well known, at least in general outline, but his handling of these themes remains outstanding. It is also the first of what may be considered a trilogy. In 1960 he published **Tribe, Caste and Nation: A Study of Political Activity and Political Change in Highland Orissa** (New York: Humanities Press, 279 p.). Three years later with a broadening interest in the centers of political power, he wrote **Politics and Social Change: Orissa in 1959** (Berkeley: University of California Press, 1963, 241 p.). Collectively these books carry the readable and believable qualities of the best gazetteer writers of the nineteenth century, enriched by developing social science insights and unsullied by technical virtuosities.

CARSTAIRS, G. MORRIS. **The Twice-Born: A Study of a Community of High Caste Hindus.** Bloomington: Indiana University Press, 1958, 343 p.

Despite the subtitle, this is not a community study in the usual sense of the word. Nor is it solely about Hindus, since Muslim case histories are included. Margaret Mead, in a brief foreword, calls it a study in national and caste character, but it seems more nearly a standard mid-twentieth-century culture and personality enterprise.

The field work, carried out in 1951–1952 in a pseudonymously designated village of some 2,500 people near Udaipur in Rajasthan, utilized participant observation, Rorschach test, word association and nonverbal intelligence tests and the collection of 45 case histories from Brahmans, Rajputs, Bania and Muslims. Self-portraits of a Brahman, a Rajput and a Bania constitute more than 40 percent of the second part of the text.

The first part summarizes and interprets findings under such chapter headings as interpersonal and family relations, Hindu body-image, and religion and fantasy, aspects of the data that the author apparently felt were salient. He concludes with two chapters that discuss those factors he found common to his caste groups and those unique to each caste. He then offers an interpretive reconstruction of conscious and unconscious processes in Hindu personality formation.

In the "personality and culture" school, there is no better or even comparable study for India. Dr. Carstairs was uniquely equipped to undertake it. As a child he lived in the Punjab where he learned Hindustani and was exposed to both British and American schools of anthropology. As a medically trained psychiatrist he is primarily a neo-Freudian. Theories and methodologies that have become fashionable in the last two decades may appear to date this work. Nevertheless, it remains insightful and useful.

BÉTEILLE, ANDRÉ. **Caste, Class and Power: Changing Patterns of Stratification in a Tanjore Village.** Berkeley: University of California Press, 1965, 238 p.

This study in social anthropology is based upon field research carried out in 1961 and 1962 in a village of Tanjore (now Thanjavur) district of Madras (now Tamil Nadu) State, an agriculturally rich district with a large population of Brahmans who owned or controlled a great deal of the best land. Sripuram village, with a population of about 1,400, was dominated economically and politically by Brahmans (24 percent of the population) until the advent of modern politics. Members of the "non-Brahman" category of castes (49 percent of the population) wrested political control from the Brahmans, which they were able to do, in large part, because the non-Brahman movement was successful at the state level. The primary empirical significance of this book is as a document of Brahman-non-Brahman political rivalry at the local level. Theoretically, it is most important as a study of the detachment from one another of the variables that enter into social stratification in a modernizing society. Caste rank, economic power and political power are shown to become increasingly independent of one another, particularly after about 1950.

This book is the work of an Indian social anthropologist who, however, has broken with the Indian tradition in such matters by working in a region of India that is linguistically and culturally quite different from his own. In both method and theory, this study belongs to British social anthropology but with leavening from contemporary sociology and political science.

DUBE, SHYAMA CHARAN. **India's Changing Villages: Human Factors in Community Development.** Ithaca: Cornell University Press, 1958, 230 p.

In this volume, Shyama Charan Dube examines "some of the important human factors involved in externally induced and State directed programmes of economic development and culture change in a technologically under-developed society." Under the Government of India's First Five-Year Plan (April 1951 to March 1956) one of the chief means for improving life in India's villages was the many-sided Community Development Program. The author describes the successes and failures of this program in western Uttar Pradesh during the first 18 months of a three-year program to meet multiple technical and social targets. Using data from one block of 153 villages in general and two villages in particular, Dube analyzes the villagers' responses to efforts at change, the effectiveness of state officials as agents of change and the problems of communication between them and the villagers. The chapter entitled "Cultural Factors in Community Development" summarizes ways in which cultural factors influenced the effectiveness of the Community Development Program—for example, villagers abandoning compost pits because composting did not fit the traditional work roles of either men or women; village élites channeling programs for their own benefit; village factions blocking improvements that might benefit their opponents. The author calls for coöperation between planners and social scientists in conducting base-line studies, controlled experiments and critical evaluations of development efforts. An appendix presents remarkable illustrations of the communication problem between planners and villagers by comparing a village-level worker's diary of his daily activities with villagers' perceptions of his activities.

MARRIOTT, McKIM, *ed.* **Village India: Studies in the Little Community.** Chicago: University of Chicago Press, 1955, 269 p.

The eight papers in this volume are products of a 1954 University of Chicago anthropology seminar on "Comparison of Cultures: The Indian Village," conducted by Professors Robert Redfield and Milton Singer, which attempt "to understand how to seek understanding of any great civilization and its enormously complex changes through anthropological studies of villages." The authors share the view that peasant villages, unlike many tribal villages, may not be considered observational isolates. Elements of village life filter outward and upward through a process Marriott terms "universalization" to become part of a great tradition, and elements of that great tradition filter downward and are "parochialized" into village practices. The downward filtration of India's classical tradition (called "Sanskritization") is often accompanied by the simultaneous filtration of Western-urban influences termed "Westernization." Several authors describe villages in which a lower group is adopting Sanskritic traits while a higher group is forsaking those same Sanskritic traits and adopting Westernized ones.

The final chapter presents a comparison of the world view of the Kota tribe with that of seven other villages, showing that, despite wide variation, the eight villages share certain processes such as kin groups uniting to protect their interests against outsiders, concern for ritual pollution, manoeuvring for heightened social standing, status sensitivity and an increasing economic and political dependence of the village on outside forces—a dependence that has weakened bonds of unity and authority within the village and opened the way for further changes.

SHILS, EDWARD. **The Intellectual between Tradition and Modernity: The Indian Situation.** The Hague: Mouton, 1961, 120 p.

Since Edward Shils wrote his book there have been many explorations of the condition of Indian intellectuals and of the problems generated for them within a society in transit from tradition to modernity, but none of them has been able to ignore his analysis or to challenge it in a serious fashion. That this is so is perhaps one of the chief validations of his insights into the character of the Indian intellectual élite. His book has been denounced at times as calumny, but it has not been answered, as would have been quite possible, by an analysis proceeding from different perceptions of Indian history and, above all, of India's social needs.

Shils argues that the Indian intellectual is a product of the nineteenth century and insists that many of the essential characteristics of the class are a result of the fact that it could not participate fully in the civil life of the country since most positions of influence were preëmpted by aliens. He finds that the sense of alienation and rejection still colors the attitudes of the intellectuals, preventing them from making a contribution to an informed public opinion commensurate with their numbers. Despite the somewhat depressing picture that he paints, the author insists on the potentialities of Indian intellectuals for creative leadership, once they are able to come to terms with the particularism of their inherited culture and the universalism of their new culture.

Memoirs and Biographies

GANDHI, MOHANDAS KARAMCHAND. **Gandhi's Autobiography.** Washington: Public
Affairs Press, 1948, 640 p.

In this introspective narrative Gandhi explores events and relationships which
influenced his life prior to 1921. These 167 short chapters in his "story of my
experiments with truth" were begun in prison (1922–1924) and continued week by
week during the mid-1920s as columns in *Navajivan,* a Gujarati weekly through
which Gandhi sought to heighten political and ethical awareness in his countrymen. It was not his purpose, he explains, to attempt a real autobiography but to
convey "the inner meaning of Satyagraha." He reflects upon social values and
recounts political highlights concluding with the crucial 1920 session of the Indian
National Congress which adopted his sociopolitical program and accepted *Satyagraha* as the means for winning Indian independence.

Gandhi refers the reader to his earlier personal history, **Satyagraha in South
Africa** (Ahmedabad: Navajivan Publishing House, rev. ed., 1950, 351 p.) for the
important years 1906–1914, which are not covered here. The uninitiated would do
well to begin with a complete biography such as **Mahatma Gandhi** by Bal Ram
Nanda, for without considerable knowledge of the political framework and cultural
setting within which Gandhi lived, the autobiography may provide as many puzzles
as it furnishes insights. Moreover, 28 years of intensive political leadership,
philosophical reflection, social experimentation and experience with *Satyagraha* lay
ahead in the eventful period which had only just begun when this account ends.
The Collected Works of Mahatma Gandhi (Delhi: Ministry of Information and
Broadcasting, Publications Division, 1958–)—a monumental series to be completed in the early 1970s—covers Gandhi's entire public life from 1884 to 1948
and is the primary reference source.

NANDA, BAL RAM. **Mahatma Gandhi: A Biography.** Boston: Beacon Press, 1959,
542 p.

Gandhi's centenary celebrations ended in 1969. Books and articles on his life
nevertheless continue to be published, as do his own words (the collected works
ultimately may number 100 stout volumes). Time has not simplified the problem of
understanding this most remarkable figure of the twentieth century. Many feel that
Bal Ram Nanda's biography approaches perfection in laying out the political life of
India's nationalist saint, leaving to the future the task of interpreting the significance of Gandhi's ideas on India and the world.

This book is based on a wide reading of Gandhi's works and of the thousands of
documents and monographs that have been written about the subject. The style of
writing is clean and unencumbered by the excessive rhetoric and adulation that
normally accompany tales of the Mahatma. Facts and common-sense interpretation
replace religiosity and sentiment. Gandhi emerges a man, faults, failings and all,
and not a revered figure to be observed from afar. The biography is strongest on
the Indian period. The author apparently believes that Gandhi's autobiography and
his major book on South Africa are more authentic sources for the early period.

Gandhi was a politician; perhaps more, but certainly not less. Bal Ram Nanda's
book is one of the two best introductions to the Indian politics of this century; the
other, Jawaharlal Nehru's autobiography, is more personal but by no means as
judicious.

ERIKSON, ERIK H. **Gandhi's Truth: On the Origins of Militant Nonviolence.** New
York: Norton, 1969, 474 p.

Erik H. Erikson's **Gandhi's Truth** represents a model of the psycho-historical
approach, of which the author has been a pioneer. The book is marked by an
avoidance of the pathological emphasis that the medical origin of psychoanalysis
has imbedded in some approaches to historical figures and by considerable cultural

empathy. Erikson recognizes an analogy to psychoanalytic ethics in Gandhi's propensity to treat political counter-players so as to elicit their better rather than their worst selves. Much of the book is a vehicle for a comprehensive normative statement stressing this theme.

The analysis focuses on the Ahmedabad textile strike of 1918, Gandhi's first major foray into urban mass mobilization and into economic issues in India. A poverty of sources, due in part to British destruction of nationalist records, makes the account of the Ahmedabad "event" more formalistic than one would like. But the book sheds much light on the psychodynamics of a critical period in Gandhi's life, when he was converted from a loyalist into the British Crown's most determined opponent. Erikson sees Gandhi as growing in effectiveness in part as he learns to treat his inner self "non-violently," allowing his overweening conscience to relent both in its treatment of himself and others.

The book is sometimes overly bold in its willingness to generalize concerning all of Indian culture—without reference to region, class and caste. It is scrupulous, however, in its Gandhi scholarship and, on the whole, successful in traversing extremely difficult cultural and historical terrain. A significant contribution to the history of Gandhi's role in conflict resolution.

NEHRU, JAWAHARLAL. **Toward Freedom.** New York: Day, 1941, 445 p.

Despite its seeming candor, Nehru's autobiography is not a very personal book, for the author uses his literary skill to conceal as well as to explain and elucidate. It will not provide the raw material for a psychoanalytic analysis, as Gandhi's story of his life did for Erikson. Nor does it even give much inside information on the Congress Party or national politics. What it does provide is an unmatched statement on what it meant to be a proud, wellborn Indian in the last decades of foreign rule. The ambiguities and doubts of a sensitive intellectual caught up in a national movement are revealed, sometimes self-consciously, sometimes by indirection, but always in a way that illumines the twentieth-century experience. One senses behind the elegant language the misgivings of a rational mind yielding unwillingly to the emotional certainties of Gandhi, but then being persuaded by the apparent political wisdom of decisions that seemed to have been based on mystical intuition. Nehru's failure to understand Jinnah and the demands of the Muslim League are also revealed throughout the book, as is the underlying premise of so much of nationalist thought—that the disappearance of the British would solve India's social and economic problems.

NEHRU, JAWAHARLAL. **The Discovery of India.** New York: Day, 1946, 595 p.

Between April and September 1944, during his ninth and longest period of imprisonment, Jawaharlal Nehru wrote **The Discovery of India,** the last volume in a remarkable trilogy which also included **Glimpses of World History,** letters to his daughter Indira, ranging over the whole course of human history, and his autobiography, **Toward Freedom.** It is a long, discursive, partly autobiographical series of essays, full of insightful and brilliant passages, beginning and ending with reflections on problems and events in India and the world at large, on philosophy and science, on the past and the present. The bulk of the book is a reflective survey, essentially within a chronological framework, of "the panorama of India's past," which, in spite of its disjointed and episodic treatment and often dubious interpretations, is probably the most stimulating commentary on Indian history that has ever been written—and almost certainly the most widely read. Particular emphasis is given to "the last phase," which Nehru described in terms of "nationalism versus imperialism," with the British as the villains and the nationalist leaders, especially Gandhi, as the heroes. The comments on developments in India during World War II are particularly full and valuable.

Jawaharlal Nehru was intrigued—one might almost say haunted—by India's past, in which he found much to praise and much to condemn. He discerned a common heritage and a basic unity in that past, and he searched diligently for his own links with it. "To know and understand India," he wrote, "one has to travel far in time and space." For such a voyage into India's past, as well as into the mind of Nehru himself, he has provided an indispensable guide.

BRECHER, MICHAEL. **Nehru: A Political Biography.** New York: Oxford University Press, 1959, 682 p.

The Nehru literature has proliferated since Panditji's death in May 1964. Yet this book remains the single most valuable volume for an understanding not only of Nehru and the post-independence period loosely called the Nehru era but of Indian history since 1920. As a history of modern India it will be rep¹aced, but as a biography of Nehru it will survive indefinitely, its staying power deriving from the detail amassed during extensive interviews with Nehru and his contemporaries, many of whom failed to produce autobiographies or to preserve their personal papers. It will serve as a source book even after the Nehru archives become available.

Brecher avoids the harsh judgments of Walter Crocker's **Nehru: A Contemporary's Estimate** (New York: Oxford University Press, 1966, 186 p.) as well as the eulogistic approach of Vincent Sheean's **Nehru: The Years of Power** (New York: Random House, 1960, 306 p.). Although he was faulted at the time for enumerating Nehru's "defects," especially his vacillation as a decision maker and his myopia as a judge of character, Brecher concluded that these were "the weaknesses of a giant." Brecher wrote—and wrote extremely well—at the apex of Nehru's popularity. It is likely that the scholar who produces the next substantial work on the subject, able to view Nehru's life and times in their entirety, including the difficulties which eroded Nehru's proudest accomplishments even before his death, will arrive at a more critical assessment. In addition, the availability of the papers of Rajendra Prasad, Maulana Azad and especially Sardar Patel should make it possible to see Nehru's role in more accurate perspective.

CHAUDHURI, NIRAD C. **The Autobiography of an Unknown Indian.** Berkeley: University of California Press, 1968, 506 p.

This fascinating and elegantly written account of the life and perceptions of India's leading intellectual demonstrates the impact of British imperialism and is a major expression of India's cultural vitality in this century. The author combines in his work the passions and sensitivities of the indigenous Bengali man of letters and the detachment and analytical skill of the Western intellectual.

His concern is with man and his natural, cultural, social and political environments—first dealing with his own life and times and then developing a general theory of Indian history. He traces his own life from its beginnings in rural East Bengal early in this century through his student days and young manhood in Calcutta. He reaches out as well to sketch and assess the cultural movements flowering in Bengal and the course of Indian nationalism. After describing early liberal Indian nationalism, he scathingly depicts how Gandhi brought to the surface an older and rancorous nationalism which spread widely but generated hates and divisions in Indian society. Through these same pages he interweaves a very useful account of Hindu-Muslim relations. He completes his picture of India under British rule by contrasting the England of his imagination (which he learned of through literature) with the behavior of Britishers in India.

Finally he presents a pessimistic and cyclical theory of the death of cultures, Aryan, Muslim, European, in an Indian environment. His very autobiography, however, by its sweep and intelligence, vivid portraiture and moral passion gives one sign among many that Indian culture still thrives.

PAKISTAN

CALLARD, KEITH B. **Pakistan: A Political Study.** New York: Macmillan (in coöperation with the Institute of Pacific Relations), 1957, 355 p.

"Pakistanis are a people united by a common will to be a nation," wrote the late Keith Callard in 1957, "but they do not yet know what kind of nation they want to be." More than any other book, this pioneering study of Pakistan's political history, constitutional confusion and social dynamics helps explain the tenuous civic culture of a divided people. It is a study of the bad "fit" between an imperial legacy, an awakening but fragmented religio-political community and the imported ideal of consensual parliamentary democracy. And if the chronicle is one of quarreling men, the absence of a disciplining public philosophy and the demise of parliamentary government, the persistence of the state alone would justify its study: as Callard said, "It is a remarkable achievement that the country has fared no worse."

The author used the skills of the social historian in analyzing an inherently quarrelsome attempt to reconcile jarringly competitive institutions, ideals and groups. Since the book was written just a year before General Ayub Khan's coup d'état of 1958, it stands as the most comprehensive analysis of the parliamentary experiment in the country. Following President Ayub Khan's fall from power, the country seems poised to resume that democratic quest. As in 1947, Pakistan faces extraordinary federal problems, its autocratic past has done little to widen the number or competence of its public men, its tryst with an Islamic ideology is still to be realized or rejected, and its relations with India remain disastrous. The Callard book, therefore, offers a definitive statement on the tasks ahead.

SAYEED, KHALID BIN. **Pakistan: The Formative Phase.** Karachi: Pakistan Publishing House (in coöperation with the Institute of Pacific Relations), 1961, 492 p.

Those who undertake to study the political processes of Pakistan do well to start with this work, which presents in some detail the events which led to the partition of the subcontinent and provides an impressive case for the establishment of this Muslim state. It also offers a comprehensive description of the initial efforts by the Muslim League leadership to build a political system and a unified nation.

Clearly the author is deeply involved in his subject—a condition which presumably helped stimulate the profound insights which abound in his work. This may also explain his willingness occasionally to move into the role of an advocate. Some such instances involve the discussion of the "first faint glimmerings of Pakistan" and a justification of Mohammad Ali Jinnah's role at the Simla Conference, 1945.

Professor Khalid, moreover, is constrained by the paucity of high quality data. Until recently, information regarding the political processes on the Indian subcontinent depended upon reports of colonial officials who generally had relatively little contact with the population and usually were somewhat less than devoted to scholarly analysis. Alternatively, such information had to be extrapolated from indigenous political tracts, contemporary literary pieces and folklore. Thus it was practically impossible for the author to demonstrate empirically one of his individual contentions that "the Muslim League bridged the gulf that yawned between the illiterate Muslim masses and the highly Westernized Muslim elite at the top." Without evidence of its popular dimension, however, it is difficult to get a perspective on the struggle for Pakistan. And it is difficult to evaluate the opportunities and alternatives available after independence when the presentation is confined to politics and policy-making at the highest level.

By now, this last problem is being corrected by several scholars, including Professor Khalid himself, but his first major published work remains a significant contribution.

VON VORYS, KARL. **Political Development in Pakistan.** Princeton: Princeton University Press (for the Princeton Center of International Studies), 1965, 341 p.

Political development, for Professor von Vorys, is the process by which political systems develop the capacity to manage social and economic problems. During and after a Fulbright year in East Pakistan, when he observed the extraordinary weakness of Pakistan's political system, he was provoked to the research and analysis resulting in this study. It is presented in a useful form of double entry bookkeeping in which government capacity and development problems are juxtaposed. The research period covered by the book was the heyday of the Ayub Khan régime, and the book is appreciative of planned and disciplined "state-building." Yet there are very clear analyses of the difficulty of effectively using coercion and of the paucity of state instruments in producing social compliance.

The author concludes that the building of state authority must *follow* the building of a sense of national identity: "In the absence of a national focus of orientation or a tradition of confidence in the political system, popular response to persuasion by government—any government—is necessarily negligible," and that "guided democracy" efforts lead to a progressive decline in the control of the political system. The author leaves the reader, as Pakistan's experience left him, with the dilemma: authoritative government is necessary for planned economic and social development, but the popular support on which it rests presupposes wide participation in the political system. Von Vorys leaves the analytical dilemma unresolved, except by noting the need for extraordinary leadership, much as Pakistan has left the operational dilemma unresolved since 1947.

HAQ, MAHBUB UL. **The Strategy of Economic Planning: A Case Study of Pakistan.** New York: Oxford University Press, 1964, 266 p.

Although Pakistan is presently the sixth most populous country in the world, the social science literature on Pakistan cannot compare in scope and depth with that available on countries a fraction of its size.

Mahbub ul Haq's book was the first significant effort to analyze economic development, and especially its planning, in Pakistan. The author was also one of the first officials of the central government to argue in print that East Pakistan was falling further behind West Pakistan in per capita income and to advocate policies to close the gap. Even more significant was his candor about the "brutal, sordid" nature of the process of economic growth. He did not blame the problems facing the country on lazy workers, ignorant tradition-bound peasants, spendthrift landlords or businessmen, nor on monopoly power or exploitation by the developed world. Using data he had developed himself, Haq demonstrated that the fundamental problem was pervasive poverty. He argued the importance of economic growth and that there were no easy options facing the planners which would permit an escape from poverty.

Nearly ten years after the book's publication, it can justifiably be criticized for its preoccupation with growth, with investment and for its mechanistic view of economic relationships, combined with its neglect of equity, of economic efficiency, of political factors and of the importance of policies. But when the book was written in 1960–1961, most scholars and planners were guilty of the same narrowness of vision (and some still are in 1970). Besides, to some extent such "narrowness" was quite appropriate at that time when Pakistan and other countries with similar problems had achieved only a negligible increase in per capita income over ten years, while income distribution had probably worsened. Since then, the Pakistan economy has been growing at nearly 6 percent, and the social and political consequences of inequality have become all too obvious. Now an emphasis on equity and efficiency is as appropriate as was the emphasis on growth in 1960.

PAPANEK, GUSTAV F. **Pakistan's Development: Social Goals and Private Incentives.** Cambridge: Harvard University Press, 1967, 354 p.

The Director of Harvard's Development Advisory Service uses this book simultaneously to describe Pakistan's economic development experience, to use its lessons to question many concepts in the development literature and to find in Pakistan's case ample evidence to demolish some of the shibboleths about traditional society. The book portrays the agents of growth, their problems and opportunities, and the pragmatic policy "mix" that passed for a growth strategy. The book was written a year before the demise of the Ayub Khan government that made economic growth its ideology, and as a case study of the primacy of economics over political equilibrium, it is a classic.

In Pakistan, the entrepreneur proved "the social utility of greed," the civil servants of the country coöperated as "gentlemen *at work*," and the peasants by their acquiescence to taxation and profiteering, and by their willingness to innovate, laid the foundation for the growth that foreign aid, good luck, good advice and the new agricultural technology made possible.. This was a development miracle, but like all miracles, it was tenuous. Many of the problems that first discredited and then toppled the régime of Ayub Khan were generated from both the magnitude and the mix of economic growth. The benefits of development were very unequally distributed, and while the distribution pattern was conducive to high rates of reinvestment, it did little to broaden the social base for continued régime support. Papanek's vigorous analysis makes clear why the government came to court disaster and why a distinctive pattern of policy trade-offs worked in Pakistan's economy.

AFGHANISTAN

FRASER-TYTLER, SIR WILLIAM KERR. **Afghanistan: A Study of Political Developments in Central and Southern Asia.** New York: Oxford University Press, 3rd ed., 1967, 362 p.

Sir William K. Fraser-Tytler was a British foreign service officer stationed in Kabul during the reigns of King Amanullah and Kings Nadir and Zahir. Rarely a disinterested observer, his political history of Afghanistan reflects his British imperial perspective, and his attitude toward the Afghans displays his affectionate condescension. The book is nevertheless indispensable for the primary observations made by the author with regard to geography, political intrigue and court manners, especially during his tenure in Kabul.

Fraser-Tytler's discussion of the first two Anglo-Afghan Wars is based upon documents of the governments of India and of Britain, as well as upon British eyewitness accounts. His descriptions of the Anglo-Afghan encounters are at times sympathetic to the Afghan position and critical of the British revenge and destruction, but the author never wavers in his belief that the British were bringing safety and stability to Central Asia.

WILBER, DONALD NEWTON and OTHERS. **Afghanistan: Its People, Its Society, Its Culture.** New Haven: Human Relations Area Files, rev. ed., 1962, 320 p.

This revised edition of **Afghanistan** is designed more for the layman or the beginning student than for the person interested either in knowing the sources of information presented or in sensing where scholars differ in their interpretations of Afghanistan's social and economic history. Well-written chapters briefly summarize such topics as "Ethnic Groups and Languages," "Religion," "Arts and Literature," "Traditional Patterns of Living," "Mass Media" and "Public Health and Welfare." Virtually no references at all are cited in the text, which might serve as a useful guidebook to the traveler going to Afghanistan without any previous knowledge of the country. It is far less comprehensive, however, than the **Area Handbook for Afghanistan** (Harvey Henry Smith and others, Washington: Government Printing Office, 1969, 435 p.) and based on many of the same source materials—the Human Relations Area Files.

FLETCHER, ARNOLD. **Afghanistan: Highway of Conquest.** Ithaca: Cornell University Press, 1965, 325 p.

Arnold Fletcher was employed by the Afghan Ministry of Education for three years and has made a number of additional trips to Afghanistan. His book opens with a brief panorama of Afghan history from the Pashtoons' legend of their descent from King Saul to 1747, when Afghan nationhood is often said to have begun. The book is a very readable but scantily documented account of the rise and fall of the Sadozi, of the British invasions and disasters, and of innumerable stories of internal intertribal strife and intrigue for the Amirship. The most useful sections of the book are those that deal with the "Pushtoonistan" dispute between Pakistan and Afghanistan and a chapter, "Afghanistan in the Cold War," which discusses the early political and social disasters of the United States' aid program in the Helmand River Valley.

CEYLON; NEPAL

WRIGGINS, WILLIAM HOWARD. **Ceylon: Dilemmas of a New Nation.** Princeton: Princeton University Press, 1960, 505 p.

W. Howard Wriggins' comprehensive and interdisciplinary textbook on Ceylonese politics represents a rare intellectual achievement in writings on the postcolonial states of Asia. In the thoroughness of his research, in his impressive documentation, in his concern for theoretical and comparative issues, and in his sober, sympathetic and impartial treatment of the full range of political, social, economic and foreign policy issues which confronted Ceylon in common with other Asian countries a decade after independence, Wriggins set a standard of scholarship of the highest order. More recent studies, such as Robert Kearney's **Communalism and Language in the Politics of Ceylon** (Durham: Duke University Press, 1967, 165 p.), have built upon but not replaced this classic work.

Of special value in Wriggins' book is the excellent discussion of the interconnections between religious and cultural revivalism, ethnic and linguistic conflict, political organization and electoral politics and relations with India on the issues of Tamil-Sinhalese relations and the status of the Indian Tamils in Ceylon. The descriptions of the leadership, organization and program of the main Ceylonese political parties and of the pivotal election of 1956 are also invaluable. The basic theme of the volume, namely, the transformation of politics, of élite conflict and of élite-mass relations by the rise to political consciousness of new social classes and forces inspired by indigenous values, makes the study still relevant beyond Ceylon.

This book is one of the outstanding studies of the past 15 years on South Asian politics and continues to be the most solid introduction to Ceylon available.

JOSHI, BHUWAN LAL and ROSE, LEO E. **Democratic Innovations in Nepal: A Case Study of Political Acculturation.** Berkeley: University of California Press, 1966, 551 p.

This is the joint work of a Nepali psychologist, now teaching in the United States, and the most informed American scholar on Nepal and the entire Himalayan area. It is a significant book that attempts for almost the first time to analyze in depth the agony of a developing nation attempting to modernize through the assimilation of alien legal and administrative systems. The book is both objective and sympathetic to the problems faced by Nepal and its modernizing élites, and the lessons which can be derived from this detailed study of a crucial 14-year period in the history of Nepal have a significance which goes well beyond the affairs of this small Himalayan kingdom. It is a case study which contains certain pervasive truths applicable to all emerging countries—the struggle between the modernizing élites and the traditional system, the difficulty of imposing a modern democracy on an archaic economic and political structure, the frustrations faced by the reformers when they actually attain power.

After establishing the setting for their study, the authors describe the political system established by the Shah kings and subsequently by the Ranas. The account of the 1950 revolution is followed by the heart of the book, a detailed discussion of the attempt to establish Western democracy in Nepal and the apparent failure of the experiment when the king assumed full power in 1960 with his own version of "guided" democracy. The book closes with a discussion of the Panchayat Raj innovation established by King Mahendra and a concluding retrospective section on patterns and trends in Nepal's political modernization.

Democratic Innovations in Nepal is without doubt the most incisive and best-documented work on modern Nepal to date, and it can be read with profit not only by Himalayan specialists but by all those concerned with the process of change in a developing society.

SOUTHEAST ASIA

GENERAL

BASTIN, JOHN and BENDA, HARRY J. **A History of Modern Southeast Asia: Colonialism, Nationalism, and Decolonization.** Englewood Cliffs: Prentice-Hall, 1968, 214 p.

The focus of this masterful introduction to Southeast Asian history is on the advent of Western influence, the evolution of colonial practices, the indigenous social reaction to foreign domination and the final process of decolonization. Little attention is given to the names and dates that dominate conventional political histories of Southeast Asia because the concern of the two authors is with deeper social and economic processes. John Bastin is the authority on colonial patterns and practices while Harry J. Benda deals with the complex Southeast Asian responses, and the two constitute an admirable team.

Aside from a general and diffuse sympathy for Southeast Asian nationalism the study lacks a central theme. The authors constantly stress the complexity of cultural, economic and imperial considerations in the evolution of Southeast Asia. In dealing with the postwar scene, the authors do advance the interesting, but not fully demonstrated, hypothesis that the countries with the greatest élite continuity— Thailand, Cambodia, Malaysia and the Philippines—have "enjoyed internal stability," while a second category of states consisting of Burma, Indonesia and Vietnam have been characterized by recently emergent élites and have been "poised on the brink of incipient social upheaval." Less open to question is their final observation about the spread of military rule in the region.

HALL, DANIEL GEORGE EDWARD. **A History of South-East Asia.** New York: St. Martin's Press, rev. ed., 1964, 955 p.

Professor Hall's book has been properly acclaimed as a monumental contribution to the understanding of the history of the area. The account is comprehensive, covering the earliest times to the 1960s with equal thoroughness. The second edition of 1964 added a discussion of the Philippines and a thoughtful chapter on the independence period. The appendix contains the listings and dates of all known rulers of the several areas down to the end of the colonial period in the 1950s. The selected bibliography is no less than 30 pages in length.

The book is destined for long and useful service as a standard historical treatise. An English reviewer suggests, however, that the book "scarcely passes over the boundary which separates reference works from literature" and that few would read it in front of the fire. It is a valuable compilation of historical information about states, rulers, colonial personalities and political events. It is less adequate as a historical interpretation of the peoples involved. Although demonstrating on the whole a remarkable degree of detachment and concern for accuracy of detail, the lack of systematic footnoting precludes any scholarly reëvaluation of sources used and interpretations hazarded. Undergraduate students find it difficult to use.

CADY, JOHN F. **Southeast Asia: Its Historical Development.** New York: McGraw-Hill, 1964, 657 p.

This is a useful volume on the chronologies of the various Southeast Asian societies. It is not as detailed as the work by D. G. E. Hall nor as imaginative as that of John S. Furnivall, but it summarizes standard information well.

Although published in 1964, this work strongly reflects a pre–World War II perspective, and the general practice of the author is to discount more recent events in favor of detailed treatment of earlier periods to the extent that the postwar period, with the ending of colonialism and the emergence of independent states throughout the region, receives only the briefest possible coverage. Cady is most informative and most authoritative when dealing with Southeast Asian societies at the time of the early advent of Europeans and during the process of establishing Western colonial authorities.

As one of the most eminent American historians of Southeast Asia, the author has masterfully maintained the European, and particularly British, tradition of Southeast Asian historical scholarship which stresses dates, names and official policies. This book, noteworthy as a classic in that tradition, will probably never be superseded since the trend is toward great appreciation of the social sciences and particularly of sociological, cultural and psychological factors in the development of Southeast Asia.

FURNIVALL, JOHN SYDENHAM. **Colonial Policy and Practice.** New York: Cambridge University Press, 1948, 568 p.

The essence of this stout volume is a distinctive reappraisal of the nature of colonialism and, in particular, of its effects upon the relationships of the diverse peoples embraced within the colonial domain. The structure of the book is rather cumbersome and lends itself to repetition, but the basic message comes through clearly. The first part is devoted to Burma (where Mr. Furnivall had been a member of the civil service) and to the Netherlands Indies (brief because he had already written an extensive study of that country), rounded out by 275 pages on colonial policy and practice in general, including Africa.

In briefest compass his thesis is that colonial rule, especially in the kind of direct rule utilized in Burma, destroys the bonds and the restraints which hold an integrated society together and produces instead a plural society with no common bond other than the cash nexus and the search for profit. "Progress" and colonially imposed reforms tend only to make the situation worse, engendering communal ill will rather than promoting the crucially needed common social will. To seek welfare through an expansion of the activity of the colonial government and the multiplication of officials, expatriate or native, is only to atomize the society further and to encourage increased resort to compulsion. More significant than the wealth of information which the book contains on Burma, the Netherlands Indies and other colonies is its fundamental challenge to the accepted canons of colonial rule and its insistence upon the destructiveness of colonialism as bringing both material and spiritual impoverishment. It may be, however, that the book appeared too close to the demise of colonialism to have the full impact which it might otherwise have had.

EMERSON, RUPERT and OTHERS. **Government and Nationalism in Southeast Asia.** New York: Institute of Pacific Relations, 1942, 242 p.

This wartime study of Southeast Asia consists of three distinct essays, closely related but not coördinated. The book is concerned with the eventual task of liberating Southeast Asia from Japanese control and in assessing the measure of support to be anticipated from the several peoples and their ultimate participation in the task of promoting the cause of self-government. In his substantial introduction, Professor Emerson treats relevant political factors in the historical background of the peoples of the area and political aspects of nationalist movements in general. Lennox Mills describes in some detail the character of prewar colonial administrations, including organizational principles, political forms and prevailing economic problems, all of which would have to be taken into account in future contingencies. Virginia Thompson clarifies the perplexing problems of political relationships, both within the respective countries and between them, which would have to be faced during the post-colonial situation. She cites the distressing tendency of élite leaderships to revert to one-party rule and then to develop factionalism within the select group. The authors advance no claims that their contributions are definitive, but their perceptive accounts are well written, and much that has happened since 1942 has vindicated the accuracy of their observations. Limited attention was accorded the relation of the peasantry to the various national movements and to their eventual role in post-colonial governments.

KAHIN, GEORGE McTURNAN, *ed.* **Governments and Politics of Southeast Asia.** Ithaca: Cornell University Press (for the Southeast Asia Program, Cornell University), 2d enl. ed., 1964, 796 p.

This book constitutes one of the major contributions of American scholarship in general and that of the Cornell Southeast Asia Program in particular to the understanding of the political realities of postwar Southeast Asia. The original edition of 1959 (531 p.) included only six states of the area. Laos and Cambodia were added in the 1964 edition. All country studies follow the same developmental pattern, namely: historical background, contemporary setting (economic, social and political), political process and major problems, plus a listing of suggested readings. The arrangement has the advantage of ensuring systematic coverage, but the organizational structure does not fit all situations equally well, and it virtually precludes efforts at comparative analysis. The several accounts quite properly reflect the viewpoints of the separate authors, but the role of Kahin as teacher and editor is everywhere present, if not always definable. All the accounts are perceptive and accurate, although reflecting some unevenness in analytical depth, mainly apparent in the treatment of chapters on the political process. Among the best sections are those by David Wilson on Thailand and Herbert Feith on Indonesia, but all of the country treatments can be recommended to students, the general reader and professionally interested persons. The whole stands as a tribute to the contribution which George Kahin has made in training the present generation of American scholars devoted to the political affairs of Southeast Asia.

EMERSON, RUPERT. **Representative Government in Southeast Asia.** Cambridge: Harvard University Press (for the Institute of Pacific Relations), 1955, 197 p.

Professor Emerson's discussion of the prospects for representative government in Southeast Asia is both informative and judicious. He is less concerned with governmental forms than with the ability of citizens to participate meaningfully in their respective governments. Chapters by Willard Elsbree and Virginia Thompson cover the Philippines and local government problems. Western democratic institutions are largely alien to the traditions of Southeast Asian peoples, and prewar colonial régimes, apart from the Philippines and Burma, afforded little training in the field. In a country-by-country examination, Professor Emerson notes the encouraging postwar support of constitutional forms by many of the nationalist élites. He also points out that this vogue will surely dissipate unless leaders are willing to accept the risks of holding genuinely free elections. The prospects for democracy in 1955 were exciting but not encouraging, for totalitarian methods provided tempting alternatives for accomplishing rapid change under authoritarian leadership. Thailand at the time was retreating from democracy in the direction of military dictatorship, President Sukarno's commitment to the democratic creed faded in 1957, and Premier Nu lost out to military rule in 1958. Malaya at the time was trying to be born as a state outside the womb of nationhood. Emperor Bao Dai and Ngo Dinh Diem in Vietnam could not, in 1955, enlist nationalist sentiment to stem disruptive tendencies, much less develop a democratic governmental system. The three authors are undogmatic and designate many topics calling for additional study.

VANDENBOSCH, AMRY and BUTWELL, RICHARD. **The Changing Face of Southeast Asia.** Lexington: University of Kentucky Press, 1966, 438 p.

This is essentially a systematic country-by-country review of post–World War II events in the eight major states of Southeast Asia which culminates in chapters on the international relations of the region, American policy toward Southeast Asia and general observations about future prospects.

The authors are well informed and present highly readable and authoritative accounts of recent political history. An earlier version of this work focused largely upon the emergence of nationalism and representative institutions in Southeast Asia; this version is based on the more pessimistic understanding that authoritarian and above all military governments are most consistent with Southeast Asian realities.

The tone is more popular and journalistic than scholarly, but in general the judgments are balanced, there is little effort at sensationalism, and the interpretations are based on sound information. Although their coverage only extends to early 1966, the authors show themselves to have been wise about the growing American involvement in Vietnam and immediately appreciative of the realities and significance of the attempted communist coup of September 30–October 1, 1965.

FIFIELD, RUSSELL H. **The Diplomacy of Southeast Asia: 1945–1958.** New York: Harper, 1958, 584 p.

This book is a study of the first phases of the shaping of foreign policies in a demanding and dangerous world by states (except for Thailand) just emerging from colonial rule in a critically important corner of the globe. Its primary focus is on the development of the relations of the newly emerging states of Southeast Asia with each other, with their neighbors and with the world at large, but it also makes constant reference to internal developments in each of the countries. Since it is the author's conclusion that Southeast Asia speaks with no single voice and that the forces separating the countries are much stronger than those favoring regional coöperation, he has ordered the bulk of the book on a country-by-country basis plus introductory chapters which set the stage and concluding chapters which include one on Southeast Asia in the United Nations. The book is a highly valuable storehouse of detailed material for the formative period with which it deals, but a shortcoming is that Professor Fifield, by so largely limiting himself to an objective presentation of the facts, has attempted so little in the way of analysis and evaluation.

PURCELL, VICTOR WILLIAM WILLIAMS SAUNDERS. **The Chinese in Southeast Asia.** New York: Oxford University Press (for the Royal Institute of International Affairs and the Institute of Pacific Relations), 1951, 801 p.

Having served for a quarter of a century in the Malayan civil service, where he dealt primarily with Chinese affairs, Victor Purcell was unusually well qualified to meet the difficult challenge posed by the writing of this book. Its subject matter was meticulously demanding in terms of the statistics, legislative and administrative practice, and racial relationships in each of the seven territories with which he was concerned, as well as in the relations of the emigrants with China. At the same time, it also required a breadth of sympathetic understanding and interpretation. The bulk of the book is composed of a country-by-country survey of the Chinese situation and problem, for the most part organized on a historical basis for each country from the earliest times to World War II and its immediate aftermath. Opening chapters contain a wide-ranging glance at the nature of Chinese civilization and at Southeast Asia as a whole, and a brief conclusion and postscript bring up the rear. It is characteristic of the author's outlook that he saw the Chinese as being held to constitute a "problem" not because of their vicious propensities but because of "their superiority in resource, ability, and industry" to the Southeast Asian peoples among whom they live.

A new revised edition in 1965 enabled the author to undertake a further examination of major issues, such as the effects of the end of colonialism, the spread and intensification of nationalism and the communist takeover of China.

FIFIELD, RUSSELL H. **Southeast Asia in United States Policy.** New York: Praeger (for the Council on Foreign Relations), 1963, 488 p.

This book, conceived within the framework of a cold war in which China has largely replaced Russia as the ever-threatening enemy, embraces a wide-ranging treatment of many aspects of the Southeast Asian countries and their relations with the world at large and the United States. Its central and recurrent theme, however, is the assumption that China is aggressively intent "through new visions and old memories" upon establishing its paramountcy over Southeast Asia. The newly independent countries are portrayed as living under the lengthening shadow of China, and the international communist movement is described as ready to capitalize dynamically on any favorable military situation. Written while Ngo Dinh Diem still reigned (though danger signals were apparent), the book reflects an interval of uncertain transition, when the United States was already much concerned with the region in general and with Vietnam in particular, but not yet as wholly committed in Vietnam. There is a familiar ring to the concluding thesis that as Asian states gain in strength and stature the maintenance of their security should be less an American responsibility and more an Asian undertaking within a broad pattern of coöperation. The author has gathered a mass of valuable material, has much sage comment as to American policy, past and future, and has leavened it all with a realistic recognition that there are no quick and easy answers to Southeast Asia's manifold problems.

INDOCHINA; VIETNAM

THOMPSON, VIRGINIA MCLEAN. **French Indo-China.** New York: Macmillan, 1937, 517 p.

The greatest interest this book holds today is for its elaborate presentation of French imperialism as an expression of Western nationalism and political theory. Written before decolonization became a political possibility, this analysis of "the contacts of civilizations" between France and Indochina is no tribute to the cultural successes of *la mission civilisatrice*. The descriptions of pre-colonial Cochin China, Tonkin, Annam, Laos and Cambodia offer rich detail about imperial and mandarin traditions imported from China and India, and the indigenous variations on them. The early village communities are also carefully described on the basis of secondary sources. The extraordinary variation in the patterns of life among these peoples succumbed to a rigid, rationalistic French rule, foreshadowing the necessity for applying force during both the colonizing and independence periods. The book is based on visits to Vietnam and many interviews there and in France, supplemented by extensive use of the imaginative literatures and memoirs as well as French scholarly studies of the region. Few official documents were then available to provide much detail about French colonial administration, for which Buttinger is a better source.

HAMMER, ELLEN JOY. **The Struggle for Indochina.** Stanford: Stanford University Press (for the Institute of Pacific Relations), 1954, 332 p.

The primary importance of this book is its early eminence as an English-language source of information about the growth of nationalism in Vietnam, Laos and Cambodia. It also includes a useful discussion of French and Japanese negotiations over Indochina during World War II and of their joint administration of the area just before Vietnamese nationalism reached its highest peak with the Bao Dai accession. It describes the waning of French political authority and legitimacy prior to the Japanese coup and military occupation. There is considerable, and still useful, background and history of the independence efforts that became the Vietminh movement. Miss Hammer dramatizes the brief moment of hope at Bao Dai's abdication and shows its sharp, almost poignant contrast to French expectations of return to prewar imperialism. The entry of Chinese troops in the immediate postwar years and the growing Vietnamese opposition to Vietminh are also described in some detail; but most of the attention focuses on French perception and disappointments. On the whole the book is somewhat more sympathetic to the American role in Indochina as a product of its anti-communist ideology than is Bernard Fall's study, but it is less detailed than subsequent works by Fall and Joseph Buttinger. Rupert Emerson's perceptive preface is still worth reading.

BUTTINGER, JOSEPH. **Vietnam: A Dragon Embattled.** New York: Praeger, 1967, 2 v.
These volumes continue Buttinger's extended history of Vietnam, which began with **The Smaller Dragon** (New York: Praeger, 1958, 535 p.). The narrative here starts with the death of Paul-Armand Rousseau as Governor General of French Indochina in 1896 and continues to the fall of Diem in 1963. This intricate, detailed, painstakingly (and controversially) documented history includes many case studies illustrating the effects of changes in the leadership and policies of French colonial officials after 1900. There are also circumstantial accounts of French colonial projects in various fields of capital infrastructure development, social and educational improvement, law enforcement, responses to early national resistance movements and administrative changes. These case histories are supplemented by comparative studies of development projects conducted under American sponsorship, notably in land tenure, industrialization and educational modernization. The cases are interspersed with personal histories of French colonial administrators and Vietnamese resistance leaders. French intransigence and brutality in the post-Japanese period are presented as consequences of political insensitivity to Vietnamese nationalism, as is the subsequent American underestimation of the nature of the nationalist and communist resistance movements. There is a detailed account of the opportunities, efforts and failures of Diem's régime and a valuable analysis of the sources of the anti-Diem movement leading to the November coup.

DEVILLERS, PHILIPPE. **Histoire du Viêt-Nam de 1940 à 1952.** Paris: Seuil, 1952, 471 p.
This history of Vietnam concentrates on political and administrative developments toward the end of the French imperial rule. It complements Paul Mus' study of the social and cultural aspects of Vietnamese life with its precise but impassioned account of the background to France's effort to subdue Ho Chi Minh. But although Devillers is highly critical of French policies (which he regards as contributing to the legitimacy of the revolution), he regards Vietminh atrocities as an equal cause for the alienation of the Vietnamese masses from the politics of accommodation. This book is still a useful source of social and administrative conditions of the French colonial period, well documented from both official and highly critical sources. It concludes with a searching inquiry into the moral basis of the French postwar intervention.

MUS, PAUL. **Viêt-Nam: Sociologie d'une Guerre.** Paris: Seuil, 1952, 373 p.
In spite of its age, this book survives as a profound interpretation of the sources of the Vietnamese national character, which is presented as its capacity to survive the military and cultural attacks on its integrity. The late Paul Mus, successively soldier, diplomat and savant, attributed the sustained originality and ambiguity of Vietnamese culture to its spirit of resisting while paradoxically engaged in assimilation. He identified its major cultural attributes in its village life, which retained its vitality by remaining indifferent to political vicissitudes in the distant capitals. These insights led him to a locally based perception of the emerging independence movements against France, in which he clearly distinguished communist from nationalist elements. In addition to his valuable description of the nature of the changing ethical base of Vietnam's Asian culture, Mus also described with insight and sympathy the contradictory impulses of French colonialism and its final contributions to the emerging nation.

DUNCANSON, DENNIS J. **Government and Revolution in Vietnam.** New York: Oxford University Press (for the Royal Institute of International Affairs), 1968, 442 p.

This compact, lucid history sympathetically treats the successive efforts of the Chinese, the French and the Americans to dominate Vietnam culturally, and displays a special compassion for the Vietnamese people. Among these contending forces, only the National Liberation Front and its communist predecessors are considered as subversive, external and undeserving. It is this latter fact which induces the writer to conclude that although "sooner or later the conflict must come to an end," "no viable settlement is possible." The historical evidence presented for this view is carefully sorted and summarized, although the early American involvement (before the fall of Diem) is slighted somewhat in his otherwise comprehensive treatment. With this exception, the reader finds a generally pro-American interpretation of the development and problems of contemporary Vietnam, whose plight Duncanson believes might have been avoided if President Diem had understood politics a little better and had been able to offer "more government" to his people.

FALL, BERNARD B. **Street without Joy: Indochina at War, 1946–1954.** Harrisburg: Stackpole, 4th ed., 1964, 403 p.

This description of the French war in Indochina, 1946–1954, spiced with grim and moving personal recollections, eloquently sets forth a startling preview of American military tactics and experience in the same area in the late 1960s. The French tactics and even their equipment were unmistakably drawn from the same field manuals and ordnance depots that supplied the later American effort. The essential lessons of the earlier "Revolutionary War" are clearly drawn in the concluding chapter. Like most of Fall's writings, this one displays somewhat more understanding of the French position than the American reprise, and the tragedy of the neglected historical lessons is apparent on every page. Fall sees the ultimate problem of the two Indochinese wars as the lack of popular support for the campaign against Ho Chi Minh. The importance of sanctuary as a support base for the "revolutionary" fighters provides insuperable odds against the counterinsurgents, he argues, especially if efforts to infiltrate the sanctuary are in turn defeated by the absence of sympathetic partisans in the enemy's base. For Bernard Fall, the first Indochina war was unavoidable; but the second, following the American interlude, is a product of misjudgment and ignorance. He therefore regards the human cost of the first, graphically detailed on these pages, as more legitimate than that of the second.

FALL, BERNARD B. **The Two Viet-Nams: A Political and Military Analysis.** New York: Praeger, 2d rev. ed., 1967, 497 p.

This readable, exuberant account of the history and politics of Vietnam is based on the author's brief residence and frequent visits there, supplemented by interviews and extensive use of official and unofficial documents, direct observation, and unpublished materials. The result is a comprehensive and compassionate account, somewhat shifting in focus and sometimes inaccurate, but always displaying the author's conviction that Vietnam's political needs have been ignored by foreigners and national leaders alike. Written at the end of Diem's presidency, it is especially valuable for its detailed account of that period and for its sympathetic treatment of French colonial policy during its declining years. The exhaustive treatment of the conditions of life in both the North and South lead Fall to the conclusion that the libertarian would have little basis for choice between them. The fact of this resemblance is taken as the greatest reproach to Western influence.

PIKE, DOUGLAS. **Viet Cong: The Organization and Techniques of the National Liberation Front of South Vietnam.** Cambridge: M. I. T. Press, 1966, 490 p.

This book offers the most precise available description of the National Liberation Front (NLF) and its predecessors and affiliates, stressing its organizational and communications techniques and its essentially manipulative approach to the mobilization of the unorganized rural masses. NLF relations with Hanoi and the communist world are explored in political perspective, and the tactical history of Vietcong warfare is presented as a new revolutionary "science." Based on captured documents, interviews, personal observation and public information, this study seeks to provide source material that would support a variety of hypotheses about the NLF. The author is an American foreign service officer, but his analysis is by no means an unqualified apology for the American position in Vietnam. His main argument is that skillful administration and communications provided the NLF with its original access to the Vietnamese rural population but proved to be insufficient to achieve the ultimate objective of political control. This failure led to its final recourse to violence.

TANHAM, GEORGE K. **Communist Revolutionary Warfare: The Vietminh in Indochina.** New York: Praeger, 1961, 166 p.

This brief and simply written RAND study traces the transition from Mao's three-stage strategy for China into the Vietminh doctrine for the struggle against the French in Indochina, 1945–1954. Tanham attributes Ho Chi Minh's successes as much to French failure to perceive the strength of the nationalist movement as to Ho's communist training, ideological convictions and popular appeal. He regards the political attractiveness of the communist movement in its nationalist dress as essential to its local successes, but he devotes most of the book to a discussion of organizational details of the Vietminh's military actions, including personnel and logistics, tactical operations and responses to French tactics and air warfare. The book also includes a brief section on the strengths and weaknesses of revolutionary war and a description by Ann M. Jonas of North Vietnamese post-armistice developments. Although the author adverts to the primacy of politics in this struggle, he presents most of his lessons in military terms of reference.

HONEY, P. J. **Communism in North Vietnam: Its Role in the Sino-Soviet Dispute.** Cambridge: M. I. T. Press, 1963, 207 p.

This short and readable study of communist foreign policies stresses North Vietnam's problems in dealing with the rising tensions between China and the Soviet Union. Even before the split had become evident, the expectation of a unified international communist foreign policy had already begun to break down, Honey argues, citing in evidence the division of the Indochinese Communist Party and Hanoi's mounting distrust of Peking. Hanoi's heavy indebtedness to Peking for economic and military aid made this underlying political distrust the source of painful ambivalence in North Vietnamese foreign policy. The author concludes that the North Vietnamese fear for continued independence as China grows in strength is fully justified. He predicts either Chinese dominance or its eventual "direct rule" in the region. There is also a useful discussion of the leadership of the Democratic Republic of Vietnam, and a prediction of political disorder following Ho's death.

ZAGORIA, DONALD S. **Vietnam Triangle: Moscow, Peking, Hanoi.** New York: Pegasus, 1967, 286 p.

Zagoria's brief, closely written book offers a subtle analysis of the conflicting and changing foreign policy objectives of the principals involved in the Vietnam War. While arguing that the United States and China have a more immediate interest in its outcome than has the Soviet Union, Zagoria believes that Moscow was unable to exploit its relative neutrality because of its rivalry with Peking over their respective roles in Southeast Asia. China's reluctant willingness to play the junior partner to Moscow is presented as a consequence of its greater fear of the United States and its long-term objective of bringing about American withdrawal from Asia. The delicate balance of forces among the three external powers also permitted the National Liberation Front to develop some degree of independence from Hanoi as

North Vietnam became more closely involved in the Moscow-Peking-Washington triangle. Miscalculations based on inadequate information about these relationships led to the American bombing of the North. This action in turn interrupted negotiations just as they were beginning to show promise, and Zagoria argues that cessation of American bombing of North Vietnam should reopen negotiations and lead to a coalition government in Saigon.

THAILAND; CAMBODIA

RIGGS, FRED W. **Thailand: The Modernization of a Bureaucratic Polity.** Honolulu: East-West Center Press, 1966, 470 p.

This book combines a historical review of Thailand, a detailing of the politics of cliques and factions, the application of public administration theory and culminates in a general theory of modernization.

The historical material provides the basis for an understanding not only of Thai developments but of the pattern of traditional kingship and rule in Southeast Asia, particularly Burma. Riggs is especially skillful in demonstrating how a traditional form of hierarchical authority was transformed in Thailand into a more functional modern bureaucracy without destroying all the positive and human features of tradition. In general Riggs is sympathetically understanding of Thai bureaucratic practices, and he indicates what he feels are the limits of appropriate change in a society that seeks to blend the old and the new.

In the final chapter Riggs turns to political theory and develops his concepts relevant for understanding political development and modernization. He advances many useful concepts, including a theory of a "bureaucratic polity" which may be particularly relevant for developing countries in which popular participation cannot be easily mobilized and there is a need for political tutelage.

PHILLIPS, HERBERT P. **Thai Peasant Personality.** Berkeley: University of California Press, 1966, 231 p.

This is a classic anthropological study based on psychological projective tests. Field work was carried out in a typical rice farming village northwest of Bangkok. Observations of village life and practices are systematically related to existing literature about Thai national character.

The unique importance of the study is the elaborate sentence completion test which Phillips designed to find out about such matters as the Thai peasant's attitudes toward authority, feelings of aggression, achievement and failure, dependency, and their notions of good and evil. Phillips' test questions have been widely utilized by other scholars working with different peasant cultures and thus have become an important standard of measurement for cross-cultural comparisons.

The findings of the study suggest that Thai peasants have a more complex and subtle personality than stereotypes of peasants might suggest. Although the peasants' life must be focused on material matters and practical considerations, there is also room for considerable cultural variation.

STEINBERG, DAVID J. and OTHERS. **Cambodia: Its People, Its Society, Its Culture.** New Haven: Human Relations Area Files, rev. ed., 1959, 350 p.

This is the most comprehensive, scholarly introduction to Cambodia published to date. Professor David Steinberg and his associates, who included Bernard B. Fall, collected a tremendous mass of information about every aspect of life in Cambodia and have presented their findings in lucid and orderly chapters that are models of summarization in each of the social science disciplines.

The essays were originally based on data of the early and mid-1950s, but Herbert H. Vreeland did seek whenever possible to update the information to 1959. Thus, the focus of the work is on the situation shortly after Cambodian independence when Norodom Sihanouk was most active in identifying his personality with the evolving character of the ancient Khmer people as they reëstablished their sense of nationhood. The political reporting is balanced and neither caters to the pretensions of the Cambodian rulers nor displays any unsympathetic sentiments about the Cambodian people.

The great strength of the work is the skill with which anthropological information, ranging from the analysis of class structure and family life to cultural values and descriptions of the Cambodian's spirit world, is related to national patterns of development.

BURMA

CADY, JOHN FRANK. **A History of Modern Burma.** Ithaca: Cornell University Press, 1958, 682 p.

This substantial history focuses on the political evolution of Burma during the last century and a half. The central theme is the growth of Burmese nationalism and the struggle for independence. Based almost entirely on English-language sources, the work nevertheless retains an admirable objectivity. Professor Cady has carefully collected and sifted a great mass of material from reports and periodical publications, with some new additions from missionary records. The result is a history of the Burmese people, and not merely the record of their rulers and exploiters. The author is particularly illuminating in his first part, "Old Burma," which provides an admirable picture of society and culture in the late eighteenth and early nineteenth centuries. The long middle section covering British rule and renascence of Burmese nationalism is a well-modulated and balanced account, which also reaches out from the capital into the countryside. The chaotic and centrifugal politics of Burma's 1920s take on an understandable pattern. The goals of such disparate persons as U Ottama, J. A. Maung Gyi, Ba Maw, U Saw and Chit Hlaing emerge compatibly, as different approaches to the common goal of self-rule. For the period up to independence, the book profits from intensive research and the author's close association with the Burmese scene. It includes a useful glossary and bibliography. A supplementary chapter carrying the story to 1960 was added to successive editions published since that date.

TINKER, HUGH. **The Union of Burma: A Study of the First Years of Independence.** New York: Oxford University Press (for the Royal Institute of International Affairs), 3rd ed., 1961, 424 p.

Professor Tinker of London's School of Oriental and African Studies provides a clarifying description of the problems confronting independent Burma as viewed in 1955, when he served as visiting lecturer at the University of Rangoon. Background data include a brief assessment of British rule since 1885 plus thoughtful introductions to the several topical chapters. The latter cover the origins and course of Burma's civil strife from 1948 to 1952, problems of economic planning, difficulties of political and governmental administration, cultural and social trends, and problems of trade, defense and external relations. The study merits a wide reading. The author's interpretations reflect his moderate Anglophile predilections regarding the character of British colonial rule and the proper status to be assigned to Burma's nationalist hero, Thakin Aung San. However, his assessment about Burma's prospects of developing a successfully functioning social democracy was over-optimistic.

Originally published in 1957, the book's third edition differs only in the addition of a few pages of new materials covering events to 1960, which are appended to the several chapters without altering the pagination.

TRAGER, FRANK N. **Burma—From Kingdom to Republic.** New York: Praeger, 1966, 455 p.

As a government official and a research scholar, Frank N. Trager has become identified as one of the most knowledgeable Westerners on contemporary Burma.

Author of numerous books, articles and bibliographies on Burma, he has in this volume produced a perceptive history that combines scholarship with highly personal interpretations. The tone is continuously sympathetic to the Burmese nationalists, possibly to the point of being, at times, unrealistically optimistic about what an independent Burma can accomplish.

Although written after the split in the nationalist ranks and after the introduction of military rule, Trager's book has little to tell about domestic Burmese politics. The focus is more on the development plans of the government, the problems of the insurgencies and, above all, on Burma's foreign relations. His review of U.S.– Burmese relations is detailed, and generally critical of American insensitivities and defensive of Burmese sensitivities. His explanation of Burmese neutralism is generally valid, but events have demonstrated that he underestimated the historic Burmese cravings for isolation.

PYE, LUCIAN WILMOT. **Politics, Personality, and Nation Building: Burma's Search for Identity.** New Haven: Yale University Press, 1962, 307 p.

This is a path-breaking book on the political psychology of leadership in the new states emerging from colonialism. Based on detailed interviews with colonially trained administrators and nationalist politicians, the result is a description of the political culture of Burma. These results are related to patterns of Burmese personality development that have been noted by anthropologists.

The book directed attention to the "crises of national identity" in societies torn between a traditional heritage and exposure to the modern world. Rapid social and political change produces psychic strains which play upon the deeper culturally implanted feelings of insecurity. The work suggests that as long as leaders and the dominant political class of a country are basically unsure of themselves they will have difficulties in establishing the stable organizations necessary for successful nation building.

Although the significance of this study extends far beyond the Burmese case, it is also noteworthy for having appeared at a time when most books were stressing a constructive version of Burmese nationalism and thus failed to foresee what has become the path of Burmese politics.

DONNISON, FRANK SIEGFRIED VERNON. **Public Administration in Burma.** New York: Royal Institute of International Affairs (in coöperation with the International Secretariat, Institute of Pacific Relations), 1953, 119 p.

The author of this brief monograph served in the Indian civil service from 1922 to 1948, ending his career as Chief Secretary for Burma. He represents the official colonial point of view, which held no brief for the disruptive but historically inevitable forces of militant Asian nationalism. He assesses favorably the achievements of the British colonial administration and raises the question of why it disappeared from Burma while it carried on in Ceylon and India. The author concludes that London's attempts to introduce steps toward self-government in Burma during the 1920s and 1930s were misguided. The Burmese were simply not ready to assume such responsibilities because of the country's relative isolation, lack of knowledge and interest in the outside world, and the prevailing low standard of education. He terms particularly disastrous the British decision of 1923 to eliminate Burmans from the Indian army in favor of minority tribal contingents. This meant, he alleged, that an effective defense against the Japanese was impossible and that the postwar Burma government lacked an indigenous army capable of preserving internal order and promoting an orderly transition to independence. Thus, London's attempted response to prewar political turmoil was all a mistake, while the traumatic experience of warfare and Japanese occupation were presumably incidental considerations. The British-Indian administration should have been more firm. The monograph itself is historically dated and significant for that reason.

WALINSKY, LOUIS JOSEPH. **Economic Development in Burma 1951–1960.** New York: Twentieth Century Fund, 1962, 680 p.

Walinsky served for six years as the ranking officer in the Robert R. Nathan Associates advisory team charged with the task of implementing Burma's economic development program. This articulate and comprehensive account of his experience in the task covers both the personal and political difficulties encountered as well as the international pressures to which the Nathan group was subjected. The author presents a narrative account of the entire nine-year period, followed by a detailed analysis of functioning difficulties encountered in particular sectors of the economy. A concluding section estimates the wider relevance of his experiences in Burma, followed by an apologetic interpretation of the American advisory role.

Actually, the requisite resources of administrative talent, capital resources and business experience were simply not available, as the candid World Bank report of 1953 had suggested. Walinsky and his associates, following the line of positive thinking, elected to encourage Burmese expectations that socialist planning would provide a short path to economic development and prosperity and would lead in turn to peace and order. However, potentially profitable enterprises faltered badly under inefficient public management, while such foolish but prestige-laden projects as a steel mill (*sans* ore and coal) were insisted upon. Much of the advice contributed by the Nathan group was not relevant to Burma's absorptive capacities, while total salary costs ran prohibitively high. General Ne Win eventually cancelled the entire program as useless. Walinsky's book is a valuable case study of the factors contributing to planning failure in Burma, underscoring the crucial importance of governmental competence. His prescription of charismatic leadership and group coördination is less than convincing, in view of the records of both Nu and Sukarno.

SCOTT, SIR JAMES GEORGE. **The Burman, His Life and Notions.** New York: Norton, 1963, 609 p.

Republication through Asia Society sponsorship of this classic description of the folkways and governmental system of pre-British Burma is an event of scholarly significance, since earlier editions of the work (1882, 1895, 1909, 1921) have long been out of print. Sir James George Scott, who used the pen name of Shway Yoe (Golden Honest), spent some 30 years among the people whom he so understandingly describes. Much that he relates is relevant not only to present-day Burma but also to neighboring Southeast Asian peoples of similar cultural antecedents. Cosmology, religion, family life, magical practices and social custom generally have been stubbornly resistant to modernistic change. The 64 chapters of **The Burman** cover a great variety of topics, ranging from circumstances of birth and childhood, schooling, life-cycle rituals, marriage and domestic life, Buddhism and animistic cults, to economic life, popular entertainment, superstitions, language and literature. The author devotes several chapters to a description of the governmental system and the royal Court of the Burma Kingdom as it functioned under King Thibaw prior to 1882. As a historical and cultural document, **The Burman** is probably unmatched in any other country of Southeast Asia and constitutes an indispensable reference for all serious students of Burma of whatever academic discipline. One must be grateful for its preservation in so convenient and attractive a form.

HTIN AUNG, MAUNG. **A History of Burma.** New York: Columbia University Press, 1967, 363 p.

The former Rector of the University of Rangoon and onetime head of the Burma Historical Commission is an authority in the area of folklore rather than history. He writes in beautiful English but in the spirit of the traditional chroniclers of the Burmese Court. Burma's Buddhist-oriented culture was contemptuous of idle talk about historical happenings, except as they might illustrate the *maya* principle of the impermanence of mundane affairs or possibly contribute moral guidance for the art of government. The successive historical chronicles sponsored by the Burmese Courts were intended to enhance dynastic prestige and ethnic pride, but paid little serious concern to factual accuracy per se. Htin Aung's traditionalist-style history similarly rejects the meticulous scholarship of Professor Gordon Luce and his students at the University of Rangoon, along with other research studies dealing with more modern times. He makes no attempt to appraise the traditional accounts in the light of available evidence and completely ignores the European sources so abundantly available from the eighteenth century onward. When the Royal Chronicles fade out after 1880, the author makes his own subjective selection of events and interpretations. Numerous factual inaccuracies mar the apparently memory-based account of the inter-war period in particular. The author avoids risking any judgment covering the independence period, where everybody attains alleged heroic proportions. Htin Aung's book illustrates the difficulties of historical interpretation within tradition-dominated countries where values other than concern for factual accuracy prevail.

JOHNSTONE, WILLIAM C. **Burma's Foreign Policy: A Study in Neutralism.** Cambridge: Harvard University Press, 1963, 339 p.

Professor Johnstone's study of the background and development of Burma's foreign policy from 1948 to 1962 is based on a series of Research Project papers prepared during the course of the 1950s by the Rangoon-Hopkins Center at the University of Rangoon. The account is well informed, but it reflects overmuch the cold-war dichotomy characteristic of the American viewpoint at the time. The historical narrative is followed by separate chapters covering Burma's relations with China, its participation in the United Nations and the author's attempted critical appraisal. Particularly useful are the full texts of the Sino-Burma border treaty of 1960 and the 1962 Manifesto of Burma's Revolutionary Council. Socialist ideology proved internally attractive as a means of realizing the goal of a welfare state. Objectives included independence from alien domination of the economy by means of state-developed industrialization and public ownership of land and other means of production. The initial pro-Western orientation of Burma's external relations did not long survive the suppression of the communist-promoted rebellion of 1948–1952. The shift to a more neutralist policy after 1953 was due in part to Burma's anger over unacknowledged American assistance to China border refugees, to the apparent ineffectiveness of United Nations intervention in Korea, and to the consequent seeming necessity of Burma's coming to terms with Communist China. Both Khrushchev and Mao Tse-tung responded favorably to Burma's neutralist orientation. The account is somewhat labored and repetitive, but Johnstone's exposition commands serious consideration.

BUTWELL, RICHARD. **U Nu of Burma.** Stanford: Stanford University Press, 1963, 301 p.

Butwell's biography of U Nu deals briefly with his boyhood and his role as student and teacher, but concentrates quite properly on his career as leader in the fight for Burma's independence, as a Buddhist, internationalist, politician and prime minister. Major emphasis is placed on Nu's relationships with colleagues within the Anti-Fascist People's Freedom League, which emerged from the wartime experience. The book is as much a political and party history of independent Burma as it is a political biography.

Following Aung San's assassination in July 1947, U Nu became the central figure in Burma's postwar struggle for nationhood. The effort involved Buddhist revival, the attempted achievement of a welfare state and industrialization, plus the promotion of internal tranquility and positive neutrality in a politically polarized world, all within the framework of a parliamentary democracy. To this staggering task Nu brought the gifts of popular leadership, courage, idealism and a refreshing sense of humor. He also brought to it grave weaknesses, including impracticality, inability to establish priorities, a lack of administrative experience and executive ability, a tendency to make impulsive decisions and lack of capacity for sustained effort. Butwell's study shows evidence of careful, painstaking research, but it falls somewhat short of capturing the full complexity of the subject's character, his great strengths and serious weaknesses. The tragedy of his eventual failure as a political leader and statesman and the consequent loss which his country sustained is here overmuch submerged in the minutiae of personal relationships.

COLLIS, MAURICE. **Last and First in Burma (1941–1948).** New York: Macmillan, 1956, 303 p.

The task of preparing this biographical apologia for Burma's wartime Governor, Sir Reginald Dorman-Smith, was assigned to a Burmophile ex-judge famous as the author of **Trials in Burma** (London: Faber, 1938, 294 p.). Collis was afforded exclusive access to Sir Reginald's official and personal papers prior to their interment in the India Office Library. Taking over the governorship in March 1941, Sir Reginald managed to reach a personal accommodation with Premier U Saw, a likeable but crafty rascal, whom he encouraged to go to London in late 1941 to ask Churchill for postwar independence. Collis is at his best in depicting the ghoulish atmosphere of the episode of the Governor's last night in Rangoon shortly thereafter, before fleeing from the Japanese invasion, and in describing the tragic overtones of the refugee flight to India, but he has little to say about the wartime government-in-exile at Simla.

He is less than candid in references to the bitter feud which developed between the returning Governor and the Supreme Allied Commander, Lord Louis Mountbatten, at the conclusion of the war. Whereas Mountbatten accepted Aung San as a bona fide nationalist leader, Dorman-Smith and his Simla entourage, both Burmese and British, viewed the AFPFL leadership as both treacherous and treasonable. Premier Atlee's eleventh-hour cancellation of the warrant to arrest Aung San in April 1946, based in part on military considerations, ended Dorman-Smith's career. Collis's book is in rejoinder to this alleged betrayal of his hero by Mountbatten and London's Labor government. The argument would be more impressive if the author had adopted a detached point of view, had taken care to document his extensive research efforts, and had been willing to acknowledge the existence of contrary evidence.

MALAYSIA

EMERSON, RUPERT. **Malaysia: A Study in Direct and Indirect Rule.** New York: Macmillan, 1937, 536 p.

This substantial monograph was one of the important early contributions of American scholarship to the study of Southeast Asian affairs. It presents an original and perceptive comparison of British rule in Malaya with Dutch rule in Indonesia during the 1930s, superior in many respects to Furnivall's classic **Colonial Policy and Practice,** which compared British Burma with Dutch Indonesia. At the time of its appearance Emerson's work was acclaimed as the first and only adequate account of the history of modern Malaya, "thorough, comprehensive, and well documented." A British reviewer commented: "While many of Professor Emerson's conclusions will not commend themselves to those in control of the colonial dependencies to which they refer, they make stimulating and often salutary reading. . . . Professor Emerson has an acute mind. . . . He writes as a good American citizen who regards imperialism with distrust."

MILLS, LENNOX ALGERNON. **British Rule in Eastern Asia.** Minneapolis: University of Minnesota Press, 1942, 581 p.

Accurately described in its subtitle as a study of contemporary government and economic development in British Malaya and Hong Kong, this book suffered the misfortune of coming to birth at an awkward time. The loss of the original copy and maps, "owing to enemy action," was a lesser mishap than that it was written before the Japanese conquest of Southeast Asia but did not appear until both the territories with which it was concerned had fallen. Inevitably, therefore, it dealt with a world already undergoing drastic changes which were barely, if at all, foreshadowed in its pages. Thus the fortifications of Singapore, so swiftly overrun by the Japanese forces, were spoken of as among the strongest in the world, and any thought of a self-governing Malaya, seen as an oasis of unnatural political calm, was held to be "utterly premature." These time-induced adversities should not, however, be allowed to obscure the fact that Lennox Mills gathered and subjected to penetrating analysis an abundance of both political and economic material, including extensive footnote reference to a wide range of official reports and documents as well as other sources. More than two-thirds of the book is devoted to Malaya and the remainder to Hong Kong, with incidental comparative reference to the Dutch in the neighboring Indies and the United States in the Philippines.

JONES, STANLEY WILSON. **Public Administration in Malaya.** New York: Royal Institute of International Affairs (in coöperation with the International Secretariat, Institute of Pacific Relations), 1953, 229 p.

Written by a long-time officer in the Malayan civil service, this book reaches well beyond the relatively narrow scope suggested by its title. While the author does pay useful and significant attention to questions of public administration in relation to the handling of such matters as health, education, social welfare, agriculture, mining, labor and police, it also embraces within the limits of its brief compass a survey both of the history of the British connection with Malaya and of the whole range of Malayan government and politics as well. Thus the author covers the speedy transition, once intervention had been decided upon, from mainland independence to "British administration for and on behalf of the Rulers" in the Federated Malay States, and the repeated efforts to achieve a greater measure of uniformity among the F.M.S., the four northern unfederated states and Johore. The latter half of the book deals with the maladroit British handling of Malaya at the close of the war and with the somewhat chaotic appearance of politics and political parties, with the Emergency in the background. The hesitant birth of the Alliance Party, which held Malaya together until 1969, lay just ahead as the book was completed. Its last sentence expresses the fear, still not to be dismissed, that in a self-governing Malaya the Malays may undergo a gradual political eclipse because of their economic insignificance.

RATNAM, K. J. **Communalism and the Political Process in Malaya.** Kuala Lumpur: University of Malaya Press (for the University of Singapore), 1965, 248 p.

The heart of the problem which Dr. Ratnam, a political scientist at the University of Singapore, tackled in this book is the basic fact that Malaya is not a nation but a plural society in which Malays and Chinese compete for supremacy and survival, with a substantial Indian population in the background. The book is concentrated primarily on the seminal period 1945–1961 when, as a result of the war and constitutional reform, politics erupted in a previously nonpolitical country. Independence in 1957 underscored the inescapable necessity of coming to grips with the question, obscured by colonialism, as to who would rule whom and on what terms. As Dr. Ratnam put it, the confrontation could be defined in two key constitutional phrases: the "special position of the Malays" in its bearing upon the "legitimate interests of the other communities," with the added provision that the Malays felt themselves too weak to compete effectively in a system of free competition. Much of the ground which the book covered is familiar to students of Malaya, but the author pulled together a valuable mass of constitutional, electoral and political material and threw useful light on how it may be interpreted and evaluated. Malaya was the principal focus of his interest with little mention of Singapore and none of the forthcoming complications of Malaysia. Aware of impending future troubles, the concluding paragraph rightly warned of the need to spread the gospel of intercommunal partnership to all sections of the society and not to confine it to the present ruling élite.

PYE, LUCIAN WILMOT. **Guerrilla Communism in Malaya.** Princeton: Princeton University Press, 1956, 369 p.

This was the first detailed study of an Asian communist movement to be based on modern social science methods and intensive life history interviews with former party members. It provides insights into the psychological motivations and the human experiences of Asian peasants and workers as they enter a communist party and seek to advance in a party hierarchy. The work was carried out during the Emergency in Malaya, and although the subjects had all fought in the jungle struggle they had become politically activated under varying conditions and thus their private experiences provide a human basis for understanding the history of communism in an Asian society.

Since the subjects were Chinese, the work is useful for understanding not only Malayan developments but also the relationships between communism and Chinese culture and psychology. Also, as a study of a "People's Liberation" movement, this work is valuable in giving deeper understanding to Vietcong motivations in the Vietnam War.

The findings suggest that the appeal of communism in Asia is largely to restless, ambitious people who find little possibility for social advancement in their lives and who perceive in the party a way to a more satisfying and exciting life.

INDONESIA

FURNIVALL, JOHN SYDENHAM. **Netherlands India: A Study of Plural Economy.** New York: Macmillan, 1944, 502 p.

This is a survey of the history of the Dutch colonial era in Indonesia from 1600 to the mid-1930s. Its comprehensive quality makes it the best single history of the colonial era in Indonesia. Rather than being a mere chronology, Furnivall's book claims general relevance by postulating the theory of "plural economy." This theory contends that the Netherlands Indies, as well as other colonies, are plural societies "comprising two or more elements or social orders which live side by side, yet without mingling, in one political unit." Racial barriers as well as differences in economic functions distinguish these separate social orders. Because of the fragmented nature of the society, governments promulgate policies taking account of the racial and cultural divisions rather than putting forth policies applying universally to all groups. Likewise, because of these divisions, interests cannot be articulated by organizations having appeal across the whole breadth of the polity; instead demands tend to be those of separate social groups. In concluding, Furnivall points to political integration as being the most difficult problem facing plural societies. The history of Southeast Asia in the years since this book's publication has attested to the critical nature of the social divisions within colonial societies and the political conflicts flowing from them.

LEGGE, J. D. **Indonesia.** Englewood Cliffs: Prentice-Hall, 1964, 184 p.

Legge's volume on the history of Indonesia is noteworthy for the brevity and clarity with which it handles many of the major issues of Indonesian history. Many controversial themes brought forth by other major works on Indonesia are evaluated and synthesized. Legge deals with the whole gamut of Indonesian history—the Hindu kingdoms, the influence of Islam, the early colonial era from the sixteenth to the nineteenth century, the apex of Dutch rule (1870–1942), the rise of nationalism and the post-independence era to 1964. Two major themes frequently recur: the influence of geographic, ethnic and economic divisions on historical development, and the pattern of interaction between the rulers and the ruled. Both the past and present effects of these factors on Indonesian politics are considered. Legge's book supplies a most useful and lucid introduction to the history of Indonesia as it affects the future of that republic.

McVey, Ruth T., ed. **Indonesia.** New Haven: Human Relations Area Files Press, rev. ed., 1967, 600 p.

This work is the product of a highly talented collective research effort that was initially inspired by Karl J. Pelzer and ultimately completed under the editorship of Ruth McVey. It was originally published in early 1963 and revised in 1967. Consequently, the general tone is one of sympathy for Sukarno's efforts at guiding Indonesia into the modern world, and there is little recognition that the country would skirt as close to communism as it did or that it would so shortly reject the direction of Sukarno's leadership.

Most of the material, however, is of far more enduring significance than reports on Djakarta politics. Karl Pelzer provides a detailed and masterful introduction to the geographical, resource and agricultural foundations of Indonesian society. Hildred Geertz has produced an encyclopedic report on the cultures and ethnic communities of all the Indonesian islands. Robert van Niel deals objectively with the early history, and Herbert Feith gives a somewhat defensive interpretation of "guided democracy" under Sukarno. Mantle Hood's report on music and the theatre on both Java and Bali is truly exceptional. Douglas S. Paauw and Everett D. Hawkins struggled with explaining aspects of the Indonesian economy, but since they were not prepared to acknowledge that conditions were as bad as they were under Sukarno, their contributions are the most dated.

Kahin, George McTurnan. **Nationalism and Revolution in Indonesia.** Ithaca: Cornell University Press (for the International Secretariat, Institute of Pacific Relations, and Southeast Asia Program, Cornell University), 1952, 490 p.

Nationalism and Revolution in Indonesia is the most extensive and exhaustive study available on the Indonesian revolution. It includes chapters on the genesis of the nationalist movement, the Japanese occupation, the military and diplomatic course of the struggle, the political infighting between revolutionary leaders and the movement away from the Dutch-sponsored federal structure to the unitary state after independence. Its strong point is the richness of the historical data presented on both the war and the internal politics of the revolution. The treatment of the revolution is strongly (some might say, uncritically) pro-nationalist, and as such it is more useful for understanding the nationalists than for understanding the motives and policies of the Dutch, the U.N. and the United States. The portrait of the nationalist leaders leaves one ill-prepared for the chaos that descended upon Indonesia under their leadership during the first 15 years of independence. A more skeptical observer might have revealed the weaknesses of the revolutionary élite as well as its strengths. In spite of these flaws, however, Kahin's work remains absolutely essential to the study of Indonesian political behavior.

Feith, Herbert. **The Decline of Constitutional Democracy in Indonesia.** Ithaca: Cornell University Press (for the Modern Indonesia Project, Southeast Asia Program, Cornell University), 1962, 618 p.

This extremely rich study, synthesizing earlier findings as well as presenting a large quantity of original information, concerns the political history of the period from December 1949 to March 1957—that is, from the conclusion of the Indonesian revolution until the replacement of parliamentary democracy with guided democracy. It supplies detailed information on the rise and fall, political composition and issues confronting each of the cabinets of the period. The introduction, conclusion and two other chapters sketch the major trends and provide an analytical framework. Feith proposes that the era can be viewed as a struggle between two groups within the Indonesian élite: the "administrators" and the "solidarity makers." The administrators were Western-educated, bureaucratically skilled and more oriented toward unexciting technical problems of economic management and administration. In contrast, the solidarity makers, as epitomized by Sukarno, concentrated on the problems of national identity, the excitements of foreign policy and the construction of mass organizations. Feith argues that the decline of constitutional democracy was a process by which the administrators lost out politically to the solidarity makers. While Feith's conceptualization may be criticized for viewing Indonesian history by starting from a Western model of democracy, his book must still be judged as the single best political history written about Indonesia since the Second World War.

VAN LEUR, JACOB CORNELIS. **Indonesian Trade and Society: Essays in Asian Social and Economic History.** The Hague: Van Hoeve, 1955, 465 p.

This volume of essays by a Dutch historian furnishes a provocative challenge for formulations of the history of Indonesia and other Asian nations which stress the lasting effects of successive waves of foreign cultural and economic influence. Van Leur argues that enduring influence upon Indonesia by Indian culture and by the Dutch colonials was much more limited than is usually assumed. Indonesia's basic political and social structures were substantially formed prior to the Indian infusion, and, at least until the nineteenth century, the impact of the Dutch upon Indonesian society was not overwhelming. The author is sharply critical of those who portray Indonesian history as suddenly evolving into a new era with the advent of the European traders and adventurers. Indonesia grew from its own traditions rather than being merely the creation of external Indian and later Dutch influences. Van Leur contends that this Euro-centric view of Asian history fails to perceive the steadfast continuity of Indonesia's traditional structures. His thesis was highly original when first espoused in Holland during the 1930s, and it has relevance today because Indonesia in many ways continues to be a nation in which traditional society seems not to be passing. The history of the post-colonial era has reinforced Van Leur's thesis that Western dominance was not nearly so permanent and penetrating as the early European colonial historians assumed.

WERTHEIM, WILLIAM FREDERICK. **Indonesian Society in Transition.** The Hague: Van Hoeve, 1956, 394 p.

The most striking aspect of Professor Wertheim's volume is its wide-ranging scope. Initially it surveys the ethnic and geographic scene, comments upon general social developments in South and Southeast Asia, and gives a general outline of Indonesian political history down to 1955. With this background, Wertheim discusses social change by appraising the economic system, changes in the status system, urban development, labor relations, cultural factors and nationalism. Each topic is dealt with by assessing the pre-colonial situation, the Dutch imperium, the Japanese occupation and the development of Indonesia after 1945. Throughout, the data brought to bear from many and varied sources is impressive, and the interpretation is stimulating. Of particular interest is Wertheim's thesis that Western individualism arrived on the scene "too late" and that social development was proceeding according to a model in which the individual's interests and identity are submerged in collective groups. Wertheim's account is, however, misleading in that he has extended this basically sound cultural insight into an inappropriate form of class analysis. Indonesian political and social behavior is not amenable to such economic determinism. However, the author's penchant for class analysis in history does not detract from the overall worth of the volume which is derived from the scope and detail of its presentation.

VAN NIEL, ROBERT. **The Emergence of the Modern Indonesian Elite.** The Hague: Van Hoeve, 1960, 314 p.

Robert van Niel's **The Emergence of the Modern Indonesian Elite** provides an in-depth historical study of the process of social change between 1900 and 1927. Concentration is placed upon the ethical policy that dominated the philosophy of

government for the first 20 years of this century in Indonesia. Through encouragement of participation in political, economic and cultural organization, and most of
all through exposure to Western education, the colonial governors sought to transform Indonesian society in the image of the West. As a result of the expansion of
education and the inclusion of increasing numbers of Indonesians in the state's
administration, the Indonesian élite became more heterogeneous, less hereditary
and more open to the organizations which eventually would control the bureaucratic and political destiny of independent Indonesia. The philosophy of governing
reverted during the 1920s to an overtly dualistic policy emphasizing separateness of
cultures, economic benefits and political privileges rather than the integrationist
orientation of the ethical era. This alternate colonial policy, along with the onset of
worldwide economic depression, provides the background for the growth of greater
radicalism and the genesis of the Indonesian nationalist movement.

Van Niel emphasizes the split within the Indonesian élite between the functional
élite (those continuing to work for limited gains within the Dutch system) and the
political élite (those who could not envision substantial improvement without
political independence from Holland). In addition, he focuses on the problems of
organizational fragmentation. The birth pangs of organizations such as *Budi
Utomo, Sarekat Islam,* the *Muhammediajah* and the *Perserakatan Nasional Indonesia* foreshadow many of the problems of political and governmental organization
that have continued to plague Indonesia in the years since independence.

SELOSOEMARDJAN. **Social Changes in Jogjakarta.** Ithaca: Cornell University Press,
(for the Modern Indonesia Project, Southeast Asia Program), 1962, 440 p.

Selosoemardjan is peculiarly well suited to write a book on social change in
Indonesia because of his experience as an Indonesian civil servant at various levels.
He served in the Jogjakarta civil administration from 1935 to 1948, and since 1947
he has been the private secretary of Sultan Hamengkubuwono IX, who has occupied high positions of national authority in the Indonesian government. The book
surveys the social changes intentionally brought about by reforms instituted by the
Sultan's government in Jogjakarta during and after the revolution. Through these
changes the centralized autocratic nature of the administrative apparatus was
transformed along more democratic lines. In addition to describing the administrative system during the Dutch, Japanese, revolutionary and post-revolutionary eras,
Selosoemardjan concludes with a set of general theoretical propositions on social
change that were drawn from this case study.

BENDA, HARRY JINDRICH. **The Crescent and the Rising Sun.** The Hague: Van Hoeve,
1958, 320 p.

The Crescent and the Rising Sun is a history of the rise of Islam as a political
force in Indonesia up to the close of World War II. It traces the development of
Dutch colonial policy toward Islam, the development of Islamic political organizations and the relationship of these organizations to the traditional *prijaji* élite and to
the secular nationalists. The book's core concerns the growing importance of
Islamic political organizations during the 40 months of Japanese occupation. The
Japanese initially cultivated the Islamic political leaders in preference to the secular
nationalists. The competition between the nationalists and the Islamic political
leaders, which had great significance during the first 20 years of independence, is
shown to have its roots in the colonial past and most of all in the history of the
Japanese occupation. Benda's book is the most detailed study available of this
occupation, and it provides data vital to all who wish to understand the postwar
role of Islam in Indonesian politics.

GEERTZ, CLIFFORD. **The Religion of Java.** New York: The Free Press, 1960, 395 p.

The Religion of Java stands out among Professor Geertz's many distinguished
contributions to the study of behavior and beliefs at the town and village levels in
Indonesia. When this book is considered along with **The Social History of an**

Indonesian Town (Cambridge: M.I.T. Press, 1965, 217 p.), **Agricultural Involution: The Process of Ecological Change in Indonesia** (Berkeley: University of California Press, for the Association of Asian Studies, 1963, 176 p.) and **Peddlers and Princes: Social Change and Economic Modernization in Two Indonesian Towns** (Chicago: University of Chicago Press, 1963, 162 p.), Geertz's work must be judged the most important contribution to understanding Indonesian culture by a single person during the past decade.

The Religion of Java presents a detailed anthropological account of the rituals, beliefs and social effects of the three distinct religious strains visible beneath the guise of nearly universal Islam in Indonesia. According to Geertz, these three variants—the *abangan,* the *santri* and the *prijaji*—dominate the life styles of three different sectors of the social structure—the village, the market place and the government bureaucracy, respectively. The *abangan* tradition, emphasizing ritual feasts and animistic beliefs, has characterized Javanese village religious orientations since long before the coming of Islam. In contrast, the *santri* variant enjoins careful adherence to Islamic doctrine and intolerance of heterodox beliefs. The *prijaji* world view descends from the traditional court culture and the Hindu-Buddhist influence predating the arrival of Islam in Indonesia. In addition to being dominant among the upper levels of the government bureaucracy, the *prijaji* life style provides a model for correct etiquette and behavior in many ways for the entire society. This threefold classification of life styles and religious orientations has provided the point of departure for much research presently in progress on religion and politics in Indonesia.

EAST ASIA

CHINA

Pre-1911 Revolution

TENG, SSU-YU and FAIRBANK, JOHN KING. **China's Response to the West: A Documented Survey, 1839–1923.** Cambridge: Harvard University Press, 1954, 296 p.

This is a seminal work in modern Chinese history, which led to the writing of many dissertations and monographs. Until it appeared, most accounts of Sino-Western relations concentrated on the diplomatic aspects and relied heavily on Western sources. This book was instrumental in ushering in a period in which institutional, social and intellectual aspects of the contact have received increasing attention.

No mere compilation of translated material, the book's introductory sections and editorial comments are themselves of high value. After discussing the Manchu dynasty's early and limited contact with the West, the book treats in turn the accelerated Western pressure on China, the beginnings of China's recognition of the need to strengthen herself, the acquisition of arms and machinery, and the many modernization efforts of the "self-strengthening" movement. It then deals with the basic political and intellectual reforms, such as the rivalry between constitutionalists and revolutionaries and the debate among the adherents of the various intellectual trends of the 1920s. Its wide use today demonstrates the continuing value of the book.

FAIRBANK, JOHN KING. **Trade and Diplomacy on the China Coast: The Opening of the Treaty Ports, 1842–1854.** Cambridge: Harvard University Press, 1953, 2 v.

The theme of this influential book, which has done more to shape the historiography of Chinese foreign relations than any other single work, is China's response to the West's intrusion in the mid-nineteenth century, regarded as not so much a shattering blow as a stimulus toward the gradual metamorphosis of Chinese institutions. Fairbank first explains the workings of the Chinese tributary system, which brought other countries under the symbolic sway of the Emperor, then the evolution of the Canton trading system and the increasing tension between Chinese authorities and Western free traders which culminated in the Opium War of 1839–1842. The most detailed portions concern the consequences of the treaty settlement: the growth of new ports and reorganization of trade, the ensuing disruption of Chinese society and the rise of the Taiping rebels, whose armies threw foreign consuls and native prefects into a mutually protective "synarchy" to rule China together. The key to this institutional coöperation was the foreign inspectorate of customs (later the Imperial Maritime Customs), established in Shanghai in 1854 and later administered for the Chinese throne by Sir Robert Hart. To Fairbank, this is proof that the treaty system had incorporated the foreigner into the universal Confucian state.

Fairbank's thesis has been heartily attacked by those who feel it deprecates the intent of Western imperialism in China. That it should still merit such debate almost 20 years after its appearance is testimony to its influence. Whether one entirely accepts its conclusions or not, **Trade and Diplomacy** will remain a monumental classic in the history of Chinese foreign relations.

WRIGHT, MARY CLABAUGH. **The Last Stand of Chinese Conservatism: The T'ung-Chih Restoration, 1862–1874.** New York: Atheneum, rev. ed., 1966, 429 p.

When this book first appeared in 1957, it was described as "the outstanding work in print on Chinese history in the second half of the nineteenth century." That assessment still stands.

During the 1840s and 1850s the Ch'ing dynasty faced two extraordinary problems: the growing encroachment of the West, facilitated by the post-Opium War treaty framework, and mushrooming internal disorders, the most threatening of which was the famous Taiping Rebellion (1850–1864). A change of emperors in 1861–1862 paved the way for a more energetic approach to China's ills; in the ensuing decade new institutions were devised to cope with the Westerners and the rebellions were gradually brought under control. The hallmark of the new reign, however, was its valiant effort to put a gravely traumatized Confucian order back together again. This effort proved in vain. But it earned for the T'ung-chih period a secure place among the great restorations of imperial Chinese history.

Professor Wright's study of the T'ung-chih Restoration is a model of exacting and thorough scholarship, supported by bold analysis and a polished, forceful prose style. It matters little whether one accepts her central thesis, frequently iterated, that the ultimate incompatibility between the requirements of modernization and the requirements of Confucian stability doomed the Restoration from the outset. The lasting value of the book lies in its bibliographical sweep and in the judicious insights it offers into virtually every aspect of the Confucian state on the eve of its disintegration in the modern era.

HSÜ, IMMANUEL C.Y. **China's Entrance into the Family of Nations: The Diplomatic Phase, 1858–1880.** Cambridge: Harvard University Press, 1960, 255 p.

Chinese and Westerners in the mid-nineteenth century were possessed of very different conceptions and systems of inter-state relations. The Westerners premised that all sovereign states were formally and legally equal. The Chinese, on the contrary, saw China as a universal state, which non-Chinese peoples could approach only as subordinates and tributaries to the Emperor, the Son of Heaven.

Immanuel C.Y. Hsü has studied the process between 1858 and 1880 through which China gradually became reconciled to the Western concept of diplomatic relations. The major contribution of this work lies in the skillful description of the cultural assumptions determining China's diplomatic responses to the West. Hsü's narrative of the diplomatic history of this period between China and the foreign powers, together with his analysis of domestic political forces affecting Chinese foreign policy, make this a major monograph on Chinese foreign relations during the modern period.

LATOURETTE, KENNETH SCOTT. **A History of Christian Missions in China.** New York: Macmillan, 1929, 930 p.

This substantial work, half of which deals with the nineteenth century and half with the first quarter of the twentieth, has not been rivalled, nor significantly continued, in Chinese or other languages, although Catholic scholarship has advanced our grasp of the seventeenth and eighteenth centuries, and the manifold reports and articles from recent years would contribute importantly if the book were to be revised and extended to the 1950s.

Latourette's scholarship was marked by wide coverage and careful use of sources, and he unhesitatingly stated his dependence on materials in Western languages, including some so written by Chinese authors and some translated. (However, it is now recognized that for the period covered Chinese-language items were less insistently necessary to useful scholarship than they have now become.) Grasp and presentation by this Protestant student of significant Roman Catholic elements in the story were so able and fair as to win respect and use in the educational circles of that tradition.

The character of this volume can best be understood in the perspective of the author's continued work on China. In his later writings Latourette updated parts of this earlier work, notably in volume IV of **History of the Expansion of Christianity** and in volumes II and III of **Christianity in a Revolutionary Age** (New York: Harper, 1958–1962, 5 v.).

COHEN, PAUL A. **China and Christianity: The Missionary Movement and the Growth of Chinese Antiforeignism, 1860–1870.** Cambridge: Harvard University Press, 1963, 392 p.

Paul A. Cohen's carefully researched and well-written book is a ground-breaking effort at putting the Christian missionary encounter with China in perspective. He treats the missionary story as important both in modern Chinese history and in the development of the modern relationship between China and the West. His conclusions in both regards, however, are rather negative. Pressures exerted and privileges gained by foreign missionaries in the nineteenth century helped to undermine the already weakened Ch'ing dynasty and also to build up a good bit of animus between Chinese and foreigners.

The book is organized in two parts. The first, "The Anti-Christian Tradition," sees Chinese opposition to Christianity as part of a long practice of resisting heterodox ideologies. From seventeenth-century doctrinal refutations, Chinese anti-Christianity became progressively more "rabid and prolific," more xenophobic.

In the second part, "The Anti-Christian Tradition in Action, 1860–1870," the author shows how the anti-Christian tradition operated in post-Treaty of Tientsin circumstances to create a "critical turning point in modern Chinese history." Moving into the interior in the 1860s, Christian missionaries came into increasing rivalry with local gentry. Local Chinese officials were caught between the anti-Christianity of their gentry constituents and the demands of the Treaty Powers (and to a lesser extent of the Peking government) that local anti-Christianity be suppressed. The tensions generated in this multi-sided encounter led in the short run to such events as the Tientsin massacre of 1870. In the longer run the missionary presence and the xenophobia it exacerbated remained "the most prominent source of Sino-foreign friction in the Chinese interior right up to the end of the Ch'ing." The very inability of the Ch'ing to resolve this friction, the author suggests, was an important factor in the dynasty's demise.

HOU, CHI-MING. **Foreign Investment and Economic Development in China, 1840–1937.** Cambridge: Harvard University Press, 1965, 306 p.

The economic modernization of China, a process begun in the latter half of the last century and not yet completed, is a vast and complex subject. The present monograph, the result of wide-ranging research and careful reasoning, contains much information on the various aspects of foreign investment in China during the century before World War II and challenges the usual view regarding the long-range impact of that investment in China's modern history.

The first chapters give factual information on the development of foreign investment in China, including the foreign loans contracted by the Chinese government, as well as direct investment by foreign interests in many fields, from trade and banking to railroads and manufacturing; the ebb and flow of capital representing different countries are indicated. The most important portions of the book explain Hou's interpretation of the role of foreign investment in China's economic modernization through linkage and other types of effects and analyze the nature of the Chinese economy during this "dualistic" period, in which the traditional sector coexisted with a slowly growing modern sector.

Hou maintains that, on the whole, foreign investment since the nineteenth century had a positive effect on China's economic modernization, reasoning that the dualistic economy of China was able to overcome the destructive effects of foreign competition, while the presence of new forms of industry stimulated greater productivity in many areas. In China this occurred without creating a lopsided export development.

Quantitatively, Hou's conclusions seem valid up to a certain point, although the absence of some necessary components of the economy (the demographic element, for example) lends the appearance of a single-dimensioned statistical account to his analysis. Statistics, however, do not tell the whole story in cases involving fundamental societal change. This book is a useful study of one of the aspects of the economic transformation of China, but it should not be read as an integrative interpretation of the process of modernization.

FEUERWERKER, ALBERT. **China's Early Industrialization: Sheng Hsuan-huai (1844–1916) and Mandarin Enterprise.** Cambridge: Harvard University Press, 1958, 311 p.

In this interesting study, Feuerwerker discusses the various forces which retarded the processes of economic modernization in China in the late Ch'ing period. He does it by examining the modern enterprises under the system of *kuan-tu shang-pan* ("official supervision and merchant management") which in his view underlay all Chinese efforts toward industrialization. The enterprises he has chosen to study were those associated with Sheng Hsuan-huai, the official-industrialist; hence the subtitle of the book.

The author concludes that "the *kuan-tu shang-pan* industries remained marginal undertakings within their own environment," representing no "fundamental break with the traditional agrarian economy and the conservative economic outlook which reflected it." He attributes this to foreign economic pressure, impotence of the government, official exactions, inadequate capital accumulation, technical backwardness, bureaucratic motivation, traditional practices such as family and local ties, low valuation of mercantile and industrial activity, and the traditional relationship between officials and merchants.

Feuerwerker is very persuasive on all these points, but one is left with some doubt as to how the China Merchants' Company, the prototype of all *kuan-tu shang-pan* enterprises, could still be able to pay dividends of more than 10 percent consistently for decades. Technical analysis is severely limited by lack of data: only one annual report of some detail is examined—hardly sufficient to identify the sources of success or failure. One would also wish that the author had dealt with more emphasis on the notion that from a long-range perspective "the industries organized by Sheng Hsuan-huai represented a chipping away at institutional barriers."

In all, this is a very useful economic and social history of a period when modernization efforts met traditional barriers head-on.

LEVENSON, JOSEPH RICHMOND. **Confucian China and Its Modern Fate: A Trilogy.**
Berkeley: University of California Press, 1968, 3 v.

Joseph Levenson's trilogy is one of a small handful of truly seminal works on modern Chinese history and, quite possibly, the most exciting one of all. A probing, exploratory, trailblazing study, it necessarily provokes disagreement, but even its critics salute the book's erudition, subtlety and wit.

The book's *leitmotif* is the desperate struggle waged by Chinese during the last 100 years to maintain continuity with their tradition even as they fought to free themselves from it. This gigantic theme, inseparable from the lengthy history of one-fifth of the human race, became in Levenson's deft and sympathetic hands an epic tone poem of creative history. Rich in counterpoint, the trilogy weaves together chords from Chinese philosophy, art, politics and historiography to convert an ambiguous theme into a polyphonic one.

From two complementary angles, one intellectual and the other institutional, the first and second volumes explain China's break with Confucianism. In the first, entitled "The Problem of Intellectual Continuity," it is held that Confucian ideas and values atrophied because, under the weight of a "total Western invasion," men came to believe in them for emotional rather than intellectual reasons. Levenson argued that an idea dies if its believers feel in their hearts it must be true instead of being confident in their minds that it is true. According to the next volume, "The Problem of Monarchical Decay," Confucianism also withered because its life depended on its connection with monarchy and bureaucracy. The third volume, "The Problem of Historical Significance," explains how continuity has been maintained with a dead past. Distinguishing between the perpetuation of a living creed and the preservation of a depleted one, Levenson held that Confucianism has been preserved rather than perpetuated; the Chinese Communists, by managing to preserve as well as to innovate, have maintained continuity amidst revolutionary change.

Levenson died in 1969 at the age of 48, and this trilogy, written between 1952 and 1964, will stand as his final large-scale work. It has stimulated an entire generation of scholars and charted new areas for research that will be fruitfully explored for many years to come.

PURCELL, VICTOR. **The Boxer Uprising.** Cambridge: Cambridge University Press, 1963, 349 p.

Purcell's study of this dramatic anti-foreign movement in China at the turn of the century focuses on the nature of the movement and the circumstances under which it changed from being anti-dynastic to being pro-dynastic. The author traces the antecedents of the Boxers to the White Lotus group of secret societies. He shows that the Boxers comprised several diverse factions, and that they derived their ideas largely from popular novels and plays and their manpower largely from youth. Venting their wrath against Christian missionaries and Chinese converts, the Boxers became allies of the xenophobic officials as a result of two contemporaneous developments: the defeat of the leader of the anti-dynastic Boxer faction by government forces in October of 1899 and the increasing anti-foreignism of the Ch'ing court.

Purcell's book contains new details on the questions with which it deals. The first few chapters, however, serve more as a sampling of the (then) recent bibliography on nineteenth-century China than as an analysis of the historical setting. Despite the author's tendency to take an equivocal stand in the face of conflicting evidence, the book provides the groundwork for further inquiry into the subject.

WRIGHT, MARY CLABAUGH, *ed.* **China in Revolution: The First Phase, 1900–1913.**
New Haven: Yale University Press, 1968, 505 p.

This volume of essays by 12 historians from seven countries represents a first attempt at synthesizing recent researches into the background of the Republican revolution of 1911. Until her untimely death in 1970, the editor had done more than anyone else to promote the study of this crucial yet neglected period of Chinese history. Like most of the contributors in this volume, she has done intensive work on nineteenth-century China and views the events leading up to 1911 from that perspective rather than from the vantage point of the Communist revolution. The essays deal with the various classes and groups in China which, emerging out of the conditions of the nineteenth century, played decisive roles in the downfall of the Manchu dynasty, as well as with individuals and their ideas as they defined the shape in which the new China would be molded.

From such a historical perspective, most of the writers here do not doubt that revolutionary change was taking place in China in the first years of the twentieth century. What most fascinates the student of international affairs, however, is the picture that emerges from this volume of the close interaction between men, events and ideas in China and those in the West and elsewhere. Chinese history had become part of world history in the age of imperialism, and there were constantly developing dialectical interrelationships between forces inside and outside China. In this sense, these essays offer indispensable empirical studies of the way in which traditional societies come to be linked to the wider world politically, economically and intellectually.

Republican Period; Kuomintang

SHERIDAN, JAMES E. **Chinese Warlord: The Career of Feng Yü-hsiang.** Stanford: Stanford University Press, 1966, 386 p.

This biography contributes significantly to our understanding of China's history during the anarchical period of "warlord" politics in the 1920s and 1930s. Feng Yü-hsiang, popularly known (to Westerners, at least) as the "Christian general," was a principal figure during these years, though not, perhaps, a typical warlord either in respect to his aspirations or to his abilities.

As Sheridan's meticulously researched and vigorously written study makes clear, Feng was a man of far greater substance than the "baptism-by-firehose" legends to which he gave rise would suggest. A militarist of extraordinary energy and stature, not only physically, he was at the same time a shrewdly insightful politician and a naturally gifted leader of men. He was moved by an instinctive nationalism and possessed an intuitive social sympathy, equally innocent of ideological bias or a very firm sense of long-range purpose. These qualities, coupled with an unusual administrative competence, set Feng apart from most of his military and political rivals and made him, in an era of conspicuously cynical political selfishness, sometimes the most prominent and effective social reformer in China.

The warlord interlude has often been decried for its wastage of wealth and human life. One comes away from Sheridan's study not only with a clearer understanding of the political and military intricacies of the period, and of the complex phenomenon of warlordism itself, but also with a sense of the tragic waste of human talent sacrificed, as was ultimately the case with Feng Yü-hsiang, to the appetite for personal power and the simple passion for survival in a chaotic world.

WILLOUGHBY, WESTEL WOODBURY. **Foreign Rights and Interests in China.** Baltimore: Johns Hopkins Press, rev. and enl. ed., 1927, 2 v.

Foreign Rights and Interests in China is a survey of the official and semi-official declarations that formed the basis of the relations of foreign states and individual foreigners with China. Willoughby wanted to provide a reference book which would be of greater use to the non-expert than a collection of treaties and similar documents and would present a more comprehensive picture than the customary monograph.

Among the most important subjects Willoughby covers in this study are the agreements, largely extracted from China by the foreign powers, which led to the establishment and maintenance of spheres of interest, leased areas, concessions and settlements, the extraterritorial system, tariff controls and the stationing of foreign troops in China.

Foreign Rights and Interests in China is still a serviceable handbook. In some respects, however, it is inevitably badly outdated. Moreover, the circumstances under which it was written must be kept in mind. A leading American political scientist, Willoughby served for a considerable time as adviser to the Chinese government, beginning in 1916. The original one-volume edition of this book appeared shortly before the Washington Conference of 1921 and had an evident purpose. Essentially it was an appeal to the foreign powers to abandon their restrictions on China's sovereignty and to provide the Chinese with the "friendly, positive aid" that Willoughby was convinced would ensure their "rapid political and economic development."

CHOW, TSE-TSUNG. **The May Fourth Movement: Intellectual Revolution in Modern China.** Cambridge: Harvard University Press, 1960, 486 p.

The May Fourth Movement, as Chow Tse-tsung defines it, was more than the 1919 student protest against imperialism. It included the literary revolution, fundamental questioning of the Confucian ethic and the search for Western guides to China's modernization, the political emergence of such groupings as the proletariat and modern industrialists, and the growth of nationalism as the most powerful doctrine in urban China. Beginning about 1917, Chow traces the evolution of these divergent trends, their temporary coalescence in nationalist demonstrations in 1919, and their divergence again by 1921. Though certain intellectuals remained committed to inculcating liberal ideals through education, many turned to building political instruments to accomplish their goals. The nationalist and socialist forces overwhelmed the individualistic trends of May Fourth, Chow argues, because of emphasis on the primacy of the nation-state, foreign interference and factionalism among revolutionary groups. Thus Chow provides insights concerning the origins of the Chinese Communist Party and Kuomintang reorganization as well as detailed analysis of the intellectual upheaval between 1917 and 1921.

Chow's monograph is the standard work on a crucial period in China's revolutionary transition. Though it should be supplemented by economic studies, it is indispensable for understanding the search for a good society by Chinese intellectuals and the development of a tradition of political activism among twentieth-century Chinese students. To accompany his study, Chow published **Research Guide to the May Fourth Movement** (Cambridge: Harvard University Press, 1963, 297 p.); together, they provide a valuable reference for many publications, organizations and individuals important in the May Fourth Movement.

SHARMAN, ABBIE MARY (LYON). **Sun Yat-sen.** New York: Day, 1934, 418 p.

This is one of the first and best biographical studies of Sun Yat-sen, father of Republican China and Asian nationalist. Written in 1934, it has remained a standard work on modern China's tortuous path toward national development. The study covers the period of Sun's life from 1866 to 1925, focusing upon the interaction between Sun and his program for China's development and the environmental-situational context of the era. Sun emerges as a symbol of the mixed success of the Western impact upon China and a representative of the "transitory man" in modern Chinese society. As such, Sharman's biographical study is less an examination of Sun and his program than a chapter in China's search for a solution toward national development.

CH'IEN, TUAN-SHENG. **The Government and Politics of China.** Cambridge: Harvard University Press (for the International Secretariat, Institute of Pacific Relations), 1950, 526 p.

A comprehensive and critical examination of politics and government during the two decades of Chiang Kai-shek's rule of China, this book was completed just before that régime had lost control of the mainland. The author, a Western-educated political scientist and leading liberal of China, systematically analyzes the administrative, legislative, judicial and financial institutions of the government under the Kuomintang, and describes the factional disputes and personal cliques that divided the party, government and army. Ch'ien portrays a Kuomintang that had lost its capacity to govern; unable to perform its mission of political "tutelage," unwilling to share its power with other groups, it fell under the sway of Chiang Kai-shek, who was able to play one faction against another and build a personal machine based on his command of troops.

This material is treated in historical perspective. Introductory chapters outline the political thought and institutions of Confucian China and the struggles of the early Republic. Sun Yat-sen is given sympathetic yet perceptive treatment. There is a useful section on minority parties and an account of the futile struggle for parliamentary democracy during and after the war with Japan. Many of the author's observations are still pertinent today.

The book, a valuable reference work for the period, also contains an extensive bibliography and nine appendices of documents.

CHIANG, KAI-SHEK. **China's Destiny.** New York: Macmillan, 1947, 260 p.; Roy, 1947, 347 p.

The ideology of the later Kuomintang receives its fullest expression in **China's Destiny,** first published in China in March 1943. Its many Chinese printings, and its wide use in schools, the Youth Corps and the Central Political Training Institute, often with a specially prepared catechism, made it a Kuomintang political bible rivaling Sun Yat-sen's *"San Min Chu-I"* (The Three Principles of the People). In emphasis that reflects Chiang's bureaucratic-élitist rule, Confucian virtues are extolled throughout as the only sound basis for the Chinese nation-state. Cast in chronological sequence, its longest sections score the harmful effects of the unequal treaties, followed by chapters highlighting more recent Kuomintang history, and concluding with a detailed statistical tabulation of a ten-year program of economic reconstruction.

The Macmillan edition, the officially authorized English translation, lacks the critical and explanatory notes and the useful commentary of the Roy edition, which also adds a translation of Chiang Kai-shek's "Chinese Economic Theory," a shorter treatise designed for members of the inner party circle.

VAN SLYKE, LYMAN P., *ed.* **The China White Paper, August 1949.** Stanford: Stanford University Press, 1967, 2 v.

This work is a reissue of the original State Department publication (3573), **United States Relations with China: With Special Reference to the Period 1944–1949** (Washington: Government Printing Office, 1949, 1,054 p.), with the addition of a map, a useful index and an illuminating introduction by Professor Lyman P. Van Slyke. The **White Paper,** prefaced by Secretary of State Acheson's letter of transmittal to President Truman, includes a historical treatment and over 600 pages of appended documents. Its value lies in the official data made public regarding such important matters as the Yalta pact and China, the Chinese civil strife of 1944–1949, the Hurley and Marshall mediation missions, the Wedemeyer fact-finding mission and the nature and extent of U.S. postwar aid to China.

In 1949, all of those topics were the subject of controversy in the American political arena, and the **White Paper** promptly became the focus of fresh contention when it appeared. Professor Van Slyke reviews the publication in a political context. He offers analyses of the U.S. China policy, the development of American partisanship on the China issue, the polemics that raged around the State Department volume, and the effects of domestic partisanship on the conduct of U.S. foreign policy. Finally, he touches briefly on parallels between the situations in China in 1944–1949 and in Vietnam at a later date, the different American approaches to the two situations, and poses crucial questions raised by the record: "Are the goals of United States Asian policy justified? Is the United States able to achieve such goals?" The **White Paper,** he observes, suggests some answers but cannot provide all; others must be given by the nation.

Tsou, Tang. **America's Failure in China, 1941–50.** Chicago: University of Chicago Press, 1963, 614 p.

The whole problem of Sino-American relations since World War II has generated so much partisan and emotional controversy—indicating in part its vital importance for the world—that any writing about it can please only some people, while exasperating others. Professor Tang Tsou has a comprehensive thesis about American policy toward China since the Open Door notes which should satisfy more people than any other and which makes it required reading for all, of whatever political persuasion, who would seek some understanding.

His thesis, in brief, is that from the beginning of the twentieth century the United States has set certain goals for itself in China, and then has been unwilling or unable to commit the human and physical resources to achieve these goals. It has also refused to change its goals to conform to resources it was willing and able to commit. The inevitable result has been persistent failure.

In his admirable study Professor Tsou has refrained from trying to explain why the United States has so long adhered to this policy.

Boorman, Howard L. and Howard, Richard C., *eds.* **Biographical Dictionary of Republican China.** New York: Columbia University Press, 1967–1971, 4 v.

This indispensable work contains almost 600 biographical sketches, and no similar publication dealing with the same era compares with it in scope, detail and accuracy. The basic criterion for inclusion in the **Dictionary** is prominence in the public life of the Republican period of China, 1912–1949. However, careers that started before that period or continued after 1949 are fully described, so that most outstanding Chinese of the twentieth century are included, including many persons still alive. The articles are full, informative, balanced; the shortest entries are about 500 words, but the majority range between 1,000 and 2,000 words. Many are longer, such as the 15,000-word essays devoted to Mao Tse-tung and Sun Yat-sen. The fourth volume contains a few biographical articles, and two types of bibliographical data: lists of sources used in preparing each article and lists of the publications of persons described in the **Dictionary.**

There are some minor inconsistencies, but as a whole the **Dictionary** not only provides accurate biographical data not available elsewhere but gives more reliable factual information about the events and movements of those tumultuous years than any other work in English.

Chinese Communism to 1949

Wilbur, Clarence Martin and How, Julie Lien-ying, *eds.* **Documents on Communism, Nationalism, and Soviet Advisers in China, 1918–1927.** New York: Columbia University Press, 1956, 617 p.

This invaluable work makes available in English translation 50 documents selected from among those salvaged from a sensational historic raid, sanctioned by the diplomatic corps, on the office of the Soviet military attaché in Peking on April 6, 1927, by the warlord Chang Tso-lin. The editors, both deeply knowledgeable on the history of the Chinese revolution in the 1920s, have done an excellent job in selecting, authenticating and arranging the documents. They have also provided introductory essays throughout the volume which offer desirable historical and contextual information and give a measure of coherence to the work.

The documents reveal information on the Chinese revolutionary movement, both Chinese Communist and Kuomintang, and the relationship of each of these parties to each other and to their Soviet advisers, to April 1927. The book focuses on actual developments within China, on the policies established on the scene and on the participating individuals.

NORTH, ROBERT CARVER. **Moscow and the Chinese Communists.** Stanford: Stanford University Press, rev. ed., 1963, 310 p.

Professor North's book combines careful textual exegesis, documentary research in Russian and Chinese sources, and penetrating analysis of the interaction between Russia and the Chinese Communists. The author is at his best in the first half, examining the origins of Bolshevik strategy and tactics toward China through theory and practice as manifest in the writings of Lenin and the workings of the Third Communist International (Comintern). He admits to severe source limitations for the period after 1929. More recent scholarly works, and others scheduled to appear in the near future, provide better insight into this later period. Except for a superb final chapter which sums up the Sino-Soviet split, the revised edition is virtually identical with the original 1953 work. The durability of Professor North's analysis testifies to his perceptive understanding of the dynamic elements in Sino-Soviet relations. His lucidity and accuracy make this a book of equal utility for scholar and layman.

ISAACS, HAROLD R. **The Tragedy of the Chinese Revolution.** Stanford: Stanford University Press, rev. ed., 1951, 382 p.

This early study of the Chinese revolution of 1925–1927 still exercises an influence upon more recent scholarship and upon public attitudes toward China. Based on four years of research, the book was first published in 1938 and was soon regarded as a classic. In the revised 1951 edition, Professor Isaacs has, he informs us, cut out polemical excesses, subjective comments and repetitious arguments. His purpose is to describe what happened in the revolution with maximum fidelity to the historical record.

It is the author's thesis that the revolution was largely a spontaneous worker-peasant uprising that was subverted and sacrificed by Stalin to Russian national interests. The tragedy was that as a consequence a reactionary Kuomintang régime under Chiang Kai-shek was imposed on China. The narrative is supported by considerable documentation, yet there are aspects of the thesis which cannot be sustained by the evidence.

The view of a largely spontaneous proletarian revolution takes scant account of the extensive organizational and ideological efforts of young communist intellectuals; it requires an exaggeration of the numbers and maturity of the proletariat as a class; and it discounts the military aspects of the revolution. The Russian-made débâcle thesis rests upon the assertion that, had the proletariat and peasantry been unleashed in the spring of 1927 to fight Chiang Kai-shek for hegemony, instead of being restrained on Stalin's orders, they would have been victorious. This is speculative.

In placing his work in a wider context, Isaacs generalizes that the subversion of indigenous social revolutionary movements by national policies and strategic interests has been a major facet of recent Asian history. In the concluding chapters, he attempts to show the consequences, for both China and Russia, of the malformation of the Chinese revolution.

SCHWARTZ, BENJAMIN I. **Chinese Communism and the Rise of Mao.** Cambridge: Harvard University Press, 1951, 258 p.

Professor Schwartz's classic study of the early years of the Chinese Communist movement combines the best features of political history and the history of ideas. His analysis illuminates many obscure doctrinal disputes without losing sight of the social forces and political intrigues which shaped those disputes. The book demonstrates how Marxism, previously neglected by the Chinese intelligentsia, became a potent force after 1919 because of the combination of nationalist fervor unleashed by the Versailles peace settlement, the appeal of Lenin's theory of imperialism and the example of Bolshevik success. Subsequently, the growth of the Chinese Communist Party (CCP), competing revolutionary strategies and intra-party power struggles in the 1920s and early 1930s are skillfully discussed. Careful attention is

given throughout to the role of the Comintern in issuing ambiguous policy directives, manipulating without fully controlling the CCP, and protecting Stalin's
political interests under cover of shifting ideological formulations. Always the
realist, Schwartz argues that none of the strategies offered in the pre-1927 period by
Stalin, Trotsky or any of the Chinese factions could succeed given the basic
political-military strength of the Kuomintang.

A major contribution of the book is its analysis of the gradual emergence of Mao
Tse-tung after 1927 as the leading figure of the movement. It examines Mao's
formulation of a new strategy of revolution—one stressing Leninist party organization, mobilizing peasant grievances, developing armed revolutionary forces and
controlling a self-sufficient territorial base. Although later scholarship has shown
that Schwartz dated Mao's ascendancy in the CCP two years too early, his conclusion that it occurred independent of Moscow in response to Chinese realities
remains unshaken.

SNOW, EDGAR. **Red Star Over China.** New York: Random House, 1938, 520 p.

Red Star Over China was a journalistic scoop in 1938; it has since become a
historical classic. When Edgar Snow made his way through Nationalist lines to the
barren reaches of Shensi in June 1936, the Communists had only recently
emerged—exhausted and decimated—from their 6,000-mile Long March. Snow
found them developing the distinctive brand of communism that governed the lives
of a hundred million people by 1945 and enabled Mao to challenge Chiang for
nationwide power.

Many of the men whom Snow interviewed in 1936, including Chou En-lai, Chu
Teh and Lin Piao, appear today in the top echelons of the Peking hierarchy. The
best known section of the book is Mao's autobiography as related to Snow, which a
leading student of Mao's life and thought still deems "the single most important
and instructive document we possess." Another section unsurpassed by subsequent
Western historians is Snow's masterful description of the Long March.

Snow's sympathetic human portrayal of the Chinese Communists exposed him to
widespread criticism during the McCarthy years. However, there is little in this
work to provide substance for allegations that the author considered Mao and his
followers to be "agrarian reformers" rather than real communists.

JOHNSON, CHALMERS A. **Peasant Nationalism and Communist Power: The Emergence of Revolutionary China, 1937–1945.** Stanford: Stanford University Press,
1962, 256 p.

This work—partly descriptive, partly theoretical—is a pioneering study of the
growth of Chinese Communist Party (CCP) power during the Sino-Japanese War.
Johnson describes Japanese activities in China, CCP armies, CCP-controlled areas
in north and central China, and—for comparative purposes—the Jugoslav guerrilla
movement. The book closes with an essay on "communism in the service of the
nation-state."

Based on evidence drawn from Japanese sources, including many translated from
Chinese, Johnson argues that Japanese aggression and cruelty created a mass
peasant nationalism which was continuously mobilized and organized by the CCP.
Out of this organized nationalism grew the genuine popular support and strength
that carried the CCP to victory in 1949. Without the Japanese invasion, therefore,
the CCP could not have gained power, for its earlier agrarian program, in his view,
had had only a narrow appeal. Johnson views Tito's Jugoslav experience as functionally similar and believes that "peasant nationalism" represents a new type of
revolutionary power.

This influential thesis has been criticized as underplaying other equally important
factors. In particular, Johnson pays little attention to the CCP's social and economic programs at the local level, nor does he adequately explain popular support
for the CCP in regions where the Japanese rarely, if ever, came. Furthermore,
Johnson's vision of CCP success during the war reduces the subsequent civil war

period (1945–1949, when the Japanese were out of the picture) to an anticlimax
during which the CCP completed the victory it had already won.

Despite such shortcomings, this work is essential to an understanding of the
expansion of CCP power, both for its content and for the questions it raises.

BARNETT, A. DOAK. **China on the Eve of Communist Takeover.** New York: Praeger,
1963, 371 p.

This is an eyewitness account as well as a frequently shrewd analysis of events
that occurred in China during the five-year-long civil war (1945–1949) between
the Communists and the Nationalists which culminated in Communist domination
of the Chinese mainland. The author traveled extensively in areas ruled by the
Nationalists or their allies, and his insights into the weaknesses of Chiang Kai-
shek's régime and the reasons why it failed to offer effective resistance to the
Communists are impressive. He describes vividly and with great perceptiveness the
deterioration in conditions in the Nationalist-held cities, as well as the ineffectual-
ness of Kuomintang rule in the countryside, and he possesses an immense knowledge both of the dynamics of student opposition to Chiang's régime and of the
animosities which by dividing the Nationalist camp contributed so greatly to the
defeat of Chiang's armies. On the other hand, owing perhaps to the brief period of
time he spent in Communist-occupied territory, the author seems to underestimate
the strength of the forces which enabled the Chinese Communist Party to mobilize
the traditionally apathetic rural masses in its support and even win the backing of
much of the initially skeptical urban population.

Two other eyewitness accounts, Jack Belden's **China Shakes the World** (New
York: Harper, 1949, 524 p.) and Derk Bodde's **Peking Diary: A Year of Revolution** (New York: Schuman, 1950, 292 p.), should be read in conjunction with this
book.

MAO, TSE-TUNG. **Selected Works.** Peking: Foreign Languages Press, 1961–1969, 4 v.

The four-volume **Selected Works**—the officially sanctioned versions of Mao's
writings—consist of 158 selections from his many essays and speeches written from
1926 to 1949. First published in Chinese from 1951 to 1960, the volumes were
then translated into English by a special committee in Peking which revised and
edited the originals. In addition to these four volumes, the Chinese government has
released a few of Mao's post-1949 writings separately. But his pre-1926 writings
and the original versions of his articles in the **Selected Works** remain scattered in
other sources.

In spite of the sometimes substantial editing, these easily available volumes
provide a reliable general guide to the beliefs of the Chinese ruler. Here are Mao's
analyses of the social structure of China, his theory of contradictions, his egalitarian and voluntaristic impulses, his views on guerrilla warfare and his strategy for
the seizure of power in China. Themes which emerge repeatedly and hence form
the core of Mao's beliefs are his dialectical view of history, his distaste for rigid
bureaucracy and his confidence that man through sheer will can overcome all
difficulties. The volumes also yield clues to the evolution in Mao's thought as he
developed new solutions to the changing opportunities and problems he confronted.
In volume IV, for example, which covers works from 1945 to 1949, one senses
Mao's genuine surprise at the rapidity and ease of his victory over Chiang Kai-shek
in the civil war, and one sees him devise programs for the takeover of China's
cities.

In sum, the **Selected Works** remain the handiest entry into the mind of Mao Tse-
tung. Until an unexpurgated, comprehensive collection of his works becomes available, these volumes will be basic to an understanding of contemporary China.

SCHRAM, STUART. **Mao Tse-tung.** New York: Simon and Schuster, 1967, 351 p.

Making judicious use of primary sources and available monographs, Stuart
Schram has written a lucid and intelligent political biography of twentieth-century

China's perpetual rebel. In considering Mao Tse-tung's public career since the First World War, Schram lays stress on two key elements in Mao's political personality: revolutionary voluntarism and militant nationalism. Mao's greatness as a political leader, in this estimate, has been his success in combining the theory and practice of Marxism-Leninism with concepts and behavior patterns drawn from China's past, to make the mixture both comprehensible and acceptable to his compatriots. His limitation is that rather than a durable synthesis of communism and traditional Chinese ideas, Mao has produced an uneven amalgam ill-suited to the demands and dynamics of China's struggle to become a modern nation.

An American scholar who directs the Contemporary China Institute at the University of London, Schram is also the editor of **The Political Thought of Mao Tse-tung** (New York: Praeger, rev. ed., 1969, 479 p.).

People's Republic of China

BARNETT, A. DOAK. **Communist China and Asia: Challenge to American Policy.** New York: Harper (for the Council on Foreign Relations), 1960, 575 p.

This volume was the first comprehensive study of Communist China's role as an Asian power in the decade after 1949. Its central theme is the "challenge" Communist China poses for Asia and the resulting implications for future U.S. policies in the area. Though now outdated, **Communist China and Asia** provides much useful background data on such substantive topics as: China's national power resources; the development of Peking's economic and trade relations; overseas Chinese affairs; the Sino-Soviet alliance; China's relations with Asian states and communist parties; and the Taiwan dispute. The study is well documented and contains an excellent annotated bibliography of English-language sources.

As with most books which seek to be "policy-relevant," many of this study's major arguments and assumptions (*i.e.* Peking's growing "threat" to Asia; the stability of the Sino-Soviet alliance; the high industrial performance of the Chinese economy; the monolithic solidarity of the CCP; and the desire of non-communist Asian states to become "free societies based on democratic values") have been invalidated or weakened in the light of subsequent developments. On the other hand, this volume has lasting significance because it represents a good statement of the overall rationale behind the "containment" doctrine which governed U.S. policy toward China after the late 1950s.

ZAGORIA, DONALD S. **The Sino-Soviet Conflict, 1956–1961.** Princeton: Princeton University Press, 1962, 484 p.

This is an unusual and important book. Unusual, because it closely reflects the detailed and sophisticated research and analysis done by the author and his colleagues during a period of several years of government service spanning the eruption of the Sino-Soviet dispute into public view. Important, because the emergence of a bitter dispute in place of the previously more or less "monolithic" relationship between the two major communist powers is one of the main features of recent international politics, and because it is the only book in any language that approaches complete coverage in depth of this startling process. Thoroughly mature in approach and readable in style, it includes detailed and valuable references. It is excellent on the ideological and party aspects of the dispute; somewhat less so, but still adequate, on the state aspects (diplomatic, economic, military). The book has attained the status of a classic in its field and is literally indispensable to anyone trying to understand, let alone do serious work on, the Sino-Soviet dispute.

LIU, TA-CHUNG and YEH, KUNG-CHIA. **The Economy of the Chinese Mainland: National Income and Economic Development, 1933–1959.** Princeton: Princeton University Press, 1965, 771 p.

During the 1950s, the Chinese government set up a large and increasingly effective statistical organization and began publishing the results it obtained. Then in 1960 publication of almost all figures was stopped and has not since been renewed.

The Liu-Yeh volume represents the most systematic attempt to use the data of the 1950s to estimate China's national income and its component parts. For the year 1957 the authors use mainly official data to construct their estimates, while for the earlier years (and 1958–1959) they use a combination of official statistics and their own estimates or "corrections" of the official figures. In order to have a standard for comparison, they also calculate national income for a year (1933) prior to the Communist rise to power.

For the period of the 1950s, the authors indicate that modern industrial growth was rapid while that of agriculture and other traditional sectors more or less matched population growth. The latter conclusion is still a source of controversy as are the authors' estimates of the rate of growth in national income for 1952–1957 of 6 percent (in 1952 prices) or 4.4 percent (in 1933 prices) per year as contrasted to estimates of 8.7 percent (in 1952 prices) when only official data are used.

Whatever one's position on these controversies, the book remains the major work on Chinese national income and is an invaluable starting point for further work on the Chinese economy, past or present.

ECKSTEIN, ALEXANDER. **Communist China's Economic Growth and Foreign Trade.** New York: McGraw-Hill (for the Council on Foreign Relations), 1966, 363 p.

This book attempts to assess the contribution of foreign trade in Communist China to her economic development in the period 1949–1963. After specifying at the outset an analytical framework to be followed in the book, the author presents a picture of economic conditions existing in China in the pre-communist period and the economic development during the Communist era, an excellent summary of the findings from major studies then available about the Chinese economy. The latter part of the book concentrates on Communist China's economic relations with other countries. Actually, the author goes beyond the scope of foreign trade by including many thoughtful analyses on international credits and technical assistances received and provided by Peking. The basic data have been compiled by the author from Chinese, Japanese, Russian and English sources, and have been carefully adjusted to remove biases. The analyses are thorough and penetrating. In conclusion, the author shows, quite convincingly, the strength and weaknesses of the Chinese economy and suggests some policy implications for the United States.

This well-written book will remain one of the basic references for students of the Chinese economy and politics for many years, though a few points in it may have to be modified in view of the developments during and after the Great Cultural Revolution.

LEWIS, JOHN WILSON. **Leadership in Communist China.** Ithaca: Cornell University Press, 1963, 305 p.

This tediously written but none the less extraordinarily perceptive book describes and analyzes the methods used by the Chinese Communists to indoctrinate and motivate their élite or "cadre." Especially revealing is its discussion of the important process known as "self-struggle." Communist cadres are taught that within themselves, as well as in the society around them, there exist innumerable contradictions which they must continually strive to resolve. This has the effect of keeping conscientious Communists perpetually tense and insecure; however, the author feels that much of the dynamism in Chinese communism is the result of the self-criticism and incessant striving for individual perfection generated by this internal conflict.

Lewis also attaches great importance to the inseparability of knowledge and action in Chinese Communist thinking. According to him, Communist leaders believe that although action without knowledge is useless, knowledge itself is imperfect unless put into actual practice. Their aim is to inculcate in their cadres a knowledge of Marxism-Leninism, especially in its Maoist form, so thorough and deep-seated that these young Communists instinctively will act in accord with the tenets of communist theory. Another salient characteristic of the Chinese Communists to which he devotes considerable attention is their determination to rule through suasion and a popular consensus instead of arbitrarily and by means of coercion. This accounts for their preoccupation with organizing the masses, whom they wish to involve in so many directed activities and structured personal relationships that every Chinese will feel obliged to conform.

This book enlarges significantly our understanding of how communism affects the thinking and behavior of the Chinese.

SCHURMANN, FRANZ. **Ideology and Organization in Communist China.** Berkeley: University of California Press, 2d enl. ed., 1968, 642 p.

First published on the eve of the Cultural Revolution, Franz Schurmann's study constitutes a significant advance in the scholarly literature on the People's Republic of China. Its seven chapters treat ideology, party, government, management, control, cities and villages. They are woven together by the theme of contradictions and by his account of the interplay of ideological and organizational principles after 1949. Utilizing comparative data and a wide variety of analytical techniques, Schurmann provides a comprehensive analysis of Communist China's quest for a mode of modernization compatible with revolutionary doctrines and experiences.

In the second edition (which adds a 90-page supplement), Schurmann acknowledges the discrepancy between his earlier judgments and later events and downgrades ideology and organization while assigning greater weight "to the resurgence of the forces of Chinese society." The supplement draws its data from the Cultural Revolution (or its antecedents) and discusses its principal manifestations: Maoism, power struggles in the Communist Party, the new army role and the revolt of the young in society. Schurmann regards even his conclusions in the supplement as tentative and believes that global conditions of war or peace will tip the balance toward further radicalism or economic development.

The Polemic on the General Line of the International Communist Movement. Peking: Foreign Languages Press, 1965, 586 p.

This collection of 13 documents represents the Chinese position on questions of ideological interpretation and political line for world communism as published between mid-1963 and late 1964, when the already strained Sino-Soviet relationship deteriorated into a period of mutual public recrimination.

Each of these articles is a brilliant example of the Marxist genre of political polemicizing. The first constitutes a direct challenge to Soviet leadership of the international communist movement through its point-by-point criticism of Khrushchev's "revisionist" policies of "peaceful coexistence," "peaceful competition" and "peaceful transition [to socialism]," and his theories of a party and state "of the whole people." The second details the evolution of Sino-Soviet tensions, beginning with Khrushchev's attack on Stalin in 1956 and revealing aspects of Sino-Soviet military and economic relations previously unknown to foreign observers. The next five articles, published in late 1963, attack Khrushchev's policies of de-Stalinization, rapprochement with Jugoslavia, the wooing of non-communist countries in the underdeveloped world, and the Soviet leader's handling of the relations with "capitalist" countries.

The final four articles, published during 1964, attack in bitter, personalized terms Khrushchev's "degenerate" leadership of the Soviet party, as the Chinese sought to place the blame for the now public split of the international communist movement on the Russian leader. The ninth of these polemical attacks, however, contains the first public hints that the Maoist leadership within China was concerned about "revisionism" and the problem of "cultivating revolutionary successors" within the Chinese Communist Party itself. These themes presaged Mao Tse-tung's Cultural Revolution by two years and thus suggest that the Sino-Soviet dispute, in part, was compounded by the growing leadership conflict within the Chinese party. The final article, written shortly after Khrushchev's fall from power, is an uncompromising assertion that the Soviet leader's demise was a result of his erroneous policies, and thus a vindication of China's position in the Sino-Soviet dispute.

VOGEL, EZRA F. **Canton under Communism: Programs and Politics in a Provincial Capital, 1949–1968.** Cambridge: Harvard University Press, 1969, 448 p.

Canton under Communism is described by its author, a sociologist, as an attempt to understand the People's Republic of China on its own terms. This objective is pursued by presenting materials in the shape of a historical narrative. Although the hand of the sociologist is conspicuous in the emphasis on institutional patterns, specific events and personalities also figure importantly. At the core of the study is the city of Kwangchow and its provincial environs, fascinating for its special meld of national Chinese characteristics and strongly local and idiosyncratic elements. Through Vogel's reconstruction, the reader is taken from a highly synoptic view of the pre-1949 background through two decades of Communist development, terminating in February 1968, after the ascendancy of the military followed the turmoil of Red Guard activity in the Great Proletarian Cultural Revolution.

The essence of the author's concern is pragmatic. He wishes to know how the social system that is mainland China survived a major shift in the locus of political power, and the steps that were taken to deal with a variety of thoroughly practical problems, such as maintenance of public order and sustenance, as well as revolutionary fervor and command. If the book has a thesis, it is expressed on the final narrative page: the leaders in the development of Kwangchow's current society have been replaced by a more routinized leadership. As the Communists put it, they fulfilled their historical mission. In the process, concludes Vogel, they left Canton with a new administrative structure far beyond anything in the past.

Readers will turn to this book in years to come, particularly for its wealth of detail on a variety of continuities that join Communist China to its past. None is more significant than the continuation of lively conflict between national policies and local interests, and no other book yet available presents this so well.

SCHURMANN, FRANZ and SCHELL, ORVILLE, *eds*. **Communist China: Revolutionary Reconstruction and International Confrontation.** New York: Vintage Books, 1967, 667 p.

This highly readable documentary history of mainland China since 1949 was compiled in the fall of 1966 by two scholars at the University of California at Berkeley. In the context of widespread misunderstanding and fear of China growing out of the frenzied Cultural Revolution and the escalating war in Vietnam, the editors sought to be both informative and relevant in their selection of documents and interpretation of trends and meanings in accompanying commentaries. The result stands as probably the best popular collection of writings thus far assembled on Communist China, as articulated by her leaders and observed by experts from outside.

Excerpts from some 52 documents are presented, chosen from a wide range of official Chinese sources and perceptive foreign comment. Besides contrasting the view from China looking outward with that of the West (especially the United States) looking in, the editors have attempted to balance the political orientations of the observers, for example pairing the foreign policy perceptions of Dean Rusk with those of Chou En-lai. Schurmann and Schell forthrightly present their own "rational and moral position" in interpretive essays and annotations linking the documents. However, this emerges, in the main, as an appreciation of the limited scope of choices available to the Chinese and a faith in the capacity of modernization and growing international contacts to modify ideological rigidities, provided an external environment conducive to pacific change can be created by greater understanding and acceptance of China in the West.

Ho, Ping-ti and Tsou, Tang, *eds*. **China in Crisis. Volume One: China's Heritage and the Communist Political System.** Chicago: University of Chicago Press, 1968, 2 v.

Tsou, Tang, *ed.* **China in Crisis. Volume Two: China's Policies in Asia and America's Alternatives.** Chicago: University of Chicago Press, 1968, 484 p.

In 1967 the University of Chicago sponsored two five-day conferences on contemporary China. The papers and commentaries of these volumes are the products of those meetings. **Volume One** is composed of 13 papers; seven concern themselves with Chinese historical trends that preceded the Communist victory, and six deal directly with contemporary Chinese political problems. Among those papers that raise and consider the broad problems of China's cultural heritage, outstanding indeed is the tour de force of Professor Ho Ping-ti. Though the Great Proletarian Cultural Revolution looms large over the more contemporarily oriented papers, both authors and editors have held down the tendency to overemphasize immediate events.

Volume Two deals with foreign policy. The title suggests equal weight to American alternatives as well as Peking policy. In fact, the book really analyzes Chinese policy in terms of (1) bi-national relations, with chapters on China and Japan, Indonesia, Vietnam and the like, and (2) selected problems, *i.e.* China and nuclear weapons, military capability, perceptions. Only a few papers, such as "Two Chinas" (Robert Scalapino) and "China and the U.S." (Hans J. Morgenthau), are specifically devoted to American alternatives.

These volumes reflect the thinking of top American academicians and must be classed as superior collections. The foreign policy volume probably will not stand the test of time as well as **Volume One,** but they both represent careful work and clear statements of the major trends in scholarship and policy of the late 1960s.

JAPAN

General; Historical

Nihon Gaikō Bunsho [Documents on Japan's Foreign Relations]. Tokyo: Nihon Kokusai Rengō Kyōkai, Gaimushō [Ministry of Foreign Affairs], 1936–1963, 91 v.

This monumental series for the reign of the Emperor Meiji (1867–1912) includes both Japanese and foreign documents, the latter usually in the original language followed by a Japanese translation. A new series for the next reign (1912–1926) began appearing in 1964 under the title **Nihon Gaikō Bunsho: Taishō Jidai** [Documents on Japan's Foreign Relations: Taishō Period]; by the end of 1969, 18 volumes had been published, covering the period 1912–1918. In addition to intergovernmental correspondence, agreements, memoranda of conversations and the Foreign Ministry's internal correspondence, the collection includes numerous memoranda exchanged between the Foreign Ministry and other agencies of the Japanese government. The cumulation is generally by calendar year, but within the one or more volumes for each year the arrangement is by subject (not country). Subjects requiring very extended treatment are presented in separate volumes either within the chronological numbering system or grouped apart with separate numbering. Within the Meiji series, these include from one to eight volumes each on revision of the extraterritoriality treaties and the commercial treaties, the Boxer Rebellion, the Russo-Japanese War and the 1911 Chinese revolution. There are no cumulative indexes, but each volume (annual or special) has an appendix listing all documents in chronological order, cross-referenced to the main text by subject number and document number.

Another Foreign Ministry compilation, **Nihon Gaikō Nempyō narabini Shuyō Bunsho** [Japan's Foreign Relations: Chronology and Principal Documents] (Tokyo: Nihon Kokusai Rengō Kyōkai, 1955; reprinted by Hara Shobō, 1965, 2 v.), is a useful companion to the long series. It is primarily a collection of the most important documents between 1854 and 1945 but also contains a detailed chronology of events (1840–1945) and lists of Japanese and foreign ambassadors, ministers and chargés d'affaires, with exact dates of appointment.

Gaimushō no Hyakunen [A Hundred Years of the Foreign Ministry]. Tokyo: Hara Shobō, Gaimushō Hyakunenshi Hensan Iinkai [Foreign Ministry Centennial History Compilation Committee], 1969, 2 v.

Though based on archives of Japan's Ministry of Foreign Affairs and prepared with the help of two researchers on the Ministry staff, this work is expressly labelled "not a representation of Foreign Ministry views." The authors are four diplomatic historians from as many universities. They also specify that the work is "a history of the Foreign Ministry, not a history of Japan's diplomatic relations," but in fact it is something of both. The organization is basically chronological, with 1,064 pages on the period 1869–1930, another 761 pages on 1931–1945 and 425 pages on 1945–1969, dealing with diplomatic events as well as with the Ministry itself.

The authors have intentionally emphasized the period (since 1920) for which the official archives have not yet been made public. They include numerous lengthy quotations from important diplomatic documents not yet available in the **Nihon Gaikō Bunsho** or elsewhere, and this alone would suffice to make this work invaluable to other scholars. In addition, chapters on Foreign Ministry organization and personnel are interspersed throughout the account, and complete rosters of Ministry personnel for 1884, 1904, 1921, 1931, 1942, 1951 and 1969 are given in an appendix. These sections are excellent sources for an institutional study. Other appendices include lists and narrative accounts of military attachés, foreign employees of the Ministry and consular police. There is even a brief but intriguing chapter on diplomatic ciphers, as well as a short account of the compilation of the **Nihon Gaikō Bunsho** and an explanation of its peculiar numbering system. In short, the 2,733 pages of this work are a rich treasure-house of information not readily available elsewhere, much of it ideally suited for exploitation by future researchers.

Taiheiyō Sensō e no Michi [The Road to the Pacific War]. Tokyo: Asahi Shimbun Sha, Nihon Kokusai Seiji Gakkai Taiheiyō Sensō Gen'in Kenkyūbu [Japan International Politics Association Research Group on the Origins of the Pacific War], 1962–1963, 8 v.

Of all the accounts of the decade preceding Pearl Harbor, this was the first to use large numbers of Japanese primary materials, private as well as official. The first seven volumes contain 19 well-coördinated studies by 14 Japanese scholars, including one volume on Japanese foreign relations for 1917–1931 and six volumes on the period 1931–1941. Through extensive interviews with participants in the events of the 1930s and discovery of numerous private papers and previously unknown military records, the authors were able to present evidence on many points that had been unclear or unproven. Each volume has chronological and biographical appendices and a detailed index. The eighth volume of the series is a collection of important documents not previously published; the 1941 section of this volume has been translated into English by Nobutaka Ike as **Japan's Decision for War: Records of the 1941 Policy Conferences.** However, only a fraction of the documents used by the authors of the seven narrative volumes appear in the documentary volume, and footnotes identifying the other documents are often quite inadequate. Fortunately, both these deficiencies have since been largely rectified by publication of a new multivolume collection, **Gendaishi Shiryō** [Documents on Contemporary History] (Tokyo: Misuzu Shobō, 1964–66), containing vast quantities of previously unpublished documents on both foreign and domestic affairs in the 1930s.

Kindai Nihon Gaikōshi Sōsho [Modern Japanese Diplomatic History Series]. Tokyo: Hara Shobō, 1968–1970, 10 v.

Two volumes in this series are translations of Akira Iriye, **After Imperialism: The Search for a New Order in the Far East, 1921–1931,** and (with some abridgment) Waldo H. Heinrichs, Jr., **American Ambassador: Joseph C. Grew and the Development of the United States Diplomatic Tradition** (Boston: Little, Brown, 1967, 460 p.). The other eight monographs are the product of Japanese scholars, including four of the authors of the **Taiheiyō Sensō e no Michi.** Their subjects are: Japan and Russia during the period of rapprochement, 1905–1917; Japan in World War I; the Paris Peace Conference; the Russian Revolution and Japan; the Washington Conference; the League of Nations; Japanese relations with China; and the events leading to the seizure of Manchuria. In comparison with the earlier series, the authors have the advantage of an even larger collection of newly available primary materials and less restricted space for exposition. There are copious extracts from the documents, and the documentary footnotes are of good quality.

TREAT, PAYSON J. **Diplomatic Relations between the United States and Japan, 1853–1905.** Gloucester: Peter Smith, 1963, 3 v.

These volumes, first published in 1938, continue to be of unique value. The published volumes of U.S. diplomatic archives include barely 10 percent of the messages exchanged between the State Department and the U.S. Legation in Japan during the period 1853–1905. In recent years, all the correspondence has been microfilmed, but the lack of an index makes it very tedious to locate material. Treat's three volumes, based on a meticulous reading of the entire file, contain, as he said, "an account of practically everything which became the subject of correspondence between the Legation and the State Department," and copious footnotes make them an invaluable guide to the new microfilm. Quite apart from this, they remain the only detailed account of Japanese-American relations for most of the period covered and also (as the author consciously intended) a striking case study of the work of a nineteenth-century American legation over a long period. As diplomatic history they now need to be supplemented by information from the Japanese archives, but as evidence for an institutional study of American diplomats and diplomatic methods in a still primitive era they are unlikely to be surpassed. Treat's choice of annual-chapter organization in preference to a more topical arrangement enhances the usefulness of the work for the purposes stated.

ESTHUS, RAYMOND A. **Theodore Roosevelt and Japan.** Seattle: University of Washington Press, 1967, 329 p.

The classic works on Japanese-American relations during the presidency of Theodore Roosevelt are Tyler Dennett's **Roosevelt and the Russo-Japanese War** (New York: Doubleday, Page, 1925, 357 p.) and Thomas A. Bailey's complementary **Theodore Roosevelt and the Japanese-American Crises: An Account of the International Complications Arising from the Race Problem on the Pacific Coast** (Stanford: Stanford University Press, 1934, 353 p.). Though their interpretations and conclusions remain generally sound, these works were necessarily based on rather limited sources. Now that Japanese, Russian and other foreign archives, as well as more Roosevelt papers, are available, many events and policies can be clarified. The latter half of John Albert White's **The Diplomacy of the Russo-Japanese War** (Princeton: Princeton University Press, 1964, 410 p.) updates Dennett, and Charles E. Neu's **An Uncertain Friendship: Theodore Roosevelt and Japan, 1906–1909** (Cambridge: Harvard University Press, 1967, 347 p.) does the same for Bailey.

Esthus has now covered the entire Roosevelt period, 1901–1909, in a careful and ably integrated account based on a wide range of sources. Though White and Neu together are somewhat longer and provide some additional detail on various points, the work by Esthus has the merit of integrating the Roosevelt period and presenting a well-rounded and judiciously balanced view of Roosevelt's attitude toward Japan and the problems he encountered. The Japanese position is also thoroughly examined, on the basis of 80,000 pages of Japanese government telegrams from the postwar American microfilming of captured Japanese archives.

JONES, FRANCIS CLIFFORD. **Extraterritoriality in Japan and the Diplomatic Relations Resulting in Its Abolition, 1853–1899.** New Haven: Yale University Press, 1931, 237 p.

It is commonly agreed that the major diplomatic problem of the first 25 years following the Restoration of 1868 was the removal of the stigma and disadvantages of the treaties concluded with Western nations in the 1850s, at the heart of which was the principle of extraterritoriality. It is a measure of the quality of this monograph, as well as commentary on the dearth of studies in English on this important subject, that the late Professor F. C. Jones' M.A. thesis of 40 years ago still stands as the best history of the origins, operations and abolition of extraterritoriality in Japan. He traces the inception of extraterritoriality, from Townsend Harris' 1858 treaty between the United States and Japan, the working of the system and the complex diplomatic negotiations which eventually regained judicial autonomy through the Aoki-Kimberley treaty of 1894 between Great Britain and Japan (both texts are included as appendices). The book relies primarily on British diplomatic documents and the accounts of foreign diplomats engaged in treaty negotiations; it does not exploit the rich Japanese archival materials on the subject. Professor Jones shows how the Western powers were able to postpone the inevitable by demanding a reform of Japan's judicial system, and how, in the end, the willingness of Britain to yield extraterritorial rights in 1899 was a product of the development of modern legal codes and laws in Japan. He also indicates how treaty negotiations were interwoven with domestic political developments.

KAMIKAWA, HIKOMATSU, *ed.* **Japan-American Diplomatic Relations in the Meiji-Taishō Era.** Tokyo: Pan-Pacific Press (Centenary Cultural Council Series), 1958, 458 p.

This is one of an extensive series of volumes published by the Centenary Cultural Council in commemoration of the one hundredth anniversary of the inauguration of Japanese-American diplomatic relations in 1854. Edited by a well-known Japanese authority on international relations, it consists of four separately authored sections devoted respectively to the last stage of the shogunate (1845–1867), the first half of the Meiji era (1867–1895), the latter half of the Meiji period (1895–1912) and the Taishō era (1912–1926). Within these rubrics organization is chronological and centered about notable episodes or events such as Hawaii and the Japanese, the United States and the Sino-Japanese and Russo-Japanese Wars, Japan and the Open Door Policy, the Manchurian railways problem, or World War I and American-Japanese relations. The treatment is strictly factual and leaves a great deal to be desired by current standards of scholarship in the field. Given the paucity of materials for this period, however, it is still a useful starting point. There is a rudimentary index, but no sources are cited.

SCHWANTES, ROBERT S. **Japanese and Americans: A Century of Cultural Relations.** New York: Harper (for the Council on Foreign Relations), 1955, 380 p.

It is now taken for granted that cultural relations are an important dimension of modern diplomacy. This was not the case when Dr. Schwantes wrote this pioneering account of the respective national "images" of each other held by the Japanese and American peoples and of the history that underlies and shapes them. His immediate stimulus was the American occupation of postwar Japan and the vastly increased flow of broad American cultural influence that accompanied this, but the real strength of the book lies in its investigation in depth of the many ways and occasions upon which the United States has influenced the course and shape of Japan's modernization since the Perry expedition of 1853–1854. This involves separate explorations of the fields of economic, institutional and ideological, and educational development in Japan followed by a systematic examination of the principal channels through which American influence has flowed, *i.e.* teachers, students, cultural materials and missionaries. The work concludes with a plea for the expanded and more systematic use of cultural interchange as a means for the improvement of international relations. There is also an excellent bibliographical essay.

NISH, IAN HILL. **The Anglo-Japanese Alliance: The Diplomacy of Two Island Empires, 1894–1907.** London: Athlone Press, 1966, 420 p.

Professor Nish of the London School of Economics and Political Science has written a masterful account of the diplomacy of the Anglo-Japanese Alliance. The book is solidly based on published and unpublished official documents, secondary works in several languages, private papers and biographies, and the author has skillfully correlated the British and Japanese sources. Divided into three parts, his study traces in great detail, first, the origins of the alliance from the Three-Power intervention of 1895 through the impact of the Boxer Rebellion in China; secondly, the signing of the alliance in 1902 against the background of the reaction of the powers to Russian activity in Manchuria and the internal struggle in Japan between Ito Hirobumi and the advocates of the 1902 agreement; and, thirdly, the conclusion of the second alliance in 1905 which modified the 1902 agreement as a result of the Russo-Japanese War. While arguing that it was Russian expansion in the Far East which brought Britain and Japan together, he denies that the alliance was directly related to the Russo-Japanese War or that it precluded a subsequent rapprochement between Japan and Russia or Britain and Russia. One of the virtues of his analysis is the identification of the individuals in Tokyo and London who were instrumental in bringing about the alliance which, he concludes, "was negotiated more or less secretly by the foreign ministries on both sides." This well-written, well-documented monograph gains additional value by the inclusion of an appendix of "Translated Documents," a useful bibliographical note and an excellent bibliography.

SATOW, SIR ERNEST. **A Diplomat in Japan.** London: Seeley, Service, 1921, 427 p.

Sir Ernest Satow's recollections of his first years in the British consular service in Japan are unmatched in English as a contemporary eyewitness account of the momentous events that led to the Restoration in 1868. A resident in Japan almost continuously from 1862 to 1882, he later served as ambassador to Tokyo (1895–1900) and to Peking (1900–1906) to crown a distinguished diplomatic career of 45 years.

This book, dealing with only a fraction of his early stay in Japan, provides a graphic account of the turbulent years of 1862–1869 during which the forces opposed to the Tokugawa government successfully brought about a restoration of Imperial rule. Based on his diaries, it recounts his experience in the foreign and diplomatic community, his observations on the Japanese people and their country and his assessment of the significant political events of the time. The central focus is on the major episodes in Anglo-Japanese relations in which he was a participant. His account is less a penetrating analysis and rounded historical narrative than a piecing together of his personal experiences to give a picture of the times, the policy of Great Britain and its influence on the restoration of the Emperor. Full of facts which throw light on the end of the old era and the beginning of the new, Satow's recollections are a valuable part of the historical records of the dawn of modern Japan.

MOORE, FREDERICK. **With Japan's Leaders: An Intimate Record of Fourteen Years as Counsellor to the Japanese Government, Ending December 7, 1941.** New York: Scribner, 1942, 232 p.

Frederick Moore's candid recollections of his experiences as a salaried adviser to the Japanese government provide a unique eyewitness footnote to Japanese-American relations between the two world wars. As a foreign counsellor on international affairs in the Japanese Foreign Office, as a member of the Japanese delegation to the Washington Conference in 1921 and to the League of Nations at the time of the Manchurian crisis, and as a trusted adviser to three successive Japanese ambassadors to Washington—Saito, Horinouchi and Nomura—he gained intimate knowledge of the men, events and documents that shaped Japan's relations with the United States for almost two decades. The emphasis of the narrative is on the three years preceding Pearl Harbor. His judgment of those he advised is often too uncritical. He attributes the deterioration of relations between the two countries wholly to the "militarists" with whom he was entirely out of sympathy. Sprinkled with anecdotes and informative insights, the narrative adds a modest but valuable dimension to the study of U.S.-Japanese diplomatic history. One gains confidence in the author's judgment by virtue of the fact that in a book written in 1942, at the height of Japanese military successes in Southeast Asia, he clearly predicts both the defeat of Japan and her postwar resurgence. "The ruin," he concludes, "will not be permanent. . . . They are a people too gifted and too willing to labor to be permanently suppressed."

RÔYAMA, MASAMICHI. **Foreign Policy of Japan: 1914–1939.** Tokyo: Institute of Pacific Relations, 1941, 182 p.

This brief survey of Japan's foreign policy by a well-known political scientist appeared as the last in a seven-volume "Far Eastern Conflict" series published by the Japan Council of the Institute of Pacific Relations. It combines two essays: the first traces the major developments in Japan's foreign relations from the end of World War I to her withdrawal from the League of Nations as a consequence of the Manchurian Incident, and the second surveys the evolution of the proclamation of a New Order in East Asia as a result of the China Incident which broke out in 1937. Both parts of the study keep close to the official documents and accounts of the Sino-Japanese conflict and stress the internal and international repercussions of the conflict. The interpretation presented argues the reasonableness and nonaggressive character of Japan's policy and the benevolent nature of the conception of the New Order, a plan which the author describes as conciliatory and at the same time "a national policy really her own" holding promise for a solution to "the age-long instability of the Far East." Subsequent scholarship makes this interpretation dubious, but its significance lies in the fact that a liberal scholar, known for his anti-military views, found much to support in his government's foreign policy on the eve of Pearl Harbor.

JONES, FRANCIS CLIFFORD. **Manchuria since 1931.** New York: Oxford University Press (for the Royal Institute of International Affairs and the Institute of Pacific Relations), 1949, 256 p.

Why and how the Japanese seized Manchuria in 1931 are questions that have been elaborately studied by a host of writers, and the end is not in sight: new documents and new interpretations continue to emerge. What the Japanese did with Manchuria thereafter, in 14 years of unchallenged rule, remains largely unstudied. F. C. Jones' monograph, written barely two years after the puppet state vanished into history (the preface is dated December 1947), stands almost alone as an attempt to review the whole range of Japanese policies and performance in occupied Manchuria. Roughly two-thirds of the book concerns economic development, including the largely unsuccessful program for Japanese agrarian immigration, and achievements and failures in communications, transport, finance, industrial planning, agriculture, trade and urbanization. Other chapters survey Japanese experimentation with political and administrative organization and the studied but often clumsy attempts to foster "Manchurian" national feeling while at the same time exploiting the aspirations of non-Chinese racial minorities within Manchuria. In all these respects—economic, political and social—Manchoukuo continues to offer, long after its demise, remarkable opportunities for institutional study of a landmark innovation in the techniques of imperialism: the modern puppet state as distinguished from the traditional colony or protectorate. This book is a succinct marshaling of an impressive quantity of data; its chief limitation is almost total reliance on English-language sources. Even in 1947, there was a staggering array of Japanese-language publications on Manchoukuo that are much more detailed and often much more revealing than any of the English sources. In recent years, the former have been augmented by new documentary collections and a growing number of nostalgic memoirs by participants in the Japanese venture.

Foreign Relations Before 1945

See also Second World War: Diplomatic Aspects; Immediate Origins, p. 302.

TAKEUCHI, TATSUJI. **War and Diplomacy in the Japanese Empire.** New York: Doubleday, 1935, 505 p.

This older book is still of substantial interest to those concerned with prewar Japanese foreign affairs. It is an attempt by Professor Takeuchi of Kwansei Gakuin University to explain to a non-Japanese audience the structure of law and institutions within which prewar Japanese diplomacy operated and to illustrate the operations of the system through a series of 18 brief case studies of major episodes in Japanese diplomatic history. These range from the struggle for the revision of the unequal treaties in the latter part of the nineteenth century to the Manchurian crisis of 1931–1933. The work concludes with a description of the treaty-making power and the war power in prewar Japan and a discussion of the formulation and control of foreign policy. A useful bibliography of works largely in Japanese is appended.

CONROY, HILARY. **The Japanese Seizure of Korea, 1868–1910: A Study of Realism and Idealism in International Relations.** Philadelphia: University of Pennsylvania Press, 1960, 544 p.

Professor Conroy's monograph is the most detailed study available of Japan's policy toward Korea from the beginning of the Meiji era to the annexation in 1910. Using original and secondary Japanese source materials, he traces the tortuous course of Korean-Japanese relations from the debate over Korea in 1873, through the Li-Ito Convention of 1885, the Sino-Japanese and the Russo-Japanese Wars, to the final takeover. In his attempt to discover why Japan seized Korea after four decades of debate and conflict, he identifies three groups within Japan with differing approaches. The "realists," the dominant Meiji statesmen, proceeded cautiously in assuring the national security; they were challenged, first, by "liberals" who demanded a more progressive policy and aimed to embarrass the ruling oligarchs and, secondly, by "reactionaries" who advocated an iron-fisted approach to Korea in order to strengthen Japan in the face of Chinese and Russian power. He concludes that annexation was not the result of a long-term plot but a product of compromises between rival domestic political groups under changing international conditions. Conroy's examination of the historical record does not take into account Korean sources, although he does admit the harshness of Japanese rule. Had he done so, greater emphasis would undoubtedly have been given to Japan's aggressive imperialism and the deep-seated hatred that the Koreans felt toward their conquerors. The impressive historical data he has marshaled, however, show convincingly that Meiji foreign policy was significantly influenced by domestic considerations which produced stopgap compromise solutions.

MORLEY, JAMES WILLIAM. **The Japanese Thrust into Siberia, 1918.** New York: Columbia University Press, 1957, 395 p.

This impressive study, solidly based on Russian, English and hitherto unused Japanese archival sources, casts new light on the 1918 Allied intervention in Siberia by explaining why Japan participated and how the decision was made. In 13 tightly packed chapters, the author analyzes the three elements involved in Japan's decision—the political situation in the Amur basin area, the attitude of the Western powers toward an expedition and the location of political power in Japan. He shows how the debate between Japanese "interventionists," who feared the encroachment of the Soviet revolution into the Far East, and the "noninterventionists" in Japan, who delayed support for fear of the consequences of independent action, was resolved by the American invitation to participate in an Allied expedition to rescue beleaguered Czech troops. Focusing on the structure of political power in Japan and its influence on this major decision, Morley convincingly shows that the decision to intervene was reached through a compromise among several centers of power—the military and civil bureaucracy, the political parties and private groups. As a study of the formulation of Japanese foreign policy, this book stands as one of the best accounts available.

IRIYE, AKIRA. **After Imperialism: The Search for a New Order in the Far East, 1921–1931.** Cambridge: Harvard University Press, 1965, 375 p.

This careful study provides a brilliant account and fresh understanding of the changes in Far Eastern international relations from the time of the Washington Conference in 1921–1922 to the Manchurian crisis of 1931. Documents from the Japanese and Chinese Foreign Ministry archives are correlated with materials in English, German and Russian. Professor Iriye demonstrates that the turbulent decade of the 1930s was an outgrowth of the failure of the major powers to develop a stable framework for international relations in the Far East. The multilateral framework erected by the powers at the Washington Conference destroyed the old system of imperialist diplomacy but failed to define a new order which could reconcile the competing interests of the major powers.

Iriye traces in turn the "initiatives" of the United States, Russia, Japan and China in the Far East. He shows how the unilateral efforts of each nation to pursue an independent course of action in China undermined "the search for a new order in the Far East;" how American interest in "self-determination," Soviet support for "a world-wide struggle against Imperialism," Japan's efforts to strengthen its position in China and the resurgence of nationalism in China were mutually irreconcilable and doomed the evolution of a new system of diplomacy in the area. The monograph not only elucidates the diplomatic and military history of the subject but also provides a method of analysis that appreciably deepens our understanding of the interactions involved.

Foreign Relations of the United States: Diplomatic Papers. Japan, 1931–1941. Washington: Government Printing Office, 1943, 2 v.

This wartime publication elaborates in great detail the thesis that the Japanese attack on Pearl Harbor and the consequent general warfare in the Pacific was the logical climax of a series of aggressive moves by Japan in eastern Asia and the western Pacific stretching back in a more or less unbroken chain to the Manchurian Incident of 1931. The case is presented in the form of texts of hundreds of official documents drawn from contemporary diplomatic communications by both American and Japanese agencies, press releases, official speeches and memoranda of conversations. It treats practically all major episodes in American-Japanese relations during the decade involved, including the Manchurian Incident, the course and development of Japanese policy and activities in China and Southeast Asia, the breakdown of the arms limitation agreements, the emergence of economic sanctions and, most extensively of all, the long series of informal conversations in Washington between Japanese and American representatives throughout 1941.

ELSBREE, WILLARD H. **Japan's Role in Southeast Asian Nationalist Movements, 1940 to 1945.** Cambridge: Harvard University Press (for the International Secretariat, Institute of Pacific Relations), 1953, 182 p.

Japanese attempts to exploit nationalist sentiment in occupied countries were probably predestined to fail with the Chinese majority in Manchuria, as described in F. C. Jones' **Manchuria since 1931,** and with the large Chinese minorities in Southeast Asia. With this exception, prospects for winning support in the south were much brighter than in the north. Elsbree's concern is to show how and why the initial spirit of coöperation with the Japanese soon evaporated in most parts of occupied Southeast Asia. The ultimate failure of Japan's "Greater East Asia Co-Prosperity Sphere" concept was due partly to military reverses, which produced not prosperity but hardship, and partly to Japanese cruelty. However, Elsbree concludes that the principal difficulty was Japan's faulty conception of the nationalist movements and underestimation of the strength of nationalism in Southeast Asia. Concessions made late in World War II, such as the appointment of non-Japanese administrators and the emphasis on "national unity," came too late. The Co-Prosperity Sphere had been built too obviously on an assumption of Japanese superiority in an unequal partnership.

Elsbree's brief survey focuses primarily on Indonesia, Burma and the Philippines, with less attention to other areas. Based chiefly on newspapers and on documents of the Tokyo war crimes tribunal, the book is a useful beginning, hampered by inadequate sources. More archives are now available, and a few studies have been completed by Japanese scholars in recent years. But no detailed and systematic study of the Japanese administration of occupied Southeast Asia is yet available and, until one appears, Elsbree's pioneer work will remain important.

CROWLEY, JAMES B. **Japan's Quest for Autonomy: National Security and Foreign Policy, 1930–1938.** Princeton: Princeton University Press, 1966, 428 p.

This excellent monograph studies from a revisionist standpoint the way in which Japan's major foreign policy decisions were made in the 1930s. On a strong central thread that challenges the "conspiracy" theory of Japanese militarism and aggression Professor Crowley of Yale University strings six beads chronologically: the controversy over the London Naval Treaty, the Manchurian crisis, Japan's withdrawal from the League, the evolution of a China policy, army factionalism and foreign policy, and the war against Nationalist China. Each topic is dissected on the basis of a careful reading of published and unpublished primary and secondary Japanese sources supplemented by interviews with some of the participants. The author uses the evidence from the Tokyo war crimes trials with greater discrimination than any previous scholar and adds depth by the use of Foreign Ministry and military archives. The study maintains a disciplined focus on the thesis that the determining factor in each foreign policy decision was an overriding concern for national security based on Japan's hegemony in northeast Asia and that it was formulated by responsible civil and political leaders. He rejects the argument of Maxon, Butow, Storry and others that field armies flouted orders from army headquarters and that the highest ranking military officials were helpless puppets of their subordinates. New light is cast on a variety of topics. He presents Prince Konoye as a stronger, more confident leader than portrayed in previous studies; he gives a convincing analysis of military factionalism; and he offers a reinterpretation of the Marco Polo Bridge incident of 1937.

MAXON, YALE CANDEE. **Control of Japanese Foreign Policy: A Study of Civil-Military Rivalry, 1930–1945.** Berkeley: University of California Press, 1957, 286 p.

Dr. Maxon is interested in the dual power structure of the Japanese government prior to defeat in 1945 and the consequences this had in the sphere of foreign policy. He perceives the government as divided into increasingly competitive civilian and military camps and as lacking any effective legal or institutional means for resolving the strife which resulted short of personal intervention by the Emperor. Since by tradition and practice the Emperor did not participate in the making of policy, such intervention did not in fact normally take place. After tracing the historical, constitutional and political antecedents of this situation, the author provides an admirable description of the emergence of dual government and the increasing political activism and power of the military element from 1930 to 1936, the efforts to adjust and control the civil-military split through devices of Liaison and Imperial Conferences, the decisions and manoeuvres leading up to the Pearl Harbor decision and, of especial interest, the way in which those elements favoring a negotiated surrender were finally able with the help of the Emperor and his advisers to bring about the acceptance of the Potsdam terms. An excellent bibliography is appended.

JONES, FRANCIS CLIFFORD. **Japan's New Order in East Asia: Its Rise and Fall, 1937–1945.** New York: Oxford University Press (for the Royal Institute of International Affairs and the Institute of Pacific Relations), 1954, 498 p.

Unlike David H. James' **The Rise and Fall of the Japanese Empire** (New York: Macmillan, 1951, 409 p.) which, except for his firsthand account of the fall of Singapore, is an ill-organized and inadequate account of Japan's military defeat, Professor Jones' detailed history of the events leading Japan to war and to surrender is a balanced, well-documented monograph. His analysis of Japan's disastrous attempt to build a New Order was the first to exploit the voluminous documentary evidence compiled for the trial of Japan's wartime rulers. This source is supplemented by the sifting of facts from the memoirs of statesmen and from the diplomatic correspondence between the major powers. It is a judicious survey, interweaving the major diplomatic and military events with domestic developments, and stands as an authoritative scholarly study of Japan's rise and fall from 1937 to the surrender in 1945. In an excellent final chapter he concludes that Japan's policy "did not represent the steady unfolding of a master-plan" but resulted from "a mixture of opportunism and blundering" reflecting conflicting rivalries at home, an ineffective alliance with the Axis powers, a war in China which she could not consummate, and a gross underrating of the determination and resources of the United States. He is critical of the inflexibility of the United States in the pre-Pearl Harbor negotiations and the formula of unconditional surrender which delayed the end of hostilities. Added value is given to the book by the inclusion of 11 key documents and a useful bibliography.

IKE, NOBUTAKA, *ed.* **Japan's Decision for War: Records of the 1941 Policy Conferences.** Stanford: Stanford University Press, 1967, 306 p.

The Japanese did not stumble inadvertently into the launching of general warfare in the Pacific on December 7, 1941. It might be called a cumulative decision, taken after long and extensive consideration by the nation's highest military and civil authorities. Professor Ike makes this completely clear in this fascinating and most unusual annotated translation of the detailed notes taken by a representative of the Japanese Army's Chief of Staff on the proceedings and decisions of the series of Liaison and Imperial conferences that preceded the outbreak of war. Liaison conferences normally brought together the Prime Minister and the Foreign, War and Navy Ministers with the Chiefs and Vice-Chiefs of the Army and Navy General Staffs. Imperial conferences added the Emperor and the President of the Privy Council. In general the former considered and agreed upon major national policy decisions; the latter gave them formal sanction of the highest sort. The present collection provides complete translations of the Army notes on 72 of the 75 Liaison conferences held between April 18 and December 4, 1941 (Nos. 19–75)— all that relate to American-Japanese relations (no notes were available for the 27th, 64th and 68th Liaison conferences)—plus those for the five pertinent Imperial conferences of September 30, 1940 (on the Tripartite Pact), and July 2, September 6, November 5 and December 1, 1941. Professor Ike adds to these texts his own very helpful comments and explanations. There are also two documentary appendices and a bibliographical note.

BUTOW, ROBERT JOSEPH CHARLES. **Tojo and the Coming of the War.** Princeton: Princeton University Press (for Princeton University Center of International Studies), 1961, 584 p.

Professor Butow presents a comprehensive account of the role of the Japanese army in the fateful events leading to war and defeat as seen through the career of General Tojo. Official documents and records, especially those presented at the Tokyo war crimes trial, are supplemented by thorough use of secondary sources, biographies and periodicals, as well as by interviews and correspondence with many Japanese. The narrative starts with Tojo's early years and his rise within the army; it broadens into a history of Japan's efforts to create a New Order which came to a climax in the decision for war against the United States; it follows the flow of military triumphs and defeats during the war; and it concludes with Tojo's imprisonment, trial and execution. The book is less a probing of Tojo's character and career than a close reëxamination of the background against which Tojo played his part. The author's conclusion that Tojo was a narrow-minded, unimaginative but able military bureaucrat, not a fanatical dictator, corrects earlier gross misinterpretations of his role. This assessment supports Butow's thesis that Japan was plunged into war by the frustrations and irresponsible ambitions of the military. However, he also contends that Tojo and "the ranking members of the military services were the robots of their subordinates." This is a judgment that has been called into question by later scholarship. Nevertheless, for any critical reëxamination of the high-level decisions which led Japan into the Pacific war, Professor Butow's readable and scholarly work is a basic study.

HATTORI, TAKUSHIRŌ. **Daitōa Sensō Zenshi** [A Complete History of the Greater East Asia War]. Tokyo: Masu Shobō, 1953, 8 v.

Military history has become an increasingly popular genre in Japan. Numerous war memoirs, studies of campaigns and war theaters, and more popular descriptions of Japan's wartime experience have appeared. Among these the eight-volume **Daitōa Sensō Zenshi,** completed in 1953 and recently reissued in two volumes, remains the most comprehensive account of the war published in Japanese. The author, a former colonel in the Japanese army with extensive experience at General Staff Headquarters, gathered a group of ex-military officers under the aegis of the Intelligence Section of the American occupation forces in order to compile this narrative history of the Pacific war. The work, based on official Japanese sources, totals over 1,600 pages with each small volume including about 200 pages of chronological narrative.

The study begins with the appointment of the second Konoye cabinet in 1940 and concludes with a brief discussion of Japan under the occupation. Its primary focus is on the overall military strategy of Japan and the major campaigns undertaken in each theater to implement that strategy. Diplomatic and internal political developments which affected strategic planning are referred to, but the result is less a probing analysis of the war than a synthesis of reports providing full descriptions of each military campaign. Illustrations and maps add value, but no bibliography or index is included. For students of the military history of the Pacific war as seen from the Japanese side this work is an important starting point.

International Military Tribunal for the Far East: Record of the Proceedings, Documents, Exhibits, Judgment, Dissenting Judgments, Preliminary Interrogations, and Miscellaneous Documents. Tokyo: International Military Tribunal for the Far East, 1946–1949, mimeo.

This enormous mass of documentation assembled in the course of the Tokyo war crimes trial of the 28 Japanese military and civilian leaders allegedly most responsible for involving Japan in the Second World War is undoubtedly the most valuable single source for research materials on Japanese domestic politics and foreign relations for the years 1928–1945. For the most part the documentation exists in both English and Japanese versions. The principal subjects treated are: the

Japanese constitution and governmental structure; preparing Japanese public opinion for war; Japanese military activities in Manchuria and China; the use of opium, other narcotics and atrocities in China; Japanese economic activities in Manchuria and China; relations with Germany and Italy; relations with France and Thailand; relations with the U.S.S.R.; preparation for war; relations with the United States, the British Commonwealth, the Netherlands and Portugal; war crimes; and the alleged relations of each of the 28 defendants to the foregoing matters. The total documentation is divided into a number of series, separately titled volumes and indexes.

A detailed description of the collection may be found in Delmer M. Brown, "Recent Japanese Political and Historical Materials," *American Political Science Review*, v. XLIII, no. 5 (October 1949), pp. 1010–1017. An analytic index of the **Proceedings** may also be found in Paul S. Dull and Michael T. Umemura, **The Tokyo Trials, a Functional Index to the Proceedings of the IMTFE** (Ann Arbor: University of Michigan Press, Center for Japanese Studies, Occasional Papers No. 6, 1957, 94 p.).

Japan After 1945

Foreign Relations

PACIFIC WAR RESEARCH SOCIETY, *comp.* **Japan's Longest Day.** Palo Alto: Kodansha International, 1968, 339 p.

This is an hour-by-hour account of developments at the heart of the Japanese government in Tokyo from noon on August 14 to noon on August 15, 1945. It is a dramatic and fascinating narrative of the last-minute debates, the manoeuvring, the reasoning and the personalities involved in the final stages of the agonizing decision to accept the Potsdam terms of surrender. The climactic events are the abortive military revolt on the night of August 14–15 and the broadcasting of the Emperor's surrender message to his people at noon on August 15. The text is based upon the available published records of the period supplemented by private diaries, contemporary notes and extensive interviews with all surviving high-level participants with the sole exception of the Emperor. It provides unique insights into the decision-making process of a government at a moment of unparalleled national crisis.

KAWAI, KAZUO. **Japan's American Interlude.** Chicago: University of Chicago Press, 1960, 257 p.

There is a curious dearth both in this country and in Japan of serious scholarly studies of the American military occupation of Japan (September 2, 1945, to April 28, 1952). Indeed, this brief account by the late Professor Kawai of Ohio State University, who also served as editor of the *Nippon Times* from 1946–1949, is practically the only existing systematic attempt at an overall assessment of this remarkable endeavor to democratize an entire society by means of a military occupation. While the author finds much to criticize about the occupation and its results, his general conclusion is that it was a remarkable success. His coverage is broad and includes very perceptive treatments of the physical and psychological setting of the occupation, Japan's state of readiness for democratization, constitutional change, the Emperor, major political reforms and their consequences, economic reform programs including the fields of labor, agriculture and industrial deconcentration, changes in the educational system and social change and democratization in general.

HELLMANN, DONALD C. **Japanese Foreign Policy and Domestic Politics: The Peace Agreement with the Soviet Union.** Berkeley: University of California Press, 1969, 202 p.

This is a case study of a particular major episode in postwar Japanese foreign policy—the negotiation and conclusion on December 11, 1956, of a joint agreement normalizing diplomatic and economic relations between Japan and the U.S.S.R. Professor Hellmann's concern is primarily with the domestic political circumstances in Japan from which the agreement emerged and in particular with factional strife among the leadership of the ruling conservative political group that in November 1955 amalgamated to form the Liberal Democratic Party. On the Japanese side this domestic factional strife, rather than the realities of the international scene, was primarily responsible for determining the timing and tactics of the negotiations. The study thus focuses on domestic decision-making processes and the manner in which they affect developments in the realm of foreign policy. It represents one of the few attempts to apply such an approach to Japan, and, while the particular case chosen for investigation may no longer be adequately representative of current Japanese practice in this respect, it provides an invaluable foundation for further work in this neglected field.

PACKARD, GEORGE R., III. **Protest in Tokyo: The Security Treaty Crisis of 1960.** Princeton: Princeton University Press, 1966, 423 p.

No single event in postwar Japanese politics has been more dramatic, more far-reaching in influence or aroused more widespread foreign interest and concern than the Security Treaty crisis which reached its peak in June 1960. Ultimately the opponents of a revised treaty with the United States failed, but only after they had forced the cancellation of President Eisenhower's projected state visit to Japan and set in train events that led rapidly to massive and sometimes violent anti-revisionist demonstrations throughout the country and finally to the fall of the Kishi cabinet on July 15, 1960. Packard's book is a careful, detailed and fascinating account of what actually took place, the background and extensive preparations involved, and the reasons why things happened as they did. It thus takes place with the Hellmann volume as one of the few case studies of enduring value devoted to the interrelationships of Japanese domestic politics and foreign policies.

REISCHAUER, EDWIN O. **The United States and Japan.** Cambridge: Harvard University Press, 3rd rev. ed., 1965, 396 p.

The praises of this book, originally published in 1950, have been sung continuously for the past 20 years. Most specialists agree that it is still the best single general introduction available to postwar Japan and its complex relationships with the United States. Its basic theme is the seven years of American occupation (1945–1952) and their consequences for Japan and for Japanese-American relations. But this theme is developed within a framework of Professor Reischauer's unique knowledge of Japanese and Far Eastern history, Japanese national character, and the inner workings of the contemporary Japanese government, economy and society in general. The result is an extraordinarily sensitive, judicious and well balanced account of the new postwar Japan. The value of the work is further enhanced by five well-chosen documentary appendices and a brief bibliographical essay.

PASSIN, HERBERT, *ed.* **The United States and Japan.** Englewood Cliffs: Prentice-Hall, 1966, 174 p.

This is a collection of six essays prepared as background papers for the Twenty-eighth American Assembly. The meetings were devoted to a consideration of the current state and prospects of American-Japanese relations. Included among the papers are a treatment of Japanese and American views of each other by Edward Seidensticker, a discussion of the legacy of the American occupation by Robert E. Ward, treatments of developments in the political and economic spheres by Lawrence Olson and William W. Lockwood respectively, and essays on "The View from Japan" by Kinhide Mushakoji and "The Future" by Herbert Passin. This collection has been supplemented and updated by a more recent volume edited by Gerald L. Curtis entitled **Japanese-American Relations in the 1970s** (Washington: Columbia Books, 1970, 203 p.). The seven papers involved were a product of the

Second Japanese-American Assembly held at Shimoda from September 4–7, 1969. Together the two volumes provide an excellent introduction to the recent circumstances, problems and prospects of American-Japanese relations.

STOCKWIN, J. A. A. **The Japanese Socialist Party and Neutralism: A Study of a Political Party and Its Foreign Policy.** Carlton, Victoria: Melbourne University Press, 1968, 197 p.

The Japan Socialist Party (JSP) stands out among its counterparts elsewhere in the world for its qualities of doctrinaire devotion to outmoded ideological issues and continued failure to adapt to the realities of politics in an affluent and decidedly non-revolutionary society. Professor Stockwin finds its only analogue in the earlier postwar phases of Nenni's Italian Socialist Party. While his particular interest lies in examining and explaining the JSP's postwar foreign policy stands in terms of the doctrines of neutralism and pacifism on which they are primarily based, this endeavor leads him to explore in considerable depth the structure and leadership of the party itself and particularly of the factions that constitute its basic components. It is in the unremitting struggle among these factions and the personalities and local support structures associated with them that he finds much of the explanation for the party's foreign policies. An appendix sets forth the results of a questionnaire on foreign policy attitudes devised and circulated by Professor Stockwin, responded to by 40 percent of the JSP's Diet delegation.

Waga Gaikō no Kinkyō [The Recent State of Our Foreign Relations]. Tokyo: Gaimushō [Ministry of Foreign Affairs], 1957–.

This official annual, released each summer, deals with events and issues of the preceding Japanese fiscal year (April through March) and is divided into three sections. The first discusses multinational and general questions and Japan's position on these. The second reviews Japan's relations with individual countries, grouped regionally. These are narrative sections, written from the official viewpoint but in relatively informal style. The third section is a collection of recent documents and foreign policy speeches, chiefly Japanese but occasionally including major documents in foreign languages. The promptness of publication makes this documentary section a convenient source. In addition to tables giving the locations of Japanese embassies, legations and consulates and their foreign counterparts in Japan, there are appendices that change from year to year and often reflect the economic emphasis of Japanese policy. For example, the 1969 edition had a statistical comparison of Japan with the five nations ranking highest in population, gross national product, income per capita and output of each major commodity. There is a fairly detailed table of contents but no index.

Economic and Social Questions

HUNSBERGER, WARREN S. **Japan and the United States in World Trade.** New York: Harper and Row (for the Council on Foreign Relations), 1964, 494 p.

The importance of the subject of this book is implicit in two facts: Japan is the only non-Western nation that has succeeded in building a first-rate industrial economy, and its massive foreign trade inevitably involves the United States in many ways. The speed and scale of changes in the Japanese economy after 1950 threaten the timeliness of any book on the subject, but Hunsberger's is less perishable than most. His statistics generally end in 1962 and his manuscript was virtually completed by mid-1963, but his concern is not static but retrospective and prospective. For this reason, the book is a valuable survey of Japan's foreign economic relations and how they involve the United States.

The first part of the book, largely historical, is an overview of Japan's position within the world economy, with a detailed examination of the balance of international payments since 1929, and problems of capital and technology. The second considers the structure, geography and politics of Japan's export and import trade since the 1930s and especially since World War II. The third deals with Japanese and American foreign economic policy since the war and the problems and possibilities of the future. In addition to statistical appendices, there is a bibliographic essay that is especially useful for its description of Japanese economic sources available in English.

HOLLERMAN, LEON. **Japan's Dependence on the World Economy: The Approach toward Economic Liberalization.** Princeton: Princeton University Press, 1967, 291 p.

Warren Hunsberger's **Japan and the United States in World Trade** was written during one of the peaks of Japan's recent economic growth; Hollerman wrote in one of the valleys. Consequently, their books differ considerably in circumstance as well as in emphasis, though both are optimistic about the future of the Japanese economy. Hollerman is especially concerned with the relationship between domestic production and foreign trade, and attaches more importance than Hunsberger does to indications of imbalance and immaturity in the Japanese economy. The first section of his book deals with changes in the structure of Japan's foreign trade in comparison with changes in the structure of industrial production since World War II and includes a thoughtful discussion of alternative definitions and measures of dependence on foreign trade. The second section, examining sources of stability and instability in the Japanese economy, concludes that postwar growth has been chiefly in the domestic market rather than abroad and that structural defects in the capital composition of Japan's modern industries are matched by an "excessive role of short-term capital in the balance of payments." The third and longest section discusses the real and imagined problems involved in "liberalization"—that is, in the relaxation of import restrictions by Japan in compliance with international agreements and the demands of its trading partners. The copious narrative and documentary footnotes indicate considerable use of Japanese-language (as well as English-language) sources, but there is no bibliography.

ALLEN, GEORGE CYRIL. **Japan as a Market and Source of Supply.** Oxford: Pergamon Press, 1967, 140 p.

While not intended for scholars, this is an extraordinarily useful account of the economic foundations of recent Japanese foreign policy. Professor Allen, one of Great Britain's foremost students of the political economy of Japan, has provided a brief but authoritative interpretation of such basic subjects as the remarkable postwar growth and structure of the Japanese economy, the role and importance therein of foreign trade, the nature of major commercial policies, the structure of the Japanese import and export markets, trading partners and recent economic trends and prospects. The text is supported and illustrated by a number of well-chosen statistical tables covering postwar economic developments through 1965. There is a brief bibliography and an index. Given the salience of economic factors in the determination of Japanese foreign policy, this is a useful point of entry to those seeking a practical introduction to the factors determining current policies in this area. For a more detailed and scholarly account of the postwar development of the domestic Japanese economy, one may consult Professor Allen's **Japan's Economic Expansion** (New York: Oxford University Press, for the Royal Institute of International Affairs, 1965, 296 p.).

HUH, KYUNG-MO. **Japan's Trade in Asia: Developments since 1926—Prospects for 1970.** New York: Praeger, 1966, 283 p.

Today the actual and potential importance of the Japanese role in contributing to both the development and the stability of eastern and southern Asia is generally accepted. So is the fact that, in the near future at least, that contribution will be largely economic. Dr. Huh, an economist with the International Monetary Fund, here provides the most extensive and systematic analysis available of Japan's economic involvements with the 11 countries that constitute the Economic Commission for Asia and the Far East (ECAFE)—Burma, Ceylon, Taiwan, India, Indonesia, Malaya and Singapore (treated as a unit), Pakistan, the Philippines, Korea and Thailand. The period under review is primarily that from 1926 to 1962. The principal topics treated are the role and importance of foreign trade in the Japanese and ECAFE economies, structural changes in the development of Japan's economy and foreign trade since 1926, changes in the extent and character of Japan's trade with the ECAFE region since the mid-1920s, the place of the ECAFE trade in Japan's global trade pattern, trade and tariff barriers in the region, Japan's balance of trade and long-term capital flows with the ECAFE group, and prospects for changes and expansion of the trading relationships involved. The text is supplemented by numerous tables and charts and has a lengthy statistical appendix and a bibliography.

YANAGA, CHITOSHI, **Big Business in Japanese Politics.** New Haven: Yale University Press, 1968, 371 p.

It is frequently claimed that big business constitutes the most influential interest group in Japan and that as a group it is capable of controlling major decisions on both foreign and domestic policy. Professor Yanaga's book, while scarcely definitive, is the only reasonably systematic attempt in English to investigate this proposition on a significant scale. In general his findings support the hypothesis. He attempts to document this viewpoint through a series of case studies, four of which relate specifically to major issues of foreign policy. These are: atomic energy policy, the Southeast Asian reparations settlements, the United States–Japan partnership and the United States–Japan treaty of mutual coöperation and security.

SCALAPINO, ROBERT A. **The Japanese Communist Movement, 1920–1966.** Berkeley: University of California Press, 1967, 412 p.

Studies of contemporary communist parties in non-communist settings inevitably involve a substantial international component. This is the case with this excellent monograph by Professor Scalapino. Following a brief treatment of the prewar antecedents of the Japan Communist Party (JCP), the author recounts in considerable detail the shifting domestic fortunes of the postwar party and the several changes in basic orientation with respect to the United States, Moscow and Peking that have occasioned extensive internecine strife. The account is admirably interwoven with major developments on the Japanese and international scenes. Professor Scalapino concludes that, since Japan has become a post-Marxist society, there is very small prospect of the JCP coming to power. Some 21 tables convey very useful information about the membership, finances and electoral record of the JCP. Readers interested in more detailed information about the prewar history of the JCP are referred to George M. Beckmann and Genji Okubo, **The Japanese Communist Party, 1922–1945** (Stanford: Stanford University Press, 1969, 453 p.).

KOREA

General; Historical

MARCUS, RICHARD, *ed.* **Korean Studies Guide**. Berkeley: University of California Press, 1954, 220 p.

Scholarly research on Korea is dependent to a great extent upon source materials in various languages. This guide, published when serious Korean studies were just starting in the United States, provides a bibliographical introduction to such basic sources. Though it gives references to some English, French and German language sources, it emphasizes works written in Korean, Chinese and Japanese. Introductions are given to some 17 topics, including four on the major historical periods.

These brief essays are themselves of value to the scholar becoming interested in Korean studies. The important source materials are then listed and annotated for each topic. The guide also contains useful chronological tables and a series of maps of historical periods. Considerable emphasis is placed on the work of Japanese scholars and on Japanese-sponsored reprints of old Korean classics.

McCUNE, SHANNON. **Korea's Heritage: A Regional and Social Geography.** Rutland: Tuttle (with the coöperation of the International Secretariat, Institute of Pacific Relations), 1956, 250 p.

The place of Korea in the society of nations is conditioned by its geographical proximity to the major powers: China, Russia and Japan. The importance of geography in Korea's heritage is emphasized in this book by Shannon McCune, who was born in Korea and has spent many years there carrying on research on various phases of Korean geography. Dr. McCune divides Korea into ten regions on the basis of geographical characteristics, describing these in some detail and noting the underlying geographical contrasts between North and South Korea. The book is illustrated with numerous pictures and maps on uniform bases useful for comparative purposes. Unfortunately, most of the economic and population data is from the 1940s; the Korean War and the subsequent rehabilitation and development of the land and economy greatly changed the geography of Korea.

In 1965 Dr. McCune wrote a short book, **Korea: Land of Broken Calm** (Princeton: Van Nostrand, 1965, 221 p.), designed for general readers, which updated his description of the geographical regions of Korea and added historical, political and cultural summaries.

Noteworthy among foreign geographers was the German scholar, Hermann Lautensach, who published in 1945 a voluminous work, **Korea: Eine Landeskunde auf Grund eigener Reisen und der Literatur** (Leipzig: Koehler Verlag, 1945, 542 p.), and subsequently published a small book, **Korea: Land, Volk, Schicksal** (Stuttgart: Koehler Verlag, 1950, 135 p.), which updated and highlighted the conclusions of his earlier work.

BROWN, ARTHUR JUDSON. **The Mastery of the Far East.** New York: Scribner, rev. ed., 1921, 671 p.

This book is revealingly subtitled "The Story of Korea's Transformation and Japan's Rise to Supremacy in the Orient." Dr. Brown was well informed on the Far East and had made two lengthy visits to Korea, first in 1901 and again in 1909, after the Japanese had taken control. His comparisons of law and order and of economic development between the periods before and after the establishment of Japanese control are strongly in favor of the Japanese, though he "sought to be fair and just" in his treatment of Korea and of Japan's role there.

Because Dr. Brown was Secretary of the Board of Foreign Missions of the Presbyterian Church and was writing his book mainly for an audience of interested pastors and laymen, he devoted much attention to the Christian missionary movement in the Far East. He considered it "one of the most potent of the enlightening and reconstructive forces" at work in Japan and Korea. He notes but does not readily explain the phenomenal success of missionary work in Korea as contrasted with that in Japan, and his comments on the anti-Japanese attitudes of some of the American missionaries in Korea are interesting. Though the hopes the book expressed for the Christianization of the Far East were never realized, it was of considerable importance in molding informed American opinion on Korea at the end of World War I.

GRAJDANZEV, ANDREW JONAH. **Modern Korea.** New York: Day, 1944, 350 p.

During World War II, and especially after the Cairo Declaration of 1943 stated that "in due course" Korea would become free and independent, only a limited amount of objective and unclassified material was available on Korea in the English language. In part this gap was filled by **Modern Korea** by Andrew J.

Grajdanzev, a graduate student at Columbia University and a research associate of the American Council of the Institute of Pacific Relations, who used mainly Japanese source materials to compile his rather encyclopedic work. By critically assessing the official Japanese statistics, he was able to draw conclusions on the plight of Korean tenant farmers and on the industrialization taking place in Korea as part of the growth of Japan's war economy.

The book, a useful compendium of information, particularly for general data on the economic situation of Korea, drew heavily for its treatment of agricultural conditions from Hoon K. Lee's **Land Utilization and Rural Economy in Korea** (Chicago: University of Chicago Press, 1936, 302 p.). The tight hold which the Japanese had on the Korean farmers who were being driven into tenancy through Japanese-sponsored credit, marketing and irrigation systems is noted in both books. The resulting constant rural unrest was a significant factor in the inability of the Japanese to win the loyalty of the Korean people throughout their decades of political control. Great economic development took place in Korea during this period, but, as Grajdanzev effectively pointed out, this was for the benefit of the Japanese rather than the Koreans.

NELSON, MELVIN FREDERICK. **Korea and the Old Orders in Eastern Asia.** Baton Rouge: Louisiana State University Press, 1945, 326 p.

Through many centuries Korea had a particularly close relationship with Imperial China, which treated Korea not as a "barbarian" country but as a "younger brother" nation within the Confucian Chinese system of international affairs. The relationship was described in this book, completed in 1944 but not published until 1945, after the defeat of Japan in World War II and the division of Korea. The book as published, therefore, makes no mention of these important events.

Dr. Nelson's study, heavily dependent upon Western-language source materials, uses many State Department documents. Despite its handicaps, the book has value because it is lucidly written and effectively develops the important theme of Korea's relation to the Confucian state system. The author makes the interesting point that at the time of the signing of Korea's first treaty with a Western power, the United States, the two nations were operating on the basis of two quite different concepts of international relations. The loss of Korea's independence at the end of the nineteenth century has been the subject of a multiplicity of theses of American and Korean students attending American universities, yet there is today no adequate scholarly treatment of the whole span of Korean history available in English.

Korea and the Old Orders in Eastern Asia was published at a time when there was concern with the immediate situation in Korea: its division at the 38th parallel and occupation by Russian and American forces. As a consequence, Dr. Nelson's book, which seemed to deal with a remote past and "the old orders," did not get the attention it deserved. But the book represents an important beginning in developing a significant theme in Korean international relations.

LEE, CHONG SIK. **The Politics of Korean Nationalism.** Berkeley: University of California Press, 1963, 342 p.

The Koreans are a distinct ethnic group of people in Northeast Asia, with their own language, customs and traditions. For centuries they were greatly influenced by their near neighbors, the Chinese, more recently by the Japanese, and now by the Russians and the Americans. The important pre-1910 background of Korean nationalism is outlined in the first part of this book, where Dr. Lee stresses Korea's close relations with Confucian China and notes the effects of the training received by members of the Korean royal court and the bureaucracy in Confucian theories of government. The most valuable part of the book is a detailed account of the activities of Korean nationalists within and outside Korea during the periods when Korea was losing its independence and when it was a Japanese colonial possession. The growth of national consciousness in Korea was complex; it varied between the élite and the masses, a variation which Dr. Lee brings out cogently. The Independence Movement of March 1, 1919, which had a profound influence on nationalist groups of Koreans abroad and on the development of a new élite political group at home, is given full treatment. Western influence was strong in this movement, largely developed through the intermediary of Christian missionaries.

Three recent scholarly studies which cover some of the same period are: C. I. Eugene Kim and Han-Kyo Kim, **Korea and the Politics of Imperialism, 1876–1910** (Berkeley: University of California Press, 1967, 260 p.); Hahn-Been Lee, **Korea: Time, Change, and Administration** (Honolulu: East-West Center Press, 1968, 240 p.); and Soon Sung Cho, **Korea in World Politics, 1940–1950: An Evaluation of American Responsibility** (Berkeley: University of California Press, 1967, 338 p.). A fourth book, John Kie-Chiang Oh, **Korea: Democracy on Trial** (Ithaca: Cornell University Press, 1968, 240 p.), a political history of the Republic of Korea from 1945 to 1967, serves somewhat as a sequel to Dr. Lee's book, though not specifically designed to do so.

MCCUNE, GEORGE MCAFEE and GREY, ARTHUR L., JR. **Korea Today.** Cambridge: Harvard University Press (for the International Secretariat, Institute of Pacific Relations), 1950, 372 p.

The late George M. McCune, a son of a missionary educator in Korea and a professor of history at the University of California, finished most of the writing of this work before his death in 1948. It was completed by his wife, Evelyn B. McCune, with the collaboration of one of his former students, Arthur L. Grey, Jr. Published by coincidence at the beginning of the Korean War, it had a wide distribution, meeting a demand for information on Korea though some of the material was slightly dated.

The book is a general survey of Korea with emphasis upon its historical development and on its postwar partition. Major attention is given to political and economic development under the respective Russian and American occupations of North and South Korea. The role of the Japanese during their control of Korea from 1910 to 1945, and the possible reëmergence of Japanese influence in Korea, is explored at length—an aspect of the story rarely noted in recent works on Korea. The appendices include key official documents, data on Korean demography, tables of economic statistics and a selected bibliography. Dr. McCune was critical of some of the political and economic actions of the American occupying authorities. The heavy hand of the Russian military and political authorities in Pyongyang also receives adverse comments. Because information on North Korea came mainly from Russian sources and North Korean propaganda materials, this area of the book has of necessity some imbalance. The book none the less set a pattern for thorough scholarship and is still much needed for any study of Korea's internal and international situation.

HENDERSON, GREGORY. **Korea: The Politics of the Vortex.** Cambridge: Harvard University Press, 1968, 479 p.

This book has a significant theme: "In Korea . . . the imposition of a continuous high degree of centralism on a homogeneous society has resulted in a vortex, a powerful, upward-sucking force active throughout the culture." The theme is stated only as a hypothesis but is supported by an impressive amount of documentation and by forceful exposition. The author, who was for some years a Korean specialist at the United States Embassy in Korea and later a Research Associate at the Harvard Center for International Affairs, has a broad and scholarly interest in Korean culture, and an empathy with Koreans that shows through all of his writing.

The book is divided into four parts. The first deals with the traditional Korean society and, of necessity briefly, with Korea's long history. The second discusses in considerable detail the politics of the Korean anti-Japanese independence movement. The third part of the book, in which the author analyzes the continuity of Korean political culture, seeking to estimate the importance of a great variety of factors and to relate them to his central theme, is difficult reading and seems at times a little contrived. The final and most interesting part of the book is an account of the search for cohesion in Korea—a search which still seems a long way from success.

This is one of the most important modern books on Korea. Though it cannot be recommended for weekend perusal, it deserves to be read by those who seek to understand the country. Readers familiar with Korea may disagree with some of its ideas, question some of its generalizations and wish that some factors had been given more emphasis. However, all who read this book (including the footnotes) will have gained a deeper knowledge of modern Korea.

OLIVER, ROBERT TARBELL. **Syngman Rhee: The Man behind the Myth.** New York: Dodd, Mead, 1954, 380 p.

Syngman Rhee's resignation in 1960 from the presidency of the Republic of Korea marked the end of a period. This sympathetic biography by Robert T. Oliver was published in 1954 when Dr. Rhee was at the high point of his career. His resiliency, stubbornness and even intransigence had successfully rallied the Korean people during the Korean War; he had complete political control of South Korea and was much admired in the United States.

Dr. Oliver, professor of speech at Pennsylvania State University, became closely associated with Dr. Rhee during World War II, when the latter was working in the United States for the cause of Korean independence. This book obviously benefits from the close association the author had with Dr. and Mrs. Rhee and is near to being an official biography. The main elements in Rhee's life are sympathetically delineated. The weaknesses in his programs for the postwar development of Korea, his ignorance of economic and military strategy, and his misplaced trust in those around him are not stressed. Because of these shortcomings, the subtitle of the book is misleading, for Dr. Rhee does not fully emerge from some of the myths.

In contrast to Dr. Oliver's account is a biography by Richard C. Allen, **Korea's Syngman Rhee: An Unauthorized Portrait** (Rutland: Tuttle, 1960, 259 p.). The author's name is a pseudonym. The book, published shortly after Syngman Rhee's fall from power, is highly critical of the Korean President.

The definitive study of Syngman Rhee's life and role in Korean history is still to be written.

Korean War

PAIGE, GLENN D. **The Korean Decision: June 24–30, 1950.** New York: Free Press, 1968, 394 p.

One of the most important political decisions of any American president in recent times was made by Harry S. Truman when he ordered American troops into Korea in 1950 to meet the North Korean invasion. There have been numerous accounts of this decision in published memoirs, congressional testimony and the letters and speeches of various key figures. Utilizing these materials plus interviews with a number of important civilian officials, Glenn Paige has developed a most significant book, important not only for the information it gives about Korea and the Korean War but also for its presentation and analysis of the decision-making process in American foreign policy. Most of the book is a day-by-day narrative of the tumultuous week, June 24–30, 1950, when the procedure of reaching a decision shifted back and forth among the State Department, the Pentagon, the United States Embassy to the United Nations, the White House and the Congress. The dramatic unfolding of events is clearly elucidated.

The author notes, "In conclusion, it must be appreciated that the efforts made in this book to describe, analyze, evaluate and extrapolate from the Korean decision by no means have produced either a scientific theory of foreign policy making or a recipe for effective statesmanship." Yet the methodology he has used is very interesting and does indicate some of the sophisticated techniques which political scientists may now employ to discern important factors in the decision-making process. In this crisis situation the response of the key leaders—civilian and military—had to be empirically analyzed and evaluated. This has been done in two chapters which may not be so absorbing as the narrative of the process, but which in the long run may be of equal importance.

The Korean decision will be discussed for many years. Certainly this book will be invaluable in giving an enlightened basis for that discussion. If only one could read similar accounting in detail of what took place in Moscow, Peking, Seoul and Pyongyang during the same period!

RIDGWAY, MATTHEW B. **The Korean War.** Garden City: Doubleday, 1967, 291 p.

Many books have been written on the Korean War, including voluminous and detailed official histories of the various branches of the United States armed forces; but this relatively brief book, which gives in terse form the major events of the Korean War, is one of the best. Among the numerous highlights in the book is the account from General Ridgway's vantage point of the dismissal of General Mac-Arthur by President Truman; the author's summation of the issues involved in the MacArthur controversy is indeed authoritative. Many personal impressions are included in the book, which lighten and bring reality to this account of strategy and of battles, political and military. Above all, however, the book is valuable for its thoughtful comments on the implications of the events it recounts. General Ridgway, one of the most important participants, has put the Korean War in its significant setting, concluding with some "Lessons Learned and Unlearned"—a trenchant and sobering evaluation of the possible future military stance of the United States and of the role and ability of the American armed forces in such a situation.

Among other excellent books on the Korean War are T. R. Fehrenbach's **This Kind of War: A Study in Unpreparedness** (New York: Macmillan, 1963, 688 p.) and those on individual battles by S. L. A. Marshall, **The River and the Gauntlet** (New York: Morrow, 1953, 385 p.) and **Pork Chop Hill: The American Fighting Man in Action, Korea, Spring, 1953** (New York: Morrow, 1956, 315 p.).

VATCHER, WILLIAM H., JR. **Panmunjom: The Story of the Korean Military Armistice Negotiations.** New York: Praeger, 1958, 322 p.

Dr. Vatcher served as Psychological Warfare Adviser to the American delegation at the armistice negotiations in Panmunjom, Korea, at the end of the Korean War, "the longest truce talks in the World's history." To summarize the words spoken and unspoken and the issues involved at Panmunjom is no easy task; this book, a chronological account complete with footnotes and quotations from the official records and 90 pages of appendices, gives the pertinent material in readable form. The negotiations were indeed protracted and frustrating.

Dr. Vatcher tries to be objective in his portrayal of the participants and of the processes, but in view of his intimate association with the negotiations his personal views at times inescapably enter. He concedes that the United Nations command made some mistakes; included in these was the lack of adequate representation of other states fighting aggression in Korea. Though the Republic of Korea was represented, "it was seldom consulted. Its representatives were merely tolerated." The communist techniques of using propaganda, constant repetition, lying "without hesitation" and manufacturing incidents as part of their negotiations are commented upon. To the communists, according to Dr. Vatcher, "negotiation proved again to be simply one weapon in their arsenal of war."

Admiral Charles Turner Joy, who was the United Nations Senior Delegate for much of the negotiations, has written an interesting account from his vantage point: **How Communists Negotiate** (New York: Macmillan, 1955, 178 p.).

North Korea

SUH, DAE-SOOK. **The Korean Communist Movement, 1918–1948.** Princeton: Princeton University Press, 1967, 406 p.

One of the critical elements in the Korean situation since 1945 has been the role of Kim Il-sung and his communist movement in North Korea. This detailed work by a Korean scholar is a notable addition to Korean studies. Dr. Suh made good use of hitherto classified Japanese archival material as well as Chinese, Russian and Korean sources, and the growth of and intrigues among the shadowy factions of the Korean communist groups are traced with skill.

According to his study, there is an important distinction to be made between the Korean communist movements which developed during the 30 years from 1918 to 1948 and the present Communist régime which captured firm control of North Korea in 1948. Kim Il-sung, the present leader, was an obscure member of a communist group which operated with certain small Chinese Communist guerrilla forces in Manchuria in the 1930s. Kim's ascension to power in North Korea was largely due, the author says, to the mistakes of the other Korean communist groups rather than to Kim's own abilities. Dr. Suh points out that the present leaders are "alien" to the main forces within the communist movement of 1918 to 1948. The book ends with the events of 1948 when Kim Il-sung took control. A sequel, as objectively written and as rich in its source materials, needs to be written.

SCALAPINO, ROBERT A., ed. **North Korea Today.** New York: Praeger, 1963, 141 p.

In June 1963 a special issue of *The China Quarterly* was devoted to North Korea, and these articles were later assembled in book form by Professor Scalapino. The political, economic, educational and military systems of North Korea are individually treated in brief contributions. Most of the authors are Koreans educated in the United States, one exception being Dong-Jun Lee, who had escaped from Pyongyang in 1959 after four years as a writer for *Pravda*. Because of the diverse origin of the articles, however, the book suffers from an unevenness of presentation and a lack of coherence. North Korea needs to be better known. This book supplies some of the needed knowledge.

OUTER MONGOLIA

BAWDEN, C. R. **The Modern History of Mongolia.** New York: Praeger, 1968, 460 p.

The best modern history of the Mongols in any European language, this book is solidly based on Mongolian primary sources and on recent Mongolian scholarship founded on those sources; the author is one of the first scholars outside Mongolia to evaluate these materials critically. For Bawden, modern Outer Mongolia begins in the seventeenth century, when Manchu control was established over the area, Tibetan Buddhism began to spread rapidly among the population and Russian contacts became regular. A great deal of the subsequent history of Outer Mongolia relates to these three events, and Bawden's treatment of their evolution down to 1921 is outstanding. The chapters covering the revolutionary and socialist periods are less satisfactory: the sources are fewer, less helpful and have been tampered with (the author spends a good deal of time on historiographical problems). The focus throughout is squarely on the Mongols and Mongolia, in contrast to earlier works, such as the still valuable Gerard M. Friters, **Outer Mongolia and Its International Position** (Baltimore: Johns Hopkins Press, for the International Secretariat, Institute of Pacific Relations, 1949, 358 p.), which treats Mongolia mainly as an object of international rivalries.

RUPEN, ROBERT A. **Mongols of the Twentieth Century.** Bloomington: Indiana University (Indiana University Publications, Uralic and Altaic Series, v. 37), 1964, 2 v.

An encyclopedic history—mainly political—of the Mongolian People's Republic.

The author has read extensively in the Russian sources on Mongolia for many years, and those materials form the basis of this book, which pays special attention to the Soviet and Chinese roles in Mongolian affairs. A great deal of factual information is presented in notes, tables and 17 appendices, and the book is enriched by more than 80 rare and fascinating photographs. The second volume is a classified (but largely unannotated) bibliography on the M.P.R. of more than 2,900 items in all languages—the largest of its kind in existence.

SANDERS, ALAN J. K. **The People's Republic of Mongolia: A General Reference Guide.** New York: Oxford University Press, 1968, 232 p.

This is the most useful recent handbook on the M.P.R. in any European language. It provides a large fund of general information on the country, particularly on the government, party, army and press, along with the names of all important (and many unimportant) officials at the time of writing—about 1966. The most recent official Mongolian statements and statistics on state finance, industry and agriculture, transport, communications, and domestic and foreign trade (to 1964) are found here in condensed form. A gazetteer of place-names, some biographical sketches, a chronology of events, and some aids for travelers round out the volume. The book is based primarily on official Mongolian sources, which the author usually accepts at face value, and should not be regarded as a critical evaluation. Its fidelity to its sources gives it a unique feature, however: it is the only book on the M.P.R. in a European language in which all personal and place-names are spelled correctly.

For extended treatment of the M.P.R.'s geography and natural resources, Sanders' book is still surpassed by Erich Thiel's **Die Mongolei: Volk und Wirtschaft der Mongolischen Volksrepublik** (Munich: Isar Verlag, 1958, 495 p.).

V. THE PACIFIC

THE PHILIPPINES

KIRK, GRAYSON LOUIS. **Philippine Independence.** New York: Farrar, 1936, 278 p.

Grayson Kirk's book deals mainly with the forces responsible for the Philippine Independence Act and includes a very perceptive discussion of the way in which the United States came to take over the Philippine Islands as well as the general course of our Philippine policy. The author, who preferred a semi-protectorate to the Tyding-McDuffie Independence Act, analyzed the moral, political and economic factors involved in U.S. policy toward the Philippines with great care and skill.

There is a valuable analysis of the special interests in American politics, such as the methods and objectives of the farm groups, as well as of the American political process, all based on contemporary sources. At the same time, the author shows an appropriate understanding of the aims and motives of the Filipino politicians. The approach is moral without being moralistic, the style is witty, graceful and clear, a model for all political scientists.

This book should be read along with George A. Malcolm's **The Commonwealth of the Philippines** (New York: Appleton-Century, 1936, 511 p.), in which some of the same issues are discussed. Malcolm, a former Justice of the Supreme Court of the Philippine Islands for 18 of the 30 years he spent there in public service, thought the Filipinos had proven that they could maintain an autonomous government when protected by the United States. But he predicted a bleak economic future and a country open to Japanese aggression for an independent Philippines. He recommended that the United States should have nothing to do with their security, not even share in a multilateral guarantee of their neutrality, in order to avoid a dangerous political alliance.

WORCESTER, DEAN CONANT and HAYDEN, RALSTON. **The Philippines, Past and Present.** New York: Macmillan, rev. ed., 1930, 862 p.

Dean Worcester's account of American administration in the Philippines first appeared in 1914. This revised edition adds a biographical study of Worcester's 14 years' experience as a member of the Philippine Commission, a summary of events since 1914 and some useful appendices. Worcester, who did scientific zoological studies in the Philippines before the American occupation, played a decisive role in formulating policy in the Commission. One virtue of his book is the well-written account of how that policy came to take shape, an account which is equally well informed as to the attitudes of Filipinos toward the American decision makers and which reveals the vital interplay between them. He deals fully with the American conquest of the Philippines and the question of the Filipinos' readiness for independence. As Secretary of the Interior, he was responsible for the bureaus of public health, public land, forestry, mining, agriculture, fisheries, the pagan and Mohammedan tribes, government laboratories, patents and copyrights, the weather bureau and guarantee service, as well as the enforcement of the pure food and drug act. Worcester had the qualities of judgment and leadership to perform this Napoleonic task. Of all he undertook, he was perhaps proudest of his work with the pagan peoples of the mountains, people who had never been within sound of the bells under Spain. This book is exciting reading, invaluable for the student of international relations, modernization, American policy, public administration and the Philippines.

FORBES, WILLIAM CAMERON. **The Philippine Islands.** Boston: Houghton Mifflin, 1928, 2 v.

Both the British and the American colonial services contained men who combined a talent for administration with a gift for sound scholarship. Forbes, like most administrators, naturally assumed that the achievements of the modernizing colonial power were well worth the cost to the colonized. He seemed to be unaware that American trade policies had serious disadvantages for the Filipinos, and, although much more generous in his estimates of Filipino capacities for self-government than most of his contemporaries, he did not believe in complete independence. He favored a "supervised Commonwealth under American sovereignty" with a reserved power of intervention entrusted to a high commissioner.

The value of this book lies in its firsthand accounts of many important aspects of Philippine life and affairs, its revelation of the official American view of the country's problems and its discussion of the alternatives for U.S. policy regarding Philippine independence. Much of the information on geography and early history is now outdated, but the chapters on government, public order, finance, justice, health and education, public works, prisons, Church and State are still useful. There is good material on political parties and elections and the role of the Filipino in administration and politics.

The work also reveals quite a lot about the nature of American colonialism in this period just before the independence movement found powerful allies in the United States. The self-image is one of the high purpose, determination and unselfishness of Americans whose rule was a blessing to the Filipinos, to the world and to America. The comparison with the rule of other imperial powers is high-minded and naïve in spite of an effort to be fair. The documentation is extensive and all the more useful because the author illuminates much of it from personal experience. These volumes are a valuable period piece.

SCAFF, ALVIN HEWITT. **The Philippine Answer to Communism.** Stanford: Stanford University Press, 1955, 165 p.

There are very few careful scholarly accounts of the Huk movement in the Philippines. In fact, there is a dearth of responsible investigation of the radical movements in the Philippines both for the American period and after. Scaff's study thus has both intrinsic merit and scarcity value. It is the most compact, inclusive and perceptive of contemporary studies of Philippine dissent and includes a very useful summary of the antecedent preparation for the Hukbalahap movement. The long history of agrarian revolt especially in central Luzon is obviously a contributing factor, and this aspect is put in perspective in an excellent study of agrarian politics by Frances Lucille Starner, **Magsaysay and the Philippine Peasantry** (Berkeley: University of California Press, 1961, 294 p.). Scaff points out that the communists brought with them the new dimension of effective organization, leadership and a sustaining ideology. The part played by the Comintern in preparing the way for a Philippine communist movement is especially revealing. It is a pity that more material was not given on this issue. The main part of Scaff's book is important for its account of how the initial use of the mailed fist gave way to the later and more successful techniques.

HAYDEN, JOSEPH RALSTON. **The Philippines.** New York: Macmillan, 1942, 984 p.

The most useful contemporary books on the American era in the Philippines (1898–1946) were written by men who held high office in the colonial government. Professor Hayden's study of the national development of the Philippine people is perhaps the best general account of this period, especially in regard to the Commonwealth, because the author combines colonial administrative experience—he was vice-governor and secretary of public instruction in 1933–1935—with highly competent professional scholarship in the field of political science. Twenty years of research went into this massive study, and the result is a work that represents the best that American political science could offer at that time in the study of the non-Western world.

The book discusses the character and history of the Filipino people, presents a formal picture of the main institutions of government and a vivid account of how politics really works. It deals extensively with problems of education, public health, language, literature and foreign relations. There is no substitute for Hayden in impressive coverage and documentation. Nor is there a better way of recovering an evaluation of American rule and of Filipino capacities made by contemporary American officialdom and political science. However, like many other involved and responsible Americans, Professor Hayden thought that the Filipinos could never solve their problems and maintain independence without continuing American help and protection. He shows little interest in the economy, especially in those gross inequalities of wealth and opportunity in the Philippines which help to explain revolutionary political developments both during and after the war.

FRIEND, THEODORE. **Between Two Empires: The Ordeal of the Philippines, 1929–1946.** New Haven: Yale University Press, 1965, 312 p.

The main recommendations for this book are that it makes use of social science as well as historical techniques and that it uses impressive amounts of Philippine materials (an advantage over an otherwise useful work by Garel A. Grunder and William E. Livezey, **The Philippines and the United States**, Norman: University of Oklahoma Press, 1951, 315 p.). The author made use of the National Library's Quezonia Collection, the Laurel papers, captured Japanese documents and the usual American collections, and did a lot of interviewing. His review of source materials at the end of the volume is first-rate.

Friend chooses to emphasize what he calls two crises: first, the combination of the Great Depression, Japanese expansion and Philippine nationalism that led to the promise of independence; second, the invasion and partial "Japanization," followed by American liberation and the final achievement of Philippine sovereignty. New material and a new approach illuminate Friend's treatment of the movement toward independence. The portraits of Quezon and Osmeña emerge as vivid, life-sized and credible. On the second crisis Friend also brings new material to bear with considerable effect. Discussion of U.S. military policy is very realistic. The failure of the United States either to leave defense to the Filipinos or to provide adequate security meant that the United States was responsible for much death and destruction in the Philippines. The Republic today, according to the author, is now between two different empires, as the Chinese Communists have taken the place of the Japanese military. Any shortcomings in the book are more than compensated for by the new material and the realistic approach.

AGONCILLO, TEODORO A. and ALFONSO, OSCAR M. **A Short History of the Filipino People.** Quezon City: University of the Philippines, 1960, 648 p.

In the study of international relations, there are times when what is related is more important than the relations themselves. This was true in every period of United States relations with the Philippines. There are several other good histories of the Philippines, essential to the student of these relations, such as those of Conrado Benitez, **History of the Philippines** (Boston: Ginn, rev. ed., 1954, 522 p.), John L. Phelan, **The Hispanization of the Philippines** (Madison: University of Wisconsin Press, 1959, 218 p.), Pedro S. de Achútegui, S. J., and Miguel S. Bernad, S. J., **The Religious Revolution in the Philippines** (Manila: Ateneo de Manila, 1960, 578 p.), and Gregorio F. Zaide, **The Philippines since Pre-Spanish Times** (Manila: Garcia, 1949, 486 p.).

The **Short History** stands out, not for scholarly qualities but because it is a statement of the position of the Filipino revisionist school of historians which emerged after World War II. To these two scholars, Filipino history begins with the revolt against Spain, what went before 1892 being a lost history. They present

Bonifacio, long overshadowed by Rizal and Aguinaldo, as the hero of the revolt against Spain because he fought for social revolution. America served, in their view, to reduce a social revolution into a mere political compromise ending with the granting of independence on July 4, 1946. According to the revisionists, Bonifacio was also a man of the masses, a hero of the people and a proletarian who understood the need for organization. The Americans immortalized Rizal, so runs the argument, because he opposed violence. The revisionists elevated Bonifacio because he understood the need for violence. The Agoncillo-Alfonso book records one of the main themes, possibly the most important theme, of postwar Philippine nationalism. To it might be added Luis Taruc's **Born of the People** (New York: International Publishers, 1953, 286 p.), Cesar Adib Majul's **The Political and Constitutional Ideas of the Philippine Revolution** (Ithaca: Cornell University Press, 1957, 304 p.), and Emilio Aguinaldo y Famy's and Vincente Pacis' **A Second Look at America** (New York: Speller, 1957, 258 p.). They all speak of the stuff of which postwar nationalism is made and help to clarify many aspects of United States–Philippine relations, particularly after independence.

JENKINS, SHIRLEY. **American Economic Policy toward the Philippines.** Stanford: Stanford University Press (for the American Institute of Pacific Relations), 1954, 181 p.

There are few books on United States economic policies toward the Philippines; most of the material is in the *Congressional Record* or institutional reports. Shirley Jenkins' examination of U.S. economic policy revolves around the Philippine Trade Act (Bell Act) of 1946 and its impact on the postwar Philippine economy. The thesis of her book is that the Bell Act put the clock back to prewar patterns and prevented the Filipinos from the industrialization and diversification that were rightly considered to be necessary conditions for an independent foreign policy. The value of the study lies in its discussion of the background of the Philippine economy—for which the eloquent introduction by Claude Buss is very helpful— and its critical evaluation of the United States attitude toward the Philippines, especially the favored position demanded for American business. It falls short, however, of an institutional analysis that would suggest an alternative program for the type of economic development that would bolster an independent republic.

There are several good books on the Philippine economy itself. Very important among these is A. V. H. Hartendorp's **History of Industry and Trade of the Philippines** (Manila: American Chamber of Commerce of the Philippines, 1958– 1961, 2 v.). But for the student of international relations, an essential analysis of the national economic development is Frank H. Golay's **The Philippines: Public Policy and National Economic Development** (Ithaca: Cornell University Press, 1961, 455 p.). While not dealing directly with foreign policy, it is a professional analysis of economic conditions and problems of the postwar period for which there is no substitute.

FISCHER, GEORGES. **Un Cas de Décolonisation.** Paris: Librairie Générale de Droit, 1960, 377 p.

Georges Fischer's book is among the more thoughtful foreign evaluations of United States policy in the Philippines. Fischer claims that the policy was doomed to failure because it was too legalistic and indifferent to the social setting of the new institutions it brought with it. In other words, the social setting in the Philippines, as with most developing countries, was such that a well-informed, responsible public opinion would never mature sufficiently to make the foreign-imposed democratic institutions work to the advantage of the people at large. Social change in such countries, says Fischer, can only come from above, from the state, and not from the pressures of public opinion. To make matters worse, the United States froze all possibilities of initiative from above by forming an alliance between dominant American political and economic interests and the small Filipino élite which benefited from the colonial connection. According to the author, the United States took care to see that this alliance survived the granting of independence. This approach not only robbed Philippine independence of its dynamism but also helped to maintain structures unadapted to the needs of development. Limitation of the suffrage to those who had the main stake in society, Fischer claims, worked against those changes that we set for ourselves as conditions for a healthy public opinion. These arguments are taken up and discussed in a somewhat different setting in George E. Taylor's **The Philippines and the United States: Problems of Partnership** (New York: Praeger, for the Council on Foreign Relations, 1964, 325 p.), an examination in depth of the relations between the two countries.

GROSSHOLTZ, JEAN. **Politics in the Philippines.** Boston: Little, Brown, 1964, 293 p.

This is an outstanding study of the cultural and psychological bases of Philippine politics. Its central theme is that the strengths and weaknesses of Philippine democracy rest largely upon the distinctive cultural attitudes of Filipinos, particularly with respect to bargaining relationships. The fluid and flamboyant character of Philippine politics is related to the constant Filipino need to seek out and establish quid pro quo relationships that will give them a degree of security. Grossholtz traces these attitudes back to educational and child-rearing practices and the features of the folk culture.

The work also provides a useful historical resumé, an analysis of the economic base of Philippine public life and an outline of the formal structures and institutions of government. Its rich treatment of the Philippine political culture extends to the style of politicians, the process of élite recruitment, the play of interest groups and the role of the mass media.

Above all, this is an understanding work about Filipinos which helps to explain why they should have found some features of American culture so congenial, and why they have such difficulties finding their national identity and making their national institutions more effective.

AUSTRALIA; NEW ZEALAND

WATT, ALAN. **The Evolution of Australian Foreign Policy 1938–1965.** New York: Cambridge University Press, 1967, 387 p.

Although Watt begins his historical and analytical account of Australian foreign policy in 1938, the year of the Munich crisis, he states in his preface that this "should not be taken to imply that Australia had no foreign policy worth examining before that year." Nevertheless, 1938 is a logical year in which to begin such a discussion, for while Australia was then led by conservatives strongly devoted to the dogma of "the diplomatic unity of the Empire," and continued to be so until 1941, events soon dictated the elaboration of positions and policies rather more particular to Australia. Watt deals with that great shift in orientation with efficiency and insight, skillfully utilizing the accumulated literature. The book is the best historical introduction to Australian foreign policy as it has evolved since 1938.

Because it is so admirably specific in reference to the facts of the unfolding story, Watt's book takes priority over but does not eliminate from consideration T. B. Millar, **Australia's Foreign Policy** (Sydney: Angus and Robertson, 1968, 361 p.), which is focused on the problems of policy as they appeared in the late 1950s and early 1960s. While Watt launches his book from Munich, he does refer back to the policy of appeasement, one of the most controversial in imperial history. For more light on the role of the dominions in the appeasement policy, see Essay 8 in D. C. Watt, **Personalities and Policies** (London: Longmans, 1965, 276 p.), and for an especially judicious assessment, see chapter 10 of Nicholas Mansergh, **The Commonwealth Experience** (New York: Praeger, 1969, 471 p.).

HALL, HENRY LINDSAY. **Australia and England.** New York: Longmans, 1934, 319 p.

Hall's book deals with Australia's imperial relations, with emphasis on the tensions between Australia's proto and actual nationalism and its active or passive sense of "loyalty" to the Empire. It therefore deals with foreign policy only as it can be said to have become involved in the tensions mentioned as detectable in the discussions of "separation" (from the imperium), neutrality in Britain's wars, imperial federation, the range of powers available to self-governing British colonies after about 1840 and the role of locally financed and commissioned defense forces (the Australian navy) in relation to imperial defense.

For a quick review of the general history of Australia, see Manning Clark, **A Short History of Australia** (London: Heinemann, rev. ed., 1969, 274 p.). Further national background is given by O. H. K. Spate, **Australia** (New York: Praeger, 1968, 344 p.).

SCOTT, ERNEST. **Australia during the War.** Sydney: Angus and Robertson, 1936, 922 p.

While it is generally agreed that the roots of Australian foreign policy run far back into its colonial past, it is also generally agreed that it first came to the surface at the time of World War I, particularly at the Peace Conference. There it was enunciated by William Morris Hughes, who emphasized the Australian concern to ensure that the neighboring islands be placed under its own or British control, and on absolute insistence that no challenge, explicit or implicit, to the country's White Australia policy be tolerated. Mr. Hughes also associated himself with the extremist demands for reparations from Germany. This multifaceted episode is treated as history in Sir Ernest Scott's volume, part of the official Australian war history series, the fullest account available. It is treated in a personal fashion by Mr. Hughes himself in **The Splendid Adventure** (London: Benn, 1929, 456 p.). See also L. F. Fitzhardinge's life of Hughes, the first volume of which is **William Morris Hughes: A Political Biography. V. I: That Fiery Particle, 1862–1914** (Sydney: Angus and Robertson, 1964, 321 p.).

EGGLESTON, SIR FREDERIC WILLIAM. **Reflections on Australian Foreign Policy.** New York: Institute of Pacific Relations (for the Australian Institute of International Affairs), 1957, 216 p.

In the last 40 years of his life, Sir Frederic William Eggleston, who called himself a liberal, became the exemplary nonacademic intellectual of his country. His experience of public life covered the years from World War I, including the Paris Peace Conference, the inter-war years (during which he was associated with the Australian Round Table group), World War II and a decade after. He was the first Australian minister to China, 1941–1944, and minister to the United States, 1944–1946.

The papers in this book, some of them reprints, mirror his last reflections on "the basics" of Australian foreign policy and the evolution of the Commonwealth out of the Empire. He speculated on how viable the Commonwealth may now be, on the problems of Asia at large and specifically (at considerable length) on the course of events in China leading up to the communist triumph in 1949 and the situation in the Pacific after the Korean War. Taken as a whole, the book is an illuminating *tour d'horizon* of Australian external relations, past and emergent, made savory by the salt of long experience and the pepper of a self-devised sociology of nations in their domestic and international relations. The book concludes with a full bibliography of Sir Frederic's writings.

EVATT, HERBERT VERE. **Foreign Policy of Australia.** Sydney: Angus and Robertson, 1945, 266 p.

Dr. Herbert Vere Evatt, Minister for External Affairs in the Labor Party's federal administrations under Prime Ministers John Curtin and Ben Chifley, 1941–1949, was President of the U.N. General Assembly, 1948–1949, and from 1950 to 1960 leader of the Opposition (Labor) to the government of Prime Minister Robert Gordon Menzies. Before entering federal politics he had served for ten years as an associate justice of the High Court of the Commonwealth.

By virtue of the coercion of events, by virtue of his own intellectual power and with the concurrence of his cabinet colleagues, Evatt gave Australian foreign policy its highest nationalistic expression. In so doing, he transformed the terms and conditions for the formulation of Australian policy without, however, in any comprehensive sense, fixing either the particulars or the generalizations in final form. Evatt's policy was a compound of nationalist, internationalist and social-democratic elements: nationalistic in that he sought to establish the reality of an Australian national personality; internationalist in that he sought the equality of all states under a rule of law strong enough to contain power politics; and social-democratic in that he sought the extension of social policies Australian Labor had found valuable to all nations. These are reflected in this and subsequently published collections of his speeches.

MILLAR, THOMAS BRUCE. **Australia's Defence.** Melbourne: Melbourne University Press, 1965, 198 p.

Millar's book is a careful statement of the Australian defense problem as it is seen today. His proposition is that Australia cannot hope to defend itself out of its own resources against an assault by an enemy of major stature and so must find a great power overseas to serve as final guarantor of security. Traditionally that power had been the United Kingdom; today it is the United States. However, within this definition of realities there is ample room for discussion and decision as to the size and composition and organization of the defense forces actually in being at any particular time, or to be striven for in the predictable future.

Millar discusses the issues in the light of the ruling decisions since World War II. He concludes that Australia has been underspending on defense, partly to favor basic economic development, partly because of the difficulty of deciding what defense-in-being is wise in the complicated present in view of the rapid obsolescence of contemporary defense technology, and partly from too acute awareness of the overarching fact that whatever Australia does, it cannot accumulate forces and material sufficient to enable it to stand alone, stopping short of nuclear capacity. Millar favors emphasis on mobility to meet Australia's own uses for defense forces on a limited scale and in coöperation with her security guarantor.

CASEY, RICHARD GARDINER. **Friends and Neighbors: Australia, the U.S. and the World.** East Lansing: Michigan State University Press, 1955, 181 p.

R. G. Casey, now Lord Casey and retired Governor General, has had a longer direct involvement in Australian foreign relations than any other person, beginning as liaison officer for foreign affairs between the Australian and United Kingdom governments between 1924 and 1931, serving as first Australian minister to the United States, and from 1951 to 1960 as Minister for External Affairs. Some of this background is reflected in his **Personal Experience, 1939–1946** (New York: McKay, 1963, 256 p.).

As shown in both the papers in this book and the record, the Casey diplomacy as Minister for External Affairs was oriented around three basic ideas: it was necessary to ensure Australia's security by cultivating the friendliest possible relations with the United States; it was basic to Australia's interests that it be on the best possible terms with its Asian neighbors; and both objectives should be realized with no serious diminution of the intimacy of the traditional ties with Britain. The severest challenge to the Casey outlook came at Suez in 1956, when his Prime Minister took the initiative in supporting the policy of Sir Anthony Eden.

STARKE, JOSEPH GABRIEL. **The ANZUS Treaty Alliance.** Melbourne: Melbourne University Press, 1965, 315 p.

The Australian–New Zealand–United States Alliance of 1951 symbolizes the great post–World War II switch from the United Kingdom to the United States for the ultimate guarantee of Australia's national security. It is regarded by the Liberal-Country Party leadership, in power when it was negotiated and still (1970) in power, as the sine qua non of Australian defense policy. The idea of the centrality of ANZUS in Australia's foreign political outlook is emphasized in this study of the alliance by J. G. Starke, an international lawyer. The book can be usefully supplemented by an account of the negotiation of the treaty by Percy Spender, Minister for External Affairs at the time, in his **Exercises in Diplomacy: The ANZUS Treaty and the Colombo Plan** (Sydney: Sydney University Press, 1969, 304 p.).

GRATTAN, C. HARTLEY. **The United States and the Southwest Pacific.** Cambridge: Harvard University Press, 1961, 273 p.

Although the history of American-Australian contacts begins with the visit to the infant settlement at Sydney of an American trading vessel in 1792, the relations, while certainly various, were peripheral for both countries until the great turntable event of World War II. Nevertheless, the earlier story is well worth examining carefully, and it is now being done both extensively, since the 1790s, and intensively, focusing on particularly significant episodes. The Grattan book, published in the American Foreign Policy Library, examines the relation in its historical context. So also, subject to the time limitations of their titles, do Werner Levi, **American-Australian Relations** (Minneapolis: University of Minnesota Press, 1947, 184 p.) and Gordon Greenwood, **Early American-Australian Relations from the Arrival of the Spaniards in America to the Close of 1830** (Melbourne: Melbourne University Press, 1944, 184 p.), which takes in relations with South as well as North America. A book which examines the relation as it has developed since 1942 from various angles is Norman Harper, *ed.,* **Pacific Orbit: Australian-American Relations since 1942** (New York: Humanities Press, 1969, 256 p.).

O'CONNELL, D. P. and VARSANYI, J., *eds.* **International Law in Australia.** Sydney: The Law Book Company, 1965, 603 p.

While this book is specifically addressed to Australian lawyers with a general interest in or professional concern with international law, it is useful to all students of foreign affairs because of the strong light it throws on the legal aspects of Australia's foreign relations, and also because professional legal men such as Evatt, Menzies and Barwick have played so large a role in the formulation and execution of Australian foreign policy.

As this book is decisively oriented toward the situation of Australia after World War II (though some of the essays include a brief statement of the pre–World War II position), it may be useful to the student to consult J. G. Starke's excellent retrospective essay on "The Commonwealth in International Affairs," in R. Else-Mitchell, *ed.,* **Essays on the Australian Constitution** (Sydney: The Law Book Company, 1952, 319 p.), in which the international position of Australia back to pre-federation days before 1901 is reviewed.

CRAWFORD, SIR JOHN GRENFELL and OTHERS. **Australian Trade Policy 1942–1966: A Documentary History.** Canberra: Australian National University Press, 1968, 641 p.

The relation between Australia's foreign economic policy and political foreign policy is as difficult to explain exactly as is the case with any other nation, but there is certainly a connection between them. In any account of Australia's economic relation to the Empire it figures as the "cash nexus" and is placed along with and as complementary to the politico-constitutional-cultural factors supporting "loyalty." The "cash nexus" was undoubtedly a factor of prime importance in imperial relations up to World War II, when the great redefinition took place. Sir John Crawford, who is Vice Chancellor of the Australian National University, traces the evolution of Australia's trade policy during a period when spectacular adjustments in political foreign policy were made and far more widely observed and assessed than the equally spectacular changes in trade policy.

An essay by Sir John, dealing specifically with Australian-American trade relations, is to be found in Norman Harper, *ed.,* **Pacific Orbit: Australian-American Relations since 1942** (New York: Humanities Press, 1969, 256 p.). For material extending the story to Europe, see H. G. Gelber, **Australia, Britain and the EEC,**

1961 to 1963 (New York: Oxford University Press, 1967, 296 p.). On Australia's world economic position a good short book is J. O. N. Perkins, **Australia in the World Economy** (Melbourne: Sun Books, 1968, 197 p.), and for a sound general account of the Australian economy, see P. H. Karmel and M. Brunt, **The Structure of the Australian Economy** (Melbourne: Cheshire, 1962, 154 p.), which necessarily emphasizes the centrality of trade to Australia's economic viability.

WOOD, FREDERICK LLOYD WHITFIELD. **New Zealand in the World.** Auckland: Whitcombe, 1940, 143 p.

Professor Wood's book is the best explication of New Zealand's place in the world—which is largely to say, its place in the British Empire—up to World War II. It is a lucid and understanding account of why, in the inter-war parlor game of ranking the dominions in order of loyalty to Britain, New Zealand was invariably placed first, ahead of its neighbor Australia. While this ranking generally corresponded with the facts, there were instances of New Zealand dissent from imperial policy and practice over the years. Little has been written since the publication of this book in 1940 that either modifies or supplements Wood's story. However, a great deal of study and assessment of the domestic history has been done, and this has invariably enriched the understanding of New Zealand's international position. A good, short, up-to-date history is Keith Sinclair, **A History of New Zealand** (New York: Oxford University Press, 1961, 305 p.). For a longer account see C. Hartley Grattan, **The Southwest Pacific to 1900** and **The Southwest Pacific since 1900** (Ann Arbor: University of Michigan Press, 1963, 2 v.).

WOOD, FREDERICK LLOYD WHITFIELD. **The New Zealand People at War: Political and External Affairs.** Wellington: Department of Internal Affairs, War History Branch, 1958, 395 p.

This admirably expert volume offers not only an account of the domestic impact of World War II on New Zealand but also demonstrates the consequences to its external relations. The reorientation of these relations closely parallels that of Australia, though both the subtle and the more obvious factors of difference in geographical position and character and the structure of the economy are qualitatively very important. In his opening chapters Professor Wood deals with the foreign political outlook during the 1920s and 1930s and devotes much attention to the Labor Party's position with regard to both imperial and foreign relations. A companion volume to Wood's in the official war history, dealing with the economic aspects, is J. V. T. Baker, **War Economy** (Wellington: Department of Internal Affairs, War History Branch, 1965, 660 p.).

MILLAR, THOMAS BRUCE, *ed.* **Australian–New Zealand Defence Co-operation.** Canberra: Australian National University Press, 1968, 125 p.

The papers in this small book were delivered at a conference held at Wellington, New Zealand, in February 1968. While they focus on the possibility of a more systematic collaboration in defense between Australia and New Zealand, the papers set out clearly the differences between the two countries, an aspect of the relation that too often escapes foreign observers. As T. B. Millar puts it, "the two states have overlapping and complementary preoccupations." They are not identical. Nevertheless, there is a decided trend toward trans-Tasman collaboration at all levels—political, economic, defense.

OCEANIA

FURNAS, JOSEPH CHAMBERLAIN. **Anatomy of Paradise.** New York: Sloane (in coöperation with the American Institute of Pacific Relations), 1948, 542 p.

Insightful, iconoclastic, entertainingly witty, remarkably provocative despite the flippancy of its style, this survey of Hawaii and the islands of the South Seas succeeds in encompassing the full sweep of Pacific history, ending with the post–

World War II period. The work's major contribution is the debunking of the myth of the South Seas savage, whether it be the idyllic account first introduced by the explorer and then embroidered by novelist and artist, or that of the degraded and inept heathen as depicted by the missionary and governmental functionary. Through the device of separating fact from fiction, the lure of the South Pacific is relentlessly dissected. Stripped of the romanticism, what emerges is a complex account of multidimensional political, economic and social change, ofttimes repetitive as the various island areas sequentially experienced the erosion of their indigenous cultures under the impact of continuing Western contact.

FUCHS, LAWRENCE H. **Hawaii Pono.** New York: Harcourt, Brace and World, 1961, 501 p.

James Michener's "Hawaii," read by many uninitiates as a true-to-life portrayal of the Hawaiian Islands, in part finds a scholarly companion in Fuchs' "social history," which covers the period between annexation at the turn of the twentieth century and statehood, six decades later. Buttressed by extensive recourse to documented sources, polling returns and 155 depth interviews, this book surveys the Islands' ethnic stratification of *haole* (Caucasians of North European ancestry), Hawaiian, Portuguese, Chinese, Japanese and Filipino, and the oligarchical control exercised by the *haole* élite. In vivid style, all of the contestants who played major roles in the unionization of labor, the democratization of politics and the successful challenge to the Island oligopoly come alive in the recounting of the changes which have restructured the Hawaiian polity. But, despite its academic attention to accuracy of detail, testified to by 40 pages of references and footnotes, this book runs afoul of the same trap that ensnared Michener, for, as Fuchs admits, it "is an *interpretation*—not a definitive history."

CARANO, PAUL and SANCHEZ, PEDRO C. **A Complete History of Guam.** Rutland: Tuttle, 1964, 452 p.

The peoples of Guam—ruled for more than 400 years under the flags of three different nations—survived only through replacement of their traditional culture by a new, hispanicized amalgam, just as intermarriage with nonnatives preserved the vestiges of the almost annihilated Chamorro stock. These peoples nevertheless still maintain their distinctiveness even though they are now American citizens and their island a territory of the United States. Their history deserves to be recorded. That is what this work sets out to do, covering the long saga from discovery through Spanish rule, the land-battleship administration of the U.S. Navy between the Spanish-American War and World War II, the interlude of Japanese occupation, to the final placement of Guam under American civilian administration at mid-twentieth century. But in the course of the endeavor, history becomes equated with chronology, to the detriment of analysis and the loss of perspective on the relative importance of events. This results in such anomalies as the itemization of island prices in 1949 in four times as much space as is given a reference to the extended defiance of the Governor by the Guam Congress' lower house which led to the adoption of the Guam Organic Act by the U.S. Congress in the following year. Useful as this work is, with its scholarly references, Guam's definitive history remains to be written.

MELLER, NORMAN. **The Congress of Micronesia.** Honolulu: University of Hawaii Press, 1969, 480 p.

Broader than the title suggests, this is a study of the introduction of the American-type legislature into the Trust Territory of the Pacific Islands and of the legislative institution which serves as the cutting edge for the development of Micronesian self-government. The book relates the numerous experiments of the American administration with structuring variant forms of district legislatures, superimposing them on indigenous political organizations, and shows how prescriptive leadership was accommodated at the same time that American forms and processes were being modified. As a capstone, the Congress of Micronesia was established in 1965, providing for the first time an all-Micronesia identity. The decisions leading to the creation of the Congress, the drafting of its charter, the application of the one-man-one-vote principle to the apportionment of the Territory, the election of its initial members and the first Congress at work are all reported fully as part of an analysis of the evolution of the legislative process. Focusing upon a single political institution—the legislature—this work highlights the emergence of a new indigenous leadership bent on using the Congress to force modification of the trusteeship relationship, with complete independence for Micronesia the potential objective.

KEESING, FELIX MAXWELL and KEESING, MARIE MARGARET. **Elite Communication in Samoa: A Study of Leadership.** Stanford: Stanford University Press, 1956, 318 p.

Self-styled as a study of communications to, from and among persons who wield influence in negotiation, the formation of public opinion and decision making, this work is a seminal inquiry into status relations within American and Western Samoa. Traditional Samoan structure and its adaptation to modern government constitute the background against which the various forms of communication and the processes of political participation are treated. In a still predominantly oral culture, sensitive to the nuances of symbolic meaning, the modern mass media have been adapted to the purposes of the traditional élite. Similarly, the *matais* (chiefs) have mastered the modern parliamentary procedures of the differing legislatures of the two Samoas. In thus expanding the scope of their communication skills, they have succeeded in preserving their élite roles in traditional society, as it has been modified, and in transferring them to the introduced governmental institutions as well.

KEESING, FELIX MAXWELL. **The South Seas in the Modern World.** New York: Day, rev. ed., 1945, 391 p.

World War II is long since over, the talented Keesings now dead, but this book on the islands of the South Pacific stands as a solid assessment of the area just prior to the bringing of modern warfare to the South Seas. Without singling out any island group for special consideration, a number of topics pertinent to the Pacific are insightfully covered: land as the crucial factor in indigenous society, health and education, the role of religion and the missions, native populations and nonnative residents, traditional leadership and introduced government, and alternatives in native policy and governance. The 61 pages of appendix and 19 of selected bibliography are testimony that the book was based on original work of Professor Keesing and a wide array of published studies, many of which he had directed.

A survey always runs the risk of either emphasizing diversity to the detriment of commonality or so searching for threads of parallelism and for universality that individual phenomena are downgraded. The book chooses a path between both extremes. The revised edition attempts to identify the effects of the war on the South Pacific, but although provocative, the Keesings were more successful as chroniclers than as prognosticators. Nevertheless, this book continues to provide a carefully documented basing point from which to commence research on the current Pacific basin.

OLIVER, DOUGLAS LLEWELLYN. **The Pacific Islands.** Garden City: Doubleday, rev. ed., 1961, 456 p.

This comprehensive survey of Oceania from the pre-contact period to the middle of the twentieth century succeeds in weaving history, geosciences, economics and ethnography into a captivating account of cultural change. Through the device of grouping the impact of the various waves of "alien" intruders on the Australian aborigines, and on Melanesians, Micronesians and Polynesians in such developmental categories as "coconut civilization" and "mining," the full scope of over 400 years of change is perceptively recounted. The very strengths of its historical and ethnographic research and its delightfully wry and sometimes iconoclastic style are the sources of its major weaknesses: too gross a gloss of the current scene and the shallowness of its predictions.

STANNER, WILLIAM E. H. **The South Seas in Transition.** Sydney: Australasian Publishing Company, 1953, 448 p.

In a suave, literate, wide-ranging survey of three Pacific dependencies—Australia's Papua and New Guinea, England's Fiji and New Zealand's Western Samoa—Stanner reconstructs the pre-contact and pre–World War II scene in each, the impact of their war experiences and their immediate postwar changes and plans. Papua and New Guinea's atomistic multiplicity of small, unintegrated social units is contrasted with Fiji's highly stratified social system of chieftainship, rank and centralized authority and with Samoa's strong emphasis upon political-ceremonial life. All three have small European populations and know economic penetration by European capital, so that they present dual economies within plural racial and cultural communities. Unlike economic development elsewhere, characterized as largely a question of encouraging capital formation and industrialization, bases for development had yet to be built here. Stanner turns a critical eye on the postwar use of political placebos instead of implementing modifications which would encourage fundamental change. Nevertheless, he found all three areas administered conscientiously within the general spirit of the U.N. Charter. The study concludes with a well-reasoned generalized treatment of development theory.

In the choice of three British areas, this work was in effect setting the stage for F. J. West's later comparative treatment of three different colonial policies in the Pacific in his **Political Advancement in the South Pacific.** And if Stanner leans toward New Zealand, in his sometimes depreciative references to Samoan character and the Samoan independence drive, this is but counterweight for J. W. Davidson's treatment of the Samoan cause in **Samoa mo Samoa.**

WEST, FRANCIS JAMES. **Political Advancement in the South Pacific.** New York: Oxford University Press, 1961, 188 p.

"Fiji, Tahiti and [Eastern] Samoa," the author notes, "belonged to a common Polynesian system of rank and authority; they experienced a similar history of European contact; but their political advancement has been molded by three different colonial practices." The British policy of association, the French tradition of assimilation and the indeterminacy of American colonial aims provide the frame within which the governmental structure and activities of these island areas are each briefly examined. All three demonstrate an acceptance of the introduced political institutions and partial success in meeting modern standards of government. Singled out for particular attention are the roles of the executive and legislative institutions and the division of power between them. Traditional leadership is found to have disappeared in Tahiti, to have been preserved in Fiji through the device of creating a government for native peoples (the Fijian Administration) within the Fijian government, and to have been adapted so as to be an integral part of the American administration of Eastern Samoa. But with this survey completed, the reader may ask why the author did not address himself more to an examination of the specific causative factors underlying differential political advancement, rather than being content with merely identifying the divergencies which separate these three territorial aspects of Polynesia.

DAVIDSON, J. W. **Samoa mo Samoa.** Melbourne: Oxford University Press, 1967, 467 p.

A history of Western Samoa in its quest for independence, the work also serves as an autobiography of the author in Samoa and his contributions to that end. (This is not to suggest impropriety in the juxtaposition, for Davidson early identified himself as champion of "Samoa for the Samoans," and he has served subsequently as constitutional adviser to other Pacific peoples seeking self-government.)

In essence, this is a sympathetic survey of Samoan political history, starting with the traditional polity and its adaptation on contact with the West. Critical of colonial paternalism, the book is long on developments within Samoa since World War II and ends briefly with the initial years of the independent state of Western Samoa. The story of the Mau rebellion between the two wars is recounted fully, premised upon a thorough examination of New Zealand and Samoan sources, some of which are still classified. Interest in the influence of basic economic and social change on the course of political events tends to be slighted in the concern for the inclusion of impressionistic detail. As a consequence, the stage of history comes alive as Davidson carefully threads his way among the complexities of Samoan titles, introducing the reader in terms of first-person intimacy to the great and near-great of Western Samoa's political society. There still remains need for a definitive treatment of the emergence of the new state of Western Samoa in which the inadequacies as well as the attributes of the Samoans receive equal consideration.

VI. AFRICA

GENERAL TREATMENTS

HISTORICAL

See also France: Colonial Questions, p. 519.

OLIVER, ROLAND ANTHONY and FAGE, J. D. **A Short History of Africa.** Baltimore: Penguin Books, 1962, 279 p.

Published in 1962 and aimed at the general reader, **A Short History of Africa** quickly took its place as the most widely used textbook of African history in the English-speaking world. Though now out of date in several important respects, it has retained its position for the sufficient reason that no better text has come forward to replace it. It was the first comprehensive survey of the history of the whole continent that stood foursquare on the assumption that Africa had an "autonomous" past—*i.e.* a past that could be viewed from an indigenous perspective and not through the distorting lens of imperial and colonial historiography. No one reading this work could retain the illusion that there was no African history before the Europeans came; it caught the rising tide of post-colonial interest in Africa at the flood and has had an impact out of all proportion to its size.

DU BOIS, WILLIAM EDWARD BURGHARDT. **The World and Africa.** New York: Viking, 1947, 276 p.

In this book, W. E. B. Du Bois, a brilliant and productive black scholar, presents a historical framework aimed at emphasizing the contributions of Africans and people of African descent to the development of world history. Dr. Du Bois has been consistent in his efforts to correct the misrepresentations and distortions of black history as portrayed by Europeans. Among his numerous works are **The Souls of Black Folk** (Chicago: McClurg, 17th ed., 1931, 264 p.), **Black Folk: Then and Now,** and **Dusk of Dawn** (New York: Harcourt, 1940, 334 p.).

The World and Africa was written at the end of World War II and is one of the last books the author wrote. In it he examines the roots of the doctrine of white supremacy in scholarly research, both exploring the reasons why Europeans ignored the contributions of black people to world history and analyzing the nature of European exploitation of people of African descent, emphasizing its connection with the development of capitalism. His use of the flashback technique is effective in presenting the historical material which deals with the origin of black people in Africa, the relationship of blacks with the civilization in the Nile valley, the growth of the Sudanic empires, the perpetuation of the slave trade, the "rape of Africa" and the economic exploitation by international capitalism.

A revised edition of the book, issued in 1965, included several new essays written by Dr. Du Bois about such important events and personalities as the Congo crisis, Patrice Lumumba, Ghanaian independence and Kwame Nkrumah.

HAILEY, WILLIAM MALCOLM HAILEY, BARON. **An African Survey: A Study of Problems Arising in Africa South of the Sahara.** New York: Oxford University Press (for the Royal Institute of International Affairs), rev. ed., 1957, 1,676 p.

Lord Hailey's monumental work remains a landmark of postwar African scholarship. Its wide scope covers almost every aspect of the physical and cultural background of the continent, albeit understandably painted with broad strokes of the brush. The information has inevitably become dated, but the historical and ethnographic material retains much of its original freshness.

Substantial sections of the volume are taken up with descriptive material, particularly dealing with the administrative system of the colonial territories, but the Republic of South Africa receives extensive treatment. A particular feature of the work is the lengthy portion devoted to natural resources, land law and custom and to development problems as seen from the period of the middle 1950s. A variety of functional problems, such as labor, justice and education, are handled less satisfactorily; but even those chapters in which the author has obviously drawn on secondary sources contain recondite information that is to be found nowhere else in so convenient a package.

A concluding chapter on research in Africa makes interesting reading not so much for its present-day relevance but as an illustration of what gigantic strides have been made in 15 years to extend the knowledge of the continent, its peoples and its future. The casual references to the beginning of African studies in the United States at Northwestern and Boston Universities may sound somewhat strange to the reader today, but in themselves they show only too clearly how greatly American sophistication about Africa has grown in little more than a decade.

MURDOCK, GEORGE PETER. **Africa: Its Peoples and Their Culture History.** New York: McGraw-Hill, 1959, 456 p.

Professor Murdock's book is concerned with outlining the history of Africa for the last 7,000 years and also determining and describing the cultural areas for the whole continent. It is an excellent source book with an all-inclusive tribal index and a large-scale tribal map. The book contains a comprehensive classification of African peoples although the ethnographic details about each cultural group are rather sparse. One of the major difficulties is that the author includes too much, resulting in weak coverage at times. Also, the usual detailed behavioral emphasis of most anthropologists is missing. Murdock's historical reconstruction correlates six sources of data: the distribution of cultivated plants, linguistics, archaeology, extant documents, botany, and ethnographic relationships and distributions.

The first part of the book is a general introduction to Africa in which the problems of race, geography, language, economics, government and history are discussed. The remaining sections are concerned with African peoples and culture areas in which the people discussed are grouped together under the headings of agriculture, hunting, pastoralism, geography and linguistics. There are three North African subdivisions concerned with agriculture, three pastoral groupings of both East and West African peoples and one division on hunting that describes Bushmen, Pygmies and East African peoples. In the remaining three subsections, the peoples are grouped around three separate concepts of Indonesian impact, Cushite expansion and Bantu languages.

This excellent source book introduces many new and novel interpretations of African relationships, migrations, crops and groupings of people. The book is difficult to use since there is no topical index; however, excellent source material is listed at the end of each chapter.

KIMBLE, GEORGE HERBERT TINLEY. **Tropical Africa.** New York: Twentieth Century Fund, 1960, 2 v.

This book, written primarily for Americans who wished to gain greater understanding of Africa at a time of swift and profound changes in the political structure of tropical Africa, ranks among the most important general studies on Africa. Its aim was to project the basic conditions which set the framework within which change occurs. By drawing upon working papers prepared by specialists in numerous fields and upon his own firsthand encounter with the continent, the author, a former director of the American Geographical Society, attains a breadth of vision and a depth of understanding brilliantly illuminated by his own lucid and imaginative pen.

Volume I, entitled "Land and Livelihood," covers primarily the environmental frame, the human and natural resource endowment of Africa and its major economic activities. Volume II, "Society and Polity," examines the dynamics of social and political change, the assault upon ignorance and sickness, the emergence of the new élite and the price of growth. This is not a country-by-country study of tropical Africa; rather the region is viewed systematically, with a common denominator in the interaction between the natural environment and the cultural background and equipment of its people. The author boldly uncovers the manifold problems of emerging Africa but equally vividly captures the mood of the region—more truly a ferment than a revolution of rising expectations—as well as the desire of its peoples to retain their individuality, to be valued for what they are and not merely for what they can do.

LUGARD, FREDERICK DEALTRY LUGARD, BARON. **The Dual Mandate in British Tropical Africa.** London: Blackwood, 2d ed., 1923, 643 p.

Lord Lugard's classic statement on the theory and practice of British colonial rule makes as interesting reading today as when it was first published. In it he details the basis of his personal philosophy of administration which became enshrined in the governance first of India and later for most of tropical Africa. The basis of the system was the concept of indirect rule—that is, the exercise of administrative authority not directly by the expatriate administrator but through the agency of the traditional ruler, whose authority in the eyes of the people must be kept intact at all times. Lugard demonstrates that the origins of indirect rule go back to the British treatment of the princely states of India and points up his own role in transferring it to Uganda and to Northern Nigeria. Unfortunately, Lugard's methods were applied by his successors to parts of Africa where the structure of indigenous authority was unsuited to indirect rule and where the rulers proved incapable of adapting to modern needs, so that by World War II the system had lost many of the virtues of flexibility with which it had earlier been identified.

The "Dual Mandate" referred to in the title derives from Lugard's view that "Europe is in Africa for the mutual benefit of her own industrial classes and of the native races to their progress to a higher plane." To the modern reader, this is the basic justification for imperialism. Lugard makes no defense of it; rather, he sees this as the duty of the England of his time. We may disagree with his ends, but his methods left a lasting imprint on modern Africa.

PERHAM, MARGERY FREDA. **Lugard: The Years of Adventure, 1858–1898.** New York: Oxford University Press, 1956, 750 p.
————. **Lugard: The Years of Authority, 1898–1945.** New York: Oxford University Press, 1960, 748 p.

Margery Perham's **Lugard** is a full-scale, definitive biography of Frederick Dealtry Lugard, first Baron Lugard of Abinger, perhaps the ablest and certainly the most famous of Britain's proconsuls in tropical Africa during the imperial age. Lugard's life falls into three main phases. After soldiering briefly in India, he made his way to Africa and worked for a succession of commercial companies, exploring new territory and extending British influence in Nyasaland, Uganda, Borgu and Bechuanaland. Only in middle life did he win appointment as an official representative of the British government, and his main field of action became Nigeria. There he created the West African Frontier Force, conquered the north and ruled it as High Commissioner, and then was given responsibility for the whole country as Governor General after the amalgamation of Northern and Southern Nigeria in 1914. After his retirement in 1918 Lugard continued to exert great influence over colonial and imperial policy-making, and not over British policy alone. Among the many organizations with which he was associated were the Permanent Mandates

Commission of the League of Nations, the Advisory Committee upon Education in Tropical Africa and the International African Institute.

This excellently written work is more than a biography. From it the reader may gain a very clear perception of what imperialism was actually like for a participant (there are plentiful extracts from Lugard's voluminous private diaries) and also of the process by which an ambitious, hardworking man-on-the-spot could impose his will on a cautious and hesitant home authority.

Miss Perham, who worked closely with Lugard in his later years, writes as a convinced, if liberal, imperialist. She is as sure as was the subject of her biography that British rule was good for Africans, and few authors today would make quite such frequent use of words like "savage," "primitive," "barbarian," "uncivilized" when describing pre-colonial Africa. The work, in short, is something of a period piece (this need not be taken as a slur on Miss Perham) which strikingly demonstrates the revolution which has overtaken African studies during the decade of the 1960s.

DELAVIGNETTE, ROBERT LOUIS. **Service Africain.** Paris: Gallimard, 1947, 281 p.

Written by a former director of the School of Overseas France, this is one of the most candid and in many ways most accurate pictures of prewar French administration in Africa. It was originally issued in 1940, censored by the Vichy government and suppressed during the German occupation.

It is simultaneously a highly critical picture of the French administration and colonial society and a tribute to the work of the administrator. Delavignette's major thesis is that the French administration had long underestimated the real powers and position of the indigenous leadership; the chiefs, because they retained the full confidence of the mass of Africans, remained the "true heads of the empire." The bureaucracy of administration crushed out the spirit of experimentation in the administrator to the point where he became little more than an executor of the orders of the central government. The author's prescription for rectification of the sins of prewar administration was to revive the traditional village government by returning real power to the village chief—not the "straw-chief" who was a creation of the administration but to the man whom the villagers recognized as their real head.

In the new postwar African world, Delavignette foresaw the entry of Africa in the community of nations, but under the fraternal leadership of France. He warned against the inherent dangers of racism and against a feeling of French superiority bred of the colonial relationship. Although his vision of independent Africa may have been limited, in this volume he touches on the most trenchant criticisms that could have been made of the administrative theory and practice in the French empire.

BUELL, RAYMOND LESLIE. **The Native Problem in Africa.** New York: Macmillan, 1928, 2 v.

Despite its somewhat unfortunate title, Buell's two-volume work remains the best and most detailed account in English of British and French colonial administration in the inter-war period. It also includes chapters on Liberian administration and government and sections on South Africa and the former Belgian Congo. His accounts of the operation of administration in British East and West Africa and in former French West and Equatorial Africa are based on personal observation and on massive documentation; many of the most important documents are reproduced as appendices. The book therefore is valuable not only for its massively detailed description but as a reference source for the history of this period of colonial development.

As might be expected, Buell displays many of the prejudices common to colonial observers in his time, but his comment and conclusions on the various systems of colonial rule remain extremely accurate. His final words comparing the British and

French systems may sound rather ironic to the modern reader: "If France . . . maintains the friendly tolerance and affability toward the colored races . . . which the British lack . . . her ultimate success in developing native races . . . may be greater than that of the British Empire." Buell's work ranks among the great classics on pre-independence Africa, essential to any full understanding of the complex motivation behind European rule of the continent.

HAILEY, WILLIAM MALCOLM HAILEY, BARON. **Native Administration in the British African Territories.** London: H.M.S.O., 1950–1951, 4 v.

These four volumes, based on research undertaken by the author immediately before and after World War II, constitute the most comprehensive survey ever done of administration at all levels in British tropical Africa. It deals in detail with local administrative organization in each subdivision of the different territories, its history and its relationship to the indigenous structure of rule. While designed for the use of administrative officers as a means of comparative study of areas with which they were not acquainted, the survey forms an invaluable source of documentation for the specialized reader on the forms of British colonial administration. In addition, Lord Hailey offers substantial information on the administration of justice and a comparative treatment of the modifications of land law and custom.

What emerges is a picture of diversity within a single framework of a theory of colonial rule. Underlying the administrative philosophy of every territory were the prescriptions of indirect rule laid down by Lord Lugard for Northern Nigeria. One of the major accomplishments of the Hailey report was to show through comparative information the degree of success with which Lugard's principles have been applied.

The final short volume offers the author's general conclusions and policy recommendations, dealing particularly with the necessity of developing a general policy by the Colonial Office to give direction to progressive local self-government. In the light of the subsequent drive for independence, Lord Hailey's views in 1947 take on a particular cogency.

POLITICAL

FORTES, MEYER and EVANS-PRITCHARD, E. E., *eds.* **African Political Systems.** New York: Oxford University Press, 1940, 301 p.

Virtually every bibliography on Africa or comparative political analysis includes this pioneering work. Although not comparative in the more recent sense of the term, it brought together studies of eight indigenous political systems at a time when the study of political institutions had been strangely subordinated (though not ignored) by the anthropologists, who then still dominated the African studies field. Introduced by a ground-breaking essay by the editors, the anthropological contributors present what are still standard analyses of the governmental systems of the Zulu (South Africa), Ngwato (Bechuanaland), Bemba (Northern Rhodesia), Ankole (Uganda), Kede (Nigeria), Bantu Kavirondo (Kenya), Tallensi (Gold Coast) and Nuer (Sudan). The introduction's principal significance lies in its identification of two major types of political systems in what had been simplistically regarded by many as "tribal Africa": state systems (with centralized authority and other obvious institutions of government) and stateless systems (lacking both permanent governmental institutions and sharp divisions of rank, status or wealth). Variations of each type are analyzed by the contributors. The introduction, like the individual studies, also emphasizes the importance of economic influences on the political systems and the interrelations among power, authority and responsibility. The study of African political institutions stimulated by these insights has modified or elaborated them without diminishing their basic utility to the understanding of traditional African politics and government.

CARTER, GWENDOLEN MARGARET, *ed.* **African One-Party States.** Ithaca: Cornell University Press, 1962, 501 p.

African One-Party States is among the first of many compendia of analyses of politics in independent African states and is the first of three that its editor produced for Cornell University Press. Professor Carter, a noted scholar of Africa and European comparative politics, has brought together individual studies of Tunisia, Senegal, Guinea, Ivory Coast, Liberia and Tanganyika, each prepared by a different author but according to a common outline. Each author gives considerable attention to the physical, cultural and historical setting of political life, as well as to the contemporary intricacies of political competition. Unfortunately, neither the common outline nor the editor's introduction produces much in the way of useful comparison among the political systems discussed, since no detailed common analytic categories are developed. The most interesting chapters, those by L. Gray Cowan on Guinea and J. Gus Liebenow on Liberia, follow different paths to provide descriptions of those complex systems which still remain among the. best available.

COLEMAN, JAMES S. and ROSBERG, CARL G., JR., *eds.* **Political Parties and National Integration in Tropical Africa.** Berkeley: University of California Press, 1964, 730 p.

This bulky volume presents a series of mostly excellent studies of political life in 12 black African countries: Senegal, Ivory Coast, Sierra Leone, Cameroon, Guinea, Mali, Ghana, Liberia, Zanzibar, Somalia, Congo (Leopoldville) and Nigeria. Each chapter is written by a specialist who completed field work in the area in the late 1950s or early 1960s and focuses on political party structure, activity and competition, particularly as they relate to the political integration of plural societies and the territorial integration of smaller political units. A section on "Control of Nonparty Groups" presents chapters on voluntary associations, trade unions, traditional rulers and students, as they are active in a variety of African contexts. The introduction and conclusions by the editors analyze the tendency toward one-party and one-party-dominant régimes in Africa. They divide these régimes into those demonstrating a "pragmatic-pluralistic pattern" and a "revolutionary-centralizing trend" and assess probable future evolutions of each sort.

The book represents the most complete statement of what might be called the early "American school" of African political studies as it developed in the years around 1960. Its virtues were those of careful field work, sympathy with the polities studied, a familiarity with social science theory and a freedom from legalistic biases dominating much of European work. Its weaknesses were an overconcentration on political parties and on the present moment, and a tendency to underestimate the latent power of nonparty groups as most blatantly illustrated by the book's lack of attention to the African military.

FRIEDLAND, WILLIAM H. and ROSBERG, CARL G., JR., *eds.* **African Socialism.** Stanford: Stanford University Press (for the Hoover Institution on War, Revolution, and Peace), 1964, 313 p.

African Socialism provides an interpretive survey of the meanings that now familiar slogan had in the early 1960s for a wide variety of African states. Warily sympathetic scholars analyze national experiences with socialist planning in Ghana, Guinea, Senegal, Mali and Tanganyika, and the appendices provide representative samplings from statements of socialist doctrine by appropriate African political figures. Of these, the excerpt from George Padmore's previously unpublished "Guide to Pan-African Socialism" is particularly welcome.

Part I of the book is intellectually the most rewarding as seven scholars analyze the phenomenon from seven different perspectives. Three of these chapters illustrate the contrasts: Margaret Roberts warmly supports the independent development of African socialist experiments from her perspective as a Fabian socialist; I. I. Potekhine, at the time the U.S.S.R.'s leading Africanist, protects Soviet orthodoxy by denying that true socialism can have a national or regional content, though he cautiously allows for one or many "African roads" toward the creation of a socialist state; Igor Kopytoff calls upon his anthropological training to dispose— with a resounding negative—of the question of whether or not the sources of contemporary African socialism should be sought in traditional African societies, an assertion dear to the hearts of many proponents of African socialist doctrine. A report on the 1962 Dakar colloquium on African socialism makes it clear that such divergent points of view are not limited to non-Africans.

Subsequent events such as Tanzania's Arusha declaration and Nkrumah's short-lived espousal of "scientific socialism" emphasize the book's oft-stated point that the idea of socialism has a genuine appeal in large parts of Africa and that this idea can combine with differing local situations to produce a wide variety of political and economic structures.

HODGKIN, THOMAS. **Nationalism in Colonial Africa.** London: Muller, 1956, 216 p.

Thomas Hodgkin's **Nationalism in Colonial Africa** has been one of the most influential books on Africa to appear in the English language. Hodgkin, a Briton who has taught both in Ghana and at Oxford, skillfully relates social movements, such as urbanization, the rise of voluntary associations, syncretist religious sects and labor unions, to the growth of nationalist political organizations and nationalist ideologies. The application to Africa of Duverger's classification of political movements, and particularly the distinctions between congresses and parties and between mass and élite or cadre parties, set a model for nearly a decade of political research in Africa. While the distinctions have been shown to be less useful than they once appeared, and subsequent monographs permit today's analyst to develop a more nuanced picture of the nationalist era, Hodgkin's work is one of the rare books producing broad generalizations about African politics that remains well worth reading 15 years after it appeared.

ZOLBERG, ARISTIDE R. **Creating Political Order: The Party-States of West Africa.** Chicago: Rand McNally, 1966, 168 p.

Aristide R. Zolberg, a University of Chicago political scientist, presents in this short volume the first mid-1960s revisionist view of the early work of the American school of African political studies. In the course of developing his own argument about the difficulties of creating political order in Africa, Zolberg sympathetically and effectively criticizes some of the less adequate underlying assumptions of earlier works, including his own. Focusing on the single-party régimes of West Africa (especially Senegal, Guinea, Mali, Ghana and the Ivory Coast), the book uses a fair amount of theoretical sophistication to point out the very real limits to the power of political organizations in these countries, some of which had previously been described by both friend and foe in terms equivalent to those used for Hitlerian Germany or Leninist Russia. Zolberg effectively criticizes the mass versus the élite party distinction first presented by Hodgkin and argues that one must distinguish sharply those areas over which any African régime can exercise power from the large "residual" sector about which it can do very little. The book discusses sensitively the political role that ideology and socialist planning play in Africa, and its final chapters effectively prefigure the rash of military coups that began as the book went to press.

DIA, MAMADOU. **The African Nations and World Solidarity.** New York: Praeger, 1961, 145 p.

Mamadou Dia, educated to be an African teacher but trained as a politician and economist under the French Fourth Republic, built the political party that made Léopold Senghor Senegal's first president and served as Prime Minister until deposed by Senghor and the party he built in 1963. Neither a work of scholarship nor a bristling polemic, **The African Nations and World Solidarity** is an eloquent and honest statement, by a practicing politician, of the dilemmas of African development in the mid-twentieth century. Dia discusses sympathetically the political revolt of the third world's "proletarian nations," analyzes and rejects imitation of both Eastern and Western models of development for Africa and projects in the context of the short-lived Mali Federation a generous vision of "complementary development" (largely inspired by the theories of the Catholic economist François Perroux) which would shut African nations off neither from one another nor from the developed world. The subsequent collapse of the Mali Federation (analyzed in an epilogue) as well as Senegal's present economic difficulties and Dia's continuing imprisonment all testify to the problems generous visions confront in Africa.

The English translation by Mercer Cook, subsequently American ambassador to Senegal, is a model of grace and accuracy.

PADMORE, GEORGE. **Pan-Africanism or Communism? The Coming Struggle for Africa.** New York: Roy, 1956, 463 p.

Historically, one of the most important concerns of black scholars has been the relationship of Africa to people of African descent in the New World. George Padmore has made a valuable contribution to an understanding of this area of scholarly research in his book entitled **Pan-Africanism or Communism?,** a work especially significant today because of the great interest in black studies and pre-occupation with the black movements in Africa, the United States and the West Indies. Padmore played a special role in the postwar development of black thought and Pan-Africanism and also in African political developments as an adviser to Dr. Nkrumah in Ghana.

In the first part of his book, Padmore ties together many threads in the Pan-African movement, back to the slave trading era when the first "Back to Africa movements" were started. He focuses on the Sierra Leone settlement, the Liberian experiment and the role of Dr. E. W. Blyden, one of the earliest Pan-Africanists. In the second part, he ties in the birth of the Garvey movement, which had an explosive effect on black urban masses in the 1920s. W. E. B. Du Bois played a unique role in the "struggle for Africa" by organizing several Pan-African Congresses which Padmore analyzes in part III, showing how the congresses were related to the African independence movement of the contemporary era, particularly in Nigeria and Ghana. Parts IV and V give historical background on the development of the various colonial systems in British, French, Belgian and Portuguese areas with specific reference to Britain's multiracial policy in Kenya which produced the Mau Mau rebellion and constitutional developments in Nigeria which fostered tribalism. This material helps give the reader an understanding of crucial events that are taking place in Africa, namely the "multi-racial" policy of Ian Smith leading to the Rhodesian crisis and the constitutional-tribal conflict in Nigeria resulting in civil war. The final chapter of the book contains a comprehensive discussion of the relationships of communism to black nationalism in the United States and Africa.

George Padmore's book ranks among the best two or three studies yet published on Pan-Africanism.

ZARTMAN, I. WILLIAM. **International Relations in the New Africa.** Englewood Cliffs: Prentice-Hall, 1966, 175 p.

Professor Zartman's valuable study is a concise analysis of the relationships of 17 states in North and West Africa with each other. To sharpen his focus, the author has largely excluded relationships of the 17 with other African states and with the states of other continents. These geographical and substantive limitations may puzzle the reader at first, but the stimulating insights of the book turn out to be quite rewarding. It is a pioneering effort to interpret the developing system of international relations in Africa.

After surveying intra-African relations between nationalist leaders and groups from 1956 to 1965, the author analyzes the criteria for foreign policy. He concludes that ideology and personal interest are used more frequently than national interest as criteria. Moreover, the predominance of political party and other "subnational interests" tends to prevent the formation of national criteria. At the same time, the leaders are under pressure to justify their actions on the basis of national goals and symbols. A third section of the book discusses the limits on violence and intervention in each other's affairs, the politics of boundary problems and the limits on African unity and coöperation.

The author stresses the continual searching by African leaders for ideologies, definitions and national interests. A corollary of this "searching process" is the predominance of ad hoc policy-making in both form and substance. A result in western Africa is a special type of international relations system. The "proto-balance-of-power (1959–1963)" ended with the formation of the Organization of African Unity. Since then conflicting alliances have been avoided in favor of an African system of "mobile relations" based on "temporary coincidence of policy on the issue of the moment."

RIVKIN, ARNOLD. **Africa and the West: Elements of Free-World Policy.** New York: Praeger, 1962, 241 p.

The author, Director of the African Economic and Political Development Project at the Center for International Studies of the Massachusetts Institute of Technology, seeks to identify the important problems of African development. A crucial question is whether the swift passage from tribal and colonial societies to independent national states can be absorbed by a world community in a nonviolent and orderly way. The author reviews the necessarily changed role of Western European powers in Africa, the challenge that Africa presents to the European Economic Community and the new interest of the United States in the continent, born out of a concern for developing countries everywhere.

A second major and intimately related question is whether African economic growth can attain sufficient momentum to match the pace and meet the needs of swift and comprehensive political change and to absorb in steadily increasing measure those elements of the technological revolution that can be adapted to the African scene and harnessed to its development. The outcome of events in Africa in the 1960s does not make less relevant the logic upon which the author's main proposals for paving the way to African economic development are made—a multilateral organization for aid to Africa on the part of the West, an international guarantee of the national security of the African states, a moratorium on outside military assistance to African states and a security role for the United Nations in Africa.

THIAM, DOUDOU. **The Foreign Policy of African States.** New York: Praeger, 1965, 134 p.

Of all the books on the development of African foreign policies up to the creation of the Organization of African Unity (OAU) in 1963, this study has the advantage of being written by the long-incumbent Foreign Minister of an important African state (Senegal); it has the unique feature of being the only such treatment by a "conventionalist" or "moderate" practitioner, standing up against more numerous statements by the "revisionists" or "radicals" (Nkrumah, Touré). As such, it begins with a discussion of micro versus macro-nationalism (state national-ism versus Pan-Africanism), recognizing the appeal of both but the predominance of the first. He then discusses various meanings attached to socialism, although with less precision; after noting the bases of African socialism, Thiam attempts to characterize its application in African state systems into Eastward and Westward-leaning varieties. He then traces the dialectics of competing African groups leading to the formation of the OAU and, most important in his eyes, to the establishment of normative rules governing intra and extra-African relations, largely on the "conventionalist" model. It is unfortunate that the discussion of economic factors in external relations that have to do with communism is a secondhand summary of some scattered Western commentators, rather than the attempt to grapple with problems and concepts in his own terms that is evident in the rest of the work.

The book originally appeared as "La Politique Étrangère des États Africains" (Paris: Presses Universitaires, 1963, 166 p.). There is no substantive difference between the two language versions; both end with the formation of the OAU.

McKay, Vernon. **Africa in World Politics.** New York: Harper and Row, 1963, 468 p.

McKay's account stands as a fact-laden monument to what seems to be a far bygone era in African world relations. The emphasis of the study is out of balance, more determined by the experience of the writer (a member of the State Department in the formative years of African policy) than by the abstract importance of things, but the resulting treatment is uniquely rich in its areas of emphasis and beyond competition. The study deals mainly with African relations with the U.N. and the United States, with lesser attention to Pan-Africanism, Eur-Africanism and relations with Russia and India. In regard to the U.N., the emphasis is on the postwar pre-independence years and the aid, encouragement and training that the international organization afforded the new states and states-to-be (plus an additional chapter on pressures through the U.N. on South Africa). American interests, policy and relations are also examined in the same, sometimes overwhelming detail, in which the strongest portions concern the making of policy and its domination by external events. The historical and ideological roots of European, Indian and Russian interest in Africa are also explained as a background for a factual account of their influence in 1960. The book rises above its factual, non-conceptual level at the end when it suggests not only the increasing importance of race in international relations (still to be proven) but the characteristics of new states' foreign policy, the impact on international law and on the U.N. and the reversal of the trends of "radicalism" and "conservatism" in Ghana and Nigeria.

Cowan, Laing Gray. **Local Government in West Africa.** New York: Columbia University Press, 1958, 292 p.

An examination of the political science literature on sub-Saharan Africa reveals a striking imbalance. Most political scientists have emphasized the macro-political in African studies. Few have directed their attention to local government and politics in general and village micro-politics in particular. As a result, we know relatively little today about modern political and administrative processes in local Africa. At the same time, however, we observe that a growing number of political scientists have begun to recognize the need for a more balanced perspective. This development augurs well for African studies.

Since colonial and independent Africa are organically linked, it behooves those who would study local political and administrative processes in the contemporary period to become thoroughly familiar with the historical record. A very useful introduction to that record may be found in L. Gray Cowan's **Local Government in West Africa,** a study which traces the history of local government in the West African territories of Great Britain and France. Especially useful is the author's examination of the interplay of traditional authority patterns and novel political party currents and the impact that this interplay had on local government developments in the terminal phase of colonial rule. In the process, Cowan highlights forces which continue to affect (plague?) policy-maker and citizen alike in independent Africa: hence the value of the study to students of modern political and administrative processes in contemporary local Africa.

ECONOMIC

Hance, William Adams. **The Geography of Modern Africa.** New York: Columbia University Press, 1964, 653 p.

This study by a professor of economic geography at Columbia University is the most comprehensive in its field and concerns mainly the geography of economic development in Africa. The author points out that the political "struggle" for independence has been far less difficult than the problems of development that the independent countries now face. The purpose of his book is thus to present the major features of the economy of Africa, to analyze the handicaps and attributes that affect economic development and to assess some of the potentialities for growth in the years ahead. Since variety is one of the keynotes of Africa, he says, the approach is regional. After background chapters on the environmental and economic settings, the population and peoples of Africa and the political scene, the rest of the book is devoted to individual countries or groups of countries. An outstanding feature of the volume is the richness of its illustrative material, in particular the series of excellently drafted economic maps of particular countries and regions and several hundred well-chosen photographs. The book is a valuable reference work on the economic geography of Africa, and its insights and the logic of its argument make it a major contribution to the understanding of the African scene.

HANCE, WILLIAM ADAMS. **African Economic Development.** New York: Praeger (for the Council on Foreign Relations), 2d ed., 1967, 326 p.

This book originated in 1958 as a collection of research papers for a discussion group on African economic development at the Council on Foreign Relations, but the dramatic and far-reaching changes in the ensuing years necessitated substantial revisions in a second edition. By means of case studies, the author critically assesses major facets of modern African economic development: agricultural (the Gezira Scheme), mining (iron ore in Liberia), industrial (the Volta River project) and economic coöperation (East Africa). He briefly measures the environmental, economic and cultural potentialities of and obstacles to Africa's advance, the role of transport, and looks regionally at Madagascar, environmentally a part of Africa but displaying some striking cultural contrasts. He concludes with a quick view of the economic problems and potentialities of some 33 tropical African countries and summarizes the continent's major needs as to aid, agriculture and ambition. The book is essentially selective in its treatment, providing in-depth studies of development projects seen within the broader framework of environmental and cultural opportunities and constraints. Africa's modern dilemma, Hance points out, is that everything needs doing at once.

DUMONT, RENÉ. **False Start in Africa.** New York: Praeger, 1966, 320 p.

This is a bold, controversial but constructive work, mainly about ex-French Africa south of the Sahara but applicable to tropical Africa as a whole. The author is an agronomist deeply experienced in the physical problems and potentialities of the underdeveloped world who also displays a sensitivity for the human issues. Slavery and colonialism must bear the blame for the fact that tropical Africa, after a tentative pre-colonial start, now seems to be marking time, he notes; but obstacles to modern development lie not only in the environmental problems of the tropics but also in traditional attitudes and, where it occurs, in a potentially dangerous self-interest among the new ruling élite. But the author's real message is that underdevelopment can be conquered in 20 years. He sees economic progress largely in a rural socioeconomic revolution which is necessary to secure any appreciable increase of purchasing power of the overwhelming mass of population, who remain—and for scores of years will remain—dependent upon agriculture. The training of peasant leaders is thus an immediate priority; industry and agriculture must be complementary; the fuller potential of Africa's ecological zones must be realized; the whole educational system must be reorganized; credit and coöperatives require improvement, and external financial and technical aid must continue.

SOCIAL AND CULTURAL

HERSKOVITS, MELVILLE JEAN. **The Human Factor in Changing Africa.** New York: Knopf, 1962, 500 p.

This last book by Herskovits stresses the human factor in assessing development in Africa, and primary emphasis is placed on the reaction of the peoples of Africa to a variety of social situations. Generally, Herskovits analyzes modern Africa with stress on the interaction of conservatism, the retention of established cultures and the acceptance of innovation. In a sense, this book is a summation of his earlier writings and experiences in Africa.

Africa's relationship to the world and her rich past and heritage are briefly discussed in the first two chapters. Pastoralism, agricultural societies and food gathering and hunting are described in general terms in the next two. These chapters form the background or base line of change against which the topical discussions are viewed.

The first major topic scrutinized is the incomers, or outsiders: Europeans, Asians, Arabs and others whom Herskovits saw as the peoples from beyond Africa who changed African behavior. This is followed by an analysis of land, which, to Herskovits, means the different ways people use, allocate or control land. Religion is then examined on three levels only, as he discusses the impact of Christianity, the Missions and the spread of Islam. A chapter reviews the development and impact of modern European education and literacy on African cultures. Under the heading of the city, urbanism is scrutinized; this section is poorly done. Independence movements, nationalism and the problems of new states are evaluated with few new insights. Herskovits sees economic change as economic development, increased productivity and the growth of labor unions. Finally, the book ends with a discussion of African art and the new values and attitudes developing in Africa today. This is a useful book with many new insights into modern Africa.

BASCOM, WILLIAM RUSSELL and HERSKOVITS, MELVILLE JEAN, *eds.* **Continuity and Change in African Cultures.** Chicago: University of Chicago Press, 1958, 309 p.

This book is a collection of papers by some of the participants at the first interdisciplinary conference on Africa in 1953, many of whom had been trained in anthropology at Northwestern University. The major theme is cultural continuity and linkage of behavior in Africa as opposed to conflict and change. The editors assume that African states or cultural entities are synthesizing Western culture with their traditional patterns of behavior instead of opposing it. This interpretation of change in Africa would be questioned by many anthropologists today.

Specifically, the book consists of 15 papers concerned with different phases of African life. Three deal with African kinship systems, two with economics, and two examine religions. A general analysis of cultural change is set forth in two papers, while one is concerned with ethnohistory and change over a long period of time. The remaining papers are much more general, analyzing such topics as language, art, music, and demography and stability in African cultures. Seven of the papers are based on studies conducted in West Africa, and three are concerned with Central, West and southeast Africa respectively. As a result, the book has a general West African bias, although nine different cultures are examined. Topically, some very interesting data and analyses are presented with regard to the position of women and polygyny in African cultures.

One of the difficulties with using the book is that all the research for the various papers was completed before 1953, while the book was published in 1958; thus much of the data and the analysis employed is comparatively dated.

SMITH, EDWIN WILLIAM. **The Golden Stool.** New York: Doubleday, 1928, 328 p.

The author, a son of missionaries, served as a missionary in Africa for many years. From this background came a wealth of writings which established him as one of the leading humanists with a deep and in many ways profound interest in Africa. This book is a series of essays on a variety of subjects—the "worth of the African," the impacts of commerce and industry, colonial rule, Christianity and Islam, and education—all of them integrated by the theme, "the conflict of cultures." The title refers to the most sacred symbol in Ashanti culture, an object made more famous because of its desecration by an imperious and culturally ignorant colonial officer. Smith's recounting of the tragic episode serves as a parable from which he derives what was, for the 1920s, an enlightened if rather patronizing set of guide-lines for the conduct of a "higher civilization" when it impinges upon a "lower one." He was deeply aware of what he called "the disintegration of African social life and its evil consequences," and he exhorted his compatriots to decry the wretched racist myths of inherent African inferiority, to respect and honor the good in African life, to strive to make the good better and to stimulate Africans to develop themselves according to their own genius.

WESTERMANN, DIEDRICH. **The African Today and Tomorrow.** New York: Oxford University Press, rev. ed., 1939, 355 p.

Westermann, truly one of the forefathers of scholarly African studies, was the first editor of *Africa,* the journal of the International Institute of African Languages and Cultures. He took the post in the midst of an outstanding career as a social anthropologist, linguist and Africanist. In 1934 he published **The African Today,** which quickly became a standard work and subsequently reappeared in this revised edition.

The book was the first credible introduction to the peoples and problems of Africa as a whole written for the general reader. It grew out of the firsthand experiences and reflections of an expert Africanist whose interests, both scientific and humane, were primarily in African people themselves rather than in the European presence in Africa. Westermann presented overviews of African economic institutions, arts and crafts, traditional and colonial governments, languages, education and race relations. The second edition appeared with only modest revisions and updating. The additional word "Tomorrow" in the title drew attention to the contemporaneity of the work, which dealt with current African life and the problems of culture contact and social development in colonial Africa. That the book is simplified and generalized need not detract from appreciation of its contribution to the history of African studies.

WILSON, GODFREY and WILSON, MONICA. **The Analysis of Social Change.** New York: Cambridge University Press, 1945, 177 p.

This general theory of society and of social change is a truly remarkable, compressed and parsimonious synthesis of abstract concepts, concrete illustrations and statement of general policy implications. The latter two elements are of special significance for Africanists, because the work grew out of the Wilsons' research among the Nyakyusa and other Central African peoples, but the theoretical concepts continue to have value for the analysis of any social groups, whether small in scale such as local communities or on as large a scale as a "world society." Out of the background of early theoretical developments in the fields of comparative sociology, social anthropology and structural-functional analysis, "scale" emerges as the principal organizing concept. After constructing their theoretical framework, the authors turn to the analysis of the nature and causes of social and cultural change as societies increase in scale. Because the scales of various African social institutions increase at differential rates in consequence of both internal and external (especially European) factors, strains or disequilibria result. Certain social policies, some rooted in traditional, some in modern institutions and practices, are incompatible with increase in scale and must be modified in the interests of a new equilibrium. If this book tends now to be overlooked in the welter of studies of social change, it is probably because it is 25 years old. Its reissuance in 1965 was deserved. Professor Monica Wilson is professor of anthropology at the University of Cape Town, South Africa.

HUNTER, GUY. **The New Societies of Tropical Africa: A Selective Study.** New York: Oxford University Press (for the Institute of Race Relations), 1962, 376 p.

This study of the societies of parts of tropical Africa in the period immediately after independence attempts to cover a wide variety of aspects of social change, with particular emphasis on post-independence development. The author was assisted by a committee appointed by the Institute of Race Relations and by a number of well-known specialists who prepared studies of discrete topics.

Any effort to depict changing societies with so broad a brush is bound to be the subject of criticism, since no one topic can be dealt with exhaustively. But for the general reader, no other volume provides so convenient and, on the whole, so accurate a discussion of the entire field as it was at the time the volume appeared.

The book contains some particularly pertinent observations on the relationships between social advance in the rural areas and the growing politicization of the rural masses. As they become more conscious of the possibilities of improvement, the author argues, they will exert greater pressures on the state to create those conditions in which individual ambition can be fulfilled. For continued economic progress, manpower planning will be needed, but Mr. Hunter warns against the danger that planning may well be aimed at the upper levels of manpower needs without sufficient attention to middle and even less skilled manpower resources. His comment appears particularly apt in the light of a possible oversupply of graduates in some African nations today.

Although completed almost a decade ago, this book can still be recommended for the insights it lends to the contemporary social problems of much of Africa.

MOUMOUNI, ABDOU. **Education in Africa.** New York: Praeger, 1968, 319 p.

Education in Africa is an ambitious effort to survey the history, present situation and future prospects of the educational systems of the independent African countries. Abdou Moumouni is well qualified to write such a volume as he has traveled extensively and taught in several West African countries. He is presently a professor at the École Normale Superieure in Bamako, Mali. The book, originally published in French, deals almost exclusively with Francophone Africa. Although this makes the title misleading, the book is more useful to an American audience whose knowledge is primarily limited to English-speaking Africa.

In reviewing the situation, Moumouni is highly critical of the irrelevancy of the colonial tradition in African education and says that, with the exception of Guinea and Mali, no countries have broken with the neo-colonialist dependence upon French patterns and technical experts. The author urges that countries reject their inherited colonial traditions and develop school systems based upon African languages and culture.

ASHBY, ERIC. **Universities: British, Indian, African: A Study in the Ecology of Higher Education.** Cambridge: Harvard University Press, 1966, 558 p.

With the possible exception of land rights, no aspect of the process of decolonization in Africa has created greater controversy than education, and a good share of this controversy has raged around higher education. Among the welter of official documents, commission reports and personal memoirs, Eric Ashby's book provides a clearer and more detailed picture than any previous publication of the export of the British university to the colonial areas.

Although he begins with a brief treatment of the university in Europe and a rather more detailed discussion of the beginning of the university in India, the bulk of the volume deals with the foundations and structure of higher education in Africa, with, as one might expect, heavy emphasis on the British model. He analyzes the evolution of British concepts of the university in Africa since the Asquith Report of 1945, pointing up not only the influence of British academics and of local African interests, but also the reluctantly accepted role of the American academic.

The book deals primarily with structure and function of the university itself, but the author devotes a substantial section to a discussion of academic freedom and the autonomy of the African university. He concludes that no constitutional device can protect the freedom of higher educational institutions in the face of a determined effort by the state to bend the university into an instrument for the accomplishment of political ends.

A thoughtful and informed presentation, the book has much that can be applied to the dilemma of the Western university today as well as to that of the university in Africa.

TRIMINGHAM, J. SPENCER. **Islam in West Africa.** New York: Oxford University Press, 1959, 262 p.

This masterfully scholarly work examines its subject from every conceivable angle and—by the nature of the treatment as well as of the subject—stands as strong today as when it was written more than a decade ago. Trimingham is interested in examining the impact of Islam on the western part of the continent and then its effect on modernization. He explains West African Islam through its beliefs, institutions, social, economic, political and legal influence, and its relation in all these areas to westernization. As a "modern" influence which reached animist Africa before the West and, because of its indigenous and flexible quality, was more readily received, Islam has served as a barrier to modernization in Western forms. Although African culture then tended to be a synthesis between pre-Islamic and Islamic influences, the subsequent dialectic is most likely to be between this culture and Western materialism, not Christianity. A particularly strong point of the book is its balanced treatment of both French and British West Africa and its skillful handling of Islam as both a structural and a belief system.

LYSTAD, ROBERT A., *ed.* **The African World: A Survey of Social Research.** New York: Praeger, 1965, 575 p.

This ambitious attempt to survey the frontiers of research on Africa in 18 disciplines of the social sciences and the humanities is the product of the coöperation of leading scholars in their own fields under the auspices of the African Studies Association.

The individual chapters will, of course, be of greatest interest to specialists in each field, but the unique contribution of the volume lies in the comparative nature of the themes treated under the various disciplines. The subject matter treated deals with the accomplishments of the disciplines in their application to the African continent, and this in itself makes fascinating reading. But equally important is the demonstration (often almost accidentally) of the interdependence of usually unrelated bodies of knowledge when they are directed toward the specific goal of illuminating our knowledge of a defined area of the world. In discussing the perimeters of a given field, the authors suggest directions in which research might be pushed not only in this specialty but in others as well so that greater complementarity of information might be achieved.

Any volume of this nature is subject to early dating, since research frontiers are rapidly expanding, but **The African World** will remain of substantial value to African studies for some years to come. It is to be hoped that, now that the utility of this type of venture has been proved, an effort will be made to keep abreast of current research progress in a second edition.

NORTH AFRICA

GENERAL

GALLAGHER, CHARLES F. **The United States and North Africa: Morocco, Algeria, and Tunisia.** Cambridge: Harvard University Press, 1963, 275 p.

In a real sense the title of this book is a misnomer. Although it is a volume of the Harvard Foreign Policy Library, it does not concern itself directly with the United States and the Maghrib until the last 20 pages. For the most part, it is a lucid survey of the history, culture, politics and world position of the three countries— Morocco, Algeria and Tunisia—that make up the Maghrib. The countries are treated as a whole, beginning with a description of the cultural and physical context of the area, its historical background from Carthaginian times and culminating in the post-colonial period of independence. The author, who spent many years in North Africa as representative of the American Universities Field Staff, demonstrates an unusual grasp of the area and its problems in this compact volume. It remains the best single introduction to North Africa in English.

ASHFORD, DOUGLAS E. **National Development and Local Reform: Political Participation in Morocco, Tunisia, and Pakistan.** Princeton: Princeton University Press, 1967, 439 p.

A basic problem of modernization, ubiquitous throughout the developing world, concerns how rural populations are mobilized into the process. The former colonial régimes, whether by design or because of traditional resistance, failed, in any real sense, to involve the rural populations in the modernization which they touched off. The newly independent régimes, dominated by "native" modernists, encounter similar difficulties in seeking to enlist the collaboration of these populations in modernizing their countries. Professor Ashford has directed himself to this basic problem in three erstwhile colonial Muslim countries—Morocco, Tunisia and Pakistan. The various factors that affect the growth of political participation at the local level, such as planning, education, local government, Islam and foreign aid, are compared in the three countries, each of which has a distinct national style: traditional monarchy in Morocco; single-party activist system in Tunisia; and political professionalism of a military bureaucracy in Pakistan.

The study does not contain any prescription for success but rather points out weak spots that emerge as it analyzes the role of government intervention in modernization. In the field of comparative modernization, this work is a pioneering effort of great value, not only for the information it imparts but also because it points to further areas of research and study needed if we are to understand this complex problem of rural social mobilization in the modern political process.

JULIEN, CHARLES ANDRÉ. **L'Afrique du Nord en Marche: Nationalismes Musulmans et Souveraineté Française.** Paris: Juilliard, 1952, 416 p.

When some 20 years ago French policy and most of France were disdainfully dismissing the nationalists of North Africa as xenophobic Muslim fanatics unrepresentative of the peoples of the Maghrib, Professor Julien presented his study of the march of events and social forces in the Maghrib that flew in the face of the official thesis and called for a change in the direction of French policy. Although his plea for a new policy that would recognize the rights and aspirations of all the peoples of North Africa, Muslim as well as French, fell on deaf ears, his levelheaded, incisive and knowledgeable analysis remains one of the earliest and best studies of the underlying factors and early history of the nationalist movements in Algeria, Morocco and Tunisia and of France's ineptness in dealing with them. The analysis of the movement of social forces and events in each Maghrib country, as well as for the area as a whole, focuses on "the triple aspects of the same problem that each nationalism [in North Africa] has to resolve within the context of local conditions," namely particular nationalism, Pan-Maghribism and Pan-Arabism.

WOOLMAN, DAVID S. **Rebels in the Rif: Abd el Krim and the Rif Rebellion.** Stanford: Stanford University Press, 1968, 257 p.

One of the first sustained colonial rebellions of the twentieth century, and the precursor of the guerrilla wars of Algeria and Vietnam, is the subject of this most interesting and well-written study. Dissident nationalism had not yet emerged in North Africa nor in most other parts of the colonial world when the Rif rebellion captured the attention of the world. This rebellion of Berber tribesmen, launched in 1921 by brothers Mohamed and Mhamed Abd el Krim against the Spanish Protectorate régime, was finally squashed in 1926 when 150,000 French troops under Marshal Pétain reinforced the 200,000 Spanish forces that were being defeated and humiliated.

This book by David Woolman, a free-lance journalist and long-time resident of Tangier, contains the most complete and detailed account of the Rif war published to date, focusing on Mohamed Abd el Krim's extraordinary gifts as a military and political strategist, as well as providing vivid insight into the colonial mentality of the 1920s and the life of a proud people under colonialism.

BRIGGS, LLOYD CABOT. **Tribes of the Sahara.** Cambridge: Harvard University Press, 1960, 295 p.

In this book, the result of 12 years of field work and library research, Lloyd Briggs dispels the popular image of the Sahara peddled by "professional purveyors of mysterious romance" because the region has always been off the beaten track of travellers and scholars. "The sober truth about the Sahara, however," writes Briggs in his preface, "is more mysterious than anything that has ever been written about it, even by the most irresponsible spinner of fairy-tales." He proceeds to replace the myths and exaggerations with factual data and information, also exciting and mysterious, the more so because it is real. This first general description ever published of all the Saharan peoples includes detailed discussion of four population groups—the Touareg, Teda, Chaamba (Arab Nomads) and Moors—considered to be representative of the larger and more important elements in the Sahara, as well as discussions of several minor but interesting subgroups such as the well-diggers of Ouargla and the Nemadi who are inland hunters. Of special interest are the opening chapters which set the ecological scene and give a concise summary of Saharan history from the early fossil days to the contemporary oil exploitation, and the concluding chapter "Retrospect and Prophecy," in which Briggs speculates about the changing nature of the Sahara. The volume, enhanced by many excellent illustrations and the readable style of the author, is of great value to the general reader as well as to the author's fellow anthropologists.

BERQUE, JACQUES. **French North Africa: The Maghrib between Two World Wars.** New York: Praeger, 1967, 422 p.

Berque has woven an analysis of rare sensitivity and intelligence, reflecting his long and intimate association with the Maghrib, where he was born and where he distinguished himself as government administrator and scholar. Concerned primarily with the single theme of interaction between French civilization and the indigenous Arabo-Berber-Islamic culture in North Africa, this remarkable volume probes deeply at the local roots and imparts the flavor of the agonizing day-to-day changes that ensued from the clash of cultures. Basically a study of acculturation, this book is not written according to any rigid mode of analysis. Its style and method are eclectic, including hard data, personal experiences and illuminating vignettes that substantiate the underlying theses that "the colonial phenomenon . . . consists of destroying and remaking;" that "the downfall of the [colonial] system was imminent in its apogee;" that "the Maghribi nation arose out of the colonial triumph;" and that "although the sons of the Maghrib still turned to religion for symbols of their resistance, and looked to the Arab last for archetypes and true images of themselves, they had more or less taken France into their inner lives."

The translation is by Jean Stewart. The original edition was published as "Le Maghreb entre Deux Guerres" (Paris: Éditions du Seuil, 1962, 444 p.).

MOROCCO

BERNARD, STÉPHANE. **The Franco-Moroccan Conflict, 1943–1956.** New Haven: Yale University Press, 1968, 2 v.

The process of decolonization in Morocco is the subject of this book in the "Case Studies of International Conflicts" series sponsored by the Carnegie Endowment for International Peace. The fact that the English edition of this comprehensive work does not contain volume III of the original French version (**Le Conflit Franco-Marocain, 1943–1956,** Brussels: Institut de Sociologie de l'Université Libre de Bruxelles, 1963, 3 v.) does not diminish the usefulness of the English edition since it contains the heart of the study, a detailed step-by-step analysis of the conflict. This ambitious undertaking methodologically attempts to combine several social sciences into a theoretical perspective upon decolonization. In essence, it is really two works—one on Morocco and the other on methodology. While one may quarrel with the author's conceptualization of the interrelationships of the social sciences in the study of international politics—particularly since political science is seen as merely part of his own discipline of sociology—this section (which constitutes the second of the English volumes) is a noteworthy contribution to theory in international relations. The other part of the study on Morocco is somewhat less impressive. It contains much detail, particularly on the attitudes and actions of those on the French side. Its major weakness is that it does not deal with the subject analytically or historically. The roots of the Franco-Moroccan conflict go back long before the year 1943 when this study's concern begins. Basically, the marriage between the theoretical sections of the book and the case study does not come off.

ZARTMAN, I. WILLIAM. **Morocco: Problems of New Power.** New York: Atherton Press, 1964, 276 p.

The subject of this book is how a former colonial dependency—in this case Morocco—has dealt with the problems of its newfound power in the years immediately after attaining independence. In a series of five case studies covering major areas of concern, the political decision-making process in the newly independent state is subjected to a carefully documented analysis of unusual depth and detail. The areas dealt with are diplomacy (the evacuation of American bases), the military (organization of the army), economic development (agrarian reform), education (Arabization of primary and secondary schools) and politics (the organization of the country's first local elections).

Because of Professor Zartman's command of the material, his intimate knowledge of the country and many of the principal participants in Morocco's political process, the volume is a major contribution to the literature on contemporary Morocco and North Africa. While it is difficult to transfer conclusions reached about politics in Morocco to other African or Arab countries, the study does raise basic questions that are pertinent to the study of political development in other newly independent states. Each of these states is "forced to govern while it undergoes transition and . . . decision-making therefore becomes both a governmental and an evolutionary process."

LE TOURNEAU, ROGER. **Fès avant le Protectorat.** Casablanca: Société Marocaine de Libraire et d'Édition, 1949, 668 p.
————. **Fez in the Age of the Marinides.** Norman: University of Oklahoma Press, 1961, 158 p.
————. **La Vie Quotidienne à Fès en 1900.** Paris: Hachette, 1965, 315 p.

The old Moorish city of Fez in Morocco stands today as a living monument to the development of Muslim and Arab civilization in the Maghrib. The eminent North African scholar, Roger Le Tourneau, has given his attention to this remarkable thousand-year-old city, which he describes as a place "not of mystery but of good sense and good living," in three excellent studies. The first and most comprehensive is **Fès avant le Protectorat** which in its eight parts—history, physical setting, population, urban institutions, economic life, intellectual life, religious life and the customs of Fez—presents a meticulous account of life in this city before France established its hegemony over Morocco. Replete with diagrams, sketches and more than 100 photographs, this is a real tour de force.

The two succeeding books follow much the same organization but present the material in a more condensed version. For the reader in English, we are indebted to the "Centers of Civilization Series" of the University of Oklahoma Press for including a book on Fez by Le Tourneau in its series. Each of the three books contains a richness of detail that enables one to see the city, its inhabitants and its life in all its vibrancy.

ALGERIA; TUNISIA

BOURDIEU, PIERRE. **The Algerians.** Boston: Beacon Press, 1962, 208 p.

This small volume by an important French sociologist, originally appearing as "Sociologie de l'Algérie" (Paris: Presses Universitaires, 1958, 126 p.), is the best background work available in English for understanding Algerian society. The first half of the book examines the component ethnic groups in Algeria—the Kabyles, the Shawia, the Mozabites and the scattered majority of Arabs. These societies are extended family groups organized to handle the problems of existence in their environment. Bourdieu's analysis is a detailed, sometimes technical anthropological treatment, supported by maps, charts and glossary (all necessary). The second part of the work shows the disruptive impact of the colonial system on these traditional structures and on the environmental setting that they were designed to handle. The result was a dislocated society, with a chasm between colonizer and colonized and an undercutting void separating Algerian society from its changing context; the society was thus free to devise new answers and a new culture. "Algeria [is] highly revolutionary because it has been highly revolutionized." That the new answers may not yet have been forthcoming does not invalidate the book (which was written in the last years of the revolutionary war); rather, it underscores the needs and tensions that still exist. On this basis, other narrower books on Algerian politics and current events become understandable.

TILLION, GERMAINE. **France and Algeria: Complementary Enemies.** New York: Knopf, 1961, 183 p.

A noted French anthropologist, active in the Resistance of World War II and with long experience in Algeria, ambles over the political landscape of the Algerian war in 1957 and 1960. Tillion is not noted for style, but the choppiness gives the text an air of having been jotted down on the run between one human encounter and the next (which may in fact be true and in any case enhances the book). A large part of the book is devoted to her account of meeting Saadi Yacef, leader of the Battle of Algiers, and her role in toning down the escalating round of terror and reprisal. The rest of the book is a sound impressionistic analysis of the phenomenon of colonization and independence, with particular exploration of the relation of double dependence between metropole and special colony. At this point, Tillion presses her compromise solution of association between the two entities, ignoring her own conclusion that "African people now flow toward their independence like rivers toward the sea—irresistibly." That it was too late for compromise is less important than the open wrestling with the problem which the book portrays. The debate is honest, typical and strewn with wisdom.

Less impressive is Tillion's earlier translated book, **Algeria: The Realities** (New York: Knopf, 1958, 115 p.), originally appearing as "L'Algérie en 1957" (Paris: Minuit, 1957, 121 p.), in which some of the dynamics of underdevelopment are presented a bit too schematically and impressionistically and the positive compromise of the time turns out to be the Constantine Plan of tangible French economic concern for Algeria—far too late. The 1958 book also suggests that Algeria is not viable as an independent state, another indication that even the best of such books are usually better as an example of the political climate at the time than as eternal truths.

GORDON, DAVID C. **The Passing of French Algeria.** New York: Oxford University Press, 1966, 265 p.

This first serious work on independent Algeria to appear in English is still among the best. Pursuing the theme so sensitively developed in his **North Africa's French Legacy, 1954–1962** (Cambridge: Harvard University Press, distributed for the Center for Middle Eastern Studies, 1962, 121 p.), Gordon interprets Algeria on the basis of its identity dichotomy: the love-hate relationship between modernism that is associated with France and native Arabo-Islamism that is traditional. The drama in the conflict between "de-Frenchifying" modernism and de-traditionalizing indigenous views and ways lies in the fact that in every source for the synthesis of new Algerian values, the part that is to be selected is inseparable from a part to be rejected. This dichotomy runs through the "self-contradictory commitment" to the Evian Accords and the Tripoli Program, and eventually through the double dangers of anarchy and apathy. Gordon's analysis of political issues, cultural debates, economic programs and colonial reactions focuses on the Ben Bella period, with the preceding three decades as background, and is drawn from a wide range of documents, articles, novels, memoirs, assembly debates, commentaries and the press. The synthesis is excellent, but the greatest strength is in the field of culture and values, without which the conflicts of politics, personality and economics would be meaningless.

FANON, FRANTZ. **The Wretched of the Earth.** New York: Grove Press, 1965, 255 p.

This major work of the Martiniquan psychiatrist who was also the prime ideologue of the Algerian revolution is a powerful combination of analysis and prescription. Fanon is an exponent of the cathartic qualities of expressive as well as instrumental violence in ridding the soul as well as the body of colonially induced denaturing. He is also an incisive critic of the modernized (as he sees it, "colonized") élites who have taken over the colonial positions of power in African states without bringing the creative capital and attitudes normally associated with the bourgeoisie in the development of Europe. The true repository of national values and the true disinherited rebel is the peasant who, as in Algeria, can be counted on to destroy the old order and create the new (or rather, recreate the original society transfigured). Black nationalist self-determination is Fanon's call, and he buttresses his prescription at the end of his study with analyses of mental disorders resulting from the colonial clash. Like many revolutionary calls, Fanon's future model is utopian, in the sense that the necessary has as yet rarely turned out to be inevitable. But his analysis of the ills of colonized society and its successor élites is true, complete and relevant. This study originally appeared in French as "Les Damnés de la Terre" (Paris: Maspéro, 1961, 242 p.). Further extensions of Fanon's thought are found in **Toward the African Revolution** (New York: Monthly Review Press, 1967, 197 p.).

QUANDT, WILLIAM B. **Revolution and Political Leadership: Algeria, 1954–1968.** Cambridge: M.I.T. Press, 1969, 313 p.

Quandt's book, a revised doctoral dissertation, is the most explicitly disciplinary work available on Algerian politics, and perhaps on all Algeria. As such, it lifts the level of debate, even though it has its weaknesses (not the least of which is, unfortunately, an overly heavy-handed theorizing). The thesis of the work is that the uneven process of revolution is not a single socializing experience that produces an élite of "new revolutionary men" but a complex process that produces differentiated, overlapping élites. These, in Algeria, were the liberals of the 1930s, the radicals of the 1940s, the revolutionaries of the 1950s and the militaries and the intellectuals of the 1960s, with the last pulling ahead (but subdividing into what?) in the 1970s. On this analytical framework, the events to, through and after the revolutionary war are portrayed. The study contains an excellent presentation of events during the war and the subsequent Ben Bella period, the decade during which these élites grew and clashed. What is not clear from the analysis is whether the élites described were categories imposed from the outside or real groups that relate, cohere and act collectively. To the general reader seeking to understand Algeria the point is unimportant, but to the analyst looking to broader processes and concepts it is crucial and its resolution can tell more about recent events (the Boumedienne period) than can Quandt's book as now written. Hence, the level of debate is raised, and with it the level of understanding.

MOORE, CLEMENT HENRY. **Tunisia since Independence: The Dynamics of One-Party Government.** Berkeley: University of California Press, 1965, 230 p.

Moore's study of Tunisia stands out as one of the finest political studies, on developed or underdeveloped countries, that has appeared in the last decade. Well written and carefully documented, it deftly combines conceptualization about one-party régimes with a rare understanding of the country to which it is applied. The central figure in Tunisia since independence has been President Bourguiba. Thus Moore rightfully and expertly analyzes the phenomenon of "Bourguibism" in the chapter "The Leader as a Nation-Builder" and its succeeding one, aptly called "Presidential Monarchy." The great virtue of the book, however, is that it properly recognizes that, despite Bourguiba, Tunisian politics is a many-faceted and complex subject; and the analyses of the party, the patterns of local politics, the national organizations and the consultative process which make up two-thirds of the book give the reader a total picture of the Tunisian polity. The author raises the fundamental questions as to whether the Tunisian political system and the "permissive party régime" which has evolved under Bourguiba's direction will lead to the development of stable political institutions in the country.

WEST AFRICA

FRENCH WEST AFRICA

HERSKOVITS, MELVILLE JEAN. **Dahomey.** New York: Augustin, 1938, 2 v.

Melville J. Herskovits' preëminence in the field of African studies both in the United States and internationally was recognized by his election as first president of the African Studies Association of the United States. A cultural anthropologist of the first rank, Herskovits was drawn to the study of West African cultures by his research among Negro groups in Haiti and Dutch Guiana. This monumental work emerged from field work conducted with his wife, Frances S. Herskovits, in southern Dahomey, the site of one of the most complex of the cultures and states of the West African forest region. Herskovits organized his rich materials and his interpretations into seven sections: the people and their setting (history and geography), economic life, social organization, the life cycle of the individual, political organization, religion and art. Although not the first to attempt to view African life "from within," he succeeded as few had before him. His detailed analysis of economic institutions, the discussion of the life cycle of individuals and the analysis of the relationship between the Dahomean world view and daily life were also unusual for the time. This and other works by Herskovits gave great impetus to the creation and development of the field of African studies in the United States.

ANSPRENGER, FRANZ. **Politik im Schwarzen Afrika: Die Modernen Politischen Bewegungen im Afrika Französischer Prägung.** Cologne: Westdeutscher Verlag, 1961, 516 p.

This book deals with political development in French-speaking West Africa, and within this compass it is one of the most comprehensive and penetrating analyses of political phenomena in Africa to be found in any language. After a brief sketch of the history of French expansion in Africa and a discussion of French colonial policy, the author concentrates on an account of the growth of political movements in former French West Africa and their role in the struggle for independence. The coverage of Guinea and the Mali Federation is particularly worthy of note, as is the discussion of the place of the labor unions in the politics of the period.

While Dr. Ansprenger is fully aware that at the time of his writing no final judgments could be made on the course of African politics (or can today, for that matter), he poses the question of the possibility of a peculiarly African democratic form. His conclusion is that without a strong leader and a party which is the vehicle for political life, no viable African democracy is possible. But the leader must derive from a popular consensus, the single party must remain dynamic and the system must remain flexible enough to permit criticism. The validity of his general judgment would appear to be borne out not only for French Africa but for most other countries as well in the years since Ansprenger's book appeared.

THOMPSON, VIRGINIA MCLEAN and ADLOFF, RICHARD. **French West Africa.** Stanford: Stanford University Press, 1958, 626 p.

Completed in the year of the *Loi-Cadre,* when French-speaking Africa began to stir under the joint impact of reform from above and intensified activity from below, the compendium assembled by Virginia Thompson and Richard Adloff, a husband-and-wife team of free-lance scholar-journalists who had already performed a similar service for Indochina, was an extremely valuable contribution. Based on some interviews in the area and in Paris, but mostly on painstakingly assembled documents, it is best summarized in their own modest words: "This book offers a survey of French West Africa which in no way purports to be exhaustive. Its authors have tried simply to give a general and balanced appraisal of the main developments in that vast and little-travelled territory—an appraisal which aims to take into account both official and non-official French and African viewpoints."

The book is divided into sections covering the political scene (with useful territory-by-territory summaries), the economy and the social and cultural fields, all of which contain a fair quota of errors but also numerous astute remarks concerning problems of lasting concern. The brief conclusions combine an obsolete flavor (Would these territories be affected by "the virus of nationalism"? Would the French Union move in the direction of a federation?) with insight into the developing conflict between the first generation of African political leaders and their youthful, better-educated successors, still a major theme in many of the countries of the area. Ultimately, the book has an eclectic quality: nowhere does one get a sense that these are societies experiencing an immensely complex transformation; nowhere does one get a sense of the problems of nation building which they would soon face. Paradoxically, that absence of analysis may well be what makes the book worthwhile reading today. Not only does it remain a useful record of important facts for the crucial decade preceding independence, but it is also an extremely important illustration of the limited point of view then shared by most intelligent and well-informed observers of the African scene.

MORGENTHAU, RUTH SCHACHTER. **Political Parties in French-Speaking West Africa.** New York: Oxford University Press, 1964, 445 p.

For several years before publication of the present book, the author generously shared her unique knowledge and understanding of political processes in former French West Africa with a whole generation of scholars. In 1956, when working on her doctorate at Oxford, she was one of only two or three non-Africans who had gained access to the inner circles of leading political groups in the area and the only one to have acquired an intimate understanding of the intricate relationships between political activity at the level of each territory, of the federal capital in Dakar and of Paris itself. Her analysis of these relationships in this book remains unsurpassed in scope and subtlety.

The work also contains case studies of Senegal, Ivory Coast, Guinea and Mali— the four most important of the eight territories which constituted the Federation. For each of them, Ruth Morgenthau provides the first intelligible analytic overview of the initial phase of political transformation, with stress on the interaction among traditional societies, contemporary discontent, the rise of critical new élites and the personalities of important leaders. The result is an identification of lasting features of the political process in these societies. As a study of contemporary history in the best tradition, this book remains a valuable record of the period, whose insights still provide useful hypotheses for further research. It concludes with an essay on the emergence of one-party states which has become a classic in the field and has stimulated nearly a decade of lively debate.

FOLTZ, WILLIAM J. **From French West Africa to the Mali Federation.** New Haven: Yale University Press, 1965, 235 p.

Although there is a voluminous literature on the unity or non-unity of African countries during the period after independence, it is often forgotten that these oscillations began in various regions of the continent during the terminal colonial period. Foltz's work is a lucid account of how the colonial administrative federation formerly known as French West Africa was transformed into eight separate countries after various attempts to maintain unity of the entire federation or of at least some of its components. In particular, he carefully reconstructs the birth and death of the Mali Federation constituted by Senegal and the former French Sudan in 1959–1960.

The book's lasting value, however, stems from the author's attempt to account for relationships between the territories by means of quantitative techniques. Applying a transactional analysis model inspired by Karl Deutsch to their trade patterns, Foltz, now teaching political science at Yale, demonstrates persuasively that only some of the eight would be inclined on economic grounds to resolve problems in terms compatible with maintaining close relationships with the others. However, political considerations may well have been determinative, as illustrated by his application of content analysis to the ideological orientation of leading newspapers in Senegal and Sudan. Another interesting aspect of the book is its revelation of the role of the military in the breakup of the Federation. In the light of subsequent events on the continent, Foltz deserves special credit for having been one of the first scholars to turn the spotlight on that important political factor.

ZOLBERG, ARISTIDE R. **One-Party Government in the Ivory Coast.** Princeton: Princeton University Press, 1964, 374 p.

There is little doubt that Professor Aristide R. Zolberg's book is the most informative political document written in English about the growth and development of the Ivory Coast government. It provides valuable material on the origins of the national movement, the development of an indigenous élite and the struggle against colonialism which produced a powerful political machine, the *Parti Démocratique de la Côte d'Ivoire,* that has resulted in one-party control of the government in the Ivory Coast. Professor Zolberg arrives at his conclusions after carefully analyzing vast amounts of material and conducting extensive interviews with key leaders as well as ordinary political participants, allowing him to provide valuable insights into Ivoirian affairs, particularly the problems and conflicts within the ruling élite.

The revised edition published in 1969 analyzes some of the important trends and problems that have manifested themselves in the Ivory Coast since independence. Zolberg points out that political scientists were preoccupied with the nationalist movement and the resultant one-party state and probably overemphasized the problem of balancing democracy and authority. He also raises the question of the effectiveness of the criteria used to evaluate new African governments. In spite of this self-criticism, the book provides valuable information and is the best description in English of the development of Ivory Coast government.

NIGERIA; GHANA

BURNS, ALAN CUTHBERT. **History of Nigeria.** London: Allen and Unwin, 1929, 360 p.

The first attempt by any author to write a history of the whole of Nigeria, this work appeared in 1929 and is still in print, having gone through no less than eight editions. During the last quarter-century of colonial rule it exercised considerable influence on colonial servants, merchants, teachers and missionaries, as well as on the general public in Europe and America. For foreigners going to West Africa for the first time it was essential reading. The author was a distinguished colonial governor, holding high office in Nigeria, the Gold Coast and the British West

Indies. His book describes the establishment of British rule and its extension throughout the country. Most of the text is devoted to the nineteenth and twentieth centuries, and small account is taken of the activities and ambitions of the ruled as opposed to the rulers. But this approach, though inappropriate for the modern historian of Africa, was the fashion of the time, and Burns' volume is an example of British colonial history at its best.

SKLAR, RICHARD L. **Nigerian Political Parties: Power in an Emergent African Nation.** Princeton: Princeton University Press, 1963, 578 p.

Professor Richard Sklar has written an extremely original and important study of Nigerian social and political development. In view of the subsequent civil strife that has tormented Africa's most populous nation-state, this work takes on an added dimension of value.

Unlike the influential "functional" approach to the study of political development, Professor Sklar approaches his subject in terms of "class action," the dynamics of class formation and its relationship to national integration in nation-states like Nigeria. In choosing this approach, Professor Sklar has made a significant theoretical contribution and simultaneously opened up a valuable debate within the profession over the conceptual tools with which political and other social scientists need to approach the study of the new societies of Africa.

Nigerian Political Parties seeks to deal with the political relationships among three central political forces: nationalism, cultural particularism and the crystallization of emergent class interests. The work's major contribution lies in its approach to an examination of power in an emergent society. Its analysis focuses on the links between the political parties and the Nigerian social structure which undergirds the party system. It seeks the social basis of power, thereby avoiding some of the pitfalls of the functional approach. The central theme is that political power rested with an emergent bourgeoisie, established in regional bastions, and that although communal interests were influential, they tended to accept the leadership of the dominant class-interest groups.

Much of the recent scholarly discourse on African political development has been retarded by far too simplistic use of the concept of tribalism. Cultural particularisms undoubtedly survive tenaciously in Africa; however, they survive within a modern complex political framework. Professor Sklar's approach begins to recognize that complexity.

COLEMAN, JAMES SAMUEL. **Nigeria: Background to Nationalism.** Berkeley: University of California Press, 1958, 510 p.

Coleman's **Nigeria** is a truly classic study of nationalism in the former colonial world, presenting a profound appraisal of the Western impact on African social institutions. The author clearly reveals the historic contradiction between divisive administrative policies and unifying economic policies which has undermined Nigerian political development. His demonstration that British policy gave rise to regionalism and the resulting politicization of tribal sentiments should be read by those who still interpret Nigerian politics in simplistic tribal terms.

The ultimate test of comparative political analysis may lie in questions of sensitivity concerning the cultural determinants of political behavior. In this regard, Coleman succeeds brilliantly. His work pioneers the systematic study of political culture in Africa. His disclosure of the disparate influence of British and American education in relation to diverse cultural tendencies was insightful. After the Biafran tragedy, we may ponder the persistently controversial Ibo affinity for American education in this British sphere of influence.

In brief, Coleman's book is a lasting and lucid introduction to the complexity of relationships that bind the Nigerian peoples to one another and to the industrial states which have shaped their destinies in the past. It is a composition of hope and fear in the finest academic form.

MACKINTOSH, JOHN P. **Nigerian Government and Politics: Prelude to the Revolution.**
Evanston: Northwestern University Press, 1966, 651 p.

This is an overall survey of government and politics, mainly during the post-independence period from 1960 to 1966, when the first republic was overthrown by a coup d'état. In addition to Mackintosh, the book includes chapters by five other authors. In substance, it largely supersedes a previous comprehensive work of comparable quality, L. Franklin Blitz, *ed.,* **The Politics and Administration of Nigerian Government** (New York: Praeger, 1965, 281 p.).

Mackintosh contributes a useful account of the 1964–1965 election crisis, a critical event in the degeneration of Nigerian politics to civil war. His standpoint is more favorable to the late Prime Minister, Abubakar Tafawa Balewa, than to the latter's rival, ex-President Nnamdi Azikiwe. The composite picture portrays an incessant struggle for power between persons who represent sectional interests. Mackintosh questions the capacity of Nigerian society to sustain democratic forms of limited government.

The book includes a notable chapter by M. J. Dent on the politics of Tiv Division in the former Northern Region, supplementing the anthropological studies of Bohannan. Its importance in the literature of Nigerian politics is magnified by the recent political emergence of so-called minority group elements under the Gowon military régime. Dent's study of Tiv politics in the "middle belt" of Nigeria heralds the rise to prominence of J. S. Tarka as a significant civilian leader during the military period.

MEEK, CHARLES KINGSLEY. **The Northern Tribes of Nigeria.** New York: Oxford University Press, 1925, 2 v.

Meek had a distinguished career as a colonial officer and government anthropologist in Northern and Eastern Nigeria. This work, an outgrowth of the 1921 Census in the north, of which he was in charge, is a major integration of ethnographic data and other information on the peoples of the north. It is based on the earlier work of O. and C. L. Temple, "Notes on the Tribes, Provinces, Emirates and States of the Northern Provinces of Nigeria" (1919), on information gathered by administrative offices and on Meek's own researches.

The work provides what was for many years the accepted racial, cultural and linguistic classification of this region. The information is presented by anthropological categories rather than by ethnic groups. In the first volume what little was known of the prehistory and history of the north is discussed, and there are substantial chapters on economic life, social organization and government and law. The second volume, by N. W. Thomas, deals with religion, folklore and language groups. Meek introduces anthropological theories of the time (for example, concerning the mother-right and the levirate) into his survey. The census figures, the value of which he doubts, are presented in about a hundred pages at the end of the second volume.

The book stood for years as the best summary of the anthropology of an important and complex region.

TALBOT, PERCY AMAURY. **The Peoples of Southern Nigeria.** New York: Oxford University Press, 1926, 4 v.

Talbot, a government anthropologist and administrator, was the author of a number of substantial ethnographic books covering the Ekoi, Ibibio, Ijaw and southern Ibo, but his most famous work is this monumental compendium on the peoples of Southern Nigeria and the southern Cameroons. Based on his own researches and on early nineteenth-century government records, it remains today the only extensive interpretation of the anthropology of the area as a whole, and it is still of considerable value.

The first volume provides general historical information (unfortunately without detailed references) on the period from the Pleistocene through supposed Greek and Egyptian influences (Talbot was something of a diffusionist) to the time of his writing, all in summary form. This is followed by brief histories of the peoples of each province. The second and third volumes, the most substantive of all, cover the ethnography of the peoples of the area, arranged by topic. The information on the southeastern Nigerian area is fuller than that on the southwestern region. The most detailed and the best anthropological materials in these two volumes are on religion and rituals, the poorest on political organization. Talbot's interest in systems of belief and in indigenous conceptions of deities comes to the fore. The last volume is a summary of the statistics of the 1921 Census, with the author's commentaries. Useful information is given on languages, ethnic groupings, religion, marriage, educational levels and the missions, as well as the population figures.

MEEK, CHARLES KINGSLEY. **Law and Authority in a Nigerian Tribe: A Study in Indirect Rule.** New York: Oxford University Press, 1937, 372 p.

The author had had 18 years' experience in Northern Nigeria as a government anthropologist and administrator and was transferred to Eastern Nigeria in 1930, following the extensive women's riots in the area in the preceding year. He then carried out anthropological research in several Ibo areas and organized the preparation of an extensive series of government intelligence reports, prepared by local administrative officers, on most of the groupings in the east.

This book is a summary of his own research and of data in the intelligence reports on the major cultural group of the region, the Ibo. It stands, even today, as the basic study of these people. While emphasizing the Awgu, Nsukka and Owerri areas, it also provides valuable information on other Ibo. There is only limited data on Ibo law, the major portion of the book consisting of a discussion of religion and of social and political structures. Meek is at his best in the discussion of Ibo leadership, descent organization and the systems of titles. Some rituals and political events are described in detail. In the conclusion he summarizes his own recommendations, and those of other government officials, which led to the reorganization of the system of native authority in the Eastern Region, in which his ideas carried considerable weight. The book is thus a valuable historical and political document on its time as well as an anthropological treatise.

APTER, DAVID ERNEST. **Ghana in Transition.** New York: Atheneum, rev. ed., 1963, 432 p.

First published in 1955 as **The Gold Coast in Transition: A Case Study of Political Institutional Transfer** (Princeton: Princeton University Press, 1955, 355 p.), this revised edition brings us through the period 1957–1963, when Ghana under Nkrumah moved rapidly toward authoritarianism and *personalismo*. Apter's last chapter, "Ghana as a New Nation," rationalizes some of his earlier conclusions and adds new ones. About one-third of the book deals with the Ghanaian traditional system and, while offering nothing new, provides a rather good background to modern political developments. Some chapters concern themselves with the pros and cons of indirect rule. The last four chapters, which are the most rewarding, describe the problems of transition from traditional authority into "constitutional democracy." Apter is especially interested in analyzing these problems. In somewhat euphoric terms, he sees the CPP (Convention People's Party) as the best means for legitimatizing the authority of the Nkrumah parliamentary structure (which did not occur). One of his main propositions is that Nkrumah's "charismatic" authority might satisfy the functional requirements of transitional leaderships among the more traditionally oriented ethnic groups. A more realistic understanding of the Ashanti and Ewe, however, might have made him more cautious about his conclusions on the nature of "charisma" in developing areas.

BOURRET, F. M. **Ghana: The Road to Independence, 1919–1957.** New York: Oxford University Press, rev. ed., 1963, 246 p.

Books dealing with the political history of Ghana outnumber all others on tropical African states. Some of them, such as David Kimble's **A Political History** of Ghana: The Rise of Gold Coast Nationalism, 1850–1928 (Oxford: Clarendon Press, 1963, 587 p.) and Dennis Austin's Politics in Ghana: 1946–1960 (New York: Oxford University Press, for the Royal Institute of International Affairs, 1964, 459 p.), are academic masterpieces, but they are too heavy for the non-specialists who want salient observations unencumbered by innumerable facts and data. For this category of readers, Bourret's work offers one of the most readable, comprehensive and accurate studies available on the emergence of Ghana from colonial status to independence.

The author refrained from conjecturing on modern Ghanaian politics. His objective was to provide the reader with a solid underpinning of the historical, social, economic and political forces which continue to shape Ghana's destiny. This he has succeeded in doing. The reader gains excellent insights into both the creative elements and deficiencies of British policies of self-government and how these have influenced the present. The roots of the historical ethnic divisions which impose themselves on current politics are effectively, if briefly, drawn in the two chapters on the Ashanti and the Northern Territories and Togoland. In sum, although the book stops at 1957, there is much of contemporary significance.

The book may be criticized for not having given more attention than it did to the role Africans played in developing the new state. But given all the factors involved, it still turns out to be one of the most objective studies of this period of Ghanaian history.

EAST AFRICA

KENYA

HUXLEY, ELSPETH JOSCELIN (GRANT) and PERHAM, MARGERY FREDA. Race and Politics in Kenya. London: Faber, 1944, 247 p.

This remarkable correspondence dates from the dark years of World War II when face-to-face argumentation over colonial policy and race relations in Kenya was unusually difficult. Mrs. Huxley, a Kenyan-born biographer and novelist whom Miss Perham called the best apologist for white settlement, suggested throughout that settlers were the only hope for a moderate and calmly evolving Kenya. She wrote of the settlers' desire to improve local race relations and of the importance—for all Kenyans—of nurturing white interest in Kenya. She stressed economic and social development, for which whites could provide good leadership, rather than political development which would be shared by Africans. Kenya, in her view, needed more, not fewer Europeans, with greater economic security and wider opportunities if the ultimate goal (which she accepted) of African economic and social as well as political independence was to be achieved.

Miss Perham, for more than 40 years a tireless investigator of African problems in situ as well as from her base as Reader in Colonial Institutions at Nuffield College, Oxford, was conscious of African resentment of white rule even in 1942–1943. Unlike Mrs. Huxley, she realized that the whites could not hope to continue to rule blacks, even in their best interest. Minority rule could only be preserved, she wrote, "by measures of racial discrimination and capitalist exploitation of one race by the other," policies which she declared were indefensible on general principles and which ran counter to Britain's professed colonial aims. Her vision of the future was clear: she saw a large African population, admittedly backward and disunited, but she believed that "powerful modern administrative and educational techniques could be used . . . to bring them forward with a speed of development hitherto unknown in human history." She wondered how a Britain committed to self-government for colonial people could long permit a handful of expatriate Britons— "in the midst of this great indigenous electorate of the future"—to maintain their present superior position.

HUXLEY, ELSPETH. **White Man's Country: Lord Delamere and the Making of Kenya.**
New York: Macmillan, 1935, 2 v.

Hugh Cholmondley, the third Baron Delamere of Cheshire, was attracted to
Africa by big game during the 1890s and later led an exploring party to what
eventually became Kenya. Not until 1903, however, when the British government
of the then East Africa Protectorate started to settle whites along the line of the
advancing railway, did Delamere and his wife take up residence. He raised sheep
and introduced new strains of wheat suitable for the highland environment near
Nairobi. Having helped to turn Kenya into a viable region suitable for European
farmers, he began championing the political rights of whites vis-à-vis Africans and
Asians and became the leading public figure in the colony—the spokesman for
whites and a tireless crusader for minority home rule. Subsequently, too, he advocated a closer union of East and Central Africa in order to unite the scattered white
settlers and provide a vehicle for the orderly transfer of power from the Colonial
Office to local Europeans. Throughout his life in Kenya, African nationalism and
British paternalism were his main antipathies and the fear of Asian and African
dominance his consuming concern. Lord Delamere thus belongs, as does this
exceedingly readable biography, to a very different era. Mrs. Huxley is herself a
product of Kenya and that period.

DILLEY, MARJORIE RUTH. **British Policy in Kenya Colony.** New York: Nelson, 1937,
296 p.

This is a standard reference work written after a close examination of all of the
relevant printed matter. As the *New Statesman* said at the time, it is an objective
and complete account of postwar political history in Kenya. "Official papers, the
relevant passages from contemporary letters and speeches, everything is included."
Such was a remarkable verdict for a book written by an American professor who
had never been to Kenya.

After a straightforward survey of the geography of the colony, Miss Dilley
turned to a discussion of racial groups, potted history and the emergence of
governmental organizations. She then traced the development and application of
the British policy of trusteeship for Africans, providing a detailed account of the
growth of white political organizations and describing each of the important crises
in the colony's political past. Largely about settler Kenya, no book more accurately
reflected its times.

MBOYA, TOM. **Freedom and After.** Boston: Little, Brown, 1963, 288 p.

Tom Mboya, assassinated in 1969 before the age of 40, already had experienced
two careers and was working on a third. He completed this book just before
Kenya's independence. In it, he permits glimpses of positions and activities in the
crowded years before he assumed official responsibility for national economic
development. He discusses his role as a trade unionist, as he mobilized a combination of international and local resources for the expression of social grievances at a
time when open political agitation was banned in Kenya. He comments on Mau
Mau and nationalist politics during the period in which he championed the cause
of the jailed Kikuyu leaders and Mau Mau detainees, despite attractive political
opportunities for articulate but coöperative non-Kikuyu politicians. Mboya established his political base in Nairobi, the center of Kikuyuland. His support for
Kenyatta and his election victory demonstrated the possibilities for transcending
tribal differences in the late 1950s, thus hastening independence. Finally, in reviewing his dramatic involvement in the education "airlift" to the United States in 1959
and in noting the conditions underlying development and socialism in Kenya,
Mboya reveals himself as a tough-minded but pragmatic militant.

Not an autobiography but rather a series of vignettes and meditations, the book
is of interest to scholars and politicians who want to ask most of the right questions
beyond the rhetoric of "neo-colonialism," "Pan-Africanism," "neutralism" and
nationalism.

ROSBERG, CARL G., JR., and NOTTINGHAM, JOHN. **The Myth of "Mau Mau": Nationalism in Kenya.** New York: Praeger (for the Hoover Institution on War, Revolution, and Peace), 1966, 427 p.

A scholarly refutation of the view held by colonial rulers and foreign journalists in the 1950s that Mau Mau was a retreat into tribal barbarism, the book traces in copious detail the rise of grievances, protests and rebellion among the Kikuyu. Rosberg, a political scientist, and Nottingham, a former colonial administrator, now a director of a publishing company in Nairobi, place Mau Mau in the context of the anti-colonial, nationalist—though not necessarily national—movements of Africa after World War II. The fact that the movement in Kenya took a tribalistic form is a reflection of differential cultural development among Kenya's ethnic groups, the character of colonial rule and the locus of the main depradations of an alien élite.

In order to explain more fully the restriction of nationalism to the Kikuyu, the authors introduce a distinction between "acquisition" movements and "integration" movements. Intense demands to "acquire" political rights and benefits—demands which clearly have national implications but brought forth within a restrictive political framework—can lead to insurrection, but one that adopts popular and immediately recognizable forms. (So the sorely beset Kikuyu were available to militants, dealing in oaths.) On the other hand, movements that "integrate" peoples on a territorial basis can count on opportunities for wider and less parochial popular involvement.

UGANDA; TANZANIA

APTER, DAVID ERNEST. **The Political Kingdom in Uganda: A Study in Bureaucratic Nationalism.** Princeton: Princeton University Press, 1961, 498 p.

The author, a political scientist at Yale, illuminates the conflicts among political groupings in the 1940s and 1950s, a formative phase in the development of nationalism in Uganda. Politics in Buganda, the strongest kingdom in the Uganda Protectorate, reflected a surface anomaly of traditional leadership in the van of modernizing tendencies. A "modernizing autocracy" was able to absorb Christianity and commercialism and yet strengthen popular identification with kingship. The analytical core of the study represents an attempt to explain, rather than merely describe, relationships between Baganda social structure and cultural values, with implications for understanding political development elsewhere in Africa.

The Baganda people discarded obsolete traditions within the existing social framework, capped by the reverential figure of the Kabaka. Instead of territorial nationalism also representing modernization, efforts to organize nationalist movements and an effective national régime in Uganda were forced to cope with Buganda nationalism, focused on the "narrow, ethnic and xenophobic" Kabaka. The efforts of post-colonial leadership in Uganda to neutralize Buganda separatism lends poignancy to the author's policy conclusions. A federal system is seen as probably appropriate to territories harboring powerful traditional political systems; territory-wide autocracy appears proportional to the degree of governmental antagonism to tradition.

LOW, DONALD ANTHONY and PRATT, ROBERT CRANFORD. **Buganda and British Overrule: 1900–1955.** New York: Oxford University Press (for East African Institute of Social Research), 1960, 373 p.

Professor Low, a historian now at the University of Sussex, writes a fascinating case study of the making and implementation of the Uganda Agreement of 1900. The Ganda chiefs, in the kingdom of Buganda, emerged with more than Sir Harry H. Johnston, the British Special Commissioner, was prepared to yield at the start of negotiations. In return for collecting taxes for the British, the chiefs were accorded proprietary individual rights over land. The result was the degradation of older cultural sanctions, enhancement of the status of chieftainship, accumulation of capital for agricultural improvement and the establishment of the Buganda assembly as a forum for powerful notables. This, in turn, led to the development of the politics of oligarchy, often in opposition to the Kabaka at the top.

Professor Pratt, a political scientist now at the University of Toronto, analyzes more than 50 years of the politics of indirect rule. British policy served to toughen tribal institutions by modifying them just sufficiently to foster prosperity and westernization. In so doing, British rulers laid the foundations for tribal separatism, which plagued efforts to foster Protectorate-wide political institutions. The study concludes with useful comparative analyses of indirect rule elsewhere in Africa, adding an appendix on the deportation of the Kabaka in 1953, an incident which brought the conflicting currents of Uganda politics to a watershed.

RICHARDS, AUDREY ISABEL, *ed.* **East African Chiefs: A Study of Political Development in Some Uganda and Tanganyika Tribes.** New York: Praeger, 1960, 419 p.

This book consists of a series of essays comparing political structures and administrative organizations of 13 different ethnic groups in Tanganyika and Uganda, each essay written by an anthropologist. The study begins by outlining the general characteristics of the people under scrutiny and indicates that there are two major groupings included in the study: the Interlacustrine Bantu of Tanganyika and the acephalous or segmentary societies of Uganda. Each essay contains a similar pattern describing the geographical environment, economic potential, population density and traditional political structure of each tribe. Major analytical emphasis is placed on the selection, training, rights and privileges of the paramount chiefs. An analysis is also made of the changes in the traditional structure introduced by the British administration and the problems that have developed in 60 years of British rule. In conclusion, comparisons are made between the various tribal groups and a number of generalizations are suggested about African political development. This is an excellent book with one drawback—its narrow orbit of comparative analysis.

NYERERE, JULIUS K. **Freedom and Unity: Uhuru na Umoja.** New York: Oxford University Press, 1967, 366 p.

————. **Freedom and Socialism: A Selection from Writings and Speeches, 1965–1967.** New York: Oxford University Press, 1968, 422 p.

These companion collections of speeches and articles, some addressed to the Tanzanian citizenry and others for the consumption of outside political observers, span 15 years of intense political activity and major changes. They reflect the movement of Nyerere's thoughts, and Tanzanian government policy, from the basis of a political order to plans for political development. Contemporary African political ideology is enriched by President Nyerere's formulations of the issues of democracy in relation to the party system and socialism in the African context. The seminal essays are included in the first volume.

From an emphasis on liberal values of nonracialism and equal rights, Nyerere turns in the second volume to a concern for collectivist values of state direction and developmental socialism. It is interesting that the frontispiece photographs show the author in a multicolored African shirt in 1965 and in a Chinese-style tunic popular in Tanzania in 1967. Nevertheless, despite the pressures of nearly two decades of political activism, certain themes are constant: a basic humanism, a hatred of élitism and its manifestations and a belief in morality as an instrument of policy. Nyerere, the founder of his country and its only president to date, invests the politics of Tanzania with significance for all of Africa, perhaps for the cause of courageous leadership the world over.

BIENEN, HENRY. **Tanzania: Party Transformation and Economic Development.** Princeton: Princeton University Press (for Center of International Studies), 1967, 446 p.

This study is crucial for the light it sheds on the gap between political doctrine and practice, on the possible perils of premature conceptualizing and on the ways of politics in a country upon which much comment has been lavished. Bienen, a political scientist at Princeton, questions the utility of models of "political mobilization" and Leninist rhetoric that claim a significant relationship among party structure, political integration and economic development. Some observers of Tanzanian affairs as well as certain militant local politicians have claimed, according to the author, far too much organization and influence for TANU, the ruling party. In this one-party state, the party depends on the government bureaucracy for maintaining a presence in the countryside and reflects rather than manages the very economic and social divisions it is supposed to transcend.

The book captures the realities of politics in Tanzania without sacrificing a challenging argument or lively detail. In revealing the weakness of party organization, ideological formulations and actual development policies, the author underlines the need for more extensive "micro" studies before generalizations about "macro" systems, and at the higher levels of comparative analysis. In effect, rather than by design, the book also raises the issue of conditions for democracy in Africa. A plurality of clusters of authority and a slowly developing economy exemplified by Tanzania may, despite doctrinal images, lay a basis for one-party or no-party democratic institutions in the future.

CENTRAL AND SOUTHERN AFRICA

RHODESIA; ZAMBIA; MALAWI

POWDERMAKER, HORTENSE. **Copper Town: Changing Africa; The Human Situation on the Rhodesian Copperbelt.** New York: Harper and Row, 1962, 391 p.

This study attempts to define the moods, tensions and symbols of Africans caught in their swiftly changing universe of Africa. The book focuses on the town of Luanshya, a mining town in the Copperbelt of Northern Rhodesia, present-day Zambia. It is based on field work carried out in Luanshya and the surrounding areas in 1954. Luanshya, a racially and culturally plural town divided into European and African districts, is completely dominated by the mining interests of the Rhodesian Selection Trust Company. The book is generally concerned with the new values, roles, ideas and symbols that Africans in Luanshya have acquired.

The first part of the book deals with the history of the town and the surrounding areas, the second with the new economic order and its racial overtones and conflicts between blacks and Europeans. Marriage, love and the shifting role of women is the major theme of the third part; and new symbols, communication and leisure are examined in the fourth section. Movies, radio broadcasts and newspapers—the major European communication media—are analyzed for the first time, and it is indicated in detail how these communication media shape and develop new values, symbols and behavior among Africans. The last chapter examines the new freedoms: individualism, nationalism, release from superstition and witchcraft, educational growth and growing economic security.

The study makes use of a novel technique of recording a series of verbatim conversations between Africans. It is through the analysis of these that the author shows the changing values, symbols and attitudes of Africans. This study is highly impressionistic, but it does reflect the changing values of Africans in a way that few other social scientists have been able to record. A major difficulty is that the analysis of politics and nationalism was out of date when the book was published.

GRAY, RICHARD. **The Two Nations: Aspects of the Development of Race Relations in the Rhodesias and Nyasaland.** New York: Oxford University Press (for the Institute of Race Relations), 1960, 373 p.

The *leitmotif* of this book is contained in the title, taken from Benjamin Disraeli: "I was told that the Privileged and the People formed Two Nations." Richard Gray, now Reader in African history at the School of Oriental and African Studies, the University of London, set out to investigate the historical evolution of racial policies and conflicts in what then was the Federation of Rhodesia and Nyasaland. He found that there had always been two nations and that by one means or another white settlers had contrived to discriminate against the black majority of the three colonies.

The book begins with a functional examination of segregation and trusteeship, includes a chapter on differential land policies by Philip Mason, and in subsequent chapters discusses labor policies, urbanization, the industrial color bar and the treatment of education. There is a survey of constitutional development and brief, but for the time detailed and accurate, accounts of both European and African political stirrings. The movement toward federation is described, but the book carries the story of political, social and economic developments only to 1953. Nevertheless, this is a book upon which a wide range of subsequent research has been based.

KAUNDA, KENNETH DAVID. **Zambia Shall Be Free.** London: Heinemann, 1962, 202 p.

Dr. Kenneth Kaunda is a modest, unpretentious man, and his qualities shine through in this little book which narrates the story of his life in the simplest of terms. It is not as full as such comparable autobiographies as that of Kwame Nkrumah, nor does it succeed in telling the reader much that was not previously known about African protest in Zambia. Its usefulness is in the insights it gives into Kaunda's character and the forces which shaped his views. Especially interesting are the earlier chapters in which Kaunda describes his boyhood in the missionary village at Lubwa and his subsequent experiences as a schoolboy and then a schoolmaster. In view of his strong stand against racialism, Kaunda's account of his earliest experiences of the color bar are also interesting, such as the indignities to which Africans were subjected by shopkeepers in the Copperbelt town of Mufulira. The humiliations increased Kaunda's militance but not his racial bitterness. A most vivid chapter is the one dealing with Kaunda's split with Harry Nkumbula, one of the first major African politicians in Northern Rhodesia.

HALL, RICHARD. **The High Price of Principles: Kaunda and the White South.** London: Hodder, 1969, 256 p.

Richard Hall is an English journalist who emigrated to Zambia in 1955 and became intimately involved in the country's struggles for independence. Zambia found itself in the awkward position of being an independent African state whose colonial past had forged economic, political and social ties with the white supremacist régimes of the south. Mr. Hall's book is a detailed account of Dr. Kaunda's refusal to sacrifice cherished political principles for the economic benefits of a more accommodationist approach to his southern neighbors. The importance of the book is that it was the first detailed analysis of the changing character of the subcontinent after the declaration of independence by the Rhodesian Front régime. Hall's analysis of Prime Minister Harold Wilson's treatment of Zambia in the Rhodesian imbroglio is a searing indictment of British policy. Wilson is bluntly accused of deceiving and betraying Kaunda.

Zambia's copper resources make it a rich state by African standards, but, as Hall shows, the dependence of the economy on this mineral makes it extremely vulnerable to the vagaries of prices on the world copper market. The acute tribal rivalries are also a source of potential instability. These factors and the real possibility of a racial war in southern Africa make Zambia's position a delicate one. Hall succeeds admirably in showing the agonizing dilemmas which Kaunda faces.

ROTBERG, ROBERT I. **The Rise of Nationalism in Central Africa: The Making of Malawi and Zambia, 1873–1964.** Cambridge: Harvard University Press, 1965, 362 p.

Rotberg's book is the first major effort by a political scientist to record the development of African nationalism in Malawi and Zambia. This particular volume is one of a trilogy on Central Africa and is based upon a wide variety of archival and other sources, including a large number of interviews with many of the main actors in the conflicts which are described. It describes the development of colonial rule in the two territories and analyzes the roots of conflict. Rotberg deals with the aspirations of the white settlers in the period between the two world wars and during the time of the Federation of Rhodesia and Nyasaland. His meticulous analysis of the rise of African protest and its culmination in mass political movements forms the heart of the book and entitles it to be ranked as one of the classic studies of African nationalism. It is also notable as a contribution to the numerous studies of the Federation and its demise.

ANGOLA; MOZAMBIQUE; MALAGASY REPUBLIC

DUFFY, JAMES. **Portuguese Africa.** Cambridge: Harvard University Press, 1959, 389 p.

A pioneering American scholarly treatise on five centuries of Portuguese African history, mainly in Angola and Mozambique, Professor Duffy's work concentrates on the era after 1875 and stresses consideration of the gap between theory and practice in Portuguese colonial policy. Colonial literature and philosophy are not neglected in the study of the internal and external debates which have raged about the Portuguese presence in Africa since the writings of Dr. David Livingstone, the missionary-traveller. **Portuguese Africa** became an essential primer for scholars as well as a catalyst for further work on topics which Duffy did not develop here: African nationalism, social history and politics. An abbreviated edition, **Portugal in Africa** (Cambridge: Harvard University Press, 1962, 239 p.), contains a new chapter bringing events to the end of 1961.

Imaginatively written and judicious in judgment, the work is a classic with few flaws. Research was derived from personal visits to the area and from a mastery of the published, secondary Portuguese works, as well as the scattered material in English; unpublished documentation was not consulted. This original study touched off an enduring debate, opened up the field of Portuguese African history for many Africanists and painted an unforgettable portrait of this region as it was in the late 1950s.

MARCUM, JOHN. **The Angolan Revolution. Volume I: The Anatomy of an Explosion (1950–1962).** Cambridge: M. I. T. Press, 1969, 380 p.

This is a scholarly study—sympathetic to African nationalist aspirations—of contemporary Angolan nationalism through 1962. A promised second volume will cover affairs through 1968. The author emphasizes the recent origins of Angolan nationalism, the "explosion" of insurgency against Portuguese rule in 1961 and the continuing crisis through 1962, when Western support in the United Nations for Angolan nationalism seriously ebbed. Included is a serious, and in large part successful, attempt to unravel the complex events of the 1961 conflicts, clearly the crucial turning point in Angola's recent history. Nearly two-thirds of the volume treats the two years 1961–1962. The rich biographical and institutional detail will aid many students, as will the index and charts of parties in the appendices.

The impressive range of sources includes a culling of recent periodical literature in English, French and Portuguese, oral history from Angolan informants, a personal visit of the author to northern Angola via insurgent paths and unpublished manuscripts of African and European observers. Here is an essential contribution to the study of Angolan nationalism which is clearly written and ably edited for scholars' use. The book contains a mass of information, the origins and interpretation of which are as controversial as they are significant.

THOMPSON, VIRGINIA and ADLOFF, RICHARD. **The Malagasy Republic: Madagascar Today.** Stanford: Stanford University Press, 1965, 504 p.

Until the appearance of this volume, information in English on contemporary Madagascar was scarce, spotty and often inaccurate. No broad treatment of the island, its people, politics and economic problems was available, but the gap has been admirably filled by the present authors.

Almost every aspect of the island, from the earliest history to modern economic planning, receives attention. The chapters dealing with the rural economy, and with education and scholarly research, are particularly useful to the specialist, but the general reader will find that the description of the country, its people and the story of the pre-independence struggle is of great value as background to the present situation in this little known part of the world. Madagascar cannot fairly be described as part of Africa (if for no other reason than that the ruling caste, the Merina, vehemently deny any connection to the continent) nor as a part of the Malayo-Polynesian world which the Merina claim as their ancestral home. It is, has been and, as the authors emphasize, wishes to continue as a world apart.

The exhaustively detailed research which went into the descriptive material in the book is remarkable. But the reader may regret that, armed with such detail, the authors did not engage in further analysis, or even speculation, on the theoretical implications of the rise to power of the present leadership. Even if the volume falls short in this respect, however, the reader cannot but be grateful for the wealth of information which it provides.

REPUBLIC OF SOUTH AFRICA

DE KIEWIET, CORNELIS WILLEM. **A History of South Africa.** New York: Oxford University Press, 1941, 292 p.

No writing of the pre-1948 period captures the essence of South Africa's tortuous development more effectively than Cornelis W. de Kiewiet's book. It is a tantalizingly compressed history which discusses only those trends and events which had long-term significance or transformational importance at a particular moment in time. Hence only the first chapter deals with the Dutch era. The second evaluates the impact of British humanitarian ideas, and the third examines the effect of the expanding frontier and the emergence, as a part of this same ongoing process, of an Afrikaner model. The ways in which South Africa was recast by the discovery of diamonds and gold are reserved for a further chapter. The Anglo-Boer war is set, as befits this kind of treatment, in an economic context, as is the ensuing struggle for unification. Only two chapters are specifically focused upon the problem of color and African strivings, but, even so, this is a book infused with liberalism, albeit the liberalism of an earlier time.

The author is a Hollander who grew up in South Africa and obtained his early university education at the University of the Witwatersrand and a doctoral degree from the University of London. He then began a long and distinguished teaching career in the United States.

For a comprehensive history of South Africa, see Eric A. Walker's massive political study, **A History of Southern Africa** (New York: Longmans, 3rd ed., 1957, 973 p.).

SCHAPERA, ISAAC, ed. **The Bantu-Speaking Tribes of South Africa: An Ethnographical Survey.** London: Routledge, 1937, 453 p.

This classic study of the Bantu-speaking peoples of South Africa is a collection of 18 essays by 13 different anthropologists. Each paper deals with a different aspect of the life of the Bantu-speaking peoples, with the greater part of the book devoted to an analysis of the traditional life of the Bantu before the intrusion of Western culture.

The first chapters are concerned with social origins, habitat and tribal groupings. Five major tribal groups are specified: the Nguni, Shangana-Tonga, Sotha, Venda and Lemba peoples who inhabit a region south of the Zambesi and east of the Kalahari Desert. The next section is concerned with social organization, child rearing and domestic and communal life. Emphasis is placed on the details of the kinship system, village life and marital relationships. Economics, political institutions and law and justice are reviewed with stress on the pattern of coercion. Religion, magic and medical practices are lumped together, indicating the major supernatural sanctions and ancestral worship that determined and controlled behavior. Three chapters deal with music, literature and language. The last chapters indicate how the traditional institutions and patterns of behavior were altered by Western culture. Some reference is made to Bantu farm workers and life in towns.

Few surveys have ever covered a group of people as thoroughly as this scientific venture. The study is a landmark and became the forerunner and model of ethnographic surveys in anthropology.

WILLOUGHBY, WILLIAM CHARLES. **Race Problems in the New Africa.** Oxford: Clarendon Press, 1923, 296 p.

This book, written after the end of World War I, has as its goal the explanation of the life of Bantu-speaking peoples under British rule. Willoughby was a missionary who had spent many years of his life living among the Bantu-speaking peoples. He divided the book into three parts, the first of which briefly discusses geography, climate and rainfall and demarcates the area of the Bantu-speaking people as the lands south of the Congo. The second section consists of five chapters in which the traditional culture of the Bantu-speaking people is discussed. Major emphasis is initially placed on an analysis of religion, magic, divination and the behavior of priests and medicine men. Tribal law, political structure, kinship systems and marital relationships are then scrutinized, followed by a detailed description of child rearing, training of youths and girls and initiation rites. The third section deals with the "Europeanization" of the culture and is an odd mixture of history, early European contacts, racial problems, religion, governmental controls and economic development. While some of the material is quite interesting, many of the theories and ideas presented are unscientific and unsubstantiated by empirical data, making it difficult to use the book as a reliable source.

KUPER, LEO. **An African Bourgeoisie: Race, Class, and Politics in South Africa.** New Haven: Yale University Press, 1965, 452 p.

Leo Kuper is a South African sociologist who, aside from his academic profession, was an activist in the liberal cause, working for a nonracial South Africa. His book reflects these two concerns: it is a sociological analysis combined with a passionate concern for racial justice. Kuper is careful to say that he is not employing the term "bourgeoisie" in any strictly analytical sense. In this context it means the African white-collar class, represented by the schoolteacher, clergyman, lawyer and other occupations. His study is based upon interviews with members of this class in Durban.

The book is a major contribution to African sociology, involving a detailed analysis of his subjects' values, life-styles, hopes, aspirations and frustrations, for Kuper does not attempt to isolate the African bourgeoisie from the society in which they live. A significant portion of the book is devoted to a critical analysis of the apartheid ideology, and Kuper succeeded in producing one of the most penetrating accounts that have appeared to date. His description of the system of Bantu education is especially good. Also notable is his study of the African advisory board system as it operated within the context of the structure of local government in Durban.

CARTER, GWENDOLEN MARGARET. **The Politics of Inequality: South Africa since 1948.** New York: Praeger, 1958, 535 p.

The significance of Professor Carter's massive book is that it is the first major treatment of South African politics by a political scientist. She sought to encompass all segments of the political system. Parliamentary and extra-parliamentary politics, white and nonwhite political movements are described in considerable detail, and a clear picture emerges of how racial inequality is built into the South African system. It is difficult to single out particular sections of the book for praise, but the portion dealing with the structures of white political parties is especially valuable. The strength of the book lies not so much in the cogency of its analysis as in the vast amount of factual data in the text and in the appendices. Another notable feature is the comprehensive bibliography which has proved a boon to subsequent scholars. Much work remains to be done on South African politics, but this book provided a valuable impetus to further study. Time has not diminished its value as an indispensable reference work.

VII. THE POLAR REGIONS

BAIRD, PATRICK D. **The Polar World.** New York: Wiley, 1964, 328 p.

Numerous geographical summaries of the polar regions have been published during the past half century. Good examples are: R. N. Rudmose Brown, **The Polar Regions: A Physical and Economic Geography of the Arctic and Antarctic** (New York: Dutton, 1927, 245 p.); Otto Nordenskjöld and Ludwig Mecking, **The Geography of the Polar Regions** (New York: American Geographical Society, 1928, 359 p.); and George H. T. Kimble and Dorothy Good, *eds.,* **Geography of the Northlands** (New York: American Geographical Society; Wiley, 1955, 534 p.).

An excellent, more current discussion of the polar regions is **The Polar World.** In this book, Mr. Baird summarizes the history of polar exploration, the polar climates and the salient characteristics of the polar seas. His discussion of the Arctic includes its landforms, its flora and fauna, its native peoples, transportation, political geography and regional characteristics. The considerably briefer section on the Antarctic includes a chapter on the Antarctic continent and one on the subantarctic islands. The book has 76 maps and diagrams which add much to its usefulness and 36 well-chosen photographs.

Much more is now known about the Antarctic, and a planned revised edition of Mr. Baird's book will undoubtedly reflect this increased knowledge.

COMMITTEE ON POLAR RESEARCH, NATIONAL RESEARCH COUNCIL. **Polar Research: A Survey.** Washington: National Academy of Sciences, 1970, 204 p.

"Polar research is almost synonymous with international scientific cooperation," as this report states. The Arctic was the scene of the first formal multinational polar effort during the first and second International Polar Years of 1882–1883 and 1932–1933. The worldwide International Geophysical Year in 1957–1958 saw extensive scientific programs carried out by many nations in both polar regions. Since the IGY, international scientific coöperation in Antarctica has continued, and a need for a renewed international effort in the Arctic is beginning to be felt.

In this survey, the Committee on Polar Research has summarized the current knowledge of the polar regions and has made recommendations for future investigations. The significance of the polar atmosphere, oceans and glaciers to the global environment is emphasized, and the importance of Arctic and Antarctic geology and geophysics to an understanding of the earth's structure is discussed. This is a valuable reference work for those concerned with scientific investigation in the polar regions.

JOERG, W. L. G., *ed.* **Problems of Polar Research.** New York: American Geographical Society, 1928, 477 p.

In the middle 1920s Isaiah Bowman, then Director of the American Geographical Society, thought that the time was ripe for a world conference on polar research. Such a meeting was not held, but "to supply an equivalent," the American Geographical Society undertook to prepare this volume—a symposium by 31 prominent students of polar problems. The articles summarize what was known about the polar regions and suggest problems for further study. The roster of authors includes most of the polar authorities then living; among them are Nansen, Stefansson, Mawson, Drygalski, Priestley, Byrd, Wilkins, Ellsworth and Nobile.

The book is of much historical interest. The role it played for its era has since been largely taken over by reports of the National Academy of Sciences in the United States, and by various official polar groups in other nations, as noted in the

Survey of the Committee on Polar Research. But the American Geographical Society volume remains a milestone in the advancement of polar research.

SMEDAL, GUSTAV CATHRINUS HOFGAARD. **Acquisition of Sovereignty Over Polar Areas.** Oslo: Dybwad, 1931, 143 p.

Four decades have passed since Smedal wrote this summary, yet it still remains a valuable reference for those who seek an insight into the foundations upon which nations have declared sovereignty in polar regions. Much space is given to the controversy between Denmark and Norway over eastern Greenland, which was settled in Denmark's favor by a decision of the Permanent Court of International Justice only two years after the appearance of Smedal's report. Denmark and Norway had each maintained territorial claims in Greenland at various times throughout a period of nearly a thousand years. The case is the only territorial dispute in the polar regions to have been settled by an international court. This historical decision is the subject of a book by Oscar Svarlien, **The Eastern Greenland Case in Historical Perspective.**

A helpful reference on sovereignty in the Antarctic is the book by J. F. da Costa, **Souveraineté sur l'Antarctique** (Paris: Librairie Générale de Droit, 1958, 249 p.), more than half of which is devoted to a list of reports and official acts related to the subject.

VICTOR, PAUL-ÉMILE. **Man and the Conquest of the Poles.** New York: Simon and Schuster, 1963, 320 p.

This is the story of how men have overcome obstacles in the way of traveling to polar regions as well as in living and working there. The author's theme is that through increasingly improved methods of transportation, and through sophistication of instruments and methods, man has at last become master of the polar regions and can now really "explore" them. As head of Expéditions Polaires Françaises, Victor has had extensive experience in organizing scientific expeditions to Greenland and Antarctica, experience which undoubtedly explains his interest in equipment and methods. He also knows the importance of the human factor in the success or failure of an expedition and discusses in his book the personal qualifications of some of the leaders of polar expeditions. He also does not overlook the social, political and economic climates that have sent man to the polar regions. The book has been translated by Scott Sullivan.

Another excellent and more conventional account of polar exploration is that by L. P. Kirwan, **A History of Polar Exploration** (New York: Norton, 1960, 374 p.). An especially interesting history of Antarctic exploration is **Quest for a Continent** by Walter Sullivan (New York: McGraw-Hill, 1957, 372 p.).

HATHERTON, TREVOR, *ed.* **Antarctica.** New York: Praeger, 1965, 511 p.

Articles by Antarctic specialists, chiefly from New Zealand and the United States, make this volume an authoritative summary of what was known about the Antarctic following the concentrated scientific investigations which began with the International Geophysical Year. The book is in four parts: "The Nations of Antarctica," "The Southern Ocean," "The Antarctic Continent" and "The South Polar Atmosphere." Maps, diagrams and photographs are used to advantage throughout.

In a sense, this volume is a revised edition of an earlier one sponsored by the New Zealand Antarctic Society: Frank A. Simpson, *ed.,* **The Antarctic Today** (Wellington: Reed, 1952, 389 p.). This earlier volume was a widely accepted treatise on Antarctica and was translated into Russian in 1957 and Spanish in 1962. As a result of the increasing interest in and knowledge of the Antarctic, the British also brought out a book on the region: Sir Raymond Priestley, Raymond J. Adie and G. deQ. Robin, *eds.,* **Antarctic Research: A Review of British Scientific Achievement in Antarctica** (London: Butterworths, 1964, 360 p.). The roster of topics in these three books is similar in many respects, but the British book is oriented more toward that country's contributions to Antarctic research.

A fourth and quite different summary on the Antarctic has resulted from Neal Potter's study of the economic potentialities of the area: **Natural Resource Potentials of the Antarctic** (New York: American Geographical Society, Occasional Publication No. 4, 1969, 97 p.). While this study has not added to the store of knowledge of the Antarctic, it is the first to assess the resources of the area in a systematic way.

NATIONAL ACADEMY OF SCIENCES. **Antarctic Research Series.** Washington: American Geophysical Union, 1964–, 15 v. to date.

Comprehensive scientific research in the Antarctic started with the International Geophysical Year and is continuing. Several of the nations participating are issuing special periodicals for the publication of the reports on their research, and many articles have found their way into established scientific journals. In addition, a number of books have appeared. Several are proceedings of Antarctic symposia; for example, Raymond J. Adie, *ed.*, **Antarctic Geology: Proceedings of the First International Symposium on Antarctic Geology** (Amsterdam: North-Holland, 1964, 758 p.) and M. W. Holdgate, *ed.,* **Antarctic Ecology** (London: Academic Press, for the Scientific Committee on Antarctic Research, 1970, 2 v.).

Perhaps the most ambitious undertaking for the publication of results of Antarctic scientific research, however, is the National Academy's **Antarctic Research Series.** Each volume of the series is devoted to one particular scientific discipline or topic; a few volumes have a single author, but most are collections of essays by several workers in the same field. Topics covered include biology of the Antarctic seas, snow and ice studies, geomagnetism and aeronomy, geology and paleontology, Antarctic soils, meteorology, entomology, bird studies and oceanology.

TAUBENFELD, HOWARD J. **A Treaty for Antarctica.** New York: Carnegie Endowment, 1961, 322 p.

The Antarctic Treaty of 1959 provides that Antarctica shall be used for peaceful purposes only; it also states that territorial claims shall remain as they existed at the time of the writing of the treaty. Mr. Taubenfeld appraises the factors that made the treaty possible and considers its potential as a precedent for peaceful settlement of such problems as world disarmament, control of nuclear explosions and neutralization of other regions such as the Arctic and outer space.

Interestingly, the author had been concerned with the analogy of Antarctica and outer space even before the Antarctic Treaty was written. A study, on which he collaborated with Philip C. Jessup, **Controls for Outer Space,** will be useful to the reader interested in an assessment of the similarity between problems of international controls in Antarctica and those in outer space.

ARMSTRONG, TERENCE. **Russian Settlement in the North.** Cambridge: Cambridge University Press, 1965, 224 p.

This is an interestingly written account of the Russian advance into the north in which the author discusses the numbers of settlers, the character of their settlements, government policy and relations with the natives. The knowledge and skills the Russians have acquired in the Arctic are becoming increasingly important to other nations because pressure of world population is making it more and more essential that marginal land areas and their resources be fully utilized. The book includes appendices giving population figures and information on the native people of the north, together with a glossary of Russian terms and an extensive bibliography. This work and two earlier ones by the same author—**The Russians in the Arctic** (Fair Lawn: Essential Books, 1958, 182 p.) and **The Northern Sea Route** (New York: Cambridge University Press, for the Scott Polar Research Institute, 1952, 162 p.)—are excellent sources of general information on Russian activities in the Arctic.

The reader seeking further presentation of the development of the Northern Sea Route will find two books by Constantine Krypton of interest: **The Northern Sea**

Route: Its Place in Russian Economic History before 1917 (New York: Research Program on the U.S.S.R., 1953, 194 p.) and **The Northern Sea Route and the Economy of the Soviet North** (New York: Praeger, for the Research Program on the U.S.S.R., 1956, 219 p.). The classic work on the Soviet advance into the Arctic is Timothy A. Taracouzio's **Soviets in the Arctic** (New York: Macmillan, 1938, 563 p.). Though not current, it is still of considerable value from a historical point of view and contains a wealth of material in its appendices and bibliography.

APPENDIX

The following list represents a selection of important collections of documents in the field of international relations published during the past half century and dealing with events of that period. The division by subject is arbitrary. The great national collections of foreign policy documents contain material on general subjects and on almost all the countries of the world; and there are individual volumes in series listed under general subjects which deal with developments in specific countries.

GENERAL COLLECTIONS

Documents on International Affairs, 1928– . New York: Oxford University Press (for the Royal Institute of International Affairs), 1929– .

INTERNATIONAL LAW

Hackworth, Green Haywood, ed. *Digest of International Law*. Washington: Department of State, 1940–1944, 8 v.

Whiteman, Marjorie M., ed. *Digest of International Law*. Washington: Department of State, 1963– , 13 v. to date.

[Publications.] Leyden: Sijthoff (for the Permanent Court of International Justice), 1922–1946. Documentation of the Permanent Court of International Justice appeared in the following series: A: *Collection of Judgments;* B: *Collection of Advisory Opinions;* A/B: *Judgments, Orders and Advisory Opinions;* C: *Acts and Documents relating to Judgments and Advisory Opinions Given by the Court;* D: *Acts and Documents concerning the Organization of the Court;* E: *Annual Reports;* F: *General Indexes.*

[Publications.] Leyden: Sijthoff (for the International Court of Justice), 1946– . The following series are published by the I.C.J.: *Reports of Judgments, Advisory Opinions and Orders; Pleadings, Oral Arguments, Documents; Acts and Documents concerning the Organization of the Court; Yearbook; The Bibliography of the International Court of Justice.*

TREATIES

List of Treaty Collections. New York: United Nations, Office of Legal Affairs, 1956, 174 p.

Treaty Series: Publications of Treaties and International Engagements Registered with the Secretariat of the League of Nations. Geneva: League of Nations, 1920–1946, 205 v.

Treaty Series: Treaties and International Agreements Registered or Filed and Recorded with the Secretariat of the United Nations. New York: United Nations, 1947– .

Hudson, Manley O. and Sohn, Louis B., eds. *International Legislation: A Collection of the Texts of Multipartite International Instruments of General Interest, 1919–1945.* Washington: Carnegie Endowment, 1931–1950, 9 v.

Bevans, Charles I., comp. *Treaties and Other International Agreements of the United States of America, 1776–1949.* Washington: Department of State, 1968–   , 7 v. to date.

United States Treaties and Other International Agreements, 1950–   . Washington: Department of State, 1950–   .

Treaties in Force: A List of Treaties and Other International Agreements of the United States, 1941–   . Washington: Department of State, 1944–   .

Slusser, Robert M. and Others. *A Calendar of Soviet Treaties, 1917–1957.* Stanford: Stanford University Press, 1959, 530 p.

Markert, Werner and Geyer, Dietrich, eds. *Sowjetunion: Verträge und Abkommen; Verzeichnis der Quellen und Nachweise 1917–1962.* Cologne: Böhlau Verlag, 1967, 611 p.

The Treaties of Peace, 1919–1923. New York: Carnegie Endowment, 1924, 2 v.

Leiss, Amelia C. and Dennett, Raymond, eds. *European Peace Treaties after World War II: Negotiations and Texts of Treaties with Italy, Bulgaria, Hungary, Rumania, and Finland.* Boston: World Peace Foundation, 1954, 341 p.

INTERNATIONAL ORGANIZATIONS

Aufricht, Hans. *Guide to League of Nations Publications: A Bibliographical Survey of the Work of the League, 1920–1947.* New York: Columbia University Press, 1951, 682 p.

Brimmer, Brenda and Others. *A Guide to the Use of United Nations Documents.* Dobbs Ferry: Oceana Publications, 1962, 272 p.

United Nations Documents Index: United Nations and Specialized Agencies Documents and Publications, 1950–   . New York: United Nations, 1951–   .

Yearbook of the United Nations, 1946/47–   . New York: United Nations, 1947–   .

FIRST WORLD WAR

British Documents on the Origins of the War, 1898–1914. London: H.M.S.O. (for the Foreign Office), 1926–1938, 11 v. in 13 pts.

Documents Diplomatiques Français, 1871–1914. Paris: Imprimerie Nationale (for the Ministère des Affaires Étrangères, Commission pour la Publication des Documents Relatifs aux Origines de la Guerre de 1914–1918), 1929–1959, 41 v.

Die Grosse Politik der Europäischen Kabinette, 1871–1914: Sammlung der Diplomatischen Akten des Auswärtigen Amtes. Berlin: Deutsche Verlagsgesellschaft für Politik und Geschichte, 1922–1927, 40 v. in 54 pts.

Die Deutschen Dokumente zum Kriegsausbruch 1914: Vollständige Sammlung der von Karl Kautsky Zusammengestellten Amtlichen Aktenstücke mit einigen Ergänzungen. Berlin: Deutsche Verlagsgesellschaft für Politik und Geschichte, 1927, 4 v.

Österreich-Ungarns Aussenpolitik von der Bosnischen Krise 1908 bis zum Kriegsausbruch 1914: Diplomatische Aktenstücke des Österreichisch-Ungarischen Ministeriums des Äussern. Vienna: Österreichischer Bundesverlag für Unterricht, Wissenschaft und Kunst, 1930, 9 v.

Mezhdunarodnye Otnosheniia v Epokhy Imperializma: Dokumenty iz Arkhivov Tsarskogo i Vremennogo Pravitel'stv 1878–1917 gg. Moscow: Gosudarstvennoe Sotsial'no-Ekonomitscheskoe Izdatel'stvo (for the Komissiia pri TsIK SSSR po Izdaniiu Dokumentov Epokhi Imperializma).

    Seriia II: 1900–1913 gg. (May 1911 to Oct. 1912), 3 v., 1938–1940.

    Seriia III: 1914–1917 gg. (Jan. 1914 to Apr. 1916), 10 v. in 13 pts., 1931–1938.

A German edition of this collection appeared as: *Die Internationalen Beziehungen im Zeitalter des Imperialismus,* Berlin: Hobbing (for the Deutsche Gesellschaft zum Studium Osteuropas).

Reihe I: Das Jahr 1914 bis zum Kriegsausbruch. (Jan. to July 1914), 1 v. in 5 pts., 1931–1934.
Reihe II: Vom Kriegsausbruch bis zum Herbst 1915. (July 1914 to Oct. 1915), 3 v. in 6 pts., 1934–1936.
Reihe III: Vom Frühjahr 1911 bis zum Ende 1913. (May 1911 to May 1912, Oct. to Dec. 1912), 3 v. in 5 pts., 1939–1943.

Stieve, Friedrich, ed. *Der Diplomatische Schriftwechsel Iswolskis, 1911–1914.* Berlin: Deutsche Verlagsgesellschaft für Politik und Geschichte, 1924, 4 v.

Stieve, Friedrich, ed. *Iswolski im Weltkriege: Der Diplomatische Schriftwechsel Iswolskis aus den Jahren 1914–1917.* Berlin: Deutsche Verlagsgesellschaft für Politik und Geschichte, 1925, 264 p.

Bogićević, Milosh, ed. *Die Auswärtige Politik Serbiens 1903–1914.* Berlin: Brückenverlag, 1928–1931, 3 v.

Gauss, Imanuel, ed. *Julikrise und Kriegsausbruch 1914: Eine Dokumentensammlung.* Hanover: Verlag für Literatur und Zeitgeschichte, 1963–1964, 2 v.

Scherer, André and Grunewald, Jacques, eds. *L'Allemagne et les Problèmes de la Paix pendant la Première Guerre Mondiale: Documents Extraits des Archives de l'Office Allemand des Affaires Étrangères.* Paris: Presses Universitaires, 1962–1966, 2 v. to date.

Zeman, Z. A. B., ed. *Germany and the Revolution in Russia, 1915–1918: Documents from the Archives of the German Foreign Ministry.* London: Oxford University Press, 1950, 157 p.

Protokolle des Gemeinsamen Ministerrates der Österreichisch-Ungarischen Monarchie (1914–1918). Budapest: Akadémiai Kiadó, 1966, 723 p.

Der Waffenstillstand, 1918–1919: Das Dokumentenmaterial der Waffenstillstandsverhandlungen von Compiègne, Spa, Trier und Brüssel. Berlin: Deutsche Verlagsgesellschaft für Politik und Geschichte (for the Deutsche Waffenstillstandskommission), 1928, 3 v.

Les Délibérations du Conseil des Quatre (24 Mars—28 Juin 1919): Notes de l'Officier Interprète, Paul Mantoux. Paris: Éditions du Centre National de la Recherche Scientifique, 1955, 2 v.

INTER-WAR YEARS

Gantenbein, James W., ed. *Documentary Background of World War II, 1931–41.* New York: Columbia University Press, 1948, 1,122 p.

Deutsch-sowjetische Beziehungen von den Verhandlungen in Brest-Litowsk bis zum Abschluss des Rapallovertrages: Dokumentensammlung. Berlin: Staatsverlag der Deutschen Demokratischen Republik (for the Ministerium für Auswärtige Angelegenheiten der UdSSR and the Ministerium für Auswärtige Angelegenheiten der DDR), 1967–1971, 2 v.

Král, Václav, ed. *Das Abkommen von München, 1938.* Prague: Academia, 1968, 369 p. (Tschechoslowakische Diplomatische Dokumente, 1937–1939.)

Nazi-Soviet Relations, 1939–1941: Documents from the Archives of the German Foreign Office. Washington: Department of State, 1948, 362 p.

Documents and Materials Relating to the Eve of the Second World War. Moscow: Foreign Languages Publishing House, 1948, 2 v.

Kerekes, Lajos, ed. *Allianz Hitler-Horthy-Mussolini: Dokumente zur Ungarischen Aussenpolitik, 1933–1944.* Budapest: Akadémiai Kiadó (for the Történttudományi Intézet), 1966, 409 p.

SECOND WORLD WAR

La Délégation Française auprès de la Commission Allemande d'Armistice: Recueil de Documents Publié par le Gouvernement Français. Paris: Costes, 1947–1959, 5 v.

Documents on Polish-Soviet Relations, 1939–1945. London: General Sikorski Institute, 1961–1968, 2 v.

Actes et Documents du Saint Siège Relatifs à la Seconde Guerre Mondiale. Vatican City: Libreria Editrice Vaticana (for the Secrétairerie d'État de sa Sainteté), 1965– , 5 v. in 6 pts. to date.

Vneshniaia Politika Sovetskogo Soiuza v Period Otechestvennoi Voiny: Dokumenty i Materialy. Moscow: Gospolitizdat, 1944–1947, 3 v.
  English translation of first two volumes appeared as: *Soviet Foreign Policy during the Patriotic War* (London: Hutchinson, 1944–1945, 2 v.).

Trial of the Major War Criminals before the International Military Tribunal, Nuremberg, 14 November 1945 – 1 October 1946. Nuremberg: International Military Tribunal, 1947–1949, 42 v.

Pearl Harbor Attack: Hearings before, and Report of, the Joint Committee on the Investigation of the Pearl Harbor Attack. Washington: G.P.O., 1946, 40 v. (79th Congress, 1st Session.)

Holborn, Louise W., ed. *War and Peace Aims of the United Nations.* Boston: World Peace Foundation, 1943–1948, 2 v.

POSTWAR PERIOD

Paris Peace Conference 1946: Selected Documents. Washington: Department of State, 1947, 1,442 p.

Ruhm von Oppen, Beate, ed. *Documents on Germany under Occupation, 1945–1954.* New York: Oxford University Press (for the Royal Institute of International Affairs), 1955, 660 p.

Documents on Germany, 1944–1970. Washington: G.P.O., 1971, 897 p. (92nd Congress, 1st Session.)

Dokumente zur Deutschlandpolitik. III Reihe: Vom 5. Mai 1955 bis 9. November 1958. Frankfurt/Main: Metzner (for the Bundesministerium für Gesamtdeutsche Fragen), 1961–1969, 4 v.

European Yearbook, 1953– . The Hague: Nijhoff (for the Council of Europe), 1955– .

Higgins, Rosalyn. *United Nations Peacekeeping, 1946–1967: Documents and Commentary.* New York: Oxford University Press (for the Royal Institute of International Affairs), 1969–1970, 2 v.

Documents on Disarmament, 1945– . Washington: Department of State. 1945 to 1959, 1 v. in 2 pts.; 1960– , annual volumes.

UNITED STATES

Foreign Relations of the United States. Washington: G.P.O. (for the Department of State), 1861– . (Title varies; coverage to date through 1946.) Supplementary volumes and series:
  1914–1918. Supplements: The World War (1928–1933, 8 v.).
  1918–1919. Russia (1931–1937, 4 v.).
  The Lansing Papers, 1914–1920 (1939–1940, 2 v.).
  Paris Peace Conference, 1919 (1942–1947, 13 v.).
  Japan, 1931–1941 (1943, 2 v.).
  The Soviet Union, 1933–1939 (1952, 1 v.).
  1942–1943. China (1956–1957, 2 v.).
  The Conferences at Malta and Yalta, 1945 (1955, 1 v.).
  The Conferences of Berlin (Potsdam), 1945 (1960, 2 v.).
  The Conferences of Cairo and Teheran, 1943 (1961, 1 v.).
  The Conferences at Washington, 1941–1942, and Casablanca, 1943 (1968, 1 v.).
  The Conferences at Washington and Quebec, 1943 (1970, 1 v.).

Peace and War: United States Foreign Policy, 1931–1941. Washington: G.P.O. (for the Department of State), 1943, 874 p.

A Decade of American Foreign Policy: Basic Documents, 1941–1949. Washington:

G.P.O. (for the Senate Committee on Foreign Relations, 81st Congress, 1st Session), 1950, 1,381 p.

American Foreign Policy, 1950–1955: Basic Documents. Washington: G.P.O. (for the Department of State), 1957, 2 v.

American Foreign Policy: Current Documents, 1956– . Washington: G.P.O. (for the Department of State), 1959– .

United States Relations with China, with Special Reference to the Period 1944–1949. Washington: G.P.O. (for the Department of State), 1949, 1,054 p.

Documents on American Foreign Relations, 1938– . Boston: World Peace Foundation, 1939–1953; New York: Council on Foreign Relations, 1953– .

Baker, Ray S. and Dodd, William E., eds. *The Public Papers of Woodrow Wilson.* New York: Harper, 1925–1927, 6 v.

Rosenman, Samuel I., ed. *The Public Papers and Addresses of Franklin D. Roosevelt.* New York: Random House; Macmillan; Harper, 1938–1950, 13 v.

Nixon, Edgar B., ed. *Franklin D. Roosevelt and Foreign Affairs.* Cambridge: The Belknap Press of Harvard University, 1969, 3 v.

Public Papers of the Presidents of the United States: Containing the Public Messages, Speeches, and Statements of the President. Washington: G.P.O., 1960– .
> *Harry S. Truman, 1945–1953* (1961–1966, 8 v.).
> *Dwight D. Eisenhower, 1953–1961* (1960–1961, 8 v.).
> *John F. Kennedy, 1961–1963* (1962–1964, 3 v.).
> *Lyndon B. Johnson, 1963–1969* (1965–1970, 10 v.).

GREAT BRITAIN

Index to the Correspondence of the Foreign Office, 1920– . Nendeln, Liechtenstein: Kraus-Thomson (by arrangement with H.M.S.O.), 1969– . Index for 1920 to 1938, 1969, 77 v.; subsequent volumes published annually.

Documents on British Foreign Policy, 1919–1939. London: H.M.S.O. (for the Foreign Office), 1947– .
> *1st Series.* 1919 to 1922 (1947–1970, 17 v.).
> *Series IA.* 1925 to 1927 (1966–1970, 3 v.).
> *2nd Series.* 1929 to 1933 (1946–1970, 11 v.).
> *3rd Series.* Mar. 1938 to Sept. 1939 (1949–1961, 10 v.).

FRANCE

Documents Diplomatiques Français, 1932–1939. Paris: Imprimerie Nationale (for the Ministère des Affaires Étrangères, Commission de Publication des Documents Relatifs aux Origines de la Guerre 1939–1945), 1963– .
> *Ire Série (1932–1935).* July 9, 1932 to Mar. 13, 1934 (1964–1970, 5 v.).
> *2e Série (1936–1939).* Jan. 1, 1936 to Sept. 29, 1937 (1963–1970, 6 v.).

Les Événements Survenus en France de 1933 à 1945. Paris: Presses Universitaires (for the Commission d'Enquêter sur les Événements Survenus en France de 1933 à 1945), 1947–1952, 2 pts. in 11 v.

ITALY

I Documenti Diplomatici Italiani. Rome: Libreria dello Stato (for the Ministero degli Affari Esteri).
> *4a Serie: 1908–1914.* V. 12: 28 Giugno – 2 Agosto 1914 (1964, 581 p.).
> *5a Serie: 1914–1918.* V. 1: 2 Agosto – 16 Ottobre 1914 (1954, 616 p.).
> *6a Serie: 1918–1922.* V. 1: 4 Novembre 1918 – 17 Gennaio 1919 (1956, 526 p.).
> *7a Serie: 1922–1935.* V. 1–7: 31 Ottobre 1922 – 12 Settembre 1929 (1953–1970, 7 v.).

8a Serie: 1935–1939. V. 12–13: 23 Maggio – 3 Settembre 1939 (1952–1953, 2 v.).
9a Serie: 1939–1943. V. 1–5: 4 Settembre 1939 – 28 Ottobre 1940 (1954–1965, 5 v.).

GERMANY

A Catalogue of Files and Microfilms of the German Foreign Ministry Archives, 1867–1920. Washington: American Historical Association, Committee for the Study of War Documents, 1959, 1,290 columns.

Kent, George O., ed. *A Catalog of Files and Microfilms of the German Foreign Ministry Archives, 1920–1945.* Stanford: Hoover Institution, 1962–1966, 3 v. (Joint project of U.S. Department of State and Hoover Institution.)

Akten zur Deutschen Auswärtigen Politik 1918–1945: Aus dem Archiv des Auswärtigen Amts.

> *Serie A: 1918–1925.* (German ed. in preparation.)
> *Serie B: 1925–1933.* Göttingen: Vandenhoeck und Rupprecht, 1966– ; 4 v. to date (Dec. 1925 to Mar. 1927).
> *Serie C: 1933–1937.* (German ed. in preparation.) English ed.: *Documents on German Foreign Policy,* Washington: G.P.O., 1957–1964, 5 v. (Jan. 1933 to Oct. 1936).
> *Serie D: 1937–1941.* Baden-Baden: Imprimerie Nationale; Göttingen: Vandenhoeck und Rupprecht, 1950–1970, 13 v. English ed.: Washington: G.P.O., 1949–1964, 13 v.
> *Serie E: 1941–1945.* Göttingen: Vandenhoeck und Rupprecht, 1969– ; 1 v. to date (Dec. 1941 to Feb. 1942).

Dokumente zur Aussenpolitik der Regierung der Deutschen Demokratischen Republik, 1949– . Berlin: Rütten und Loening (for the Ministerium für Auswärtige Angelegenheiten), 1954– .

U.S.S.R.

Dokumenty Vneshnei Politiki SSSR. Moscow: Gospolitizdat (for the Ministerstvo Inostrannykh Del SSSR), 1957– . 16 v. (1917 to 1933) to date.

Vneshniaia Politika Sovetskogo Soiuza: Dokumenty i Materialy, 1945– . Moscow: Izdatel'stvo Politicheskoi Literatury, 1949– .

Vneshniaia Politika Sovetskogo Soiuza i Mezhdunarodnye Otnosheniia: Sbornik Dokumentov, 1961– . Moscow: Izdatel'stvo Instituta Mezhdunarodnykh Otnoshenii, 1962– .

Degras, Jane, comp. *Calendar of Soviet Documents on Foreign Policy, 1917–1941.* New York: Royal Institute of International Affairs, 1948, 248 p.

Degras, Jane, ed. *Soviet Documents on Foreign Policy, 1917–41.* New York: Oxford University Press, 1951–1953, 3 v.

Eudin, Xenia J. and Fisher, Harold H. *Soviet Russia and the West, 1920–1927: A Documentary Survey.* Stanford: Stanford University Press, 1957, 450 p.

Eudin, Xenia and North, Robert C. *Soviet Russia and the East, 1920–1927: A Documentary Survey.* Stanford: Stanford University Press, 1957, 478 p.

Eudin, Xenia J. and Slusser, Robert M. *Soviet Foreign Policy 1928–1934: Documents and Materials.* University Park: Pennsylvania State University Press, 1966–1967, 2 v.

INDEX TO AUTHORS

INDEX TO TITLES

RECENT PUBLICATIONS

FOREIGN AFFAIRS (quarterly), edited by Hamilton Fish Armstrong.

THE UNITED STATES IN WORLD AFFAIRS (annual), by Richard P. Stebbins.

DOCUMENTS ON AMERICAN FOREIGN RELATIONS (annual), by Richard P. Stebbins and Elaine P. Adam.

THE UNITED STATES AND THE INDUSTRIAL WORLD: FOREIGN ECONOMIC POLICY FOR THE '70s, by William Diebold, Jr. (1972).

AMERICAN AID FOR DEVELOPMENT, by Paul G. Clark (1972).

THE CARIBBEAN COMMUNITY: CHANGING SOCIETIES AND U.S. POLICY, by Robert D. Crassweller (1972).

INDIA, PAKISTAN, AND THE GREAT POWERS, by William J. Barnds (1972).

CONGRESS, THE EXECUTIVE, AND FOREIGN POLICY, by Francis O. Wilcox (1971).

THE REALITY OF FOREIGN AID, by Willard L. Thorp (1971).

POLITICAL HANDBOOK AND ATLAS OF THE WORLD, 1970, edited by Richard P. Stebbins and Alba Amoia (1970).

JAPAN IN POSTWAR ASIA, by Lawrence Olson (1970).

THE CRISIS OF DEVELOPMENT, by Lester B. Pearson (1970).

THE GREAT POWERS AND AFRICA, by Waldemar A. Nielsen (1969).

A NEW FOREIGN POLICY FOR THE UNITED STATES, by Hans J. Morgenthau (1969).

MIDDLE EAST POLITICS: THE MILITARY DIMENSION, by J. C. Hurewitz (1969).

THE ECONOMICS OF INTERDEPENDENCE: Economic Policy in the Atlantic Community, by Richard N. Cooper (1968).

HOW NATIONS BEHAVE: Law and Foreign Policy, by Louis Henkin (1968).

THE INSECURITY OF NATIONS, by Charles W. Yost (1968).

PROSPECTS FOR SOVIET SOCIETY, edited by Allen Kassof (1968).

THE AMERICAN APPROACH TO THE ARAB WORLD, by John S. Badeau (1968).

U.S. POLICY AND THE SECURITY OF ASIA, by Fred Green (1968).

NEGOTIATING WITH THE CHINESE COMMUNISTS: The U.S. Experience, by Kenneth T. Young (1968).

FROM ATLANTIC TO PACIFIC: A New Interocean Canal, by Immanuel J. Klette (1967).

TITO'S SEPARATE ROAD: America and Yugoslavia in World Politics, by John C. Campbell (1967).

U.S. TRADE POLICY: New Legislation for the Next Round, by John W. Evans (1967).

TRADE LIBERALIZATION AMONG INDUSTRIAL COUNTRIES: Objectives and Alternatives, by Bela Balassa (1967).

THE CHINESE PEOPLE'S LIBERATION ARMY, by Brig. General Samuel B. Griffith II U.S.M.C. (ret.) (1967).

THE ARTILLERY OF THE PRESS: Its Influence on American Foreign Policy, by James Reston (1967).

TRADE, AID AND DEVELOPMENT: The Rich and Poor Nations, by John Pincus (1967).

BETWEEN TWO WORLDS: Policy, Press and Public Opinion on Asian-American Relations, by John Hohenberg (1967).

THE CONFLICTED RELATIONSHIP: The West and the Transformation of Asia, Africa and Latin America, by Theodor Geiger (1966).

THE ATLANTIC IDEA AND ITS EUROPEAN RIVALS, by H. van B. Cleveland (1966).

EUROPEAN UNIFICATION IN THE SIXTIES: From the Veto to the Crisis, by Miriam Camps (1966).

THE UNITED STATES AND CHINA IN WORLD AFFAIRS, by Robert Blum, edited by A. Doak Barnett (1966).

THE FUTURE OF THE OVERSEAS CHINESE IN SOUTHEAST ASIA, by Lea A. Williams (1966).

ATLANTIC AGRICULTURAL UNITY: Is it Possible?, By John O. Coppock (1966).

TEST BAN AND DISARMAMENT: The Path of Negotiation, by Arthur H. Dean (1966).

COMMUNIST CHINA'S ECONOMIC GROWTH AND FOREIGN TRADE, by Alexander Eckstein (1966).

POLICIES TOWARD CHINA: Views from Six Continents, edited by A. M. Halpern (1966).

THE AMERICAN PEOPLE AND CHINA, by A. T. Steele (1966).

INTERNATIONAL POLITICAL COMMUNICATION, by W. Phillips Davison (1965).

ALTERNATIVE TO PARTITION: For a Broader Conception of America's Role in Europe, by Zbigniew Brzezinski (1965).

THE TROUBLED PARTNERSHIP: A Re-appraisal of the Atlantic Alliance, by Henry A. Kissinger (1965).